THE LEAGUE CLUB DIRECTORY 1985

Editor: Tony Williams

NEWNES BOOKS

The compiler and publishers wish
to thank the following:
Mei Lim for ground drawings, the AA for
'how to get there' directions

Published by Newnes Books
84-88, The Centre, Feltham, Middlesex, England
and distributed for them by
The Hamlyn Publishing Group Limited
Rushden, Northants, England

This edition first published 1984

ISBN 0 600 35783 X (softback)
ISBN 0 600 35852 6 (hardback)

Phototypeset by New Rush Filmsetters Ltd, London
Printed in Finland

Front cover Liverpool's Alan Kennedy attempts to stop Manchester United's Bryan Robson firing in a shot.
Photo: Bob Thomas

ACKNOWLEDGEMENTS

When a book is as comprehensive as 'The League Club Directory', a large and experienced team of compilers is a necessity.

The club statisticians for The Directory, who are all members of Ray Spillers' Association of Football Statisticians, have given great support, while I have also been most grateful for the enthusiastic support of the Secretaries, Commercial Managers and Programme editors at all League clubs.

The editorial committee have taken a great deal of responsibility upon themselves with Tony Pullein and Barry Hugman concentrating on the match by match analysis and the players pages.

The advice and photographic contributions of Simon Inglis and Stuart Ashby, who helped so much with the pages featuring the League club grounds, and the incredibly thorough statistical research of Julian Barker have been invaluable.

The Football League administrative staff have, as usual, been extremely helpful, and amongst the many other contributors who have helped are: Tony Matthews, A. Jenkins, Peter Holton, Kevin Pullein.

I am also particularly grateful to assistant editor Bill Mitchell and to the publishers, Newnes Books, who had the confidence that this mammoth task could be successfully completed and consistently gave much appreciated support and encouragement through Tony Bagley, Peter Arnold, Chris Pow, James Hughes and Steve Ridout. Also to photographers Ged Murray and Martin Parr.

While fully appreciating all the contributions and helpers, their work would have come to nothing if it had not been for the gargantuan effort of Dave Williams and the New Rush typesetters who produced superb results under severe pressure. Teamwork is very important in football and the team who produced this book were an inspiration. Thank you all very much.

Tony Williams

Editor: Tony Williams

Editorial Committee: Tony Williams, Bill Mitchell (Assistant Editor), Tony Bagley, Chris Pow (Newnes Books), Peter Arnold (House Editor), Tony Pullein and Barry Hugman.

Editorial Office: 4 Rosen Court, Turners Drive, Thatcham, Newbury, Berkshire RG13 4DF.

PREFACE

The League Club Directory is a completely original book and has been prepared to appeal to all categories of the game's supporters.

For the **Statistician:** Full match-by-match details for League and Cups in 1983-4 for all 92 league clubs.

For the **TV Supporter:** Every player's full details listed in the clubs with whom they started the season **including summer transfers.**

For the **Historian:** A review of the season for all clubs, plus club records and statistics since their inception.

For the **Ground 'Traveller':** Photos, ground plans, directions, prices and ground statistical records for all 92 clubs.

For **Players:** Full details of career records and honours since they entered the League, up to date at the beginning of this season plus **this season's** club photographs.

For **Journalists:** The most comprehensive club and players records ever presented with players as contracted on the first day of the season.

For **Programme Collectors:** Every club programme cover for this season is shown with basic details.

This Directory is a reference book which I hope will be both useful and extremely enjoyable. Having had the thrill of being the founder compiler of the **Rothmans Football Yearbook** in 1970 I am equally excited about this very different publication which has been so well supported and promoted by Newnes Books. How they have kept the price so low I really don't know but hopefully the exciting new concept of the book will give the publishers the bestseller they deserve.

TONY WILLIAMS

CONTENTS

EDITORIAL

As a soccer-mad youngster who hero-worshipped the Birmingham City side of the 1950s, I was rewarded by some sparkling cup runs and emotional days at St Andrews. My special moments in those days were collecting the Sports Argus and Blue Mail on Saturday evening to read about 'The Blues', and rushing out to buy many of the 'nationals' the day after a cup success.

Even if I had watched the match I couldn't wait to read the wonderful descriptions of my heroes' exploits as portrayed by the likes of Desmond Hackett and Roy Peskett. Everything seemed to be larger than life and I literally got 'the tingles' as much from reading these reports as I did from being emotionally drained as a packed St Andews sang 'Keep right on to the end of the road'.

I kept the cuttings, and many years later was able to thank Desmond and Roy for the pleasure they had given me. When asked why they wrote such uplifting reports the answer was: 'to sell newspapers.' They wrote the stories that the fans wanted to read about their club and national sides.

Since that day, our national winter sport has suffered from all types of bad publicity (some admittedly deserved), but I cannot imagine that an on-field or off-field flare-up is 'news' that deserves better coverage than a brilliant hat trick or superb goalkeeping display. Football in this country still provides a very spectacular, highly skilled and often very emotional spectacle that many more people would go to watch if the good in the game was presented as efficiently as all the bad aspects are publicised.

I mentioned 'the tingles' which I am sure all sportsmen and their supporters have experienced when they watch a moving or exciting incident. Last season I enjoyed just that emotion at Wembley when the whole crowd chanted 'Merseyside' as one, at the end of the Milk Cup Final. The sportsmanship and humour of all those Liverpudlians was a fine example throughout the day.

My return to St Andrews for Watford's visit in the Sixth Round of the F.A. Cup brought the hairs out on the back of my neck when the Blues ran on to their old anthem but it was John Barnes' first goal which was as uplifting as anything I saw last season, and thanks to television we could all see it again and again.

The sight of the Everton players led by skipper Ratcliffe applauding and shaking hands with the disappointed Watford players as they came down the Wembley steps, and the general atmosphere at Villa Park when little Plymouth just lost to Graham Taylor's side in the semi-final were two more memories to treasure.

But perhaps the sight of the sparkling eyes and sheer happiness of Plymouth manager John Hore and match winner Andy Rogers, when interviewed by an equally ecstatic Barry Davies, caught everything that the game means to me and I suspect, millions of others. Our game which we love very much can still thrill and excite us but we do resent the wrong people claiming the sports headlines. Such contrasting characters as Graham Taylor and Brian Clough burst with this love and pride for their sport and I only hope they and their managerial colleagues will be able to inspire their sides to give us many more moments to cherish this season.

There's nothing like a good 'tingle'!

TONY WILLIAMS

CANON LEAGUE TABLES 1983-84

First Division

		HOME					AWAY						
	P	W	D	L	F	A	W	D	L	F	A	Df	Pts
Liverpool	42	14	5	2	50	12	8	9	4	23	20	+41	80
Southampton	42	15	4	2	44	17	7	7	7	22	21	+28	77
Nottm Forest	42	14	4	3	47	17	8	4	9	29	28	+31	74
Man Utd	42	14	3	4	43	18	6	11	4	28	23	+30	74
Q.P.R.	42	14	4	3	37	12	8	3	10	30	25	+30	73
Arsenal	42	10	5	6	41	29	8	4	9	33	31	+14	63
Everton	42	9	9	3	21	12	7	5	9	23	30	+2	62
Tottenham	42	11	4	6	31	24	6	6	9	33	41	−1	61
West Ham	42	10	4	7	39	24	7	5	9	21	31	+5	60
Aston Villa	42	14	3	4	34	22	3	6	12	25	39	−2	60
Watford	42	9	7	5	36	31	7	2	12	32	46	−9	57
Ipswich	42	11	4	6	34	23	4	4	13	21	34	−2	53
Sunderland	42	8	9	4	26	18	5	4	12	16	35	−11	52
Norwich	42	9	8	4	34	20	3	7	11	14	29	−1	51
Leicester	42	11	5	5	40	30	2	7	12	25	38	−3	51
Luton	42	7	5	9	30	33	7	4	10	23	33	−13	51
W.B.A.	42	10	4	7	30	25	4	5	12	18	37	−14	51
Stoke	42	11	4	6	30	23	2	7	12	14	40	−19	50
Coventry	42	8	5	8	33	33	5	6	10	24	44	−20	50
Birmingham	42	7	7	7	19	18	5	5	11	20	32	−11	48
Notts County	42	6	7	8	31	36	4	4	13	19	36	−22	41
Wolves	42	4	8	9	15	28	2	3	16	12	52	−53	29

Second Division

		HOME					AWAY						
	P	W	D	L	F	A	W	D	L	F	A	Df	Pts
Chelsea	42	15	4	2	55	17	10	9	2	35	23	+50	88
Sheff Wed	42	16	4	1	47	16	10	6	5	25	18	+38	88
Newcastle	42	16	2	3	51	18	8	6	7	34	35	+32	80
Man City	42	13	3	5	43	21	7	7	7	23	27	+18	70
Grimsby	42	13	6	2	36	15	6	7	8	24	32	+13	70
Blackburn	42	9	11	1	35	19	8	5	8	22	27	+11	67
Carlisle	42	10	9	2	29	13	6	7	8	19	28	+7	64
Shrewsbury	42	13	5	3	34	18	4	5	12	15	35	−4	61
Brighton	42	11	6	4	42	17	6	3	12	27	43	+9	60
Leeds Utd	42	13	4	4	33	16	3	8	10	22	40	−1	60
Fulham	42	9	6	6	35	24	6	6	9	25	29	+7	57
Huddersfield	42	8	6	7	27	20	6	9	6	29	29	+7	57
Charlton	42	13	4	4	40	26	3	5	13	13	38	−11	57
Barnsley	42	9	6	6	33	23	6	1	14	24	30	+4	52
Cardiff	42	11	3	7	32	27	4	3	14	21	39	−13	51
Portsmouth	42	8	3	10	46	32	6	4	11	27	32	+9	49
Middlesbrough	42	9	8	4	26	18	3	5	13	15	29	−6	49
Crystal P	42	8	5	8	18	18	4	6	11	24	34	−10	47
Oldham	42	10	6	5	33	27	3	2	16	14	46	−26	47
Derby Co	42	9	5	7	26	26	2	4	15	10	46	−36	42
Swansea	42	7	4	10	20	28	0	4	17	16	57	−49	29
Cambridge Utd	42	4	7	10	20	33	0	5	16	8	44	−49	24

Third Division

		HOME					AWAY						
	P	W	D	L	F	A	W	D	L	F	A	Df	Pts
Oxford Utd	46	17	5	1	58	22	11	6	6	33	28	+41	95
Wimbledon	46	15	5	3	58	35	11	4	8	39	41	+21	87
Sheff Utd	46	14	7	2	56	18	10	4	9	30	35	+33	83
Hull City	46	16	5	2	42	11	7	9	7	29	27	+33	83
Bristol R	46	16	5	2	47	21	6	8	9	21	33	+14	79
Walsall	46	14	4	5	44	22	8	5	10	24	39	+7	75
Bradford City	46	11	9	3	46	30	9	2	12	27	35	+8	71
Gillingham	46	13	4	6	50	29	7	6	10	24	40	+5	70
Millwall	46	16	4	3	42	18	2	9	12	29	47	+6	67
Bolton	46	13	4	6	36	17	5	6	12	20	43	−4	64
Orient	46	13	5	5	40	27	5	4	14	31	54	−10	63
Burnley	46	12	5	6	52	25	4	9	10	24	36	+15	62
Newport	46	11	9	3	35	27	5	5	13	23	48	−17	62
Lincoln	46	11	4	8	42	29	6	6	11	17	33	−3	61
Wigan	46	11	5	7	26	18	5	8	10	20	38	−10	61
Preston	46	12	5	6	42	27	3	6	14	24	39	0	56
Bournemouth	46	11	5	7	38	27	5	2	16	25	46	−10	55
Rotherham	46	10	5	8	29	17	5	4	14	28	47	−7	54
Plymouth	46	11	8	4	38	17	2	4	17	18	45	−6	51
Brentford	46	8	9	6	41	30	3	7	13	28	49	−10	49
Scunthorpe	46	9	9	5	40	31	0	10	13	14	42	−19	46
Southend	46	8	9	6	34	24	2	5	16	21	52	−21	44
Port Vale	46	10	4	9	33	29	1	6	16	18	54	−32	43
Exeter	46	4	8	11	27	39	2	7	14	23	45	−34	33

Fourth Division

		HOME					AWAY						
	P	W	D	L	F	A	W	D	L	F	A	Df	Pts
York City	46	18	4	1	58	16	13	4	6	38	23	+57	101
Doncaster	46	15	6	2	46	22	9	7	7	36	32	+28	85
Reading	46	17	6	0	51	14	5	10	8	33	42	+28	82
Bristol City	46	18	3	2	51	17	6	7	10	19	27	+26	82
Aldershot	46	14	6	3	49	29	8	3	12	27	40	+7	75
Blackpool	46	15	4	4	47	19	6	5	12	23	33	+18	72
Peterborough	46	15	5	3	52	16	3	9	11	20	32	+24	68
Colchester	46	14	7	2	45	14	3	9	11	24	39	+16	67
Torquay	46	13	7	3	32	18	5	6	12	27	46	−5	67
Tranmere	46	11	5	7	33	26	6	10	7	20	27	0	66
Hereford	46	11	6	6	31	21	5	9	9	23	32	+1	63
Stockport	46	12	5	6	34	25	5	6	12	26	39	−4	62
Chesterfield	46	10	11	2	34	24	5	4	14	25	37	−2	60
Darlington	46	13	4	6	31	19	4	4	15	18	31	−1	59
Bury	46	9	7	7	34	32	6	7	10	27	32	−3	59
Crewe	46	10	8	5	35	27	6	3	14	21	40	−11	59
Swindon	46	11	7	5	34	23	4	6	13	24	33	+2	58
Northampton	46	10	8	5	32	32	3	6	14	21	46	−25	53
Mansfield	46	9	7	7	44	27	4	6	13	22	43	−4	52
Wrexham	46	7	6	10	34	33	4	9	10	25	41	−15	48
Halifax	46	11	6	6	36	25	1	6	16	19	64	−34	48
Rochdale	46	8	9	6	35	31	3	4	16	17	49	−28	46
Hartlepool	46	7	8	8	31	28	3	2	18	16	57	−38	40
Chester	46	7	5	11	23	35	0	8	15	22	47	−37	34

F.A. CHALLENGE CUP

FIRST ROUND PROPER

Boston United v Bury	0-3
Hyde United v Burnley	0-2
Rotherham United v Hartlepool United	0-0
Halifax Town v Whitby Town	2-3
Frickley Athletic v Altrincham	0-1
Tranmere Rovers v Bolton Wanderers	2-2
Rochdale v Crewe Alexandra	1-0
Penrith v Hull City	0-2
Northwich Victoria v Bangor City	1-1
Darlington v Mossley	5-0
Gainsborough Trinity v Blackpool	0-2
Bradford City v Wigan Athletic	0-0
Telford United v Stockport County	3-0
Wrexham v Sheffield United	1-5
Chester City v Chesterfield	1-2
Scunthorpe United v Preston North End	1-0
Macclesfield Town v York City	0-0
Mansfield Town v Doncaster Rovers	3-0
Port Vale v Lincoln City	1-2
Southend United v Plymouth Argyle	0-0
Oxford United v Peterborough United	2-0
AFC Bournemouth v Walsall	4-0
Chelmsford City v Wycombe Wanderers	0-0
Barnet v Bristol Rovers	0-0
Exeter City v Maidstone United	1-1
Aldershot v Worcester City	1-1
Burton Albion v Windsor & Eton	1-2
Corinthian Casuals v Bristol City	0-0
Poole Town v Newport County	0-0
Kettering Town v Swindon Town	0-7
Millwall v Dartford	2-1
Barking v Farnborough Town	2-1
Reading v Hereford United	2-0
Wimbledon v Orient	2-1
Torquay United v Colchester United	1-2
Wealdstone v Enfield	1-1
Dagenham v Brentford	2-2
Northampton Town v Waterlooville	1-1
AP Leamington v Gillingham	0-1
Yeovil Town v Harrow Borough	0-1

Replays

Hartlepool United v Rotherham United	0-1
Bolton Wanderers v Tranmere Rovers	4-1
Bangor City v Northwich Victoria	1-0
Wigan Athletic v Bradford City	4-2
York City v Macclesfield Town	2-0
Plymouth Argyle v Southend United	2-0
Wycombe Wanderers v Chelmsford City	1-2
Bristol Rovers v Barnet	3-1
Maidstone United v Exeter City	2-1
Worcester City v Aldershot	2-1
Bristol City v Corinthian Casuals	4-0
Newport County v Poole Town	3-1
Enfield v Wealdstone	2-2
Brentford v Dagenham	2-1
Waterlooville v Northampton Town	1-1

Second Replays

Wealdstone v Enfield	2-0
Northampton Town v Waterlooville	2-0

SECOND ROUND PROPER

Rotherham United v Hull City	2-1
York City v Rochdale	0-2
Darlington v Altrincham	0-0
Bangor City v Blackpool	1-1
Bolton Wanderers v Mansfield Town	2-0
Lincoln City v Sheffield United	0-0
Wigan Athletic v Whitby Town	1-0
Scunthorpe United v Bury	2-0
Chesterfield v Burnley	2-2
Harrow Borough v Newport County	1-3
Colchester United v Wealdstone	4-0
Gillingham v Chelmsford City	6-1
Maidstone United v Worcester City	3-2
Windsor & Eton v AFC Bournemouth	0-0
Millwall v Swindon Town	2-3
Brentford v Wimbledon	3-2
Reading v Oxford United	1-1
Bristol Rovers v Bristol City	1-2
Plymouth Argyle v Barking	2-1
Northampton Town v Telford United	1-1

Replays

Altrincham v Darlington	0-2
Blackpool v Bangor City	2-1
Sheffield United v Lincoln City	1-0
Burnley v Chesterfield	3-2
AFC Bournemouth v Windsor & Eton	2-0
Oxford United v Reading	3-0
Telford United v Northampton Town	3-2

continued opposite

1983-84

THIRD ROUND (January 7)

*Luton	(2)3	
Watford	**(2)4**	
*Colchester	0	
Charlton	1	
*Brighton	2	
Swansea	0	
*Liverpool	4	
Newcastle	0	
*Bolton	0	
Sunderland	3	
*Sheffield Utd	(1)0	
Birmingham	(1)2	
*Crystal Palace	1	
Leicester	0	
*West Ham	1	
Wigan	0	
*Rotherham	(0)0	
WBA	(0)3	
*Leeds Utd	(1)(1)2	
Scunthorpe	(1)(1)4	
*Plymouth A.	(2)1	
Newport	(2)0	
*Darlington	4	
Maidstone U.	1	
*Cambridge U.	0	
Derby Co.	3	
*Rochdale	1	
Telford	4	
*Fulham	(0)0	
Tottenham	(0)2	
*Aston Villa	(1)0	
Norwich	(1)3	
*Huddersfield	2	
QPR	1	
*Notts County	(2)2	
Bristol City	(2)0	
*Middlesbrough	3	
Arsenal	2	
*Bournemouth	2	
Man United	0	
*Stoke City	0	
Everton	**2**	
*Gillingham	5	
Brentford	3	
*Shrewsbury	3	
Oldham	0	
*Cardiff City	0	
Ipswich T.	3	
*Burnley	(0)1	
Oxford U.	(0)2	
*Blackpool	2	
Man City	1	
*Sheff Wed.	1	
Barnsley	0	
*Coventry	(1)(1)3	
Wolves	(1)(1)0	
*Carlisle	(1)1	
Swindon	(1)3	
*Blackburn	1	
Chelsea	0	
*Portsmouth	2	
Grimsby	1	
*Nott'm Forest	1	
Southampton	2	

FOURTH ROUND (January 28)

Watford	**2**
*Charlton	0
*Brighton	2
Liverpool	0
*Sunderland	1
Birmingham	2
*Crystal Palace	(1)0
West Ham	(1)2
*WBA	1
Scunthorpe	0
*Plymouth A.	2
Darlington	1
*Derby Co.	3
Telford	2
*Tottenham	(0)1
Norwich	(0)2
*Huddersfield	1
Notts County	2
*Middlesbrough	2
Bournemouth	0
***Everton**	**(0)(0)3**
Gillingham	(0)(0)0
*Shrewsbury	2
Ipswich T.	0
*Oxford U.	2
Blackpool	1
*Sheff Wed	3
Coventry	2
*Swindon	1
Blackburn	2
*Portsmouth	0
Southampton	1

FIFTH ROUND (February 18)

***Watford**	**3**
Brighton	1
*Birmingham	3
West Ham	0
*WBA	0
Plymouth A.	1
*Derby Co.	2
Norwich	1
*Notts County	1
Middlesbrough	0
***Everton**	**3**
Shrewsbury	0
*Oxford U.	0
Sheff Wed	3
*Blackburn	0
Southampton	1

SIXTH ROUND (March 10)

Watford	**3**
*Birmingham	1
*Plymouth A.	(0)1
Derby	(0)0
*Notts County	1
Everton	**2**
*Sheff Wed	(0)1
Southampton	(0)5

SEMI-FINALS (April 14)

Watford	**1**
Plymouth Arg.	0
(At Villa Park)	
Everton	**1**
Southampton	0
(At Highbury)	

FINAL (May 19)

WATFORD	**0**
EVERTON	**2**

(*Club drawn at home)

THE MILK CUP

First Leg

Bradford City	0	Sheffield United	1
Millwall	3	Northampton Town	0
Southend United	1	Wimbledon	0
Aldershot	3	Orient	1
Blackpool	2	Walsall	1
Bolton Wanderers	3	Chester*	0
Bournemouth	1	Bristol Rovers	2
Brentford	3	Charlton Athletic	0
Colchester United†	3	Reading	2
Crewe Alexandra	1	Burnley	0
Crystal Palace	3	Peterborough United*	0
Gillingham	1	Chelsea	2
Halifax Town	0	Darlington	1
Hull City	0	Lincoln City	0
Mansfield Town	1	Huddersfield Town	2
Middlesbrough	0	Chesterfield*	1
Newport County	2	Torquay United	3
Preston North End	1	Tranmere Rovers	0
Rochdale	0	Stockport County	3
Rotherham United	0	Hartlepool United	0
Scunthorpe United	1	Doncaster Rovers	1
Swindon Town	1	Plymouth Argyle	0
Wigan Athletic	1	Bury	1
York City	2	Grimsby Town	1
Exeter City	2	Cardiff City	3
Hereford United	3	Portsmouth	2
Oxford United	1	Bristol City	1
Port Vale	3	Wrexham	1

Second Leg

Sheffield United	1	Bradford City	1
Northampton Town	1	Millwall	2
Wimbledon	6	Southend United	4
Orient	3	Aldershot	3
Walsall	3	Blackpool	1
Chester*	3	Bolton Wanderers	0
Bristol Rovers	2	Bournemouth	2
Charlton Athletic	2	Brentford	1
Reading	4	Colchester United†	3
Burnley	3	Crewe Alexandra	4
Peterborough United*	3	Crystal Palace	0
Chelsea	4	Gillingham	0
Darlington	3	Halifax Town	2
Lincoln City	3	Hull City	1
Huddersfield Town	5	Mansfield Town	1
Chesterfield*	0	Middlesbrough	1
Torquay United	1	Newport County	0
Tranmere Rovers	0	Preston North End	0
Stockport County	2	Rochdale	2
Hartlepool United	0	Rotherham United	1
Doncaster Rovers	3	Scunthorpe United	0
Plymouth Argyle	4	Swindon Town	1
Bury	2	Wigan Athletic	0
Grimsby Town	2	York City	0
Cardiff City	2	Exeter City	1
Portsmouth	3	Hereford United	1
Bristol City	0	Oxford United	1
Wrexham	1	Port Vale	5

† won on away goals
* won on penalty shoot-out

1983-84

SECOND ROUND

Team	Score	Opponent	Score
Liverpool	**4:4**	*Brentford	1:0
Fulham	3:3	*Doncaster	1:1
Birmingham	3:4	*Derby C.	0:0
Notts County	4:4	*Aldershot	2:1
*Sheffield Wed	3:4	Darlington	0:2
Preston N.E.	3:1	*Wolves	2:0
*Stoke City	0:2	Peterborough	0:1
*Huddersfield	2:2	Watford	1:2
*Walsall	1:2	Barnsley	0:0
*Shrewsbury	2:2	Sheffield United	1:2
Arsenal	1:1	*Plymouth	1:0
*Tottenham	3:1	Lincoln	1:2
*Rotherham	2:2	Luton Town	3:0
Southampton	0:3	*Carlisle Utd	2:0
*Wimbledon	2:1	Nott'm. Forest	0:1
Oldham Ath.	2:2	*Stockport Co.	0:2
Aston Villa	2:3	*Portsmouth	2:2
Manchester C.	0:6	*Torquay	0:0
WBA	0:5	*Millwall	3:1
†Chelsea	2:0	*Leicester City	0:2
Norwich City	0:3	*Cardiff City	0:0
Sunderland	3:4	*Cambridge	2:3
*Ipswich Town	4:2	Blackburn R.	3:1
*QPR	8:0	Crewe Alex.	0:3
Oxford Utd.	1:2	*Newcastle Utd.	1:1
*Leeds United	0:4	Chester	1:1
Manchester Utd.	1:2	*Port Vale	0:0
Colchester	1:1	*Swansea	1:0
West Ham	2:10	*Bury	1:0
*Brighton	4:1	Bristol Rovers	2:2
Coventry	0:2	*Grimsby	0:1
Everton	**1:2**	*Chesterfield	0:2

THIRD ROUND

Team	Score	Opponent	Score
Liverpool	**1:1:1**	*Fulham	1:1:0A
*Birmingham	2:0:0:3	Notts C.	2:0:0:1B
Sheffield Wed	2	*Preston N.E.	0
*Stoke City	0:2	Huddersfield	0:0
*Walsall	2	Shrewsbury	1
Arsenal	2	*Tottenham	1
*Rotherham	2	Southampton	1
*Wimbledon	3	Oldham	1
*Aston Villa	3	Manchester C.	0
WBA	1	*Chelsea	0
*Norwich City	0:2	Sunderland	0:1
*Ipswich Town	3	QPR	2
Oxford United	1:4	*Leeds United	1:1
Manchester United	2	*Colchester	0
*West Ham	1	Brighton	0
Coventry	1	***Everton**	**2**

FOURTH ROUND

Team	Score	Opponent	Score
Liverpool	**1:3**	*Birmingham	1:0
Sheffield Wed.	1	*Stoke City	0
Walsall	2	*Arsenal	1
*Rotherham	1	Wimbledon	0
Aston Villa	2	*WBA	1
Norwich City	1	*Ipswich Town	0
*Oxford Utd	1:1:2	Manchester U.	1:1:1C
*West Ham	2:0	**Everton**	**2:2**

FIFTH ROUND

Team	Score	Opponent	Score
Liverpool	**2:3**	*Sheffield Wed	2:0
Walsall	4	*Rotherham	2
Aston Villa	2	*Norwich City	0
*Oxford United	1:1	**Everton**	**1:4**

SEMI-FINAL

Team	Score	Opponent	Score
***Liverpool**	**2:2**	Walsall	2:0
Aston Villa	0:1	***Everton**	**2:0**

FINAL

LIVERPOOL	**0:1**
EVERTON	**0:0**

*Denotes club drawn at home. †won 4-3 on penalties. A—Third match at Fulham. B—Third match at Birmingham, Fourth at Notts County. C—Third match at Oxford.

INTRODUCTION TO CLUB PAGES

Page One Basic reviews of the 1983-4 season are featured and as some have been submitted by club statisticians, styles should vary. Club 'personalities' have been sent to us by club officials and there is no order of 'seniority' intended. The team photos are of this season's squads.

Pages Two and Three Match details are given for each club's full season, including cup-ties. Clubs who enjoyed outstanding cup seasons are given special features of their own. Players who were 'ever present' in their League programme in 1983-4 have their **42** or **46** totals in bold type. Players sent off in a match have † by their position number. Players who represent clubs while on loan have (L) behind their name.

Page Four Players' details include League, Milk Cup, F.A. Cup and, for Division One and Two clubs, European appearances and goals, while players in Division Three and Four have details of their Associate Members' Cup matches.

Honours won by players are shown by the following examples: Div. 1 80 means Division One Championship 1979-80; FAC — F.A. Cup winners; Lg.C — League Cup winners; EC — European Cup winners; ECWC — European Cup Winners Cup winners; ES — European Super Cup winners; EF — European Fairs Cup winners; SPD — Scottish Premier Division champions; S DIV 1 — Scottish Division One champions; etc. International honours for England (E), Scotland (S), Northern Ireland (NI), Wales (W), Eire (E) and overseas countries are shown thus: E (10) B(2) U21 (2) Y,S. This indicates that the player has won ten full caps, made two 'B' international appearances, two for the Under 21 team and was a Youth and Schoolboy International.

Other initials used are A.S. for Anglo-Scottish; Tex for Texaco; D for Dryborough Cup; FAYC for FA Youth Cup.

Other symbols on this page are † for Player of The Year 1983-4 and * for Club Captain 1984-5.

Page Five Photos of this season's club programmes are included with basic details. Club facts and figures will become increasingly comprehensive as years go by.

Page Six Ground details are self explicit, but we will be pleased to receive photos of League Grounds taken by readers for possible publication in future.

KEY TO GROUND PLANS

- Open Terrace
- Covered Terrace
- Open Seats
- Covered Seats
- Turnstile
- Main Entrance/Exit
- PE Players'/Officials' Entrance
- PR Press Entrance
- RLY Railway

SUPPORTERS' CLUBS

Details of supporters' clubs may be obtained from

Malcolm Gamlen
National Federation of Football Supporters' Clubs
69 Fourth Avenue
CHELMSFORD
Essex
Tel: 0245-63305

and for **Provincial Football Supporters' Clubs in London:**

Rupert Metcalf
Press and Publicity Officer
A.P.F.S.C.I.L.
1a Gordon Road
Ealing
London W5 2AD
Tel: 01-998 1676 (H); 01-328 5641 (W)

ALDERSHOT Division 4

Chairman
RJ Driver

Directors
FG Wiltshire
Major A Dobson, MBE
T Lewis
RR Potter
R Clifford
A English

Secretary/Commercial Manager
THC Green, FAAI (0252 20211)

Manager
Len Walker

Coach
Ian Gillard

Physiotherapist
J Lange

Trainer
J Anderson

Seven new faces appeared in the Aldershot line-up that opened the new season in August, with a further two making their debut the following Saturday. All were free transfers – reflecting the financial problems being experienced by many clubs.

Early season form at home was disappointing, but progress was made in the Milk Cup with a 6-3 aggregate win over Third Division high-flyers Orient before bowing to First Division Notts County in the second round. Away results were more encouraging at the beginning, but this run was spoilt with three fruitless journeys up the M1 in October – the only bright spot in between being a home victory over table toppers Bristol City.

Teenage goalkeeper David Coles played a significant part in a seventeen match unbeaten home run in the league which stretched from September until the middle of April. Several outstanding performances earned him the club 'Player of the Year' award.

November brought success in league games with four consecutive wins and a rapid climb to fifth position. However, the team came crashing down to earth in the FA Cup losing to non-league Worcester City in a replay.

After two poor results at the beginning of December Dale Banton scored the goal that secured the points at Darlington despite being involved in a car crash the previous day. A Boxing Day clash with local rivals Reading was notable for attracting the biggest league crowd to Aldershot for 3½ years and not for the goalless draw it produced. The Club's 2000th league match ended in a 4-1 defeat at Colchester and, despite ending the year on a winning note, worse was to come in the pouring rain at Blackpool with the home side scoring five without reply just two days into 1984.

Seven successive home wins saw Aldershot remain amongst the leaders while other promotion candidates began to fade away. February saw Aldershot score eighteen goals in five games and this included a 7-1 thrashing of Mansfield Town with the ever improving Glen Burvill scoring four.

Les Lawrence emulated this feat against Chester after vital midweek away wins had been secured at Northampton and Peterborough.

Five defeats in the remaining twelve matches saw the promotion dream fade away for yet another season although a final placing of fifth was a vast improvement on the previous year (18th) and a creditable achievement for Len Walker and his skeleton squad.

Patrick Worrall
The League Directory's Statistician for the Club

Back Row: G. Mazzon, P. Foley, C. Day, D. Coles, I. Gillard (Coach), D. Banton, D. Souter. **Front Row:** J. Anderson (Trainer), A. Massey, I. McDonald, P. Shrubb, G. Peters, G. Burvill, M. Foyle, C. Fielder, L. Walker (Manager).

'THE SHOTS'

Formed: 1926 **Turned Professional:** 1927 **Ltd Co:** 1927
Previous Managers: 1932-7 Angus Seed 1937-49 Bill McCracken 1950-5: Gordon Clark 1955-9 Harry Evans 1959-67 Dave Smith 1967-8 Tom McAnearney 1968 Dick Connor 1968-72 Jimmy Melia 1972 Cliff Huxford 1972-81 Tom McAnearney
Honours: None
League Career: Elected to Division 3 (South) 1932 Joined Division 4 1958 Promoted to Division 3 1972-3 Relegated to Division 4 1975-6
Colours: Red and blue striped shirts, blue trim on collar and cuffs, blue shorts, red stockings with two blue hoops
Change Colours: White shirt, red trim on collar and cuffs, white shorts with blue stripe, white stockings with two blue hoops

CLUB RECORDS

Most Appearances for Club: Murray Brodie: Football League 461 + F.A. Cup 32 + 18 League Cup **Total 511**
Most Capped Player: Peter Scott, 1, Northern Ireland **For England:** None
Record Goalscorer in a Match: Harry Brooks, 5 v Reading (7-3, F.A. Cup) 24.11.45
Harry Brooks, 5 v Newport (I.O.W.) (7-0, F.A. Cup) 08.12.45 Charlie Mortimore, 5 v Orient (Div 3S) (A, 7-2) 25.02.50
Dale Banton, 5 v Halifax Town (Div 4) 07.05.83
Tommy Lawton scored 6 on two occasions for Aldershot in Football League South games during the war
Record League Goalscorer in a season: John Dungworth, 26, Div 4, 1978-9 **In All Competitions:** John Dungworth, 34 (League 26, F.A. Cup 8), 1978-9
Record League Goalscorer in a career: Jack Howarth, 171, 1965-71, 1972-7 **In All Competitions:** Jack Howarth, 196 (League 171, F.A. Cup 19, League Cup 6), 1965-71
Record Transfer Fee Received: £100,000 from Shrewsbury Town for John Dungworth, Nov 1979
Record Transfer Fee Paid: £54,000 to Portsmouth for Colin Garwood, Feb 1980
Best Performances: League: 8th Div 3 1973-4 **F.A. Cup:** 5th Round Replay **League/Milk Cup:** Never past 2nd Round
Most League Points: 75 in Div 4, 1983-4
Record League Victory: 8-1 v Gateshead, Div 4, 13 Sept 1958
Record League Defeat: 0-9 v Bristol City, Div 3 South, 28 Dec 1946
Club Statistician for the Directory: Patrick Worrall

Programme Editor
T.H.C. Green

Price	Number of Pages
40p	16

Subscriptions
£14.00 per season for home matches (postage included)

ALDERSHOT

PLAYERS NAME Ht Wt Birthdate	Honours	Birthplace Transfers	Clubs	APPEARANCES League	Milk Cup	F.A.C.	A.M.C.	GOALS League	Milk Cup	F.A.C.	A.M.C.
GOALKEEPERS											
David Coles†		Wandsworth	Birmingham C. (A)								
5-10 12.0 15.6.64		F	Mansfield T.	3							
		F	Aldershot	45	4	2	1				
DEFENDERS											
Ian Gillard	E.(3), U.23(5)	Hammersmith	Q.P.R. (A)	403+5	32	36	8E	9	1	1	
6-0 13.5 9.10.50		F	Aldershot	65	4	2		2			
Georgio Mazzon		Cheshunt	Tottenham H.	3+1	+2	1					
5-10 11.9 4.9.60		F	Aldershot	45	4	2	1	3			
Don Souter		Hammersmith	Ipswich T. (A)								
5-11 11.8 1.12.61		F	Barnsley	19+2	4						
		F	Aldershot	39	3	2					
Gary Peters*		Carshalton	Aldershot (A)								
5-11 11.12 3.8.54		F	Reading	150+6	15	9+1		7			
		F	Fulham	57+4	4	4		5			
		F	Wimbledon	83	2		1	4			1
MIDFIELD											
Glen Burvill	FAYC 81	Camden Town	West Ham Utd. (A)								
5-9 10.10 26.10.62		F	Aldershot	33+5	1+1			12	1		
Clive Day		Orsett	Fulham (A)	2+8							
5-11 12.9 27.1.61			Mansfield T. (L)	10+2	2	2					
		F	Aldershot	28+3	3		1		1		
Ian McDonald	Div. 3. 77	Barrow	Barrow (A)	30+5	1	2		2			
5-9 11.9 10.5.53		£3,000	Workington	42	2	1		4	1		
		£35,000	Liverpool								
			Colchester U. (L)	5				2			
		£19,000	Mansfield T.	47+9	6+1	6		4	3	1	
		F	York C.	175	9	11		29	1	1	
		F	Aldershot	123	6	8	1	19	2		
Andy Massey	E. I. Y. AM	London	Millwall	73+15	2+1	8		8		1	
5-10 10.9 20.10.61			Port Vale (L)	4				1			
		Player Exchange	Aldershot								
Paul Shrubb		Guildford	Fulham (A)	1							
5-8 10.8 1.8.55		F	Hellenic								
		F	Brentford	170+12	9	6+1		8			
		F	Aldershot	66+6	4	3+1	1	1			
FORWARDS											
Dale Banton		Kensington	West Ham Utd. (A)	2+3	1						
5-10 10.5 15.5.61			Aldershot	90+1	6	5	1	43	4	4	
Peter Foley	Ei. Y	Bicester	Oxford U. (A)	262+15	26	13		70	8	9	
5-11 11.12 10.9.56			Gillingham (L)	5							
			Hong Kong								
			Aldershot								
Martin Foyle		Salisbury	Southampton	6+6	0+2			1	2		
5-10 11.2 2.5.62		£10,000	Aldershot								

NON-CONTRACT PLAYERS 1984-85

Mark Brown **Colin Fielder** (4+5) **Doug Hatcher** (1 Lg+1 AMC) **Gary McFarlane**

ALDERSHOT

DIVISION FOUR 5TH **FA CUP** 1ST ROUND **MILK CUP** 2ND ROUND

MATCH	DATE	COMPETITION	VENUE	OPPONENTS	RESULT	HALF TIME	L'GUE POS'N	GOALSCORERS	ATTENDANCE
1	A 27	CL	H	Hereford U	L1-4	0-2		Lawrence	2,001
2	**30**	**MC 1**	**H**	**Orient**	**W3-2**	**2-1**		**Banton 2, Burvill**	**1,978**
3	S 3	CL	A	Hartlepool U	W1-0	0-0	15	Banton	1,831
4	6	CL	A	Crewe Alex	D0-0	0-0			2,039
5	10	CL	H	Bury	L1-2	1-1	18	Lucas	1,908
6	**12**	**MC 1**	**A**	**Orient**	**D3-3**	**2-1**		**Lawrence 2, Lucas**	**2,236**
7	17	CL	A	Torquay U	W1-0	0-0	13	Banton	1,812
8	24	CL	H	Wrexham	D1-1	1-1	14	McDonald	2,007
9	27	CL	H	Swindon T	W2-1	2-1		Banton, McDonald (pen)	2,644
10	O 1	CL	A	Mansfield T	L2-5	1-2	13	Banton, Lucas	1,836
11	**4**	**MC 2**	**H**	**Notts Co**	**L2-4**	**1-1**		**Day, McDonald**	**4,458**
12	8	CL	H	Tranmere R	D1-1	1-0	14	McDonald (pen)	1,769
13	15	CL	A	Doncaster R	L1-3	0-1	19	Banton	2,299
14	17	CL	A	Stockport Co	D2-2	0-0		Lawrence, Lucas	1,935
15	22	CL	H	Bristol C	W1-0	1-0	17	Lawrence	3,195
16	**25**	**MC 2**	**A**	**Notts Co**	**L1-4**	**0-2**		**McDonald (pen)**	**3,439**
17	29	CL	A	Halifax T	L0-1	0-1	17		1,242
18	N 1	CL	H	Northampton T	W1-0	0-0		Gage (og)	1,711
19	5	CL	H	Peterborough U	W3-2	2-1	8	Banton, Lucas, Lawrence	1,856
20	12	CL	A	Chester C	W2-1	2-0	6	Banton, Lawrence	975
21	**19**	**FAC 1**	**H**	**Worcester C**	**D1-1**	**1-1**		**Burvill**	**3,553**
22	**21**	**FAC 1R**	**A**	**Worcester C**	**L1-2**	**1-1**		**Banton**	**5,353**
23	26	CL	H	Rochdale	W2-1	0-0	5	Burvill, Mazzon	1,686
24	D 3	CL	A	York C	L0-2	0-1	8		3,951
25	10	CL	H	Stockport Co	D1-1	0-1	7	Burvill	1,349
26	17	CL	A	Darlington	W1-0	0-0	6	Banton	1,273
27	26	CL	H	Reading	D0-0	0-0	8		6,270
28	27	CL	A	Colchester U	L1-4	1-3	10	McDonald	3,123
29	31	CL	H	Chesterfield	W2-1	2-1	8	Lawrence, Briley	1,899
30	J 2	CL	A	Blackpool	L0-5	0-2	9		3,193
31	7	CL	H	Hartlepool	W2-1	0-1	5	Banton, Lawrence	1,637
32	14	CL	A	Hereford U	L1-2	1-1	7	Burvill	2,008
33	21	CL	H	Torquay U	W3-1	1-0		Burvill, Banton 2	1,543
34	F 4	CL	H	Mansfield T	W7-1	4-0	6	Burvill 4, Lawrence, McDonald (pen),	
								Nicholson (og)	1,629
35	11	CL	A	Wrexham	D1-1	1-1	6	McDonald	1,898
36	14	CL	A	Northampton T	W4-1	3-1	4	Banton 2, Lawrence, Burvill	1,573
37	18	CL	H	Halifax T	W5-2	4-1	4	Banton 2, Lawrence 2, McDonald (pen)	2,382
38	**21**	**AMC 1**	**A**	**AFC Bournemouth**	**L0-4**	**0-0**			**1,706**
39	25	CL	A	Bristol C	L1-2	1-2	5	Lawrence	6,849
40	M 7	CL	A	Peterborough U	W2-1	0-0		McDonald (pen), Mazzon	3,568
41	10	CL	H	Chester C	W5-2	3-0	4	Lawrence 4, McDonald (pen)	2,879
42	17	CL	A	Tranmere R	L0-3	0-2	5		1,761
43	24	CL	H	Doncaster R	W2-1	2-1	5	Lawrence 2	3,636
44	31	CL	H	Crewe Alex	D0-0	0-0	5		2,865
45	A 7	CL	A	Swindon T	W2-0	0-0	5	Bailie (og), Lawrence	2,834
46	14	CL	H	York C	L1-4	0-1	5	McDonald (pen)	5,071
47	21	CL	A	Reading	L0-1	0-0	5		7,645
48	23	CL	H	Colchester U	W5-1	3-1	5	Burvill, Lawrence, Banton 2, Lucas	2,446
49	28	CL	A	Rochdale	L1-3	1-2	5	Banton	970
50	M 1	CL	A	Bury	W3-0	1-0		Lawrence, Banton, Burvill	1,231
51	5	CL	H	Blackpool	W3-2	1-1	5	Burvill, Mazzon, Lawrence	2,936
52	7	CL	A	Chesterfield	L1-3	0-1	5	McDonald	1,991
53	12	CL	H	Darlington	D0-0	0-0	5		1,798
								Av Home Att	**2,483**

Goal Scorers

League (76): Lawrence 22, Banton 19, Burvill 12, McDonald 11 (7 pens), Lucas 5, Mazzon 3, Briley 1, opponents 3
FA Cup (2): Banton 1, Burvill 1
Milk Cup (9): Banton 2, Lawrence 2, McDonald 2 (1 pen), Burvill 1, Day 1, Lucas 1
AMC (-): —

1983-84

Hatcher	Fielder	Gillard	Burvill	Ampofo	Souter	Day	Banton	Lawrence	McDonald	O'Sullivan	Lucas	Coles	Shrubb	Mazzon	Briley	Jopling	Wooler	Compton	Berry **(L)**	REFEREE	
1	2*	3	4	5	6	7	8	9	10	11	12									A Moules	1
		3	**12**		**6**	**2**	**8**	**9***	**10**	**11**	**7**	**1**		**5**	**4**					**A Crickmore**	**2**
		3	9		6	2	8		10	11	7	1	4	5						I Hendrick	3
		3	9		5	2	8		10	11	7	1		6	4					A Challinor	4
		3	9*		5	2	8		10	11	7	1	12	6	4					A Gunn	5
		3			**5**	**2**	**8**	**9**	**10**	**11**	**7**	**1**		**6**	**4**					**K Baker**	**6**
		3*	12		5	2	8	9	10	11	7	1		6	4					B Stevens	7
		3*	12		5	2	8	9	10	11	7	1		6	4					D Vickers	8
					5	2	8	9	10	11	7	1	3	6	4					M Taylor	9
			9		5	2*	8		10	11	7	1	3	6	4	12				N Midgley	10
					5	**2**	**8**	**9**	**10**	**11**	**7**	**1**	**3**	**6**	**4**					**E Read**	**11**
					5	2	8	9	10	11	7	1	3	6	4					E Scales	12
			11	5			8	9	10		7	1	3	2	4	6				T Jones	13
			11	5		12	8	9	10		7	1	2	3	4*	6				D Hutchinson	14
			11	5			8	9	10	12	7	1	2	3	4*	6				D Axcell	15
			4				**8**	**9**	**10**	**11**	**7**	**1**	**2**	**3**		**6**	**5**			**D Shaw**	**16**
			9			4	8		10	11	7	1	2	3		6	5†			N Glover	17
			4			2	8	9	10		7	1	3	11		6	5			D Hedges	18
			4			2	8	9	10	11	7	1		3			6	5		M Bodenham	19
	2		4			3	8	9	10	11	7	1		6				5		C Thomas	20
			11		**6**	**2**	**8**	**9**	**10**	**12**	**7**	**1**		**3***	**4**			**5**		**M Taylor**	**21**
					6	**2**	**8**	**9**	**10**	**11**	**7**	**1**	**12**	**4**			**3***	**5**		**M Taylor**	**22**
			12		6*	2	8	9	10		7	1	11	4			3	5		M Dimblebee	23
			11		6	2	8	9†	10			1		7	4		3	5		D Scott	24
			7		6	2	8	9	10			1		11	4		3	5		J Ashworth	25
			7		6	2	8		10			1	9	11	4		3	5		C Seel	26
					6	2	8		10	11		1	7	9	4		3	5		C Downey	27
					6	2	8	9	10			1	7	11	4		3	5		J Bray	28
			7		6*		8	9	10		11	1	12	2	4		3	5		T Ward	29
			7		6		8	9	10		11*	1	12	2	4		3	5		M Heath	30
			12		6	2	8	9	10		7	1		11	4		3*	5		R Milford	31
			4		6	2	8	9	10		7	1	3	11*		12		5		V Callow	32
		3	7		6		8	9	10			1	2	11	4			5		K Salmon	33
		3	7		6	12	8	9	10			1	2	11	4*	5				K Cooper	34
		3	7		5		8	9	10			1	2	11	4	6				R Guy	35
		3	7		5		8	9	10			1	2	11	4	6				J Lovatt	36
		3	7		5		8	9	10			1	2	11	4	6				E Scales	37
	12					**3**	**8**	**9**	**10**		**7**	**1**	**2***	**11**	**4**	**6**	**5**			**B Stevens**	**38**
		3	7		5		8	9	10			1	2	11	4	6				L Shapter	39
		3	7		5		8	9	10			1	2	11	4	6				P Tyldesley	40
		3	7		5		8	9	10			1	2	11	4	6				B Hill	41
		3	7		5	12	8	9	10			1	2	11	4	6*				K Walmsley	42
		3			5	2	8	9	10			1	4	11		6			7	J Moules	43
		3			5	2	8	9	10		12	1		11	4	6			7*	D Vickers	44
		3			5	2	8	9	10			1		11	4	6			7	H King	45
		3	12		5	2	8	9	10			1		11	4	6			7*	D Axcell	46
		3			5	2	8	9	10			1		11	4	6			7	M Robinson	47
		3	7		5	2	8	9	10		12	1	4	11		6				K Barratt	48
		3	7*		5	2	8	9	10			1	12	11	4	6				F Roberts	49
		3	7		5		8	9	10			1	2	11	4	6				D Owen	50
		3	7		5		8	9	10			1	2	11*	4	6			12	D Brazier	51
		3	7		5		8	9	10			1	2	11	4	6				A Robinson	52
		3	7*		5		8	9	10			1	2	11	4	6			12	K Baker	53
1	2	26	33	4	39	28	**46**	39	**46**	13	20	45	29	45	36	24	12	13	5	League Appearances	
			+5S			+3S				+1S	+3S		+4S			+2S			+2S		
			1		2	2	2	2	2	1+1S	2	2	1S	2	1				1	FA Cup Appearances	
	2		1+1S		3	3	4	4	4	4	4	4	2	4	3		1	1		Milk Cup Appearances	
	1S					1	1	1	1		1	1	1	1	1		1	1		AM Cup Appearances	

RECREATION GROUND

Official Address: Recreation Ground, High Street, Aldershot GU11 1TW. Telephone (0252) 20211

Ground Capacity: 16,000 (14,000 under cover)

Record Attendance: 19,138 v. Carlisle United, F.A Cup 4th Round Replay, 28 Jan 1970

Record Receipts: £11,850 v. Shrewsbury Town, F.A. Cup 5th Round, 20 Feb 1979

Size of Playing Area: 117yds × 76 yds

Season Tickets: Stand: £52.50/£57.20, Ground: £39.50 (£17.50 juveniles/OAP)

Executive Box Season Tickets: V.I.P. Club (Members only)

Cost of Stand Tickets: £2.80, £2.90, £3.00; **Terraces:** £2.25 (juveniles/OAPs)

Match and Ticket Information: Telephone ground two weeks before match

Car Parking: Within ¾ mile of ground

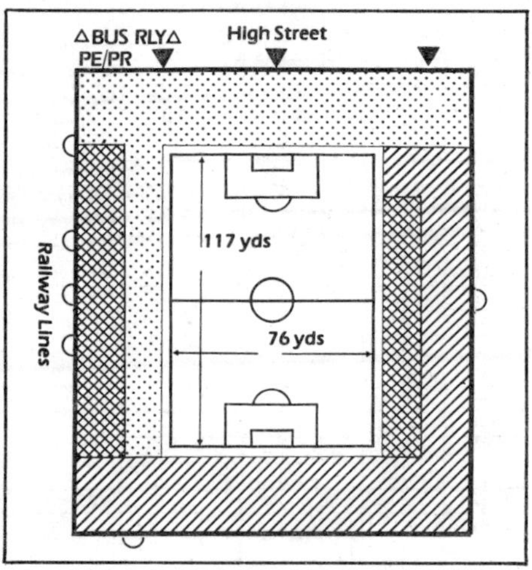

For key see page 12

How to get to the ground

From London: Leave M3 at junction 4, then follow signs Aldershot A325. In 5 miles at roundabout take 1st exit A323 into Wellington Avenue. In 0.8 miles at roundabout take 2nd exit into High Street for Recreation Ground (on left)
From East: From Guildford follow signs Aldershot and enter via A323 High Street for Recreation Ground (on right)
From South & West: From Farnham follow signs Farnborough A325. Then at roundabout take 2nd exit into Wellington Avenue A323. In 0.8 miles at roundabout take 2nd exit into High Street for Recreation Ground (on left)

ARSENAL Division 1

President
Sir Stanley Rous CBE

Chairman
P D Hill-Wood

Directors
Sir Robert Bellinger
S C McIntyre MBE, FCIS
A Wood
R G Gibbs
C E B L Carr
R C L Carr
D Dein

Secretary/Managing Director
K J Friar

Assistant Secretary
D Miles

Commercial Manager
A J Kelsey (01-226 9562)

Manager
D Howe

First Team Coach
R Burton

Reserve Team Coach
T Coleman

Youth Team Coach
P Rice

Chief Scout
S Burtenshaw

Physiotherapist
R Johnson

Groundsman
J Hosie

Amidst the euphoria of Charlie Nicholas's arrival from Celtic Arsenal started the season with the much publicised aim of introducing a new attacking style to satisfy the Highbury regulars.

A change in character of that magnitude is just not possible in a short time, however, and with the pressure building up on the young Scottish hero as every opponent gave him very special 'treatment' results just did not come and the fans applied their own brand of 'pressure' to Manager Terry Neill and the board of Directors.

To those not involved, it appeared that circumstances took control of the club and poor Terry Neill just could not prevent the wave of frustration sweeping him out. The defeat by Walsall in the Milk Cup was the last straw and Don Howe took over as the 'caretaker'. Some sound league results were not helped by an early FA Cup exit at Middlesbrough but the arrival of Tommy Caton and later Paul Mariner lifted morale throughout the club.

Indeed it was the arrogance and obvious happiness of Mariner plus the return from injury of Stewart Robson that helped 'The Gunners' to a comfortable run in at the end of the season and there is no doubt that Arsenal will once again fancy their chances to be the South's main contenders for all the domestic competitions again next season.

With a potentially strong international 'strike-force' there should be no problems encountered in scoring goals and the midfield with Charlie Nicholas given freedom to roam should also be very impressive. Last season there was considerable inconsistency at the back with some unforced errors in defence bringing some bad results. If these can be eliminated Arsenal could well be a real force from now onwards and trophies may return once more to Highbury. The club's loyal supporters deserve something in return for their steadfast and, on the whole, well-behaved backing for their favourites.

In these inflationary days it is good to record that the cost of watching 'The Gunners' remains most modest by modern standards. The various charges in fact represent very good value indeed. If the results improve the Highbury investment for any intending season-ticket holder will be most sound.

Back Row L to R: David Cork, Brian Talbot, Ian Allinson, Tony Woodcock, Colin Hill. **Middle Row:** Terry Burton (Coach), Paul Davis, Viv Anderson, John Lukic, Pat Jennings, Stewart Robson, Kenny Sansom, Roy Johnson (Physio). **Front Row:** Charlie Nicholas, Tommy Caton, Raphael Meade, Don Howe (Manager), David O'Leary, Graham Rix, Paul Mariner.

'THE GUNNERS'

Sponsored by
JVC

Formed: 1886 **Turned Professional:** 1891 **Ltd Co:** 1893
Previous Names: Royal Arsenal 1886-91, Woolwich Arsenal 1891-1914
Previous Managers: 1897-98 T B Mitchell 1898-99 Mr Ellcoat 1899-1904 H Bradshaw 1904-8 P Kelso 1908-15 G Morrell 1919-25 A L Knighton 1925-34 Herbert Chapman 1934-47 George Allison 1947-56 Tom Whittaker 1956-58 Bill Crayston 1958-62 George Swindon 1962-6 Billy Wright 1966-76 Bertie Mee 1976- Terry Neill
Honours: League Champions (8), F.A. Cup Winners (5), League + Cup 'Double' 1970-71, European Fairs Cup Winners
League Career: Elected to Division 2 1893 Promoted to Division 1 1904-13 Relegated to Division 2 1913 Promoted to Division 1 1919
Colours: Red shirts, white sleeves, shorts with red and white socks
Change Colours: Yellow shirts, blue shorts, yellow socks

CLUB RECORDS

Most Appearances for Club: George Armstrong: Football League 490 + 10 subs = 600, F.A. Cup 58 + 2 subs = 60, F.Lg/Milk Cup 35 = 35, European Cup 5 = 5, Fairs Cup 19 + 2 subs = 21 **Total 621**
Most Capped Player: Pat Rice, Northern Ireland 49 **For England:** Kenny Sansom 35
Record Goalscorer in a Match: Ted Drake, 7 v Aston Villa (A), Div 1, 7-1, 14.12.35
Record League Goalscorer in a season: Ted Drake, 42, Div 1, 1934-35 **All competitions:** Ted Drake, 42 League + 1 F.A. Cup = 43 (Season 1934-35)
Record League Goalscorer in a career: Cliff Bastin, 150, 1930-47 **In all competitions:** Cliff Bastin, 150 League + 26 F.A. Cup = 176 (Season 1929-46)
Record Transfer Fee Received: £1,250,000 from Crystal Palace for Clive Allen, Aug 80
Record Transfer Fee Paid: £1,250,000 to Queens Park Rangers for Clive Allen, June 80
Best Performances: League: Champions 1931, 1933, 1934, 1935, 1938, 1948, 1953, 1961 **F.A. Cup:** Winners 1930, 1936, 1950, 1971, 1979 **League/Milk Cup:** Runners-Up 1968, 1969
Most League Points: 71 in Div 1, 1981-2 **Most League Goals:** 127, Div 1, 1930-31
Record League Victory: 12-0 v Loughborough Town, Div 2, 12 March 1900
Record League Defeat: 0-8 v Loughborough Town, Div 2, 12 Dec 1896
European Competitions: European Cup 1971-72, European Cup Winners Cup 1979-80 (R-up), Fairs Cup 1963-64, 1969-70 (winners), 1970-71, U.E.F.A. Cup 1978-79, 1981-82, 1982-83
Club Statistician for the Directory: Joe Waters

Programme Editor
Kevin Connolly

Price	Number of Pages
50p	24

Subscriptions
Subscription price on application to club shop.

ARSENAL

PLAYERS NAME Ht Wt Birthdate	Honours	Birthplace Transfers	Clubs	APPEARANCES League	Milk Cup	F.A.C.	E. Cups	GOALS League	Milk Cup	F.A.C.	E. Cups
GOALKEEPERS											
Pat Jennings	N.I.(105). U.23(1)	Newry	Newry T.								
6-0 12.6 12.6.45	Y. UEFAC. 72	£30,000	Watford	48	1	3					
	FAC. 67. 79	£25,000	Tottenham H.	472	39	43	40				
	FC. 71. 73	£50,000	Arsenal	222	29	38	19				
John Lukic	E. U.21(7). Y	Chesterfield	Leeds U. (A)	146	7	9	3				
6-4 13.7 11.12.60		£70,000	Arsenal	4							
Rhys Wilmot	W. U.21(3)	Newport	Arsenal (A)								
6-1 12.0 21.2.61			Hereford U. (L)	9							
DEFENDERS											
Tony Adams	E.Y	Romford	Arsenal (A)	3							
6-2 12.0 10.10.66											
Viv Anderson	E.(11). B.(7).	Nottingham	Nottingham F. (A)	323 + 5	39	23 +	28	15	5	1	1
5-11 10.4 28.8.56	U.21(1). Div. 1. 78	£200,000	Arsenal								
	EC. 80. ESC. 79.										
	FC. 78										
Tommy Caton	E. U.21(14). Y. S	Kirby	Manchester C. (A)	164 + 1	21	12		8			
6-2 12.10 6.10.62			Arsenal	26		1					
David O'Leary	Ei.(28). FAC. 79	London	Arsenal (A)	308	37	38	20	9	1	1	
5-11 11.3 2.5.58											
Stewart Robson	E.U.21(1). Y	Billericay	Arsenal (A)	79	13	9	2	10	2		1
5-11 11.13 6.11.64											
Kenny Sansom	E.(44). B.(2).	Camberwell	Crystal Palace (A)	172	11	17		3		1	
5-6 11.8 26.9.58	U.21(8). Y. S.	£800,000	Arsenal	164	21	11	6	4			
	Div. 2. 79.										
	FAYC. 77										
MIDFIELD											
David Cork		Doncaster	Arsenal (A)	5 + 2		1		1			
5-9 11.8 28.10.62											
Paul Davis	E.U.21(6)	London	Arsenal (A)	118 + 8	14 + 2	7 + 1	3 + 1	10	2	2	2
5-8 9.7 9.12.61											
Colin Hill		Uxbridge	Arsenal (A)	44	4	1		1			
5-11 11.11 12.11.63											
Graham Rix*	E.(16). B.(3)	Doncaster	Arsenal (A)	262 + 5	33	37 +	21	34	1	4	1
5-9 11.0 23.7.53	U.21(7). FAC. 79										
Brian Talbot	E.(6). B.(8).	Ipswich	Ipswich T. (A)	177	12	23	15	25	1	3	3
5-10 12.0 21.7.53	U.21(1).	£450,000	Arsenal	208 + 5	23	17 + 1	15	30	1	2	
	FAC. 78. 79										
FORWARDS											
Ian Allinson		Hitchin	Colchester U. (A)	291 + 17	22 + 1	25 + 1		69	6	5	
5-10 11.0 1.10.57		F	Arsenal	7 + 2	1						
Brian McDermott	E. Y	Slough	Arsenal (A)	38 + 23	3 + 1	0 + 1	0 + 1	12			1
5-9 11.7 1.7.53			Fulham (L)	0 + 3							
Paul Mariner	E.(33). B.(7).	Bolton	Chorley								
6-0 12.2 22.5.53	UEFAC. 81.	£22,500	Plymouth A.	134 + 1	12	11		56	2	3	
	FAC. 78	£200,000 + P/E	Ipswich T.	260	20	28	27	97	8	19	12
		£150,000	Arsenal	15				7			
Raphael Meade		London	Arsenal (A)	19 + 14	3	1		11	1		
5-10 11.9 22.11.62.											
Charlie Nicholas	S.(8). U.21(6). Y. S	Glasgow	Celtic	68 + 3	15 +	8	8 + 1	48	22	7	5
5-10 11.10 30.12.61	SPD.(1). SLC.(1)	£750,000	Arsenal	41	4	1		11	1	1	
Tony Woodcock†	E.(35). B.(1).	Nottingham	Nottingham F. (A)	125 + 4	21	14	13	36	12	10	3
5-10 11.0 6.12.55	U.21(2).		Lincoln C. (L)	2 + 2				1			
	Lg.C. 78. 79.		Doncaster R. (L)	6				2			
	Div. 1. 78. EC. 79.	£650,000	Cologne	81				28			
	ESC. 79	£500,000	Arsenal	71	12	9	2	35	4	4	

CONTRACT PLAYERS WHO HAVE NO FIRST TEAM APPEARANCES: Caesar (D), **Campbell** (MF), **Hayes** (MF), **Isaacs** (MF), **Keown** (D), **Lee** (F), **Quinn** (F)

APPRENTICES: Gregg Allen, Jon Purdie, David Rocastle, Mike Thomas, Allan Caven, Paul Merson, David Sykes

NON-CONTRACT PLAYERS 1984-85: Donato Russo, John Say

ARSENAL

DIVISION ONE 60TH **FA CUP** 3RD ROUND **MILK CUP** 4TH ROUND

MATCH	DATE	COMPETITION	VENUE	OPPONENTS	RESULT	HALF TIME	L'GUE POS'N	GOALSCORERS	ATTENDANCE
1	A 27	CL	H	Luton T	W2-1	1-1		Woodcock, McDermott	39,348
2	29	CL	A	Wolverhampton W	W2-1	1-1		Nicholas 2 (1 pen)	18,671
3	S 3	CL	A	Southampton	L0-1	0-0	9		19,377
4	6	CL	H	Manchester U	L2-3	1-3		Woodcock, Talbot	42,704
5	10	CL	H	Liverpool	L0-2	0-1	12		41,896
6	17	CL	A	Notts Co	W4-0	2-0	11	Rix, Hunt (og), Talbot, Woodcock	10,217
7	24	CL	H	Norwich C	W3-0	1-0	8	Chapman, Sunderland 2	24,438
8	O 1	CL	A	QPR	L0-2	0-1	12		26,293
9	**4**	**MC 2**	**A**	**Plymouth Arg**	**D1-1**	**0-1**		**Rix**	**20,983**
10	15	CL	H	Coventry C	L0-1	0-0	14		20,290
11	22	CL	H	Nottingham F	W4-1	2-0	12	Sunderland, Hill, Woodcock 2	22,870
12	**25**	**MC 2**	**H**	**Plymouth Arg**	**W1-0**	**1-0**		**Sunderland**	**22,640**
13	29	CL	A	Aston Villa	W6-2	4-1	8	Woodcock 5, McDermott	23,678
14	N 5	CL	H	Sunderland	L1-2	0-1	12	Woodcock	26,064
15	**9**	**MC 3**	**A**	**Tottenham H**	**W2-1**	**1-0**		**Nicholas, Woodcock**	**48,200**
16	12	CL	A	Ipswich T	L0-1	0-0	13		21,652
17	19	CL	H	Everton	W2-1	2-1	11	Sunderland, Robson	24,338
18	26	CL	A	Leicester C	L0-3	0-2	13		14,777
19	**29**	**MC 4**	**H**	**Walsall**	**L1-2**	**1-0**		**Robson**	**22,406**
20	D 3	CL	H	WBA	L0-1	0-0	15		22,271
21	10	CL	A	West Ham U	L1-3	0-1	16	Whyte	25,118
22	17	CL	H	Watford	W3-1	1-0	12	Meade 3	25,104
23	26	CL	A	Tottenham H	W4-2	1-1	12	Nicholas 2, Meade 2	38,756
24	27	CL	H	Birmingham C	D1-1	0-0	12	Nicholas (pen)	25,642
25	31	CL	H	Southampton	D2-2	1-0	13	Cork, Nicholas (pen)	27,596
26	J 2	CL	A	Norwich C	D1-1	0-0	11	Woodcock	20,482
27	**7**	**FAC 3**	**A**	**Middlesbrough**	**L2-3**	**1-1**		**Woodcock, Nicholas**	**17,813**
28	10	CL	A	Luton T	W2-1	1-0	11	Sansom, Woodcock	16,320
29	21	CL	H	Notts Co	D1-1	1-0	11	Nicholas	20,110
30	28	CL	A	Stoke C	L0-1	0-0	11		12,840
31	F 4	CL	H	QPR	L0-2	0-0	11		31,014
32	11	CL	A	Liverpool	L1-2	1-1	14	Rix	34,642
33	18	CL	H	Aston Villa	D1-1	1-0	13	Rix	26,640
34	25	CL	A	Nottingham F	W1-0	0-0	13	Mariner	20,045
35	M 3	CL	A	Sunderland	W2-2	1-1	12	Nicholas (pen), Woodcock	15,370
36	10	CL	H	Ipswich T	W4-1	1-0	8	Mariner 2, Talbot, Woodcock	24,000
37	17	CL	A	Manchester U	L0-4	0-2	12		48,942
38	24	CL	H	Wolverhampton W	W4-1	2-0	11	Woodcock, Rix, Nicholas (pen), Robson	18,612
39	31	CL	A	Coventry C	W4-1	1-1	8	Whyte, Robson, Talbot, Mariner	10,550
40	A 7	CL	H	Stoke C	W3-1	0-0	7	Nicholas, Mariner, Woodcock	21,211
41	9	CL	A	Everton	D0-0	0-0			21,174
42	21	CL	H	Tottenham H	W3-2	1-0	8	Robson, Nicholas, Woodcock	48,831
43	23	CL	A	Birmingham C	D1-1	1-0	8	Woodcock	11,164
44	28	CL	H	Leicester C	W2-1	0-0	6	Woodcock, Davis	24,143
45	M 5	CL	A	WBA	W3-1	2-1	6	Talbot, Mariner, Robson	13,566
46	7	CL	H	West Ham U	D3-3	2-3	6	Talbot, Woodcock, Mariner	33,347
47	12	CL	A	Watford	L1-2	1-1	6	Robson	22,007
								Av Home Att	**28,139**

Goal Scorers

League (74): Woodcock 21, Nicholas 11 (5 pens), Mariner 7, Robson 6, Talbot 6, Meade 5, Rix 4, Sunderland 4, McDermott 2, Whyte 2, Chapman 1, Cork 1, Davis 1, Hill 1, Sansom 1, opponent 1
FA Cup (2): Nicholas 1, Woodcock 1
Milk Cup (5): Nicholas 1, Rix 1, Robson 1, Sunderland 1, Woodcock 1

1983-84

Jennings	Robson	Sansom	Talbot	O'Leary	Hill	McDermott	Davis	Nicholas, C	Woodcock	Rix	Sunderland	Whyte	Chapman	Adams	Gorman	Meade	Kay	Caton	Madden	Allinson	Cork	Mariner	Sparrow	Lukic	REFEREE	
1	2	3	4	5	6	7	8	9	10	11															J Martin	1
1	2	3	4	5	6	7	8	9	10	11															A Challinor	2
1	2	3	4	5	6	7*	8	9	10	11		12													G Napthine	3
1	2	3	4	5	6	7*	8	9	10	11	12														H Bodenham	4
1	2	3	4	5	6		8	10	9	11	7														A Seville	5
1	2	3	12	6	7		4	10*	9	11	8	5													K Redfern	6
1	2	3		5	6	12	8	10*		11	7	4	9												H Taylor	7
1	2	3		5	6		7	10		11	8	4	9												LC Shapter	8
1	**2**	**3**	**12**	**5**	**6**		**8**	**10**	**9***	**11**	**7**	**4**													**T Spencer**	**9**
1	2	3		5	6	12	8	10		11	7	4*	9												A Gunn	10
1	2	3		5	6	12	8	10*	9	11	7	4													K Cooper	11
1	**2**	**3**		**5**	**6**		**8**	**10**	**9**	**11**	**7**	**4**													**Alan Robinson**	**12**
1	2	3		5	6	12	7	11	9	10	8	4													A Robinson	13
1	2	3	8		6	12		10	9	7*	4			5											D Hedges	14
1	**2**	**3**		**5**	**6**		**8**	**10**	**9**	**11**	**7**	**4**													**K Hackett**	**15**
1	2	3		5	6		8	10	9	11	7*	4			12										K Baker	16
1	2	3		5	6	9		10		11	7*	4			8	12									J Bray	17
1	2	3		5			8	10	9	11*	7	4	12				6								R Guy	18
1	**2**	**3**		**5**	**6**		**8**	**10**	**9**		**7**	**4**								**11**					**L Burden**	**19**
1	2	3*			6		8	10	9					5		12		4	7	11					T Bone	20
1		3			2*		8	10	9			5				12	4†	6	7	11					E Read	21
1		3			2		8	10	9			5				7		6		11	4				C Thomas	22
1	4*	3		5	2		8	10	9							7		6		11	12				R Lewis	23
1		3			2	12	8	10	9			5				7		6*		11	4				M James	24
1		3		5	2		8	10	9							7		6		11	4				M Scott	25
1		3		5	2		8	10	9							7		6		11	4				T Holbrook	26
1		**3**	**12**	**5**	**2**		**8**	**10**	**9**	**11**						**7**		**6**			**4***				**M Heath**	**27**
1		3	4	5			8	10	9	11						7	2	6							K Hackett	28
1		3	4			12	8	10	9	11				5*		7	2	6							A Crickmore	29
1		3	4	5		7	8	10	9	11							2	6							K Walmsley	30
1		3	4	5			8	10	9	11						7*	2	6			12				B Hill	31
1		3	4	5	2		8	10	9	11								6		12	7*				C Seel	32
1		3	4	5	2		8	10	9	11								6				7			M Taylor	33
1		3	4	5	2		7	8	10	11								6				9			D Owen	34
1		3	4	5	2		7	8	10	11								6				9			R Dilkes	35
1		3	4	5	2		7	8	10	11*								6		12		9			Alan Robinson	36
1	7	3	4	5†	2			8	10	11								6				9			G Courtney	37
1	7	3	4	5	2			8	10	11								6				9			D Axcell	38
1*	7		4	5	2			8	10	11		6†					12					9	3		D Shaw	39
	7		4	5	2			8*	10	11						12		6				9	3	1	I Borrett	40
	7	3	4	5	2			8	10	11								6				9		1	N Ashley	41
	7	3	4	5	2		12	8	10	11*								6				9		1	J Hunting	42
	7	3	4	5	2		11	8	10									6				9		1	J Key	43
1	7	3	4*	5	2		12	8†	10	11								6				9			M Bodenham	44
1	7*	3	4	5	2		12	8	10	11								6				9			J Worrall	45
1	7	3	4	5	2		12	8	10	11*								6				9			R Lewis	46
1	7	3	4	5	2		8			11						10		6				9			E Read	47
38	28	40	26	36	37	6	31	41	37	34	11	14	3	3	1	9	6	26	2	7	5	15	2	4	League Appearances	
			+1S			+7S	+4S				+1S	+1S	+1S		+1S	+4S	+1S			+2S	+2S					
1		1	1S	1	1		1	1	1	1						1		1			1				FA Cup Appearances	
4	4	4	1S	4	4		4	4	4	3	4	4								1					Milk Cup Appearances	

ARSENAL STADIUM, HIGHBURY

Official Address: Arsenal Stadium, Highbury, London N.5. Telephone: 01-226 0304

Telegraphic: Gunneretic London N.5.

Ground Capacity: 60,000

Record Attendance: 73,295 v. Sunderland, Division 1, 9 Mar 1935

Record Receipts: £116,498 v. Juventus, Cup-Winners Cup Semi-Final 1st Leg, 9 Apr 1980

Size of Playing Area: 110yds × 71 yds

Season Tickets: Stands: £98.00, £112.00, £126.00, £182.00; Ground: £44.00

Executive Box Season Tickets: £650.00 with Private Restaurant & Bars

Cost of Stand Tickets: £4.00, £4.50, £5.50, £7.50; **Terraces:** £2.50

Match and Ticket Information: Ansafone Service, 01-359 0131

Car Parking: Parking is permitted in adjacent streets

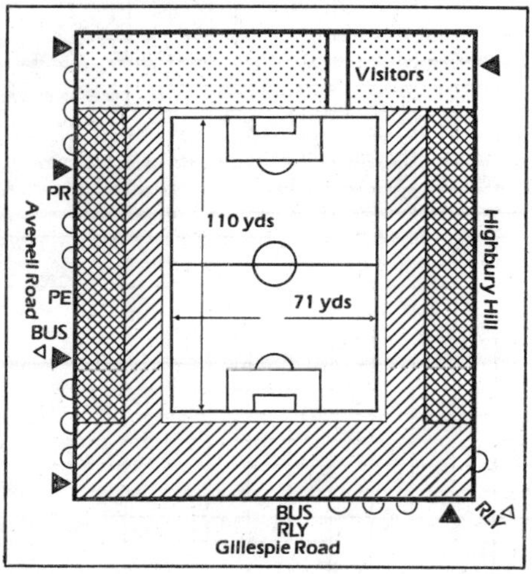

For key see page 12

How to get to the ground

From North: Leave Motorway M1 at junction 2 and follow signs City. In 6.2m pass Holloway Road Station and then take 3rd turning on left into Drayton Park Road. In 0.7m to right into Avenue Road for Arsenal F.C.

From South: From London Bridge follow signs, to Bank of England, then follow signs to Angel (Islington). At traffic signals turn right (S.P. The North) and in 1m at Highbury roundabout forward into Holloway Road. Then take 3rd turning on right into Drayton Park Road. In 0.07m turn right into Avenue Road for Arsenal F.C.

From West: Leave Motorway M4 at junction 1 (Chiswick and follow A315 (S.P. Chiswick). In 0.9m turn left A40 then follow signs City to join Motorway M41, then A40(m) at end forward into Ring Road A501. At Angel (Islington) turn left to Highbury roundabout, keep forward into Holloway Road. Then take 3rd turning on right into Drayton Park Road. In 0.07m turn right into Avenue for Arsenal F.C.

ASTON VILLA Division 1

President
A T Gill

Chairman
D Ellis

Directors
H Kartz
T Alderson
Dr D Targett

Secretary
Steven Stride

Assistant Secretary
Arthur Moseley

Manager
Graham Turner

First Team Coach
Malcolm Beard

Reserve Team Coach
Bill Shorthouse

Youth Team Coach
Brian Little

Commercial Manager
Tony Stephens
(021 327 5399)

Physiotherapist
Jim Williams

Groundsman
Tony Eden

With the added spice of a season 'in Europe', Villa appeared to have a happy time in front of them but off the field power struggles did not help, as the club could not achieve any sort of consistency.

A very good Moscow Spartak side eliminated them from the UEFA Cup and after an exciting Milk Cup run Everton just edged into the Final and gained revenge for the 1977 Final result.

Tony Morley, a hero when on form, but a frustration to many when things were not going well, left to join local rivals West Bromwich Albion but Mark Walters continued to improve while Peter Withe was as dominating as ever. However, the injured Gary Shaw was badly missed and then, after a disappointing early exit from the FA Cup and a quiet end of the League season, the future of manager Tony Barton was well and truly in the balance.

Eventually it was decided to look for a new 'boss' and Tony moved on to Northampton while John Toshack and Ron Atkinson were reported to have turned down a move to Villa Park. Eventually Graham Turner, who had performed miracles at Shrewsbury, and had been Chairman Doug Ellis's first choice all along, was appointed.

With the unlucky Gordon Cowans expected to return after a season's rehabilitation and the promising Paul Rideout challenging for a regular place, the squad should be amongst the strongest in the country and Aston Villa should be challenging for all the honours once again. With a wonderful tradition behind them, a superb ground and excellent support Villa need honours to give satisfaction and there is no reason why they should not do this again. With more steadiness in defence and a return to top form by goalkeeper Spink, this might be achieved.

Back Row L to R: Ray Walker, Alan Curbishley, Nigel Spink, Steve Foster, Mervyn Day, Paul Rideout, Brendan Ormsby. **Middle Row:** Jim Williams (Physio), Steve McMahon, Mark Walters, Gary Shaw, Dennis Mortimer, Eamonn Deacy, Colin Gibson, Gordon Cowans. **Front Row:** Paul Birch, Gary Williams, Allan Evans, Graham Turner (Manager), Peter Withe, Des Bremner, Tony Dorigo.

'THE VILLA'

Sponsored by
Mita

Formed: 1874 **Turned Professional:** 1885 **Ltd Co:** 1896
Previous Managers: 1934-6 Jimmy McMullen 1936-9 Jimmy Hogan 1945-50 Alex Massie 1950-3 George Martin 1953-8 Eric Houghton 1958-64 Joe Mercer 1964-7 Dick Taylor 1967-8 Tommy Cummings 1968 Arthur Cox 1968-70 Tommy Docherty 1970-4 Vic Crowe 1974-82 Ron Saunders 1982-4 Tony Barton
Honours: Champions Division 1 (7) 1893-4, 1895-6, 1896-7, 1898-9, 1899-1900, 1909-10, 1980-1 Champions Division 2 (2) 1937-8, 1959-60 Champions Division 3 1971-2 Winners F.A. Cup (7) 1887, 1895, 1897, 1905, 1913, 1920, 1957 (joint Record Holders) Winners League/Milk Cup (3) 1961, 1975, 1977 Winners European Cup 1981-2 Winners European Super Cup 1982-3
League Career: Original Members of The Football League 1888 Relegated to Division 2 1935-6 Promoted to Division 1 1937-8 Relegated to Division 2 1958-9 Promoted to Division 1 1959-60 Relegated to Division 2 1966-7 Relegated to Division 3 1969-70 Promoted to Division 2 1971-2 Promoted to Division 1 1974-5
Colours: Claret shirts with light blue sleeves and trim, white shorts with light blue trim, blue stockings
Change Colours: White shirt with faint yellow/claret hoops, white shorts with yellow/claret stripe, white stockings with yellow/claret hoops

CLUB RECORDS

Most Appearances for Club: Charlie Aitken: Football League 559 + 2 + F.A. Cup 33 + League Cup 59 + UEFA Cup 2 **Total 653 + 2 subs**
Most Capped Player: Peter McParland, 33, N Ireland. **For England:** Billy Walker, 18, 1921-33
Record Goalscorer in a Match: Harry Hampton, 5 v Sheffield Wednesday (10-0), 05.10.12
Len Capwell, 5 v Burnley (10-0), 29.08.25
George Brown, 5 v Leicester City (8-3) (A), 02.01.32
Gerry Hitchins, 5 v Charlton Athletic (11-1), 14.11.59
Record League Goalscorer in a season: Pongo Waring, 49, Div 1, 1930-1 **All competitions:** Pongo Waring, 50 (League 49, F.A. Cup 1), 1930-1
Record League Goalscorer in a career: Harry Hampton (1904-20) and Billy Walker (1919-34), 213
All competitions: Harry Hampton, 247 (League 213, F.A. Cup 34), 1904-20
Record Transfer Fee Received: £1,469,000 (£1,175,000 basic fee) from Wolverhampton Wanderers for Andy Gray, Sept 1979
Record Transfer Fee Paid: £500,000 to Newcastle United for Peter Withe, May 1980
Best Performances: As in Honours
Most League Points: (2pts for win) 70, Div 3, 1971-2
Most League Goals: 128, Div 1, 1930-1
Record League Victory: 12-2 v Accrington Stanley, Div 1, 12 March 1892; 11-1 v Charlton Ath, Div 2, 24 Nov 1959; 10-0 v Sheffield Wed, Div 1, 5 Oct 1912; 10-0 v Burnley, Div 1, 29 Aug 1925
Record League Defeat: 0-7 v Blackburn Rov (A), Div 1, 19 Oct 1889; 0-7 v Everton (A), Div 1, 4 March 1890; 0-7 v WBA (H), Div 1, 19 Oct 1935; 0-7 v Manchester United (A), Div 1, 8 March 1950; 0-7 v Manchester United (A), Div 1, 24 Oct 1964
European Competitions Entered: European Cup 1981-2, 1982-3 UEFA Cup 1975-6, 1977-8
World Club Championship 1982-3 European Super Cup 1982-3

Club Statistician for the Directory: Dave Hodges

Production & Design
Sports Projects & Tony Matthews

Price	Number of Pages
50p	24

Subscriptions
Please apply to Commercial Department

ASTON VILLA

PLAYERS NAME Ht Wt Birthdate	Honours	Birthplace Transfers	Clubs	APPEARANCES League	Milk Cup	F.A.C.	E. Cups	GOALS League	Milk Cup	F.A.C.	E. Cups
GOALKEEPERS											
Mervyn Day	E.U.23(5). Y.	Chelmsford	West Ham U.	194	14	14					
6-2 15.1 26.6.55	FAC. 75	£100,000	Orient	170	10	8					
		£15,000	Aston Villa	14							
Nigel Spink	E.(1). EC. 82	Chelmsford	Chelmsford C.								
6-1½ 14.6 8.8.58	ESC. 82	£6,000	Aston Villa	51	7	6	8+1				
DEFENDERS											
Tony Dorigo		Australia	Aston Villa (A)	0+1							
5-10 11.0 31.12.65											
Allan Evans*	S.(4). Y. Div. 1. 81	Dunfermline	Dunfermline A.	94+4	20+	2		14			
6-1½ 13.2 12.10.56	EC. 82. ESC. 82	£30,000	Aston Villa	232+2				35			
Steve Foster	E.(3). U.21(1)	Portsmouth	Portsmouth (A)	101+8	10	8		6		2	
6-0 14.0 24.9.57			Brighton	171+1	13	16		6	2		
			Aston Villa	7				1			
Colin Gibson	E.U.21(1).	Bridport	Aston Villa (A)	134+4	20	11	13+1	4	3	1	2
5-8 10.10 6.4.60	Div. 1. 81. EC. 82.										
	ESC. 82										
Brendan Ormsby	E. Y. S.	Birmingham	Aston Villa (A)	69+2	7+1	2+1	7	2			1
5-11 11.3 1.10.60	EC. 82										
Ray Walker	E. Y. FAYC. 80	North Shields	Aston Villa (A)	6+3	0+1	2					
5-10 11.9 28.9.63	ESC. 82										
Gary Williams	Div. 1. 81. EC. 82	Wolverhampton	Aston Villa (A)	146+5	18	9					
5-9 11.1 17.6.60	ESC. 83		Walsall (L)	9							
MIDFIELD											
Paul Birch	FAYC. 80. ESC. 82	Birmingham	Aston Villa (A)	22	2	2	0+1	2			
5-6 10.6 20.11.62											
Des Bremner	S.(1). U.23(9). Y.	Abirchirder	Hibernian	198	26+	26	11	18	2	2	
5-10 11.11 17.9.52	S. Div. 1. 81.	£275,000	Aston Villa	166+4	13	14	19		1		
	EC. 82. ESC. 82										
Gordon Cowans	E.(7). B.(1). U.21(5)	Durham	Aston Villa	247+9	17+3	18+1		41	4	3	
5-7½ 10.5½ 27.10.58	Y. FC. 77. Div. 1.										
	81. EC. 82. ESC. 82										
Alan Curbishley	E. U.21(1). Y	Forest Gate	West Ham U. (A)	78+7	3	5	1+1	5			
5-10½ 11.6 8.11.57		£275,000	Birmingham C.	128+2	12	10		11	3	1	
		£100,000	Aston Villa	31+2	5		2	1			
Eamonn Deacy	Ei.(4). AM	Galway	Galway R.	39	5	3		1			
5-9 10.10 1.10.58	Div. 1. 81	F	Aston Villa	27+6	2+3	1	0+1				
			Derby Co.	5							
Steve McMahon	E. U.21(6)	Liverpool	Everton (A)	99+1	11	9		11		3	
5-9 12.1½ 20.8.61		£175,000	Aston Villa	37	6	2	4	5			
Dennis Mortimer†	E. B(3). U.23(6). Y.	Liverpool	Coventry C. (A)	179+14	18	8+1		10			
5-10 12.0 5.4.52	FC. 77. Div. 1. 81.		Aston Villa	311	31	21	28	31	2		
	EC. 82. ESC. 82										
FORWARDS											
Paul Kerr		Portsmouth	Aston Villa (A)	1+1							
5-8½ 11.3½ 7.6.64											
Gary Shaw	E. U.21(7). Y. S.	Birmingham	Aston Villa (A)	146+2	16+	11	16	58	5	4	9
5-10 11.9 12.1.62	Div. 1. 81. EC.										
	ESC. 82. PFAYP										
Mark Walters	E. U.21(2). Y. S.	Birmingham	Aston Villa (A)	51+9	5	4+1	4+3	9	2	1	2
5-9 11.5 2.6.64	FAYC. 80. ESC. 82										
Peter Withe	E.(10). Div. 1. 78.	Liverpool	Southport	3							
6-2 13.0 30.8.51	81. FC 78. EC. 82.	F	Barrow	1							
	ESC. 82	F	Arcadia S.								
		F	Wolverhampton W.	12+5				3			
		£50,000	Birmingham C.	35	3	2		9			
		£40,000	Nottingham F.	74+1	21	14		28	12	10	
		£225,000	Newcastle U.	76	3	4		25		2	
		£500,000	Aston Villa	142	17	8	21	61	5	2	8

CONTRACT PLAYERS WHO HAVE NO FIRST TEAM APPEARANCES:
Steve Poole (G), Dean Glover (D), Darren Bradley (D), Tony Obi (F), Leigh Palin (M), Andy Greenhalgh (F), David Norton (MF)

APPRENTICES:
Dale Belford, Bernard Gallagher, Matt Hellin, Peter Howell, Paul Hutchings, Greg McKenzie, David McMahon, Derek Mitchell, Jerry O'Connell, Phil Robinson, Paul Shipley, Mark Daley, Matt Foreman, Paul Grainger, Stuart Ritchie

NON-CONTRACT PLAYERS 1984-85: Darren Giles, Carl Foster, Darren English, S. Vacanti

ASTON VILLA

DIVISION ONE 10TH **FA CUP** 3RD ROUND **MILK CUP** SEMI-FINAL **UEFA CUP** 2ND ROUND

MATCH	DATE	COMPE-TITION	VENUE	OPPONENTS	RESULT	HALF TIME	L'GUE POS'N	GOALSCORERS	ATTEN-DANCE
1	A 27	CL	H	WBA	W4-3	3-3		Evans, Walters, Shaw, Ormsby	29,522
2	29	CL	H	Sunderland	W1-0	0-0		Walters	20,390
3	S 3	CL	A	QPR	L1-2	0-1	13	Withe	16,922
4	7	CL	A	Nottingham F	D2-2	1-1		Withe, Shaw	16,363
5	10	CL	H	Norwich C	W1-0	1-0	6	Mortimer	18,887
6	**14**	**UEFA 1**	**A**	**Vitoria Guimaraes**	**L0-1**	**0-0**			**30,000**
7	17	CL	A	Liverpool	L1-2	0-0	8	Gibson	34,236
8	24	CL	H	Southampton	W1-0	1-0	6	Withe	21,207
9	**28**	**UEFA 1**	**H**	**Vitoria Guimaraes**	**W5-0**	**1-0**		**Withe 3, Ormsby, Gibson**	**23,732**
10	O 1	CL	A	Luton T	L0-1	0-0	11		12,747
11	**4**	**MC 2**	**A**	**Portsmouth**	**D2-2**	**0-1**		**Gibson, Evans**	**18,484**
12	15	CL	H	Birmingham C	W1-0	1-0	8	Withe	39,318
13	**19**	**UEFA 2**	**H**	**Spartak Moscow**	**D2-2**	**0-0**		**Gibson, Walters**	**50,000**
14	23	CL	A	Wolverhampton W	D1-1	1-0		Withe	13,202
15	**26**	**MC 2**	**H**	**Portsmouth**	**W3-2[1]**	**1-1**		**Evans (pen), Withe, Walters**	**20,898**
16	29	CL	H	Arsenal	L2-6	1-4	14	Morley, Evans (pen)	23,678
17	**N 2**	**UEFA 2**	**H**	**Spartak Moscow**	**L1-2**	**1-0**		**Withe**	**29,511**
18	5	CL	A	Manchester U	W2-1	1-0	11	Withe 2	45,077
19	**9**	**MC 3**	**H**	**Manchester C**	**W3-0**	**1-0**		**Gibson, Evans, Mortimer**	**23,922**
20	12	CL	H	Stoke C	D1-1	0-1	8	Withe	19,272
21	19	CL	H	Leicester C	W3-1	2-1	6	Withe, Rideout, McMahon	19,024
22	26	CL	A	Notts Co	L2-5	0-2	9	Mortimer, Evans (pen)	8,960
23	**30**	**MC 4**	**A**	**WBA**	**W2-1**	**1-1**		**Walters, Mortimer**	**31,114**
24	D 3	CL	H	West Ham U	W1-0	0-0	7	Rideout	21,297
25	10	CL	A	Everton	D1-1	0-0	10	Rideout	15,810
26	17	CL	H	Ipswich T	W4-0	1-0	7	Mariner (og), Rideout, McMahon, Evans (pen)	16,548
27	26	CL	A	Watford	L2-3	0-2	9	Curbishley, Walters	18,226
28	27	CL	H	Tottenham H	D0-0	0-0	12		30,125
29	31	CL	H	QPR	W2-1	0-0	7	Evans, McMahon	19,978
30	J 2	CL	A	Southampton	D2-2	1-0	7	McMahon, Shaw	18,963
31	**7**	**FAC 3**	**H**	**Norwich C**	**D1-1**	**1-1**		**Withe**	**21,454**
32	**11**	**FAC 3R**	**A**	**Norwich C**	**L0-3**	**0-1**			**16,420**
33	14	CL	A	WBA	L1-3	0-0	8	Shaw	20,399
34	**17**	**MC 5**	**A**	**Norwich C**	**W2-0**	**2-0**		**Shaw, Rideout**	**21,568**
35	20	CL	H	Liverpool	L1-3	1-0	9	Mortimer	19,566
36	F 4	CL	H	Luton T	D0-0	0-0	9		18,656
37	11	CL	A	Norwich C	L1-3	0-0	12	Shaw	14,392
38	**15**	**MC SF1**	**A**	**Everton**	**L0-2**	**0-1**			**40,006**
39	18	CL	A	Arsenal	D1-1	0-1	11	Evans (pen)	26,640
40	**22**	**MC SF2**	**H**	**Everton**	**W1-0**	**0-0**		**Rideout**	**42,426**
41	25	CL	H	Wolverhampton W	W4-0	1-0	10	Withe 2, Birch, Walters	18,257
42	M 3	CL	H	Manchester U	L0-3	0-1	11		32,874
43	10	CL	A	Stoke C	L0-1	0-0	12		13,967
44	13	CL	A	Coventry C	D3-3	2-2		Evans (pen), Withe, Rideout	11,098
45	17	CL	H	Nottingham F	W1-0	0-0	8	McMahan	16,270
46	24	CL	A	Sunderland	W1-0	1-0	8	Walters	11,908
47	31	CL	A	Birmingham C	L1-2	1-1	10	Withe	23,993
48	A 7	CL	H	Coventry C	W2-0	1-0	9	Ormsby, Birch	15,318
49	14	CL	A	Leicester C	L0-2	0-1	9		13,666
50	18	CL	A	Tottenham H	L1-2	1-2		Walters	18,668
51	21	CL	H	Watford	W2-1	1-1	9	Mortimer, Foster	16,110
52	28	CL	H	Notts Co	W3-1	1-1	9	Walters 2, Withe	13,059
53	M 5	CL	A	West Ham U	W1-0	1-0	8	Mortimer	17,390
54	7	CL	H	Everton	L0-2	0-0	9		16,792
55	12	CL	A	Ipswich T	L1-2	1-1	9	Withe	20,043

[1]After Extra Time

Av Home Att **21,243**

Goal Scorers

League (59): Withe 15, Walters 8, Evans 7 (6 pens), McMahon 5, Mortimer 5, Rideout 5, Shaw 5, Birch 2, Ormsby 2, Curbishley 1, Foster 1, Gibson 1, Morley 1, opponent 1
FA Cup (1): Withe 1
Milk Cup (13): Evans 3 (1 pen), Gibson 2, Mortimer 2, Rideout 2, Walters 2, Shaw 1, Withe 1
UEFA Cup (8): Withe 4, Gibson 2, Ormsby 1, Walters 1

1983-84

Spink	Williams	Gibson	Evans	Ormsby	Mortimer	Curbishley	Shaw	Withe	McMahon	Walters	Blair	Birch	Rideout	Morley	Bremner	Jones	Day	Deacy	Walker	Kerr	Foster	Dorigo	Glover	REFEREE	
1	2	3	4	5	6	7	8	9	10	11														N Ashley	1
1	2	3	4	5		7	8	9		11	6	10												J Deakin	2
1	2	3	4	5	6	7	8	9	10	11*			12											D Hedges	3
1	2	3	4	5	6	7	8*	9	10	11			12											J Hough	4
1	2	3	4	5	6	7		9	10	11			9											N Midgley	5
1	2	3	4	5	6	7		9	10	13	11*		8*	12										**Quinlou**	6
1	2	3	4	5	6	7		9	10†	11*			8	12										D Hutchinson	7
1	2	3	4	5	6	7		9	10	8				11										J Key	8
1	2	3	4	5	6	7		9	10	8				11										**Fockler**	9
1	2	3	4	5	6	7	12	9		8				11*	10									I Borrett	10
1	2	3	4	5	6	7*	8	9	10	11					12									**J Moules**	11
1	2	3†	4	5	6	7		9	10	8				11*	12									D Allison	12
1	2	3	4	5	6			9	10	8				11	7									**Schoeters**	13
1	2	3	4	5	6			9	10	8			12	11	7									JB Worral	14
1	2	3	4	5	6			9	10	8				11	7									**D Richardson**	15
1	3		4	5	6			9	10	8				11	7	2								A Robinson	16
1		3	4	5	6			9	10	8				11	7	2								**E Mulder**	17
1	2	3	4	5	6			9	10			8	11			7								C Seel	18
1	3	11	4	5	6			9	10			7	8			2								**L Burden**	19
	2	3*	4	5	6			9	10	12		8	11			7	1							M Scott	20
1	3*		4	5	6	12		9	10	8		7	11			2								F Roberts	21
1	3	11	4	5	6	10		9		12		7*	8			2								G Tyson	22
1	2	3	4	5	6	10		9*		11		7	8						12					**C Thomas**	23
1	2	3*	4	5	6					8		7	9	11				12	10					N Glover	24
	2		4	5	6				10	11		7	9				1	3	8					D Shaw	25
1	2		4	5	6	7		9	10	11			8					3						D Scott	26
1	2		4	5	6	7		9	10	11			8					3†						J Martin	27
1	2*		4	5	6	7		9	10	11			8					3	12					R Milford	28
1			4	5	6	7	8	9	10	11					2			3						A Banks	29
1			4	5	6		8	9	10	11		7			2				3					A Gunn	30
1			4	5	6		8	9	10	11		7			2				3					**R Bridges**	31
1			4		6		8*	9	10	11		7	12		2				3				5	**D Brazier**	32
1	2	3	4		6	7	8	9	10				11		5									A Ward	33
1	2	3*	4		6	7	8	9	10				11		5			12						**T Mills**	34
1	2	3	4		6	7	8	9	10				11		5									R Lewis	35
1	2	3	4		6	7	8		10	11			9		5									L Dilkes	36
	2	11	4		6	7	8						9		5		1	3	10					E Scales	37
1	2	3	4		6	7	8	9	10	11					5									**A Saunders**	38
1	2	3	4		6	7	8	9	10	11					5									M Taylor	39
1	2	3	4		6	7	8	9	10	11*			12		5									**K Hackett**	40
1	2	3		4	6	7		9	10	12		8	11*		5									N Wilson	41
1	2	3		4	6	7*		9	10	12		8	11		5									K Salmon	42
1	2	3	4	5	6			9	10	8		7	11											G Courtney	43
1*	2	3	4	5		6		9	10	8		7	11						12					D Vickers	44
	2	3	4	5		6		9	10	8		7	11				1							H King	45
	2	3	4	5		6		9	10	8		7	11				1							K Walmsley	46
	2	3*	4	5		6		9	10	8		7	11		12		1							J Hunting	47
	2		4	5	6				10	11	9	8			7		1	3						B Stevens	48
	2		4		6				10	11	9	8			7		1	3*		12	5			A Challinor	49
	2	3	4		6			9	10	11	8	7					1				5			L Shapter	50
	2	3	4		6			9	10	11	7	8					1				5			I Hendrick	51
	2			4	6			9	10	11	7	8					1	3			5			D Hedges	52
	2			4	6			9	10	11*	8	7					1	3	12		5			B Hill	53
	2			4	6			9	10		8				12		1	3	7	11*	5			T Bune	54
	2			4	6			9	10	11*	7	8					1	3			5	12		M Bodenham	55
28	40	28	36	34	37	25	11	36	37	33	9	22	22	6	14	5	14	12	5	1	7	0		League Appearances	
						+1S	+1S			+4S			+3S	+1S	+3S			+1S	+3S	+1S		+1S			
2			2	1	2		2	2	2	2		2	1S		2				2				1	FA Cup Appearances	
7	7	7	7	4	7	5	4	7	6	5		2	3+1S	1	4+2S		1S	1S						Milk Cup Appearances	
4	3	4	4	4	4	2		4	4	3+1S	1		1	3+1S	2	1								UEFA Cup Appearances	

VILLA PARK

Official Address: Villa Park, Trinity Road, Birmingham B6 6HE. Telephone: 021-327 6604, 24 hr answering service: 021-328 1722

Telegraphic: Villa Birmingham 6

Ground Capacity: 48,000

Record Attendance: 76,588 v. Derby County, F.A. Cup Round 6, 2 Mar 1946

Record Receipts: £165,481 v. Juventus, European Cup Semi-Final, 2 Mar 1983

Size of Playing Area: 115yds × 75 yds

Season Tickets: Stand, Shareholders: £60.80, £68.40, £76.00, £91.20; Stand, Non-Shareholders: £64, £72, £80, £96 (£32, £36, £40, £48 juveniles)

Executive Box Season Tickets: 57 boxes leased on three year basis. Information can be obtained from Secretary.

Cost of Stand Tickets: £4.00, £4.50, £5.00, £6,00; **Terraces:** £2.50 (£1.50 juveniles)

Match and Ticket Information: By post or in person, applications accepted any time during season.

Car Parking: Asda Park in Aston Hall Road. Street parking also available.

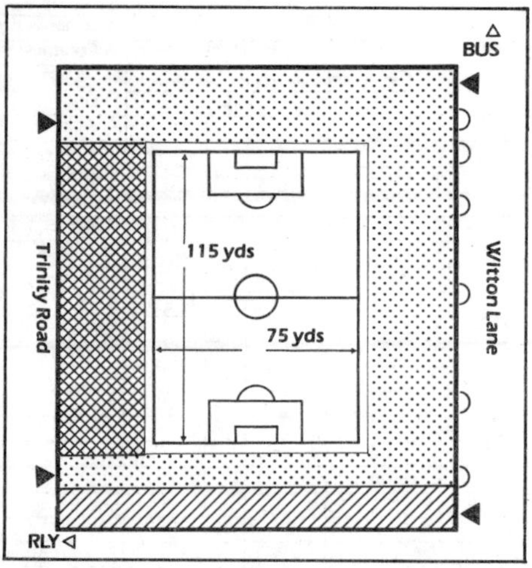

For key see page 12

How to get to the ground

From North, East, South and West: Use Motorway M6 with Junction 6. Leave Motorway and follow signs Birmingham (NE). Shortly at roundabout take 4th exit A38 (S.P. Alston). In 0.5m turn right into Aston Hall Road for Aston Villa F.C.

BARNSLEY Division 2

Chairman
G Buckle LLB

Directors
J A Dennis
N W B Moody
G Pallister
A Raynor
R F Potter
J Steele
C B Taylor
C Williams

Secretary
M J Spinks

Manager
R Y Collins

Reserve Team Coach
E Winstanley

Youth Team Coaches
E Winstanley
M Wadsworth

Commercial Manager
G Whewall (0226-86718)

Physiotherapist
N Rimmington

Groundsman
L Clayton

By finishing in 14th position, Barnsley completed a somewhat disappointing season after finishing 6th and 10th respectively during the last two campaigns following their successful Third Division promotion of 1980-81.

The main event at the club was the sacking of Manager Norman Hunter following a run which brought only one win in ten games, and after a 3-2 home defeat to Cardiff City, his last game in charge, Bobby Collins the youth team coach took over as caretaker manager.

The team improved considerably under Collins, taking 12 points out of a possible 15, and by staving off a possible relegation threat virtually assured Collins permanent appointment as Manager.

A total of 15 players made their debut for Barnsley during the season. The new signings were Stuart Gray, Larry May, David Geddis, Simon Lowe, Gwyn Thomas, Paul Futcher and Calvin Plummer, whilst in addition the six youngsters made their first team appearance, namely Andy Rhodes, Mark Fletcher, Alan Semley, Steve Agnew, Dean Whitehouse and Simon Jeffels. On loan players who also made their debut were Jake Findlay from Luton and David Johnson from Everton, whilst the most appearances were by Larry May with an overall total of 44.

The leading goal scorer for the season was David Geddis with 12 goals and Ronnie Glavin, who finished second with 11 goals, had scored 92 goals in 205 League and Cup appearances in his five years at the club.

Mick McCarthy, the very popular Barnsley defender, created a new club record when in December he was transferred to Manchester City for £200,000, after making 272 League appearances for the Reds.

The average home gate at Oakwell was 9,645 which showed a drop of 2,745 on the previous season and 5,451 lower than the figures recorded in their first season back in Division Two a couple of seasons ago. The Reds had a disastrous time in the two major Cup Competitions. They were knocked out in the second round of the Milk Cup Competition by Third Division Walsall, and were beaten in the third round of the F.A. Cup by their local rivals, Sheffield Wednesday.

Whilst it had been a somewhat disappointing season for the first team, both the reserve and junior sides finished on a good note.

The Reserves were promoted to Division One of the Central League due to an influx of new teams in the league, whilst the Juniors reached the semi-final of the F.A. Youth Cup before losing to the eventual winners, Everton, in extra time at Oakwell.

Arthur Bower, The League Directory's Statistican for the Club

Back Row L to R: Wayne Goodison, Paul Futcher, Larry May, Nicky Law, Carl Airey, David Geddis. **Middle Row:** Eric Winstanley (Coach), Michael Fielding, Winston Campbell, Stuart Gray, Clive Baker, Andy Rhodes, Ian Walsh, Calvin Plummer, Gwyn Thomas, Lew Clayton (Physiotherapist). **Front Row:** Billy Ronson, Mick McGuire, David Wilkes, Bobby Colins (Manager), Gordon Owen, Joe Joyce, Phil Chambers.

'THE TYKES' or 'THE REDS'

Sponsored by
F. Haselden Ltd

Formed: 1887 **Turned Professional:** 1888 **Ltd Co:** 1899
Previous Name: Barnsley St. Peter's
Previous Managers: 1901-4 John McCartney 1904-12 Arthur Fairclough 1912-4 John Hastie 1914-9 Harry Percy Lewis 1919-26 Peter Sant 1926-9 John Commins 1929-30 Arthur Fairclough 1930-7 Brough Fletcher 1937-53 Angus Seed 1953-60 Tim Ward 1960-71 Johnny Steel 1971-72 John McSeveney 1972-3 Johnny Steel (caretaker) 1973-8 Jim Iley 1978-80 Allan Clarke 1980-84 Norman Hunter
Honours: Division Three (North) Champions 1933-4, 1938-9, 1954-55
FA Cup Winners 1912
League Career: Elected to Division 2 1898 Moved to Division 3 (North) 1932
Promoted to Division 2 1933-4 Relegated to Division 3 (North) 1937-8
Promoted to Division 2 1938-9 Relegated to Division 3 (North) 1952-3
Promoted to Division 2 1954-5 Relegated to Division 3 1958-9
Relegated to Division 4 1964-5 Promoted to Division 3 1967-8
Relegated to Division 4 1971-2 Promoted to Division 3 1980-1
Promoted to Division 2 1981-2
Colours: Red shirts, white shorts, red stockings
Change Colours: White shirts, black shorts, white stockings.

CLUB RECORDS

Most Appearances for Club: Barry Murphy: Football League 509 + F.A. Cup 26 + League Cup 29 **Total 564**
Most Capped Player: Eddie McMorran 9, N. Ireland **For England:** G. Utley 1
Record Goalscorer in a Match: P. Cunningham, 5 v Darlington (6-2) H. Div 3 (N) 4 Feb 1933 B. Asquith 5 v Darlington (7-1) H. Div 3 (N) 12.11.38 C. McCormack 5 v Luton Town (6-1) H. Div 2 9 Sep 1950
Record League Goalscorer in a season: Cecil McCormack 33, Div 2, 1950-1 **In All Competitions:** Cecil McCormack, 34 (League 33, F.A. Cup 1) 1950-1
Record League Goalscorer in a career: Ernie Hine, 122, 1921-6 and 1934-5 **In All Competitions:** Ernie Moss (80 League, 2 F.A. Cup in 1921-6 and 42 League, 5 F.A. Cup in 1934-5)
Record Transfer Fee Received: £200,000 from Manchester City for Mick McCarthy, Dec 1983
Record Transfer Fee Paid: £110,000 to Leicester City for Larry May, Aug 1983
Best Performances: League: 3rd Div 2 1914-15, 1921-2 **F.A. Cup:** Winners 1912 **League/Milk Cup:** 5th Round 1981-2
Most League Points: (2pts for win) 67 Div 3 (N) 1938-39, (3pts for win) 67 Div 2 1981-82
Record League Victory: 9-0 v Loughborough Town, Div 2, 28 Jan 1899 9-0 v Accrington Stanley (a) Div 3 (N) 3 Feb 1934
Record League Defeat: 0-9 v Notts County, Div 2, 19 Nov 1927
Club Statistician for the Directory: Arthur Bower

Programme Editor
Keith Lodge

Price	**Number of Pages**
45p	32

Subscriptions
Rates on request

BARNSLEY

PLAYERS NAME Ht Wt Birthdate	Honours	Birthplace Transfers	Clubs	APPEARANCES League	Milk Cup	F.A.C.	E. Cups	GOALS League	Milk Cup	F.A.C.	E. Cups
GOALKEEPERS											
Andy Rhodes†		Doncaster	Barnsley	31	2	1					
6-1 12.9 23.8.64											
Clive Baker		North Walsham	Norwich C.	14		2					
5-9 11.0 14.2.59		F	Barnsley								
DEFENDERS											
Phil Chambers*	E. S.	Barnsley	Barnsley (A)	436 + 1	28	23		8			
5-7½ 11.1 10.11.53											
Paul Cross		Barnsley	Barnsley (A)								
5-7 9.6 31.10.65											
Paul Futcher	E. U.21(11)	Chester	Chester (A)	20		1					
6-0 12.3 25.9.56		£100,000	Luton T.	131	4	6		1			
		£350,000	Manchester C.	36 + 1	3 + 1	3		1			
		£150,000	Oldham A.	98	9	4					
		£44,000	Derby Co.	35	1	4					
		£30,000	Barnsley	10							
Wayne Goodison		Wakefield	Barnsley (A)	3							
5-8 11.7 23.9.64											
Simon Jeffels	E. Y	Darton	Barnsley (A)	3							
6-1 11.8 18.1.66											
Joe Joyce		Consett	Barnsley	131 + 2	15 +	10		2	1		
5-9 10.5 18.3.61											
Nicky Law		Greenwich	Arsenal (A)								
6-0 13.5 8.9.61			Barnsley	77 + 1	4	3		1			
Larry May	Div. 2, 80	Sutton Coldfield	Leicester C. (A)	180 + 7	8	12		12		3	
6-0 12.6 26.12.58			Barnsley	41	2	1		1			
MIDFIELD											
Winston Campbell		Sheffield	Barnsley (A)	53 + 4	6	1 + 1		5			
5-8 11.6 9.10.62			Doncaster R. (L)	3							
Stuart Gray		Withernsea	Nottingham F.	48 + 1	5 + 1	3		3			
5-9 11.10 19.4.60			Bolton W. (L)	7							
		£40,000	Barnsley	16 + 1				8			
Mick McGuire	E. Y	Blackpool	Coventry C.	60 + 12	3	5		1			
5-7 10.5 4.9.52		£50,000	Norwich C.	172 + 10	11	7 + 1		11	1		
		£30,000	Barnsley	43	2	1		6			
Billy Ronson		Fleetwood	Blackpool (A)	124 + 4	10	4		12	1		
5-6 9.9 22.1.57		£135,000	Cardiff C.	90	9	3		4			
		£100,000	Wrexham	31 + 1		4		1	1		
		£50,000	Barnsley	70 + 1	5 + 1	3		3			
Gwyn Thomas	W. U.21(3)	Swansea	Leeds U. (A)	79 + 10	9 + 1	4 + 1		3			
5-8 11.0 26.9.57		£40,000	Barnsley	13							
FORWARDS											
Steve Agnew		Shipley	Barnsley	0 + 1							
5-9 10.6 9.11.65											
Carl Airey		Barnsley	Barnsley (A)	30 + 8	1	1		5			
5-11 11.6 6.2.65			Bradford C. (L)	4 + 1							
David Geddis	E. B(1), Y,	Carlisle	Ipswich T. (A)[1]	26 + 17	+ 1	2 + 1	2 + 5	5		1	
5-10½ 12.2 12.3.58	FAC. 78,	£300,000	Aston Villa[2]	43 + 4	4	4 + 1		12		4	
	FAYC. 75	£50,000	Barnsley	31				15			
Gordon Owen		Barnsley	Sheffield W.[3]	33 + 15	7 + 4	1 + 1		5			
5-8 10.9 14.6.59		F	Cardiff C.	38 + 1	2	1		14			
Calvin Plummer		Nottingham	Nottingham F.	10 + 2				2			
5-8 10.7 14.2.63		Player Exchange	Chesterfield	28				7			
		£10,000	Derby Co.	23 + 4	2	3 + 1		3			
		£10,000	Barnsley	1 + 1				1			
Alan Semley		Barnsley	Barnsley (A)	1 + 3		1					
6-0½ 11.0 21.2.66											
Ian Walsh	W.(18), U.21(1),	St Davids	Crystal Palace (A)	101 + 16	1 + 3	11	1 + 1	23	2	2	
5-9½ 11.6 4.9.58	Div. 2, 79,	Player Exchange	Swansea C.	32 + 5				5			
	FAYC. 77										
David Wilkes		Barnsley	Barnsley (A)	14 + 3		2		2			
5-8 10.2 10.3.64			Halifax T. (L)	4							

CONTRACT PLAYERS WITH NO APPEARANCES: Ironside (G), Fielding (D), Marshall (MF)

NON-CONTRACT PLAYERS 1984-85: Andrew Duggan, Bob Jones, Andy Kiwomya, Wayne Scargill, Derek Tiffany, Andy Wood, Martin Yates

APPRENTICES: Dean Croft, Ian Knight, Mark Ogley, Colin Peel, David Hurst

Loan Periods: [1]Luton T. (9 + 4 Lg, 4G). [2]Luton T. (4). [3]Rotherham U. (9), Doncaster R. (9 Lg, 2 FAC (1G)), Chesterfield (6 Lg, 2G).

BARNSLEY

DIVISION TWO 14TH **FA CUP** 3RD ROUND **MILK CUP** 2ND ROUND

MATCH	DATE	COMPETITION	VENUE	OPPONENTS	RESULT	HALF TIME	L'GUE POS'N	GOALSCORERS	ATTENDANCE
1	A 27	CL	H	Fulham	W3-0	1-0		Wilkes 2, Gray	9,851
2	S 3	CL	A	Manchester C	L2-3	1-2	13	Chambers, Gray	25,105
3	6	CL	A	Portsmouth	L1-2	0-1	13	Gray	12,804
4	10	CL	H	Middlesbrough	L0-2	0-0	19		10,039
5	17	CL	A	Shrewsbury T	L2-3	1-2	20	Gray, Cunningham	3,867
6	24	CL	H	Newcastle U	D1-1	0-0	20	Cunningham	14,085
7	27	CL	H	Grimsby T	W3-1	2-0		Gray, Geddis 2	10,966
8	O 1	CL	A	Cardiff C	W3-0	1-0	11	Glavin 2, Geddis	6,433
9	**4**	**MC 2**	**A**	**Walsall**	**L0-1**	**0-0**			**3,681**
10	8	CL	A	Derby Co	W2-0	0-0	6	Cunningham, Glavin	12,696
11	15	CL	H	Huddersfield T	D2-2	2-0	7	Geddis, Cunningham	14,096
12	22	CL	H	Leeds U	L0-2	0-0	10		18,236
13	**25**	**MC 2**	**H**	**Walsall**	**L0-2**	**0-1**			**7,844**
14	29	CL	A	Crystal Palace	W1-0	1-0	9	May	6,377
15	N 5	CL	A	Sheffield W	L0-2	0-1	13		27,491
16	12	CL	H	Swansea C	W3-2	1-0	8	Glavin, Gray 2 (1 pen)	8,161
17	19	CL	A	Charlton Ath	L2-3	1-1	11	Geddis 2	4,582
18	26	CL	H	Brighton & HA	W3-1	3-1	9	Gray (pen), Airey 2	7,705
19	D 3	CL	A	Oldham Ath	L0-1	0-1	10		5,475
20	10	CL	H	Chelsea	D0-0	0-0	11		10,300
21	17	CL	A	Carlisle U	L2-4	2-3	13	Airey, Joyce	4,812
22	26	CL	H	Cambridge U	W2-0	0-0	11	McGuire, Law	7,486
23	28	CL	A	Blackburn R	D1-1	1-0	12	Glavin,	8,954
24	31	CL	H	Manchester C	D1-1	0-1	11	Geddis	17,184
25	J 2	CL	A	Newcastle U	L0-1	0-1	13		29,833
26	**7**	**FAC 3**	**A**	**Sheffield W**	**L0-1**	**0-1**			**29,638**
27	14	CL	H	Fulham	L0-1	0-0	14		5,085
28	F 4	CL	H	Cardiff C	L2-3	0-1	16	McGuire, Geddis	7,107
29	11	CL	A	Middlesbrough	L1-2	0-0	18	Glavin	7,480
30	18	CL	H	Crystal Palace	D1-1	1-0	18	Geddis	6,239
31	25	CL	A	Leeds U	W2-1	0-1	14	Glavin, Johnson	19,138
32	M 3	CL	H	Sheffield W	L0-1	0-1	17		20,322
33	10	CL	A	Swansea C	L0-1	0-0	18		4,864
34	13	CL	H	Shrewsbury T	W3-0	1-0		Geddis, Glavin, Campbell	5,576
35	17	CL	H	Portsmouth	L0-3	0-1	17		7,030
36	31	CL	H	Derby Co	W5-1	1-0	17	McGuire 2 (1 pen), Plummer, Ronson, Glavin	6,500
37	A 7	CL	A	Huddersfield T	W1-0	1-0	15	Geddis	9,657
38	10	CL	A	Grimsby T	L0-1	0-0			6,934
39	14	CL	H	Charlton Ath	W2-0	0-0	14	Glavin, McGuire (pen)	6,321
40	21	CL	A	Cambridge U	W3-0	1-0	12	Geddis 2, Ronson	2,200
41	23	CL	H	Blackburn R	D0-0	0-0	12		7,123
42	28	CL	A	Brighton & HA	L0-1	0-0	13		8,975
43	M 5	CL	H	Oldham Ath	L0-1	0-1	15		5,539
44	7	CL	A	Chelsea	L1-3	0-1	15	Geddis	29,541
45	12	CL	H	Carlisle U	W2-1	0-1	14	Geddis, Campbell	4,512
								Av Home Att	**9,730**

Goal Scorers

League (57): Geddis 15, Glavin 10, Gray 8 (2 pens), McGuire 5 (2 pens), Cunningham 4, Airey 3, Campbell 2, Ronson 2, Wilkes 2, Chambers 1, Johnson 1, Joyce 1, Law 1, May 1, Plummer 1

FA Cup (-): —

Milk Cup (-): —

1983-84

Horn	Joyce	Chambers	Glavin	Law	McCarthy	Wilkes	Campbell	Ronson	Cunningham	Gray	May	Findlay **(L)**	McGuire	Airey	Geddis	Rhodes	Thomas	Whitehouse	Semley	Futcher	Pickering	Plummer	Johnson **(L)**	Jeffels	REFEREE	
1	2	3	4	5	6	7	8	9	10	11															N Midgley	1
1	2	3	4		6	7	8	9	10	11	5														M Robinson	2
1	2	3	4		6†	7	8	9	10	11	5														KG Salmon	3
1	2	3	4		6	7	8*	9	10	11	5			12											T Holbrook	4
1	2	3			6	7		9	10	11	5		4	8											R Guy	5
	2	3	4	6		7			10	11	5	1	8	9											K Walmsley	6
	2	3	4	6		7			10	11	5	1	8	12	9*										K Barratt	7
	2	3	4	6		7			10	11	5	1	8		9										A Crickmore	8
	2	**3**	**4**	**6**		**7***		**12**	**10**	**11**	**5**		**8**		**9**	**1**									**F Roberts**	**9**
	2	3	4	6				7	10	11	5	1	8		9										D Vickers	10
	2	3	4	6				7	10	11	5	1	8		9										A Saunder	11
	2	3		6		12	7	4	10	11*	5	1	8		9										P Willis	12
	2			**3**	**6**	**7***	**11**		**10**		**5**		**8**		**9**	**1**		**12**							**G Courtney**	**13**
	4	3		2	6	7	11†		10		5		8		9	1									J C Deakin	14
	4	3	12	2	6	7*	11		10		5		8		9	1									D Shaw	15
	7	3	4	2	6					11	5		8	10	9	1									A Banks	16
	7	3	4	2	6					11	5		8	10	9	1									H Taylor	17
	4	3		2	6		7			11	5		8	10	9	1									I Hendrick	18
	7	3	4	2*	6			12		11	5		8	10	9	1									J Hough	19
	2	3	4	12	6		7	8		11*	5			10	9	1									N Wilson	20
	7	3	4	6				8			5			10	9	1		11							D Owen	21
	2	3	4	6			11	8			5		7	10	9	1									J Lovatt	22
	2	3	4	6*			11	8			5		7	10	9	1			12						K Redfern	23
	2	3	4				11	8			5		7	10*	9	1			12		6				J Bray	24
	2	3	4				11	8			5		7	10*	9	1			12		6				D Scott	25
	2	**3**	**4**	**6**			**11***	**8**			**5**		**7**	**10**	**9**	**1**			**12**						**G Napthine**	**26**
	4	3		2			11	8			5		7		9	1		12			6		10		T Spencer	27
	2	3	4	6			11	8			5		7		9	1							10		N Ashley	28
	2*	3	4	6			11	8			5		7	12	10	1							9		T Fitzharris	29
		3	4	2			11	8			5		7	9	10	1								6	G Tyson	30
		3	4	2			11	8			5		7	9		1							10	6	J Worrall	31
	12	3	4	2			11	8			5		7			1			9				10	6	M Peck	32
	2	3	4	6			11	8			5		7		10	1	9								C Downey	33
	2	3	4	6			11				5		7	10	9	1	8								P Tyldesley	34
	2	3	4*	6			11			12	5		7	9	10	1	8								A Robinson	35
	2	3	4					7			5		8	12	10	1	9			6		11			D Allison	36
	2	3*	4				11	7			5		8	12	9	1	10			6					M Heath	37
	2		4*	3			11	7			5		8	12	10	1	9			6					N Glover	38
	2		4	3			11	7			5		8	9*		1	10			6					R Bridges	39
	2		4	3			11	7			5		8	12	10*	1	9			6					M James	40
	2		4	3			11	7			5		8	9*		1	10			6		12			M Robinson	41
	2	3	4				11	7			5		8	9		1	10			6					L Burden	42
	2	3	4				11	7			5		8		10	1	9			6					J Hunting	43
	2	3					11	7			5		8	4	10	1	9			6					V Callow	44
	2			3			11	7			5		8		10	1	4			6					G Napthine	45
5	39	37	34	30	12	10	31	31	13	16	41	6	36	20	31	31	13	1	1	10	3	1	4	3	League Appearances	
	+1S		+1S	+1S		+1S		+1S		+1S				+7S				+1S	+3S			+1S				
	1	1	1	1			1	1			1		1	1	1	1			1S						FA Cup Appearances	
	2	1	1	2	1	2	1	1S	2	1	2		2		2	2		1S							Milk Cup Appearances	

Also Played: Agnew match 39, no.12. Fletcher match 21, no.2 Lowe match 27, no.10; 45, no.9 Shutt match 13, no.4.

OAKWELL GROUND

Official Address: Oakwell Ground, Grove Street, Barnsley. Telephone: 0226 295353

Ground Capacity: 35,554 (15,000 under cover)

Record Attendance: 40,225 v. Stoke City, F.A. Cup 5th Round, 15 Feb 1936

Record Receipts: £16,146 v. Rotherham United, F.A. Cup Round 2, 16 Dec 1978

Size of Playing Area: 111yds × 75 yds

Season Tickets: Stand: £68.00 (juveniles/OAP £52.00); Ground: £40.00 (juveniles/OAP £28)

Cost of Stand Tickets: £4.00 (all seats); **Terraces:** £2.30 (£1.60 juveniles/OAP)

Match and Ticket Information: Phone ground. Available two weeks in advance

Car Parking: Two official club parks adjacent ground for 1,200 vehicles (fee 25p). Visiting supporters should use Queens Road free park — two minutes from ground
in side streets and at the Molyneux Hotel.

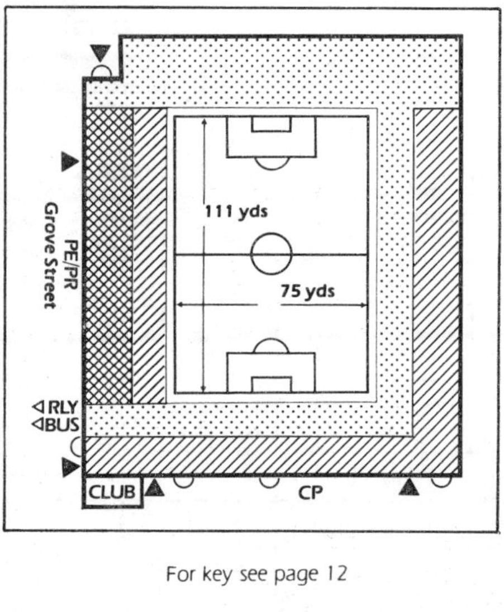

For key see page 12

How to get to the ground

From North: Leave Motorway M1 at junction 37 and follow signs into Barnsley A628. Then follow signs Pontefract into Pontefract Road. In 0.3m turn left into Grove St. for Barnsley F.C.
From East: From A1(M) and Doncaster, follow signs Barnsley A635, then 107m after Ardsley turn right into Pontefract Road. In 0.3m turn left into Grove Street for Barnsley F.C.
From South: Leave Motorway M1 at junction 36 and follow signs into Barnsley A628. Then follow signs Pontefract into Pontefract Road. In 0.3m turn left into Grove Street for Barnsley F.C.
From West: Follow signs Barnsley to enter via A628 or A635 then follow signs Pontefract into Pontefract Road. In 0.3m turn left into Grove Street for Barnsley F.C.

BIRMINGHAM CITY Division 2

Chairman
C K Coombs

Directors
J F Wiseman
H Parkes
N B A Bosworth

Secretary
A R Waterhouse

Coach
K Leonard

Manager
R Saunders

Reserve Team Coach
S Fleet

Youth Team Coach
K Bradley

Chief Scout
N Bodell

Promotions Manager
D Blee (021 772 0101)

Lottery Manager
R Kernick

Physiotherapist
G Doig

Groundsman
A Clarke

A season, which for most of its run promised a great deal, ended in total disaster with the Blues losing their hard-earned First Division status. But it could have been much different for although at no time did the team seem likely to do anything special in the League, they were a respectable eighth position in late September. So, until the latest moments it did seem that survival was 'on' until everything fell apart and the last match of the campaign arrived with victory over Southampton at St. Andrews being essental for retention of senior status. There was only a draw and back to Division Two goes the club although if previous stays there are any guide it should not be for long — but nothing can be taken for granted.

In the cups the team did reasonably well with Derby being despatched in the second round of the Milk Cup very easily. In the next round Notts County provided stern opposition and excitement. Draws at St. Andrews and Meadow Lane were followed in the end with a fine win for the Blues in Nottingham, which brought holders Liverpool to St. Andrews for the next stage, where the visitors shared two goals and won by three clear goals in the Anfield replay.

The F.A. Cup campaign started with a draw at Bramall Lane and a two goal replay win over the Third Division team; this was followed by a very good traditional success at Roker Park, a first half goal for Sunderland being overtaken by efforts from Kuhl and Harford in the last five minutes. West Ham, amidst disgraceful supporters' behaviour, were then thrashed at St. Andrews (3-0) so all was set for a last eight confrontation at home to Watford, who played superbly on the day and were worthy winners (3-1). No Wembley, no cups.

To add to the embarrassment the club's disciplinary record left much to be desired and Manager Ron Saunders has much hard work on his hands to change the luck and the team's image so that loyal supporters may have something to admire.

Back Row L to R: Graham Doig (Physiotherapist), Mick Halsall, Mick Ferguson, Noel Blake (now with Portsmouth), Mick Harford, Tony Coton, Jim Blyth, Jim Hagan, Kevan Broadhurst, Byron Stevenson, Pat Van Den Hauwe, Keith Leonard (First Team Coach). **Front Row:** Gerry Daly, Brian Roberts, David Giles, Paul Gormon, Billy Wright, Robert Hopkins, Martin Kuhl, Tony Rees.

'THE BLUES'

Formed: 1875 **Turned Professional:** 1885 **Ltd Co:** 1888
Previous Names: Small Heath Alliance (1875-88), Small Heath (1888), Birmingham (1905-45)
Previous Managers: Since 1946: Ted Goodier Harry Storer Bob Brocklebank Arthur Turner Pat Beasley Gil Merrick Joe Mallett Stan Cullis Fred Goodwin Willie Bell Sir Alf Ramsey Jim Smith
Honours: Division 2 Champions 1892-3, 1920-1, 1947-8, 1954-5 Football League Cup Winners 1962-3
League Career: Elected to Division 2 1892 Promoted to Division 1 1894
Relegated to Division 2 1896 Promoted to Division 1 1901 Relegated to Division 2 1902
Promoted to Division 1 1903 Relegated to Division 2 1908 Promoted to Division 1 1921
Relegated to Division 2 1939 Promoted to Division 1 1948 Relegated to Division 2 1950
Promoted to Division 1 1955 Relegated to Division 2 1965 Promoted to Division 1 1972
Relegated to Division 2 1979 Promoted to Division 1 1980 Relegated to Division 2 1984
Colours: Royal blue shirts with three white vertical stripes on sleeves, white shorts with blue trim, white stockings with blue hoops on turnover
Change Colours: Yellow shirts with three blue vertical stripes on sleeves, yellow shorts with blue trim, yellow stockings with blue hoops on turnover

CLUB RECORDS

Most Appearances for Club: Gil Merrick: Football League 486 + F.A. Cup 42 **Total 528** (1946-80)
Most Capped Player: Malcolm Page, 28, Wales. **For England:** Harry Hibbs, 25
Record Goalscorer in a Match: Trevor Francis, 5
Record League Goalscorer in a season: Joe Bradford, 29, Div 1, 1927-8 **All competitions:** Joe Bradford, 32, 1929-30
Record League Goalscorer in a career: Joe Bradford, 249 **All competitions:** Joe Bradford, 270 (League 249, F.A. Cup 21), 1920-35
Record Transfer Fee Received: £975,000 from Nottingham Forest for Trevor Francis, Feb 1979
Record Transfer Fee Paid: £350,000 to Derby Co. for David Langan, June 1980
Best Performances: League: 6th Div 1 1955-6 **F.A. Cup:** Finalists (2) **League/Milk Cup:** Winners (1)
European Fairs Cup: Finalists
Most League Points: 59 in Div 2, 1947-8
Most League Goals: 103, Div 2, 1893-4
Record League Victory: 12-0 v Walsall Town Swifts, Div 2, 17.12.1892
12-0 v Doncaster Rovers, Div 2, 11.4.1903
Record League Defeat: 1-9 v Sheffield Wednesday, Div 1, 13.12.30
1-9 v Blackburn Rovers, Div 1, 5.1.1895
European Competitions Entered: European Fairs Cup 1955-8, 1958-60, 1960-1, 1960-2

Club Statistician for the Directory: Dave Drage

Programme Editors
Bill Galden & Andrew Waterhouse

Price	Number of Pages
50p	24

Subscriptions
£14.00 per season (U.K.) — League matches only

BIRMINGHAM CITY

PLAYERS NAME Ht Wt Birthdate	Honours	Birthplace Transfers	Clubs	APPEARANCES League	Milk Cup	F.A.C.	E. Cups	GOALS League	Milk Cup	F.A.C.	E. Cups
GOALKEEPERS											
Jim Blyth	S.(2)	Perth	P.N.E. (A)	1							
6-1¼ 13.3 28.7.44		F	Coventry C.	151	13	10					
			Hereford U. (A)	7							
		F	Birmingham C.	14	2						
Tony Coton		Tamworth	Mile Oak R.								
6-1 11.10 19.5.64			Birmingham C.	87	10	10					
DEFENDERS											
Jim Hagan	N.I. Y	Monkstown	Larne								
5-11 11.9 10.8.56		£20,000	Coventry C.	12+1							
			Detroit & Hong Kong (L)								
			Torquay U. (L)	7							
		F	Birmingham C.	60+5	10						
Brian Roberts		Manchester	Coventry C. (A)	209+6	19+	13					
5-8 11.3 6.11.55			Hereford U. (L)	5							
		£10,000	Birmingham C.	11							
Pat Van Der Hauwe		Dendermonde.	Birmingham C.	113+4	12	5		1			
5-10 10.6 16.12.60		Belgium									
Billy Wright†	E. B.(2). U.21(6)	Liverpool	Everton	164+2	13	13		10			
5-11 12.7 28.4.58		F	Birmingham C.	40	8	5		5		3	
MIDFIELD											
David Giles	W.(12). U.21(4).	Cardiff	Cardiff C. (A)	51+8	6	4	1+1	3	1	1	
5-7 10.4 21.9.56	Y. S	£30,000	Wrexham	38	3	3	2	2			
		£70,000	Swansea C.	49+5	2	5+1	+2	13		4	
			Orient (L)	3				2			
		Player Exchange	Crystal Palace	83+5	5	5		6			
Kevan Broadhurst*		Dewsbury	Birmingham C.	148+6	7	13		10			
5-9½ 11.2 3.6.59			Walsall (L)	3							
Gerry Daly	Ei.(37). Div. 2. 75	Dublin	Bohemians								
5-10 10.6 30.4.54			Manchester U.	107+4	17	9	4	23	4	5	
		£175,000	Derby Co.	111+1	5	5		31	1	2	
		£310,000	Coventry C.	82+2	10+	6		15	1	4	
			Leicester C. (L)	17							
Mike Halsall		Bootle	Liverpool (A)								
5-10 11.4 21.7.61		F	Birmingham C.	33	6+1	3		3			
Martin Kuhl		Frimley	Birmingham C. (A)	22+2	3	5		1		1	
5-11 11.9 10.1.65											
Byron Stevenson	W.(15). U.21(3)	Llanelli	Leeds U.	88+7	7+1	6		4	3	1	
6-1 11.0 7.9.56		Player Exchange	Birmingham C.	63+5	9+1	6		3			
Paul Gorman		Dublin	Arsenal (A)	5+1				1			
5-10 11.8 6.8.63		F	Birmingham C.								
FORWARDS											
Wayne Clarke	E. Y. S	Wolverhampton	Wolverhampton W. (A)	129+19	8+2	9+2	0+1	30	2	1	
5-11¼ 10.6 28.2.61		£80,000	Birmingham C.								
Steve Cooper		Birmingham	Moor Green								
5-11 11.4 22.6.64			Birmingham C.								
			Halifax T. (L)	7				1			
Mike Ferguson		Newcastle	Coventry C. (A)	121+6	10+	3		51	3		
6-1 12.8 3.10.54		£280,000	Everton	7+1	3+1			4	2		
		£60,000	Birmingham C.	20	2			8			
			Coventry C. (L)	7				3			
Mick Harford		Sunderland	Lincoln C.	109+6	8	3		41	5		
6-1 12.4 12.2.59		£180,000	Newcastle U.	18+1				4			
		£160,000	Bristol C.	30	5	5		11	6	2	
		£100,000	Birmingham C.	80	6	7		23		7	
Robert Hopkins	FAYC. 80	Birmingham	Aston Villa (A)	1+2				1			
5-7 10.5 25.10.61		F	Birmingham C.	43	6	5		7	2	1	
Tony Rees	W.(1). U.21(1). S.	Merthyr Tydfil	Aston Villa (A)								
5-8½ 11.0 1.8.64	FAYC. 80		Birmingham C.	22+3		3		2		1	

APPRENTICES: Peter Shearer, Mike Clarke, Tom Devesey, Julian Dicks

NON CONTRACT PLAYERS: Ian Brown, Ian Gore, Mark Hopkins Robin Judd, Andy Poole, Guy Russell, David Smith, Stuart Storer, Martin Weir, Lee Williams, Roger Willis, Tom Woolley

BIRMINGHAM CITY

DIVISION ONE 20TH **FA CUP** 6TH ROUND **MILK CUP** 4TH ROUND

MATCH	DATE	COMPE-TITION	VENUE	OPPONENTS	RESULT	HALF TIME	L'GUE POS'N	GOALSCORERS	ATTEN-DANCE
1	A 27	CL	A	West Ham U	L0-4	0-3			19,792
2	S 30	CL	A	Notts Co	L1-2	1-1		Harford	11,031
3	3	CL	H	Watford	W2-0	1-0	17	Hopkins, Halsall	11,931
4	6	CL	H	Stoke C	W1-0	1-0		Blake (pen)	13,728
5	10	CL	A	Wolverhampton W	D1-1	1-1	10	Wright (pen)	15,933
6	17	CL	H	Ipswich T	W1-0	0-0	10	Gayle	13,159
7	24	CL	A	Everton	D1-1	1-0	12	Gayle	15,253
8	O 1	CL	H	Leicester C	W2-1	2-0	8	Rees, Harford	15,212
9	**5**	**MC 2**	**A**	**Derby Co**	**W3-0**	**2-0**		**Watson (og), Rees, Gayle**	**13,114**
10	15	CL	A	Aston Villa	L0-1	0-1	12		39,318
11	22	CL	H	Tottenham H	L0-1	0-0	15		19,016
12	**25**	**MC 2**	**H**	**Derby Co**	**W4-0**	**2-0**		**Harford 3, Gayle**	**7,786**
13	29	CL	A	WBA	W2-1	1-0	13	Gayle, Harford	20,224
14	N 5	CL	H	Coventry C	L1-2	1-1	14	Blake	16,169
15	**8**	**MC 3**	**H**	**Notts Co**	**D2-2**	**1-0**		**Handysides, Phillips**	**10,484**
16	12	CL	A	Luton T	D1-1	1-1	14	Hopkins	11,111
17	19	CL	A	QPR	L1-2	0-0	15	Harford	10,824
18	**22**	**MC 3R**	**A**	**Notts Co**	**D0-0[1]**	**0-0**			**8,268**
19	26	CL	H	Sunderland	L0-1	0-0	16		11,948
20	**29**	**MC 3R2**	**H**	**Notts Co**	**D0-0[1]**	**0-0**			**9,678**
21	D 3	CL	A	Liverpool	L0-1	0-0	17		24,791
22	**5**	**MC 3R3**	**A**	**Notts Co**	**W3-1**	**3-0**		**Hopkins 2, Harford**	**7,361**
23	10	CL	H	Norwich C	L0-1	0-1	17		9,971
24	17	CL	A	Southampton	L1-2	1-1	17	Stevenson	15,248
25	**20**	**MC 4**	**H**	**Liverpool**	**D1-1**	**0-1**		**Harford**	**17,405**
26	**22**	**MC 4R**	**A**	**Liverpool**	**L0-3**	**0-1**			**11,638**
27	26	CL	H	Nottingham F	L1-2	1-0	19	Rogers	14,482
28	27	CL	A	Arsenal	D1-1	0-0	19	Hopkins	25,642
29	31	CL	A	Watford	L0-1	0-0	19		14,359
30	J 2	CL	H	Everton	L0-2	0-0	19		10,004
31	**7**	**FAC 3**	**A**	**Sheffield U**	**D1-1**	**1-0**		**Wright (pen)**	**17,202**
32	**10**	**FAC 3R**	**H**	**Sheffield U**	**W2-0**	**0-0**		**Harford, Wright (pen)**	**10,888**
33	14	CL	H	West Ham U	W3-0	1-0	19	Harford, Halsall, Hopkins	10,334
34	21	CL	A	Ipswich T	W2-1	1-1	19	Harford, Butcher (og)	12,900
35	**28**	**FAC 4**	**A**	**Sunderland**	**W2-1**	**0-1**		**Kuhl, Harford**	**21,226**
36	F 4	CL	A	Leicester C	W3-2	2-0	19	Peake (og), Gayle, Wright (pen),	13,776
37	7	CL	H	Manchester U	D2-2	1-1	18	Hopkins, Wright (pen)	19,975
38	11	CL	H	Wolverhampton W	D0-0	0-0	18		14,319
39	**18**	**FAC 5**	**H**	**West Ham U**	**W3-0**	**2-0**		**Hopkins, Rees, Wright (pen)**	**29,570**
40	25	CL	A	Tottenham H	W1-0	0-0	15	Harford	23,564
41	28	CL	H	WBA	W2-1	2-0		Rees, Broadhurst	16,780
42	M 3	CL	A	Coventry C	W1-0	1-0	14	Gayle	13,705
43	**10**	**FAC 6**	**H**	**Watford**	**L1-3**	**0-1**		**Terry (og)**	**40,220**
44	17	CL	A	Stoke C	L1-2	0-1	15	Gayle	13,506
45	20	CL	H	Luton T	D1-1	0-1		Wright (pen)	9,592
46	24	CL	H	Notts Co	D0-0	0-0	13		9,040
47	31	CL	H	Aston Villa	W2-1	1-1	12	Stevenson, Gayle	23,993
48	A 7	CL	A	Manchester U	L0-1	0-1	15		39,891
49	14	CL	H	QPR	L0-2	0-1	15		10,255
50	21	CL	A	Nottingham F	L1-5	0-2	17	Harford	15,323
51	23	CL	H	Arsenal	D1-1	0-1	17	Kuhl	11,164
52	28	CL	A	Sunderland	L1-2	0-1	18	Wright (pen)	13,061
53	M 5	CL	H	Liverpool	D0-0	0-0	19		18,809
54	7	CL	A	Norwich C	D1-1	0-0	18	Gayle	13,601
55	12	CL	H	Southampton	D0-0	0-0	20		16,445
								Av Home Att	**14,108**

Goal Scorers

League (39): Gayle 8, Harford 8, Hopkins 5, Wright 5 (5 pens), Blake 2 (1 pen), Halsall 2, Rees 2, Stevenson 2, Broadhurst 1, Kuhl 1, Rogers 1, opponents 2
FA Cup (9): Wright 3 (3 pens), Harford 2, Hopkins 1, Kuhl 1, Rees 1, opponent 1
Milk Cup (13): Harford 5, Gayle 2, Hopkins 2, Handysides 1, Phillips 1, Rees 1, opponent 1

1983-84

Coton	Hagan	Stevenson	Blake	Wright	Broadhurst	Handysides	Phillips	Harford	Van den Hauwe	Hopkins	Rees	Halsall	McCarrick	Gayle	Mumford	Rogers	Kuhl	Muir	Linton	Roberts	Kendall	REFEREE	
1	2	3	4	5	6	7*	8	9	10	11	12											A Robinson	1
1	2		4	5	6	12	8	9	3	11†	7*	10										T Jones	2
1	2		4	5	6		8	9	3	11	7	10										R Guy	3
1	2		4	5	6		8	9	3	11	7*	10	12									C Downey	4
1	2		4	5	6		8	9	3	11	7*	10		12								C Thomas	5
1		12	4	5	6		8	9	3		11*	10		7	2							Alan Robinson	6
1		12	4	5	6*		8	9	3		11	10		7	2							A Saunders	7
1	2		4	5			8	9	3	11	6	10		7								K Walmsley	8
1	**2**	**12**	**4**	**5**			**8**	**9**	**3**	**11**	**6***	**10**		**7**								**N Ashley**	**9**
1	2	12	4	5	6*			9	3	11	8	10		7								D Allison	10
1	2	6	4	5			12	9	3	11	8*	10		7								D Shaw	11
1	**2**	**6**	**4**	**5**			**8**	**9**	**3**	**11**		**10**		**7**								**R Milford**	**12**
1	2	6	4	5			8	9	3	11		10		7								D Hutchinson	13
1	2	6	4	5			8	9*	3	11		10		7		12						J Lovatt	14
1	**2**	**6**	**4**	**5**		**9**	**8**		**3**	**11**		**10**		**7**								**R Bridges**	**15**
1	2	6	4	5		10	8		3	11				7			9					T Spencer	16
1	2	6	4	5		10	8	9	3	11				7								D J Axcell	17
1	**2**	**6**	**4**	**5**			**8***	**9**	**3**	**11**		**12**		**7**			**10**					**J Worrall**	**18**
1	2	6	4	5		10	8	9	3	11				7								L F Burden	19
1	**2**	**6**	**4**	**5**			**8**	**9**	**3**	**11**				**7**			**10**					**B Stevens**	**20**
1	2			5			8	9	3	11		6		7			4	10				K Redfern	21
1	**2**		**4**	**5**			**8**	**9**	**3**	**11**		**6**		**7**			**10**					**P Willis**	**22**
1	2	5	4	6			9	10	3			7		8			11					J Hough	23
1	2	6	4	5			8	9	3		10			7*			11		12			D Vickers	24
1	**2**	**6**	**4**	**5**			**8**	**9**	**3**		**11***	**7**	**12**				**10**					**B Hill**	**25**
1	**2**	**6**	**4**	**5**			**8**	**9**	**3**	**11**	**10**	**7**										**K Hackett**	**26**
1	2		4	5				9	3	11	7				12	10	8*		6			D Richardson	27
1	2*	8	4	5				9	3	11	7				12	10			6			M James	28
1		6	4	5	3			9	8	11	7			10					2			D Brazier	29
1		8	4	5	6		12	9	3	11	7				2	10*						J Deakin	30
1		**2**	**4**	**5**	**6**			**9**	**3**	**11**	**7**	**10**					**8**					**C Downey**	**31**
1		**2**	**4**	**5**	**6**			**9**	**3**	**11**	**7**	**10**					**8**					**C Downey**	**32**
1		2	4	5	6			9	3	11		10		7			8					D Hedges	33
1			4	5	6			9	3	11*	12	10	2	7			8					M Dimblebee	34
1			**4**	**5**	**6**			**9**	**3**	**11**		**10**	**2**	**7**			**8**					**D Richardson**	**35**
1			4	5	6			9	3	11		10	2	7			8					I Borrett	36
1		12	4	5	6			9	3	11		10	2	7			8*					H King	37
1		8	4	5	6		10	9	3	11	7		2									G Napthine	38
1		**10**	**4**	**5**	**6**			**9**	**3**	**11**	**7**		**2**				**8**					**G Courtney**	**39**
1	6	10	4	5			11	9	3		7		2				8					D Letts	40
1	12	10	4	5	6			9	3		11*		2	7			8					L Shapter	41
1	12	10	4	5	6			9	3*	11			2	7			8					C Downey	42
1		**10**	**4**	**5**	**6**			**9**	**3**	**11**			**2**	**7**			**8**					**T Bune**	**43**
1	3		4	5	6			9†	10	11			12	7			8*			2		P Tyldesley	44
1	3		4	5	6			9	8	11	10			7						2		E Read	45
1	3		4		6*			9	5	11	10		12	7			8			2		D Reeves	46
1	3	6	4						8	11		10	9	7			5			2		J Hunting	47
1	3	6	4	5				9	8			10	11*	7			12			2		T Mills	48
1	12	8	4	5	6*			9	3		11	10		7						2		N Glover	49
1	11	8	4	5	12			9	3				10*	7			6			2		J Moules	50
	4			5	6*			9	3	11			2	7		10	12			8	1	J Key	51
1	4			5				9†	3		11		2	7		10	8			6		D Scott	52
1	2		4	5				9	3	11				7		10	8			6		K Salmon	53
1	2		4	5				9	3	11	12			7		10	8*			6		A Gunn	54
1	2		4	5					3	11	9	6		7		10	8					N Wilson	55
41	30	21	39	40	22	4	18	39	**42**	32	22	21	12	32	3	8	20	1	3	11	1	League Appearances	
	+3S	+4S			+1S	+1S	+2S				+3S		+3S	+1S	+2S	+1S	+2S		+1S				
5		4	5	5	5			5	5	5	3	3	3	2			5					FA Cup Appearances	
8	8	6+1S	8	8		1	8	7	8	7	3	6+1S	1S	6			4					Milk Cup Appearances	

ST. ANDREWS

Official Address: St. Andrews, Birmingham B9 4NH. Telephone: 021-772 0101/2689

Ground Capacity: 44,500 (9,009 seated)

Record Attendance: 66,844 v. Everton, F.A. Cup Round 5, 11 Feb 1939

Record Receipts: £110,450.72 v. Watford, F.A. Cup Round 6, 10 Mar 1984

Size of Playing Area: 115yds × 75 yds

Season Tickets: Centre Stand £112.00; Wing Stand £90.00; City Stand £78.00; Main Stand Paddock £72.00; City Stand Paddock £61.00; Terraces: £45.00; juveniles/OAP (except Centre Stand) approx half-price

Cost of Stand Tickets: £3.00, £3.50, £4.00, £5.00, £6.00; **Terraces:** £2.50

Match and Ticket Information: 021-773 7161

Car Parking: Public car park in Coventry Road and Cattell Road

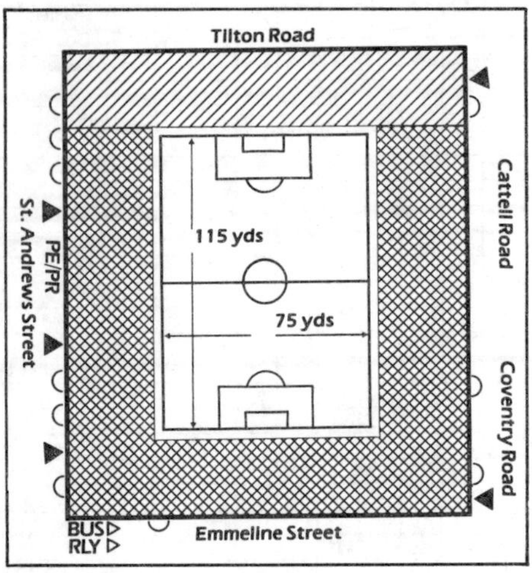

For key see page 12

How to get to the ground

From North and East: Use Motorway M6 until Junction 6. Leave motorway and follow signs Birmingham Central A38M. In 1.9m branch left and at roundabout take 1st exit A45 along Dartmouth Middleway. In 1.2m turn left A45 into St. Andrews Road for Birmingham City F.C.

From South: Leave M5 at Junction 4 or use A435 or A41 to enter Birmingham. Then follow signs Coventry A45 to enter Coventry Road, then in 0.3m turn left into St. Andrews Road for Birmingham City F.C.

From West: Follow signs Birmingham A456, then follow signs The South A41 then Coventry A45 to enter Coventry Road, then in 0.3m turn left into St. Andrews Road for Birmingham City F.C.

BLACKBURN ROVERS Division 2

President
W H Bancroft

Chairman
W Fox

Directors
R D Coar BSc (Vice Chairman)
Dr M Jeffries TD
T W Ibbotson LLB
L Neale
K C Lee
I R Stanners

Secretary
J W Howarth FAAI

Commercial Department
(0254 5542/3/4)

Manager
Bobby Saxton

Reserve Team Manager
Jim Furnell

Coach
T Parkes

Physiotherapist
T G Long

Groundsman
S Grime

Rovers won nothing and stay in the Second Division, but few who saw them play would allow a summary of the season to end with those few terse comments. With little cash available and modest attendance figures owing to the local unemployment problems among other things, the team managed to make the best of its own circumstances and imposed limitations and a final position of sixth was most creditable, although a promotion place was never really in sight.

The Milk Cup challenge ended early with an aggregate defeat against Ipswich Town after two most attractive matches. In the away leg Rovers led by two clear goals at half-time and later went ahead again after Town had equalised, but the defence was shaky on the night and the East Anglian club went to Ewood Park with a single goal lead which had been increased to two by half-time — and there it stayed. The F.A. Cup was more productive with Brotherston's first-half goal dismissing Chelsea in Round Three. Swindon led at half-time at the County Ground in the next session but Keeley netted with his first touch as a late substitue and then made a winner for top scorer Garner, so optimism was felt with Southampton and the television cameras at Ewood Park for the Fifth Round. But there was to be no advance as the visitors won a splendid match rather fortunately with an early second-half goal. Thereafter good defence and bad luck thwarted Rovers.

Being an attractive team to watch is not in itself consolation for a blank sideboard but with a number of talented players, particularly Brotherston and Garner, and a sound defence, quiet optimism for the future can justly be felt by Manager Saxton and his staff. If only cash resources were better so that the occasional star could be added, First Division football would be back in Blackburn. Even so the good organisation could still bring that and fans in most places would applaud it. It would also be just reward for such marvellously loyal club men as Fazackerly who is still playing as well as ever.

Back Row L to R: Mick Rathbone, David Byrom, Jimmy Quinn, Glenn Keeley, John Lowey, Chris Thompson, Mark Patterson. **Middle Row:** Tony Long (Remedial Therapist), Bobby Saxton (Manager), David Glenn, Jim Branagan, Terry Gennoe, Vice O'Keefe, David Mail, Simon Barker, Jim Furnell (Reserve Team Manager), Tony Parkes (Coach). **Front Row:** David Hamilton, Colin Randell, Derekk Fazackerley, William Fox (Chairman), Ian Miller, Noel Brotherston, Simon Garner.

'THE BLUE & WHITES' or 'ROVERS'

Formed: 1875 **Turned Professional:** 1880 **Ltd Co:** 1897
Previous Names: Blackburn Grammar School O.B.
Previous Managers: (Since 1946) Eddie Hapgood Will Scott Jack Bruton Jackie Bestall John Carey Dally Duncan Jack Marshall Eddie Quigley John Carey Ken Furphy Gordon Lee Jim Smith Jim Iley Howard Kendall
Honours: Division 1 Champions 1911-12, 1913-14 Division Two Champions 1938-9 Division 3 Champions 1974-5 F.A. Cup Winners 1884, 1885, 1886, 1890, 1891, 1928
League Career: Original Members of the League 1888 Relegated to Division 2 1935-6 Promoted to Division 1 1938-9 Relegated to Division 2 1946-7 Promoted to Division 1 1956-7 Relegated to Division 2 1965-6 Relegated to Division 3 1970-1 Promoted to Division 2 1974-5 Relegated to Division 3 1978-9 Promoted to Division 2 1979-80
Colours: Blue and white halved shirts, white shorts, blue stockings with red and white tops

CLUB RECORDS

Most Appearances for Club: Ronnie Clayton: (Football League 580 + F.A. Cup 40) **Total 620** (1950-69
Most Capped Player: Bob Crompton, 41, England
Record Goalscorer in a Match: Tommy Briggs, 7 v Bristol Rovers (Div 2 record) 05.02.55
Record League Goalscorer in a season: Ted Harper, 43, Div 1, 1925-6 **All competitions:** Ted Harper, 45 (League 43, F.A. Cup 2), 1925-6
Record League Goalscorer in a career: Tommy Briggs, 140, 1952-8 **All competitions:** Tommy Briggs, 150 (League 140, F.A. Cup 10)
Record Transfer Fee Received: £357,000 from Leeds United for Kevin Hird, Feb 1979
Record Transfer Fee Paid: £100,000 to Chelsea for Duncan McKenzie, March 1979
Best Performances: League: Champions (2) **F.A. Cup:** Winners (6) **League/Milk Cup:** Semi-Final 1961-2
Most League Points: (3pts for win) 67, Div 2 (2pts for win) 60, Div 3, 1974-5
Most League Goals: 114, Div 2, 1954-5
Record League Victory: 9-0 v Middlesbrough, Div 2, 6 Nov 1954
Record League Defeat: 0-8 v Arsenal, Div 1, 25.2.33

Club Statistician for the Directory: H. Berry

Programme Editor
John W. Howarth

Price
40p

Number of Pages

Subscriptions
Not available

BLACKBURN ROVERS

PLAYERS NAME Ht Wt Birthdate	Honours	Birthplace Transfers	Clubs	APPEARANCES League	Milk Cup	F.A.C.	E.Cups	GOALS League	Milk Cup	F.A.C.	E. Cups
GOALKEEPERS											
Terry Gennoe		Shrewsbury	Bury	3							
6-2½ 13.5 16.3.53		F	Halifax T.	78	8	8					
		£40,000	Southampton	36	10	5					
			Crystal Palace (L)	3							
		£60,000	Blackburn R.	98	6	5					
Vince O'Keefe		Birmingham	Exeter C.[1]	53	11	3					
6-0 11.0 2.4.57		£30,000	Torquay U.	108	4	6					
		£15,000	Blackburn R.	21							
		F	Bury (L)	2							
DEFENDERS											
Jim Branagan		Barton	Oldham A.	24+3	2						
5-10 11.6 3.7.55		F	Cape Town								
		F	Huddersfield T.	37+1		+1					
		£20,000	Blackburn R.	190+1	10	13		3			
David Byrom		Padiham	Blackburn R. (A)								
5-10 12.0 6.1.65											
Derek Fazackerley*	Div. 3, 75	Preston	Blackburn R. (A)	511+2	30	32		18	1	1	
5-11 11.6 5.11.51											
David Glenn		Wigan	Wigan Ath. (A)	68+4	7	+1		4			
5-10 10.10 30.11.62			Blackburn R.	21+1		3					
Glen Keeley	E. Y	Basildon	Ipswich T. (A)	4							
6-0 12.0 1.9.54		£70,000	Newcastle U.	43+1	12	8+1		2	2		
		£30,000	Blackburn R.	258+5	14	14+1		16		1	
			Everton (L)	1							
David Mail	FAYC 80	Bristol	Aston Villa (A)								
5-11 11.12 12.9.62		F	Blackburn R.	42+3	2+1	3		1			
Mike Rathbone	E. Y	Birmingham	Birmingham C (A)	17+3	1	2					
5-10 11.13 6.11.58		£40,000	Blackburn R.	162+2	5	7		2			
MIDFIELD											
Simon Barker		Farnworth	Blackburn R. (A)	28		2					
5-9 11.0 4.11.64											
David Hamilton	E. Y	South Shields	Sunderland (A)								
5-8 9.12 7.11.60		F	Blackburn R.	70+8	6	1		4			
Colin Randell	W. U.23(1), Y S	Skewen	Coventry C. (A)								
5-9 10.8 12.12.52		F	Plymouth A.	137+2	10	8		9		2	
		£10,000	Exeter C.	78	5	5		4		2	
		£60,000	Plymouth A.	110	12	3		8			
		£40,000	Blackburn R.	42+1	4	1		4			
			Newport Co. (L)	15							
FORWARDS											
Noel Brotherstone	N.I.(25), U.21(1)	Belfast	Tottenham H. (A)	1							
5-9 10.8 18.11.56	Y. S. FAYC 74	F	Blackburn R.	241+6	15	16+1		32	2	2	
Simon Garner†		Boston	Blackburn R.	194+11	14+2	10+1		76	6	5	
5-8 11.3 23.11.59											
John Lowey		Manchester	Sheffield W.[2]	35+7		7		4		2	
5-11 12.7 7.3.58		£25,000	Blackburn R.	95+2	4	3		8		1	
Ian Miller		Perth	Bury								
5-9 11.7 13.5.55			Nottingham F.								
		Player Exchange	Doncaster R.	124	10	4		14			
		£25,000 + P/E	Swindon T.	123+4	19+	12		9	2	2	
		£67,000	Blackburn R.	108+2	5+1	3		10	1		
Mark Patterson		Darwen	Blackburn R. (A)	27+2		2		7			
5-6 10.10 24.5.65											
Jimmy Quinn		Belfast	Oswestry T.								
6-0½ 12.2 18.11.59		£10,000	Swindon T.	34+15	1+1	5+2		10		2	
		£32,500	Blackburn R.								
Chris Thompson	E. Y	Walsall	Bolton W. (A)	66+7	4+1	3+1		18	1	1	
5-10 11.6 24.1.60			Lincoln C. (L)	5+1							
		F	Blackburn R.	31+2	2	3		8			

CONTRACT PROFESSIONAL WITH NO FIRST TEAM APPEARANCES: P. Rigby

NON-CONTRACT PLAYERS 1984-85: I. Arthur, G. Mather, M. Tiplady, S. Wallace, A. Diamond, A. Haydock, M. Henshaw, S. Marrow, C. Taylor, M. Walker, J. Willis

[1] Previously on books of Birmingham C. and Walsall (no appearances) and joined Exeter from AP Leamington

[2] Previously on books of Manchester U. (A), Blackburn R., Port Vale (no appearances)

BLACKBURN ROVERS

DIVISION TWO 6TH **FA CUP** 5TH ROUND **MILK CUP** 2ND ROUND

MATCH	DATE	COMPETITION	VENUE	OPPONENTS	RESULT	HALF TIME	L'GUE POS'N	GOALSCORERS	ATTENDANCE
1	A 27	CL	H	Huddersfield T	D2-2	1-0		Keeley, Thompson	7,700
2	29	CL	A	Carlisle U	W1-0	1-0		Randell	4,470
3	S 3	CL	A	Cambridge U	L0-2	0-0	11		2,636
4	7	CL	H	Chelsea	D0-0	0-0			5,873
5	10	CL	H	Derby Co	W5-1	3-0	6	Garner 5 (1 pen)	6,837
6	17	CL	A	Manchester C	L0-6	0-3	9		25,433
7	24	CL	H	Brighton & HA	D2-2	1-1	11	Thompson, Garner (pen)	5,060
8	O 1	CL	A	Sheffield W	L2-4	1-1	15	Thompson 2	16,849
9	**5**	**MC 2**	**A**	**Ipswich T**	**L3-4**	**2-0**		**Garner 2, Miller**	**11,478**
10	8	CL	A	Middlesbrough	W2-1	0-0	11	Keeley, Garner	7,062
11	16	CL	H	Shrewsbury T	D1-1	1-0		Garner	5,777
12	22	CL	H	Oldham Ath	W3-1	0-1	9	Randell, Miller, Thompson	5,863
13	**26**	**MC 2**	**H**	**Ipswich T**	**L1-2**	**1-2**		**Garner**	**8,990**
14	29	CL	A	Swansea C	W1-0	0-0	8	Garner	10,588
15	N 5	CL	A	Charlton Ath	L0-2	0-2	10		4,563
16	12	CL	H	Leeds U	D1-1	0-1	9	Devine	9,556
17	19	CL	H	Portsmouth	W2-1	0-1	8	Devine, Garner	5,551
18	26	CL	A	Fulham	W1-0	0-0	7	Miller	5,647
19	D 4	CL	H	Grimsby T	D1-1	0-0		Patterson	6,409
20	10	CL	A	Cardiff C	W1-0	0-0	7	Patterson	5,200
21	17	CL	H	Crystal Palace	W2-1	2-0	7	Garner, Mail	4,794
22	26	CL	A	Newcastle U	D1-1	1-0	8	Barker	33,802
23	28	CL	H	Barnsley	D1-1	0-1		Garner	8,954
24	31	CL	H	Cambridge U	W1-0	0-0	7	Miller	5,675
25	J 2	CL	A	Brighton & HA	D1-1	1-0	8	Garner,	9,844
26	**7**	**FAC 3**	**H**	**Chelsea**	**W1-0**	**1-0**		**Brotherston**	**10,940**
27	14	CL	A	Huddersfield T	W2-0	1-0	7	Patterson, Thompson	8,203
28	21	CL	H	Manchester C	W2-1	1-1	6	Brotherston, Fazackerly (1pen)	18,199
29	**28**	**FAC 4**	**A**	**Swindon T**	**W2-1**	**0-1**		**Garner, Keeley**	**11,143**
30	F 3	CL	H	Sheffield W	D0-0	0-0	6		16,158
31	11	CL	A	Derby Co	D1-1	0-1	6	Keeley	13,922
32	**17**	**FAC 5**	**H**	**Southampton**	**L0-1**	**0-0**			**15,357**
33	25	CL	A	Oldham Ath	D0-0	0-0	7		6,855
34	M 7	CL	H	Swansea C	W4-1	2-1		Fazackerley, Evans (og), Thompson, Patterson	5,554
35	10	CL	A	Leeds U	L0-1	0-0	7		12,857
36	16	CL	A	Chelsea	L1-2	0-2		Garner	18,905
37	21	CL	H	Charlton Ath	D1-1	1-1		Thompson	4,784
38	24	CL	H	Carlisle U	W4-1	2-1	7	Garner, Barker, Hamilton, Fazackerley (pen)	6,171
39	30	CL	A	Shrewsbury T	L0-1	0-1			3,352
40	A 7	CL	H	Middlesbrough	W1-0	1-0	7	Patterson	4,910
41	14	CL	A	Portsmouth	W4-2	0-2	7	Garner 3, Patterson	8,915
42	20	CL	H	Newcastle U	D1-1	0-0		Fazackerley (pen)	19,196
43	23	CL	A	Barnsley	D0-0	0-0	6		7,123
44	29	CL	H	Fulham	L0-1	0-0			4,301
45	M 5	CL	A	Grimsby T	L2-3	0-1	6	Garner, Barker	4,826
46	7	CL	H	Cardiff C	D1-1	1-1	6	Patterson	3,107
47	12	CL	A	Crystal Palace	W2-0	0-0	6	Keeley, Hamilton	5,078
								Av Home Att	**7,591**

Goal Scorers

League (57): Garner 19 (2 pens), Thompson 8, Patterson 7, Fazackerley 4 (3 pens), Keeley 4, Barker 3, Miller 3, Devine 2, Hamilton 2, Randell 2, Brotherston 1, Mail 1, opponent 1
FA Cup (3): Brotherston 1, Garner 1, Keeley 1
Milk Cup (4): Garner 3, Miller 1

1983-84

Gennoe	Branagan	Rathbone	Randell	Keeley	Fazackerley	Miller	Lowey	Bell	Garner	Hamilton	Thompson	O'Keefe	Brotherston	Patterson	Mail	Barker	Devine	Glenn	REFEREE	
1	2	3	4	5	6	7	8	9*	10	11	12								T Holbrook	1
	2	3	4	5	6	7	8		10	11	9	1							J Key	2
1	2	3	4		6	7	8		10	11	9		5						M James	3
	2	3	4		6	7	8		10	11	9	1	5						R Nixon	4
	2	3	4	5	6	7	8		10	11		1	9						C Seel	5
	2	3	4*	5	6	7	8		10	11	9	1		12					G Courtney	6
	2	3		5	6	7	8		10	4	9	1		11					D Owen	7
	2	3*	12		6	7	8		10	4	9	1		11	5				G Tyson	8
1	**2**		**4**	**5**	**6**	**7**	**8**		**10**	**3**	**9**		**11**						**D Vickers**	**9**
1	2		4	5*	6	7	8		10	3	9		11		12				A Challinor	10
1	2		4	5	6	7	8		10	3	9			11					K Hackett	11
1	2		4	5	6	7	8		10	3	9		11						N Ashley	12
1	**2**		**4**	**5***	**6**	**7**	**8**		**10**	**3**	**9**		**11**		**12**				**R Bridges**	**13**
1	2			5	6	7	8		10	3	9		11			4			G Napthine	14
1	2		4	5	6	7	8		10	3	9		11						K Barratt	15
1	2			5	6	7	8		10	3				11		4	9		M Heath	16
1	2			5*	6	7	8		10	3				11		4	9	12	D Shaw	17
1	2			5		7	8		10	3*				11	12	4	9	6	A Crickmore	18
1	2			5		7	8		10				12	11	3	4	9*	6	J Lovatt	19
1	3			5	6	7	8		10					11		4	9	2	D Brazier	20
1	3			5	6	7	8		10					11	2	4	9		T Mills	21
1	3			5	6	7	8		10					11	12	4	9*	2	D Hutchinson	22
1	3			5	6	7	8		10		9			11		4		2	K Redfern	23
1	3				6	7*	8		10		9		12	11	5	4		2	F Roberts	24
1	3				6		8		10		9		7	11	5	4		2	M Taylor	25
1	**3**				**6**		**8**		**10**		**9**		**7**	**11**	**5**	**4**		**2**	**G Courtney**	**26**
1	3				6		8		10		9		7	11	5	4		2	J Ashworth	27
1	3				6		8		10		9		7	11	5	4		2	M Peck	28
1	**3**			**12**	**6**		**8**		**10**		**9**		**7**	**11**	**5**	**4**		**2***	**K Baker**	**29**
1	3			5	6	7	8		10		9		11			4		2	R Nixon	30
1	3			5	6	7	8		10	4	9		11					2	T Jones	31
1	**3**			**5**	**6**	**7**	**8**		**10**	**4**	**9**		**11**					**2**	**N Ashley**	**32**
				5		7	8		10	4	9	1		11	3	6		2	A Seville	33
1	3			5	6	7	8		10	4	9		11*	12				3	G Tyson	34
1	2			5	6	7	8		10	3	9			11		4			J Hunting	35
1	3			5	6		8		10	4	9			11		7		2	H Taylor	36
1	3			5	6	7	8		10	12	9			11		4		2*	P Willis	37
1	2			5	6	7	8		10	3	9			11		4			K Hackett	38
1	3			5	6	7*	8		10		9		12	11		4		2	C Thomas	39
1	3			5	6		8		10		9		7	11		4		2	C Seel	40
	3			5	6		8		10		9	1	7	11		4		2	A Ward	41
	3			5	6	12	8		10		9	1	7	11*		4		2	J Key	42
	3			5	6	11	8		10		9	1	7			4		2	M Robinson	43
	3			5	6	11	8		10		9	1		7		4		2	J Lovatt	44
	3	2		5	6	7*	8		10	12	9	1	11			4			T Bray	45
1	3	2		5	6	7	8		10	9				11		4			K Redfern	46
1	3	2		5	6	7	8		10*	9	12			11		4			K Cooper	47
30	41	11	10	35	39	35	**42**	1	**42**	24	31	12	18	27	8	28	7	21	League Appearances	
			+1S			+1S				+2S	+2S		+3S	+2S	+3S			+1S		
3	3			1+1S	3	1	3		3	1	3		3	2	2	2		3	FA Cup Appearances	
2	2		2	2	2	2	2		2	2	2		2		1S				Milk Cup Appearances	

EWOOD PARK

Official Address: Ewood Park, Blackburn BB2 4JF. Telephone: 0254-55432 (4 lines)

Telegraphic: Rovers Blackburn

Ground Capacity: 23,400

Record Attendance: 61,783 v. Bolton Wanderers, F.A. Cup Round 6, 2 Mar 1929

Record Receipts: £36,262.61 v. Newcastle United, Division 2, 20 Apr 1984

Size of Playing Area: 116yds 2ft × 72 yds 2ft

Executive Box Season Tickets: £115.00 which includes admission into '100 Club' lounge & bar facilities

Cost of Stand Tickets: £3.00, £4.00 (£1.50/£2.00 juveniles/OAP); £2.00/£2.20 (£1.40 under 12's)

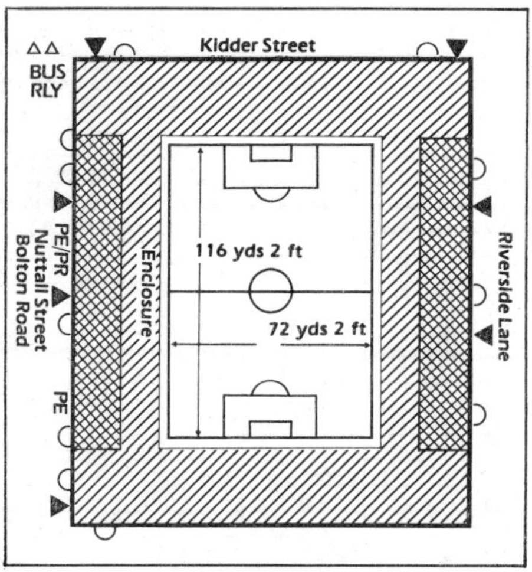

For key see page 12

How to get to the ground

From North and West: Leave motorway M6 at junction 31, and follow signs Blackburn, or use A666 into Blackburn. Then follow signs Bolton A666 into Bolton Road. In 1.5m turn left into Kidder Street for Blackburn Rovers F.C.
From East: Follow signs Blackburn A679 or A677. Then follow signs Bolton A666 into Bolton Road. In 1.5m turn left into Kidder Street for Blackburn Rovers F.C.
From South: Use M6, junction 31 as route from North or via Bolton and A666, when follow signs Blackburn 2.7m after Darwen turn right into Kidder Street for Blackburn Rovers F.C.

BLACKPOOL Division 4

Chairman
K Chadwick, LL.B.

Directors
G Bloor
M H Melling
R P Gibrail
T White

Secretary
D Johnson

Manager
Sam Ellis

Physiotherapist
A Smith

Commercial Manager
Mrs D Howarth
(0253 404331)

After the traumas of the previous season – the worst in the club's history – there were only two possibilities – improvement or extinction. The latter was unthinkable and under a bright young manager, Sam Ellis, a promotion challenge did take place, although in the end sixth place in the lowest division had to be accepted with a deficit of ten points behind the last promoted team, Bristol City. Those mindful of the 'great' days of Matthews, Mortensen, Johnston and Wembley will not be consoled but life must go on and the really loyal supporters will surely find Bloomfield Road a good place to visit this season.

If nothing is won then a season must be viewed in terms of 'might-have-beens' but there were some good days especially when Manchester City visited Blackpool for the FA Cup Third Round, but more of that later. In the Milk Cup the challenge was very brief with Walsall the opposition. A win at home (2-1) was not enough to take away to the West Midlands where the Saddlers in an inspired second half managed an aggregate win. As they then went on to beat Arsenal and reach the semi-finals against Liverpool the result can be seen in perspective. The FA Cup (as mentioned) was a better affair, although the early performances were none too impressive. The opposition in the first two rounds came from outside the League and after a comfortable but not overwhelming home win over Gainsborough Trinity the team struggled to beat Bangor City of the Alliance Premier League who were narrowly beaten in the home replay after taking a first-half lead. A match against Manchester City, even though the latter were in the Second Division, offered no consolations but by half-time a lead of two goals to one had been established and that was the final score. A visit to Oxford in the Fourth Round produced the same score – in favour of the home team – so out went the Tangerines, but with honour.

The need now is for consistency and better defensive work particularly in away matches and if this can be achieved even such a modest success as a rise to the Third Division would make supporters happy for the moment. In Hetzke, Britton and Mercer there is the experience available to bring the best out of the young players who will probably form the nucleus of the team this coming season; shrewd management may well do the rest. The club belongs in the higher spheres of the League.

WLM

Back Row L to R: Barry Wolstenholme, Stewart Diggle, Stephen Hornby, Billy O'Rourke, Phil Clark, Lee Howarth, Paul Swan, Neil Matthews. **Middle Row:** Billy Haydock (Physio), Colin Greenall, Dave Moore, Kevin Stonehouse, Mike Walsh, Paul Stewart, Mike Davis, Alex Dyer, Jack Chapman (Coach). **Front Row:** Bobby Downes (Coach), Phil Ferns, Steve Hetzke (Captain), Sam Ellis (Manager), Brian Butler, John Deary, Ian Britton.

'THE SEASIDERS'

Formed: 1887 **Turned Professional:** 1887 **Ltd Co:** 1896
Previous Names: In 1899 South Shore amalgamated with Blackpool who had been formed when Blackpool St John disbanded in 1887
Previous Managers: (Since 1946) Joe Smith Ron Stuart Stan Mortenson Les Shannon Jimmy Meadows Bob Stokoe Harry Potts Allan Brown Jimmy Meadows Bob Stokoe Stan Ternent Alan Ball (jnr) Allan Brown
Honours: Division 2 Champions 1929-30 F.A. Cup Winners 1953 Anglo-Italian Cup Winners 1971
League Career: Elected to Division 2 1896 Failed to gain re-election 1899
Re-elected to Division 2 1900 Promoted to Division 1 1929-30 Relegated to Division 2 1932-3
Promoted to Division 1 1936-7 Relegated to Division 2 1966-7 Promoted to Division 1 1969-70
Relegated to Division 2 1970-1 Relegated to Division 3 1977-8 Relegated to Division 4 1980-1
Colours: Tangerine shirts with white trim, white shorts, tangerine stockings with white tops
Change Colours: White shirts, tangerine shorts and stockings

CLUB RECORDS

Most Appearances for Club: Jimmy Armfield: Football League 568 + Cup ties 101 **Total 659**
Most Capped Player: Jimmy Armfield, 43, England
Record League Goalscorer in a season: Jimmy Hampson, 45, Div 2 **All competitions:** Jimmy Hampson, 50 (League 45, F.A. Cup 5), 1929-30
Record League Goalscorer in a career: Jimmy Hampson, 247 **All competitions:** Jimmy Hampson, 271 (League 247, F.A. Cup 24), 1927-38
Record Transfer Fee Received: £325,000 from Everton for Mickey Walsh, Aug 1978
Record Transfer Fee Paid: £110,000 to Peterborough United for Bobby Doyle, July 1979
Best Performances: League: 2nd Div 1 1955-6 **F.A. Cup:** Winners (1) **League/Milk Cup:** Semi-Final 1962
Most League Points: (3pts for win) 72, Div 4, 1983-4 (2pts for win) 58, Div 2, 1929-30 58, Div 2, 1967-8
Record League Victory: 7-0 v Preston, Div 1, 1 May 1948
Record League Defeat: 1-10 v Small Heath, Div 2, 2.3.01
1-10 v Huddersfield Town, Div 1, 13.12.30

Programme Editor
John Keal

Price	Number of Pages
40p	16

Subscriptions
Apply to club for details

BLACKPOOL

PLAYERS NAME Ht Wt Birthdate	Honours	Birthplace Transfers	Clubs	APPEARANCES League	Milk Cup	F.A.C.	A.M.C.	GOALS League	Milk Cup	F.A.C.	A.M.C.
GOALKEEPERS											
Billy O'Rourke		Nottingham	Burnley (A)	14							
6-0 12.7 2.4.60		F	Chester	5							
		F	Blackpool	6	2						
DEFENDERS											
Brian Butler		Salford	Blackpool (A)	0+2							
5-6½ 10.6 4.7.66											
Phil Ferns		Liverpool	Bournemouth (A)	94+1	3	4					
5-11 11.4 12.9.61		£25,000	Charlton Ath.	35+3	3+1	1					
		F	Wimbledon (L)	7							
		F	Blackpool	37+1	2	3	1				
Colin Greenall†	E. Y	Billinge	Blackpool (A)	89+4	4	5	1	5			
5-11 11.10 30.12.63											
Steve Hetzke*	Div. 4. 79	Marlborough	Reading (A)	254+7	28	8+3		23	5	1	
6-2 11.10 3.6.55			Blackpool	87	6	7		9	1		
Dave Moore		Grimsby	Grimsby T. (A)	136	9	8		2			
5-10 13.0 14.10.56		F	Carlisle U.	13	2			1			
		£3,500	Blackpool	28				1			
Mick Walsh	Ei.(5)	Manchester	Bolton W.	169+8	13	10+		4	1		
6-0 12.0 20.6.56		£90,000+P/E	Everton	20	2						
			Norwich C. (L)	5							
			Burnley (L)	3							
			Fort Lauderdale								
			Manchester C.	3+1							
		£6,000	Blackpool	20			1				
MIDFIELD											
Ian Britton		Dundee	Chelsea (A)	253+10	11	14		33			
5-5 9.2 19.5.54		F	Dundee U.	7+3	6			1	1		
		F	Blackpool	29+1		5	1	9			
Mike Conroy	SPD.81. 82.		Celtic	58+9	8+5	5+1	2E	9	3	1	
5-9½ 11.2 31.7.57	SC.80		Hibernian	31+1	6	1		2	2		
			Blackpool								
John Deary		Ormskirk	Blackpool (A)	104+9	6	5+2	1	12	1	1	
5-8 11.2 18.10.62											
Alex Dyer		West Ham	Watford (A)								
5-11 11.12 14.11.65			Blackpool	4+5	1	1+1	1				
FORWARDS											
Mike Davies		Stretford	Blackpool	3			1				
5-7 10.7 19.1.66											
Keith Mercer	Div. 4. 78.	Lewisham	Watford (A)	109+25	10+	6		46	3	4	
5-9 13.0 14.10.56	Div. 4. 81	£80,000	Southend U.	132	6	7		35		1	
			Blackpool	31	2	5		9		3	
Paul Stewart	E. Y	Manchester	Blackpool (A)	83+13	6	4		20	2	1	
5-11 11.10 7.10.64											
Kevin Stonehouse		Bishop Auckland	Shildon								
5-11 11.10 20.9.59		F	Blackburn R.	77+8	1	2		27	1		
		£25,000	Huddersfield T.	20+2	3+1	2		4		2	
		£25,000	Blackpool	13				5			
David Windridge		Atherstone	Sheffield U.								
5-9 11.0 7.12.61		F	Chesterfield	66+12	1+1	3+1		14	1		
		F	Blackpool	32+2	2	3	1	6			

NON-CONTRACT PLAYERS 1984-85:

Andy Brand (3 Lg), **Gary Hudson**

BLACKPOOL

DIVISION FOUR 6TH **FA CUP** 4TH ROUND **MILK CUP** 1ST ROUND

MATCH	DATE	COMPE-TITION	VENUE	OPPONENTS	RESULT	HALF TIME	L'GUE POS'N	GOALSCORERS	ATTEN-DANCE
1	A 27	CL	H	Reading	W1-0	1-0		Mercer	3,429
2	**30**	**MC 1**	**H**	**Walsall**	**W2-1**	**1-0**		**Bardsley, McNiven**	**3,353**
3	S 3	CL	A	Colchester U	L1-2	0-1	11	Serella	2,169
4	6	CL	A	Bury	D0-0	0-0			2,993
5	10	CL	H	Northampton T	L2-3	1-2	17	McNiven, Serella	3,216
6	**13**	**MC 1**	**A**	**Walsall**	**L1-3**	**1-1**		**Stewart**	**2,879**
7	17	CL	A	Swindon T	D0-0	0-0	18		2,867
8	24	CL	A	Crewe Alex	W3-0	0-0	13	Deary (pen), Greenall, Windridge	4,198
9	27	CL	H	Mansfield T	W2-0	0-0		Hetzke, Mercer	3,461
10	O 1	CL	A	York C	L0-4	0-1	12		4,058
11	8	CL	H	Rochdale	L0-2	0-0	15		3,126
12	18	CL	A	Wrexham	W1-0	1-0		Deary (pen)	2,005
13	22	CL	H	Chesterfield	W1-0	1-0	12	McNiven	4,206
14	29	CL	A	Stockport Co	W2-1	1-0	9	Mercer, McNiven	2,602
15	N 1	CL	H	Bristol C	W1-0	1-0		Windridge	3,434
16	5	CL	H	Darlington	W3-1	2-0	4	Grenall, Hetzke, Mercer	3,843
17	9	CL	A	Chester C	W2-0	1-0		Stewart, Mercer	2,286
18	12	CL	A	Doncaster R	L1-2	0-2	3	Greenall	4,604
19	**19**	**FAC 1**	**A**	**Gainsborough T**	**W2-0**	**2-0**		**Mercer, McNiven**	**2,557**
20	26	CL	A	Hereford U	W2-1	1-0	2	Windridge, Mercer	2,801
21	D 3	CL	H	Peterborough U	L1-2	0-1		Deary	4,439
22	**10**	**FAC 2**	**A**	**Bangor C**	**D1-1**	**0-0**		**Mercer**	**5,000**
23	**13**	**FAC 2R**	**H**	**Bangor C**	**W2-1**	**0-1**		**Deary, Stewart**	**5,013**
24	17	CL	H	Torquay U	W1-0	0-0	2	Hetzke (pen)	3,955
25	26	CL	A	Tranmere R	L2-3	0-2	3	Mercer, Windridge	3,492
26	27	CL	H	Hartlepool U	W1-0	0-0	2	Hetzke (pen)	4,562
27	31	CL	A	Halifax T	L0-1	0-0	4		1,958
28	J 2	CL	H	Aldershot	W5-0	2-0	3	McNiven, Hetzke (pen), Windridge, Britton 2	3,193
29	**7**	**FAC 3**	**H**	**Manchester C**	**W2-1**	**2-1**		**McNiven McNab (og)**	**15,377**
30	14	CL	A	Reading	L0-2	0-0	4		4,923
31	21	CL	H	Swindon T	D1-1	0-1	4	Stewart	3,474
32	**28**	**FAC 4**	**A**	**Oxford U**	**L1-2**	**0-1**		**Mercer**	**10,759**
33	F 4	CL	H	York C	W3-0	2-0	5	Mercer, Britton, Moore	6,010
34	11	CL	A	Crewe Alex	L1-2	0-0	7	Stewart	4,042
35	14	CL	A	Bristol C	D1-1	1-0		Hetzke	7,413
36	**22**	**AMC 1**	**A**	**Chester C**	**L1-2[1]**	**1-1**		**Serella**	**1,046**
37	25	CL	A	Chesterfield	D1-1	1-1	7	Windridge	3,281
38	M 3	CL	H	Wrexham	W4-0	2-0	7	Wright (og), Britton 2, Walsh	3,798
39	10	CL	H	Doncaster R	W3-1	2-0	7	Mercer, Stewart 2	6,062
40	17	CL	A	Rochdale	L0-1	0-0	7		3,115
41	20	CL	A	Northampton T	W5-1	3-0	6	Walker 3, Greenall, Stewart	1,318
42	24	CL	H	Chester C	D3-3	1-0	6	Stewart 3	4,746
43	31	CL	A	Mansfield T	D1-1	0-1	6	Hetzke (pen)	2,007
44	A 7	CL	H	Bury	D1-1	1-0	6	Stewart	4,513
45	10	CL	H	Stockport Co	D1-1	0-0		Stonehouse	3,971
46	14	CL	A	Peterborough U	L0-4	0-1	7		2,921
47	20	CL	A	Hartlepool U	W1-0	0-0		Stonehouse	1,817
48	21	CL	H	Tranmere R	L0-1	0-0	6		4,055
49	28	CL	H	Hereford U	W3-1	1-0	6	Deary 3	2,143
50	M 1	CL	H	Colchester U	W3-2	2-2		McNiven, Stonehouse 2	3,111
51	5	CL	A	Aldershot	L2-3	1-1	6	McNiven, Britton	2,936
52	7	CL	H	Halifax T	W4-0	1-0	6	Britton 3, Stonehouse	2,324
53	12	CL	A	Torquay U	L0-1	0-1	6		1,592
54	15	CL	A	Darlington	L0-2	0-1			1,177

[1]After Extra Time **Av Home Att 3,881**

Goal Scorers

League (70): Stewart 10, Britton 9, Mercer 9, Hetzke 7 (4 pens), Deary 6 (2 pens), McNiven 6, Windridge 6, Stonehouse 5, Greenall 4, Walker 3, Serella 2, Moore 1, Walsh 1, opponent 1
FA Cup (8): Mercer 3, McNiven 2, Deary 1, Stewart 1, opponent 1
Milk Cup (3): Bardsley 1, McNiven 1, Stewart 1
AMC (1): Serella 1

1983-84

O'Rourke (L)	Bardsley	Pritchett	Rodaway	Hetzke	Greenall	Windridge	Mercer	Stewart	Ferns	McNiven	Serella	Deary	Steele (L)	Dyer	Siddall (L)	Britton	Pierce	Moore	Downes	Walsh	Walker (L)	Stonehouse	Brand	Davies	REFEREE	
1	2	3	4	5	6	7	8	9	10	11															D Owen	1
1	**2**	**3**	**4**	**5**	**6**	**7***	**8**		**10**	**11**		**9**		**12**											**J Worrell**	**2**
1	2	3	4	5		7	8	12	10	11*	6	9													J Ashworth	3
1	2	3	4	5		7	8	9	10		6	11													R Bridges	4
1	2	3	4	5		7*	8	12	10	11	6	9													P Tyldesley	5
1	**2**	**3**	**4**	**5**		**7***	**8**	**9**	**10**	**12**	**6**	**11**													**T Jones**	**6**
1	2	3	4	5	6	7	8	9	10			11													B Hill	7
1	2	3	4	5	6	7	8	9*	10	12		11													B Hutchison	8
	2	3	4	5	6	7*	8	12	10	9		11	1												P Willis	9
	2	3	4	5	6	7		8	10	9		11	1												A Saunders	10
	2	3	4	5	6	7	8	9	10				1	11											G Courtney	11
	2		4	5	6	7	8	9	3	11		10			1										H Taylor	12
	2		4	5	6	7	8	9	3	11		10			1										R Nixon	13
	2		4	5	6	7	8	9	3	11		10			1										K Barratt	14
	2		4	5	6	7	8	9†	3	11		10			1										N Ashley	15
	2		4	5	6	7	8*	9	3	11		10		12	1										F Roberts	16
	2		4	5	6	7	8	9	3	11		10			1										A Seville	17
	2		4*	5	6	7	8	9	3	11		10			1	12									I Borrett	18
			4	**5**	**6**	**7***	**8**		**3**	**11**		**10**		**12**		**9**	**1**		**2**						**A Robinson**	**19**
			4	5	6	7	8		3	11	2	10				9	1								J Martin	20
			4	5	6	7	8	12	3*	11	2	10				9	1								G Tyson	21
		3	**4**	**5**	**6**		**8**	**9**		**11**	**2**	**10**				**7**	**1**								**A Challinor**	**22**
			4	**5**	**6**		**8**	**9**	**3**	**11**	**2**	**10**				**7**	**1**								**A Challinor**	**23**
			4	5	6		8	9	3	11		10*		12		7	1	2							J Lovatt	24
		10*	4†	5	6	12	8	9	3	11						7	1	2							J Hough	25
			4	5	6	10	8	9	3*	11				12		7	1	2							D Shaw	26
			4	5	6	10	8	9	3	11*			12		7	1	2								T Holbrook	27
			4	5	6	10	8	9	3	11						7	1	2							M Heath	28
			4	**5**	**6**	**10**	**8**	**9**	**3**	**11**						**7**	**1**	**2**							**K Redfern**	**29**
				5	6	10	8	9	3	11				4		7	1	2							L Burden	30
				5	6		8	9		11	3			4		7	1	2	10						A Challinor	31
				5	**6**	**10***	**8**	**9**		**11**	**3**	**12**		**4**		**7**	**1**	**2**							**J Bray**	**32**
			4	5	6	10	8	9*		11		12				7	1	2		3					P Tyldesley	33
			4	5		10	8	9	3	11						7	1	2		6					T Mills	34
			4	5		10	8	9	3	11				12		7*	1	2		6					D Hedges	35
					6	**8**			**10**	**12**	**5**	**4**		**7**		**11***	**1**			**3**				**13**	**K Baker**	**36**
			4	5	6	11	8	9	10*			12				7	1	2		3					C Downey	37
			4	5	6	11	8	9*		12		10				7	1	2		3					K Hackett	38
				5	6	11	8	9	10			4				7	1	2		3					N Ashley	39
				5	6	11	8*	9	10	12		4				7	1	2		3					G Napthine	40
			4	5	6			9		11		10				7	1	2		3	8				D Axcell	41
			4	5	6			9		12		10				7*	1	2		3	8	11			G Courtney	42
			4	5	6	12		9				10				7	1	2		3	8*	11			I Borrett	43
			4	5	6	7		9	12	8		10					1	2		3*		11			D Allison	44
			4	8	5	10*		9	3							7	1	2		6	12	11			M Peck	45
			4	10	5			9	3							7	1	2		6	8	11			V Callow	46
			4	10	6			9	3							7	1	2		5	8	11			D Hutchinson	47
			4	10	6			9	3			12				7*	1	2		5	8	11			A Saunders	48
			4					9	3		6	8		10		7	1	2		5		11			R Nixon	49
			4*	5				9	3	10		8				7	1	2		6	12	11			C Seel	50
		12	4	5	6	8				10	3*				7	1	2			9	11				D Brazier	51
			4	5	6			9								7		2		3	10	11	1	8	R Bridges	52
			4	5	6			9								7		2		3	10	11	1	8	R Bridges	53
				5	6			9	10			4				7		2		3		11	1	8	J Key	54
6	16	10	41	45	39	32	31	40	37	28	8	27	3	4	7	29	27	28	1	20	8	13	3	3	League Appearances	
		+1S				+2S		+4S	+1S	+4S		+4S		+5S		+1S					+2S					
		1	4	5	5	3	5	4	3	5	3	3+1S		1+1S		5	5	2	1						FA Cup Appearances	
2	2	2	2	2	1	2	2	1	2	1+1S	1	2		1S											Milk Cup Appearances	
					1	1			1	1S	1	1		1		1	1			1				1S	AM Cup Appearances	

Also Played: Butler match 36, no.2. Bramhall match 36, no.9*

BLOOMFIELD ROAD

Official Address: Bloomfield Road Ground, Blackpool FY1 6JJ. Telephone: Blackpool (0253) 404331

Telegraphic: Football Blackpool

Ground Capacity: 18,000

Record Attendance: 39,118 v. Manchester U, Div 1, 19 Apr 1952

Record Receipts: £28,986 v. Everton, League Cup Round 2, 2nd Leg, 3 Sept 1980

Size of Playing Area: 111yds × 73 yds

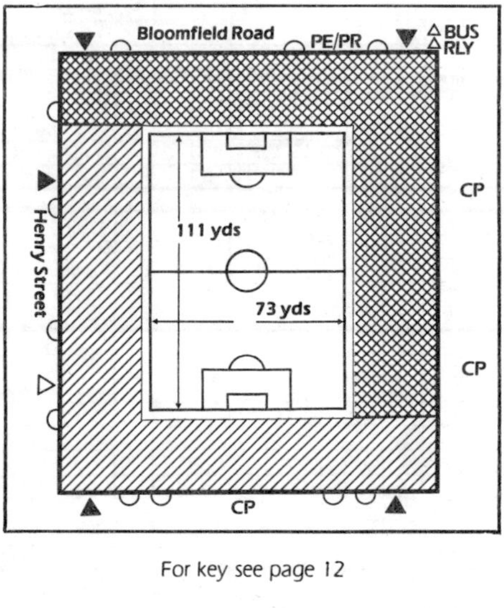

For key see page 12

Season Tickets: Stand: £60 (West & South); Paddock: £43 (adults), £20 (Junior/OAP); Ground: £36, £18 (OAP/Juniors)

Executive Box Season Tickets: £138.00

Cost of Stand Tickets: £3.00, £3.30, £1.20 (Juveniles/OAP), £2.50 (New Stand); **Terraces:** £1.80, £1.00 (Junior/OAP)

Match and Ticket Information: Bookable four weeks prior to match

Car Parking: Parking for 1,000 cars. Street parking available

How to get to the ground

From North, East and South: Leave M6 Motorway at junction 32 and follow signs Blackpool M55. At end of Motorway join A583. In 2m at traffic signals turn left into Waterloo Road (S.P. South Shore). In 0.7m turn right into Central Drive. Then take 3rd turning on left into Bloomfield Road for Blackpool F.C.

BOLTON WANDERERS Division 3

President
J Battersby

Chairman
N Riley

Directors
G Ball
T Edge
G Hargreaves
S Jones
G Seymour
G Warburton

Secretary
D McBain

Assistant Secretary
K Gardiner

Manager
John McGovern

Assistant Manager
Charlie Wright

Reserve & Youth Team Manager
W Joyce

Commercial Manager
A Davies (0204 389200)

Physiotherapist
P Nightingale

Groundsman
A Whittle

Season 1983/84 saw plenty of ups and downs for Bolton Wanderers and ended with the club finishing in their lowest ever league position but at the same time showing plenty of promise for the future.

For the first time in five years the club were not involved in a battle against relegation and up until the end of March had an outside chance of promotion, but the side with an average age of just 20 couldn't find the consistency, especially in the latter stages of the season.

The season started well enough including an 8-1 thumping of Walsall at Burnden Park. Non-league signing Tony Caldwell netted five times to set a new club record and if Ally Brown had not pulled a goal back in the final minute the Wanderers would have equalled their record league victory set in 1934.

The Milk Cup saw a disappointing exit at the hands of Chester City with the game at Burnden producing the club's lowest attendance on record of 2665.

After going down to their first home defeat of the season at the hands of Newport, the Wanderers embarked on their best period with just one defeat in fourteen games including victories in the first two rounds of the FA Cup.

The highlights of this run were the wins at Wigan Athletic on Boxing Day which saw a record league gate of £10,045 and the victory over Oxford United the following day which produced Burnden Park's best league gate of the season of 11,059.

Manager John McGovern had promised that the side would take some hammerings due to their inexperience and he was proved right when the spell came to an end with a 5-0 defeat at Sheffield United on New Years Eve.

The Wanderers bowed out of the cup by giving Sunderland a run for their money at Burnden but the shortcomings of the side were again emphasized a week later when they crashed 4-0 at Wimbledon.

The month of March saw them produce some of their best football which was unfortunately away from home, notably in defeat at Orient and in victory at Newport.

After the win in South Wales the Wanderers hit their worst spell of the season, picking up just four points from nine games and scoring in only two. To make matters worse the club's lowest ever league gate of 3,045 saw the game with Bournemouth.

The final home game of the season was worth the wait, as the Wanderers "got it together" and outplayed Sheffield United to win 3-1 and prove that with a little luck they are capable of a stronger challenge in 1984/85.

The League Directory's Statistician for the Club

Back Row: Peter Valentine, Jimmy Phillips, Mark Came, Gerry McElhinney, Neil Berry, Paul Booth, George Oghani. **Centre:** Walter Joyce (Coach), Brian Borrows, Steve Thompson, Tony Caldwell, Simon Farnworth, John Platt, Ray Deakin, Paul Lodge, Warren Joyce, Peter Nightingale (Physio). **Front:** Wayne Foster, Charles Wright (1st Team Coach), Jeff Chandler, Simon Rudge, Steve Saunders, John McGovern (Manager), Graham Bell.

Sponsored by
HB
Electronics

'THE TROTTERS'

Formed: 1874 **Turned Professional:** 1880 **Ltd Co:** 1895
Previous Names: Christ Church F.C. from 1874-1877
Previous Managers: 1910-5 Will Settle 1915-9 Tom Mather 1919-45 Charles Foweraker 1945-50 Walter Rowley 1950-68 Bill Ridding 1968-70 Nat Lofthouse 1970-71 Jimmy McIlroy 1971 Jimmy Meadows 1971 Nat Lofthouse 1971-4 Jimmy Armfield 1974-80 Ian Greaves 1980-1 Stan Anderson 1981-2 George Mulhall
Honours: Division 2 Champions 1908-9, 1977-8 Division 3 Champions 1972-3
F.A. Cup Winners 1923, 1926, 1929, 1958
League Career: Founder Members of the League 1888 Relegated to Division 2 1898-9 Promoted to Division 1 1899-1900 Relegated to Division 2 1902-3 Promoted to Division 1 1904-5 Relegated to Division 2 1907-8 Promoted to Division 1 1908-9 Relegated to Division 2 1909-10 Promoted to Division 1 1910-1 Relegated to Division 2 1932-3 Promoted to Division 1 1934-5 Relegated to Division 2 1963-4 Relegated to Division 3 1970-1 Promoted to Division 2 1972-3 Promoted to Division 1 1977-8 Relegated to Division 2 1979-80 Relegated to Division 3 1982-3
Colours: White shirts, navy blue shorts, white stockings
Change Colours: Red shirts, white shorts, red stockings

CLUB RECORDS

Most Appearances for Club: Eddie Hopkinson: Football League 519 + F.A. Cup 59 **Total 578**
Most Capped Player: Nat Lofthouse, 33, England
Record Goalscorer in a Match: J Cassidy, 5 v Sheff Utd (13.0), 2nd Round F.A. Cup 1980
Tony Caldwell, 5 v Walsall (8-1), Division 3 1983
Record League Goalscorer in a season: Joe Smith, 38, Div 1, 1920-1 **All competitions:** Joe Smith, 38, 1920-1
Record League Goalscorer in a career: Nat Lofthouse, 255, 1946-61 **All competitions:** Nat Lofthouse, 285 (League 255, F.A. Cup 30)
Record Transfer Fee Received: £340,000 from Birmingham City for Neil Whatmore, Aug 1974
Record Transfer Fee Paid: £350,000 to West Bromwich Albion for Len Cantello, May 1979
Best Performances: League: 3rd, 1891-2, 1920-1, 1924-5 **F.A. Cup:** Winners 1922, 1926, 1929, 1958 **League/Milk Cup:** Semi-Final 1976-7
Most League Points: 61 in Div 3, 1974-5
Most League Goals: 96 in Div 2, 1934-5
Record League Victory: 9-0 v Loughborough, Div 2, 28 Jan 1899
Record League Defeat: 0-7 v Manchester City, Div 1, 21.3.36
Club Statistician for the Directory: Simon Marland

Programme Editor
Commercial Department

Price	**Number of Pages**
50p	24

Subscriptions
No subscriptions

BOLTON WANDERERS

PLAYERS NAME Ht Wt Birthdate	Honours	Birthplace Transfers	Clubs	APPEARANCES League	Milk Cup	F.A.C.	A.M.C.	GOALS League	Milk Cup	F.A.C.	A.M.C.
GOALKEEPERS											
Simon Farnworth	E. S	Chorley	Bolton W. (A)	36	2	4					
5-11 10.11 28.10.63											
John Platt		Ashton	Ashton U.								
5-10 11.7 22.8.54			Oldham Ath.	109	3	9					
		F	Bury	20	3						
		F	Bolton W.	10			1				
DEFENDERS											
Graham Bell	E. Y	Middleton	Chadderton								
5-9 10.6 30.3.55			Oldham Ath.	166 + 4	9	6 + 1		9		1	
		£80,000	P.N.E.	140 + 3	11 +	1 + 1		9	1		
			Huddersfield T. (L)	2							
			Carlisle U.	11 + 3	2	1 + 1					
			Bolton W.	20			1	1			
Neil Berry	S. Y	Edinburgh	Bolton W. (A)	19 + 7	2 + 2	1					
5-11 10.4 6.4.63											
Brian Borrows†		Liverpool	Everton	27	2						
5-10 10.12 20.12.60		£6,000	Bolton W.	71	2	3	1				
Ray Deakin*		Liverpool	Everton (A)								
5-8 11.1 19.6.59		F	Port Vale	21 + 2	4			6	1		
		F	Bolton W.	71	3	5	1	2			
George Elhinney	N.I. (5)	Londonderry	Distillery								
6-2 13.0 19.9.56		£25,000	Bolton W.	94 + 1	5	8	1	2			
			Rochdale (L)	20				1			
Jim Phillips		Bolton	Bolton W. (A)	0 + 1							
6-0 11.12 8.2.66											
Peter Valentine		Huddersfield	Huddersfield T. (A)	19	2	1		1			
5-10 12.0 16.4.63			Bolton W.	42	2	4	1	1			
MIDFIELD											
Paul Booth		Bolton	Bolton W. (A)								
7.12.65											
Mark Came		Exeter	Bolton W.								
14.9.61											
Warren Joyce		Oldham	Bolton W.	50 + 3	2	4	1	3	1	1	
5-8½ 11.5 20.1.65											
Paul Lodge	E. S	Liverpool	Everton (A)	20 + 4	5	6					
5-9 11.9 13.2.61			Wigan A. (L)	5							
			Rotherham U. (L)	4							
			P.N.E.	36 + 2	5	3					
Steve Thompson		Oldham	Bolton W. (A)	43	1	4	1	3			
5-8½ 11.0 2.11.64											
FORWARDS											
Tony Caldwell		Salford	Horwich R.M.I.								
5-9 11.7 21.3.58			Bolton W.	32 + 1	1	3	1	19		1	1
Jeff Chandler		Hammersmith	Blackpool (A)	31 + 6	2 + 1	0 + 1		7		1	
5-7 10.1 19.6.59		F	Leeds U.	21 + 5	1	1		2			
		£40,000	Bolton W.	113 + 3	5	7		20		3	
Wayne Foster	E. Y	Leigh	Bolton W. (A)	68 + 9	2 + 1	5	1	9		2	
5-8½ 11.0 11.9.63											
George Obhani		Manchester	Bury								
5-10½ 12.3 2.9.60			Hyde U.								
			Bolton W.	1 + 2							
Simon Rudge		Warrington	Bolton W. (A)	48 + 7	4	3 + 1		10		2	
5-6½ 10.6 30.12.64											
Steve Saunders		Warrington	Bolton W. (A)	3	1 + 1	0 + 1					
5-7½ 10.6 21.9.64											

APPRENTICES: Paul Bolton, Dean Roberts

NON-CONTRACT PLAYERS 1984-85: R. Coghiel, P. Crooks, S. Darby, P. Howard. G. Jakeman, J. McGovern, R. Walker, A. Zelem

BOLTON WANDERERS

DIVISION THREE 10TH **FA CUP** 3RD ROUND **MILK CUP** 1ST ROUND

MATCH	DATE	COMPETITION	VENUE	OPPONENTS	RESULT	HALF TIME	L'GUE POS'N	GOALSCORERS	ATTENDANCE
1	A 27	CL	H	Wimbledon	W2-0	0-0		Rudge, Chandler (pen)	3,992
2	**30**	**MC 1**	**H**	**Chester C**	**W3-0**	**2-0**		**Joyce, Caldwell 2**	**2,665**
3	S 3	CL	A	Bradford C	W2-0	0-0	4	Caldwell, Rudge	3,324
4	6	CL	A	Gillingham	L0-2	0-1			3,087
5	10	CL	H	Walsall	W8-1	4-0	4	Caldwell 5, Deakin, Rudge, Valentine	4,375
6	**14**	**MC 1**	**A**	**Chester C**	**L0-3[5]**	**0-1**			**1,502**
7	16	CL	A	Scunthorpe U	L0-1	0-0	4		4,406
8	24	CL	H	Rotherham U	W2-0	2-0	4	Caldwell, Redfearn	5,592
9	27	CL	H	Burnley	D0-0	0-0			9,709
10	O 1	CL	A	Bristol R	L1-2	0-2	6	Rudge	5,651
11	8	CL	A	Exeter C	D2-2	1-0	6	Caldwell 2	3,478
12	15	CL	H	Newport Co	L2-3	1-1	10	Caldwell, Chandler	4,928
13	18	CL	H	Hull C	D0-0	0-0			6,397
14	22	CL	A	Port Vale	W2-1	2-1	10	Chandler, Caldwell	4,269
15	29	CL	H	Southend U	W2-0	1-0	8	Caldwell 2	5,366
16	N 2	CL	A	Lincoln C	D0-0	0-0			3,988
17	5	CL	H	Orient	W3-2	1-1	7	McElhinney, Foster, Joyce	5,859
18	12	CL	A	Plymouth Arg	L0-2	0-1	9		4,624
19	**19**	**FAC 1**	**A**	**Tranmere R**	**D2-2**	**1-1**		**Joyce, Chandler (pen)**	**5,497**
20	**22**	**FAC 1R**	**H**	**Tranmere R**	**W4-1[1]**	**1-1**		**Chandler 2 (1 pen), Rudge, Caldwell**	**6,305**
21	26	CL	A	AFC Bournemouth	D2-2	0-2	11	Chandler, Thompson	3,941
22	D 3	CL	H	Brentford	W1-0	0-0	11	Chandler	5,416
23	**10**	**FAC 2**	**H**	**Mansfield T**	**W2-0**	**2-0**		**Foster, Rudge**	**6,934**
24	17	CL	H	Preston NE	D2-2	2-1	8	Foster, Chandler	6,275
25	26	CL	A	Wigan Ath	W1-0	0-0	7	Chandler	10,045
26	27	CL	H	Oxford U	W1-0	0-0	6	Chandler	11,059
27	31	CL	A	Sheffield U	L0-5	0-2	9		14,252
28	J 2	CL	H	Millwall	W2-0	1-0	7	Rudge, Joyce	7,054
29	**7**	**FAC 3**	**H**	**Sunderland**	**L0-3**	**0-1**			**14,018**
30	14	CL	A	Wimbledon	L0-4	0-1	8		2,955
31	21	CL	H	Scunthorpe U	D0-0	0-0	8		5,379
32	28	CL	A	Walsall	L0-1	0-0	9		7,812
33	F 4	CL	H	Bristol R	W3-0	1-0	7	Caldwell 2, Chandler (pen)	5,399
34	6	CL	A	Southend U	W1-0	0-0		Caldwell	1,594
35	11	CL	A	Rotherham U	D1-1	1-1	7	Rudge	5,043
36	14	CL	H	Lincoln C	L0-2	0-0			5,450
37	**21**	**AMC 1**	**A**	**Burnley**	**L1-2**	**0-1**		**Caldwell**	**3,355**
38	25	CL	H	Port Vale	W2-0	1-0	7	Caldwell 2	5,818
39	M 3	CL	A	Hull C	D1-1	0-0	7	Chandler	6,869
40	6	CL	A	Orient	L1-2	0-0		Chandler	2,449
41	17	CL	H	Exeter C	W1-0	0-0	7	Foster	5,161
42	24	CL	A	Newport Co	W3-2	3-0	7	Whatmore, Thompson, Joyce	2,436
43	27	CL	H	Bradford C	L0-2	0-1			5,994
44	31	CL	A	Burnley	D2-2	1-1	8	Thompson, Whatmore	8,359
45	A 7	CL	H	Gillingham	L0-1	0-1	8		4,815
46	14	CL	A	Brentford	L0-3	0-2	9		3,831
47	16	CL	H	Plymouth Arg	W2-1	1-0		Chandler (pen), Bell	3,266
48	20	CL	A	Oxford U	L0-5	0-4			9,788
49	21	CL	H	Wigan Ath	L0-1	0-1	7		6,142
50	28	CL	H	AFC Bournemouth	L0-1	0-0	10		3,045
51	M 5	CL	A	Millwall	L0-3	0-2	12		2,346
52	7	CL	H	Sheffield U	W3-1	2-0	10	Chandler 2, Caldwell	9,036
53	12	CL	A	Preston NE	L1-2	1-1	10	Rudge	5,077

[1]After Extra Time [5]Lost on Penalties

Av Home Att **5,890**

Goal Scorers

League (56): Caldwell 19, Chandler 14 (3 pens), Rudge 7, Foster 3, Joyce 3, Thompson 3, Whatmore 2, Bell 1, Deakin 1, McElhinney 1, Redfearn 1, Valentine 1
FA Cup (8): Chandler 3 (2 pens), Rudge 2, Caldwell 1, Foster 1, Joyce 1
Milk Cup (3): Caldwell 2, Joyce 1
AMC (1): Caldwell 1

1983-84

Farnworth	Borrows	Deakin	Joyce	McElhinney	Valentine	Saunders	Chandler	Rudge	Caldwell	Redfearn	Berry	Thompson	Foster	Snookes	Oghani	McGovern	Bell	Platt	Whatmore (L)	Phillips	REFEREE	
1	2	3	4	5	6	7	8	9	10	11											T Mills	1
1	2	3	4	5	6	7	8*	9	10	11			12								**K Hackett**	**2**
1	2	3	4	5	6	7	8	9	10	11											V Callow	3
1	2	3	4	5	6	7*	8	9	10	11	12										D Brazier	4
1	2	3	4	5	6		8	9	10	11		7									G Tyson	5
1	2	3	4	5	6*	12	8	9		11		7	10								**H Taylor**	**6**
1	2	3	4	5	6		8	9	10	11		7									M Scott	7
1	2	3	4	5	6		8	9	10	11		7									N Ashley	8
1	2	3	4	5	6		8	9	10	11		7									D Allison	9
1	2	3	4*	5	6		8	9	10	11	12	7									A Buksh	10
1	2	3	4	5	6		8	9	10	11		7									K Cooper	11
1	2	3	4	5	6		8	9	10	11		7									J Key	12
1	2	3	4	5	6		8	9	10	11		7									R Bridges	13
1	2	3	4	5	6		8*	9	10	11		7	12								J Ashworth	14
1	2	3	4	5	6		8	9*	10	11		7	12								A Challinor	15
1	2	3	4	5	6		8	9	10	11		7									B Hill	16
1	2	3	4	5	6		8		10	11		7	9								D Owen	17
1	2	3	4	5	6		8		10	11	12	7	9*								B Stevens	18
1	2	3	4	5	6		8	9	10	11		7									**N Ashley**	**19**
1	2	3	4	5	6	12	8	9	10*	11		7									**N Ashley**	**20**
1	2	3	4	5	6		8		10	11		7	9								E Scales	21
1	2	3	4	5	6		8		10	11		7	9								P Willis	22
1	2	3	4	5	6		8	12	10*	11		7	9								**T Holbrook**	**23**
1	2	3	4		6		8	10		11	5	7	9								K Hackett	24
1	2	3	4		6		8	10		11	5	7	9								R Nixon	25
1	2	3	4	5			8	10		11	6	7	9								A Saunders	26
1	2	3	4	5	6		8	10		11		7	9								M Robinson	27
1		3	4	5	6		8	10		11	2	7	9								M Peck	28
1		3	4	5	6		8	10		11	2	7	9								**D Hutchinson**	**29**
1		6	4	5			8	10		11	2	7	9*	3	12						K Barratt	30
1	2	3	4	5	6		8	10*	12	11		7	9								J Lovatt	31
1	7		4	5	6		8		10†		2		9	3		11					T Ward	32
1	2		4	5	6		8		10			7	9	3			11				M Heath	33
1	2		4	5	6		8		10			7	9	3			11				K Salmon	34
1*	2		4	5	6		8	12				7	9	3	10		11				J Hunting	35
	2		4	5	6		8	10				7*	9	3	12		11	1			D Hutchinson	36
	2	3	4	5	6		8		10			7	9				11	1			**D Owen**	**37**
	2	3	4	5	6		8		10			7	9				11	1			T Mills	38
	2	3	4	5	6		8	10				7	9				11	1			T Holbrook	39
	2	3	4	5	6		8	10*			12	7	9				11	1			D Brazier	40
	2	3	4	5	6		8	12				7*	9				11	1	10		C Seel	41
1	2	3	4	5	6		8	12				7	9				11		10*		M Dimblebee	42
1	2	3	4	5	6		8	12				7	9				11		10*		J Hough	43
1	2	3	4	5	6		8		9*			7	12				11		10		A Seville	44
1	2	3*	4	5	6		8		10			7					11		9	12	G Courtney	45
1	2	3	4	5	6		8		10			7					11		9		A Crickmore	46
1	2	3	4	5	6		8		9			7					11		10		K Redfern	47
1	2	3	4*	5	6		8		10		12	7	9				11				A Gunn	48
	2	3	4	5	6		8	12	10			7*	9				11	1			N Ashley	49
	2	3		5	6		8		10			7	9			4	11	1			D Shaw	50
	2	3	4		6		8	9	10		5		7				11	1			D Hedges	51
	2	3	4	5			8	9	10		6		7				11	1			F Roberts	52
	2	3	4	5			8	9	10		6	7					11	1			G Tyson	53
36	44	41	45	43	42	3	**46**	27	32	25	9	40	27	6	1	2	20	10	7	0	League Appearances	
								+5S	+1S		+5S		+3S		+2S					+1S		
4	3	4	4	4	4	1S	4	3+1S	3	4	1	4	2								FA Cup Appearances	
2	2	2	2	2	2	1+1S	2	2	1	2		1	1+1S								Milk Cup Appearances	
	1	1	1	1	1		1		1			1	1				1	1			AM Cup Appearances	

BURNDEN PARK

Official Address: Burnden Park, Bolton BL3 2QB. Telephone: 0204 389200

Ground Capacity: 43,000

Record Attendance: 69,912 v. Manchester City, F.A. Cup Round 5, 18 Feb 1933

Record Receipts: £53,931 v. Everton, League Cup Semi-Final 2nd Leg, 15 Feb 1977

Size of Playing Area: 113yds × 76 yds

Season Tickets: Stand: £34.25 (Great Lever), £67.75 (Burnden), £47.75 (Block 'A' Wing), £65.75 (Manchester Road), Juveniles/OAP £20, £37.75, £28.00, £37.75 respectively. Manchester Road Terrace/Burnden Terrace £34.25 (juveniles/OAP £20)

Executive Box Season Tickets: £300

Cost of Stand Tickets: Manchester Road & Burnden £3.65 (OAP/juveniles £2.10), Block A £2.65 (£1.55), Great Lever £2.00 (£1.10); **Terraces:** £2.00 (£1.10), Visitors (Embankment) £2.00

Match and Ticket Information: 0204 21101

Car Parking: Private car parking only in forecourt. Large car park 200 yards from ground. Limited street parking nearby. Multi-storey car parks are in town centre

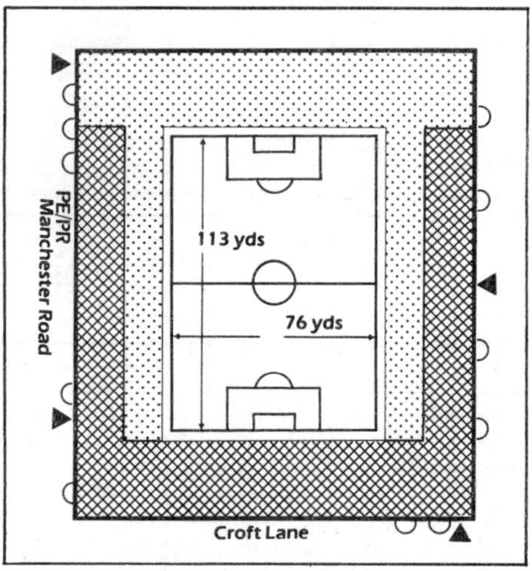

For key see page 12

How to get to the ground

From North: Leave M61 at junction 5 or enter Bolton via A666 or A676. Then follow signs Farnworth B653 into Manchester Road. In 0.6m turn left into Croft Lane to Bolton Wanderers F.C.

From South, East and West: Use M62 until junction 14 then join M61. In 2.1m leave Motorway and at roundabout take 1st exit B6536. In 2.1m turn right into Croft Lane for Bolton Wanderers F.C.

AFC BOURNEMOUTH Division 3

President
CM Pardy

Chairman
RJC Barton

Directors
PW Hayward (V Chairman)
B Tiler (Managing Director)
GP Pound
EG Keep
P McDonagh
JP Nolan
W Oakley
MP McDonagh
AWA Stock

Secretary
Mrs CB Dowsett

Assistant Secretary
KRJ McAlister

Manager
Harry Redknapp

Coach
Stuart Morgan

Chief Scout
M Ennals

Commercial Manager
Dickie Dowsett (0202 37777)

Physiotherapist
J Kirk

Groundsman
J Harriss

One swallow does not make a summer and one match does not make a Football Season. True or false? Bournemouth will say that it is the latter and Manchester United would wholeheartedly endorse that without any reservations, although it would be more accurate to say that it was a season of contrasting halves for Bournemouth and, in the end, they had a slightly bizarre reward.

The League programme might well be given an 'X-Certificate' and left at that since for most of the time it was a long and painful struggle, which might have ended in total disaster had the 'Fulham Connection' not happened and former player Roger Brown along with his club colleague O'Driscoll (on loan) appeared on the scene. Their presence possibly helped to inspire the consistent members of the team such as Sulley and Thompson and in the end relegation back to the Fourth Division was avoided comfortably (on paper by nine points with a semi-respectable seventeenth place in the table).

A close pair of matches in the First Round of the Milk Cup brought dismissal at the hands of Bristol Rovers. The F.A. Cup was a different story with a glorious initial success at home to Walsall by four clear goals. In the next round a visit to Windsor and Eton was postponed by the weather for a few days by which time it was known that a match at home to Manchester United was the prize. This may explain why the tie was a difficult struggle and the Isthmian team kept a clean scoresheet (as did Bournemouth) until the second half of the replay at Dean Court when Beck and Ian Thompson finally broke through and enabled the club to have a prospect of a big home gate. It was better than that and a mixture of home inspiration and First Division blunders produced yet another surprise for Football historians to record. It was Middlesbrough next but this time a visit to the North East failed although the point had been made. It was well underlined in the new Associate Members Cup, which was won against huge odds at Hull in as brave a performance as any in the club's history. For the record Bournemouth won after overtaking a first half Hull City lead.

Which form is the best guide to the team's potential? If the Cup form provided it then a promotion challenge can be expected. We shall see, but there must be quiet confidence felt by Harry Redknapp (replacement for Don Megson early in the season) and his staff.

Back Row L to R: John Kirk (Trainer/Physio), Milton Graham, Bill Rafferty, Roger Brown, John Smeulders, Paul Morrell, Ian Leigh, Mark Nightingale, Phil Brignull, John Beck, Stuart Morgan (Assistant Manager). **Front Row:** Everald La Ronde, Chris Shaw, Colin Russell, Bobby Savage, Morgan Lewis, Harry Redknapp (Manager), Keith Williams, Chris Sulley, Mark Schiavi, Sean O'Driscoll, Ian Thompson.

'THE CHERRIES'

Formed: 1899 **Turned Professional:** 1912 **Ltd Co:** 1914
Previous Names: Boscombe St Johns 1890-9 Boscombe F.C. 1899-1923 Bournemouth & Boscombe Athletic F.C. 1923-72
Previous Managers: -1925 Harry Kinghorn 1925-8 Leslie Knighton 1928-30 Frank Richards 1930-5 Billy Birrell 1935-6 Bob Crompton 1936-9 Charles Bell 1939-47 Harry Kinghorn 1947-50 Harry Lowe 1950-6 Jack Bruton 1956-8 Freddie Cox 1958-61 Don Welsh 1961-3 Billy McGarry 1963-5 Reg Flewin 1965-70 Freddie Cox 1970-3 John Bond 1973-5 Trevor Hartley 1975-9 John Benson 1979-80 Alec Stock 1980-2 David Webb 1983 Don Megson
Honours: Associate Members Cup Winners 1983-4
League Career: Elected to Division 3 (South) 1923 Transferred to Division 3 1958 Relegated to Division 4 1969-70 Promoted to Division 3 1970-1 Relegated to Division 4 1974-5 Promoted to Division 3 1981-2
Bournemouth's stay in the Third Division from 1923 until 1970 is a record for consecutive years membership of that Division.
Colours: All red with white pinstripe on shirt and white side stripes on shorts
Change Colours: All yellow

CLUB RECORDS

Most Appearances for Club: Ray Bumstead: Football League **Total 511**
Most Capped Player: Tommy Godwin, 4, Eire. **For England:** None
Record Goalscorer in a Match: Ted MacDougall, 9 v Margate, F.A. Cup 1st Round, 20.11.71
Record League Goalscorer in a season: Ted MacDougall, 42, Div 4, 1970-1 **All competitions:** Ted MacDougall, 79 (League 42, F.A. Cup 7)
Record League Goalscorer in a career: Ron Eyre, 202 (Cup goals not known), 1924-33
Record Transfer Fee Received: £195,000 from Manchester United for Ted MacDougall, Sept 1972
Record Transfer Fee Paid: £70,000 to Cardiff City for Brian Clark, Oct 1972
Best Performances: League: 3rd Div 3 1961-2 2nd Div 3 (S) 1947-8 **F.A. Cup:** 6th Round, 1956-7
League/Milk Cup: 4th Round, 1962, 1964
Most League Points: (3pts for win) 88, Div 4, 1981-2 (2pts for win) 62, Div 3, 1971-2
Record League Victory: 10-1 v Northampton Town, Div 3 (S), Sept 1939
Record League Defeat: 0-9 v Lincoln City, Div 3, 1 Dec 1982
Club Statistician for the Directory: John Treleven

Programme Editor
Brian Tiler

Price	Number of Pages
50p	16

Subscriptions
£15

AFC BOURNEMOUTH

PLAYERS NAME Ht Wt Birthdate	Honours	Birthplace Transfers	Clubs	APPEARANCES League	Milk Cup	F.A.C.	A.M.C.	GOALS League	Milk Cup	F.A.C.	A.M.C.
GOALKEEPERS											
Ian Leigh		Ilfracombe	Swaythling A.								
5-11 12.3 11.6.62			Bournemouth	105	2	8	5				
John Smeulders	E. Y	Hackney	Orient (A)								
5-10 13.0 28.3.57			Bournemouth	14							
			Trowbridge T.								
			Bournemouth	1							
DEFENDERS											
Phil Brignull†	E. S	Stratford	West Ham U. (A)	10+1							
6-0 11.2 2.10.60		F	Bournemouth	119	6	7	4	10	2		
Roger Brown*		Tamworth	AP Leamington								
6-1 11.10 12.12.52		£5,000	Bournemouth	63	2	3		3	1		
		£85,000	Norwich C.	16	2	3					
		£100,000	Fulham	141	8	8		18	1		
		£40,000	Bournemouth	23		3	4	2			
Everald Laronde	FAYC. 81	East Ham	West Ham U. (A)	6+1		2					
5-9 10.12 24.1.63		£12,000	Bournemouth	18			2				1
John McLaughlin	E. Y. Div. 3. 83	Edmonton	Colchester U. (A)	66	2	4		2			
5-8 10.10 29.10.54			Swindon T.	199+3	15	21		8			
		£45,000	Portsmouth	172	13	7		1			
		F	Bournemouth								
Mark Nightingale	E. Y	Salisbury	Bournemouth (A)	44+5	2	8		4			
5-10 10.7 1.2.57			Crystal Palace								
			Norwich C.	28+7							
			Bulova H.K.								
			Bournemouth	70+2	2	4	6	4			
Chris Sulley		Camberwell	Chelsea (A)								
5-8 10.0 3.12.59			Bournemouth	145+1	8	9	4	3			
MIDFIELD											
John Beck		Edmonton	Q.P.R. (A)	32+8	2	4		1			
5-11 11.9 25.5.54			Coventry C.	60+9	5	3		6			
			Fulham	113+1	6	6		13	1		
			Bournemouth	59+1	2	3	6	7		2	1
Milton Graham		Hackney	Bournemouth	41+14	2	3+1	4	9	1	1	1
5-11 12.6 2.11.62											
Paul Morrell		Poole	Weymouth								
23.3.61			Bournemouth	19+3	1	3	6	2			1
Sean O'Driscoll	Ei. (3)	Wolverhampton	Alvechurch								
5-8 10.6 1.7.57			Fulham	141+7	13+	11+		13			
		£20,000	Bournemouth	19			6	1			
Bob Savage		Liverpool	Liverpool (A)								
5-7 11.1 8.1.60			Wrexham (L)	27		2		10		1	
			Stoke C.	5+2							
		£20,000	Bournemouth	22+1			5	5			3
Mark Schiavi	E. Y	London	West Ham U. (A)								
5-7½ 10.6 1.5.64			Bournemouth	10							
Chris Shaw		Bourne	Bournemouth	3+2			0+1				1
5-6 9.8 23.8.65											
Keith Williams		Burtwood	Aston Villa (A)								
5-9 11.7 12.4.57		F	Northampton T.	128+3	8	2+1		6	1		
		F	Bournemouth	78+3	8	5	2	1			
FORWARDS											
Morgan Lewis		Bournemouth	Bournemouth								
5-8½ 10.12											
Bill Rafferty	Div. 3. 83	Glasgow	Coventry C.	27	3	1		3		1	
6-0 12.6 30.12.50		Player Exchange	Blackpool	35+1		1		9			
		£25,000	Plymouth A.	89+1	5	6		35	1	4	
		£19,000	Carlisle U.	72	7	6		27	5	7	
		£125,000	Wolverhampton W.	41+3	3	3		6	5	2	
		£175,000	Newcastle U.	34+5	2	1		6			
		£85,000	Portsmouth	98+4	5	4		40	2		
		£4,000	Bournemouth	17				5	1	2	
Colin Russell		Liverpool	Liverpool (A)	0+1							
5-7 10.7 21.1.61		F	Huddersfield T.	64+2	10	4+1		23	1	1	
			Stoke C. (L)	11				2			
Ian Thompson		Dartford	Salisbury								
6-1 11.0 8.6.58		£16,000	Bournemouth	42+2	1	4	5	12		3	2

NON-CONTRACT PLAYERS 1984-85: David Coleman, Paul Jones (0+1 A.M.C.)

AFC BOURNEMOUTH

DIVISION THREE 17TH **FA CUP** 4TH ROUND **MILK CUP** 1ST ROUND

MATCH	DATE	COMPE-TITION	VENUE	OPPONENTS	RESULT	HALF TIME	L'GUE POS'N	GOALSCORERS	ATTEN-DANCE
1	A 27	CL	H	Preston NE	L0-1	0-1			4,163
2	**30**	**MC 1**	**H**	**Bristol R**	**L1-2**	**1-1**		**Morgan (pen)**	**3,473**
3	S 3	CL	A	Burnley	L1-5	1-4	23	Duffield	5,512
4	6	CL	A	Wimbledon	L2-3	0-2		Graham, Morgan (pen)	2,345
5	10	CL	H	Wigan Ath	L0-1	0-1	24		3,161
6	**13**	**MC 1**	**A**	**Bristol R**	**D2-2**	**1-1**		**Graham, Brignull**	**4,564**
7	17	CL	A	Millwall	L1-3	1-1	24	Graham	4,774
8	24	CL	H	Gillingham	W2-0	1-0	23	Beck 2	3,045
9	27	CL	H	Bristol R	L0-1	0-1			3,328
10	O 1	CL	A	Lincoln C	L0-3	0-1	24		3,586
11	8	CL	H	Plymouth Arg	W2-1	2-1	22	Morgan, Thompson I	3,759
12	15	CL	A	Sheffield U	L0-2	0-1	23		8,984
13	18	CL	A	Walsall	L1-3	0-1		Morgan	3,782
14	22	CL	H	Oxford U	W2-1	1-0	21	Thompson I, Morgan	4,758
15	29	CL	A	Brentford	D1-1	1-1	21	Morgan	4,630
16	N 1	CL	H	Rotherham U	W4-2	2-1		Lee 2, Morgan, Thompson I	3,495
17	5	CL	H	Hull C	L2-3	0-3	20	Brignull, Thompson I	4,644
18	11	CL	A	Southend U	D0-0	0-0			3,277
19	**19**	**FAC 1**	**H**	**Walsall**	**W4-0**	**2-0**		**Thompson I, Beck, Morgan, Lee**	**4,298**
20	26	CL	H	Bolton W	D2-2	2-0	20	Morgan 2	3,941
21	D 3	CL	A	Scunthorpe U	W2-1	1-0	18	Morgan 2	2,344
22	**13**	**FAC 2**	**A**	**Windsor & Eton**	**D0-0**	**0-0**			**3,451**
23	17	CL	A	Bradford C	L2-5	1-1	20	Thompson I 2	2,802
24	**19**	**FAC 2R**	**H**	**Windsor & Eton**	**W2-0**	**0-0**		**Beck, Thompson I**	**6,008**
25	26	CL	H	Newport Co	D1-1	1-0	21	Morgan	7,220
26	27	CL	A	Orient	L0-2	0-1	21		4,077
27	31	CL	H	Exeter C	W3-1	3-1	19	Savage, Morgan, Thompson I	5,133
28	J 2	CL	A	Port Vale	L1-2	0-2	21	Tartt (og)	4,008
29	**7**	**FAC 3**	**H**	**Manchester U**	**W2-0**	**0-0**		**Graham, Thompson I**	**15,000**
30	14	CL	A	Preston NE	L0-2	0-0	21		3,476
31	21	CL	H	Millwall	D1-1	1-1	20	Thompson I	4,242
32	**31**	**FAC 4**	**A**	**Middlesbrough**	**L0-2**	**0-1**			**20,175**
33	F 4	CL	H	Lincoln C	W3-0	2-0	19	Morgan, Brignull, Graham	3,597
34	11	CL	A	Gillingham	L1-2	1-1	19	Savage (pen)	4,891
35	18	CL	H	Brentford	L0-3	0-1	21		4,308
36	**21**	**AMC 1**	**H**	**Aldershot**	**W4-0**	**0-0**		**Williams, Morgan, La Ronde, Savage**	**1,706**
37	25	CL	A	Oxford U	L2-3	1-1	21	Sulley, Thompson 1	6,535
38	M 3	CL	H	Walsall	W3-0	1-0	18	Brignull, Raferty 2	3,913
39	6	CL	A	Hull C	L1-3	1-2		Swann (og)	8,047
40	10	CL	H	Southend C	W1-0	1-0	18	Savage (pen)	3,615
41	**13**	**AMC 2**	**A**	**Millwall**	**D2-2***	**0-0**		**Shaw, Beck**	**2,099**
42	17	CL	A	Plymouth Arg	L0-1	0-1	18		7,235
43	20	CL	A	Wigan Ath	W3-1	0-1		Brignull, Rafferty, Thompson I	2,910
44	24	CL	H	Sheffield U	L0-1	0-1	18		4,767
45	31	CL	H	Wimbledon	L2-3	2-2	18	Thompson I 2	3,538
46	**A 3**	**AMC SQF**	**H**	**Wrexham**	**W2-0**	**1-0**		**Thompson I, Savage**	**1,909**
47	7	CL	A	Bristol R	W3-1	2-0	18	Savage, Brignull, Beck	5,032
48	9	CL	H	Burnley	W1-0	1-0		Brown	4,113
49	14	CL	H	Scunthorpe U	D1-1	1-0	17	Savage (pen)	3,501
50	17	CL	A	Rotherham U	L0-1	0-1			3,937
51	21	CL	A	Newport Co	L1-2	1-1	18	Graham	2,356
52	24	CL	H	Orient	W3-2	0-0		Sulley, Nightingale, Brignull	3,736
53	28	CL	A	Bolton W	W1-0	0-0	17	Rafferty	3,045
54	M 5	CL	H	Port Vale	D1-1	1-1	17	Brown	3,305
55	7	CL	A	Exeter C	W2-0	0-0	17	Morrell, O'Driscoll	2,790
56	12	CL	H	Bradford C	W4-1	1-0	17	Campbell (og), Morrell, Raferty, Nightingale	3,608
57	**14**	**AMC SSF**	**H**	**Bristol R**	**W1-0**	**0-0**		**Savage (pen)**	**2,810**
58	**21**	**AMC SF**	**H**	**Millwall**	**W2-1**	**1-0**		**Thompson I, O'Driscoll**	**4,058**
59	**24**	**AMC F**	**A**	**Hull C**	**W2-1**	**1-1**		**Graham, Morrell**	**6,544**

*Won 7-6 on Penalties, After Extra Time

Av Home Att **4,000**

Goal Scorers

League (63): Morgan 13 (1 pen), Thompson I 12, Brignull 6, Rafferty 5, Savage 5 (3 pens), Graham 4, Beck 3, Brown 2, Lee 2, Morrell 2, Nightingale 2, Sulley 2, Duffield 1, O'Driscoll 1, opponents 3
FA Cup (8): Thompson I 3, Beck 2, Graham 1, Lee 1, Morgan 1
Milk Cup (3): Brignull 1, Graham 1, Morgan 1 (1 pen)
AMC (13): Savage 3 (1 pen), Thompson I 2, Beck 1, Graham 1, La Ronde 1, Morrell 1, Morgan 1, O'Driscoll 1, Shaw 1, Williams 1

1983-84

Leigh	Nightingale	Morrell	Brignull	Thompson M	Beck	Williams	Sulley	Morgan	Thompson I	Carter	Dawtry	Ramsbottom	Lee	Duffield	Graham	Shaw	La Ronde	Schiavi (L)	Train (L)	Brown	Savage	Smeulders	O'Driscoll (L)	Rafferty	REFEREE	
1	2	3	4*	5	6	7	8	9	10	11	12														M Bodgnham	1
1	**2**	**3**	**4**	**5**	**6**	**7**	**8**	**9**	**10**		**11***		**12**												**D Letts**	**2**
	2	3	4*	5	6	7	8	9	10			1	12	11											D Owen	3
	2	3*		5†	6	7	8	9	10			1	12	4	11										D Axcell	4
	2*		4	5	6	7	3	9	10			1		11	8	12									A Buksh	5
	2		**4**	**5**	**6**	**7**	**3**	**9**		**10**		**1**		**11**	**8**										**H King**	**6**
	2		4	5	6		3	9	12	11		1		8*	10		7								DA Hedges	7
1	4		5		6	8*	3	9	11					7	10	12	2								C Thomas	8
1	5	12	4		6		3	9	11					7*	10	8	2								C Downey	9
1	6		5		4	8	3	9	11						10		2	7							A Robinson	10
1	6		5		4	8	3	9	11						10		2	7							R Lewis	11
1	6	10	5		4	8*	3	9	11						12		2	7							D Scott	12
1	6	10	5		4	8	3	9	11								2	7							A Banks	13
1	6		5		4	8	3	9	11						10		2	7							K Salmon	14
1	6		5		4	8	3	9	11				10				2	7							D H Brazier	15
1	6		5	8	4		3	9	11				10				2	7							RG Milford	16
1	6		5	8*	4		3	9	11				10		12		2	7							J Moules	17
1	6		5		4	8	3	9	11				10				2	7							D Reeves	18
1	**6**	**8**	**5**		**4**		**3**	**9**	**11**				**12**		**10**		**2***		**7**						**D Hedges**	**19**
1	6	2	5		4		3	9	11				12		10*			8	7						E Scales	20
1	2	8	6		4		3	9	11						10				7	5					T Mills	21
1	**2**	**8**	**6**		**4**		**3**	**9**	**11**				**12**		**10***				**7**	**5**					**K Salmon**	**22**
1	2	8	6		4		3	9	11	10									7	5					N Midgley	23
1	**2**	**8**	**6**		**4**		**3**	**9**	**11**	**10**									**7**	**5**					**K Salmon**	**24**
1	5	8	6		4		3	9	11	10*					12		2		7						L Shapter	25
1	5	8*	6		4	10	3	9	11	12							2		7						A Gunn	26
1	5		6	2	4		3	9	11						10				7		8				D Vickers	27
1	5		6	2	4		3	9	11	12					10*				7		8				R Bridges	28
1	**8**		**6**				**3**	**9**	**11**						**10**		**2**		**7**	**5**	**4**				**B Stevens**	**29**
1	8	12	6		7		3	9	11						10*		2			5	4				N Ashley	30
1	8		6		4		3	9	11						10		2			5	7				T Bune	31
1	**8**	**10**	**6**		**4**		**3**	**9**	**11**	**12**							**2***			**5**	**7**				**K Hackett**	**32**
1	2	7	6		12	8*	3	9	11						10					5	4				A Ward	33
	2	7	6		8		3	9	11						10					5	4	1			D Letts	34
1	5	7	6		8		3	9*	12						10		2				4		11		J Deakin	35
1	**5**	**6***			**8**	**7**	**3**	**9**	**11**	**12**							**2**				**4**		**10***		**B Stevens**	**36**
1	5		6		4	7*	3	9	11	12					10		2						8		G Napthine	37
1	2	10	6		4	8	3		11											5			7	9	M Dimblebee	38
1	2	10	6		4	7*	3		11											5	12		8	9	K Walmsley	39
1	2	10	6		4*	12	3								11					5	8		7	9	D Hedges	40
	2	**10**			**4**	**8**	**3**			**11***					**9**	**12**	**6**			**5**		**1**	**7**		**M James**	**41**
1	2		6		4	10	3								11					5	8		7	9	R Milford	42
1	2*		6		4	10	3		11						12					5	8		7	9	G Courtney	43
1	2		6			4	3		11						10					5	8		7	9	E Read	44
1	2		6		10	4*	3		11						12					5	8		7	9	Alan Robinson	45
1	**2**	**5**	**6**		**4**		**3**		**11**						**10**						**8**		**7**	**9**	**C Downey**	**46**
1	2		6		10	4	3		11											5	8		7	9	K Salmon	47
1	2		6		10	4	3		11											5	8		7	9	A Crickmore	48
1	2		6		10	4	3		11											5	8		7	9	D Reeves	49
1	2		6		10	4*	3		11						12					5	8		7	9	T Holbrook	50
1	2		5		8		3		11						9					4	7		6	10	R Lewis	51
1	2		6		4		3		11						10					5	8		7	9	T Bune	52
1	2	10	6		4		3		11											5	8		7	9	D Shaw	53
1	2	12	6		4		3		11						10*					5	8		7	9	E Scales	54
1	2	10	6		4		3		11											5	8		7	9	H Taylor	55
1	2	10			4		3		11											5	8		7	9	J Moules	56
1	**2**	**10**	**6**		**4**		**3**		**11**						**9**					**5**	**8**		**7**		**D Vickers**	**57**
1	**2**	**10**	**6**		**4**		**3**		**11**											**5**	**8**		**7**	**9**	**J Martin**	**58**
1	**2**	**10**	**6**		**4**		**3**		**11**						**9**					**5**	**8**		**7**		**G Courtney**	**59**
41	**46**	19	44	9	44	25	**46**	29	42	4	0	4	4	6	24	1	18	10	7	23	22	1	19	17	League Appearances	
		+3S			+1S	+1S			+2S	+3S	+1S		+3S		+6S	+2S					+1S					
5	5	4	5		4		5	5	5	1+1S			2S		3		3		4	4	2				FA Cup Appearances	
1	2	1	2	2	2	2	2	2	1	1	1	1	1S	1	1										Milk Cup Appearances	
5	6	6	4		6	2	6	1	5	1+1S					4	1S	2			4	5	1	6	2	AM Cup Appearances	

Also Played: Lewis match 56, no.6. Jones match 36, no.13.

DEAN COURT

Official Address: Dean Court Ground, Bournemouth. Telephone: (0202) 35381

Telegraphic: Football Bournemouth

Ground Capacity: 19,086

Record Attendance: 28,799 v. Manchester United, F.A. Cup Round 6, 2 Mar 1957

Record Receipts: £33,723 v. Manchester United, F.A. Cup Round 3, 7 Jan 1984

Size of Playing Area: 112yds × 75 yds

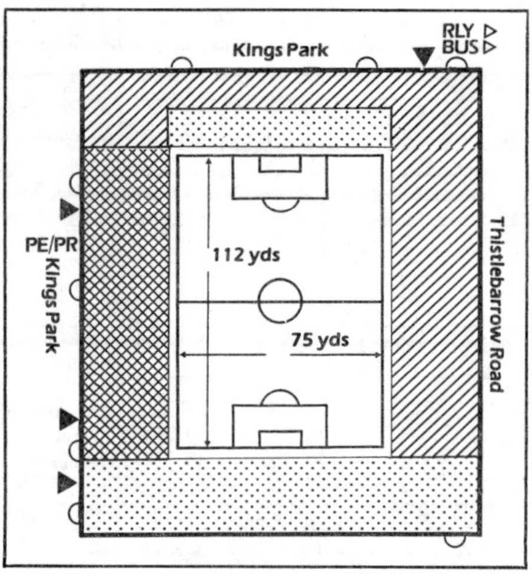

For key see page 12

Season Tickets: Centre Stand: £80.00, B or E Block £70.00

Executive Box Season Tickets: None

Cost of Stand Tickets: Centre Stand £4, B or E Block £3.50, F Block (Wing Stand) £3.00 (juveniles/OAP £1.50), A Block (visiting supporters) £3.50; **Terraces:** £2.50 (juveniles/OAP £1.50)

Match and Ticket Information: Phone Club

Car Parking: Adequate for 1,500 vehicles

How to get to the ground

From North and East: Use A338 (S.P. Bournemouth) and at roundabout junction with A3060 take 2nd exit. At next roundabout take 1st exit into Kings Park Drive, then turn left into Thistlebarrow Road for A.F.C. Bournemouth.
From West: Follow signs Bournemouth A3049, 0.7m after Wallisdown (traffic signals) turn left into Talbot Road. In 2m at roundabout take 1st exit into Queens Park South Drive then at roundabout take 2nd exit into Kings Park Drive, then turn left into Thistlebarrows Road for A.F.C. Bournemouth.

BRADFORD CITY Division 3

Chairman
Stafford Heginbotham

Directors
Jack Tordoff
Peter Flesher, FCA

Secretary
Terry Newman

Manager
Trevor Cherry

Assistant Manager
Terry Yorath

Chief Scout
Maurice Lindley

Commercial Manager
Mike Ryan (0274-306062)

Physiotherapist
Brian Edwards

Groundsman
Alan Gilliver

After the promising form of 1982/83 it was hoped that there would be great things last season, but Bradford City were almost not in existence even to start it off. Financial problems and a 'winding-up' exercise took place during the summer and the new season started with Bradford City (1983) Ltd being the new title. It also started without star striker Bobby Campbell.

A former clubmate of Trevor Cherry at Leeds United, John Hawley, was bought from Hong Kong to replace him but the club's early season form — just 8 points from their first 15 games — showed how much their top scorer would be missed.

At the beginning of November, City were firmly entrenched in the bottom four, and relegation seemed a formality. It was then that the big affable Irishman returned after his unhappy stay at Derby in the hope of stemming the flow of bad results. His presence pepped up the side, in particular young Stuart McCall, and the fans were slowly charmed back to the terraces.

A shock 4-1 away win at Brentford late in November was the turning point and started a club record breaking run of ten consecutive victories. This brought the club to within a whisker of the promotion chasers and erased the memories of first round exits from the major cups. The scalps of high flying Wimbledon and Sheffield United were amongst those captured and in December the 'Bantams' scored 18 goals to win a Canon award.

A final assault on the top places ended as the end of season fixture congestion proved too much to handle. Nevertheless, the club had regained their team spirit and but for a dismal start, promotion might well have been gained.

A creditable seventh place creates a good launching pad for next season and certainly expectations and confidence are high.

Terry Frost, The League Directory's Statistician for the Club

Back Row L to R: Mark Fletcher, David Evans, Chris Withe, Bobby Campbell, Eric McManus, Melvin Gwinnett, John Hawley, Peter Jackson, Tony Clegg, Don Goodman, Mike Holmes, Bryan Edwards (Physiotherapist). **Front Row:** Terry Gray, John Hendrie, Gary Haire, Trevor Cherry (Player Manager), Mr Tordoff (Vice-Chairman), Mr Heginbotham (Chairman), Mr Flesher (Director), Terry Yorath (Assistant Manager), Stuart McCall, Mark Ellis, Greg Abbott.

'THE BANTAMS'

Sponsored by **Bradford Mythbreakers**

Formed: 1903 **Turned Professional:** 1903 **Ltd Co:** 1908
Previous Managers: 1903-5 Robert Campbell 1905-21 Peter O'Rourke 1921-6 David L Menzies 1926-8 Colin Campbell Mckechnie Veitch 1928-30 Peter O'Rourke 1930-5 Jack G Peart 1935-8 Richard Ray 1938-43 Fred Westgarth 1943-6 Councillor Robert Sharp 1946-7 Jack Barker 1947-8 John Milburn 1948-52 David M Steele 1952 Albert V Harris 1952-5 Ivor V Powell 1955-61 Peter Jackson 1961-4 Robert Brocklebank 1965-6 William Harris 1966-8 William Watson 1968 Grenville Hair 1968-71 Jimmy Wheeler 1971-5 Bryan Edwards 1975-8 Robert Kennedy 1978 John Napier 1978-81 George Mulhall 1981-2 Roy McFarland
Honours: Division 2 Champions 1907-8 Division 3 (N) Champions 1928-9 F.A. Cup Winners 1911
League Career: Elected to Division 2 1903 Promoted to Division One 1907-8 Relegated to Division 2 1921-2 Relegated to Division 3 (N) 1926-7 Promoted to Division 2 1928-9 Relegated to Division 3 1936-7 Relegated to Division 4 1960-1 Promoted to Division 3 1968-9 Relegated to Division 4 1971-2 Promoted to Division 3 1976-7 Relegated to Division 4 1977-8 Promoted to Division 3 1981-2
Colours: White shirts with claret and amber shoulders, claret shorts, white stockings
Change Colours: Amber shirts with white and claret shoulders, amber shortsand stockings

CLUB RECORDS

Most Appearances for Club: Cyril Podd: Football League 494 + 8 + F.A. Cup 30 + League Cup 33 + 1 **Total 557 + 9 subs**
Most Capped Player: Harry Hampton, 9, N Ireland. **For England:** Evelyn Lintott, 4
Record Goalscorer in a Match: Albert Whitehurst, 7 v Tranmere Rovers (8-0) (H), Div 3 (N), 6 March 1929
Record League Goalscorer in a season: David Layne, 34 **All competitions:** David Layne 36 (League 34, F.A. Cup 2) 1961-2
Record League Goalscorer in a career: Frank O'Rourke 88, 1906-13 **All competitions:** Bobby Campbell 96 (League 85, F.A. Cup 2, League Cup 9) 1979-83, 1984-
Record Transfer Fee Received: £50,000 from Walsall for Steve Baines, July 1980
Record Transfer Fee Paid: £31,000 to Burnley for Billy Ingham, August 1980
Best Performances: League: 5th Div 1 1910-1 **F.A. Cup:** Winners **League/Milk Cup:** 5th Round 1965
Most League Points: (3pts for win) 91, Div 4, 1981-2 (2pts for win) 63, Div 3 (S), 1971-2
Record League Victory: 11-1 v Rotherham United, Div 3 (N), 25 Sept 28
Record League Defeat: 1-9 v Colchester United, Div 4, 30 Dec 61

Club Stastician for the Directory: Terry Frost

Programme Editor
David Markham

Price	Number of Pages
40p	16

Subscriptions
Subscriptions on request to club

BRADFORD CITY

PLAYERS NAME Ht Wt Birthdate	Honours	Birthplace Transfers	Clubs	APPEARANCES League	Milk Cup	F.A.C.	A.M.C.	GOALS League	Milk Cup	F.A.C.	A.M.C.
GOALKEEPERS											
Eric McManus	N.I. AM	Limavady	Coleraine								
6-1 12.12 14.11.50			Coventry C.	6							
			Notts Co.	229	13	9					
			Stoke C.	4							
			Lincoln C. (L)	21							
			Bradford C.	73	8	6	2				
DEFENDERS											
Greg Abbott		Coventry	Coventry C. (A)								
5-9 10.7 14.12.63			Bradford C.	41 + 5	2	2		3			
Trevor Cherry	E.(27), Div. 2, 70,	Huddersfield	Huddersfield T.	184 + 2	7	13		10	1		
5-9 11.0 23.2.48	Div. 1, 74,	£90,000	Leeds U.	393 + 6	36	28+1	19+1	24	4	1	2
	F.Lg.XI(2)	£10,000	Bradford C.	72	2	2	1				
Tony Clegg		Bradford	Bradford C. (A)	2							
6-0 11.5 8.11.65											
David Evans		Solihull	Aston Villa (A)	2							
5-11 12.6 6.5.61		£25,000	Halifax T.	18	8	11	1	9	1		
		F	Bradford C.								
Greg Fee		Halifax	Bradford C.	6 + 1	1						
6-2 13.6 24.6.64											
Mark Fletcher		Barnsley	Barnsley (A)	1							
5-8 11.0 1.4.65											
Peter Jackson*		Bradford	Bradford C. (A)	170 + 11	17	5 + 1	2	16			
6-1 12.6 6.4.61											
Chris Withe†		Liverpool	Newcastle U. (A)	2							
5-10 11.3 25.9.62		F	Bradford C.	45	2	2	2	1			
MIDFIELD											
Terry Gray	E. Y	Bradford	Ashley Rd.								
5-6 10.5 3.6.54			Huddersfield T.	146 + 17	7 + 2	9		36	3	2	
		£45,000	Southend U.	106 + 4	8	2		28	1	1	
		F	Bradford C.	65 + 4	7	4		15		1	
Stuart McCall		Leeds	Bradford C. (A)	71 + 3	4	2	2	9			1
5-6 10.2 10.6.64											
Terry Yorath	W.(59), U.23(7)	Cardiff	Leeds U. (A)	120 + 23	10+1	18+2	20+7	10		1	1
5-10 11.10 27.3.50	Div. 1, 74,	£135,000	Coventry C.	99	7	3		3			
	E.F. 71	£300,000	Tottenham H.	44 + 4	7	7		1			
		£140,000	Vancouver W.								
		F	Bradford C.	21 + 3	1	2	1				
John Hendrie	S. Y	Lennox Town	Coventry C. (A)	15 + 6	2			2			
5-8½ 10.11 24.10.63			Hereford U. (L)	6							
FORWARDS											
Bobby Campbell	N.I.(2), Y	Belfast	Aston Villa (A)	7 + 3	1			1			
6-0 12.7 13.9.56			Halifax T. (L)	14 + 1							
		F	Huddersfield T.	30 + 1	3			9	1		
		£10,000	Sheffield U.	35 + 2	1			11			
		F	Huddersfield T.	7				3			
		F	Halifax T.	19 + 3		1		3			
		F	Brisbane C.								
		F	Bradford C.	147 + 1	15	6		76	9	2	
		£70,000	Derby C.	11				4			
			Bradford C.	32		1	2	9			1
Mark Ellis		Bradford	Bradford C.	81 + 3	8	4 + 1	1	12	1		
5-9 10.5 6.1.62											
Don Goodman		Leeds	Bradford C.	0 + 2							
5-9 10.8 9.5.66											
Gary Haire		Sedgefield	Oxford U. (A)								
5-7 10.8 24.7.63			Whitley Bay								
			Bradford C.	39 + 4	1 + 1	2	1	13			
John Hawley		Withernsea	Hull C.	101 + 13	10 +	5		22	2	1	
6-0 13.12 8.5.54		£75,000	Leeds U.	30 + 3	6	3		16	1		
		£200,000	Sunderland	25	3	3		11			
		£50,000	Arsenal	14 + 6	1			3			
			Orient (L)	4				1			
			Hull C. (L)	3				1			
			Bradford C.	43	1	2		22			

NON-CONTRACT PLAYERS 1984-85: Paul Allen, Nigel Beaumont, David Cheshire, Stewart Ferrebee, Mel Gwynnett, Mike Holmes (0 + 1 A.M.C.), **Carl Hudson, Andy Lawrence, Gary Peat, Alan Starling, Paul Williamson, Paul Hodgson, Phil Kitching, Mike Nevison, Chris Reade**

APPRENTICE: Shane Beeby

BRADFORD CITY

DIVISION THREE 7TH **FA CUP** 1ST ROUND **MILK CUP** 1ST ROUND

MATCH	DATE	COMPETITION	VENUE	OPPONENTS	RESULT	HALF TIME	L'GUE POS'N	GOALSCORERS	ATTENDANCE
1	A 27	CL	A	Orient	L0-2	0-2			2,675
2	**29**	**MC 1**	**H**	**Sheffield U**	**L0-1**	**0-0**			**4,401**
3	S 3	CL	H	Bolton W	L0-2	0-0	21		3,324
4	7	CL	H	Hull C	D0-0	0-0			3,391
5	10	CL	A	Newport Co	L3-4	1-2	23	Gray, McCall, Hawley	2,462
6	**13**	**MC 1**	**A**	**Sheffield U**	**D1-1**	**1-1**		**Podd**	**8,658**
7	17	CL	H	Southend U	D1-1	0-0	21	Ellis	2,574
8	24	CL	A	Port Vale	W2-1	1-1	19	Haire 2	4,897
9	27	CL	A	Sheffield U	L0-2	0-0			10,040
10	O 1	CL	H	Exeter C	L1-3	1-2	22	Haire	2,505
11	8	CL	H	Scunthorpe U	D2-2	1-1	21	Haire, Hawley	2,476
12	15	CL	A	Bristol R	L0-1	0-0	22		3,861
13	19	CL	A	Oxford U	L0-2	0-1			5,624
14	22	CL	H	Walsall	D0-0	0-0	23		2,474
15	29	CL	A	Rotherham U	L0-1	0-0	23		4,506
16	N 5	CL	A	Wimbledon	L1-4	0-1	23	Ellis	2,408
17	12	CL	H	Millwall	D3-3	0-1	23	McCall, Haire, Hawley	3,548
18	**19**	**FAC 1**	**H**	**Wigan Ath**	**D0-0**	**0-0**			**4,559**
19	26	CL	A	Brentford	W4-1	3-1	23	Hawley, Ellis, McCall, Campbell	3,738
20	**28**	**FAC 1R**	**A**	**Wigan Ath**	**L2-4**	**1-0**		**Hawley Haire**	**4,741**
21	D 3	CL	H	Plymouth Arg	W2-0	0-0	22	Hawley (pen), Haire	2,955
22	17	CL	H	AFC Bournemouth	W5-2	1-1	22	Hawley 2, Haire, Ellis, Campbell	2,802
23	26	CL	A	Burnley	W2-1	0-1	19	Campbell, Ellis	12,136
24	27	CL	H	Wigan Ath	W6-2	3-0	16	Ellis, Hawley 3 (1 pen), Gray 2	5,176
25	31	CL	A	Lincoln C	W3-2	1-1	15	Hawley, Abbott, Jackson	3,983
26	J 2	CL	H	Preston NE	W3-2	1-1	14	Jackson, Hawley, Withe	6,405
27	7	CL	H	Wimbledon	W5-2	3-2	14	Haire, Hawley 4 (1 pen)	4,563
28	14	CL	H	Orient	W4-1	2-1	11	Gray 2, Ellis, Campbell	3,950
29	F 3	CL	A	Exeter C	W2-0	0-0		Gray, Hawley	3,105
30	11	CL	H	Port Vale	D2-2	1-2	12	Hawley (pen), Abbott	5,340
31	14	CL	A	Gillingham	D0-0	0-0			4,390
32	18	CL	H	Rotherham U	W1-0	0-0	11	Campbell	5,020
33	**22**	**AMC 1**	**H**	**Hartlepool U**	**W3-2**	**3-2**		**Campbell, Ellis, Abbott**	**1,178**
34	25	CL	A	Walsall	W2-1	0-1	10	Haire, McCall	6,013
35	M 3	CL	H	Oxford U	D2-2	0-1	11	Campbell, McCall	7,322
36	10	CL	A	Millwall	D0-0	0-0	11		3,259
37	**13**	**AMC 2**	**A**	**Sheffield U**	**L1-2**	**1-0**		**McCall**	**3,175**
38	17	CL	A	Scunthorpe U	L1-2	0-1	12	Hawley	3,274
39	27	CL	A	Bolton W	W2-0	1-0		Campbell, Hawley	5,994
40	31	CL	A	Hull C	L0-1	0-1	11		7,743
41	A 7	CL	H	Sheffield U	W2-1	0-1	10	Ellis, Haire	9,262
42	11	CL	H	Gillingham	W3-2	1-2		Campbell, Hawley (pen), Haire	3,465
43	16	CL	A	Southend U	L1-2	1-1		Gray	2,035
44	21	CL	H	Burnley	W2-1	1-1	8	Miller (og), Kennedy (og)	5,578
45	23	CL	A	Wigan Ath	W1-0	1-0	7	Haire	3,470
46	25	CL	H	Newport Co	W1-0	0-0		Hawley (pen)	3,347
47	28	CL	H	Brentford	D1-1	0-0	7	Jackson	3,739
48	M 2	CL	H	Bristol R	L0-1	0-0	7		3,271
49	5	CL	A	Preston NE	W2-1	1-1	7	Haire, Campbell	3,242
50	7	CL	H	Lincoln C	D0-0	0-0	7		3,085
51	9	CL	A	Plymouth Arg	L0-3	0-1			5,744
52	12	CL	A	AFC Bournemouth	L1-4	0-1	7	Abbot (pen)	3,608
								Av Home Att	**4,155**

Goal Scorers

League (73): Hawley 22 (6 pens), Haire 13, Campbell 9, Ellis 8, Gray 7, McCall 5, Abbott 3 (1 pen), Jackson 3, Withe 1, opponents 2
FA Cup (2): Haire 1, Hawley 1
Milk Cup (1): Podd 1
AMC (4): Abbott 1, Campbell 1, Ellis 1, McCall 1

1983-84

McManus	Abbott	Withe	McCall	Jackson	Cherry	Ellis	Gray	Cooke	Haire	Yorath	Hill	Podd	Hawley	Fee	Watson	Mellor	Airey (L)	Pickering (L)	Lampkin	Campbell	Griffiths (L)	Holmes	Goodman	Clegg	REFEREE	
1	2	3	4	5	6	7	8	9*	10	11	12														L Shapter	1
1	7	3	4	5	6		8		10	11	9	2													**D Allison**	2
1	7	3	4	5	6		8		10	11		2	9												V Callow	3
1	7	3	4	10	6	11	8*		12			2	9	5											G Courtney	4
1	7*	3	4	5	6	11			12			2	9	10											J Martin	5
1	11	3	4	5	6	7*	8		12			2	9	10											**A Seville**	6
1	7	3	4	5	6	11	8		12			2	9	10*											J Worrall	7
1		3	4	5	6		8	10	7			2	9		11										R Guy	8
1		3*	4	5	6		8	10	7			2	9		11	12									D Richards	9
1		3	4	5	6		8	10*	7			2	9		11	12									N Wilson	10
1		3	4	5	6		8*		7			2	9		11	10	12								J Hough	11
1	12	3	4	5	6		8		7			2*	9			10	11								D Reeves	12
1	8	3	4	5	6		7		11			2	9				10								D Axcell	13
1	11	3*	4	5	6		8		7			2	9			12	10								N Glover	14
1	11	3	4	5	6		8*		7	9		2				12	10								R Nixon	15
1	2	3	4		6	11	8		7*	10								5	12	9					T Spencer	16
1		3	4		6	11			7	10		2	8					5		9					J Ashworth	17
1		3	4		6	11	9		7	10		2	8					5							**J Lovatt**	18
1		3	4		6	11			7	10		2	8					5		9					B Stevens	19
1		3	4		6	11			7	10		2	8					5		9					**J Lovatt**	20
1		3	4		6	11*	12		7	10		2	8					5		9					N Ashley	21
1		3	4	5	6	11			7	10		2	8							9					N Midgley	22
1		3	4	5	6	11			7	10		2	8							9					P Tyldesley	23
1	12	3	4	5	6	11	10		7*			2	8							9					P Willis	24
1	12	3	4	5	6	11	10		7*			2	8							9					H Taylor	25
1	12	3	4	5	6	11	10		7*			2	8							9					G Tyson	26
1		3	4	5	6	11	10		7			2	8							9					T Fitzharris	27
1		3	4	5	6	11	10		7			2	8							9					K Redfern	28
1	12	3	4	5	6	11*	10		7			2	8							9					L Burden	29
1	10	3	4	5	6	11			7	12		2*	8							9					K Walmsley	30
1	10	3	4	5	6	11				7		2	8							9					A Gunn	31
1	10	3	4	5	6	11				7		2	8							9					C Seel	32
1	10	3	4	5		11		6	7*			2	8							9		12			**N Glover**	33
1	10	3	4	5	6	11			7			2	8							9					R Milford	34
1	10	3	4	5	6	11			7			2	8							9					M Heath	35
1	10	3	4	5	6	11*				12		2	8							9	7				G Napthine	36
1	10	3	4	5	6					11		2	8							9	7				**A Saunders**	37
1	10		4	5	6	11			12	3		2	8							9	7*				N Wilson	38
1	10	3	4	5	6	11			7	2			8							9					J Hough	39
1	10	3	4	5	6	11			7	2			8							9					J Bray	40
1	2	3	4	5	6	11	10		7				8							9					A Banks	41
1	2*	3	4	5	6	11	10	12	7				8							9					T Jones	42
1	2	3	4	5	6	11	10		7				8							9					A Buksh	43
1	2	3	4	5	6	11	10		7				8							9					B Hill	44
1	2	3	4	5	6	11	10		7				8							9					M Peck	45
1	2	3	4	5	6	11	10		7				8*							9			12		I Hendrick	46
1	2	3	4	5	6	11*	10		7	12			8							9					R Guy	47
1	2	3	4	5	6	11*	10	9	7				8										12		R Bridges	48
1	2	3	4	5		11			7	10			8							9				6	L Robinson	49
1	2	3	4	5	6	11			7	10			8							9					D Owen	50
1	2	3	4	5		11	12		7	10			8*							9				6	R Lewis	51
1	2	3	4	5	6	11*	10		7	8				12						9					J Moules	52
46	30	45	46	42	44	37	28	5	39	18	0	30	43	3	4	2	4	4	0	32	2	0	0	2	League Appearances	
	+5S						+2S	+1S	+4S	+3S	+1S			+1S		+4S	+1S		+1S				+2S			
2		2	2		2	2	1		2	2		2	2					2		1					FA Cup Appearances	
2	2	2	2	2	2	1	2		1+1S	1	1	2	1	1											Milk Cup Appearances	
2	2	2	2	2	1	1		1	1	1		2	2							2	1	1S			AM Cup Appearances	

VALLEY PARADE GROUND

Official Address: Valley Parade Ground, Bradford BD8 7DY. Telephone: 0274 306062

Ground Capacity: 16,000

Record Attendance: 39,146 v. Burnley, F.A. Cup Round 4, 11 Mar 1911

Record Receipts: £27,000 v. Southampton, F.A. Cup Round 6, 6 Mar 1976

Size of Playing Area: 110yds × 76 yds

Season Tickets: Stand: £80.00 (juvenile/OAP £50.00); Ground: £50.00 (juvenile/OAP £30)

Executive Box Season Tickets: £150

Cost of Stand Tickets: £3.50, £4.00 (juvenile/OAP £2.00, £2.50); **Ground:** £2.50 (juvenile/OAP £1.50)

Match and Ticket Information: Bradford 306062 (2 weeks prior)

Car Parking: Street parking in nearby side streets. None at Valley Parade or South Parade

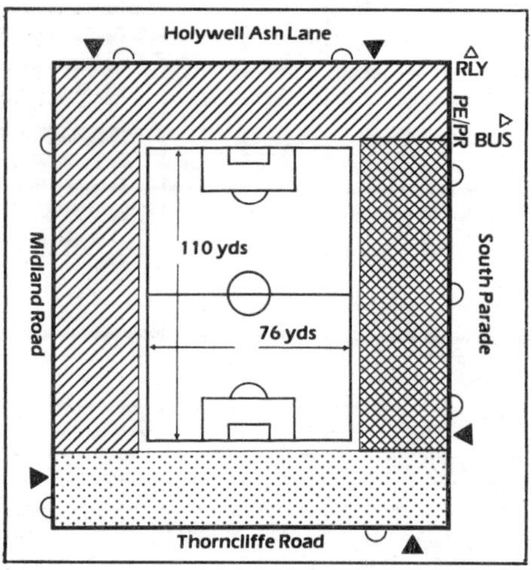

For key see page 12

How to get to the ground

From North: Follow signs Bradford A650. 0.3m after junction with A6036 (Ring Road) turn left into Valley Parade for Bradford City.
From East: Follow signs Bradford A647 then at cross roads turn right A6036 (S.P. Keighley). In 2.2m at cross roads turn left A650. In 0.3m turn left into Valley Parade for Bradford City.
From South, West: Use M62 and A606(M) (S.P. Bradford) then at roundabout take 4th exit into Ring Road A6036 (S.P. Keighley). In 4.8m at crossroads turn left A650. In 0.3m turn left into Valley Parade for Bradford City.

BRENTFORD — Division 3

President
W Wheatley

Chairman
M M Lange

Directors
R J J Blindell, LL.B.
E J Radley-Smith, M.S., F.R.C.S., L.R.C.P.
D Tana
G V Totter

Commercial Department
(01-560 2021)

Chief Development Officer
Miss C Mathews

Manager
Frank McLintock

Physiotherapist
Eddie Lyons

Poor seasons for 'The Bees' are sadly no novel experience and the latest campaign followed familiar patterns with few happy moments to relieve the gloom. In the end the only 'success' to record was the escape from relegation to the Fourth Division by three points (i.e. one win) after nine months during which a position of thirteenth was the highest achieved.

In such circumstances it was no surprise that there was a change of management early in 1984 with Fred Callaghan being replaced by Frank McLintock, who possibly ensured survival by bringing three people from Cambridge — deposed Manager John Docherty (ex-Bees), Tom Finney and Bobby Fisher. Certainly, performances seemed to improve but only time will show whether this was an illusion.

A very heavy veil should be drawn over the League results and in the Cups there was not much more to celebrate. The Milk Cup produced a good first round aggregate win over Charlton Athletic, which meant a second round against Liverpool, and also a very nice home gate as a consolation for the inevitable defeat by a large margin on aggregate. The F.A. Cup at least produced some successful ties and excitement with Dagenham of the Alliance Premier League despatched shakily in a replay and a better show against promotion-seeking Wimbledon who went down at Griffin Park by the odd goal in five (Kamara, G. Roberts and Joseph). A visit to Gillingham in the next round ended all that as the home team turned a one-nil first half deficit into a good win (5-3).

After such a season supporters can only hope that things will improve, but this will not be easy to achieve with money in short supply for the purchase of the kind of players who are essential for the production of better things. After all other teams will have exactly the same hopes and everyone cannot do well and no-one will envy the task of Frank McLintock with his problems. Perhaps, a new stand to replace the old destroyed edifice will see better luck, but no-one who saw the team last season will claim that the blend of talent available looks good enough for any success to arrive.

(Photo: David Crump)

Back Row L to R: Eddie Lyons (Physio), Tom Finney, Chris Kamara, Gary Roberts, Trevor Swinburne, Richard Key, Bob Booker, Steve Wignall, David Salman. **Middle Row:** Frank McLintock (Manager), Terry Bullivant, Keith Cassells, Bobby Fisher, Terry Hurlock, Jamie Murray, Francis Joseph, Paul Roberts, John Docherty (Assistant Manager). **Front Row:** Alan Myers, Glenn Bropley, Tony Lynch, Keith Mullen, Tony Spencer, Terry Rowe.

Brentford FC

Sponsored by
KLM

'THE BEES'

Formed: 1889 **Turned Professional:** 1899 **Ltd Co:** 1901
Previous Managers: A committe handled team matters until 1903
1903-6 Richard Molyneux (Secretary/Manager) 1906-8 W G Brown (Secretary/Manager)
1908-12 Fred Halliday (Secretary/Manager) 1912-5 Ephraim 'Dusty' Rhodes (Player/Manager)
1915-21 Fred Halliday (Secretary/Manager) 1921-4 Archie Mitchell (Player/Manager 1921/22 then Secretary/Manager) 1924-6 Fred Halliday (Secretary/Manager) 1926-49 Harry Curtis (Secretary/Manager)
1949-52 A H 'Jackie' Gibbons (Secretary/Manager) 1952-3 Jim Bain 1953 Tommy Lawton (Player/Manager) 1953-7 Bill Dodgin (Senior) 1957-65 Malcolm McDonald 1965-6 Tommy Cavanagh
1966-7 Billy Gray 1967-9 Jimmy Sirrel 1969-73 Frank Blunstone 1973-5 Mike Everitt
1975-6 John Docherty 1976-80 Bill Dodgin (Junior) 1980-4 Fred Callaghan
Honours: Champions Division 2 1934-5 Champions Division 3 (S) 1932-3
Champions Division 4 1962-3
League Career: Founder Members of Division 3 1920 Division 3 (S) 1921-33
Promoted to Division 2 1932-3 Promoted to Division 1 1934-5 Relegated to Division 2 1946-7
Relegated to Division 3 (S) 1953-4 Division 4 1962-3 Promoted to Division 3 1962-3
Relegated to Division 4 1965-6 Promoted to Division 3 1971-2 Relegated to Division 4 1972-3
Promoted to Division 3 1977-8
Colours: Red and white striped shirts, black shorts, black stockings with red and white hooped tops
Change Colours: All blue

CLUB RECORDS

Most Appearances for Club: Ken Coote: Football League 514 + F.A. Cup 35 + League Cup 10 **Total 559**
Most Capped Player: Idris Hopkins, 10, Wales. **For England:** Billy Scott and Leslie Smith, one each
Record Goalscorer in a Match: Jack Holliday 5, v Luton Town (5-5), Div 3 (S) (A), 28.01.33
Billy Scott 5, v Barnsley (8-1), Div 2 (H), 15.12.34
Peter McKennan 5, v Bury (8-2), Div 2 (H), 18.02.49
Record League Goalscorer in a season: Jack Holliday, 38, Div 3 (S), 1932-3 **All competitions:** Jack Holliday, 39, (League 38, F.A. Cup 1), 1932-3
Record League Goalscorer in a career: Jim Towers, 153 1954-61 **All competitions:** Jim Towers, 163 (League 153 + F.A. Cup 9 + League Cup 1), 1954-61
Record Transfer Fee Received: £60,000 from Sheffield Wednesday for Andy McCulloch, June 1979
Record Transfer Fee Paid: £78,000 to Bury for Alan Whitehead, July 1981
Best Performances: League: 5th Div 1 1935-6 **F.A. Cup:** 6th Round, 1938, 1946, 1949 **League/Milk Cup:** 4th Round 1982-3
Most League Points: (2pts for a win): 62, Div 3 (S), 1932-3 62, Div 4, 1962-3
(3pts for a win): 68, Div 3, 1981-2
Record League Victory: 9-0 v Wrexham, Div 3, 15 Oct 63
Record League Defeat: 0-7 v Walsall, Div 3 (S), 19 Jan 57

Club Statistician for the Directory: Graham Haynes

Programme Editor
Eric White

Price	Number of Pages
50p	24

Subscriptions
Apply to club for details

BRENTFORD

PLAYERS NAME Ht Wt Birthdate	Honours	Birthplace Transfers	Clubs	APPEARANCES League	Milk Cup	F.A.C.	A.M.C.	GOALS League	Milk Cup	F.A.C.	A.M.C.
GOALKEEPERS											
Trevor Swinburne	FAYC. 69	East Rainton	Sunderland (A)	10							
6-0 12.12 20.6.53		F	Carlisle U.	248	17	7					
		Player Exchange	Brentford	21	4	1	2				
DEFENDERS											
Ian Bolton	Div. 4. 78	Leicester	Birmingham C. (A)								
6-2 12.7 13.7.53			Notts. Co.	61 + 9	4 + 1	3		4			
			Lincoln C. (L)	1							
		£12,500	Watford	231 + 1	29+1	15	3E	28	5	2	
		£5,000	Brentford	14		1	2	1			
Bobby Fisher		Wembley	Orient	302 + 6	19+1	26		4	1		
5-8 11.2 3.8.56		F	Cambridge U.	42	1	4					
		£5,000	Brentford	17			2				
Jamie Murray		Glasgow	Cambridge U.	213 + 16	11+2	10+2		3			
5-9 10.12 27.12.58			Sunderland (L)	1							
		£27,500	Brentford								
Paul Roberts†	FAYC. 79	London	Millwall (A)	142 + 4	7 + 1	9					
5-10 12.0 27.4.62			Brentford	34		4	1				
Terry Rowe		Fulham	Brentford	62 + 3	8 + 1	5	1	1			
5-7 9.7 8.6.64											
Danis Salman	E. Y	Famagusta	Brentford (A)	233 + 9	12 +	11 +	1	5			
5-10 11.8 12.3.60											
Tony Spencer		Chiswick	Brentford (A)	17 + 1	2						
5-9 11.7 27.4.65											
Steve Wignall		Liverpool	Liverpool (N-C)								
5-11 11.11 17.9.54			Doncaster R.	127 + 3	6	8		1			
			Colchester U	279 + 2	17	26	2	22	3	3	
		£12,000	Brentford								
MIDFIELD											
Bob Booker		Watford	Bedmond Social								
6-2 12.4 25.1.58		F	Brentford	120 + 27	10 +	7 + 2	2	27		1	
Terry Bullivant		London	Fulham (A)	94 + 7	8	5					
5-7½ 10.11 23.9.56		£220,000	Aston Villa	10 + 3		1					
		£90,000	Charlton A.	30	6	4		3			
		F	Brentford	24				1			
			Reading (L)								
Chris Kamara		Middlesbrough	Portsmouth (A)	56 + 7	1	4		7		1	
6-1 12.0 25.12.57		£20,000	Swindon	133 + 14	18 +	14		21	1	4	
		£50,000	Portsmouth	11	3				1		
		Player Exchange	Brentford	112 + 1	11	9	1	22			
Terry Hurlock*		Hackney	Leytonstone								
5-9 13.2 22.9.58		£6,000	Brentford	153	9	13	2	13	1	1	
FORWARDS											
Keith Cassells		London	Wembley								
5-10 11.12 10.7.57		£500	Watford	6 + 6	2	1 + 1					
			Peterborough (L)	8							
		£5,000	Oxford U.	43 + 2	5	8		13	4	7	
		£115,000	Southampton	13 + 6	5	1		4	1		
		£25,000	Brentford	42 + 4	2	1	0 + 2	17		1	
Tom Finney	N.I. (14)	Belfast	Crusaders								
5-10 11.8 6.11.52	Div. 4. 77	£17,000	Luton T.	13 + 1	4	2 + 1		5	1		
		£50,000	Sunderland	8 + 7		6		1		1	
		£10,000	Cambridge U.	259 + 9	16	12		56	4		
		F	Brentford	14 + 1			1	2			
Francis Joseph		London	Hillingdon Boro.								
5-10 12.0 6.3.60		£1,000	Wimbledon	42 + 9	2	1		14			
		£3,000	Brentford	85 + 1	11	7	2	41	1	1	
Tony Lynch		Paddington	Brentford	2			2				
5-10 11.9 20.1.66											
Gary Roberts	W. U.21 (1)	Rhyl	Wembley								
6-0 11.6 5.4.60		£6,000	Brentford	138 + 7	12	9	1 + 1	33	3	3	

NON-CONTRACT PLAYERS 1984-85:

Paul Dawson, Vince Deritis, Mark Hopson, Keith Miller, Tony Tillbrook

BRENTFORD

DIVISION THREE 20TH **FA CUP** 3RD ROUND **MILK CUP** 2ND ROUND

MATCH	DATE	COMPE-TITION	VENUE	OPPONENTS	RESULT	HALF TIME	L'GUE POS'N	GOALSCORERS	ATTEN-DANCE
1	A 27	CL	H	Millwall	D2-2	2-1		Joseph, Kamara	6,224
2	**30**	**MC 1**	**H**	**Charlton Ath**	**W3-0**	**2-0**		**Roberts G, Joseph, Berry (og)**	**4,868**
3	S 3	CL	A	Preston NE	D3-3	2-1	15	Joseph, Roberts G, Cassells	3,799
4	6	CL	A	Bristol R	L1-3	1-1		Joseph	5,148
5	10	CL	H	Lincoln C	W3-0	1-0	13	Houghton (og), Joseph 2	4,712
6	**12**	**MC 1**	**A**	**Charlton Ath**	**L1-2**	**1-0**		**Joseph**	**3,622**
7	17	CL	A	Wigan Ath	L1-2	1-0	17	Garner	3,034
8	24	CL	H	Burnley	D0-0	0-0	17		8,042
9	O 1	CL	A	Gillingham	L2-4	0-2	20	Kamara, McNicholl	3,268
10	**5**	**MC 2**	**H**	**Liverpool**	**L1-4**	**1-1**		**Roberts G**	**17,859**
11	8	CL	A	Oxford U	L1-2	0-0	20	Kamara	7,140
12	15	CL	H	Hull C	D1-1	1-0	21	Joseph	4,258
13	18	CL	H	Port Vale	W3-1	1-0		Bullivant, Roberts G, McNicholl	3,903
14	22	CL	A	Sheffield U	D0-0	0-0	18		9,848
15	**25**	**MC 2**	**A**	**Liverpool**	**L0-4**	**0-1**			**9,092**
16	29	CL	H	AFC Bournemouth	D1-1	1-1	19	Joseph	4,630
17	31	CL	A	Southend U	L0-6	0-2			2,902
18	N 5	CL	H	Plymouth Arg	D2-2	1-1	19	Mahoney, Cassells	4,183
19	12	CL	A	Orient	L0-2	0-2	21		3,650
20	**19**	**FAC 1**	**A**	**Dagenham**	**D2-2**	**1-1**		**Joseph, Roberts P**	**2,100**
21	**22**	**FAC 1R**	**H**	**Dagenham**	**W2-1**	**1-0**		**Mahoney, Roberts G**	**3,936**
22	26	CL	H	Bradford C	L1-4	0-3	21	Roberts G	3,738
23	D 3	CL	A	Bolton W	L0-1	0-0	23		5,416
24	**10**	**FAC 2**	**H**	**Wimbledon**	**W3-2**	**1-1**		**Kamara, Roberts G, Joseph**	**5,666**
25	17	CL	A	Walsall	L0-1	0-1	23		3,965
26	24	CL	H	Wimbledon	L3-4	2-1		Kamara, McNicholl, Hurlock	6,689
27	27	CL	A	Exeter C	W2-1	0-0	23	Cassells, Roberts G	4,252
28	31	CL	H	Newport Co	W2-0	2-0	21	Hurlock, Roberts G	4,631
29	J 2	CL	A	Scunthorpe U	D4-4	1-1	22	Mahoney, Cassells (pen), McNichol, Joseph	2,239
30	**7**	**FAC 3**	**A**	**Gillingham**	**L3-5**	**1-0**		**Roberts G, Hurlock, Cassells**	**6,109**
31	15	CL	A	Millwall	W2-1	1-0	22	Joseph 2	5,370
32	21	CL	H	Wigan Ath	L0-1	0-0	19		3,972
33	F 1	CL	A	Lincoln C	L0-2	0-0	19		2,266
34	4	CL	H	Gillingham	L2-3	1-1	21	Joseph, Bolton	4,317
35	11	CL	A	Burnley	D2-2	0-2	21	Cassells, Kamara	6,994
36	14	CL	H	Southend U	D0-0	0-0	21		3,901
37	18	CL	A	AFC Bournemouth	W3-0	1-0	18	Cassells 3	4,308
38	**21**	**AMC 1**	**H**	**Orient**	**W3-2**	**3-1**		**Finney, Joseph 2**	**2,301**
39	25	CL	H	Sheffield U	L1-3	1-2	18	Roberts G	5,100
40	M 3	CL	A	Port Vale	L3-4	2-3	19	Roberts G, Gray, Joseph	3,704
41	6	CL	A	Plymouth Arg	D1-1	0-0		Hurlock	4,332
42	10	CL	H	Orient	D1-1	0-0	19	Joseph	4,358
43	17	CL	H	Oxford U	L1-2	1-0	19	Roberts G	5,936
44	20	CL	H	Rotherham U	W2-1	1-0		Booker, Mahoney (pen)	3,391
45	24	CL	A	Hull C	L0-2	0-1	19		6,158
46	**26**	**AMC 2**	**A**	**Plymouth Arg**	**L0-2[1]**	**0-0**			**2,308**
47	31	CL	H	Bristol R	D2-2	0-2	19	Booker, Hurlock	4,067
48	A 3	CL	H	Preston NE	W4-1	1-0		Kamara, Finney, Roberts G, Booker	3,446
49	7	CL	A	Rotherham U	L0-4	0-2	19		3,635
50	14	CL	H	Bolton W	W3-0	2-0	19	Joseph 2, Deakin (og)	3,831
51	20	CL	H	Exeter C	W3-0	1-0		Joseph, Booker, Finney	5,620
52	21	CL	A	Wimbledon	L1-2	0-1	17	Joseph	5,487
53	28	CL	A	Bradford C	D1-1	0-0	18	Cassells	3,739
54	M 5	CL	H	Scunthorpe U	W3-0	1-0	19	Rowe, Joseph, Roffey	4,561
55	7	CL	A	Newport Co	D1-1	1-0	19	Roberts G	2,154
56	12	CL	H	Walsall	D1-1	1-1	20	Caswell (og)	5,281

[1] After Extra Time

Av Home Att 4,583

Goal Scorers

League (69): Joseph 18, Roberts G 10, Cassells 9 (1 pen), Kamara 6, Booker 4, Hurlock 4, McNichol 4, Mahoney 3 (1 pen), Finney 2, Bolton 1, Bullivant 1, Garner 1, Gray 1, Roffey 1, Rowe 1, opponents 3
FA Cup (10): Roberts G 3, Joseph 2, Cassells 1, Hurlock 1, Kamara 1, Mahoney 1, Roberts P 1
Milk Cup (5): Joseph 2, Roberts G 2, opponent 1
AMC (3): Joseph 2, Finney 1

1983-84

Swinburne	Rowe	Spencer	McNichol	Whitehead	Hurlock	Kamara	Joseph	Cassells	Bullivant	Roberts G	Booker	Salman	Garner	Roberts P	Fisher	Wilkins	Lynch	Mahoney	Gray **(L)**	Roche	Roffey **(L)**	Bowles	Bolton	Finney	REFEREE	
1	2	3	4	5	6	7	8	9	10	11															K Baker	1
1		**3**		**5**	**6**	**7**	**8**	**9**	**10**	**11**	**2**	**4**													**D Hedges**	**2**
1		3		5	6	7	8	9*	10	11	2	4	12												T Mills	3
1	12	3		5	6	7	8	9	10	11*	2	4													A Crickmore	4
1	2		12	5	6	7	8	9*	10		11	4		3											T Spencer	5
1	**2**	**3**	**4**	**5**	**6**	**7**	**8**		**10**		**9**														**B Hill**	**6**
1	2	12	4	5	6	7	8*		10		11		9	3											F Roberts	7
1	2		4	5		7		9	10		11		8*	3		12									HW King	8
1	2	3	9	5		7			10†	11	6	4		8											D Axcell	9
1	**3**		**2**	**5**		**7**	**8**		**10**	**11**	**12**	**4**						**9***							**J Martin**	**10**
1			2	5		7	8		10	11	12	4				3	7*								RG Milford	11
1			2	5		7	8	9		11	10	4				3									M Robinson	12
1			2	5		7	8		10	11	6	4				3	9								E Read	13
1	2		9	5		7†	8		10	11	6	4				3									I Hendrick	14
1	**12**		**2**	**5**		**7**	**8**	**9**	**10**	**11**	**6***	**4**				**3**									**P Tyldesley**	**15**
1			2	5		7	8	9	10	11*	6	4				3		12							DH Brazier	16
1	2	3		5		7	8	9	10	11	6*	4						12							J Bray	17
1	2			5			8	9	10	11	5	4		3				7							MJ Taylor	18
1				5		7	8		10	11		4		2		6		9							M Bodenham	19
			2	**5**	**6**	**7**	**8**		**10**	**11**		**4**		**3**				**9**		**1**					**A Gunn**	**20**
			2	**5**	**6***	**7**	**8**		**10**	**11**		**4**		**3**		**12**		**9**		**1**					**A Gunn**	**21**
	12		2			7	8		10	11		4		3				9		1					B Stevens	22
1	2		4	5		7	8			11				6		3		9				10			P Willis	23
1	**2**		**4**	**5**	**6**	**7**	**8**			**11**				**3**				**9**				**10**			**R Bridges**	**24**
			2	5	6	7	8			11	12			3				9*		1		10	4		J Hunting	25
1			2	5	6	7*	8	12		11				3				9				10	4		J Moules	26
	2		5		6		8	12	7	11				3				9		1		10*	4		V Callow	27
	2		5		6		8	12	7*	11				3				9		1		10	4		I Borrett	28
	2		5		6*		8	10	7	11	12			3				9		1			4		D Owen	29
	2		**5**		**6**		**8**	**10**	**7**	**11***	**12**			**3**				**9**		**1**			**4**		**M James**	**30**
	2				6		8	10	7	11		5		3				9		1			4		A Seville	31
	2				6		8	10	7	11		5		3				9*		1		12	4		Alan Robinson	32
			5		6		8	9	7	11*	2					3		12		1		10	4		T Mills	33
			5			6*	8	9	7	11	3					2		12		1		10	4		T Bune	34
			2			7	8	9	10	11		4		6		3				1			5		M Scott	35
					6	7	9	10		11		4		2		3				1			5	8	C Thomas	36
					6	7	9	10		11		4		3	2					1			5	8	J Deakin	37
1					**6**		**9**	**12**		**11**	**2**	**4**			**3**		**7***	**10**					**5**	**8**	**M Bodenham**	**38**
					6	7	9	10*		11		4		3	2			12		1			5	8	L Burden	39
1					6	7	10	9		11				3	2				4				5	8	L Robinson	40
					6	7	9	10*		11				4	2	3		12	5	1				8	T Spencer	41
					6	12	9		7*	11		2		4	3			10	5	1				8	M Dimblebee	42
					6	7	9			11				4	2			10	5	1	3			8	J Martin	43
					6	7	9				11	4			2			10	5	1	3			8	H King	44
	12				6	7	9	10*			11			4	2				5	1	3			8	D Shaw	45
1	**8**				**6**	**7**	**9***	**12**		**13**	**10**			**3**	**2**		**11***		**4**				**5**		**J Hunting**	**46**
	10*				6	7	12			9	11			4	2				5	1	3			8	B Hill	47
	2				6	7	9			11	10			4					5	1	3			8	L Shapter	48
					6	7	9			11	10			4	2				5	1	3			8	H Taylor	49
					6	7	9	12		11*	10			4	2				5	1	3			8	A Crickmore	50
					6	7	9			11	10			4	2				5	1	3			8	J Ashworth	51
	8				6	7	9	11*		12	10			4	2				5	1	3				R Milford	52
					6	7	9	8		11*	10			4	2			12	5	1	3				R Guy	53
1	7*				6		9	8		11	10			4	2			12	5		3				I Borrett	54
1					6	7		8		11	10			4	2			9	5		3				B Stevens	55
1					6	7	9*	8		11	10			4	2				5		3			12	A Gunn	56
21	18	5	19	18	32	37	42	26	24	40	26	21	2	34	17	12	2	15	16	25	13	7	14	14	League Appearances	
	+3S	+1S	+1S			+1S	+1S	+4S		+1S	+3S		+1S			+1S		+8S				+1S		+1S		
1	2		4	3	4	3	4	1	3	4	1S	2		4		1S		4		3		1	1		FA Cup Appearances	
4	2+1S	2	3	4	2	4	4	2	4	3	3+1S	3				1		1							Milk Cup Appearances	
2	1				2	1	2	2S		1+1S	2	1		1	2		2	1	1				2	1	AM Cup Appearances	

Also Played: Davies **(L)** match 19, no.3; 22, no 6. Harris matches 8, 10, 11, 12, no.6; 6, no.11. Rollings match 22, no.5*

GRIFFIN PARK

Photo: David Crumb

Official Address: Griffin Park, Braemar Road, Brentford, Middlesex TW8 0NT. Telephone: 01-847 2511-2, 01-560 2021, 01-847 8235 (Restaurant)

Ground Capacity: 37,000 (30,500 under cover)

Record Attendance: 39,626 v. Preston N.E., F.A. Cup Round 6, 5 Mar 1938.

Record Receipts: £55,002 v. Liverpool, Milk Cup Round 2, 4 Oct 1983.

Size of Playing Area: 114yds × 75 yds

Season Tickets: Stand: £88; Ground: £50

Executive Box Season Tickets: £250 (Executive Boxes)

Cost of Stand Tickets: £4.00; **Terraces:** £2.80 (£1.00 Juveniles/OAPs), (under 12's free subject to identity card)

Match and Ticket Information: Postal applications with SAE for Block 'B' only 14 days prior to each match by post or personal application.

Car Parking: Street parking available.

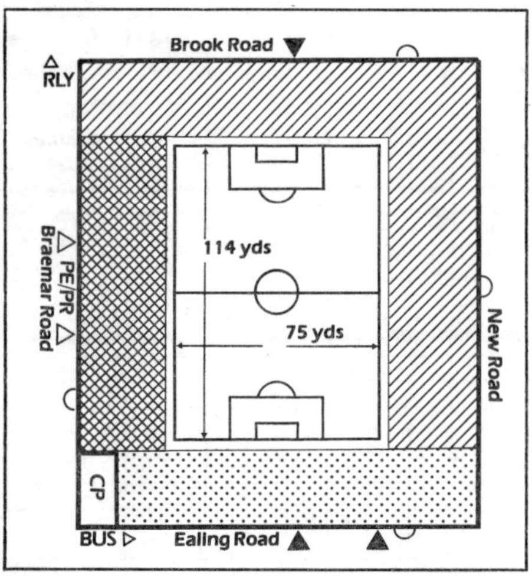

For key see page 12

How to get to the ground

From North: Use M1 or A1 then A406 North Circular Road to Chiswick then follow signs South Circular Road. In 0.3m turn right A315. (S.P. Brentford). In 0.5m turn right into Ealing Road for Brentford F.C.

From East: Use either A406 North Circular Road then as above or South Circular Road A205. Cross Kew Bridge and turn left A315 (S.P. Brentford) A315. In 0.5m turn right into Ealing Road for Brentford F.C.

From South: Use A240/A3/M3/ or A316 to junction with South Circular Road A205. Cross Kew Bridge and turn left A315 (S.P. Brentford) A315. In 0.5m turn right into Ealing Road for Brentford F.C.

From West: Use M4 until junction 1, leave Motorway and follow signs South Circular Road. In 0.3m turn right A315 (S.P. Brentford). In 0.5m turn right into Ealing Road for Brentford F.C.

BRIGHTON & HOVE ALBION Division 2

Chairman
B Bedson

Directors
T Appleby
J Campbell
D Sizen
R Crown
P Kent
R Bloom

Secretary
K Calver

Manager
Chris Catlin

Club Coach
Sammy Nelson

Youth Development Officer
G Petchey

Commercial Manager
R A Pavey (0273 778230)

Defeats in their opening three games put a damper on Brighton's hopes of making a quick return to the First Division. Though they showed more consistency during the second part of the season the Seagulls were too far behind to make any impression on the leaders.

The highlight of the season was, of course, their splendid 2-0 victory over Liverpool at the Goldstone Ground in the fourth round of the F.A. Cup. It was the second successive season that Brighton had booted Liverpool out of this competition.

They had scored an easy win over Swansea City in the third round and the Liverpool game attracted the Goldstone's biggest crowd (19,057) of the season. Second-half goals from Gerry Ryan and Terry Connor gave them their exciting win over the League Champions.

Sadly, Brighton bowed out in the next round at Watford.

In the Milk Cup they ousted Bristol Rovers 5-4 on aggregate and then lost 0-1 at West Ham.

After their poor opening in the Second Division, Brighton quickly showed an improvement and embarked upon an unbeaten run of five games, culminating in an extraordinary 7-0 victory over Charlton at the Goldstone Ground. The first five goals came within the space of just over half-an-hour in the opening half and Jimmy Case completed a hat-trick after the break.

Then came another string of defeats and a period of instability. They crashed 0-5 at Grimsby and 0-4 at Manchester City and it wasn't until the season was into its second phase that the side began to show some consistency.

Manager Chris Cattlin made many new signings during the course of the season. Former England international Joe Corrigan, once of Manchester City, took over in goal, left-back Chris Hutchings was signed from Chelsea for £50,000 and was later joined by right-back Mark Jones, a £50,000 buy from Aston Villa.

Midfield man Danny Wilson joined the club from Nottingham Forest for £40,000 and winger Steve Penney came from Ballymena United. Striker Alan Young was recruited from Sheffield United for £140,000.

Brighton began to settle during the latter weeks of the season though they still, occasionally, collapsed as at Fratton Park where they were hammered 5-1 by Portsmouth.

In the end they took ninth place and looked forward with considerably more confidence to the 1984/85 campaign. TP

Back Row L to R: Mark Jones, Steve Penney, Steve Jacobs, Alan Young, Graham Pearce, Kieran O'Regan, Gary Howlett. **Middle Row:** Sammy Nelson (Coach), Hans Kraay, Eric Young, Joe Corrigan, Perry Digweed, Frank Worthington, Terry Connor, George Petchey (Youth Development Officer). **Front Row:** Neil Smillie, Chris Hutchings, Jimmy Case, Chris Cattlin (Manager), Steve Gatting, Gerry Ryan, Danny Wilson.

'THE SEAGULLS'

Formed: 1900 **Turned Professional:** 1900 **Ltd Co:** 1904
Previous Names: Brighton & Hove Rangers
Previous Managers: Charles Webb Tommy Cook Don Welsh Billy Lane George Curtis Archie MacAuley Freddie Goodwin Pat Saward Brian Clough Peter Taylor Alan Mullery MBE Mike Bailey
Honours: Division Three (South) Champions 1957-8 Division Four Champions 1964-5
League Career: Original members of Division Three 1920 Transferred to Division Three (S) 1921 Promoted to Division Two 1978-9 Relegated to Division Three 1961-2 Relegated to Division Four 1962-3 Promoted to Division Three 1964-5 Promoted to Division Two 1971-2 Relegated to Division Three 1972-3 Promoted to Division Two 1976-7 Promoted to Division One 1978-9 Relegated to Division Two 1982-3
Colours: Blue shirts with red and white trim, white shorts with blue trim, blue stockings with white tops
Change Colours: All yellow

CLUB RECORDS

Most League Appearances for Club: 'Tug' Wilson, 509, 1922-6
Most Capped Player: Mark Lawrenson, 14, Eire **For England:** Steve Foster, 3
Record Goalscorer in a Match: Adrian Thorne, 5 v Newport County (9-1), Div 3(S), 18.05.1951 Jack Doran, 5 v Northampton Town (7-0), Div 3(S), 05.11.1921
Record League Goalscorer in a season: Peter Ward, 32, Div 3, 1976-7 **In all competitions:** Peter Ward, 36
Record League Goalscorer in a career: Tommy Cook, 113, 1922-9 **In all competitions:**
Record Transfer Fee Received: £900,000 from Liverpool for Mark Lawrenson, August 1981
Record Transfer Fee Paid: £500,000 to Manchester United for Andy Ritchie, October 1980
Best Performances: League: 13th Div 1 1981-2 **F.A. Cup:** Finalists 1982-3 **League/Milk Cup:** 5th Round 1978-9
Most League Points: 65 in Div 3(S), 1955-6, Div 3 1971-2 **Most League Goals:** 112 Div 3(S) 1955-6
Record League Victory: 9-1 v Newport County, Div 3(S), 18 April 1951
Record League Defeat: 0-9 v Middlesbrough, Div 2, 23 Aug 1958

Club Statistician for the Directory: Tim Carder

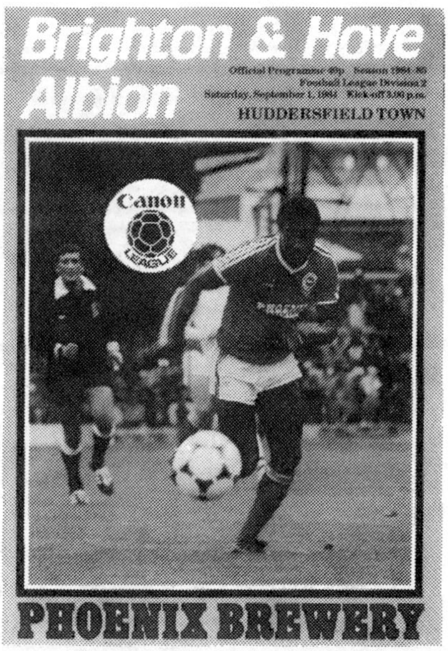

Programme Editor
Tony Millard

Price	Number of Pages
40p	32

Subscriptions

BRIGHTON

PLAYERS NAME Ht Wt Birthdate	Honours	Birthplace Transfers	Clubs	APPEARANCES League	Milk Cup	F.A.C.	E. Cups	GOALS League	Milk Cup	E. Cups	
GOALKEEPERS											
Joe Corrigan	E.(9), B.(10),	Manchester	Manchester C.	476							
6-5 14.12 18.11.48	U.23(1), U.21(1),		Seattle S.								
	FC. 70, 76		Brighton	36	3	3					
Perry Digweed		London	Fulham (A)	15							
6-0 11.4 26.10.59		£150,000	Brighton	46							
Graham Molesey	E. Y	Manchester	Blackburn R. (A)								
6-0 11.8 16.11.53			Derby Co.	32	4	4					
			Aston Villa (L)	3							
			Walsall (L)	3							
		£120,000	Brighton	138	14	15					
DEFENDERS											
Steve Gatting		Willesden	Arsenal (A)	50 + 8	3	9		5		1	
5-11 11.11 25.9.59		£200,000	Brighton	114	8	13		11	1		
Chris Hutchings		Winchester	Harrow Borough								
5-10 11.0 5.7.57		£10,000	Chelsea	83 + 4	7	7		3			
		£50,000	Brighton	26		3		1			
Mark Jones	ESC. 82,	Warley	Aston V. (A)	24	2	1	3 + 1				
5-6 10.1 22.10.61	FAYC. 80	£50,000	Brighton	6							
Kieran O'Reagan	Ei.(2)	Cork	Tramore Ath.								
5-7 10.8 9.11.63			Brighton	31 + 1	3			1			
Graham Pearce		London	Barnet								
5-9 11.0 8.7.59		£10,000	Brighton	31 + 1	4	5		1			
Chris Ramsey		Birmingham	Bristol C. (N-C)								
5-9 10.12 23.4.62		F	Brighton	30	1	6					
Eric Young		Singapore	Slough								
6-3 12.6 25.3.60		£10,000	Brighton	30	3	2		4			
MIDFIELD											
Jimmy Case*†	E. U.23(1),	Liverpool	South Liverpool								
5-9 12.7 18.5.54	ESC. 77, FC. 81,		Liverpool	170 + 16	21 + 1	20 + 1	28 + 3	23	3	7	13
	Div. 1, 73, 77, 78,		Brighton	103	6	12		10		4	
	79, EC. 77, 78, 81										
	UEFAC. 76										
Gary Howlett	Ei. Y	Dublin	Home Farm								
5-8 10.4 2.4.63			Coventry C.								
			Brighton	24 + 2	2	3		1			
Steve Jacobs		West Ham	Coventry C. (A)	94 + 7	5 + 3	2 + 2					
5-8 11.0 5.7.61			Brighton								
Gary O'Reilly	Ei. Y, S	Isleworth	Tottenham H.	39 + 6	4	2	2 + 2				
6-0 12.12 21.3.61											
Giles Stille		London	Kingstonian								
5-9 11.9 10.11.58			Brighton	20 + 7		3					
Danny Wilson		Wigan	Wigan Ath.								
5-7 10.3 1.1.60			Bury	87 + 3	4	11		8			
			Chesterfield	100	8	9		13			
			Nottingham F.	9 + 1			0 + 1	1			
			Scunthorpe U. (L)	6				3			
			Brighton	26		2		10			
FORWARDS											
Terry Connor	E. Y	Leeds	Leeds U.	83 + 13	4 + 2	5		19	1	1	
5-7 10.0 9.11.62				45 + 2	3	3		14	2	2	
Steve Penney			Ballymena								
5-9 10.4 16.1.64			Brighton	22 + 3		2		1			
Gerry Ryan	Ei.(15)	Dublin	Bohemians								
5-10 10.12 4.10.55		£50,000	Derby Co.	30	2	2		4		1	
		£80,000	Brighton	114 + 36	6 + 5	8 + 4		27	2	3	
Neil Smillie		Barnsley	Crystal P. (A)	71 + 12	7	7		7			
5-6 10.7 19.7.58			Brentford (L)	3							
		Player Exchange	Brighton	47 + 4	2	8 + 1		2			
Frank Worthington	E.(8), U.23(2),	Halifax	Huddersfield T. (A)	166 + 5	9	12		42	2	5	
5-10 11.10 23.11.48	F.Lg.XI(1),		Leicester C.	209 + 1	10 +	18		72	2	4	
	Div. 2, 70,		Bolton W.	81 + 3	2 + 1	5		35	2	1	
	Div. 2, 78		Birmingham C.	71 + 4	6	7		30	2	2	
			Leeds U.	32	3			14	1		
			Sunderland	18 + 1				2			
			Southampton	34	2	6		4			

CONTRACT PLAYERS WITH LESS THAN TEN FIRST TEAM APPEARANCES

Mark Fleet (D), (1 FAC), **Hans Kraay (MF),** (2 + 3 Lg), **Martin Lambert (F)** (2 + 1 Lg), **Ian Muir (F)** (QPR 2 Lg), Burnley (L) (1 + 1), Birmingham C. (1 Lg).

APPRENTICES: Darrow Gearing, Gary Mitchell, Kevin Russell, Mark Wakefield, Sean Edwards, Daren Newman, Chris Murphy

BRIGHTON & HOVE ALBION

DIVISION TWO 9TH **FA CUP** 5TH ROUND **MILK CUP** 3RD ROUND

MATCH	DATE	COMPETITION	VENUE	OPPONENTS	RESULT	HALF TIME	L'GUE POS'N	GOALSCORERS	ATTENDANCE
1	A 27	CL	A	Oldham Ath	L0-1	0-0			5,750
2	29	CL	A	Leeds U	L2-3	1-2		Grealish, Connor	13,303
3	S 3	CL	H	Chelsea	L1-2	0-1	21	Young A	20,874
4	6	CL	H	Derby Co	W1-0	1-0		Smith (pen)	10,891
5	10	CL	A	Swansea C	W3-1	2-0	12	Young A, Connor 2	7,643
6	17	CL	H	Carlisle U	D1-1	0-1	11	Moore (og)	11,735
7	24	CL	A	Blackburn R	D2-2	1-1	12	Case, Smith (pen)	5,060
8	O 1	CL	H	Charlton Ath	W7-0	5-0	14	Ryan 2, Smith, Case 3, Connor	11,517
9	**4**	**MC 2**	**H**	**Bristol R**	**W4-2**	**2-2**		**Ryan, Connor, Smith 2**	**9,417**
10	8	CL	H	Portsmouth	L0-1	0-1	12		17,582
11	15	CL	A	Grimsby T	L0-5	0-3	14		5,469
12	22	CL	H	Sheffield W	L1-3	0-2	16	Ryan	14,827
13	**25**	**MC 2**	**A**	**Bristol R**	**L1-2[1]**	**1-1**		**Connor**	**9,936**
14	29	CL	A	Cambrige U	W4-3	3-1	14	Young A 2, Grealish, Pearce	3,905
15	N 5	CL	H	Huddersfield T	W3-1	0-1	12	Gatting (pen), Connor, Young A	11,063
16	**8**	**MC 3**	**A**	**West Ham U**	**L0-1**	**0-0**			**17,082**
17	12	CL	A	Manchester C	L0-4	0-3	16		24,562
18	19	CL	H	Shrewsbury T	D2-2	1-0	16	Connor, Young A	9,746
19	26	CL	A	Barnsley	L1-3	1-3	17	Young A	7,705
20	D 3	CL	H	Cardiff C	W3-1	1-0	14	Wilson 2, Connor	9,924
21	10	CL	A	Middlesbrough	D0-0	0-0	14		6,037
22	17	CL	H	Newcastle U	L0-1	0-0	14		13,896
23	26	CL	A	Crystal Palace	W2-0	0-0	12	Wilson, Smillie	13,781
24	27	CL	H	Fulham	D1-1	0-0	14	Ryan	15,076
25	31	CL	A	Chelsea	L0-1	0-0	14		18,542
26	J 2	CL	H	Blackburn R	D1-1	0-1	14	Wilson (pen)	9,844
27	**7**	**FAC 3**	**H**	**Swansea C**	**W2-0**	**0-0**		**McQuillan (og), Connor**	**11,330**
28	14	CL	H	Oldham Ath	W4-0	1-0	13	Connor, Wilson, Ryan, Foster	10,203
29	21	CL	A	Carlisle U	W2-1	2-0	10	Wilson, Connor	5,169
30	**29**	**FAC 4**	**H**	**Liverpool**	**W2-0**	**0-0**		**Ryan, Connor**	**19,057**
31	F 4	CL	A	Charlton Ath	L0-2	0-0	10		7,435
32	11	CL	H	Swansea C	D1-1	0-0	11	Gatting	11,979
33	**18**	**FAC 5**	**A**	**Watford**	**L1-3**	**0-2**		**Wilson (pen)**	**28,000**
34	25	CL	A	Sheffield W	L1-2	0-1	13	O'Reagan	21,614
35	28	CL	H	Cambridge U	W3-0	2-0		Connor, Gatting, Wilson	8,167
36	M 3	CL	A	Huddersfield T	W1-0	1-0	9	Young A	6,985
37	10	CL	H	Manchester C	D1-1	0-0	10	Grealish	14,132
38	17	CL	A	Derby Co	W3-0	0-0	10	Penney, Young A, Smith	11,560
39	24	CL	H	Leeds U	W3-0	2-0	9	Wilson (pen), Young E, Connor	12,605
40	31	CL	A	Portsmouth	L1-5	1-0	9	Wilson (pen)	12,724
41	A 7	CL	H	Grimsby T	W2-0	1-0	9	Young A 2	10,610
42	14	CL	A	Shrewsbury T	L1-2	0-1	9	Young E	3,332
43	21	CL	H	Crystal Palace	W3-1	2-0	9	Young A, Connor, Young E	15,214
44	23	CL	A	Fulham	L1-3	0-3	9	Connor	7,742
45	28	CL	H	Barnsley	W1-0	0-0	9	Gatting	8,975
46	M 5	CL	A	Cardiff C	D2-2	0-1	9	Hutchings, Wilson	4,366
47	7	CL	H	Middlesbrough	W3-0	1-0	9	Smillie, Nattrass (og), Young E	9,168
48	12	CL	A	Newcastle U	L1-3	1-1	9	Ryan	36,415

[1] After Extra Time

Av Home Att **12,287**

Goal Scorers

League (69): Connor 13, Young A 12, Wilson 10 (3 pens), Ryan 6, Case 4, Gatting 4 (1 pen), Smith 4 (2 pens), Young E 4, Grealish 3, Smillie 2, Foster 1, Hutchings 1, O'Reagan 1, Pearce 1, Penney 1, opponents 2

FA Cup (5): Connor 2, Ryan 1, Wilson 1 (1 pen)

Milk Cup (5): Connor 2, Smith 2, Ryan 1

1983-84

Moseley	O'Reagan	Pearce	Grealish	Foster	Gatting	Case	Howlett	Ryan	Connor	Smillie	Smith	Kraay	Lambert	Digweed	Young A	Corrigan	Young E	Ring	Young W (L)	Ramsey	Hutchings	Penney	Wilson	Jones	REFEREE	
1	2	3	4	5	6	7	8*	9	10	11	12														R Nixon	1
	2	3	4	5	6	7			10	11	8		9												K Redfern	2
	2	3	4*	5	6	7			10	11	8		12	1	9										K Baker	3
	2	3		5	6	7	4		10	11	8			1	9										T D Spencer	4
	2	3	12	5	6	7	4*		10	11	8			1	9										R Milford	5
	2	3	4*	5	6	7	12		10	11	8				9	1									T Ward	6
	2	3	4		6	7	12		10	11*	8				9	1	5								D Owen	7
	2	3	4		6	7*	11	9	10		8					1	5	12							P Letts	8
	2	**3**	**4**		**6**	**7**	**11**	**9**	**10**		**8**					**1**	**5**								**D Axcell**	**9**
	2	3	4			7	11	9	10		8					1	5	12							C Downey	10
	2	3			6	7	11	9	10		8					1	5			4*					G Napthine	11
	2	3	4		6	7		9	10	11	8					1	5								E Scales	12
	2	**3**	**4**		**6**	**7**		**9**	**10**	**11**	**12**				**8**	**1**	**5***								**J Deakin**	**13**
	2	3	4		6	7		9	10	11*	12				8	1	5†								H Taylor	14
	7	3	4		6		11	9	10						8	1	5			2					K Cooper	15
	7	**3**	**4**		**6**		**11**	**9**	**10**						**8**	**1**	**5**			**2**					**M Scott**	**16**
	7	3	4		6	5	11	9*	10		12				8	1				2					P Willis	17
	7	3	4		6	8	11		10*						9	1	5	12		2					J Moules	18
	11		4	5	6	8			10*		12				9	1	2				3	7			I Hendrick	19
	2		4*	5	6	8		11	10						9†	1					3	12	7		K Salmon	20
	2			5	6	8		9*	10						12	1					3	11	7		J Key	21
	2		4*	5	6			12	10				9			1					3	11	7		D Reeves	22
			2	5		8		9	10	4						1	6				3†	11	7		D Hedges	23
				5		8		9	10	4		2				1	6				3	11	7		Alan Robinson	24
			2		6	8†		9	10	4						1	5				3	11	7		A Seville	25
			2	5	6	8			10	4					9	1					3	11	7		M Taylor	26
			2	**5**	**6**	**8**		**12**	**10**						**9***	**1**					**3**	**11**	**7**		**L Burden**	**27**
	2			5	6		4	9	10	8		12				1	3					11	7*		L Buksh	28
	2				6		8	9	10	4						1	5				3	11	7		R Dilkes	29
			4	**5**	**3**			**9**	**10**	**8**						**1**	**6**				**2**	**11**	**7**		**B Stevens**	**30**
			4	5	3			9	10	8						1	6				2	11	7		E Read	31
			4	5	3			9	10	8						1	6				2	11	7		M Dimblebee	32
			4	**5**	**3**	**12**		**9***	**10**	**8**						**1**	**6**				**2**	**11**	**7**		**R Lewis**	**33**
	2		4		6	8			10*			12			9	1	5				3	11	7		G Courtney	34
	2		12		6	4			10	7					9	1	5*				3	11	8		A Crickmore	35
	2		8		6	4	11		10						9*	1	5				3	12	7		C Seel	36
	2		8			4	11		10*						9	1	5		6		3	12	7		C Thomas	37
	2					4	8				10			1	9		5		6		3	11	7		R Banks	38
	2					4			10	8					9	1	5		6		3	11	7		L Shapter	39
	2				5	4			10	8						1			6		3	11	7		B Stevens	40
					6	4		12	10*	8					9	1	5				3	11	7	2	J Moules	41
					6	4		12		8					9	1	5				3	11*	7	2	D Allison	42
	2				6	4		12	10	8*					9	1	5				3	11	7		D Letts	43
	2				6	4		8	10						9	1	5				3	11	7		I Borrett	44
					6		4		10	8*		12			9	1	5				3	11	7	2	L Burden	45
	12	8			6	4			10						9	1	5				3	11*	7	2	K Baker	46
		11				4		9	10	8		6				1	5				3		7	2	D Axcell	47
		11			6	4		8	10*	12					9	1	5				3		7	2	K Walmsley	48
1	30	18	23	16	35	35	15	20	40	25	11	2	2	4	25	36	30	0	4	4	26	22	26	6	League Appearances	
	+1S		+2S				+2S	+4S		+1S	+4S	+3S	+1S		+1S			+3S				+3S				
			3	3	3	1+1S		2+1S	3	2					1	3	2				3	3	3		FA Cup Appearances	
	3	3	3		3	2	2	3	3	1	1+1S				2	3	3			1					Milk Cup Appearances	

Also Played: Steel match 2, no.1. Stille match 10, no.6*; 11, no.12. Wilkins match 21, no.4; 22, no.8; 27, no.4. Muir match 40, no.9; 42, no.10.

THE GOLDSTONE GROUND

Official Address: Goldstone Ground, Old Shoreham Road, Hove, Sussex BN3 7DE. Telephone: Brighton (0273) 739535

Ground Capacity: 32,500

Record Attendance: 36,747 v. Fulham, Division 2, 27 Dec 1958

Record Receipts: £66,000 v. Norwich City, FA Cup Round 4, 29 Jan 1983

Size of Playing Area: 112yds × 75 yds

Season Tickets: Stand: seats up to £150.00

Executive Box Season Tickets: £500.00

Cost of Stand Tickets: £5.00, £4.00 (£3.00 Family Stand); **Terraces:** £2.50

Match and Ticket Information: Postal bookings depending on availability four weeks before each match.

Car Parking: Available at the Greyhound Stadium (Nevill Road) and in Hove Station Goods Yard (Sackville Road). Limited parking adjacent to ground.

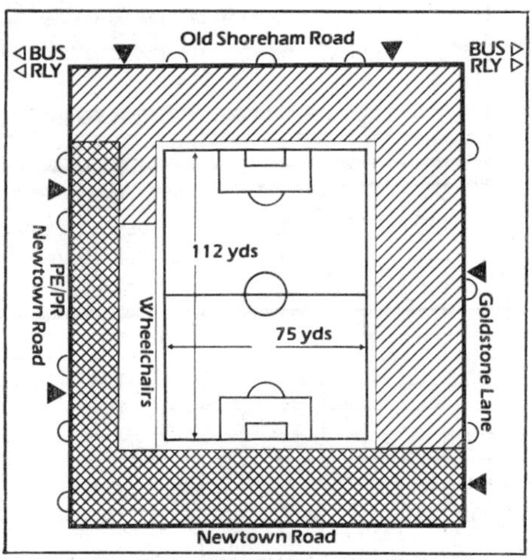

For key see page 12

How to get to the ground

From North: Use A23 with Pyecombe, then in 2m turn right (S.P. Hove). In 1.1m bear left into Nevill Road A2023. In 0.9m at cross roads turn left A27 into Old Shoreham Road for Brighton and Hove Albion.
From East: From Lewes use A27 to Brighton then follow signs Worthing A27 along Old Shoreham Road for Brighton and Hove Albion
From West: Use A27 (S.P. Brighton) along Old Shoreham Road for Brighton and Hove Albion.

BRISTOL CITY Division 3

Chairman
D Williams

Directors
O Newland
D Russe
P Manning
M Fricker
T Cooper
W Williams

Secretary
Bob Twyford

Lottery Manager
Brian White (0272-632812)

Manager
Terry Cooper

Assistant Manager
Clive Middlemass

Reserve Team Manager
Mike Gibson

Physiotherapist
Alex Lockhart

Chief Scout
Jock Rae

After the nightmares of recent seasons a modest start was made on the road to respectability with fourth place being achieved in the ultimate Canon League division and this will bring better teams to Ashton Gate in the new season. In other respects there were signs that the 'Dark Ages' were over for this once-great club, but a slice of luck was still to be needed to consolidate since the playing staff does probably need to be strengthened and money to do this is virtually unavailable.

However, promotion was Manager Terry Cooper's aim for the season and this was won so who can complain? It was always 'on' particularly from the New Year onwards and the final margin over Aldershot, the fifth club, was a fairly comfortable seven points.

The Cup campaigns did not start too well with immediate dismissal from the Milk Cup by a narrow aggregate against Oxford United. This was disappointing since the hard work had already been done with a draw at the Manor Ground only for United to score the only goal of the return match to counter the initial drawn effort. The F.A. Cup was a better showing even though Corinthian Casuals were no 'soft touch' in the first round; they drew at home but were well beaten at Ashton Gate. Round Two produced great satisfaction — at least parochially — as a visit to Eastville brought a thriller and a very late winner by Martyn Hirst, a Bath University student! A visit to Meadow Lane saw City share four goals with Notts County, but there was to be no shock result in the replay as County went through with two second half goals.

So what are the chances? Terry Cooper, who was a virtually permanent No.12 for his side last season, does have some useful experience in John Shaw, Forbes Phillipson-Masters, Alan Crawford, Glyn Riley, Trevor Morgan, Howard Pritchard and the returned Tom Ritchie. But there is a veteran look about some of them and if new local talent is not found to step into the breach should any of them need replacing there could be problems.

One could say that City's loyal support deserves success but the behaviour of some young louts at Reading late in the season is a nasty reminder of the fact that all clubs have to suffer such nonsense with few signs that this is likely to change until drastic deterrents are officially introduced.

Back Row: Gary Marshall, Howard Pritchard, Tom Ritchie, Bruce Halliday, Nigel Smith. **Middle Row:** Rob Newman, Trevor Morgan, Alan Walsh, John Shaw, Keith Curle, Forbes Phillipson-Masters, Alan Nicholls. **Front Row:** Paul Stevens, Bob Hutchinson, Alan Crawford, Terry Cooper (Manager), Andy Llewellyn, Martin Hirst, Glyn Riley.

'THE ROBINS'

Formed: 1894 **Turned Professional:** 1897 **Ltd Co:** 1897
Previous Names: Bristol South End 1894-7
Previous Managers: Bob Hewison Bob Wright Pat Beasley Peter Doherty Fred Ford Alan Dicks Bob Houghton Roy Hodgson
Honours: Division Two Champions 1905-6 Division Three (S) Champions: 1922-3, 1926-7, 1954-5 Welsh Cup Winners Anglo-Scottish Cup Winners 1977-8
League Career: Elected to Division 2 1901 Promoted to Division 1 1905-6
Relegated to Division 2 1910-1 Relegated to Division3 (S) 1921-2
Promoted to Division 2 1922-3 Relegated to Division 3(S) 1923-4
Promoted to Division 2 1926-7 Relegated to Division 3(S) 1931-2
Promoted to Division 2 1954-5 Relegated to Division 3 1959-60
Promoted to Division 2 1964-5 Promoted to Division 1 1979-80
Relegated to Division 2 1980-1 Relegated to Division 3 1981-2
Relegated to Division 4 1982-3 Promoted to Division 3 1983-4
Colours: Red shirts, white shorts, red and white stockings
Change Colours: White shirts, black shorts, white stockings

CLUB RECORDS

Most Appearances for Club: John Atyeo, 1951-66 League 597, F.A. Cup 42, League Cup 6, Total 645
Most Capped Player: Billy Wedlock, 26, England
Record Goalscorer in a Match: "Tot" Walsh, 6 v. Gillingham (H) 9-4, Div 3(S), 15.01.1927
Record League Goalscorer in a season: in all competitions, Don Clark, 41 (League 36, Fairs Cup 5) 1946-7
Record League Goalscorer in a career: in all competitions: John Atyeo, 350 (League 315, Fairs Cup 30, League Cup 5) 1951-66
Record Transfer Fee Received: £325,000 from Coventry City for Gary Collier, July 1979
Record Transfer Fee Paid: £235,000 to St Mirren for Tony Fitzpatrick, July 1979
Best Performances: League: 2nd Div 1 1906-7 **F.A. Cup:** Finalists 1909 **League/Milk Cup:** Semi-Final 1970-1
Most League Points: 82 in Div 4, 1983-4 **Most League Goals:** 104, Div 3(S), 1926-7
Record League Victory: 9-0 v. Aldershot, Div 3(S), 28 Dec 1946
Record League Defeat: 0-9 v Coventry City, Div 3(S), 28 April 1934

Club Statistician for the Directory: David Woods

Programme Editor
John Cox

Price	**Number of Pages**
40p	32

Subscriptions
Rates obtainable from club

BRISTOL CITY

PLAYERS NAME Ht Wt Birthdate	Honours	Birthplace Transfers	Clubs	APPEARANCES League	APPEARANCES Milk Cup	APPEARANCES F.A.C.	APPEARANCES A.M.C.	GOALS League	GOALS Milk Cup	GOALS F.A.C.	GOALS A.M.C.
GOALKEEPERS											
Mike Hooper		Bristol	Bristol C								
6-3 12 7 10.2.64											
John Shaw		Stirling	Leeds U (A)				2E				
6-1 13.7 4.2.54		F	Bristol C	254	9	13					
DEFENDERS											
Terry Cooper	E.(20). Div 1. 69.	Castleford	Leeds U (A)	239 + 10	21	30 +	49	7		2	
5-8 10.9 12.7.44	Lg.C. 68.		Middlesbrough	105	11	7		1			
	EFC. 68, 71		Bristol C.	11							
			Bristol R.	53 + 6	6 + 1	2					
			Doncaster R.	20		3					
			Bristol C	38 + 21	3	1 + 5	1				
Bruce Halliday		Sunderland	Newcastle U (A)	32							
5-11 11.2 3.1.61			Darlington (L)	4							
			Bury	29							
		F	Bristol C		2	5	1				
Andy Llewellyn	E Y	Bristol	Bristol C. (A)	5 + 2			0 + 1				
5-7 11 12 26.2.66											
Alan Nicholls		Plymouth	Bristol C (A)	79	2	3		5			
6-2 12.0 10.2.63											
Forbes Phillipson-Masters		Bournemouth	Southampton (A)	9							
			Exeter C. (L)	6							
6-1 12.10 14.1.55			Bournemouth (L)	7				2			
			Luton T (L)	10							
		£50,000	Plymouth A.	119	8	6					
		F	Bristol C	69	2	3	1	3			
Paul Stevens		Bristol	Bristol C (A)	116 + 1	8	7	1	3			
5-7 9 9 4 4 60											
MIDFIELD											
Martyn Hirst	E. Y	York	Bath University								
5-9 11 7 26.10.61			Bristol C	22 + 2		4		1		1	
Bobby Hutchinson		Glasgow	Hibernian								
5-9 11.4 19.6.57			Wigan A	34 + 1	4	2		3	1		
			Tranmere R.	42 + 3	7	2		6	3		
			Mansfield	25		3		3			
			Tranmere R.	21			5	4			2
Rob Newman		Bradford-on-Avon	Bristol C. (A)	86 + 8	5	3	1	7	1		
6-2 12.0 13.12.63											
Nigel Smith		Bath	Bristol C. (A)	2							
6-0 12 7 12.1.66											
FORWARDS											
Alan Crawford		Rotherham	Rotherham U. (A)	233 + 4	17	15		49	6	9	
5-7 9.10 30.10.53			Mansfield T (L)	1 + 1							
		£30,000	Chesterfield	88 + 6	7	6		20	1	1	
		F	Bristol C.	75 + 1	5	4		22		1	
Keith Curle		Bristol	Bristol R. (A)	21 + 11	3	1		4			
6-0 11.9 14.11.63		£5,000	Torquay U.	16		1		5			
		£5,000	Bristol C.	5 + 1			1	8			
Gary Marshall			Bristol C.	0 + 1							
5-11½ 10.10 20.4.64											
Trevor Morgan		Forest Gate	Leytonstone								
6-1 13.1 30.9.56		£3,000	Bournemouth	53	2	2		13			
		£10,000	Mansfield T.	12	1			6			
		£10,000	Bournemouth	88	8	7	1	33	3	3	1
		£12,000	Bristol C.	15				5			
Howard Pritchard†	W. Y	Cardiff	Bristol C. (A)	31 + 7	1	5 + 1		2		2	
5-10 12.7 18.10.58		F	Swindon T.	59 + 6	2 + 1	8		11		8	
		F	Bristol C.	46	2	5		10		3	
Glyn Riley		Barnsley	Barnsley (A)	103 + 27	9	5		16	2	1	
5-10 11.1 24.7.58			Doncaster R.	7 + 1							
		F	Bristol C.	85 + 1	6	4		32	1	1	
Tom Ritchie*		Edinburgh	Bridgend Th.								
5-11 12.8 2.1.52			Bristol C.	308 + 13	21 +	17 +		77	2	2	
		£185,000	Sunderland	32 + 3	2	3		8	2		
			Carlisle U.	14 + 1							
		F	Bristol C.	82	5	5		24	1	2	
Alan Walsh		Hartlepool	Horden C.W.								
6-0 12.8 9.12.56		F	Middlesbrough	0 + 3							
		F	Darlington	245 + 6	12	14 +		87	7	6	
		£18,000	Bristol C.								

NON-CONTRACT PLAYERS 1984-85: Paul Derrick, Wayne Morris

APPRENTICES: Jon Osborne, Lee Rogers

BRISTOL CITY

DIVISION FOUR 4TH **FA CUP** 3RD ROUND **MILK CUP** 1ST ROUND

MATCH	DATE	COMPE-TITION	VENUE	OPPONENTS	RESULT	HALF TIME	L'GUE POS'N	GOALSCORERS	ATTEN-DANCE
1	A 27	CL	H	Mansfield T	W4-0	2-0		Crawford 2, Riley 2	5,758
2	**31**	**MC 1**	**A**	**Oxford U**	**D1-1**	**0-0**		**Riley**	**3,924**
3	S 3	CL	A	Bury	L1-2	1-2	9	Kerr	2,015
4	6	CL	A	Colchester U	D0-0	0-0			2,120
5	10	CL	H	Hartlepool U	W2-0	0-0	6	Pritchard, Riley	5,390
6	**12**	**MC 1**	**H**	**Oxford U**	**L0-1**	**0-1**			**5,163**
7	16	CL	A	Wrexham	L1-3	0-1	7	Crawford	1,731
8	24	CL	H	Torquay U	W5-0	1-0	6	Crawford 3, Riley, Ritchie	4,266
9	27	CL	H	Reading	W3-1	0-1		Ritchie, Pritchard 2	6,322
10	O 1	CL	A	Hereford U	W2-0	1-0	2	Ritchie, Kerr	5,875
11	8	CL	H	Halifax T	W3-0	3-0	2	Riley, Crawford, Kerr	6,739
12	14	CL	A	Tranmere R	L0-2	0-1			2,518
13	18	CL	H	York C	W1-0	1-0		Stevens	10,837
14	22	CL	A	Aldershot	L0-1	0-1	1		3,195
15	29	CL	H	Peterborough U	L0-1	0-0	2		7,380
16	N 1	CL	A	Blackpool	L0-1	0-1			3,434
17	5	CL	H	Doncaster U	L1-2	1-1	7	Stroud	5,963
18	12	CL	A	Darlington	W1-0	0-0	5	Kerr	1,888
19	**19**	**FAC 1**	**A**	**Corinthian Casuals**	**D0-0**	**0-0**			**2,116**
20	**23**	**FAC 1R**	**H**	**Corinthian Casuals**	**W4-0**	**2-0**		**Riley, Pritchard 3**	**5,339**
21	26	CL	H	Chesterfield	W2-0	0-0	4	Ritchie, Pritchard	5,797
22	D 3	CL	A	Northampton T	L0-1	0-1	7		2,823
23	**10**	**FAC 2**	**A**	**Bristol R**	**W2-1**	**0-0**		**Ritchie, Hirst**	**16,200**
24	17	CL	A	Rochdale	W1-0	0-0	7	Pritchard	1,496
25	26	CL	H	Stockport Co	W3-1	2-0	4	Riley, Crawford, Stroud	8,888
26	28	CL	A	Crewe Alex	D2-2	1-2		Ritchie (pen), Pritchard	3,457
27	31	CL	H	Chester C	W4-2	0-1	3	Crawford, Stevens, Ritchie, Riley	7,293
28	**J 8**	**FAC 3**	**A**	**Notts Co**	**D2-2**	**1-1**		**Crawford, Ritche**	**11,042**
29	**10**	**FAC 3R**	**H**	**Notts Co**	**L0-2**	**0-0**			**16,107**
30	21	CL	H	Wrexham	W2-1	1-0	6	Ritchie (pen), Crawford	6,441
31	24	CL	A	Swindon T	D1-1	0-0		Riley	6,493
32	28	CL	A	Hartlepool U	D2-2	1-2	4	Riley, Pritchard	1,881
33	31	CL	H	Bury	W3-2	1-0		Ritchie (pen), Riley, Crawford	7,759
34	F 4	CL	H	Hereford U	W1-0	1-0	3	Crawford	7,184
35	11	CL	A	Torquay U	L0-1	0-0	3		4,188
36	14	CL	H	Blackpool	D1-1	0-1		Stroud	7,413
37	18	CL	A	Peterborough U	L1-4	1-1	5	Crawford	3,356
38	**22**	**AMC 1**	**A**	**Exeter C**	**L1-3**	**0-1**		**Ritchie (pen)**	**1,754**
39	25	CL	H	Aldershot	W2-1	2-1	4	Ritchie (pen), Riley	6,849
40	M 3	CL	A	York C	D1-1	0-0	3	Morgan	5,096
41	6	CL	A	Doncaster R	L0-1	0-1			4,954
42	10	CL	H	Darlington	W1-0	0-0	5	Morgan	6,579
43	13	CL	H	Rochdale	D1-1	0-1		Riley	6,996
44	17	CL	A	Halifax T	W2-1	0-0	4	Pritchard, Riley	1,204
45	24	CL	H	Tranmere R	D1-1	0-0	4	Morgan	6,548
46	27	CL	A	Mansfield T	W1-0	0-0		Newman	1,826
47	31	CL	H	Colchester U	W4-1	1-0	2	Ritchie 2 (1 pen), Riley 2	6,504
48	A 7	CL	A	Reading	L0-2	0-2	2		8,528
49	14	CL	H	Northampton T	W4-1	1-1	2	Crawford 2, Riley, Ritchie (pen)	6,620
50	17	CL	H	Crewe Alex	W2-1	2-0		Hirst, Pritchard	8,139
51	21	CL	A	Stockport Co	D0-0	0-0	2		2,645
52	28	CL	A	Chesterfield	D1-1	0-0	2	Phillipson-Masters	2,975
53	M 5	CL	H	Swindon T	W1-0	0-0	3	Pritchard	12,786
54	7	CL	A	Chester C	W2-1	1-0	3	Morgan 2	3,900

Av Home Att 7,149

Goal Scorers

League (70): Riley 16, Crawford 15, Ritchie 12 (8 pens), Pritchard 10, Morgan 5, Kerr 4, Stroud 3, Stevens 2, Hirst 1, Newman 1, Phillipson-Masters 1
FA Cup (8): Pritchard 3, Ritchie 2, Crawford 1, Hirst 1, Riley 1
Milk Cup (1): Riley 1
AMC (1): Ritchie 1 (1 pen)

1983-84

Shaw	Stevens	Williams G	Phillipson-Masters	Halliday	Riley	Pritchard	Ritchie	Kerr	Musker	Crawford	Williams P	Newman	Economou	Cooper	Stroud	Hirst	Marshall	Morgan	Curle	Hooper	Llewellyn	Williams T	REFEREE	
1	2	3	4	5	6	7	8	9*	10	11	12												H King	1
1	**2**	**3**	**5**	**4**	**6**	**7**	**8**	**9***	**10**	**11**	**12**												**E Scales**	**2**
1	2	5		4	10	6	7	11*	8	9	12												J Key	3
1	10	3	5	4	6*	7	8	9		11	12	2											M James	4
1	12	5*	4	3	10	6	7	11		9		2	8										D Reeves	5
1		**3**	**5**	**4**	**6**	**7**	**8***	**9**		**11**	**12**	**2**	**10**										**L Burden**	**6**
1	8	3	5	4	6	7			12	11	9*	2	10										D Allison	7
1	2	3	5	4	6	7	8	9		11			10										L Robinson	8
1	2	3	5	4	6	7	8	9*		11			10	12									J Deakin	9
1	2	3	5	4	6	7	8	9		11			10										K Baker	10
1	2	3	5	4	6	7	8	9		11			10*	12									J Martin	11
1	2	3	5	4	6	7	8	9		11			10*	12									M Peck	12
1	2	3	5	4*	6	7	8	9		11			10	12									K Cooper	13
1	2	3	5		6	7	8	9*		11		4†	10	12									D Axcell	14
1	2	3	5	4	6	7	8			11		12	10*		9								J Worrall	15
1	2	12	5	4	6*	7	8			11	10	3			9								N Ashley	16
1	2	3	5	4*	6	7	8			11	10		12		9								A Buksh	17
1	2	3	5	4	6*	7	8	12			11		10		9								A Challinor	18
1	**2**	**3**		**4**		**7**	**8**	**6**			**9**	**5**	**10***	**12**		**11**							**M James**	**19**
1	**2**	**3**		**4**	**9**	**7**	**8**	**10**				**5**	**6***	**12**	**11**								**M James**	**20**
1	2	3		4		7	8	10			11*	5			9	6	12						D Vickers	21
1	2	3		4†	11*	7	8	10				5		12	9	6							A Ward	22
1	**2**	**3**	**5**	**4**	**10**	**7**	**8**			**11***				**12**	**6**	**9**							**K Baker**	**23**
1	2	3	5		10	7	8			11*		4		12	9	6							R Nixon	24
1	2	3	5	4	10	7	8*			11				12	6	9							T Spencer	25
1	2	3	5	4	10	7	8			11				12	6	9*							D Richardson	26
1	2	3	5	4	6	7	8			11				12	10	9*							T Bune	27
1	**2**	**3**	**5**	**4**	**6**	**7**	**8**			**11***				**12**	**9**	**10**							**N Glover**	**28**
1	**2**	**3**	**5**	**4**	**6**	**7**	**8**			**11***				**12**	**9**	**10**							**N Glover**	**29**
1	2	3	5	4	10	7	8			11				12	6	9*							J Moules	30
1	2	3	5	4	9	7	8			11				12	6	10*							C Downey	31
1	2	3	5	4	9	7	8			11*				12	6	10							D Allison	32
1	2	3	5		10	7	8			11		4			6	9							A Robinson	33
1	2	3	5		10	7	8			11		4		12	6	9*							C Thomas	34
1	2	3	5	4		7	8			11*		9		12	6	10							V Callow	35
1	2	3	5	4		7	8			11		10		12	6	9*							D Hedges	36
1	2	3	5	4		7	8			11*		9		12	6	10							A Gunn	37
	2	**12**	**5**	**4***		**7***	**8**				**9**	**3**	**6**	**11**		**10**				**1**	**12**		**J Martin**	**38**
1	2		5	4	9	7	8					3		11	6	10							L Shapter	39
1	2		5	4	9	7	8					3			6			10	11				I Hendrick	40
1	2		5	4	10*	7	8					3			6	12		9	11				A Robinson	41
1	2		5	4	9	7	8					3			6			10	11				D Letts	42
1	2		5	4	9	7	8					3			6	12		10	11*				R Lewis	43
1	2		5	4	10	7	8					3			6			9	11				J Lovatt	44
1	2		5	4	9	7	8					3		12	6*	11		10					A Seville	45
1	2		5	4	9	7	8					3			6	11		10					D Shaw	46
1	2		5	4	9	7	8					3			6	11		10					M Heath	47
1	2		5	4	9	7	8					3		12	6	11*		10					D Vickers	48
1	2		5	4	9	7	8			11*		3		12	6			10					K Cooper	49
1	2		5		9	7	8			11		3			6	4		10					E Scales	50
1	2		5	4	9	7	8					3			6	11		10					D Scott	51
1	2		5*	4	9	7	8					3			6	11		10	12				K Baker	52
1	2		5	4	9	7	8			11		3			6			10					B Stevens	53
1	2		5	4	9	7	8			11		3			6			10					P Scott	54
46	45	29	44	41	42	**46**	45	13	2	31	5	29	11	1	34	22	0	15	5				League Appearances	
	+1S	+1S						+1S	+1S		+3S	+1S	+1S	+20S		+2S	+1S		+1S					
5	5	5	3	5	4	5	5	2		3	1	2	2	5S	4	4							FA Cup Appearances	
2	1	2	2	2	2	2	2	2	1	2	2S	1	1										Milk Cup Appearances	
	1	1S	1	1		1	1					1	1	1		1				1	1S		AM Cup Appearances	

ASHTON GATE

Official Address: Ashton Gate, Bristol BS3 2EJ. Telephone: Bristol (0272) 632812 (5 lines)

Telegraphic: City Bristol

Ground Capacity: 30,868

Record Attendance: 43,335 v. Preston N.E., F.A. Cup Round 5, 16 Feb 1935

Record Receipts: £45,000 v. Aston Villa, F.A. Cup Round 4, 23 Jan 1982

Size of Playing Area: 115yds × 75 yds

Season Tickets: £75 Adults (£35 juveniles/OAP), £55 (£25 juveniles/OAP) (Stands); Family (2 adults, 2 children) £160, £110.

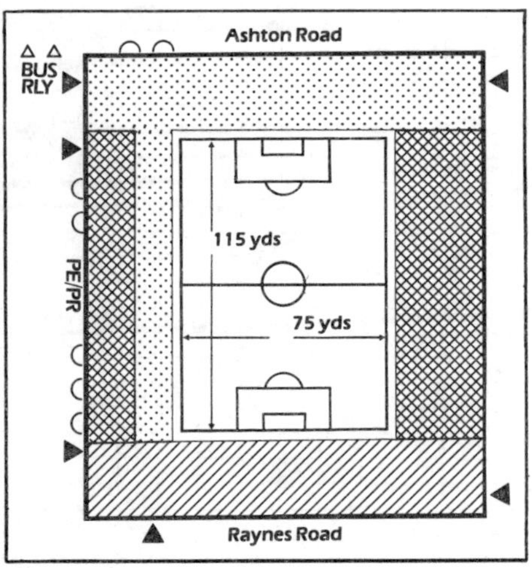

For key see page 12

Executive Box Season Tickets: none

Cost of Stand Tickets: £4.00 (Grand Stand) (£2.00 juveniles/OAP); £3.50 (£1.50 juveniles/OAP); **Enclosure:** £2.20 (£1.00 juveniles/OAP); **Covered standing:** £2.00 (£1.10 juveniles/OAP); **Uncovered standing:** £2.00 (£1.00 juveniles/OAP)

Match and Ticket Information: any time before match applications by post (with sae) are accepted. Personal applications four weeks prior to each match.

Car Parking: season car park tickets for season ticket holders. Coaches park at Cannons March. There is limited street parking around ground.

How to get to the ground

From North/West: Use Motorway M5 until junction 16, leave motorway and follow signs Bristol A38. Follow signs to City Centre then follow signs Taunton A38. In 1.2m cross Cumberland Basin swing bridge, then branch left into Winterstoke Road for Bristol City F.C.
From East: Use Motorway M4, then M32 and follow signs to City Centre, then follow signs Taunton A38. In 1.2m cross Cumberland Basin swing bridge, then branch left into Winterstoke Road for Bristol City F.C.
From South: Use Motorway M5 with junction 18. Leave motorway and follow signs Bristol A4 along Portway then turn right and follow signs Taunton over Cumberland Basin swing bridge, then branch left into Winterstoke Road for Bristol City F.C. To use Bristol City F.C. park and ride scheme follow AA signs to "Bristol City F.C. car park", which is in Anchor Road.

BRISTOL ROVERS Division 3

President
To be announced

Vice-Presidents
E W H Godfrey
H E L Brown
Dr W T Cussen
G A W Holmes
A I Seager
Con A L Stevens

Chairmen (Joint)
Martin R Flook
B W Bradshaw

Director
G J Bennett (Managing)

Honorary Company Secretary
A E Hill FCA, MBA

Player-Manager
David Williams

Assistant Manager
P W Jones

Club Coach
Harold Jarman

Physiotherapist
R Gingell

Commercial Manager
Commercial Department (0272 573687)

After the surprise departure of manager Bobby Gould to his home town club Coventry City, Rovers' directors selected David Williams in preference to experienced England international Alan Ball or ex-Rover Larry Lloyd. Williams, a talented Welsh schoolteacher, had notched up a decade at Eastville as a player and at 28 became the youngest manager in the football league. Williams's first appointment was Shrewsbury assistant manager Wayne Jones who had won a Welsh International cap during his playing career with Rovers. Two other ex Rovers players were also to return – striker Steve White £35,000 from Charlton and utility defender Phil Bater £10,000 from Wrexham.

Rovers started their league campaign in consistent style and after winning at Orient on 23 September went top of the Third Division table. In the first third of the season Rovers knocked Bournemouth out of the Milk Cup and also held onto the Gloucestershire Professional Cup with a 3-2 win over rivals Bristol City for the third consecutive year.

With eight consecutive home wins Rovers achieved the distinction of being the last team in the league to be defeated at home when Hull City won 3-1. Probably Rovers' best performances of the season were the Milk Cup ties with Brighton. Although the Second Division club were overall victors over the two legs, it took an extra time goal from Terry Conner to clinch the tie by a 5-4 aggregate.

In the FA cup competition Rovers saw off non-league Barnet after a replay before being drawn at home in an intriguing all Bristol derby match. This was an all ticket affair which stretched the ground capacity to 14,396 fans who paid £31,809 and new record receipts for a match at Eastville. Bristol City's part-time university student Martin Hirst scored the winning goal in injury time. This defeat had a lasting effect over the next couple of months as Rovers slipped to sixth position. After a spell of 48 consecutive league matches in which time Rovers had failed only once to score they were held to two successive goalless draws by Port Vale and Orient. Manager David Williams signed striker Paul Bannon from Carlisle to add goalpower to an unsettled combination of strikers in a determined effort to improve the promotion prospects but ultimately the prize was primarily missed by Rovers' inability to retain goal leads in away matches at Plymouth, Wimbledon, Rotherham, Scunthorpe and notably Brentford where they took a two goal lead. All these matches resulted in draws when each should have produced full points. But 1984/85 is another season!

The League Directory's Statistician of the Club

Back Row: Ray Kendall (Kit Manager), Roy Dolling (Youth Officer/Trainer), Steve White, Paul Bannon, Ray Cashley, Phil Kite (now Southampton), Tim Parkin, Aidan McCaffery, Geraint Williams, Harold Jarman (Youth Coach), Wayne Jones (Assistant Manager). **Front Row:** Phil Bater, Neil Slatter, Brian Williams, David Williams (Player-Manager), Ian Holloway, Archie Stephens, Paul Randall.

'ROVERS'

Formed: 1883 **Turned Professional:** 1897 **Ltd Co:** 1896
Previous Managers: 1889-1920 Alf Homer (Secretary-Manager) 1920-1 Ben Hall 1921-6 Andrew Wilson 1926-9 Joe Palmer 1929-30 David McLean 1930-6 Captain Albert Prince-Cox 1936-7 Percy Smith 1938-49 Brough Fletcher 1950-8 Bert Tann 1968-9 Fred Ford 1969-72 Bill Dodgin (Snr) 1972-7 Don Megson 1978-9 Bobby Campbell 1979-80 Harold Jarman 1980-1 Terry Cooper 1981-3 Bobby Gould
Honours: Division Three (South): Champions
League Career: Original Members of Division Three 1920 Transferred to Division Three (South) 1921 Promoted to Division Two 1952-3 Relegated to Division Three 1961-2 Promoted to Division Two 1973-4 Relegated to Division Three 1980-1
Colours: Blue shirts with blue and white quartered fronts and white trim, blue shorts and blue stockings with white trim
Change Colours: Orange shirts with navy pin stripe, navy blue shorts with navy and blue stockings

CLUB RECORDS

Most Appearances for Club: Stuart Taylor, 1965-80: League 548 + F.A. Cup 16 + League Cup 36 **Total 600**
Most Capped Player: Matt O'Mahoney, 6 Eire and 1 N. Ireland **For England:** Geoff Bradford 1
Record Goalscorer in a Match: A player has scored 4 on eleven occasions
Record League Goalscorer in a season: Geoff Bradford, 33, Div 3(S) 1952-3 **In all competitions:** Geoff Bradford, 34 (League 33, F.A. Cup 1)
Record League Goalscorer in a career: Geoff Bradford, 245, 1949-64 **In all competitions:** Geoff Bradford, 260 (League 245, F.A. Cup 12, League Cup 3)
Record Transfer Fee Received: £200,000 from Luton Town for Steve White, Dec 1979
Record Transfer Fee Paid: £100,000 to Birmingham City for Stewart Barrowclough, July 1979
Best Performances: League: 6th Div 2 1955-6, 1958-9 **F.A. Cup:** 6th Round, 1950-1, 1957-8 **League/Milk Cup:** 5th Round 1970-1, 1971-2
Most League Points: (3 pts for a win) 79, Div 3, 1983-4, (2 pts for win) 64, Div 3(S), 1952-3 **Most League Goals:** 92, Div 3(S) 1952-3
Record League Victory: 7-0 v Swansea Town, Div 2, 2 Oct 1954
7-0 v Brighton & Hove Albion, Div 3(S), 29 Nov 1952
7-0 v Shrewsbury Town, Div 3, 21 March 1964
Record League Defeat: 0-12 v Luton Town, Div 3(S), 13 April 1936

Club Statistician for the Directory: Mike Jay

Programme Editor
Gordon Bennett

Price	**Number of Pages**
50p	36

Subscriptions

BRISTOL ROVERS

PLAYERS NAME Ht Wt Birthdate	Honours	Birthplace Transfers	Clubs	APPEARANCES League	Milk Cup	F.A.C.	A.M.C.	GOALS League	Milk Cup	F.A.C.	A.M.C.
GOALKEEPER											
Ray Cashley		Bristol	Bristol C.	227	16	3					
5-10 11.0 23.10.51			Hereford U. (L)	20							
		F	Bristol R.	27			2				
DEFENDERS											
Phil Bater	W. U.21(2)	Cardiff	Bristol R. (A)	211 + 1	13	13					
5-10½ 12.12 26.10.55		£50,000	Wrexham	73	5	6					
		£10,000	Bristol R.	30 + 2		3					
Aidan McCaffery*	E. Y	Newcastle	Newcastle U. (A)	57 + 2	3 + 1	5		4		1	
5-11 11.2 30.8.57		£25,000	Derby Co.	31 + 6	4			4			
		£40,000	Bristol R.	156 + 1	15	9	4	11	1		
			Bristol C. (L)	6				1			
Tim Parkin		Penrith	Blackburn R. (A)	13	3						
6-2 13.3 31.12.57			Malmo								
			Almondsbury Greenway								
			Bristol R.	119 + 3	8	6	2	7	1		
Neil Slatter	W (3). U.21(6). Y	Cardiff	Bristol R. (A)	110 + 1	10	6	3	2	1	1	
5-11 10.10 30.5.64											
Brian Williams†		Salford	Bury (A)	148 + 11	11	12		19			
5-8 12.12 5.11.55		£70,000	Q.P.R.	9 + 10	1 + 1	0 + 2					
		£50,000	Swindon T.	89 + 10	14	9		8			
			Bristol R.	126 + 2	9	7	4	10	1		1
MIDFIELD											
Steve Bailey		Bristol	Bristol R. (A)	15 + 1				1			
5-10 11.7 12.3.64											
Ian Holloway		Kingswood	Bristol R. (A)	63 + 6	6	5	3	8		1	
5-7 9.12 12.3.63											
David Williams	W. U.23(1). U.21(1)	Cardiff	Bristol R.	308 + 7	27	14 +	4	60	4	6	
5-10 11.8 11.3.55											
Geraint Williams	W. U.21(2)	Cwmpark	Bristol R. (A)	110 + 3	9	8	3	8		2	
5-7 10.8 5.1.62											
FORWARDS											
Paul Bannon		Dublin	Bridgend								
6-2½ 12.4 15.11.56		£8,500	Carlisle U.	127 + 12	5	13 +		45	1	5	
			Darlington (L)	2							
		£8,000	Bristol R.	11				3			
Paul Randell		Liverpool	Frome T.								
5-11 12.6 16.2.58			Bristol R.	49 + 3	2	4		37			
		£180,000	Stoke C.	38 + 8	2 + 2	1		7			
		£55,000	Bristol R.	111 + 13	10 +	6	1	41	2		
Archie Stevens		Liverpool	Melksham T.								
5-11 12.7 19.5.54		£3,000	Bristol R.	78 + 25	6 + 4	5 + 1	2 + 1	30	3	2	1
Paul Vassell	(Monthly Contract)	Bristol	Bristol R.								
5-11 11.2 11.1.66											
Steve White	Div. 2. 82	Chipping Sodbury	Mangotsfield U.	46 + 4	2	3		20	1	3	
5-11 11.10 2.1.59			Bristol R.	63 + 9	3 + 1	2		25	1		
				29	2			12			
				2 + 1							
				4							
				38 + 5	4	2 + 1	2 + 1	9	1		

APPRENTICES:
Mark Brain, Craig Harding, Steve Hare, Wayne Noble (0 + 1), **Lee Portch, Tim Carter, Ian Weston**

BRISTOL ROVERS

DIVISION THREE 5TH **FA CUP** 2ND ROUND **MILK CUP** 2ND ROUND

MATCH	DATE	COMPE-TITION	VENUE	OPPONENTS	RESULT	HALF TIME	L'GUE POS'N	GOALSCORERS	ATTEN-DANCE
1	A 27	CL	A	Newport Co	L1-2	0-1		Stephens	5,015
2	**30**	**MC1**	**A**	**AFC Bournemouth**	**W2-1**	**1-1**		**Randall, Holloway**	**3,473**
3	S 3	CL	A	Southend U	W2-1	1-1	12	Holloway, Randall	4,410
4	6	CL	H	Brentford	W3-1	1-1		White, Williams B, Barrett	5,148
5	10	CL	A	Port Vale	L0-2	0-1	11		4,308
6	**13**	**MC 1**	**H**	**AFC Bournemouth**	**D2-2**	**1-1**		**Williams B, Stephens**	**4,564**
7	17	CL	H	Exeter C	W2-0	1-0	10	Parkin, Stephens	4,813
8	23	CL	A	Orient	W1-0	1-0		Pulis	4,206
9	27	CL	A	AFC Bournemouth	W1-0	1-0		White	3,328
10	O 1	CL	H	Bolton W	W2-1	2-0	3	Barrett, Randall	5,651
11	**4**	**MC 2**	**A**	**Brighton & HA**	**L2-4**	**2-2**		**Barrett Slatter**	**9,417**
12	8	CL	A	Wimbledon	D1-1	1-0	3	Barrett	3,462
13	15	CL	H	Bradford C	W1-0	0-0	3	Randall	3,861
14	18	CL	A	Plymouth Arg	D1-1	0-0		Williams, G	4,896
15	22	CL	H	Scunthorpe U	W4-1	1-1	2	Williams B (pen), Barrett, Stephens, Green (og)	5,324
16	**25**	**MC 2**	**H**	**Brighton & HA**	**W2-1[1]**	**1-1**		**Barrett, White**	**9,936**
17	29	CL	A	Walsall	L1-2	0-1	2	Stephens	4,964
18	N 1	CL	H	Preston NE	W3-1	1-1		Williams G, Barrett, Randall	5,635
19	5	CL	A	Rotherham	D2-2	1-1	1	Willaims B 2	3,957
20	12	CL	H	Burnley	W2-1	2-1	1	Bater, Williams B (pen)	7,021
21	**19**	**FAC 1**	**A**	**Barnet**	**D0-0**	**0-0**			**2,650**
22	**22**	**FAC 1R**	**H**	**Barnet**	**W3-1**	**2-0**		**Holloway, Barrett, Slatter**	**5,338**
23	26	CL	A	Lincoln C	L0-4	0-2	2		3,709
24	D 3	CL	H	Sheffield U	D1-1	1-0	2	Williams B	7,472
25	**10**	**FAC 2**	**H**	**Bristol C**	**L1-2**	**0-0**		**Stephens**	**16,200**
26	17	CL	A	Hull C	L1-3	0-1	5	Parkin	5,673
27	26	CL	A	Oxford U	L2-3	1-2	6	Stephens 2	12,748
28	27	CL	H	Gillingham	W3-0	1-0	5	Stephens, Williams D, White	5,996
29	30	CL	A	Millwall	L0-1	0-1			4,885
30	J 9	CL	A	Southend U	W2-1	1-0		Williams B, Barrett	2,564
31	14	CL	H	Newport Co	W4-0	2-0	5	Stephens 2, Williams G 2	6,041
32	21	CL	A	Exeter C	W2-1	1-1	3	Webster (og), Slatter	5,310
33	28	CL	H	Port Vale	D0-0	0-0	4		6,502
34	F 4	CL	A	Bolton W	L0-3	0-1	6		5,399
35	11	CL	A	Orient	D0-0	0-0	6		4,741
36	14	CL	A	Preston NE	L0-1	0-0	5		3,813
37	18	CL	H	Walsall	W4-2	3-1	5	Bannon, Williams D, Hart (og), Randall	5,643
38	25	CL	A	Scunthorpe U	D2-2	2-1	4	White 2	2,737
39	**28**	**AMC 1**	**A**	**Newport Co**	**W1-0**	**0-0**		**Bannon**	**2,116**
40	M 3	CL	H	Plymouth Arg	W2-0	1-0	5	Bannon, White	5,619
41	6	CL	H	Rotherham U	W2-0	2-0		Williams D, Bannon	5,264
42	10	CL	A	Burnley	D0-0	0-0	5		6,296
43	**13**	**AMC 2**	**H**	**Port Vale**	**W2-0**	**0-0**		**Williams B, Stephens**	**2,585**
44	17	CL	H	Wimbledon	D1-1	0-0	5	White	5,383
45	27	CL	H	Wigan Ath	W2-1	1-1		Williams B, Walsh (og)	7,072
46	31	CL	A	Brentford	D2-2	2-0	5	Williams B, White	4,067
47	**A 3**	**AMC SQF**	**A**	**Southend U**	**W2-1**	**1-1**		**Hughes, Adams**	**1,480**
48	7	CL	H	AFC Bournemouth	L1-3	0-2	6	Pulis	5,032
49	14	CL	A	Sheffield U	L0-4	0-0	6		12,688
50	17	CL	A	Wigan Ath	D0-0	0-0			2,665
51	21	CL	H	Oxford U	D1-1	1-0	5	Stephens	6,397
52	23	CL	A	Gillingham	W2-1	0-0	5	Stephens 2	3,400
53	28	CL	H	Lincoln C	W3-1	1-1	5	White, Barrett 2	3,254
54	M 2	CL	A	Bradford C	W1-0	0-0		Stephens	3,271
55	8	CL	H	Millwall	W3-2	1-1		Williams B (pen), Randall, Barrett	5,347
56	12	CL	A	Hull C	D0-0	0-0	5		11,657
57	**14**	**AMC SSF**	**A**	**AFC Bournemouth**	**L0-1**	**0-0**			**2,810**

[1] After Extra Time

Av Home Att 5,534

Goal Scorers

League (68): Stephens 13, Williams B 10 (3 pens), Barrett 9, White 9, Randall 6, Willims G 4, Bannon 3, Williams D 3, Parkin 2, Pulis 2, Bater 1, Holloway 1, Slatter 1, opponents 4

FA Cup (4): Barrett 1, Holloway 1, Slatter 1, Stephens 1

Milk Cup (8): Barrett 2, Slatter 1, Holloway 1, Randall 1, Stephens 1, White 1, Williams B 1

AMC (5): Adams 1, Bannon 1, Hughes 1, Stephens 1, Williams B 1

1983-84

Kite	Slatter	Williams B	Williams G	Parkin	McCaffery	Holloway	Williams D	White	Randall	Barrett	Stephens	Pulis	Bater	Cashley	Bannon	Hughes	Noble	Vassall	Metcalfe	Adams	REFEREE	
1	2	3	4	5	6	7	8*	9	10	11	12										G Napthine	1
1	**2**	**3**	**4**	**5**	**6**	**7**		**9**	**10**	**11**		**8**									**D Letts**	**2**
1	2	3	4	5	6	7		9	10	11		8									K Barratt	3
1	2	3	4	5	6	7		9	10	11		8									A Crickmore	4
1	2	3	4	5	6	7		9	10	11*	12	8†									D Richardson	5
1	**2**	**3**	**4**	**5**	**6**	**7**		**9**	**12**	**11**	**10***	**8**									**H King**	**6**
1	2	3		5	6	7		9*	12	11	10	8	4								T Holbrook	7
1	2	3		5	6	7		9		11	10	8	4								T Bune	8
1	2	3	8	5	6	7		9	12	11	10*		4								C Downey	9
1	2	3	8	5	6	7		9	10	11			4								A Buksh	10
1	**2**	**3**	**4**	**5**	**6**	**7**		**9**	**10***	**11**	**12**	**8**									**D Axcell**	**11**
1	2	3		5	6	7		9*	10	11	12	8	4								M Taylor	12
1	2	3	11*	5	6	7		12	10		9	8	4								D Reeves	13
1	2	3	11	5	6	7		12	10		9	8	4*								A Seville	14
1	2	3	8	5	6	7		12	10*	11	9		4								L Burden	15
1	**2**	**3**	**4**	**5**	**6**	**7**		**8**	**10**	**11**	**9**										**J Deakin**	**16**
1	2	3	8	5	6	7		9	10*	11	12		4								R Guy	17
1	2	3	8	5	6	7		9	12	11	10*		4								V G Callow	18
1	2	3	8	5	6	7		10	9	11			4								N Midgley	19
1	2	3	8	5	6	7		9	10	11			4								T Ward	20
1	**2**	**3**	**8**	**5**	**6**	**7**		**9**	**10***	**11**	**12**		**4**								**D Letts**	**21**
1	**2**	**3**	**8**	**5**	**6**	**7**		**9**	**10**	**11**			**4**								**A Crickmore**	**22**
1	2	3	8	5	6	7		9*	10	11	12		4								JB Worrall	23
1	2	3	8	5	6	7*		12	10	11	9		4								J Moules	24
1	**2**	**3**	**8**	**5**	**6**	**7**		**12**	**10***	**11**	**9**		**4**								**K Baker**	**25**
1	2	3		5	6	7*	8	12	10	11	9		4								J Martin	26
	2	3	8	5	6		7	11			9	10	4	1							J Ashworth	27
	2	3	8	5	6		7	11		12	9*	10	4	1							L Shapter	28
	2*	3	8	5	6		7	11		12	9	10	4	1							J Hunting	29
	2	3	8	5	6			11		7	9	10	4	1							D Letts	30
	2	3	8	5	6	7	12	10*		11	9	4		1							D Vickers	31
	2	3	8	5	6	7		10		11	9	4		1							H Taylor	32
	2	3	8	5	6	7	12	9*	10	11		4		1							R Lewis	33
	2	3	4*	5	6	7	12	9	10	11		8		1							M Heath	34
	2	3	8	5	6		7			11	9†	4		1	10						J Bray	35
	2	3	12	5	6	4	7		11*		9	8		1	10						M Dimblebee	36
	2	3		5	6	8	7		12	11	9	4		1	10*						Alan Robinson	37
	2	3		5	6	7		9	12	11		4	8	1	10*						A Saunders	38
	2	**3**		**5**	**6**	**8**	**7**	**9**				**4**	**11**	**1**	**10**						**A Seville**	**39**
	2	3		5	6	7	11	9	12			4	8	1	10*						H King	40
	2	3		5	6*	7	11	9	12			4	8	1	10						J Deakin	41
		5		4		6	8	10	9		12	7	2	1	11*	3					D Shaw	42
1		**11**	**4**	**5**	**6**		**8**	**12**		**7**	**9**		**3**			**2***	**13**	**10***			**D Hedges**	**43**
		11	7*	5	6		8	10		12	9	4	3	1		2					M Robinson	44
	2	11		5	6		8	9	7		12	4	3	1	10*						C Thomas	45
	2	11		5	6		8	10	7		12	4	3	1	9*						B Hill	46
1	**2**	**3**	**4**		**6***	**7**	**8**			**11**	**9**					**5**			**12**	**10**	**A Gunn**	**47**
	2	11		5	6		8	9*	7		12	4	3	1	10						K Salmon	48
	2	11	7	5	6			9		8	12	4	3	1	10*						K Baker	49
	2	11	4		6	7		9		8	10		3	1		5					J Key	50
	2	3	4		6	7*	8	10	12	11	9			1		5					L Burden	51
	2	3	4		6	7	8	10		11	9			1		5					M James	52
	2	3	4		6	7	8	10		11	9			1		5					J Moules	53
		3	4		6	7	8	10		11	9		2	1		5					R Bridges	54
	2	3	4		6	7	8	9	10	11			12	1		5*					E Crickmore	55
	2	3	4		6	7*	8	9	10	11			12	1		5					P Tyldesley	56
	2	**3**	**4**		**6**	**7***	**8**	**10**	**9**	**11***	**12**		**13**	**1**		**5**					**D Vickers**	**57**
19	43	**46**	33	39	45	36	21	38	24	33	24	28	30	27	11	9					League Appearances	
			+1S				+3S	+5S	+8S	+3S	+10S		+2S									
3	3	3	3	3	3	3		2+1S	3	3	1+1S		3								FA Cup Appearances	
4	4	4	4	4	4	4		4	3+1S	4	2+1S	3									Milk Cup Appearances	
2	3	4	3	2	4	3	4	2+1S	1	3	2+1S	1	2+1S	2	1	3	1S	1	1S	1	AM Cup Appearances	

EASTVILLE STADIUM

Official Address: Bristol Stadium, Eastvilte, Bristol BS5 6NN. Telephone: Bristol (0272) 573687

Ground Capacity: 12,500 (7,500 covered)

Record Attendance: 38,472 v. Preston N.E., F.A. Cup Round 4, 30 Jan 1960

Record Receipts: £23,275 v. Southampton, F.A. Cup Round 4, 28 Jan 1978

Size of Playing Area: 110yds × 70 yds

Season Tickets: Stand (Main): £90, £65 (Juveniles/OAPs), £195 (family of three); Tip-Up Seats: £70, £35 (Juveniles/OAPs), £140 (family of three); £45 (North Enclosure), £22.50 (Juveniles/OAPs); £40 (South Enclosure), £20 (Juveniles/OAPs)

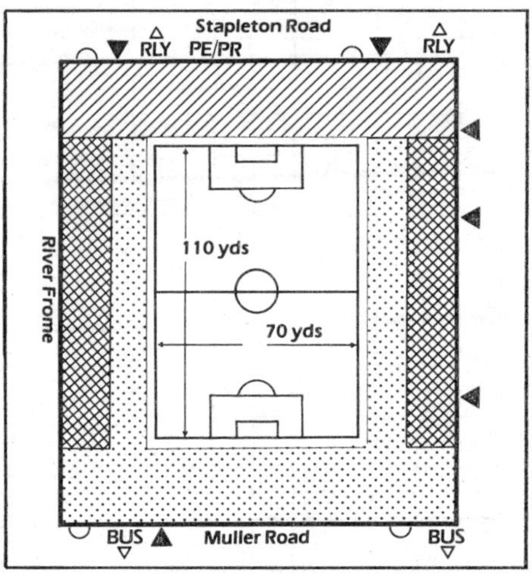

For key see page 12

Executive Box Season Tickets: Presidents Club. Consult Mr Roy Cowell (0454 778577)

Cost of Stand Tickets: £5, £4 (£3, £2 Juveniles/OAPs); **Terraces:** £2.50 (North Enclosure), £1.25 (Juveniles/OAPs); £2.20 (South Enclosure), £1.10 (Juveniles/OAPs)

Match and Ticket Information: Stand tickets available two weeks before each match.

Car Parking: Large parks at Stapleton Road and Muller Road entrances.

How to get to the ground

From North, East, South and West: Use M4 or M5 then M4 to Motorway M32. Follow signs Bristol until junction 2. Leave Motorway and at roundabout take 2nd exit into Stapleton Road for Bristol Rovers F.C.

BURNLEY — Division 3

Chairman
JE Jackson

Directors
Dr RD Iven, MRCS(Eng), LRCOP(Lond), MRCGP
(Vice Chairman)
D Gill, FCA (Managing Director)
AR Hutchinson

Secretary
R Bradshaw

Manager
John Benson

Reserve Team Coach
John Sainty

Youth Team Coach
A Bellamy

Commercial Manager
W Dore (0282 27777)

Chief Scout
John Docherty

A final position of twelth in the Third Division meant just about the poorest season in the club's history and this was 'achieved' by a team which was not lacking in big names (mostly veteran), many of whom will not be around in the new campaign. Manager John Bond having seen success with Norwich City and Manchester City discovered the realities of being in charge of struggling sides.

At no time were freshly-relegated Burnley really serious contenders for promotion although after a seven clear goal win over Port Vale in November they reached sixth place only to slump to a final position of twelfth. In fact, the most exciting match in the League was the final game — at home to Hull City. The Humberside team needed to win by three clear goals to gain promotion and with thirty minutes to go needed just one for that honour, which eluded them thanks to home pride and a resolute defence. A repeat of such bravery might augur well for the future.

Good cup results were also elusive with an early exit on aggregate in the Milk Cup against Crewe Alexandra, who won both legs. In the F.A. Cup non-League Hyde United provided stout resistence in the First Round and a replay at Turf Moor was needed before Chesterfield were ousted in the next, which brought Oxford United to Turf Moor in Round Three. There were no goals this time and a controversial winner saw the end of the Cup for Burnley at the Manor Ground.

Numerous 'name' players wore the claret and blue of the club during the season and failed to produce anything worthwhile, but an exception to any criticism must be Tommy Hutchison, who at the age of thirty-six played his heart out. Billy Hamilton also did his best in a struggling team, but John Bond was forced to spend the summer break (with no money at his disposal) looking for bargain players of modest ages who must be able to restore former glories to the club. Good youngsters are not thick on the ground, but they are still badly needed. Bond left the club after a disagreement in August 1984, and previous Assistant Manager John Benson took over.

Back Row L to R: Wayne Biggins, Steve Kennedy, David Miller, Phil Malley, Neil Whatmore, Alan Taylor. **Middle Row:** Derek Scott, Micky Phelan, Vince Overson, John Turner, Roger Hansbury, Barry Powell, Andy Kilner, Peter Hampton. **Front Row:** Kevin Hird, Peter Devine, Tommy Hutchison, Neil Grewcock, Brian Flynn.

'CLARETS'

Formed: 1882 **Turned Professional:** 1883 **Ltd Co:** 1897
Previous Name: Burnley Rovers 1881-2
Previous Managers: 1945-9 Cliff Britton 1949-54 Frank Hill 1954-7 Alan Brown 1957-8 Billy Dougal 1958-70 Harry Potts 1970-6 Jimmy Adamson 1976-7 Joe Brown 1977-9 Harry Potts 1979-83 Brian Miller 1983 Frank Casper (Caretaker) 1983-4 John Bond
Honours: Division 1 Champions 1920-1, 1959-60 Division 2 Champions 1897-8, 1972-3 Division 3 Champions 1981-2 F.A. Cup Winners 1913-4 Anglo-Scottish Cup Winners 1978-9
League Career: Original Members of Football League 1888 Relegated to Division 2 1896-7 Promoted to Division 1 1897-8 Relegated to Division 2 1899-1900 Promoted to Division 1 1912-3 Relegated to Division 2 1929-30 Promoted to Division 1 1946-7 Relegated to Division 2 1970-1 Promoted to Division 1 1972-3 Relegated to Division 2 1975-6 Relegated to Division 3 1979-80 Promoted to Division 2 1982-3
Colours: Claret shirts with light blue sleeves, white shorts and stockings
Change Colours: All Yellow

CLUB RECORDS

Most Appearances for Club: Jerry Dawson:1907-28, League 522 + F.A. Cup 45 + F.A. Charity Shield 1 **Total 568**
Most Capped Player: Jimmy McIlroy, 51, N Ireland. **For England:** Bob Kelly, 11
Record Goalscorer in a Match: Louis Page, 6 v Birmingham City (A) 7-1, Div 1, 10.04.26
Record League Goalscorer in a season: George Beel, 35, Div 1, 1927-8 **All competitions:** Jimmy Robson, 37 (League 25, F.A. Cup 5, League Cup 4, European Cup 3) 1960-1; Willie Irvine 37 (League 29, F.A. Cup 5, League Cup 3) 1965-6
Record League Goalscorer in a career: George Beel, 178, 1923-4 **All competitions:** George Beel, 187 (League 178, F.A. Cup 9)
Record Transfer Fee Received: £300,000 from Everton for Martin Dobson, Aug 1974
£300,000 from Derby County for Leighton James, Nov 1975
Record Transfer Fee Paid: £165,000 to Queen's Park Rangers for Leighton James, Sept 78
Best Performances: League: Champions (2) **F.A. Cup:** Winners **League/Milk Cup:** Semi-Finalist 1960-1, 1968-9
European Cup: Quarter Final **European Fairs Cup:** Quarter Final
Most League Points: (3pts for win) 80, Div 3, 1981-2 (2pts for win) 62, Div 2, 1972-3
Most League Goals: 102, Div 1, 1960-1
Record League Victory: 9-0 v Darwen, Div 1, 9 Jan 1892
Record League Defeat: 0-10 v Aston Villa, Div 1, 29 Aug 25 0-10 v Sheffield United, Div 1, 19 Jan 57
European Competitions Entered: European Cup 1960-1 European Fairs Cup 1966-7

Club Statistician for the Directory: W G Chadwick

Programme Editor
W. Dore

Price	Number of Pages
50p	24

Subscriptions
No subscriptions

BURNLEY

PLAYERS NAME Ht Wt Birthdate	Honours	Birthplace Transfers	Clubs	APPEARANCES League	Milk Cup	F.A.C.	A.M.C.	GOALS League	Milk Cup	F.A.C.	A.M.C.
GOALKEEPERS											
Roger Hansbury		Barnsley	Norwich C.	78	4						
5-11 12.0 26.1.55			Cambridge U. (L)	11							
		Hong Kong	Burnley	46	2	5	4				
John Turner		Peterlee	Reading'	31	5						
6-0 12.8 23.12.54		£3,000	Torquay U.	76	6	6					
		£30,000	Chesterfield	132	8	9					
		F	Torquay U.	34	4	i	1				
		Weymouth	Burnley								
DEFENDERS											
Joe Gallagher	E. B	Liverpool	Birmingham C. (A)	281+5	16	21		17	4	3	
6-1 12.0 11.1.55		£350,000	Wolverhampton W.	31	2	1					
		F	West Ham U.	8+1	1	1					
		£25,000	Burnley	1	1						
			Halifax T. (L)	4							
Peter Hampton	E. Y	Oldham	Leeds U. (A)	63+5	5+1	5	3+1E	2			
5-7½ 10.9 12.9.54		£165,000	Stoke C.	144+4	11	7		4			
		F	Burnley								
Kevin Hird		Colne	Blackburn R. (A)	129+3	7+1	8		20	1		
5-7 10.6 11.2.55		£357,000	Leeds U.	165+16	7+1	9+2	3E	19		2	
Vince Overson	E. Y. Div. 3. 82	Kettering	Burnley (A)	137+4	3	16	4	5			
6-0 13.0 15.5.62											
Mickey Phelan†	E. Y. Div. 3. 82	Nelson	Burnley (A)	123+2	12	13	4	6	2		
5-10½ 11.11 24.9.62											
Barry Powell	E. U 23(4).	Kenilworth	Wolverhampton W. (A)	58+6				7			
5-8 11.0 29.1.54	FC. 74		Coventry C.	162+2				28			
			Derby C.	52				5			
		Hong Kong	Burnley								
MIDFIELD											
Brian Flynn	W.(66). U.23(2)	Port Talbot	Burnley (A)	115+5	11+	5		8	2		1
5-4 12.3 12.10.55		£175,000	Leeds U.	152+2	12	6+1	4E	11			
		£60,000	Burnley	71	6	12	4	10	2		1
Tommy Hutchinson*	S.(17). U.23(1)	Alloa	Alloa A.	68				4			
5-11½ 11.2 22.9.47			Blackpool	163+2	17	6		10	2	1	
			Coventry C.	312+2	18	23		24	2	4	
		£45,000	Manchester C.	46	3+1	10		4		1	
		Hong Kong	Burnley	46	2	5		4			
Steve Kennedy		Audenshaw	Burnley (A)	7	1		1				
6-0¼ 11.11 22.7.65											
Phil Malley		Felling	Sunderland (A)								
5-7½ 11.2 1.11.65		F	Hartlepool U.	0+1							
		F	Burnley	1+1							
David Miller		Burnley	Burnley (A)	15+3			2+1	2			
5-10½ 10.3 8.1.64			Crewe A. (L)	3							
FORWARDS											
Wayne Biggins		Sheffield	Lincoln C.	8				1			
5-10½ 12.0 20.11.61			Matlock T.								
			Burnley	20			4	8			3
Peter Devine		Chorley	Chorley								
5-7½ 12.0 25.5.60			Bristol C.	19+2	1+1	5		1			
		Vancouver W.	Blackburn R.	8				2			
Neil Grewcock			Shepshed Charterhouse								
5-5¾ 11.11¼			Burnley								
Andy Kilner	E. Y		Burnley (A)								
5-11 12.0											
Kevin Reeves	E.(2). B(3).	Burley	Bournemouth (A)	6+3	2	4		20			
5-9 11.4 20.10.57	U.21(10). Y	£50,000	Norwich C.	118+1	9	5		37	5		
		£1,250,000	Manchester C.	129+1	15	13		34	1	4	
		£100,000	Burnley	20+1	2	5		12			
Alan Taylor		Hinckley	Morecambe								
5-9¼ 10.12½ 14.11.53			Rochdale	55	3	3		7	1	1	
			West Ham U.	88	8	7	6+1E	25	2	6	3
			Norwich C.	20				5			
		America	Cambridge U.	8	2			2			
			Hull C.	13+1				3			
			Burnley								
Neil Whatmore		Ellesmere Port	Bolton W. (A)	262+15	22+1	20		102	7	6	
5-9½ 11.8 17.5.55		£340,000	Birmingham C.	24+2							
			Bolton W. (L)	10							
		£25,000	Oxford U.	33+3	3+1	2+2	1	15	1		
			Bolton W. (L)	7							

APPRENTICES: Carl Coloran, Darren Heesom

'Previously Derby Co. (A). Doncaster R. (L) (4 Lg). Huddersfield T. (L) (1 Lg)

BURNLEY

DIVISION THREE 12TH **FA CUP** 3RD ROUND **MILK CUP** 1ST ROUND

MATCH	DATE	COMPE-TITION	VENUE	OPPONENTS	RESULT	HALF TIME	L'GUE POS'N	GOALSCORERS	ATTEN-DANCE
1	A 27	CL	A	Hull C	L1-4	1-2		Reeves	9,764
2	**30**	**MC 1**	**A**	**Crewe Alex**	**L0-1**	**0-0**			**2,043**
3	S 3	CL	H	AFC Bournemouth	W5-1	4-1	11	Dobson, Reeves (pen), Hamilton 3	5,512
4	6	CL	H	Newport Co	W2-0	0-0		Reeves (pen), Hamilton	6,719
5	10	CL	A	Oxford U	D2-2	0-0	9	Hamilton, Flynn	5,637
6	**13**	**MC 1**	**H**	**Crewe Alex**	**L3-4**	**1-4**		**Flynn 2 (1 pen), Wharton**	**5,653**
7	24	CL	A	Brentford	D0-0	0-0	13		8,042
8	27	CL	A	Bolton W	D0-0	0-0			9,709
9	O 1	CL	H	Plymouth Arg	D2-1	0-1	8	Hamilton, Scott	6,766
10	9	CL	A	Millwall	L0-2	0-1			6,709
11	15	CL	H	Gillingham	L2-3	0-0	15	Dobson, Hamilton	5,462
12	18	CL	H	Southend U	W3-0	1-0		Hamilton, Miller, Reeves	5,301
13	22	CL	A	Lincoln C	L1-3	1-1	15	Hamilton	3,793
14	29	CL	H	Wigan Ath	W3-0	2-0	13	Flynn, Hutchinson, Reeves	7,410
15	N 2	CL	A	Exeter C	D1-1	1-1		Flynn	3,714
16	5	CL	H	Preston NE	W2-1	2-0	11	Reeves, Hamilton	7,915
17	8	CL	H	Sheffield U	W2-1	1-0		Dobson, Donachie	9,551
18	12	CL	A	Bristol R	L1-2	1-2	10	Reeves	7,021
19	**19**	**FAC 1**	**A**	**Hyde U**	**W2-0**	**1-0**		**Waldron, Reeves (pen)**	**7,723**
20	26	CL	H	Port Vale	W7-0	6-0	6	Hamilton, Reeves 3, Hutchinson, Flynn, Donachie	6,358
21	D 3	CL	A	Rotherham U	D1-1	1-1	10	Flynn	5,544
22	**10**	**FAC 2**	**A**	**Chesterfield**	**D2-2**	**2-1**		**Dobson, Reeves**	**5,788**
23	17	CL	A	Wimbledon	W4-1	2-1	7	Reeves, Hamilton, Scott 2	2,883
24	**19**	**FAC 2R**	**H**	**Chesterfield**	**W3-2**	**2-1**		**Reeves, Hamilton 2**	**8,286**
25	26	CL	H	Bradford C	L1-2	1-0	10	Jackson (og)	12,136
26	27	CL	A	Walsall	D1-1	0-0	10	Hamilton	8,131
27	31	CL	H	Scunthorpe U	W5-0	3-0	8	Flynn, Hutchinson, Dobson, Reeves, Tueart	7,632
28	J 2	CL	A	Orient	W2-1	1-1	6	Flynn, Hamilton	4,470
29	**7**	**FAC 3**	**H**	**Oxford U**	**D0-0**	**0-0**			**11,672**
30	**11**	**FAC 3R**	**A**	**Oxford U**	**L1-2**	**0-1**		**Hamilton**	**10,497**
31	21	CL	A	Sheffield U	D0-0	0-0	7		13,892
32	F 4	CL	A	Plymouth Arg	D1-1	0-0	8	Tueart	5,104
33	11	CL	H	Brentford	D2-2	2-0	8	Hamilton, Tueart	6,994
34	14	CL	H	Exeter C	W4-0	1-0		Tueart (pen), Flynn, Phelan, Biggins	5,951
35	18	CL	A	Wigan Ath	L0-1	0-1	8		7,509
36	**21**	**AMC 1**	**H**	**Bolton W**	**W2-1**	**1-0**		**Donachie, Biggins**	**3,355**
37	25	CL	H	Lincoln C	W4-0	2-0	8	Biggins 3, Flynn	6,584
38	M 2	CL	A	Southend U	D2-2	1-1		Hutchinson, Hamilton	2,567
39	6	CL	A	Preston NE	L2-4	1-1		Donachie, Tueart	8,745
40	10	CL	H	Bristol R	D0-0	0-0	9		6,296
41	**13**	**AMC 3**	**H**	**Darlington**	**W2-1**	**0-1**		**Biggins, Baker**	**1,978**
42	17	CL	H	Millwall	W1-0	1-0	8	Biggins	5,061
43	**20**	**AMC NQF**	**A**	**Doncaster R**	**W3-1**[1]	**1-1**		**Flynn, Daley, Biggins**	**3,504**
44	24	CL	A	Gillingham	W1-0	0-0	8	Biggins	4,319
45	27	CL	H	Oxford U	D1-1	1-0		Daley (pen)	7,993
46	31	CL	H	Bolton W	D2-2	1-1	7	Hamilton, Miller	8,359
47	A 7	CL	A	Newport Co	L0-1	0-0	7		2,306
48	9	CL	A	AFC Bournemouth	L0-1	0-1			4,113
49	14	CL	H	Rotherham U	D2-2	1-2	7	Biggins, Scott	4,591
50	**17**	**AMC NSF**	**A**	**Tranmere R**	**L0-2**[1]	**0-0**			**3,968**
51	21	CL	A	Bradford C	L1-2	1-1	11	Biggins	5,578
52	23	CL	H	Walsall	L0-2	0-1	11		3,953
53	28	CL	A	Port Vale	W3-2	1-1	8	Daley 3	3,061
54	M 5	CL	H	Orient	L2-3	2-1	11	Hamilton, Phelan	3,256
55	7	CL	A	Scunthorpe U	L0-4	0-2	12		2,620
56	12	CL	H	Wimbledon	L0-2	0-2	12		3,340
57	15	CL	H	Hull C	L0-2	0-1			8,045

[1]After Extra Time **Av Home Att 6,573**

Goal Scorers

League (76): Hamilton 18, Reeves 12 (3 pens), Flynn 9, Biggins 8, Tueart 5 (1 pen), Daley 4 (1 pen), Dobson 4, Hutchinson 4, Scott 4, Donachie 3, Miller 2, Phelan 2, opponents 1
FA Cup (8): Hamilton 3, Reeves 3 (1 pen), Dobson 1, Waldron 1
Milk Cup (3): Flynn 2, Wharton 1
AMC (7): Biggins 3, Baker 1, Daley 1, Donachie 1, Flynn 1

1983-84

Hansbury	Dixon	Donachie	Phelan	Gallagher	Flynn	Scott	Reeves	Hamilton	Young	Hutchison	Wharton	Overson	Dobson	Gow	Donovan	Miller	Waldron	Daley	Tueart	Kennedy	Biggins	Baker (L)	Glendon	Malley	REFEREE	
1	2	3	4	5	6	7	8	9	10	11															K Hackett	1
1	**2***	**12**	**4**		**6**	**7**	**8**	**9**		**11**	**3**	**5**	**10**												**F Roberts**	**2**
1			4		6	2	8	9		11	3*	5	7	10	12										D Owen	3
1		2	4		6		8	9		11	3	5	7	10											J Lovatt	4
1		2	4		6	12	8	9		11	3*	5	7	10											H Taylor	5
1		**2**	**4**	**5**	**6**	**7**	**8***	**9**		**11**	**3**			**10**						**12**					**K Redfern**	**6**
1			4		6	2		9	11*	7	3	5	8	10		12									HW King	7
1			4		6	2		9		11	3	5	7	8			10								D Allison	8
1			4		6	2	12	9		11	3	5	7	8			10*								JD Hough	9
1			4		6	2	8	9		7	3		11	10			5								K Barratt	10
1		3	4		6	12	8	9		7		5*	11	10			2								C Seel	11
1		3	4		6		8	9		7		5	11			10	2								TJ Holbrook	12
1		3	4		6	2	8	9		7		5	11	12		10*									A Buksh	13
1		3	4		6	2	8	9		7		5	11			10									A Saunders	14
1		3	4		6	2	8	9		7		5				10	11								E Read	15
1		3	4		6	2	8	9		7		5	11				10								P Willis	16
1		3	4		6	2	8	9		11		5	10				7								RF Nixon	17
1		3	4		6	2	8	9		7		5	11*				10	12							T Ward	18
1		**3**	**4**		**6**	**2**	**8**	**9**		**7**		**5**	**11**				**10**								**K Walmsley**	**19**
1		3	4		6	2	8	9		7		5	11				10*	12							D Hutchinson	20
1		3	4		6	2	8	9		7		5					11	10							T Jones	21
1		**3**	**4**		**6**	**2**	**8**	**9**		**7**		**5**	**11**					**10**							**F Roberts**	**22**
1		3	4			2	8	9		7		5	11				6	10							J Ashworth	23
1		**3**	**4**		**6**	**2**	**8**	**9**		**7**		**5**					**11**	**10**							**D Hutchinson**	**24**
1		3	4		6	2	8	9		7		5					11	10							P Tyldesley	25
1		3	4		6	2	8	9		7		5	11					10							R Bridges	26
1		3	4		6	2	8	9		7		5	11				10		12						M Peck	27
1			3		6		8	9		7		4	5				2	10	11						D Letts	28
1		**3**	**4***		**6**	**2**	**8**	**9**		**7**		**5**	**11**					**12**	**10**						**P Willis**	**29**
1		**3**			**6**	**2**	**8***	**9**		**7**		**5**	**11**				**4**	**12**	**10**						**J Deakin**	**30**
1		3			6	2		9		7		5	11					8	10	4					G Napthine	31
1		3	4		6	2		9		11		5	8					10	7						C Downey	32
1		3	4		6	2		9		7		5	8						11		10				M Scott	33
1		3	4		6	2		9		7		5	8						11		10				M Heath	34
1		5	3		6*	2		10		9		4	8				7	12			11				K Redfern	35
1		**3**	**4**		**6**	**9**				**11**		**5**	**2**			**7**		**8**			**10**				**D Owen**	**36**
1		3	4		6	8		9		11			5					7			10	2			N Ashley	37
1		3	4		6*	8		9		11			5			12		7			10	2			R Lewis	38
1		3	4			8		9		11			5					6	7		10	2			A Saunders	39
1		5	3		6	8		10		9			4					7			11	2			D Shaw	40
1		**3**	**4**		**6***	**8**		**9**		**11**		**5**				**12**		**7***	**13**		**10**	**2**			**J Worrall**	**41**
1		5	4		6	8*		11		9		3				7			12		10	2			J Key	42
1		**3**	**4**		**6**			**9**		**11**		**5**				**8***		**7**	**12**		**10**	**2**			**T Holbrook**	**43**
1		3	4		6*			9		11		5				8		7	12		10	2			J Bray	44
1		3	4		6			9		11		5				8*		7	12		10	2			A Challinor	45
1		3	4		6			9		11		5				8		7*	12		10	2			A Seville	46
1		3	4		6*	8		9		11		5							12		10	2	7		V Callow	47
1		3				8		9		11		5				6			7	4	10	2			A Crickmore	48
1		3	4		6	8		9		11		5						7		2	10				J Lovatt	49
1		**3**	**4**		**6**	**8**		**9**		**11**		**5**						**7**		**2**	**10**				**J Hough**	**50**
1		3*	4		6	2		9		11		5				8			12	7	10				B Hill	51
1		3	4		6*	8		9		11						5			7	2	10			12	P Willis	52
1			4		6	8		9		11						5		7		2	10		3		B Stevens	53
1			4		6	2		9		11		5				8		7		10			3		R Nixon	54
1			4		6	2		9		11		5				8		7			10		3		L Robinson	55
1		3	4		6	2		9		11		5				8		7			10				T Mills	56
1		3	4		6	2		9		11		5						7			10			8	K Baker	57
46	1	37	44	1	43	38	20	**46**	2	**46**	7	38	28	8	0	15	16	20	8	7	20	10	4	1	League Appearances	
						+2S	+1S							+1S	+1S	+2S		+3S	+7S					+1S		
5		5	4		5	5	5	5		5		5	4				3	2+2S	2						FA Cup Appearances	
2	1	1+1S	2	1	2	2	2	2		2	2	1	1	1						1S					Milk Cup Appearances	
4		4	4		4	3		3		4		4	1			2+1S		4	2S	1	4	2			AM Cup Appearances	

TURF MOOR

Official Address: Turf Moor, Burnley BB10 4BX. Telephone: Burnley (0282) 27777/38021

Ground Capacity: 23,000

Record Attendance: 54,775 v. Huddersfield Town, F.A. Cup Round 3, 23 Feb 1924

Size of Playing Area: 115yds × 73 yds

Season Tickets: Bob Lord Stand £74 (£40 juveniles/OAP); Burnley Building Society Stand £50 (£32 juveniles/OAP); Ground: £37 (£20 juveniles/OAP)

Cost of Stand Tickets: £4.00, £3.00; **Terraces:** £2.50

Match and Ticket Information: As for Club

Car Parking: Parks in Church Street and Fulledge Recreation Ground for approx 500 vehicles each (chargeable). Both are 5 minutes walk from ground

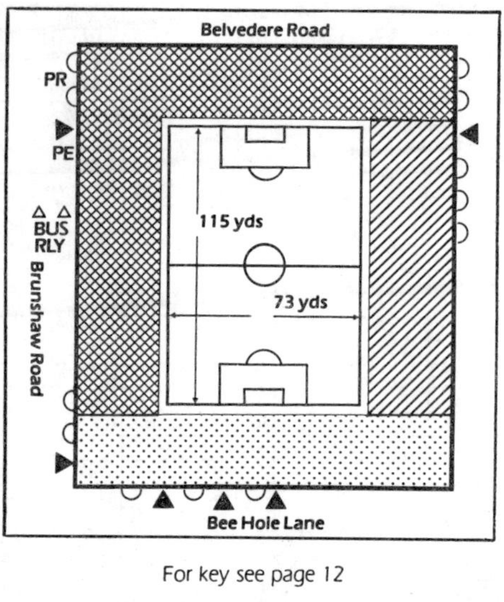

For key see page 12

How to get to the ground

From North: Follow signs Burnley A56 into Town Centre, then at roundabout take 1st exit into Yorkshire Street, shortly over crossroads into Brunshaw Road for Burnley F.C.
From East: Follow signs Burnley A646 then join A671 enter city centre by Todmorden Road and at end at crossroads turn right into Brunshaw Road for Burnley F.C.
From South: (or use route from west). Use M62, M66 and A56 signposted Burnley into town centre, then at roundabout take 3rd exit into Yorkshire Street, shortly at crossroads forward into Brunshaw Road for Burnley F.C.
From West and South: Use M6 to junction 31, then Blackburn bypass and A679 into Burnley town centre and at roundabout take 3rd exit into Yorkshire Street, shortly over crossroads into Brunshaw Road for Burnley F.C.

BURY

Division 4

Chairman
T Robinson

Vice-Chairman
Canon J R Smith, M.A.

Directors
A Jacks
A Metcalfe
Mrs A Allen
J Smith
I Pickup

Secretary
J Heap

Player/Manager
Martin Dobson

Club Coach
W McGuinness

Physiotherapist
J Cunningham

Commercial Manager
G Harrison (061 764 7475)

Unlike the previous season Bury never threatened to escape from the lowest of the Canon League divisions and there was little to recall with any satisfaction. Early good form promised better but it was not maintained and a final position in the lower half of the table was the result, although a re-election spot was comfortably avoided. The local supporters expected better as did the directors and this led to another managerial casualty; Jim Iley departed and was replaced by Martin Dobson.

When League results are modest it is nice to be able to show some consolatory news from Cup competitions, but even this was denied to 'The Shakers'. Instead, there was a match which all Bury fans would like to forget. The Milk Cup in fact started well with both legs of the first round tie with Wigan being won, but the next experience was tragic as West Ham were the opposition and after a close match at Gigg Lane they scored five goals in each half at Upton Park for a most humiliating aggregate of twelve goals to one against a club which holds the record for a victory in the F.A. Cup Final. How times can change. Last season's F.A. Cup started with a good away win at Boston, who are always a danger to League clubs in cup games, but Bury's name did not appear in the Third Round draw as Scunthorpe scored two goals without reply at the Old Show Ground, which left a bleak New Year to face.

Martin Dobson has problems, which could be eased if Craig Madden could recover his goal-scoring form of recent seasons, although he never let the side down. Others who could help to bring back former glories could be Jacub, Bramhall and Pashley and there are also some promising young players who might, with experience, do the trick. But no-one should expect too much and it would be a brave person who would forecast promotion for Bury in 1985.

WLM

Back: Frank Casper, Wilf McGuinness, Leighton James, Andy Hill, Wayne Entwistle, David Brown, Marcus Phelan, John Bramhall, Chris Cutler, Terry Pashley, Martin Dobson, Ray Pointer. **Middle:** Heath Reynolds, Trevor Ross, Gary Buckley, Joe Jakub, Winston White, Craig Madden, John Uttley, Kevin Young. **Front:** Tony Conlon, David Lee, Callum O'Shea, Alex Nair, Andy Wood, Joey Rose.

'THE SHAKERS'

Formed: 1885 **Turned Professional:** 1885 **Ltd Co:** 1897
Previous Managers: Since 1946
Norman Bullock John McNeil Dave Russell Bob Stokoe Bert Head Les Shannon Jack Marshall Les Hart Colin McDonald Tommy McAnearney Allan Brown Bobby Smith Bob Stokoe Dave Hatton Dave Connor Jim Iley
Honours: Division Two Champions 1894-5 Division Three Champions 1960-1
F.A. Cup Winners 1900, 1903
League Career: Elected to Division 2 1894 Promoted to Division 1 1894-5
Relegated to Division 2 1911-2 Promoted to Division 1 1923-4
Relegated to Division 2 1928-9 Relegated to Division 3 1956-7
Promoted to Division 2 1960-1 Relegated to Division 3 1966-7
Promoted to Division 2 1967-8 Relegated to Division 3 1968-9
Relegated to Division 4 1970-1 Promoted to Division 3 1973-4
Relegated to Division 4 1979-80
Colours: White shirts, royal blue shorts, blue stockings
Change Colours: All yellow

CLUB RECORDS

Most Appearances for Club: Norman Bullock, 1920-35 (League 506 + F.A. Cup 33) **Total 539**
Most Capped Player: Bill Gorman, 11, Northern Ireland and Eire
Record Goalscorer in a Match: Ray Pointer, 5 v Rotherham United, Div 2, 02.10.65
Eddie Quigley, 5 v Millwall (H), Div 2 (5-2), 15.02.47
Record League Goalscorer in a season: Craig Madden, 35, Div 4, 1981-2 **In all competitions:** 42 (League 35, F.A. Cup 4, League Cup 3)
Record League Goalscorer in a career: Norman Bullock, 124, Div 4, 1920-35 **In all competitions:** Wally Amos, (121 League, 9 F.A. Cup) 1921-35
Record Transfer Fee Received: £150,000 from Chesterfield for Danny Wilson, July 1980 £150,000 from Everton for Neville Southall, July 1981
Record Transfer Fee Paid: £30,000 to Port Vale for Ken Beamish, Sept 1978 £30,000 to Stoke City for David Gregory, Sept 1978
Best Performances: League: 4th Div 1 1925-6 **F.A. Cup:** Winners (2) **League/Milk Cup:** Semi-Final 1963
Most League Points: 81 in Div 4, 1982-3 **Most League Goals:** 108, Div 3, 1960-1
Record League Victory: 8-1 v Burnley, Div 1, 16 Sept 1925
Record League Defeat: 0-8 v Sheffield United, Div 1, 6 April 1896
0-8 v Swindon Town, Div 3, 8 Dec 1949

Club Statistician for the Directory: Paul Greenlees

Programme Editor
Peter Cullen

Price	Number of Pages
40p	16

Subscriptions
Apply to club for details

BURY

PLAYERS NAME Ht Wt Birthdate	Honours	Birthplace Transfers	Clubs	APPEARANCES League	Milk Cup	F.A.C.	A.M.C.	GOALS League	Milk Cup	F.A.C.	A.M.C.
GOALKEEPERS											
David Brown		Hartlepool	Horden CW								
6-1 12.8 28.1.57			Middlesbrough	10							
			Plymouth A. (L)	5							
		£40,000	Oxford U.	21	2						
		£5,000	Bury	100	5	6	2				
Marcus Phelan	E. Y		Burnley (A)								
6-1 12.7			Bury								
DEFENDERS											
John Bramhall		Warrington	Tranmere R.	164 + 6	16	8		7	1		
6-2 13.6 20.11.56		£10,000	Bury	100	5	3	2	12	1		
Terry Pashley	E. S	Chesterfield	Burnley (A)	16 + 2							
5-8 12.0 11.10.56			Blackpool	201	19	15	1	7	2	1	
			Bury	40							
John Uttley		Barnsley	Barnsley (N-C)								
5-7 10.12		F	Bury								
MIDFIELD											
Gary Buckley		Manchester	Manchester C. (A)	4 + 2	2						
5-6 10.6 3.3.61		£35,000	P.N.E.	27 + 8	2	1		2			
		F	Bury	8 + 1							
Martin Dobson	E.(5), Div. 2, 73	Blackburn	Bolton W.								
5-9 11.7 14.2.48	Div. 3, 82	F	Burnley	220 + 4	17	12		43	2	5	
		£300,000	Everton	190	22	13		29	8	2	
		£100,000	Burnley	186	17	19	1	20	2	1	
		F	Bury	10							
Yanek Jacub		Falkirk	Burnley (A)	42	2						
5-6 9.6 7.12.56		£19,000	Bury	169 + 2	7	12	2	17	2	1	
Heath Reynolds		Barnsley	Barnsley (N-C)								
5-7 10.10		F	Bury								
Trevor Ross	S. U.21(1)	Ashton-u-Lyne	Arsenal (A)	57 + 1	6	3		5	3	1	
5-9½ 11.10 16.1.57		£150,000	Everton	120 + 6	8	13		16	3	1	
			Portsmouth (L)	5							
			Sheffield U. (L)	4							
			AEK Athens								
			Sheffield U. (L)	4							
			Bury								
Winston White		Leicester	Leicester C. (A)	10 + 2				1			
5-8 11.2 26.10.58			Hereford U.	169 + 6				21			
			Stockport Co.[1]	4							
			Bury	29			2	1			1
Kevin Young	Div. 3, 82	Sunderland	Burnley (A)	114 + 6	10 + 7	17 + 1		11	1		
5-9 10.9 12.8.61			Port Vale (L)	28				4			
			Torquay U. (L)	4			2	1			
			Bury								
FORWARDS											
Chris Cutler		Manchester	Bury	7 + 12		0 + 1	2	2			
5-11 11.0 7.4.64											
Wayne Entwistle	E. Y	Bury	Bury (A)	25 + 6	4 + 2	0 + 2		7	2		
5-11 11.8 6.8.58		£30,000	Sunderland	43 + 2	1	4		12		1	
		£60,000	Leeds U.	7 + 4		0 + 1		2			
		F	Blackpool	27 + 5		2 + 1		6		2	
		F	Wimbledon	4 + 5		2		3		1	
		F	Bury	35 + 3	3	1	1 + 1	11	1	2	
Andy Hill		Ilkeston	Kimberley T.								
6-1 12.0 10.11.60			Carlisle U.	26	2	0 + 1		3			
			Derby Co. (L)	19 + 3	3	3		2	1	1	
			Bury								
Leighton James	W.(54), U.23(7)	Llwchwyr	Burnley (A)	180 + 1	14	10		44	6	1	
5-9½ 12.6 16.2.53		£140,000	Derby Co.	67 + 1	7	11		15	2	2	
		£180,000	Q.P.R.	27 + 1		5		4		2	
		£165,000	Burnley	76	3	5		9		1	
		£130,000	Swansea C.	88 + 10	6	1		27			
		F	Sunderland	50 + 2	4	1		4			
		F	Bury								
Craig Madden		Manchester	Northern Nomads								
5-8 10.2 25.9.58			Bury	198 + 19	12	10 + 1	2	93	6	7	

[1] After Hereford United, played for Hong Kong R, Chesterfield (1 sub, Lg), Port Vale (1 sub Lg)

BURY

DIVISION FOUR 15TH **FA CUP** 2ND ROUND **MILK CUP** 2ND ROUND

MATCH	DATE	COMPE-TITION	VENUE	OPPONENTS	RESULT	HALF TIME	L'GUE POS'N	GOALSCORERS	ATTEN-DANCE
1	A 27	CL	A	Tranmere R	D1-1	0-0		Madden	2,133
2	**30**	**MC 1**	**A**	**Wigan Ath**	**W2-1**	**1-1**		**Jakub, Bramhall**	**3,071**
3	S 3	CL	H	Bristol C	W2-1	2-1	7	Madden 2	2,015
4	6	CL	H	Blackpool	D0-0	0-0			2,993
5	10	CL	A	Aldershot	W2-1	1-1	4	Bramhall, Madden	1,908
6	**13**	**MC 1**	**H**	**Wigan Ath**	**W2-0**	**1-0**		**Entwistle, Madden**	**2,558**
7	18	CL	H	Halifax T	W3-0	2-0	3	Potts, Evans (og), Hilton	3,258
8	24	CL	A	Doncaster R	L1-3	0-2	5	Bramhal (pen)	2,777
9	27	CL	A	Darlington	W2-1	2-1		Jakub, Madden	1,654
10	**O 4**	**MC 2**	**H**	**West Ham U**	**L1-2**	**0-1**		**Madden**	**8,050**
11	8	CL	H	Mansfield T	D2-2	0-1	3	Hilton, Spence	2,468
12	18	CL	A	Colchester U	L0-1	1-0			1,969
13	22	CL	H	Wrexham	W2-0	1-0	8	Coleman (og), Hilton	2,320
14	**25**	**MC 2**	**A**	**West Ham U**	**L0-10**	**0-5**			**10,896**
15	29	CL	A	Hartlepool U	W3-1	2-0	5	Madden, Bramhall, Jakub	1,125
16	N 1	CL	H	Stockport Co	W2-1	1-0		Bramhall, Hilton	2,547
17	5	CL	A	Torquay U	L0-2	0-2	5		1,530
18	13	CL	H	Crewe Alex	D1-1	0-0		Madden	3,078
19	**19**	**FAC 1**	**A**	**Boston U**	**W3-0**	**2-0**		**Entwistle 2, Madden**	**2,624**
20	26	CL	H	Reading	L2-3	1-2	9	Entwistle, Hilton	2,220
21	29	CL	H	Peterborough U	D2-2	1-1		Entwistle, Jakub (pen)	2,013
22	D 3	CL	A	Chester C	L1-2	0-0	11	Madden	1,341
23	**10**	**FAC 2**	**A**	**Scunthorpe U**	**L0-2**	**0-2**			**3,246**
24	17	CL	A	Swindon T	D0-0	0-0	11		3,551
25	26	CL	H	Rochdale	W3-1	1-1	9	Jacub (pen), Entwistle, Park	4,096
26	27	CL	A	Chesterfield	W5-1	3-0	8	Entwistle 2, Jakub 2, Madden	4,916
27	31	CL	H	York C	L1-3	0-3	9	Madden	3,864
28	J 2	CL	A	Northampton T	L0-1	0-1	10		2,525
29	18	CL	A	Hereford U	W2-1	1-0		Entwistle, Madden	2,013
30	21	CL	A	Halifax T	D0-0	0-0	11		1,728
31	31	CL	A	Bristol C	L2-3	0-1		Hilton, Jakub	7,759
32	F 4	CL	A	Peterborough U	L1-2	0-1	12	Bramhall	2,507
33	7	CL	H	Tranmere R	D0-0	0-0			1,502
34	11	CL	H	Doncaster R	L2-3	0-2	15	Madden 2	2,400
35	13	CL	A	Stockport Co	D1-1	1-1		Entwistle	2,281
36	18	CL	H	Hartlepool U	W3-0	2-0	10	Cutler, Carrodus, Madden	1,565
37	**21**	**AMC 1**	**H**	**Wigan Ath**	**W1-0**	**1-0**		**White**	**1,613**
38	25	CL	A	Wrexham	L0-3	0-1	13		1,874
39	M 3	CL	H	Colchester U	D1-1	0-0	12	Madden	1,756
40	6	CL	H	Torquay U	D0-0	0-0			1,329
41	10	CL	A	Crewe Alex	L1-2	1-0	14	Cutler	2,405
42	**13**	**AMC 2**	**A**	**Hull C**	**L0-1**	**0-0**			**4,222**
43	17	CL	A	Mansfield T	D1-1	1-0	14	Madden	1,873
44	24	CL	H	Hereford U	L1-4	0-2	16	Entwistle	1,497
45	A 1	CL	H	Darlington	L0-3	0-1			1,255
46	7	CL	A	Blackpool	D1-1	0-1	17	Entwistle	4,513
47	14	CL	H	Chester C	W2-1	1-1	15	Bramhall, Jakub	1,414
48	21	CL	A	Rochdale	W2-0	0-0	16	White, Entwistle (pen)	2,027
49	23	CL	H	Chesterfield	W2-0	2-0	14	Entwistle, Jakub	1,616
50	28	CL	A	Reading	D1-1	1-1	15	Jakub	4,307
51	M 1	CL	H	Aldershot	L0-3	0-1			1,231
52	5	CL	H	Northampton T	L1-2	1-0	15	Jakub	1,096
53	7	CL	A	York C	L0-3	0-2	16		8,023
54	12	CL	H	Swindon T	W2-1	1-0	14	Madden, Potts	1,214

Av Home Att **2,111**

Goal Scorers

League (61): Madden 17, Entwistle 11 (1 pen), Jakub 11 (2 pens), Bramhall 6 (1 pen), Hilton 6, Cutler 2, Potts 2, Carrodus 1, Park 1, Spence 1, White 1, opponents 2
FA Cup (3): Entwistle 2, Madden 1
Milk Cup (5): Madden 2, Bramhall 1, Entwistle 1, Jakub 1
AMC (1): White 1

1983-84

Brown	Gardner	Pashley	Coleman	Hilton P	Bramhall	Potts	Madden	Entwistle	Jakub	Carrodus	Spence	Deacy	O'Keefe (L)	Mountford (L)	Park	Cutler	Butcher (L)	White	Buckley	Dobson	Hilton G	Jones	REFEREE	
1	2	3	4	5	6	7	8	9	10	11													A Seville	1
1	**2**	**3**	**4**	**5**	**6**	**7**	**8**	**9**	**10**	**11**													**J Lovatt**	**2**
1	2	5	7	3	4	9*	11	10	8	6	12												J Key	3
1	2	3	4	5	6	7	8	9*	10	11	12												R Bridges	4
1	2	3*	4	5	6	7	8	9	10	11	12												A Gunn	5
1	**2**	**3**		**5**	**6**	**7**	**8**	**9**	**10**	**11***	**4**	**12**											**M Dimblebee**	**6**
1	2	5	6	7	4	9	11	10	8			3											N Ashley	7
1	2	3	4*	5	6	7	8	9	10		12	11											J Bray	8
1	2	3		5	6	7	8		10	4	9	11											T Mills	9
1	**2**	**3***	**12**	**5**	**6**	**7**	**8**		**10**	**4**	**9**	**11**											**M Heath**	**10**
1	2	5*	12	7	4	9	10		8	6	11	3											F Roberts	11
1	3	3	12	5	6	7*	8		10	4	9	11											I Borrett	12
1	2	5	12	7	4	9	11*		8	6	10	3											A Saunders	13
1	**2**	**3**	**4**	**5**	**6**	**7**		**8**	**10**		**9**	**11**											**D Letts**	**14**
	2	3	7	5	6		8	11	10	4	9		1										M Scott	15
	2	3	7	5	6	12	8	11*	10	4	9		1										K Redfern	16
	2	3	7	4	5		11	10	8	6	9*	12		1									H King	17
	2	3	4	5	6	7	8		10	11	9			1									M Peck	18
	2	**3**	**4**	**5***	**6**	**7**	**8**	**9**	**10**			**11**		**1**	**12**								**M Scott**	**19**
	2	3	4	5	6	7	8	9*	10			11		1	12								D Shaw	20
	2	3	4		5	7	8	9	10	11		6		1									R Nixon	21
1	2	3	4*		5		8		10	11	9	6			12	7							V Callow	22
	2	**3**	**6**	**1**	**5**	**7***	**8**		**10**		**9**	**11**			**4**	**12**							**K Hackett**	**23**
	2	3			5		8	9	10	11		6			4		1	7					K Cooper	24
	2	5		7*	4		11	10	8	12		3			6		1	9					N Wilson	25
	2	3			5		8	9	10	11		6			4		1	7					D Brazier	26
	2	3			5		8	9	10	6		11			4		1	7					K Baker	27
	2	3	12		5		8	9*	10	11		6			4		1	7					E Read	28
	2	3		11	5		8	9	10			6			4		1	7					A Buksh	29
	2	3		5	6		8	9	10			11			4		1	7					G Tyson	30
	2	3		5	6		8	9*	10	12		11			4		1	7					Alan Robinson	31
	2	3	6		5		8	9*	10	11					4	12	1	7					M Robinson	32
	2	3			5		8	9	10	11*		6			4	12	1	7					C Seel	33
	2	5	7		3		10	11	8			4			6*	12	1	9					F Roberts	34
1	2	3	11		5		8	9	10	4		6						7					A Challinor	35
1		3	2		5	11*	8	12	10	4		6				9		7					J Hough	36
1	**12**	**3***	**2**		**5**		**8**	**9**	**10**	**4**		**6**				**11**		**7**					**K Walmsley**	**37**
1	2*		3		5		8	11	10	4		6			12	9		7					J Key	38
1	2		3		5		8		10	4		5			11	9		7					D Hutchinson	39
1	2		3		5		8	12	10	4		6			11*	9		7					M Heath	40
1	2		3		5		8		10	4*		6			11	9		7	12				H Taylor	41
1	**2**		**4**		**3**		**11**	**12**	**9**			**5***			**7**	**10**		**6***	**8**			**13**	**J Ashworth**	**42**
1	2		3		5		8	12	10			6			11	9*		7		4			K Barratt	43
1	2		3		5		8	9	10			6			11	12		7		4*			P Willis	44
1	2	3			5	4	8	9	10			6			11			7					K Hackett	45
1	2	3			5	4	8	9	10									7	11	6			D Allison	46
1	2	5			4	8*	11	10	7	12								9	6	3			K Redfern	47
1	2	3			5		8	9	10	4								7	11	6			D Shaw	48
1	2	3			5		8	9	10	4								7	11	6			N Ashley	49
1	2	3			5		8	9	10	4								7	11	6			M Dimblebee	50
	2	3			5		8	9	10	4						12		7	11*	6	1		D Owen	51
1		3	2			4	8	9	10			5			11			7		6			T Mills	52
1	2	3	12		5		8	9	10	4		6						7	11				J Hunting	53
1	2	3			5	4	8	9	10									7	11	6			J Lovatt	54
28	44	40	24	19	45	19	**46**	35	**46**	31	9	30	2	4	18	7	11	29	8	10	1		League Appearances	
			+5S			+1S		+3S		+3S	+4S	+1S			+3S	+5S			+1S					
	2	2	2	2	2	2	2	1	2		1	2		1	1+1S	1S							FA Cup Appearances	
4	4	4	2+1S	4	4	4	3	3	4	3	3	2+1S											Milk Cup Appearances	
2	1+1S	1	2		2		2	1+1S	2	1		2			1	2		2	1			1S	AM Cup Appearances	

GIGG LANE

Official Address: Gigg Lane, Bury BL9 9HR, Greater Manchester. Telephone: 061-764 4881/2.

Ground Capacity: 22,500

Record Attendance: 35,000 v. Bolton Wanderers, F.A. Cup Round 3, 9 Jan 1960

Record Receipts: £22,000 v. Nottingham Forest, League Cup Quarter-Final, 17 Jan 1978

Size of Playing Area: 112yds × 72 yds

Season Tickets: Reserved Chairs £57, Ground £38 (£28 juveniles/OAP)

Executive Box Season Tickets: £135 per season

Cost of Stand Tickets: £3.50, £3.00; **Terraces:** £2.00 (£1.50 juveniles/OAP)

Match and Ticket Information: 500 seats in reserved chair section bookable two weeks before each match.

Car Parking: available for use of season ticket holders only. Ample side-street parking is available.

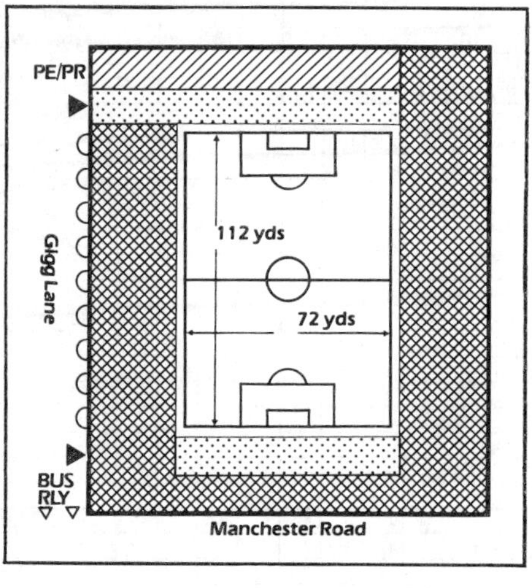

For key see page 12

How to get to the ground

From North: Use Motorway M66 until junction 2, then leave motorway and follow signs Bury A58. In 0.5m turn left into Heywood Street and at end forward into Parkhills Road. At end turn left A56 into Manchester Road, then shortly turn left into Gigg Lane for Bury F.C.

From East, South and West: Use Motorway M62 until junction 17. Leave Motorway and follow signs Bury A56. In 3.1m turn right into Gigg Lane for Bury F.C.

CAMBRIDGE UNITED Division 3

President
AE Harris

Chairman
DA Ruston

Directors
CR Brett (Vice Chairman)
JEK Barnes
NH Benton
AR Douglas
JE Cooke

Secretary
PM Daw

Manager
John Ryan

Assistant Manager/Coach
John Cozens

Youth Team Coach
Malcolm Webster

Commercial Manager
J Carter (0223 241237)

Physiotherapist
P Melville

Groundsman
I Darler

Last season started with hope but then sadly turned sour and ended with Cambridge United relegated to Division Three after six seasons in Division Two.

Two promising wins and two draws in the first seven games were followed by nine games without a victory — seven in the League and two in the Milk Cup — and it was to be nearly seven months before they won another match.

The depressing facts of that run were that the team played 34 games and drew ten, losing the remaining 24, and they also broke a record previously held by Crewe Alexandra from the 1956/57 season, playing 31 league games without a win, and beating Crewe's record of 30 games. The run was eventually ended on April 28th when they beat promotion chasing Newcastle United 1-0 at the Abbey Stadium, thanks to a Kevin Smith penalty, and then to round the season off they won the final home game to leave the team with four wins and twelve draws from the 42 matches.

One consequence of the poor run was that the club parted company with manager John Docherty in December 1983. He had become manager in February 1978 and guided the club through the early years of Second Division football. For a short while after Docherty's departure John Cozens was caretaker manager before John Ryan took over as manager in January 1984.

The financial constraints of the game also affected the club and during the season they parted with a number of senior players, including Chris Turner, Tom Finney and Bobby Fisher, and they were forced to rely heavily on youth in the form of players such as Andy Sinton, Kevin Smith, Andy Beattie, Keith Lockhart and Dean Greygoose who took over as goalkeeper from long serving Malcolm Webster. Indeed for the game against Cardiff City on March 10 ten players were aged twenty-one or under and the average age of the side was twenty years and five months. The youth side performed well in their first season in the senior section of the South Eastern Counties League, and in the F.A. Youth Cup they beat holders Norwich City and progressed to the fourth round for the first time before losing to Arsenal.

All in all it was a disappointing season but the youth team and the younger players provide hope for next year and a quick return to the Second Division.

Colin Faiers, The League Directory's Statistician for the Club

Back Row L to R: Kevin Smith, Graham Daniels, Keith Lockhart, Mark Cooper, Dean Greygoose, Andy Beattie, Keith Branagan, David Moyes, Steve Fallon, Steve Clark, Robbie Cooke. **Front Row:** Peter Melville (Physiotherapist), Andy Sinton, Steve Pyle, Michael Bennett, John Ryan (Manager), Steve Spriggs, John Cozens (Assistant Manager), Kevin Massey, Les Cartwright, Malcolm Webster (Youth Coach).

'UNITED'

Sponsored by
Benskins

Formed: 1919 **Turned Professional:** 1946 **Ltd Co:** 1948
Previous Name: Until 1949 Abbey United
Previous Managers: From 1951: 1951-5 Bill Whittaker 1955 Gerald Williams 1955-9 Ben Johnson 1959 Bill Craig 1960-3 Alan Moore (was player-coach from 1959-60) 1963-4 Roy Kirk (Caretaker) 1964-6 Roy Kirk 1966-7 Math Wynn (Caretaker) 1967-74 Bill Leives 1974 Ray Freeman (Caretaker) 1974-8 Ron Atkinson 1978-83 John Docherty John Cozens (Caretaker)
Honours: Champions Division 4 1976-7
League Career: Elected to Division 4 1970 Promoted to Division 3 1972-3 Relegated to Division 4 1973-4 Promoted to Division 3 1976-7 Promoted to Division 2 1977-8 Relegated to Division 3 1983-4
Colours: Amber shirts with black trim, black shorts with amber stockings with black trim
Change Colours: All sky blue

CLUB RECORDS

Most Appearances for Club: Steve Fallon: Football League 366 + 5 subs F.A. Cup 15 + League/Milk Cup 19 **Total 400 + 5 subs**
Most Capped Player: Tom Finney, 7, N Ireland. **For England:** None
Record Goalscorer in a Match: Brian Greenhalgh, 4 v Darlington (6-0), Div 4, 18.09.71
Record League Goalscorer in a season: Alan Biley, 21, 1977-8 **In all competitions:** Alan Biley, 24 (League 21, F.A. Cup 2, Lg/Milk Cup 1) 1977-8
Record League Goalscorer in a career: Alan Biley, 74 **In all competitions:** Alan Biley, 81 (League 74, F.A. Cup 3, Lg/Milk Cup 4)
Record Transfer Fee Received: £350,000 from Derby County for Alan Biley, Jan 1980
Record Transfer Fee Paid: £140,000 to Northampton Town for George Riley, Nov 1979
Best Performances: League: 8th Div 2 1979-80 **F.A. Cup:** 5th Round 1982-3 **League/Milk Cup:** 4th Round, 1980-1
Most League Points: 65 in Div 4, 1976-7
Most League Goals in a season: 87, Div 4, 1976-7
Record League Victory: 6-0 v Darlington, Div 4, 18 Sept 1971
Record League Defeat: 0-6 v Bristol City, Div 3 South, 28 Apr 74 0-6 v Darlington, Div 4, 28 Sept 74 0-6 v Chelsea, Div 2, 15 Jan 83

Club Statistician for the Directory: Colin Faiers

Programme Editors
Paul Douglas & Colin Faiers

Price	Number of Pages
40p	16

Subscriptions
Please apply to club

CAMBRIDGE UNITED

PLAYERS NAME Ht Wt Birthdate	Honours	Birthplace Transfers	Clubs	APPEARANCES League	Milk Cup	F.A.C.	A.M.C.	GOALS League	Milk Cup	F.A.C.	A.M.C.
GOALKEEPERS											
Keith Branagan		Fulham	Cambridge U.	1							
6-0 11.10 10.7.66											
Dean Greygoose	E. Y	Torquay	Cambridge U.	16							
5-11 11.5 18.12.64											
DEFENDERS											
Steve Fallon*	Div. 4. 77	Whittlesey	Kettering T.								
6-1 12.7 3.8.56			Cambridge U.	366 + 5	19	15		25	2	1	
David Moyse	S. S. SPD. 82	Blythswood	Celtic	19 + 8	7 + 1		2 + 1				
6-1 11.5 25.4.63			Cambridge U.	30		1					
MIDFIELD											
Andy Beattie		Lincoln	Cambridge U. (A)	21							
6-2 11.6 9.2.64											
Les Cartwright	W. (7). U.23(4).	Aberdare	Coventry C.	50 + 18	8	7 + 4		3	2		
5-9 10.13 4.3.52	Div. 3. 78	£40,000	Wrexham	111 + 4	14	14		6	1		
		F	Cambridge U.	47 + 6		4		1		1	
			Southend U. (L)	2 + 2	1						
Steve Spriggs	Div. 4. 77	Doncaster	Huddersfield T. (A)	2 + 2	1						
5-3 10.2 16.2.56			Cambridge U.	319 + 5	20	12		46	2	1	
FORWARDS											
Steve Clark		Baldock	Cambridge U. (A)	16	0 + 1						
5-11 11.2 20.9.64											
Robbie Cooke		Rotherham	Mansfield T. (A)	7 + 8		1		1			
5-9 10.8 16.2.57		F	Grantham								
		£12,000	Peterborough U.	115	9	13		51	7	10	
		£13,000	Cambridge U.	46 + 3	2	1		8	2		
David Daniels	W. S	Farnborough	Cardiff Univ.								
5-10 11.5 9.4.62			Cambridge U.	20		1		2			
Keith Lockhart		Wallsend	Cambridge U. (A)	28 + 2	2	1		11			
6-0 11.0 19.7.64											
Kevin Massey		Gainsborough	Cambridge U. (A)	1							
5-6½ 9.5 30.11.65											
Andy Sinton†	E. S	Newcastle	Cambridge U. (A)	45 + 2	2	1		11			
5-7 10.7 19.3.66											
Kevin Smith		Wallsend	Cambridge U. (A)	28 + 8	1			4	1		
5-8 11.5 20.4.65											

APPRENTICES:
Richard Anton, Mark Chandler, Mark Cooper, David Massingham, Karl Rutherford, Jonathan Taylor

NON-CONTRACT PLAYERS 1984-85:
Russell Griggs, George Measures

CAMBRIDGE UNITED

DIVISION TWO 22ND **FA CUP** 3RD ROUND **MILK CUP** 2ND ROUND

MATCH	DATE	COMPETITION	VENUE	OPPONENTS	RESULT	HALF TIME	L'GUE POS'N	GOALSCORERS	ATTENDANCE
1	A 27	CL	A	Carlisle U	D0-0	0-0			3,738
2	S 3	CL	H	Blackburn R	W2-0	0-0	7	Sinton, Cooke	2,636
3	6	CL	A	Sheffield W	L0-1	0-1			14,947
4	10	CL	A	Chelsea	L1-2	1-1	15	Goldsmith	14,425
5	17	CL	H	Charlton Ath	D2-2	1-0	17	Christie, Cooke	3,526
6	24	CL	A	Swansea C	L1-2	0-1	16	Pyle	7,197
7	O 1	CL	H	Oldham Ath	W2-1	1-0	16	Sinton (pen), Spriggs	2,696
8	**4**	**MC 2**	**H**	**Sunderland**	**L2-3**	**0-1**		**Cooke, Goldsmith**	**4,835**
9	8	CL	H	Crystal Palace	L1-3	1-2	18	Cooke	4,323
10	14	CL	A	Leeds U	L1-3	0-1		Christie	9,923
11	18	CL	H	Huddersfield T	L0-3	0-2			3,513
12	**26**	**MC 2**	**A**	**Sunderland**	**L3-4**	**2-3**		**Fallon, Smith, Cooke**	**9,059**
13	29	CL	H	Brighton & HA	L3-4	1-3	20	Smith, Sinton (pen), Pyle	3,905
14	N 1	CL	A	Portsmouth	L0-5	0-2			10,852
15	5	CL	H	Derby Co	L0-1	0-1	21		3,638
16	12	CL	A	Cardiff C	L0-5	0-4	21		4,730
17	19	CL	H	Middlesbrough	D0-0	0-0	21		2,819
18	26	CL	A	Newcastle U	L1-2	0-1	21	Daniels	25,005
19	D 3	CL	H	Fulham	D1-1	1-1	21	Fallon	3,031
20	10	CL	A	Shrewsbury T	L0-1	0-0	21		2,457
21	17	CL	H	Manchester C	D0-0	0-0	21		5,204
22	26	CL	A	Barnsley	L0-2	0-0	21		7,486
23	28	CL	H	Grimsby T	D2-2	1-0		Cooke, Sinton (pen)	4,319
24	31	CL	A	Blackburn R	L0-1	0-0	22		5,675
25	J 2	CL	H	Swansea C	D1-1	0-1	22	Daniels	2,500
26	**7**	**FAC 3**	**H**	**Derby Co**	**L0-3**	**0-2**			**6,309**
27	14	CL	H	Carlisle U	L0-2	0-0	21		2,203
28	21	CL	A	Charlton Ath	L2-5	0-2	22	Christie, Cooke	5,252
29	F 4	CL	A	Oldham Ath	D0-0	0-0	22		3,646
30	11	CL	H	Chelsea	L0-1	0-1	22		10,602
31	25	CL	H	Portsmouth	L1-3	0-2	22	Sinton	4,359
32	28	CL	A	Brighton & HA	L0-3	0-2			8,167
33	M 3	CL	A	Derby Co	L0-1	0-0	22		12,007
34	10	CL	H	Cardiff C	L0-2	0-0	22		2,512
35	17	CL	H	Sheffield W	L1-2	0-1	22	Spriggs	5,562
36	24	CL	A	Huddersfield T	L0-3	0-2	22		6,037
37	A 1	CL	A	Crystal Palace	D1-1	1-1		Lockhart	5,276
38	7	CL	H	Leeds U	D2-2	0-0	22	Lockhart, Sinton (pen)	4,700
39	14	CL	A	Middlesbrough	D1-1	1-1	22	Lockhart	5,121
40	21	CL	H	Barnsley	L0-3	0-1	22		2,200
41	23	CL	A	Grimsby T	D0-0	0-0	22		5,828
42	28	CL	H	Newcastle U	W1-0	1-0	22	Smith (pen)	7,720
43	M 5	CL	A	Fulham	L0-1	0-0	22		4,914
44	7	CL	H	Shrewsbury T	W1-0	1-0	22	Cooke	2,208
45	12	CL	A	Manchester C	L0-5	0-3	22		20,787

Av Home Att **4,017**

Goal Scorers

League (28): Cooke 6, Sinton 6 (4 pens), Christie 3, Lockhart 3, Daniels 2, Pyle 2, Smith 2 (1 pen), Spriggs 2, Fallon 1, Goldsmith 1
FA Cup (-): —
Milk Cup (5): Cooke 2, Fallon 1, Goldsmith 1, Smith 1

1983-84

Webster	Fisher	Murray	Turner	Fallon	Pyle	Finney	Sinton	Cooke	Goldsmith	Christie	Spriggs	Smith	Donaldson	Cartwright	Greygoose	Bennett	Nicholls	Moyes	Daniels	Davies **(L)**	Horn **(L)**	Beattie	Lockhart	Clark	**REFEREE**	
1	2	3	4	5	7	6	8	9	10	11															N Wilson	1
1	2	3	4	5		6	8	9		11	7	10													M James	2
1	2	3	4	5	12	6	8	9	10*	11	7														N Glover	3
1	2	3	4	5		6	8	9	10	11	7														M Bodenham	4
1	2	3	4*	5	12	6	8	9	10	11	7														GJ Napthine	5
1	2	3		5	4	6	8	9	10	11	7														L Burden	6
1	2	3	4	5		6	8	9	10	11	7														A Gunn	7
1	**2**	**3**	**4**	**5**	**12**	**6***	**8**	**9**	**10**	**11**	**7**														**C Downey**	**8**
1	2	3	4	5	12	6	8	9	10	11	7*														JE Bray	9
1	2	3	4	5		6	8	9		11			7	10											NJ Ashley	10
1		3	4	5		6	8	9	10	11*		12	2												KG Salmon	11
1		**3**		**5**	**4**	**6**	**8***	**9**				**10**	**2**				**11**							**12**	**A Challinor**	**12**
1		3		5	4	6	8	9				10	2				11								H Taylor	13
1		3		5	7	6	12	9			8*	10	2				11	4							D Reeves	14
1		3		5	7	6	8	9*				10	2				12	4	11						AW Ward	15
1		3		5	8	6			9	7		10	2					4	11						Alan Robinson	16
	2	3		5		6			9		8	10						4	11		1	7			AN Buksh	17
	2	3		5		6			9		8	10						4	11		1	7			T Mills	18
	2	3		5		6			9		8	10						4	11		1	7			D Axcell	19
	2	3		5			12		10	7*	8							4	11		1	6	9		H King	20
	2	3		5				9	12		8	10*		6				4	11		1		7		R Lewis	21
1	2	3		5				9	12		8	10*		6				4	11				7		J Lovatt	22
	2	3		5		10	8*	9				12		6				4	11		1		7		D Letts	23
	2*	3		5		10		9		12		8		6				4	11		1		7		F Roberts	24
		3		5		8		9		12		10		6				4	11		1		7*	2	D Vickers	25
1	**2**	**3**		**5**		**8**	**10**	**9**		**12**				**6**				**4**	**11**				**7***		**M Dimblebee**	**26**
		3*		5	12	8	10	9		7			2	6				4				11			M Moules	27
1				5		8	10	9		7			2					4	11			3		6	V Callow	28
1				5			10	9		7	8		2	12				4	11*	6		3			K Hackett	29
				5			10	9		7	8		12	2*	1			4		6		3			J Ashworth	30
				5			4	9		7	8			11	1			2		3		6			B Hill	31
				5			4	9		8		12			1			2		3		6	11	7	A Crickmore	32
					2		4	9				12		7	1			5		3		6	11	8	S Wilson	33
					7		4	12			8	9			1	3		5				6	11	2	M Taylor	34
					7		4*	12			8	9			1	3		5				6	11	2	M Bodenham	35
					7		4	12			8	9			1	3		5				6	11	2	R Nixon	36
							4	11			8	12	2		1	3†			7			6†	10	5	K Barratt	37
							4	11					8		1	3		5	7			6	10	2	A Gunn	38
							4	10			12		7*		1	3		5	11			6	8	2	I Hendrick	39
					12		4	6			8		3		1			5	11				10	2	M James	40
				6	12		4	9*			8	10			1	3		5	11			7		2	M Scott	41
				6	12		4	9			8	10			1	3		5	11*			7		2	A Seville	42
					6		4	9		12	8	10			1	3		5	11*			7		2	T Holbrook	43
				6	12		4	9		11*	8	10			1	3		5				7		2	D Brazier	44
				7			4	9		11	8	10		6	1	3*		5						2	M Peck	45
17	17	24	9	33	11	22	32	34	13	20	27	20	13	11	16	11	2	30	20	5	8	21	15	16	League Appearances	
					+8S		+2S	+3S	+2S	+3S	+1S	+5S	+1S	+1S			+1S									
1	1	1		1		1	1	1		1S				1				1	1				1		FA Cup Appearances	
2	1	2	1	2	1+1S	2	2	2	1	1	1	1	1				1							1S	Milk Cup Appearances	

Also Played: Branagan match 27, no.1. Cooper match 40, no.7; 45, no.12. Evans match 11, no.7. Heward matches 12, 13, no.7. Mardenborough match 31, 35, no.10; 32, 33, 34, 36, no.10*. Massey match 30, no.11. Measures matches 37, 40, no.9*; 38, 39, no.9

ABBEY STADIUM

Official Address: Abbey Stadium, Newmarket Road, Cambridge. Telephone: Teversham (0233) 241237

Ground Capacity: 12,000

Record Attendance: 14,000 v. Chelsea (friendly), 1 May 1970

Record Receipts: £25,134 v. Chelsea, Second Division, 11 Feb 1984

Size of Playing Area: 110yds × 74 yds

Season Tickets: Seats: A,B,C £70; D,Y £60; F,G,H,T,U,W £50; V (OAP) £30; Terraces: £34 (juvenile/OAP £18)

Cost of Stand Tickets: A,B,C £4.50; D,Y £3.70; F,G,H,T,U,W £3.20; **Terraces:** £2.20 (juvenile/OAP £1.10)

Match and Ticket Information: Cambridge 241237 (Postal applications with payment & SAE two weeks in advance)

Car Parking: Limited parking at main entrance. Off-street parking permitted. Also at Coldhams Common

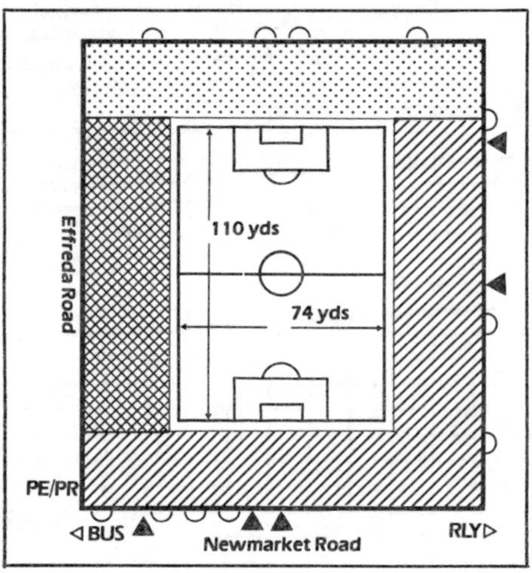

For key see page 12

How to get to the ground

From North: Use A1 and A604 S.P. Cambridge into City Centre, then follow signs Newmarket A45 into Newmarket Road for Cambridge United F.C.
From East: Follow signs Cambridge A45 into Newmarket Road for Cambridge United F.C.
From South: Use A10 or A130 into Cambridge, then follow signs Newmarket A45 into Newmarket Road for Cambridge United F.C.
From West: Follow signs Cambridge A422, into Cambridge via A45 then keep forward S.P. Newmarket into Newmarket Road for Cambridge United F.C.

CARDIFF CITY Division 2

Chairman
J P Leonard

Directors
J A Clemo, Dip PE (Vice-Chairman)
G Edwards, JP, MA

Managing Director/Secretary
R Jones

Commercial Manager
Mrs Susan Wynne (0222 398636/7/8)

Manager
Jimmy Goodfellow

Chief Scout
H Joy

Pysiotherapist
Jimmy Goodfellow

A final league position outside the crucial relegation spots was perhaps the best Cardiff could expect and this was achieved with nine points (or three wins) to spare over Derby County. In fact, with the limited resources at his disposal Len Ashurst did well to create that situation. The point was not missed by the directors of his former club, Sunderland, where he succeeded Alan Durban in March. The vacancy was filled at Ninian Park by Jimmy Goodfellow, who may have to work hard to keep Cardiff in the Second Division during the coming season.

In fact, the season was always a struggle and it was not relieved by any cup successes even in the domestic Welsh competition with its entry into Europe. Cardiff failed to reach that final and the Cup was won by the English club, Shrewsbury Town, leaving Wrexham, the other finalist, to gain a place in the Cup-Winners Cup. In the Milk Cup both legs of the First Round tie against Exeter City were won, but then Norwich followed a goalless match at Ninian Park with three clear goals at Carrow Road. It was another East Anglian team, Ipswich Town, which ended the F.A. Cup hopes in the Third Round at Ninian Park — again by three clear goals.

With such disappointing results it is not easy to give out too much praise but the veteran Dwyer continued to give his 'all' for the cause and was ably supported by a good young goalkeeper in Dibble, with good support from Bodin, Tong, Gibbins and, when fit, Vaughan, one of the few Welsh players in the club. It has been something of a tradition for Cardiff to be dominated by 'imports' and results might improve if a greater effort were made to find and exploit local talent. The contrary argument is that the Cup was won in 1927 at Wembley with a pre-dominance of 'foreigners' so which policy is correct? The fans really will not mind providing they give better results and First Division Football.

WLM

Back Row L to R: Karl Elsey, Roger Gibbons, Gary Plumley, Phil Dwyer, Lee Smelt, Colin Smith, Melvyn Rees, David Grant, Paul Bodin. **Front Row:** David Tong, Vaughan Jones, Jimmy Mullen, Nigel Vaughan, John Woods, Kevin Summerfield.

'THE BLUEBIRDS'

Sponsored by
Merthyr Motor Auctions

Formed: 1899 **Turned Professional:** 1910 **Ltd Co:** 1910
Previous Name: Riverside F.C. (1899-1910)
Previous Managers: 1910-1 Davy McDougall 1911-33 Fred Stewart 1933-4 Bartley Wilson 1934-7 B Watts Jones 1937-9 Bill Jennings 1939-46 Cyril Spiers 1946-8 Billy McCandless 1948-54 Cyril Spiers 1954-8 Trevor Morris 1958-62 Bill Jones 1962-4 George Swindon 1964-73 Jimmy Scoular 1973-4 Frank O'Farrell 1974-8 Jimmy Andrews 1978-81 Richie Morgan 1981-82 Graham Williams 1982-84 Len Ashurst 1984 Jimmy Goodfellow & Jimmy Mullen (caretakers)
Honours: Champions Division 3(S) 1946-7, F.A. Cup Winners 1926-7, Welsh F.A. Cup Winners (19)
League Career: Elected to Division 2 Promoted to Division 1 1920-1
Relegated to Division 2 1928-9 Relegated to Division 3(S) 1930-1 Promoted to Division 2 1946-7
Promoted to Division 1 1951-2 Relegated to Division 2 1956-7
Promoted to Division 1 1959-60 Relegated to Division 2 1961-2
Relegated to Division 3 1974-5 Promoted to Division 2 1975-6
Relegated to Division 3 1981-2 Promoted to Division 2 1982-3
Colours: Royal blue shirts and white shorts, white stockings
Change Colours: All yellow

CLUB RECORDS

Most Appearances for Club: Phil Dwyer: League 434 + 5s + F.A. Cup 22 + League/Milk Cup 24 + Welsh Cup 41 + Anglo-Scottish Cup 3 + European Cup Winners Cup 6 **Total 530 + 5 subs**
Most Capped Player: Alf Sherwood, 39 **For England:** None
Record Goalscorer in a Match: Derek Tapscott, 6 v Knighton Town (Welsh F.A. Cup) 28.01.61
Record League Goalscorer in a season: Stan Richards, 31, 1946-7 **All Competitions:** John Toshack, 31, 1968-9
Record League Goalscorer in a career: Len Davies, 127, 1921-9
Record Transfer Fee Received: £110,000 from Liverpool for John Toshack, Nov 1970
Record Transfer Fee Paid: £200,000 to San Jose Earthquakes for Godfrey Ingram, Sept 1982
Best Performances: League: Division One Runners-Up, 1923-4 **F.A. Cup:** Winners 1926-7 **League/Milk Cup:** Semi-Final 1965-66 **Welsh Cup:** Winners (19) **European Cup Winners Cup:** Semi-Final, 1967-8
Most League Points: 86 in Div 3, 1982-3
Record League Victory: 9-2 v Thames, Div 3(S), 6 Feb 1932
Record League Defeat: 2-11 v Sheffield United, Div 1, 1 Jan 1926
European Competitions Entered: European Cup Winners Cup 1964-5, 1965-6, 1967-8, 1968-9, 1969-70, 1970-1, 1971-2, 1973-4, 1974-5, 1976-7, 1977-8
Club Statistician for the Directory: Allan Jenkins

Programme Editor
B.A. Enos

Price
50p

Number of Pages
20

Subscriptions
£22.00 per season (postage included for U.K.) for home matches

CARDIFF CITY

PLAYERS NAME Ht Wt Birthdate	Honours	Birthplace Transfers	Clubs	APPEARANCES League	Milk Cup	F.A.C.	A.M.C.	GOALS League	Milk Cup	F.A.C.	A.M.C.
GOALKEEPER											
Gary Plumley		Birmingham	Leicester C. (A)								
6-0 12.0 24.3.56			Newport Co.	182	12	11					
			Hereford U.	13		1					
			Newport Co.	2							
			Cardiff C.	1							
DEFENDERS											
Paul Bodin	W. U.21(1)	Cardiff	Chelsea (N-C)								
5-10 10.11 13.9.64			Newport Co.								
			Cardiff C.	53+4	6	4		3			
Phil Dwyer	W.(10), U.23(5)	Cardiff	Cardiff C.	435+5	22	22	6	38	1		1
6-0 13.0 28.10.53	U.21(1),										
	W.Cup(3)										
Jim Mullen		Jarrow	Sheffield W. (A)	222+7	23	9+1		10			
5-10½ 11.12 8.11.52		£25,000	Rotherham U.	49	3	2		1			
			P.N.E. (L)	1							
		£10,000	Cardiff C.	59+4	5	32		2			
David Grant		Sheffield	Sheffield W.	132+1	11	4+2		4	1		
6-0 12.8 2.6.60		F	Oxford U.	24							
			Chesterfield (L)	7							
		F	Cardiff C.	12							
Vaughan Jones	W. U.21(2)	Tunirefail	Bristol R.	93+8	5+3	11		3			
5-6 10.8 5.3.61			Newport Co.	67+1	6	10	1	4			
Colin Smith		Ruddington	Nottingham F.								
6-0 12.0 3.11.58			Norwich C.	2+2	2						
			Cardiff C.	34				2			
MIDFIELD											
Karl Elsey		Swansea	Pembroke Boro								
5-10 11.6 20.11.58			Q.P.R.	6+1							
		F	Newport Co.	114+9	8+3	8	6	15	1		
		Player Exchange	Cardiff C.	29				1			
David Tong	Div. 3, 79	Blackpool	Blackpool (A)	70+8	5	1		7			
5-8 10.1 21.9.55		£25,000	Shrewsbury T.	156+4	8	16		8			
		F	Cardiff C.	85+1	6	4		2		1	
Nigel Vaughan	W.(8), U.21(2),	Newport	Newport Co. (A)	215+9	13+1	15+1	6	32	3		
5-5 8.10 20.5.59	Y, W.Cup(1)	Player Exchange	Cardiff C.	36				8			
FORWARDS											
Roger Gibbins	E. S, FAYC. 74	Enfield	Tottenham H. (A)								
5-11 11.11 6.9.55		F	Oxford U.	16+3				2			
		F	Norwich C.	47+1	1	2		12		1	
		£60,000	New England T.								
		F	Cambridge U.	97+3	7	2+1		12	3		
		F	Cardiff C.	88	6	4		12	3	1	
Kevin Summerfield	FAYC. 76, E. Y	Walsall	W.B.A. (A)	5+4	2	1+1		4		1	
6-0 10.7 7.1.59		F	Birmingham C.	2+3	1			1			
			Walsall	42+12	5+2	1		17	2		
			Cardiff C.								

NON-CONTRACT PLAYERS 1984-5:

Russell Heycock (1 MC), **Mel Rees, Chris Townsend** (2 + 3 SL, 1 + 1 SMC)

APPRENTICE:

Andy Battle

CARDIFF CITY

DIVISION TWO 15TH **FA CUP** 3RD ROUND **MILK CUP** 2ND ROUND

MATCH	DATE	COMPETITION	VENUE	OPPONENTS	RESULT	HALF TIME	L'GUE POS'N	GOALSCORERS	ATTENDANCE
1	A 27	CL	A	Charlton Ath	L0-2	0-2			4,525
2	29	CL	H	Manchester C	W2-1	1-0		Bodin 2	8,899
3	**31**	**MC 1**	**A**	**Exeter C**	**W3-2**	**0-0**		**Dwyer, Owen, Crawford**	**4,005**
4	S 3	CL	H	Grimsby T	W3-1	0-1	5	Owen 2 (1 pen), Crawford	5,135
5	6	CL	A	Shrewsbury T	L0-1	0-1			4,405
6	10	CL	A	Leeds U	L0-1	0-0	13		12,336
7	**12**	**MC 1**	**H**	**Exeter C**	**W2-1**	**0-0**		**Crawford, Bennett**	**2,721**
8	17	CL	H	Portsmouth	D0-0	0-0	12		9,033
9	O 1	CL	H	Barnsley	L0-3	0-1	18		6,433
10	**4**	**MC 2**	**H**	**Norwich C**	**D0-0**	**0-0**			**4,425**
11	8	CL	H	Carlisle U	W2-0	2-0	16	Owen, Vaughan	4,596
12	15	CL	A	Chelsea	L0-2	0-1	17		15,459
13	19	CL	H	Newcastle U	L0-2	0-1			9,926
14	**26**	**MC 2**	**A**	**Norwich C**	**L0-3**	**0-1**			**9,887**
15	31	CL	A	Fulham	W2-0	0-0		Bennett, Owen	5,959
16	N 5	CL	A	Middlesbrough	L0-2	0-0	16		7,686
17	8	CL	A	Crystal Palace	L0-1	0-0			5,299
18	12	CL	H	Cambridge U	W5-0	4-0	17	Gibbins 2, Vaughan, Fallon (og), Owen	4,730
19	19	CL	A	Oldham Ath	L1-2	0-1	17	Dwyer	3,587
20	26	CL	H	Huddersfield T	W3-1	1-0	16	Laws (og), Bodin, Owen	6,067
21	D 3	CL	A	Brighton & HA	L1-3	0-1	17	Baird	9,924
22	10	CL	H	Blackburn R	L0-1	0-0	17		5,200
23	17	CL	A	Sheffield W	L2-5	0-3	14	Baird 2	14,580
24	26	CL	H	Swansea C	W3-2	2-1	16	Gibbins, Vaughan, Lee	14,580
25	27	CL	A	Derby Co	W3-2	1-2	15	Baird 2, Dwyer	16,054
26	31	CL	A	Grimsby T	L0-1	0-0	15		7,164
27	**J 7**	**FAC 3**	**H**	**Ipswich T**	**L0-3**	**0-1**			**10,118**
28	21	CL	A	Portsmouth	D1-1	1-0	17	Lee	11,938
29	31	CL	H	Charlton Ath	W2-1	0-0		Owen, Bennett	4,680
30	F 4	CL	A	Barnsley	W3-2	1-0	13	Baird, Owen, May (og)	7,107
31	11	CL	H	Leeds U	L0-1	0-0	15		9,407
32	19	CL	H	Fulham	L0-4	0-2			7,149
33	25	CL	A	Newcastle U	L1-3	0-2	18	Vaughan	27,909
34	M 3	CL	H	Middlesbrough	W2-1	2-1	15	Elsey, Goldsmith	4,422
35	10	CL	A	Cambridge U	W2-0	0-0	14	Smith, Vaughan	2,512
36	17	CL	H	Shrewsbury T	W2-0	1-0	13	Vaughan, Owen	3,870
37	24	CL	A	Manchester C	L1-2	1-0	14	Owen	20,140
38	31	CL	H	Chelsea	D3-3	3-0	15	Gibbins, Owen (pen), Vaughan	11,060
39	A 7	CL	A	Carlisle U	D1-1	0-0	14	Goldsmith	4,704
40	14	CL	H	Oldham Ath	W2-0	1-0	13	Owen (pen), Lee	4,637
41	17	CL	H	Crystal Palace	L0-2	0-1			4,901
42	21	CL	A	Swansea C	L2-3	2-1	14	Smith, Owen	10,275
43	23	CL	H	Derby Co	W1-0	0-0	13	Owen	5,056
44	28	CL	A	Huddersfield T	L0-4	0-0	14		5,599
45	M 5	CL	H	Brighton & HA	D2-2	1-0	14	Lee, Vaughan	4,366
46	7	CL	A	Blackburn R	D1-1	1-1	14	Lee	3,107
47	12	CL	H	Sheffield W	L0-2	0-0	15		14,171
								Av Home Att	**7,053**

Goal Scorers

League (53): Owen 14 (3 pens), Vaughan 8, Baird 6, Lee 5, Gibbins 4, Bodin 3, Bennett 2, Dwyer 2, Goldsmith 2, Smith 2, Crawford 1, Elsey 1, opponents 3

FA Cup (-): —

Milk Cup (5): Crawford 2, Bennett 1, Dwyer 1, Owen 1

1983-84

Dibble	Jones	Bodin	Dwyer	Bennett	Tong	Owen	Gibbins	Crawford	Rodon **(L)**	Lewis	Matthews	Mullen	Elsey	Walker **(L)**	Vaughan	Townsend	Smith	Baird **(L)**	Grant	Evans	Burke **(L)**	Lee	Hemmerman	Goldsmith	REFEREE	
1	2	3	4	5	6	7	8	9	10*	11	12														T Bune	1
1	2	3	4	5	6	7	8	10	9	11															T Spencer	2
1	**2**	**3***	**4**	**5**	**6**	**7**	**8**	**9**	**10**	**11**		**12**													**J Bray**	**3**
1	2	3*	4	5	6	7	8	9	10	11		12													L Shapter	4
1	2	3	4	5	6	7	8	9	10*	11		12													A Banks	5
1	2	3	4	5	6	7*	8	9		11	12	10													A Worrell	6
1		**3**	**4**	**5**	**6**	**7**	**8**	**9**	**2**	**11***	**12**	**10**													**K Barratt**	**7**
1	2	3	4	5	6	7	8	9*		11	12	10													V Callow	8
1		3	4	11*	6	7	8				12	5	2	9	10										A Crickmore	9
1		**3**	**4**		**6**	**7**	**8**	**10**			**11**	**5**				**9**	**2**								**K Baker**	**10**
1		3	4		6	7	8					5	2	9*	10	12	11								A Seville	11
1		3	6		5	7	10				12	4	9		8	11*	2								M Scott	12
1		3	4		6	7	8				12	5	11		10	9*	2								RG Milford	13
1		**3**	**4**	**9**	**6***	**7**	**8**				**11**	**5**				**12**	**2**								**B Hill**	**14**
1		3	4	9	6*	7	8				12	5	11		10		2								M Bodenham	15
1		3	4	9	6	7	8				12	5*	11		10		2								J Hough	16
1		3	5	9	6*	7	8				4		11		10	12	2								DJ Axcell	17
1		3	5	9	6*	7	8				4		11		10	12	2								A Robinson	18
1		3	4	5	6	7	8				12		11		10		2*	9							T Holbrook	19
1		3	4	5	6	7	8				12		11*		10		2	9							D Letts	20
1		3	4	5	6	7	8						11		10		2	9							K Salmon	21
		3	4	5	6	7	8				11*				10		2	9		12					D Brazier	22
1		3*	4	5	6	7	8								10		2	9		12	11				R Guy	23
1		3	4	5	6	7	8								10		2	9				11			E Read	24
1		3	4	5	6		8								10		2	9			7	11			L Dilkes	25
1		3	4	5	6	12	8								10		2	9			7*	11			A Challinor	26
1		**3**	**4**	**5**	**6**	**7**	**8**						**2**		**10**					**9**	**11**				**A Ward**	**27**
1		3	4	5	6	7	8						2		10			9				11			A Gunn	28
1			4	5	6	7	8						2		10		3	9				11			M Heath	29
1			4	5	6	7	8						2		10		3	9				11			N Ashley	30
1			4	5	6	7	8						2		9		3						10	11	J Martin	31
1			4	5	6	7	8						2		9		3	11*					10	12	K Barratt	32
1			4	5	6	7	8						2		9		3					11	10		A Robinson	33
1			4	5*	6	7	8						10		9		2		3			11		12	L Burden	34
1			4		6	7	8						2		9		5		3			10	12	11*	M Taylor	35
1			4		6	7	8						2		9		5		3			11	10		A Crickmore	36
1			4		6	7	8						2		9		5		3			11	10		H Taylor	37
1			4		6	7	8						2		9		5		3			11	10*	12	R Nixon	38
1			4		6	7	8						2		9		5		3			11	10	12	N Wilson	39
1			4		6	7	8						2		9		5		3			11	10		C Downey	40
1			4		6	7	8						2		9		5*		3			11	10	12	L Robinson	41
1			4	10	6	7	8						2		9		5		3*			11		12	B Stevens	42
1			4	3	6	7	8					12	2†		9		5					11*	10		D Hedges	43
1		7*	4	3	6		8					12	2		9		5					11		10	G Tyson	44
1			4	5	6	7	8						10		9		2		3			11			K Baxter	45
1		2	4	10	6		8				7				9		5		3			11			K Redfern	46
1		10	4	5	6	7	8								9		2		3			11			R Milford	47
41	6	26	**42**	32	**42**	38	**42**	6	4	6	4	8	29	2	36	2	34	12	12	0	3	21	10	3	League Appearances	
						+1S					+10S	+4S				+3S				+2S			+1S	+6S		
1		1	1	1	1	1	1						1		1					1	1				FA Cup Appearances	
4	1	4	4	3	4	4	4	3	2	2	2+1S	3+1S				1+1S	2								Milk Cup Appearances	

Also played: Plumley match 22, no.1. Heycock match 14, no.10.

NINIAN PARK

Official Address: Ninian Park, Cardiff CF1 8SX. Telephone: Cardiff (0222) 398636/7/8

Telegraphic: Soccer Cardiff

Ground Capacity: 42,000

Record Attendance: 61,566, Wales v. England, 14 Oct 1961; 57,893 v. Arsenal, Division 1, 22 Apr 1953

Record Receipts: £33,164.01 v. Sheffield Wednesday, Division 2, 12 May 1984

Size of Playing Area: 114yds × 78 yds

Season Tickets: Stand: £80.00 (Grandstand), (£50.00 OAP/juveniles); Canyon Stand & Family Enclosure £55.00 (£31.00 OAP/juveniles), £80.00 (Adult, 1 child), £90.00 (1 adult, 2 children), £100.00 (1 adult, 3 children); Ground: £50.00 (£29.00 OAP/juveniles)

Executive Box Season Tickets: None available

Cost of Stand Tickets: £4.50 (£3.00 OAP/ juveniles) Grandstand; Canyon Stand & Family Enclosure £3.00 (adult), £4.50 (adult & 1 child), £6.00 (adult & two children), £7.50 (adult & 3 children); **Standing:** £2.50 (£2.00 OAP/ juveniles)

Match and Ticket Information: Bookable in advance.

Car Parking: Surrounding streets.

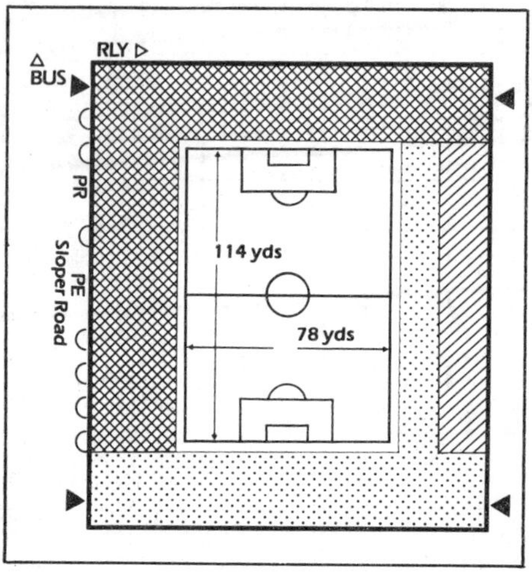

For key see page 12

How to get to the ground

From North: Follow signs Cardiff A470 until junction with Cardiff bypass. At roundabout take 3rd exit A48 (S.P. Port Talbot). In 2m at roundabout take 1st exit A4161 into Cowbridge Road. In 0.5m turn right along Lansdowne Road. At end at crossroads turn right A4055 into Leckwith Road. In 0.2m turn left into Sloper Road to Cardiff City F.C.
From East: Use Motorway M4, then A48 into Cardiff bypass. Follow signs Port Talbot then in 2m at roundabout take 1st exit A4161 into Cowbridge Road. In 0.5m turn right along Lansdowne Road. At end at crossroads turn right A4055 into Leckwith Road. In 0.2m turn left into Sloper Road for Cardiff City F.C.
From West: Follow signs Cardiff City Centre A4161 into Cowbridge Road. In 0.5m turn right along Lansdowne Road. At end at crossroads turn right A4055 into Leckwith Road. In 0.2m turn left into Sloper Road for Cardiff City F.C.

CARLISLE UNITED Division 2

Chairman
H A Jenkins

Managing Director
C Hutchinson

Directors
R S Liddell
J R Sheffield
J C Monkhouse
Dr T Gardner
T A Bingley

Match Secretary
N Irving

Commercial Manager
Susan Greenhall (0228-24014)

Administrator
Linda Allen

Manager
Bob Stokoe

Player Coach
Tommy Craig

Chief Scout
Jack Watson

Groundsman
Bill Hullock

The Cumbrians recovered from a poor start to make a strong bid for promotion. In March they held third place for a while and a return to the First Division was very much on the cards. Then, just as suddenly as they had earlier hit form, they collapsed and failed to win any of their closing ten games.

Carlisle's success was surprising in view of the fact that manager Bob Stokoe had had so many previous contract problems with his players. His team for the opening match of the season included five new players — David McKeller, David Moore, Donald O'Riordan, Graham Bell and Kevin Dixon. Soon after the start of the season, Mr Stokoe signed Andy Hill and Mike Buckley.

The Cumbrians were also one of the oldest teams in the Football League. But, though the odds seemed to be stacked so heavily against them, Carlisle's new-look team quickly settled after failing to score in its opening four games.

Malcolm Poskett, who scored four times at Derby, maintained a good scoring rate throughout with Alan Shoulder and O'Riordan giving him good support.

An unbeaten run of 15 games took the Cumbrians to within five points of the third club in January. That run ended when Brighton became only the second visiting team to win at Brunton Park and the Cumbrians were not beaten again on their own ground.

Another good run culminated in a 3-0 home win over Charlton and that shot the Cumbrians into third place in the table. But, with the First Division beckoning, Carlisle failed to win another game.

Heavy defeats at Blackburn, Newcastle and Leeds helped to send them tumbling down to seventh position.

Carlisle were just getting into confident mood when the Milk Cup came around and a 2-0 home-leg lead over Southampton gave them an excellent chance of making progress. Even though they conceded a fourth-minute goal in the return at The Dell, Carlisle seemed to be holding out and it wasn't until five minutes from time that the Saints equalised. During extra-time the home side scored the goal it needed to put them into round three.

The Cumbrians were a disappointment in the F.A. Cup. At a time when they were riding high in the Second Division, they were held at home in round three by Fourth Division Swindon Town and then lost the replay. TP

Back Row: Paul Haigh, Don O'Riordan, Malcolm Poskett, Garry MacDonald, Steve Tupling, Dave Rushbury. **Centre:** Bob Stokoe (Manager), Andy Hill, Jack Ashurst (Captain), Dave McKellar, David McAughtrie, Bill Wilson (Physiotherapist), Colin Hutchinson (Managing Director). **Front Row:** Alan Shoulder, Bryan Robson, Andrew Jenkins (Chairman), Tommy Craig (Player Coach), Mike McCartney.

Sponsored by
McEwan-Younger

'CUMBRIANS' or 'BLUES'

Formed: 1904 **Turned Professional:** **Ltd Co:** 1921
Previous Managers: W Clark Ivor Broadis Bill Shankly Fred Emery Andy Beattie Ivor Powell Alan Ashman Tim Ward Bob Stokoe Ian MacFarlane Alan Ashman Dick Young Bobby Moncur Martin Harvey
Honours: Division Three Champions 1964-5
League Career: Elected to Division Three (N) 1928 Transferred to Division Four 1958
Promoted to Division Three 1961-2 Relegated to Division Four 1962-3
Promoted to Division Three 1963-4 Promoted to Division Two 1964-5
Promoted to Division One 1973-4 Relegation to Division Two 1974-5
Relegation to Division Three 1976-7 Promotion to Division Two 1981-2
Colours: Blue shirts with white pinstripe, white collar with red and blue trim, blue shorts and white stockings
Change Colours: Yellow shirts, blue shorts, yellow stockings

CLUB RECORDS

Most Appearances for Club: Alan Ross, 466, 1963-79
Most Capped Player: Eric Walsh, 4, Northern Ireland **For England:** None
Record Goalscorer in a Match: Jim Whitehouse, 5 v Scunthorpe United (8-0), Div 3(N), 25.12.52
Record League Goalscorer in a season: Jimmy McConnell, 42, Division 3(N), 1928-9
Record League Goalscorer in a career: Jimmy McConnell, 126, 1928-32
Record Transfer Fee Received: £275,000 from Vancouver Whitecaps for David Beardsley
Record Transfer Fee Paid: £120,000 to York City for Gordon Staniforth, Oct 1979
Best Performances: League: 22nd Div 1 1974-5 **F.A. Cup:** 6th Round 1974-5 **League/Milk Cup:** Semi-Final 1969-70
Most League Points: 80 in Div 3, 1981-2 **Most League Points:** 113, Div 4, 1963-4
Record League Victory: 8-0 v Hartlepool, Div 3(N), 1 Sept 1928, v Scunthorpe United, Div 3(N), 25 Dec 1952
Record League Defeat: 1-11 v Hull City, Div 3(N), 14 Jan 1939

Club Statistician for the Directory: B. Rodgers

Programme Editor
N. Irving

Price	Number of Pages
40p	20

Subscriptions
Prices on request from Commercial Department

CARLISLE UNITED

PLAYERS NAME Ht Wt Birthdate	Honours	Birthplace Transfers	Clubs	APPEARANCES League	APPEARANCES Milk Cup	APPEARANCES F.A.C.	APPEARANCES E. Cups	GOALS League	GOALS Milk Cup	GOALS F.A.C.	GOALS E. Cups
GOALKEEPER											
David McKellar	FAYC. 73	Irvine	Ipswich T. (A)								
6-0 11.8 22.5.56		F	Ardrossan W.								
		£2,500	Derby Co.	41		2					
		£30,000	Brentford	84	2	5					
		Player Exchange	Carlisle U.	42							
DEFENDERS											
Jack Ashurst*	Div. 2. 76	Coatbridge	Sunderland (A)	129 + 11	7	8		4			
6-0 12.4 12.10.54		£110,000	Blackpool	53	2	4		3			
		£40,000	Carlisle U.	117	8	8		2	1	1	
Paul Halgh	E. U.21(1)	Scarborough	Hull C. (A)	179 + 1	13	7		8	2	1	
5-11 12.6 4.5.58		£102,000	Carlisle U.	121 + 4	7	14 +		1	1		
David McAughtrie	S. Y.	Cumnock	Stoke C. (A)	47 + 3	6	1		1			
6-1 12.3 30.1.63			Carlisle U.								
Mike McCartney	S. S	Edinburgh	W.B.A. (A)								
5-7 10.12 28.9.54		F	Carlisle U.	148 + 8	11	7		17		1	
		£30,000	Southampton	22	2			1			
		£50,000	Plymouth A.	49	4	6		5		1	
		Player Exchange	Carlisle U.	30							
Donal O'Riordent†	Ei. U.21	Dublin	Derby Co. (A)	2 + 4	0 + 1			1			
5-11 12.0 14.5.57			Doncaster R. (L)	2							
			Tulsa Roughnecks								
		£30,000	P.N.E.	153 + 5	10			8		1	
		£30,000	Carlisle U.	42	2			8			
Dave Rushbury		Wolverhampton	W.B.A. (A)	28		3					
5-10 11.0 20.2.56		£60,000	Sheffield W.	111 + 1	8	13		7		1	
		£60,000	Swansea C.	51 + 1	6	6					
		£55,000	Carlisle U.	101 + 7	6	6		1			
MIDFIELD											
Tommy Craig	S.(1), U.21(1),	Glasgow	Aberdeen								
5-8 11.9 21.11.50	U.23(9), Y. S	£100,000	Sheffield W.	210 + 4	9	9 + 1		38	1	1	
		£120,000	Newcastle U.	122 + 2	13	14		23	2	2	
		£275,000	Aston Villa	27	4	1		2			
		£150,000	Swansea C.	47 + 5	5	5		9	1		
		F	Carlisle U.	82 + 6	2 + 1	4		9			
FORWARDS											
Gary MacDonald		Middlesbrough	Middlesbrough	40 + 12	26+5	4 + 1		5		1	
6-0 12.1 26.3.62											
Malcolm Poskett		Middlesbrough	South Bank								
6-0 11.11 19.7.53		F	Middlesbrough	0 + 1							
		F	Whitby Town								
		£25	Hartlepool U.	50 + 1	3	3		20	1		
		£60,000	Brighton	33 + 12	4 + 1	1		16	1		
		£110,000	Watford	57 + 6	9	5 + 1		17	6	6	
		£25,000	Carlisle U.	77	4	4		31	2	1	
Bryan Robson	E. U.23( )	Sunderland	Newcastle U.	205 + 1	4	8		81	2	4	
5-7 11.8 11.11.45	EFC. 69	£125,000	West Ham U.	120	13	6		47	5	1	
		£145,000	Sunderland	90	5	7		34	1	4	
		£80,000	West Ham U.	107	2	6		47	1	3	
		£40,000	Sunderland	49 + 3	4 + 1	1		23	2		
		£10,000	Carlisle U.	48	2	4		21		3	
		F	Chelsea	11 + 4	1 + 1	3		2			
			Carlisle U. (L)	11				4			
		F	Sunderland								
Alan Shoulder		Bishop Auckland	Blyth Spartans								
5-5 10.5 4.2.53		£20,000	Newcastle U.	99 + 8	4 + 2	6 + 1		35	2	1	
		F	Carlisle U.	82	3	4		29		2	

NON-CONTRACT PLAYERS 1984-85: Raymond Blackhall, Ian Davies, Craig Gordon, Vincent Hartley, David Ramage, Gary Robinson, Simon Smith, Stephen Tupling

CARLISLE UNITED

DIVISION TWO 7TH **FA CUP** 3RD ROUND **MILK CUP** 2ND ROUND

MATCH	DATE	COMPE-TITION	VENUE	OPPONENTS	RESULT	HALF TIME	L'GUE POS'N	GOALSCORERS	ATTEN-DANCE
1	A 27	CL	H	Cambridge U	D0-0	0-0			3,738
2	29	CL	H	Blackburn R	L0-1	0-1			4,470
3	S 3	CL	A	Sheffield W	L0-2	0-1	19		14,544
4	6	CL	A	Charlton Ath	L0-1	0-0			3,770
5	10	CL	H	Shrewsbury T	W1-0	0-0	16	O'Riordan	3,164
6	17	CL	A	Brighton & HA	D1-1	1-0	16	Shoulder	11,735
7	24	CL	H	Huddersfield T	D0-0	0-0	15		5,481
8	O 1	CL	A	Derby Co	W4-1	2-1	13	Poskett 4	12,041
9	**4**	**MC 2**	**H**	**Southampton**	**W2-0**	**1-0**		**Poskett 2**	**8,570**
10	8	CL	A	Cardiff C	L0-2	0-2	17		4,596
11	15	CL	H	Fulham	W2-0	2-0	11	Buckley, O'Riordan	3,712
12	22	CL	H	Chelsea	D0-0	0-0	12		6,774
13	**25**	**MC 2**	**A**	**Southampton**	**L0-3**[1]	**0-1**			**12,438**
14	29	CL	A	Oldham Ath	W3-2	1-1	11	Moore, O'Riordan, Shoulder	4,087
15	N 5	CL	A	Swansea C	D0-0	0-0	14		6,938
16	12	CL	H	Portsmouth	D0-0	0-0	13		4,814
17	19	CL	H	Manchester C	W2-0	0-0	9	Shoulder, Poskett	8,745
18	26	CL	A	Grimsby T	D1-1	1-0	11	Buckley	5,665
19	D 3	CL	H	Leeds U	W1-0	0-0	9	Poskett	6,845
20	11	CL	A	Crystal Palace	W2-1	0-1		Shoulder, O'Riordan	6,460
21	17	CL	H	Barnsley	W4-2	3-2	9	Bannon, Rushbury, Poskett 2	4,812
22	26	CL	A	Middlesbrough	W1-0	1-0	7	Ashurst	11,147
23	27	CL	H	Newcastle U	W3-1	1-1	5	Shoulder (pen), Coughlin, Craig	14,756
24	31	CL	H	Sheffield W	D1-1	0-0	6	O'Riordan	10,475
25	J 2	CL	A	Huddersfield T	D0-0	0-0	7		10,131
26	**7**	**FAC 3**	**H**	**Swindon T**	**D1-1**	**1-0**		**Ashurst**	**5,778**
27	**10**	**FAC 3R**	**A**	**Swindon T**	**L1-3**	**0-1**		**Shoulder (pen)**	**8,077**
28	14	CL	A	Cambridge U	W2-0	0-0	6	Hill, Poskett	2,203
29	21	CL	H	Brighton & HA	L1-2	0-2	8	Poskett	5,169
30	F 4	CL	H	Derby Co	W2-1	1-0	8	Shoulder, Hill	4,915
31	11	CL	A	Shrewsbury T	D0-0	0-0	7		3,439
32	18	CL	H	Oldham Ath	W2-0	0-0	5	Poskett, Shoulder	4,389
33	25	CL	A	Chelsea	D0-0	0-0	6		16,543
34	M 3	CL	H	Swansea C	W2-0	0-0	6	Poskett 2	4,280
35	10	CL	A	Portsmouth	W1-0	0-0	5	Shoulder	10,748
36	17	CL	H	Charlton Ath	W3-0	1-0	3	Poskett, O'Riordan, Craig	4,375
37	24	CL	A	Blackburn R	L1-4	1-2	4	Parker	6,171
38	31	CL	A	Fulham	D0-0	0-0	4		6,018
39	A 7	CL	H	Cardiff C	D1-1	0-0	5	Poskett	4,704
40	14	CL	A	Manchester C	L1-3	1-1	6	Hill	20,760
41	20	CL	H	Middlesbrough	D1-1	1-0		O'Riordan	5,674
42	23	CL	A	Newcastle U	L1-5	0-2	7	Coughlin	33,386
43	28	CL	H	Grimsby T	D1-1	1-0	7	Coughlin	3,512
44	M 5	CL	A	Leeds U	L0-3	0-0	7		8,278
45	7	CL	H	Crystal Palace	D2-2	2-0	7	Poskett 2	3,013
46	12	CL	A	Barnsley	L1-2	1-0	7	O'Riordan	4,512

[1] After Extra Time

Av Home Att **5,602**

Goal Scorers

League (48): Poskett 17, O'Riordan 8, Shoulder 8 (1 pen), Coughlin 3, Hill 3, Buckley 2, Craig 2, Ashurst 1, Bannon 1, Moore 1, Parker 1, Rushbury 1
FA Cup (2): Ashurst 1, Shoulder 1 (1 pen)
Milk Cup (2): Poskett 2

1983-84

McKellar	Moore	Rushbury	Ashurst	O'Riordan	McCartney	Bell	Coughlin	Poskett	Dixon	Shoulder	Haigh	Horswill	Parker	Craig	Bannon	Hill	Buckley			REFEREE	
1	2	3	4	5	6*	7	8	9	10	11	12									N Wilson	1
1	2	3	4	5		7*	8	9	10	11	12	6								J Key	2
1	2	3	4	5		7	8*	9	10	11	6		12							H Taylor	3
1	2	3	4	5		7		9	12	11	6			8	10*					J Martin	4
1	2	3	4	5	10			9	7	11	6			8						K Redfern	5
1	2	3		5	10	7	4	9*	12	11	6			8						T Ward	6
1	2	3	4	5	10+			9		11	6			8		7				D Allison	7
1	2		4	5				9		11	6		3	8		7	10			M Dimblebee	8
1	**2**		**4**	**5**		**8**	**10**	**9**		**11**	**6**		**3**			**7**				**D Scott**	**9**
1	2*	12	4	5		8		9		11	6		3			7	10			A Seville	10
1	2		4	5		8		9		11	6		3			7	10			J Worrall	11
1	2		4	5		8	12	9		11*	6		3			7	10			D Richardson	12
1	**2**		**4**	**5**		**8**	**10**	**9**	**11***		**6**		**3**	**12**		**7**				**D Reeves**	**13**
1	2		4	5		12		9		11	6*		3	8		7	10			M Heath	14
1	2		4	5				9		11	6		3	8		7	10			L Shapter	15
1		2	4	5			12	9		11	6		3	8*		7	10			G Courtney	16
1		2	4	5			12	9		11	6		3	8		7	10*			G Tyson	17
1		2	4	5				9		11	6		3	8		7	10			J Ashworth	18
1		2	4	5			12	9		11	6		3	8		7*	10			A Banks	19
1		2	4	5			12	9		11	6		3	8		7*	10			M Bodenham	20
1		2	4	5		12	7	9		11	6		3	8	10*					D Owen	21
1		2	4	5		10	7	9		11	6		3	8						M Scott	22
1		2	4	5		12	7	9		11	6		3	8	10*					T Fitzharris	23
1		2	4	5		10*	7	9		11	6		3	8	12					N Midgley	24
1		2	4	5		10	7	9		11	6		3	8						F Roberts	25
1		**2**	**4**	**5**		**12**	**7**	**9**		**11**	**6**		**3**	**8**	**10***					**T Mills**	**26**
1		**2**	**4**	**5**		**10**	**7**	**9**		**11**	**3**			**8**		**12**	**6***			**T Mills**	**27**
1		2	4	5			7	9		11	6		3	8		10				J Moules	28
1		2	4	5			7	9		11	6*		3	8		10	12			R Dilkes	29
1		2	4	5	6			9		11			3	8		10	7			I Hendrick	30
1		2	4	5	6			9		11			3	8		10	7			R Bridges	31
1		2	4	5	6		12	9		11			3	8		10*	7			D Hutchinson	32
1		2	4	5	6			9		11			3	8		10	7			D Hedges	33
1		2	4	5	6		12	9		11			3	8		10*	7			N Glover	34
1		2	4	5	6		10	9		11			3	8			7			J Deakin	35
1		2	4	5	6		10	9		11			3	8			7			A Saunders	36
1		2	4	5	6		10	9		11			3	8			7			K Hackett	37
1			4	5	6		10	9		11	2		3	8			7			R Milford	38
1			4	5	6		10	9		11	2		3	8			7			N Wilson	39
1			4	5	6		10	9	12	11	2		3			8	7*			P Willis	40
1			4	5	6		12		9*	11	2		3	10		8	7			R Nixon	41
1			4	5	6		10	9		11	2		3	8		7				N Midgley	42
1			4	5	6		10	9		11	2		3	8		7				K Walmsley	43
1			4	5	6		10	9	12		2		3	8		7*		11		N Ashley	44
1			4	5	6		10	9		11	2		3	8		7*			12	J Hough	45
1			4	5	6		8	9			2		3			11	7		10	G Napthine	46
42	13	27	41	**42**	21	11	22	41	5	40	32	1	35	34	3	26	24	1	1	League Appearances	
		+1S				+3S	+8S		+4S		+2S		+1S		+1S		+1S		+1S		
2		2	2	2		1+1S	2	2		2	2		1	2	1	1S	1			FA Cup Appearances	
2	2		2	2		2	2	2	1	1	2		2	1S		2				Milk Cup Appearances	

BRUNTON PARK

Official Address: Brunton Park, Carlisle CA1 1LL. Telephone: 0228 26237)

Ground Capacity: 18,000

Record Attendance: 27,500 v. Birmingham City, F.A. Cup Round 3, 5 Jan 1957 and v. Middlesbrough, F.A. Cup Round 5, 7 Feb 1970

Record Receipts: £30,616 v. Newcastle United, Division 2, 20 Nov 1982

Size of Playing Area: 117yds × 78 yds

Season Tickets: Stands: £65.00, £72.00, £75.00 (£34 juveniles). Ground: £40, £45 (£21, £23 juveniles)

Cost of Stand Tickets: £4.00, £4.50, £5.00 (£2.00 juveniles); **Terraces:** £2.30, £2.50, £2.80 (£1.30 juveniles)

Match and Ticket Information: Bookable 1 to 3 weeks before matches by postal or personal applications

Car Parking: Car park for 1,500 vehicles next to ground. Limited street parking permitted

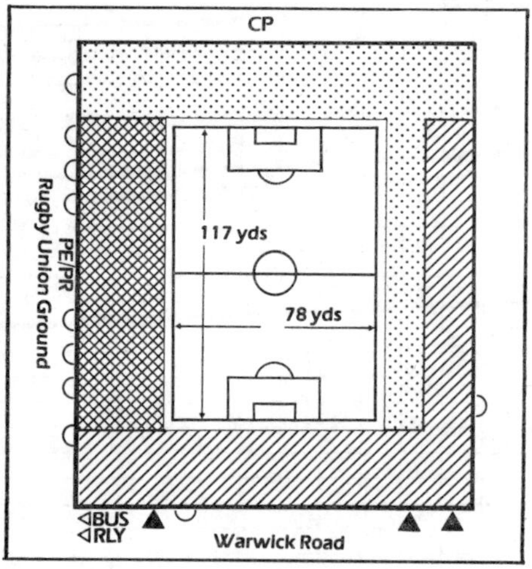

For key see page 12

How to get to the ground

From North, East, South: Use Motorway M6 until junction 43. Leave motorway and follow signs Carlisle A69 into Warwick Road for Carlisle United F.C.

From West: Follow signs into Carlisle then forward A69 along Warwick Road for Carlisle United F.C.

CHARLTON ATHLETIC Division 2

Chairman
J A E Fryer

Directors
Richard D Collins
Michael John Norris
Derek Ufton

Secretary
G I S Hortop

Commercial Department
(01-853 0444)

Manager
R M Lawrence

Assistant Manager
E C May

Physiotherapist
C A Hall

Reserve Team Coach
T F Taylor

Chief Scout
Les Gore

Club Captain
Derek Hales

Groundsman
Maurice Banham

On paper Charlton Athletic, remembered by many as F.A. Cup Winners in 1947, having been runners-up the previous season, had an undistinguished season. A final position below half-way in the Second Division was not relieved by any good cup performances, with Brentford eliminating the team in the Milk Cup First Round on aggregate and a Third Round single goal F.A. Cup victory at Colchester United being followed immediately by an exit at home by two clear goals against eventual Cup Finalists, Watford.

But that is only the superficial story and at the end of the season Manager Lawrence and his players could justifiably hold their heads high and say 'That was our Finest Hour', because early in March the club was virtually 'dead' and a match against Blackburn Rovers was postponed as the South East London club faced total extinction. The Chairman, Mark Hulyer, tried everything he knew but the courts were unrelenting. That Charlton did survive is now history and Mark Hulyer deserves all the credit he has been given for that fact, but no praise can be too high for the manager and playing staff who all retained a fierce loyalty and determination to do their bit to save the situation. Survival in the Second Division was in such circumstances a tremendous achievement — possibly better than those 1940s F.A. Cup performances.

It is now almost realistic to make forecasts about the future since that brave playing staff does contain some very talented players including some of the most prolific strikers in the country in Hales, Moore, Flanagan and Robinson. Add in a sound goal-keeper in Johns and useful defenders in Dickenson and Berry plus the eccentric genius of Carl Harris (if fit) and there should be the potential at the Valley to be as successful in the London scene as West Ham and QPR. With a more stable financial background success could be theirs. WLM

Back Row: Robert Lee, Steve Gritt, Mark Aizelwood, Steve Dowman, Mike Flanagan, Paul Curtis, Martin Robinson. **Middle Row:** David Madden, Shane Westley, Nicky Johns, Tony Lange, Les Berry, Darren Anderson. **Front Row:** Tony Towner, Derek Hales (Captain), Lennie Lawrence (Manager), Eddie May (Asst Manager), Ronnie Moore, Kevin Dickenson.

'HADDICKS', 'ROBINS' or 'VALIANTS'

Formed: 1905 **Turned Professional:** 1920 **Ltd Co:** 1919
Previous Managers: 1920-5 Walter Rayner 1925-8 Alex MacFarlane 1928-8 Albert Lindon 1928-32 Alex MacFarlane 1932-3 Albert Lindon 1933-56 Jimmy Seed 1956-61 Jimmy Trotter 1961-5 Frank Hill 1965-7 Bob Stokoe 1967-70 Eddie Firmani 1970-4 Theo Foley 1974-80 Andy Nelson 1980-1 Mike Bailey 1981-2 Alan Mullery 1982-2 Ken Craggs
Honours: Division Three (South) Champions 1928-9, 1934-5 F.A. Cup Winners 1947
League Career: Elected to Division 3(S) 1921 Promoted to Division 2 1928-9
Relegated to Division 3(S) 1932-3 Promoted to Division 2 1934-5
Promoted to Division 1 1935-6 Relegated to Division 2 1956-7
Relegated to Division 3 1971-2 Promoted to Division 2 1974-5
Relegated to Division 3 1979-80 Promoted to Division 2 1980-1
Colours: Red shirts, white shorts, red stockings
Change Colours: Yellow and blue

CLUB RECORDS

Most Appearances for Club: Sam Bartram: Football League 582 + F.A. Cup 44 **Total 626**
Most Capped Player: John Hewie (Scotland) 19 **For England:** Don Welsh 3
Record Goalscorer in a Match: W Lennox, 5 v Exeter City (a) 5-2, Div 3(S) 02.02.29
Eddie Firmani, 5 v Aston Villa (h) 6-1, Div 1 05.02.55 J Summers, 5 v Huddersfield Town (h) 6-6, Div 2
Record League Goalscorer in a season: Ralph Allen, 32, Div 3(S) 1934-5 **In All Competitions:** Ralph Allen 33 (32 League + 1 F.A. Cup)
Record League Goalscorer in a career: Stuart Leary, 153, 1953-62 **In All Competitions:** Stuart Leary 163 (153 League + 8 F.A. Cup + 2 League Cup)
Record Transfer Fee Received: £650,000 from Crystal Palace for Mike Flanagan, Aug 1979
Record Transfer Fee Paid: £324,000 to Barcelona for Allan Simonson, Nov 1982
Best Performances: League: 2nd Div 1 1936-7 **F.A. Cup:** Winners 1947 **League/Milk Cup:** 4th Round 1962-3, 1964-5, 1978-9
Most League Points: 61 in Div 3(S), 1934-5 **Most League Goals:** 107, Div 2, 1957-8
Record League Victory: 8-1 v Middlesbrough, Div 1, 12 Sept 1953
Record League Defeat: 1-11 v Aston Villa, Div 2, 14 Nov 1959
Club Statistician for the Directory: Colin Cameron

Programme Editors
Peter Burrowes, Colin Cameron, Alan Honey

Price	Number of Pages
50p	16

Subscriptions
Available from club

CHARLTON ATHLETIC

PLAYERS NAME Ht Wt Birthdate	Honours	Birthplace Transfers	Clubs	APPEARANCES League	Milk Cup	F.A.C.	E. Cups	GOALS League	Milk Cup	F.A.C.	E. Cups
GOALKEEPERS											
Nicky Johns		Bristol	Minehead								
6-3½ 11.8 8.6.57		£6,000	Millwall	50	6	5					
		£200,000	Tampa Bay R.								
			Sheffield U. (L)	1							
		£125,000	Charlton A.	199	10	11					
Tony Lange		London	Charlton A. (A)	6							
6-1 12.12 10.12.64											
DEFENDERS											
Les Berry		Plumstead	Charlton A. (A)	320 + 5	16 +	15		11			
6-2 12.5 4.8.56											
Paul Curtis		London	Charlton A. (A)	42 + 2	3 + 1	2		4			
5-9 11.2 1.7.63											
Kevin Dickinson		London	Tottenham H. (A)								
5-6 10.6 24.11.61		F	Charlton A.	59 + 3	3	2		1			
Steve Dowman		Manor Park	Colchester U. (A)	150 + 4	10+1	21		21	2	3	
5-11 12.4 15.4.58		£75,000	Wrexham	87	7	6		2			
			Charlton A.	35				3			
Geoff Scott		Birmingham	Highgate U.								
5-10½ 12.5 31.10.55			Stoke C.	76 + 2	7	3		3			
		£80,000	Leicester C.	39	3	2					
		£50,000	Birmingham C.	18 + 1							
		£40,000	Charlton A.	2							
MIDFIELD											
Mark Aizlewood	W. U.21(2)	Newport	Newport Co. (A)	35 + 3		2		1			
6-0 12.8 1.10.59	Div. 2. 82		Luton T.	90 + 8	7	5		3		1	
			Charlton A.	53	2	3		2	1		
Darren Anderson		Merton	Coventry C. (A)								
6-1 12.5 6.9.66			Charlton A.	1							
Steve Gritt		Bournemouth	Bournemouth (A)	4 + 2	4			3			
5-9 10.10 31.10.57			Charlton A.	219 + 19	14+1	12		18			
Dave Madden		Dublin	Southampton (A)								
6-0 12.0 6.1.63			Bournemouth (L)	5							
		F	Arsenal	2							
		F	Charlton A.								
Peter Mountford		Stoke	Norwich C. (A)	1 + 3	0 + 1						
5-10 10.6 13.9.60		F	Charlton A.	10 + 1				1			
Kevin Smith		St Pauls Cray	Charlton A. (A)	79 + 25	7	2 + 1		14			
5-8 10.7 5.12.62											
Shane Westley		Canterbury	Charlton A. (A)	8							
6-2½ 12.7 16.6.65											
FORWARDS											
Mike Flanagan	E. B(3), Y.	Ilford	Tottenham H. (N-C)								
5-10 12.4 9.11.52	FAYC. 70.		Charlton A.	241 + 13	23	16+1		85	7	3	
	Div. 2. 83		Crystal Palace	56	7	1		8	4		
			Q.P.R.	71 + 7	3	12		20	2		
			Charlton A.	18		1		2			
Derek Hales		Lower Halstow	Dartford								
5-9½ 11.11 15.12.51			Luton T.	5 + 2				1			
		£4,000	Charlton A.	126 + 3				72	6		
		£300,000	Derby Co.	22 + 1				4	1	2	
		£110,000	West Ham U.	23 + 1				10			
		£75,000	Charlton A.	174 + 3				68	8	5	
Carl Harris	W. (24), U.21(1)	Neath	Leeds U. (A)	124 + 30	8 + 6	5		26	1	1	
5-9 11.0 3.11.56	S	£100,000	Charlton A.	66	2	3		7			
Bobby Lee		West Ham	Charlton A.	10 + 1				4			
5-8 11.6 1.2.66											
Ronnie Moore	Div. 3. 81	Liverpool	Tranmere R.	248 + 1	18	12		72	4	1	
6-0 12.13 29.1.53		£120,000	Cardiff C.	54 + 2	2	2		6			
		£100,000	Rotherham U.	124 + 1	9	5		51	2		
		£35,000	Charlton A.	27 + 1		2		8			
Martin Robinson	FAYC. 74	Ilford	Charlton A.	213 + 9	16+2	8 + 1		56	6	2	
5-8½ 11.5 17.7.57			Reading (L)	2							

CONTRACT PLAYER 1984-85: Mark Stuart

MONTHLY CONTRACT PLAYER 1984-85: John Friar

APPRENTICES: Paul Collins, Joseph Francis, Lee Harmsworth, Stephen Harris, Duncan Horton, Sean McFadden, Mike Paye, David Spittle

CHARLTON ATHLETIC

DIVISION TWO 13TH **FA CUP** 4TH ROUND **MILK CUP** 1ST ROUND

MATCH	DATE	COMPE-TITION	VENUE	OPPONENTS	RESULT	HALF TIME	L'GUE POS'N	GOALSCORERS	ATTEN-DANCE
1	A 27	CL	H	Cardiff C	W2-0	2-0		Jones, Smith	4,525
2	**30**	**MC 1**	**A**	**Brentford**	**L0-3**	**0-2**			**4,868**
3	S 3	CL	A	Huddersfield T	D0-0	0-0	8		8,113
4	6	CL	H	Carlisle U	W1-0	0-0		Hales	3,770
5	10	CL	H	Sheffield W	D1-1	1-1	7	Hales (pen)	6,904
6	**12**	**MC 1**	**H**	**Brentford**	**W2-1**	**0-1**		**Jones, Aizlewood**	**3,622**
7	17	CL	A	Cambridge C	D2-2	0-1	8	Mountford, Harris	3,526
8	24	CL	H	Derby Co	W1-0	0-0	4	Moore	5,638
9	27	CL	A	Oldham Ath	D0-0	0-0			3,679
10	O 1	CL	A	Brighton & HA	L0-7	0-5	6		11,517
11	8	CL	A	Newcastle U	L1-2	1-0	9	Curtis	23,247
12	15	CL	H	Manchester C	W1-0	0-0	6	Hales	7,639
13	22	CL	H	Swansea C	D2-2	0-0	7	Hales (pen), Gritt	5,737
14	29	CL	A	Chelsea	L2-3	0-2	10	Robinson, Moore	17,789
15	N 5	CL	H	Blackburn R	W2-0	2-0	6	Moore, Smith	4,563
16	12	CL	A	Grimsby T	L1-2	1-0	10	Robinson	5,584
17	15	CL	H	Chelsea	D1-1	0-0		Harris	14,393
18	19	CL	H	Barnsley	W3-2	1-1	7	Moore 2, Smith	4,582
19	26	CL	A	Shrewsbury T	D1-1	0-0	8	Robinson	3,141
20	D 3	CL	H	Middlesbrough	W2-0	0-0	6	Smith 2 (2 pens)	5,053
21	10	CL	A	Fulham	W1-0	0-0	5	Curtis	6,140
22	15	CL	H	Leeds U	W2-0	1-0		Smith, Dowman	6,285
23	26	CL	A	Portsmouth	L0-4	0-2	9		15,331
24	27	CL	H	Crystal Palace	W1-0	1-0	6	Hales	10,224
25	31	CL	H	Huddersfield T	L1-2	0-1	9	Hales	5,972
26	J 2	CL	A	Derby Co	W1-0	1-0	6	Dowman	12,808
27	**7**	**FAC 3**	**A**	**Colchester U**	**W1-0**	**0-0**		**Houston (og)**	**6,296**
28	21	CL	H	Cambridge U	W5-2	2-0	17	Hales 2 (1 pen), Curtis, Moore 2	5,252
29	**28**	**FAC 4**	**H**	**Watford**	**L0-2**	**0-1**			**22,392**
30	31	CL	A	Cardiff C	L1-2	0-0		Dickinson	4,680
31	F 4	CL	H	Brighton & HA	W2-0	0-0	7	Robinson 2	7,435
32	11	CL	A	Sheffield W	L1-4	0-1	8	Moore	18,510
33	25	CL	A	Swansea C	L0-1	0-1	8		5,222
34	M10	CL	H	Grimsby T	D3-3	1-0	8	Hales, Lee, Robinson	7,626
35	17	CL	A	Carlisle U	L0-3	0-1	8		4,375
36	21	CL	A	Blackburn R	D1-1	1-1		Hales	4,784
37	24	CL	H	Oldham Ath	W2-1	2-0	8	Flanagan, Robinson	4,535
38	31	CL	A	Manchester C	W1-0	0-0	8	Jones	19,147
39	A 7	CL	H	Newcastle U	L1-3	1-1	8	Dowman	15,289
40	14	CL	A	Barnsley	L0-2	0-0	8		6,321
41	21	CL	H	Portsmouth	W2-1	0-1	8	Lee 2	6,328
42	23	CL	A	Crystal Palace	L0-2	0-0	8		7,818
43	28	CL	H	Shrewsbury T	L2-4	0-0	8	Flanagan, Aizlewood	3,786
44	M 5	CL	A	Middlesbrough	L0-1	0-0	10		4,720
45	7	CL	H	Fulham	L3-4	2-2	11	Robinson, Lee, Parker (og)	6,151
46	12	CL	A	Leeds U	L0-1	0-0	13		13,254

Av Home Att **6,761**

Goal Scorers

League (53): Hales 10 (3 pens), Moore 8, Robinson 8, Smith 6 (2 pens), Lee 4, Curtis 3, Dowman 3, Flanagan 2, Harris 2, Jones 2, Aizlewood 1, Dickinson 1, Gritt 1, Mountford 1, opponents 1

FA Cup (1): Opponent 1

Milk Cup (2): Aizlewood 1, Jones 1

1983-84

Johns	Naylor	Dickenson	Gritt	Smith	Berry	Curtis	Hales	Jones	Aizlewood	Robinson	Dowman	Harris	Moore	Mountford	Lange	Westley	Flanagan	O'Shea **(L)**	Lee	Paye	Anderson	**REFEREE**	
1	2	3	4	5	6	7	8	9	10	11												T Bune	1
1		**3**	**2**	**4**	**6**	**7***	**8**	**9**	**10**	**11**	**5**			**12**								**D Hedges**	**2**
1	2	3	4	11	6	12	8	9*	10		5	7										J Hough	3
1	2	3	4	11*	6		8	9	10	12	5	7										J Martin	4
1	2	3	4	11	6		8	9	10		5	7										M Taylor	5
1	**2**	**3**	**4**	**5**	**6**	**12**	**8**	**9**	**10**	**11***		**7**										**B Hill**	**6**
1	2	3	4	11	6		8	12			5*	7	9	10								G Napthine	7
1	2*	3	4	11	6		8	12			5	7	9	10								K Cooper	8
1		3	4	11	6	2	8				5	7	9	10								F Roberts	9
1		3	4		6*	2	8	12	11		5	7	9	10								D Letts	10
1		3	4	12	6	2	8		11		5	7	9	10*								R Tyldesley	11
1		3	4		6	2	8	12	11*	10	5	7	9									H King	12
1		3	4	12	6	2	8	10*		11	5	7	9									M James	13
1		3	4		6	2	8			11	5	7	9	10								L Burden	14
1		3	2	4	6		8			11	5	7	9	10								K Barratt	15
1		3	2	4	6		8			11	5	7	9	10†								N Wilson	16
1		3	10	4	6	2	8			11	5	7	9									K Hackett	17
1		3	10	4	6	2	8			11	5	7	9									H Taylor	18
1		3	10	4	6	2	8			11	5	7	9									R Dilkes	19
1		3	4	10	6	2		8		11	5	7	9									R Milford	20
		3	4	10	6	2		8	11		5	7	9		1							J Bray	21
		3	4*	10	6	2	12	8	11		5	7	9		1							A Crickmore	22
		3	4*	10	6	2		8	11		5	7	9	12	1							D Allison	23
		3		10	6	2	12	8	11			7	9	4*	1	5						M Dimblebee	24
		3		4	6	2	11	8	10		5	7	9		1							Alan Robinson	25
		3		4	6	2	11		10		5	7	9		1	8						J Worrall	26
1		**3**	**4**		**6**	**2**		**10**	**11**		**5**	**7**	**9**			**8†**						**T Spencer**	**27**
1		3	4		6	2	8		10		5	7	9				11					V Callow	28
1		**3**	**4***		**6**	**2**	**8**	**12**	**10**		**5**	**7**	**9**				**11**					**M Bodenham**	**29**
1		3	4	7	6	2	8	12	10		5*		9				11					M Heath	30
1		3	4		6	2	8		10	7	5		9				11					E Read	31
1		3	2	4	6		8		10	7	5		9				11					Alan Robinson	32
1		3	4	7*	6		8	9	10	12	5						11	2				T Spencer	33
1		3	4	12	6		8		10	7	5						11	2*	9			I Borrett	34
1		3	9		6		8		10	7	5					4	11	2				A Saunders	35
1		3	9	4	6		8		10	7	5						11	2				P Willis	36
1		3	9	4	6		8		10	7	5						11	2*	12			J Ashwood	37
1		3		4	6			9	10	7	5						11	2	8			G Napthine	38
1		3		4	6			9	10	7	5						11	2	8			T Bune	39
1		3		4	6			9	10	7	5		12				11*	2	8			R Bridges	40
1		3		4	6			12	10	7	5*		9				11	2	8			K Cooper	41
1		3		12	6			4*	10	7			9			5	11		8	2		A Seville	42
1		3		12	6				10	7			9	4*		5	11		8	2		L Shapter	43
1		3	7	4	6	2			10	11						5	9		8			A Challinor	44
1		5	10	6	4	2			9	11						3	7		8			M Taylor	45
1		3	9	12	6	2*			10	11						5	7		8		4	I Hendrick	46
36	6	**42**	33	30	**42**	23	27	17	31	25	35	24	27	10	6	8	18	9	10	2	1	League Appearances	
				+6S		+1S	+2S	+6S		+2S			+1S	+1S					+1S				
2		2	2		2	2	1	1+1S	2		2	2	2			1	1					FA Cup Appearances	
2	1	2	2	2	2	1+1S	2	2	2	2	1	1		1S								Milk Cup Appearances	

THE VALLEY

Official Address: The Valley, Floyd Road, Charlton, London SE7 8AW. Telephone: 01-853 0444)

Ground Capacity: 20,000

Record Attendance: 75,031 v. Aston Villa, F.A. Cup Round 5, 12 Feb 1938

Record Receipts: £38,963 v. Ipswich Town, F.A. Cup Round 3, 3 Jan 1983

Size of Playing Area: 113yds × 78 yds

Season Tickets: Stand: (before 31.5.84) £76.50 (£43.75 juveniles & OAP); Ground: £42.00 (£19.20 juveniles & OAP) (before 31.5.84)

Executive Box Season Tickets: £225 for cinema type seats and bar facilities (before 31.5.84)

Cost of Stand Tickets: £5.00; **Terraces:** £3.00

Car Parking: in ground only for season ticket holders. Off-street parking is available.

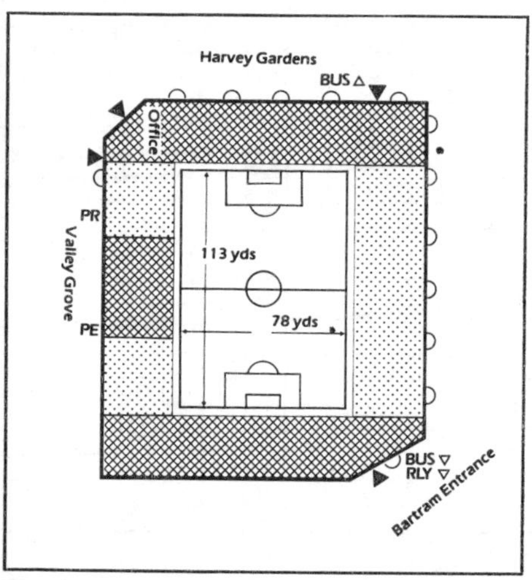

For key see page 12

How to get to the ground

From North: Use Motorway M1 and A1 follow signs London A1, then City. Then follow signs Shoreditch then Whitechapel to A13. Follow signs Tilbury then Blackwall Tunnel to cross R. Thames. Forward A102M. In 1m branch left and at T road turn left A206. In 0.5m turn right into Charlton Church Lane. Then turn left into Floyd Road for Charlton Athletic F.C.

From East: Use A2 to Eltham then follow signs Blackwall Tunnel to join A102M. Then as above.

From South: Use A21 and A20 then follow signs Blackwall Tunnel to join A102M. Then as above.

From West: From Motorway M4. Follow signs Central London A4. Then Westminster to the Embankment. Follow signs Dover A2, then pass Deptford and join A206. (S.P. Woolwich) then turn right into Charlton Church Lane. Then turn left into Floyd Road for Charlton Athletic F.C.

CHELSEA

Division 1

President
G M Thompson

Chairman
K W Bates

Directors
S S Tollman
B D Spears

Secretary
Sheila Marson

Commercial Manager
Robert Bates (01-385 5546)

Manager
John Neal

Assistant Manager
Ian McNeill

First Team Coach
John Hollins

Youth Development Officer
Gwyn Williams

Physiotherapist
Norman Medhurst

Reserve Team Trainer
Jimmy Hendry

Groundsman
John Ayling

Top place in the Second Division denoted only one thing — that Chelsea had a memorable season in the playing sense. Promotion had at last been achieved and with the bonus of being Champions by overtaking Sheffield Wednesday at the eleventh hour on goal difference (in fact by scoring more goals) celebrations have been very much in order.

Unlike the season of 1962/63 when Sunderland were miraculously overtaken in the 'run-in' Chelsea were always likely to go up and erase the poor playing memories of the previous season. There were hitches but a lowest position of sixth in September and then a brief spell in fourth place in October and November were only temporary lulls in a consistent season, which was not confused by any real cup successes as the best that was achieved was a Milk Cup Third Round place (and home defeat by West Bromwich by a single goal). Prior to that Gillingham (on aggregate) and Leicester City (on penalties) had been dismissed. In the F.A. Cup a visit to Ewood Park in the Third Round began and ended the campaign so the League struggle was not obscured by any distractions. Manager Neal has collected a good blend of experience and youth and there is no reason why there should be any fears for more success in the First Division. There is a good goalkeeper in Niedzwiecki aided by fellow-Welshman Joey Jones with potential stars in Pates, Spackman, the prolific scoring Kerry Dixon and the clever young ball-player Nevin. Prospects look good.

Former Chelsea admirers and present loyal fans will feel apprehensive about the trouble certain unruly elements may cause during any First Division campaign. It would be foolish not to mention that some of the 'fans' at the Bridge would be less trouble to the public if they were placed permanently in straight-jackets and members of the public would be very relieved to hear reassurances this season from the Chelsea directors that any form of hooliganism (even when they are apparently doing some 'harmless' celebrating) meets with their unqualified disapproval and the strongest possible disciplinary action.

It would be tragic if some outside authority were to force the Football authorities to take exemplary disciplinary action against one of their own clubs but unless matters improve in certain places this might tragically happen. WLM.

Back Row L to R: Norman Medhurst (Physio), Jimmy Hendry (Head Trainer), Joey Jones, Colin Lee, Keith Dublin, Willie Watson, Derek Johnstone, Duncan Shearer, Nigel Spackman, Eddie Niedzwiecki, Micky Droy, Steve Francis, Doug Rougvie, Joe McLaughlin, Kerry Dixon, Colin Pates, Paul Canoville, Terry Howard, Tony McAndrew, John Bumstead, Dale Jasper, Gwyn Williams (Youth Development Officer). **Middle Row:** Ian McNeill (Ass. Manager), Keith Jones, Robin Beste, Mickey Thomas, Phil Priest, John Millar, John Neal (Manager), Leo Donnellan, Pat Nevin, Robert Isaacs, David Speedie, Martin Nolan, John Hollins (Player-Coach). **Front Row:** Micky Bodley, Colin West, Simon Chandler, Stockley Sawyers, Perry Baldacchino, Scott Clifford, Grant Lunn, Gary Baker, Andy Hodgetts, Gary Graham, Ian Braithwaite, Paddy McCarthy, Gary Hogan.

'THE BLUES'

Formed: 1905 **Turned Professional:** 1905 **Ltd Co:** 1905
Previous Managers: 1905-6 John Tait Robertson 1907-33 David Calderhead 1933-9 Leslie Knighton 1939-52 Billy Birrell 1952-62 Ted Drake 1962-7 Tommy Docherty 1967-74 Dave Sexton 1974-5 Ron Suart 1975-7 Eddie McCreadie 1977-8 Ken Shellito 1978-9 Danny Blanchflower 1979-81 Geoff Hurst
Honours: Division 1 Champions F.A. Cup Winners 1970 European Cup Winners Cup Winners Football League Cup Winners
League Career: Elected to Division 2 1905 Promoted to Division 1 1906-7 Relegated to Division 2 1909-10 Promoted to Division 1 1911-12 Relegated to Division 2 1923-4 Promoted to Division 1 1929-30 Relegated to Division 2 1961-2 Promoted to Division 1 1962-3 Relegated to Division 2 1974-5 Promoted to Division 1 1976-7 Relegated to Division 2 1978-9 Promoted to Division 1 1983-4
Colours: Royal blue with thin horizontal striped shirts, blue shorts with white stripe on shorts, white stockings
Change Colours: Yellow shirts, blue shorts, yellow stockings

CLUB RECORDS

Most Appearances for Club: Ron Harris: Football League 646 + 9 + F.A. Cup 63 + League Cup 46 + 2 + Charity Shield 1 + ECWC 13 + Fairs Cup 14 + Anglo-Scottish 7 + 1 **Total 790 + 12 subs**
Most Capped Player: Ray Wilkins, 24, England
Record Goalscorer in a Match: George Hilsdon, 6 v Worksop, F.A. Cup 1907-8
Record League Goalscorer in a season: Jimmy Greaves, 41, 1960-1 **All competitions:** Jimmy Greaves, 43 (League 41, F.A. Cup 2)
Record League Goalscorer in a career: Bobby Tambling, 164 **All competitions:** Bobby Tambling, 202 (League 164, F.A. Cup 25, League Cup 10, Fairs Cup 3)
Record Transfer Fee Received: £825,000 from Manchester United for Ray Wilkins, Aug 1979
Record Transfer Fee Paid: £225,000 to Celtic for David Hay
Best Performances: League: Champions (1) **F.A. Cup:** Winners (1) **League/Milk Cup:** Winners (1) **European Cup Winners Cup:** Winners (1) **European Fairs Cup:** Semi-Final
Most League Points: (3pts for win) 88, Div 2, 1983-4 (2pts for win) 57, Div 2, 1906-7 **Most League Goals:** 98, Div 1, 1960-61
Record League Victory: 7-0 v Lincoln City, Div 2, 29 Oct 1910
Record League Defeat: 1-8 v Wolverhampton Wanderers, Div 1, 26.9.53
European Competitions Entered: European Cup Winners Cup: 1970-1, 1971-2 **European Fairs Cup:** 1958-60, 1965-6, 1968-9
Club Statistician for the Directory: D. Fletcher

Programme Editor & Photographer
Hugh Hastings

Price	Number of Pages
60p	28

Subscriptions
£17.50 (U.K. postage) for members per season, £19.00 (U.K. postage) for non-members per season

CHELSEA

PLAYERS NAME Ht Wt Birthdate	Honours	Birthplace Transfers	Clubs	APPEARANCES League	Milk Cup	F.A.C.	E. Cups	GOALS League	Milk Cup	F.A.C.	E. Cups
GOALKEEPERS											
Steve Francis	E. Y	Billericay	Chelsea (A)	66	5	10					
5-11 11.5 29.5.64											
Eddie Niedzwiecki	W. S. Div. 3. 78	Bangor	Wrexham	111	10	7					
6-0 11.0 3.5.59	Div. 2. 84		Chelsea	42	5	1					
DEFENDERS											
Micky Droy		Highbury	Slough T.								
6-4½ 15.5 7.5.51			Chelsea	262+8	17+2	21		13	2	4	
Keith Dublin											
5-7 10.0 29.1.66											
John Hollins	E. (1). B. (5).	Guildford	Chelsea (A)	436	43	50	27	47	7	4	5
5-8 11.7 16.7.46	U. 23(12). Y.	£80,000	Q.P.R.	148+3	11+2	10+1	8	5			
	F. Lg. XI. FAC. 70.	£75,000	Arsenal	123+4	19+1	12	10+3	9	3		1
	FC. 65.	F	Chelsea	29	5	1		1			
	ECWC. 71.										
	Div. 2. 84										
Joey Jones	W. (62). EC. 77.	Llandudno	Wrexham	98	3	8		2			
5-10 11.7 4.3.55	Div. 1. 76. 77.	£110,000	Liverpool	72	4	9	15	3			
	Div. 2. 84.	£210,000	Wrexham	145+1	15	14		6	1	2	
	ESC. 77	£34,000	Chelsea	62	4	4		2			
Joe McLaughlin	S. U. 21(10)	Greenock	Morton	134	17	5		3			
6-1 11.4 2.6.60	Div. 2. 84		Chelsea	41	5	1					
Colin Pates*	E. Y.	Carshalton	Chelsea (A)	150	10	12		6			
6-0 11.0 10.8.61	Div. 2. 84										
Doug Rougvie	S. (1). SPD. (2)		Aberdeen	161+8	38+5	26	26+2	20	2		
	SC. (3). ECWC. 83		Chelsea								
MIDFIELD											
John Bumstead	Div. 2. 84	Rotherhithe	Chelsea (A)	159+6	13+1	10		20	1	2	
5-7 10.0 27.11.58											
Dale Jasper		Croydon	Chelsea (A)	3							
5-6 11.1 14.1.64											
Tony McAndrew	AS. 76	Lanark	Middlesbrough (A)	245+2	13+2	20+4		13	1	1	
5-10 12.4 11.4.56		£92,000	Chelsea	20	2	1		4			
Nigel Spackman	Div. 4. 84	Romsey	Andover								
6-1 12.4 2.12.60			Bournemouth	118+1	5	7		10			
			Chelsea	40	5	1		3			
Micky Thomas	W. (42). U. 23(1).	Mochore	Wrexham	217+13	17+1	20+4	8	33	2	2	
5-6 10.7 2.12.60	U. 21(1). WC. (2).	£300,000	Manchester U.	90	5	13	4	11	2	2	
	Div. 3. 78.	£450,000	Everton	10						1	
	Div. 2. 84	£400,000	Brighton	18+2		6			1		
		£200,000	Stoke C.	57	7			14			
		£75,000	Chelsea	17				4			
FORWARDS											
Paul Canoville	Div. 2. 84	Hillingdon	Hillingdon Boro								
5-10 11.0 4.3.62			Chelsea	34+8	6	1		9	1		
Kerry Dixon	Div. 2. 84	Luton	Dunstable T.								
6-0 13.0 24.7.61		£20,000	Reading	116	6+1	2+1		51			
		£175,000	Chelsea	42	5	1		28	6		
Derek Johnstone	S. (14). U. 23(6). Y.	Dundee	Rangers	233+11	73+2	50+1	28+3	139	37	30	9
5-11 11.6 4.11.53	S. SPD. (2).		Chelsea	0+2							
	S. Div. 1(1). SC. (5).		Dundee U. (L)	2+2	1+1					2	
	SLC. (5).										
	ECWC. 72										
Keith Jones	E. Y. S	Dulwich	Chelsea (A)	0+2							
5-9 10.11 14.10.65											
Colin Lee	Div. 2. 84	Torquay	Bristol C. (A)								
6-1 11.9 12.6.56			Hereford U. (L)	7+2	0+1	2					
		£8,000	Torquay U.	35	3			14	1		
		£60,000	Tottenham H.	57+5	2	6+1		18		3	
		£80,000	Chelsea	134+14	10+2	10		35		2	
Pat Nevin†	S. Y. SD2. (1)	Glasgow	Clyde	60+13	5+3	9		17		3	
5-6 10.0 6.9.63	Div. 2. 84	£95,000	Chelsea	38	3+1	1		14			
David Speedie	Div. 2. 84	Glenrothes	Barnsley	10+13							
5-7 10.4 20.2.60			Darlington	88	4	3		21		1	
			Chelsea	66+5	5+1	4		20	2		

CONTRACT PLAYERS WITH NO FIRST TEAM APPEARANCES: Robin Beste (F), Leo Donnellan (MF), Terry Howard (D), Bob Isaac (D), Martin Nolan (MF), Phil Priest (MF), Duncan Shearer (F), Billy Watson (D)

APPRENTICES: Michael Bodley, Ian Braithwaite, Simon Chandler, Andrew Hodgetts, Grant Lunn, Stokley Sawyers, Colin West

NON-CONTRACT PLAYER 1984-85: R. Baldacchino

CHELSEA

DIVISION TWO 1ST **FA CUP** 3RD ROUND **MILK CUP** 3RD ROUND

MATCH	DATE	COMPETITION	VENUE	OPPONENTS	RESULT	HALF TIME	L'GUE POS'N	GOALSCORERS	ATTENDANCE
1	A 27	CL	H	Derby Co	W5-0	1-0		Spackman, Walker, Hutchings, Dixon 2	17,338
2	**30**	**MC 1**	**A**	**Gillingham**	**W2-1**	**1-1**		**Walker, Dixon**	**8,633**
3	S 3	CL	A	Brighton & HA	W2-1	1-0	2	Dixon 2 (1 pen)	20,874
4	7	CL	A	Blackburn R	D0-0	0-0			5,873
5	10	CL	H	Cambridge U	W2-1	1-1	2	Bumstead, Walker	14,425
6	**13**	**MC 1**	**H**	**Gillingham**	**W4-0**	**2-0**		**Dixon 4**	**9,704**
7	17	CL	A	Sheffield W	L1-2	1-0	6	Walker	20,596
8	24	CL	H	Middlesbrough	D0-0	0-0	6		15,822
9	O 1	CL	A	Huddersfield T	W3-2	1-0	3	Dixon 2, Canoville	13,280
10	**4**	**MC 2**	**A**	**Leicester C**	**W2-0**	**2-0**		**Dixon, Canoville**	**7,825**
11	8	CL	A	Fulham	W5-3	2-2	3	Dixon 2, Jones, Nevin, Lee	24,787
12	15	CL	H	Cardiff C	W2-0	1-0	3	Nevin, Lee	15,459
13	22	CL	A	Carlisle U	D0-0	0-0	4		6,774
14	**25**	**MC 2**	**H**	**Leicester C**	**L0-2***	**0-1**			**15,646**
15	29	CL	H	Charlton Ath	W3-2	2-0	4	Speedie 2, Dixon	17,789
16	N 5	CL	A	Oldham Ath	D1-1	0-0	4	Bumstead	5,807
17	**8**	**MC 3**	**H**	**WBA**	**L0-1**	**0-0**			**22,932**
18	12	CL	H	Newcastle U	W4-0	2-0	4	Spackman, Rhoades-Brown, Speedie 2	30,628
19	15	CL	A	Charlton Ath	D1-1	0-0		Nevin	14,393
20	19	CL	H	Crystal Palace	D2-2	1-2	3	Hollins, Speedie	19,060
21	22	CL	A	Swansea C	W3-1	3-1		Bumstead, Dixon, Nevin	7,840
22	26	CL	A	Leeds U	D1-1	0-0	2	Dixon	20,680
23	D 3	CL	H	Manchester C	L0-1	0-1	3		29,142
24	6	CL	H	Swansea C	W6-1	3-0		Canoville 3, Nevin, Dixon, Bumstead	12,389
25	10	CL	A	Barnsley	D0-0	0-0	2		10,300
26	17	CL	H	Grimsby T	L2-3	1-0	2	Dixon (pen), Bumstead	13,151
27	26	CL	A	Shrewsbury T	W4-2	0-1	2	Dixon (pen), Speedie, Bumstead 2	7,582
28	27	CL	H	Portsmouth	D2-2	2-2	2	Canoville, Dixon	25,440
29	31	CL	H	Brighton & HA	W1-0	0-0	1	Speedie	18,542
30	J 2	CL	A	Middlesbrough	L1-2	0-1	2	McAndrew	11,579
31	**7**	**FAC 3**	**A**	**Blackburn R**	**L0-1**	**0-1**			**10,940**
32	14	CL	A	Derby Co	W2-1	1-0	2	Cherry (og), McAndrew (pen)	16,727
33	21	CL	H	Sheffield W	W3-2	2-0	1	Thomas 2, Nevin	35,147
34	F 4	CL	H	Huddersfield T	W3-1	2-0	1	Dixon 2, Speedie	17,922
35	11	CL	A	Cambridge U	W1-0	1-0	1	McAndrew	10,602
36	25	CL	H	Carlisle U	D0-0	0-0	2		16,543
37	M 3	CL	H	Oldham Ath	W3-0	1-0	1	Speedie, Dixon, McAndrew (pen)	12,736
38	10	CL	A	Newcastle U	D1-1	0-0	1	Speedie	36,504
39	16	CL	H	Blackburn R	W2-1	2-0		Nevin, Speedie	18,905
40	31	CL	A	Cardiff C	D3-3	0-3	1	Dixon, Lee, Spackman (pen)	11,060
41	A 7	CL	H	Fulham	W4-0	3-0	1	Dixon 2, Speedie, Nevin	31,947
42	14	CL	A	Crystal Palace	W1-0	0-0	2	Nevin	20,540
43	21	CL	H	Shrewsbury T	W3-0	2-0	2	Dixon 2, Nevin	17,295
44	24	CL	A	Portsmouth	D2-2	1-0		Thomas, Nevin (pen)	19,267
45	28	CL	H	Leeds U	W5-0	3-0	2	Thomas, Dixon 3, Canoville	33,447
46	M 4	CL	A	Manchester C	W2-0	0-0		Nevin, Dixon	21,713
47	7	CL	H	Barnsley	W3-1	1-0	1	Speedie, Nevin 2	29,541
48	12	CL	A	Grimsby T	W1-0	1-0	1	Dixon	13,000

*Won On Penalties

Av Home Att **21,079**

Goal Scorers

League (90): Dixon 28 (3 pens), Nevin 14 (1 pen), Speedie 13, Bumstead 7, Canoville 6, McAndrew 4 (2 pens), Thomas 4, Lee 3, Spackman 3 (1 pen), Walker 3, Hollins 1, Hutchings 1, Jones 1, Rhoades-Brown 1, opponents 1

FA Cup (-): —

Milk Cup (8): Dixon 6, Canoville 1, Walker 1

1983-84

Niedzwiecki	Hollins	Hutchings	Pates	McLaughlin	Bumstead	Walker	Spackman	Dixon	Lee	Canoville	Speedie	Jones	Nevin	Rhoades-Brown	McAndrew	Thomas	Johnstone	Jasper	Dublin	REFEREE	
1	2	3	4	5	6	7	8	9	10	11										A Gunn	1
1	**2**	**3**	**4**	**5**	**6**	**7**	**8**	**9**	**10**	**11**										**J Martin**	**2**
1	2	3	4	5	6	7	8	9	10	11†										K Baker	3
1	2	3	4	5	6	7*	8	9	10	11	12									R Nixon	4
1	2		5	6	4	7	8	9	10	11		3								H Bodenham	5
1	**2**		**4**	**5**	**6**	**7**	**8**	**9**	**10**			**3**	**12**	**11***						**T Spencer**	**6**
1	2		4	5	6	7	8	9	10		12	3	11							AR Bridges	7
1	2		4	5	6	7	8	9	10*		12	3	11							D Brazier	8
1	2		4	5	6*		8	9	10	7		3	11							J Lovatt	9
1	**2**		**4**	**5**	**6**		**8**	**9**	**10**	**7***	**12**	**3**	**11**							**J Key**	**10**
1	2		4	5	6		8	9	10	11	12	3	7*							TG Bune	11
1	2		4	5	6		7	9	10	8		3	11							M Scott	12
1	2		4	5	6		8	9	10*	7	12	3	11							D Richardson	13
1	**2**		**4**	**5**			**8**	**9**	**10**	**7**	**6**	**3**	**11**							**L Shapter**	**14**
1	2		4	5	6		8	9		7	10	3	11							L Burden	15
1	2		4	5	6		8	9	12	7	10*	3	11							A Saunders	16
1	**2**		**4**	**5**	**6**		**8**	**9**	**12**	**7***	**10**	**3**	**11**							**Alan Robinson**	**17**
1	2		4	5	6		8	9	12		10	3	7	11*						H King	18
1	2	3	4	5	6		8	9			10		7	11						K Hackett	19
1	2		4	5	6*		8	9	12		10	3	7	11						R Milford	20
1	2		4	5	6		8	9			10	3	7	11						L Robinson	21
1	2		4	5	6		8	9	12		10	3	7	11*						N Midgley	22
1	2		4	5	6		8	9	12		10	3	7	11*						I Borrett	23
1	2		4	5	6		8	9		11	10	3	7							JE Bray	24
1	2		4	5	6		8	9		11	10	3	7							N Wilson	25
1	2		4	5	6		8	9	12	11	10*	3	7							D Axcell	26
1	2		4	5	6			9		11	10	3	7		8					I Hendrick	27
1	2		4	5	6*			9	12	11	10	3	7		8					M Taylor	28
1	2		4	5			8	9		11	10	3	7		6					A Seville	29
1	2		4	5			8	9	12	11*	10	3	7		6					T Jones	30
1	**2**		**4**	**5**			**8**	**9**		**11**	**10**	**3**	**7**		**6**					**G Courtney**	**31**
1			4	5			8	9	2		10	3	7		6	11				N Glover	32
1			4	5			8	9	2		10	3	7		6	11				B Stevens	33
1			4	5			8	9	2		10	3	7		6	11				J Deakin	34
1			4	5			8	9	2		10	3	7		6	11				J Ashworth	35
1	3		4	5			8	9	2		10		7		6*	11	12			D Hedges	36
1	3		4	5			8	9	2		10		7		6	11				C Thomas	37
1			4	5			8	9	2		10	3	7		6	11				J Hough	38
1			4	5			8	9	2		10	3	7		6	11*	12			H Taylor	39
1			4		12		8	9	2		10	3	7		6*	11		5		R Nixon	40
1			4	5	6		8	9	2		10	3	7			11				J Martin	41
1			4	5	6		8	9	2	12	10	3	7			11*				B Hill	42
1			4	5	6		8	9	2		10	3	7			11				T Spencer	43
1			4	5	6		8	9	2		10	3	7			11				M Bodenham	44
1			4	5	6*		8	9	2	12	10	3	7			11				G Napthine	45
1			4	5	6		8	9	2	12	10	3*	7			11				A Saunders	46
1	2		4	5			8	9			10		7			11		6	3	V Callow	47
1	2		4	5	6		8	9			10		7			11		3		D Shaw	48
42	29	4	**42**	41	30	6	40	**42**	25	17	32	34	38	6	13	17	0	3	1	League Appearances	
					+1S				+8S	+3S	+5S						+2				
1	1		1	1			1	1		1	1	1	1		1					FA Cup Appearances	
5	5	1	5	5	4	2	5	5	4+1S	4	2+1S	4	3+1S	1						Milk Cup Appearances	

STAMFORD BRIDGE

Official Address: Stamford Bridge, London S.W.6. Telephone: 01-385 5545/6. Information Service: 01-381 0111

Telegraphic: Chelstam London SW6

Ground Capacity: 44,200

Record Attendance: 82,905 v. Arsenal, Division 1, 12 Oct 1935

Record Receipts: £158,277 v. Tottenham Hotspur, F.A. Cup Round 6, 6 Mar 1982

Size of Playing Area: 114yds × 75 yds

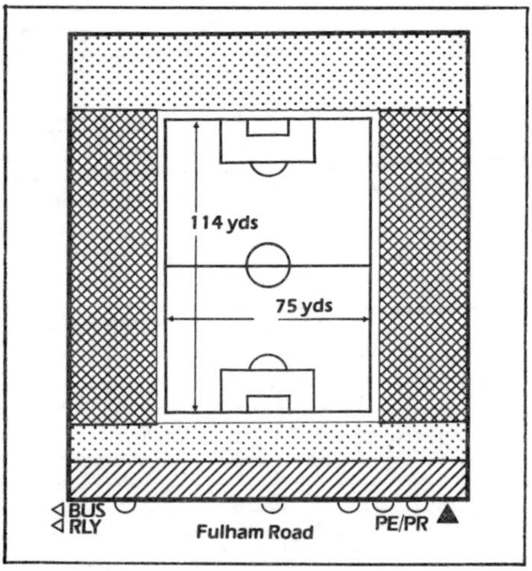

For key see page 12

Season Tickets: Stand: £96.00, £120.00, £144.00, £192.00. Ground: £72.00 (adults), £36.00 (juveniles/OAP)

Executive Box Season Tickets: £600; £5,000-£7,000 (includes use of restaurant)

Cost of Stand Tickets: £5.00, £6.00, £8.00; **Terraces:** £3.00 (£1.50 juveniles/OAP)

Match and Ticket Information: Personal or postal bookings are accepted in advance. No telephone bookings

Car Parking: Street parking only available

How to get to the ground

From North: From Motorway M1 and A1. Follow signs Central London to Hyde Park Corner, then follow signs Guildford (A3) into Knightsbridge A4. In 1m turn left A308 into Fulham Road for Chelsea F.C.
From East: Via Hyde Park Corner as above or via Embankment and Cheyne Walk A3212. Follow signs Chelsea A322C then at crossroads turn left A308 into Fulham Road for Chelsea F.C.
From South: Use A13 or A24 then A219 to cross Putney Bridge. Follow signs West End A304, then join A308 into Fulham Road for Chelsea F.C.
From West: From Motorway M4. Follow signs Central London, then Westminster A3220. In 0.8m at crossroads turn right A308 into Fulham Road for Chelsea F.C.

CHESTER CITY Division 4

President
R Rowlands

Chairman
AE Barnes, JP, TCA

Directors
G Thompson, Vice Chairman
RH Crofts
L Lloyd
RH Tressider
D Darlington
F Summers

Secretary
JA Eckersley

Assistant Secretary
I Ireland

Manager
John McGrath

Reserve & Youth Manager
Cliff Sear

Commercial Manager
B Fawkes (0244 378162)

Club Captain
A Holden

Groundsman
R Spencer

The 1983/84 season can, at best, be described as traumatic. The club finished rooted firmly at the bottom of the Fourth Division and had to apply for re-election to The Football League.

The writing was on the wall before the season started when manager John Sainty was only allowed to sign two new players despite having had a clear out at the end of the previous season. Chester started with many non-contract players and even recruited one off the dole. So under these circumstances there was no way a successful season could be expected.

The only bright spot early on was in the Milk Cup where Bolton Wanderers were defeated in the First Round and a superb 1-0 victory was achieved at Leeds before losing at home 1-4 in the Second Round second leg.

Poor league form was the order of the day due to an inability to score goals and a number of late goals being conceded. This, combined with an early exit from the FA Cup, led to the dismissal of John Sainty. This was a not unexpected move, but much sympathy was felt for a man who could not expect any financial support for new players.

The longest serving player Trevor Storton took over as caretaker coach but, despite an initial improvement, the side again struggled and Storton resigned and shortly after left the club altogether. A sad exit for a player who had given Chester ten years of tremendous service.

John McGrath, the ex-Port Vale manager, arrived early in the year and at least the club started to 'buzz' again.

Lee Dixon and Andy Wharton from Burnley made an immediate impact and for the first time optimism filtered through to the long suffering supporters on the terrace.

Goalscoring was still a problem but there was hope for things to come although defenders Andy Holden and Peter Zelem finished as leading goalscorers.

The future under John McGrath certainly looks promising. In Andy Holden he has a player of real quality who in his first season attracted scouts from the big clubs to Sealand Road. If a couple more goalscorers can be found to round off the good approach work then 1984/85 could see Chester City regain its pride and once again be a challenger at the top of the table.

Derrick Orme
The League Directory's Statistician for the Club

Back Row L to R: Mick Speight, Nigel Walker, Bobby Coy, Dave Evans, Alan Morris, Andy Higgins, Andy Holden, Paul Sanderson, Peter Zelem, Paul Blackwell. **Front Row:** Ronnie Hildersley, Andy Wharton, Peter Sayer, Martin Lane, Phil Harrington, Steve Fox, Lee Dixon, Peter Bulmer, Dave Brett.

'THE BLUES'

Sponsored by **Chester Engineering**

Formed: 1884 **Turned Professional:** 1902 **Ltd Co:** 1909
Previous Names: Chester until 1983
Previous Managers: 1930-36 Charles Hewitt 1936-38 Alex Raisbeck 1938-53 Frank Brown 1953-56 Louis Page 1956-59 John Harris 1959-61 Stan Pearson 1961-63 Bill Lambton 1963-68 Peter Hauser 1968-76 Ken Roberts 1976-82 Alan Oakes 1982-82 Cliff Sears* 1982-83 John Sainty*
* Includes period as caretaker manager
Honours: Welsh Cup Winners (3) Debenhams Cup Winners, 1977
League Career: Elected to Division 3 (N) 1931 Division Four 1957-58 Promoted to Division 3 1974-75 Relegated to Division 4 1981-82
Colours: Royal Blue shirts with white pin stripe, white shorts and blue stockings
Change Colours: All Yellow

CLUB RECORDS

Most Appearances for Club: Trevor Storton: Football League 396, 23 F.A. Cup, 28 League Cup, 3 Football League Trophy, 3 Group Cup, **Total 453**
Most Capped Player: Bill Lewis, 7 for Wales. **For England:** None
Record Goalscorer in a Match: Barry Jepson, 5 v York City in Division 4 08.02.58
Record League Goalscorer in a season: Dick Yates, 36, Div 3 (N), 1946-47 **All Competitions:** Dick Yates, 44, (36 League, 8 in other first team fixtures) 1946-47
Record League Goalscorer in a career: Gary Talbot, 83, 1963-66 **All Competitions:** Gary Talbot, 100 (83 League and 17 Cup goals), 1963-6
Record Transfer Fee Received: £300,000 from Liverpool for Ian Rush, May 1980
Record Transfer Fee Paid: £45,000 to Carlisle United for Steve Ludlam, May 1980
Best Performances: League: 5th Div 3 1977-78 **F.A. Cup:** 5th Round Replay, 1976-77, 1979-80 **League/Milk Cup:** Semi-Final 1974-75 **Welsh Cup:** Winners (3)
Most League Goals: 119, Div 4, 1964-65
Most League Points: (2pts for win) 56 in Div 3(N), 1946-47, 56 in Sic 4, 1964-5; (3pts for win) 56 in Div 4, 1982-3
Record League Victory: 12-0 v York City, Div 3 (N), 1 Feb 1936
Record League Defeat: 2-11 v Oldham Athletic, Div 3 (N), 19 Jan 1952
Club Statistician for the Directory: Derek Orme

Programme Editor & Photographer
Hugh Hastings

Price	Number of Pages
60p	28

Subscriptions
£17.50 (U.K. postage) for members per season, £19.00 (U.K. postage) for non-members per season

CHESTER CITY

PLAYERS NAME Ht Wt Birthdate	Honours	Birthplace Transfers	Clubs	APPEARANCES League	Milk Cup	F.A.C.	A.M.C.	GOALS League	Milk Cup	F.A.C.	A.M.C.
GOALKEEPER											
John Butcher		Newcastle	Blackburn R.	104	9	5					
6-2 12.3 27.5.56			Oxford U.	16	1	4	1				
			Bury (L)	11							
			Chester C.								
Phil Harrington	W. Y	Bangor	Chester	70	4	1	1				
5-10 11.4 20.11.63											
DEFENDERS											
Bobby Coy		Birmingham	Wolverhampton W. (A)	40+13	4						
5-11 11.12 30.11.61			Chester	14							
Lee Dixon		Manchester	Burnley	4	1						
5-9½ 10.12 17.3.64			Chester	16			2	1			
David Evans		Chester	Chester (A)	10							
6-0 11.3 4.4.67											
Andy Higgins		Bolsover	Chesterfield	1							
6-3 12.4 12.2.60			Port Vale	11+3	0+1	2					
			Hartlepool U.	3+1	1			1			
			Rochdale	31+2	2	2		6			
			Chester								
Martin Lane		Altrincham	Manchester U.								
5-9 11.4 12.4.61			Chester	79	6	3	2	2			
Paul Sanderson		Leeds	Manchester C. (A)								
6-0 11.7 16.2.66			Chester	24							
Peter Zelem		Manchester	Chester (A)	109+5	6	4	2	11	2	1	
6-0 11.6 13.2.62											
MIDFIELD											
Paul Blackwell		Mancot	Chester	80+5	2	2+1	2	3			
5-10 11.5 13.1.63											
David Brett		Chester	Chester C.	24+5	0+1	1+1	2				
5-8 10.7 8.4.61											
Andy Holden*†	W.(1), U.21(1)	Flint	Chester	44	4	1	2	7	1		1
6-1 13.2 14.9.62											
Peter Sayer	W.(7), U.21(2)	Cardiff	Cardiff C.	70+12	7	4		14	2	2	
5-7 11.0 2.5.55		£100,000	Brighton	46+9	7	1+1		6			
		£80,000	P.N.E.	42+3	0+1	2		6			
			Cardiff C. (L)	4				1			
			Rotherham U.	4							
			Chester								
Micky Speight	E. B(4)	Upton	Sheffield U. (A)	184+15	6+1	8+2		14	1		
5-10½ 12.7 1.11.51		£60,000	Blackburn R.	50+1	6			4			
		£25,000	Grimsby T.	35+3	2	2		2			
Nigel Walker		Gateshead	Newcastle U.	65+5	1	3					
5-10 11.11 7.4.59		F	San Diego								
			Sunderland								
			Crewe A. (N-C)	20		5					
			Sunderland	0+1							
			Blackpool (L)	8+2							
			Chester								
Andy Wharton		Rossendale	Burnley (A)	63+2	7	6+3		6	2	1	
5-6 11.6 21.12.61			Torquay U. (L)	10							
			Chester C.	15							
Alan Morris			Bangor C.								
FORWARDS											
Peter Bulmer		Liverpool	Chester (A)	19+14	2+2	1		1			
5-9 11.4 31.8.65											
Terry Cooke		Wrexham	Chester (A)	37+12	2+1	1		11			
5-10 10.8 21.2.62											
Steve Fox		Tamworth	Birmingham C. (A)	26+3				1			
5-8 11.2 17.2.58		£90,000	Wrexham	136+6	7+1	15		10			
		F	Port Vale	71+3	4	2	2	6			
		F	Chester C.								
Ronnie Hildersley		Kirkcaldy	Manchester C. (A)	1			3				
5-4 9.2 6.4.65			Chester	9			1				

NON-CONTRACT PLAYERS 1984-85:

Dennis Burke (G), Peter Donnelly

CHESTER CITY

DIVISION FOUR 24TH **FA CUP** 1ST ROUND **MILK CUP** 2ND ROUND

MATCH	DATE	COMPE-TITION	VENUE	OPPONENTS	RESULT	HALF TIME	L'GUE POS'N	GOALSCORERS	ATTEN-DANCE
1	A 27	CL	H	Northampton T	D1-1	1-1		Williams P	1,680
2	**30**	**MC 1**	**A**	**Bolton W**	**L0-3**	**0-2**			**2,665**
3	S 3	CL	A	Swindon T	L0-4	0-1	20		2,891
4	7	CL	A	Hereford U	L1-2	1-1		Allen	3,480
5	10	CL	H	Crewe Alex	L0-1	0-0	23		2,090
6	**14**	**MC 1**	**H**	**Bolton W**	**W3-0[4]**	**1-0**		**Holden, Zelem (pen), Phillips**	**1,502**
7	17	CL	A	York C	L1-4	1-3	24	Holden	3,037
8	24	CL	H	Reading	W2-1	1-1	22	Parker, Blackwell	1,367
9	28	CL	H	Torquay U	L1-2	0-1		Elliott	1,356
10	O 1	CL	A	Colchester U	L0-1	0-0	24		1,976
11	**5**	**MC 2**	**A**	**Leeds U**	**W1-0**	**1-0**		**Elliott**	**8,106**
12	8	CL	A	Darlington	L1-2	0-0	24	Gilbert (og)	1,117
13	19	CL	A	Hartlepool U	D1-1	0-0		Parker	1,150
14	22	CL	H	Stockport Co	L2-4	1-2	24	Storton, Williams M	1,495
15	**26**	**MC 2**	**H**	**Leeds U**	**L1-4**	**0-1**		**Zelem**	**8,044**
16	29	CL	A	Rochdale	D1-1	0-0	24	Parker	1,481
17	N 2	CL	H	Halifax T	D1-1	0-0		Parker	1,211
18	5	CL	A	Chesterfield	D1-1	0-1	23	Parker	3,513
19	9	CL	H	Blackpool	L0-2	0-1			2,286
20	12	CL	H	Aldershot	L1-2	0-2	23	Holden	975
21	**19**	**FAC 1**	**H**	**Chesterfield**	**L1-2**	**0-1**		**Holden**	**1,774**
22	26	CL	A	Doncaster R	D0-0	0-0	23		2,967
23	D 3	CL	H	Bury	W2-1	0-0	23	Allen, Camden	1,341
24	17	CL	H	Peterborough U	D1-1	1-0	23	Waddle (og)	1,191
25	26	CL	A	Wrexham	L0-2	0-1	23		5,756
26	27	CL	H	Mansfield T	L0-4	0-3	23		1,431
27	31	CL	A	Bristol C	L2-4	1-0	24	Camden, Brett	7,293
28	J 2	CL	H	Tranmere R	D0-0	0-0	23		2,672
29	14	CL	A	Northampton T	L1-2	1-1	23	Phillips	2,198
30	28	CL	A	Crewe Alex	D1-1	1-1	23	Phillips	3,096
31	F 4	CL	H	Colchester U	L1-4	0-2	24	Blackwell	1,179
32	8	CL	H	Swindon T	L0-3	0-3			880
33	11	CL	A	Reading	L0-1	0-0	24		3,280
34	14	CL	A	Halifax T	D2-2	2-1		Elliott, Holden	911
35	18	CL	H	Rochdale	W1-0	0-0	24	Zelem	1,423
36	**22**	**AMC 1**	**H**	**Blackpool**	**W2-1[1]**	**1-1**		**Zelem (pen), Serella (og)**	**1,046**
37	24	CL	A	Stockport Co	L1-2	1-1		Holden	2,006
38	M 3	CL	H	Hartlepool U	W4-1	3-1	24	Wharton, Holden, Zelem (pen), Sanderson	1,241
39	7	CL	H	Chesterfield	L0-2	0-1			1,334
40	10	CL	A	Aldershot	L2-5	0-3	24	Dixon, Holden	2,879
41	**12**	**AMC 2**	**A**	**Tranmere R**	**L1-4**	**0-1**		**Holden**	**2,116**
42	17	CL	H	Darlington	W2-1	1-0	24	Zelem 2 (2 pens)	981
43	24	CL	A	Blackpool	D3-3	0-1	24	Zelem, Wharton, Sanderson	4,746
44	A 7	CL	H	Hereford U	L0-1	0-0	24		1,346
45	14	CL	A	Bury	L1-2	1-1	24	Holden	1,414
46	18	CL	H	York C	D1-1	1-1		Brett	1,750
47	21	CL	H	Wrexham	W1-0	0-0	24	Sanderson	3,486
48	24	CL	A	Mansfield T	L1-3	1-0		Zelem	2,346
49	28	CL	H	Doncaster R	W1-0	1-0	24	Elliott	1,549
50	M 2	CL	A	Torquay U	L0-1	0-1			967
51	5	CL	A	Tranmere R	D2-2	1-1	24	Blackwell, Allen	1,592
52	7	CL	H	Bristol C	L1-2	0-1	24	Zelem	3,900
53	12	CL	A	Peterborough U	L0-1	0-0	24		1,679

[4]Won On Penalties [1]After Extra Time — **Av Home Att** **1,659**

Goal Scorers

League (45): Holden 7, Zelem 7 (3 pens), Parker 5, Allen 3, Blackwell 3, Elliott 3, Sanderson 3, Brett 2, Camden 2, Phillips 2, Wharton 2, Dixon 1, Storton 1, Williams M 1, Williams P 1, opponents 2
FA Cup (1): Holden 1
Milk Cup (5): Zelem 2 (1 pen), Elliott 1, Holden 1, Phillips 1
AMC (3): Holden 1, Zelem 1 (1 pen), opponent 1

1983-84

Harrington	Coy (L)	Lane	Brett	Zelem	Holden	Bulmer	Allen	Manns	Blackwell	Williams P (L)	Elliott	Dixon	Phillips	Storton	Williams M	Parker	Wharton	Ryan	Wann	Sutcliffe	Camden	Evans	Hildersley (L)	Sanderson	REFEREE	
1		3	4*	5	6	7	8	9	10	11		12													K Walmsley	1
1		**3**		**5**	**6**	**7**	**8**	**9**	**10**	**11**	**4**														**D Letts**	**2**
1		3		5	6	7	8	9	11		4														A Buksh	3
1		3		5	6		8	7	10		4		9		12										E Read	4
1		3		5	6	12	8	7	11		4		9		2										K Barratt	5
1		**3**		**5**	**10**	**12**	**8**	**7**	**11**		**4**		**9**	**6***	**2**										**H Taylor**	**6**
1		3		5	10	12	8	7	11		4		9*	6	2										M Peck	7
1		3		5	6		8	7	10	11	12			2	4*	9									J Hendrick	8
1		3		5	6	12	8	7*	10	11	4			2		9									D Scott	9
1		3		5	6	12	8		10*	11	4				2	9		7							M Bodenham	10
1		**3**	**12**	**5**	**6**	**7**	**8**			**11**	**4**		**10***		**2**	**9**									**A Saunders**	**11**
1		3	4	5	6		8		10	11	9				2			7							D Richardson	12
1			4*	5	6	11	9	7		12				8	2	10		3							M Dimblebee	13
1		3			6	7*	12	8	10	11	4			5	2	9									C Seel	14
1		**3**		**5**	**6**	**12**	**9**			**7**	**4**		**8***	**2**		**10**			**11**						**A Robinson**	**15**
1		3		5	6		8	4*	10		12				7	9		2	11						K Redfern	16
1		3		8	6	9		7			4			5	2	10			11						D Allison	17
1		3		8	6	9	11	7*	4		12			5	2	10									J Bray	18
1		3		8	6		11*	7	12		4			5	2	10				9					A Seville	19
1		3	4	5	6	11		10						8	2				12	7*	9				C Thomas	20
1		**3**	**4**	**5**	**6**	**11**	**7**	**10**	**8**						**2**						**9**				**L Dilkes**	**21**
1		3	4	5	6		7	10						8						11	9	2			G Courtney	22
1		3	4	5	6		7	10*			12			8						11	9	2			V Callow	23
1		3	4*	5	6		7		12				10	8						11	9	2			D Hutchinson	24
1		3	4	5	6		7		12				10	8						11	9*	2			T Holbrook	25
1			12	5	9		7		6		4*		10	8	3					11		2			J Deakin	26
1			4	5†	6		7		3		10			8						11†	9	2			T Bune	27
1			8	5			11		3						4					7	9	2	6	10	G Napthine	28
1			7		6		11		3				8		5						10	2	4	9	E Scales	29
1		3		5	10		11						9	4						7		2	6	8	L Robinson	30
1		3		5	10		11		2				9*	4	12					7			6	8	J Key	31
1		3		5*	10		11		9		12			4	7							2	6	8	A Robinson	32
1		3	7	5	10	11*	12		2		4										9		6	8	L Shapter	33
1		3	7	5	9	2	11		10		4												6	8	R Banks	34
1		3		5	4		9		11		7	2					10						6	8	J Ashworth	35
1		**3**	**12**	**5**	**4**		**9**		**11**		**7***	**2**					**10**						**6**	**8**	**K Baker**	**36**
1		3	12	5	4		9		11		7*	2					10						6	8	K Walmsley	37
1		3	7	5	4		9		11		12	2					10							8	A Taylor	38
1	3		4	5	7	12	9*		11			2					10							8	T Fitzharris	39
1	5		7		4	12	9		3		6	2					10							8*	B Hill	40
	9	**3**	**7**	**5**	**4**				**11**			**2**					**10**							**8**	**I Hendrick**	**41**
	9	3	7	5	4				11			2					10							8	K Cooper	42
	5	3	7	4	11				9		12	2					8							10	G Courtney	43
	5	3	7*	5	4		9		11		12	2					10							8	J Hunting	44
	4		7*	3	5	12	10		9		8	2					6							11	K Redfern	45
1	10	3	7		6	2	9		11		4				5									8	N Wilson	46
1	9	3	12	5	4		7		11		6*	2					10							8	N Glover	47
1	9	3	12	5	4		7		11		6	2					10							8*	A Saunders	48
1	9	3		5	4		7		11		6†	2					10							8	D Richardson	49
	9	3	12	5	4		7		11		6*	2					10†							8	T Spencer	50
1	9	3	6	5	4		7		11			2					10							8	M Peck	51
1	9	3	11	5		12	7				6	2			4		10*							8	P Scott	52
1	9	3	10	5	6	12	7		11*			2												8	A Buksh	53
41	14	38	24	42	44	10	40	16	36	6	24	16	9	18	17	9	15	4	2	11	9	10	9	24	League Appearances	
			+5S			+9S	+2S		+3S	+1S	+8S				+2S				+1S							
1		1	1	1	1	1	1	1	1						1						1				FA Cup Appearances	
4		4	1S	4	4	2+2S	4	2	2	3	4		3	2	2	2			1						Milk Cup Appearances	
1	1	2	1+1S	2	2		1		2		1	2					2						1	2	AM Cup Appearances	

Also Played: Raynor matches 1, 2, 3, 4, no.2. Burke match 3, no. 10; 4, no.11*; 5, no.10*; 41, no.1. Manns match 8, no.7. Bowler match 45, no.12. O'Rourke matches 42, 43, 44, 45, 50, no.1. Donnerly match 53, no.4. Wintersgill **(L)** matches 38, 43, no.6*; 39, 41, 42, no.6; 40, no.11.

THE STADIUM, SEALAND ROAD

Official Address: Sealand Road, Chester CH1 4LW. Telephone: Chester (0244) 371376

Ground Capacity: 20,000

Record Attendance: 20,500 v. Chelsea, F.A. Cup Round 3 Replay, 16 Jan 1952

Record Receipts: £15,854 v. Aston Villa, League Cup Semi-Final 1st Leg, 15 Jan 1975

Size of Playing Area: 114yds × 76 yds

Season Tickets: Stand: £54.00

Executive Box Season Tickets: £75.00 exclusive lounge, car park and seats

Cost of Stand Tickets: £3.00, **Terraces:** £1.80

Match and Ticket Information: No advance booking

Car Parking: Extensive at ground

For key see page 12

How to get to the ground

From North: Use Motorway M56, A41 or A56 S.P. Chester into town centre, then follow signs Queensferry A548 into Sealand Road for Chester F.C.
From East: Use A54 or A51 S.P. Chester into town centre, then follow signs Queensferry A548 into Sealand for Chester F.C.
From South: Use A41 or A483 S.P. Chester into town centre then follow signs Queensferry A548 into Sealand for Chester F.C.
From West: Use A55, A494 or A548 S.P. Chester, then follow signs to Queensferry. Follow signs Birkenhead A494 then in 1.2m branch left to join A548 S.P. Chester into Sealand Road for Chester F.C.

CHESTERFIELD — Division 4

President
His Grace The Duke of Devonshire, MC, DL, JP

Chairman
BW Hubbard

Directors
DP Kelly
E Brocklehurst
P Taylor
KR Unwin
B Watson
RAC Woodhead
D Wright

Secretary
Bob Pepper

Manager
John Duncan

Trainer/Coach
Kevin Randall

Player/Coach
Steve Baines

Youth Team Coach
Derek Cluley

Commercial Manager
Alan Humphreys (0246 31535)

A position in the lower half of the Fourth Division and early elimination from both cup competitions suggests a most moderate season for Chesterfield. With limited financial resources at the club's disposal this could be a permanent summary, but Football is not always predictable and each club can find factors which can break monotonies.

Such excitement as there was for the 'Spireites' was created in the early part of the season when four Milk Cup games brought considerable credit. First, Middlesbrough lost by a single goal at Ayresome Park in the First Round and although they redeemed that deficit at Saltergate the penalty 'shoot-out' went in favour of the home team, who then met Everton and after losing again by a single goal in the home leg, the visitors gave the Goodison Park crowd many anxious moments in a drawn return; another Chesterfield goal, being away from home, would have eliminated Everton. The FA Cup was less good, as a fine win over Chester City away from home was followed in the Second Round by a replay defeat and elimination at Turf Moor. This left the players to try their best to draw and entertain reasonable crowds in the League – a most difficult task.

Manager John Duncan, who had a good record at Scunthorpe, has a gigantic job on his hands without much in the way of talent to be successful. The consistent Baines, Kendal and Newton provide his best prospects with, perhaps, a shrewd use of bargain signings in the transfer market.

WLM

Back Row L to R: Shaun O'Neill, Brian Scrimgeour, Gary Bellamy, Jim Brown, Les Hunter, Ernie Moss, Chris Marples, Dan Divers, John Matthews, Barrie Stimpson. **Front Row:** Phil Brown, Steve Kendal, Steve Baines (Player-Coach), John Duncan (Manager), Bob Newton, Kevin Randall (Trainer-Coach), Neil Brown, Steve Spooner, Mick Hoskins.

'THE BLUES' OR 'THE SPIREITES'

Sponsored by **Coalite**

Formed: 1866 **Turned Professional** 1891 **Ltd Co** 1871
Previous Managers Bob Brocklebank Bob Marshall 1952-8 Ted Davison 1958-62 Dugald Livingstone 1962-7 Tony McShane 1967-73 Jimmy McGuigan 1973-76 Joe Shaw 1976-80 Arthur Cox 1980-3 Frank Barlow
Honours: Champions Division 3(N) 1930-31 Champions Division 4 1969-36 Anglo Scottish Cup Winners 1980-81
League Career: Elected to Division 2 1899 Failed re-election 1908-09 Re-elected to Division 3(N) 1921-22 Promoted to Division 2 1930-31 Relegated to Division 3(N) 1932-33 Promoted to Division 2 1935-36 Relegated to Division 3(N) 1950-51 Transferred to Division 3 1958 Relegated to Division 4 1960-61 Promoted to Division 3 1969-70 Relegated to Division 4 1982-83
Colours: Royal Blue shirts with white pin stripe, White shorts with blue stripeat sides, white stockings
Change Colours: Red shirt with white pin stripe, black shorts and stockings

CLUB RECORDS

Most Appearances for Club: Dave Blakey: Football League 613 + F.A. Cup 32 + 6 League Cup **Total 651**
Most Capped Player: Walter McMillan, 4. **For England:** None
Record Goalscorer in a Match: No player has ever scored more than 4 goals in a match and this feat has been achieved on 19 occasions
Record League Goalscorer in a season: Jimmy Cookson, 44, Div 3(N), 1925-6 **In All Competitions:** Jimmy Cookson (League 44, F.A. Cup 2), 1925-6
Record League Goalscorer in a career: Ernie Moss, 128, 1968-76, 1979-81 **In All Competitions:** Ernie Moss, 158 (League 128, F.A. Cup 11, League/Milk Cup 12, Anglo-Scottish Cup 3), 1968-76, 1979-81
Record Transfer Fee Received: £200,000 from Wolverhampton Wanderers for Alan Birch, Aug 1981
Record Transfer Fee Paid: £150,000 to Carlisle United for Phil Bonnyman, Mar 1980
Best Performances: League: 4th Div 2 1946-7 **F.A. Cup:** 5th Round **League/Milk Cup:** 4th Round 1964-5
Most League Points: 64, Div 4, 1969-70, Div 3, 1981-82 **Most Goals in a Season:** 102, Div 3(N), 1930-1
Record League Victory: 10-0 v Glossop, Div 2, 13 Jan 1903
Record League Defeat: 1-9 v Port Vale, Div 2, 24 Sept 1932
Club Statistician for the Directory: R West

Programme Editor
P.J. Tooley

Price	**Number of Pages**
40p	16

Subscriptions
For subscription apply to club office

CHESTERFIELD

PLAYERS NAME Ht Wt Birthdate	Honours	Birthplace Transfers	Clubs	APPEARANCES League	Milk Cup	F.A.C.	A.M.C.	GOALS League	Milk Cup	F.A.C.	A.M.C.
GOALKEEPERS											
Jim Brown	S.(1), U.23(4)	Coatbridge	Albion R.	79	5	5					
5-11 12.4 11.5.52			Chesterfield	47	2	2					
			Sheffield U.	170	7	6					
			U.S.A.								
			Cardiff C.	3							
			Kettering								
			Chesterfield	40	4	3	1	1			
Chris Marples		Chesterfield	Chesterfield								
5-11 12.0 3.8.64											
DEFENDERS											
Gary Bellamy		Worksop	Chesterfield (A)	105+3	8	4	1	1			
6-2 11.5 4.7.62											
Neil Brown		Sheffield	Chesterfield (A)	5							
5-10 10.6 16.1.66											
Steve Baines*		Newark	Nottingham F. (A)	2							
6-0 12.12 23.6.54			Huddersfield T.	113+1	11	7		10	1	1	
		£15,000	Bradford C.	98+1	8	4		17	1	2	
		£50,000	Walsall	47+1	2	1		5			
			Bury (L)	7							
		£5,000	Scunthorpe U.	37+1							
			Chesterfield	45	4	3	1	2	1		
Les Hunter		Middlesbrough	Chesterfield (A)	156+9	15+	13+		8	2	1	
6-2 11.10 15.1.55			Scunthorpe U.	61	4	4		7			
			Chesterfield	21				2			
Steve Kendal		Birtley	Nottingham F. (A)	1							
5-10 11.2 4.8.61			Chesterfield	65	3+1	3	1	9			
Brian Scrimageur		Dundee	Dundee	24+10	3+3	1					
6-0 12.13 11.8.59			Chesterfield	41	4	3	1	3	1		
Barry Stimpson		Billingham	Hartlepool U. (A)	66+2	6	5		2			
5-10 11.10 8.2.64			Chesterfield	27		2	1				
MIDFIELD											
Bryan Klug	E. Y	Coventry	Ipswich T. (A)								
5-8 10.10 8.10.60			Wimbledon (L)	10+1							
		F	Chesterfield	27+7	3	1	1	2			
John Matthews		London	Arsenal (A)	38+7	6	4		2	2	1	
6-0 12.6 1.11.55		£90,000	Sheffield U.	98+5	5	5		14			
			Mansfield T.	70+2	3	5	1	6			
			Chesterfield								
Steve Spooner		London	Derby Co. (A)	7+1							
5-11 12.10 25.1.61		F	Halifax T.	71+1	6	4		13			
			Chesterfield	20				3			
FORWARDS											
Phil Brown		Sheffield	Chesterfield	16+1				6			
5-6 9.7 16.1.66											
Ernie Moss	Div. 4, 70	Chesterfield	Chesterfield	271	14+	14		94	6	8	
6-1½ 13.2 19.10.49		£16,000	Peterborough U.	34+1	5	2		9	2	1	
		£20,000	Mansfield T.	56+1	2			21			
		£16,000	Chesterfield	105+2	9	5		33	6		
		£15,000	Port Vale	74	4	5		23	3	2	
		F	Lincoln C.	10+1				2			
		F	Doncaster R.	41+3	4	1	3	15	2		
		F	Chesterfield								
Bob Newton†		Chesterfield	Huddersfield T. (A)	37+5	3+1	3		7	3	2	
5-11 12.6 23.11.56		£5,000	Hartlepool U.	150	5	12		48	2	10	
		£20,000	Port Vale	48	2	1		22	2		
			Chesterfield	33		3		14		3	

NON-CONTRACT PLAYERS 1984-85:

John Duncan, Mike Hoskin, Jim O'Neill (31 app. 2g.), **Kevin Randell, Leslie Robinson, Colin Thacker, Simon Taylor, David Walsh, Andy Crowther, Adee Davison, John Foster, Jim Hewitt, Lee Pressley, Andy Taylor, Andy Wood**

CHESTERFIELD

DIVISION FOUR 13TH **FA CUP** 2ND ROUND **MILK CUP** 2ND ROUND

MATCH	DATE	COMPETITION	VENUE	OPPONENTS	RESULT	HALF TIME	L'GUE POS'N	GOALSCORERS	ATTENDANCE
1	A 27	CL	H	Swindon T	W1-0	1-0		Birch	4,161
2	**30**	**MC 1**	**A**	**Middlesbrough**	**W1-0**	**0-0**		**Baines**	**7,126**
3	S 3	CL	A	Crewe Alex	L1-2	0-1	12	Klug	2,298
4	7	CL	A	Hartlepool U	D2-2	1-2		Kendal 2	1,661
5	10	CL	H	York C	W2-1	1-0	8	Clayton 2	4,041
6	**13**	**MC 1**	**H**	**Middlesbrough**	**L0-1**[4]	**0-0**			**5,949**
7	17	CL	A	Reading	D1-1	0-0	8	Spooner	2,985
8	24	CL	H	Colchester U	D1-1	0-0	10	Birch	4,106
9	27	CL	H	Hereford U	D0-0	0-0			4,040
10	O 1	CL	A	Northampton T	D1-1	0-0	11	Birch	2,733
11	**4**	**MC 2**	**H**	**Everton**	**L0-1**	**0-1**			**10,713**
12	8	CL	H	Stockport Co	W2-0	0-0	8	Brown J, Spooner	3,846
13	15	CL	A	Rochdale	W4-2	2-0	4	Bellamy, Newton 2, Spooner	1,762
14	18	CL	H	Doncaster R	D0-0	0-0			6,488
15	22	CL	A	Blackpool	L0-1	0-0	9		4,206
16	**26**	**MC 2**	**A**	**Everton**	**D2-2**	**0-1**		**Scrimgeour, Birch (pen)**	**8,067**
17	29	CL	H	Darlington	D1-1	0-0	11	Bell	3,200
18	N 2	CL	A	Torquay U	D1-1	0-0		Bell (pen)	1,542
19	5	CL	H	Chester C	D1-1	1-0	10	Bell	3,513
20	12	CL	A	Peterborough U	L0-2	0-1	14		3,807
21	**19**	**FAC 1**	**A**	**Chester C**	**W2-1**	**1-0**		**Newton 2**	**1,774**
22	26	CL	A	Bristol C	L0-2	0-0	16		5,797
23	D 3	CL	H	Tranmere R	D3-3	1-2	18	Clayton, Birch (pen), Kendal	2,796
24	**10**	**FAC 2**	**H**	**Burnley**	**D2-2**	**1-2**		**Newton, Birch (pen)**	**5,788**
25	17	CL	H	Wrexham	D1-1	0-1	15	Clayton	2,616
26	**19**	**FAC 2R**	**A**	**Burnley**	**L2-3**	**1-2**		**Birch (pen), Bellamy**	**8,286**
27	26	CL	A	Mansfield T	W1-0	1-0	16	Kendal	6,734
28	27	CL	H	Bury	L1-5	0-3	16	Newton	4,196
29	31	CL	A	Aldershot	L1-2	1-2	16	Kendal	1,899
30	J 2	CL	H	Halifax T	D0-0	0-0	16		2,298
31	7	CL	H	Crewe Alex	L1-3	1-0	19	Kendal	2,470
32	14	CL	A	Swindon T	W2-1	1-1	15	Kendal, Newton	3,936
33	21	CL	H	Reading	W2-1	0-0	14	Newton 2	3,010
34	31	CL	A	York C	L0-1	0-1			4,782
35	F 4	CL	H	Northampton T	W2-1	0-0	14	Clayton, Scrimgeour	3,280
36	11	CL	A	Colchester U	L0-2	0-2	16		2,358
37	18	CL	A	Darlington	L1-2	1-0	16	Waddington	1,350
38	**21**	**AMC 1**	**A**	**Scunthorpe U**	**L1-2**	**1-1**		**Birch (pen)**	**2,507**
39	25	CL	H	Blackpool	D1-1	1-1	16	Brown P	3,281
40	M 3	CL	A	Doncaster R	L1-2	0-0	17	Birch (pen)	4,162
41	7	CL	A	Chester C	W2-0	1-0		Scrimgeour 2	1,334
42	10	CL	H	Peterborough U	W1-0	1-0	16	Hunter	2,853
43	16	CL	A	Stockport Co	L0-2	0-2			2,010
44	18	CL	H	Torquay U	W3-2	0-2		Newton 2 (1 pen), Brown P	3,142
45	24	CL	H	Rochdale	W3-0	1-0	12	Brown P, Newton 2 (1 pen)	2,955
46	31	CL	A	Hereford U	L1-3	1-1	13	Newton	2,211
47	A 7	CL	H	Hartlepool U	W4-1	4-0	13	Newton, Klug, Hunter, Baines	2,263
48	14	CL	A	Tranmere R	W3-0	2-0	11	Baines, Newton, Kendal	1,929
49	21	CL	H	Mansfield T	D0-0	0-0	12		4,364
50	23	CL	A	Bury	L0-2	0-2	12		1,616
51	28	CL	H	Bristol C	D1-1	0-0	14	Kendal	2,975
52	M 4	CL	A	Halifax T	L1-2	0-1		O'Neill	1,001
53	7	CL	H	Aldershot	W3-1	1-0	12	Brown P 2, Newton	1,991
54	12	CL	A	Wrexham	L2-4	0-1	13	O'Neill, Brown P	1,039

[4]Won On Penalties — **Av Home Att 2,483**

Goal Scorers

League (59): Newton 14 (2 pens), Kendal 9, Brown P 6, Birch 5 (2 pens), Clayton 5, Bell 3 (1 pen), Scrimgeour 3, Spooner 3, Baines 2, Hunter 2, Klug 2, O'Neill 2, Bellamy 1, Brown J 1, Waddington 1
FA Cup (6): Newton 3, Birch 2 (2 pens), Bellamy 1
Milk Cup (3): Birch 1 (1 pen), Baines 1, Scrimgeour 1
AMC (1): Birch 1 (1 pen)

1983-84

Brown J	Scrimgeour	O'Neill	Klug	Baines	Bellamy	Birch	Spooner	Bell	Henderson	Waddington	Clayton	Kendal	Brown N	Grant (L)	Newton	King (L)	Boxall	Stimpson	Hornsby (L)	Higginbottom	Walker	Hunter	Gregory	Brown P	REFEREE	
1	2	3	4	5	6	7	8	9	10	11															I Hendrick	1
1	2	3	4	5	6	7	8	10		11*	9	12													**C Seel**	**2**
1	2	3	4	5	6	7	8	10	9*		12	11													N Wilson	3
1	2*	3	4	5	6	7	8	10			9	11													D Hutchinson	4
1	2	3	4	5	6	7	8	10			9	11													J Ashworth	5
1	2	3	4	5	6	7	8	10			9	11													**N Ashley**	**6**
1	2	3	4	5	6	7	8	10			9	11													M James	7
1	4	3		5	6	7	8	10		11	9	2													D Scott	8
1	4		12	5	6	7	8	10		11*	9	2		3											R Bridges	9
1	4		11	5	6	7	8	10	9			2		3											T Bune	10
1	4	3	11	5	6	7	8	9*	10		12	2													**H Taylor**	**11**
1	4		11	5	6	7*	8	10		12	9	2		3											G Tyson	12
1	4		11*	5	6	7	8			12	10	2		3	9										D Owen	13
1	4		11	5	6	7	8				10	2		3	9										J Lovatt	14
1	4		11*	5	6	7	8			12	10	2		3	9										R Nixon	15
1	4	3		5	6	7	8	10		11*	9	2				12									**M Peck/E Hart**	**16**
1	4			5	6	7		10		8	12	2		3	9	11*									K Baker	17
1	4	3		11	6	12		10		7	8*	2			9		5								L Burden	18
1	4	3		11	6	7	8	10			12	2*			9		5								J Bray	19
1	4*	3		11	6	7	8	10		12		2			9		5†								D Letts	20
1	4	3	5*	11	6	7	8	12			10	2			9										**L Dilkes**	**21**
1	4	3*	12	11	6	7	8				10	2			9			5							D Vickers	22
1	4			11	6	7	8				10	2			9			5	3						M Robinson	23
1	4			11	6	7	8				10	2			9			5*	3	12					**F Roberts**	**24**
1	4			11	6	7	8				10	2			9			5		3					E Scales	25
1	4			11	6	7	8				10	2			9			5		3					**D Hutchinson**	**26**
1	2			5	6	7	8	11			10	4			9			3							A Seville	27
1	2			5	6	7		12		8*	10	4			9			3			11				D Brazier	28
1	11	2			6	7*	8	12			10	4			9		5	3							T Ward	29
1	11	2		5	6		8	7				4			9			3			10				J Hough	30
1	8	2	12	5		7				11	10*	4			9			3				6			J Hunting	31
	8*	2	12	5		7				11	10	4			9			3				6	1		J Deakin	32
	8	2	12	5		7				11	10*	4			9			3				6	1		N Midgley	33
	8	2	4	5		7				11	10*				9			3		12		6	1		D Richardson	34
	8	2	4	5		7				11	10				9			3				6	1		T Holbrook	35
	8	2	12	5		7				11*	10	4			9			3				6	1		R Lewis	36
	8	2	10	5		7				11*	12	4			9			3				6	1		N Glover	37
1	8	2	10*	5	11	7*				12		4			9			3			13	6			**K Redfern**	**38**
1		2	10	5	11	7						4						3			8	6		9	C Downey	39
1		2	10	5	11	7						4						3			8	6		9	R Nixon	40
1	8	2	10	5	11							4			9†			3				6		7	T Fitzharris	41
1	8	2	10	5	11							4			9			3				6		7	I Hendrick	42
1	8	2	10	5	11	12						4			9			3				6		7*	G Tyson	43
1	8	2	12	5	11							4			9			3		10*		6		7	D Shaw	44
1	8	2	10	5	11							4			9			3				6		7	A Buksh	45
1	8		10	5	2						12	4			9			3		11*		6		7	J Lovatt	46
1	8*	11	10	5	2						12	4			9†			3				6		7	D Owen	47
1		11	10	5	2						8	4			9			3				6		7	D Hutchinson	48
1	8	11	10	5	2						12	4						3			9*	6		7	M Heath	49
1	8	11	10	5	2						12	4						3			9*	6		7	N Ashley	50
1	8	11	10	5	2							4	3		9							6		7	K Baker	51
1	8	11	10	5	2							4	3		9							6		7	R Guy	52
1		11	10	5	2						8	4	6		9			3						7	A Robinson	53
1		11	10	5	2						8	4	6		9			3						7*	D Allison	54
40	41	34	27	45	38	30	20	15	3	14	25	43	5	7	33	1	4	27	1	4	6	21	6	16	League Appearances	
			+7S			+2S		+4S	+8S						+1S			+1S								
3	3	1	1	3	3	3	3	1S			3	3			3			2	1	1+1S					FA Cup Appearances	
4	4	4	3	4	4	4	4	4	1	2	3+1S	3+1S				1S									Milk Cup Appearances	
1	1	1	1	1	1	1				1S		1			1			1			1S	1			AM Cup Appearances	

Also Played: White match 4, no.12. Hoskins match 54, no.12.

RECREATION GROUND

Official Address: Recreation Ground, Chesterfield S40 4SX. Telephone: Chesterfield (0246) 209765

Ground Capacity: 19,750 (12,000 covered)

Record Attendance: 30,968 v. Newcastle United, Division 2, 7 April 1939

Record Receipts: £26,640 v. Barnsley, Division 3, 26 Dec 1980

Size of Playing Area: 114yds × 72 yds

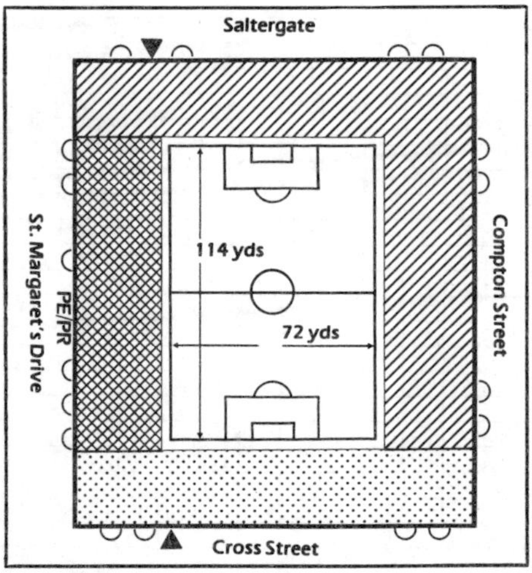

For key see page 12

Season Tickets: Stand: £55.00 (£38 juveniles/OAP), £35 Ground (£29 juvenile/OAP)

Executive Box Season Tickets: None

Cost of Stand Tickets: £3.00 (adults), £2.50 (juveniles/OAP), Terraces: £1.60 (adults), £1.20 (juveniles/OAP)

Match and Ticket Information: Centre and Wing stands bookable in advance

Car Parking: Street parking near ground allowed. Car parks ½ mile from ground in Saltergate

How to get to the ground

From North: Use Motorway M1 until junction 30, then follow signs Chesterfield A619. In town centre follow signs Old Brampton into Salter Gate for Chesterfield F.C.
From East and South: Follow signs Chesterfield A617 into town centre then follow signs Old Brampton into Salter Gate for Chesterfield F.C.
From West: Follow signs Chesterfield 619 then at roundabout take 1st exit into Foljambe Road at end turn right into Salter Gate for Chesterfield F.C.

COLCHESTER UNITED Division 4

Chairman
MJ Cadman

Directors
HR Piper
JW Rippingale
RF West

Secretary
Martyn R Bennett

Commercial Manager
E J Keegan (0206 572202)

Manager
Cyril Lea

Player Coaches
Stewart Houston
Mike Walker

Youth Team Manager
Roy Massey

Physiotherapist
Charlie Simpson

A final Fourth Division place of eighth was an ultimate disappointment after a first half of the season when a top-four place looked likely. In fact, it was a season when much was promised and less was achieved although there were exciting moments.

Since it must be said that the League challenge faded badly after a good start it can also be mentioned that without anything very special the club did adequately well in the Cups. The Milk Cup First Round against Reading was thrillingly won on away goals over the two legs and this was followed by a narrow Second Round aggregate success over Swansea City, which then brought Manchester United and a bumper gate to Layer Road. Two first half goals made sure that there would be no second 'pay-day', but the FA Cup soon arrived and a fine away win at Torquay was followed by a comfortable home success against Alliance Premier club Wealdstone. Charlton were at Layer Road in the Third Round and a second half goal by the visitors was enough to end the cup interest for the season apart from the new Associate Members Cup where there was limited satisfaction.

Colchester needs Third Division Football or better and there is the potential at Layer Road for Manager Cyril Lea to bring this about even after losing the services through injury of the veterans, Cook and Leslie. With consistent performers such as Chamberlain, Hadley, Bowen and Adcock still around aided by some promising young players the coming season might bring about the success local fans urgently require.

WLM

Back Row L to R: Steven Allen, Noel Parkinson, Perry Groves, Alec Chamberlain, David Gadsdon, Rudi Hedman, Andy Farrell, Tony Adcock. **Centre Row:** Roger Osborne, Russell Irving, Keith Bowen, Michael Whytock, Alex Chappell, Simon Burman. **Front Row:** Ian Phillips, Jeff Hull, Cyril Lee (Manager), Stewart Houston (Player/Coach), Mike Walker (Player/Coach), Stuart Youngman, Robin Reid.

'THE U's'

Sponsored by **The Royal London Mutual Insurance Society**

Formed: 1937 **Turned Professional:** 1937 **Ltd Co:** 1937
Previous Managers: Since joining the Football League:
Ted Fenton Jimmy Allen Jack Butler Benny Fenton Neil Franklin Dick Graham Jim Smith Bobby Roberts Allan Hunter
Honours: None
League Career: Elected to Division Three (S) 1950 Transferred to Division Three 1958
Relegated to Division Four 1960-1 Promoted to Division Three 1961-2
Relegated to Division Four 1964-5 Promoted to Division Three 1965-6
Relegated to Division Four 1967-8 Promoted to Division Three 1973-4
Relegated to Division Four 1975-6 Promoted to Division Three 1976-7
Relegated to Division Four 1980-1
Colours: Blue and white striped shirts, blue shorts, white stockings
Change Colours: Red shirts, black shorts and stockings

CLUB RECORDS

Most Appearances for Club: Micky Cook: Football League 609 + 4 subs + F.A. Cup 46 + League/Milk Cup 36 **Total 691 + 4**
Most Capped Player: None
Record Goalscorer in a Match: No one has scored more than four
Record League Goalscorer in a season: Bobby Hunt, 37, Div 4, 1961-2 **In all competitions:** Bobby Hunt, 38 (League 37, F.A. Cup 1)
Record League Goalscorer in a career: Martyn King, 131, 1959-65
Record Transfer Fee Received: £90,000 from Gillingham for Trevor Lee, Jan 1981
Record Transfer Fee Paid: £25,000 to Ipswich Town for Roger Osborne, Feb 1981
Best Performances: League: 3rd Div 3(S) 1956-7 **F.A. Cup:** 6th Round (shared record for Div 4) 1970-1 **League/Milk Cup:** 5th Round 1974-5
Most League Points: 81 in Div 4, 1982-3 **Most League Goals:** 104, Div 4, 1961-2
Record League Victory: 9-1 v Bradford City, Div 4, 30 Dec 1961
Record League Defeat: 0-7 v Leyton Orient, Div 3(S), 5 Jan 1953 0-7 v Reading, Div 3(S), 18 Sept 1957
Club Statistician for the Directory: Mick Middleton

Programme Editor
E. Keegan

Price	Number of Pages
40p	36

Subscriptions
Rates available from club

COLCHESTER UNITED

PLAYERS NAME Ht Wt Birthdate	Honours	Birthplace Transfers	Clubs	APPEARANCES League	Milk Cup	F.A.C.	A.M.C.	GOALS League	Milk Cup	F.A.C.	A.M.C.
GOALKEEPERS											
Alec Chamberlain		Ely	Ramsey T.								
6-2 11.11 20.6.64			Ipswich T.								
		F	Colchester U.	50	4	3	3				
Mike Walker	W. U.23(4),	Colwyn Bay	Reading (A)								
6-1 13.2 28.11.45	Div. 3, 69	F	Shrewsbury T.	6							
			York C.	60	1	7					
		£6,000	Watford	137	8	14					
			Charlton A. (L)	1							
			Colchester U.	451	34	35					
DEFENDERS											
Keith Day			Aveley								
6-1 11-10			Colchester								
Andy Farrell		Colchester	Colchester U. (A)	15	4	1					
5-11 11.0 7.10.65											
Daryl Godbold			Norwich C (A)	0+2							
5-0 11-10			Colchester								
Stewart Houston*	S.(1), U.23(2),	Dunoon	Port Glasgow Jrs.								
5-11 12.3 20.8.49	Div. 2, 75,		Chelsea	6+3	1+1	3					
	Div. 4, 82		Brentford	77	3	2		9			
		£40,000	Manchester U.	204+1	17	22		13	2	1	
		F	Sheffield U.	93+1	8	10		1			
		F	Colchester U.	42	4	3	1	4		1	
Ian Phillips		Edinburgh	Ipswich T.								
5-8 12.2 23.4.59		F	Mansfield T.	18+5		1+1		5			
		F	Peterborough U.	97	7	7		3			
		F	Northampton T.	42	4			1		2	
		£3,000	Colchester U.	43		3	2	5			
MIDFIELD											
Simon Burman		Ipswich	Colchester U. (A)								
5-10 11.0 26.4.65											
Jeff Hull		Rochford	Southend U.	10+5							
5-6 9.11 25.8.60		F	Basildon U.								
		F	Colchester U.	60	4		2	5		2	
Roger Osborne	FAC. 78	Ottley	Ipswich T.	109+15	2+1	8+4		9		1	
5-9 10.11 9.3.50		£25,000	Colchester U.	129+3	11	9	1	8			
Stuart Youngman		Beccles	Colchester U.								
5-7 10.9 15.10.65											
FORWARDS											
Tony Adcock		Bethnal Green	Colchester U. (A)	99+15	9+1	5+2	2	48	5		2
5-10 11.0 1.10.57											
Keith Bowen	W. U.21(1)	Northampton	Northampton T. (N-C)	61+4	8+1	2		25	1		
6-1 11.2 26.2.58			Brentford	42+9	0+1	3+2		9		3	
		£10,000	Colchester U.	59	3	3	2	15	1	5	
Perry Groves		London	Colchester U.	55+13	5	2	1	4	1		
5-11 11.12 19.4.65											
Russell Irving		Wallsend	Ipswich T.								
5-9 11.2½ 4.1.64			Colchester U.								

NON-CONTRACT PLAYERS 1984-85:

Steve Allen, Rudi Hedman (3 + 1), **Dave Hubbick** (3 + 7), **Robin Reid, Mike Whytock**

Player of the Year 1983-84: Steve Wignall (now Brentford)

COLCHESTER UNITED

DIVISION FOUR 8TH **FA CUP** 3RD ROUND **MILK CUP** 3RD ROUND

MATCH	DATE	COMPETITION	VENUE	OPPONENTS	RESULT	HALF TIME	L'GUE POS'N	GOALSCORERS	ATTENDANCE
1	A 27	CL	A	Darlington	W2-0	0-0		Adcock, Houston	1,411
2	**30**	**MC 1**	**H**	**Reading**	**W3-2**	**2-1**		**Adcock 2, Wignall**	**2,418**
3	S 3	CL	H	Blackpool	W2-1	1-0	3	Adcock (pen), Serella (og)	2,169
4	6	CL	H	Bristol C	D0-0	0-0			2,120
5	9	CL	A	Stockport Co	D0-0	0-0	2		2,077
6	**14**	**MC 1**	**A**	**Reading**	**L3-4[2]**	**2-1**		**Adcock, Wignall, Bowen**	**3,460**
7	17	CL	H	Rochdale	W4-0	2-0	2	Bowen, Adcock 2, Wignall	1,955
8	24	CL	A	Chesterfield	D1-1	0-0	4	Wignall	4,106
9	26	CL	A	Tranmere R	L1-2	0-1		Adcock (pen)	1,866
10	O 1	CL	H	Chester C	W1-0	0-0	3	Adcock	1,976
11	**4**	**MC 2**	**A**	**Swansea C**	**D1-1**	**1-1**		**Adcock**	**3,758**
12	7	CL	A	York C	L0-3	0-1			6,207
13	15	CL	H	Northampton T	D2-2	1-1	5	Houston, Cook	1,964
14	18	CL	H	Bury	W1-0	1-0		Adcock	1,969
15	22	CL	A	Swindon T	L1-2	1-0	4	Adcock (pen)	3,079
16	**25**	**MC 2**	**H**	**Swansea C**	**W1-0**	**1-0**		**Adcock**	**5,204**
17	29	CL	H	Crewe Alex	W2-0	0-0	4	Adcock 2 (1 pen)	3,402
18	N 1	CL	A	Doncaster R	D3-3	2-1		Bowen, Humphries (og), Adcock (pen)	3,451
19	5	CL	H	Reading	W3-0	2-0	2	Houston, Leslie, Adcock	2,433
20	**8**	**MC 3**	**H**	**Manchester U**	**L0-2**	**0-2**			**13,031**
21	12	CL	A	Mansfield T	D0-0	0-0	4		3,042
22	**19**	**FAC 1**	**A**	**Torquay U**	**W2-1**	**1-0**		**Bowen 2**	**2,126**
23	26	CL	A	Torquay U	L1-2	1-2	7	Cook	1,364
24	D 3	CL	H	Hartlepool U	W6-0	1-0	5	Wignall 2, Phillips 2, Groves, Nichols	1,935
25	**10**	**FAC 2**	**H**	**Wealdstone**	**W4-0**	**4-0**		**Bowen 3, Houston**	**2,673**
26	17	CL	H	Halifax T	W4-1	2-0	3	Houston, Adcock, Bowen 2	1,866
27	26	CL	A	Peterborough U	L0-2	0-0	6		6,527
28	27	CL	H	Aldershot	W4-1	3-1	4	Adcock 2, Wignall, Bowen	3,123
29	J 2	CL	H	Wrexham	D1-1	1-0	6	Adcock	3,182
30	**7**	**FAC 3**	**H**	**Charlton Ath**	**L0-1**	**0-0**			**6,296**
31	14	CL	H	Darlington	W2-1	0-0	5	Adcock 2 (1 pen)	2,151
32	28	CL	H	Stockport C	D1-1	1-1	7	Adcock	2,213
33	F 4	CL	A	Chester C	W4-1	2-0	7	Bowen 2, Phillips, Mutrie	1,179
34	11	CL	H	Chesterfield	W2-0	2-0	5	Adcock, Wignall	2,358
35	14	CL	H	Doncaster R	D1-1	1-0		Bowen	2,821
36	18	CL	A	Crew Alex	D1-1	1-0	6	Bowen	2,532
37	**21**	**AMC 1**	**H**	**Wimbledon**	**W2-1**	**1-0**		**Adcock 2 (2 pens)**	**1,888**
38	25	CL	H	Swindon T	D0-0	0-0	6		2,448
39	M 3	CL	A	Bury	D1-1	0-0	6	Adcock (pen)	1,576
40	7	CL	A	Reading	L0-1	0-0			3,360
41	10	CL	H	Mansfield T	W1-0	0-0	6	Bowen	2,007
42	**13**	**AMC 2**	**H**	**Southen U**	**L0-2**	**0-0**			**2,841**
43	17	CL	H	York C	L1-3	0-2	6	Bowen	3,032
44	24	CL	A	Northampton T	L1-3	1-1	7	Phillips	1,499
45	31	CL	A	Bristol C	L1-4	0-1	9	Wignall	6,504
46	A 4	CL	A	Hereford U	D1-1	1-0		Wignall	2,501
47	7	CL	H	Tranmere R	L0-1	0-0	9		1,679
48	14	CL	A	Hartlepool U	D0-0	0-0	9		1,001
49	17	CL	A	Rochdale	D0-0	0-0			1,020
50	21	CL	H	Peterborough U	D1-1	1-0	9	Adcock	1,746
51	23	CL	A	Aldershot	L1-5	1-3	10	Adcock	2,446
52	28	CL	H	Torquay U	W3-0	2-0	9	Compton (og), Phillips (Pen), Adcock	1,226
53	M 1	CL	A	Blackpool	L2-3	2-2		Hull, Adcock	3,111
54	5	CL	A	Wrexham	W2-0	0-0	8	Osborne, Groves	1,016
55	7	CL	H	Hereford U	W3-0	1-0	7	Bowen, Adcock, Larkin (og)	1,286
56	11	CL	A	Halifax T	L1-4	0-2		Mutrie	1,248
								Av Home Att	**2,220**

Goal Scorers

League (69): Adcock 26 (8 pens), Bowen 12, Wignall 8, Phillips 5 (1 pen), Houston 4, Cook 2, Groves 2, Mutrie 2, Hull 1, Leslie 1, Nichols 1, Osborne 1, opponents 4
FA Cup (6): Bowen 5, Houston 1
Milk Cup (8): Adcock 5, Wignall 2, Bowen 1
AMC (2): Adcock 2 (2 pens)

1983-84

Chamberlain	Cook	Farrell	Hadley	Wignall	Houston	Groves	Osborne	Bowen	Adcock	Hull	Phillips	Oldfield	Leslie	Hubbick	Nichols	Mutrie	Hedman	Coleman	Taylor	REFEREE	
1	2	3	4	5	6	7	8	9	10	11										L Dilkes	1
1	**2**	**3**	**4**	**5**	**6**	**7**	**8**	**9**	**10**	**11**										**M Scott**	**2**
1	2	3	4	5	6	7*	8	9	10	11		12								J Ashworth	3
1	2	3	4	5	6	7	8	9	10	11										M James	4
1	2		4	5	6	7	8	9	10	11	3									V Callow	5
1	**2**	**3**	**4**	**5**	**6**	**7***	**8**	**9**	**10**	**11**									**12**	**A Ward**	**6**
1	2		4	5	6	7	8	9	10	11*	3	12								C Downey	7
1	2		4	5	6	7	8	9	10	11	3									D Scott	8
1	2		4	5	6	7*	8	9	10	11	3	12								MJ Heath	9
1	2		4		6	7	8	9	10	11	3		5							MJ Bodenham	10
1	**2**	**3**	**4**	**5**	**6**	**7**		**9**	**10**	**11**			**8**							**A Seville**	**11**
1	2		4		6	7	8	9	10	11	3		5							R Guy	12
1	2		4		6	7*	8	9	10	11	3		5	12						D Letts	13
1	2		4	5		7*	8	9	10	11	3		6		12					IJ Borrett	14
1	2		4	5*		7	8	9	10	11	3		6		12					A Crickmore	15
1	**2**	**3**	**4**		**6**	**7**	**8**		**10**	**11**				**9**	**5**					**A Seville**	**16**
1	2		4		6	7	8	9	10	11*	3			12	5					MJ Taylor	17
1		2	4		6	7*	8	9	10		3		11	12	5					I Hendrick	18
1	2		4	5	6	12	8*	9	10		3		11	7						BJ Scales	19
1	**2**	**3**	**4**	**5**	**6**	**12**	**8**	**9**	**10**				**7**	**11***						**T Bune**	**20**
1	2	8	4	5	6			9	10		3		11	7						JD Hough	21
1	**2**		**4†**	**5**	**6**		**8**	**9**	**10**		**3**		**11**	**7**						**K Cooper**	**22**
1	2	8	4	5	6			9	10		3		11	7						J Deakin	23
1	2			5	6	7	8	9	10		3		11		4					A Gunn	24
1	**2**		**4**	**5**	**6**	**7**	**8**	**9**	**10**		**3**		**11**							**M Bodenham**	**25**
1	2†		4	5	6	7	8	9	10*		3		11	12						A Buksh	26
1	2		4	5	6	7*	8	9	10		3		11	12						H Taylor	27
1	2		4	5	6	7	8	9	10		3		11							JE Bray	28
1		2	4	5	6	7	8	9	10		3			12	11*					D Hedges	29
1		**2**	**4**	**5**	**6**	**7**	**8**	**9**	**10**		**3**		**11**							**T Spencer**	**30**
1	2		4	5	6	7*	8	9	10		3		11	12						J Martin	31
1	2	5	4		6	12		9	10	8	3		11			7*				D Reeves	32
1	2		4	5	6	12		9	10	8	3		11			7				J Key	33
1	2		4	5	6	7		9	10	8	3		11							R Leslie	34
1	2		4	5	6	7		9	10	8	3		11							A Ward	35
1	2		4	5	6		12	9	10*	8	3		11			7				M Scott	36
1	**2**		**4**	**5**	**6**			**9**	**10**	**8**	**3**	**12**	**11**			**7***				**M Taylor**	**37**
1	2		4	5	6	12		9	10	8	3		11			7*				I Borrett	38
1	2		5	3	4			10	11*	8	6		7			9	12			D Hutchinson	39
1	2		4	5	6	7	12	9*		8	3		11			9				M Bodenham	40
1	2		4	5	6	7	11	9		8	3					10				M James	41
1	**2**		**4**	**5**		**7**	**11**	**9**	**10**	**8***	**3**		**12**			**13**		**6***		**K Hackett**	**42**
1	2		4	5	6	7	8	9	10*		3		11			12				T Spencer	43
1	2		4*		6	7	8	9	12		3		11			10		5		N Ashley	44
1	2		12	5	6	7	8	9	10		3*		11				4			M Heath	45
1	2		11	5	6	7		9		8	3					10	4			I Worrall	46
1	2		11	5	6	7*		9	12	8	3					10	4			L Burden	47
1	2		4		6	7	8	9	10	11	3							5		A Robinson	48
1			4	5	6	7	8	9	10	11	3							2		P Willis	49
1		6	4	5		7	8	9	10	11	3							2		M Dimblebee	50
1		6	4	5		7	8*	9	10	11	3					12		2		K Barratt	51
1		5	4		6	7*	8	9	10	11	3					12		2		J Hunting	52
1		5	4		6	7	8	9	10	11	3							2		C Seel	53
1		4	2	5	6	7*	8	9	10	11	3							12		T Fitzharris	54
1		4	2	5	6	7	8	9	10	11	3									D Letts	55
1		4	2	5	6	7*	8	9	10	11	3					12				D Owen	56
46	36	15	44	36	42	38	34	**46**	41	33	43	0	25	3	4	10	3	7		League Appearances	
			+1S			+4S	+2S		+2S			+3S		+7S	+2S	+4S	+1S	+1S			
3	2	1	3	3	3	2	3	3	3		3		3	1						FA Cup Appearances	
5	5	5	5	4	5	4+1S	4	4	5	4			2	2	1					Milk Cup Appearances	
2	2		2	2	1	1	1	2	2	2	2	1S	1+1S			1+1S		1		AM Cup Appearances	

LAYER ROAD GROUND

Official Address: Layer Road Ground, Colchester. Telephone: (0206) 574042)

Telegraphic: United Colchester

Ground Capacity: 14,000

Record Attendance: 13,031 v. Manchester United, Milk Cup Round 3, 8 Nov 1983

Record Receipts: £22,754 v. Manchester United, Milk Cup Round 3, 8 Nov 1983

Size of Playing Area: 110yds × 71 yds

Season Tickets: B & C Block: £70 (£50 juveniles/OAP), A & D: £60 (£40 juveniles/OAP), Bench Seats: £50 (£40 juveniles/OAP), Ground Season tickets: £35 (juveniles/OAP £20)

Executive Box Season Tickets: None

Cost of Stand Tickets: B & C: £4.00, A & D £3.50, Bench £2.50, Terraces: £2.00 (adults), £1.00 (juveniles/OAP)

Match and Ticket Information: 0206 572202 or 574042 (Bookable two weeks in advance and retained if paid for until 48 hours before kick-off)

Car Parking: available in Butts Road and Layer Road (150 yards from ground South side of Colchester). Also in Army Barracks (150 yards from ground)

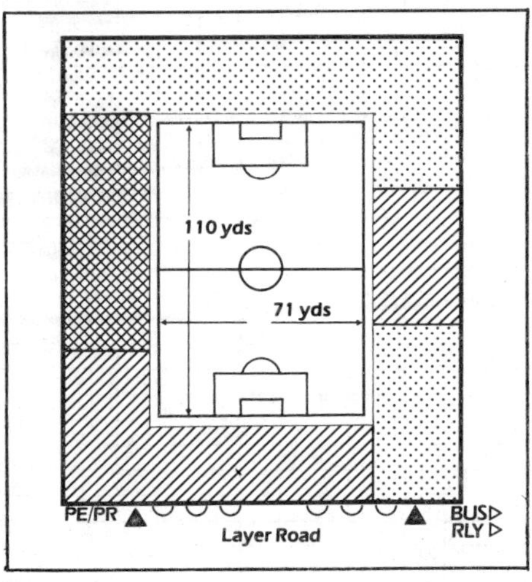

For key see page 12

How to get to the ground

From North: Follow signs in Colchester on A133/B1508 or A12, then follow signs Layer B1026 into Layer Road for Colchester United F.C.
From East: Follow signs into Colchester on A604 or A133 then follow signs Layer B1026 into Layer Road for Colchester United F.C.
From South and West: Follow signs into Colchester on A604 or A12 then follow signs Layer B1026 into Layer Road for Colchester United F.C.

COVENTRY CITY Division 1

Life President
Derrick H Robins

Chairman
J Poynton

Directors
M F French FCA
P D H Robins
T Sergeant FRCS
G W Curtis

Secretary
G P Hover

Commercial Manager
G W Curtis (0203 57171-7)

Manager
Bobby Gould

Physiotherapist
George Dalton

Perennial relegation favourites, the Sky Blues looked in even more trouble than usual as the 1983/84 season approached when the problem was not "would the players be good enough" but "where are the players?" Bobby Gould, who succeeded Dave Sexton on the final day of the previous season was faced with the unenviable task of rebuilding from scratch as one by one the young starlets who had formed the backbone of Sexton's team, refused new contracts and moved on to pastures new, some for what must be considered rock bottom prices. The foothills of the mountain were climbed as a collection of players were assembled from the lower divisions, an area that Gould knew and understood, and reserve team players with some First Division experience.

Surprisingly, they were able to clear a large overdraft, build a squad and still have some left over for emergencies as the players ran out at Runners Up Watford for the first match of the season. A shock first victory set them up quite nicely as a run of luck, few injuries and the surprise element that always accompanies unknowns propelled them to fifth place by mid season including a 4-0 humiliation of champions Liverpool in front of BBC's Match of the Day cameras. Some of the new signings had settled down very quickly and Peake and Pearce, solid as rocks at the back, Gibson's prolific scoring; Platnauer and Gynn in midfield certainly did not look out of place in the top bracket. It could'nt last and didn't. The luck that accompanied them in the first half of the season left them, injuries began to pile up, the surprise element had gone and after the usual early exit from the F.A. Cup at Sheffield Wednesday, the usual post Christmas slide began. This time it was longer and steeper than usual and by the time the final day of the season arrived they had slid fifteen places in the table and faced Norwich needing to win to have any chance of staying up. Recent heavy defeats at Southampton and Liverpool had shattered what little confidence they had left. Manager Gould managed to galvanise them into a unit for this final match and they scraped home amid wild scenes of enthusiasm thanks to the thickness of the right hand post in the 89th minute.

It had been their closest escape in seventeen seasons of uninterrupted 1st Division football (a marvellous achievement when one considers the low level of support and the generally depressed condition of the City) and one feels that the worst might be over although another difficult season is in prospect. With the division of riches in our league now even more pronounced clubs like Coventry, with a hardcore average crowd of around 13,000, are always going to be at a disadvantage but Football would be a duller place without the miracle that they achieved last season.

Rod Dean
The League Directory's Statistician for the Club

Back Row L to R: Trevor Peake, Martin Jol, Steve Ogrizovic, Brian Kilcline, Perry Suckling, Graham Withey, Ian Butterworth. **Middle Row:** Kirk Stephens, Stuart Pearce, Nicky Platnauer, Bob Latchford, Andy Spring, Kenny Hibbitt, Dave Bennett, Peter Hormantschuk. **Front Row:** Keith Thompson, Terry Gibson, Micky Adams, Bobby Gould (Manager), Micky Gynn, Martin Singleton, Lloyd McGrath.

'SKY BLUES'

Sponsored by
Glazepta

Formed: 1883 **Turned Professional:** 1893 **Ltd Co:** 1907
Previous Managers: Until 1914 the secretary and commitee undertook all manageral duties
1914-5 F Scott-Walford 1917-9 W Clayton 1919-20 H Pollitt 1920-4 A J Evans 1924-8 J Kew
1928-31 J McIntyre 1931-45 H Storer 1945-7 R Bayliss 1947-8 W Frith 1948-53 H Storer
1954 J Fairbrother 1954-5 C Elliott 1955-6 J Carver 1956-7 H Warren 1957-61 W Frith
1961-7 J W T Hill 1967-72 N Cantwell 1972 R Dennison 1972-81 G Milne 1981-3 D Sexton
1983 — to date R Gould
Honours: Division 2 Champions 1966-7 Division 3 Champions 1963-4
Division 3 (S) Champions 1935-6
League Career: Elected to Division 2 1925-6 Relegated to Division 3 (N) 1924-5
Transferred to Division 3 (S) 1926 Promoted to Division 2 1935-6 Relegated to Division 3 (S) 1951-2
Relegated to Division 4 1957-8 Promoted to Division 3 1958-9 Promoted to Division 2 1963-4
Promoted to Division 1 1966-7
Colours: Sky blue shirts and shorts with navy and white trim, sky blue stockings
Change Colours: Red shirts and shorts with navy and white trim, red stockings

CLUB RECORDS

Most Appearances for Club: George Curtis: Football League 486 + F.A. Cup 29 + League Cup 20 **Total 535**
Most Capped Player: Dave Clements, 21, N Ireland. **For England:** Reg Matthews, 5
Record Goalscorer in a Match: C Bourton, 5 v Bournemouth (6-1) (H), Div 3 (S), 17.10.31
A Bacon, 5 v Gillingham (7-3) (A), Div 3 (S), 30.12.34
Record League Goalscorer in a season: Clarrie Bourton, 49 **All competitions:** Clarrie Bourton, 50 (League 49, F.A. Cup 1), 1931-2
Record League Goalscorer in a career: Clarrie Bourton, 171 **All competitions:** Clarrie Bourton, 180 (League 171, F.A. Cup 9)
Record Transfer Fee Received: £1,250,000 from Nottingham Forest for Ian Wallace, July 1980
Record Transfer Fee Paid: £325,000 to Bristol City for Gary Collier, July 1979
Best Performances: League: 6th Div 1 1969-70 **F.A. Cup:** 6th Round 1962-3 **League/Milk Cup:** Semi-Final 1970-1 **European Fairs Cup:** 2nd Round
Most League Points: 60 in Div 4, 1958-9 60 in Div 3, 1963-4
Most League Goals: 108, Div 3 (S)
Record League Victory: 9-0 v Bristol City, Div 3 (S), 28.4.34
Record League Defeat: 2-10 v Norwich City, Div 3 (S), 15.3.30
European Competitions Entered: European Fairs Cup 1970-1
Club Statistician for the Directory: R. Deane

Programme Editor
Mike Dale (Coventry News Service)

Price	Number of Pages
40p	24

Subscriptions
Subscriptions on request to club

COVENTRY CITY

PLAYERS NAME Ht Wt Birthdate	Honours	Birthplace Transfers	Clubs	APPEARANCES League	Milk Cup	F.A.C.	E. Cups	GOALS League	Milk Cup	F.A.C.	E. Cups
GOALKEEPERS											
Steve Ogrizovic		Mansfield	Chesterfield	16	2						
6-3 14.7 12.9.57		£70,000	Liverpool	4							
		Player Exchange	Shrewsbury	84	5	5					
		£72,500	Coventry C.								
Perry Suckling		Leyton	Coventry C.	27	1						
6-1½ 11.2 12.10.65											
DEFENDERS											
Mike Adams	E. Y	Sheffield	Gillingham (A)	85 + 7	5	10		4			
5-6 10.4 8.11.61		£75,000	Coventry C.	10 + 1				1			
Ian Butterworth		Crewe	Coventry C. (A)	61 + 7	3	5 + 1					
6-1 12.6 25.1.65											
Peter Hormantschuk		Coventry	Coventry C. (A)	18 + 6	1	3 + 1		1	1		
5-10 10.8 11.9.62											
Brian Kilcline	E. U.21(2)	Nottingham	Notts. Co. (A)	156 + 2	16	10		9	1	1	
6-2 12.0 7.5.62		£60,000	Coventry C.								
Lloyd McGrath	E. Y	Birmingham	Coventry C. (A)								
5-8 10.6 24.2.65											
Trevor Peake*	E.S-P	Nuneaton	Nuneaton B.								
6-0 12.9 10.2.57		£27,750	Lincoln C.	171	16	7		7		2	
		£100,000	Coventry C.	33	3	4		3		1	
Stuart Pearce		London	Wealdstone								
5-10 12.2 24.4.62		£15,000	Coventry C.	23							
Kirk Stevens	Div. 2, 82	Coventry	Nuneaton B.								
5-9 11.8 27.2.55		£15,000	Luton T.	226 + 1	13	8		2			
		£75,000	Coventry C.								
MIDFIELD											
Micky Gynn		Peterborough	Peterborough U. (A)	152 + 4	12	13		33	1	2	
5-5 10.6 19.8.61		£60,000	Coventry C.	20 + 3							
Kenny Hibbitt	E. U.23(1),	Bradford	Bradford	13 + 2	1						
5-10 12.0 3.1.51	Div. 2, 77,	£10,000	Wolverhampton W.	446 + 19	34 +	46	16 +	88	12	10	3
	FC. 74, 80	F	Coventry C.								
Martin Jol		Hague	F.C. Twente								
5-11 11.2 14.1.56			W.B.A.	63 + 1	10	4		4			
		F	Coventry C.								
Jim McDonald		Glasgow	Coventry C. (A)								
5-7½ 10.12 31.12.65											
Nicky Platnauer†		Leicester	Bedford T.								
5-11 12.10 10.6.61		F	Bristol R.	21 + 3	1	0 + 1		7	1		
		£50,000	Coventry C.	29 + 5	3	4		6			
Martin Singleton	E. Y	Banbury	Coventry C. (A)	18 + 3	3 + 1			1			
5-9 10.0 2.8.63											
FORWARDS											
Dave Bennett		Manchester	Manchester C.	43 + 9	7	5 + 1		9	5	1	
6-0 11.2 11.7.59		£120,000	Cardiff C.	75 + 2	4	4		18	1		
		£100,000	Coventry C.	32 + 2	3	3		6	1		
Terry Gibson	E. Y	Walthamstow	Tottenham H. (A)	16 + 2	1	5		4	1	1	
5-5 10.0 23.12.62		£70,000	Coventry C.	35 + 1	2	3		17		2	
Bob Latchford	E.(12), U.23(6)	Birmingham	Birmingham C. (A)	157 + 2	15 +	11		68	6	6	
6-0 13.6 18.1.51		£350,000	Everton	235 + 1	28	17		106	19	10	
		£125,000	Swansea C.	87	5	1		35	4		
			NAC Breda								
		F	Coventry C.								
Andy Spring		Gateshead	Coventry C. (A)	0 + 1							
5-10 13.2 17.11.65											
Keith Thompson		Birmingham	Coventry C. (A)	8 + 2		1					
5-8½ 11.2 24.4.65			Wimbledon (L)	0 + 3							
Graham Withey		Bristol	Bath City								
6-1 11.12 11.6.60		£5,000	Bristol R.	19 + 3	1	1 + 1		10			
		£5,000	Coventry C.	10 + 10	1	4		4		3	

APPRENTICES

Jeff Doyle, Tony English, Gareth Evans, Don Bethfield, Jon Hillson, Tony Mahan, Karlton Stratford, Paul Whittington, Bobby Keates, Terry Merriman, Ian Rock, Steve Sedgley, David Smith

COVENTRY CITY

DIVISION ONE 19TH **FA CUP** 4TH ROUND **MILK CUP** 3RD ROUND

MATCH	DATE	COMPETITION	VENUE	OPPONENTS	RESULT	HALF TIME	L'GUE POS'N	GOALSCORERS	ATTENDANCE
1	A 27	CL	A	Watford	W3-2	1-0		Bolton (og), Rice (og), Gibson	15,333
2	29	CL	A	Tottenham H	D1-1	0-1		Withey	35,854
3	S 3	CL	H	Everton	D1-1	1-1	10	Adams	12,532
4	6	CL	H	Notts Co	W2-1	0-1		Gibson, Platnauer	10,912
5	10	CL	A	West Ham U	L2-5	2-3	7	Peake, Platnauer	22,195
6	17	CL	H	Leicester C	W2-1	1-0	6	Platnauer, Gibson	12,377
7	24	CL	A	Sunderland	L0-1	0-0	11		11,612
8	O 1	CL	H	Ipswich T	L1-2	0-2	14	Gibson	10,492
9	**4**	**MC 2**	**A**	**Grimsby T**	**D0-0**	**0-0**			**6,088**
10	15	CL	A	Arsenal	W1-0	0-0	10	Bamber	20,290
11	22	CL	H	WBA	L1-2	0-1	14	Withey	13,441
12	**25**	**MC 2**	**H**	**Grimsby T**	**W2-1**	**1-0**		**Bennett, Grimes**	**8,705**
13	29	CL	A	Stoke C	W3-1	2-1	10	Bennett, Gibson, Bamber	11,836
14	N 5	CL	A	Birmingham C	W2-1	1-1	9	Gibson, Bennett	16,169
15	**8**	**MC 3**	**A**	**Everton**	**L1-2**	**0-0**		**Bamber**	**9,080**
16	12	CL	H	QPR	W1-0	1-0	6	Bamber	11,755
17	19	CL	A	Wolverhampton W	D0-0	0-0	5		11,419
18	26	CL	H	Southampton	D0-0	0-0	6		11,578
19	D 3	CL	A	Luton T	W4-2	2-0	5	Gibson 2, Gynn, Bennett	10,698
20	10	CL	H	Liverpool	W4-0	3-0	4	Platnauer, Gibson 3	20,586
21	17	CL	A	Norwich C	D0-0	0-0	5		16,646
22	26	CL	H	Manchester U	D1-1	1-1	7	Gibson	21,453
23	28	CL	A	Nottingham F	L0-3	0-1	7		22,169
24	31	CL	A	Everton	D0-0	0-0	8		13,659
25	J 2	CL	H	Sunderland	W2-1	2-0	6	Withey, Daly	13,249
26	**7**	**FAC 3**	**H**	**Wolverhampton W**	**D1-1**	**1-1**		**Withey**	**15,817**
27	**10**	**FAC 3R**	**A**	**Wolverhampton W**	**D1-1[1]**	**0-0**		**Peake**	**19,204**
28	14	CL	H	Watford	L1-2	1-1	6	Peake	13,307
29	**16**	**FAC 3R2**	**H**	**Wolverhampton W**	**W3-0**	**2-0**		**Withey 2, Hunt**	**18,000**
30	21	CL	A	Leicester C	D1-1	1-0	8	Daly	16,262
31	**30**	**FAC 4**	**A**	**Sheffield Wed**	**L2-3**	**2-1**		**Gibson 2**	**26,154**
32	F 4	CL	A	Ipswich T	L1-3	0-2	8	Gibson	13,406
33	11	CL	H	West Ham U	L1-2	0-1	10	Hunt	13,271
34	18	CL	H	Stoke C	L2-3	1-1	10	Bennett, Gibson	9,752
35	25	CL	A	WBA	D1-1	0-0	12	Gibson	10,900
36	M 3	CL	H	Birmingham C	L0-1	0-1	13		13,705
37	10	CL	A	QPR	L1-2	1-0	13	Daly (pen)	10,284
38	13	CL	H	Aston Villa	D3-3	2-2		Daly, Alladyce, Gibson	11,098
39	17	CL	A	Notts Co	L1-2	0-0	13	Peake	6,564
40	24	CL	H	Tottenham H	L2-4	0-2	16	Withey, Daly (pen)	12,803
41	31	CL	H	Arsenal	L1-4	1-1	17	Bennett	10,550
42	A 7	CL	A	Aston Villa	L0-2	0-1	17		15,318
43	14	CL	H	Wolverhampton W	W2-1	1-1	16	Daly (pen), Ferguson	8,246
44	17	CL	H	Nottingham F	W2-1	1-0		Ferguson, Platnauer	9,818
45	21	CL	A	Manchester U	L1-4	0-1	15	Daly	38,524
46	28	CL	A	Southampton	L2-8	0-2	17	Grimes, Gynn	16,746
47	M 5	CL	H	Luton T	D2-2	1-0	18	Platnauer, Gibson	9,391
48	7	CL	A	Liverpool	L0-5	0-2	19		33,393
49	12	CL	H	Norwich C	W2-1	1-1	19	Ferguson, Bennett	14,007

[1]After Extra Time

Av Home Att **12,586**

Goal Scorers

League (57): Gibson 17 (1 pen), Daly 7 (3 pens), Bennett 6, Platnauer 6, Withey 4, Bamber 3, Ferguson 3, Peake 3, Gynn 2, Adams 1, Allardyce 1, Grimes 1, Hunt 1, opponents 2

FA Cup (7): Withey 3, Gibson 2, Hunt 1, Peake 1

Milk Cup (3): Bamber 1, Bennett 1, Grimes 1

1983-84

Suckling	Hormantschuk	Roberts	Grimes	Butterworth	Jacobs	Gynn	Daly	Bamber	Gibson	Thompson	Platnauer	Singleton	Peake	Adams	Withey	Avramovic **(L)**	Bennett	Allardyce	Hendrie	Hunt	Pearce	Langley	Ferguson **(L)**	McGrath	REFEREE	
1	2	3	4	5	6	7*	8	9	10	11	12														M Taylor	1
1	2	3	7		6			9	10		8	4	5	11*	12										I Borrett	2
1	2	3	4		6		8		10		9	7*	5	11	12										D Axcell	3
1	2	3	4		6		8		10		9	7*	5	11	12										T Bune	4
1	2	3	4	7	6				10		9	12	5	11*	8										A Crickmore	5
	2	3		4	6		8		10	11*	9		5		7	1	12								D Reeves	6
	2	3		4			8		10	11*	9		5		7	1	12	6							C Seel	7
	2	3	4				8		10		9		5		7	1	11	6	12						N Glover	8
		3	**9**		**6**				**10**		**7**	**4**	**5**		**8**	**1**	**11**	**2**							**D Hutchinson**	**9**
		3	10	2				7	8		9	4	5		12	1	11	6							A Gunn	10
		2	4	3		7		9	10		11	8*	5		12	1		6							E Read	11
		2	**11**			**4**		**9**	**10†**		**3**	**8**	**5**			**1**	**7**	**6**							**J Hough**	**12**
		2	4			8		9	10		11	3	5			1	7	6							D Scott	13
		2	11			8		9	10*		3	4	5			1	7	6		12					J Lovatt	14
1		**2**	**4**			**3**		**9**			**11**	**12**	**5**				**7**	**6**	**10***	**8**					**A Challinor**	**15**
1		2	4			8		9			12		5				7	6	10*	11	3				R Guy	16
1		2	4			8		9	10*		12		5				7	6		11	3				R Nixon	17
1		2	4			8		9	10*		12		5				7	6		11†	3				D Owen	18
1		2				8		9	10		4		5				7	6		11	3				B Hill	19
		2				8	11	9*	10		4		5		12	1	7	6			3				D Letts	20
		2				8	4	9	10		11		5			1	7	6			3				M James	21
		2	12			8	11	9	10		4*		5			1	7	6			3				R Milford	22
		2	10	12		8	4				11		5		9*	1	7	6			3				T Jones	23
		2	10				4				11		5		9	1	7	6		8	3				K Hackett	24
		2	10*	5	6	12	8				4				9	1	7			11	3				E Scales	25
		2*				**12**	**4**		**10**		**11**		**5**	**3**	**9**	**1**	**7**	**6**		**8**					**J Martin**	**26**
		2		**5**		**4**	**12**		**11**		**10**		**6**	**3**	**9***	**1**	**7**			**8**					**J Martin**	**27**
		2		6		4	12		9*		8		5	11		1	7			7	3				L Shapter	28
		2		**6**		**4**	**7**			**10**	**11**		**5**	**3**	**9**	**1**				**8**					**J Martin**	**29**
		2		6			7				11		5	10	9	1	4			8	3				J Worrall	30
		2		**4**			**8**	**12**	**3**		**10**		**5**	**11**	**9***	**1**	**7**			**6**					**D Hutchinson**	**31**
		2		6		4*		9	8		12		5	3		1	7			10	11				K Salmon	32
		2	11				4	9	10				5			1	7	6		8	3				L Burden	33
		2	11			4			10	9			5		12	1	7	6		8	3*				J Martin	34
1		2	7			4*			10			11	5	3	12		9	6		8					P Tyldesley	35
1		2	7	6				12	10			11*	5	3	4		9			8					C Downey	36
1		2	7	6			4	8	10*			11	5	3	12		9								A Gunn	37
1			11		2		4	9	10	8*			5	3			7	6		12					D Vickers	38
1			8	12	2		4*	9	10	11			5	3			7	6							K Redfern	39
1			8*	11	2		4						5	12	9		7	6			3	10			L Dilkes	40
1				2			4		10		9	8*	5	11	12		7	6			3				D Shaw	41
1			12	2	6		4		10		9	8	5*				7				3	11			B Stevens	42
1			8	2	6		4		10·		11			7				5			3		9		M Dimblebee	43
1			7	2	6	12	4		10*		8			3			11	5					9		A Ward	44
1			8	2	6	10	4		12		11			3*			7	5					9		D Hutchinson‡	45
1			8	2	6	10	4		7		11								12		3		9	5*	H King	46
1			8*	2	6	12	4		10		11						7	5			3		9		R Bridges	47
1				2	5	11	4		10		8						7	6			3		9*		A Challinor	48
1			12	2	6	8	4*		10		11						7	5			3		9		N Ashley	49
24	8	30	29	22	18	20	27	18	35	6	29	12	33	16	10	18	32	28	1	13	23	2	7	1	League Appearances	
			+3S	+2S		+3S	+1S	+1S	+1S		+5S	+1S		+1S	+10S		+2S		+2S	+2S						
		4		3		2+1S	3+1S	1S	3	1	4		4	4	4	4	3	1		4					FA Cup Appearances	
1		3	3		1	2		2	2		3	2+1S	3		1	2	3	3	1	1					Milk Cup Appearances	

Also Played: Spring match 48, no.12. ‡ Replaced by D Maurice

HIGHFIELD ROAD

Official Address: Highfield Road Stadium, King Richard Street, Coventry CV2 4FW. Telephone: 0203 57171. Telex: 312132-AB: COV AFC-G

Telegraphic: City Football Coventry

Ground Capacity: 20,500 (all seated)

Record Attendance: 51,455 v. Wolverhampton Wanderers, Div 2, 29 Apr 1967

Record Receipts: £68,029.70 v. West Ham United, League Cup Semi-Final 1st Leg, 27 Jan 1981

Size of Playing Area: 115yds × 75 yds

Season Tickets: £45, £50, £55, £60, £80, £90 (half-price juveniles/OAP); Terraces: £40 (half-price juveniles/OAP)

Executive Box Season Tickets: £4,500 per annum (for ten), £2,000 per annum (for ten) (ground level)

Cost of Stand Tickets: £5.30, £4.50, £4.20 (visitors), £3.50, £3.20, £2.70 (respective prices for juveniles/OAP £2.50, £2.20); **Terraces:** (passes only): £2.10 (£1.00 juveniles/OAP), £2.00 (visitors), £1.70, £1.50, £1.30

Match and Ticket Information: Postal applications for stand tickets accepted (with SAE) 21 days before each match by the Ticket Office manager at the Stadium, Highfield Road, Coventry

Car Parking: Street parking around ground permitted. Special park — cars & coaches is situated at Gosford Green on Walsgrave Road (A46) 200 yards from stadium.

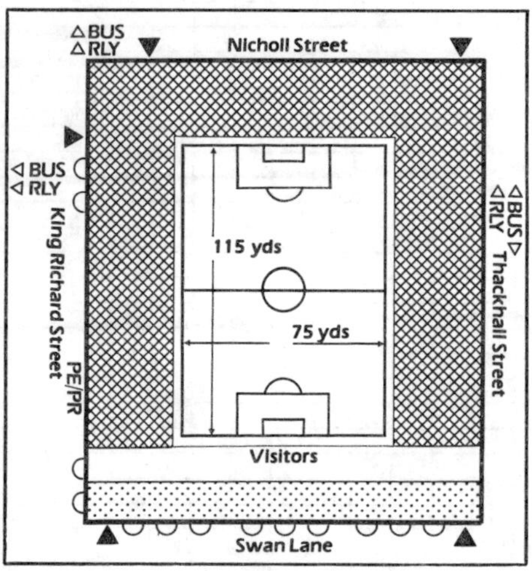

For key see page 12

How to get to the ground

From North: Use Motorway M6 until junction 3. Leave Motorway and follow signs Coventry A444. In 3.5m turn left into Eagle Street B4110, then forward over all crossroads into Swan Lane for Coventry City F.C.
From East: Use Motorway M45 then A45 to Ryton on Dunsmore. In 1.5m at roundabout take 3rd exit A423. In 1.2m turn right B4110. Over crossroads and at T road turn left then shortly right into Swan Lane for Coventry City F.C.
From South: Use Motorway M1 then M45 and route from East or A46 (S.P. Coventry) into City Centre, then follow signs Market Harborough A427 into Binley Road and on nearside of railway bridge turn left into Swan Lane for Coventry City F.C.
From West: Use Motorway M6 and route from North or A45 (S.P. Coventry) into City Centre, then follow signs Market Harborough, A427 into Binley Road and on nearside of railway bridge turn left into Swan Lane for Coventry City F.C.

CREWE ALEXANDRA Division 4

President
D Godfrey

Chairman
N Rowlinson

Directors
J McHugh
K Potts
D Rowlinson
R Clayton
J McMillan
J Bowler

Managing Director/Manager
Dario Gradi

Secretary
Mrs Gill Palin

Commercial Manager
M Challis
(0270 256557)

Lottery Manager
T Connor

Physiotherapist
M Allen

Chief Scout
P Slack

A season when Crewe Alexandra do not have to apply for re-election may be cited as being a reasonable success in recent years, and this did happen in 1983/84. In fact 'Alex' had eleven points in hand over the nearest troubled team and at no time during the season did they in fact seem likely to face the humiliating prospect of finishing in the 'basement'. That success apart there was little at Gresty Road to encourage supporters to feel too much enthusiasm.

The cups certainly provided little to bring any solace apart from two very good performances against Burnley — semi-finalists the previous season — in the Milk Cup. Both legs were won and then reality had to be faced against QPR, who won over the two legs by an aggregate of eleven goals to one — an improvement on Bury's performance at the same time against West Ham. The F.A. Cup challenge began and ended in November at Rochdale where a single goal was enough to see the Lancashire club side through to another round. Thereafter apart from a brief flirtation with the new Associate Members Cup there was very little to provide inspiration.

What hopes does Manager Dario Gradi have to provide encouragement? Not too much. But there was consistency from Scott, Leonard and Waller and that may give some hope of better things to come. Crewe have been in the Third Division and no-one would begrudge their happy staff the satisfaction of another season of excitement when it comes.

WLM

Back Row L to R: Steve Davis, Paul Brady, Dave Waller, Mark Leonard, Nick Longley, Nigel Hart, Vernon Allatt, Geoff Thomas, Gary Blissett, Dave Pullar. **Middle Row:** Tony Cliss, Neil Aldridge, Andy Mason, Dario Gradi (Manager), Bob Scott (Captain), Peter King, Paul Shaw. **Front Row:** Lee Broomhead, Andy Green, Steve Crompton, Alan Milne.

'RAILWAYMEN'

Sponsored by
County Glass

Formed: 1877 **Turned Professional:** 1893 **Ltd Co:** 1892
Previous Managers: Since 1946
George Lillycrop Frank Hill Arthur Turner Harry Catterick Ralph Ward Maurice Lindley Harry Ware Jimmy McGuigan Ernie Tagg Dennis Viollet Jimmy Melia Ernie Tagg Harry Gregg Warwick Rimmer Tony Waddington Arfon Griffiths
Honours: Welsh Cup Winners 1936, 1937
League Career: Original members of Division Two 1892 Failed to gain re-election 1896
Re-joined the League in Division 3(N) 1921 Transferred to Division Four 1958
Promoted to Division Three 1962-3 Relegated to Division Four 1963-4
Promoted to Division Three 1967-8 Relegated to Division Four 1968-9
Colours: Red shirts, white shorts, red stockings
Change Colours: All white

CLUB RECORDS

Most Appearances for Club: Tommy Lowrie, 1966-78 (League 436 + F.A. Cup 20 + League Cup 18 + Watney Cup 1 **Total 475**
Most Capped Player: Bill Lewis, 12, Wales **For England:** J H Pearson 1
Record Goalscorer in a Match: No one has scored more than four goals
Record League Goalscórer in a season: Terry Harkin, 35, Div 4, 1964-5 **In all competitions:** Terry Harkin, 35
Record League Goalscorer in a career: Bert Swindells, 126, 1928-37 **In all competitions:** Bert Swindells, 134 (League 126, F.A. Cup 7)
Record Transfer Fee Received: £40,000 from Port Vale for Paul Bowles, Sept 1979
Record Transfer Fee Paid: £10,000 to Derby County for Colin Chesters, Sept 1979 £10,000 to Sheffield United for Mike Guy, Sept 1979
Best Performances: League: 10th Div 2 1892-3 **F.A. Cup:** Semi-Final 1888 **League/Milk Cup:** 3rd Round 1974-5, 1975-6, 1978-9 **Welsh Cup:** Winners (2)
Most League Points: (3 pts for win) 59, Div 4, 1983-4; (2 pts for win) 59, Div 4, 1962-3
Record League Victory: 8-0 v Rotherham United, Div 3(N), 1 Oct 1932
Record League Defeat: 1-11 v Lincoln City, Div 3(N), 29 Sept 1951

Club Statistician for the Directory: H. Finch

Programme Editor
H. Finch

Price	**Number of Pages**
40p	20

Subscriptions
Subscription rates on request from club

CREWE ALEXANDRA

PLAYERS NAME Ht Wt Birthdate	Honours	Birthplace Transfers	Clubs	APPEARANCES League	Milk Cup	F.A.C.	A.M.C.	GOALS League	Milk Cup	F.A.C.	A.M.C.
GOALKEEPER											
Nick Longley		Mexborough	Crewe A. (part-time)	3							
6-1 13.0 21.5.61											
DEFENDERS											
Neil Aldridge		Manchester	Manchester C (A)								
5-9½ 11.6 10.1.66		F	Crewe A.								
Paul Brady		Birmingham	Birmingham C. (A)								
5-11 10.8 26.3.61		F	Northampton T.	49+2	8	7		3			
		F	Crewe A.	42+1	2	1		1			
Steve Davis	E. Y	Birmingham	Stoke C (A)								
6-0 12.7 26.7.65		F	Crewe A.	23+1	3	1	1+1		1		
Nigel Hart		Golborne	Wigan A.	1							
6-3 12.13 1.10.58		F	Leicester C.								
		F	Blackpool	36+1	4+1	3					
		F	Crewe A.	64+1	2	1	3	3			
Bob Scott*†		Liverpool	Wrexham	15+4							
6-2½ 13.4 22.2.53			Reading (L)	5							
		F	Hartlepool U.	37	2	1					
		F	Rochdale	71	5	2		3			
		F	Crewe A.	224+1	12	6	3	15			
MIDFIELD											
John Crabbe		Weymouth	Southampton (A)	8+4							
5-8 11.0 20.10.54			Gillingham	181	10	12		12	1		
		F	Carlisle U.	26	4	3		4			
		F	Hereford U.	15+1	2	1		2			
		F	Crewe A.	37	4	1	3	4	1		
Peter King		Liverpool	Liverpool (A)								
5-8 10.7 5.7.64		F	Crewe A.	38+4	3	1	2+1	4	1		
David Pullar		London	Portsmouth (A)	84+9	3	9					
5-11 11.8 13.2.59		£12,000	Exeter C.	124+6	12+	7		22	2	3	
			Crewe A.	33+1	2	1	1	6			
Geoff Thomas		Manchester	Rochdale	10+1					1		
6-1 12.0 5.8.64			Crewe A.	5+3	3	1	2+1	1	1		
FORWARDS											
Vernon Allatt		Hednesford	Hednesford T.								
5-11 11.8 28.5.59		£2,000	Halifax T.	93+5	3	9		14		1	
		F	Rochdale	40	2	3	1	8			
		F	Crewe A.								
Gary Blissett		Manchester	Crewe A.	20+2	4	1	1+1	3	1		
6-0 12.7 29.6.64											
Tony Cliss		March	Peterborough U.	65+20	4+1	1+2		11			
5-9 11.0 27.9.62		F		66+1	3		3	7			
Mark Leonard		St Helens	Witton Alb.								
5-11 11.10 27.9.62			Everton	-							
		F	Tranmere R.	6+1							
		F	Crewe A.	36+2	2	1	3	10			
David Waller		Urmston	Crewe A.	78+2	3	2	3	27	4		
5-10 10.0 20.12.63											

NON-CONTRACT PLAYERS 1984-85

Ian Bowers, Dario Gradi

CREWE ALEXANDRA

DIVISION FOUR 17TH **FA CUP** 1ST ROUND **MILK CUP** 2ND ROUND

MATCH	DATE	COMPETITION	VENUE	OPPONENTS	RESULT	HALF TIME	L'GUE POS'N	GOALSCORERS	ATTENDANCE
1	A 27	CL	A	Rochdale	L0-1	0-0			1,673
2	**30**	**MC 1**	**H**	**Burnley**	**W1-0**	**0-0**		**Bowers**	**2,043**
3	S 3	CL	H	Chesterfield	W2-1	1-0	13	Scott, Brady	2,298
4	6	CL	H	Aldershot	D0-0	0-0			2,039
5	10	CL	A	Chester C	W1-0	0-0	9	Leonard	2,090
6	**13**	**MC 1**	**A**	**Burnley**	**W4-3**	**4-1**		**Leonard, Crabbe, Waller (pen), Blissett**	**5,653**
7	17	CL	H	Darlington	W2-1	2-1	4	Waller, Leonard	2,514
8	24	CL	A	Blackpool	L0-3	0-0	9		4,198
9	28	CL	A	Peterborough U	L0-1	0-1			3,783
10	30	CL	H	Stockport Co	L0-3	0-1			2,965
11	**O 4**	**MC 2**	**A**	**QPR**	**L1-8**	**1-3**		**King**	**8,911**
12	8	CL	H	Swindon T	W2-0	1-0	12	Spittle, Scott	2,111
13	14	CL	A	Reading	L0-5	0-3			3,039
14	18	CL	A	Halifax T	L0-1	0-0			1,352
15	22	CL	H	Northampton T	W3-2	2-0	18	King, Scott, Blissett	2,107
16	**25**	**MC 2**	**H**	**QPR**	**W3-0**	**2-0**		**Waller 3**	**3,662**
17	29	CL	A	Colchester U	L0-2	0-2	18		3,402
18	N 1	CL	H	Hartlepool U	W2-0	2-0		Hart 2	2,117
19	5	CL	H	York C	L0-3	0-0	16		2,785
20	13	CL	A	Bury	D1-1	0-0		Leonard	3,078
21	**19**	**FAC 1**	**A**	**Roachdale**	**L0-1**	**0-1**			**2,465**
22	26	CL	A	Tranmere R	W3-2	3-1	14	Blissett 2, Pullar	2,210
23	D 18	CL	H	Doncaster R	D1-1	0-0		Pullar	2,515
24	26	CL	A	Hereford U	W1-0	0-0	15	Waller	3,099
25	28	CL	H	Bristol C	D2-2	2-1		Crabbe, King (pen)	3,457
26	31	CL	A	Mansfield T	D3-3	1-2	15	Scott 2, Cliss	2,652
27	J 2	CL	H	Torquay U	W2-1	2-0	12	King (pen), Cliss	2,489
28	7	CL	A	Chesterfield	W3-1	0-1	11	Waller, King, Leonard	2,470
29	14	CL	H	Rochdale	L0-1	0-1	11		2,640
30	28	CL	H	Chester C	D1-1	1-1	12	Leonard	3,096
31	F 3	CL	A	Stockport Co	W3-2	2-1		Waller, Pullar, Crabbe	2,775
32	11	CL	H	Blackpool	W2-1	0-0	8	Williams, Leonard	4,042
33	15	CL	A	Hartlepool U	L1-2	0-0		Williams	2,059
34	18	CL	H	Colchester U	D1-1	0-1	9	Crabbe (pen)	2,532
35	**22**	**AMC 1**	**A**	**Stockport Co**	**D2-2[4]**	**0-0**		**Waller, King (pen)**	**1,692**
36	25	CL	A	Northampton T	L0-2	0-1	12		1,696
37	M 3	CL	H	Halifax T	W6-1	2-0	9	Williams, Waller 3, Leonard, Pullar	2,058
38	6	CL	A	York C	L2-5	1-1		Cliss, Sbragia (og)	4,106
39	10	CL	H	Bury	W2-1	0-1	10	Waller, Crabbe (pen)	2,405
40	**13**	**AMC 2**	**A**	**Scunthorpe U**	**D4-4[5]**	**0-1**		**Blisset, Waller, Crabbe (pen), King**	**1,524**
41	18	CL	A	Swindon T	L0-1	0-1			2,960
42	**20**	**AMC NQF**	**A**	**Tranmere R**	**D0-0[6]**	**0-0**			**2,246**
43	23	CL	H	Reading	D1-1	1-1		Hart	2,435
44	27	CL	A	Darlington	L0-2	0-1			1,275
45	31	CL	A	Aldershot	D0-0	0-0	11		2,865
46	A 7	CL	H	Peterborough U	L0-1	0-1	14		2,024
47	14	CL	A	Wrexham	W1-0	0-0	13	Pullar	2,102
48	17	CL	A	Bristol C	L1-2	0-2		Leonard	8,139
49	21	CL	H	Hereford U	D1-1	0-0	14	Leonard	2,139
50	28	CL	H	Tranmere U	W3-0	1-0	12	Waller, Thomas, Scott	2,066
51	M 5	CL	A	Torquay U	L1-3	0-1	13	Pullar	1,167
52	7	CL	H	Mansfield T	L1-3	0-3	15	Waller	1,810
53	12	CL	A	Doncaster R	L0-1	0-0	16		3,879
54	15	CL	H	Wrexham	D1-1	0-1		Leonard	1,811

[4]Won 3-0 on Penalties, AET. [5]Lost 6-7 on Penalties, AET [6]Lost 3-4 on Penalties, AET. **Av Home Att** **2,454**

Goal Scorers

League (56): Leonard 10, Waller 10, Pullar 6, Scott 6, Crabbe 4 (2 pens), King 4 (2 pens), Blissett 3, Cliss 3, Hart 3, Williams 3, Brady 1, Spittle 1, Thomas 1, opponent 1
FA Cup (-): —
Milk Cup (9): Waller 4 (1 pen), Blissett 1, Bowers 1, Crabbe 1, King 1, Leonard 1
AMC (6): King 2 (1 pen), Waller 2, Blissett 1, Crabbe 1 (1 pen)

1983-84

Smith	Edwards	Bowers	King	Scott	Davis	Spittle	Crabbe	Bissett	Leonard	Cliss	Brady	Waller	Williams	Newell	Pullar	Naylor (L)	Hart	Thornhill	Sheldon	Bishop (L)	Thomas	Grimshaw	REFEREE	
1	2	3	4	5	6	7	8	9	10	11							12						C Seel	1
1	**2**	**3**	**4**	**5**	**6**	**7***	**8**	**9**	**10**	**11**													**F Roberts**	**2**
1	2	3	4	5	6	7*	8	9	10	11	12												N Wilson	3
1	2	3	4	5	6		8*	9	10	11	7	12											A Challinor	4
1	2	3	4*	5	6		8	12	10	7	11	9											K Barratt	5
1	**2**	**3**		**5**	**6**		**8**	**11**	**10**	**7**	**4**	**9**											**K Redfern**	**6**
1	2	3*	12	5	6		8	11	10	7	4	9											J Key	7
1	2*	3	12	5	6		8	11	10	7	4	9											D Hutchinson	8
1	2		4	5	6	12	8		10*	7	3	9			11								R Lewis	9
1	2		4	5	6	12	8	10*		7	3	9			11								G Napthine	10
1	**2**		**4**	**5**	**6**		**8**	**10**		**7**		**9**			**11**		**3**						**I Borrett**	**11**
	5		2	3		6	7	8		11				10	9	1	4						N Glover	12
	2	3	4	5			8			7	6	12		9*	11	1		10					J Moules	13
	2		4	5		8				7	3	9		10	11	1	6						G Courtney	14
	2		4	5			8	10		7	3	9			11	1	6						A Robinson	15
	2		**4**	**5**		**12**	**8***	**10**			**3**	**9**			**11**	**1**	**6**			**7**			**K Hackett**	**16**
	2		4	5			8	10		7	3	9			11	1	6						M Taylor	17
	2	12	4	5			8	10*			3	9			11	1	6		7				D Brazier	18
	2	12	4	5			8		10		3	9			11	1	6		7*				T Holbrook	19
	2		4	5			8	12	10	7*	3	9			11	1	6						M Peck	20
	2		**4**	**5**			**8**	**7**	**10**		**3**	**9**			**11**	**1**	**6**						**D Allison**	**21**
	2	8	4	5				7	10		3	9			11	1	6						K Walmsley	22
		3	4	5			8	11	10		2	9			7	1	6						B Hill	23
		3	4	5			8		10	11	2	9			7	1	6						B Stevens	24
	12	3	4	5			8		10	11	2	9			7*	1	6						D Richardson	25
		3	4	5	7*		8		10	11	2	9	12			1	6						R Dilkes	26
		3	4	5			8		10	11	2	9			7	1	6						I Hendrick	27
		3	4	5			8		10	11	2	9			7	1	6						J Hunting	28
		3	4	5			8		10	11	2	9	12		7*	1	6						H King	29
	3		4	5			8		10	11	2	9*	12		7	1	6						L Robinson	30
	3		4	5			8		10	11	2	9			7	1	6						D Owen	31
	3		4	5			8		10	11	2*	9	12		7	1	6						T Mills	32
	3*		4	5	2		8		10	11		9	7		12	1	6						R Banks	33
	3		4*	5	2		8		10	11		9	12		7	1	6						M Scott	34
	3		**4**	**5**	**2**		**8**		**10**	**11***		**9**	**12**		**7**	**1**	**6**						**F Roberts**	**35**
	3		4	5	2		8		10	11*		9	12		7	1	6						A Buksh	36
	2	3		4			8		10	6		9	11		7	1	5						V Callow	37
	2	3	12	5			8		10	4		9	11		7*	1	6						D Allison	38
	2	3	12	5			8	7*	10	4		9	11			1	6						H Taylor	39
	2	**3**	**12**	**5**	**13**		**8**	**7***	**10**	**4**		**9**	**11***			**1**	**6**						**G Tyson**	**40**
		3	2	5	6		8	9	10	4			11		7*	1	12						A Ward	41
	2	**3**	**4**	**5**			**8**	**12**	**10**	**7***		**9**	**11**			**1**	**6**						**N Glover**	**42**
	3		4	5	2		8	7	10	11		9				1	6						T Fitzharris	43
	3			5	2		8	7	10			9			11	1	6			4			D Scott	44
	3			5	2		8	10				9*	11		7	1	6			4	12		D Vickers	45
	3		4	5	2		8	10*	12			9	11		7	1	6						N Midgley	46
	3		4	5	2		8		10*	12		9	11		7	1	6						C Thomas	47
	3		4	5	2				10*	7		9	11			1	6			8	12		E Scales	48
	3		4	5	2				10	7		9	11*			1	6			8	12		A Challinor	49
	3		2	5					10	4		9	11*		7	1	6				8	12	J Key	50
	3		2	5	12				10	4*		9	11		7	1	6				8		K Cooper	51
	3		4	5	2				10*			9	11		7	1	6				8	12	N Wilson	52
	3		4	5	2			10*	12	11		9			7	1	6				8		I Borrett	
	3			5	2			10	4			9	11			1	6				8	7	D Hutchinson	54
8	38	19	38	**46**	23	4	37	20	36	36	24	40	14	3	33	38	36	1	2	4	5	1	League Appearances	
	+1S	+2S	+4S		+1S	+2S		+2S	+2S	+1S	+1S	+2S	+6S		+1S		+1S				+3S	+2S		
	1		1	1			1	1	1		1	1			1	1	1						FA Cup Appearances	
3	4	2	3	4	3	1+1S	4	4	2	3	2	3			2	1	2			1			Milk Cup Appearances	
	3	2	2+1S	3	1+1S		3	1+1S	3	3		3	2+1S		1	3	3						AM Cup Appearances	

GRESTY ROAD

Official Address: Gresty Road, Crewe Cheshire. Telephone: Crewe (0270) 213014

Telegraphic: Alex Football Crewe

Ground Capacity: 17,000

Record Attendance: 20,000 v. Tottenham Hotspur, F.A. Cup Round 4, 30 Jan 1960

Record Receipts: £5,388 v. Wigan Athletic, League Cup Round 1, 13 Aug 1980

Size of Playing Area: 112yds × 74 yds

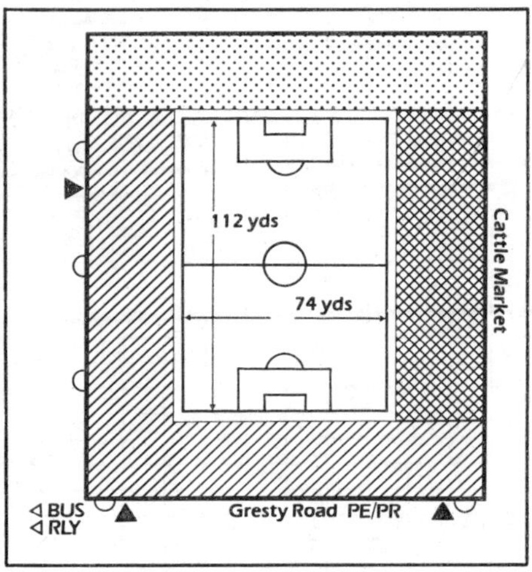

For key see page 12

Season Tickets: Ground £32.00 (£18.00 juveniles/OAP), Paddock £41 (£25), Stand A & D £48 (£38), Stand C £55, B £60

Executive Box Season Tickets: none

Cost of Stand Tickets: £2.80 (A, D) (£2.00 juveniles/OAP), C £3.00, B £3.30; **Terraces:** £2.00 (£1.20 juveniles/OAP); Paddock: £2.50 (£1.60 juveniles/OAP)

Match and Ticket Information: advance bookings for important cup matches only.

Car Parking: parking at the ground for 200 cars.

How to get to the ground

From North: Use Motorway M6 until junction 17 and follow signs Crewe A534. At Crewe roundabout follow signs Chester into Nantwich Road. Then take next turning on left into Gresty Road for Crewe Alexandra F.C.
From East and South: Use A52 then A5020 (S.P. Crewe) then at Crewe roundabout follow signs Chester into Nantwich Road. Then take next turning on left into Gresty Road for Crewe Alexandra F.C.
From West: Use A534 (S.P. Crewe) and immediately before Crewe Railway Station turn right into Gresty Road for Crewe Alexandra F.C.

CRYSTAL PALACE Division 2

President
S Stephenson

Chairman
R G Noades

Directors
B Coleman
A De'Souza
C D Richards
R S Briggs
J Rose
R M Marsden

Secretary
Alan Leather

Commercial Manager
Graham Drew (01-731 9502)

Sales & Marketing Manager
Graham Drew

Manager
Steve Coppell

Assistant Manager
Ian Evans

Youth Team Coach
Alan Smith

Youth Development Officer
Peter Prentice

Chief Scout
John Griffin

Groundsman
Len Chatterton

A final league position of eighteenth in the Second Division and early elimination from both cup competitions suggests it was a disappointingly bad season for Palace. In fact, at times the club kept in the public eye more through failures and managerieal outbursts than for their achievements on the field of play. There were occasional bright moments such as the occasion late November when the unbeaten record of Sheffield Wednesday was ended at Selhurst Park by a Giles goal and the large defender Gilbert's solo effort sent Leicester City out of the F.A. Cup in the Third Round, but there was little else to cheer.

In the end Second Division status was preserved by a five point margin from Derby County after a season when the drop was never an impossibility. A season, which started disastrously at least ended with that small consolation — a chance to do better at the same level in 1984/85. A poor position at the end of the previous campaign meant that the Milk Cup started at Round One and a tie against Peterborough, who succumbed by three clear goals at Selhurst Park, and then recovered that deficit exactly at London Road and won on penalties to provoke an outburst from the Palace Manager, Alan Mullery, about a lack of effort from his team (that is a polite version about what was alleged to have been said!) Possibly good relations with his team were difficult to maintain thereafter and Mullery departed at the end of the season.

The F.A. Cup win over Leicester was followed by a good effort against West Ham, who needed a replay before despatching Palace at Upton Park. Then, survival was the target which was ultimately achieved. In an inconsistent season good marks were earned by the eccentric Wood in goal, Gilbert, Hughton and the inevitable Hilaire, who will be at Luton this coming season.

Perhaps a broad new managerial 'team' will lift this club to a more meaningful and happier season.

W.L.M.

Back Row L to R: Tony Mahoney, Bob Horn, Ian Evans (Assistant Manager), George Wood, Trevor Aylott. **Second Row:** Alan Smith (Youth Coach), David Boyce, Jimmy Carter, Gary Stebbing, Alan Irvine, Gary Locke, Gavin Nebbeling, John Lacy, Jim Cannon, Chris Whyte, Phil Barber, David Lindsay, Tony Haistead, Owen Harris (Physiotherapist). **Third Row:** Henry Hughton, Kevin Mabbutt, Peter Nicholas, Steve Coppell (Manager), Brian Sparrow, Jerry Murphy, Stan Cummins. **Front Row:** Mark Sutcliffe, John Day, Paul Blade, Paul Martin, Lee Byne, Mark Howe, Stephen Boys, George Barry, Graham Steele.

'THE EAGLES'

Formed: 1905 **Turned Professional:** 1905 **Ltd Co:** 1905
Previous Managers: 1905-7 John Robson 1907-25 Eddie Goodman 1925-7: Alec Maley 1927-30 Fred Maven 1930-5 Jack Tresarden 1935-6 Tom Bromilow 1936 R S Moyse 1937-9 Tom Bromilow 1939-47 George Irwin 1947-9 Jack Butler 1949-50 Ronnie Rooke 1950-1 Fred Dawes & Charlie Slade 1951-4 Lawrie Scott 1954-8 Cyril Spiers 1958-60 George Smith 1960-3 Arthur Rowe 1963-6 Dick Graham 1966 Arthur Rowe 1966-72 Bert Head 1972-6 Malcolm Allison 1976-80 Terry Venables 1980-1 Malcolm Allison 1981 Dario Gradi 1981-2 Steve Kember 1982-4 Alan Mullery May 1984 Dave Bassett
Honours: Division 2: Champions 1978-9 Division 3 (S): Champions 1920-1
League Career: Original Members of Division 3 1920
Promoted to Division 2 1920-1 Relegated to Division 3 (S) 1924-5
Relegated to Division 4 1957-8 Promoted to Division 3 1960-1
Promoted to Division 2 1963-4 Promoted to Division 1 1968-9
Relegated to Division 2 1972-3 Relegated to Division 3 1973-4
Promoted to Division 2 1976-7 Promoted to Division 1 1978-9
Relegated to Division 2 1980-1
Colours: Red shirts with royal blue three vertical stripes with plain royal blue sleeves with three red stripes, royal blue trim, shorts and stockings.
Change Colours: Sky Blue

CLUB RECORDS

Most Appearances for Club: Terry Long: Football League 432 + F.A. Cup 31 + 9 subs **Total 463 + 9 subs**
Most Capped Player: Peter Nicholas, 16 Wales **For England:** Kenny Sansom 9
Record Goalscorer in a Match: Peter Simpson, 6 v Exeter C (h) 7-2, Div 3(S) 04.10.30
Record League Goalscorer in a season: Peter Simpson, 46, Div 3 (S), 1930-1 **All Competitions:** Peter Simpson, 54 (League 46, F.A. Cup 8) 1930-31
Record League Goalscorer in a career: Peter Simpson, 154 **All Competitions:** Peter Simpson 164 (League 154, F.A. Cup 12) 1930-36
Record Transfer Fee Received: £800,000 (Nett) from Arsenal for Kenny Sansom, August 1980
Record Transfer Fee Paid: £800,000 to Arsenal for Clive Allen, August 1980
Best Performances: League: 13th Div 1 1979-80 **F.A. Cup:** Semi-Final 1975-6 **League/Milk Cup:** 5th Round 1968-9, 1970-1
Most League Points: 64 in Div 4, 1960-1
Most League Goals: 110 Division 4, 1960-1
Record League Victory: 9-0 v Barrow, Div 4, 10 Oct 1959
Record League Defeat: 0-8, v Coventry City, Div 3 (S), 6 Feb 1932; 2-10 v Reading, Div 3 (S), 4 Sept 1946

Club Statistician for the Directory: Mike Purkiss

Programme Editor
Colin Benson

Price	**Number of Pages**
50p	24

Subscriptions
£18.00 from Programme Department C.P.F.C.

CRYSTAL PALACE

PLAYERS NAME Ht Wt Birthdate	Honours	Birthplace Transfers	Clubs	APPEARANCES League	Milk Cup	F.A.C.	E. Cups	GOALS League	Milk Cup	F.A.C.	E. Cups
GOALKEEPERS											
George Wood	S.(4)	Douglas	East Stirling	44	4	1		1			
6-3 14.0 26.9.53			Blackpool	117	8	4					
			Everton	103	13	4	2				
		£150,000	Arsenal	60	4	1					
		F	Crystal Palace	42	2	3					
Bobby Horn	E. Y	Westminster	Crystal Palace (A)								
6-2 14.6 15.12.61			Barnsley	67	13	1					
			Cambridge U. (L)	8							
DEFENDERS											
Jim Cannon*	Div. 2. 79	Glasgow	Crystal Palace (A)	404 + 3	31	36		22	3	1	
6-0 13.0 2.10.53											
Henry Hughton	Ei. U.21	Stratford	Orient (A)	104 + 7	4	9		2	1		
5-8½ 11.10 18.11.59		F	Crystal Palace	75	5	5		1			
John Lacy		Liverpool	Kingstonian								
6-1 12.4 14.8.51			Fulham	164 + 4	9	16		7	1		
			Tottenham H.	99 + 5	11	12		2	1		
			Crystal Palace	24 + 3	2	1					
Gary Locke	E. Y	Kingsbury	Chelsea (A)	270 + 2	21	24		3		1	
5-11 11.5 12.7.54		F	Crystal Palace	49	2	6		1			
Gavin Nebbeling		South Africa	Arcadia Shepherds								
6-0 12.4 15.5.63			Crystal Palace	40 + 5	3 + 1	1		1			
Brian Sparrow		London	Arsenal (A)	19							
5-7 10.2 24.6.66			Wimbledon (L)	17				1			
			Millwall (L)	5				2			
			Gillingham (L)	5				1			
Chris Whyte	E. U.21(4)	London	Arsenal (A)	82 + 1	14	5	3 + 1	7			
6-1 11.10 2.9.61	FAYC. 77	£90,000	Crystal Palace								
MIDFIELD											
David Lindsay		Havering	Crystal Palace (A)	1							
5-7½ 10.7 17.5.66											
Stan Cummins		Durham	Middlesbrough (A)	39 + 5	0 + 1	7		9		1	
5-9 9.1 6.12.58		£300,000	Sunderland	132 + 1	6	8		29	3		
		F	Crystal Palace	17 + 1	2			4			
Jeremy Murphy	Ei.(3).	Stepney	Crystal Palace (A)	179 + 14	18	13 +		17	5		
5-9 11.0 23.9.59	Div. 2. 79.										
	FAYC. 77. 78										
Peter Nicholas	W.(33)	Newport	Crystal Palace (A)	127	10	7		7			
5-8½ 11.8 10.11.51	U.21(3)	£400,000	Arsenal	57 + 3	8	8		1	1	1	
		£150,000	Crystal Palace	25		3		3			
Gary Stebbing	E. Y	Croydon	Crystal Palace	30 + 1		3		2			
5-8 11.0 11.8.65											
FORWARDS											
Trevor Aylott		London	Chelsea (A)	26 + 3	2	1		2			
6-1½ 14.0 26.11.57		£60,000	Barnsley	93 + 3	11	9		26	7	1	
		£150,000	Millwall	32				5			
		£55,000	Luton T.	32	2	1		10	1		
		Player Exchange	Crystal Palace								
Phil Barber		Tring	Crystal Palace	8 + 1				2			
5-11 12.7 10.6.65											
Paul Blades	S. Y	Peterborough	Derby Co. (A)	10	1						
6-0 10.11 5.1.65			Crystal Palace								
Alan Irvine	SD.2. 81	Glasgow	Queen's Park	83 + 5	4 + 1	3		9	1		
5-8 11.4 17.7.58			Everton	51 + 9	10+1	8		4		2	
		£30,000	Crystal Palace								
Andy McCulloch	S. U.23(1)	Northampton	Walton & Hersham								
6-2 13.11 3.1.51			Q.P.R.	30 + 12	3	0 + 1		10	1		
		£45,000	Cardiff C.	58	3	5	2	24	3	3	
		£70,000	Oxford U.	41	1	1		9			
		£25,000	Brentford	115 + 2	2	3		48			
		£70,000	Sheffield W.	122 + 3	14	10		44	1	4	
		£20,000	Crystal Palace	25	1	3		3		1	
Kevin Mabbutt	E. Y. S	Bristol	Bristol C. (A)	112 + 17	11	8		29	3	7	
5-7 10.2 5.12.58		£100,000 + P/E	Crystal Palace	64 + 3	5	8		21	2		
Tony Mahoney		Barking	Fulham (A)	53 + 6	4	8 + 2		10	1	5	
6-0 11.12 29.9.59		F	Brentford	33 + 8	8	4		11	3	3	
			Crystal Palace								

CONTRACT PLAYERS WITH NO FIRST TEAM APPEARANCES: David Boyce (F), Jimmy Carter (F), Tony Halstead (D)

APPRENTICES: George Barry, Steve Boys, Tony Halstead, John Day, Mark Sutcliffe

PLAYER OF THE YEAR 1983-84: Billy Gilbert (now with Portsmouth)

CRYSTAL PALACE

DIVISION TWO 18TH **FA CUP** 4TH ROUND **MILK CUP** 1ST ROUND

MATCH	DATE	COMPE-TITION	VENUE	OPPONENTS	RESULT	HALF TIME	L'GUE POS'N	GOALSCORERS	ATTEN-DANCE
1	A 27	CL	H	Manchester C	L0-2	0-1			13,382
2	**30**	**MC 1**	**H**	**Peterborough U**	**W3-0**	**1-0**		**Hilaire 2, Brooks**	**3,975**
3	S 3	CL	A	Shrewsbury T	D1-1	0-0	18	Cummins	3,849
4	6	CL	A	Huddersfield T	L1-2	1-0		Cummins	7,814
5	11	CL	H	Fulham	D1-1	0-1	20	Wilson (og)	11,327
6	**13**	**MC 1**	**A**	**Peterborough U**	**L0-3[5]**	**0-2**			**3,504**
7	17	CL	A	Newcastle U	L1-3	0-1	21	Evans	22,774
8	27	CL	H	Portsmouth	W2-1	1-0		Wilkins, Hateley (og)	8,486
9	O 1	CL	A	Middlesbrough	W3-1	2-1	17	Hilaire, Evans 2	8,927
10	8	CL	A	Cambridge U	W3-1	2-1	13	Hilaire, Giles, Evans	4,323
11	15	CL	H	Derby Co	L0-1	0-0	15		7,081
12	22	CL	A	Grimsby T	L0-2	0-1	17		6,075
13	29	CL	H	Barnsley	L0-1	0-1	17		6,377
14	N 5	CL	A	Leeds U	D1-1	1-0	17	Giles	14,847
15	8	CL	H	Cardiff C	W1-0	0-0		Murphy	5,299
16	12	CL	H	Oldham Ath	W2-1	2-0	14	McCulloch, Murphy	5,481
17	19	CL	A	Chelsea	D2-2	2-1	14	Locke, Evans	19,060
18	26	CL	H	Sheffield W	W1-0	0-0	12	Giles	11,263
19	D 3	CL	A	Swansea C	L0-1	0-1	13		6,304
20	11	CL	H	Carlisle U	L1-2	1-0		Stebbing	6,460
21	17	CL	A	Blackburn R	L1-2	0-2	15	Evans	4,794
26	26	CL	H	Brighton & HA	L0-2	0-0	17		13,781
23	27	CL	A	Charlton Ath	L0-1	0-1	18		10,224
24	31	CL	H	Shrewsbury T	D1-1	1-0	18	Stebbing	5,275
25	**J 7**	**FAC 3**	**H**	**Leicester C**	**W1-0**	**0-0**		**Gilbert**	**11,497**
26	14	CL	A	Manchester C	L1-3	0-1	19	Giles	20,144
27	21	CL	H	Newcastle U	W3-1	3-0	18	McCulloch, Mabbutt, Gilbert	9,464
28	**28**	**FAC 4**	**H**	**West Ham U**	**D1-1**	**1-1**		**McCulloch**	**27,590**
29	**31**	**FAC 4R**	**A**	**West Ham U**	**L0-2**	**0-1**			**27,127**
30	F 4	CL	H	Middlesbrough	W1-0	0-0	17	Nicholas (pen)	5,819
31	11	CL	A	Fulham	D1-1	0-0	17	McCulloch	9,119
32	18	CL	A	Barnsley	D1-1	0-1	17	Nicholas (pen)	6,239
33	25	CL	H	Grimsby T	L0-1	0-1	19		5,956
34	M 3	CL	H	Leeds U	D0-0	0-0	19		8,077
35	10	CL	A	Oldham Ath	L2-3	1-2	19	Barber, Cummins	4,138
36	17	CL	H	Huddersfield T	D0-0	0-0	19		5,003
37	24	CL	A	Portsmouth	W1-0	1-0	19	Evans	10,237
38	A 1	CL	H	Cambridge C	D1-1	1-1		Murphy	5,276
39	7	CL	A	Derby Co	L0-3	0-2	18		10,903
40	14	CL	H	Chelsea	L0-1	0-0	18		20,540
41	17	CL	A	Cardiff C	W2-0	1-0		Smith (og), Cummins	4,901
42	21	CL	A	Brighton & HA	L1-3	0-2	18	Nicholas	15,214
43	23	CL	H	Charlton Ath	W2-0	0-0	17	Cannon, Mabbutt	7,818
44	28	CL	A	Sheffield W	L0-1	0-0	18		27,287
45	M 5	CL	H	Swansea C	W2-0	2-0	18	Cannon, Mabbutt	5,318
46	7	CL	A	Carlisle U	D2-2	0-2	17	Giles, Barber	3,013
47	12	CL	H	Blackburn R	L0-2	0-0	18		5,078

[5]Lost On Penalties

Av Home Att **8,325**

Goal Scorers

League (42): Evans 7, Giles 5, Cummins 4, McCulloch 3, Mabbutt 3, Murphy 3, Nicholas 3 (2 pens), Barber 2, Cannon 2, Hilaire 2, Stebbing 2, Gilbert 1, Locke 1, Wilkins 1, opponents 3

FA Cup (2): Gilbert 1, McCulloch 1

Milk Cup (3): Hilaire 2, Brookes 1

1983-84

Wood	Locke	Gilbert	Hughton	Lacy	Cannon	Evans	Murphy	Cummins	McCulloch	Hilaire	Brooks	Giles	Nebbeling	Stebbing	Fashanu **(L)**	Strong	Wilkins	Nicholas **(L)**	Lindsay	Martin	Mabbutt	Barber	**REFEREE**	
1	2	3	4†	5	6	7	8*	9	10	11	12												K Barratt	1
1	**2**	**3**	**4**	**5**	**6**	**7***		**9**	**10**	**11**	**8**	**12**											**E Read**	**2**
1	2	3	6	4	5			9	10	11	8	7											TA Jones	3
1	2	3	4	5	6			9	10	11	8	7											N Ashley	4
1	2*	3			5		10	8		11	7	12	4	6	9								L Shapter	5
1	**2**	**3**		**6**	**5***		**10**	**8**		**11**	**4**	**7**	**12**		**9**								**J Hough**	**6**
1		2	4	5		11	8	10	9			7	6			3							N Midgley	7
1		2	4	5		8	10			11		7	6			3	9						I Borrett	8
1			4	5		8		10		11		7	6	2		3	9						P Tyldesley	9
1	10		4	5		8				11		7	6	2		3	9						J Bray	10
1	2*	12	4	5	9	10	8			11		7	6			3							Alan Robinson	11
1		2	3	5	6	8	4			11		7					9	10					D Owen	12
1			3	12	6	8				11		7	5	2		4*	9	10					J Deakin	13
1	4	5	3		6	8				11		7		2			9	10					G Napthine	14
1	2	6	3		5	8	12		9	11		7		4*				10					D Axcell	15
1	2	6	3		5*	8	4		9	11		7		12				10					D Brazier	16
1	2	6	3	10	5	8	7		9	11				4									R Milford	17
1	2	6	3	8	5		4		9	11		7		10									B Hill	18
1	2	6	3	12	5*	8	4		10	11		7		9									R Guy	19
1	2	6	3	4			5		9*	11			12	10					7	8			M Bodenham	20
1	2	6	3	5		10	8		9	11			12	4		7*							T Mills	21
1	2	6	3	5		8	7		10	11			12	4*				9					D Hedges	22
1	2	6	3	5			4		9	11*		7	8	10							12		M Dimblebee	23
1	2	6	3	5			4					7	9	8				11			10		J Ashworth	24
1	**2**	**6**	**3**	**5**					**9**	**11**		**7**		**4**				**10**			**8**		**D Vickers**	**25**
1	2		3				6		9	11		7	5	4				10			8		J Key	26
1	2	6	3		5		12		9*	11		7		4				10			8		T Spencer	27
1	**2**	**6**	**3**		**5**				**9**	**11**		**7**		**4**				**10**			**8**		**J Hunting**	**28**
1	**2**	**6**	**3***		**5**	**12**			**9**	**11**		**7**		**4**				**10**			**8**		**J Hunting**	**29**
1	2	6†	3		5				9	11		7		4				10			8†		B Stevens	30
1	2*	6			5	12	3		9	11		7		4				10			8		H King	31
1	2				5	8	3		9	11		7	6	4				10						32
1	2			12	5*		3	8		11		7	6	4				10				9	J Martin	33
1	2	6			5	12	3	8	9*	11		7		4				10					Alan Robinson	34
1	2	6		9	5		3	8		11				4				10				7	M Scott	35
1	2	6		10	5		3	8		11				4			9					7	M Taylor	36
1	2	6	9		5	8	3			11				4				10				7	K Baker	37
1	2	6	9		5	8	3	12		11				4*				10				7	K Barratt	38
1	2	6	9		5	8*	3	4	7	11								10				12	P Willis	39
1	2	6	3	7	5				9	11				4				10				8	B Hill	40
1	2	6	3	10	5			7	9	11				8				4					L Robinson	41
1	2	6	3	8	5			7	9	11		12		4*				10					D Letts	42
1	2	6	3		5		4	8	9	11		7*						10			12		A Seville	43
1	2	6	3		5		4	8	9	11								10			7		R Banks	44
1			3	6	5		4	7*		11		12		2				10			8	9	H Taylor	45
1	2	6	3	5			4			11		8						10			7	9	J Hough	46
1	2		3	5			10	9		11		7	6	4							8		K Cooper	47
42	36	33	35	24	30	19	30	17	25	40	3	26	13	30	1	7	7	25	1	1	9	8	League Appearances	
		+1S		+3S		+2S	+2S	+1S			+1S	+3S	+3S	+1S							+2S	+1S		
3	3	3	3	1	2	1S			3	3		3		3				3			3		FA Cup Appearances	
2	2	2	1	2	2	1	1	2	1	2	2	1+1S	1S		1								Milk Cup Appearances	

SELHURST PARK

Official Address: Selhurst Park, London SE25 6PU. Telephone: 01-653 4462

Ground Capacity: 38,500 (18,000 covered)

Record Attendance: 51,482 v. Burnley, Div. 2, 11 May 1979

Record Receipts: £103,173 v. West Ham U, F.A. Cup, Round 4, 28 Jan 1984

Size of Playing Area: 110yds × 74 yds

Season Tickets: Stand: £90.00 (AB & HJ), £108 (C & G), £126 (D & F), £54 (OAP & juveniles); £90 (Block V) (£45 OAP & juveniles); £90 (other seats) (£45 OAP & juveniles); £63 (enclosure) (£36 OAP & juveniles); Terraces: £54 (£27 OAP & juveniles).

Executive Box Season Tickets: £4,000 per season (£250 per match); £2,000 Associate Directors (double); £1,200 Associate Directors (single); £375 Vice Presidents' Club; £275 Strikers Lounge (£15 per match); £200 Executive Lounge (£12 per match); £175 Tudor Lounge (£12 per match).

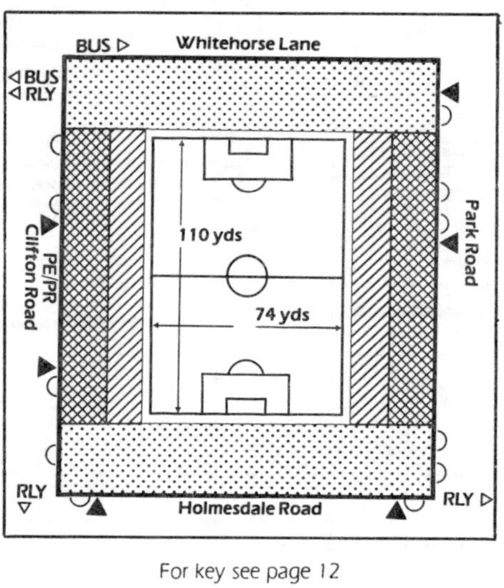

For key see page 12

Cost of Stand Tickets: £7.00, £6.00, £5.00; **Terraces:** £3.00 (£1.50 for registered members of "Palace Club" only)

Match and Ticket Information: Seats bookable in advance, one month by post (with sae) and two weeks for personal applications. Cheques should be made payable to Crystal Palace F.C. and should record the name and address of applicant on back. Separate applications for each match.

Car Parking: by prior arrangement only through the Secretary. Street parking is available. Supporters may use Club Car Park (for 600 cars) for £2 per day.

How to get to the ground

From North: From Motorway M1 or A1, use A406 North Circular Road to Chiswick. Follow signs South Circular Road A205 to Wandsworth. Then use A3 to A214 and follow signs to Streatham. Join A23. In 1m turn left B273. At end turn left into High Street then forward into Whitehorse Lane for Crystal Palace F.C.

From East: Use A232 (S.P. Croydon) to Shirley then join A215 (S.P. Norwood). In 2.2m turn left B266 into Whitehouse Lane.

From South: Use A23 (S.P. London) then follow signs Crystal Palace B266 via Thornton Heath into Whitehouse Lane.

From West: Use Motorway M4 to Chiswick then route from North or A232 (S.P. Croydon) to Beddington, then follow signs London A23. After follow signs Crystal Palace B266 via Thornton Heath into Whitehouse Lane.

DARLINGTON Division 4

President
JL Moore

Chairman
KW Warne

Directors
JB Hawley
A Brown
W Mason
CH Parias
A Heaton
P Bowwy
A Moore

Secretary
DA Thorne

Manager
Cyril Knowles

Reserve Team Coach
Brian Swift

Commercial Manager
Alice Burton (0325 465097)

Physiotherapist
Bob Farrelly

Groundsman
Colin Gray

There have been worse seasons at the Feethams but a final Fourth Division position of sixteenth suggests correctly that the local supporters did not have too many joyous moments, which came mostly in the domestic cup competitions. The League was mostly a typical dour struggle to avoid the need at the end of the season to produce yet another collection of begging letters to colleagues so the avoidance of that must have given some relief to the hard working directors.

The Milk Cup was given a good start in both first-round 'legs' against Halifax, but this brought a second round draw against Sheffield Wednesday and elimination with the Owls taking both legs comfortably. The FA Cup produced a run as far as Round Four after three wins against Non-League opposition. Mossley went first by five clear goals at The Feethams, Walsh scoring three; Altrincham then drew at Darlington but failed in the home replay by two clear goals (Walsh again scoring once); in the Third Round it was Maidstone at home and a good winning margin (4-1) with Walsh again amongst the scorers. Defeat at Plymouth by the odd goal in three at the next hurdle was no disgrace as the West Country side were the heroes of the competition and reached the semi-finals.

Manager Cyril Knowles has one of the less envious tasks in Football but has made the best out of the limited resources at his disposal. He will start the new season without the successful striker, Walsh, and will need to rely on the consistency of Barber in goal, the veteran Craggs, McLean and Smith for next season's results. Perhaps a raid on the Non-League clubs in the North-East may unearth some useful talent, but he has a difficult job ahead of him. WLM

Back Row L to R: Phil Lloyd, Kevan Smith, Phil Laycock, Chris Anthony, Phil Shute, Kevin Todd. **Middle Row:** Mike Angus, Dave McLean, Chris Sanders, Fred Barber, Steve Smith, Dave Hawker, John Hannah. **Seated:** Bob Farrelly (Physio), Colin Ross, Guy Ulliott, Cyril Knowles (Manager), Peter Johnson, Mark Miller, John Craggs.

'THE QUAKERS'

Formed: 1883 **Turned Professional:** 1908 **Ltd Co:** 1891
Previous Managers: Since 1946
Bill Forrest George Irwin Bob Gurney Dick Duckworth Eddie Carr Lol Morgan
Jimmy Greenhalgh Ray Yeoman Len Richley Frank Brennan Allan Jones Ralph Brand
Dick Conner Billy Horner Peter Madden Len Walker
Honours: Division Three (North) Champions 1924-5
League Career: Original member of Division Three (N) 1921 Promoted to Division Two 1924-5
Relegated to Division Three (N) 1926-7 Transferred to Division Four 1958
Promoted to Division Three 1965-6 Relegated to Division Four 1966-7
Colours: White shirts with black trim, black shorts and black stockings with white hoop at top
Change Colours: All blue or all red

CLUB RECORDS

Most Appearances for Club: Ron Greener, 442, 1955-68
Most Capped Player: None
Record Goalscorer in a Match: Tom Ruddy, 5 v South Shields, Div 2, 23.04.27
Maurice Wellock, 5 v Rotherham United, Div 3(N), 15.02.30
Record League Goalscorer in a season: David Brown, 39, Div 3(N), 1924-5
Record League Goalscorer in a career: Alan Walsh, 90, 1978-84 **In all competitions:** Alan Walsh 100 (87 League + 6 F.A. Cup + 7 Milk Cup) 1978-84
Record Transfer Fee Received: £65,000 from Chelsea for David Speedie, May 1982
Record Transfer Fee Paid: £17,000 to Notts County for Eric Probert, Oct 1978
Best Performances: League: 15th Div 2 1925-6 **F.A. Cup:** 3rd Round 1910-1, 5th Round 1957-8 (both last 16)
League/Milk Cup: 5th Round 1967-8
Most League Points: 59 in Div 4, 1965-6
Record League Victory: 9-2 v Lincoln City, Div 3(N), 7 Jan 1928
Record League Defeat: 0-10 v Doncaster Rovers, Div 4, 25 Jan 1964

Club Statistician for the Directory: F. Tweddle

Programme Editors
D. Thorne, F. Tweddle, P. Boddy

Price	Number of Pages
35p	12

Subscriptions
£8.05 + postage for home League games.
Cup games on application

DARLINGTON

PLAYERS NAME Ht Wt Birthdate	Honours	Birthplace Transfers	Clubs	APPEARANCES League	Milk Cup	F.A.C.	A.M.C.	GOALS League	Milk Cup	F.A.C.	A.M.C.
GOALKEEPER											
Fred Barber		Ferryhill	Darlington (A)	58	4	5	2				
6-0 11.10 26.8.63											
DEFENDERS											
John Craggs*	E. Y	Flint Hill	Newcastle U. (A)	50	1	2		1			
5-8½ 12.4 31.10.48		£60,000	Middlesbrough	408 + 1	31	33		12	1		
		F	Newcastle U. (A)	10 + 2	0 + 1						
		F	Darlington	44	4	5	2				
Peter Johnson		Harrogate	Middlesbrough	42 + 1		7					
5-8 10.4 5.10.58		£60,000	Newcastle U.	16							
			Bristol C. (L)	20		1		1			
		F	Doncaster R.	12							
		F	Darlington	44	1	5	2	1			
Kevan Smith†		Eaglescliffe	Stockton								
6-3 11.10 13.12.59			Darlington	206 + 3	8 + 1	12	2	9	1		
MIDFIELD											
Mitchel C. Cook			Scarborough								
5-7 10.10											
Dave Hawker		Hull	Hull C.	35	2	2		2			
5-7 9.12 29.11.58		F	Darlington	77	3	1		2			
David McLean	E. S	Newcastle	Newcastle (A)	7 + 2	1						
5-8 11.0 24.11.57		£10,000	Carlisle U.	9 + 6							
		F	Darlington	208 + 4	10	12	2	27	3 2		
Colin Ross		Daily	Middlesbrough (A)	37 + 1		2					
5-7 11.0 29.8.62			Chesterfield (L)	6	2						
			Darlington	7							
FORWARDS											
Mike Angus		Middlesbrough	Middlesbrough	35 + 2	4	1 + 1		1	1		
5-10 12.3 28.10.68			Scunthorpe U. (L)	20				2			
			Southend U.								
			Darlington	13				7			
Carl Airey		Barnsley	Barnsley (A)	30 + 8	1	1		5			
5-11 11.6 6.2.65			Bradford C. (L)	4 + 1							
		£6,000	Darlington								
Mark Forster		Cleveland	Guisborough								
5-11½ 11.11 1.11.64			Leicester C.								
			Darlington	10 + 2				4			
Mark Miller		Tynemouth	Whitley Bay								
5-8 11.0 22.9.62			Doncaster R.	21 + 9	4	1	1 + 1	4		1	
			Darlington								
Kevin Todd		Sunderland	Ryehope C.A								
5-9 12.1 28.2.58		£5,000	Newcastle U.	5 + 2	1	2 + 1		3			
		F	Darlington	56 + 1	2	4	2	17	2	1	

NON-CONTRACT PLAYERS 1984-85

John Hannah (9 + 4 Lg., 3g., 1 AMC), **Phil Lloyd, Kevin Wolfe**

DARLINGTON

DIVISION FOUR 14TH **FA CUP** 4TH ROUND **MILK CUP** 2ND ROUND

MATCH	DATE	COMPETITION	VENUE	OPPONENTS	RESULT	HALF TIME	L'GUE POS'N	GOALSCORERS	ATTENDANCE
1	A 27	CL	H	Colchester U	L0-2	0-0			1,411
2	**30**	**MC 1**	**A**	**Halifax T**	**W1-0**	**0-0**		**Honour**	**1,331**
3	S 3	CL	A	Northampton T	L0-2	0-1	22		2,009
4	7	CL	A	Torquay U	W1-0	1-0		Walsh	2,038
5	10	CL	H	Swindon T	W1-0	0-0	15	Walsh (pen)	1,091
6	**12**	**MC 1**	**H**	**Halifax T**	**W3-2**	**0-1**		**Pugh, Walsh 2**	**1,793**
7	17	CL	A	Crewe Alex	L1-2	1-2	16	Walsh	2,614
8	24	CL	H	York C	D0-0	0-0	17		2,181
9	27	CL	H	Bury	L1-2	1-2		Gilbert	1,654
10	O 1	CL	A	Reading	L0-1	0-0	21		2,422
11	**4**	**MC 2**	**A**	**Sheffield W**	**L0-4**	**0-3**			**9,060**
12	8	CL	H	Chester C	W2-1	0-0	18	Barton, Gilbert	1,117
13	15	CL	A	Stockport Co	L0-2	0-0	21		1,360
14	19	CL	A	Hereford U	L0-1	0-0			3,024
15	22	CL	H	Rochdale	W1-0	0-0	20	Todd	1,307
16	**25**	**MC 2**	**H**	**Sheffield W**	**L2-4**	**1-0**		**Walsh, Cartwright**	**3,615**
17	29	CL	A	Chesterfield	D1-1	0-0	20	Walsh	3,200
18	N 1	CL	H	Tranmere R	W1-0	0-0		Johnson	1,776
19	5	CL	A	Blackpool	L1-3	0-2	21	Todd	3,843
20	12	CL	H	Bristol C	L0-1	0-0	21		1,888
21	**19**	**FAC 1**	**H**	**Mossley**	**W5-0**	**3-0**		**Barton, Walsh 3 (1 pen), McLean**	**1,863**
22	25	CL	A	Halifax T	W2-0	1-0		Walsh 2	1,018
23	D 3	CL	H	Mansfield T	W3-0	1-0	16	Smith, Kearney (og), Walsh	1,630
24	**10**	**FAC 2**	**H**	**Altrincham**	**D0-0**	**0-0**			**2,634**
25	**14**	**FAC 2R**	**A**	**Altrincham**	**W2-0**	**1-0**		**Johnson, Walsh**	**2,142**
26	17	CL	H	Aldershot	L0-1	0-0	16		1,273
27	26	CL	A	Hartlepool U	L1-2	1-0	17	Davies	2,968
28	27	CL	H	Doncaster R	L1-2	1-0	18	Todd	2,457
29	31	CL	A	Wrexham	D1-1	1-1	18	Cartwright	2,200
30	J 2	CL	H	Peterborough U	W1-0	0-0	17	Todd	1,471
31	**7**	**FAC 3**	**H**	**Maidstone U**	**W4-1**	**1-1**		**Davies, Walsh, Cartwright, McLean**	**3,509**
32	14	CL	A	Colchester U	L1-2	0-0	19	Walsh	2,151
33	**28**	**FAC 4**	**A**	**Plymouth Arg**	**L1-2**	**1-1**		**Todd**	**8,918**
34	F 4	CL	H	Reading	D1-1	1-1	19	Todd	1,395
35	11	CL	A	York C	L0-2	0-1	19		4,773
36	13	CL	A	Tranmere R	W1-0	0-0		Cartwright	1,606
37	18	CL	H	Chesterfield	W2-1	0-1	17	Honour, Hannah	1,350
38	**21**	**AMC 1**	**A**	**Mansfield T**	**W3-1**	**1-0**		**Honour 2, Todd**	**1,086**
39	25	CL	A	Rochdale	L0-2	0-0	17		1,048
40	28	CL	H	Northampton T	W5-3	2-1		Walsh 2, Hannah 2, Smith	1,328
41	M 3	CL	H	Hereford U	D0-0	0-0	16		1,520
42	10	CL	A	Bristol C	L0-1	0-0	18		6,579
43	**13**	**AMC 2**	**A**	**Burnley**	**L1-2**	**1-0**		**Hannah**	**1,978**
44	17	CL	A	Chester C	L1-2	0-1	18	McLean	981
45	27	CL	H	Crew Alex	W2-0	1-0		Angus, McLean	1,275
46	A 1	CL	A	Bury	W3-0	1-0		Angus 2, Forster	1,225
47	7	CL	H	Torquay U	L0-1	0-0	18		1,322
48	14	CL	A	Mansfield T	L0-1	0-1	18		2,084
49	17	CL	A	Swindon T	L0-1	0-1			1,681
50	21	CL	H	Hartlepool U	W2-0	0-0	18	Todd, McLean	2,625
51	24	CL	A	Doncaster R	L2-3	2-1		Cartwright, Forster	4,741
52	28	CL	H	Halifax T	W3-2	0-1	17	Forster, Angus 2	1,161
53	M 2	CL	H	Stockport Co	W1-0	0-0		Forster	1,102
54	5	CL	A	Peterborough U	D2-2	1-0	17	Angus, Todd	1,925
55	8	CL	H	Wrexham	D2-2	0-1		Angus, Todd	1,123
56	12	CL	A	Aldershot	D0-0	0-0	17		1,798
57	15	CL	H	Blackpool	W2-0	1-0		Todd, Hetzke (og)	4,177
								Av Home Att	**1,496**

Goal Scorers

League (49): Walsh 10 (1 pen), Todd 9, Angus 7, Forster 4, Cartwright 3, Hannah 3, McLean 3, Gilbert 2, Smith 2, Barton 1, Davies 1, Honour 1, Johnson 1, opponents 2
FA Cup (12): Walsh 5 (1 pen), McLean 2, Barton 1, Cartwright 1, Davies 1, Johnson 1, Todd 1
Milk Cup (6): Walsh 3, Cartwright 1, Honour 1, Pugh 1
AMC (4): Honour 2, Hannah 1, Todd 1

1983-84

Barber	Craggs	Gilbert	McLean	Smith	Barton	Johnson	Ross	Lee	Walsh	Honour	Wakefield	Cartwright	Pugh	Hulse	Todd	Wilson	Bannon (L)	Young	Davies	Hannah	Forster (L)	Lloyd	Angus (L)	REFEREE	
1	2	3	4	5	6	7*	8	9	10	11	12													L Dilkes	1
1	**2**	**3**	**4**	**5**	**6**		**8**	**9**	**10**	**11**		**7**												**R Nixon**	**2**
1	2	3		5	6	4*	8	9	10	11	12	7												I Borrett	3
1	2	3		5	6	4	8	9	10	11		7												D Letts	4
1	2	3	4	5	6		8	9	10	11		7												A Robinson	5
1	**2**	**3**	**11**	**5**	**6**		**8***	**9**	**10**	**4**		**7**	**12**											**K Walmsley**	**6**
1	2	3	11	5	6	8		9*	10	4		7	12											J Key	7
1	2	3	11	5	6	8			10	4		7*	12	9†										TA Jones	8
1	2	3	11	5	6	8			10	4	12			7*	9									T Mills	9
1	2	3	11	5	6	8*	7		10	4				12	9									E Read	10
1	**2**	**3**	**11**	**5**	**6**		**7**		**10**	**4**	**12**	**8***			**9**									**G Napthine**	**11**
1	2	3	11	5	6		7*		10	4	8	12			9									D Richardson	12
1			11	5	6	3			10	4	8	7		2	9									H Taylor	13
1	8		11	5	6	3*			10	4	12	7			9	2									14
1	2		7	5	6	3			11	4					10	8	9							M Peck	15
1	**2**		**11**	**5**	**6**	**3**			**10**	**4**	**8**	**12**			**9**		**7***							**D Allison**	**16**
1	2		11	5	6	3			10	4	8	7			9									K Baker .	17
1	2		11	5	6	3			10	4*	12	7			9		8							M Dimblebee	18
1	2			5	6	3			10	4	8*	7			9	11		12						F Roberts	19
1	2		8	5	6	3			11	4*	12	7			10				9					A Challinor	20
1	**2**		**11**	**5**	**6**	**3**			**10**	**4**	**12**	**7**			**8**				**9***					**N Wilson**	**21**
1	2		11	5	6	3			10	4		7			8			12	9*					M Scott	22
1	2		11	5	6	3			10	4	12	7			8				9*					I Hendrick	23
1	**2**	**8**	**11**	**5**	**6**	**3**			**10**	**4***	**12**	**7**							**9**					**N Glover**	**24**
1	**2**	**8**	**11**	**5**	**6**	**3**			**10**	**4**		**7**			**9**									**N Glover**	**25**
1	2	12	11	5		3			10	4		7			8	6			9*					C Seel	26
1	2		11	5		3			10	4	12	7				6		8*	9					K Redfern	27
1	2		11	5	6	3			10	4	12	7			9*				8					P Tyldesley	28
1	2		11	5	6	3			10	4		7			12	8*			9					J Hough	29
1	2	4	11	5	6	3			10	12		7			9				8*					K Hackett	30
1	**2**	**4**	**11**	**5**	**6**	**3**			**10**			**7**			**9**				**8**					**D Richardson**	**31**
1	2	4	11	5	6	3			10	12		7			9				8*					J Martin	32
1	**2**	**9**	**11**	**5**	**6**	**3**			**10**	**4***		**7**			**8**				**12**					**R Milford**	**33**
1	2	4	11	5	6	3			10	12		7			8				9*					R Banks	34
1	2	9	11	5	6	3			10	4*	12	7			8									M Robinson	35
1	2	4	11	5	6	3			10	9*	12	7			8									D Allison	36
1	2	9	11*	5	6	3			10	4		7			8					12				N Glover	37
1	**2**	**9**	**11**	**5**	**6**	**3**			**10**	**4**	**7**				**8**									**A Robinson**	**38**
1	2	9	11	5	6	3			10	4*	12	7			8									J Bray	39
1	2	4	11	5	6	3			10	12		7			8					9*				R Guy	40
1	2	4	11	5	6	3			10*	12		7			8					9				D Owen	41
1	2	4	11*	5	6	3				12		7			8	10				9				D Letts	42
1	**2**		**11**	**5**	**6***	**3**				**4**	**7**				**8**	**10**		**12**		**9**				**J Worrall**	**43**
1	2	12	11	5		3						7			8	10*				9	4	6		K Cooper	44
1	2	4	11	5		3						7			8					9	12*	6	10	D Scott	45
1	2	4	11	5		3						7			8					9*	12	6	10	K Hackett	46
1	2	4	11	5		3*			12			7								9	8	6	10	T Fitzharris	47
1	2	7	11	5		3				4		12								9*	8	6	10	T Holbrook	48
1	2		11	5		3				12		7			8					9*	4	6	10	L Shapter	49
1	2		11	5		3			8*	4					7					12	9	6	10	P Tyldesley	50
1	2		11	5		3			12	4		7			8						9*	6	10	R Bridges	51
1	2		11	5		3				4*		8			7					12	9	6	10	I Hendrick	52
1	2		11	5		3				9*		7			8					12	4	6	10	N Wilson	53
1	2		11	5		3			10	12		7			8						9*	6	4	R Lewis	54
1	2		11	5		3			10	12		7			8						4*	6	9	C Seel	55
1		2	11			3	4		10			7			8	5						6	9	K Baker	56
1	2*	9	11			3			10	6		7			8	12						5	4	J Key	57
46	44	25	43	44	30	44	7	5	36	32	4	39	0	3	36	9	2	1	10	9	10	14	13	League Appearances	
		+2S							+2S	+9S	+12S	+2S	+2S	+1S	+1S	+1S		+2S		+4S	+2S				
5	5	4	5	5	5	5			5	4	2S	5			4				3+1S					FA Cup Appearances	
4	4	3	4	4	4	1	3	2	4	4	1+1S	3+1S	1S		2		1							Milk Cup Appearances	
2	2	1	2	2	2	2			1	2	2				2	1		1S		1				AM Cup Appearances	

FEETHAMS

Official Address: Feethams Ground, Darlington. Telephone: Darlington (0325) 465097/467712)

Ground Capacity: 20,000

Record Attendance: 21,023 v. Bolton Wanderers, League Cup Round 3, 14 Nov 1960

Record Receipts: £15,059 v. Sheffield Wednesday, Division 4, 15 May 1982

Size of Playing Area: 110yds × 74 yds

Cost of Stand Tickets: £2.60 (adults), £1.80 (juveniles/OAP), Terraces: £2.00 (adults), £1.20 (juveniles/OAP)

Match and Ticket Information: Postal and telephone one month in advance (P A Thorne, Secretary, 0325 465097)

Car Parking: Very adequate in adjacent side streets.

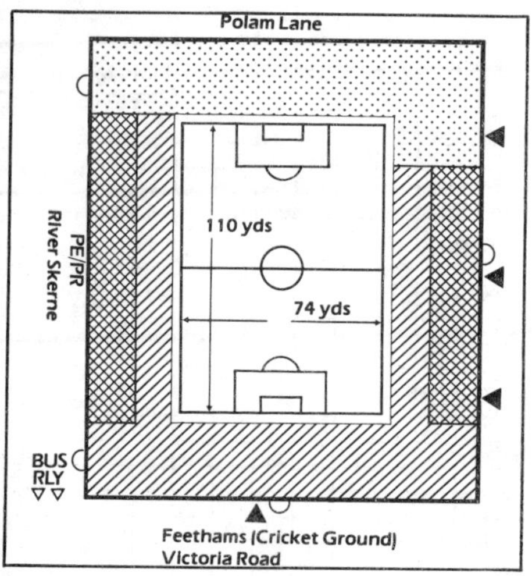

For key see page 12

How to get to the ground

From North: Use Motorway A1M then A167 S.P. Darlington into town centre then follow signs Northallerton into Victoria Road for Darlington F.C.
From East: Use A67 S.P. Darlington into town centre, then follow signs Northallerton into Victoria Road for Darlington F.C.
From South: Use Motorway A1M and A66M then A66 S.P. Darlington and at roundabout take 4th exit into Victoria Road for Darlington F.C.
From West: Use A67 (S.P. Darlington) into town centre and at roundabout take 3rd exit into Victoria Road for Darlington F.C.

DERBY COUNTY   Division 3

President
S Longson OBE

Chairman
AS Webb

Directors
FW Fern
JN Kirkland BSc, CEng, MICE
W Hart
TJ East
G Glossop
C Charlton
C McKerrow

Secretary
MJ Dunford

Manager
Arthur Cox

Assistant Manager
Roy McFarland

Chief Scout/Youth Team Coach
K Gutteridge

Commercial Manager
SFT Crooks (0332 40105)

Physiotherapist
G Guthrie

Groundsman
R Martin

When Judgement Day arrives (if it ever does) and Football clubs take stock of their histories, the season just ended will figure prominently in the Derby County annals, but mostly for reasons which they would like to have erased. But

The Moving finger writes and having writ
Moves on . . . (Fitzgerald)

We should start with the playing results and in these we can first note that twentieth position in the Second Division was the final result and this means Third Division fare at the Baseball Ground next season for a second time. Apart from a brief spell early in the season this was always a likely outcome especially as Oldham and Crystal Palace seemed likely to muster enough points for their own survival. The FA Cup did provide some consolation while The Milk Cup challenge ended abruptly in Round Two on aggregate against Birmingham City, who won both legs easily. But in the big one, the Sixth Round was achieved with some very good performances starting with a three clear goals win at Cambridge. Telford United of the Alliance provided stern resistance at the Baseball Ground in the next round, but they had to depart and this brought First Division Norwich, who fancied their chances for a Wembley trip until Derby shattered such illusions. Things really looked good with a draw against strugglers Plymouth of the Third. Here a lucky goalless draw at Home Park should have been the prelude to a semi-final place but a stupid goal put an end to that dream with Second Division survival then eluding the team as a final blow.

So much for the playing side of things. The domestic problems have been well discussed in the media but the continued fight for physical survival as a club could not have given the players much inspiration. The shaky finances as much as anything also led to the departure of Peter Taylor as Manager. Much reliance will be placed on the ability of Davison to strike well in the lower division, but boardroom stability led by the determined efforts of Stuart Webb to keep the finances healthy will also be a very important part of the club's future.

Now manager Arthur Cox at least has the very great encouragement of excellent season ticket sales and guaranteed enthuiastic support. WLM

Back Row L to R: Roy McFarland (Assistant Manager), Billy Livingstone, Paul Blades, Charlie Palmer, Rob Hindmarch, Eric Steele, Richard Pratley, Andy Garner, Mark Clifford, Steve Buckley, Gordon Guthrie (Physiotherapist). **Front Row:** Steve Devine, Paul Hooks, Kevin Taylor, Bobby Davison, Kenny Burns, Arthur Cox (Manager), Steve Powell, Kevin Wilson, John Robertson, Graham Harbey, Andy Irvine.

'THE RAMS'

Formed: 1884 **Turned Professional:** 1884 **Ltd Co:** 1896
Previous Managers: Since 1946:
Stuart McMillan Jack Barker Harry Storer Tim Ward Brian Clough Dave Mackay Colin Murphy Tommy Docherty Colin Addison John Newman
Honours: Division One Champions 1971-2, 1974-5 Division Two Champions 1911-2, 1914-5, 1968-9 Division 3(N) Champions 1956-7 F.A. Cup Winners 1945-6 Charity Shield Winners 1975 Texaco Cup Winners 1971-2
League Career: Founder member of Football League 1888 Relegated to Division 2 1906-7
Promoted to Division 1 1911-2 Relegated to Division 2 1913-4
Promoted to Division 1 1914-5 Relegated to Division 2 1920-1
Promoted to Division 1 1925-6 Relegated to Division 2 1952-3
Relegated to Division 3(N) 1954-5 Promoted to Division 2 1956-7
Promoted to Division 1 1968-9 Relegated to Division 2 1979-80
Relegated to Division 3 1983-4
Colours: White shirts with blue, gold and brown centenary sash, blue shorts and white stockings
Change Colours: Blue shirts with white, brown and gold centenary sash, white shorts, blue stockings

CLUB RECORDS

Most Appearances for Club: Kevin Hector, 486, 1966-8, 1980-2
Most Capped Player: Roy MacFarland, 28, England
Record Goalscorer in a Match: Steve Bloomer, 6, v. Sheffield Wednesday, Div 1, 02.01.1899
Record League Goalscorer in a season: Jack Bowers, 37, Div 1, 1930-1 Ray Straw, 37, Div 3(N), 1956-7
Record League Goalscorer in a career: Steve Bloomer, 291, 1892-1906, 1910-4
Record Transfer Fee Received: £400,000 from Southampton for Charlie George, Dec 1978
Record Transfer Fee Paid: £41,000 to Crystal Palace for David Swindlehurst, April 1980
Best Performances: League: Champions (2) **F.A. Cup:** Winners (1) **League/Milk Cup:** Semi-Final 1967-8
European Cup: Semi-Final **U.E.F.A. Cup** 3rd Round **Texaco Cup:** Winners
Most League Points: 63 in Div 2, 1968-9, Div 3(N) 1958-9, Div 3(N) 1956-7
Record League Victory: 9-0 v. Wolverhampton W, Div 1, 10 Jan 1891; 9-0 v. Sheffield Wednesday, Div 1, 2 Jan 1899
European Competitions Entered: European Cup: 1972-3, 1975-6 U.E.F.A. Cup: 1974-5, 1976-7

Club Statistician for the Directory: S. McGhee

Programme Editor
Harry Brown (Derby 551172)

Price	Number of Pages
50p	16

Subscriptions
50p plus postage per match

DERBY COUNTY

PLAYERS NAME Ht Wt Birthdate	Honours	Birthplace Transfers	Clubs	APPEARANCES League	Milk Cup	F.A.C.	E. Cups	GOALS League	Milk Cup	F.A.C.	E. Cups
GOALKEEPERS											
Scott Mackay			Ayr United								
			Derby Co.								
Eric Steele	Div. 4. 74	Newcastle	Newcastle U.								
6-0 12.8 14.5.54			Peterborough U.	124	11	13					
		£19,000	Brighton & H.A.	87	9	2					
		£100,000	Watford	51	7	4					
			Cardiff C. (L)	7	1						
			Derby Co.								
DEFENDERS											
Steve Buckley		Brinsley	Burton Alb.								
5-11 12.4 16.10.53		£2,000	Luton T.	123	7	5		9			
		£165,000	Derby Co.	231	12	9		13	2		
Kenny Burns*	S.(20). U.23(2).	Glasgow	Birmingham C.	163+7	12+	11		45	2	3	
5-10 11.0 23.9.53	Div. 1. 78.	£150,000	Nottingham F.	137	25	13		13	1		
	Euro Cup 79.	£400,000	Leeds U.	54+2	3	3		2			
	80. ESC.79	F	Derby Co.	17+1		2		1			
Rob Hindmarch	E. Y	Stannington	Sunderland (A)	114+1	6+2	5		2	1		
6-1½ 13.4 27.4.61			Portsmouth (L)	2							
		F	Derby Co.								
Charlie Palmer		Aylesbury	Watford (A)	10	2		4	1			
5-11 11.9 10.7.63		F	Derby Co.								
Steve Powell	E. U.23(1).	Derby	Derby Co. (A)	317+9	20	30+		19			
5-9 12.0 20.9.55	Y. S										
Richard Pratley		Banbury	Banbury U.								
6-1 12.6 12.1.63		£1,500	Derby Co.	1+1							
			Scunthorpe U.(L)	10			2AM				
MIDFIELD											
Mark Clifford		Derby	Derby Co. (A)								
6-1 10.1 31.12.65											
Steve Devine	NI. Y	Strabane	Wolverhampton (A)								
5-7 10.9 11.12.64			Derby Co.	9+1							
Graham Harbey		Chesterfield	Derby Co. (A)	19	2						
5-7 10.2 29.8.64											
Paul Hooks		Wallsend	Notts Co. (A)	144+29	15+	6+3		30	5	1	
5-8 10.11 30.5.59			Derby Co.	25	2	2		3			
Kevin Taylor		Wakefield	Sheffield W. (A)	118+7	11+	7		22	5	1	
5-8 11.11 22.1.61			Derby Co.								
FORWARDS											
Bobby Davison		South Shields	Seaham C.W.								
5-10 11.5 17.7.59		£1,000	Huddersfield T.	1+1							
		£20,000	Halifax T.	63	5	3		29	3		
		£60,000	Derby Co.	63+3	2	5		22		4	
Andrew Garner		Chesterfield	Derby Co. (A)	13		1		5			
5-11 11.9 8.3.66											
Billy Livingstone	S. Y	Coventry	Wolverhampton	10+2	1			3			
5-10 11.3 13.8.64			Derby Co.								
John Robertson	S.(28). Y. S.	Uddingston	Nottingham F.	374+12	45+	35+	20	61	16	10	5
5-8 10.9 20.1.53	Lg.C. 78. 79.	£135,000	Derby Co.	31	2	4		2			
	E.Cup 79. 80.										
	ESC. 79. Div.1. 78										
Kevin Wilson		Banbury	Banbury U.								
5-7 10.7 18.4.61		£20,000	Derby Co.	93+16	4+3	8		22	2	3	

NON-CONTRACT PLAYERS 1984-85: John Chamberlain, Andy Cockhill, Gordon Tucker, Steve White

APPRENTICES

Neil Bailey, Richard Butler, Andy Irvine, Andy Roberts, Eddie Briscoe, Brian McCord, Steve Parsons

PLAYER OF THE SEASON 1983-84: Archie Gemmell (retired)

DERBY COUNTY

DIVISION TWO 20TH **FA CUP** 6TH ROUND **MILK CUP** 2ND ROUND

MATCH	DATE	COMPETITION	VENUE	OPPONENTS	RESULT	HALF TIME	L'GUE POS'N	GOALSCORERS	ATTENDANCE
1	A 27	CL	A	Chelsea	L0-5	0-1			17,338
2	29	CL	H	Sheffield W	D1-1	1-0		Davison	10,241
3	S 3	CL	H	Swansea C	W2-1	1-0	12	Davison, Campbell	9,711
4	6	CL	A	Brighton & HA	L0-1	0-1			10,891
5	10	CL	A	Blackburn R	L1-5	0-3	18	Campbell	5,837
6	17	CL	H	Oldham Ath	D2-2	2-1	19	Campbell 2	12,521
7	24	CL	A	Charlton Ath	L0-1	0-0	19		5,638
8	O 1	CL	H	Carlisle U	L1-4	0-2	21	Davison	12,041
9	**5**	**MC 2**	**H**	**Birmingham C**	**L0-3**	**0-2**			**13,114**
10	8	CL	H	Barnsley	L0-2	0-0	21		12,696
11	15	CL	A	Crystal Palace	W1-0	0-0	21	Robertson	7,081
12	22	CL	A	Huddersfield T	L0-3	0-1	21		10,752
13	**25**	**MC 2**	**A**	**Birmingham C**	**L0-4**	**0-2**			**7,786**
14	29	CL	H	Grimsby T	L1-2	1-1	21	Davison	11,531
15	N 5	CL	A	Cambridge U	W1-0	1-0	19	Davison	3,638
16	12	CL	H	Middlesbrough	W1-0	0-0	18	Davison	12,495
17	19	CL	H	Leeds U	D1-1	0-0	18	Davison	16,726
18	26	CL	A	Manchester C	D1-1	1-1	19	Plummer	22,689
19	D 3	CL	H	Newcastle U	W3-2	0-2	19	Davison 2, Gemmill (pen)	18,691
20	10	CL	A	Portsmouth	L0-3	0-2	19		11,834
21	17	CL	H	Shrewsbury T	W1-0	0-0	17	Plummer	11,265
22	26	CL	A	Fulham	D2-2	0-0	15	Wilson 2	7,480
23	27	CL	H	Cardiff C	L2-3	2-1	17	McAlle, Hooks	16,054
24	31	CL	A	Swansea C	L0-2	0-0	19		6,578
25	J 2	CL	H	Charlton Ath	L0-1	0-1	19		12,808
26	**7**	**FAC 3**	**A**	**Cambridge U**	**W3-0**	**2-0**		**Wilson, Plummer, McAlle**	**6,309**
27	14	CL	H	Chelsea	L1-2	0-1	20	Plummer	16,727
28	21	CL	A	Oldham Ath	L0-3	0-2	20		4,564
29	**F 1**	**FAC 4**	**H**	**Telford U**	**W3-2**	**1-1**		**Davison 3**	**21,488**
30	4	CL	A	Carlisle U	L1-2	0-1	20	Powell	4,915
31	11	CL	H	Blackburn R	D1-1	1-0	20	Gemmill (pen)	13,922
32	**18**	**FAC 5**	**H**	**Norwich C**	**W2-1**	**0-0**		**Gemmill (pen), Davison**	**25,793**
33	21	CL	A	Grimsby T	L1-2	1-1		Garner	8,530
34	25	CL	H	Huddersfield T	D1-1	0-0	20	Robertson (pen)	14,529
35	M 3	CL	H	Cambridge U	W1-0	0-0	20	Davison	12,007
36	**10**	**FAC 6**	**A**	**Plymouth Arg**	**D0-0**	**0-0**			**34,365**
37	**14**	**FAC 6R**	**H**	**Plymouth Arg**	**L0-1**	**0-1**			**26,906**
38	17	CL	H	Brighton & HA	L0-3	0-0	20		11,560
39	20	CL	A	Middlesbrough	D0-0	0-0			5,735
40	31	CL	A	Barnsley	L1-5	0-1	20	Davison	6,500
41	A 7	CL	H	Crystal Palace	W3-0	2-0	20	Garner 3	10,903
42	10	CL	A	Sheffield W	L1-3	0-1		Davison	21,792
43	14	CL	A	Leeds U	D0-0	0-0	20		12,549
44	21	CL	H	Fulham	W1-0	1-0	20	Garner	12,178
45	23	CL	A	Cardiff C	L0-1	0-0	20		5,056
46	28	CL	H	Manchester C	W1-0	1-0	20	Watson	14,470
47	M 5	CL	A	Newcastle U	L0-4	0-2	20		35,850
48	9	CL	H	Portsmouth	W2-0	0-0		Davison 2	10,189
49	12	CL	A	Shrewsbury T	L0-3	0-1	20		5,562
								Av Home Att	**12,998**

Goal Scorers

League (36): Davison 14, Garner 5, Campbell 4, Plummer 3, Gemmill 2 (2 pens), Robertson 2 (1 pen), Wilson 2, Hooks 1, McAlle 1, Powell 1, Watson 1
FA Cup (8): Davison 4, Gemmill 1 (1 pen), McAlle 1, Plummer 1, Wilson 1
Milk Cup (-): —

1983-84

Cherry	Barton	Buckley	Gemmill	Powell	Futcher	Plummer	Davison	Campbell	Hooks	Robertson	Attley	McAlle	O'Brien **(L)**	McFarland	Hill	Harbey	Watson	Blades	Wilson	Garner	Deacy **(L)**	Lane	Devine	Burns	REFEREE	
1	2	3*	4	5	6	7	8	9	10	11	12														A Gunn	1
1	2		4	5*	6	7	8	9	10	11	3	12													D Reeves	2
1	2		4		6	7	8	9	10	11			3	5											D Hutchinson	3
1	2		4		6	7		9	10	11		12	3	5*	8										TD Spencer	4
1	7		4		6	8		9	10	11	2	5	3												C Seel	5
1	2		4		6	7	8	9	10	11			3												K Hackett	6
1	2		4	7	6		8*	9	10†	11				12		3	5								K Cooper	7
1	2*		4	7	6	12	8	9	10	11						3	5								M Dimblebee	8
1			**4**	**6**		**7**	**8**		**10**	**11**	**2**					**3**	**5**		**9**						**N Ashley**	**9**
1			4	10		7	8			11				6		3	5	2	9						D Vickers	10
1			4	2	6	7	8	9		11						3	5		10						Alan Robinson	11
1			4	2	6	7	8	9		11						3	5		10						R Guy	12
1					**6**	**7**	**8**	**9**	**2**	**11**				**4**		**3**	**5**		**10**						**R Milford**	**13**
1				4	6	7	8	9	10	11						3	5		12		2*				PN Willis	14
1		3	4	6			8		10	11	7						5		9		2				AW Ward	15
1		3	4	6		10	8			11*	7			12			5		9		2				C Downey	16
1		3	4		6	10	8				7			12			5		9		2	11*			KG Salmon	17
1		3	4	6		10	8					7		12		11*	5		9		2				R Bridges	18
1		3	4	6		10	8				2	7				11	5		9						R Nixon	19
1		3	4	6		10	8				2	7		12		11*	5		9						A Buksh	20
1		3	4	6		10	8		11		2	7					5		9						A Robinson	21
1		3	4	6		10	8		11		2	7					5		9						I Borrett	22
1		3	4	6		10	8		11		2	7					5		9						L Dilkes	23
1		3	4	6		10	8		11		2	7					5		9						A Crickmore	24
	2	3	4	6		10	8		11			7					5		9						J Worrall	25
1	**2**	**3**	**4**	**6**		**10**	**8**		**11**			**7**					**5**		**9**						**M Dimblebee**	**26**
1	2	3	4	6		10	8		11			7					5		9						N Glover	27
1	2	3	4	6	7	10	8			11							5		9						K Redfern	28
1	**2**	**3**	**4**	**6**	**7**	**10**	**8**			**11**							**5**		**9**						**N Midgeley**	**29**
1	2	3	4	6	7	12	8			11						10*	5		9						I Hendrick	30
1	2	3	4	6	7		8		10	11							5		9						T Jones	31
1	**2**	**3**	**4**	**6**	**7**	**12**	**8**			**11**							**5**		**9**	**10***					**A Saunders**	**32**
1	2	3	4	6*	7	12	8			11							5		9	10					D Shaw	33
1	2	3	4		7		8			11		6							9	10				5	C Thomas	34
1	2	3	4	6	7	12	8			11									9	10*				5	S Wilson	35
1	**2**	**3**	**4**	**6**	**7**		**8**		**10***	**11**							**12**		**9**					**5**	**B Stevens**	**36**
1	**2**	**3**	**4**	**6**	**7**	**10**	**8***			**11**							**12**		**9**					**5**	**B Stevens**	**37**
	2	3		4		7	8					11					5		9	10				6	R Banks	38
	2	3		4			8			11	7	10					5		9					6	N Midgley	39
	2	3		4			8			11	7	10*					5		9				12	6†	D Allison	40
1		3	4	6			8			11						10*	5		12	9			7	2	P Willis	41
1		3	4	6			8			11						10	5			9			7	2	D Owen	42
1		3	4	6			8			11*						10	5	2	12	9			7		P Tyldesley	43
1		3	4	6			8			11						10	5	2	12	9*			7		J Hough	44
1		3	4	6			8			11						10	5	2*		9			7		D Hedges	45
1		3	4	6			8			11						10	5		12	9*			7	2	M Heath	46
1		3	4	6			8			11						10	5		12	9*			7	2	D Richardson	47
1		3	4	6			8			11						10	5		12	9			7*	2	D Scott	48
1		3	4	6			8			11						10	5		12	9*			7	2	D Hutchinson	49
38	19	31	38	36	18	23	40	11	17	31	13	14	4	3	1	19	34	4	24	13	5	1	9	11	League Appearances	
						+4S					+1S	+2S		+5S					+8S				+1S			
5	5	5	5	5	4	3+1S	5		2	4		1					3+2S		5	1				2	FA Cup Appearances	
2			1	1	1	2	2	1	2	2	1			1		2	2		2						Milk Cup Appearances	

Also Played: Findlay **(L)** match 25, no.1. Banovic matches 38, 39, 40, no.1. Pratley match 6, no.5; 45, no.12.

BASEBALL GROUND

Official Address: Baseball Ground, Shaftesbury Crescent, Derby DE3 8NB. Telephone: Derby (0332) 40105

Telegraphic: Football Derby

Ground Capacity: 33,301

Record Attendance: 41,826 v. Tottenham Hotspur, Division 1, 20 Sept 1969

Record Receipts: £108,000 v. Manchester United, F.A. Cup Round 5, 19 Feb 1983

Size of Playing Area: 110yds × 71 yds

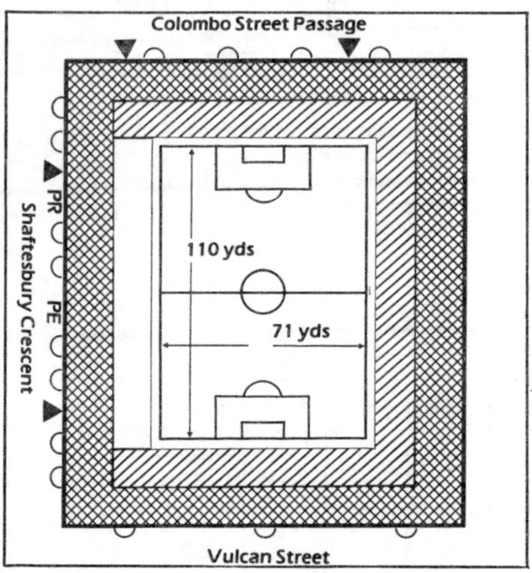

For key see page 12

Season Tickets: Stand: From £50.00 to £100.00. Terraces: £50.00 (adults), £30 (juveniles); OAP any stand £50

Cost of Stand Tickets: Home supporters £4.00, £4.50, £5.00; Visitors £4.00 (Clay Stand juveniles/OAP £3.00); Terraces: Home £2.50, Visitors £3.00

Match and Ticket Information: Available 14 days prior to match

Car Parking: Eight parks within ½ mile of ground run by club in cooperation with local corporation. Street parking within same distance

How to get to the ground

From North: Follow signs Derby A38 into Town Centre, then follow signs Melbourne A514. Then on nearside of Railway Bridge turn right into Shaftesbury Street for Derby County F.C.

From East, South and West: Use Derby Ring Road from East and South (S.P. Burton) and from West (S.P. Nottingham) as far as junction with A514, then follow signs town centre into Osmaston Road. In 1.3m turn left into Shaftesbury Street for Derby County F.C.

DONCASTER ROVERS Division 3

President
J C Morris

Vice President
R Jones

Chairman
I M Jones

Directors
H Bates
K Jackson
B E Boldry
G Smith
N. Taylor

Secretary
L Holloway

Commercial Manager
N Johnson (0302 539679)

Manager
Billy Bremner

Assistant Manager
David Bentley

Youth Team Coach
David Pugh

Physiotherapist
Gerry Delahont

This was a thoroughly satisfying season for the Rovers from South Yorkshire, who well deserved to make an early return to the Third Division with a record which would have left them as divisional champs in any normal season; it was not normal as York chose this occasion to break all records.

Consistency, an essential ingredient in any good campaign, was always present and only in the early stages of the season were Rovers outside a promotion place. Thereafter it was only a question of where the final position would be and second place must have given Manager Billy Bremner great satisfaction. His genuine youth policy has won the rewards it has deserved and the signing of Scotsman Philliben (for a record fee) and Dobbin showed the club meant business.

The major cups did not provide much excitement but they also removed any distractions from the main target — promotion. The First Round of the Milk Cup was passed successfully and comfortably on aggregate against Scunthorpe United (a three goal margin), but Fulham were too good and won both legs by the same score (3-1). The F.A. Cup campaign was even briefer with a First Round defeat by three clear goals being suffered at Mansfield. But no-one was demanding the head of Billy Bremner at the end of the season and the fans must now wonder whether the team is good enough to progress even further.

The manager has many plusses in his favour in terms of playing consistency. Peacock has been sound in goal and reliability can be guaranteed from the Snodins, Russell, Lister and Humphries — to name but a few. Crowds were once large and loyal. It could be like that again soon.

WLM

Back Row L to R: E. Brailsford (Physio), S. Lister, G. Lee, N. Saddington, D. Peacock, P. Gregory, C. Douglas, J. Philliben, S. Yates, B. Bremner (Manager), D. Bentley (Asst Manager). **Front Row:** I. Snodin, B. Russell, J. Buckley, J. Dobbin, G. Snodin, G. Humphries, D. Harle. **Kneeling:** N. Woods, A. Kowalski, A. Brown.

Doncaster Rovers Football Club Ltd.
(Founded 1879)

'ROVERS'

Formed: 1879 **Turned Professional:** 1885 **Ltd Co:** 1905 & 1920
Previous Managers: Since 1946: Bill Marsden Jackie Bestall Peter Doherty Jack Hodgson Syd Bycroft Jack Crayston Jack Bestall Norman Curtis Danny Malloy Oscar Hold Bill Leivers Keith Kettleborough George Raynor Lawrie McMenemy Maurice Setters Stan Anderson
Honours: Division 3 (N) Champions 1934-5, 1946-7, 1949-50 Division 4 Champions 1965-6, 1968-9
League Career: Elected to Division 2 1901 Failed to gain re-election 1903 Re-elected to Division 2 1904 Failed to gain re-election 1905 Re-elected to Division 3 (N) 1923 Promoted to Division 2 1934-5 Relegated to Division 3 (N) 1936-7 Promoted to Division 2 1946-7 Relegated to Division 3 (N) 1947-8 Promoted to Division 2 1949-50 Relegated to Division 3 1957-8 Relegated to Division 4 1958-9 Promoted to Division 3 1965-6 Relegated to Division 4 1966-7 Promoted to Division 3 1968-9 Relegated to Division 4 1970-1 Promoted to Division 3 1980-1 Relegated to Division 4 1982-3 Promoted to Division 3 1983-4
Colours: Red and white hooped shirts with one thin green hoop, white shorts with red, white and green stripes on sides, white stockings with red and green tops
Change Colours: Green shirts with white sleeves and red trim, green shorts with white and red stripe on sides, red stockings with green and white tops

CLUB RECORDS

Most Appearances for Club: Fred Emery: Football League 422 + F.A. Cup 19, 1924-36 **Total 441**
Most Capped Player: Len Graham, 14, N Ireland. **For England:** None
Record Goalscorer in a Match: Tom Keetley, 6 v Ashington (A) (7-4), Div 3 (N), 16.02.29
Record League Goalscorer in a season: Clarrie Jordan, 42, Div 3 (N), 1946-7 **In all competitions:** Clarrie Jordan, 44 (League 42 + F.A. Cup 2) 1946-7
Record League Goalscorer in a career: Tom Keetley, 175, 1923-9 **In all competitions:** Tom Keetley, 180 (League 175 + F.A. Cup 5)
Record Transfer Fee Received: £70,000 from P.N.E. for Mike Elwiss, Feb 1974 £70,000 from Bolton Wanderers for Dennis Peacock, March 1980
Record Transfer Fee Paid: £60,000 to Stirling Albion for John Philliben, March 1984
Best Performances: League: 7th Div 2 1901-2 **F.A. Cup:** 5th Round 1951-2, 1953-4, 1954-5, 1955-6
League/Milk Cup: 5th Round 1975-6
Most League Points: (3pts for win) 85, Div 4, 1983-4 (2pts for win) 72, Div 3 (N), 1946-7
Most League Goals: 123, Div 3 (N), 1946-7
Record League Victory: 10-0 v Darlington, Div 4, 25 Jan 64
Record League Defeat: 0-12 v Small Heath, Div 2, 11 Apr 03

Club Statistician for the Directory: E Wiles

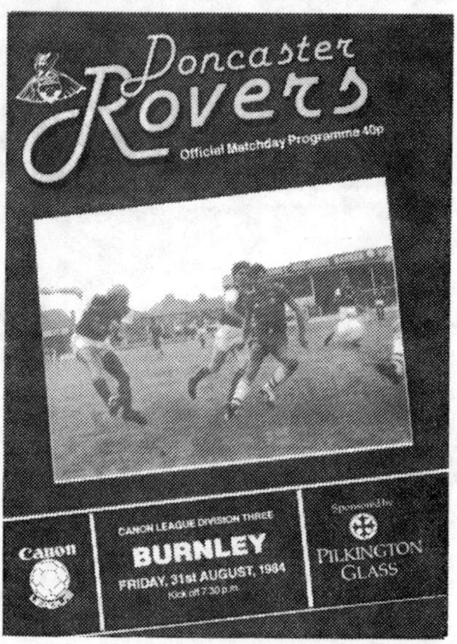

Programme Editor
Geoff Haley

Price	Number of Pages
40p	12

Subscriptions
Apply to club for details

DONCASTER ROVERS

PLAYERS NAME Ht Wt Birthdate	Honours	Birthplace Transfers	Clubs	APPEARANCES League	Milk Cup	F.A.C.	A.M.C.	GOALS League	Milk Cup	F.A.C.	A.M.C.
GOALKEEPERS											
Paul Gregory		Sheffield	Chesterfield (A)	23		1					
5-10 11.7 26.7.61		F	Doncaster R.								
Dennis Peacock		Lincoln	Nottingham F. (A)	22	2						
6-2 14.1 19.4.53			Walsall (L)	10							
		Player Exchange	Doncaster R.	199	18	8					
		£70,000	Bolton W.	16	2	2					
		F	Doncaster R.	77	5	2	3				
DEFENDERS											
Bill Green		Newcastle	Hartlepool U.	128+3	5	4		9			
6-3 12.8 22.12.50		£15,000	Carlisle U.	119	8	8		4			
		£90,000	West Ham U.	35	3	2		1			
		£50,000	Peterborough U.	30	8						
		£40,000	Chesterfield	160	11	12		5	1	2	
		F	Doncaster R.	10+1	2	1		1			
Glenn Humphries	E. Y	Hull	Doncaster R. (A)	94+5	7+1	2	3	7	1		
6-0 12.0 11.8.64											
Steve Lister		Doncaster	Doncaster R.	193+8	14	11		28			
6-1 11.10 18.11.61											
Billy Russell	S. Y	Glasgow	Everton (A)								
5-10 11.4 14.9.59		F	Celtic								
		£15,000	Doncaster R.	203+3	15	15	3	15			
Steve Yates		Burton	Leicester C. (A)	12+7	1	1					
6-0 12.13 8.12.53		£15,000	Southend U.	223+1	13	12		8	1		
		F	Doncaster R.	27			2	1			
MIDFIELD											
David Harle	E. Y	Denaby	Doncaster R.	48+13	4	1		3			
5-9 10.7 15.8.63		F	Exeter C.	42+1	4	1		6			
		F	Doncaster R.	28+1			3	6			1
Andy Kowalski		Mansfield	Worksop T.								
5-10 11.0 26.2.53			Chesterfield	354+11	23+	18+		30	5		
		F	Doncaster R.	32	4	1		1			
John Philliben	S. Y	Stirling	Stirling Alb.	109	11	2		1	1		
5-11 12.0 14.3.64		£70,000	Doncaster R.	12			1				
Glynn Snodin		Rotherham	Doncaster R. (A)	245+21	10+	11	3	43			1
5-6 9.5 14.2.60											
Ian Snodin	E. Y	Rotherham	Doncaster R. (A)	140+7	8	7+1	2	17	1		
5-7 8.12 15.8.63											
Neil Woods		York	Doncaster R. (A)	6+5			2+1	1			2
6-0 11.11 30.7.66											
FORWARDS											
Alan Brown		Easington	Sunderland (A)	87+26	7	4		21	4		
5-11½ 12.10 22.5.59			Newcastle U.	5				3			
		Player Exchange	Shrewsbury T.	65	4	2		15	3		
		£35,000	Doncaster R.	9				2			
John Buckley			Partick Thistle	42+3	1	1					
5-9 10.7 18.5.62			Doncaster R.								
Colin Douglas		Hurlford	Celtic								
6-1 11.0 9.9.62		F	Doncaster R.	115+9	9+1	6	3	25	3		
Jim Dobbin	S. Y		Celtic	2	1				1		
5-9½ 11.7 17.9.63			Motherwell (L)	2							
		£25,000	Doncaster R.	11			1	2			

NON-CONTRACT PLAYERS 1984-85

Ashley Tomlinson (2&25), **Simon Bradshaw, Darren Fletcher, Sean Joyce, Gary Lee, Dale Parkinson, Lee Rogers, Phil Sharpe**

APPRENTICES 1984-85

Matt Burleigh, Sean Fowler, Paul Holmes

DONCASTER ROVERS

DIVISION FOUR 2ND **FA CUP** 1ST ROUND **MILK CUP** 2ND ROUND

MATCH	DATE	COMPE-TITION	VENUE	OPPONENTS	RESULT	HALF TIME	L'GUE POS'N	GOALSCORERS	ATTEN-DANCE
1	A 27	CL	H	Wrexham	W3-0	2-0		Douglas, Humphries, Moss	2,035
2	**30**	**MC 1**	**A**	**Scunthorpe U**	**D1-1**	**1-1**		**Moss**	**4,295**
3	S 3	CL	A	Mansfield T	W2-1	1-1	1	Moss, Snodin I	2,967
4	7	CL	A	Reading	L2-3	2-2		Miller, Moss	3,688
5	11	CL	H	Hereford U	W3-0	2-0	1	Moss, Douglas, Russell	3,532
6	**13**	**MC 1**	**H**	**Scunthorpe U**	**W3-0**	**2-0**		**Humphries, Douglas, Snodin I (pen)**	**4,377**
7	17	CL	A	Hartlepool	L0-1	0-0	5		1,611
8	24	CL	H	Bury	W3-1	2-0	3	Moss, Lister, Douglas	2,777
9	27	CL	H	York C	D2-2	0-1		Moss, Douglas	4,996
10	O 1	CL	A	Torquay U	L1-4	0-2	7	Green	1,814
11	**5**	**MC 2**	**H**	**Fulham**	**L1-3**	**1-2**		**Douglas**	**4,843**
12	8	CL	A	Peterborough U	D1-1	1-0	7	Snodin I	4,400
13	15	CL	H	Aldershot	W3-1	1-0		Humphries, Harle, Douglas	2,299
14	18	CL	A	Chesterfield	D0-0	0-0			6,488
15	21	CL	H	Halifax T	W3-2	3-0		Snodin G 2, Russell	3,299
16	**26**	**MC 2**	**A**	**Fulham**	**L1-3**	**0-2**		**Moss**	**3,891**
17	29	CL	A	Tranmere R	D1-1	0-1	3	Snodin G	2,789
18	N 1	CL	H	Colchester U	D3-3	1-2		Douglas, Miller, Snodin I (pen)	3,451
19	5	CL	A	Bristol C	W2-1	1-1	3	Kowalski, Harle	5,963
20	12	CL	H	Blackpool	W2-1	2-0	2	Douglas 2	4,604
21	**19**	**FAC 1**	**A**	**Mansfield T**	**L0-3**	**0-2**			**5,027**
22	26	CL	H	Chester C	D0-0	0-0	3		2,967
23	D 3	CL	A	Swindon T	L1-2	1-1		Snodin I (pen)	3,545
24	18	CL	A	Crewe Alex	D1-1	0-0		Moss	2,515
25	26	CL	H	Northampton T	W1-0	0-0	5	Douglas	3,127
26	27	CL	A	Darlington	W2-1	0-1	3	Mutrie, Moss	2,457
27	31	CL	H	Stockport C	W2-1	1-0	2	Moss 2	3,736
28	J 2	CL	A	Rochdale	D3-3	1-0	2	Higgins (og), Douglas, Moss	1,978
29	7	CL	H	Mansfield T	W3-1	1-0	2	Russell, Miller, Snodin G	3,804
30	14	CL	A	Wrexham	W2-1	1-1	2	Snodin G, Lister	2,266
31	28	CL	A	Hereford U	W3-0	2-0	2	Harle, Miller, Russell	2,540
32	F 4	CL	H	Torquay U	D1-1	1-1	2	Snodin G (pen)	3,727
33	11	CL	A	Bury	W3-2	2-0	2	Harle, Moss, Snodin G	2,400
34	14	CL	A	Colchester U	D1-1	0-1		Snodin G	2,821
35	18	CL	H	Tranmere R	D1-1	0-0	2	Harle	3,781
36	**22**	**AMC 1**	**A**	**Lincoln C**	**W2-0**	**2-0**		**Harle, Woods**	**1,941**
37	25	CL	A	Halifax T	W2-1	2-1	2	Woods, Snodin I	2,408
38	M 3	CL	H	Chesterfield	W2-1	0-0	2	Douglas, Yates	4,162
39	6	CL	H	Bristol C	W1-0	1-0		Douglas	4,954
40	10	CL	A	Blackpool	L1-3	0-2	2	Russell	6,062
41	**13**	**AMC 2**	**H**	**Preston NE**	**W2-1**	**1-0**		**Miller, Woods**	**2,098**
42	17	CL	H	Peterborough U	D1-1	0-1	2	Douglas	3,672
43	**20**	**AMC NQF**	**H**	**Burnley**	**L1-3[1]**	**1-1**		**Snodin G**	**3,504**
44	24	CL	A	Aldershot	L1-2	1-2	2	Dobbin (pen)	3,636
45	A 8	CL	A	York C	D1-1	1-1		Snodin G	11,297
46	14	CL	H	Swindon T	W3-0	1-0	3	Snodin G, Snodin I (pen), Russell	3,804
47	21	CL	A	Northampton T	W4-1	3-1	3	Harle, Snodin G, Dobbin, Douglas	1,912
48	24	CL	H	Darlington	W3-2	1-2		Snodin I (pen), Snodin G 2	4,741
49	28	CL	A	Chester C	L0-1	0-1	2		1,549
50	M 1	CL	H	Reading	L2-3	1-2		Brown, Douglas	4,972
51	5	CL	H	Rochdale	W3-0	2-0	2	Snodin I, Brown, Moss	3,396
52	7	CL	A	Stockport Co	W2-0	1-0	2	Snodin I, Moss	2,993
53	12	CL	H	Crewe Alex	W1-0	0-0	2	Moss	3,879
54	15	CL	H	Hartlepool U	L0-1	0-0			3,770

[1] After Extra Time

Av Home Att **3,718**

Goal Scorers

League (82): Douglas 15, Moss 15, Snodin G 13 (1 pen), Snodin I 9 (4 pens), Harle 6, Russell 6, Miller 4, Brown 2, Dobbin 2 (1 pen), Humphries 2, Lister 2, Green 1, Kowalski 1, Mutrie 1, Woods 1, Yates 1, opponents 1
FA Cup (-): —
Milk Cup (6): Douglas 2, Moss 2, Humphries 1, Snodin I 1 (1 pen)
AMC (5): Woods 2, Harle 1, Miller 1, Snodin G 1

1983-84

Peacock	Russell	Breckin	Snodin I	Lister	Humphries	Miller	Moss	Douglas	Kowalski	Snodin G	Woods	Green	Bukovina	Harle	Boyd	Tomlinson	Allanson	Yates	Mutrie **(L)**	Philliben	Brown	Dobbin	Lee	REFEREE	
1	2	3	4	5	6	7	8	9*	10	11	12													D Richardson	1
1	**2**	**3**	**4**	**5**	**6**	**7**	**8**	**9**	**10**	**11**														**A Saunders**	**2**
1	2	3	4	11	6	7	8	9	10			5												J Worrall	3
1	2	3	4	11*	6	7	8	9	10	12		5												R Milford	4
1	2	3	4	12	6	7	8	9	10	11*		5												R Banks	5
1	**2**	**3**	**4**	**11**	**6**	**7***	**8**	**9**	**10**	**12**		**5**													**6**
1	2	3	4	11	6	7	8		10	12		5	9*											N Glover	7
1	2		4	11	6	7	8	9	10	3		5												J Bray	8
1	2		4	11	6	7	8	9	10	3		5												J Hough	9
1	2		4	11	6	7	8*		10	3	12	5		9										J Martin	10
	2		**4**	**11**	**6**	**7**	**8**	**9**	**10**	**3**		**5**			**1**									**N Wilson**	**11**
	2	3	4	11	6		8	9		10		5		7	1									D Hedges	12
	2	3	4	11	6	12	8	9		10		5*		7	1									T Jones	13
	2	3	4	11	6	12	8	9	5	10				7*	1									J Lovatt	14
	2	3	4	5	6	7*	8	9	10	11				12	1									L Robinson	15
1	**2**	**3**	**4**	**5**	**6**	**7**	**8**	**9**	**10**	**11**														**M Taylor**	**16**
	2	3	4	5	6	12	8	9	10	11				7*	1									N Midgley	17
	2	3	4	5	6	7	8	9	10	11					1									I Hendrick	18
	2		4	5	6	7	8	9	10	11				3	1									A Buksh	19
	2		4	5	6	7	8	9	10	11				3*	1	12								I Borrett	20
	2	**3**	**4**	**5**	**6**	**7**	**8***	**9**	**10**	**11**					**1**		**12**							**K Barratt**	**21**
1	2	3	4	5	6		8	9	10	11				7*			12							R Courtney	22
1	2	3	4†	5	6	12	8	9	10							7*	11							L Burden	23
1	2			5	6		8	9	10	11				4				3	7					B Hill	24
1	2			5	6	12	8	9	10	11				4*				3	7					D Scott	25
1	2		4	5	6	12	8	9	10	11								3*	7					P Tyldesley	26
1	2		4	5	6	7	8	9		11								3	10					D Allison	27
1	2		4	5	6	7	8	9		11								3	10					A Saunders	28
1	2		4	5	6	7	8	9	10	11								3						D Owen	29
1	2		4	5	6	7		9		11				10				3	8					K Cooper	30
1	2	12		5	6	7	8	9*	10	11				4				3						K Barratt	31
1	2			5	6	7	8	9	10	11				4				3						P Willis	32
1	2		8	4	3		10	9	7	11				6				5						F Roberts	33
1	2		4	5	6		8	9	10	11				7				3						A Ward	34
1	2		4	5	6	12	8	9	10*	11				7				3						L Dilkes	35
1	**2**	**5**	**4**		**6**		**8**	**9**		**11**	**10**			**7**				**3**						**L Robinson**	**36**
1	2		4	5	6		8	9		11	10			7				3						K Redfern	37
1		2	4		6	12	8	9		11	10*	5		7				3						R Nixon	38
1		3	4		6	7*	8	9	10	11	12			5				2						A Robinson	39
1	2	7*	4		6		8	9	10	11	12			5				3						N Ashley	40
1	**2**		**4**		**6**	**7**	**8**	**9**		**11**	**10**			**5**				**3***						**M Heath**	**41**
1	2		4		6	7	8	9		11	10*	12		5						3				R Guy	42
1	**2***				**6**	**12**	**8**	**9**		**11**	**13**	**5**		**7***						**4**		**10**	**3**	**T Holbrook**	**43**
1	2	6				7	8	9						4				3		5	10	11		J Moules	44
1	2				5		8	9	10	11								3		6	7	4		K Walmsley	45
1	2		4		5		12	9		11				7*				3		6	8	10		J Hough	46
1	2		4		5			9		11				7				3		6	8	10		C Downey	47
1	2		4		5		8	9		11				7				3		6		10		R Bridges	48
1	2		4		5		12	9		11				7				3*		6	8	10		D Richardson	49
1	2		4		5		12	9	7*	11								3		6	8	10		M Scott	50
1	2*		4			12	8	9	5	11								3		6	7	10		A Seville	51
1			4		2		8	9	5	11								3		6	7	10		K Baker	52
1					2		8	9	5*	11				4		12		3		6	7	10		I Borrett	53
1			4		2		8	9		11				5		7		3		6		10		J Ashworth	54
38	41	17	39	30	44	21	41	44	32	41	3	10	1	28	8	2	1	27	6	12	9	11		League Appearances	
		+1S		+1S		+9S	+3S			+2S	+4S	+1S		+1S		+2S	+1S								
	1	1	1	1	1	1	1	1	1	1					1		1S							FA Cup Appearances	
3	4	3	4	4	4	4	4	4	4	3+1S		2			1									Milk Cup Appearances	
3	3	1	2		3	1+1S	3	3		3	2+1S	1		3				2		1		1	1	AM Cup Appearances	

BELLE VUE GROUND

Official Address: Belle Vue Ground, Doncaster. Telephone: Doncaster (0302) 539441

Telegraphic: Rovers Doncaster

Ground Capacity: 21,150

Record Attendance: 37,149 v. Hull C, Div 3 (N), 2 Oct 1948

Record Receipts: £15,220.66 v. Huddersfield T, Div 3, 6 Nov 1981

Size of Playing Area: 111yds × 75 yds

Season Tickets: Terrace: £35; Main Stand: £55

Executive Box Season Tickets: None

Cost of Stand Tickets: £3.80 (£2.00 juniors if accompained by an adult); **Terraces:** £2.60 (£1.50 junior/OAP); **Ground:** £2.00 (£1.50 junior/OAP)

Match and Ticket Information: No advance bookings except for Cup matches.

Car Parking: Very large car and coach park adjacent to ground; entrance direct from Great North Road.

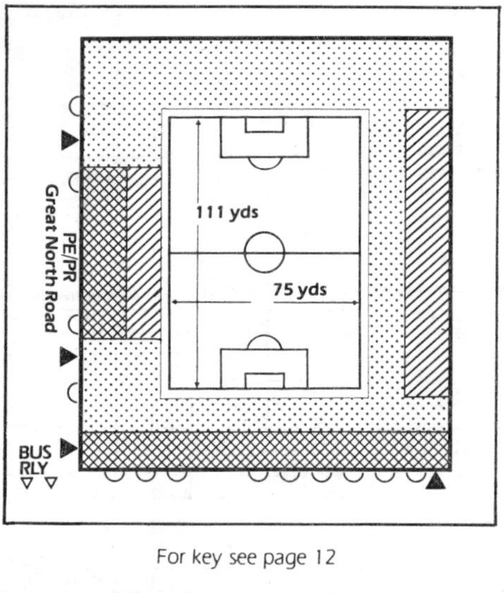

For key see page 12

How to get to the ground

From North: Use Motorway A1 (N) then A638 S.P. Doncaster into Town Centre, then follow signs Bawtry (A638) and in 1.2m at roundabout take 3rd exit into Bawtry Road for Doncaster F.C.
From East: Use Motorway M18 then A630 S.P. Doncaster. In 2.7m at roundabout take 1st exit A18. In 2.5m at roundabout take 1st exit into Bawtry Road A638 for Doncaster F.C.
From South: Use Motorway M1, then M18 and A1 (M) and follow signs Doncaster A630. In 1.8m branch right A S.P. Bawtry and in 1.2m at roundabout take 3rd exit A638 into Bawtry Road for Doncaster F.C.
From West: Use A635 in Doncaster Town Centre then follow signs Bawtry A638 and in 1.2m at roundabout take 3rd exit into Bawtry Road for Doncaster F.C.

EVERTON Division 1

Chairman
P D Carter CBE

Directors
T H W Scott (Vice Chairman)
G A Watts
A W Waterworth
K M Tamlin
J Search
D A B Newton

Secretary
J Greenwood

Assistant Secretary
B Forsyth

Commercial Manager
R Williams

Manager
H Kendall

Coaches
M Heaton
C Harvey

Youth Development Officer
R Minshull

Youth Team Coach
G C Smith

Reserve Team Coach
T Darracott

Physiotherapist
J Clinkard

Chief Scout
H Cooke

Groundsman
A Storey

A season that started disastrously ended in a double Wembley triumph for the Toffees. Everton ended 1983 with a run of five games without a win and were then in serious danger of relegation. But, with manager Howard Kendall's position looking precarious, they suddenly found luck changing for them.

Concerned at his team's lack of goalscoring power, Mr Kendall invested £250,000 in Wolves' Scotland international striker Andy Gray in November and, once he had aligned himself with the team's tactics, Gray helped to transform the outlook.

Having already played for Wolves in the Milk Cup, Gray could not play for Everton as they made steady progress to the final of that competition. The Toffees had disposed of Chesterfield and Coventry during the period when they were struggling in the League. But they were unlucky not to beat West Ham at the first attempt at Upton Park, though they made quite sure in the replay.

Everton's Milk Cup run looked to be ending away to Third Division Oxford in round five. They were trailing 0-1 with only nine minutes left at The Manor when Adrian Heath equalised. There was a fine 4-1 win in the replay and, by then, confidence was running high.

They ran up a 2-0 first-leg lead over Aston Villa in the semi-final and did enough at Villa Park to win the tie 2-1 on aggregate. They then faced the exciting prospect of meeting neighbouring Liverpool in the Wembley final.

Missed chances cost Everton possible victory at Wembley and they lost the Maine Road replay by 0-1. But, having tasted Wembley, Mr Kendall was convinced his team could return for the F.A. Cup Final. They had had a fairly easy passage up to the semi-final, defeating Stoke, Gillingham, Shrewsbury and Notts County. They then had to face a Southampton side that was also at its peak.

At Highbury the Everton goal survived several early scares and the tie was just three minutes from the end of extra-time when Heath nipped in to score a golden winner.

This time Everton went to Wembley as favourites and they were nearly always in command against Watford. Goals from Graeme Sharp and Andy Gray produced a deserved 2-0 victory.

It was a particularly fine season for Peter Reid and Kevin Sheedy in midfield though the latter missed the final weeks through injury.

Everton's great Cup runs inspired the side to better things in the League, too, and they were beaten only three times in their closing 22 League matches, ending with a run of three successive victories which took them into seventh place in the table — that situation looked quite impossible at the half-way stage.

Back Row L to R: Derek Mountfield, Neville Southall, Jim Arnold, Andy Gray. **Middle Row:** John Clinkard (Physio), Paul Bracewell, John Bailey, Kevin Richardson, Graeme Sharp, Gary Stevens, Alan Harper, Terry Curran, Peter Reid, Colin Harvey (Coach), Mick Heaton (Coach). **Front Row:** Kevin Sheedy, Trevor Steven, Mark Higgins (Club Captain), Howard Kendall (Manager), Kevin Ratcliffe (Team Captain), Adrian Heath, Alan Irvine.

'THE BLUES' or 'TOFFEEMEN'

Sponsored by **Hafnia**

Year Formed: 1878 **Turned Professional:** 1885 **Ltd Co:** 1892
Previous Managers: Since 1946: Theo Kelly Cliff Britton Ian Buchan John Carey Harry Catterick Billy Bingham Gordon Lee
Honours: Division 1 Champions 1890-1, 1914-5, 1927-8, 1931-2, 1938-9, 1962-3, 1969-70 Division 2 Champions 1930-1 F.A. Cup Winners 1906, 1933, 1966, 1984
League Career: Founder Member of Football League 1888 Relegated to Division 2 1929-30 Promoted to Division 1 1930-31 Relegated to Division 2 1950-51 Promoted to Division 1 1953-54
Colours: Blue shirts with shadow stripe and white trim, white shorts, white stockings with blue hoops
Change Colours: All silver grey

CLUB RECORDS

Most Appearances for Club: Ted Sager 465, 1929-53
Most Capped Player: Alan Ball, 39 for England
Record Goalscorer in a Match: Jack Southworth, 6 v. W.B.A., Div 1, 30.12.1893
Record League Goalscorer in a season: Bill 'Dixie' Dean 60, Div 1 1927-28
In all competitions: Bill 'Dixie' Dean 63 (League 60 + F.A. Cup 3)
Record League Goalscorer in a career: Bill 'Dixie' Dean 377 (League 349 + F.A. Cup 28)
Record Transfer Fee Received: £450,000 from Manchester United for John Gidman, Aug 1981
Record Transfer Fee Paid: £700,000 to Stoke City for Adrian Heath, Jan 1982
Best Performances: Football League: Champions(7) **F.A. Cup:** Winners(4) **League/Milk Cup:** Finalists 1976-77, 1983-4, **European Cup:** Quarter Final **European Cup Winners Cup:** 2nd Round **Fairs Cup/U.E.F.A. Cup:** 3rd Round
Most League Points: 66 Div 1, 1969-70 **Most League Goals:** 121 Div 2, 1930-31
Record League Victory: 9-1 v. Manchester C, Div 1, 03.09.1906, 9-1 v. Plymouth Argyle, Div 2, 1930
Record League Defeat: 4-10 v Tottenham Hotspur Div 1, 11 Oct 1958
European Competitions Entered: European Cup: 1963-4, 1970-1 European Cup Winners Cup: 1966-7, 1984-5, European Fairs Cup: 1962-3, 1964-5, 1965-6, U.E.F.A. Cup: 1978-9, 1979-80.

Club Statistician for the Directory: G Smailes

Programme Editor
Mike Beddow

Price	Number of Pages
50p	24

Subscriptions
£21.90 (postage paid U.K.), £29.70 (Scandinavia), £29.70 (surface U.S.A., Canada, Saudi Arabia, Australia), £52.80 (airmail U.S.A., Canada), £55.80 (airmail Australia), £45.90 (airmail Saudi Arabia)

EVERTON

PLAYERS NAME Ht Wt Birthdate	Honours	Birthplace Transfers	Clubs	APPEARANCES League	Milk Cup	F.A.C.	E. Cups	GOALS League	Milk Cup	F.A.C.	E. Cups
GOALKEEPERS											
Jim Arnold	E.S-P(2)	Stafford	Stafford R.								
6-1 11.5 6.8.50		£20,000	Blackburn R.	58	3	7					
		£175,000	Everton	48	6	6					
			P.N.E. (L)	6							
Neville Southall†	W.(16),	Llandudno	Winsford U.								
6-0 12.0 16.9.58	FAC. 84	£6,000	Bury	39		5					
		£150,000	Everton	78	13	9					
			Port Vale (L)	9							
DEFENDERS											
John Bailey	FAC. 84	Liverpool	Blackburn R. (A)	115 + 5	8	8		1			
5-8 11.3 1.4.57		£300,000	Everton	155	18	22		3			
Mark Higgins*	E. Y	Buxton	Everton (A)	150 + 2	20	7		6			
6-1 13.4 29.9.58											
Darren Hughes	FAYC. 84	Prescot	Everton (A)	1							
5-9 10.9 6.10.65											
Derek Mountfield	E. U.21(1),	Liverpool	Tranmere R. (A)	26	1	1		1			
6-1 12.7 2.11.62	FAC. 84	£30,000	Everton	32	8	8		3			
Kevin Ratcliffe*	W.(26), U.21(2)	Newcastle	Everton (A)	114 + 1	17	10		1			
5-7 10.2 4.12.62	Y, S, FAC. 84										
Gary Stevens	E. U.21(1),	Barrow	Everton (A)	73 + 1	14	14		2			
5-11 10.12 27.3.63	FAC. 84										
MIDFIELD											
Paul Bracewell	E. U.21(12)	Stoke	Stoke C. (A)	123 + 6	6	6		5			
5-8 10.9 19.7.62		£250,000	Sunderland	38	4	2		4			
		£425,000	Everton								
Ian Bishop		Liverpool	Everton (A)	0 + 1							
5-7 10.1 29.5.65			Crewe A. (L)	4							
Alan Harper	E. Y, FAC. 84	Liverpool	Liverpool (A)								
5-8 9.7 1.11.60			Everton	26 + 3	6 + 1	1 + 1		1			
Peter Reid	E. U.21(6),	Huyton	Bolton W. (A)	223 + 3	18+1	17		23	1	1	
5-7 11.5 20.6.56	FAC. 84	£60,000	Everton	41 + 1	9 + 1	11		2	1		
Kevin Richardson	FAC. 84	Newcastle	Everton (A)	64 + 11	7 + 3	8		9	2	1	
5-7 9.2 21.10.59											
Kevin Sheedy†	Ei.(2), U.21(1),	Builth Wells	Hereford U. (A)	47 + 4	2 + 1	2		4		1	
5-7 9.2 21.10.59	Y	£80,000	Liverpool	1 + 2	2				2		
		£100,000	Everton	68	13	11		15	4	4	
Trevor Steven	E. Y, FAC. 84,	Berwick	Burnley (A)	74 + 2	10	13		11	1	4	
5-10 11.7 29.9.63	Div. 3, 82		Everton	23 + 4	3	2		1	1		
FORWARDS											
Terry Curran		Kinsley	Doncaster R.	67 + 1	4	3 + 1		11			
5-10 12.6 20.3.55		£60,000	Nottingham Forest	46 + 2	2			12	1		
			Bury (L)	2							
		£50,000	Derby Co.	26		3		2			
		£60,000	Southampton	25 + 1	8	5			1		
		£100,000	Sheffield Wed.	122 + 3	8	3		35	4		
		£100,000	Sheffield U.	31 + 2	4	4		3			
			Everton	15		1		1			
Andy Gray	S.(19), U.23(4),	Glasgow	Dundee U.	61 + 1	6	8		36	5	3	
5-11 11.7 30.11.55	Y, S, FC. 77, 80,	£110,000	Aston Villa	112 + 1	18	6		54	10	3	
	FAC. 84	£1,525,000	Wolverhampton W.	130 + 3	13	13		38	3	3	
		£200,000	Everton	23		7 + 1		5		3	
Adrian Heath	E. U.21(8),	Stoke	Stoke C. (A)	94 + 1	9	4		16		1	
5-6 10.1 11.1.61	FAC. 84		Everton	95 + 1	14	12		28	4	3	
Stuart Rimmer	E. Y	Southport	Everton (A)	3							
5-7 9.2 12.10.64											
Graeme Sharp	S. U.21(1),	Glasgow	Dumbarton	37 + 3	2	3		17		2	
6-1 11.8 16.10.60	FAC. 84	£125,000	Everton	96 + 8	16	11+2		36	3	1	
Bob Wakenshaw	FAYC. 84		Everton (A)	1				1			
5-8 9.11 22.12.65											

CONTRACT PLAYERS WITH NO FIRST TEAM APPEARANCES: Ian Marshall, Ian Macowat, John Morrissey

NON-CONTRACT PLAYERS 1984-85: Graham Brinsley, Peter Byrne, Neil Deamer, Gary Parkinson, Jason Dansley

APPRENTICES: Darren Oldroyd, Neill Rimmer, Derek Walsh, David O'Brien

*Mark Higgins is Club Captain and Kevin Ratcliffe is Team Captain. †Both players won awards.

EVERTON

DIVISION ONE 7TH **FA CUP** WINNERS **MILK CUP** FINALISTS

MATCH	DATE	COMPE-TITION	VENUE	OPPONENTS	RESULT	HALF TIME	L'GUE POS'N	GOALSCORERS	ATTEN-DANCE
1	A 27	CL	H	Stoke C	W1-0	1-0		Sharp	22,658
2	29	CL	H	West Ham U	L0-1	0-0			20,375
3	S 3	CL	A	Coventry C	D1-1	1-1	12	Sheedy	12,532
4	6	CL	A	Ipswich T	L0-3	0-0			16,543
5	10	CL	H	WBA	D0-0	0-0	17		15,548
6	17	CL	A	Tottenham H	W2-1	2-0	15	Reid, Sheedy	29,125
7	24	CL	H	Birmingham C	D1-1	0-1	14	Sharp (pen)	15,253
8	O 1	CL	A	Notts Co	W1-0	1-0	13	Reid	7,949
9	5	MC 2	A	Chesterfield	W1-0	1-0		Sharp	10,713
10	15	CL	H	Luton T	L0-1	0-0	15		14,325
11	22	CL	H	Watford	W1-0	1-0	13	Johnson	13,571
12	26	MC 2	H	Chesterfield	D2-2	1-0		Heath, Steven	8,067
13	29	CL	A	Leicester C	L0-2	0-2	15		10,953
14	N 6	CL	A	Liverpool	L0-3	0-1			40,875
15	9	MC 3	H	Coventry C	W2-1	0-0		Heath, Sharp	9,080
16	12	CL	H	Nottingham F	W1-0	1-0	16	Heath	17,546
17	19	CL	A	Arsenal	L1-2	1-2	17	King (pen)	24,338
18	26	CL	H	Norwich C	L0-2	0-0	17		14,016
19	30	MC 4	A	West Ham U	D2-2	1-1		Reid, Sheedy	19,702
20	D 3	CL	A	Manchester U	W1-0	0-0	16	Sheedy	43,664
21	6	MC 4R	H	West Ham U	W2-0[1]	0-0		King, Sheedy	21,609
22	10	CL	H	Aston Villa	D1-1	0-0	14	Gray	15,810
23	17	CL	A	QPR	L0-2	0-1	16		11,608
24	26	CL	H	Sunderland	D0-0	0-0	16		18,683
25	27	CL	A	Wolverhampton	L0-3	0-1	16		12,781
26	31	CL	H	Coventry	D0-0	0-0	16		13,659
27	J 2	CL	A	Birmingham	W2-0	0-0	16	Stevens, King	10,004
28	7	FAC 3	A	Stoke C	W2-0	0-0		Gray, Irvine	16,462
29	14	CL	A	Stoke C	D1-1	0-0	18	Heath	7,935
30	18	MC 5	A	Oxford U	D1-1	0-0		Heath	14,333
31	21	CL	H	Tottenham H	W2-1	1-0	14	Heath 2	18,003
32	24	MC 5R	H	Oxford U	W4-1	2-0		Richardson, Sheedy, Heath, Sharp	31,011
33	28	FAC 4	H	Gillingham	D0-0	0-0			22,380
34	31	FAC 4R	A	Gillingham	D0-0[1]	0-0			15,339
35	F 4	CL	H	Notts Co	W4-1	3-1	14	Heath 3, Sheedy (pen)	13,016
36	6	FAC 4R2	A	Gillingham	W3-0	3-0		Sheedy 2, Heath	15,943
37	11	CL	A	WBA	D1-1	0-0	13	Mountfield	10,313
38	15	MC SF	H	Aston Villa	W2-0	1-0		Sheedy, Richardson	40,006
39	18	FAC 5	H	Shrewsbury T	W3-0	1-0		Irvine, Reid, Griffin (og)	27,106
40	22	MC SF	A	Aston Villa	L0-1	0-0			42,426
41	25	CL	A	Watford	D4-4	0-1	14	Sharp 2, Gray, Heath	16,987
42	M 3	CL	H	Liverpool	D1-1	0-1	15	Harper	51,245
43	10	FAC 6	A	Notts Co	W2-1	1-1		Richardson, Gray	19,534
44	14	CL	A	Nottingham F	L0-1	0-0			13,647
45	17	CL	H	Ipswich T	W1-0	1-0	14	Mountfield	18,013
46	20	CL	H	Leicester C	D1-1	1-0		Richardson	15,142
47	25	MC F	N	Liverpool	D0-0[1]	0-0			100,000
48	28	MC FR	N	Liverpool	L0-1	0-1			52,089
49	31	CL	H	Southampton	W1-0	1-0	13	Gray	20,244
50	A 7	CL	A	Luton T	W3-0	0-0	11	Mountfield, Heath 2 (1 pen)	9,224
51	14	FAC SF	N	Southampton	W1-0[1]	0-0		Heath	46,587
52	9	CL	H	Arsenal	D0-0	0-0			21,174
53	17	CL	A	Southampton	L1-3	0-0		Richardson	16,978
54	21	CL	A	Sunderland	L1-2	1-1	14	Heath	15,876
55	23	CL	H	Wolverhampton W	W2-0	1-0		Gray, Steven	17,185
56	28	CL	A	Norwich C	D1-1	1-0	11	Gray	13,624
57	M 5	CL	H	Manchester U	D1-1	0-0	11	Wakenshaw	28,817
58	7	CL	A	Aston Villa	W2-0	0-0	10	Richardson, Sharp	16,792
59	12	CL	H	QPR	W3-1	1-0	10	Heath, Sharp 2	20,679
60	14	CL	A	West Ham U	W1-0	1-0		Richardson	25,452
61	19	FAC F	N	Watford	W2-0	1-0		Sharp, Gray	100,000

[1]After Extra Time **Av Home Att** 19,343

Goal Scorers

League (44): Heath 12 (1 pen), Sharp 7 (1 pen), Gray 5, Richardson 4, Sheedy 4 (1 pen), Mountfield 3, King 2 (1 pen), Reid 2, Harper 1, Johnson 1, Steven 1, Stevens 1, Wakenshaw 1

1983-84

Arnold	Harper	Bailey	Mountfield	Higgins	Richardson	Steven	Heath	Sharp	King	Sheedy	Johnson	Ratcliffe	Reid	Curran	Southall	Irvine	Gray	Hughes	Rimmer	Stevens	Wakenshaw	Bishop	REFEREE	
1	2	3	4	5	6	7	8	9	10	11													G Tyson	1
1	2	3	4	5	6*	7	8	9	10	11	12												P Tyldesley	2
1	2	3		5	6	7	8*	9	10	11	12	4											D Axcell	3
1	2	3*		5	6	8		9		11	10	4	12	7									T Ward	4
1	2	3		5	12	6	8	9		11	10	4		7*									P Willis	5
1	2	3		5	12	7	8	9		11	10	4	6*										EA Read	6
1	2	3		5		7*	8	9	12	11	10	4	6										A Saunders	7
	2	3		5		7	8	9		11		4	6		1	10							TJ Holbrook	8
	2	**3**		**5**	**10**	**7**	**8**	**9**		**11**		**4**	**6**		**1**								**H Taylor**	**9**
	2	3		5		7	8	9	10	11		4	6		1								J Hough	10
	2	3		5	6	7*		9	10	11	8	4			1	12							K Redfern	11
	2	**3**		**5**	**6**	**10**	**8**	**9**		**11**		**4**			**1**	**7**							**M Peck/E Hart**	**12**
	2	3		5	6	7	8	9	10	11*		4			1	12							K Salmon	13
	2	3		5		6	8	9	10	11		4			1	7							G Courtney	14
	2	**3**		**5**		**6***	**8**	**9**	**10**	**11**		**4**	**12**		**1**	**7**							**A Challinor**	**15**
	2	3		5			8		10	11		4	6		1	7	9						C Seel	16
	2	3	5				8		10	11		4	6		1	7	9						J Bray	17
	2	3	5				8*		10	11		4	6		1	7	9			12			M Heath	18
			4	**5**			**8**	**9**	**10**	**11**		**3**	**6**		**1**	**7**				**2**			**A Gunn**	**19**
			4	5				9	8	11		3	6		1	7	10			2			K Walmsey	20
			4	**5**			**8**	**9**	**10**	**11**		**3**	**6**		**1**	**7**				**2**			**T Mills**	**21**
	12	3	5				8		10*	11		4	6		1	7	9			2			D Shaw	22
	3		5				8		10	11	9	4	6		1	7				2			B Stevens	23
	3		5				8			11	9	4	6		1	7	10			2			K Barratt	24
			5		8	12				11*		4	6		1	7	9	3	10	2			N Ashley	25
		3	5		12		8*		10	11		4	6		1	7	9			2			K Hackett	26
		3	5				8		10	11		4	6		1	7	9			2			J Deakin	27
		3	**5**				**8**	**9**		**11**		**4**	**6**		**1**	**7**	**10**			**2**			**M Peck**	**28**
		3	5		2		8	9		11		4	6		1	7	10						B Hill	29
	3		**5**		**12**		**8**	**9**		**11**	**10***	**4**	**6**		**1**	**7**				**2**			**J Hunting**	**30**
	3		5		10		8	9		11		4	6		1	7				2			D Hutchinson	31
	3		**5**		**10**		**8**	**9**		**11**		**4**	**6**		**1**	**7**				**2**			**P Willis**	**32**
	3		**5**				**8**	**9**		**11**		**4**	**6**		**1**	**7**	**10**			**2**			**G Courtney**	**33**
		3	**5**		**10**		**8**	**9***		**11**		**4**	**6**		**1**	**7**	**12**			**2**			**I Borrett**	**34**
		3	5		10		8			11		4	6		1	7	9			2			F Roberts	35
		3	**5**		**10**		**8**			**11**		**4**	**6**		**1**	**7**	**9**			**2**			**R Lewis**	**36**
		3	5		10		8			11		4	6		1	7	9			2			D Reeves	37
		3	**5**		**10**		**8**	**9**		**11**		**4**	**6**		**1**	**7**				**2**			**A Saunders**	**38**
		3	**5**				**8***	**12**	**10**	**11**		**4**	**6**		**1**	**7**	**9**			**2**			**G Napthine**	**39**
		3	**5**				**8**	**9**	**10**	**11**		**4**	**6**		**1**	**7**				**2**			**K Hackett**	**40**
		3	5				8	9		11		4	6		1	7	10			2			V Callow	41
	12	3	5			7*	8	9		11		4	6		1		10			2			G Tyson	42
	12	**3**	**5**		**8**			**9**		**11***		**4**	**6**		**1**	**7**	**10**			**2**			**J Martin**	**43**
	11	3	5		8			9				4	6		1	7	10			2			A Buksh	44
	3		5		11	12	8	9*				4	6		1	7	10			2			A Seville	45
		3	5		11	7	8		10			4	6		1		9			2			J Lovatt	46
	12	**3**	**5**		**10**		**8**	**9**		**11***		**4**	**6**		**1**	**7**				**2**			**Alan Robinson**	**47**
	11	**3**	**5**		**10**		**8**	**9**	**12**			**4**	**6**		**1**	**7***				**2**			**Alan Robinson**	**48**
	7*	3	5		11	12	8	9				4	6		1		10			2			K Redfern	49
	4	3	5		11	10	8	9					6	7	1					2			J Ashworth	50
		3	**5**		**11**	**10***	**8**	**12**				**4**	**6**	**7**	**1**		**9**			**2**			**G Courtney**	**51**
		3	5		11	12	8	9*				4	6	7	1		10			2			N Ashley	52
	3		5		11	10	8					4	6	7	1		9			2			C Downey	53
	12	3	5		11	10	8	9				4	6*	7	1					2			M Peck	54
		3	5		11	10	8					4	6	7	1		9			2			C Seel	55
		3	5		11	10	8	12				4	6	7*	1		9			2			D Vickers	56
	4	3	5		11	10		9	8				6		1					2	7*	12	D Shaw	57
		3	5		11	10	8	9	7			4	6		1					2			T Bune	58
	3		5		11	7	8	9				4	6		1		10			2			J Key	59
	3		5		8	9	10	11	7			4	6		1					2			M Taylor	60
		5	**3**		**11**	**6**	**8**	**10**				**4**	**7**		**1**		**9**			**2**			**J Hunting**	**61**
7	26	33	31	14	25	23	36	27	19	28	7	38	34	8	35	19	23	1	1	26	1	0	League Appearances	
	+3S				+3S	+4S		+1S	+1S		+2S		+1S			+2S				+1S		+1S		

GOODISON PARK

Official Address: Goodison Park, Liverpool L4 4EL. Telephone: 051 521 2020. Match Ticket Information: 051 523 6042 — 24 hour service.

Ground Capacity: 53,419 (25,000 seats)

Record Attendance: 78,299 v. Liverpool, Div 1, 18 Sept 1948.

Record Receipts: £174,945, Liverpool v. Manchester United, F.A. Cup Semi-Final Replay, 4 Apr 1979

Size of Playing Area: 112yds × 78 yds

Season Tickets: Stand: £75 & £85 Ground: £41 & £43

Executive Box Season Tickets: £6,500 pa — Box for 10 persons with restaurant and waiter service in boxes

Cost of Stand Tickets: £4.20 & £4.40; **Terraces:** £2.10 & £2.20

Match and Ticket Information: Box office open each weekday 0900 to 1700. Except matches v. Liverpool reserved stand seats can be purchased for all home fixtures any time during season by post (with remittance and SAE) or personally from the box office at the Goodison Road side of the ground. Postal applications to the Box Office Manager.

Car Parking: Extensive parking is available on site at the corner of Prior and Utting Avenue.

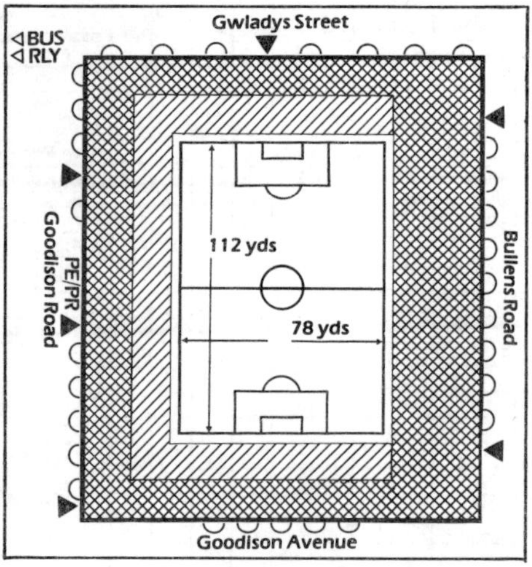

For key see page 12

How to get to the ground

From North: Use Motorway M6 until junction 28 then follow signs Liverpool on A58 then A580 and forward into Walton Hall Avenue for Everton F.C.

From East, South: Use Motorway M6 then M62 until end of Motorway then turn right A5058 into Queens Drive. In 3.7m turn left A580 into Walton Hall Avenue for Everton F.C.

From West: Use Mersey into Liverpool City Centre, then follow signs Preston A580 into Walton Hall Avenue for Everton F.C.

EXETER CITY — Division 4

President
FEJ Dart

Chairman
WC Hill

Directors
R Williams
G Vece
B Snell
I Doble
P Read
A Minter

Secretary
C Davey

Manager
J Iley

Assistant Manager
M Musgrove

Reserve & Youth Teams Coach
M Radford

Commercial Manager
ER Ellis

Groundsman
L Clarke

When it was announced that Gerry Francis, the former England captain had been appointed Player/Manager of Exeter City, unusual enthusiasm at St. James Park greeted his arrival. Nine months later Francis had gone and the season that had promised so much had been a disaster after relegation to Division Four and unfortunate boardroom squabbles.

A quick exit was made from the Milk Cup competition when Cardiff City triumphed 5-3 on aggregate in the First Round.

A first League victory did not come until October, when Bradford City were beaten on their Valley Parade ground 3-1. It was even worse at home where Exeter did not win until the visit of Hull City on December 3rd (It was Hull's first away defeat!). Before this, City had disappeared from the F.A. Cup in the First Round, after Maidstone United had held them to a 1-1 draw at home and then inflicted a humiliating 2-1 defeat in the replay.

A director decided action was needed and offered to inject a substantial amount of money whilst becoming chairman. Some of this money was promised to Francis for new players. However, after a disturbing 'press', the supporters were surprised that the director was removed; he has made repeated attempts to return since.

Francis was left to struggle on with a small staff. He introduced a succession of 'loan players', the most successful of which was Mark O'Connor from Queen's Park Rangers.

At times the League side contained non-contract players to make up the numbers and City were heading for inevitable relegation. Indeed as early as December supporters had resigned themselves to this probability.

There were few bright spots in a dismal season but the consistent defender Keith Viney was the 'player of the year' for the second consecutive season.

Unfortunately the season created a string of unwanted club records such as: the lowest number of League victories in a season, the fewest points registered in a season and the lowest total of goals scored at home.

Exeter City face the coming season with Jim Iley in charge. Will his managerial experience change the club's fortunes? We all hope so!

Jim Blackstone, The League Directory's Statistician for the Club

Note: Since this photograph, Jeff Wood, the ex-Charlton Athletic goalkeeper, was signed from Enfield.

Back Row L to R: Graeme Kirkup, Jim McNichol, John Sims, Roy McDonough, Nick Marker, Frank Howarth, Steve Harrower. **Front Row:** Martin Rogers, Steve Neville, Martin Ling, Jim Iley (Manager), Keith Viney, Danny O'Shea, Ray Pratt.

'THE GRECIANS'

Formed: 1904 **Turned Professional:** 1908 **Ltd Co:** 1908
Previous Managers: 1908-23 Arthur Chadwick 1923-7 Fred Mavin 1927-30 David Wilson 1930-6 Billy McDevitt 1936-9 Jack English 1945-52 George Roughton 1952-3 Norman Kirkman 1953 Tim Ward 1953-7 Norman Dodgin 1957-8 Bill Thompson 1958-60 Frank Broome 1960-2 Glen Wilson 1962-3 Cyril Spiers 1963-5 Jack Edwards 1965-6 Ellis Stuttard 1966-7 Jock Basford 1967-9 Frank Broome 1969-76 John Newman 1977-9 Bobby Saxton 1979-83 Brian Godfrey 1983-4 Gerry Francis
Honours: None
League Career: Elected to Division 3 1920 Transferred to Division 3(S) 1921
Relegated to Division 4 1957-8 Promoted to Division 3 1963-4
Relegated to Division 4 1965-6 Promoted to Division 3 1976-7
Relegated to Division 4 1983-4
Colours: Red and white striped shirts, black shorts, red stockings with white tops
Change Colours: All yellow with red trim

CLUB RECORDS

Most Appearances for Club: Arnold Mitchell (1952-66): League 494 + F.A. Cup 17 + League Cup 4 **Total 515**
Most Capped Player: Dermot Curtis, 1 (Eire) **For England:** None
Record Goalscorer in a Match: James Bell, 6 v Weymouth, 1st Prelim Round F.A. Cup 1908
Fred Whitlow v Crystal Palace, Div 3(S) Cup 1934
Record League Goalscorer in a season: Fred Whitlow, 34, Div 3(S), 1932-3, 1963-6, 1967-73 **In All Competitions:** Rod Williams 36 (League 32, F.A. Cup 4)
Record League Goalscorer in a career: Alan Banks, 105 **In All Competitions:** Tony Kellow, 120 (League 101, F.A. Cup 10, League Cup 9)
Record Transfer Fee Received: £105,000 from Blackpool for Tony Kellow, Nov 1978
Record Transfer Fee Paid: £65,000 to Blackpool for Tony Kellow, Mar 1980
Best Performances: League: 8th Div 3 1979-80 **F.A. Cup:** 6th Round Replay 1930-1 **League/Milk Cup:** Never beyond 4th Round
Most League Points: 62 in Div 4, 1976-7 **Most League Goals:** 88 in Div 3(S), 1932-3
Record League Victory: 8-1 v Coventry, Div 3(S), 4 Dec 1926 v Aldershot, Div 3(S), 4 May 1935
Record League Defeat: 0-9 v Notts County, Div 3(S), 16 Oct 1948 v Northampton Town, Div 3(S), 12 Apr 1958
Club Statistician for the Directory: Jim Blackstone

Programme Editor
J.W. Dimond

Price	Number of Pages
45p	24

Subscriptions
£15 plus postage per season

EXETER CITY

PLAYERS NAME Ht Wt Birthdate	Honours	Birthplace Transfers	Clubs	APPEARANCES League	Milk Cup	F.A.C.	A.M.C.	GOALS League	Milk Cup	F.A.C.	A.M.C.
GOALKEEPER											
Len Bond		Ilminster	Bristol C. (A)	30	1	4					
6-0 12.10 12.2.54			Exeter C. (L)	30		1					
			Torquay U. (L)	3							
			Scunthorpe U. (L)	8							
			Colchester U. (L)	3							
		£8,000	Brentford	122	6	4					
		£10,000	Exeter C.	138	5	11	2				
DEFENDERS											
Graeme Kirkup		Cramlington	Exeter C.	59+2	3	3	1+1	1			
5-10 12.2 31.5.65											
Nick Marker		Budleigh	Exeter C. (A)	57+6	1	1	2	2			
6-0 12.11 3.5.65		Salterton									
Jim McNichol	S. U.21(7)	Glasgow	Ipswich T. (A)								
6-0 12.10 9.6.58		F	Luton T.	13+2							
		F	Brentford	151+4	7	8		22		1	
Martyn Rogers	E. Y	Bristol	Bristol C. (A)								
		F	Bath C.								
		£10,000	Exeter C.	120+2	7	9		5		1	
Keith Viney*†		Portsmouth	Portsmouth (A)	160+6	14	13		3			
5-11 11.9 26.10.57		F	Exeter C.	86	4	3	3	4			
MIDFIELD											
Steve Harrower		Exeter	Dawlish								
9.10.61			Exeter C.	10+3			2	1			
Martin Ling		London	Exeter C.	23+7	2		2				
5-7 9.12 15.7.66											
FORWARDS											
Frankie Howarth		Budleigh	Exeter C. (A)	10+8	2	1					
5-9 10.10 19.11.64		Salterton									
Roy McDonough		Solihull	Birmingham C. (A)	2				1			
6-1 11.11 16.10.58		£15,000	Walsall	76+6	4	5		15			
		£15,000	Chelsea								
		£15,000	Colchester U.	89+4	9	6		24	2		
			Southend U.	22	2	2		4		1	
			Exeter C.	15+1			2+1				
Steve Neville	Div. 4, 82	Walthamstow	Southampton (A)	5				1			
5-9½ 11.0 18.9.57			Exeter C.	90+3	9	3		22	3	1	
			Sheffield U.	40+9	4	5+1		6			
			Exeter C.	73+3	2	3		26		1	
Ray Pratt	W. Y	Merthyr Tydfil	Merthyr Tydfil								
5-10 12.4 11.11.55		£12,000	Exeter C.	83+38	2	0+6	3	40			2
John Sims		Belper	Derby Co. (A)	2+1							
6-0 12.0 14.8.52			Luton T. (L)	3	1			1			
			Oxford U. (L)	6+1				1			
			Colchester U. (L)	2							
		£10,000	Notts Co.	48+13	4	2		13	1		
		£12,000	Exeter C.	33+1	5	2		11	1		
			Plymouth A.	161+2	8	11		43	2	2	
			Torquay U.	30	4	1		8	1		
			Exeter C.	12+2			2	3			

NON-CONTRACT PLAYERS 1984-85

Simon Burgher, Richard Crabtree (1 Lg. 1 AMC), **Steve Guppy, Wayne Hackman, Damian Keeley, Robin M Martin Musgrove, Adrian Robson, Leon Smith**

APPRENTICES 1984-85

Darren Clifford, Phil King, Michael Lane

EXETER CITY

DIVISION THREE 24TH **FA CUP** 1ST ROUND **MILK CUP** 1ST ROUND

MATCH	DATE	COMPETITION	VENUE	OPPONENTS	RESULT	HALF TIME	L'GUE POS'N	GOALSCORERS	ATTENDANCE
1	A 27	CL	H	Walsall	L0-1	0-1			4,742
2	**31**	**MC 1**	**H**	**Cardiff C**	**L2-3**	**0-0**		**Kellow, Rogers**	**4,005**
3	S 3	CL	A	Scunthorpe U	L1-3	0-1	20	McEwan (pen)	2,768
4	6	CL	A	Wigan Ath	D1-1	0-1		McEwan	2,569
5	10	CL	H	Rotherham U	L0-1	0-1	22		3,193
6	**13**	**MC 1**	**A**	**Cardiff C**	**L1-2**	**0-0**		**McEwan**	**2,721**
7	17	CL	A	Bristol R	L0-2	0-1	23		4,813
8	24	CL	H	Wimbledon	L0-3	0-1	24		3,046
9	28	CL	H	Lincoln C	L0-3	0-0			2,775
10	O 1	CL	A	Bradford C	W3-1	2-1	23	McEwan, Rogers 2	2,505
11	8	CL	H	Bolton W	D2-2	0-1	24	McEwan 2 (1 pen)	3,478
12	15	CL	A	Southend U	W3-0	1-0	20	Rogers, Francis, Pratt	2,342
13	18	CL	A	Gillingham	L1-3	1-2		Rogers	4,013
14	22	CL	H	Newport Co	L1-2	1-0	22	Kirkup	3,970
15	29	CL	A	Orient	D2-2	1-1	22	Neville, Pratt	3,190
16	N 2	CL	H	Burnley	D1-1	1-1		McEwan (pen)	3,714
17	5	CL	H	Port Vale	D1-1	1-1	21	Francis	3,301
18	12	CL	A	Sheffield U	D2-2	0-1	22	Rogers, Neville	10,334
19	**19**	**FAC 1**	**H**	**Maidstone U**	**D1-1**	**1-1**		**O'Connor**	**3,615**
20	**23**	**FAC 1R**	**A**	**Maidstone U**	**L1-2**	**1-1**		**Neville**	**4,381**
21	26	CL	A	Preston NE	L1-2	1-1	22	Neville	3,373
22	D 3	CL	H	Hull C	W2-1	0-0	20	O'Connor, Pratt	3,099
23	17	CL	H	Millwall	W3-2	2-0	18	Pratt 2, Neville	2,854
24	26	CL	A	Plymouth Arg	D2-2	0-1	20	Neville, Pratt	10,387
25	27	CL	H	Brentford	L1-2	0-0	20	Pratt	4,252
26	31	CL	A	AFC Bournemouth	L1-3	1-3	22	McEwan	5,133
27	J 2	CL	H	Oxford U	W3-1	0-0	19	McEwan (pen), O'Connor, Neville	4,557
28	14	CL	A	Walsall	L1-4	1-1	20	Harrower	5,028
29	21	CL	H	Bristol R	L1-2	1-1	22	Pratt	5,310
30	F 3	CL	H	Bradford C	L0-2	0-0			3,105
31	11	CL	A	Wimbledon	L1-2	1-0	22	Smith (og)	3,013
32	14	CL	A	Burnley	L0-4	0-1			5,951
33	18	CL	H	Orient	L3-4	1-1	24	Pratt 2, McEwan (pen)	2,347
34	**22**	**AMC 1**	**H**	**Bristol C**	**W3-1**	**1-0**		**Pratt 2, Neville**	**1,754**
35	25	CL	A	Newport Co	L0-1	0-1	24		2,465
36	M 3	CL	H	Gillingham	D0-0	0-0	24		2,801
37	5	CL	A	Port Vale	D2-2	1-1		Pratt, Neville	4,338
38	10	CL	H	Sheffield U	L1-2	0-0	24	Pratt	3,274
39	**14**	**AMC 2**	**A**	**Wrexham**	**L0-2**	**0-1**			**834**
40	17	CL	A	Bolton W	L0-1	0-0	24		5,161
41	23	CL	H	Southend U	D3-3	1-0		Pratt 2, Neville	1,782
42	31	CL	A	Lincoln C	D1-1	0-0	24	Neville	1,498
43	A 7	CL	H	Wigan Ath	D1-1	0-1	24	Sims	2,412
44	11	CL	H	Scunthorpe U	D1-1	0-1		Francis	2,003
45	14	CL	A	Hull C	L0-1	0-0	24		8,238
46	20	CL	A	Brentford	L0-3	0-1			5,620
47	21	CL	H	Plymouth Arg	D1-1	1-0	24	Pratt	6,870
48	**24**	**AMC SQF**	**A**	**Plymouth Arg**	**L1-2**	**0-1**		**O'Connor**	**3,715**
49	28	CL	H	Preston NE	W2-1	1-0	24	Pratt (pen), Sims	2,005
50	M 1	CL	A	Rotherham U	L0-1	0-1			3,636
51	5	CL	A	Oxford U	D1-1	0-1	24	Sims	8,056
52	7	CL	H	AFC Bournemouth	L0-2	0-0	24		2,790
53	12	CL	A	Millwall	L0-3	0-2	24		2,898
								Av Home Att	**3,376**

Goal Scorers

League (50): Pratt 16 (1 pen), Neville 9, McEwan 9 (5 pens), Rogers 5, Francis 3, Sims 3, O'Connor 2, Harrower 1, Kirkup 1, opponent 1
FA Cup (2): Neville 1, O'Connor 1
Milk Cup (3): Kellow 1, McEwan 1, Rogers 1
AMC (4): Pratt 2, Neville 1, O'Connor 1

1983-84

Bond	Kirkup	Viney	Evans **(L)**	Harle	McEwan	Neville	Rogers	Kellow	Francis	Ling	Dennis	Sims	Pratt	Howarth	Marker	Auguste	Hicks	Taylor	O'Connor **(L)**	Musker **(L)**	Atkinson	Webster **(L)**	Harrower	McDonagh	**REFEREE**	
1	2	3	4	5	6	7	8	9	10	11*	12														D Letts	1
1	**10**	**3**	**4**	**5**	**6**	**7**	**8**	**9**		**11**															**J Bray**	**2**
1		3*	4	5	6	7	8	9	10	11			12												PA Tyldesley	3
1	2	3	4	5	6	7	8*	9	10	12	11														G Tyson	4
1	2	3	4	5	6	7		9	10	12	11		8*												B Stevens	5
1		**3**		**5**	**6**	**7**		**9**	**10**	**11**	**8**			**2**	**4**										**K Barratt**	**6**
1		3		5	6	10			8*	11	7		12	2	4	9									T Holbrook	7
1		3		8	6	7		9		11				2	4*	12	5	10							J Deakin	8
1		3			6	7	8	12	10	4*					2	9	5	11							L Burden	9
1	2	3			6	12	8	9	10	4				7	5	11*									N Wilson	10
1	2	3			6	12	8	9	10	7*					5	11			4						K Cooper	11
1		3			6	12	8		10*				9	2	5			11	4	7					JE Martin	12
1		3			6		8		10				9	2	5			11	4	7					C Downey	13
1	2	3			6		8		10				9		5	12		11*	4	7					Alan Robinson	14
1	2	3			6	10							9		5	11			4	7	8				A Seville	15
1	2	3			6	10	8						12		5	9*		11	4	7					E Read	16
1	2	3			6	11	8		10				9*		5	12			4	7					M James	17
1	2	3			6	7	8		10							9		11	4			5			N Ashley	18
1	**2**	**3**			**6**	**7**	**8**		**10**				**12**			**9***		**11**	**4**		**5**				**L Burden**	**19**
1	**2**	**3**			**6**	**7**	**8**		**10**				**12**	**9***				**11**	**4**		**5**				**L Burden**	**20**
1	2	3			6	7	8		10				12					11*	4		9†	5			J Lovatt	21
1	2	3				7	8		10				9	11*	12				4		6	5			D Hedges	22
1	2	3			6	7	8		10*	12			9		11				4			5			T Spencer	23
1	2	3			6	7	8			10			9	12	11*				4			5			T Bune	24
1	2	3			6	7	8			10			9						4		11	5			V Callow	25
1	2	3			6	7	8		10*				9				5		4		11		12		D Vickers	26
1	2	3			6	7	8			11			9						4		5		10		R Milford	27
1	2				6	7	8			11*			9	12					4		3	5	10		D Reeves	28
1	2				6	7				11			9	12	10*				4		3	5		8	H Taylor	29
1	2	3			6	7				11*			9		12				4		8	5		10	L Burden	30
1	2	3			6	7				11			12		9				4		8	5*		10†	D Brazier	31
1	2	3			6	7				11			12		10*				4		9	5		8	M Heath	32
1	2	3			6	7				11			9		12				4		10	5*		8	M Robinson	33
1		**2**				**9**	**10**			**7**			**8**		**3**				**6**		**5**	**4**		**11**	**J Martin**	**34**
1		3				7	8		10			9	11		2				4		6	5			A Ward	35
1		3				7	8		10			9	11		2				4		6	5			J Hunting	36
1		3				7	8		10			12	9		2				4		6	5	11*		M Peck	37
1	2	3				7	8		10				9						4		6	5		11	D King	38
1	**12**	**3**				**7**	**8**		**10**			**11***	**9**						**4**		**6**	**5**	**2***	**13**	**R Banks**	**39**
1	2	3				7	8		10	12			9						4		6	5		11*	C Seel	40
1		3				7			10	8			9		2				4		6	5		11	J Deakin	41
1	2	3				7			10	8		12	9						4		6	5		11*	K Salmon	42
1	2	3				7			10	8		11	9*						4		6	5		12	M James	43
1	2	3				7			10			8							4		6	5	11	9	R Lewis	44
1	2	3				7			10			8			5				4		6		11	9	G Tyson	45
1	2	3				7*			10			8			9				4		6	5	12	11	J Ashworth	46
	2	3								7*		8	9	12	6				4			5	10	11	G Napthine	47
	2	**3**							**12**	**7***		**8**	**9**		**6**				**4**		**13**	**5***	**10**	**11**	**D Letts**	**48**
1	2	3				7				11*		8	9	12	5				4		6		10		E Scales	49
1	2	3				7				11		8	9		5				4		6		10		P Willis	50
1	2					7				12		8	9		5				4		6	3	10*	11	M Scott	51
1	2					7				11*		8	9		5				4		6	3	12	10	H Taylor	52
1	2	3				7				12		8	9		6				4		10	5*	11		T Spencer	53
45	36	42	4	6	28	40	25	7	28	23	3	12	30	6	28	7	3	8	38	6	28	26	10	15	League Appearances	
						+3S		+1S		+6S	+1S	+2S	+6S	+5S	+3S	+3S							+3S	+1S		
2	2	2			2	2	2		2	2				1		1		2	2		2				FA Cup Appearances	
2	1	2			2	2	1	2	2		1		3	1	1										Milk Cup Appearances	
2	1+1S	3	1	2		2	2		1S	2		2	2S		1				3		2+1S	3	2	2+1S	AM Cup Appearances	

Also Played: Lane matches 2, 3, no.2. Crabtree matches 47, 48, no.1.

ST. JAMES' PARK

Official Address: St James Park, Exeter EX4 6PX. Telephone: (0392) 54073/59466

Ground Capacity: 17,500

Record Attendance: 20,984 v. Sunderland, F.A. Cup 6th Round replay, 4 March 1931

Record Receipts: £32,007 v. Newcastle United, F.A. Cup 5th Round replay, 18 Feb 1981

Size of Playing Area: 114yds × 73 yds

Season Tickets: Stand seat: £75, Ground: £42

Executive Box Season Tickets: None

Cost of Stand Tickets: £3.50; **Terraces:** £2.00

Match and Ticket Information: Tickets usually bookable up to two weeks prior to each match. Clubhouse 'Centre Spot' behind goal at opposite end to St James Road, refreshments in grandstand and 'Cowshed'.
Car Parking: Limited street parking.

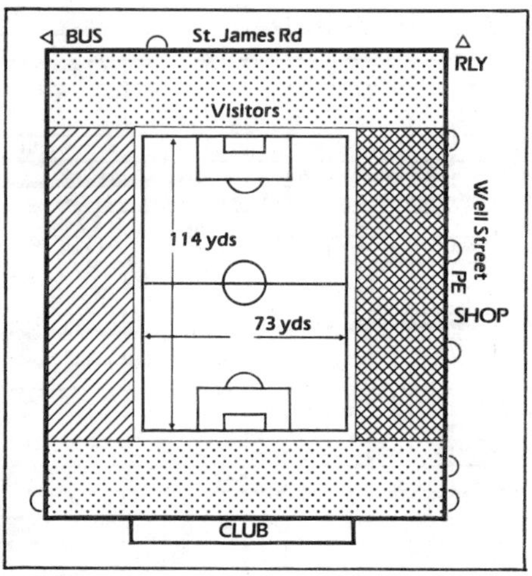

For key see page 12

How to get to the ground

From North: Use Motorway M5 until junction 30. Leave Motorway and follow signs City Centre along Sidmouth Road for Heavitree Road, then at roundabout take 4th exit into Western Way and at roundabout take 2nd exit into old Tiverton Road, then take next turning left into St. James Road for Exeter F.C.
From East: Use A30 (S.P. Exeter) into Heavitree Road, then at roundabout take 4th exit into Western Way and at roundabout take 2nd exit into Old Tiverton Road, then take next turning left into St James Road for Exeter F.C.
From South and West: Use A38 and follow signs City Centre into Western Way and at roundabout take 3rd exit passing Coach Station, then at next roundabout take 2nd exit into Old Tiverton Road, and turn left into St. James Road for Exeter City.

FULHAM Division 2

Chairman
E Clay

Directors
B Dalton
G C Clay
G P Clay

Secretary
Mrs Y Haines

Commercial Manager
Miss J Baldwin (01-736 0366)

Manager
Ray Harford

Assistant Manager
Terry Mancini

Youth Team Coach
Brian Nicholls

Physiotherapist
Derek Wright MSRG, SRG

After the near-miss season of 1982/83 when promotion was lost during the closing matches of the season it was no surprise that a reaction set in for the Cottagers in 1983-84 and there were times when it seemed possible that a position in the bottom three might be the final situation, but this was avoided and the team finished in eleventh place after a late rally; fans could feel that it might have been a great deal worse.

The season could hardly have started with more indifferent form which might well have been a backlash after the disappointments of the previous season. By the beginning of January 1984 the club were precariously placed in the last three and hopes of a compensatory FA Cup run ended in the Third Round with a two goal defeat at White Hart Lane against a very physical Spurs team after a goalless draw at the Cottage. Could the players 'lift' themselves after this and escape? Without the distraction of a cup run they did and the final position was — in the circumstances — most creditable.

That Fulham were no bad team was clearly shown in the Milk Cup where a Second Round win over Doncaster Rovers (3-1 in each leg) was followed by good draws at Anfield and the Cottage in the Third Round before a single goal in the second replay (again at home) saw the advance of the Merseysiders towards their fourth consecutive success in the competition.

Morale was not helped during the season by the resignation of Manager Malcolm Macdonald for domestic reasons, but his successor, Ray Harford, would seem to have the right ideas and a very promising squad to put them into practice. The defence has lost Gale, but there is great potential in such young men as Carr, Hopkins (already an established Welsh International) and Parker, with Houghton and Lewington (in midfield) and Coney and Davies (the strikers) always ready to give opponents many problems.

Fulham are always fun to watch and they would be good for the First Division.

WLM

Back Row L to R: Derek Wright (Physio), Steve Tapley, Brian Cottington, Kevin Lock, Leroy Rosenior, Jim Stannard, Gerry Peyton, Dean Coney, Jeff Hopkins, Gary Elkins, John Marshall, Terry Mancini (Assistant Team Manager). **Front Row:** Robert Wilson, Tony Sealy, Gordon Davies, Kenny Achampong, Ray Lewington, Ray Harford (Team Manager), Ray Houghton, Clifford Carr, Peter Scott, Paul Parker, Wayne Kerrins.

'THE COTTAGERS'

Sponsored by **Youngers Breweries**

Formed: 1879 **Turned Professional:** 1898 **Ltd Co:** 1903
Previous Managers: Jack Peart Frank Osborne Doug Livingstone Bill Dodgin (Snr) Bedford Jezzard Vic Buckingham Bobby Robson Johnny Haynes Bill Dodgin (Jnr) Alec Stock Bobby Campbell Malcolm Macdonald
Honours: Division Two Champions 1948-9 Division Three (S) Champions 1931-2
League Career: Elected to Division Two 1907 Relegated to Division Three (S) 1927-8
Promoted to Division Two 1931-2 Promoted to Division One 1948-9
Relegated to Division Two 1951-2 Promoted to Division One 1958-9
Relegated to Division Two 1967-8 Relegated to Division Three 1968-9
Promoted to Division Two 1970-1 Relegated to Division Three 1979-80
Promoted to Division Two 1981-2
Colours: White shirts with black trim, black shorts and white stockings with three black hoops on tops
Change Colours: Red shirts, red shorts and black stockings with three red hoops on tops

CLUB RECORDS

Most Appearances for Club: Johnny Haynes, 594, 1952-70
Most Capped Player: Johnny Haynes, 56, England
Record Goalscorer in a Match: Fred Harrison, 5 v Stockport County, Div 2, 05.09.1908
Bedford Jezzard, 5 v Hull City, Div 2, 08.10. 1955
Jimmy Hill, 5 v Doncaster Rovers (A), Div 2, 15.03.1958
Steve Earl, 5 v Halifax Town, Div 3, 16.09.1969
Record League Goalscorer in a season: Frank Newton, 41, Div 3(S), 1931-2
Record League Goalscorer in a career: Bedford Jezzard, 154, 1948-56
Record Transfer Fee Received: £333,333 from Liverpool for Richard Money, May 1980
Record Transfer Fee Paid: £150,000 to Orient for Peter Kitchen, Feb 1979 £150,000 to Brighton for Teddy Maybank, Dec 1979
Best Performances: League: 10th Div 1 1959-60 **F.A. Cup:** Finalists 1974-5 **League/Milk Cup:** 5th Round 1967-8, 1970-1
Most League Points: 78 in Div 3, 1981-2 **Most League Goals:** 111, Div 3(S), 1931-2
Record League Victory: 10-1 v Ipswich Town, Div 1, 26 Sept 1963
Record League Defeat: 0-9 v Wolverhampton Wanderers, Div 1, 16 Sept 1959

Club Statistician for the Directory: Dennis Turner

Programme Editor
Dennis Turner

Price	Number of Pages
50p	28

Subscriptions
£16.50 (postage paid U.K.) for season

FULHAM

PLAYERS NAME Ht Wt Birthdate	Honours	Birthplace Transfers	Clubs	APPEARANCES League	Milk Cup	F.A.C.	E. Cups	GOALS League	Milk Cup	F.A.C.	E. Cups
GOALKEEPERS											
Gerry Peyton	Ei.(20)	Birmingham	Atherstone U.								
6-2 13.11 20.5.56			Burnley	30	1	1					
		£40,000	Fulham	277	19	19					
			Southend U. (L)	10							
Jim Stannard		London	Fulham (A)	34	3						
6-0 13.1 6.10.62											
DEFENDERS											
Cliff Carr		London	Fulham (A)	42+5	6	2		5			
5-4 10.4 19.6.64											
Jeff Hopkins	W.(11), U.21(5),	Swansea	Fulham (A)	104+6	16	7		1	1		
6-0 11.9 14.4.64	Y										
Kevin Lock	E. U.23(4), Y,	Plaistow	West Ham U. (A)	122+10	13	11+		2			
6-0 11.6 27.12.53	FAC 75	£60,000	Fulham	180+1	14+	9+1		22	2		
John Marshall			Fulham (A)	21+4	3	2					
5-9 11.4 18.8.64											
Paul Parker	E. Y	London	Fulham (A)	43+13	6	5					
5-7 10.8 4.4.64											
Steve Tapley		London	Fulham (A)	1							
5-11 11.0 3.10.63											
MIDFIELD											
Rod Braithwaite		Middlesex	Fulham (A)								
5-9½ 10.10 19.12.65											
Brian Cottingham		London	Fulham (A)	0+1							
5-8 10.4 14.2.65											
Gary Elkins	E. Y	Wallingford	Fulham (A)								
5-8¼ 11.0 4.5.66											
Ray Houghton		Glasgow	West Ham U.	0+1							
5-7 10.10 9.1.62		F	Fulham	82	9	3		8	1	1	
Ray Lewington*		Lambeth	Chelsea (A)	80+5	3	4		4			
5-6 10.5 7.9.56			Vancouver W.								
			Wimbledon (L)	23	2	5					
		£50,000	Fulham	134+2	17	9+1		15	2	1	
John Reeves		London	Fulham (A)	10+2	1	2					
5-7 9.10 8.7.63											
Peter Scott		London	Fulham	32+1	2	2		4	1		
5-8 11.0 1.10.63											
Robert Wilson	Ei. U.21	Kensington	Fulham	129+7	13+	7+1		23	3		
5-10 11.2 5.6.61											
FORWARDS											
Kenny Achampong		London	Fulham (A)								
5-8 10.3½ 26.6.66											
Dean Coney		Dagenham	Fulham (A)	112+1	13	5		27	5	4	
6-0 12.6 18.9.63											
Gordon Davies	W.(13)	Merthyr Tydfil	Merthyr Tydfil								
5-7 10.6 3.8.55		£2,000	Fulham	234+2	21	18		108	8	4	
Wayne Kearns			Fulham								
5-7 11.1 5.8.65											
Leroy Rosenoir	E. S	London	Fulham	23+1		2		8			
6-1 11.10 24.3.64											
Dale Tempest		Leeds	Fulham (A)	25+9	1			6	1		
5-11 12.0 30.12.63											

APPRENTICES: Jeff Willis, Steve Freeman, David Harlow, Paul Mortimer

No Player of the Year Award for 1983-84 season.

FULHAM

DIVISION TWO 11TH **FA CUP** 3RD ROUND **MILK CUP** 3RD ROUND

MATCH	DATE	COMPE-TITION	VENUE	OPPONENTS	RESULT	HALF TIME	L'GUE POS'N	GOALSCORERS	ATTEN-DANCE
1	A 27	CL	A	Barnsley	L0-3	0-1			9,861
2	S 3	CL	H	Portsmouth	L0-2	0-1	22		10,672
3	7	CL	A	Manchester C	D0-0	0-0			23,356
4	11	CL	A	Crystal Palace	D1-1	1-0	21	Tempest	11,327
5	17	CL	H	Leeds U	W2-1	0-0	17	Lock (pen), Tempest	10,055
6	24	CL	A	Grimsby T	L1-2	1-1	17	Davies	5,769
7	27	CL	H	Middlesbrough	W2-1	1-0		Houghton, Tempest	6,432
8	O 1	CL	H	Swansea C	W5-0	1-0	15	Gale, Davies 2, Houghton, Tempest	7,253
9	**5**	**MC 2**	**A**	**Doncaster R**	**W3-1**	**2-1**		**Tempest, Davies, Scott**	**4,843**
10	8	CL	H	Chealsea	L3-5	2-2	14	Davies 3	24,787
11	15	CL	A	Carlisle U	L0-2	0-2	16		3,712
12	22	CL	A	Shrewsbury T	D0-0	0-0	15		4,767
13	**26**	**MC 2**	**H**	**Doncaster R**	**W3-1**	**2-0**		**Davies 2, Lewington**	**3,891**
14	31	CL	H	Cardiff C	L0-2	0-0			5,959
15	N 5	CL	A	Newcastle U	L2-3	1-1	18	Wilson 2	31,568
16	**8**	**MC 3**	**H**	**Liverpool**	**D1-1**	**0-0**		**Lock (pen)**	**20,142**
17	11	CL	H	Sheffield W	D1-1	0-1		Davies	9,687
18	19	CL	A	Huddersfield T	L0-2	0-0	19		8,914
19	**22**	**MC 3R**	**A**	**Liverpool**	**D1-1**[1]	**0-0**		**Lock (pen)**	**15,783**
20	26	CL	H	Blackburn R	L0-1	0-0	20		5,647
21	**29**	**MC 3R2**	**H**	**Liverpool**	**L0-1**[1]	**0-0**			**20,905**
22	D 3	CL	A	Cambridge U	D1-1	1-1	20	Lock (pen)	3,031
23	10	CL	H	Charlton Ath	L0-1	0-0	20		6,140
24	17	CL	A	Oldham Ath	L0-3	0-1	20		4,916
25	26	CL	H	Derby Co	D2-2	0-0	20	Rosenoir	7,480
26	27	CL	A	Brighton & HA	D1-1	0-0	20	Sealy	15,076
27	31	CL	A	Portsmouth	W4-1	2-1	20	Carr (pen), Davies 2, Rosenoir	15,649
28	J 2	CL	H	Grimsby T	D1-1	1-0	20	Carr (pen)	7,351
29	**7**	**FAC 3**	**H**	**Tottenham H**	**D0-0**	**0-0**			**23,398**
30	**11**	**FAC 3R**	**A**	**Tottenham H**	**L0-2**	**0-2**			**32,898**
31	14	CL	H	Barnsley	W1-0	0-0	18	Carr (pen)	5,085
32	21	CL	A	Leeds U	L0-1	0-1	19		11,421
33	F 5	CL	A	Swansea C	W3-0	0-0		Davies 2, Coney	7,350
34	11	CL	H	Crystal Palace	D1-1	0-0	19	Davies	9,119
35	19	CL	A	Cardiff C	W4-0	2-0		Coney 2, Rosenoir 2	7,149
36	25	CL	H	Shrewsbury T	W3-0	0-0	15	Coney, Stevens (og), Rosenoir	5,149
37	M 3	CL	H	Newcastle U	D2-2	2-1	16	Scott, Davies	12,290
38	7	CL	A	Sheffield W	D1-1	0-0		Rosenoir	20,440
39	17	CL	H	Manchester C	W5-1	4-0	15	Davies 3, McCarthy (og), Rosenoir	9,684
40	24	CL	A	Middlesbrough	W2-0	0-0	13	Davies, Coney	5,435
41	31	CL	H	Carlisle U	D0-0	0-0	14		6,018
42	A 7	CL	A	Chelsea	L0-4	0-3	16		31,947
43	14	CL	H	Huddersfield T	L0-2	0-2	16		5,265
44	21	CL	A	Derby Co	L0-1	0-1	16		12,178
45	23	CL	H	Brighton & HA	W3-1	3-0	15	Scott, Davies, Coney	7,742
46	29	CL	A	Blackburn R	W1-0	0-0		Davies	4,301
47	M 5	CL	H	Cambridge U	W1-0	0-0	13	Wilson	4,914
48	7	CL	A	Charlton Ath	W4-3	2-2	13	Scott, Houghton, Davies, Carr	6,151
49	12	CL	H	Oldham Ath	W3-0	2-0	11	Davies, Coney, Scott	5,089

[1] After Extra Time

Av Home Att **8,182**

Goal Scorers

League (60): Davies 21, Rosenoir 8, Coney 7, Carr 4 (3 pens), Scott 4, Tempest 4, Houghton 3, Wilson 3, Lock 2 (2 pens), Gale 1, Sealy 1, opponents 2

FA Cup (-): —

Milk Cup (8): Davies 3, Lock 2 (2 pens), Lewington 1, Scott 1, Tempest 1

1983-84

Stannard	Hopkins	Lock	O'Drisoll	Brown	Gale	Tempest	Wilson	Coney	Houghton	Parker	Carr	Marshall	Davies	Scott	Lewington	Tapley	Rosenoir	Peyton	Sealy **(L)**	Foley **(L)**	Reeves	Cottington			REFEREE	
1	2*	3	4	5	6	7	8	9	10	11	12														M Midgley	1
1		3		5	6*	12	8	9	10	2		4	7	11											D Brazier	2
1		3*		5	6	9	8		10	2	12	4	7	11											A Jeville	3
1			12	5	6	9*	8		10	2	3	4	7	11											L Shapter	4
1		3		5	6	9			10	2	8	4	7	11											C Thomas	5
1	12	3		5	6	9			10	2	8	4*	7	11											A Robinson	6
1		3*	4	5	6	9	8		10	2	12		7	11											J Martin	7
1	12		4	5*	6	9	8		10	2	3		7	11											D Hedges	8
1	**5**		**4**		**6**	**9**	**8**		**10**	**2**	**3**		**7**	**11**											**N Wilson**	**9**
1			4	5	6	9	8*		10	2	3		7	11	12										TG Bune	10
1			4	5	6	9*	8	12	10	2	3		7	11											J Worrall	11
1	5		4		6		8*	9	10	2	3		7	12	11										B Stevens	12
1	**5**		**4***		**6**			**9**	**10**	**2**	**3**		**7**	**8**	**11**							**12**			**M Taylor**	**13**
1	5	6	4					9*	10	2	3	12	7	8	11										MJ Bodenham	14
1	4	6		5			8	9*	10	2	3	12	7		11										D Richardson	15
1	**2**	**3**			**6**		**8**		**10**	**5**	**4**	**8**	**7**		**11**										**K Baker**	**16**
1		3		5	6		8		10	2	4	9	7		11										A Gunn	17
1		3		5	6		8	7	10	2	4	9			11										K Redfern	18
	2	**3**	**12**		**6**		**8**		**10**	**5***	**4**	**9**	**7**		**11**			**1**							**F Roberts**	**19**
	2	3			6		8		10		4	9*	7		11	5	12	1							A Crickmore	20
	2	**3**			**6**		**8**	**9**	**10**		**4**	**5**	**7**		**11**			**1**							**G Napthine**	**21**
	2	3	6				8	9	10		4	5	7		11			1							D Axcell	22
	5	3	4		6			9	10		8	2	7		11			1							J Bray	23
	5	3			6				10		4	2			11		9	1	7	8					G Tyson	24
	5	3*			6				10		4	2		8	11		9	1	7	12					I Barratt	25
	5				6				10*		3	2	12	8	11		9	1	7	4					Alan Robinson	26
	5				6				10		3	2	4	8	11		9	1	7						L Burden	27
	5				6			7	10*		3	2	4	8	11		9	1			12				K Cooper	28
	5				**6**					**2**	**3**	**7**	**4**	**8**	**11**		**9**	**1**			**10**				**T Bune**	**29**
	5		**12**		**6**					**2**	**3**	**7**	**4**	**8**	**11**		**9**	**1**			**10***				**T Bune**	**30**
	5		4		6					2	3	7		8	11		9	1			10				T Spencer	31
	5		12		6					2	3	4		8	11		9	1	7		10*				D Allison	32
	5				6			11	9	2	3		4	7	10		8	1							V Callow	33
	5				6			8	10	2	3		7	4	11		9	1							H King	34
	5				6			8	11	2	3		7	4	10		9	1							K Barratt	35
	5				6			8	10	2	3		7	4	11		9	1							M James	36
	5				6		12	8	10	2	3		7	4	11		9*	1							E Read	37
	5				6			8	10	2	3		7	4	11		9	1							L Robinson	38
	5				6	12		8	10	2	3		7	4	11*		9	1							B Hill	39
	5				6			8	10	2	3		7	4	11		9	1							D Richardson	40
	5				6			8	10	2	3		7	4	11		9	1							R Milford	41
	5				6	4		8	10	2	3		7		11		9	1							J Martin	42
	5				6	4*		8	10	2	3		7		11		9	1				12			A Robinson	43
	5				6			8	10*	2	3	12	7	4	11		9	1							J Hough	44
	5				6*			8	10	2	3	12	7	4	11		9	1							I Borrett	45
	5							8	10	2	3	6	7	4	11		9	1							J Lovatt	46
	5						12	8	10	2	3	6	7	4	11		9*	1							T Holbrook	47
	5					9		8	10	2	3	6	7	4	11			1							M Taylor	48
	5					9		8	10	2	3	6	7	4	11			1							L Burden	49
15	31	15	10	13	35	13	14	26	40	34	38	21	35	31	32	1	22	27	5	2	2	0			League Appearances	
	+2S		+2S			+2S	+2S	+1S			+3S	+4S	+1S	+1S	+1S		+1S			+1S	+1S	+1S				
	2		1S		2					2	2	2	2	2	2		2	2			2				FA Cup Appearances	
3	5	3	2+1S		5	1	4	2	5	4	5	3	5	2	4			2				1S			Milk Cup Appearances	

CRAVEN COTTAGE

Official Address: Craven Cottage, Stevenage Road, Fulham, London S.W.6. Telephone: 01-736 6561/2/3, Pools Office: 01-736 6561

Telegraphic: Fulhamish London S.W.6.

Ground Capacity: 25,680

Record Receipts: £80,247 v. Chelsea, Division 2, 8 Oct 1983

Size of Playing Area: 100yds × 75 yds

Season Tickets: Stand: £84.00 to £115.50; Ground: £52.50

Executive Box Season Tickets: Riversiders' Club £157.50

Cost of Stand Tickets: £4.50, £5.00, £5.50, £6.00; **Terraces:** £2.80 (enclosure £3.00)

Match and Ticket Information: Computerised. Bookable daily during season 9.30-4.30

Car Parking: Ample in adjacent streets

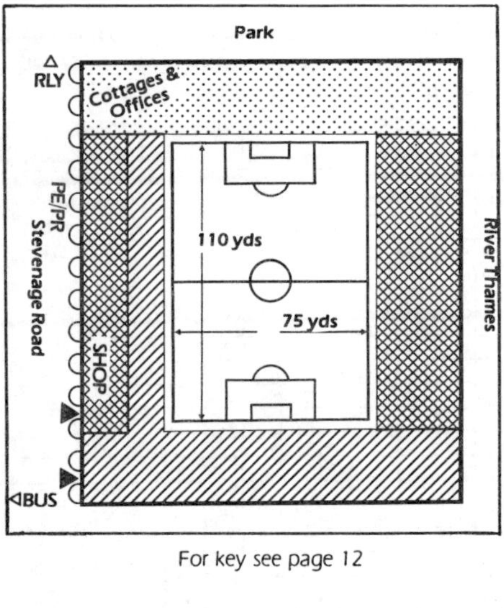

For key see page 12

How to get to the ground

From North: Use Motorway M1 S.P. London then take North Circular Road A406 S.P. West to Neasden follow signs Harledon A404, then Hammersmith A219 and at Broadway follow sign Fulham and in 1m turn right into Harbord Street and at end turn left for Fulham F.C.
From East and South: Use South Circular Road A205 and take sign Putney Bridge A219. Cross Bridge and follow sign Hammersmith and in 0.5m turn left into Bishops Park Road and at end turn right for Fulham F.C.
From West: Use Motorway M4 then A4 and in 2m branch left S.P. other routes into Hammersmith Broadway, follow sign Fulham A219 and in 1m turn right into Harbord Street and at end turn left for Fulham F.C.

GILLINGHAM Division 3

Chairman
CAL Cox

Directors
JW Leech
BB Moore

Secretary
Richard Dennison

Commercial Department
(0634 51462)

Manager
Keith Peacock

Coach
Paul Taylor

Chief Scout
Ted Buxton

Groundsman
Bill Wood

A final Third Division position of eighth and a more than useful cup run in the F.A. Cup provided the highlights of a satisfactory season at Priestfield and in a game where fortunes can change without warning it would not be incautious to say that Gillingham must be looking ahead with confidence.

With a deficit of thirteen points behind the last promotion place the Gills never seriously threatened an ascent to higher things but at the same time the League never produced any anxious moments so that with tranquility at home it was not difficult to see why the F.A. Cup produced plenty of excitement. The Milk Cup started with a First Round against Chelsea who were too good in both legs, but when the older competition started the events were most satisfying even though the first tie at Leamington was only won by a single Handford goal. Chelmsford at Priestfield suffered for that in the next round; a single goal lead at half-time for the Gills became an overwhelming win by six goals to one with five players appearing on the scoresheet. There were goals galore at Priestfield in the Third Round also with five players again scoring against Brentford — all in the second half after a single goal lead for the Bees at the interval. This brought a trip to Goodison Park and a goalless draw earned through sound defensive work. The same scoreline was recorded in the replay when the 'Gills' had their chances, but the third attempt to obtain a result at Priestfield was successful as the eventual Cup Winners scored three without reply. Even so it gave the home fans some fun and the final good league position was a nice bonus.

Manager Keith Peacock has collected a well balanced squad and the improvement should be maintained although the opposition — at least on paper — is formidable this season and promotion may be beyond the club. But with such good players available as Leslie (player of the year in his first season at Gillingham), Mehmet and Weatherly (to mention just three of several worthy men) prospects look good and they should also remain an attractive team to watch.

WLM

Back Row L to R: Joe Hinnigan, Peter Shaw, Tony Cascarino, Dave Fry, Ron Hillyard, Keith Oakes, John Sitton. **Centre Row:** Paul Taylor (Assistant Manager), Bill Collins (Youth Team Coach), Mel Sage, Dave Shearer, John Sharpe, Paul Shinners, Paul Collins, Mark Weatherly, Ted Buxton (Chief Scout). **Front Row:** John Leslie, Tarki Micallef, Russell Musker, Keith Peacock (Manager), Dave Mehmet, Jeff Johnson, Terry Cochrane.

'THE GILLS'

Sponsored by
Zanussi

Formed: 1893 **Turned Professional:** 1894 **Ltd Co:** 1893
Previous Name: New Brompton 1893-1913
Previous Managers: since 1946: Archie Clark Harry Barratt Freddie Cox Basil Hayward Andy Nelson Len Ashurst Gerry Summers
Honours: Division 4 Champions 1963-4
League Career: Original Members of Division 3 1920 Transferred to Division 3 (S) 1921 Failed to gain re-election 1938 Southern League 1938-44 Kent League 1944-6 Southern League 1946-50 Re-elected to Division 3 (S) 1949 Transferred to Division 4 1958 Promoted to Division 3 1963-4 Relegated to Division 4 1970-1 Promoted to Division 3 1973-4
Colours: Royal blue shirts, white shorts and stockings with blue trim
Change Colours: All red

CLUB RECORDS

Most Appearances for Club: John Simpson: Football League 571 + F.A. Cup 27 + League Cup 19 **Total 617**
Most Capped Player: Damien Richardson, 2, Eire **For England:** None
Record Goalscorer in a Match: Fred Cheesemuir, 6, v Merthyr Tydfil (H) Div 3 (S) (6-0), 26.04.30
Record League Goalscorer in a season: Ernie Morgan, 31, Div 3 (S), 1954-5 Brian Yeo, 31, Div 4, 1973-4 **In all competitions:** Ernie Morgan, 33 (League 31 + F.A. Cup 2) 1954-5
Record League Goalscorer in a career: Brian Yeo, 136, 1963-75 **In all competitions:** Brian Yeo, 149 (League 136 + F.A. Cup 9 + League Cup 4) 1963-75
Record Transfer Fee Received: £85,000 from Coventry City for Micky Adams, July 1983
Record Transfer Fee Paid: £90,000 to Colchester United for Trevor Lee, Jan 1981
Best Performances: League: 4th Div 3 1978-9 **F.A. Cup:** 5th Round 1969-70 **League/Milk Cup:** 4th Round 1964
Most League Points: (3pts for a win) 70, Div 3, 1983-4 (2pts for a win) 62, Div 4, 1973-4
Record League Victory: 6-0, v Brentford, Div 3 (S), 19 March 1924, v Merthyr Tydfil, Div 3 (S), 26 April 1930.
Record League Defeat: 2-9 v Nottingham Forest, Div 3 (S), 18 Nov.1950

Club Statistician for the Directory: Roger Triggs

Programme Editors
Andy Bradley, David Garth, Roger Triggs, David Taylor, Alan Liptrott

Price	Number of Pages
50p	20

Subscriptions
Rates obtainable from club

GILLINGHAM

PLAYERS NAME Ht Wt Birthdate	Honours	Birthplace Transfers	Clubs	APPEARANCES League	Milk Cup	F.A.C.	A.M.C.	GOALS League	Milk Cup	F.A.C.	A.M.C.
GOALKEEPERS											
David Fry	FAYC. 77, 78	Bournemouth	Crystal Palace (A)	40		5					
6-1 12.7 5.1.60			Gillingham	38		6					
Ron Hillyard		Folkestone	York C.	61	2	9					
5-11 11.4 31.3.52			Hartlepool U. (L)	23							
			Gillingham	382	27	22	1				
DEFENDERS											
Keith Oakes		Bedworth	Peterborough U. (A)	48 + 13	7 + 2	4 + 1		2			
5-10 12.2 3.7.56		£15,000	Newport Co.	232	14	13+1	1	27	1	1	
		F	Gillingham								
Joe Hinnigan		Liverpool	South Liverpool								
6-0½ 12.7 3.12.55		£1,000	Wigan A.	66	4	7		10			
		£80,000	Sunderland	63	1	1					
		£15,000	P.N.E.	51 + 1	3	1	1	8	2		
			Gillingham								
Mel Sage		Gillingham	Gillingham (A)	44 + 6			1	2			
5-8 10.4 24.3.64											
John Sharpe		Portsmouth	Southampton (A)	21		1					
5-11 11.5 9.10.57		£30,000	Gillingham	191 + 2	16	14	1	2			
Peter Shaw		Northolt	Staines T.								
6-2½ 13.11 9.1.56		£19,000	Charlton A.	100 + 5	9	8		5		1	
			Exeter C. (L)	3							
			Gillingham	76 + 2	7	4		1	1	1	
John Sitton		Hackney	Chelsea (A)	11 + 2							
5-11 12.4 21.10.59		£10,000	Millwall	43 + 2	2	2		1			
		£10,000	Gillingham	97 + 5	5	11 +	1	5			
Mark Weatherly		Ramsgate	Gillingham (A)	280 + 26	21 +	18 +		33	1	5	
6-0 11.12 18.1.58											
MIDFIELD											
Terry Cochrane	NI.(26)	Killyleagh	Coleraine								
5-7½ 10.8 23.1.53			Burnley	62 + 5	7	4 + 1		13	4		
		£238,000	Middlesbrough	96 + 15	5	12		7	1		
			Gillingham	34		6		6		1	
Jeff Johnson	W. U.23(2), S	Cardiff	Manchester C. (A)	4 + 2							
5-8 11.12 26.11.53			Swansea C. (L)	37 + 2	2			4			
		£12,000	Crystal Palace	82 + 5	5 + 1	5		4	1		
		F	Sheffield Wed.	177 + 5	17	14		6	2	1	
		£60,000	Newport Co.	34	3			2			
		£8,000	Gillingham	61 + 2	4	3		4	1	1	
Dave Mehmet*	FAYC. 79	London	Millwall	97 + 17	6 + 1	9 + 1		15			
5-9 11.9 2.12.60		£120,000	Tampa Bay								
		£80,000	Charlton Ath.	29	1			2			
		F	Gillingham	55 + 1	2	6		19		1	
FORWARDS											
Tony Cascarino		St Paul's Cray	Crocken Hill								
6-2 11.10 1.9.62			Gillingham	89 + 10	6	2 + 1	1	32	3	2	2
John Leslie†		London	Dulwich Hamlet								
5-8 11.2 25.10.55			Wimbledon	242 + 11	20 +	14 +		86	10	5	
			Gillingham	44 + 1	2	6	1	9		2	
Russell Musker		Plymouth	Bristol C. (A)	44 + 2	4	3		1			
5-7 10.0 10.7.62			Exeter C. (L)	6							
		£5,000	Gillingham	23 + 4				5			

NON-CONTRACT PLAYER 1984-85: Alen Cotting (3Lg. 1AMC)

APPRENTICES: Paul Collins (1AMC), **Paul Edwards**

GILLINGHAM

DIVISION THREE 8TH **FA CUP** 4TH ROUND **MILK CUP** 1ST ROUND

MATCH	DATE	COMPETITION	VENUE	OPPONENTS	RESULT	HALF TIME	L'GUE POS'N	GOALSCORERS	ATTENDANCE
1	A 27	CL	A	Sheffield U	L0-4	0-1			10,405
2	**30**	**MC 1**	**H**	**Chelsea**	**L1-2**	**1-1**		**Shaw**	**8,633**
3	S 3	CL	H	Hull C	L1-2	0-1	23	Leslie	3,019
4	6	CL	H	Bolton W	W2-0	1-0		Mehmet, Weatherly	3,087
5	10	CL	A	Plymouth Arg	D1-1	0-0	17	Sitton	3,192
6	**13**	**MC 1**	**A**	**Chelsea**	**L0-4**	**0-2**			**9,702**
7	17	CL	H	Oxford U	L2-3	1-3	19	Johnson, Sitton	3,370
8	24	CL	A	AFC Bournemouth	L0-2	0-1	22		3,045
9	O 1	CL	H	Brentford	W4-2	2-0	19	Leslie 2, Mehmet 2 (1 pen)	3,268
10	8	CL	H	Preston NE	W2-0	1-0	16	Cochrane, Weatherly	3,725
11	15	CL	A	Burnley	W3-2	0-0	13	Cochrane, Cascarino, Mehmet	5,462
12	18	CL	H	Exeter C	W3-1	2-1		Bruce, Weatherly 2	4,013
13	22	CL	A	Wigan Ath	W2-1	2-0	9	Cochrane, Weatherly	4,189
14	24	CL	A	Orient	D1-1	0-1		Cascarino	4,013
15	29	CL	H	Millwall	D3-3	2-1	10	Leslie, Sage, Mehmet	6,226
16	N 5	CL	H	Lincoln C	W2-0	1-0	10	Johnson, Mehmet	4,428
17	12	CL	A	Walsall	L1-3	0-1	11	Cascarino	4,639
18	**19**	**FAC 1**	**A**	**AP Leamington**	**W1-0**	**1-0**		**Handford**	**2,600**
19	26	CL	H	Rotherham U	W4-2	2-0	9	Weatherly 2, Mehmet 2	4,052
20	D 3	CL	A	Port Vale	W1-0	1-0	8	Cochrane	3,086
21	**10**	**FAC 2**	**H**	**Chelmsford C**	**W6-1**	**1-0**		**Shaw, Weatherly 2, Sage, Mehmet, Leslie**	**4,812**
22	17	CL	A	Scunthorpe U	L0-2	0-1	10		2,127
23	26	CL	H	Southend U	W5-1	2-1	9	Weatherly, Musker, Mehmet 2, Bruce	5,511
24	27	CL	A	Bristol R	L0-3	0-1	11		5,996
25	31	CL	H	Wimbledon	L0-1	0-1	11		5,024
26	**J 7**	**FAC 3**	**H**	**Brentford**	**W5-3**	**0-1**		**Cochrane, Musker, Cascarino,**	
								Weatherly, Leslie	**6,109**
27	14	CL	H	Sheffield U	W4-2	2-2	10	Bruce 2, Weatherly, Cochrane	5,408
28	**28**	**FAC 4**	**A**	**Everton**	**D0-0**	**0-0**			**22,380**
29	**31**	**FAC 4R**	**H**	**Everton**	**D0-0[1]**	**0-0**			**15,339**
30	F 4	CL	A	Brentford	W3-2	1-1	10	Musker, Cascarino, Leslie	4,317
31	**6**	**FAC 4R2**	**H**	**Everton**	**L0-3**	**0-0**			**15,942**
32	11	CL	H	AFC Bournemouth	W2-1	1-1	9	Mehmet, Leslie	4,891
33	14	CL	H	Bradford C	D0-0	0-0			4,390
34	19	CL	A	Millwall	D2-2	1-0		Cascarino, Cochrane	6,344
35	25	CL	H	Wigan Ath	W3-0	1-0	9	Mehmet 2, Cascarino	4,013
36	**28**	**AMC 1**	**A**	**Millwall**	**L3-4[1]**	**2-2**		**Cascarino 2, Sparrow**	**2,364**
37	M 3	CL	A	Exeter C	D0-0	0-0	9		2,801
38	7	CL	A	Lincoln C	L0-4	0-2			1,574
39	10	CL	H	Walsall	L1-3	0-1	12	Cascarino	4,544
40	14	CL	A	Oxford U	W1-0	1-0		Cavener	7,433
41	17	CL	A	Preston NE	D2-2	2-0	10	Musker, Sparrow	3,874
42	24	CL	H	Burnley	L0-1	0-0	10		4,319
43	27	CL	A	Newport Co	L0-1	0-0			1,849
44	31	CL	H	Orient	W3-1	1-0	9	Leslie, Cascarino, Mehmet	3,090
45	A 7	CL	A	Bolton W	W1-0	1-0	9	Cascarino	4,815
46	11	CL	A	Bradford C	L2-3	2-1		Mehmet, Clarke	3,465
47	14	CL	H	Port Vale	D1-1	0-0	8	Leslie	3,323
48	17	CL	A	Hull C	D0-0	0-0			9,179
49	20	CL	A	Southend U	L1-3	0-2		Sage	3,218
50	23	CL	H	Bristol R	L1-2	0-0	9	Musker	3,400
51	28	CL	A	Rotherham U	L0-3	0-2	12		3,198
52	M 1	CL	H	Plymouth Arg	W2-1	1-0		Leslie, Shaw	3,103
53	5	CL	H	Newport Co	W4-1	3-1	8	Musker, Cascarino 2, Bruce (pen)	3,073
54	7	CL	A	Wimbledon	W3-1	0-1	8	Bruce, Cascarino, Sitton	6,009
55	12	CL	H	Scunthorpe U	D1-1	0-1	8	Mehmet	3,513

Av Home Att 4,034

Goal Scorers

League (74): Mehmet 16 (1 pen), Cascarino 12, Leslie 9, Weatherly 9, Bruce 6 (1 pen), Cochrane 6, Musker 5, Sitton 3, Johnson 2, Sage 2, Cavener 1, Clarke 1, Shaw 1, Sparrow 1
FA Cup (12): Weatherly 3, Leslie 2, Cascarino 1, Cochrane 1, Handford 1, Mehmet 1, Musker, Sage 1, Shaw 1
Milk Cup (1): Shaw 1
AMC (3): Cascarino 2, Sparrow 1

1983-84

Hillyard	Sage	Duncan	Sitton	Shaw	Handford	Woodhead	Tydeman	Leslie	Mehmet	Weatherly	Stokes	Sharpe	Daniel **(L)**	Johnson	Garner **(L)**	Cascarino	Fry	Bruce	Cochrane	Cavener	Musker	Armstrong	Sparrow **(L)**	Clarke **(L)**	**REFEREE**	
1	2	3	4	5	6	7*	8	9	10	11	12														V Callow	1
1	**3**		**4**	**5**	**6**	**12**	**7**	**9**	**10**	**11**		**2**													**J Martin**	**2**
1	3		4	5	12		8	9	10	11*		2	6	7											T Bune	3
1	2		4	5	6			9	10	11			7	8	3*	12									D Brazier	4
1	2		4	5	6			9	10	11			7*	8	3	12									E Read	5
1	**3**		**4**	**5***	**6**		**12**	**9**	**10**	**11**		**2**		**7**		**8**									**T Spencer**	**6**
1	6		4					9	10	5		2	7	8	3	11									R Lewis	7
			4		6			9	10	5		2	7*	8	3	11	1	12							C Thomas	8
	7		6					9	10	5		2		8	3	11	1	4							D Axcell	9
	3		6			12		9	10	5		2		8		11	1	4	7*						J Ashworth	10
	3		6					9	10	5		2		8		11	1	4	7						C Seel	11
	3		6					9	10	5		2		8		11	1	4	7*	12					C Downey	12
	5		4					9	7	10		2		6		8	1	3	11						G Napthine	13
	3		6					9	10	5		2		8		11	1	4	7						B Hill	14
	3		6					9	10	5		2		8		11	1	4	7						M Bodenham	15
	3		6					9	10	5		2		8		11	1	4	7						M James	16
	3		6					9	10	5		2		8		11	1	4	7						I Hendrick	17
	3		**6**		**11**			**9**	**10**	**5**		**2**		**8**			**1**	**4**	**7**						**J Martin**	**18**
	3		6					9	10	5		2		8†			1	4	7		11				D Reeves	19
	3		6	12				9	10	5		2*		8			1	4	7		11				D Allison	20
	3		**6**					**9**	**10**	**5**		**2**				**11***	**1**	**4**	**7**		**8**	**12**			**R Milford**	**21**
1			6	2	11			9	10	5								4	7	12	8	3*			M Heath	22
1			3	6	12			9	10	5		2		8				4	7*		11				A Ward	23
1			3	6				9	10	5		2		8				4	7		11				L Shapter	24
			2	6				9	10	5				8		12	1	4	7		11	3*			D Hedges	25
			2	**6**				**9**	**10***	**5**				**8**		**12**	**1**	**4**	**7**		**11**	**3**			**M James**	**26**
			2	6				9	10*	5				8		11	1	4	7		12	3			B Stevens	27
			2	**6**				**9**	**10**	**5***				**8**		**11**	**1**	**4**	**7**		**12**		**3**		**G Courtney**	**28**
	3		**2**	**6**				**9**	**10**					**8**		**11**	**1**	**4**	**7**		**5**				**I Borrett**	**29**
	3		2*	6				9	10					8		11	1	4	7		5	12			T Bune	30
	2			**6**				**9**	**10**					**8**		**11**	**1**	**4**	**7**		**5**		**3**		**R Lewis**	**31**
	2			6				9	10					8		11	1	4	7		5	3			D Letts	32
	2		12	6				9	10					8*		11	1	4	7		5	3			A Gunn	33
	8		2*	6	5			9	10							11	1	4	7	12		3			M Dimblebee	34
	2			6	5			9	10							11	1	4	7		8	3			J Moules	35
1	**2**		**5**		**12**	**13**		**9***				**4**				**11**				**7**	**8**		**3**		**D Axcell**	**36**
	2			6	5			9*	10							11	1	4	7	12	8		3		J Hunting	37
	2		12	6	5			9	10							11*	1	4	7		8		3		R Banks	38
	2		5	6				9	10							11	1	4	7	12	8		3*		R Lewis	39
	2		5	6				9								11	1	4	7	10	8		3		L Robinson	40
	2		5	6				9*	12							11	1	4	7	10	8		3		D Hutchinson	41
	2		3	6	12			9	10							11	1	4		7	5			8*	J Bray	42
	3		2*	6	11			9	10							12	1	4	7		5			8	L Burden	43
	3		2	6	8			9	10							11	1	4	7		5				K Baker	44
	3		2	6				9	10							11	1	4	7		5			8	G Courtney	45
	3		2	5				9	10	12				6		11	1	4*		7				8	T Jones	46
	3		2	6				9	10	12				5		11	1	4	7					8*	I Borrett	47
	3		2	6	7			9*	10	4				5		11	1				12			8	N Midgley	48
	3		2	6					10	9				5		11*	1	4	7		12			8	D Reeves	49
	2			6*				12	10	9				5			1	4	7		11			8	M James	50
	2		5		6			10		9				8			1	4	7†		11				N Glover	51
	2		3	6	5			9	10	12						11*	1	4	7		8				K Salmon	52
	3		2	6	8			9		10*				12		11	1	4	7		5				C Downey	53
	3		2	6	5			9	10*	7				8		11	1	4		12					E Read	54
	3		2	6	5			9*	10	7				8		11	1	4			12				Alan Robinson	55
8	40	1	40	32	17	1	2	44	42	29	0	16	5	31	5	33	38	39	34	4	23	7	5	8	League Appearances	
			+2S	+1S	+3S	+1S		+1S	+1S	+3S	+1S			+1S		+4S		+1S		+6S	+4S	+1S				
	4		5	4	1			6	6	4		2		5		4+1S	6	6	6		4+1S	1+1S	2		FA Cup Appearances	
2	2		2	2	2	1S	1+1S	2	2	2		2		1		1									Milk Cup Appearances	
1	1		1		1S	1S		1				1				1				1	1		1		AM Cup Appearances	

Also Played: Bowman match 2, no.8. Collins match 36, no.10. Scutting matches 50, 51 no.3; 36, no.6.

PRIESTFIELD STADIUM

Official Address: Priestfield Stadium, Gillingham. Telephone: Medway (0634) 51854

Telegraphic: Football Gillingham Kent

Ground Capacity: 16,000

Record Attendance: 23,002 v. Queens Park Rangers, F.A. Cup Round 3, 10 Jan 1948

Record Receipts: £35,074 v. Everton, Milk Cup Quarter Final, 1984

Size of Playing Area: 114yds × 75 yds

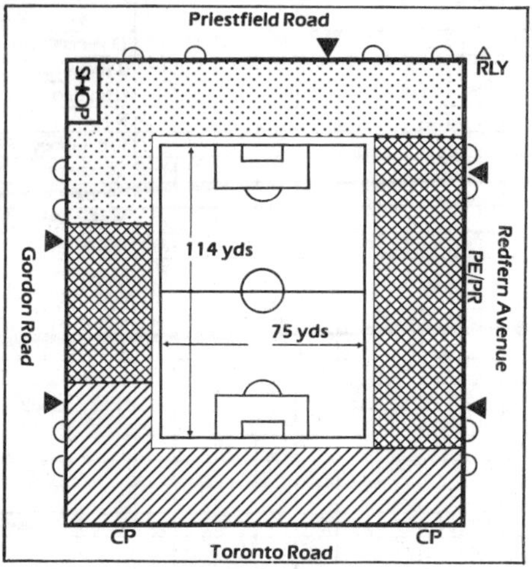

For key see page 12

Season Tickets: Stand: £65.00 and £75.00; Ground: £45.00 or £50.00

Executive Box Season Tickets: Match sponsors lounge £500 (25 seats)

Cost of Stand Tickets: £4.00 & £4.50; **Terraces:** £2.50 & £3.00

Match and Ticket Information: Can reserve by postal application with payment and SAE

Car Parking: For 500 cars near ground, entry by Toronto Road

How to get to the ground

From East, South and West: Use Motorway M2 until junction 4. Leave Motorway and follow signs Gillingham A27, then A2. In 1.3m turn right A231 into Nelson Road. Pass Bus Station then turn right into Gillingham Road, then turn right into Gordon Road for Gillingham F.C.

GRIMSBY TOWN Division 2

Life President
J Evans MBE

Chairman
R K Middleton

Directors
T J Lindley (Vice Chairman)
T W Bygott
D P Everitt FCA
P Sheffield
D B Ramsden
W R Ramsden
T Wilkinson

Secretary
Bernard Fleming

Commercial Consultant
Alec King (0472-697111)

Assistant Commercial Manager
John Waite

Manager
David Booth

Assistant Team Manager
Chris Nicholl

Youth Coach
Alan Woodward

Chief Scout
Tony Askew

Physiotherapist
John Fraser

Groundsman
Frank Bridge

It is doubtful whether many of the five thousand who turned up at Blundell Park on the opening day of the season looked forward to the coming months with much optimism.

Many of last season's squad had left and new faces were Dave Shearer, Paul Emson and (surprisingly) Chris Nichol, whose appointment as player and assistant manager meant three staff were supervising a first team squad of twelve.

Early home form was sound with four wins and a draw but the first five away games produced only two points. Hopes that the away jinx had been broken, when a 2-1 win at Derby was the first away success for thirteen months, were quickly dashed by a 0-4 defeat at Portsmouth.

Trevor Whymark soon asked to be relieved of his coaching duties and some weeks later asked for a move but gradually on the field organisation improved. The experience of Chris Nicholl at the heart of the defence helped Kevin Moore, Bob Cumming and the ever relieable Dean Crombie form one of the best defences in the division.

Up front Paul Emson and the "in-form" Tony Ford gave width to the attack in which Kevin Drinkell again finished as top scorer.

After the 'Pompey' disaster the club enjoyed a run of sixteen games without defeat. Victories over Newcastle (away) and Sheffield Wednesday, plus a superb win at Chelsea, having been 0-2 down at one time, put the club into the promotion race but it was the 'bogy' team from Hampshire, who having also knocked 'The Mariners' out of the F.A. Cup, completed a spectacular league double with an exciting 4-3 victory at Blundell Park and the tension set in.

One point from the Easter programme put paid to any lingering promotion hopes but the flowing football returned, albeit too late; but a final position of fith was the club's best since dropping out of the First Division in 1948.

The introduction into the side of further home nurtured talent such as Andy Moore and Gary Lund plus the achievement of the junior side in taking the Northern Intermediate League title augurs well for the future. The disappointingly low level of support does not.

Les Triggs, The League Directory's Statistican for the Club

Back Row: Dean Crombie, Paul Wilkinson, Peter Grotier, Nigel Batch, Andy Moore, Neil Matthews. **Middle Row:** David Booth (Manager), Kevin Moore (Captain), Gary Lund, Paul Emson, Michael Rowbotham, Gary Henshaw, Tony Ford, Steve Foley, Chris Nicholl (Asst Manager). **Front Row:** Mark Hine, Phil Bonnyman, Kevin Drinkell, Bob Cumming, Chris Seagraves, Paul Agnew.

Sponsored by
NISA

'THE MARINERS'

Formed: 1878 **Turned Professional:** 1890 **Ltd Co:** 1890
Previous Names: Grimsby Pelham
Previous Managers: 1920-1 Haydn Price 1921-5 George Fraser 1925-32 Wilf Gillow 1932-6 Frank Womack 1937-51 Charlie Spencer 1951-4 Bill Shankly 1954-5 Billy Walsh 1955-9 Allenby Chilton 1960-2 Tim Ward 1962-4 Tom Johnston 1964-7 Jimmy McGuigan 1967-8 Don McEvoy 1968-9 Bill Harvey 1969-71 Bobby Kennedy 1971-3 Lawrie McMenemy 1973-5 Ron Ashman 1975-6 Tom Casey 1976-9 John Newman 1979-82 George Kerr
Honours: Division Two Champions 1900-1, 1933-4 Division Three (N) Champions 1925-6, 1955-6 Division Three Champions 1979-80 Division Four Champions 1971-2
League Career: Original Member of Division 2 1892 Promoted to Division 1 1900-1 Relegated to Division 2 1902-3 Failed re-election 1910 Re-elected to Division 2 1911 Relegated to Division 3 1919-20 Transferred to Division 3(N) 1921 Promoted to Division 2 1925-6 Promoted to Division 1 1928-9 Relegated to Division 2 1931-2 Promoted to Division 1 1933-4 Relegated to Division 2 1947-8 Relegated to Division 3(N) 1950-1 Promoted to Division Two 1955-6 Relegated to Division 3 1958-9 Promoted to Division 2 1961-2 Relegated to Division 3 1963-4 Relegated to Division 4 1967-8 Promoted to Division 3 1971-2 Relegated to Division 4 1976-7 Promoted to Division 3 1978-9 Promoted to Division 2 1979-80
Colours: Black and white striped shirts, black shorts and white stockings
Change Colours: All red

CLUB RECORDS

Most Appearances for Club: Keith Jobling: Football League 450 + F.A. Cup 23 + League Cup 19 **Total 492**
Most Capped Player: Pat Glover, 4, Wales **For England:** H Betmead, J Bestall, G Tweedy (1 each)
Record Goalscorer in a Match: Tommy McCairns, 6 v Leicester Fosse (h) 7-1 Div 2, 11.04.1896
Record League Goalscorer in a season: Pat Glover, 42, Div 2, 1933-4 **In All Competitions:** Pat Glover 43 (League 42 + F.A. Cup 1) 1933-4
Record League Goalscorer in a career: Pat Glover, 180, 1930-9 **In All Competitions:** Pat Glover, 197 (League 180 + F.A. Cup 17)
Record Transfer Fee Received: £125,000 from Aston Villa for Terry Donovan, July 1979
Record Transfer Fee Paid: £80,000 to Vancouver Whitecaps for Trevor Whymark, Dec 1980
Best Performances: League: 5th Div 1 1934-5 **F.A. Cup:** Semi-Final 1936, 1939 **League/Milk Cup:** 5th Round 1979-80
Most League Points: 70 in Div 2, 1983-4 **Most League Goals:** 103, Div 2, 1933-4
Record League Victory: 9-2 v Darwen, Div 2, 15 Apr 1899
Record League Defeat: 1-9 v Arsenal, Div 1, 28 Jan 1931
Club Statistician for the Directory: Les Triggs

Programme Editor
Patrick Conway

Price	Number of Pages
40p	24

Subscriptions
£16.50 per season (home matches postage included)

GRIMSBY TOWN

PLAYERS NAME Ht Wt Birthdate	Honours	Birthplace Transfers	Clubs	APPEARANCES League	Milk Cup	F.A.C.	E. Cups	GOALS League	Milk Cup	F.A.C.	E. Cups
GOALKEEPERS											
Nigel Batch	Div. 3, 80	Huddersfield	Derby Co. (A)								
5-10 12.5 9.11.57			Grimsby T.	274	22	17					
Peter Grotier		Stratford	West Ham U.	50	4						
5-11 12.0 18.10.50			Cardiff C. (L)	2							
		£16,666	Lincoln C.	233	16	14					
		£25,000	Cardiff C.	38	5						
		£5,000	Grimsby T.	4	2						
DEFENDERS											
Paul Agnew	N.I. Y. S	Lisburn	Grimsby T. (A)	1							
5-9½ 10.4 15.8.65											
Dean Crombie	Div. 3, 80	Lincoln	Ruston Bucyrus								
5-11 11.7 9.8.54			Lincoln C.	33	1 + 1						
		F	Grimsby T.	225 + 3	17	13		2			
Bob Cumming	Div. 3, 80	Airdrie	Baillieston								
5-8 11.4 7.12.55		F	Grimsby T.	280 + 18	22 +	16		49	5	2	
Andy Moore		Cleethorpes	Grimsby T. (A)	8 + 1							
6-0 12.0 14.11.65											
Kevin Moore*	E. S	Grimsby	Grimsby T.	311 + 2	29	20		16	1	2	
5-11 11.7 29.4.58	Div. 3, 80										
Chris Nicholl†	N.I.(51),	Wilmslow	Burnley								
6-2 12.13 12.10.46	FC. 75, 77,	F	Witton Alb.								
	Div. 3, 72		Halifax T.	42	2	6		3			
		£25,000	Luton T.	98	4	4		6			
		£90,000	Aston Villa	210	27	12	2E	11	5	4	
		£90,000	Southampton	228	21	17	2E	8	1		
			Grimsby T.	39	4	1					
MIDFIELD											
Phil Bonnyman		Glasgow	Hamilton Ac.	71	17	3		7	2		
6-0 12.0 6.2.54		£20,000	Carlisle U.	149 + 3	10	14		26	2	5	
		£150,000	Chesterfield	98 + 1	6	8		25	1	2	
		£80,000	Grimsby T.	67 + 2	5	3		4			
Steve Foley		Liverpool	Liverpool (A)								
5-7 10.12 4.10.62			Fulham (L)	2 + 1							
			Grimsby T.								
Mark Hine		Middlesbrough									
5-8½ 9.0 18.5.64											
Gary Henshaw		Leeds	Grimsby T. (A)	3 + 1							
5-9½ 9.10 18.2.65											
FORWARDS											
Kevin Drinkell	Div. 3, 80	Grimsby	Grimsby T. (A)	212 + 23	20 +	2 + 3		75	8	5	
5-10 11.10 18.6.60											
Paul Emson		Lincoln	Brigg T.								
5-11 11.3 22.10.58		£5,000	Derby Co.	112 + 15	4 + 3	1 + 3		13			
			Grimsby T.	39	4	1		6			
Tony Ford	Div. 3, 80	Grimsby	Grimsby T.	247 + 31	22 +	11 +		45	4		
5-9 12.2 14.5.59											
Gary Lund		Grimsby	Grimsby T.	4 + 3				4			
5-11 11.0 13.9.64											
Paul Wilkinson		Louth	Grimsby T.	39 + 2	4	1 + 2		13	2		
5-11½ 11.0 30.10.64											

APPRENTICES

Andy Foster, Shawn Holgeth, Neil Matthews, Kevin Topliss

GRIMSBY TOWN

DIVISION TWO 5TH **FA CUP** 3RD ROUND **MILK CUP** 2ND ROUND

MATCH	DATE	COMPE-TITION	VENUE	OPPONENTS	RESULT	HALF TIME	L'GUE POS'N	GOALSCORERS	ATTEN-DANCE
1	A 27	CL	H	Shrewsbury T	D1-1	0-0		Drinkell	5,177
2	**30**	**MC 1**	**A**	**York C**	**L1-2**	**0-1**		**Wilkinson**	**3,505**
3	S 3	CL	A	Cardiff C	L1-3	1-0	17	Waters	5,135
4	6	CL	H	Leeds U	W2-0	1-0		Drinkell, Waters (pen)	7,000
5	10	CL	H	Newcastle U	D1-1	1-0	14	Speight	9,000
6	**13**	**MC 1**	**H**	**York C**	**W2-0**	**0-0**		**Drinkell 2**	**3,529**
7	17	CL	A	Middlesbrough	D1-1	1-1	14	Waters	10,239
8	24	CL	H	Fulham	W2-1	1-1		Wilkinson, Emson	5,769
9	28	CL	A	Barnsley	L1-3	0-2		Wilkinson	10,966
10	O 1	CL	A	Manchester C	L1-2	0-0		Emson	25,080
11	**4**	**MC 2**	**H**	**Coventry C**	**D0-0**	**0-0**			**6,088**
12	8	CL	A	Huddersfield T	D0-0	0-0			8,897
13	15	CL	H	Brighton & HA	W5-0	3-0		Wilkinson 2, Ford, Lund, Emson	5,469
14	22	CL	H	Crystal Palace	W2-0	1-0		Waters, Ford	6,075
15	**25**	**MC 2**	**A**	**Coventry C**	**L1-2**	**0-1**		**Wilkinson**	**8,705**
16	29	CL	A	Derby Co	W2-1	1-1		Drinkell 2	11,531
17	N 5	CL	A	Portsmouth	L0-4	0-2			12,906
18	12	CL	H	Charlton Ath	W2-1	0-1		Drinkell, Whymark	5,684
19	19	CL	A	Swansea C	W1-0	1-0		Moore	6,178
20	26	CL	H	Carlisle U	D1-1	0-1		Waters (pen)	5,665
21	D 4	CL	A	Blackburn R	D1-1	0-0		Bonnyman	6,409
22	13	CL	H	Oldham Ath	W3-0	2-0		Ford, Speight, Wilkinson	4,825
23	17	CL	A	Chelsea	W3-2	0-1		Waters, Emson, Ford	13,151
24	26	CL	H	Sheffield W	W1-0	0-0		Wilkinson	16,197
25	28	CL	A	Cambridge U	D2-2	0-1		Emson, Ford	4,319
26	31	CL	H	Cardiff C	W1-0	0-0		Emson	7,164
27	J 2	CL	A	Fulham	D1-1	0-1		Drinkell	7,351
28	**7**	**FAC 3**	**A**	**Portsmouth**	**L1-2**	**0-0**		**Drinkell**	**12,707**
29	14	CL	A	Shrewsbury T	W2-1	1-1		Drinkell, Wilkinson	3,343
30	21	CL	H	Middlesbrough	D0-0	0-0	5		7,342
31	F 4	CL	H	Manchester C	D1-1	0-1	5	Wilkinson	11,986
32	11	CL	A	Newcastle U	W1-0	1-0	4	Drinkell	28,526
33	21	CL	H	Derby Co	W2-1	1-1		Wilkinson, Drinkell	8,530
34	25	CL	A	Crystal Palace	W1-0	1-0	3	Ford	5,956
35	M 3	CL	H	Portsmouth	L3-4	2-2	5	Drinkell, Ford, Cumming	8,729
36	10	CL	A	Charlton Ath	D3-3	0-1	6	Drinkell 2, Ford	7,626
37	17	CL	A	Leeds U	L1-2	1-1	6	Wilkinson	14,412
38	31	CL	H	Huddersfield T	W2-1	2-0	6	Waters (pen), Bonnyman	7,541
39	A 7	CL	A	Brighton & HA	L0-2	0-1	6		10,610
40	10	CL	H	Barnsley	W1-0	0-0		Wilkinson	6,934
41	14	CL	H	Swansea C	W3-0	1-0	5	Drinkell 3	5,851
42	21	CL	A	Sheffield W	L0-1	0-0	5		25,828
43	23	CL	H	Cambridge U	D0-0	0-0	5		5,828
44	28	CL	A	Carlisle U	D1-1	0-1	4	Wilkinson	3,512
45	M 5	CL	H	Blackburn R	W3-2	1-0	4	Bonnyman (pen), Lund 2	4,826
46	7	CL	A	Oldham Ath	L1-2	1-1	4	Lund	4,156
47	12	CL	H	Chelsea	L0-1	0-1	5		13,000

Av Home Att **7,586**

Goal Scorers

League (60): Drinkell 15, Wilkinson 12, Ford 8, Waters 7 (3 pens), Emson 6, Lund 4, Bonnyman 3 (1 pen), Speight 2, Cumming 1, Moore 1, Whymark 1
FA Cup (1): Drinkell 1
Milk Cup (4): Drinkell 2, Wilkinson 2

1983-84

Batch	Cumming	Crombie	Waters	Nicholl	Moore K	Ford	Wilkinson	Drinkell	Bonnyman	Emson	Cooper	Whymark	Speight	Lund	Henshaw	Moore A	Shearer	Agnew	REFEREE	
1	2	3	4	5	6	7	8	9	10	11									A Saunders	1
1	**2**	**3**	**4**	**5**	**6**	**7**	**8**	**9**	**10**	**11**									**D Richardson**	**2**
1	2	3	4		6	7	8*	9	10	11	5	12							L Shapter	3
1		5	7	3	4	6		11	8	9	2	10							H Taylor	4
1		5	7	3	4	6		11		9	2	10	8						MJ Heath	5
1	**12**	**3**	**4**	**5**	**6**	**7**	**8**	**9**		**11**	**2***		**10**						**P Tyldesley**	**6**
1		3	4	5	6	7	8	9		11	2		10						D Scott	7
1	12	5	7	4	3	6	11	10*		9	2		8						A Robinson	8
1	12	3	4	5	6	7	8			11	2		10	9*					K Barratt	9
1	12	3	4*	5	6	7	8	9		11	2		10						K Redfern	10
1	**2**	**3**	**4**	**5**	**6**	**7**	**8**	**9**		**11**					**10**				**D Hutchinson**	**11**
1	2	3	4	5	6	7	8	9		11			10						V Callow	12
1	2	3	4	5	6	7	9			11			10*	8	12				G Napthine	13
1	2	3	4	5	6	7	8	9	10	11									D Owen	14
1	**2**	**3**	**4**	**5†**	**6**	**7**	**8**	**9**	**10**	**11**									**J Hough**	**15**
1	2	3	4	5	6	7	8	9		11			10						P Willis	16
1	2	3	4	5	6	7		9		11*		12	10				8		R Lewis	17
1	2	5	7		4	6	10	11		9		3	8						N Wilson	18
1	2	3	4	5	6	7	8	9		11			10						T Bune	19
1	2	3	4	5	6	7	8	9		11			10						J Ashworth	20
1	2	3	4	5	6	7	8*	9	12	11			10						J Lovatt	21
1	2	3	4	5	6	7	8		12	11		9	10*						J Key	22
1	2	3	4	5	6	7	8		10	11		9							D Axcell	23
1	5		7	3	4	6	11		8	9		10				2			D Brazier	24
1	3		4	5	6	7	8*	12	10	11		9				2			D Letts	25
1	2	3	4	5	6	7		9	10	11		8							A Challinor	26
1	2	3	4	5	6	7		9	10	11		8							K Cooper	27
1	**2**	**3**	**4**	**5**	**6**	**7**	**8**	**9**	**10**	**11**									**J Moules**	**28**
1		3	4	5	6	7	8	9	10	11						2			R Nixon	29
1	2	3	4	5	6	7	8	9	10	11									A Banks	30
1	2*	3	4	5	6	7	8	9	10	11			12						G Courtney	31
1	2	3	4	5	6	7	8	9	10	11									D Allison	32
1	2	3	4	5	6	7	8	9	10	11									D Shaw	33
1	2	3	4	5	6	7	8	9	10	11									J Martin	34
1	2	3	4	5	6	7	8	9	10	11									J Worrall	35
1	2	3	4	5	6	7	8	9	10	11*			12						I Borrett	36
1		3	4	5	6	7	8	9	10	11			2						T Holbrook	37
1		3	4	5	6	7	8	9	10	11						2			J Scales	38
1		3	4	5	6	7	8*	9	10	11						2	12		J Moules	39
1		3	4	5	6	7	8	9	10*	11			2				12		N Glover	40
1		3	4	5	6	7	8	9	10	11*			2				12		T Jones	41
1		3	4*	5	6	7	8		10	11			2	9		12			F Roberts	42
1	2	3		5*	6	7	8	9		11			4	12	10				M Scott	43
1	2	3		5	6	7	8	9	10	11			4						K Walmsley	44
1	2*	3			6	7	8	9	10				4	12	11	5			T Bray	45
1		6		5		7	8	9	10				4	11		2		3	N Ashley	46
1		3		5	6	7	8	9	10				4	12	11*	2			D Shaw	47
42	27	40	37	39	41	**42**	37	35	27	39	7	9	23	4	3	8	1	1	League Appearances	
	+3S							+1S	+2S			+2S	+2S	+3S	+1S	+1S	+3S			
1	1	1	1	1	1	1	1	1	1	1									FA Cup Appearances	
4	3+1S	4	4	4	4	4	4	4	2	4	1		1		1				Milk Cup Appearances	

BLUNDELL PARK

Official Address: Blundell Park, Cleethorpes, South Humberside DN35 7PY. Telephone: Cleethorpes (0472) 697111.

Telegraphic: Football Grimsby

Ground Capacity: 22,146

Record Attendance: 31,657 v. Wolverhampton Wanderers, Football League Cup Round 5, 4 Dec 1979

Record Receipts: £39,530 v. Sheffield Wednesday, Division 2, 26 Dec 1983

Size of Playing Area: 111yds × 74 yds

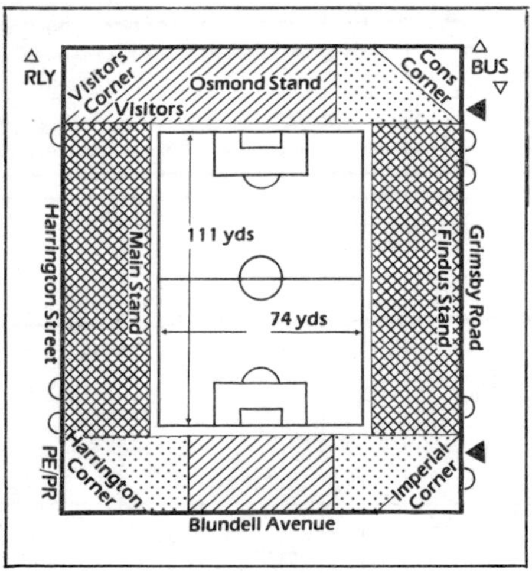

For key see page 12

Season Tickets: Findus Stand: £79.50 (all classes), £69.50 (off-centre & wings), £49.50 juveniles/OAP; Main Stand: £59.50 (£45.00 juveniles/OAP), £79.95 (1 adult, 1 child), £99.95 (1 adult, 2 children); Ground: £37.50 (£25 juveniles/OAP)

Executive Box Season Tickets: Consult Commercial Manager

Cost of Stand Tickets: Findus Stand: £4.75 (all classes), £4.00 (wings, off-centre), (£3.00 juveniles/OAP), Main Stand: £3.50 (£2.50 juveniles/OAP), Osmond Stand £3.00 (all classes); **Terraces:** £2.50 (£1.50 children/OAP)

Match and Ticket Information: Seats bookable two weeks in advance of each match.

Car Parking: Street parking available.

How to get to the ground

From North and West: Use Motorway M180 then A18 (S.P. Grimsby) then follow signs to Cleethorpes and at roundabout take 1st exit into Grimsby Road A1098 for Grimsby Town F.C.

From South: Use A1 then A16 and follow signs to Cleethorpes and at roundabout take 1st exit into Grimsby Road A1098 for Grimsby Town F.C.

HALIFAX TOWN Division 4

President
TH Scott

Chairman
J Turner

Directors
JS Crowther
F Hinchcliffe
T McLean
P Dawson
Dr D Lord
D Sharp
C Wood
T Dawson
R Newby
D Wilkinson

Secretary
Mrs C Bell

Assistant Secretary
Mrs A Pettifor

Manager
Micky Bullock

Commercial Manager
T Thwaites (0422 66593)

Physiotherapist
A Sutton

Horrific seasons for Halifax Town have been nothing exceptional and too often letters asking their League colleagues to re-elect them have been a necessity. It was the same story in 1983/84 although twenty-first position in the Fourth Division was only the thin end of goal difference which ended in Wrexham's favour. The happiest day for the club happened after the season ended when they were reelected for another season, which will mean many more days and nights of hard work for the brave directors and staff of The Shay.

The playing story is quickly told. A re-election place was always possible and there was no cup win to relieve the gloom with Darlington winning both legs of their Milk Cup First Round match and the FA Cup campaign ending at the same stage at home to Whitby Town of the Northern League after the home team had failed to safeguard a two-goal lead. As North Shields had won at Halifax in the previous campaign, 'Town' will wish to avoid Drybrough Northern League clubs this season.

Since most of the staff will be new for the coming season it would be invidious to mention any players as having been consistent, since that would clearly not be the view of the manager, Micky Bullock and his small staff. The heroes of clubs like Halifax are almost always the Chairman such as Mr Turner, who provides the resources to keep a club alive, plus the volunteers who dedicate themselves to the task of survival. Better days for 1984/85 – let us hope so for their sake. WLM

Back Row L to R: Alan Sutton (Physio), Simon Lowe, Alan Little, Stephen Ward, Billy Ayre (Player/Coach), Paddy Roche, Barry Gallagher, Paul Kendall, Alan Knill, Paul Sanderson. **Front Row:** *Dean Martin, *Paul Fleming, Garry Watson, Jeff Cook, Stephen Thornber, Mark Greenway, Chris Moyses, Cec Podd.
*Youth Training Scheme

'THE SHAYMEN'

Sponsored by
Paul Madeley Ltd/MacDee

Formed: 1911 **Turned Professional:** 1911 **Ltd Co:** 1911
Previous Managers: Since 1946
Jack Breedon W Wooton Jimmy Thompson Gerald Henry Bobby Browne Willie Watson
Billy Burnicle Harry Hooper Willie Watson Vic Metcalfe Alan Ball (Snr) George Kirby
Ray Henderson George Mulhall John Quinn Alan Ball (Snr) Jimmy Lawson George Kirby
Honours: None
League Career: Original members of Division Three (N) 1920 Transferred to Division 3 1958
Relegated to Division Four 1962-3 Promoted to Division Three 1968-9
Relegated to Division Four 1975-6
Colours: Royal blue shirts with white trim, white shorts with blue trim, blue stockings with white tops
Change Colours: Yellow shirts with blue trim, blue shorts, yellow stockings with blue tops

CLUB RECORDS

Most Appearances for Club: John Pickering, 367, 1965-74
Most Capped Player: None
Record Goalscorer in a Match: William Chambers, 5 v Hartlepool United, Div 3(N), 07.04.34
Albert Valentine, 5 v New Brighton, Div 3(N), 09.03.35
Record League Goalscorer in a season: Albert Valéntine, 34, Div 3(N), 1934-5
Record League Goalscorer in a career: Ernie Dixon, 129, 1922-30
Record Transfer Fee Received: £55,000 from Huddersfield Town for Mick Kennedy, Aug 1980
Record Transfer Fee Paid: £25,000 to Huddersfield Town for Kevin Johnson, Aug 1978
Best Performances: League: 3rd Div 3 1970-1 **F.A. Cup:** 5th Round 1932-3, 1952-3 **League/Milk Cup:** 4th Round, 1964
Most League Points: 60 in Div 4, 1982-3
Record League Victory: 6-0 v Bradford (P.A.), Div 3(N), 3 Dec 1955
Record League Defeat: 0-13 v Stockport County, Div 3(N), 6 Jan 1934

Club Statistician for the Directory: M. Belshaw

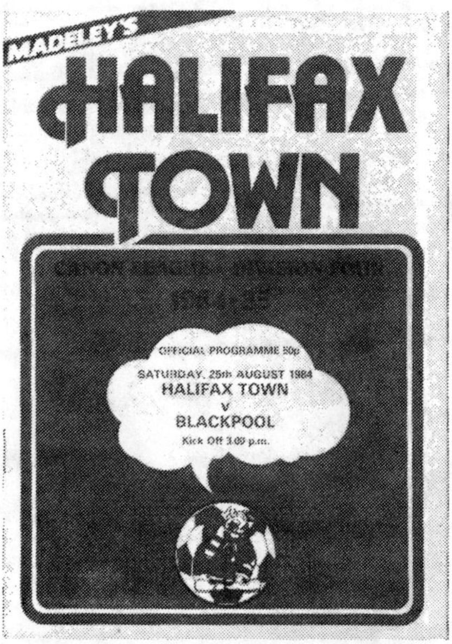

Programme Editor
Tony Thwaites

Price	Number of Pages
50p	16

Subscriptions
Apply to club for details

HALIFAX TOWN

PLAYERS NAME Ht Wt Birthdate	Honours	Birthplace Transfers	Clubs	APPEARANCES League	Milk Cup	F.A.C.	A.M.C.	GOALS League	Milk Cup	F.A.C.	A.M.C.
GOALKEEPER											
Paddy Roche	Ei.(7)	Dublin	Shelbourne								
6-1 11.9 4.1.51		£15,000	Manchester U.	46	5						
			Brentford	71	7	6					
DEFENDERS											
Billy Ayre		Crookhill	Scarborough								
5-11 12.10 7.5.52			Hartlepool	141	6	8		27			
			Halifax T.	63	2	1		5			
		£15,000	Mansfield T.	67	2	3	1	7			
Mark Greenway		Halifax	Halifax T. (A)	10+1				1			
5-8 11.0 19.4.66											
Paul Kendall		Halifax	Halifax T. (A)	50+12	1	1	1	2	1		
6-10 12.6 19.10.64											
Alan Little*	FAYC. 72	Newcastle	Aston Villa	2+1	2						
5-11½ 12.12 5.2.55		F	Southend U.	102+1	4	11		12	1		
			Barnsley	91	9	4		14	1		
		£30,000	Doncaster R.	84+1	2	6		11		1	
		Player Exchange	Torquay U.	51	3	6		4	1	1	
		F	Halifax T.	27			1	3			
Alan Knill		Slough	Southampton								
6-2½ 10.9 8.10.64											
'Cec' Podd		St. Kitts, W.I.	Bradford C. (A)	494+8	33+1	30	2	3	1		
5-9 10.0 7.8.52											
Gary Watson		Bradford	Bradford C.	246+17	18+	9+1					
5-8 10.6 7.10.65			Doncaster R. (L)	13							
		F	Halifax T.								
MIDFIELD											
Barry Gallagher†		Bradford	Bradford (A)	66+5	11+	3		22	5	1	
5-11 12.3 7.4.61			Mansfield T. (L)	2+1							
			Halifax T.	42+3	2		1	14			
Steve Ward		Derby	Brighton & HA (A)								
6-0 12.12 21.7.59		F	Northampton T.	13+2	4						
		F	Halifax T.	166+3	5	4+1	1	12			
Chris Moyses		Lincoln	Lincoln City								
5-9 11.4 1.11.65		F	Halifax T.								
FORWARDS											
Jeff Cook		Hartlepool	Hellenic S.A.								
5-9 11.3 14.3.52			Stoke C.	22+8	1	2+1		5		2	
			Bradford C. (L)	8				1			
		£25,000	Plymouth A. (L)	58+4	3	4		26			
		F	Halifax T.	25+5	2	1	1	6			
Simon Lowe		London	Barnsley								
5-11 12.11 26.12.62		F	Halifax T.								

HALIFAX TOWN

DIVISION FOUR 21ST **FA CUP** 1ST ROUND **MILK CUP** 1ST ROUND

MATCH	DATE	COMPETITION	VENUE	OPPONENTS	RESULT	HALF TIME	L'GUE POS'N	GOALSCORERS	ATTENDANCE
1	A 27	CL	H	Torquay U	D2-2	1-1		Cook, Hendrie	1,448
2	**30**	**MC 1**	**H**	**Darlington**	**L0-1**	**0-0**			**1,331**
3	S 3	CL	A	Hereford U	D0-0	0-0	16		3,188
4	6	CL	A	Swindon T	W3-2	2-0		Kendall, Staniforth, Cook	3,635
5	9	CL	H	Mansfield T	D0-0	0-0	7		1,728
6	**13**	**MC 1**	**A**	**Darlington**	**L2-3**	**1-0**		**Kendall, Staniforth**	**1,793**
7	18	CL	A	Bury	L0-3	0-2	15		3,258
8	23	CL	H	Hartlepool U	W3-2	1-2		Mell 2, Staniforth	1,416
9	27	CL	H	Northampton T	D2-2	0-1		Staniforth, Mell	1,519
10	O 1	CL	A	Wrexham	L0-1	0-0	16		5,472
11	8	CL	A	Bristol C	L0-3	0-3	19		6,739
12	15	CL	H	Peterborough U	W2-1	1-0	14	Mell, Nuttall	1,079
13	18	CL	H	Crewe Alex	W1-0	0-0		Ward	1,352
14	21	CL	A	Doncaster R	L2-3	0-3		Staniforth, Cook (pen)	3,299
15	29	CL	H	Aldershot	W1-0	1-0	12	Gallagher	1,242
16	N 2	CL	A	Chester C	D1-1	0-0		Cook (pen)	1,211
17	4	CL	H	Tranmere R	L1-2	1-2		Hendrie	1,735
18	11	CL	A	Stockport Co	L0-4	0-1			2,134
19	**19**	**FAC 1**	**H**	**Whitby T**	**L2-3**	**1-0**		**Ward, Evans**	**2,588**
20	25	CL	H	Darlington T	L0-2	0-1			1,018
21	D 2	CL	A	Reading	L0-1	0-0			3,930
22	17	CL	A	Colchester U	L1-4	0-2	21	Greenway	1,866
23	26	CL	H	York C	L1-2	1-1	21	Little	2,457
24	27	CL	A	Rochdale	D1-1	0-1	22	Cook	1,896
25	31	CL	H	Blackpool	W1-0	0-0	19	Little (pen)	1,958
26	J 2	CL	A	Chesterfield	D0-0	0-0	18		2,298
27	7	CL	H	Hereford U	W2-1	2-0	16	Cooper, Little	1,037
28	14	CL	A	Torquay U	D1-1	0-1	17	Nuttall	1,369
29	21	CL	H	Bury	L0-2	0-0	17		1,728
30	F 4	CL	H	Wrexham	L1-2	1-2	17	Smith	1,184
31	11	CL	A	Hartlepool U	L0-3	0-1	17		1,658
32	14	CL	H	Chester C	D2-2	1-2		Gallagher, Thornber	911
33	18	CL	A	Aldershot	L2-5	1-4	18	Staniforth, Gallagher (pen)	2,832
34	**20**	**AMC 1**	**A**	**Tranmere R**	**L0-2**	**0-0**			**937**
35	25	CL	H	Doncaster R	L1-2	1-2	21	Harle (og)	2,408
36	M 3	CL	A	Crew Alex	L1-6	0-2	21	Gallagher (pen)	2,058
37	5	CL	A	Tranmere R	L2-3	0-2		Staniforth, Cook	1,486
38	9	CL	H	Stockport Co	W2-0	2-0		Gallagher 2	1,261
39	17	CL	H	Bristol C	L1-2	0-0	21	Evans	1,204
40	24	CL	A	Peterborough U	L0-4	0-1	21		2,304
41	30	CL	H	Swindon T	W2-1	1-0		Kendall, Gallagher	1,008
42	A 7	CL	A	Northampton T	D1-1	0-0	21	Evans	1,356
43	10	CL	A	Mansfield T	L1-7	0-0		Foster (og)	1,696
44	13	CL	H	Reading	L0-1	0-1			1,113
45	20	CL	A	York C	L1-4	0-3		Mell	7,123
46	23	CL	H	Rochdale	W5-0	2-0	20	Mell, Gallagher 4	1,422
47	28	CL	A	Darlington	L2-3	1-0	21	Ward, Nuttall	1,161
48	M 4	CL	H	Chesterfield	W2-1	1-0		Mell, Gallagher (pen)	1,001
49	7	CL	A	Blackpool	L0-4	0-1	21		2,324
50	11	CL	H	Colchester U	W4-1	2-0		Ward, Gallagher 2, Mell	1,248
								Av Home Att	**1,368**

Goal Scorers

League (55): Gallagher B 14 (3 pen), Mell 8, Cook 6 (2 pen), Staniforth 6, Little 3 (1 pen), Nuttall 3, Ward 3, Evans 2, Hendrie 2, Kendall 2, Cooper 1, Greenway 1, Smith 1, Thornber 1, opponents 2
FA Cup (2): Evans 1, Ward 1
Milk Cup (2): Kendall 1, Staniforth 1
AMC (-): —

1983-84

Smelt	Nobbs	Wood	Evans	Smith	Hendrie	Ward	Cook	Mell	Hanson	Staniforth	Kendall	Gallagher B	Nuttall	Gallagher J **(L)**	Vessey	Little	Greenway	Cooper **(L)**	Thornber	REFEREE	
1	2	3	4	5	6	7	8	9*	10	11	12									J Ashworth	1
1	**2**	**3**	**4**	**5**	**6**		**8**	**9***	**10**	**11**		**7**	**12**							**R Nixon**	**2**
1	2	3	4	5	6	9	8			11	10	7								J Deakin	3
1	2	3	4	5	6	9	8	12		11	10	7*								J Moules	4
1	2	3	4	5	6	9*	8	12		11	10	7								R Guy	5
1	**2**	**3**	**4**	**5**	**6**	**9**	**8***	**12**		**11**	**10**	**7**								**K Walmsley**	**6**
1	2	5	3	4	8	9	10*			11	7	6	12							N Ashley	7
1	2	3	4	5	6	11		8		9	10	7								J Lovatt	8
1	2	3	4	5	6	11		8		9	10	7								C Seel	9
1	2	3	4	5	6	11*	12	8		9	10	7								T King	10
1	2	3	4	5†	6	11		8		9	10		7							J Martin	11
1	2	3	4	5	6	11	9	8			10*	12	7							P Willis	12
1	2	3	4	5	6	11	9	8			10	12	7*							G Courtney	13
1	2	3	4	5	6	11	9	8		12	10		7*							L Robinson	14
1	2	3	4		6	11	10	8		9		7		5						N Glover	15
1	2	3	4		6	11	10	8*		9		7	12	5						D Allison	16
	2	3	4	10*	6	11	9	8				7	12	5	1					H Taylor	17
1		3	4	2	6	11		8			10	7	9	5						A Seville	18
1	**2**	**3**	**4**		**6**	**11**	**8**	**12**			**10**	**7**	**9***	**5**						**C Seel**	**19**
1	2	3	4	5	6	11	9		12		10	7*				8				M Scott	20
1	2	5	3	4	6	8	11*	10			12					7	9			T Spencer	21
1	2	3	4	5	6	11	12				10		9			8	7*			A Buksh	22
1	2	3	4	5	6	11	12				10					8†	7*	9		A Challinor	23
1	2	3	4	5	6	11	10				7					8	12	9*		M Heath	24
1	2		4	5*	6	11				10	12		7			8	3	9		T Holbrook	25
1	2		4		6	11				10	5		7			8	3	9		J Hough	26
1	2		4		6	11				10	5		7			8	3	9		N Wilson	27
1	2	12	4	5	6	11				10	8		7				3	9*		C Downey	28
1	2	6	4			11		12		10	5	8	7				3	9*		G Tyson	29
1	2	6	4	12		11		9		10	5	8	7*				3			J Worrall	30
1	2	3	4	5		11*		9		10	6	7	12			8				M Peck	31
1	2	10	4		6	11*				9	5	7				8	3		12	R Banks	32
1	2	3	4		6	11				9	5	7				8			10	E Scales	33
1	**2**	**3**	**4**		**5**	**11**	**9**	**12**			**6**	**7**				**8**			**10***	**M Heath**	**34**
1	2	3	4	12	6	11	9*				5	7				8			10	K Redfern	35
1	2	3	4	5*	6	11	12			9		7				8			10	V Callow	36
1		3	4	5	6	11	10	12		9*	2	7				8				N Midgley	37
1		3	4	5	6	11	10	9*		12	2	7				8				N Glover	38
1		3	4	5	6	11	10*	12		9	2	7				8				J Lovatt	39
1	2	3	4	5	6	11				9	10	7				8				I Borrett	40
1	6	3	2	5		11	10	12		9	4	7*				8				A Saunders	41
1	6	3	2	5		11*	10	12		9	4	7				8				L Shapter	42
	6	3	2	5		11	10*	12		9	4	7			1	8				G Courtney	43
1	10	3	2	5	6	11				9	4	12	7			8*				D Shaw	44
1	7	3	2	5	6	11		10			4	9				8				M Scott	45
1	2	3	4	5	6	11	7*	10				9	12			8				R Nixon	46
1	2	3	4	5	6	11	7	10*				9	12			8				I Hendrick	47
1	2	3	4	5	6	11	7	10				9				8				R Guy	48
1		3	4	5	6	11	7*	10			2	9	12			8				R Bridges	49
1	7	3	4	5	6	11		10			2	9*	12			8				D Owen	50
44	41	42	**46**	37	40	**46**	25	22	1	28	36	32	13	4	2	27	10	7	3	League Appearances	
		+1S		+2S			+5S	+8S	+1S	+2S	+3S	+3S	+8S				+1S		+1S		
1	1	1	1		1	1	1	1S			1	1	1	1						FA Cup Appearances	
2	2	2	2	2	2	1	2	1+1S	1	2	1	2	1S							Milk Cup Appearances	
1	1	1	1		1	1	1	1S			1	1				1			1	AM Cup Appearances	

THE SHAY

Official Address: Shay Ground, Halifax HX1 2YS. Telephone: 0422 53423

Ground Capacity: 16,500

Record Attendance: 36,885 v. Tottenham Hotspur, F.A. Cup Round 5, 14 Feb 1953

Record Receipts: £14,000 v. Manchester City, F.A. Cup Round 3, 5 Jan 1980

Size of Playing Area: 110yds × 70 yds

Season Tickets: Main Stand: £55.00 (£27.00 OAP/juveniles); Patrons & 160 Stand £60.00 (£30.00 juveniles/OAP); Ground: £39.00 (£19.00 juveniles/OAP)

Executive Box Season Tickets: 50 Club £100, Vice-Presidents £100

Cost of Stand Tickets: £5.00 (50 Club & Vice Presidents), £2.50 Main Stand (£1.25 juveniles/OAP); £2.70 (Patrons & 160 Stand), £1.35 (juveniles/OAP); **Terraces:** £2.00 (£1.00 juveniles/OAP)

Match and Ticket Information: Applications in advance may be sent to secretary.

Car Parking: Car park available with entrance in Shaw Hill.

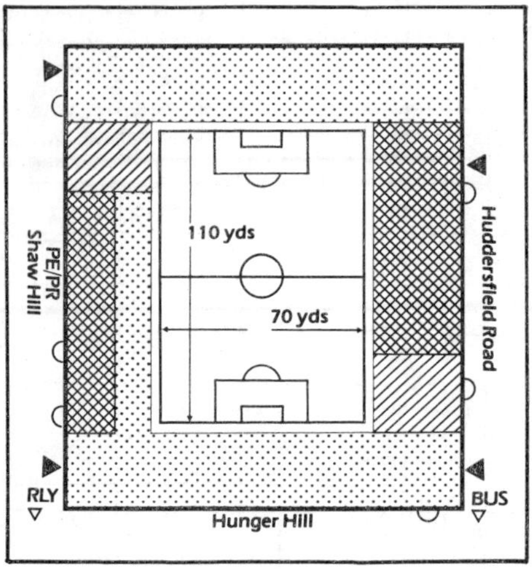

For key see page 12

How to get to the ground

From North: Use A629 into Halifax town centre, then at roundabout take 2nd exit into Broad Street and follow signs Huddersfield A629 into Skircoat Road for Halifax Town F.C.
From East, South and West: Use Motorway M62 until junction 24, leave Motorway and follow signs Halifax A629, then follow signs to town centre into Skircoat Road for Halifax Town F.C.

HARTLEPOOL UNITED Division 4

President
E Leadbitter, M.P.

Executive Vice-President
E Ord

Chairman
J W Smart

Vice-Chairman
J S Fullard

Directors
D Jukes
F Mulcaster (Financial)
J V Barker

Secretary
Mrs Linda Holmes

Manager
W Horner

Commercial Manager
S Lavelle
(0429 222077)

Club Coach
J Bird

Physiotherapist
T Johnson

Twenty-third position (i.e. 91st in the whole League) was achieved by Hartlepool in the Fourth Division last season and that meant a 'cap-in-hand' visit to the League A.G.M. for the umpteenth time. The question was now whether the ambitious Kent club, Maidstone United, would take their place and the North-Eastern outfit could thank the Southern directors for an earlier boardroom squabble, which may well have gone against them in the vote and made sure of Hartlepool's survival yet again.

There were no redeeming features on the playing side with a bottom-four place being virtually assured at an early stage of the season. There was also an early exit from each of the two cup competitions – both times against Rotherham United. In the Milk Cup only one goal was scored and that was in the second leg at home and in the F.A. Cup a replay after a good draw at Millmoor brought a single goal success for the 'Millers'.

The club, which started Brian Clough on his successful managerial career, needs another genius like him very badly if there are to be some improvement in fortunes. Can Billy Horner with backing from a new board achieve that? It is a daunting task and we wish them all well. We would also hope that the good people of Hartlepool value League Football enough to rally round their team.

WLM

Back Row L to R: John Brownlie, Graeme Hedley, Harry Wilson, Dave Robinson, Eddie Blackburn, John Bird (Player-Coach), Tony Smith, Phil Brown, Roy Hogan, Tommy Johnson (Physio). **Middle Row:** Brian Liddle, Les Mutrie, Paul Dobson, Billy Horner (Manager), Kevin Dixon, Barrie Wardrobe, Mark Taylor. **Front Row:** Mark Venus, Craig Farnaby, Mike Finch, Ian Ferguson.
Photograph courtesy Frank Reid

'THE POOL'

Formed: 1908 **Turned Professional:** 1908 **Ltd Co:** 1908
Previous Names: Until 1968 Hartlepools United; 1968-77 Hartlepool
Previous Managers: 1908-15 Fred Priest 1919-20 Jack Manners 1920-22 Cecil Potter 1922-24 David Gordon 1924-27 Jack Manners 1927-31 Bill Norman 1932-35 Jackie Carr 1935-39 Jimmy Hamilton 1943-57 Fred Westgarth 1957-59 Ray Middleton 1959-62 Bill Robinson 1962-63 Allenby Chilton 1963-64 Bob Gurney 1964-65 Alvan Williams 1965 Geoff Twentyman 1965-67 Brian Clough 1967-70 Angus McLean 1970-71 John Simpson 1971-74 Len Ashurst 1974-76 Ken Hale 1976-83 Billy Horner 1983 John Duncan 1983 Mick Docherty
Honours: None
League Career: Original members of Division 3(N) 1921 Transferred to Division Four 1958 Promoted to Division Three 1967-8 Relegated to Division Four 1968-9
Colours: Blue and white striped shirts, white shorts, blue stockings
Change Colours: All red with thin white stripes on shirt

CLUB RECORDS

Most Appearances for Club: Wattie Moore, 473, 1948-64 (League 448, F.A. Cup 25)
Most Capped Player: Ambrose Fogarty, 1, Eire **For England:** None
Record Goalscorer in a Match: Harry Simmons, 5 v Wigan Borough (6-1), Div 3(N), 01.01.1931 Bobby Folland, 5 v Oldham Athletic (5-1), Div 3(N), 15.04.1961
Record League Goalscorer in a season: Billy Robinson, 28, Div 3(N), 1927-8 **In all competitions:** Billy Robinson, 28
Record League Goalscorer in a career: Ken Johnson, 98, 1949-60 **In all competitions:** 106, Ken Johnson (League 98, F.A. Cup 6, League Cup 2)
Record Transfer Fee Received: £60,000 from Brighton for Malcolm Poskett, Feb 1978
Record Transfer Fee Paid: £10,000 to Sunderland for Ambrose Fogarty, Nov 1963
Best Performances: League: 22nd Div 3 1968-9 **F.A. Cup:** 4th Round 1954-5, 1977-8 **League/Milk Cup:** 4th Round 1974-5
Most League Points: 60 in Div 4, 1967-8 **Most League Goals:** 90, Div 3(N), 1956-7
Record League Victory: 10-1 v Barrow, Div 4, 4 Apr 1959
Record League Defeat: 1-10 v Wrexham, 3 Mar 1962

Club Statistician for the Directory: Gordon Small

Programme Editor
Stan Gate

Price	Number of Pages
40p	16

Subscriptions
Please apply to club

HARTLEPOOL UNITED

PLAYERS NAME Ht Wt Birthdate	Honours	Birthplace Transfers	Clubs	APPEARANCES League	Milk Cup	F.A.C.	A.M.C.	GOALS League	Milk Cup	F.A.C.	A.M.C.
GOALKEEPER											
Eddie Blackburn		Houghton-Le-	Hull C. (A)	68	2	5					
5-9 10.5 18.4.57		Spring £6,000	York C.	76	6	5					
		F	Hartlepool U.	61	2		1				
DEFENDERS											
Alan Barker		Newcastle	Newcastle U.	21+2							
5-10 10.8 18.12.55		£45,000	Gillingham	64				2			
		F	Ferryhill A.								
		F	Bishop Auckland								
		F	Hartlepool U.	59+1	2	3	1	1	2		
Phil Brown		Hartlepool	Hartlepool U.	169+6	10	9	1	7			
5-11 11.6 30.5.59											
John Brownlie	S.(7), U.23(5)	Caldercruix	Hibernian	206	35	18	13E	14	6		3E
5-11 11.0 11.3.52	SLC. 73, SL	N/D	Newcastle U.	124	4	7+1		2			
	D.C 72	£30,000	Middlesbrough	12	2	1					
		F	Hartlepool U.								
Bryan Liddle			Brandon U.								
5-9 11.0			Hartlepool U.								
Tony Smith*	E. S	Sunderland	Newcastle U.	1+1							
5-10 11.11 20.2.57		£10,000	Peterborough U.	68	3	4		5			
		F	Halifax T.	44	4	1		2			
		F	Hartlepool U.								
Harry Wilson	E. Y. S	Hetton	Burnley	10							
5-9½ 10.12 29.11.53		£35,000	Brighton	130	9	7		4			
		Player Exchange	P.N.E.	38+4	8						
		F	Darlington	82+3	2	3					
		F	Hartlepool U.	16	2	2					
MIDFIELD											
Paul Dobson		Hartlepool	Newcastle U. (N-C)								
5-11 10.2 17.12.62		F	Hartlepool U.	50+8			1	20			
Graham Hedley			Horden								
5-9 10.5											
Roy Hogan		Hartlepool	Hartlepool U.	150+10	6+1	6+1	1	17			
5-8 10.6 24.9.60											
David Linighan		Hartlepool	Hartlepool U.	31+4	0+1	3		1			
6-2 11.12 9.1.65											
FORWARDS											
Kevin Dixon		Consett	Carlisle U.	5+4							
5-10 11.0 27.7.60			Hartlepool U. (L)	6				3			
		F	Hartlepool U.								
Les Mutrie	E.S-P	Newcastle	Gateshead								
6-1 11.6 1.4.52			Carlisle U.	4+1							
			Blyth Spartans								
		£30,000	Hull City	114+1	6+2	8		49		1	
			Doncaster (L)	6				1			
		£10,000	Colchester U.	10+4			1+1	2			
			Hartlepool U.								
David Robinson		Cleveland	Hartlepool U.	6+1	2	2					
6-1 11.0 14.1.65											
Barry Wardrobe		Newcastle	Sunderland								
5-8½ 11.4 3.7.63		F	Hartlepool U.								

HARTLEPOOL UNITED

DIVISION FOUR 23RD **FA CUP** 1ST ROUND **MILK CUP** 1ST ROUND

MATCH	DATE	COMPETITION	VENUE	OPPONENTS	RESULT	HALF TIME	L'GUE POS'N	GOALSCORERS	ATTENDANCE
1	A 27	CL	A	Peterborough U	L 1-3	0-2		Robinson	3,213
2	**30**	**MC 1**	**A**	**Rotherham U**	**D 0-0**	**0-0**			**4,384**
3	S 3	CL	H	Aldershot	L 0-1	0-0	21		1,831
4	7	CL	H	Chesterfield	D 2-2	2-1		Waddle, Linighan A	1,661
5	10	CL	A	Bristol C	L 0-2	0-0	22		5,390
6	**14**	**MC 1**	**H**	**Rotherham U**	**L 0-1**	**0-0**			**2,321**
7	17	CL	H	Doncaster R	W 1-0	0-0	20	Staff	1,611
8	23	CL	A	Halifax T	L 2-3	2-1		Waddle, Lowe	1,416
9	27	CL	A	Rochdale	L 0-2	0-0			1,381
10	O 1	CL	H	Tranmere R	L 0-1	0-1	23		1,226
11	8	CL	A	Torquay U	D 0-0	0-0	23		1,936
12	15	CL	H	Wrexham	D 1-1	0-1	23	Bird	982
13	19	CL	H	Chester C	D 1-1	0-0		Bird	1,150
14	22	CL	A	Mansfield T	L 0-5	0-4	23		1,906
15	29	CL	H	Bury	L 1-3	0-2	23	Dixon	1,125
16	N 1	CL	A	Crewe Alex	L 0-2	0-2			2,117
17	5	CL	H	Hereford U	D 0-0	0-0	24		1,021
18	12	CL	A	Swindon T	L 2-3	1-1	24	Gibson (og), Ray	3,072
19	**19**	**FAC 1**	**A**	**Rotherham U**	**D 0-0**	**0-0**			**3,325**
20	**23**	**FAC 1R**	**H**	**Rotherham U**	**L 0-1[1]**	**0-0**			**2,635**
21	26	CL	H	York C	L 2-3	2-1	24	Dixon 2	2,012
22	D 3	CL	A	Colchester U	L 0-6	0-1	24		1,935
23	17	CL	A	Reading	L 1-5	1-3	24	Kennedy	2,737
24	26	CL	H	Darlington	W 2-1	0-1	24	Dobson 2	2,968
25	27	CL	A	Blackpool	L 0-1	0-0	24		4,562
26	31	CL	H	Northampton T	W 2-0	1-0	23	Burrows (og), Hogan (pen)	1,706
27	J 2	CL	A	Stockport Co	L 0-1	0-0	24		1,799
28	7	CL	A	Aldershot	L 1-2	1-0	24	Staff	1,637
29	28	CL	H	Bristol C	D 2-2	2-1	24	Dobson, Staff	1,881
30	F 3	CL	A	Tranmere R	W 1-0	1-0		Linacre P	1,774
31	11	CL	H	Halifax T	W 3-0	1-0	23	Linacre P, Kennedy, Hogan	1,658
32	15	CL	H	Crewe Alex	W 2-1	0-0		Lowe, Dobson	2,059
33	18	CL	A	Bury	L 0-3	0-2	23		1,565
34	**22**	**AMC 1**	**A**	**Bradford C**	**L 2-3**	**2-3**		**Dobson, Linighan**	**1,178**
35	25	CL	H	Mansfield T	W 4-1	0-1	23	Kennedy, Linacre P (pen), Dobson 2	1,734
36	M 3	CL	A	Chester C	L 1-4	1-3	23	Staff (pen)	1,241
37	7	CL	A	Hereford U	L 0-5	0-4			2,071
38	10	CL	H	Swindon T	L 0-1	0-1	23		1,274
39	17	CL	H	Torquay U	W 2-1	1-1	23	Bird, Dobson	969
40	24	CL	A	Wrexham	W 4-1	2-1	23	Dobson 3, Barker	1,181
41	27	CL	H	Peterborough U	D 1-1	1-1		Robinson	1,689
42	31	CL	H	Rochdale	L 1-2	0-1	22	Linacre P (pen)	1,245
43	A 7	CL	A	Chesterfield	L 1-4	0-4	23	Linacre P	2,263
44	10	CL	A	Northampton T	D 1-1	1-0		Staff	1,109
45	14	CL	H	Colchester U	D 0-0	0-0	23		1,001
46	20	CL	H	Blackpool	L 0-1	0-0			1,817
47	21	CL	A	Darlington	L 0-2	0-0	23		2,625
48	28	CL	A	York C	L 0-2	0-0	23		6,063
49	M 5	CL	H	Stockport Co	L 1-2	0-1	23	Linacre P	790
50	12	CL	H	Reading	D 3-3	1-1	23	Linighan A, Linacre P, Dobson	1,214
51	15	CL	A	Doncaster R	W 1-0	0-0		Dobson	3,770

[1] After Extra Time **Av Home Att 1,505**

Goal Scorers

League (47): Dobson 12, Linacre P 7 (2 pens), Staff 5 (1 pen), Bird 3, Dixon 3, Kennedy 3, Hogan 2 (1 pen), Linighan A 2, Lowe 2, Robinson 2, Waddle 2, Barker 1, Ray 1, opponents 2
FA Cup (-): —
Milk Cup (-): —
AMC (2): Dobson 1, Linighan A 1

1983-84

Blackburn	Brown	Wilson	Smithies	Linighan A	Bainbridge	Staff	Whitfield	Waddle	Johnson	Robinson M	Weir	Lowe	Linighan D	Lawrence	Bird	Hogan	Bassett	Linacre J	Dixon **(L)**	Linacre P	Dobson	Barker	Borthwick	Kennedy	REFEREE	
1	2	3		5	6	7	8	9	10	11															A Buksh	1
1	**2**	**3**		**5**	**6**	**7***	**8**	**9**	**10**	**11**		**12**													**R Guy**	**2**
1	2	3		5	6	7	8	9	10	11															I Hendrick	3
1	2	3		5	6*		8	9	10	11	12	7													D Hutchinson	4
1	2	3		5		12	8	9*	10	11	6	7													D Reeves	5
1	**2**	**3**		**5**		**7**	**8**		**10***	**11**	**6**	**9**	**12**												**M Peck**	**6**
1	2	3		5		7	8	9		11	6	10													N Glover	7
1	2	3		5		7	8	9		11†	6	10*	12												J Lovatt	8
1	2	3		5		7	8	9			6	10	11	4											TJ Holbrook	9
1	2	3		5		7	8	9		11	6	10*	12	4											K Hackett	10
1	2	3		5				9	11		7	8	6	10	4										E Read	11
1	2	3		5				9	11*		7	8	6	10	4		12								T Mills	12
1	2			5		8*	6	9	11	7				10	4		12								M Dimblebee	13
1	2*			5		7	6	9		8			11	10	4		12								I Borrett	14
1	2	3		5		7*	6			8				11	4		10		9						MP Scott	15
1*		3		5	12		6			8	7				4		10		9						DA Brazier	16
	12	3		5			6			8*	2	11			4		10		9		1				LR Dilkes	17
	7	3		5		10†	6			8		11	4						9						K Salmon	18
	7	**3**		**5**		**10**	**6**			**8**		**11**	**4**				**9***								**J Ashworth**	**19**
	7	**3**		**5**		**10**	**6**			**8**		**11***	**4**				**9**								**N Glover**	**20**
	7	3		5			12		11	8			4						9			6	10*		C Seel	21
1	7	3		5		10			11	8			4						9			6			A Gunn	22
1	4				5	10	2*					11	3				9					8		7	K Baker	23
1	2			5		11			12				6*			4		8			10	3	9	7	K Redfern	24
1	2			5	6	11										4		8			10	3	9	7	D Shaw	25
1	2			5	6	11										4		8			9	3	10	7	N Wilson	26
1	2			5	6	11			7							4		8			10	3	9		J Bray	27
1	2		12	5	6	11										4		8			10	3	9*	7	R Milford	28
1			2	5		11							6			4		8		9	10	3		7	D Allison	29
1			2	5		11							6			4		8		9	10	3		7	A Challinor	30
1			2	5		11						8	6			4				9	10	3		7	M Peck	31
1			2	5	6	11						8				4				9	10	3		7	R Banks	32
1	12		2	5	6							8				4		11		9	10	3		7	J Hough	33
1	**6**		**2**	**5**					**11**			**8**				**4**				**9**	**10**	**3**		**7**	**N Glover**	**34**
1	6		2	5		11						8				4				9	10	3		7	D Richardson	35
1	6		2	5		11			12			8				4					10*	3†	9	7	A Taylor	36
1			2	5		11			8				6			4				9	10	3		7	A Seville	37
1	2*			5		11						7			6	4		8		9	10	3		12	T Fitzharris	38
1				5		11				8*		7	3		6	4		2		9	10			12	D Scott	39
1				5		11			8			7*			6	4		2		9	10	3		12	T Jones	40
1				5		11*			8	7			6			4		2		9	10	3		12	K Walmsley	41
1				5					8	7		11	6*			4		2		9	10	3		12	J Key	42
			6	5		11†			8*				12			4		2		9	10	3		7	D Owen	43
1			6	5		11						8				4				9	10	3		7	L Robinson	44
1			6	5								8				4				9	10	3		7	A Robinson	45
1			3	5								8			6	4				9	10			7	D Hutchinson	46
1			3	5								8	12		6	4					10		9	7*	P Tyldesley	47
1	7		3	5								8			6	4				9	10	2	12		L Dilkes	48
1	7		2*									8	5		6	4		11		9	10	3			C Seel	49
1	8					7							6		5	4				9	10	3			J Worrall	50
	8*				5	7						9	6			4					10	3			J Ashworth	51
41	29	16	15	42	11	32	15	12	15	18	9	27	19	7	15	27	4	15	6	19	27	27	8	18	League Appearances	
	+2S		+1S		+1S	+1S	+1S		+2S		+1S		+4S				+3S						+1S	+5S		
	2	2		2		2	2			2		2	2				2								FA Cup Appearances	
2	2	2		2	1	2	2	1	2	2	1	1+1S	1S												Milk Cup Appearances	
1	1		1	1					1			1				1				1	1	1		1	AM Cup Appearances	

Also Played: Campbell matches 15, 23, no.12; 16, no.11. Stimpson 13, 14, no.3. Prudhoe **(L)** 17, 18, 21, no.1. Ray **(L)** 16, 18, 19, 20, 21, 22, no.2; 17, no.7. Buckley 1, 2, 3, 4, 5, 6, 7, 8, no.4. Moore 33, no.6. Roberts 19, 20, 43, no.1. Finch 51, no.1. Taylor M 45, 46, 47, 51, no.11, 48, 50, no.11*. Harrington 50, 51, no.12. Robinson D 44, 45, 46, 47, no.2; 49, no.12. Malley 22, no.12. Taylor D 45, no.11. Dixon 23, no.6.

THE VICTORIA GROUND

Official Address: The Victoria Ground, 18 Scarborough Street, Hartlepool. Telephone: 0429 72584 (0429 222077 - Office)

Ground Capacity: 18,000

Record Attendance: 17,426 v. Manchester United, F.A. Cup Round 3, 18 Jan 1957

Record Receipts: £17,000 v. Leeds United, F.A. Cup Round 3, 18 Jan 1979

Size of Playing Area: 113yds × 77 yds

Season Tickets: £47 (Stand) £35 (juveniles/OAP), £37 (Stand) £26 (juveniles/OAP)

Executive Box Season Tickets: none

Cost of Stand Tickets: £2.20 (£1.70 juveniles/OAP), Ground £1.70 (£1.20 juveniles/OAP)

Match and Ticket Information: No pre-booking of tickets.

Car Parking: side street parking is ample

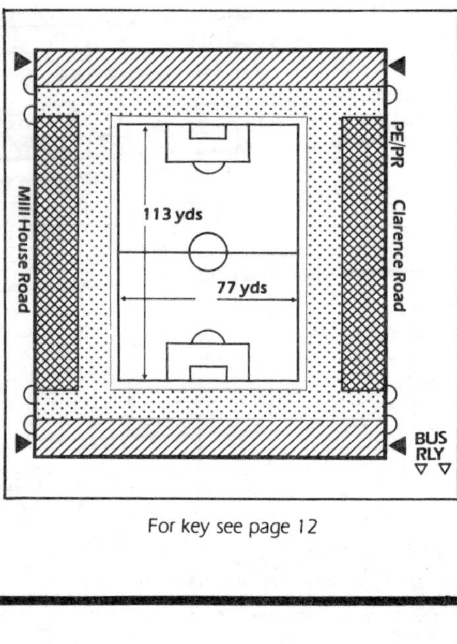

For key see page 12

How to get to the ground

From North: Use A1, A19 then A179 S.P. Hartlepool to Hart. In 2.5m at traffic signals forward, then at crossroads turn right into Clarence Road for Hartlepool United F.C.
From South, West: Use A1, A19 and A689 into Hartlepool town centre, then bear right into Clarence Road for Hartlepool United F.C.

HEREFORD UNITED Division 4

Chairman
PS Hill, FRICS

Directors
MB Roberts (Vice Chairman)
D Vaughan
J Jackson
AJ Phillips
GRE Rivers
GCE Hales

Football Admin Secretary
Jim Finney

Manager
John Newman

Assistant Manager
Alan Ashman

Commercial Manager
C Wyatt (0432 273155)

Physiotherapist
Peter Isaac

Groundsman
David James

For a club whose very existence has been seriously threatened in recent seasons, the latest campaign with a final Fourth Division position of eleventh was a distinct improvement, and now Third Division Football must be the aim of the management.

A good second half of the season produced a spot above half-way and the fans will hope that the upward trend will be maintained. The cups, the major English crowd pulling competitions, saw United exit early on both occasions. Portsmouth survived on aggregate by four goals to three in the Milk Cup First Round and with luck there could have been a better result there, but the First Round of the FA Cup took Hereford to Reading and defeat by two clear goals. In the Welsh Cup the semi-final was reached, which was a minor consolation.

As always the team needs players of consistency and dedication to maintain any momentum and money for new players is in short supply, but manager John Newman is one who has frequently shown a capacity for making 'bricks with straw' as a 'Manager of the Month' award during the recent season will indicate. In playing terms people like goalkeeper Rose, Maddy, Pejic and Dalziel would seem to provide a basis for producing the necessary consistency.

Even with limited resources the club should improve and thus tempt back local supporters who do not have much other local Football to act as a distraction if the results from Edgar Street are right. WLM

Back Row L to R: Leonard, Rose, Mullen, Kearns. **Middle Row:** Isaac (Trainer), Pejic, Larkin, Dalziel, Hicks, Maddy, Beacock, Carter. **Front Row:** Phillips, Price, Bray, Newman (Manager), Delve, Harvey, Emery.

'UNITED'

Sponsored by
Twenty's Holidays

Formed: 1924 **Turned Professional:** 1924 **Ltd Co:** 1939
Previous Managers: Since joining the Football League
Colin Addison John Sillett Tony Ford Mike Bailey Frank Lord
Honours: Division Three 1975-6
League Career: Elected to Division Four 1972 Promoted to Division Three 1972-3
Promoted to Division Two 1976-7 Relegated to Division Three 1976-7
Relegated to Division Four 1977-8
Colours: White shirts with red and black trim, black shorts, white stockings with red and black tops
Change Colours: All red

CLUB RECORDS

Most Appearances for Club: Tommy Hughes, 240, 1973-82
Most Capped Player: Brian Evans, 1, Wales **For England:** None
Record Goalscorer in a Match: No player has scored more than four goals
Record League Goalscorer in a season: 'Dixie' McNeil, 35, Div 3, 1975-6 **In all competitions:**
Record League Goalscorer in a career: 'Dixie' McNeil, 85, 1974-7 **In all competitions:**
Record Transfer Fee Received: £100,000 from Derby County for Steve Emery, Sept 1979
Record Transfer Fee Paid: £25,000 to Aston Villa for David Cunningham, Aug 1979
Best Performances: League: 22nd Div 2 1976-7 **F.A. Cup:** 4th Round 1971-2, 1976-7, 1981-2 **League/Milk Cup:** 3rd Round 1974-5 **Welsh Cup:** Finalists (3)
Most League Points: 67 in Div 4, 1981-2 **Most League Goals:** 86, Div 3, 1975-6
Record League Victory: 5-0 v Chesterfield, Div 3, 28 Sept 1974
5-0 v Chester, Div 3, 10 Aug 1975
6-1 v Crewe Alexandra, Div 4, 16 Sept 1978
5-0 v Hartlepool, Div 4, 7 March 1984
Record League Defeat: 0-5 v Wrexham, Div 3, 22 Dec 1973 1-6 v Tranmere Rovers, Div 3, 29 Nov 1974
1-6 v Wolverhampton Wanderers, Div 2, 2 Oct 1976

Club Statistician for the Directory: L. Appleby

Programme Editor
Ted Woodriffe

Price 40p

Number of Pages 20

Subscriptions
Contact Ron Parrott c/o Club

HEREFORD UNITED

PLAYERS NAME Ht Wt Birthdate	Honours	Birthplace Transfers	Clubs	APPEARANCES League	Milk Cup	F.A.C.	A.M.C.	GOALS League	Milk Cup	F.A.C.	A.M.C.
GOALKEEPER											
Kevin Rose		Evesham	Ledbury T.								
5-11 12.12 23.11.60			Lincoln C.								
		F	Hereford U.	61	2	2	1				
DEFENDERS											
Ian Bray		Neath	Hereford U.	63 + 3		3	1	3			
5-9 11.2 6.12.62											
Ian Dalziel		Sunderland	Derby Co. (A)	22	5 + 1	2 + 1		4			
5-8 11.10 24.10.62		F	Hereford U.	30	2			4			
Keith Hicks	E. Y, Div. 3, 74	Oldham	Oldham A. (A)	240 + 2	12	15	1	11			
6-0 13.2 9.8.54		F	Hereford U.	163				1			
Tony Larkin	Div. 3, 79	Wrexham	Wrexham								
6-0 11.2 12.1.56		F	Shrewsbury T.	54 + 1	2	5					
		£7,000	Carlisle U.	47 + 2	3	4		2			
		F	Hereford U.	20 + 1	1		1	1			
Carleton Leonard	Div. 3, 79	Oswestry	Shrewsbury T.	224 + 3	9	20		1		1	
5-9 10.3 3.2.58		F	Hereford U.	24 + 1	2	1	1				
Mel Pejic†		Newcastle-u-	Stoke C.	1							
5-7½ 10.6 27.4.59		Lyme F	Hereford U.	129	5 + 1	2	1	1	2		
Chris Price	E. Y	Hereford	Hereford U. (A)	245 + 3	12	12	0 + 1	18			
5-7 10.2 30.3.60											
MIDFIELD											
John Delve*		London	Q.P.R. (A)	9 + 6	0 + 1	1					
5-7 11.0 27.9.53		£25,000	Plymouth A.	127 + 5	8	8					
		£15,000	Exeter C.	215	17	13		20	3		
		F	Hereford U.	35 + 1	2			3			
Steve Emery	Div. 3, 76	Ledbury	Hereford U. (A)	203 + 1	17	11		10	1		
5-10 11.10 7.2.56		£100,000	Derby Co.	73 + 2	2	3		4			
		F	Newport Co.								
		F	Hereford U.	32 + 2	2	1	1		1		
Jimmy Harvey	N.I. U.23(1)	Lurgan	Glenavon								
5-9½ 11.4 2.5.58		£20,000	Arsenal	2 + 1							
		£35,000	Northampton T.								
		F	Hereford U.	166 + 2	8	8 + 1	1	19		1	
Paul Maddy	W. U.21(2), Y	Cwmcarn	Cardiff C. (A)	35 + 8		3		3			
5-10 10.9 17.8.62			Hereford U. (L)	9							
		F	Swansea C.	18 + 2				3			
		£10,000	Hereford U.	10				1			
FORWARDS											
Gary Beacock		Scunthorpe	Holland								
5-10 11.10 22.1.60		F	Grimsby T.	12 + 3		1 + 1					
		F	Hereford U.	13 + 1	2	1	1	3			
Mike Carter		Warrington	Bolton W. (A)	37 + 12	3 + 1	3		8			
5-9 10.7 18.4.60			Mansfield T. (L)	18				4			
			Swindon T. (L)	4 + 1							
		F	Plymouth A.	6 + 6	0 + 1			1			
		F	Hereford U.	10							
Ollie Kearns	Div. 4, 79	Banbury	Banbury U.								
6-2 12.9 12.6.56			Reading	75 + 11	4 + 2	6 + 1		40	1	2	
		F	Oxford U.	9 + 9	0 + 2	0 + 1		4			
		F	Walsall	31 + 7	2	2		11		1	
		F	Hereford U.	39 + 2	1	1	1	10			
Stuart Phillips		Halifax	Hereford U.	152 + 6	5 + 1	7		46	3	2	
6-0½ 11.7 30.12.61											

NON-CONTRACT PLAYERS 1984-85

Richard Mullen, Alan Riches, Martin Thomas, Shaun Bufton, Nick Isaac, Ian Maude, Martin Pearce, Ian Rodgerson, Alan Savoury

HEREFORD UNITED

DIVISION FOUR 11TH **FA CUP** 1ST ROUND **MILK CUP** 1ST ROUND

MATCH	DATE	COMPETITION	VENUE	OPPONENTS	RESULT	HALF TIME	L'GUE POS'N	GOALSCORERS	ATTENDANCE
1	A 27	CL	A	Aldershot	W4-1	2-0		Beacock, Dalziel, Phillips 2	2,001
2	**31**	**MC 1**	**H**	**Portsmouth**	**W3-2**	**1-1**		**Phillips 2, Pejic**	**4,631**
3	S 3	CL	H	Halifax T	D0-0	0-0	4		3,188
4	7	CL	H	Chester C	W2-1	1-1		Kearns, Phillips	3,480
5	11	CL	A	Doncaster R	L0-3	0-2	7		3,532
6	**13**	**MC 1**	**A**	**Portsmouth**	**L1-3**	**1-2**		**Beacock**	**8,363**
7	17	CL	H	Peterborough U	W2-1	2-0	3	Kearns, Harvey (pen)	3,172
8	23	CL	A	Tranmere R	W1-0	0-0		Price	1,984
9	27	CL	A	Chesterfield	D0-0	0-0			4,040
10	O 1	CL	H	Bristol C	L0-2	0-1	5		5,875
11	8	CL	A	Wrexham	D0-0	0-0	5		3,190
12	19	CL	H	Darlington T	W1-0	0-0		Phillips	3,024
13	22	CL	A	Torquay U	D1-1	1-0	5	Harvey	1,951
14	29	CL	H	Mansfield T	D0-0	0-0	8		3,110
15	N 1	CL	A	Swindon T	L0-3	0-3			3,645
16	5	CL	A	Hartlepool U	D0-0	0-0	11		1,021
17	12	CL	H	Northampton T	D0-0	0-0	12		3,007
18	**19**	**FAC 1**	**A**	**Reading**	**L0-2**	**0-0**			**4,453**
19	26	CL	H	Blackpool	L1-2	0-1	15	Phillips	2,801
20	D 3	CL	A	Rochdale	D3-3	1-0	15	Beacock, Phillips 2	1,261
21	17	CL	A	York C	L0-4	0-2	17		2,722
22	26	CL	H	Crewe Alex	L0-1	0-0	18		3,099
23	27	CL	A	Stockport Co	L0-1	0-1	19		2,287
24	J 2	CL	A	Reading	L1-3	0-1	21	Dalziel	4,548
25	7	CL	A	Halifax T	L1-2	0-2	21	Harvey	1,037
26	14	CL	H	Aldershot	W2-1	1-1	19	Dalziel, Emery	2,008
27	18	CL	H	Bury	L1-2	0-1		Kearns	2,013
28	21	CL	A	Peterborough U	D1-1	1-0	20	Kearns	2,559
29	28	CL	H	Doncaster R	L0-3	0-2	20		2,540
30	F 4	CL	A	Bristol C	L0-1	0-1	21		7,184
31	11	CL	H	Tranmere R	L0-1	0-0	21		2,188
32	15	CL	H	Swindon T	W2-1	1-1		Phillips, Kearns	2,002
33	18	CL	A	Mansfield T	D1-1	1-1	19	Bray	1,868
34	**22**	**AMC 1**	**H**	**Port Vale**	**L0-1**	**0-1**			**1,605**
35	25	CL	H	Torquay U	D1-1	0-0	20	Phillips	1,978
36	M 3	CL	A	Darlington	D0-0	0-0	19		1,520
37	7	CL	H	Hartlepool U	W5-0	4-0		Kearns 2, Linigham D (og), Phillips, Butler	2,071
38	10	CL	A	Northampton T	W3-0	0-0	17	Harvey, Kearns, Phillips	1,592
39	17	CL	H	Wrexham	W3-0	1-0	17	Dalziel, Harvey, Kearns	2,570
40	24	CL	A	Bury	W4-1	2-0	17	Butler, Harvey (pen), Phillips, Delve	1,497
41	31	CL	H	Chesterfield	W3-1	1-1	15	Phillips 2, Kearns	2,211
42	A 4	CL	H	Colchester U	D1-1	0-1		Phillips	2,501
43	7	CL	A	Chester C	W1-0	0-0	12	Harvey	1,346
44	14	CL	H	Rochdale	W2-1	1-1	10	Harvey, Delve	2,686
45	21	CL	H	Crew Alex	D1-1	0-0	11	Phillips	2,139
46	23	CL	H	Stockport C	W2-0	2-0	11	Phillips, Harvey (pen)	3,560
47	28	CL	A	Blackpool	L1-3	0-1	10	Larkin	2,143
48	M 5	CL	H	Reading	D1-1	0-0	12	Delve	3,611
49	7	CL	A	Colchester U	L0-3	0-1	13		1,286
50	12	CL	H	York C	W2-1	2-0	10	Maddy, Beacock	4,333

Av Home Att **2,914**

Goal Scorers

League (54): Phillips 17, Kearns 10, Harvey 9 (3 pens), Dalziel 4, Beacock 3, Delve 3, Butler 2, Bray 1, Emery 1, Larkin 1, Maddy 1, Price 1, opponent 1

FA Cup (-): —

Milk Cup (4): Phillips 2, Beacock 1, Pejic 1

AMC (-): —

1983-84

Rose	Emery	Leonard	Hicks	Larkin	Delve	Harvey	Beacock	Phillips	Black	Dalziel	Pejic	Kearns	Price	Bray	Hendrie **(L)**	Francis **(L)**	Butler **(L)**	Maddy	REFEREE	
1	2	3	4	5	6	7	8	9	10	11									A Moules	1
1	**2**	**3**	**4**	**5***	**6**	**7**	**8**	**9**	**10**	**11**	**12**								**K Cooper**	**2**
1	2	3	4		6	7	8*	9	10	11	5	12							J Deakin	3
1	2	3	4		6	7*		9	10	11	5	8	12						E Read	4
1	2	3	4		6	7	11	9	10		5	8							R Banks	5
1	**12**	**3**	**4**		**6**	**7**	**8**		**10***	**11**	**5**	**9**	**2**						**M Bodenham**	**6**
1	8	3	4		6	7		9	12	11*	5	10	2						M Heath	7
1	8	3	4		6	7		9	11		5	10	2						N Glover	8
1	8	3	4		6	7		9	11		5	10	2						R Bridget	9
1	8*	3	4		6	7	12	9	11		5	10	2						K Baker	10
1	8	3	4		6	7		9	11		5	10	2						I Hendrick	11
1	2	3	4		6	7	8	9		11	5	10								12
1	2	3	4		6	7	8	9		11	5	10							T Spencer	13
1	2	3	4		6	7	8	9		11	5	10							D Reeves	14
1	8	3*	4		6	7		9		11	5	10	2	12					D Letts	15
1	8	3	4		6	7		9		11	5	10	2						L Dilkes	16
1	8	3	4		6	7		9		11	5	10	2						L Shapter	17
1	**8**	**3**	**4**			**7**	**6**	**9**		**11**	**5**	**10**	**2**						**A Ward**	**18**
1	7	3	4		6	12	8	9		11	5	10*	2						J Martin	19
1	8	3	4		6	7	10	9		11	5		2						F Roberts	20
1	8		4		6	7	10	9		11*	5	12	2	3					G Courtney	21
1	6		4		12	7	10*	9		11	5	8	2	3					B Stevens	22
1	8	3	4		6	7		9		11	5	10	2						R Guy	23
1	6	3		4		8	10	9		11	5		2			7			Alan Robinson	24
1	12	3	4	6		8	10	9		11†	5		2*			7			N Wilson	25
1	6	3	4			8		9		11	5	10	2			7			V Callow	26
1	6	3	4			8		9		11	5	10	2			7			A Buksh	27
1	6	3	4			8		9			5	10	2		11	7			T Mills	28
1	6	3	4			8		9			5	10	2		7		11		K Barratt	29
1	2		4	6		8		9		3*	5	10		12	7		11		C Thomas	30
1	2		4	6		8		9			5	10*	12	3	7		11		T Bune	31
1	8		4	6				9			5	10	2	3	7		11		N Ashley	32
1	8		4	6				9			5	10	2	3	7		11		D Vickers	33
1	**8***	**2**	**4**	**6**		**7**		**9**			**5**	**10**	**12**	**3**			**11**		**E Crickmore**	**34**
1				4	8	7		9		6	5	10	2	3			11		N Midgley	35
1			4		8	7		9		6	5	10	2	3			11		D Owen	36
1			4		8	7		9		6	5	10	2	3			11		A Seville	37
1			4		8	7		9		6	5	10	2	3			11		L Burden	38
1			4		8	7		9		6	5	10	2	3			11		D Brazier‡	39
1				4	7	6		9		8	3	10	2	5			11		P Willis	40
1			4		8	7		9		11	5	10	2	3				6	J Lovatt	41
1			4		8	7		9			5	10	2	3			11	6	I Worrall	42
1			4		8	7		9			5	10	2	3			11	6	J Hunting	43
1			4		8	7		9			5	10	2	3			11	6	D Hedges	44
1			4		8	7		9			5	10	2	3			11	6	A Challinor	45
1	12		4		8	7		9			5	10	2†	3			11*	6	K Cooper	46
1	6		4	12	8*	7		9			5	10	2	3				11	R Nixon	47
1			3		8	7		9		11	4	10	2	5				6	F Roberts	48
1	2		4	5	8	7		9		11		10		3				6	D Letts	49
1	2	12	4		8	7	10*	9		11	5			3				6	B Hill	50
46	32	24	43	10	35	43	13	**46**	8	30	44	39	35	21	6	5	16	10	League Appearances	
	+2S	+1S		+1S	+1S	+1S	+1S		+1S			+2S	+2S	+2S						
1	1	1	1			1	1	1		1	1	1	1						FA Cup Appearances	
2	1+1S	2	2	1	2	2	2	1	2	2	1+1S	1		1					Milk Cup Appearances	
1	1	1	1	1		1		1			1	1	1S	1			1		AM Cup Appearances	

‡Injured referee replaced by D Shadwick

EDGAR STREET

Official Address: Edgar Street, Hereford. Telephone: (0432) 276666

Ground Capacity: 17,500

Record Attendance: 18,114 v. Sheffield Wednesday, F.A. Cup Round 3, 4 Jan 1958

Record Receipts: £12,666 v. Bristol City, F.A. Cup Round 4, 26 Jan 1974

Size of Playing Area: 111yds × 80 yds

Season Tickets: Merton Stand: £62.00 (£50.00 juveniles/OAPs); Len Weston Stand: £57.00 (£41.00 juveniles/OAPs); Ground: £42.00 (£24.50 juveniles/OAPs)

Executive Box Season Tickets: None available

Cost of Stand Tickets: £3.00; **Terraces:** £2.00 (juveniles/OAPs £1.30)

Match and Ticket Information: Bookable in advance

Car Parking: available near ground for 1,000 cars (approx)

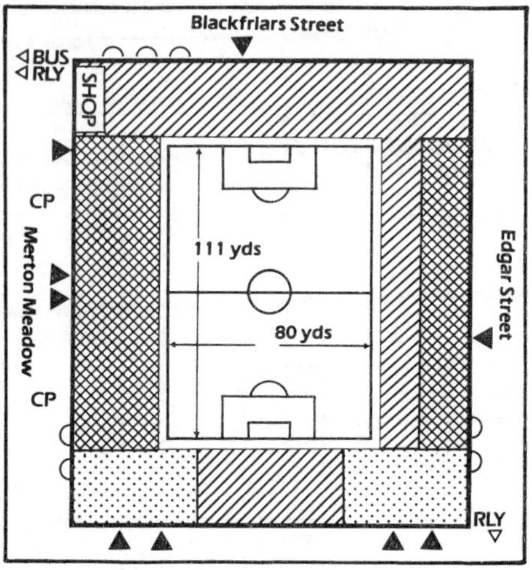

For key see page 12

How to get to the ground

From North: Use Motorway A49 (S.P. Hereford) into Edgar Street for Hereford United F.C.
From East: Use A465 or A438 (S.P. Hereford) into town centre, then follow signs Leominster A49 into Edgar Street for Hereford United F.C.
From South: Use A49 or A465 (S.P. Hereford) into town centre, then follow signs Leominster A49 into Edgar Street for Hereford United F.C.
From West: Use A438 (S.P. Hereford) into town centre, then follow signs Leominster A49 into Edgar Street for Hereford United F.C.

HUDDERSFIELD TOWN Division 2

Chairman
K Longbottom

Directors
J Christie (Vice-Chairman)
E Lodge
C Senior
F L Thewlis
B Buckley

Secretary
G S Binns

Assistant Secretary
Mrs M Baldwin

Commercial Manager
Maurice Porter

Promotions Manager
Steve Kindon (0484 34867)

Manager
Mick Buxton

Assistant Manager/Physiotherapist
John Haselden

Reserve Team Coach
Jimmy Robson

Youth Team Coach
Steve Smith

Chief Scout
Steve Smith

Groundsman
Raymond Chappell

The rehabilitation of Huddersfield Town continued during the recent season even though a position of twelfth in the Second Division might have been considered modest by their own great standards of the past. But since those great days there has been a spell right down in the Fourth Division and all the indications are that a season of consolidation may well lead to even better achievements.

It is true that at no time during the season did Town mount a serious promotion challenge and in the end the cup campaigns produced nothing very exciting, but the club scored more goals than were conceded and generally played attractively. It was a pity perhaps that League form fell away latterly when a move upwards was out of the question. In the major cups, success was limited but there were satisfying moments. In the Milk Cup Mansfield were beaten in both legs in the First Round and then Watford of the First Division were despatched on aggregate. It needed a replay to lose in the Third Round to Stoke City and this was a disappointment since a draw was achieved at the Victoria Ground before the men from the Potteries scored twice without reply at Leeds Road. The Third Round of the F.A. Cup brought the talented First Division players of Queen's Park Rangers to Yorkshire and the West London interest in the competition ended there thanks to goals by Lillis and Stonehouse. This should have meant a good cup run but Notts County shattered any ideas in that direction by winning (again 2-1) at Leeds Road in the Fourth Round.

Manager Mick Buxton has gathered a good squad together at Leeds Road with players like Burke, Sutton, Lillis, Stanton, Cowling and Wilson providing stability. An upward change of pace could be the small ingredient necessary for greater things and a reward for the patient and loyal local supporters.

WLM.

Back Row: Charlie Cooper, Mark Lillis, Dave Sutton, Sam Allardyce, Paul Jones, Ian Measham. **Middle Row:** Peter Butler, Stephen Doyle, Julian Winter, Brian Cox, Keith Mason, David Burke, Dale Tempest, Brian Stanton. **Front Row:** Liam Robinson, Phil Wilson, Brian Laws, Mick Buxton (Manager), John Haselden (First Team Coach), Dave Cowling, Graham Cooper, Daral Pugh.

'THE TERRIERS'

© 1973

Sponsored by **Daihatsu**

Formed: 1908 **Turned Professional:** 1908 **Ltd Co:** 1908
Previous Managers: F Walker R Puden J Howie A Fairclough A Langlry 1921 H Chapman 1925 C B Potter C Stephenson D Steele G Stephenson A Beattie E Boot T Johnston I Greaves R Collins T Johnston (reappointed)
Honours: Division One Champions 1923-4, 1924-5, 1925-6 (first of only three clubs to win the Championship three years in succession), Division Two Champions 1969-70, Division Four Champions 1979-80, F.A. Cup Winners 1922
League Career: Elected to Division 2 1910 Promoted to Division 1 1919-20
Relegated to Division 2 1951-2 Promoted to Division 1 1952-3
Relegated to Division 2 1955-6 Promoted to Division 1 1969-70
Relegated to Division 2 1971-2 Relegated to Division 3 1972-3
Relegated to Division 4 1974-5 Promoted to Division 3 1979-80
Promoted to Division 2 1982-3
Colours: Blue and white striped shirts, white shorts and white stockings
Change Colours: All yellow

CLUB RECORDS

Most Appearances for Club: W H Smith: Football League 519 + F.A. Cup 53 **Total 572**
Most Capped Player: Jimmy Nicholson, 31, Northern Ireland **For England:** Ray Wilson 30
Record Goalscorer in a Match: D Mangall, 5 v Derby County (h) 6-0 Div 1, 21.11.31 A.P. Lythgoe, 5 v Blackburn Rovers (h) 6-0 Div 1, 13.04.35
Record League Goalscorer in a season: Sam Taylor, 35, Div 2, 1919-20 **In All Competitions:** Dave Mangnall, 42 (League 33, F.A. Cup 9) 1931-2
Record League Goalscorer in a career: Jimmy Glazzard, 142, 1946-56 George Brown, 142, 1921-29
In All Competitions: George Brown, 161 (League 142, F.A. Cup 19)
Record Transfer Fee Received: £100,000 from Leeds United for Trevor Cherry, June 1972
Record Transfer Fee Paid: £110,000 to Mansfield for Terry Austin, Dec 1980
Best Performances: League: Champions (3) **F.A. Cup:** Winners (1) **League/Milk Cup:** Semi-Final 1967-8
Most League Points: 82 in Div 3, 1982-3
Record League Victory: 10-1 v Blackpool, Div 1, 13 Dec 1930
Record League Defeat: 0-8 v Middlesbrough, Div 1, 30 Sept 1950
Club Statistician for the Directory: J D Loughrey

Programme Editor

Price	**Number of Pages**
45p	24

Subscriptions
Apply to club

HUDDERSFIELD TOWN

PLAYERS NAME Ht Wt Birthdate	Honours	Birthplace Transfers	Clubs	APPEARANCES League	Milk Cup	F.A.C.	E. Cups	GOALS League	Milk Cup	F.A.C.	E. Cups
GOALKEEPERS											
Brian Cox		Sheffield	Sheffield Wed. (A)	22	4						
6-0 13.3 7.5.61		F	Huddersfield T.	82	12	4					
Keith Mason		Leicester	Huddersfield T.	20		2					
6-0 12.7 19.7.58											
DEFENDERS											
David Burke	E. Y	Liverpool	Bolton W. (A)	65+4	5	1+1		1			
5-10 10.7 6.8.60		F	Huddersfield T.	127	15	8		2			
Paul Jones†	Div. 3, 73	Ellesmere Port	Bolton W. (A)	440+4	30	31		38	4	1	
6-1½ 12.9 13.5.53	Div. 2, 78	F	Huddersfield T.	36	6			7		2	
Brian Laws	Div. 3, 82	Wallsend	Burnley (A)	125	14	15		12	2	1	
5-8 11.0 14.10.61		£10,000	Huddersfield T.	31	5						
Ian Measham		Barnsley	Huddersfield T. (A)								
5-10 11.8 14.12.64											
David Sutton*	Div. 4, 80	Tarleton	Plymouth A. (A)	60+1	2+1	3					
6-1 12.2 21.1.57			Reading (L)	9							
		£10,000	Huddersfield T.	242	23	19		11	1	3	
MIDFIELD											
Sam Allardyce		Dudley	Bolton W. (A)	180+4	15	14+		21	1	2	
6-1½ 14.0 19.10.54			Sunderland	24+1	2			2			
		£95,000	Millwall	63	3	5		2			
			Coventry C.	28	3	1		1			
			Huddersfield T.								
Charles Cooper		Huddersfield	Huddersfield T. (A)								
5-9 11.8 22.5.62											
David Cowling	Div. 4, 80	Doncaster	Mansfield T. (A)								
5-7 10.6 27.11.58		F	Huddersfield T.	224+5	18+	18		34	1	2	
Steve Doyle	W. U.21(2)	Neath	P.N.E. (A)	178+19	16+	17+		8			
5-9½ 11.1 2.6.58		F	Huddersfield T.	75+3	9			4			
Daral Pugh	W. U.21(2)	Sunderland	Doncaster R. (A)	136+18	12	9+1		15	1	1	
5-8 10.7 5.6.61		Player Exchange	Huddersfield T.	28+28	1+1	2		6			
Brian Stanton	Div. 4, 80	Liverpool	Bury	72+11	5	5		14			
5-7 10.7 7.2.56			Huddersfield T.	189+4	14	15		43	2	7	
Phil Wilson		Hemsworth	Bolton W. (A)	35+4	1	2		4			
5-6 10.4 16.10.60		F	Huddersfield T.	117+3	16	7		11	1		
Julian Winter		Huddersfield	Huddersfield T. (A)								
5-10 11.10 6.9.65											
FORWARDS											
Graham Cooper		Huddersfield	Huddersfield T. (A)	3				1			
5-9 11.8 22.5.62											
Mark Lillis		Manchester	Huddersfield T.	164+7	15	16+		42		4	
6-0 12.12 17.1.60											
Liam Robinson		Bradford	Huddersfield T.	4+1							
5-7 11.5 29.12.65											

NON-CONTRACT PLAYER FOR 1984-85

Steve Stoutt (3 Lg + 1 MC)

APPRENTICES

Phil Burns, Peter Butler, Bob Ragiste, Bob Turner, Ian Wadsworth, Andy Watson, Darren Wardman, Karl Buxton, Shaun Lynch, Graham Mitchell, Simon Trevitt

HUDDERSFIELD TOWN

DIVISION TWO 12TH **FA CUP** 4TH ROUND **MILK CUP** 3RD ROUND

MATCH	DATE	COMPETITION	VENUE	OPPONENTS	RESULT	HALF TIME	L'GUE POS'N	GOALSCORERS	ATTENDANCE
1	A 27	CL	A	Blackburn R	D2-2	0-1		Stonehouse (pen), Lillis	7,700
2	**30**	**MC 1**	**A**	**Mansfield T**	**W2-1**	**1-1**		**Sutton, Russell**	**3,734**
3	S 3	CL	H	Charlton Ath	D0-0	0-0	16		8,113
4	6	CL	H	Crystal Palace	W2-1	0-1		Lillis 2	7,814
5	10	CL	A	Oldham Ath	W3-0	0-0	5	Stanton, Cowling, Lillis	8,543
6	**13**	**MC 1**	**H**	**Mansfield T**	**W5-1**	**4-0**		**Lillis 2, Jones, Stanton, Sutton**	**5,190**
7	17	CL	H	Swansea C	W1-0	1-0	3	Stanton	10,116
8	24	CL	A	Carlisle U	D0-0	0-0	3		5,481
9	O 1	CL	H	Chelsea	L2-3	0-1	7	Stanton, Lillis	13,280
10	**4**	**MC 2**	**H**	**Watford**	**W2-1**	**0-0**		**Cowling, Bolton (og)**	**10,631**
11	8	CL	H	Grimsby T	D0-0	0-0	6		8,897
12	15	CL	A	Barnsley	D2-2	0-2	8	Lillis, Russell (pen)	14,096
13	18	CL	A	Cambridge U	W3-0	2-0		Lillis, Stanton, Russell (pen)	3,513
14	22	CL	H	Derby Co	W3-0	1-0	5	Lillis, Russell, Cowling	10,752
15	**25**	**MC 2**	**A**	**Watford**	**D2-2**	**1-2**		**Sutton, Jones**	**13,006**
16	29	CL	A	Sheffield W	D0-0	0-0	5		27,824
17	N 5	CL	A	Brighton & HA	L1-3	1-0	5	Sutton	11,063
18	**8**	**MC 3**	**A**	**Stoke C**	**D0-0**	**0-0**			**14,175**
19	12	CL	H	Shrewsbury T	W1-0	1-0	5	Wilson	8,798
20	19	CL	H	Fulham	W2-0	0-0	5	Stanton, Russell (pen)	8,914
21	**22**	**MC 3R**	**H**	**Stoke C**	**L0-2**	**0-1**			**14,191**
22	26	CL	A	Cardiff C	L1-3	0-1	5	Russell (pen)	6,067
23	D 3	CL	H	Portsmouth	W2-1	1-0	5	Pugh, Stonehouse	8,724
24	10	CL	A	Newcastle U	L2-5	2-2	6	Wilson, Jones	25,652
25	17	CL	H	Middlesbrough	D2-2	0-1	8	Cowling, Stonehouse (pen)	7,889
26	26	CL	A	Leeds U	W2-1	2-0	6	Russell, Lillis	23,791
27	27	CL	H	Manchester C	L1-3	0-2	8	Stonehouse	23,497
28	31	CL	A	Charlton Ath	W2-1	1-0	8	Hanvey, Russell	5,972
29	J 2	CL	H	Carlisle U	D0-0	0-0	9		10,131
30	**7**	**FAC 3**	**H**	**QPR**	**W2-1**	**1-0**		**Lillis, Stonehouse**	**7,984**
31	14	CL	H	Blackburn R	L0-2	0-1	9		8,203
32	18	CL	A	Swansea C	D2-2	1-1		Pugh, Lillis	4,944
33	**F 1**	**FAC 4**	**H**	**Notts Co**	**L1-2**	**1-2**		**Stonehouse**	**13,634**
34	4	CL	A	Chelsea	L1-3	0-2	9	Doyle	17,922
35	11	CL	H	Oldham Ath	L0-1	0-1	9		8,162
36	25	CL	A	Derby Co	D1-1	0-0	9	Stanton	14,529
37	M 3	CL	H	Brighton & HA	L0-1	0-1	10		6,985
38	10	CL	A	Shrewsbury T	L0-1	0-0	11		3,627
39	17	CL	A	Crystal Palace	D0-0	0-0	12		5,003
40	24	CL	H	Cambridge U	W3-0	2-0	11	Eves 2, Jones (pen)	6,037
41	31	CL	A	Grimsby T	L1-2	0-2	12	Jones (pen)	7,541
42	A 7	CL	H	Barnsley	L0-1	0-1	13		9,657
43	14	CL	A	Fulham	W2-0	2-0	12	Lillis, Eves	5,265
44	21	CL	H	Leeds U	D2-2	0-1	13	Eves, Doyle	16,270
45	23	CL	A	Manchester C	W3-2	2-2	10	Jones (pen), Pugh, Wilson	23,247
46	28	CL	H	Cardiff C	W4-0	0-0	11	Jones 3 (2 pens), Pugh	5,599
47	M 1	CL	H	Sheffield W	L0-1	0-0			18,488
48	5	CL	A	Portsmouth	D1-1	0-1	12	Robinson	7,738
49	7	CL	H	Newcastle U	D2-2	2-2	12	Cooper, Carney (og)	25,101
50	12	CL	A	Middlesbrough	D0-0	0-0	12		5,687
								Av Home Att	**11,020**

Goal Scorers

League (56): Lillis 11, Jones 7 (5 pens), Russell 7 (4 pens), Stanton 6, Eves 4, Pugh 4, Stonehouse 4 (2 pens), Cowling 3, Wilson 3, Doyle 2, Cooper 1, Hanvey 1, Robinson 1, Sutton 1, opponents 1

FA Cup (3): Stonehouse 2, Lillis 1

Milk Cup (11): Sutton 3, Jones 2, Lillis 2, Cowling 1, Russell 1, Stanton 1, opponent 1

1983-84

Cox	Bird	Burke	Stanton	Jones	Hanvey	Lillis	Stonehouse	Russell	Wilson	Cowling	Pugh	Laws	Sutton	Doyle	Mason	Robinson	Greenwood	Stoutt	Eves **(L)**	Eastoe **(L)**	Cooper	REFEREE	
1	2	3	4	5	6*	7	8	9	10	11	12											J Holbrook	1
1		**3**	**4**	**6**		**7**	**8**	**9**	**10***	**11**	**12**	**2**	**5**									**M Robinson**	**2**
1		3	4	6		7	8*	9		11	12	2	5	10								J Kough	3
1		3	4	6		7		9	10	11		2	5	8								N Ashley	4
1		3	4	6		7		9	10	11		2	5	8								R Bridges	5
1		**3**	**4**	**6**		**7**		**9**	**10**	**11**		**2**	**5**	**8**								**N Wilson**	**6**
1		3	4	6		7		9	10	11		2	5	8								PN Willis	7
1		3	4	6		7		9	10	11	12	2*	5	8								D Allison	8
1		3	4	6		7		9	10	11	2		5	8								J Lovatt	9
1		**3**	**4**	**6**		**7**		**9**	**10**	**11**		**2**	**5**	**8**								**R Nixon**	**10**
1		3	4	6		7		9*	10	11	12	2	5	8								V Callow	11
1		3	4	6		7		9	10	11		2	5	8								A Saunders	12
1		3	4	6		7		9	10	11		2	5	8								KG Salmon	13
1		3	4	6		7		9	10	11		2	5	8								R Guy	14
1		**3**	**4**	**6**			**7**	**9**	**10**	**11**		**2**	**5**	**8**								**T Bune**	**15**
1		3	4	6		7	12	9	10	11		2	5	8*								K Walmsley	16
1		3	4	6		7	8	9	10	11*	12	2	5									K Cooper	17
1		**3**	**4**	**6**		**7**	**8**	**9**	**10**	**11**		**2**	**5**									**D Hedoes**	**18**
1		3	4	6		7		9	10	11		2	5	8								J Worrall	19
1		3	4	6		7		9	10	11		2	5	8								K Redfern	20
1		**3**	**4**	**6**		**7**	**12**	**9**	**10**	**11**	**2**		**5***	**8**								**N Midgley**	**21**
1		3	4	6		7		9	10	11	12	2	5	8*								D Letts	22
1		3	4	6			8	9	10	11	7	2	5									MG Peck	23
1		3	4	6		7	8	9	10	12	11	2*	5									I Hendrick	24
1		3	4	6*		7	8	9	10	11	2		5	12								G Napthine	25
1		3	4		6	7	12	9*	10	11	2		5	8								G Courtney	26
1		3	4		6	7	9		10	11	2		5	8								M Scott	27
		3	4		6	7	8	9	10	11	2		5		1							Alan Robinson	28
		3	4		6*	7	8	9	10	11	2		5	12	1							F Roberts	29
		3	**4**		**6**	**7**	**9**		**10**	**11**	**2**		**5**	**8**	**1**							**K Barratt**	**30**
		3	4		6	7	9	12	10	11*	2		5	8	1							J Ashworth	31
		3	4*			7	9		10	11	2		5	8	1	12	6					R Bridges	32
		3			**6**	**7**	**9**	**12**	**10**	**11***	**4**		**5**	**8**	**1**			**2**				**A Saunders**	**33**
1		3		11	6		9	7	10		4		5*	8			12	2				J Deakin	34
1*		3	4	5	6	7	9	12	10	11	2			8								K Baker	35
		3	4	6		7			10	11	12	2	5	8	1	9*						C Thomas	36
		3	4	6		7			10	11	12	2	5	8	1	9*						C Seel	37
		3	4	6		7	9		10	11	12	2	5	8*	1							K Barratt	38
		3	4*	6		7	9		10	11	12	2	5	8	1							M Taylor	39
		3	4	6					10	11		2	5	8	1				7	9		R Nixon	40
		3	4	6		7			10	11		2	5	8	1					9		J Scales	41
		3	4	6		12			10	11		2	5	8	1				7	9*		M Heath	42
		3		6		9			10	11	4	2	5	8	1				7			Alan Robinson	43
		3		6	5*	9			10	11	4	2		8	1				7	12		N Wilson	44
		3		6		9			10	11	4	2	5*	8	1				7	12		D Owen	45
		3		6		5			10	11	4	2		8	1				7	9		G Tyson	46
		3		6		5			10	11	4	2		8	1				7	9		N Glover	47
		3		6					10	11	4*	2			1	7	12	5		9	8	M Dimblebee	48
		3		6					10	11		2		8	1	7*	12	5		9	4	J Lovett	49
		3		6		5			10	11	7	2		8	1					9	4	J Hough	50
23	1	**42**	33	36	9	36	15	23	41	40	19	31	34	34	19	4	1	3	7	8	3	League Appearances	
						+1S	+2S	+2S		+1S	+10S			+2S		+1S	+3S			+2S			
		2	1		2	2	2	1S	2	2	2		2	2	2			1				FA Cup Appearances	
6		6	6	6		5	3+1S	6	6	6	1+1S	5	6	4								Milk Cup Appearances	

LEEDS ROAD

Official Address: Leeds Road, Huddersfield HD1 6PE. Telephone: 0484 20335/6

Ground Capacity: 32,000

Record Attendance: 67,037 v. Arsenal, F.A. Cup Round 6, 27 Feb 1932

Record Receipts: £52,607 v. Newcastle United Division 2, 7 Mar 1984

Size of Playing Area: 115yds × 75 yds

Season Tickets: Centre Stand: £69 (£35 Juniors/OAP), £59 Outer Centre Stand (£30 Juniors/OAP), £50 Wing Stand (£25 Juniors/OAP), £40 Ground (£20 Juniors/OAP).

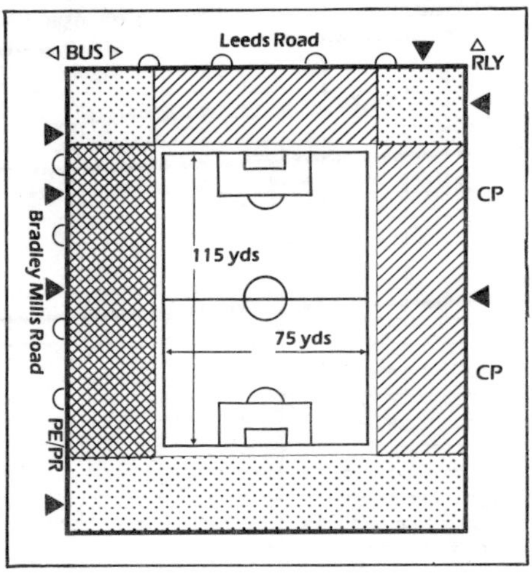

For key see page 12

Executive Box Season Tickets: consult Secretary

Cost of Stand Tickets: £3.20, £4.20 (£2.10 Juniors/OAP); **Terraces:** £2.30 (£1.30 Juniors/OAP)

Match and Ticket Information: Advance reservations only for special matches, otherwise admission to ground and stands on days of matches.

Car Parking: ample parking on all sides of the ground for 6,000 cars approx. All within 200 yards of ground.

How to get to the ground

From East and M1 (Junction 38): Use A642 (S.P. Huddersfield) into town centre, then follow signs Leeds A62 into Leeds Road for Huddersfield Town F.C.
From South: Use A616 (S.P. Huddersfield) into town centre, then follow signs Leeds A62 into Leeds Road for Huddersfield Town F.C.
From West: Use Motorway M62 until junction 23 then A640 or A62 into town centre, then follow signs Leeds A62 into Leeds Road for Huddersfield Town F.C.

HULL CITY

Division 3

Chairman
D Robinson

Vice-Chairman
T C Waite FIM, MIRTE

Directors
J Johnson MP
G H C Needler BA, ACA
C M Thorpe
H Bermitz
R Chetham

Secretary
To be appointed

Commercial Department
(0482-51119)

Player-Manager
Brian Horton

Assistant Manager/Coach
Chris Chilton

Reserve Team Player Manager
Dennis Booth

Physiotherapist
Jeff Radcliffe

So near and yet so far! That is the story of Hull City in 1983/84 when much was promised and nothing was won, but it could all have been very different. The last Third Division match of the season at Burnley was decisive and a three-clear-goal win was needed for promotion for the second successive season. With thirty minutes remaining Hull had a two goal lead but a resolute Burnley defence held out and Sheffield United took that remaining spot.

For long periods Hull were well in contention for that third promotion place and it was tragic that the reward for much hard work should have been taken away at the last moment — but that is Football. Even the cups could provide no consolation for that bitter disappointment with early departures from both the major competitions. In the Milk Cup, a goalless match at Boothferry Park was followed by a second leg defeat at Lincoln (1-3) and First Round elimination, whilst the F.A. Cup produced only a slight improvement in the form of a First Round win at Penrith through goals by G. Roberts and Whitehurst followed by a narrow defeat at Rotherham in the Second Round. The Tigers also won the Northern Section of the New Associate Members Cup and with a draw at home for the Final they were strong favourites to win against Bournemouth, but the latter had other ideas and an early Hull lead was overtaken by the fine South Coast cup fighters.

The big question is whether the club without the inspiration of Colin Appleton can recover from two disappointments and gain promotion to the Second Division. The playing staff looks good enough with a sound goalkeeper in Norman and impressive players outside him such as McNeil, Hollifield and Skipper but the brilliant young striker Marwood has left for First Division football at Hillsborough. If the team performs as well as it undoubtedly can the support will be excellent yet again and the right results will surely come. WLM

Back Row L to R: Gary Swann, Paul Olsson, Andy Flounders, Lawrie Pearson, Bobby McNeil, Ian Davis, Neil Williams. **Middle Row:** Chris Chilton (Assistant Manager), Mick Hollifield, John Davies, Billy Whitehurst, Tony Norman, Stan McEwan, Pete Skipper, Dennis Booth (Player/Coach). **Front Row:** Dale Roberts, Steve Massey, Garreth Roberts, Brian Horton (Player/Manager), Don Robinson (Chairman), Steve McClaren, Billy Askew, Jeff Radcliffe (Physiotherapist).

'THE TIGERS'

Formed: 1904 **Turned Professional:** 1904 **Ltd Co:** 1904
Previous Managers: 1905-13 Ambrose Langley 1913-4 Harry Chapman 1914-6 F G Stringer 1916-21 David Menzies (1) 1921-3 Harry Lewis 1923-31 Bill McCracken 1931-4 Haydn Green 1934-6 Jack Hill 1936 David Menzies (2) 1936-46 Ernie Blackburn 1946-8 Frank Buckley 1948-51 Raich Carter 1952-5 Bob Jackson 1955-61 Bob Brocklebank 1961-70 Cliff Britton 1970-4 Terry Neill 1974-7 John Kaye 1977-8 Bobby Collins 1978-9 Ken Houghton 1980-2 Mike Smith 1982-4 Colin Appleton
Honours: Champions Div 3 (N) 1932-3, 1948-9 Champions Div 3, 1965-6
League Career: Elected to Division 2 1905 Relegated to Division 3 (N) 1929-30 Promoted to Division 2 1932-3 Relegated to Division 3 (N) 1935-6 Promoted to Division 2 1948-9 Relegated to Division 3 (N) 1955-6 Division 3 1958 Promoted to Division 2 1958-9 Relegated to Division 3 1959-60 Promoted to Division 2 1965-6 Relegated to Division 3 1977-8 Relegated to Division 4 1980-1 Promoted to Division 3 1982-3
Colours: Amber shirts with red pin stripe and black trim, black shorts with amber and red stripe, black stockings with red and amber tops
Change Colours: All white.

CLUB RECORDS

Most Appearances for Club: Andy Davidson: Football League 520 + 43 F.A. Cup + 16 League Cup **Total 579**
Most Capped Player: Terry Neill, 15, Northern Ireland. **For England:** The following all went on dominions tours — Stan Alexander (Canada, 1931) Chris Chilton (Australia, 1971) David Mercer (South Africa, 1920) Ken Wagstaff (Australia, 1971). Gordon Wright won 20 caps at Amateur level — including one for the 1912 Olympic Games. He also won a full England cap on 19th March 1906 against Wales, which was just three weeks before his first appearance for Hull City. Most lists of international appearances show Portsmouth as his club, but the City management had been negotiating with Wright since the turn of the year. It may be that he was already a Hull City player when he won that full cap.
Record Goalscorer in a Match: Ken McDonald, 5 v Bristol City (5-1), Div 2 17.11.28
Sim Raleigh, 5 v Halifax Town (10-0), Div 3 (N) 26.12.30
Record League Goalscorer in a season: Bill McNaughton 41, Div 3 (N), 1932-3 **In all competitions:** Bill McNaughton, 42 (League 41, F.A. Cup 1) 1931-2
Record League Goalscorer in a career: Chris Clifton, 194, 1960-71 **In all competitions:** Chris Chilton, 220 (League 194, F.A. Cup 16, League Cup 10)
Record Transfer Fee Received: £200,000 from Manchester United for Stuart Pearson, May 1974
Record Transfer Fee Paid: £150,000 to Carlisle for Mick Tait, Sept 1979
Best Performances: League: 3rd Div 2 1909-10 **F.A. Cup:** Semi-Final 1930 **League/Milk Cup:** 4th Round, 1973-4, 1975-6, 1977-8
Most League Points: (2pts for a win): 69, Div 3 1965-6 (3pts for a win): 90, Div 4 1982-3
Most League Goals in a season: 109, Div 3 1965-6
Record League Victory: 11-1 v Carlisle United, Div 3 (N), 14 Jan 39
Record League Defeat: 0-8 v Wolverhampton Wanderers, Div 2 4 Nov 11 (At the time this game was played, Hull City were top of Division 2)

Club Statistician for the Directory: Chris Elton

Programme Editor
Andy Cochrane

Price	**Number of Pages**
30p	20

Subscriptions
£15.00 (postage paid U.K.) for season

HULL CITY

PLAYERS NAME Ht Wt Birthdate	Honours	Birthplace Transfers	Clubs	APPEARANCES League	Milk Cup	F.A.C.	A.M.C.	GOALS League	Milk Cup	F.A.C.	A.M.C.
GOALKEEPERS											
John Davies		Llandyssul	Cardiff C. (A)	7							
6-3 13.2 18.11.59		£12,000	Hull C.	24	1	2					
Tony Norman	W. Y	Mancot	Burnley								
6-1½ 12.8 24.2.58		£30,000	Hull C.	179	9	14	5				
DEFENDERS											
Dennis Booth		Stanley	Charlton A. (A)	67 + 10	1	4		5			
5-7½ 11.3 9.4.49		£7,000	Blackpool	12	3						
		£7,000	Southend U.	77 + 1	3	3		1			
		£9,000	Lincoln C.	162	18+1	13		9			
		£10,000	Watford	97 + 3	11	6		2			
		£40,000	Hull C.	121 + 1	6	12		2			
Mike Hollifield		Middlesbrough	Wolverhampton W. (A)	21		4					
5-10½ 11.0 2.5.61			Hull C.	33	2	2	3	1			
Bobby McNeil		Bellshill	Hull C.	111 + 3	7	14	4	3			1
5-8½ 10.9 1.11.62											
Dale Roberts	E. Y, FAYC. 73, 75	Newcastle	Ipswich T. (A)	17 + 1	1	4					
5-10½ 11.5 8.10.56	Y World Cup, 75		Hull C.	138 + 4	6	9	4	6			
Peter Skipper		Hull	Hull C.	22 + 1							
5-11 12.6 11.4.48			Scunthorpe U. (L)	+ 1							
		£10,000	Darlington	91	4	5		4			
		£10,000	Hull C.	92	6	2	5	5			
Gary Swann		York	Hull C. (A)	99 + 7	5	7	5	4			
5-8½ 10.10 11.4.62											
MIDFIELD											
Billy Askew		Lumley	Middlesbrough (A)	10 + 2							
5-6½ 10.2 2.10.59		F	Gateshead								
		F	Hull C.	65 + 4	3	3	3 + 2	7			
Ian Davis		Hull	Hull C. (A)	25 + 3			1	1			
5-11½ 12.6½ 1.2.65											
Brian Horton	Div. 2, 80, 82	Hednesford	Hednesford T.								
5-9 11.4 4.2.49			Port Vale	232 + 4	6	16		33		3	
		£30,000	Brighton	217 + 1	24	10		33	6	2	
		£100,000	Luton T.	118	8	6		8		2	
			Hull C.								
Steve McClaren		Fulford	Hull C. (A)	131 + 7	3 + 2	13	5	12		2	1
5-7½ 9.4 3.5.61											
Stan McEwan		Cambuskenneth	Blackpool (A)	204 + 10	16	13		24	6	2	
5-11 12.8 8.6.57		F	Exeter C.	65	4	3		15	1		
			Hull C.	16			4	1			1
Gareth Roberts*†		Hull	Hull C. (A)	192 + 2	9 + 2	18	4 + 1	29	1	2	2
5-4 10.2 15.11.60											
Neil Williams	E. Y	Watford (A)									
5-10 11.0 23.10.64	FAYC. 82										
FORWARDS											
Andy Flounders		Hull	Hull C. (A)	54 + 17	1 + 1	2 + 2	1 + 2	27	1	1	
5-7½ 10.0 13.12.63											
Steve Massey		Denton	Stockport Co. (A)	87 + 14	8	5		20	3	1	
5-11 11.5 28.3.58		F	Bournemouth	85 + 12	4	4 + 1		19	1	2	
		F	Peterborough U.	13 + 5		1 + 1		3			
		F	Northampton T.	60	4	5		26	3	1	
		F	Hull C.	11 + 2	2		1 + 1	4			
Paul Olsson		Hull	Hull C. (A)				1				1
5-10 10.7 24.12.65											
Mike Ring	1 Cup	Brighton	Brighton	15	1 + 1						
5-10 11.7 13.2.61		F	Morton	6							
		F	Ballymena	2	1						
			Hull City								
Billy Whitehurst		Thurnscoe	Mexborough								
6-0 13.0 10.6.59		£2,500	Hull C.	118 + 17	7 + 1	9	5	20	1	3	

HULL CITY

DIVISION THREE 4TH **FA CUP** 2ND ROUND **MILK CUP** 1ST ROUND

MATCH	DATE	COMPETITION	VENUE	OPPONENTS	RESULT	HALF TIME	L'GUE POS'N	GOALSCORERS	ATTENDANCE
1	A 27	CL	H	Burnley	W4-1	2-1		Whitehurst 2, Massey 2	9,764
2	**30**	**MC 1**	**H**	**Lincoln C**	**D0-0**	**0-0**			**7,036**
3	S 3	CL	A	Gillingham	W2-1	1-0	3	Mutrie, Marwood	3,019
4	7	CL	A	Bradford C	D0-0	0-0			3,391
5	10	CL	H	Millwall	W5-0	3-0	1	Roberts G, Mutrie 2, McNeil, Marwood (pen)	7,338
6	**13**	**MC 1**	**A**	**Lincoln C**	**L1-3**	**1-0**		**Skipper**	**4,630**
7	17	CL	A	Preston NE	D0-0	0-0	2		6,661
8	24	CL	H	Lincoln C	W2-0	0-0	1	Whitehurst 2	8,323
9	27	CL	H	Wimbledon	W1-0	0-0		Whitehurst	9,633
10	O 1	CL	A	Wigan Ath	D1-1	0-0	2	Flounders	4,858
11	8	CL	H	Sheffield U	W4-1	1-1	2	McClaren, Marwood 2, Mutrie	16,728
12	15	CL	A	Brentford	D1-1	0-1	2	Mutrie	4,258
13	18	CL	A	Bolton W	D0-0	0-0			6,397
14	22	CL	H	Plymouth Arg	L1-2	1-0	3	McClaren	8,807
15	29	CL	A	Oxford U	D1-1	1-0	3	Marwood	7,884
16	N 1	CL	H	Walsall	D2-2	2-0		Askew, Marwood	8,375
17	5	CL	A	AFC Bournemouth	W3-2	3-0	2	Marwood, Hollifield, Whitehurst	4,644
18	12	CL	H	Newport Co	D0-0	0-0	3		7,853
19	**19**	**FAC 1**	**A**	**Penrith**	**W2-0**	**2-0**		**Roberts G, Whitehurst**	**1,828**
20	26	CL	H	Orient	W2-1	0-0	3	Whitehurst 2	6,857
21	D 3	CL	A	Exeter C	L1-2	0-0	4	McNeill	3,099
22	**10**	**FAC 2**	**A**	**Rotherham U**	**L1-2**	**0-0**		**Flounders**	**6,885**
23	17	CL	A	Bristol R	W3-1	1-0	3	Marwood (pen), Roberts G 2	5,673
24	26	CL	H	Scunthorpe U	W1-0	1-0	3	Massey (pen)	18,461
25	27	CL	A	Rotherham U	W1-0	1-0	2	Skipper	6,298
26	31	CL	H	Port Vale	W1-0	0-0	2	Roberts G	9,431
27	J 2	CL	A	Southend U	D2-2	0-2	2	Flounders 2	2,737
28	28	CL	A	Millwall	L0-1	0-1	5		3,991
29	F 4	CL	H	Wigan Ath	W1-0	1-0	4	Marwood	6,841
30	11	CL	A	Lincoln C	W3-1	0-1	3	Marwood, Swann 2	5,370
31	**21**	**AMC 1**	**A**	**York C**	**W2-1**	**0-1**		**Taylor, McClaren**	**5,674**
32	25	CL	A	Plymouth Arg	L0-2	0-1	5		10,023
33	28	CL	H	Oxford U	L0-1	0-1			11,790
34	M 3	CL	H	Bolton W	D1-1	0-0	6	Roberts D	6,869
35	6	CL	H	AFC Bournemouth	W3-1	2-1		Flounders, McNeill, Taylor	8,047
36	10	CL	A	Newport Co	D1-1	0-0	6	Roberts G	2,813
37	**13**	**AMC 2**	**H**	**Bury**	**W1-0**	**0-0**		**McEwan**	**4,222**
38	17	CL	A	Sheffield U	D2-2	1-1	6	McClaren, Marwood	15,374
39	**20**	**AMC NQF**	**H**	**Preston NE**	**W3-0**	**2-0**		**Taylor, Roberts G 2**	**4,377**
40	24	CL	H	Brentford	W2-0	1-0	5	Marwood, Roberts D	6,158
41	27	CL	A	Walsall	L1-2	0-1		Flounders	6,851
42	31	CL	H	Bradford C	W1-0	1-0	6	Roberts G	7,743
43	A 7	CL	A	Wimbledon	W4-1	2-0	4	Marwood, Flounders, Roberts G,	
								McEwan (pen)	4,495
44	10	CL	H	Preston NE	W3-0	1-0		Roberts G, Flounders, Taylor	8,134
45	14	CL	H	Exeter C	W1-0	0-0	3	Taylor	8,238
46	17	CL	H	Gillingham	D0-0	0-0			9,179
47	21	CL	A	Scunthorpe U	L0-2	0-1	4		8,286
48	23	CL	H	Rotherham U	W5-0	3-0	3	Marwood, Whitehurst, Johnson (og),	
								Flounders 2	9,799
49	28	CL	A	Orient	L1-3	1-1	4	Whitehurst	3,020
50	**M 2**	**AMC NSF**	**H**	**Sheffield U**	**W1-0**	**0-0**		**Olsson**	**3,800**
51	5	CL	H	Southend U	W2-1	2-1	4	Roberts G, Massey	6,757
52	7	CL	A	Port Vale	L0-1	0-1	4		3,958
53	12	CL	H	Bristol R	D0-0	0-0	4		11,657
54	15	CL	A	Burnley	W2-0	1-0		Marwood 2	8,045
55	**18**	**AMC NF**	**H**	**Tranmere R**	**W4-1**	**1-0**		**Taylor 2, Roberts G 2**	**5,478**
56	**24**	**AMC F**	**H**	**AFC Bournemouth**	**L1-2**	**1-1**		**McNeill**	**6,544**
								Av Home Att	**9,251**

Goal Scorers

League (71): Marwood 16 (2 pens), Whitehurst 10, Flounders 9, Roberts G 9, Mutrie 5, Massey 4 (1 pen), McClaren 3, McNeill 3, Taylor 3, Roberts D 2, Swann 2, Askew 1, Hollifield 1, McEwan 1 (1 pen), Skipper 1, opponent 1
FA Cup (3): Flounders 1, Roberts D 1, Whitehurst 1
Milk Cup (1): Skipper 1
AMC (12): Roberts G 4, Taylor 4, McClaren 1, McEwan 1, McNeill 1, Olsson 1

1983-84

Norman	McNeil	Roberts D	Booth	Skipper	Wassell	Roberts G	McClaren	Marwood	Whitehurst	Massey	Mutrie	Hollifield	Askew	Swann	Flounders	Gill (L)	Saville	Cockin	Taylor	McEwan	Blackburn	Olsson	Davis	REFEREE	
1	2	4	6*	5	3	11	8	7	9	10	12													K Hackett	1
1	**2**	**4**		**5**		**11**		**7**	**9**	**10**	**12**	**3**		**8***				**6**						**N Glover**	**2**
1	2	4		5		11		7	9	10	8	3	6											T Bune	3
1	2	4		5		11		7	9		10	3	6	8										G Courtney	4
1	2	4		5		11		7	9*	12	10	3	6	8										L Dilkes	5
1	**2**	**4**		**5**		**12**		**7**	**9**	**11**	**10**	**3**	**6**	**8***										**I Borrett**	**6**
1	2	4		5		11		7	9		10*	3	6	8	12									J Hough	7
1	2	4		5		11*	12	7	9		10	3	6	8										R Nixon	8
1	2	4		5			8	7	9		10	3	6	11										N Midgley	9
1	2	4		5			8	7	9			3	6	11	10									K Barratt	10
1	2	4		5			8	7	9		10	3	6	11										K Redfern	11
1	2	4		5			8	7	9		10	3*	6	11	12									L Robinson	12
1	2	4		5			8	7			10	3	6	11	9									R Bridges	13
1	2	4		5			8	7	9		10	3	6	11*	12									P Tyldesley	14
1	2	4		5		12	8	7	9			3	6	11	10*									L Shapter	15
1	2	4		5		11	8	7	9			3	6		10									A Challinor	16
1	2	4		5		11	8	7	9			3	12	6*	10									J Moules	17
1	2	4	6	5		11	8	7	9		10	3												R Richardson	18
1	**2**	**4**	**6**	**5**		**11**		**7**	**9**			**3**	**8**		**10**									**D Hutchinson**	**19**
1	2	4	6	5		11	12	7	9	10		3	8*											NL Wilson	20
1	2	4	6	5		11	8	7	9	10				3										D Hedges	21
1	**2**		**3**	**5**		**11**	**8**	**7**	**9**			**4**	**6**		**10**									**R Nixon**	**22**
1	2		6	5		11	8	7	9			4		3	10									J Martin	23
1	2		6	5		11	8		9	10		3		4	7									T Jones	24
1	2		6	5		11	8		9	10*		3		4	7	12								D Hutchinson	25
1	2		6	5		11	8	7				3		4	9		10							A Saunders	26
1	2		6	5		11	8	7		10		3		4	9									M Dimblebee	27
1	2		6	5		11	12	7	9	4*			8	3	10									M Taylor	28
1	2		6	5		11	8	7	9			3		4					10					H Taylor	29
1	2		6	5			8	7	9			3	11	4					10					A Seville	30
1	**2**		**6**	**5**		**12**	**8**	**7**	**9**			**3**	**11***	**4**	**13**				**10***					**T Mills**	**31**
1	2		6	5		11	8	7	9			3		4					10					E Read	32
1	2		6	5		11	8	7	9			3		4	12				10*					D Scott	33
1	2	4		5		11	8	7	9				6	3	10									T Holbrook	34
1	2	4		5		11	8		9				6	3	10				7					K Walmsley	35
1	2	4		5		11		7		10*			6	3	9				12	8				E Scales	36
1	**2**	**4**		**5**		**11**		**7**		**12**			**6**	**3**	**9***				**10**	**8**				**J Ashworth**	**37**
1	2	4		5		11	9	7		12			6*	3					10	8				M Heath	38
1	**2**	**4**		**5**		**11**	**8**	**7**	**9**					**3**					**10**	**6**				**K Redfern**	**39**
1	2	4		5		11	8	7	9*				12	3					10	6				D Shaw	40
1	2	4		5		11	8	7					12	3	9				10*	6				B Hill	41
1	2			5		11	8	7				4	10	3	9					6				J Bray	42
1	2	12		5		11	8	7*				3	10	6	9					4				D Axcell	43
1	2			5		11	8					3	10	7	9				6	4				G Napthine	44
1	2			5		11	8		12			3	10	6	9				7*	4				G Tyson	45
1	2	10		5			8		9			3*	11	6	12				7	4				N Midgley	46
1	2			5		11	8*	7	9			3	12	6	10					4				T Fitzharris	47
1	2	3		5		11		7	9				10	6	8					4				R Banks	48
1	2	3		5		11	12	7*	9				10	6	8					4				V Callow	49
			6				**7**		**9**	**8**		**3**	**10**					**5**	**11**		**1**	**2**	**4**	**D Richardson**	**50**
1	2			5		11	8	7	9	10			6	3						4				D Allison	51
1	2	4		5		11	8	7	9	10*				3	12					6				L Dilkes	52
1	2			5		11	8		9			4	10*	3	12				7	6				P Tyldesley	53
1	2			5		11	8	7	9			4		3	12				10*	6				K Baker	54
1		**2**		**5**		**11**	**8***	**7**	**9**			**4**	**12**	**3**					**10**	**6**				**P Willis**	**55**
1	**2**	**4***		**5**		**11**	**8**	**7**	**9**				**12**	**3**	**13**				**10***	**6**				**G Courtney**	**56**
46	**46**	28	14	**46**	1	37	36	39	36	11	11	33	29	41	22	0	1	0	13	16				League Appearances	
		+1S				+1S	+4S		+1S	+2S	+1S		+4S		+8S	+1S			+1S						
2	2	1	2	2		2	1	2	2			2	2		2									FA Cup Appearances	
2	2	2		2		1+1S		2	2	2	1+1S	2	1	2				1						Milk Cup Appearances	
5	4	4	2	5		4+1S	5	5	5	1+1S		3	3+2S	5	1+2S			1	6	4	1	1	1	AM Cup Appearances	

BOOTHFERRY PARK

Official Address: Boothferry Park, Hull HU4 6EU. Telephone: (0482) 51119

Telegraphic: Tigers Hull

Ground Capacity: 34,000

Record Attendance: 55,019 v. Manchester United, F.A. Cup Round 6, 26 Feb 1949

Record Receipts: £28,863 v. Scunthorpe United, Division 3, 26 Dec 1983

Size of Playing Area: 112yds × 75 yds

Season Tickets: Stand: £75.00 (Main Stand), £50.00 (South), £35.00, £26.00 respectively juveniles/OAP; Ground: £30.00 (£22.00 juveniles/OAP)

Executive Box Season Tickets: None available

Cost of Stand Tickets: £5.00, £4.00 (£3.00, £2.00 respectively juveniles/OAP); **Terraces:** £2.50 (£1.20 juveniles/OAP)

Match and Ticket Information: Pay at turnstiles only except for special matches

Car Parking: At Kempton Park opposite Three Tuns Hotel, five minutes walk from ground.

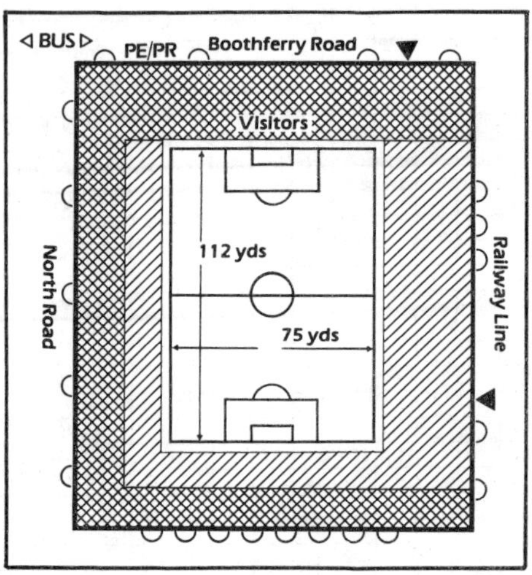

For key see page 12

How to get to the ground

From North: Use A1 or A19 then A1079 S.P. Hull into town centre then follow signs Leeds A63 into Anlaby Road, then at roundabout take 1st exit into Boothferry Road for Hull City F.C.
From West: Use Motorway M62 then A63 S.P. Hull into Boothferry Road for Hull City F.C.
From South: Use Motorway M1, M18 then M62 and A63 S.P. Hull into Boothferry Road for Hull City F.C.

IPSWICH TOWN Division 1

President
Lady Blanche Cobbold

Chairman
Patrick Cobbold

Directors
Kenneth Brightwell
John Kerr
John Kerridge
Murray Sangster
Harold Smith

Secretary
David Rose

Assistant Secretary
Peter Smith

Public Relations Officer
Mel Henderson

Commercial Manager
Tommy Parker (0473-221276)

Manager
Bobby Ferguson

Reserve Team Coach
Brian Owen

Coach
Charlie Woods

Youth Team Coach
Peter Trevivian

Physiotherapist
Tommy Eggleston

Chief Scout
Ron Gray

Groundsman
Winston Chapman

After years of success Ipswich Town alm[illegible] experienced disaster, but when relegation seemed inevitable a late rally brought a final position of twelfth, far better than might have been expected. A fair start was followed by a slump particularly in the first three months of 1984 and at one stage a bottom three situation existed with few signs of a revival, which only came at a time when a very difficult programme on paper had to be faced. Then excellent performances away to Liverpool and Manchester United and at home to Sunderland and Aston Villa completed the escape. The win at Old Trafford helped to deny United a top three place.

Problems were numerous; injuries to key players such as Butcher, Burley and Mariner and financial problems became public knowledge which not only reduced morale amongst the players but also made it necessary for players to be transferred to produce extra funds. Mariner (when finally fit) was transferred to Arsenal and a Liverpool bid for Wark had to be accepted. The team was now too inexperienced and it was not until the later matches that replacements in Zondervan (from WBA) and Alan Sunderland (on loan from Arsenal) made their ability count.

In the cups the Town form was moderate with a Second Round victory over Blackburn Rovers (both legs being won narrowly) being followed by a good Third Round Milk Cup win over Queen's Park Rangers. Norwich won in another home match for Ipswich in the Fourth Round and that was that. The FA Cup challenge ended quickly after a Third Round match at Cardiff had been impressively won with a Gates hat-trick. They next met Shrewsbury Town at the Gay Meadow for the third time in four years and there was a second successive cup defeat there by two late but well deserved goals.

Since cash is now short at Portman Road, Town must rely on the products of their good scouting and youth policies. Already Barnes, Yallop, Putney and Brennan can break through to regular first team places and if Burley, Osman, Butcher, Cooper (in goal) and Gates can recover previous form and (in some cases) fitness, Bobby Ferguson and his staff may expect better in the new season. The permanent signing of Alan Sunderland is a calculated gamble, but another season of struggle might well be experienced.

WLM

Back Row L to R: Iain Sankey, Romeo Zondervan, Frank Yallop, Keith Gorman, Michael Cole, Anthony Humes, Tommy Parkin, Robin Turner, Mark Brennan, Ian Cranson, Mick Stockwell. **Middle Row:** Bobby Ferguson (Manager), Charlie Woods (First Team Coach), Kevin Steggles, Russell Osman, Mark Grew, Jon Hallworth, Paul Cooper, Mich D'Avray, Jon Linford, Brian Owen (Reserve Coach), Peter Trevivian (Youth Coach). **Front Row:** David Barnes, Steve McCall, George Burley, Trevor Putney, Terry Butcher (Captain), Kevin O'Callaghan, Alan Sunderland, Irvin Gernon, Eric Gates.
Photo: I.T. Foto Sales

'BLUES' or 'TOWN'

Sponsored by **Pioneer**

Formed: 1887 **Turned Professional:** 1936 **Ltd Co:** 1936
Previous Managers: Since the club turned professional:
1936-7 M T O'Brien 1937-55 A Scott-Duncan 1955-63 Sir A E Ramsey 1963-4 J E T Milburn 1964-8 W H McGarry 1969-82 R W Robson
Honours: Division 1 Champions 1961-2 Division 2 Champions 1960-61, 1967-8 Division 3 (S) Champions 1953-4, 1956-7 UEFA Cup Winners 1980-1 F.A. Cup Winners 1977-8
League Career: Elected to Division 3 (S), 1954-5 Promoted to Division 2 1953-4 Relegated to Division 3 (S) 1954-5 Promoted to Division 2 1956-7 Promoted to Division 1 1960-1 Relegated to Division 2 1963-4 Promoted to Division 1 1967-8
Colours: Royal blue shirts with red horizontal band and three white stripes, white shorts, blue stockings with three white hoops
Change Colours: White shirt with red horizontal band and three blue stripes, black shorts and white stockings

CLUB RECORDS

Most Appearances for Club: Mick Mills **Total 737 + 4 subs**
Most Capped Player: Alan Hunter, 47, N Ireland. **For England:** Mick Mills, 40 + 2 subs
Record Goalscorer in a Match: Ray Crawford, 5 v Floriana (10-1), European Cup, 25.9.62
Record League Goalscorer in a season: Ted Phillips, 41, Div 3 (S), 1956-7 **All competitions:** Ted Phillips, 46 (League 41, F.A. Cup 5), 1956-7
Record League Goalscorer in a career: Ray Crawford, 203 **All competitions:** Ray Crawford, 244, 1958-63, 1966-9
Record Transfer Fee Received: £500,000 from Tottenham Hotspur for Alan Brazil, March 1983
Record Transfer Fee Paid: £250,000 to Millwall for Kevin O'Callaghan, Jan 1980
Best Performances: League: Champions (2) **F.A. Cup:** Winners **League/Milk Cup:** Semi-Final 1981-2
Most League Points: 64 in Div 3 (S), 1954-5
Most League Goals: 106, Div 3 (S), 1955-6
Record League Victory: 7-0 v Portsmouth, Div 2, 7 Nov 1964
7-0 v Southampton, Div 1, 2 Feb 1974
7-0 v W.B.A., Div 1, 6 Nov 1976
Record League Defeat: 1-10 v Fulham, Div 1, 16.12.63
European Competitions Entered: European Cup: 1962-3 **European Cup Winners Cup:** 1978-9 **UEFA Cup:** 1973-4, 1974-5, 1975-6, 1977-8, 1979-80, 1980-1, 1981-2, 1982-3

Club Statistician for the Directory: P. Voller

Programme Editor
Mel Henderson

Price	**Number of Pages**
50p	24

Subscriptions
£17.00 (home matches), £34.00 (home and away matches) per season (postage included).
1983-84 'Programme of the Year'.

IPSWICH TOWN

PLAYERS NAME Ht Wt Birthdate	Honours	Birthplace Transfers	Clubs	APPEARANCES League	Milk Cup	F.A.C.	E. Cups	GOALS League	Milk Cup	F.A.C.	E. Cups
GOALKEEPERS											
Paul Cooper	FAC. 78	Brierley Hill	Birmingham C. (A)	17	1	4	1				
5-11 12.7 21.12.53	UEFAC. 81	£27,000	Ipswich T.	339	26	35	34				
Mark Grew	FAYC. 76	Bilston	W.B.A.	33	8	5	+1				
5-10 11.3 15.2.58			Wigan A. (L)	4							
		£25,000	Leicester C.	5							
			Oldham A. (L)	5							
		£60,000	Ipswich T.								
DEFENDERS											
David Barnes	E. Y	London	Coventry C. (A)	9		4					
5-10 10.8 16.11.61			Ipswich T.	16+1							
George Burley	S.(11), U.23(2),	Cumnock	Ipswich T. (A)	351	26	40	27	6		3	1
5-9½ 11.0 3.6.56	U.21(5), Y, S.										
	FAC. 78,										
	UEFAC. 81										
Terry Butcher*	E.(24), B(1),	Singapore	Ipswich T.	203	19	18	22	10			3
6-4 14.0 28.12.58	U.21(7),										
	UEFAC. 81										
Ian Cranson		Easington	Ipswich T. (A)	8							
5-11¼ 12.4 2.7.64											
Irvin Gernon	E. U.21(1), Y	Birmingham	Ipswitch T. (A)	49	4	4					
6-0 11.13 30.12.62											
Russell Osman	E.(11), B(1),	Ilkeston	Ipswich T. (A)	265	22	28	29+	14	2	1	
6-0 11.10 14.2.59	U.21(7), Y,										
	UEFAC. 81,										
	FAYC. 75										
Kevin Steggles		Ditchingham	Ipswich T. (A)	38	4	3	2	1	1		
6-0 11.1 19.3.61			Southend U. (L)	3			1 AMP				
Frank Yallop	E. Y	Watford	Ipswich T. (A)	6							
5-10½ 10.3 4.4.64											
MIDFIELD											
Mark Brennan	E. Y	Bicester	Ipswich T. (A)	19	1+1			1			
5-9 11.1 4.10.65											
Steve McCall	E. U.21(6), Y	Carlisle	Ipswich T. (A)	159+8	15	12+		7		1	2
5-11 11.3 15.10.60	UEFAC. 81										
Tommy Parkin	FAYC. 73	Gateshead	Ipswich T. (A)	32+10	2	2	1+1				
5-7 10.4 1.2.56			Grimsby T. (L)	6	1						
			Peterborough U. (L)	3	2						
Trevor Putney†		Harold Hill	Brentwood								
5-9½ 10.3 11.2.61		F	Ipswich T.	49+6	3	1		5			
Romeo Zondervan	Hol.(6)	Surinam	F.C. Twente								
5-9½ 11.2 4.3.59		£225,000	W.B.A.	82+2	6	5		5			
		£70,000	Ipswich T.	8				2			
FORWARDS											
Mich D'Avray	E. U.21(2)	South Africa	Ipswich T. (A)	44+16	3	1+2	1+2	11		1	
6-1 15.0 19.2.62											
Eric Gates	E.(2), FAYC. 73,	Ferryhill	Ipswich T.	226+29	20+	19+	26+	60	5	5	7
5-6 10.4 28.6.55	UEFAC. 81										
John Linford		Norwich	Gorleston/Ipswich T.								
6-2 11.12 6.2.57			Colchester U. (L)	7							
			Southend U. (L)	6				3			
Kevin O'Callaghan	Ei.(14), U.21(1)	London	Millwall (A)	15+5	2	3+1		3	2	1	
5-8½ 10.9 29.10.61	Y, FAYC. 79	£220,000	Ipswich T.	62+38	8+3	3+5	1+7	3	1		
Alan Sunderland	E.(1), B(7),	Mexborough	Wolverhampton W. (A)	139+9	13+	16		29	4		
5-9 11.7 1.7.53	U.23(1), U.21(1),	£320,000	Arsenal	204+2	26	34	13	55	13	15	7
	FC. 74	F	Ipswich T.	15				3			
Robin Turner	E. Y, FAYC. 73	Carlisle	Ipswich T. (A)	22+26	1+2	5+1	1+3	1	2	2	1
5-9 10.8 10.9.55											

CONTRACT PLAYERS WITH NO FIRST TEAM APPEARANCES

Andy Crane, Tony Humes, Mike Stockwell, Mike Culls, Keith Gorman, Ian Sankey, John Hallworth, Mike Cole

APPRENTICES

Danny Brown, John Clinch, Jason Dozzell, Mark Rogers, Dallan Atkinson, Peter Grant, Chris Nunn, Chris O'Donnell, Martin Young

IPSWICH TOWN

DIVISION ONE 12TH **FA CUP** 4TH ROUND **MILK CUP** 4TH ROUND

MATCH	DATE	COMPETITION	VENUE	OPPONENTS	RESULT	HALF TIME	L'GUE POS'N	GOALSCORERS	ATTENDANCE
1	A 27	CL	H	Tottenham H	W3-1	1-0		Gates 2, Mariner	26,185
2	30	CL	A	Watford	D2-2	2-2		Mariner, Gates	15,388
3	S 3	CL	A	Notts Co	W2-0	0-0	2	Fashanu (og), Mariner	9,023
4	6	CL	H	Everton	W3-0	0-0		Mariner, Wark, Turner	16,543
5	10	CL	H	Stoke C	W5-0	3-0	2	Burley, Gatey, Wark 2 (1 pen), Mariner	16,315
6	17	CL	A	Birmingham C	L0-1	0-0	4		13,159
7	24	CL	H	WBA	L3-4	2-2	5	Wark (pen), Gates, Mariner	16,611
8	O 1	CL	A	Coventry C	W2-1	2-0	3	Mariner, O'Callaghan	10,492
9	**5**	**MC 2**	**H**	**Blackburn R**	**W4-3**	**0-2**		**Mariner, Wark 3 (1 pen)**	**11,478**
10	15	CL	H	QPR	L0-2	0-1	6		17,959
11	22	CL	H	Leicester C	D0-0	0-0	5		14,944
12	**26**	**MC 2**	**A**	**Blackburn R**	**W2-1**	**2-1**		**Hamilton (og), Wark**	**8,990**
13	29	CL	A	Southampton	L2-3	2-1	9	Mariner 2	18,515
14	N 5	CL	A	West Ham	L1-2	1-2	12	Osman	20,682
15	**9**	**MC 3**	**H**	**QPR**	**W3-2**	**1-1**		**Wark 2 (1 pen), Mariner**	**12,341**
16	12	CL	H	Arsenal	W1-0	0-0	10	Gates	21,652
17	19	CL	A	Nottingham F	L1-2	0-0	12	Butcher	14,979
18	26	CL	H	Liverpool	D1-1	0-0	12	Wark	23,826
19	**30**	**MC 4**	**H**	**Norwich C**	**L0-1**	**0-0**			**25,570**
20	D 3	CL	A	Sunderland	D1-1	1-1	13	Gates	15,555
21	10	CL	H	Manchester U	L0-2	0-1	13		19,779
22	17	CL	A	Aston Villa	L0-4	0-1	14		16,548
23	26	CL	H	Wolverhampton W	W3-1	1-0	13	Mariner, O'Callaghan, McCall	14,477
24	27	CL	A	Norwich C	D0-0	0-0	14		25,679
25	31	CL	H	Notts Co	W1-0	1-0		Mariner	14,146
26	J 2	CL	A	WBA	L1-2	1-1		Gates	11,199
27	**7**	**FAC 3**	**A**	**Cardiff C**	**W3-0**	**1-0**		**Gates 3**	**10,118**
28	14	CL	A	Tottenham H	L0-2	0-2	15		25,832
29	21	CL	H	Birmingham C	L1-2	1-1	17	D'Avray	12,900
30	**28**	**FAC 4**	**A**	**Shrewsbury T**	**L0-2**	**0-0**			**11.110**
31	F 4	CL	H	Coventry C	W3-1	2-0	15	Mariner, Brennon, Dozzell	13,406
32	11	CL	A	Stoke C	L0-1	0-0	15		10,315
33	21	CL	H	Southampton	L0-3	0-3			14,934
34	25	CL	A	Leicester C	L0-2	0-1	17		11,399
35	M 3	CL	H	West Ham U	L0-3	0-1	19		17,297
36	10	CL	A	Arsenal	L1-4	0-1	19	Gates	24,000
37	13	CL	A	Luton T	L1-2	0-1		Putney	8,776
38	17	CL	A	Everton	L0-1	0-1	20		18,013
39	24	CL	H	Watford	D0-0	0-0	20		14,956
40	31	CL	H	Luton T	W3-0	0-0	20	Gates, Putney, D'Avray	14,750
41	A 7	CL	A	QPR	L0-1	0-0	20		12,251
42	14	CL	H	Nottingham F	D2-2	0-1	20	Zondervan, D'Avray	15,429
43	21	CL	A	Wolverhampton W	W3-0	2-0	20	D'Avray, Osman, Sunderland	6,611
44	23	CL	H	Norwich C	W2-0	1-0	19	Zondervan, Sunderland	22,135
45	28	CL	A	Liverpool	D2-2	1-2	19	Gates 2	32,069
46	M 5	CL	H	Sunderland	W1-0	1-0	16	Osman	17,657
47	7	CL	A	Manchester U	W2-1	0-1	15	D'Avray, Sunderland	44,257
48	12	CL	H	Aston Villa	W2-1	1-1	12	Gates, D'Avray	20,043
								Av Home Att	**17,422**

Goal Scorers

League (55): Gates 13, Mariner 12, D'Avray 6, Wark 5 (2 pens), Osman 3, Sunderland 3, O'Callaghan 2, Putney 2, Zondervan 2, Brennan 1, Burley 1, Butcher 1, Dozzell 1, McCall 1, Turner 1, opponent 1
FA Cup (3): Gates 3
Milk Cup (9): Wark 6 (2 pens), Mariner 2, opponent 1

1983-84

Cooper	Burley	Gernon	Parkin	Osman	Butcher	Wark	McCall	Mariner	Gates	Putney	O'Callaghan	Turner	D'Avray	Kinsella	Steggles	Brennan	Barnes	Cranson	Sivell	Dozzell	Sunderland (L)	Yallop	Zondervan		REFEREE	
1	2	3	4	5	6	7	8	9	10	11*	12														M Scott	1
1	2	3	12	5	6	7	8*	9	10	4	11														B Stevens	2
1	2	3	12	5	6	7	8	9	10	4*	11														D Allison	3
1	2	3	4	5	6	7	8	9	10*		11	12													T Ward	4
1	2	3	4*	5	6	7	8	9	10	12	11														K Salmon	5
1	2	3*	4	5	6	7	8	9	10	12	11														A Robinson	6
1		3	2	5	6	7	8	9	10	4	11														J Moules	7
1	2	3		5	6	7	8	9*	10	4	11		12												N Glover	8
1	**2**	**3***		**5**	**6**	**7**	**8**	**9**	**10**	**4**	**11**		**12**												**D Vickers**	**9**
1	2	3		5	6	7	8	9	10	4*	11		12												K Barratt	10
1	2	3	4	5	6	7	8	9	10		11*	12													D Letts	11
1	**2**	**3**	**4**	**5**	**6**	**7**	**8**	**9**			**11**			**10**											**R Bridges**	**12**
1	2	3	4	5†	6	7	8	9			11			10											LM Robinson	13
1	2			5	6	7	3	9	8	4	11	12		10*											T Bune	14
1	**2**	**3***		**5**	**6**	**7**	**8**	**9**	**10**	**4**	**11**					**12**									**J Martin**	**15**
1	2				6	7	3	9	10	4	11				5	8									K Baker	16
1	2				6	7	3	9	10	4	11				5	8									A Saunders	17
1	2				6	7	3	9	10	4	11*		12		5	8									M Bodenham	18
1	**2**				**6**	**7**	**3**	**9**	**10**	**4**	**11**		**12**		**5**	**8***									**M Taylor**	**19**
1	2		4		6	7	8	9	10			12	11*		5		3								K Hackett	20
1	2		4		6	7	8	9	10	12	11				5*		3								B Hill	21
1		3*	2	6		7	8	9	10	4	11		12					5							D Scott	22
	2*	3		5	6	7	8	9	10	4	11		12						1						D Reeves	23
		3	2	5	6	7	8	9	10		11			4					1						J Hunting	24
		3	2	5	6	7	8	9	10		11			4					1						C Downey	25
		3	2	5	6	7	8	9	10	4*	11		12						1						J Lovatt	26
	2	**3**	**4**	**5**	**6**	**7**	**8**	**9**	**10**		**11***		**12**						**1**						**A Ward**	**27**
	2	3	4	5	6	7	8		10	11*	12		9						1						C Thomas	28
1	2	3	4*	5	6	7	8		10		11	12	9												M Dimblebee	29
1	**2**		**4**	**5**	**6**	**7**	**3**		**10**		**11**		**9**	**8**											**N Ashley**	**30**
1	2			5	6	7	3	9	10*	4	11					8				12					K Salmon	31
1	2	3*		5	6	7	11			4		10	9			8				12					J Worrall	32
	2		11	5	6	7	3			4*		12	9			8			1		10				D Axcell	33
1	2			5	6	7	3			4	11		9			8					10				D Vickers	34
1			2	5	6	7	3		11	4			9			8*				12	10				J Bray	35
1	2			5	6	7	8		11	4		9					3				10				Alan Robinson	36
1	2			5	6	7	8		11	4		9*					3			12	10				H Taylor	37
1				5	6	7	8			4*			9			11	3			12	10	2			A Seville	38
1				5	6		8		9	7						11	3				10	2	4		M James	39
1	2			5	6		3		11	7			9			8	12				10		4*		R Lewis	40
1	2			5			4		11	7			9	12		8*	3	6			10				J Deakin	41
1	2			5	6		10		11	7*		12	9			8	3						4		A Gunn	42
1				5			10		11	2			9			8	3	6			7		4		R Guy	43
1				5			7		11	2			9			8	3	6			10		4		A Challinor	44
1				5			3		11	7			9			8		6			10	2	4		T Mills	45
1				5			3		11	7			9			8		6			10	2	4		A Ward	46
1			12	5			3		11	7			9			8		6			10	2	4*		G Tyson	47
1			4	5			3		11	7			9			8		6			10	2			M Bodenham	48
36	28	19	18	37	34	32	**42**	23	37	32	23	3	17	4	5	19	10	8	6	0	15	6	8		League Appearances	
			+3S							+3S	+2S	+7S	+6S	+1S			+1S			+5S						
1	2	1	2	2	2	2	2	1	2		2		1+1S	1					1						FA Cup Appearances	
4	4	3	1	3	4	4	4	4	3	3	4		2S	1	1	1+1S									Milk Cup Appearances	

PORTMAN ROAD

Official Address: Portman Road, Ipswich, Suffolk IP1 2DA. Telephone: (0473) 219211

Ground Capacity: 37,000

Record Attendance: 38,010 v. Leeds United, F.A. Cup Round 6, 8 Mar 1975

Record Receipts: £105,950 v. AZ Alkmaar, UEFA Cup Final 1st Leg, 6 May 1981

Size of Playing Area: 112yds × 72 yds

Season Tickets: Stand: £65.00 (lowest), £82 (highest); Ground: £36 (adults), £18 (OAP/ juveniles)

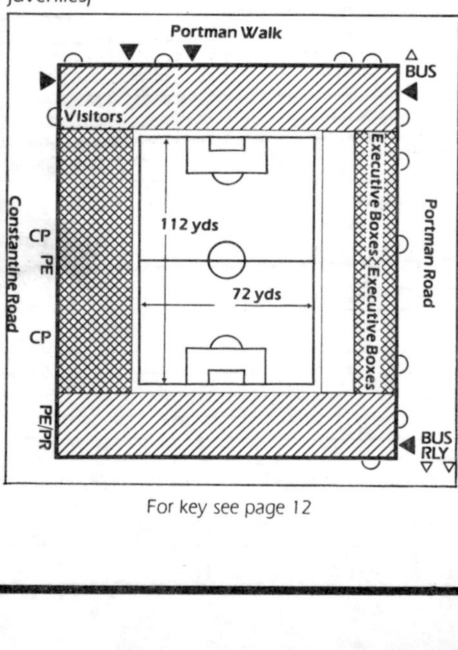

For key see page 12

Executive Box Season Tickets: Box rental £5,500 per year

Cost of Stand Tickets: £5.25, £4.70; **Terraces:** £2.20 (£1.10 OAP/juveniles)

Match and Ticket Information: On sale twelve days prior to each match. Postal bookings accepted

Car Parking: Large parks in Portman Road, Portman's Walk and off Princess Street at Greyfriars Park

How to get to the ground

From North and West: Use A45 (S.P. Ipswich) into Town Centre then follow signs Manningtree A137 then at roundabout take 3rd exit into Princes Street. In 0.2m turn right into Portman Road for Ipswich Town F.C.
From South: Use A12 S.P. Ipswich into town centre and follow signs Manningtree A137 then at roundabout take 3rd exit into Princes Street. In 0.2m turn right into Portman Road for Ipswich Town F.C.

LEEDS UNITED Division 2

President
Rt Hon Earl of Harewood

Chairman
L Silver OBE

Directors
M Cussins (Vice Chairman)
R Barker MCIT, MBIM
W J Fotherby
P J Gilman
G M Holmes
J W G Marjason
B Woodward

Chief Executive
T J Nash

Secretary
D J Dowse

Commercial Manager
T J Nash (0532 716037)

Manager
Eddie Gray MBE

Assistant Manager
J Lumsden

Reserve Team Coach
P Gunby

Youth Team Coach
K Mincher

Chief Scout
T Fawthrop

Physiotherapist
G Ladley

Groundsman
J Reynolds

Another Second Division season is ahead for the Peacocks after a very modest campaign and tenth place in 1983-84. Add in the fact that cup results were very poor and it all looks very bad for the future, but it could have been even worse since around the turn of the year relegation to the Third Division was a distinct danger. At this stage Manager Eddie Gray introduced some very promising youngsters such as Wright and brought back several experienced veterans like the two Peters — Barnes and Lorimer. With help from another veteran in goal (David Harvey) and the experienced striker Andy Ritchie disaster was somehow averted and with the 'player' part removed from his managerial title Eddie Gray may be able to blend the various ingredients into a fair combination for the new season.

So the league results could have been worse, but this could not be said for the cup performances, which were very poor. In the Milk Cup the ultimate basement team in the League, Chester City, left Elland Road with a lead after the first leg of the First Round and it needed a strong second half effort in the return for Leeds to survive for a meeting with Oxford United, which brought a promising draw at the Manor Ground and another humiliation at home (1-4). The F.A. Cup produced more disaster as Scunthorpe United follwed draws at Elland Road and the Old Show Ground with a decisive home win in the third match. This at least left the club with the chance to concentrate on safety, which was achieved, and 1984-85 is another season.

Prospects have been discussed already. The days of Leeds United being able to buy success are in the past so survival depends on shrewd signings where needs arise. The support is very demanding and only First Division football will satisfy Leeds people. One good feature of the season was the excellent support given by them without the regular instances of hooliganism which had brought a bad name to the club in recent seasons. WLM

Back Row L to R: Martin Dickinson, Neil Aspin, Andy Linighan, Tony Brown, George McCluskey, John Donnelly. **Middle Row:** Geoff Ladley (Physiotherapist), Keith Mincher (Youth Team Coach), John Stiles, John Sheridan, David Harvey, Philip Hughes, Denis Irwin, Peter Lorimer, Mark Gavin, Peter Gunby (Reserve Team Coach). **Front Row:** Andy Ritchie, Frank Gray, Scott Sellars, Eddie Gray (Manager), Jimmy Lumsden (Assistant Manager), Tommy Wright, Gary Hamson, Andy Watson.

'THE PEACOCKS' or 'THE WHITES'

Formed: 1919 **Turned Professional:** 1919 **Ltd Co:** 1920
Previous Names: Leeds City 1904-19 (disbanded on order by F.A.)
Previous Managers: 1920-7 Arthur Fairclough 1927-35 Dick Ray 1935-47 Billy Hampson 1947-48 Willis Edwards 1948-53 Major Frank Buckley 1953-8 Raich Carter 1958-9 Bill Lambton 1959-61 Jack Taylor 1961-74 Don Revie, OBE 1974 Brian Clough 1974-8 Jimmy Armfield 1978 Jock Stein 1978-80 Jimmy Adamson 1980-2 Allan Clarke
Honours: Division One Champions 1968-9, 1973-4 Division Two Champions 1923-4, 1963-4 F.A. Cup Winners 1972 Football League Cup Winners 1967-8 European Fairs Cup Winners 1967-8, 1970-1
League Career: Elected to Division 2 1920 Promoted to Division 1 1923-4
Relegated to Division 2 1926-7 Promoted to Division 1 1927-8
Relegated to Division 2 1930-1 Promoted to Division 1 1931-2
Relegated to Division 2 1946-7 Promoted to Division 1 1955-6
Relegated to Division 2 1959-60 Promoted to Division 1 1963-4
Relegated to Division 2 1981-2
Colours: All white with blue and yellow trim
Change Colours: All yellow with blue or yellow shorts and white trim

CLUB RECORDS

Most Appearances for Club: Jack Charlton, 1953-73 (League 629, F.A. Cup 52, League Cup 35, European Cups 56, Charity Shield 1) **Total 773**
Most Capped Player: Billy Bremner, 54, Scotland **For England:** Jack Charlton, 35
Record Goalscorer in a Match: Gordon Hodgson, 5 v Leicester City (H), Div 1 (8-2), 1 Oct 1938
Record League Goalscorer in a season: John Charles, 42, Div 2, 1953-4 **In All Competitions:** John Charles, 43 (League 42 + F.A. Cup 1)
Record League Goalscorer in a career: Peter Lorimer, 156, 1962-79, 1983- **In all competitions:** Peter Lorimer, 224 (156 League + 20 F.A. Cup + 8 League Cup + 30 European Cups)
Record Transfer Fee Received: £500,000 from Nottingham Forest for Frank Gray, July 1979
Record Transfer Fee Paid: £930,000 (gross fee) to Manchester City for Peter Barnes, Aug 1981
Best Performances: League: Champions (2) **F.A. Cup:** Winners (1) **League/Milk Cup:** Winners (1) **European Cup:** Finalists **European Cup Winners Cup:** Finalists **Fairs/U.E.F.A. Cup:** Winners (2)
Most League Points: 67 in Div 1, 1968-9 **Most League Goals:** 98, Div 2, 1927-8
Record League Victory: 8-0 v Leicester City, Div 1, 7 April 1934
Record League Defeat: 1-8 v Stoke City, Div 1, 27 Aug 1934
European Competitions Entered: European Cup: 1969-70, 1974-5 European Cup Winners Cup: 1972-3 European Fairs Cup: 1965-6, 1966-7, 1967-8, 1968-9, 1970-1 U.E.F.A. Cup: 1971-2, 1973-4, 1979-80

Club Statistician for the Directory: Julian Barker

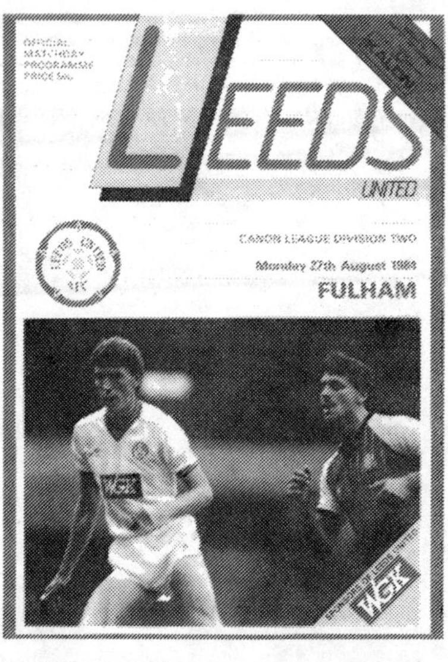

Programme Editor
T.J. Nash

Price	Number of Pages
50p	32

Subscriptions
£15.70 (U.K. postage included)

LEEDS UNITED

PLAYERS NAME Ht Wt Birthdate	Honours	Birthplace Transfers	Clubs	APPEARANCES League	Milk Cup	F.A.C.	E. Cups	GOALS League	Milk Cup	F.A.C.	E. Cups
GOALKEEPERS											
David Harvey*	S.(16), FAC. 72,	Leeds	Leeds U.	276	31	28	25+2				
5-11 12.10 7.2.48	Div. 1, 74	£40,000	Vancouver W.								
		F	Leeds U.	53	4	3					
Philip Hughes	N.I. Y	Belfast	Manchester U. (A)								
5-11½ 11.11 19.11.64		F	Leeds U.	2							
DEFENDERS											
Neil Aspin		Gateshead	Leeds U. (A)	36+1	2	7		1			
6-0 12.3 12.4.65											
Tony Brown		Bradford	Thackley								
6-2 12.7 17.9.58			Leeds U.	23				1			
Martin Dickinson		Leeds	Leeds U. (A)	71+1	4	5		1			
5-10 11.9 14.3.63											
Frank Gray	S.(32), U.23(5), S.	Glasgow	Leeds U.	188+5	18+1	19+1		17	4	3	
5-10 11.10 27.10.54	EC. 80, ESC. 79	£500,000	Nottingham F.	81	14	8		5	2	1	
		£300,000	Leeds U.	102+1	9	9		6			
Gary Hamson		Nottingham	Sheffield U. (A)	107+1	3	5		8	1		
5-9 11.11 24.8.59		£140,000	Leeds U.	65+8	2	8+1	1+1	3		1	
Dennis Irwin	Ei. Y, S	Cork	Leeds U. (A)	12		1					
5-7 10.3 31.10.65											
Andy Linigham		Hartlepool	Hartlepool U.	110	7+1	8	1 AMC	4	1		1 AM
6-3¾ 12.6 18.6.62		£20,000	Leeds U.								
Nigel Thompson		Leeds	Leeds U. (A)	1							
5-7 10.7 1.3.67											
MIDFIELD											
John Donnelly		Glasgow	Notts. Co. (A)								
5-11 11.5 8.3.61			Motherwell	21+4	1	+1		2			
			Dumbarton	73+5	8+4	5		17	5	2	
		£10,000	Leeds U.	36+3	3	1		4			
Peter Lorimer	S.(21), U.23(2), Y,	Dundee	Leeds U.	429+21	36+1	53+2	74+1	152	18	20	30
5-10 12.0 14.12.46	AM.S. FAC. 72,	Toronto B	York C.	29		3		8		1	
	Div. 1, 69, 74,		Toronto B								
	Lg.C. 68,		Vancouver W.								
	EFC. 68, 71		Leeds U.	20+2		2+1		4			
Scott Sellars		Sheffield	Leeds U. (A)	20		2		3			
5-8 10.0 27.11.65											
John Sheridan	Ei. Y	Stretford	Leeds U. (A)	38		2		3		1	
5-9 10.8 1.10.64											
Andy Watson	S. Y. SC.(1),	Aberdeen	Aberdeen	66+31	13+3	5+4	11	12	2	1	1E
5-10 11.0 3.9.59	SPD.(1), U.21(4),	£10,000	Leeds U.	30+1	4	1		7			
	ECWC. 83, SC.83										
FORWARDS											
Peter Barnes	E.(22), B.(1),	Manchester	Manchester C.	108+7	15+	6	9	15	4	2	1E
5-10 11.0 10.6.57	U.21(9), Y, S,	£748,000	W.B.A.	76+1	9+1	4	1	23	1	1	
	FC. 76, F.L.XI.	£930,000	Leeds U.	30	2			1			
		£115,000	Real Betis								
		F	Leeds U.	25+2	3	1		4	1		
Aidan Butterworth	E. S	Leeds	Leeds U.	54+10	4	6		15	1	1	
5-8 11.0 7.11.61											
Mick Gavin		Holytown	Leeds U. (A)	13+6	1+1			2			
5-9 11.4 10.12.63											
George McCluskey	S. U.21(7), S.	Hamilton	Celtic	109+31	21+6	12+3	9+3	54	11	12	5E
5-11 12.4 19.9.57	SPD.(3), SC.(1)	£140,000	Leeds U.	24+8	3+1			8			
Andy Ritchie	E. U.21(1), Y, S	Manchester	Manchester U. (A)	26+7	3	3		13			
5-9½ 11.11 28.11.60		£500,000	Brighton	82+7	3+1	9		23	1	2	
		Player Exchange	Leeds U.	48	4	3		10	2	1	
Tommy Wright†	S. Y	Fife	Leeds U. (A)	26+3	+1	3		9		3	
5-7 9.9 10.1.66											

CONTRACTED PLAYERS WITH NO FIRST TEAM APPEARANCES

Roger Eli (D), B. Bradford, John Stiles (MF)

NON-CONTRACT PLAYERS 1984-85

Terry Phelan, Peter Swan

APPRENTICES

Tom McDermott, Mark Russell, Bob Simm, Nigel Thompson

LEEDS UNITED

DIVISION TWO 10TH **FA CUP** 3RD ROUND **MILK CUP** 3RD ROUND

MATCH	DATE	COMPETITION	VENUE	OPPONENTS	RESULT	HALF TIME	L'GUE POS'N	GOALSCORERS	ATTENDANCE
1	A 27	CL	H	Newcastle U	L0-1	0-1			30,806
2	29	CL	H	Brighton & HA	W3-2	2-1		Watson, Gray F (pen), Sheridan	13,303
3	S 3	CL	A	Middlesbrough	D2-2	1-0	10	Gray F (pen), McCluskey	12,793
4	6	CL	A	Grimsby T	L0-2	0-1			7,723
5	10	CL	H	Cardiff C	W1-0	0-0	10	McCluskey	12,336
6	17	CL	A	Fulham	L1-2	0-0	13	Ritchie	10,005
7	24	CL	H	Manchester C	L1-2	0-0	14	Ritchie	21,918
8	O 1	CL	A	Shrewsbury T	L1-5	1-0	19	Ritchie	6,289
9	**5**	**MC 2**	**H**	**Chester**	**L0-1**	**0-1**			**8,106**
10	8	CL	A	Sheffield W	L1-3	0-1	19	Gray F (pen)	26,814
11	14	CL	H	Cambridge U	W3-1	1-0		Hird, Watson, Donnelly	9,923
12	22	CL	A	Barnsley	W2-0	0-0	13	Donnelly, Barnes	18,236
13	**25**	**MC 2**	**A**	**Chester C**	**W4-1**	**1-0**		**Ritchie 2, Burns, Barnes**	**8,044**
14	29	CL	H	Portsmouth	W2-1	1-0	12	Watson, Barnes	16,254
15	N 5	CL	H	Crystal Palace	D1-1	0-1	15	McCluskey	14,847
16	**8**	**MC 3**	**H**	**Oxford U**	**D1-1**	**0-1**		**McCluskey**	**13,349**
17	12	CL	A	Blackburn R	D1-1	1-0	15	Donnelly	9,556
18	19	CL	A	Derby Co	D1-1	0-0	15	Ritchie	16,726
19	**23**	**MC 3R**	**A**	**Oxford U**	**L1-4**	**0-3**		**Burns**	**13,389**
20	26	CL	H	Chelsea	D1-1	0-0	15	McCluskey	20,680
21	D 3	CL	A	Carlisle U	L0-1	0-0	16		6,845
22	15	CL	A	Charlton Ath	L0-2	0-1			6,283
23	26	CL	H	Huddersfield T	L1-2	0-2	19	Wright	23,791
24	27	CL	A	Oldham Ath	L2-3	1-0	19	Wright, Gray F	8,393
25	31	CL	H	Middlesbrough	W4-1	1-0	16	Sellers, McCluskey 2, Wright	14,125
26	J 2	CL	A	Manchester C	D1-1	0-1	17	Bond (og)	34,477
27	**7**	**FAC 3**	**H**	**Scunthorpe U**	**D1-1**	**1-0**		**Wright**	**17,130**
28	**10**	**FAC 3R**	**A**	**Scunthorpe U**	**D1-1**[1]	**0-0**		**Wright**	**13,129**
29	**16**	**FAC 3R2**	**A**	**Scunthorpe U**	**L2-4**	**1-2**		**Wright, Ritchie**	**13,312**
30	21	CL	H	Fulham	W1-0	1-0	16	Watson	11,390
31	F 4	CL	H	Shrewsbury T	W3-0	2-0	15	Watson 2, Brown	10,628
32	11	CL	A	Cardiff C	W1-0	0-0	12	McCluskey	9,407
33	15	CL	H	Swansea C	W1-0	0-0		Lorimer	10,031
34	18	CL	A	Portsmouth	W3-2	1-2	10	Wright, Watson, Lorimer (pen)	13,911
35	25	CL	H	Barnsley	L1-2	1-0	10	Wright	19,138
36	M 3	CL	A	Crystal Palace	D0-0	0-0	11		8,077
37	10	CL	H	Blackburn R	W1-0	0-0	9	Butterworth	12,857
38	17	CL	H	Grimsby T	W2-1	1-1	9	Aspin, Sellars	14,412
39	24	CL	A	Brighton & HA	L0-3	0-2	10		12,605
40	28	CL	A	Newcastle U	L0-1	0-1			30,877
41	31	CL	H	Sheffield W	D1-1	0-0	10	Ritchie	25,343
42	A 7	CL	A	Cambridge U	D2-2	0-0	10	Barnes, Sellars	4,700
43	14	CL	H	Derby Co	D0-0	0-0	10		12,549
44	21	CL	A	Huddersfield T	D2-2	1-0	10	Wright, Barnes	16,270
45	24	CL	H	Oldham Ath	W2-0	0-0		Ritchie, Lorimer (pen)	9,576
46	28	CL	A	Chelsea	L0-5	0-3	12		33,447
47	M 5	CL	H	Carlisle U	W3-0	0-0	11	Gavin, Ritchie, McCluskey	8,278
48	7	CL	A	Swansea C	D2-2	1-0	10	Wright, Lorimer	5,498
49	12	CL	H	Charlton Ath	W1-0	0-0	10	Wright	13,254

[1] After Extra Time

Av Home Att **15,5[illegible]1**

Goal Scorers

League (55): McCluskey 8, Wright 8, Ritchie 7, Watson 7, Barnes 4, Gray F 4 (3 pens), Lorimer 4 (2 pens), Donnelly 3, Sellars 3, Aspin 1, Brown 1, Butterworth 1, Gavin 1, Hird 1, Sheridan 1, opponent 1
FA Cup (4): Wright 3, Ritchie 1
Milk Cup (6): Burns 2, Ritchie 2, Barnes 1, McCluskey 1

1983-84

Harvey	Thomas	Gray F	Sheridan	Brown	Dickinson	Watson	McCluskey	Ritchie	Donnelly	Barnes	Butterworth	Irwin	Hamson	Aspin	Gavin	Hughes	Gray E	Burns	Wright	Thompson	Hird	McGoldrick (L)	Sellars	Lorimer	REFEREE	
1	2	3	4	5	6	7*	8	9	10	11	12														R Bridges	1
1	2	3	7	5	6	4	8	9		11	12		10*												K Redfern	2
1	10	3	7	5	6	4	8	9	12	11*				2											D Shaw	3
1	10	3	7	5	6	4	8		12		11			2*	10										H Taylor	4
	2	3	10*	5	6	4	8	9			12				11	1	7								A Worrell	5
	2	3	10	5	6	4	8	9			12				11	1	7*								C Thomas	6
1	2	3	7	5	6		8*	9	10						11			4	12						K Baker	7
1	2	3	7	5*	6	12	8	9	10						11			4							J Deakin	8
1	**10**	**3**		**5**	**6**	**4**	**12**	**9**			**8**				**11***						**7**	**2**			**A Saunders**	**9**
1	11	3	7		6	4*	8	9	10	12								5			2				R Nixon	10
1	11	3	7		6	4	8	9	10									5			2				NJ Ashley	11
1	11	3	7*		6	4	8	9	10	12								5			2				P Willis	12
1	**7**	**3**		**5**	**6**	**4**	**8**	**9**	**10**	**11**				**2**											**A Robinson**	**13**
1	7	3		6		4	8	9	10	11				2				5							GM Tyson	14
1	7	3			6	4*	8	9	10	11	12			2				5							G Napthine	15
1	**7**	**3**		**5**	**6**	**4**	**8**	**9***	**10**	**11**				**2**	**12**										**D Richardson**	**16**
1		3			6	4	8	9	10	11				2				5	7						M Heath	17
1	7	3			6	4	8	9	10	11								5				2			K Salmon	18
1	**7**	**3**		**5**	**6**	**4**	**8**	**9**	**10**	**11**									**12**			**2***			**M Bodenham**	**19**
1	7	3			6	4	8	9	10	11								5				2			N Midgley	20
1	7*	3		6	2	4	8	9	10	11			12					5							A Banks	21
1		3			6	4*	8	9	10	11			12					5	7			2			E Crickmore	22
1		3			6		8	9	10*				4					5	7		12	2	11		G Courtney	23
1		3			6		8*	9	10				4	5					7		12	2	11		C Seel	24
1		3			6†		8	9	10*				4	5					7			2	11	12	K Walmsley	25
1		3			6		8*	9	10				4	5					7			2	11	12	V Callow	26
1		**3***			**6**		**8**	**9**	**10**				**4**	**5**					**7**			**2**	**11**	**12**	**J Worrall**	**27**
1					**6**	**4**	**8**	**9**					**3**	**5**					**7**			**2**	**11**	**10**	**J Worrall**	**28**
1		**4**					**8**	**9**		**11**		**6**	**3**	**5†**			4		**7**			**2**		**10**	**G Tyson**	**29**
1						4		9		11		6	3	5					7		2		8	10	D Allison	30
1				5	6	4	12	9		11			3						7		2		8*	10	D Scott	31
1				5	6	4	12	9		11*			3						7		2		8	10	J Martin	32
1				5	6	4	12	9		11*			3						7		2		8	10	D Owen	33
1				5	6	4	12	9*		11			3						7		2		8	10	T Bune	34
1		6		5		4	9*			11			3		12				7		2		8	10	J Worrall	35
1	12			5		4				11		6			9		3*		7		2		8	10	Alan Robinson	36
1					6	4*		9		11	12		3	5					7		2		8	10	J Hunting	37
1				5	6			9		11			3	4					7		2		8	10	T Holbrook	38
1		3*		5	6			9		11	12			4					7		2		8	10	L Shapter	39
1					6			9		11	7	4	3	5							2		8	10	M Peck	40
1					6			9		11	7	4	3	5							2		8	10	D Richardson	41
1				6				9		11	7	4	3	5					12		2*		8	10	A Gunn	42
1					6			9	4*	11		2	3	5	12				7				8	10	P Tyldesley	43
1					6	4	12	9	10*	11		2	3	5					7					8	N Wilson	44
1					6	4		9	8			2	3	5	11				7					10	J Bray	45
1					6	4	12	9				2	3	5	11				7				8*	10	G Napthine	46
1				6		4	12	9	8			2	3	5*	11				7					10	N Ashley	47
1				6		4	12	9*	8			2	3		11				7	5				10	L Burden	48
1				6		4	9		8			2	3	5			11		7					10	I Hendrick	49
40	16	24	11	22	34	30	24	38	23	25	4	12	23	21	10	2	4	13	23	1	16	7	19	20	League Appearances	
	+1S					+1S	+8S		+2S	+2S	+7S		+2S		+2S				+2S		+2S			+2S		
3		1			2	1	3	3	1	1		1	3	3			1		3			3	2	2+1S	FA Cup Appearances	
4	4	4		4	4	4	3+1S	4	3	3	1			2	1+1S				1S		1	2			Milk Cup Appearances	

ELLAND ROAD

Official Address: Elland Road, Leeds LS11 0ES. Telephone: Leeds (0532) 716037 (3 lines).

Telegraphic: Football Leeds

Ground Capacity: 39,622

Record Attendance: 57,892 v. Sunderland, F.A. Cup Round 5 Replay, 15 Mar 1967

Record Receipts: £146,483, F.A. Cup Semi-Final Replay, Everton v. West Ham United, 16 Apr 1980

Size of Playing Area: 117yds × 76 yds

Season Tickets: Stands: From £83.00 to £102.00 (half price for juveniles & OAP)

Executive Box Season Tickets: £5,000 per annum (box of 8); £250 per annum, Executive Suite Membership

Cost of Stand Tickets: £5.00, £6.00 (£3.50 unreserved), half-price before 12 noon;**Terraces:** £2.50

Match and Ticket Information: Computerised for sale match by match. 24-hr answer phone: 0532 716037/8

Car Parking: Leeds Greyhound Association has park for 1000 cars (approx), one minute walk from ground.

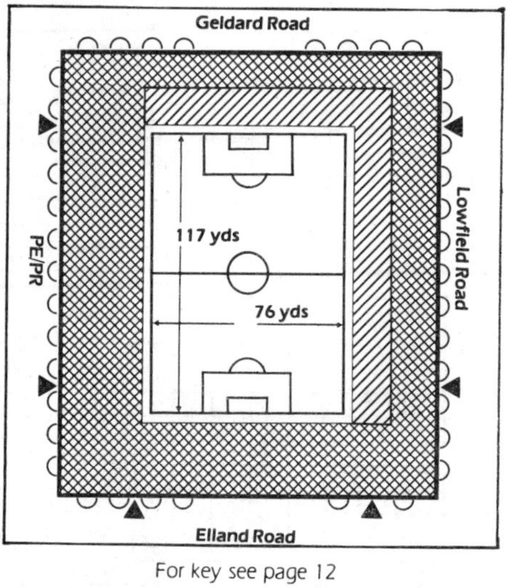

For key see page 12

How to get to the ground

From North: Use A58 or A61 into Leeds City Centre, then follow signs Motorway M621 to join Motorway. In 1.6m leave motorway and at roundabout join A643 into Elland Road for Leeds United F.C.
From East: Use A63 or A64 into Leeds City Centre, then follow signs Motorway M621 to join Motorway. In 1.6m leave motorway and at roundabout join A643 into Elland Road for Leeds United F.C.
From South: Use Motorway M1 then M621 until junction with A643, leave motorway and at roundabout join A643 into Elland Road for Leeds United F.C.
From East: Use Motorway M62 then M621 until junction with A643. Leave motorway and at roundabout join A643 into Elland Road for Leeds United F.C.

LEICESTER CITY Division 1

Chairman
T W Shipman

Vice-Chairman
T E Bloor

Directors
W G Page
D E Sharp
W K Shooter FCA
T Smeaton

General Secretary
A K Bennett

P.R.O.
Graham Clark

Manager
Gordon Milne

Assistant Manager/Club Coach
Gerry Summers

Youth Team Coach
Dave Richardson

Physiotherapist
John McVey

Commercial Manager
P Hill (0533) 555000

Goalless after three games, pointless after six and a record of one draw and nine defeats from the first ten, including the Milk Cup! This was by far and away Leicester's worst ever start to a season which had them firmly installed as everybody's favourites for relegation by late October. When taking into account the fact that Manager Gordon Milne had to operate on a shoestring budget, with a small first team pool, it was not surprising that most observers had the club favoured for quick relegation. Yet out of adversity a rare kind of fighting spirit is often born. Milne resisted the temptation to throw many untried youngsters into the fray, believing that the players who had put the club into the mess would just rescue them. The Manager's faith was rewarded when the players did that. Spirits rose dramatically following the first victory and the team's form between November and April was on a par with any of the challengers for European places.

Milne could not make any dramatic moves into the transfer market, but the two players he brought to Filbert Street during the season made an important impact. Bob Hazell's immense presence not only added much needed stability to the back four, but also helped John O'Neill to regain his best form and, eventually, his place in the Northern Ireland squad. Peter Eastoe, who came on loan from WBA, only played six games before sustaining a bad facial injury, but his effect on Alan Smith was equally dramatic. The young striker, who had been playing with Alvechurch only two seasons earlier, capped a fine season with his selection for the England Under-21 squad. Other notable successes included Mark Wallington, player-of-the-season Steve Lynex, Paul Ramsey, who also gained international recognition with Northern Ireland, and top scorer Gary Lineker, who finished the season as a member of the full England squad.

Although there were early exits in both cup competitions, there were some fine performances in the league campaign – particularly the two clashes with Liverpool, the home win over West Ham and, oddly enough, the away defeat by Aston Villa, which was the selection of many players as the best performance of the season.

All in all there seems to be every reason to be optimistic about 1984/85.

Dave Smith, The League Directory's Statistician for the Club

Back Row L to R: Robert Kelly, Andy Feeley, Andy Peake, Bob Hazell, Alan Smith, John O'Neill, Mark Bright, Tommy Williams. **Middle Row:** Dave Richardson (Youth Team Manager), Ian Banks, Paul Ramsey, Kevin MacDonald, Mark Wallington, Ian Andrews, Dave Rennie, Gary Lineker, Robert Jones, John McVey (Physiotherapist). **Front Row:** Scott Burnside, Steve Lynex, Gerry Summers (1st Team Coach), Gordon Milne (Manager), Bobby Smith, Ian Wilson.

Photograph: Neville Chadwick

'THE FILBERTS' or 'THE FOXES'

Sponsored by
Ind Coope

Formed: 1884 **Turned Professional:** 1894 **Ltd Co:** 1894
Previous Names: Leicester Fosse 1884-1919
Previous Managers: From 1884-1919 the club secretary took charge of all team matters. The first full time manager was appointed in 1919. The full list is:-
1919-26 Peter Hodge 1926-32 Willie Orr 1932-4 Peter Hodge 1934-6 Arthur Lockhead
1936-9 Frank Womack 1939-45 Tom Bromilow 1945-6 Tom Mather 1946-9 John Duncan
1949-55 Norman Bullock 1955-8 David Halliday 1959-68 Matt Gillies 1968-71 Frank O'Farrell
1971-7 Jimmy Bloomfield 1977-8 Frank McLintock 1978-82 Jock Wallace
Honours: Division 2 Champions 1924-5, 1936-7, 1953-4, 1956-7, 1970-1, 1979-80
Football League Cup Winners 1964
League Career: Elected to Division 2 1894 Promoted to Division 1 1907-8
Relegated to Division 2 1908-9 Promoted to Div 1 1924-5 Relegated to Div 2 1934-5
Promoted to Div 1 1936-7 Relegated to Div 2 1938-9 Promoted to Div 1 1953-4
Relegated to Div 2 1954-5 Promoted to Div 1 1956-7 Relegated to Div 2 1968-9
Promoted to Div 1 1970-1 Relegated to Div 2 1977-8 Promoted to Div 1 1979-80
Relegated to Div 2 1980-1 Promoted to Div 1 1982-3
Colours: Royal blue shirts with white pin stripe and trim, white shorts with blue side stripe, white stockings with blue stripes at top
Change Colours: Green shirts with yellow pin stripe and trim, green shorts with yellow side stripe, green stockings with yellow rings at top

CLUB RECORDS

Most Appearances for Club: Graham Cross: Football League 495 + 3 + F.A. Cup 59 + League Cup 40 + European Cup Winners Cup 2 **Total 596 + 3 subs**
Most Capped Player: Gordon Banks, 37, England
Record Goalscorer in a Match: John Duncan, 6 v Port Vale (7-0) (H), Div 2, 25.12.24
Arthur Chandler, 6 v Portsmouth (10-0) (H), Div 1, 20.10.28
Record League Goalscorer in a season: Arthur Rowley, 44 (5 pens), Div 2, 1956-7 **All competitions:** Arthur Rowley, 44 (all League)
Record League Goalscorer in a career: Arthur Chandler, 259, 1923-35 **All competitions:** Arthur Chandler, 273 (League 259, F.A. Cup 14)
Record Transfer Fee Received: £325,000 from Stoke City for Peter Shilton, Nov 1974
Record Transfer Fee Paid: £250,000 to F.C. Bruges for Roger Davies, Dec 1977
£250,000 to Oldham Athletic for Alan Young, July 1979
£250,000 to Patrick Thistle for Jim Melrose, July 1980
Best Performances: League: Runners Up Div 1 1928-9 **F.A. Cup:** Finalists 1949, 1961, 1963, 1969 **League/Milk Cup:** Winners **European Cup Winners Cup:** 2nd Round
Most League Points: (3pts for win) 70, Div 2, 1982-3 (2pts for win) 61, Div 2, 1956-7
Most League Goals: 109, Div 2, 1956-7
Record League Victory: 10-0 v Portsmouth, Div 1, 20 Oct 28
Record League Defeat: 0-12 v Nottingham Forest, Div 1, 21 Apr 09 (as Leicester Fosse)
European Competitions Entered: European Cup Winners Cup 1961-2 (Tottenham Hotspur, the winners of the F.A. Cup, were competing in the European Cup as League Champions)

Club Statistician for the Directory: Dave Smith

Programme Editor
Edited by Leicester News Service

Price	**Number of Pages**
50p	24

Subscriptions
£18.00 (home programmes) per season
(U.K. postage included)

LEICESTER CITY

PLAYERS NAME Ht Wt Birthdate	Honours	Birthplace Transfers	Clubs	APPEARANCES League	Milk Cup	F.A.C.	E. Cups	GOALS League	Milk Cup	F.A.C.	E. Cups
GOALKEEPERS											
Ian Andrews	E. Y	Nottingham	Leicester C. (A)	2							
6-2 12.12 1.12.64			Swindon T. (L)	1							
Mark Wallington	E. U.23(2). Y.	Sleaford	Walsall	11		1					
6-1 14.2½ 17.9.52	Div. 2. 80	£35,000	Leicester C.	401	21	25					
DEFENDERS											
Bob Hazell	E. B(1). U.21(1)	Jamaica, W.I.	Wolverhampton W. (A)	32 + 1		3		1			
6-1½ 14.1 14.6.59	Y. Div. 2. 83	£240,000	Q.P.R.	100 + 6	11 +	6		8		1	
		£100,000	Leicester C.	27	2	1		2			
John O'Neill	N.I.(25). U.21(1)	Lanark	Leicester C.	201	9	14		6		1	
6-0 13.3 11.3.58	Div. 2. 80										
Paul Ramsey	N.I.(3)	Londonderry	Leicester C. (A)	84 + 2	5	1		2			
5-10 12.0 3.9.62											
David Rennie	S. Y	Edinburgh	Leicester C. (A)	15	1						
5-11¾ 12.0 29.8.64											
Bobby Smith	Div. 2. 80	Dalkeith	Hibernian	146 + 6	13 +	8 + 1	11	19	2	2	
5-7 11.8 21.12.53		£85,000	Leicester C.	132 + 5	6 + 1	5		20		1	
			Peterborough U. (L)	5							
			Hibernian (L)	5				1			
Tommy Williams	Div. 2. 80	Leicester	Leicester C. (A)	201 + 5	9	14		10			
5-10 10.12 18.12.57											
Ian Wilson	Div. 2. 80	Aberdeen	Elgin C.								
5-7 10.11 27.3.58		£20,000	Leicester C.	170 + 6	11	10		11			
MIDFIELD											
Ian Banks		Mexborough	Barnsley (A)	158 + 6	20	11		37	3		
5-10½ 12.2 9.1.61			Leicester C.	22 + 4	1	1		3			
Mark Bright		Stoke	Leek T.								
6-0 11.0 6.6.62			Port Vale	18 + 11	1 + 1	0 + 1	2	10		1	
		£30,000	Leicester C.								
Andy Feeley		Hereford	Hereford U. (A)	50 + 1				3			
5-9 10.10 30.9.61		F	Trowbridge T.								
		£10,000	Leicester C.	2 + 1							
Mark Hutchinson	FAYC. 80	Stoke	Aston Villa (A)								
5-8 10.0 2.11.63			Leicester C.								
Robert Kelly		Birmingham	Leicester C. (A)	1							
5-9 10.13 25.11.65											
Kevin MacDonald		Inverness	Inverness Caley								
6-0¼ 11.11 27.12.60		£40,000	Leicester C.	120 + 5	8	4		8			
Andy Peake	E. U.21(1). Y.	Market	Leicester C. (A)	120 + 6	3 + 1	9		12			
5-9½ 11.2 1.11.61	Div. 2. 80	Harborough									
FORWARDS											
Robert Jones	W. Y	Coventry	Manchester C. (A)								
5-6½ 10.2 17.11.64			Leicester C.	8 + 2	1			3			
Gary Lineker	E.(1). Div. 2. 80	Leicester	Leicester C. (A)	146 + 7	6	9		71		3	
5-10 11.11 30.11.60											
Steve Lynex†	FAYC. 76	West Bromwich	W.B.A. (A)								
5-9 11.5 23.1.58		F	Shamrock R.								
			Birmingham C.	28 + 18	3	1 + 3		9	1		
		£60,000	Leicester C.	123 + 8	8	7		36	1		
Alan Smith	E.S-P(1)	Bromsgrove	Alvechurch								
6-2¾ 12.0 2.11.62			Leicester C.	74 + 5	2 + 1	2		28	1	1	

CONTRACTED PLAYERS WITH NO FIRST TEAM APPEARANCES

Mike Ford, B. Springfield

NON-CONTRACT PLAYERS 1984-85

Peter Bradley, Simon Morgan, Jon Pearson, Tony Robinson, Mahesh Thackrar, Jeremy Roberts

APPRENTICES

Paul Bunce, Derek Christopher, Bob Cooper, Wayne Homer, Phil Homer, Dean Meason, Steve Snaith

LEICESTER CITY

DIVISION ONE 15TH **FA CUP** 3RD ROUND **MILK CUP** 2ND ROUND

MATCH	DATE	COMPETITION	VENUE	OPPONENTS	RESULT	HALF TIME	L'GUE POS'N	GOALSCORERS	ATTENDANCE
1	A 27	CL	H	Notts Co	L0-4	0-2			14,838
2	31	CL	H	Luton T	L0-3	0-2			11,929
3	S 3	CL	A	WBA	L0-1	0-1	22		12,016
4	6	CL	A	West Ham U	L1-3	1-1		Lineker	22,131
5	10	CL	H	Tottenham H	L0-3	0-2	22		15,538
6	17	CL	A	Coventry C	L1-2	0-1	22	Lineker	12,377
7	24	CL	H	Stoke C	D2-2	2-2	22	Jones, Lineker	10,215
8	O 1	CL	A	Birmingham C	L1-2	0-2	22	Lineker	15,212
9	**5**	**MC 2**	**H**	**Chelsea**	**L0-2**	**0-2**			**7,825**
10	19	CL	A	Norwich C	L1-3	1-1		Eastoe	14,566
11	**25**	**MC 2**	**A**	**Chelsea**	**W2-0[5]**	**1-0**		**Smith A, English**	**15,646**
12	22	CL	A	Ipswich T	D0-0	0-0	22		14,944
13	29	CL	H	Everton	W2-0	2-0	21	Smith A, Ramsey	10,953
14	N 5	CL	A	Watford	D3-3	1-2	21	Lynex 2 (1 pen), Banks	15,807
15	12	CL	H	Manchester U	D1-1	0-1	21	Lynex	23,012
16	19	CL	A	Aston Villa	L1-3	1-2	21	Lynex (pen)	19,024
17	26	CL	H	Arsenal	W3-0	2-0	21	Lineker, Lynex, Smith A	14,777
18	30	CL	H	Southampton	W2-1	1-0		Smith A, Lineker	14,181
19	D 4	CL	A	Nottingham F	L2-3	0-2		Jones, Smith A	23,248
20	10	CL	H	Wolverhampton W	W5-1	4-1	20	Lineker, Smith A 3, Lynex	10,969
21	18	CL	A	Sunderland	D1-1	0-0		Hazell	16,993
22	26	CL	H	QPR	W2-1	1-0	17	Lineker, Lynex	17,460
23	27	CL	A	Liverpool	D2-2	1-0	17	Smith A, Banks	33,664
24	31	CL	H	WBA	D1-1	0-0	18	Lynex (pen)	15,146
25	J 2	CL	A	Stoke C	W1-0	1-0	18	Smith A	13,728
26	**7**	**FAC 3**	**A**	**Crystal Palace**	**L0-1**	**0-0**			**11,497**
27	14	CL	A	Notts Co	W5-2	1-2	17	McDonald, Lineker 3, Peake	10,607
28	21	CL	H	Coventry C	D1-1	0-1	18	Lineker	16,262
29	F 4	CL	H	Birmingham C	L2-3	0-2	18	Smith A 2	13,770
30	11	CL	A	Tottenham H	L2-3	0-2	19	Lineker 2	24,810
31	25	CL	H	Ipswich T	W2-0	1-0	18	Smith A, O'Neill	11,399
32	M 3	CL	H	Watford	W4-1	1-1	16	Peake 2, Lineker, Smith A	13,295
33	10	CL	A	Manchester U	L0-2	0-0	17		39,473
34	17	CL	H	West Ham U	W4-1	1-0	16	Hazell, Lynex 2 (2 pens), Lineker	13,533
35	20	CL	A	Everton	D1-1	0-1		Lineker	15,142
36	24	CL	A	Luton T	D0-0	0-0	15		10,509
37	31	CL	H	Norwich C	W2-1	2-0	14	Smith A 2	11,278
38	A 7	CL	A	Southampton	D2-2	0-0	14	Lineker 2	17,445
39	14	CL	H	Aston Villa	W2-0	1-0	13	O'Neill, Banks	13,666
40	18	CL	H	Liverpool	D3-3	2-1		Peake, Lynex, Lineker	26,553
41	21	CL	A	QPR	L0-2	0-1	13		12,360
42	28	CL	A	Arsenal	L1-2	0-0	14	Lineker	24,143
43	M 5	CL	H	Nottingham F	W2-1	2-0	12	Lynex, Lineker	16,600
44	7	CL	A	Wolverhampton W	L0-1	0-1	12		7,405
45	12	CL	H	Sunderland	L0-2	0-2	14		12,627

[5]Lost On Penalties

Av Home Att 14,667

Goal Scorers

League (65): Lineker 22, Smith A 15, Lynex 12 (5 pens), Peake 4, Banks 3, Hazell 2, Jones 2, O'Neill 2, Eastoe 1, McDonald 1, Ramsey 1
FA Cup (-): —
Milk Cup (2): English 1, Smith A 1

1983-84

Grew	Ramsey	Smith B	MacDonald	Banks	O'Neill	Lynex	Lineker	Smith A	Jones	Wilson	Peake	Rennie	English	Wallington	Williams	Hazell	Feeley	Eastoe **(L)**	Andrews	Kelly	**REFEREE**	
1	2	3	4	5	6	7	8	9	10	11											R Milford	1
1	2	3	4	5	6	7	8	9		11	10										D Shaw	2
1	2	5	6	7*	4	8	11	10	12	9		3									D Scott	3
1	2	3	4			7	8	9	10*	11	6	5	12								L Burden	4
1	2	3	4			7*	8	9	10	11	6	5	12								D Owen	5
	2	3	4		5		8	9	7	11	10*	6		1	12						D Reeves	6
	2	3	4		6	7	8	9*	10	11	12			1	5						T Spencer	7
	10	3	4		6	7	8		9*	11	12			1	2	5					K Walmsley	8
	10	**3**	**4**		**6***	**7**	**8**	**12**	**9**	**11**				**1**	**2**	**5**					**J Key**	**9**
	10		4	6		7	8			3			11	1	2	5		9			A Ward	10
	10		**4**	**6***		**7**		**8**		**3**		**11**	**12**	**1**	**2**	**5**		**9**			**L Shapter**	**11**
	10		4	6		7	8*	12		3		11		1	2	5		9			D Letts	12
	10		4	6		7		8		3		11		1	2	5		9			K Salmon	13
	10	12	4	6		7		8		3		11		1	2	5*		9			A Gunn	14
	10		4	11	6	7	12	9		3		5		1	2*			8			J Moules	15
	10		4	11	6	7	8	9		3		5*	12	1	2						F Roberts	16
	10	2	4	11	6	7	8	9		3				1		5					R Guy	17
	10	2	4	11	6	7	8*	9		3			12	1		5					R Nixon	18
	10	2	4	11	6	7		9	12	3			8*	1		5					A Robinson	19
	10	2	4	11	6	7	8	9		3				1		5					N Midgley	20
	10	2	4	11	6	7	8	9		3				1		5					T Fitzharris	21
	10	2	4	11	6	7*	8	9		3			12	1		5					M Heath	22
	10*	2	4	11	6	7	8	9		3		5	12	1							M Peck	23
		2	4	11	6	7	8	9		3			12	1	10*	5					T Mills	24
		2	4	11	6	7	8	9		3	10†			1		5					N Glover	25
		2	**4**	**11**	**6**	**7**	**8**	**9**		**3**	**10***		**12**	**1**		**5**					**D Vickers**	**26**
		2	4	11	6	7	8	9		3	10			1		5					D Hutchinson	27
	10	2	4	11	6	7	8	9		3				1		5					J Worrall	28
	10	2		11	6	7	8	9		3	4*		12	1		5					I Borrett	29
		2		11	6	7	8	9		3	4	10*	12	1		5					K Childs	30
	10	2	4		6	7	8	9		3	11			1		5					D Vickers	31
	10	2	4		6	7	8	9		3	11			1		5					D Allison	32
		2	4		6	7	8	9		3	11		12	1		5	10*				P Willis	33
		2	4		6	7	8	9		3	11			1	10	5					D Richardson	34
			4		6	7	8	9		3	11		12	1	10	5	2*				J Lovatt	35
		2	4		6	7	8	9		3	11			1	10	5					A Crickmore	36
	10	2	4		6	7	8	9			11			1	3	5					P Tyldesley	37
		2	4		6	7	8	9		3	11			1	10	5					A Ward	38
	4	2		12	6		8	9		3	11		7	1	10	5*					C Challinor	39
	10	2	6	12	5*	7	8	9		3	11			1	4						C Downey	40
	10	2	4	12		7	8	9*		3	11	6		1	5						M Taylor	41
	10	2	4			7	8	9		3	11†	6		1	5						M Bodenham	42
	10	2	4			7	8	9		3	11*		12	1	6	5					D Reeves	43
	10	2	4	12		7	8	9		3*	11	6			5				1		D Shaw	44
	10	2				7	8*	9		3		6	11		5		12		1	4	H King	45
5	33	35	38	22	31	40	38	39	6	41	22	15	4	35	21	27	2	5	2	1	League Appearances	
		+1S		+4S			+1S	+1S	+2S		+2S		+12S		+1S		+1S					
		1	1	1	1	1	1	1		1	1		1S	1		1					FA Cup Appearances	
	2	1	2	1	1	2	1	1+1S	1	2		1	1S	2	2	2		1			Milk Cup Appearances	

CITY STADIUM, FILBERT STREET

Official Address: City Stadium, Filbert Street, Leicester LE2 7FL. Telephone: Leicester (0533) 555000. Match Information: (0533) 551155

Ground Capacity: 32,000

Record Attendance: 47,298 v. Tottenham Hotspur, F.A. Cup Round 5, 18 Feb 1928

Record Receipts: £70,733 v. Shrewsbury Town, F.A. Cup Round 6, 6 Mar 1982

Size of Playing Area: 112yds × 75 yds

Season Tickets: Stand: £98.00, £90.00, £72.00, £70.00; £50.00 Family Enclosures (£30.00 OAP)

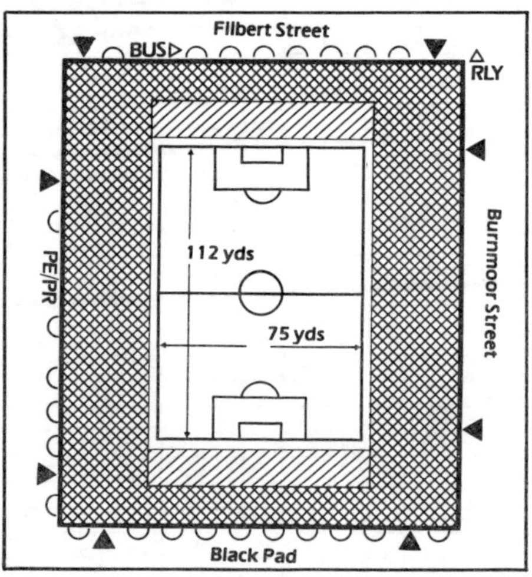

For key see page 12

Executive Box Season Tickets: £5,000 per annum (19 people each), (3 year contracts), 20 boxes have been constructed

Cost of Stand Tickets: £5.00, £4.50, £4.00, £3.50 (match days); **Terraces:** £2.50, (£1.50 juveniles if purchased three hours before kick-off)

Match and Ticket Information: Applications with SAE are accepted two months prior to each match

Car Parking: Parking adjacent to stadium for season ticket holders only. Street parking is available and there is also a public car park five minutes walk from the ground

How to get to the ground

From North: Use Motorway M1 until junction 22 or A46/A607 into Leicester City Centre. Follow signs Rugby into Almond Road, then at end turn right into Aylestone Road. Shortly turn left into Walnut Street, then turn left into Filbert Street for Leicester City F.C.
From East: Use A47 into Leicester City Centre. Follow signs Rugby into Almond Road, then at end turn right into Aylestone Road. Shortly turn left into Walnut Street, then turn left into Filbert Street for Leicester City F.C.
From South: Use Motorway M1 or M69 until junction 21 then A46 (S.P. Leicester). Under railway bridge and in 0.2m turn right into Upperton Road, then turn right into Filbert Street for Leicester City F.C.
From West: Use Motorway M69 or A50 into Leicester City centre and follow signs Rugby into Almond Road, then at end turn into Aylestone Road. Shortly turn left into Walnut Street, then turn left into Filbert Street for Leicester City F.C.

LINCOLN CITY Division 3

President
ED Walker

Chairman
DW Houlston

Directors
MB Pryor (Vice Chairman)
JK Reames
DG Overton

Secretary
PM Hough

Manager
Colin Murphy

Assistant Manager
J Pickering

Commercial Manager
C Rodman (0522 42333)

Physiotherapist
B Loxley

After the late slump of the previous season Lincoln City might have been the choice of a few experts as relegation candidates, but although it was a fairly quiet season a reasonable position just below mid-way in the Third Division was achieved. If the truth is told this was as good as anything that could have been expected. After an uncertain start the best results were mostly achieved before Christmas and by the turn of the year there was little to keep the supporters excited.

The cup performances were modest also, except that Hull City were despatched on aggregate from the Milk Cup, which brought a tie with Tottenham, who were very hard pressed to hold on to a narrow aggregate lead (4-3) at Sincil Bank. The F.A. Cup was a similar affair with a good first round win at Burslem against Port Vale being followed by a tough tie against Sheffield United, who played a goalless match at Lincoln and then won the replay in the second half at Bramall Lane. A League programme without anything ambitious being possible was the fare for Lincoln supporters from then onwards.

Recent seasons have shown Lincoln in a good light and Manager Colin Murphy should be able to restore the will to fight for promotion in the coming campaign. The talent and consistency is there with such players as Felgate, Houghton and Jack having given their colleagues a good lead. Consistency over a complete season could bring its rewards.

One of the interesting facets of Colin Murphy's team building has been his successful use of non-league talent. His own experience of this level of the game encouraged him to sign players of this pedigree and he certainly hasn't been let down by Gordon Simmonite (ex England Semi-Professional and Boston United) and Keith Houghton (ex England Semi-Professional and Blyth Spartans), Alan Walker (ex Telford United), Steve Thompson (ex Boston United) and Mark McGarrick (ex Witton Albion). WLM

Back Row L to R: Phil Neale, Steve Thompson, Keith Houghton, Stuart Naylor, John Fashanu, David Felgate, Alan Walker, Gary Strodder, Gordon Simmonite. **Front Row:** Mark McCarrick, Gordon Hobson, John Thomas, Bert Loxley (Physio), Colin Murphy (Manager), John Pickering (Assistant Manager), Ross Jack, George Shipley, Phil Turner. **Foreground:** Stuart Hall, Willie Gamble.

'THE RED IMPS'

Formed: 1883 **Turned Professional:** 1892 **Ltd Co:** 1892
Previous Managers: Bill Anderson Bob Chapman Ron Gray Bert Loxley David Herd Graham Taylor George Kerr Willie Bell
Honours: Division Three (N) Champions 1931-2, 1947-8, 1951-2 Division Four Champions 1975-6
League Career: Original members of Division 2 1892 Not re-elected to Division 2 1908
Re-elected to Division 2 1909 No re-elected to Division 2 1911 Re-elected to Division 2 1912
Not re-elected 1920 Elected to Division 3(N) 1921 Promoted to Division 2 1931-2
Relegated to Division 3(N) 1933-4 Promoted to Division 2 1947-8
Relegated to Division 3(N) 1948-9 Promoted to Division 2 1951-2
Relegated to Division 3 1960-1 Relegated to Division 4 1961-2
Promoted to Division 3 1975-6 Relegated to Division 4 1978-9
Promoted to Division 3 1980-1
Colours: Red shirts with white sleeves, red pinstripe on white sleeves and white pin stripe on body, black trim, white shorts and stockings
Change Colours: Royal blue with red pinstripe, black shorts and royal blue stockings

CLUB RECORDS

Most Appearances for Club: Tony Emery, 402, 1946-59
Most Capped Player: David Pugh, 3, Wales George Moulson, 3, Eire
Record Goalscorer in a Match: Andy Graver, 6 v. Crewe Alex (H) 11-1, Div 3(N) 29.09.1951, Frank Keetley, 6 v. Halifax T (H) 9-1, Div 3(N) 16.01.1932
Record League Goalscorer in a season: Allan Hall, 42, Div 3(N), 1931-2
Record League Goalscorer in a career: Andy Graver, 144, 1950-1 & 1958-61
Record Transfer Fee Received: £180,000 from Newcastle United for Mick Harford, Dec 1980
Record Transfer Fee Paid: £45,000 to Southampton for George Shipley, Jan 1980
Best Performances: League: 5th Div 2 1901-2 **F.A. Cup:** Equivalent of 5th Round 1886-7, 1889-90, 1901-2
League/Milk Cup: 4th Round 1967-8
Most League Points: (3 pts for win) 77, Div 3, 1981-2 (2 pts for win) Div 4, 1975-6
Record League Victory: 11-1 v Crewe Alexandra, Div 3(N), 29 Sept 1951
Record League Defeat: 3-11 v Manchester City, Div 2, 23 March 1895

Club Statistician for the Directory: John Holland

Programme Editors
C.J.N. Rodman & P.M. Hough

Price	Number of Pages
40p	24

Subscriptions
Contact club

LINCOLN CITY

PLAYERS NAME Ht Wt Birthdate	Honours	Birthplace Transfers	Clubs	APPEARANCES League	APPEARANCES Milk Cup	APPEARANCES F.A.C.	APPEARANCES A.M.C.	GOALS League	GOALS Milk Cup	GOALS F.A.C.	GOALS A.M.C.
GOALKEEPERS											
David Felgate†	W.(1), S	Blaenau	Bolton W.								
6-1 13.3 4.3.60		Festiniog	Rochdale (L)	35							
			Crewe A. (L)	14							
			Rochdale (L)	12							
		£25,000	Lincoln C.	177	13	7	1				
Stuart Naylor	E. Y. Div. 4, 76	Leeds	Yorkshire Amateurs								
6-2 11.13 6.12.62			Lincoln C.	4	2	1					
			Peterborough U. (L)	8							
			Crewe A. (L)	38							
DEFENDERS											
Keith Houghton	E.S-P(1)	Backworth	Blyth Spartans								
6-2 12.4 10.3.56			Carlisle U.	82 + 5	5	5		2			
			Lincoln C.	26	2	2			1		
Mark McCarrick		Liverpool	Witton Alb.								
5-9 11.0 4.2.62			Birmingham C.	12 + 3	1	3					
		F	Lincoln C.								
Phil Neale		Scunthorpe	Scunthorpe U. (N-C)								
5-10 11.5 5.6.54			Lincoln C.	300 + 7	11 +	13 +		22			
Gordon Simmonite*	E.S-P(2)	Sheffield	Sheffield W.	1							
5-10 11.4 25.4.57			Boston U.								
		£15,000	Blackpool	63	6	4		1			
		£5,000	Lincoln C.	59 + 1	3	1	1				
Steve Thompson		Sheffield	Boston U.								
5-9 12.0 28.7.55		£15,000	Lincoln C.	112 + 1	14	7		7		1	
Alan Walker		Ashton-u-Lyme	Telford U.								
6-1 12.2 17.12.59			Lincoln C.	32 + 1	1	2	1	2			
MIDFIELD											
Gordon Mair	S. S	Coatbridge	Notts. Co. (A)	123 + 8	10+44			18	2		
5-9 10.6 18.12.58			Lincoln C.								
Neil Redfern		Dewsbury	Nottingham F. (A)								
5-10 11.6 20.6.65			Bolton W.	35	2	4		1			
			Lincoln C.	10				1			
George Shipley		Newcastle	Southampton (A)	2 + 1							
5-7 10.3 7.3.59			Reading (L)	11 + 1							
		£45,000	Lincoln C.	199	19	8		35	8		
Gary Strodder		Spenborough	Lincoln C.	26 + 4	1			1			
6-1 11.3½ 1.4.65											
Phil Turner		Sheffield	Lincoln C.	160 + 2	15	8	1	12		1	
5-8 10.7 12.2.62											
FORWARDS											
John Fashanu		Kensington	Cambridge U. (N-C)								
6-1 11.12 18.9.62		F	Norwich C.	6 + 1		2		1			
			Crystal Palace (L)	1							
		F	Lincoln C.	22 + 4			1	7			
Gordon Hobson		Sheffield	Lincoln C.	224 + 10	18	6 + 1	1	66	3		
5-8 10.5 27.11.57											
Ross Jack		Inverness	Everton (A)	1				1			
5-10 11.2 21.3.59		£20,000	Norwich C.	31 + 25	9 + 1	4 + 1	1	10	2	2	
		£17,000	Lincoln C.	34 + 2				9	1		
John Thomas		Wednesbury	Everton								
5-8 11.3 5.8.58			Tranmere R. (L)	10 + 1				2			
			Halifax T. (L)	5							
		F	Bolton W.	18 + 4	1	2		6	1		
		F	Chester C.	44	2			20	1		
		£22,000	Lincoln C.	31 + 6	2 + 1	1	1	13	3		

NON-CONTRACT PLAYERS 1984-85

Neil Clark, Gavin Smith

APPRENTICES

Stuart Hall, Simon Gamble

LINCOLN CITY

DIVISION THREE 14TH **FA CUP** 2ND ROUND **MILK CUP** 2ND ROUND

MATCH	DATE	COMPETITION	VENUE	OPPONENTS	RESULT	HALF TIME	L'GUE POS'N	GOALSCORERS	ATTENDANCE
1	A 27	CL	A	Oxford U	L0-3	0-1			4,239
2	**30**	**MC 1**	**A**	**Hull C**	**D0-0**	**0-0**			**7,036**
3	S 3	CL	H	Sheffield U	L0-2	0-0	24		6,686
4	7	CL	H	Orient	W2-0	1-0		Jack 2 (1 pen)	2,899
5	10	CL	A	Brentford	L0-3	0-1	18		4,712
6	**14**	**MC 1**	**H**	**Hull C**	**W3-1[1]**	**0-1**		**Shipley, Thomas, Houghton**	**4,630**
7	17	CL	H	Plymouth Arg	W3-1	1-1	14	Holson 2, Jack	3,103
8	24	CL	A	Hull C	L0-2	0-0	18		8,323
9	28	CL	A	Exeter C	W3-0	0-0		Jack 2 (1 pen), Shipley	2,775
10	O 1	CL	H	AFC Bournemouth	W3-0	1-0	9	Cockerill 2, Jack (pen)	3,586
11	**5**	**MC 2**	**A**	**Tottenham H**	**L1-3**	**1-2**		**Thomas**	**20,241**
12	8	CL	A	Wigan Ath	L0-2	0-0	11		3,864
13	15	CL	H	Millwall	D2-2	1-2	14	Turner, Thompson	3,190
14	18	CL	A	Newport Co	L0-1	0-1			3,450
15	22	CL	H	Burnley	W3-1	1-1	13	Shipley, Turner, Fashanu	3,792
16	**25**	**MC 2**	**H**	**Tottenham H**	**W2-1**	**1-0**		**Thomas, Jack (pen)**	**12,088**
17	29	CL	A	Preston NE	W2-1	1-1	11	Thomas 2	4,435
18	N 2	CL	H	Bolton	D0-0	0-0			3,988
19	5	CL	A	Gillingham	L0-2	0-1	13		4,428
20	12	CL	H	Scunthorpe U	W2-1	0-1	13	Carling (og), Jack (pen)	4,657
21	**19**	**FAC 1**	**A**	**Port Vale**	**W2-1**	**2-0**		**Jack, Shipley**	**3,647**
22	26	CL	H	Bristol R	W4-0	2-0	12	Fashanu 3, Jack	3,709
23	D 3	CL	A	Wimbledon	L1-3	0-1	13	Shipley	2,434
24	**10**	**FAC 2**	**H**	**Sheffield U**	**D0-0**	**0-0**			**7,554**
25	17	CL	A	Port Vale	W1-0	0-0	12	Cockerill	2,861
26	**19**	**FAC 2R**	**A**	**Sheffield U**	**L0-1**	**0-0**			**12,547**
27	26	CL	H	Walsall	W2-1	0-1	10	Hobson, Thomas	4,886
28	27	CL	A	Southend U	L0-2	0-0	12		2,824
29	31	CL	H	Bradford C	L2-3	1-1	13	Strodder, Shipley	3,983
30	J 2	CL	A	Rotherham U	D1-1	0-0	12	Johnson (og)	4,595
31	14	CL	H	Oxford U	D2-2	2-2	12	Saxby, Thomas	3,345
32	21	CL	A	Plymouth Arg	D2-2	0-1	12	Thomas, Cockerill	3,804
33	F 1	CL	H	Brentford	W2-0	0-0		Cockerill, Jack	2,266
34	4	CL	A	AFC Bournemouth	L0-3	0-2	12		3,597
35	7	CL	A	Sheffield U	D0-0	0-0			9,765
36	11	CL	H	Hull C	L1-3	1-0	13	Turner	5,370
37	14	CL	A	Bolton W	W2-0	0-0		Hobson, Thomas	5,450
38	18	CL	H	Preston NE	W2-1	1-1	9	Thomas, Fashanu	2,780
39	**22**	**AMC 1**	**H**	**Doncaster R**	**L0-2**	**0-2**			**1,941**
40	25	CL	A	Burnley	L0-4	0-2	12		6,584
41	M 3	CL	H	Newport Co	L2-3	2-2	13	Walker, Thomas	1,780
42	7	CL	H	Gillingham	W4-0	2-0		Hobson, Neale, Walker, Cockerill (pen)	1,574
43	10	CL	A	Scunthorpe U	D0-0	0-0	10		3,889
44	17	CL	H	Wigan Ath	L0-1	0-1	11		2,030
45	31	CL	H	Exeter C	D1-1	0-0	14	Burke	1,498
46	A 7	CL	A	Orient	D1-1	0-0	14	Thomas	2,174
47	14	CL	H	Wimbledon	L1-2	1-0	15	Redfearn	1,986
48	21	CL	A	Walsall	W1-0	0-0	15	Fashanu	3,660
49	23	CL	H	Southend U	L1-2	1-1	15	Thomas	1,834
50	28	CL	A	Bristol R	L1-3	1-1	15	Burke (pen)	3,254
51	M 1	CL	A	Millwall	W2-0	0-0		Fashanu, Hobson	2,825
52	5	CL	H	Rotherham U	L0-1	0-0	15		2,140
53	7	CL	A	Bradford C	D0-0	0-0	14		3,085
54	12	CL	H	Port Vale	W3-2	1-1	14	Thomas 3 (1 pen)	1,372

[1] After Extra Time

Av Home Att 3,177

Goal Scorers

League (59): Thomas 13 (1 pen), Jack 9 (4 pens), Fashanu 7, Cockerill 6 (1 pen), Hobson 6, Shipley 4, Turner 3, Burke 2 (1 pen), Walker 2, Neale 1, Redfearn 1, Saxby 1, Strodder 1, Thompson 1, opponents 2

FA Cup (2): Jack 1, Shipley 1

Milk Cup (6): Thomas 3, Houghton 1, Jack 1 (1 pen), Shipley 1

AMC (-): —

1983-84

Felgate	Simmonite	Johnson **(L)**	Cockerill	Houghton	Thompson	Strodder	Turner	Hobson	Jack	Shipley	Thomas	Burke	Neale	Fashanu	Walker	Saxby **(L)**	Williamson **(L)**	Webb **(L)**	Redfearn **(L)**	Moyes	**REFEREE**	
1	2	3	4	5	6	7*	8	9	10	11	12										M Dimblebee	1
1	**3**		**4**	**5**	**6**		**2**	**9**	**10**	**11**	**8**	**7**									**N Glover**	**2**
1	3	2*	4	5	6		8	9	10	11	12	7									E Scales	3
1	3	2	4	5	6	7†	8	9	10	11											T Jones	4
1	3	2	4	5	6	7	8*	9	10	11	12										T Spencer	5
1	**2**		**4**	**5**		**6**	**8**	**9**	**10**	**11**	**12**	**7***	**3**								**I Borrett**	**6**
1	2		4	5	6	12	8	9	10	11	7*		3								J Lovatt	7
1	2		4	5	6		8	9	10	11			3	7							R Nixon	8
1	2		4	5	6		8	9	10	11			3	7†							L Burden	9
1	2		4	5	6		8	9*	10	11	12		3	7							A Robinson	10
1	**2**		**4**	**5**	**6**		**8**	**9**	**10**	**11**	**7**		**3**								**A Gunn**	**11**
1	2		10	3†	4		6	11	7	8			5	9							M Heath	12
1	2		4	5	6		8	9	10	11	7		3								NL Wilson	13
1	2		4	5	6		8	9	10	11	7		3								V Callow	14
1	2		4		6		8	9	10	11			3	7	5						A Buksh	15
1	**2***		**4**		**6**		**8**	**9**	**10**	**11**	**7**	**12**	**3**		**5**						**N Midgley**	**16**
1	2			4	6		8		10	11	7		3	9	5						F Roberts	17
1	2		4		6		8		10	11	7		3	9	5						B Hill	18
1	2*		4	7	6		8		10	11	12		3	9	5						M James	19
1	2		4	7	6		8		10	11			3	9	5						L Robinson	20
1	**2**		**4**	**7**	**6***		**8**		**10**	**11**	**12**		**3**	**9**	**5**						**R Guy**	**21**
1	2		4	7			8		10	11			3	9	5	6					J Worrall	22
1	2		4	7			8	12	10	11			3	9	5	6*					A Crickmore	23
1	**2**		**4**	**7**			**8**	**9***	**10**	**11**			**3**	**12**	**5**	**6**					**G Napthine**	**24**
1			4	7			8	2	10	11			3	9	5	6					L Dilkes	25
1			**4**	**7**			**8**	**2**	**10**	**11**			**3**	**9**	**5**	**6**					**G Napthine**	**26**
1	2*		4	7			8	9	10	11	12		3		5	6					K Hackett	27
1			4	7		6	8	9	10	11	2		3		5						M Bodenham	28
1				7		2	8	9	10	11	4		3		5	6					H Taylor	29
1				7		2	8	9	10	11	4		3		5	6					D Shaw	30
1			4	7		2		9	10	11	8		3		5	6					J Hough	31
1	2		4	7		9*			10	11	8	12	3		5	6					J Martin	32
1	2		4	7			8		10	11	9		3		5	6					T Mills	33
1	2		4				8	7	10	11	9		3	12	5	6*					A Ward	34
1	2		4			6	8	7	10	11	9			3	5						P Tyldesley	35
1	6		4				8	7	10	11	9		3	12	5		2*				A Seville	36
1	5		4	6*			8	7		11	10		3	9	12		2				D Hutchinson	37
1	6		4				8	7	10	11	9		3	5			2				K Baker	38
1	**6**		**4**				**8**	**7**	**10**		**9**	**2**		**11**	**5**		**3**				**L Robinson**	**39**
1	3		7				4	6	8	9	11		5	10			2				N Ashley	40
1	6		4				8	7		11	10		3	9	5		2				D Reeves	41
1	6		4	7			8	10	12	11	9	2*	3		5						R Banks	42
1	6*		4			7	8	10	12	11	9	2	3		5						D Scott	43
1			4			7	8	10		11	9	2*	3	12	5			6			J Bray	44
1						2		10		11	9	4	3	8	5			6	7		K Salmon	45
1						2	8	10		11	9	4	3		5			6	7		K Cooper	46
1						2	8		10	11*	9	4	3	12	5			6	7		D Richardson	47
1						2	8		7		10	4	3	9	5			6	11		J Worrall	48
1						2	8		7		10	4	3	9	5			6	11		G Tyson	49
1	6					2	8	9			10	4		11	5			3	7		J Moules	50
1	6					2	8	9			10	4		11*	5			3	7	12	A Gunn	51
1	6					2	8	9		11	10	4*			5			3	7	12	J Ashworth	52
1	6					2		9		11	10	4			5			3	7	8	D Owen	53
1	3					6	12	9		11	10	4*			5			2	7	8	G Courtney	54
46	35	4	33	26	16	21	41	35	34	42	31	14	36	22	32	10	5	11	10	2	League Appearances	
						+1S	+1S	+1S	+2S		+6S	+1S		+4S	+1S					+2S		
3	2		3	3	1		3	2	3	3	1S		3	2+1S	3	2					FA Cup Appearances	
4	4		4	3	3	1	4	4	4	4	3+1S	2+1S	3		1						Milk Cup Appearances	
1	1		1				1	1	1		1	1		1	1		1				AM Cup Appearances	

SINCIL BANK

Official Address: Sincil Bank, Lincoln LN5 8LD. Telephone: Lincoln (0522) 22224. Commercial Dept: Lincoln 42333

Record Attendance: 23,196 v. Derby County, League Cup Round 4, 15 Nov 1967

Ground Capacity: 16,225

Record Receipts: £34,843.30 v. Tottenham Hotspur, Milk Cup, 26 Oct 1983

Size of Playing Area: 110yds × 75 yds

Season Tickets: £55.00, £45.00 (St. Andrews); £55.00, £35.00 (South Park); Ground: £37.50 (concession £20)

Cost of Stand Tickets: £3.00 (concessions £2.00), Terraces: £2.00 (concessions £1.00)

Match and Ticket Information: Contact Club

Car Parking: Street parking available

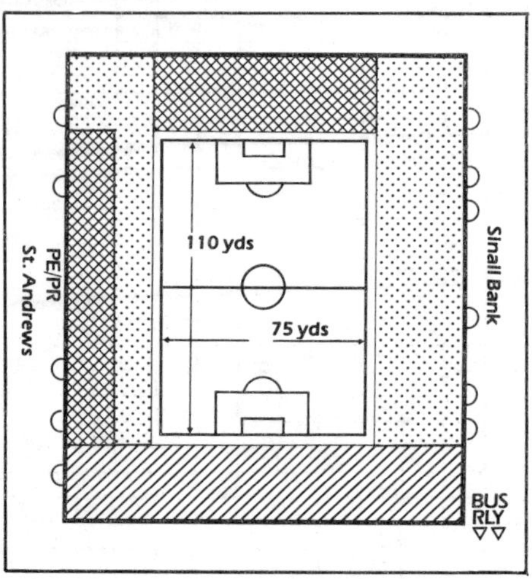

For key see page 12

How to get to the ground

From North, East and West: Use A15, A57, A46 or A158 into Lincoln City Centre then follow Newark (A46) into High Street. Under railway bridge then take next turning left into Queen Street for Lincoln City F.C.
From South: Use A1 then A46 (S.P. Lincoln) then following signs City Centre into High Street and on nearside of railway bridge turn right into Queen Street for Lincoln City F.C.

LIVERPOOL Division 1

Chairman
J W Smith CBE, JP, DL

Directors
H Cartwright
S C Reakes JP
C J Hill
J T Cross
W D Corkish
Coun S T Moss JP
R Paisley OBE

Chief Executive General Secretary
P B Robinson

Assistant Secretary
R E Jones

Commercial Manager
K Addison (051-263 6391)

Stadium Manager
B Johnson

Manager
Joe Fagan

Chief Coach
Ronnie Moran

First Team Assistant Coach
Roy Evans

Reserve Team Coach
Chris Lawler

Youth Team Coaches
Tom Saunders
J Bennison

Chief Scout
Geoff Twentyman

Groundsman
R Summers

The Change of manager following the retirement of the successful Bob Paisley allowed Joe Fagan to take over and naturally although he did things his own way he was wise enough to follow the guidelines and principles laid down back in 1959 by Bill Shankly. Fagan enjoyed more success in his first season than most managers experience in their entire careers.

The first trophy to be won — for the fourth consecutive season (a record) — was the Milk Cup, where the 'Derby' match at Wembley, although exciting, remained scoreless. The replay was won by Liverpool thanks to a fierce drive from Souness, and although it was somewhat fortuitous the result was undoubtedly just.

The Reds were on top of the League by now and had reached the semi-finals of the European Cup, due largely to two brilliant victories away from Anfield, 1-0 in Bilbao and 4-1 in Lisbon, over Benfica. New recruit from Ipswich, John Wark, scored on his League debut at Watford, and the following week West Ham were comprehensively beaten 6-0 at Anfield which kept the momentum going at the top. Four days after the Hammers' visit, Liverpool entertained Dinamo Bucharest in the first leg of the European Cup semi-final, Lee's goal after 25 minutes proving decisive. Would this be enough to take Liverpool to another final? All fears were dispelled when the Reds won emphatically in Romania, Rush scoring twice.

Back to the league and two draws against lowly Ipswich and Birmingham were followed by a 5-0 win over Coventry, where the inimitable Rush hit four. Liverpool could only draw 0-0 at Meadow Lane, but on a day when Manchester United again dropped vital points the Reds were champions again – for the third successive season, emulating the feats achieved by Huddersfield and Arsenal, over half a century ago.

The European Cup Final on May 30 in Rome was dramatic. Phil Neal shot Liverpool ahead after only 14 minutes, but Pruzzo gave AS Roma a psychological boost two minutes before half-time when he equalised. The score remained at 1-1, and a penalty shoot-out was needed to decide who would be European Champions. When Graziani missed, it was up to Alan Kennedy to score. His kick sealed victory. The European Cup was won for the fourth time. A fourth round FA Cup exit at the Goldstone Ground, where Brighton thoroughly deserved their 2-0 win, was all forgotten in those dramatic moments in Italy.

Not since the days of Roger Hunt had Liverpool unearthed a striker of Rush's calibre, whose 48 goals in all competitions set a new record for the Club.

Thus ended another successful season. How can they follow that? Fagan is shrewd enough to realise that yesterday's prizes become tomorrow's dreams, and all games will present new challenges to the men from Anfield.

Brian Pead, The League Directory's Statistician for the Club

Back Row L to R: Mike Robinson, Gary Gillespie, Bob Bolder, Alan Hansen, Bruce Grobbelaar, Mark Lawrenson, John McGregor. **Middle Row:** Ronnie Moran (Coach), John Wark, Ronnie Whelan, Ian Rush, Steve Nicol, Dave Hodgson, Roy Evans (Trainer). **Front Row:** Sammy Lee, Phil Thompson, Phil Neal (Captain), Joe Fagan (Manager), Kenny Dalglish, Alan Kennedy, Paul Walsh.

'THE REDS or POOL'

Sponsored by
Crown Paint

Formed: 1892 **Turned Professional:** 1892 **Ltd Co:** 1892
Previous Managers: 1892-6 John McKenna 1896-1920 Tom Watson 1920-3 David Ashworth 1923-8 Matthew McQueen 1938-45 George Patterson 1935-51 George Kay 1951-6 Don Welsh 1956-9 Phil Taylor 1959-74 Bill Shankly 1974-84 Bob Paisley
Honours: Division 1 Champions 1900-1, 1905-6, 1921-2, 1922-3, 1946-7, 1963-4, 1965-6, 1972-3, 1975-6, 1976-7, 1978-9, 1979-80, 1981-2, 1982-3, 1983-4 (Third club to win the Championship in three consecutive years) Division 2 Champions 1893-4, 1895-6, 1904-5, 1961-2 F.A. Cup Winners 1965-6, 1974 Football League Cup/Milk Cup 1981, 1982, 1983, 1984 European Cup Winners 1976-7, 1977-8, 1980-1, 1983-4 UEFA Cup Winners 1972-3, 1975-6
European Super Cup Winners 1977
League Career: Elected to Division 2 1893 Promoted to Division 1 1893-4
Relegated to Division 2 1894-5 Promoted to Division 1 1895-6 Relegated to Division 2 1903-4
Promoted to Division 1 1904-5 Relegated to Division 2 1953-4 Promoted to Division 1 1961-2
Colours: All red with white trim
Change Colours: All yellow with red trim

CLUB RECORDS

Most Appearances for Club: Ian Callaghan: Football League 640 + F.A. Cup 77 + League Cup 42 + European Cups 87 **Total 846**
Most Capped Player: Emlyn Hughes, 59, England
Record Goalscorer in a Match: Andy McGuigan, 5 v Stoke C (7-0) (H), Div 1, 04.01.02
John Evans, 5 v Bristol R (5-3) (H), Div 2, 15.09.54
Record League Goalscorer in a season: Roger Hunt, 41, Div 2, 1961-2 **All competitions:** Ian Rush, 47 (League 32, F.A. Cup 2, Milk Cup 8, European Cup 5) 1983-4
Record League Goalscorer in a career: Roger Hunt, 245, 1959-69 **All competitions:** Roger Hunt, 285 (League 245, F.A. Cup 18, League Cup 5, European Cups 17)
Record Transfer Fee Received: £650,000 from Sampdoria for Graeme Souness, June 1984
Record Transfer Fee Paid: £900,000 to Brighton for Mark Lawrenson, Aug 1981
Best Performances: As in honours **Most League Points:** (3pts for win) 87, Div 1, 1982-3 (record)
(2pts for win) 68, Div 1, 1978-9
Most League Goals: 106, Div 2, 1895-6 (30 games)
Record League Victory: 10-1 v Rotherham United, Div 2, 18 Feb 1896
Record League Defeat: 1-9 v Birmingham City, Div 2, 11 Dec 1954
European Competitions Entered: European Cup: 1964-5, 1966-7, 1973-4, 1976-7, 1977-8, 1978-9, 1979-80, 1980-1, 1981-2, 1982-3, 1983-4 European Cup Winners Cup: 1965-6, 1971-2, 1974-5
European Fairs Cup: 1967-8, 1968-9, 1969-70, 1970-1 UEFA Cup: 1972-3, 1975-6
European Super Cup: 1977, 1978 World Club Championship: 1981, 1983
Club Statistician for the Directory: Brian Pead

Programme Editor

Price	Number of Pages
45p	24

Subscriptions
£17.00 (home matches), £18.00 (away matches) per season. Overseas & Eire — add £3.00 per season
(Apply for old & current programmes to Manchester Programme Shop, 784 Wilmslow Road, Didsbury, Manchester 20. (061-434 6324)

LIVERPOOL

PLAYERS NAME Ht Wt Birthdate	Honours	Birthplace Transfers	Clubs	APPEARANCES League	Milk Cup	F.A.C.	E. Cups	GOALS League	Milk Cup	F.A.C.	E. Cups
GOALKEEPERS	**										
Bob Bolder		Dover	Sheffield Wed.	196	16	12					
6-1 14.8 2.10.58		£125,000	Liverpool								
Bruce Grobbelaar		South Africa	Vancouver W.								
6-1 12.0 6.10.57			Crewe A.	24				1			
			Vancouver W.								
		£250,000	Liverpool	126	18	8	21				
Bob Wardle		Halifax	Bristol C. (A)								
5-11 11.2 5.3.55			Shrewsbury T.	131	4	16					
			Liverpool								
			Wrexham (L)	13	1						
DEFENDERS											
Gary Gillespie		Stirling	Falkirk	22	2	1					
6-2 12.1 5.7.60		£75,000	Coventry C.	171 + 1	15	1		6			
		£325,000	Liverpool								
Alan Hansen		Alloa	Partick Thistle	82 + 4	14	4		6	1		
6-1 13.0 13.6.55		£100,000	Liverpool	247	32	22 +	33 +	7	1	2	
Alan Kennedy		Sunderland	Newcastle U. (A)	155 + 3	16	20 +		9			
5-9 10.7 31.8.54		£300,000	Liverpool	209 + 2	29	16	28	14	2		
Mark Lawrenson		Preston	P.N.E.	73	2	5		2			
6-0 11.7 2.6.57		£100,000	Brighton	152	15	7		5	1	1	
		£900,000	Liverpool	119 + 2	18	8	17 +	7	2	1	
John McGregor		Airdrie	Queen's Park	103	9	5		19	2	1	
5-11 12.0 5.1.63			Liverpool								
Phil Neal*†		Irchester	Northampton T. (A)	182 + 4	9	8 + 2		29	1	1	
5-11 12.2 20.2.51		£65,000	Liverpool	400	49	41	60	36	3	2	12
Phil Thompson		Liverpool	Liverpool (A)	337 + 3	42 +	36	47 +	7	1		2
6-0 11.8 21.1.54											
MIDFIELD											
Craig Johnston		Johannesburg	Middlesbrough (A)	61 + 3	4 + 2	5 + 2		16			
5-9 11.2 8.12.60		£575,000	Liverpool	71 + 9	6 + 2	4 + 2	12 +	15	2	2	2
Sammy Lee		Liverpool	Liverpool (A)	161 + 4	21	13	29	13	2		4
5-7 10.1 7.2.59											
Jan Molby	Denmark	Kolding, Jutland	Ajax								
6-1 13.8		£225,000	Liverpool								
Steve Nicol		Irvine	Ayr United	57 + 2	9	3		5			
5-10 11.0 11.12.61		£300,000	Liverpool	21 + 6		2	2 + 2	5			
John Wark		Glasgow	Ipswich T. (A)	295 + 1	24 +	36 +	25	94	12	10	18
5-10½ 11.12 4.8.57		£475,000	Liverpool	9				2			
Ronnie Whelan		Dublin	Home Farm								
5-9 10.13 25.9.61			Liverpool	78 + 6	11 +	4	13 +	17	5		6
FORWARDS											
Jim Beglin		Waterford	Shamrock Rovers								
5-11 11.0 29.7.63			Liverpool								
Kenny Dalglish		Glasgow	Celtic	200 + 4	59 +	28	22	112	34	11	7
5-8 11.13 4.3.51		£440,000	Liverpool	277	42	23	39 +	103	22	12	10
Mike Robinson		Leicester	P.N.E.	45 + 3	4	2		15	1		
6-0 13.4 12.7.58		£750,000	Manchester C.	29 + 1	4	1		8	1		
		£400,000	Brighton	111 + 2	8	12		37	3	3	
		£200,000	Liverpool	23 + 1		2	5 + 1	6		1	2
Ian Rush		St. Asaph	Chester (A)	33 + 1		5		14		3	
6-0½ 12.6 25.10.61		£300,000	Liverpool	114	19	8	18 +	73	10	5	10
Paul Walsh		Plumstead	Charlton A. (A)	85 + 2	9	4		24	6	1	
5-8 10.1 1.10.62		£400,000	Luton T.	80	5	4		24	1	2	
		£700,000	Liverpool								
David West		Leicester	Dorchester T.								
5-10 11.0 16.11.64		£30,000	Liverpool								

CONTRACT PLAYERS WITH NO FIRST TEAM APPEARANCES

Gary Abbott, Sean Curry, Ian Fairbrother, Ken De Manoe, Brian Mooney, Chris Pile, Mark Seagraves, Paul Jewell

NON-CONTRACT PLAYERS 1984-85

David Lock, Gary McGowan, Darren Rogers, Ian Vernon

APPRENTICES

Owen Devine, Neil Edwards, Jim Mulvehill, Dan MacMaster, Ian Toale, Alex Watson

**Liverpool players honours are to be found in a special feature on page 565.

LIVERPOOL

DIVISION ONE CHAMPIONS **FA CUP** 4TH ROUND **MILK CUP** WINNERS **EUROPEAN CUT** WINNERS

MATCH	DATE	COMPETITION	VENUE	OPPONENTS	RESULT	HALF TIME	L'GUE POS'N	GOALSCORERS	ATTENDANCE
1	A 27	CL	A	Wolverhampton W	D1-1	0-1		Rush	26,249
2	31	CL	A	Norwich C	W1-0	1-0		Souness	23,859
3	S 3	CL	H	Nottingham F	W1-0	0-0	3	Rush	31,376
4	6	CL	H	Southampton	D1-1	0-0		Rush	26,331
5	10	CL	A	Arsenal	W2-0	1-0	4	Johnston, Dalglish	41,896
6	17	CL	H	Aston Villa	W2-1	0-0	3	Dalglish, Rush	34,246
7	24	CL	A	Manchester U	L0-1	0-0	4		56,121
8	O 1	CL	H	Sunderland	L0-1	0-1	6		29,534
9	15	CL	A	West Ham U	W3-1	2-0	5	Robinson 3	32,557
10	22	CL	A	QPR	W1-0	0-0	2	Nicol	27,140
11	29	CL	H	Luton T	W6-0	4-0	2	Rush 5, Dalglish	31,940
12	6	CL	H	Everton	W3-0	1-0		Rush, Robinson, Nicol	40,875
13	12	CL	A	Tottenham H	D2-2	1-1	1	Robinson, Rush	45,032
14	19	CL	H	Stoke C	W1-0	0-0	1	Rush	26,529
15	26	CL	A	Ipswich T	D1-1	0-0	1	Dalglish	23,826
16	D 3	CL	H	Birmingham C	W1-0	0-0	1	Rush	24,791
17	10	CL	A	Coventry C	L0-4	0-3	1		20,586
18	17	CL	H	Notts Co	W5-0	3-0	1	Nicol, Souness 2 (1 pen), Hunt (og), Rush	22,436
19	26	CL	A	WBA	W2-1	1-0	1	Nicol, Souness	25,139
20	27	CL	H	Leicester C	D2-2	0-1	1	Lee, Rush	33,664
21	31	CL	A	Nottingham F	W1-0	1-0	1	Rush	29,692
22	J 2	CL	H	Manchester U	D1-1	0-1	1	Johnston	45,122
23	14	CL	H	Wolverhampton W	L0-1	0-1	1		23,325
24	20	CL	A	Aston Villa	W3-1	0-1		Rush 3	19,566
25	F 1	CL	H	Watford	W3-0	3-0		Rush, Neal, Whelan	20,746
26	4	CL	A	Sunderland	D0-0	0-0	1		25,646
27	11	CL	H	Arsenal	W2-1	1-1	1	Kennedy, Neal	34,642
28	18	CL	A	Luton T	D0-0	0-0	1		14,877
29	25	CL	H	QPR	W2-0	1-0	1	Rush, Robinson	32,206
30	M 3	CL	A	Everton	D1-1	1-0	1	Rush	51,245
31	10	CL	H	Tottenham H	W3-1	2-1	1	Dalglish, Whelan, Lee	36,718
32	16	CL	A	Southampton	L0-2	0-1			19,698
33	31	CL	A	Watford	W2-0	0-0	1	Wark, Rush	21,293
34	A 7	CL	H	West Ham U	W6-0	4-0	1	Rush 2, Delglish, Whelan, Souness 2	38,359
35	14	CL	A	Stoke C	L0-2	0-1	1		24,372
36	18	CL	A	Leicester C	D3-3	1-2		Whelan, Rush, Wark	26,553
37	21	CL	H	WBA	W3-0	3-0	1	McNaught (og), Souness, Dalglish	35,320
38	28	CL	H	Ipswich T	D2-2	2-1	1	Kennedy, Rush	32,069
39	M 5	CL	A	Birmingham C	D0-0	0-0	1		18,809
40	7	CL	H	Coventry C	W5-0	2-0	1	Rush 4 (1 pen), Hansen	33,393
41	12	CL	A	Notts Co	D0-0	0-0	1		18,745
42	15	CL	H	Norwich C	D1-1	1-1	1	Rush	38,837

A SPECIAL CUP TRIBUTE TO LIVERPOOL ON PAGE 566

Av Home Att 31,986

Goal Scorers

League (73): Rush 32 (1 pen), Dalglish 7, Souness 7 (1 pen), Robinson 6, Nicol 5, Whelan 4, Johnston 2, Kennedy 2, Lee 2, Wark 2, Hansen 1, Neal 1, opponents 2

1983-84

Grobbelaar	Neal	Kennedy	Lawrenson	Hansen	Dalglish	Lee	Rush	Robinson	Souness	Johnston	Hodgson	Nicol	Whelan	Wark	Gillespie	REFEREE	
1	2	3	4	6	7	8	9	10	11	5						A Ward	1
1	2	3	4	6	7	8	9	10	11	5						D Axcell	2
1	2	3	4	6	7	8	9	10*	11	5	12					J Lovatt	3
1	2	3	4	6	7	8	9	10	11	5						T Holbrook	4
1	2	3	4	6	7	8	9	10	11	5						A Seville	5
1	2	3	4	6	7	8	9	10	11	5						D Hutchinson	6
1	2*	3	4	6	7	8	9	10	11	5		12				K Hackett	7
1		3	4	6	7	8	9	10	11	5		2				M Heath	8
1	2	3	4	6	7	8	9*	10	11	5†	12					L Shapter	9
1	2	3	4	6	7	8	9	10	11	5*		12				C Thomas	10
1	2	3	4	6	7	8	9	10	11			5				JM Key	11
1	2	3	4	6	7	8	9	10	11			5				G Courtney	12
1	2	3	4	6	7	8	9	10	11			5				M Taylor	13
1	2	3	4	6	7	8	9	10	11			5				A Challinor	14
1	2	3	4	6	7	8	9		11			5	10			M Bodenham	15
1	2	3	4	6		8	9	10*	11	7		5	12			K Redfern	16
1	2	3	4	6	7	8	9		11			5	10			D Letts	17
1	2	3	4	6	7	8	9		11	10		5				N Ashley	18
1	2	3	4	6	7	8	9		11	10		5				H King	19
1	2	3	4	6	7	8	9		11	10*	12	5				M Peck	20
1	2	3	4	6	7*	8	9		11	10		5	12			M Dimblebee	21
1	2	3	4	6	7*	8	9		11	10	12	5				D Richardson	22
1	2	3	4	6		8	9	7	11	10		5*	12			A Saunders	23
1	2	3	4	6		8	9	7	11	10		5				R Lewis	24
1	2	3	4	6		8	9	7		10		5	11			L Robinson	25
1	2	3	4	6		8	9	7		10		5	11			J Hough	26
1	2	3	4	6		8	9	7		10		5	11			C Seel	27
1	2	3	4	6		8	9		11	10	7		5			J Bray	28
1	2	3	4	6		8	9	7	11	10			5			D Shaw	29
1	2	3	4	6		8*	9	7	11	10		12	5			G Tyson	30
1	2	3	4	6	7	8		9	11	10			5			T Jones	31
1	2	3	4	6	7	8	9	12		10		11*	5			B Stevens	32
1	2	3	4	6	7	8	9		11				5	10		T Holbrook	33
1	2	3	4	6	7	8	9		11				5	10		D Hutchinson	34
1	2	3	4	6	7*	8	9		11	12			5	10		E Read	35
1	2	3	4	6	7	8	9		11				5	10		C Downey	36
1	2	3	4	6	7	8	9		11				5	10		K Redfern	37
1	2	3	4*	6	7	8	9			11		12	5	10		T Mills	38
1	2	5	3	4	9	6	10		8				11	7		K Salmon	39
1	2	3	4	6	7	8	9		11				5	10		A Challinor	40
1	2	3	4	6	7	8	9		11				5	10		D Vickers	41
1	2	3	4	6	7	8	9		11	10			5			V Callow	42
42	41	**42**	**42**	**42**	33	**42**	41	23	37	28	1	19	20	9		League Appearances	
								+1S		+1S	+4S	+4S	+3S				

ANFIELD

Official Address: Anfield Road, Liverpool 4. Telephone: 051-263 2361

Telegraphic: Goalkeeper Liverpool

Ground Capacity: 45,600

Record Attendance: 61,905 v. Wolverhampton Wanderers, F.A. Cup Round 4, 2 Feb 1952

Record Receipts: £131,033 v. Bucharest, European Cup Semi-Final 1st Leg, 11 Apr 1984

Size of Playing Area: 110yds × 75 yds

Season Tickets: Stand: £67.00, £80.00; Ground: £40.00 (adult)

Cost of Stand Tickets: £4.40 Main Stand/ Hemlyn Road/Paddock; £3.75 Anfield Road, £5.25 combined Adult/Juvenile; **Terraces:** £2.20 adults, £1.50 OAP/juveniles

Match and Ticket Information: Postal applications nineteen days before match

Car Parking: Limited street parking. Mainly privately-owned car park in Priory Road (5 minutes walk from ground)

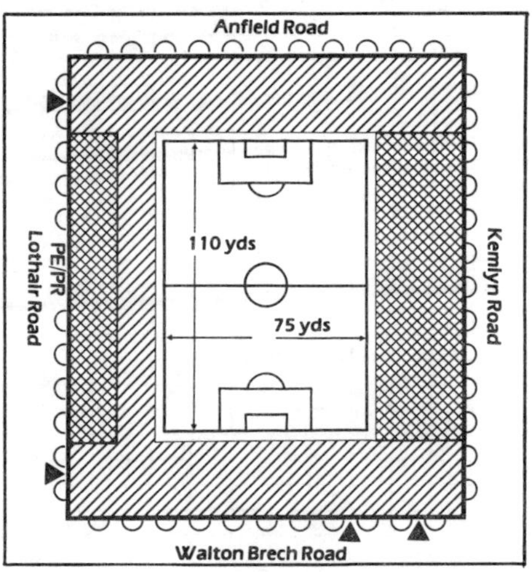

For key see page 12

How to get to the ground

From North: Use Motorway M6 until junction 28 then follow signs Liverpool on A58 and forward into Walton Hall Avenue pass Stanley Park and turn left into Anfield Road for Liverpool F.C.
From East and South: Use Motorway M6 then M62 until end of Motorway then turn right A5058 into Queens Drive. In 3m turn left into Utting Avenue. In 1m turn right into Anfield Road for Liverpool F.C.
From West: Use Mersey tunnel into Liverpool City Centre then follow signs Preston A580 into Walton Hall Avenue, then on nearside of Stanley Park turn right into Anfield Road for Liverpool F.C.

LUTON TOWN Division 1

President
Tom Hodgson

Chairman
D Mortimer

Directors
R J Smith
E S Pearson, LLM, BSC
R L Banks
D J Evans

Executive Director
J R Smith

General Secretary
G H Mackrell, FCCA

Manager
David Pleat

Club Coach
David Coates

Physiotherapist
John Sheridan

Commercial Manager
W J Tomlins (0582 411622)

The Hatters' delightful brand of attacking football won them friends everywhere. Inspired from midfield by Brian Horton, Luton's two main strikers Paul Walsh and Brian Stein revelled in the service even though they didn't score as many goals as they often promised to do.

Sometimes Luton's positive approach back-fired. Against such talented sides as Liverpool and Manchester United, they left far too much space at the back. Liverpool crashed six goals into their net at Anfield and United played with them to the tune of 5-0 before their own Kenilworth Road fans.

As a result of those experiences, manager David Pleat adopted a more cautious approach during the latter weeks of the season. But, just as it had done the previous season, the change proved alien to the players' nature and Luton won only once in 12 games and there were some fears that they might be sucked into the relegation battle.

They scored 14 goals in their first six games and it was only against the very best sides that they found themselves in difficulties — Manchester United, Liverpool, Spurs and Coventry (during their purple early patch). Mr Pleat opted to maintain his faith in an attacking policy, so after the Hatters had won 3-0 away to Notts County on Boxing Day, they held third place in the table, only five points behind leaders Liverpool.

It was after that disastrous home defeat by Manchester United in February, watched by a live TV audience, that the Luton manager felt he would have to pull more men back. After all, too many morale-shattering experiences like that would completely have eroded the team's confidence.

Though the switch in tactics tended to bring a small reduction in the number of goals conceded, Luton's own output dropped dramatically. Results, in fact, got worse as the slide took them to the very brink of relegation.

There were early disappointments in both Cups. Luton ran up what looked like a winning 3-2 lead away to Third Division Rotherham United in the second round of the Milk Cup. But they were beaten 0-2 at Kenilworth Road and so went out of that tournament.

The third round F.A. Cup draw gave them a derby clash with Watford. After a 2-2 draw at Kenilworth Road, Luton were beaten in extra-time at Vicarage Road in a 3-4 thriller.

So there were no trophies for Luton. Yet their performances during the early part of the campaign in particular brought a sparkle to the eyes of their supporters. TP

Back Row: Mark Stein, Rob Johnson, Tim Breacker, Stacey North, Mark North, Gary Parker, Wayne Turner, Ray Daniel. **Second Row:** John Moore (Reserve Coach), Emeka Nwajiobi, Frank Bunn, Jake Findlay, Paul Elliott, Andrew Dibble, Clive Goodyear, Mitchell Thomas, David Coates (Youth Coach). **Third Row:** Trevor Hartley (First Team Coach), Steve Elliot, David Moss, Ricky Hill, Mal Donaghy, David Pleat (Manager), Brian Stein, Ashley Grimes, Vince Hilaire, John Sheridan (Physiotherapist). **Front Row:** Michael Doughty, David Oldfield, Ricky McEvoy, Alec Ellisdon.

'THE HATTERS'

Sponsored by
Bedford Trucks

Formed: 1885 **Turned Professional:** 1890 **Ltd Co:** 1897
Previous Managers: 1925 George Thomson 1927-9 John McCartney 1929-31 George Kay 1931-5 Harold Wightman 1936-8 Edward Liddell 1938-9 Neil McBain 1939-47 George Martin 1947-58 'Dally' Duncan 1959-60 Syd Owen 1960-2 Sam Bartram 1962 Jack Crompton 1962-4 Bill Harvey 1965-6 George Martin 1966-8 Allan Brown 1968-72 Alec Stock 1972-8 Harry Haslam
Honours: Division 2 Champions 1981-2 Division 4 Champions 1967-8 Division 3 (S) Champions 1936-7
League Career: Elected to Division 2 1897 Failed to gain re-election 1900 Re-elected to Division 3 1920 Transferred to Division 3 (S) 1921 Promoted to Division 2 1936-7 Promoted to Division 1 1954-5 Relegated to Division 2 1959-60 Relegated to Division 3 1962-3 Relegated to Division 4 1964-5 Promoted to Division 3 1967-8 Promoted to Division 2 1969-70 Promoted to Division 1 1973-4 Relegated to Division 2 1974-5 Promoted to Division 1 1981-2
Colours: White shirts with orange sleeves and shoulders with three white and two navy stripes across shoulders and sleeves, white shorts with two orange and three navy vertical stripes down sides, orange stockings with white and navy trim
Change Colours: Orange shirts with navy blue sleeves and shoulders with white and navy stripes across shoulders and sleeves, navy shorts with white and orange trim, orange stockings with white and navy trim

CLUB RECORDS

Most Appearances for Club: Bob Morton: Football League 494 + F.A. Cup 48 + League Cup 7 **Total 549**
Most Capped Player: Mal Donaghy, 31. **For England:** Bob Hawkes, 5
Record Goalscorer in a Match: Joe Payne, 10 v Bristol Rovers (12-0) (H), Div 3 (S), 13.04.36
Record League Goalscorer in a season: Joe Payne, 55, Div 3 (S), 1936-7 **All competitions:** Joe Payne, 58 (League 55 + F.A. Cup 3
Record League Goalscorer in a career: Gordon Turner, 243 **All competitions:** Gordon Turner, 265 (League 243, F.A. Cup 18, League Cup 44), 1949-64
Record Transfer Fee Received: £350,000 from Manchester City for Paul Futcher, June 1978
Record Transfer Fee Paid: £200,000 to Mansfield Town for Mike Saxby, July 1979
£200,000 to Bristol Rovers for Steve White, Dec 1980
Best Performances: League: 8th Div 1 1957-8 **F.A. Cup:** Finalists 1959 **League/Milk Cup:** 5th Round 1978-9
Most League Points: (3pts for win) 88, Div 2, 1981-2 (record) (2pts for win) 66, Div 4, 1967-8
Most League Goals: 103, Div 3 (S), 1936-7
Record League Victory: 12-0 v Bristol Rovers, Div 3 (S), 13 Apr 1936
Record League Defeat: 0-9 v Small Heath, Div 2, 12 Nov 1898
Club Statistician for the Directory: R Wash

Programme Editor
Bill Tomlins

Price	**Number of Pages**
50p	24

Subscriptions
£18.00 (postage paid U.K.) home matches, £33.00 (postage paid U.K.) home and away matches

LUTON TOWN

PLAYERS NAME Ht Wt Birthdate	Honours	Birthplace Transfers	Clubs	APPEARANCES League	Milk Cup	F.A.C.	E. Cups	GOALS League	Milk Cup	F.A.C.	E. Cups
GOALKEEPERS											
Andy Dibble	W. U.21(3). Y. S	Cwmbran	Cardiff C. (A)	62	5	1					
6-2½ 13.7 8.5.65		£125,000	Luton T.								
Jake Findlay	Div. 2. 82	Blairgowrie	Aston Villa (A)	14	2						
6-1 14.1 13.7.54	FAYC. 72	£100,000	Luton T.	164	11	8					
			Barnsley (L)	6							
			Derby C. (L)	1							
Les Sealey		Bethnal Green	Coventry C. (A)	158	11	9					
6-1 11.6 29.9.57		£100,000	Luton T.	42	2	2					
DEFENDERS											
Mal Donaghy	N.I.(31). U.21(1)	Belfast	Larne								
5-10 12.7 13.9.57	Div. 2. 82	£20,000	Luton T.	246	17	10		14		1	
Paul Elliott	E. Y	London	Charlton A. (A)	61 + 2	2	1		1			
6-1½ 12.8 18.3.64		£145,000	Luton T.	51	2	2		3			
Mark North		Ware	Luton T.								
5-11 11.0 29.5.66											
Stacey North		Luton	Luton T.	1							
6-2 12.6 25.11.64											
Mitchell Thomas	E. Y	Luton	Luton T. (A)	30	1	3					
6-0 12.0 2.10.64											
Wayne Turner	Div. 2. 82	Luton	Luton T. (A)	58 + 2	4			2			
5-9 12.4 9.3.61			Lincoln C. (L)	16	1	5					
MIDFIELD											
Tim Breaker		Bicester	Luton T. (A)	2							
6-0 12.6 2.7.65											
Frankie Bunn		Birmingham	Luton T. (A)	35 + 4	2 + 1	2		4	2		
5-11 10.6 6.11.62											
Ray Daniel		Luton	Luton T. (A)	8 + 2				2			
5-10 10.11 10.12.64			Gillingham (L)	5							
Ashley Grimes	Ei.(16). U.21(2).	Dublin	Bohemians								
5-11½ 11.7 2.8.57	FAC. 83		Manchester U.	62 + 28	8	5		10		1	
		£200,000	Coventry C.	29 + 3	3			1	1		
		Player Exchange	Luton T.								
Vince Hilaire	E. U.21(9). B(1). Y.	Forest Gate	Crystal Palace (A)	239 + 16	20	16 +		29	4	3	
5-6 10.0 10.10.59	Div. 2. 79.	Player Exchange	Luton T.								
	FAYC. 77, 78										
Ricky Hill	E.(2). Y.	London	Luton T. (A)	273 + 6	20	12		42	1	1	
5-10 11.10 5.3.59	Div. 2. 82										
Bob Johnson		Bedford	Luton T. (A)	2							
5-6 9.12 22.2.62			Lincoln C. (L)	4							
FORWARDS											
Steve Elliott		Haltwhistle	Nottingham F. (A)	4	2						
5-11½ 11.10 15.9.58		£95,000	P.N.E.	202 + 6	11 +	5	3	70	2	2	3
			Luton T.								
David Moss	Div. 2. 82	Witney	Witney T.								
5-10½ 11.7 18.3.57			Swindon T.	217 + 13	13	25		60	7	14	
		£110,000	Luton T.	201 + 1	14	6		81	2	3	
Garry Parker	E. Y	Oxford	Luton T. (A)	14		1		2			
5-8 11.0 7.9.65											
Brian Stein	E.(1). U.21(3)	South Africa	Edgware T.								
5-10 11.8 19.10.57	Div. 2. 82		Luton T.	237 + 10	18	9		74	5	1	
Mark Stein		South Africa	Luton T.	1							
5-6 10.0 29.1.66											
Chuk Nwajiobi		Nigeria	Dulwich Hamlet								
5-7 12.2 25.5.59			Luton T.	2 + 2							

NON-CONTRACT PLAYERS 1984-85: Danny Driscoll, Alex Ellisdon, Trevor Parker

APPRENTICE: Richard McEvoy, Mick Doughty, David Oldfield

Kirk Stephens (now Coventry City) was Player of the Year 1983-84

LUTON TOWN

DIVISION ONE 16TH **FA CUP** 3RD ROUND **MILK CUP** 2ND ROUND

MATCH	DATE	COMPE-TITION	VENUE	OPPONENTS	RESULT	HALF TIME	L'GUE POS'N	GOALSCORERS	ATTEN-DANCE
1	A 27	CL	A	Arsenal	L1-2	1-1		Robson (og)	39,348
2	31	CL	A	Leicester C	W3-0	2-0		Bunn, Moss, Hill	11,929
3	S 3	CL	H	Sunderland	W4-1	0-0	5	Hill, Walsh, Munro (og), Stein	10,846
4	6	CL	H	Norwich C	D2-2	0-2		Elliott, Stein	11,095
5	10	CL	A	Manchester U	L0-2	0-0	8		41,013
6	17	CL	H	Wolverhampton W	W4-0	1-0	7	Walsh, Stein, Moss, Horton	10,975
7	24	CL	A	Nottingham F	L0-1	0-0	13		16,296
8	O 1	CL	H	Aston Villa	W1-0	0-0	9	Moss (pen)	12,747
9	**4**	**MC 2**	**A**	**Rotherham U**	**W3-2**	**2-0**		**Walsh, Bunn, Aylott**	**4,035**
10	15	CL	A	Everton	W1-0	0-0	7	Walsh	14,325
11	22	CL	H	Southampton	W3-1	2-1	4	Aylott 2, Stein	12,389
12	**25**	**MC 2**	**H**	**Rotherham U**	**L0-2**[1]	**0-1**			**6,755**
13	29	CL	A	Liverpool	L0-6	0-4	7		31,940
14	N 5	CL	A	QPR	W1-0	1-0	4	Elliott	15,053
15	12	CL	H	Birmingham C	D1-1	1-1	5	Stein	11,111
16	19	CL	H	Tottenham H	L2-4	0-1	10	Stein, Walsh	17,275
17	26	CL	A	Watford	W2-1	1-1	5	Stein, Bunn	17,791
18	D 3	CL	H	Coventry C	L2-4	0-2	10	Pearce (og), Aylott	10,698
19	10	CL	A	Stoke C	W4-2	2-1	8	Walsh 3, Daniel	10,329
20	18	CL	H	WBA	W2-0	1-0		Horton (pen), Aylott	11,566
21	26	CL	A	Notts Co	W3-0	1-0	3	Aylott 2, Daniel	9,786
22	27	CL	H	West Ham U	L0-1	0-0	5		16,343
23	31	CL	A	Sunderland	L0-2	0-0	6		19,482
24	J 2	CL	H	Nottingham F	L2-3	1-3	9	Walsh, Nwajiobi	12,126
25	**7**	**FAC 3**	**H**	**Watford**	**D2-2**	**2-2**		**Nwajiobi, Stein**	**15,007**
26	**10**	**FAC 3R**	**A**	**Watford**	**D3-4**[1]	**1-2**		**Donaghy, Walsh 2**	**20,586**
27	14	CL	H	Arsenal	L1-2	0-1	9	Kay (og)	16,320
28	21	CL	A	Wolverhampton W	W2-1	1-1	7	Parker, Walsh	11,594
29	F 4	CL	A	Aston Villa	D0-0	0-0	7		18,656
30	12	CL	H	Manchester U	L0-5	0-2			11,265
31	18	CL	H	Liverpool	D0-0	0-0	8		14,877
32	25	CL	A	Southampton	L1-2	0-2	11	Donaghy	17,947
33	M 3	CL	H	QPR	D0-0	0-0	10		11,922
34	13	CL	H	Ipswich T	W2-1	1-0		Aylott 2 (1 pen)	8,776
35	17	CL	A	Norwich C	D0-0	0-0	7		14,181
36	20	CL	A	Birmingham C	D1-1	1-0		Stein	9,592
37	24	CL	H	Leicester C	D0-0	0-0	10		10,509
38	31	CL	A	Ipswich T	L0-3	0-0	11		14,750
39	A 7	CL	H	Everton	L0-3	0-0	12		9,224
40	14	CL	A	Tottenham H	L1-2	0-1	14	Parker	25,390
41	17	CL	A	West Ham U	L1-3	0-2		Walsh	15,430
42	21	CL	H	Notts Co	W3-2	0-0	10	Moss, Horton (pen), Bunn	8,181
43	28	CL	H	Watford	L1-2	0-2	11	Walsh	12,594
44	M 5	CL	A	Coventry C	D2-2	0-1	13	Antic, Stein	9,391
45	7	CL	H	Stoke C	L0-1	0-1	13		9,867
46	12	CL	A	WBA	L0-3	0-0	16		12,400

[1] After Extra Time

Av Home Att **11,966**

Goal Scorers

League (53): Walsh 11, Stein B 9, Aylott 8 (1 pen), Moss 4 (1 pen), Bunn 3, Horton 3 (2 pens), Daniel 2, Elliott 2, Hill 2, Parker 2, Antic 1, Donaghy 1, Nwajiobi 1, opponents 4
FA Cup (5): Walsh 2, Donaghy 1, Nwajiobi 1, Stein 1
Milk Cup (3): Aylott 1, Bunn 1, Walsh 1

1983-84

Sealey	Stephens	Turner	Horton	Elliott	Donaghy	Hill	Stein B	Walsh	Bunn	Moss	Antic	Aylott	Thomas	Parker	Johnson	Goodyear	Daniel	Nwajiobi	Breaker	Stein M	North	REFEREE	
1	2	3	4	5	6	7	8	9	10	11												J Martin	1
1	2	3	4	5	6	7	8	9	10	11												D Shaw	2
1	2	3	4	5	6	7	8	9	10	11												A Lewis	3
1	2	3	4	5	6	7	8	9*	10	11	12											A Gunn	4
1	2	3	4	5	6	7	8	9	10*	11	12											F Roberts	5
1	2	3	4	5	6	7	8	9	10	11												D Letts	6
1	2	5	7	3	4	6	10	11	8*	9	12											J Worrall	7
1	2	3	4	5	6	7	8	9	10	11*	12											I Borrett	8
1	**2**	**3**	**4**	**5**	**6**	**7**	**8**	**9†**	**10**			**11**										**D Owen**	**9**
1	2	3	4	5	6	7	8	9	10	11												J Hough	10
1	2	3	4	5	6	7	8		10*	11	12	9										V Callow	11
1	**2**	**3**	**4**	**5**	**6**	**7**	**8**				**10**	**9**					**11**					**K Barratt**	**12**
1	2	10	4	5	6	7	8	9			11		3									JM Key	13
1	2	3	4	5	6	7	8	9				10		11								L Burden	14
1	2	10		5	6	7	8	9			12		3	11*	4							T Spencer	15
1	2	3		5	6	7	8	9			11	10				4						L Robinson	16
1	2	3	4	5	6	7	8	9	11			10										D Hedges	17
1	2	3	4	5	6	7	8	9	11*		12	10										B Hill	18
1	2		4	5	6	7	8	9				10	3				11					C Thomas	19
1	2		4	5	6	7	8	9				10	3				11					M Taylor	20
1	2		4	5	6	7	8	9				10	3				11					T Mills	21
1	2	12	4	5	6	7	8	9				10*	3				11					K Baker	22
1		3	4	5	6	7	8	9	10		12				2*		11					A Robertson	23
1	2		4	5	6	7	8	9	10*		12		3					11				D Axcell	24
1	**2**		**4**	**5**	**6**	**7**	**8**	**9**	**10**		**12**		**3**					**11***				**A Gunn**	**25**
1	**2**		**4**	**5**	**6**		**8**	**9**	**11**			**10**	**3**	**7**								**A Gunn**	**26**
1	2		4	5	6		8	9	11			10	3	7*				12				K Hackett	27
1	2		4	5	6*		8	9	11			10	3	7		12						H King	28
1	2		4	5	6		8	9	11			10	3	7								L Dilkes	29
1	2		4	5	6	7	8	9	11		12	10	3*									A Robinson	30
1	2		4	5	10	7	8	9					3			6	11					J Bray	31
1	2		4	5	6	7	8	9					3			12	10	11*				K Cooper	32
1	2		4	5	10	7	8	9				11	3			6						N Midgley	33
1	2			5	7		8	9	11		4	10	3			6						H Taylor	34
1	2			5	7		8	9	11		4	10	3			6						M Scott	35
1	2			5	7		8	9	11		4	10	3			6						E Read	36
1	2		4	5	7		8	9		11			3	10		6						A Crickmore	37
1	2		4		7		8	9	12	11*	5		3			6			10			R Lewis	38
1	2		4	5	6†		8		11			10	3			12			7	9*		J Ashworth	39
1	2		4	5	6		8		10	11	12	9*	3	7								M Bodenham	40
1	2		4	5	6		8	9	10*	11			3	7		12						D Reeves	41
1	2		4	5			8	9	10	11*	12		3	7		6						J Martin	42
1	2		4	5†			8	9	10	11*	12		3	7		6						R Milford	43
1	2		4		6		8	9	10		11		3	7		5						R Bridges	44
1	2		4		6		8	9	10*		11		3	7		5		12				M James	45
1		3	4		2		8	9	11		12	10		7		5					6	K Hackett	46
42	40	18	**37**	38	40	26	**42**	39	29	16	8	20	26	13	2	13	7	2	2	1	1	League Appearances	
		+1S							+1S		+14S					+4S		+2S					
2	2		2	2	2	1	2	2	2		1S	1	2	1				1				FA Cup Appearances	
2	2	2	2	2	2	2	2	1	1		1	2					1					Milk Cup Appearances	

KENILWORTH ROAD

Official Address: 70-72 Kenilworth Road, Luton. Telephone: Luton (0582) 411622. 24 hour information service: 0582 30748. Travel Club: 0582 412418

Ground Capacity: 20,000 (12,000 covered)

Record Attendance: 30,069 v. Blackpool, FA Cup Round 6 replay, 4 Mar 1959

Record Receipts: £55,906 v. Manchester U, FA Cup Round 4, 29 Jan 1983

Size of Playing Area: 112 × 72 yds

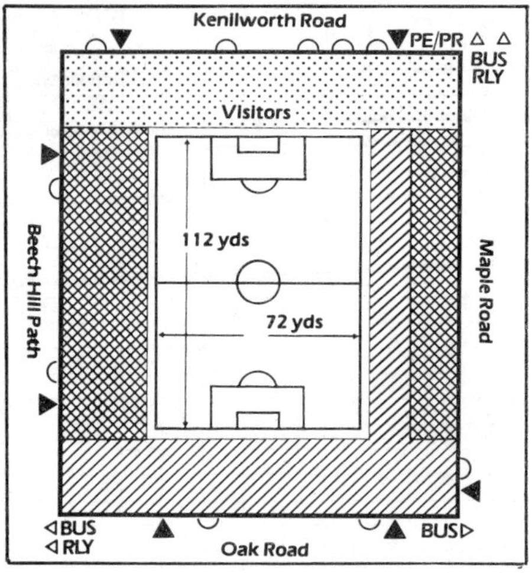

For key see page 12

Season Tickets: £80 (£40 OAPs), £75, £55 (£35 Juveniles/OAPs), £30 for Junior Hatters Club Enclosure

Executive Box Season Tickets: 'Club 82' £1,000 (for two seats, meal and bar); 'Century Club' £225 (existing members), £300 (new members) (includes buffet); 'Vice-President's Suite' £1,000 (for two seats, meal and bar)

Cost of Stand Tickets: £5.00, £4.00 (Visitors), £3.00 (£2.00 Juveniles); **Terraces:** £3.00 (Visitors), £2.50 (£1.50 Juveniles)

Match and Ticket Information: Seats bookable two weeks prior to each match

Car Parking: Street parking near ground only available

How to get to the ground

From North and West: Use Motorway M1 until junction 11 then follow signs Luton A505 into Dunstable Road. Forward through one-way system and then turn right into Kenilworth Road for Luton Town F.C.

From South and East: Use Motorway M1 until junction 10 or A6/A612 into Luton town centre, then follow signs Dunstable into Dunstable Road A505. Under railway bridge then turn left into Kenilworth Road for Luton Town F.C.

MANCHESTER CITY Division 2

Executive President
S Cussons FCACC

Chairman
P J Swales

Directors
I L G Niven MBE
C B Muir
M T Horwich
W C Adams
F Sellors
A Thomas
G Doyle
W A Miles
F Pye
J F Smith

Secretary
J B Halford

Commercial Manager
P Critchley (061 226 3143)

Curator-Statistician
W H Miles

Manager
W McNeill MBE

Assistant Manager
J Frizzell

Youth & Reserve Team Coaches
T Book & G Pardoe

Chief Scout
K Barnes

Physiotherapist
R Bailey

Groundsman
S Gibson

Under new management City promised for much of the season to make a quick return to the top flight but in the end they had to be content (if that is the right word) with a position 'outside the frame', which was the same fate that befell their Manchester rivals, who were in the top division. This was a big disappointment to Billy McNeill, but it might have been a good thing for the club since the team would not seem to be good enough yet.

Billy McNeill signed several players and had an early emphasis on Scots, of whom Jim Tolmie was the most impressive. Early results were encouraging and promotion was always possible until a late slump. The high spot was a victory at Chelsea by a single goal on the first Saturday of December (Tolmie scored), but there were also some bad results including a thrashing at St. James' Park, which could have done nothing for morale. Too many silly performances ensued and these were not relieved by anything great in the cup competitions. The Milk Cup ended at Villa Park in the Third Round with a sound beating (3-0) after Torquay had been savagely despatched in the Second Round (0-0 and 6-0 at Maine Road). The F.A. Cup was worse with a trip to Blackpool bringing a bad shock as the home team scored twice for themselves, enough to win, and once for City. Without any problems of fixture congestion City should have been able to mount an effective promotion challenge but did not from here onwards.

The question supporters will now ask is whether the new side can improve and bring back First Division Football. There are some good players apart from Tolmie, with Williams in goal a model of consistency. Others to do well were May, McCarthy, Parlane and Baker and there are good young players who could make the transition to League Football soon. But City supporters are likely to make their feelings known forcefully if good results in the new season do not come quickly.

WLM

Back Row L to R: Billy McNeill (Manager), Andy May, Derek Parlane, Tony Cunningham, Mick McCarthy, Alex Williams, Kevin Bond, Gordon Smith, Graham Baker, Roy Bailey (Physio), Jimmy Frizzell (Assistant Manager). **Front Row:** Nicky Reid, Neil McNab, Steve Kinsey, Paul Power, Clive Wilson, Jim Tolmie, David Phillips, Ray Ranson.

'CITY' or 'BLUES'

Sponsored by
Phillips Major Appliances

Formed: 1887 **Turned Professional:** 1887 **Ltd Co:** 1894
Previous Names: Ardwick 1887 until reformed as Manchester City in 1894
Previous Managers: 1892-3 L W Furniss 1893-5 W J Parlby 1895-1902 S Ormrod
1902-6 T E Maley 1906-12 H W Newbould 1912-26 J E Magnell
1926-32 P Hodge 1932-1946 W Wild
1946-7 S Cowan 1947-50 J R Thompson 1950-63 L McDowell
1963-5 G Poysor 1965-71 J Mercer 1971-3 M Allison
1973 Mar-Nov J Hart 1973-4 R Saunders 1974-9 T Book
1979-80 M Allison 1980-3 J Bond 1983 Feb-Jun J Benson
Honours: Division One Champions 1936-7, 1967-8 Division Two Champions 1898-9, 1902-3
FA Cup Winners 1904, 1934, 1956, 1969 Football League Cup Winners 1970, 1976
European Cup Winners Cup: Winners 1969-70
League Career: Elected as Ardwick as founder members of Division 2 1892
Manchester City elected to Division 2 1894
Promoted to Division 1 1898-9 Relegated to Division 2 1901-2
Promoted to Division 1 1902-3 Relegated to Division 2 1908-9
Promoted to Division 1 1909-10 Relegated to Division 2 1925-6
Promoted to Division 1 1927-8 Relegated to Division 2 1938-8
Promoted to Division 1 1946-7 Relegated to Division 2 1949-50
Promoted to Division 1 1950-1 Relegated to Division 2 1962-3
Promoted to Division 1 1965-6 Relegated to Division 2 1982-3
Colours: All sky blue with white trim and stripe down sleeve
Change Colours: White shirts with red/black diagonal stripes across chest, black shorts and stockings

CLUB RECORDS

Most Appearances for Club: Alan Oakes: Football League 564 + F.A. Cup 41 + League Cup 46 + European Cup 2 + European Cup Winners Cup 13 + UEFA Cup 2 + Charity Shield 3 + Texaco Cup 3 + Anglo-Scottish Cup 2 + Anglo-Italian 2 **Total 679**
Most Capped Player: Colin Bell, 48, England
Record Goalscorer in a Match: Denis Law, 6 v Luton Town, 4th Round F.A. Cup, 28.01.61 (match abandoned) Tommy Johnson, 5 v Everton, (H, 5-1), Div 1, 15.09.28 George Smith, 5 v Newport County, (H, 5-1), Div 2, 14.06.47
Record League Goalscorer in a season: Tommy Johnson, 38, Div 2, 1928-9 **In All Competitions:** Tommy Johnson, 38 (all League)
Record League Goalscorer in a career: Eric Brook, 159, 1927-39 (including one goal in season 1939-40)
In All Competitions: Eric Brook 178 (League 159, F.A. Cup 19)
Record Transfer Fee Received: £800,000 from Sampdoria for Trevor Francis, July 1982
Record Transfer Fee Paid: £1,150,000 to Wolverhampton Wanderers for Steve Daley, Sept 1979
Best Performances: League: Champions (2) **F.A. Cup:** Winners (4) **League/Milk Cup:** Winners (2)
European Cup Winners Cup: Winners **European Cup:** 1st Round **U.E.F.A. Cup:** Quarter Final
Most League Points: 70 in Div 2, 1983-4 **Most League Goals:** 108, Div 2, 1926-7
Record League Victory: 11-3 v Lincoln City, Div 2, 23 Mar 1895
Record League Defeat: 1-9 v Everton, Div 1, 3 Sept 1906
European Competitions Entered: European Cup 1968-9, European Cup Winners Cup 1969-70, 1970-1, UEFA Cup 1972-3, 1976-7, 1977-8, 1978-9
Club Statistician for the Directory: Ray Goble

Programme Editor
Paul Doherty

Price	Number of Pages
50p	24

Subscriptions
£19.00 (postage); (£3 extra abroad & Eire)

MANCHESTER CITY

PLAYERS NAME Ht Wt Birthdate	Honours	Birthplace Transfers	Clubs	APPEARANCES League	Milk Cup	F.A.C.	E. Cups	GOALS League	Milk Cup	F.A.C.	E. Cups
GOALKEEPER											
Alex Williams	E. Y	Moss Side	Manchester C.	64	4	1					
6-2½ 13.4 13.11.61											
DEFENDERS											
Kevin Bond	E. B(2)	West Ham	Bournemouth (A)								
6-1½ 13.7 22.6.57		F	Norwich C.	137+5	12	7		12		2	
		£200,000	Seattle Sounders								
		£350,000	Manchester C.	105+2	8	6		10			
Geoff Lomax		Droylsden	Manchester C.	17+1		1		1			
5-9 11.8 6.7.64											
Dave Phillips	W.(3), U.21(4), Y	Welborg, W.G.	Plymouth A.	65+8	2+1	9+1		15			
5-10 11.2 29.7.63		£65,000	Manchester C.								
Mick McCarthy†		Barnsley	Barnsley (A)	272	27	16		7	3		
6-1½ 13.3 7.2.59		£200,000	Manchester C.	24		1		1			
Ray Ransom	E. U.21(11), Y, S	St. Helens	Manchester C. (A)	181+2	22	13		1			
5-9½ 12.1 12.6.60											
Nicky Reid	E. U.21(6)	Ormston	Manchester C. (A)	144+4	14	13		2			
5-10 11.10 30.10.60											
MIDFIELD											
Graham Baker	E. U.21(2)	Southampton	Southampton (A)	111+2	6+1	3		22	2	1	
5-9 10.12 3.12.58		£200,000	Manchester C.	63	7	1		12			
Neil McNab	S. U.21(1), S.	Greenock	Morton	11+3	4+1	1			1		
5-7 10.10 6.6.57	FAYC. 74	£75,000	Tottenham	63+9	5	2		3			
		£250,000	Bolton W.	33+2	2	2		4			
		£220,000	Brighton	100+3	3	5		4		1	
			Leeds U. (L)	5		1					
		£30,000	Manchester C.	33	2	1		1			
Andy May		Bury	Manchester C. (A)	49+8	3			5			
5-8 11.1 26.2.64											
Paul Power*	E. B(1)	Manchester	Manchester C. (A)	280+7	29+	23		24	2	5	
5-10 11.6 30.10.53											
Paul Simpson		Carlisle		1+2	3	1			3		
5-6 10.5 26.7.66											
FORWARDS											
Tony Cunningham		Jamaica	Stourbridge								
6-1 13.2 12.11.57		£20,000	Lincoln C.	111+12	13	5+1		32	7		
		£85,000	Barnsley	40+2	4	5+1		11			
			Sheffield W.	26+2				5			
			Manchester C.								
Gordon Dalziel	SLC. 82	Motherwell	Glasgow Rangers	22+10	2+1	2+1		9	1	1	
5-10½ 12.0		£25,000	Manchester C.	4+1		+1					
Steve Kinsey	U.21(1)	Gorton	Manchester C.	42+11	1+1	3		8			
5-7 10.2 2.1.63			Chester C. (L)	3				1			
			Chesterfield (L)	3	1						
Derek Parlane	S.(12), U.23(5), Y,	Helensburgh	Glasgow Rangers	186+16	39+	19	16+	80	16	8	1
6-0 11.12 5.5.53	S.Lg(2), U.21(1),		Leeds U.	45+5	1	2		10			
	SD.1(1), SPD.(2),		Manchester C.	40+1				16			
	SC.(2), SLC.(3)										
Gordon Smith	S. U.21(1),	Kilwinning	Kilmarnock	158+5	31+1	9		36	7	1	
5-11 12.0 29.12.54	SPD.(1), SC.(2),		Glasgow Rangers	85+13	20+	15+3	15+	35	12	1	3
	SLC.(2), U.23(4)	£400,000	Brighton	97+12	8+1	5+1		22	2	1	
		£30,000	Manchester C.	9				1			
Jim Tolmie	S. U.21(1), SL.(1)	Glasgow	Morton	72	4+2	6+3		10	1	2	
5-6 10.10 20.11.60			Lokeren								
			Manchester C.	38+3	3	1		13	2		
Clive Wilson		Greenleys	Manchester C.	14+1	1						
5-7 9.10 13.11.61			Chester C. (L)	21				2			

CONTRACTED PLAYERS NOT YET ESTABLISHED IN FIRST TEAM: Richard Adams (D), **John Beresford** (MF), **Jamie Hoyland** (MF), **Gary Jackson** (MF), **Eric Nixon** (F)

NON-CONTRACT PLAYERS 1984-85: Carl Lewis, David White

APPRENTICES: Earl Barrett, Darren Beckford, Glen Sanderson, Paul Mouldon, Ian Scott, David Born, Steve Redmond

MANCHESTER CITY

DIVISION TWO 4TH **FA CUP** 3RD ROUND **MILK CUP** 3RD ROUND

MATCH	DATE	COMPETITION	VENUE	OPPONENTS	RESULT	HALF TIME	L'GUE POS'N	GOALSCORERS	ATTENDANCE
1	A 27	CL	A	Crystal Palace	W2-0	1-0		May, Parlane	13,382
2	29	CL	A	Cardiff C	L1-2	0-1		Tolmie	8,899
3	S 3	CL	H	Barnsley	W3-2	2-1	4	Tolmie 2, Parlane	25,105
4	7	CL	H	Fulham	D0-0	0-0			23,356
5	10	CL	A	Portsmouth	W2-1	2-1	4	Tolmie (pen), Parlane	18,852
6	17	CL	H	Blackburn R	W6-0	3-0	2	May, Parlane 3, Tolmie, Baker	25,433
7	24	CL	A	Leeds U	W2-1	0-0	2	Baker, Parlane	21,918
8	O 1	CL	H	Grimsby T	W2-1	0-0	2	Caton, Tolmie	25,080
9	**5**	**MC 2**	**A**	**Torquay U**	**D0-0**	**0-0**			**6,439**
10	8	CL	H	Swansea C	W2-1	1-1	2	Parlane, Davidson	23,571
11	15	CL	A	Charlton Ath	L0-1	0-0	2		7,639
12	22	CL	H	Middlesbrough	W2-1	0-1	2	Parlane, Tolmie	24,466
13	**25**	**MC 2**	**H**	**Torquay U**	**W6-0**	**1-0**		**Tolmie 2 (1 pen), Parlane 3, Hoyland**	**14,021**
14	29	CL	A	Newcastle U	L0-5	0-2	3		33,588
15	N 5	CL	A	Shrewsbury T	W3-1	0-0	3	May, Caton, Kinsey	9,471
16	**9**	**MC 3**	**A**	**Aston Villa**	**L0-3**	**0-1**			**23,922**
17	12	CL	H	Brighton & HA	W4-0	3-0	2	Baker 2, Tolmie, Parlane	24,562
18	19	CL	A	Carlisle U	L0-2	0-0	2		8,745
19	26	CL	H	Derby Co	D1-1	1-1	4	Parlane	22,689
20	D 3	CL	A	Chelsea	W1-0	1-0	2	Tolmie	29,142
21	10	CL	H	Sheffield W	L1-2	1-1	4	Bond	41,862
22	17	CL	A	Cambridge U	D0-0	0-0	4		5,204
23	26	CL	H	Oldham Ath	W2-0	0-0	4	Kinsey, Parlane	35,898
24	27	CL	A	Huddersfield T	W3-1	2-0	3	Kinsey, Baker, Lomax	23,497
25	31	CL	A	Barnsley	D1-1	1-0	3	Parlane	17,148
26	J 2	CL	H	Leeds U	D1-1	0-1	4	Tolmie (pen)	34,441
27	**7**	**FAC 3**	**A**	**Blackpool**	**L1-2**	**1-2**		**Hetzke (og)**	**15,377**
28	14	CL	H	Crystal Palace	W3-1	1-0	3	Power, Baker, Kinsey	20,144
29	21	CL	A	Blackburn R	L1-2	1-1	3	Tolmie (pen)	18,199
30	F 4	CL	A	Grimsby T	D1-1	1-0	3	Parlane	11,986
31	11	CL	H	Portsmouth	W2-1	0-1	3	Tolmie (pen), Reid	23,138
32	18	CL	H	Newcastle U	L1-2	0-2	3	Kinsey	41,767
33	25	CL	A	Middlesbrough	D0-0	0-0	5		9,343
34	M 3	CL	H	Shrewsbury T	W1-0	0-0	4	Reid	20,144
35	10	CL	A	Brighton H&A	D1-1	0-0	4	Hartford	14,132
36	17	CL	A	Fulham	L1-5	0-4	5	McNab	9,684
37	24	CL	H	Cardiff C	W2-1	0-1	5	Johnson, Baker	20,140
38	31	CL	H	Charlton Ath	L0-1	0-0	5		19,147
39	A 7	CL	A	Swansea C	W2-0	2-0	4	Parlane, Kinsey	6,261
40	14	CL	H	Carlisle U	W3-1	1-1	4	May, Smith, Parlane	20,760
41	20	CL	A	Oldham Ath	D2-2	1-1		McCarthy, Bond (pen)	20,320
42	23	CL	H	Huddersfield T	L2-3	2-2	4	Bond 2 (2 pen)	23,247
43	28	CL	A	Derby Co	L0-1	0-1	5		14,470
44	M 4	CL	H	Chelsea	L0-2	0-0			21,713
45	7	CL	A	Sheffield W	D0-0	0-0	5		36,763
46	12	CL	H	Cambridge U	W5-0	3-0	4	Tolmie, May, Baker, Kinsey, Power	20,787
								Av Home Att	**25,592**

Goal Scorers

League (63): Parlane 16, Tolmie 13 (4 pens), Baker 8, Kinsey 7, May 5, Bond 4 (3 pens), Caton 2, Power 2, Reid 2, Davidson 1, Hartford 1, Johnson 1, Lomax 1, McCarthy 1, McNab 1, Smith 1
FA Cup (1): Opponent 1
Milk Cup (6): Parlane 3, Tolmie 2 (1 pen), Hoyland 1

1983-84

Williams	Ranson	May	Bond	Power	Caton	McNab	Reid	Parlane	Hartford	Tolmie	Kinsey	Baker	Davies	Davidson	Walsh	Wilson	Hoyland	Lomax	Dalziel	McCarthy	Smith	Johnson	Sullivan	REFEREE	
1	2	3	4	5	6	7	8	9	10	11														K Barratt	1
1	2	3	4	5	6	7	8	9	10*	11	12													T Spencer	2
1	2	3	4	5	6	7	8	9		11		10												M Robinson	3
1	2	3	4	5	6	7	8	9		11		10												A Seville	4
1	2	7	4	5	6		8	9		11		10	3											D Vickers	5
1	2	3	4	5	6	7	8*	9		11		10		12										G Courtney	6
1	2	8*		5	6	7	4	9		11		10	3	12										KW Baker	7
1	2	8		5	6	7	4	9		11		10	3											K Redfern	8
1	**2**	**8**		**5**	**6**		**4**	**9**		**11**		**10**	**3**										**7**	**D Hedges**	**9**
1	2	8*		5	6	7	4	9		11		10	3	12										T Holbrook	10
1	2	8*		5	6	7	4	9		11		10	3	12										H King	11
1	2	3		5	6	7		9		11		10		8	4									F Roberts	12
1	**2**	**3**		**5**	**6**	**7**		**9***		**11**		**10**		**8**	**4**		**12**							**T Mills/J Caulkin***	**13**
1	2	3		5	6	7		9		11	12	10		8*	4									C Steel	14
1	2	3		5	6	7	4	9		11	8	10												E Read	15
1	**2**	**3**		**5**	**6**	**7**	**4**	**9**		**11**	**8***	**10**			**12**									**L Burden**	**16**
1	2	8		5	6	7	4	9		11		10				3								P Willis	17
1	2	8*	12	5	6	7	4†	9		11		10				3								G Tyson	18
1	2*	8	4	5	6	7		9		11					12	3	10							R Bridges	19
1		3	4	5		7		9	10	11	12				6*			2	8					I Borrett	20
1	2	6	4	5		7		9	10	11	12							3	8*					A Saunders	21
1		3	4	5		7		9	10	11		8						2		6				R Lewis	22
1		3	4	5		7		9		11	10	8						2		6				K Walmsley	23
1		3	4	5		7		9		11	10	8						2		6				M Scott	24
1	12	3	4	5		7		9		11	10*	8						2		6				J Bray	25
1		3	4	5		7		9		11		8						2	10	6				V Callow	26
1	**10**		**4**	**5**		**7***		**9**		**11**		**8**			**3**			**2**	**12**	**6**				**K Redfern**	**27**
1		3	4	5		7		9		11	10	8						2		6				J Key	28
1		3	4	5		7		9		11	10	8						2		6				M Peck	29
1		3	4	5		7		9		11	10	8						2		6				G Courtney	30
1		3	4	5		7	12	9*		11	10	8						2		6				K Hackett	31
1		3	4	5		7	2	9*		11	10	8						12		6				J Hunting	32
1	2	9	4	5		7	8	12		11*	10							3		6				D Hutchinson	33
1		3	4	5		7	2	9		11*	10	8							12	6				A Challinor	34
1		3	11	5			4		10		9	8						2	7	6				C Thomas	35
1		3	4	5		7	2	9	10	11		8								6				B Hill	36
1	2	3*	4	5		7		9		12		10								6	8	11		H Taylor	37
1	2	3	4	5		7*		9		11	12	10								6*		8		G Napthine	38
1		5	4					9		11	10	8				3		2		6	7			R Milford	39
1		5	4					9		11*	10	8				3		2		6	7	12		P Willis	40
1		5	4					9		12	10	8				3		2*		6	7	11		T Mills	41
1	2	5	4					9		12	10	8				3				6	7	11*		D Owen	42
1	2	5	4			10		9*		11	12	8				3				6	7			M Heath	43
1	2	11*	4	6				9		7		8				3				5	10	12		A Saunders	44
1	2	7	4	5				9		11		8				3				6	10			T Holbrook	45
1	2	7	4	5				9*		11	12	8				3				6	10			M Peck	46
42	25	**42**	33	37	16	33	18	40	7	38	16	36	5	2	3	11	1	16	4	24	9	4		League Appearances	
	+1S		+1S				+1S	+1S		+3S	+7S			+4S	+1S			+1S	+1S			+2S			
1	1		1	1		1		1		1		1			1			1	1S	1				FA Cup Appearances	
3	3	3		3	3	2	2	3		3	1	3	1	1	1+1S		1S						1	Milk Cup Appearances	

*Original Referee injured

MAINE ROAD

Official Address: Maine Road, Moss Side, Manchester M14 7WN. Telephone: 061-226 1191/2

Telegraphic: Football Manchester 14

Ground Capacity: 52,500

Record Attendance: 84,569 v. Stoke City, F.A. Cup Round 6, 3 Mar 1934 (record in Britain for match outside London or Glasgow)

Record Receipts: £240,000 Liverpool v. Everton, Milk Cup Final Replay, Mar 1984

Size of Playing Area: 119yds × 79 yds

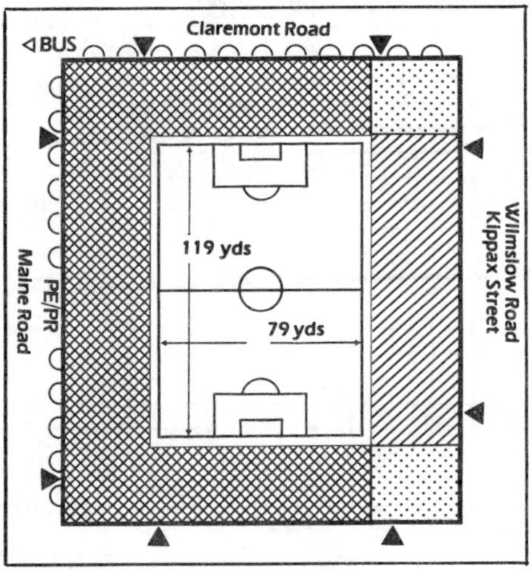

For key see page 12

Season Tickets: Stands: £50.00, £55.00, £70.00, £90.00 (£23.00, £32.00 juveniles/OAP); Ground £25.00, £36.00 (£14.00, £15.00, £22.00 juveniles/OAP)

Cost of Stand Tickets: £3.50, £5.00 (Reserved); £3.00, £3.50 (unreserved); Ground: £2.00 (£1.50 juveniles/OAP); £2.00 under 14's & OAP unreserved

Match and Ticket Information: Advance booking 14 days prior to matches

Car Parking: Kippax Street car park holds 400 vehicles (approx). Some street parking is permitted

How to get to the ground

From North: Use Motorway M61 then M63 until junction 9. Leave Motorway and follow signs Manchester A5103. In 2.8m at crossroads turn right into Claremont Road. In 0.4m turn right into Maine Road for Manchester City F.C.
From East: Use Motorway M62 until junction 17 then A56 into Manchester. Follow signs Manchester Airport then turn left to join Motorway A57(M). Follow signs Birmingham to join A5103. Then in 1.3m turn left into Claremont Road. In 0.4m turn right into Maine Road for Manchester City F.C.
From South: Use Motorway M6 until junction 19 then A556 and M56 until junction 3. Keep forward A5103 S.P. Manchester. In 2.8m at crossroads turn right into Claremont Road. In 0.4m turn right into Maine Road for Manchester City F.C.
From West: Use Motorway M62 then M63 as from north. Or use M56 as from south.

MANCHESTER UNITED Division 1

President
Sir Matt Busby CBE

Chairman
C M Edwards

Directors
R Charlton CBE
E M Watkins
D D Haroun JP
J G Gulliver
R L Edwards
J M Edelson

Secretary
R L Olive

Assistant Secretary
K R Merrett

Commercial Manager
J Lillie (061 872 1661/2/3)

Ticket Officer
K Ramsden

Manager
R Atkinson

Assistant Manager
M Brown

Reserve Team Coach
Brian Whitehouse

Youth Team Coach
E Harrison

Chief Scout
T Collins

Physiotherapist
J McGregor

Groundsman
G Loughnane

Manchester United spent most of the season chasing champions Liverpool but a disastrous run at the end meant a drop to fourth place in the League. The Reds suffered two major blows in the domestic Cups but were desperately unlucky not to reach the final of the European Cup-Winners' Cup.

Manager Ron Atkinson signed Arthur Graham from Leeds to replace the retired Steve Coppell and he did a thoroughly professional job. With Arnold Muhren operating well on the opposite flank and Frank Stapleton looking as sharp as ever up front United had a Championship look about them, particularly as England's Ray Wilkins and Bryan Robson hit peak form in midfield.

In one spell in mid-season United played 16 League games without defeat. Away form was superb with only one defeat – at Southampton (0-3) – in their opening 15 away League matches.

Disappointing performances at Old Trafford and too many drawn games ultimately cost United the title. United dropped home points to mid table sides Aston Villa (1-2), Everton (0-1), Notts County (3-3), Norwich (0-0) and Ipswich (1-2) though they scored fine wins over leading clubs like Liverpool and Southampton. Indeed, United took four points from Liverpool, winning 1-0 at Old Trafford and drawing 1-1 at Anfield and remained in contention until the end of Easter when, with five games remaining, they were only two points behind Liverpool. Sadly, they failed to win any of those matches.

They had the "luck" to be drawn against Third and Fourth Division clubs in each of the first three stages of the Milk Cup. Though they scored comfortable wins over Port Vale and Colchester United they found a tough obstacle in Oxford United. Following 1-1 draws both at The Manor and Old Trafford, United returned to the Third Division ground to lose 1-2, but worse was to follow. As holders of the FA Cup, they appeared to have a simple first defence of that trophy away to Bournemouth, fourth from bottom of the Third Division. In the event, United were outplayed. The Cherries rose splendidly to the challenge, played the more intelligent football and won with two excellent goals within two minutes mid-way through the second-half. That was one of the greatest humiliations in United's history. But they were still in the European Cup-Winners' Cup. Following wins over Dukla Prague (on away goals) and Spartak Varna (4-1), United made a disastrous start to their quarter-final tie in Barcelona. Graeme Hogg conceded an own-goal and United seemed on the way out after losing 0-2, but that inspired one of their finest-ever performances at Old Trafford. Two goals from Bryan Robson and another from Frank Stapleton transformed the situation and United advanced to the semi-final tie with Juventus.

Though ravaged by injuries – they missed Wilkins, Robson and Muhren – United did draw the first-leg 1-1 at Old Trafford. Still without Robson in the return, United recovered from an early set-back to make it 1-1. Tragically, Juventus snatched the winner in the last minute. A season that had promised so much ended in some disappointment.

TP

Back Row: Mike Duxbury, Mark Hughes, Paul McGrath, Gordon McQueen, Graeme Hogg, Norman Whiteside, John Gidman. **Middle Row:** Mick Brown (Assistant Manager), Kevin Moran, Arnold Muhren, Jeff Wealands, Stephen Pears, Gary Bailey, Alan Brazil, Frank Stapleton, Jim McGregor (Physio). **Front Row:** Arthur Albiston, Jesper Olsen, Bryan Robson, Ron Atkinson (Manager), Remi Moses, Arthur Graham and Gordon Strachan.

'UNITED REDS or RED DEVILS'

Sponsored by **Sharp Electronics (UK) Ltd**

Year Formed: 1878 **Turned Professional:** 1902 **Ltd Co:** 1907
Previous Name: Newton Heath 1880-1902
Previous Managers: Since 1946: Matt Busby Wilf McGuiness Sir Matt Busby Frank O'Farrell Tommy Docherty Dave Sexton
Honours: Division 1 Championships 1907-8, 1910-11, 1951-2, 1955-6, 1956-57,1964-5,1966-7 Division 2 Champions 1935-6, 1974-5. F.A. Cup Winners 1909, 1948, 1963, 1977, 1983 European Cup Winners 1967-8
League Career: Elected to Division 1 1892 Relegated to Division 2 1893-4 Promoted to Division 1 1905-6 Relegated to Division 2 1921-2 Promoted to Division 1 1924-5 Relegated to Division 2 1930-1 Promoted to Division 1 1935-6 Relegated to Division 2 1936-7 Promoted to Division 1 1937-8 Relegated to Division 2 1973-4 Promoted to Division 1 1974-5
Colours: Red shirts with white and black trim, white shorts, black stockings with red top with three white hoops
Change Colours: White shirts with black and red trim, black shorts with white trim, white stockings with three black hoops on tops

CLUB RECORDS

Most Appearances for Club: Bobby Charlton, 1956-73 604 + 2 subs League + 78 F.A. Cup + 24 League Cup + 45 European Cups + 3 F.A. Charity Shield **Total 754 + 2 subs**
Most Capped Player: Bobby Charlton 106 England
Record Goalscorer in a Match: R Smith, 6 for Newton Heath v. Walsall Town Swifts, Div 2, 9 March 1895.
Record League Goalscorer in a season: Dennis Viollet, 32, Div 1, 1959-60 **All competitions:** Denis Law, 46 (League 30, F.A. Cup 10, European Cup Winners Cup 6), 1963-4
Record League Goalscorer in a career: Bobby Charlton **All competitions:** Bobby Charlton, 248 (League 198, F.A. Cup 19, League Cup 7, European Cup 22, Charity Shield 2)
Record Transfer Fee Received: £1,500,000 from A.C. Milan for Ray Wilkins, June 1984
Record Transfer Fee Paid: £1,500,000 to W.B.A. for Bryan Robson, Oct 1981
Best Performances: Football League: Champions(7) **F.A. Cup** Winners(5) **League/Milk Cup:** Finalists **European Cup** Winners **European Cup Winners Cup** Semi-Finalists **European Fairs Cup/U.E.F.A Cup:** Semi-Finalists
Most League Points: (3pts for win)78 Div 1, 1981-2 (2 points for win) 64 Div 1 1956-7
Most League Goals: 103 Div 1 1956-7, 103 Div 1 1958-9
Record League Victory: 10-1 v. Wolverhampton Wanderers, Division 2, 15 Oct 1892 (as Newton Heath)
Record League Defeat: 0-7 v Wolverhampton Wanderers Div 2 26 Dec 1931 0-7 v Blackburn Rovers Div 1 10 Apr 1926 0-7 v Aston Villa Div 1 27 Dec 1931
European Competitions Entered: European Cup: 1956-7, 1957-8, 1965-6, 1967-8, 1968-9, European Cup Winners Cup: 1963-64, 1977-78, 1983-84, European Fairs/U.E.F.A. Cup: 1964-5, 1976-7, 1980-1, 1982-3
Club Statistician for The Directory: John Hewitt

Programme Editor
Ken Ramsden

Price	Number of Pages
35p	24

Subscriptions
£15 (UK) and £19 (overseas)

MANCHESTER UNITED

PLAYERS NAME Ht Wt Birthdate	Honours	Birthplace Transfers	Clubs	APPEARANCES League	Milk Cup	F.A.C.	E. Cups	GOALS League	Milk Cup	F.A.C.	E. Cups
GOALKEEPERS											
Gary Bailey	E. B(2), U.21(14),	Ipswich	Manchester U.	226	21	21	10				
6-1½ 12.10 9.8.58	FAC. 83										
Steve Pears		Brandon	Manchester U. (A)								
5-11½ 11.10 22.1.62			Middlesbrough (L)	12							
Jeff Wealands		Darlington	Wolverhampton W. (A)								
6-0½ 12.0 26.8.51		F	Darlington	28	1	2					
		£10,000	Hull C.	240	19	11					
		£30,000	Birmingham C.	102	10	5					
			Manchester U.	7	1						
			Oldham A. (L)	10							
DEFENDERS											
Arthur Albiston	S.(6), U.21(5),	Edinburgh	Manchester U. (A)	264 + 6	30 +	24	16 +	5	1		
5-7½ 10.13 14.7.57	FAC. 77, 83										
Mike Duxbury	E.(8), U.21(7),	Blackburn	Manchester U. (A)	127 + 11	15 +	1 + 2	9 + 1	3		1	
5-9 10.12 1.9.59	FAC. 83										
John Gidman	E.(1), B.(2), Y,	Liverpool	Liverpool (N-C)								
5-11 12.2 10.1.54	U.23(4), Lg.C. 77,		Aston Villa	196 + 1	21	12		9			
	FAYC. 72	£650,000	Everton	64	6	11		2	1		
		£450,000	Manchester U.	43 + 1	3	1	1	1			
Graeme Hogg	S. U.21(1)	Aberdeen	Manchester U. (A)	16		1	4	1			
6-1 12.12 19.6.64											
Paul McGrath		Ealing	St. Patrick's Ath.								
6-0 13.2 4.12.59		£30,000	Manchester U.	23	1		2	4			
Gordon McQueen	S.(30), FAC. 83,	Kilbirnie	St. Mirren	57	13	6		5	1		
6-3 13.7 26.6.52	Div. 1, 74	£40,000	Leeds U.	140	5	13	12 + 1	15		1	3
		£495,000	Manchester U.	172	18	20		19	4	1	
Kevin Moran	Ei.(17), FAC. 83	Dublin	Manchester U.	139	13	9	8 + 1	17	2	1	
5-10½ 12.8 29.4.58											
MIDFIELD											
Alan Davies	W.(4), U.21(6),	Manchester	Manchester U.	6 + 1		2					
5-8 10.4 5.12.61	FAC. 83										
Remi Moses	E. U.21(8)	Manchester	W.B.A.	63	7	2	1	5	1		
5-6 10.7 14.11.60		£650,000	Manchester U.	80 + 5	14 +	7	5	4	2		
Arnold Muhren	Hol., FAC. 83,	Volendam	FC Twente								
5-11 11.1 2.6.51	UEFAC. 81	£150,000	Ipswich T.	161	15	19	19	21	2	3	3
			Manchester U.	58	10	7	5	13	1	1	
Jesper Olsen	Denmark	Fakse	Ajax								
5-6 10.0			Manchester U.								
Bryan Robson*	E.(36), U.21(7),	Chester-le-Street	W.B.A. (A)	193 + 4	17 +	10 +		39	2	2	
5-10½ 11.9 11.1.57	B(2), Y, S, FAC. 83	£1,500,000	Manchester U.	98	15	8	18	27	1	3	4
Gordon Strachan	S.28, U.21(1), Y		Dundee	56 + 13	10 + 1	7		13	1	1	
5-6 10.8	SPD.80, 84, SC. 82		Aberdeen	175 + 9	43 + 2	29 + 1	30 + 4	55	20	7	8
	83, 84, ECWC.83		Manchester U.								
FORWARDS											
Clayton Blackmore	W. U.21(3), Y, S	Neath	Manchester U. (A)	1							
5-9 11.3 23.9.64											
Alan Brazil	S.(13), U.21(8),	Glasgow	Ipswich T. (A)	143 + 11	14 +	18 +	21	70	3	6	1
6-0 12.4 15.6.59	UEFAC. 81	£500,000	Tottenham	29 + 2	+ 1	1	3 + 2	9			4
		£700,000	Manchester U.								
Arthur Graham	S.(10), U.23(3),	Glasgow	Aberdeen	217 + 7	41	16 + 1	9	32	5		2
5-8 11.10 26.10.52	SC.(1), SLC.(1)	£125,000	Leeds U.	222 + 1	22	12	3	37	4	3	3
			Manchester U.	33 + 4	5	1	6 + 1	5	1		1
Mark Hughes	W.(2), U.21(5), Y	Wrexham	Manchester U.	7 + 4	1 + 1		2 + 3	4	1		
5-9 11.2 1.11.63											
Frank Stapleton	Ei.(38), Y,	Dublin	Arsenal (A)	223 + 2	26	32	15	75	14	15	4
5-11 13.0 10.7.56	FAC: 79, 83	£900,000	Manchester U.	124	17	9	8	40	4	3	4
Norman Whiteside	NI.(15), Y, S,	Belfast	Manchester U.	70 + 8	13 +	8	6 + 1	19	4	3	1
6-0 12.3 8.5.65	FAC. 83										

CONTRACTED PLAYERS WITH NO FIRST TEAM APPEARANCES

Bill Garton, Mark Dempsey, Pat Kelch, Andy Robinson, Martin Russell, Ken Scott, Nick Wood, David Platt, David Wynn (monthly)**, Steve Welsh, Paul McGuiness**

APPRENTICES

Denis Cronin, Fraser Digby, Jon Hardy, Alan McLoughlin, Stuart Brooks, Steve Gardner, Karl Goddard, Andy McBride, Aiden Murphy, Bob Philpot, Simon Ratcliffe, Gary Worthington, Andy Mathieson, Tony Gill, Paul Harvey

Ray Wilkinson (now A.C. Milan) was Player of the Year 1983-84

MANCHESTER UTD

DIVISION ONE 4TH **FA CUP** 3RD ROUND **MILK CUP** 4TH ROUND **EUROPEAN CUP WINNERS CUP** SEMI-FINAL

MATCH	DATE	COMPE-TITION	VENUE	OPPONENTS	RESULT	HALF TIME	L'GUE POS'N	GOALSCORERS	ATTEN-DANCE
1	A 27	CL	H	QPR	W3-1	2-0		Muhren 2 (1 pen), Stapleton	48,742
2	29	CL	H	Nottingham F	L1-2	1-0		Moran	43,005
3	S 3	CL	A	Stoke C	W1-0	0-0	7	Muhren	23,704
4	6	CL	A	Arsenal	W3-2	3-1		Moran, Stapleton, Robson	42,704
5	10	CL	H	Luton T	W2-0	0-0	3	Muhren (pen), Albiston	41,013
6	**14**	**ECWC 1**	**H**	**Dukla Prague**	**D1-1**	**0-0**		**Wilkins (pen)**	**39,765**
7	17	CL	A	Southampton	L0-3	0-2	5		20,674
8	24	CL	H	Liverpool	W1-0	0-1	2	Stapleton	56,121
9	**27**	**ECWC 1**	**A**	**Dukla Prague**	**D2-2[2]**	**1-1**		**Robson, Stapleton**	**28,000**
10	O 1	CL	A	Norwich C	D3-3	1-0	4	Whiteside 2, Stapleton	19,680
11	**3**	**MC 2**	**A**	**Port Vale**	**W1-0**	**1-0**		**Stapleton**	**19,855**
12	15	CL	H	WBA	W3-0	2-0	1	Graham, Whiteside, Albiston	42,221
13	**19**	**ECWC 2**	**A**	**Spartak Varna**	**W2-1**	**1-1**		**Robson (pen), Graham**	**37,500**
14	22	CL	A	Sunderland	W1-0	1-0	1	Wilkins (pen)	26,826
15	**26**	**MC 2**	**H**	**Port Vale**	**W2-0**	**1-0**		**Whiteside, Wilkins (pen)**	**23,589**
16	29	CL	H	Wolverhampton W	W3-0	3-0	1	Stapleton 2, Robson	41,880
17	**N 2**	**ECWC 2**	**H**	**Spartak Varna**	**W2-0**	**2-0**		**Stapleton 2**	**39,079**
18	5	CL	H	Aston Villa	L1-2	0-1	1	Robson	45,077
19	**8**	**MC 3**	**A**	**Colchester U**	**W2-0**	**2-0**		**McQueen, Moses**	**13,031**
20	12	CL	A	Leicester C	D1-1	1-0	3	Robson	23,012
21	19	CL	H	Watford	W4-1	2-0	3	Stapleton 3, Robson	43,111
22	27	CL	A	West Ham U	D1-1	0-0		Wilkins	23,355
23	**30**	**MC 4**	**A**	**Oxford U**	**D1-1**	**1-1**		**Hughes**	**13,711**
24	D 3	CL	H	Everton	L0-1	0-0	3		43,664
25	**7**	**MC 4R**	**H**	**Oxford U**	**D1-1[1]**	**0-0**		**Stapleton**	**27,459**
26	10	CL	A	Ipswich T	W2-0	1-0	3	Graham, Crooks	19,779
27	16	CL	H	Tottenham H	W4-2	1-0		Graham 2, Moran 2	33,616
28	**19**	**MC 4R2**	**A**	**Oxford U**	**L1-2[1]**	**1-1**		**Graham**	**13,912**
29	26	CL	A	Coventry C	D1-1	1-1	2	Muhren (pen)	21,453
30	27	CL	H	Notts Co	D3-3	0-0	2	Crooks, McQueen, Moran	41,544
31	31	CL	H	Stoke C	W1-0	0-0	2	Graham	40,164
32	J 2	CL	A	Liverpool	D1-1	0-1	2	Whiteside	45,122
33	**7**	**FAC 3**	**A**	**AFC Bournemouth**	**L0-2**	**0-0**			**15,000**
34	13	CL	A	QPR	D1-1	0-1	2	Robson	16,309
35	21	CL	H	Southampton	W3-2	2-2	2	Robson, Stapleton, Muhren	40,371
36	F 3	CL	H	Norwich C	D0-0	0-0	2		36,851
37	7	CL	A	Birmingham C	D2-2	1-1	2	Whiteside, Hogg	19,975
38	12	CL	A	Luton T	W5-0	2-0	3	Robson 2, Stapleton, Whiteside 2	11,265
39	18	CL	A	Wolverhampton W	D1-1	0-1	3	Whiteside	20,676
40	25	CL	H	Sunderland	W2-1	1-1	2	Moran 2	40,615
41	M 3	CL	A	Aston Villa	W3-0	1-0	2	Moses, Whiteside, Robson	32,874
42	**7**	**ECWC 3**	**A**	**Barcelona**	**L0-2**	**0-1**			**90,000**
43	10	CL	H	Leicester C	W2-0	0-0	2	Moses, Hughes	39,473
44	17	CL	H	Arsenal	W4-0	2-0	1	Muhren 2 (1 pen), Stapleton, Robson	48,942
45	**21**	**ECWC 3**	**H**	**Barcelona**	**W3-0**	**1-0**		**Robson 2, Stapleton**	**58,350**
46	31	CL	A	WBA	L0-2	0-1	2		27,954
47	A 7	CL	H	Birmingham C	W1-0	1-0	2	Robson	39,891
48	**11**	**ECWC 4**	**H**	**Juventus**	**D1-1**	**1-1**		**Davies**	**58,231**
49	14	CL	A	Notts Co	L0-1	0-0	2		13,911
50	17	CL	A	Watford	D0-0	0-0			20,764
51	21	CL	H	Coventry C	W4-1	1-0	2	Hughes 2, McGrath, Wilkins	38,524
52	**25**	**ECWC 4**	**A**	**Juventus**	**L1-2**	**0-1**		**Whiteside**	**64,655**
53	28	CL	H	West Ham U	D0-0	0-0	2		44,124
54	M 5	CL	A	Everton	D1-1	0-0	2	Stapleton	28,817
55	7	CL	H	Ipswich T	L1-2	1-0	2	Hughes	44,257
56	12	CL	A	Tottenham H	D1-1	0-0	2	Whiteside	39,790
57	16	CL	A	Nottingham F	L0-2	0-1			23,651

Av Home Att 44,546

Goal Scorers

League (71): Stapleton 13, Robson 12, Whiteside 10, Muhren 8 (4 pens), Moran 7, Graham 5, Hughes 4, Wilkins 3 (1 pen), Albiston 2, Crooks 2, Moses 2, Hogg 1, McGrath 1, McQueen 1

FA Cup (-): —

Milk Cup (8): Stapleton 2, Graham 1, Hughes 1, McQueen 1, Moses 1, Whiteside 1, Wilkins 1 (1 pen)

ECWC (12): Robson 4, Stapleton 4, Davies 1, Graham 1, Whiteside 1, Wilkins 1 (1 pen)

1983-84

Bailey	Duxbury	Albiston	Wilkins	Moran	McQueen	Robson	Muhren	Stapleton	Whiteside	Graham	Macari	Gidman	Moses	McGrath	Crooks	Wealands	Hogg	Hughes	Davies	Blackmore	Dempsey	REFEREE	
1	2	3	4	5	6	7	8	9	10*	11	12											J Bray	1
1	2*	3	4	5	6	7	8	9	10	11	12											R Bridges	2
1		3	4	6	5	7	8	9	10	11		2										M Dimblebee	3
1		3	4	5	6	7	8	9	10	11*		2	12									M Bodenham	4
1		3	4	5	6	7*	8	9	10	11		2	12									F Roberts	5
1	**2**	**3**	**4**	**5**	**6**	**7**	**8**	**9**		**11**	**10**												**6**
1	2	3	4	5	6		8	9	10	11			7									L Shapter	7
1	2	3	4	5	6	7	8	9	10	11												KS Hackett	8
1	**2**	**3**	**4**	**5**	**6**	**7**	**8**	**9**	**10**	**11**												**H Fawler**	**9**
1	2	3	4	5		7	8*	9	10	11			12	6								R Lewis	10
1	**2***	**3**	**4**	**5**		**7**	**8**	**9**	**10**	**11**			**12**	**6**								**V Callow**	**11**
1	2	3	4	5	6	7	8	9	10	11												A Challinor	12
1	**2**	**3**	**4**	**5**	**6**	**7**	**8**	**9**	**10**	**11**												**Eschweiler**	**13**
1	2	3	4	5*	6	7		9	10	11	12		8									D Hutchinson	14
1	**5**	**3**	**4**		**6**	**7**		**9**	**10***	**11**		**2**	**8**					**12**				**G Tyson**	**15**
1	5	3	4		6	7	8	9	10	11		2*	12									G Courtney	16
1	**2**	**3**		**5***	**6**	**7**		**9**	**10***	**11**	**8**		**4**					**12**			**13**	**Eriksson**	**17**
1	2	3	4	5	6	7		9	10*	11	12		8									C Seel	18
1	**2**	**3**	**4**	**5**	**6**	**7**		**9**	**10***	**11**	**12**		**8**									**T Bune**	**19**
1	2	3	4	5	6	7		9	10	11			8									J Moules	20
1	5	3	4		6	7	8	9		11			2		10							G Napthine	21
1	5	3	4		6	7	8*	9	12	11			2		10							C Thomas	22
1	**2**	**3**	**4**	**5**	**6**	**7**		**9**	**10**				**8**					**11**				**C Downey**	**23**
1	2	3	4	5	6	7		9	11				8		10							K Walmsley	24
1	**2**	**3**	**4**	**5**	**6**	**7**		**9**	**10**	**11**			**8**									**K Redfern**	**25**
1	2	3	4	5	6	7		9		11			8		10							B Hill	26
1	6	3	4	5		7	8	9*	10	11	12		2									A Saunders	27
	6	**3**	**4**	**5**		**7***	**8**	**9**	**10**	**11**	**12**		**2**			**1**						**T Spencer**	**28**
	2	3	4	5	6		8	9		11			7		10	1						R Milford	29
	2	3	4	5	6		8	9	12	11			7		10*	1						D Owen	30
1	2	3	4	5	6		8	9	10	11			7									J Key	31
1	2	3	4	5	6*		8	9	10	11			7		12							D Richardson*	32
1	**6**	**3***	**4**			**7**	**8**	**9**	**10**	**11**	**12**		**2**				**5**					**B Stevens**	**33**
1	2		6	5		8	7	10	9	11			3				4					J Hunting	34
1	2		4	5		7	8	9	10*	11			3				6	12				A Seville	35
1	6	3	4	5		7	8	9	10	11			2									M Peck	36
1	2	3	4	5		7		9	10	11			8				6					M King	37
1	2	3	4	5		7*	8	9	10	12			11				6					A Robinson	38
1	2	3	4*	5		7	8	9	10	12			11				6					D Brazier	39
1	2	3	4	5*		7	8	9	10	12			11				6					H Taylor	40
1	2	3	4			7	8	9	10*	12			11	5			6					K Salmon	41
1	**2**	**3**	**4**	**5**		**7**	**8**	**9**		**12**			**11**				**6**	**10***				**Vautrot (F)**	**42**
1	2	3	4	5		7	8	9					11				6	10				P Willis	43
1	2	3	4	5		7	8	9	10*				11				6	12				G Courtney	44
1	**2**	**3**	**4**	**5**		**7**	**8**	**9**	**10***				**11**				**6**	**12**				**Casarin (IT)**	**45**
1	2	3	4	5		7		9	10	8			11				6					D Letts	46
1	2	3	4	5		7		9	10*	8			11				6	12				T Mills	47
1	**2**	**3**		**5**				**9**	**10**	**8**		**4***	**11**	**7**			**6**	**12**				**Kelzer (HOL)**	**48**
1	2	5	6	3				9	10				7	8			4	12	11*			R Lewis	49
1	2	3	4	5				9	10	11				8			6		7			K Barratt	50
1	2	3	4*	5				9	12	11			8	7			6	10				D Hutchinson‡	51
1	**2**	**3**	**4**	**5**				**9***	**12**	**11**			**8**	**7**			**6**	**10**				**Ponnett (BEL)**	**52**
1	2	3	4	5				9	12	11			8	7*			6	10				K Hackett	53
1	2	3	4	5		7		9	12				8				6	10	11*			D Shaw	54
1	2	3	4	5		7		9		11			8	6				10				G Tyson	55
1	2	3	4	5		7		9*	12	11			8	6				10				M Taylor	56
1	2	3	4	5		7		9	12	11*				6				10		8		D Vickers	57
40	39	40	**42**	38	20	33	26	**42**	30	33	0	4	31	9	6	2	16	7	3	1		League Appearances	
									+7S	+4S	+5S		+4S		+1S			+4S					
1	1	1	1			1	1	1	1	1	1S		1				1					FA Cup Appearances	
5	6	6	6	5	4	6	2	6	6	5	2S	1	5+1S	1		1		1+1S				Milk Cup Appearances	
8	8	8	6	8	4	6	5	8	5+1S	6+1S	2	1	5	2			4	2+3S			15	ECWC Appearances	

‡Replaced by D Marre

OLD TRAFFORD

Official Address: Old Trafford, Manchester M16 0RA. Telephone: 061-872 1661/2

Telegraphic: Stadium Manchester

Ground Capacity: 58,544

Record Attendance: 76,962, Wolverhampton Wanderers v Grimsby Town, F.A. Cup Semi-Final, 25 March 1939

Record Receipts: £221,899.60 v. Juventus, 11 Apr 1984

Size of Playing Area: 116yds × 76 yds

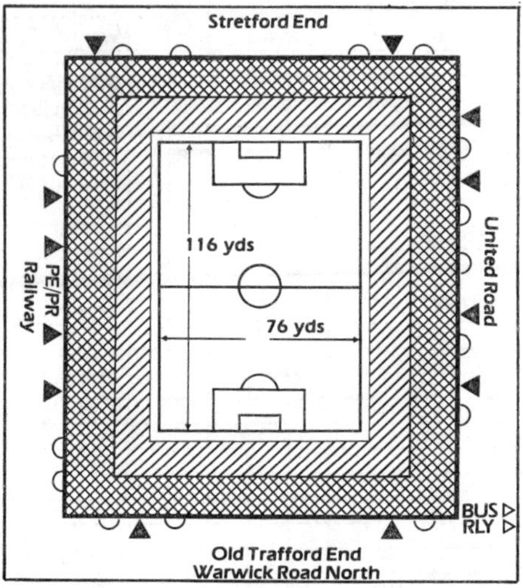

For key see page 12

Season Tickets: Stand: £62.00, £69.00, £76.00, £82.00, £88.00; Ground: £40.00, £36.00 (half-price for children)

Executive Box Season Tickets: Executive Seat: £525; Boxes: £2,700-£3,000

Cost of Stand Tickets: £4.50 (on match days); **Terraces:** £2.20, £2.40 (£2.00 for children)

Match and Ticket Information: For up-to-date information, phone 061-872 7771, 24-hour service. Seats can be reserved up to one calendar month before a match. Any unsold by the Monday before a Saturday match can be reserved by personal application

Car Parking: Several large parks:— 1. Lancashire County Cricket Ground, Talbot Road and Great Stone Road (1200), 2. White City Stadium, Chester Road (900)

How to get to the ground

From North: Use Motorway M61 then M63 until junction 4. Leave Motorway and follow signs Manchester A5081. In 2.5m turn right into Warwick Road, then turn right into United Road for Manchester United F.C.
From East: Use Motorway M62 until junction 17 then A56 into Manchester. Follow signs South then Chester into Chester Road. In 2m turn right into Warwick Road, then turn left into United Road for Manchester United F.C.
From South: Use Motorway M6 until junction 19 then follow signs Stockport A556 then Altrincham A56. From Altrincham follow signs Manchester. In 6m turn left into Warwick Road, then turn left into United Road for Manchester United F.C.
From West: Use Motorway M62 then M63 and route from north or as route from south.

MANSFIELD TOWN Division 4

Chairman
R C Hartley

Vice-Chairman
J B Almond, J.P.

Directors
J W Pratt
Ian Greaves

Secretary
J D Eaton

Manager
Ian Greaves

Assistant Manager
John Jarman

Commercial Manager
S J Burgan (0623 25877)

A margin of four points separated Mansfield Town and Halifax, who finished in twenty-first place in the Fourth Division and with no joy coming from the Cup Competitions this could fairly be described as a very poor season. Like every other club with cash problems the 'Stags' fans must have few optimistic thoughts about the future if the bare facts of 1983-84 are to be taken as a guide.

At no time during the season did it seem likely that anything exciting would be achieved once a bad start had been experienced. It was not until the seventh match that a win was achieved — by a single goal at home to Tranmere — and by then it was clear that avoidance of an application for re-election would be the team's only League target. By that time too the Milk Cup was already a shattered dream as Huddersfield won both first round legs for an aggregate score of seven goals to two. There was a brief rally when five unbeaten matches were enjoyed late in October and early in the next month, during which Doncaster were also dismissed from the F.A. Cup — 3-0 at the Field Mill Ground. But this was all rather flattering and the next Cup Round was to be the last for The Stags as a visit to Burnden Park saw the team lose by two clear goals.

That was that and with January producing only one victory there was little the supporters could do other than hope for better times in the new season, when Manager Ian Greaves will need all his shrewdness and experience to effect an improvement. There will be new faces to support the experience of Whitworth, Lowery and Foster and it can only be hoped that some of the youngsters will prove to be future stars. WLM

Back Row L to R: Mike Galloway, Mark Kearney, Kevin Hitchcock, Steve Whitworth, Andy Beasley, Gary Pollard, Colin Calderwood, Bill Dearden (Physio). **Middle Row:** John Jarman (Assistant Manager), Noel Luke, Stewart Barrowclough, Tony Lowrie, George Foster, Simon Woodhead, David Logan, Dave Caldwell, Ian Greaves (Manager). **Front Row:** Simon Coleman, Lee Howard, Paul Kee, John Cunningham, Nigel Foster, Craig McKernan.

'THE STAGS'

Formed: 1905 **Turned Professional:** 1905 **Ltd Co:** 1905
Previous Managers: 1931-3 J Hickling 1933-5 H Martin 1935 C Bell 1936 H Whiteman 1936-8 H Parkes 1938-9 J Poole 1939-45 C Barke 1945-9 R Goodall 1949-51 F Steele 1952-3 G Jobey 1953-5 S Mercer 1956-8 C Mitten 1958-60 S Weaver 1960-3 R Carter 1963-7 T Cummings 1967-70 T Eggleston 1970-1 J Basford 1971-4 D Williams 1974-6 D Smith 1976-8 P Morris 1978-9 B Bingham 1979-81 M Jones 1981-3 S Boam
Honours: Division 3 Champions 1976-7 Division 4 Champions 1974-5
League Career: Elected to Division 3 (South) 1931 Transferred to Division 3 (N) 1932 Transferred to Division 3 (S) 1936 Transferred to Division 3 (N) 1947 Transferred to Division 3 1958 Relegated to Division 4 1959-60 Promoted to Division 3 1962-3 Relegated to Division 4 1971-2 Promoted to division 3 1974-5 Promoted to Division 2 1976-7 Relegated to Division 3 1977-8 Relegated to Division 4 1979-80
Colours: Amber shirts with dark blue trim, blue shorts and stockings
Change Colours: All white with blue and amber trim

CLUB RECORDS

Most Appearances for Club: Rod Arnold: Football League 440 + F.A. Cup 29 + League/Milk Cup 24 **Total 493**
Most Capped Player: John McClelland, 6, N Ireland. **For England:** None
Record Goalscorer in a Match: Ted Harston, 7 **Record League Goalscorer in a season:** Ted Harston, 58
Record League Goalscorer in a career: Harold Johnson, 104
Record Transfer Fee Received: £200,000 from Luton Town for Mike Saxby, July 1979
Record Transfer Fee Paid: £75,000 to Luton Town for Steve Taylor, July 1979
Best Performances: League: 21st Div 2 1977-8 **F.A. Cup:** 6th Round, 1968-9 **League/Milk Cup:** 5th Round 1975-6
Most League Points: 68 in Div 4, 1974-5
Most League Goals: 108, Div 4, 1962-3
Record League Victory: 9-2 v Rotherham United, Div 3 (N), 27 Dec 32
Record League Defeat: 1-8 v Walsall, Div 3 (N), 19 Jan 34

Club Statistician for the Directory: Pete Stevenson

Programme Editor
Stuart Burgan

Price	Number of Pages
40p	16

Subscriptions
£13 per season for home matches

MANSFIELD TOWN

PLAYERS NAME Ht Wt Birthdate	Honours	Birthplace Transfers	Clubs	Appearances League	Appearances Milk Cup	Appearances F.A.C.	Appearances A.M.C.	Goals League	Goals Milk Cup	Goals F.A.C.	Goals A.M.C.
GOALKEEPERS											
Andy Beasley		Wolverhampton	Luton T. (A)								
6-2 12.2 5.2.64		F	Mansfield T.								
Kevin Hitchcock		Custom House	Nottingham F.								
6-1 12.2 5.10.62			Mansfield T.								
DEFENDERS											
Colin Calderwood		Glasgow	Mansfield T.	56 + 3	2	4	1	1		1	
6-0 12.0 20.1.65											
George Foster*†		Plymouth	Plymouth A. (A)	201 + 11	19	10		6			
5-10 11.2 26.9.56			Torquay U. (L)	6				3			
			Exeter C. (L)	28							
		£40,000	Derby Co.	30	7	5					
			Mansfield T.	42			1				
Mark Kearney		Ormskirk	Marine								
5-10 11.0 12.6.62		£23,000	Everton								
		F	Mansfield T.	28	2	+ 1		3			
David Logan		Whitley	Mansfield T.								
5-9 10.11 5.12.63											
Gary Pollard		Staveley	Chesterfield	83 + 4	4 + 1	9					
6-1 11.10 30.12.59			Port Vale	17 + 1	1	1	1 + 1				
			Mansfield T.								
Steve Whitworth	E.(7), U.23(6),	Coalville	Leicester C. (A)	352 + 1	18	29					
6-0 12.0 20.3.52	Y, S	£125,000	Sunderland	83	8	3					
		£25,000	Bolton W.	67	3	3					
			Mansfield T.	41	2	2	1				
MIDFIELD											
Mike Galloway	S, Y	Oswestry	Mansfield T.	12 + 5	1		1				
5-10 10.9 30.5.65											
Tony Lowery		Wallsend	Ashington								
5-9½ 10.6 6.7.61		£3,500	W.B.A.	1							
			Walsall (L)	4 + 2				1			
		F	Mansfield T.	46	2	2	1	6			
Noel Luke		Birmingham	W.B.A.	8 + 1	1	2 + 2		1		1	
5-11 10.11 28.12.61											
Simon Woodhead		Dewsbury	Mansfield T.	87 + 11	2 + 1	2 + 1	1	4			
5-10 11.0 26.12.62											
FORWARDS											
Stewart Barrowclough	E. U.23(5)	Barnsley	Barnsley (A)	9		1					
5-9 10.5 29.10.51		£40,000	Newcastle U.	201 + 18	14 +	13 +		20		2	
		Player Exchange	Birmingham C.	26 + 3	1			2			
		£100,000	Bristol R.	60 + 1	6	3		14	1	2	
		£50,000	Barnsley	46 + 6	7 + 1	1 + 1		1	1		
		F	Mansfield T.	36 + 2	1 + 1	2	1	10	1	1	1
David Caldwell		Aberdeen	Inverness Caley								
5-10 11.6 31.7.60			Mansfield T.	126 + 11	11	10	+ 1	48	2	3	
Mick Vinter	Div. 3, 84	Boston	Boston U.								
5-9 11.0 23.5.54			Notts. Co.	135 + 31	8 + 2	7 + 1		53	2	5	
		£150,000	Wrexham	90 + 12	9	10+1		25	5	7	
		£25,000	Oxford U.	67 + 2	12 + 1	11		21	3	4	
			Mansfield T.								

NON-CONTRACT PLAYER 1984-85

Adrian Thorpe

APPRENTICE

Paul Kee (1 appearance)

MANSFIELD TOWN

DIVISION FOUR 19TH **FA CUP** 2ND ROUND **MILK CUP** 1ST ROUND

MATCH	DATE	COMPE-TITION	VENUE	OPPONENTS	RESULT	HALF TIME	L'GUE POS'N	GOALSCORERS	ATTEN-DANCE
1	A 27	CL	A	Bristol C	L0-4	0-2			5,758
2	**30**	**MC 1**	**H**	**Huddersfield T**	**L1-2**	**1-1**		**Barrowclough (pen)**	**3,734**
3	S 3	CL	H	Doncaster R	L1-2	1-1	23	Lister (og)	2,957
4	6	CL	H	Stockport Co	L1-2	1-0		Thorpe (og)	2,166
5	9	CL	A	Halifax T	D0-0	0-0	24		1,725
6	**13**	**MC 1**	**A**	**Huddersfield T**	**L1-5**	**0-4**		**Caldwell**	**5,190**
7	17	CL	H	Tranmere R	W1-0	0-0	22	Nicholson	2,002
8	24	CL	A	Peterborough U	L0-3	0-2	23		3,490
9	27	CL	A	Blackpool	L0-2	0-0			3,461
10	O 1	CL	H	Aldershot	W5-2	2-1	22	Caldwell 3, Lowery, Barrowclough	1,836
11	8	CL	A	Bury	D2-2	0-1	22	Barrowclough (pen), Caldwell	2,468
12	15	CL	H	Torquay U	L1-3	0-2	22	Lowery	1,939
13	19	CL	A	Reading	L0-4	0-3			3,551
14	22	CL	H	Hartlepool U	W5-0	4-0	22	Lowery, Caldwell 4	1,906
15	29	CL	A	Hereford U	D0-0	0-0	22		3,110
16	N 1	CL	H	Rochdale	W3-0	1-0		Caldwell 2, Dungworth	2,535
17	5	CL	A	Wrexham	W3-2	2-0	17	Nicholson 2, Keegan	1,633
18	12	CL	H	Colchester U	D0-0	0-0	18		3,042
19	**19**	**FAC 1**	**H**	**Doncaster R**	**W3-0**	**2-0**		**Calderwood, Caldwell, Barrowclough**	**5,027**
20	26	CL	H	Swindon T	D2-2	1-1	18	Nicholson, Dungworth (pen)	3,327
21	D 3	CL	A	Darlington T	L0-3	0-1	19		1,630
22	**10**	**FAC 2**	**A**	**Bolton W**	**L0-2**	**0-2**			**6,934**
23	18	CL	A	Northampton T	L1-2	1-0		Lowery	2,628
24	26	CL	H	Chesterfield	L0-1	0-1	19		6,734
25	27	CL	A	Chester C	W4-0	3-0	17	Barrowclough, Lowery, Caldwell, Nicholson	1,431
26	31	CL	H	Crewe Alex	D3-3	2-1	17	Woodhead, Kearney, Caldwell	2,682
27	J 2	CL	A	York C	L1-2	1-1	20	Barrowclough	5,682
28	7	CL	A	Doncaster R	L1-3	0-1	20	Kearney	3,804
29	30	CL	A	Tranmere R	L0-1	0-0			1,482
30	F 4	CL	A	Aldershot	L1-7	0-4		Barrowclough	1,629
31	11	CL	H	Peterborough U	D0-0	0-0	22		2,179
32	14	CL	A	Rochdale	D0-0	0-0			1,095
33	18	CL	H	Hereford U	D1-1	1-1	22	Barrowclough	1,868
34	**21**	**AMC 1**	**H**	**Darlington**	**L1-3**	**0-1**		**Barrowclough (pen)**	**1,086**
35	25	CL	A	Hartlepool U	L1-4	1-0	22	Ayre	1,734
36	M 3	CL	H	Reading	W2-0	0-0	22	Nicholson, Barrowclough	1,950
37	6	CL	H	Wrexham	L3-4	1-1		Ayre 2, Caldwell	1,986
38	10	CL	A	Colchester U	L0-1	0-0	22		2,007
39	17	CL	H	Bury	D1-1	0-1	22	Ayre	1,673
40	24	CL	A	Torquay U	L0-1	0-0	23		1,447
41	27	CL	H	Bristol C	L0-1	0-0			1,826
42	31	CL	H	Blackpool	D1-1	1-0	23	Juryeff	2,007
43	A 6	CL	A	Stockport Co	W4-0	1-0		Barrowclough, Matthews, Caldwell, Juryeff	1,933
44	10	CL	H	Halifax T	W7-1	1-0		Barrowclough, Juryeff 3, Lowery, Matthews, Caldwell	1,696
45	14	CL	H	Darlington	W1-0	1-0	19	Caldwell	2,084
46	21	CL	A	Chesterfield	D0-0	0-0	19		4,364
47	24	CL	H	Chester C	W3-1	0-1	19	Matthews, Barrowclough, Nicholson	2,346
48	29	CL	A	Swindon T	D1-1	0-1		Nicholson	1,941
49	M 5	CL	H	York C	L0-1	0-0	19		3,355
50	7	CL	A	Crewe Alex	W3-1	3-0	19	Caldwell 3	1,810
51	12	CL	H	Northampton T	W3-1	0-1	19	Caldwell 2, Calderwood	2,141
								Av Home Att	**2,443**

Goal Scorers

League (66): Caldwell 21, Barrowclough 10 (1 pen), Nicholson 8, Lowery 6, Juryeff 5, Ayre 4, Matthews 3, Dungworth 2 (1 pen), Kearney 2, Calderwood 1, Keegan 1, Woodhead 1, opponents 2
FA Cup (3): Calderwood 1, Caldwell 1, Barrowclough 1
Milk Cup (2): Barrowclough 1 (pen), Caldwell 1
AMC (1): Barrowclough 1 (pen)

1983-84

Arnold	Whitworth	Kearney	Matthews	Foster	Calderwood	Barrowclough	Hutchinson	Dungworth	Caldwell	Lowery	Woodhead	Sindall	Nicholson	Galloway	Partridge (L)	Keegan	Daines	Storer	Ayre	Frain (L)	Taylor	Hitchcock (L)	Juryeff (L)	Kee	REFEREE	
1	2	3	4	5	6	7	8	9*	10	11	12														H King	1
1	**2**	**3**		**5**	**6**	**7**	**8**	**12**	**10**	**11**	**9***	**4***													**M Robinson**	**2**
1	2	3		5	6	7*	8	12	10	11	9	4													J Worrall	3
1	2	3	7	5	6		9	11	10	4		8*	12												E Scales	4
1	2	3	7	5	6	12	8	9	10	4			11*												R Guy	5
1	**2**	**3**	**7**	**5**	**6**	**12**	**8**	**9**	**10***	**4**			**11**												**N Wilson**	**6**
1	2	3	7	5			8	9		4	12	10*	11	6											AN Buksh	7
1	2		10*	5		7	8	9	12	4			11	6	3										KG Salmon	8
1	2			5	6	12	8	9*	10	4	3	7	11												PM Willis	9
1	2			5	6	9	8		10*	4	3	7	11	12											N Midgley	10
1	5			4	3	9	8		10	6	2	7	11												F Roberts	11
1	2		12	5	6		8	9*	10	4	3	7	11												Alan Robinson	12
1	2		7	5	6	9			10†	4	3		11			8									BT Stevens	13
	2		7	5	6	9			10*	4	3		11			8	1	12							I Borrett	14
	2		7	5	6	9		10		4	3		11			8	1								DV Reeves	15
	2		7	5	6	9		12	10*	4	3		11			8	1								D Hutchinson	16
	2		7	5	6	9*		10		4	3	12	11			8	1								N Glover	17
	2		7	5	6			10		4	3		11	9		8	1								JD Hough	18
	2		**7**	**5**	**6**	**9**			**10**	**4**	**3**		**11**			**8**	**1**								**K Barratt**	**19**
	2	3	7	5				9	10		4		11			8	1		6						V Callow	20
	2	3	7	5					10	9	4		11	6		8	1								IA Hendrick	21
	2	**12**	**7**	**5**		**9**			**10**	**4**	**3**		**11**	**6**		**8**	**1**								**T Holbrook**	**22**
	2		7	5		9			10	4	3		11			8	1		6						J Moules	23
	2		7	5		9			10	4	3		11			8	1		6						A Seville	24
	2	8		5		9			10	4	3		11	7			1		6						J Deakin	25
	3	4		5				9	10	8	2		11	7			1		6						R Dilkes	26
	2	8		5		9			10	4	3		11	7			1		6						K Redfern	27
	2	8		5		9		12	10	4	3		11*	7			1		6						D Owen	28
	2	8				9		10		4	3		12	7		5*	1		6	11					T Jones	29
	2	3†				8		9		4	7*	10	11	6			1		5	12					K Cooper	30
	2	9	8	6		7			10	4	3		11				1		5						J Lovatt	31
	2	9	7	6		8			10	4	3		11				1		5						C Seel	32
	2		8	6	9	7			10	4	3		11				1		5						D Vickers	33
	2		**8**	**9**	**6**	7			12	4	10		11	3*			1		5						A Robinson	34
	2*		8	6†	9	7			10	4	3		11	12			1		5						D Richardson	35
			8	6		9			10	4	2		11			7	1		5		3				N Ashley	36
			8	6	12	9			10	4	2		11*			7	1		5		3				J Ashworth	37
			8		6	9			10	4	2		11			7			5		3	1			M James	38
		3	8		6	9			10	4	2		11			7			5			1			K Barratt	39
		3*	8	6		11			10	4	2		12			7			5			1	9		J Martin	40
	3		8	6	12	7			10	4	2		11*						5			1	9		D Shaw	41
	3		8	6	7				10	4	2		11	12					5*			1	9		I Borrett	42
	3		8	6	5	7			10	4	2					11						1	9		M Robertson	43
	3		8	6	5	7			10	4	2					11						1	9		G Courtney	44
	3		8	6	12	7			10*	4	2	11							5			1	9		T Holbrook	45
	3		8	6	7	11				4	2		10						5			1	9		M Heath	46
	3		8	5	10	7				4	2		11	6								1	9*	12	A Saunders	47
	3			5	4	11			10	6	7		9	2								1	8		A Crickmore	48
	3			5	2	7			10	4	8		11	12					6			1	9*		N Glover	49
	3			5	2	7			10	4	8		11						6			1	9		N Wilson	50
	3			5	2	7			10	4	8		11	12					6†			1	9*		R Banks	51
11	41	17	31	42	27	36	10	14	37	45	41	9	38	12	1	18	21	1S	25	1	3	14	12	1S	League Appearances	
			+1S		+3S	+2S		+3S	+1S		+2S	+1S	+3S	+5S						+1S						
	2	1S	2	2	1	2			2	2	2		2	1		2	2								FA Cup Appearances	
2	2	2	1	2	2	1+1S	2	1+1S	2	2	1	1	1												Milk Cup Appearances	
	1		1	1	1	1			1S	1	1		1	1			1		1						AM Cup Appearances	

FIELD MILL GROUND

Official Address: Field Mill Ground, Quarry Lane, Mansfield. Telephone: Mansfield (0623) 23567.

Telegraphic: Football Mansfield

Ground Capacity: 23,500

Record Attendance: 24,467 v. Nottingham Forest, F.A. Cup Round 3, 10 Jan 1963

Record Receipts: £19,227 v. Sheffield Wednesday, Div 3, 15 Mar 1980

Size of Playing Area: 115yds × 72 yds

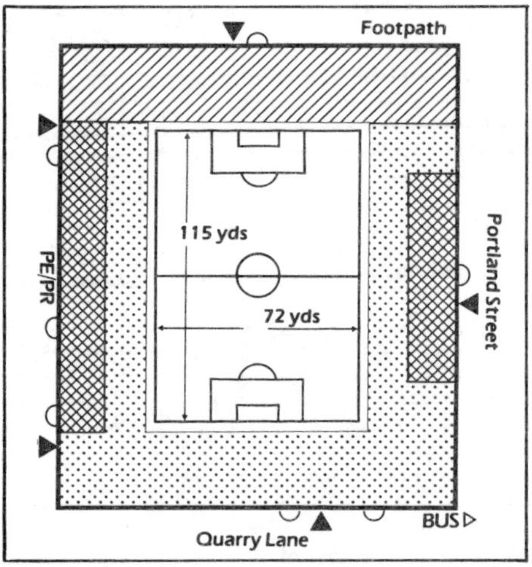

For key see page 12

Season Tickets: £53 (£38 juniors/OPA), £47.50 (£33 juniors/OAP); Ground: £30 (£16 juniors/ OAP)

Executive Box Season Tickets: Vice-Presidents £125 single, Vice-Presidents £200 double.

Cost of Stand Tickets: £3.20, £2.60; Ground £2.00 (£1.00 ground)

Match and Ticket Information: advance booking for five days prior to match.

Car Parking: space for 500 cars at the ground and for another 3,000 within 500 yards.

How to get to the ground

From North: Use Motorway M1 until junction 29. Leave Motorway and follow signs Mansfield A617. In 6.3m turn right into Rosemary Street B6030. In 1m turn right into Quarry Lane for Mansfield Town F.C.
From East: Use A617 to Rainworth. In 3m at crossroads turn left B6030 into Windsor Road. At end turn right into Nottingham Road. Shortly turn left into Portland Street, then turn left into Quarry Lane for Mansfield Town F.C.
From South, West: Use Motorway M1 until junction 28 then follow signs Mansfield A38. In 6.4m at crossroads turn right into Belvedere Street B6030. In 0.4m turn right into Quarry Lane for Mansfield Town F.C.

MIDDLESBROUGH Division 2

President
E Varley

Chairman
M McCullagh

Vice-Chairman
E K Varley

Directors
P Cook
D Gaster
J D Hatfied (Associate)
G T Kitching (Associate)

Secretary
T Edon

Manager
Willie Maddren

Club Coach
George Armstrong

Chief Scout
Ted Davies

Physiotherapist
Lew Clayton

Commercial Manager
D Gibson (0642 826664)

Hope springs eternal everywhere and this must have been the way Malcolm Allison felt at Ayresome Park during August 1983, but a good start was not maintained and a shortage of cash led to a major crisis in the club, which led to a public row in March 1984 between Allison and his board chairman. The latter won and away went the flamboyant Malcolm with Willie Maddren taking over as caretaker manager — a position confirmed in June. The trouble was that the board decided the only way to make ends meet would be by selling players and Allison refused to co-operate, arguing that selling players would not lead to better results.

Apart from the public wrangling the league results brought a season of constant anxiety for the fans and the final position of seventeenth was not only poor but it also was achieved with a margin of five points over Derby County, who were relegated from twentieth place. At times an even worse final position was possible.

The domestic cups brought some satisfaction, but not enough. The Milk Cup started with defeat by penalties against Chesterfield after two goalless matches, but the F.A. Cup started well for 'Boro' with victory after a thriller in the Third Round tie with Arsenal. That triumph was at Ayresome Park and there was another home tie in Round Four when giant-killers Bournemouth came and left without replying to Sugrue's brace of goals. The next round match was at Meadow Lane and Notts County managed a single goal to despatch Boro' from the competition.

Prospects for the future do not look bright and Willie Maddren will have to find a new side after staff cuts including the departure of two players to Portsmouth (Baxter and Kennedy) with other departures in the offing. He can still rely on the experience of Nattrass and Sugrue and the talent of Wood and Otto, but for the rest he will need to do some shrewd scouting whilst hoping that replacements for absent stars will not be too expensive. He will also hope that a return to his starting point will inspire David Mills to produce his best form, but few will envy the manager his task.

WLM

Back Row L to R: David Mills, Darren Wood, David Currie, Heine Otto, Tony Mowbray, Kelham O'Hanlan, Gary Gill, Paul Ward, Geoff Scott. **Front Row:** Gary Hamilton, Stephen Bell, Paul Sugrue, Steve Smelt (Physio), Willie Maddren (Manager), Irving Nattrass (Capt), Mick Buckley, Alan Roberts.

'THE BORO'

Formed: 1892 **Turned Professional:** 1889 (amateur 1992-99) **Ltd Co:** 1892
Previous Managers: Since 1946
David Jack Walter Rowley Bob Dennison Raich Carter Stan Anderson Jack Charlton OBE John Neal Bobby Murdoch
Honours: Division Two Champions 1926-7, 1928-9, 1973-4 Anglo-Scottish Cup Winners 1975-6 F.A. Amateur Cup Winners 1895, 1898
League Career: Elected to Division Two 1899 Promoted to Division One 1901-2
Relegated to Division Two 1923-4 Promoted to Division One 1926-7
Relegated to Division Two 1927-8 Promoted to Division One 1928-9
Relegated to Division Two 1953-4 Relegated to Division Three 1965-6
Promoted to Division Two 1966-7 Promoted to Division One 1973-4
Relegated to Division Two 1981-2
Colours: Red shirts with three narrow stripes down sleeves, red shorts with 'hummel' style white trim and stockings
Change Colours: All blue with same style white trim

CLUB RECORDS

Most Appearances for Club: Tim Williamson, 563, 1902-23
Most Capped Player: Wilf Manion, 26, England
Record Goalscorer in a Match: Andy Wilson, 5 v Nottingham Forest, Div 1 (H, 5-2), 06.10.53
George Camsell, 5 v Manchester City, Div 2 (A, 5-3), 25.12.26
George Camsell, 5 v Aston Villa, Div 1 (A, 7-2), 09.09.35
Brian Clough, 5 v Brighton, Div 2 (H, 9-0), 23.08.58
Record League Goalscorer in a season: George Camsell, 59, Div 2, 1926-7 (a record for the division)
Record League Goalscorer in a career: George Camsell, 326, 1925-39
Record Transfer Fee Received: £600,000 from Southampton for David Armstrong, Aug 1981
Record Transfer Fee Paid: £475,000 to Newcastle for Irving Natrass, Aug 1979
Best Performances: League: 3rd Div 1 1913-4 **F.A. Cup:** 6th Round 1935-6, 1946-7, 1969-70, 1974-5, 1976-7, 1977-8; last eight 1900-1, 1903-4 **League/Milk Cup:** Semi-Final 1975-6
Most League Points: 65 in Div 2, 1973-4 **Most League Goals:** 122, Div 2, 1926-7
Record League Victory: 9-0 v Brighton, Div 2, 23 Aug 1958
Record League Defeat: 0-9 v Blackburn Rovers, Div 2, 6 Nov 1954
Club Statistician for the Directory: I. Tewson

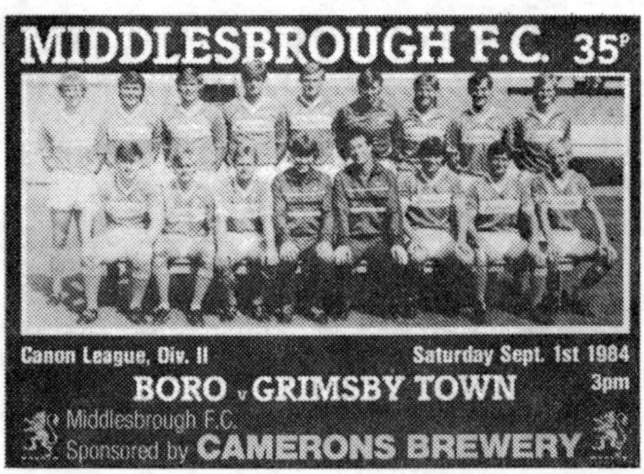

Programme Editor
Peter Cook (CPS Products, Guisborough)

Price	Number of Pages
35p	16

Subscriptions
On request from club (£14.00 per season approximately subject to confirmation)

MIDDLESBROUGH

PLAYERS NAME Ht Wt Birthdate	Honours	Birthplace Transfers	Clubs	APPEARANCES League	Milk Cup	F.A.C.	E. Cups	GOALS League	Milk Cup	F.A.C.	E. Cups
GOALKEEPER											
Kel O'Hanlon	E. U.21	Saltburn	Middlesbrough (A)	49	2	3					
6-0 12.0 16.5.62											
DEFENDERS											
Peter Beagrie		Middlesbrough	Middlesbrough								
5-8¼ 9.10											
Tony Mowbray		Saltburn	Middlesbrough (A)	58+3	2+2	6		1			
6-1 12.2 22.11.63											
Irving Nattrass*	E. U.23(1)	Fishburn	Newcastle U. (A)	236+12	21	23		16	3	1	
5-11 12.0 12.12.52		£475,000	Middlesbrough	137+5	8+1	15		2			
Geoff Scott		Birmingham	Highgate U								
5-10½ 12.5 31.10.55			Stoke C.	76+2	7	3		3			
		£80,000	Leicester C.	39	3	2					
		£50,000	Birmingham C.	18+1							
		£40,000	Charlton A.	2							
Paul Ward		Sedgefield	Chelsea (A)								
5-11 12.5 15.9.63			Middlesbrough	37+6	2	1+1		1			
Darren Wood	E. S	Scarborough	Middlesbrough	95	4	5		6			
5-10 11.8 9.6.64											
MIDFIELD											
Mike Buckley	E. U.23(2)	Manchester	Everton (A)	128+7	12	7		10	1	1	
5-6 10.7 4.11.53		£90,000	Sunderland	117+4	8	5		7	1	1	
			Hartlepool (N-C)								
		F	Carlisle U.	24+1		1					
			Middlesbrough								
Steve Corden		Middlesbrough	Middlesbrough								
5-8 10.7											
Gary Gill		Middlesbrough	Middlesbrough (A)	4+2							
5-10 10.9 28.11.64			Hull City (L)	0+1							
Gary Hamilton		Glasgow	Middlesbrough (A)	34+6		3		5			
5-9 11.2 27.12.65											
Heine Otto	Hol.	Holland	F.C. Twente								
6-0 12.0 24.8.54		£125,000	Middlesbrough	122+2	7	10		20	2	1	
Alan Roberts		Newcastle	Middlesbrough	7+1	1+1			1			
5-8½ 9.12½ 8.12.64											
FORWARDS											
Stephen Bell	E. Y	Middlesbrough	Middlesbrough (A)	64+4	2	5		10		2	
5-7 10.4 13.3.65											
Colin Cooper		Trimdon	Middlesbrough (A)								
5-8 9.3½ 28.2.67											
David Currie		Stockton	Middlesbrough	39+9	2	3		15			
6-0 11.13 27.11.62											
Boro Jankovic	Yug.	Yugoslavia	Zeljeznicar								
6-0 13.4 22.5.51		£100,000	Middlesbrough	42+8	3+2	7		16	1	1	
John McMahon		Middlesbrough	Middlesbrough								
5-7 10.13											
David Mills	E. U.23(8)	Whitby	Middlesbrough (A)	278+17	21+	27		76	8	10	
5-8 11.0 6.12.57	Div. 2, 74	£500,000	W.B.A.	44+12	6+2	2+2		5			
			Newcastle U. (L)	23				4			
		£30,000	Sheffield Wed.	15	0+2	4		3			
		£20,000	Newcastle U.	10+6				5			
		F	Middlesbrough								
Paul Sugrue†		Coventry	Nuneaton Boro								
5-7 9.10 6.11.60		£30,000	Manchester C.	5+1							
		F	Cardiff C.	2+3							
			Kansas								
		F	Middlesbrough	61+1	3	8		6		5	

APPRENTICES

Martyn Angus, Graeme Bartliff, Alan Kernaghan, Andy Strong

MIDDLESBROUGH

DIVISION TWO 17TH **FA CUP** 5TH ROUND **MILK CUP** 1ST ROUND

MATCH	DATE	COMPETITION	VENUE	OPPONENTS	RESULT	HALF TIME	L'GUE POS'N	GOALSCORERS	ATTENDANCE
1	A 27	CL	A	Portsmouth	W1-0	1-0		Otto	17,547
2	**30**	**MC 1**	**H**	**Chesterfield**	**L0-1**	**0-0**			**7,126**
3	S 3	CL	H	Leeds U	D2-2	0-1	9	Currie 2	12,793
4	6	CL	H	Newcastle U	W3-2	1-0		Currie 2, Hamilton	19,648
5	10	CL	A	Barnsley	W2-0	0-0	3	Wood, Otto	10,039
6	**13**	**MC 1**	**A**	**Chesterfield**	**W1-0**[5]	**0-0**		**Otto**	**5,949**
7	17	CL	H	Grimsby T	D1-1	1-1	4	Baxter	10,239
8	24	CL	A	Chelsea	D0-0	0-0	5		15,822
9	27	CL	A	Fulham	L1-2	1-1		Currie	6,432
10	O 1	CL	H	Crystal Palace	L1-3	1-2	8	MacDonald	8,927
11	8	CL	H	Blackburn R	L1-2	0-0	10	Currie	7,062
12	15	CL	A	Oldham Ath	L1-2	0-0	12	MacDonald	3,994
13	22	CL	A	Manchester C	L1-2	1-0	14	Roberts	24,466
14	29	CL	H	Shrewsbury T	W4-0	0-0	13	Otto, Currie 2, Ward	6,362
15	N 5	CL	H	Cardiff C	W2-0	0-0	11	Currie, Crawford	7,686
16	12	CL	A	Derby Co	L0-1	0-0	12		12,495
17	19	CL	A	Cambridge U	D0-0	0-0	13		2,819
18	26	CL	H	Swansea C	W1-0	1-0	10	Otto	6,804
19	D 3	CL	A	Charlton Ath	L0-2	0-0	11		5,053
20	10	CL	H	Brighton & HA	D0-0	0-0	13		6,037
21	17	CL	A	Huddersfield T	D2-2	1-0	12	Baxter, Sugrue	7,889
22	26	CL	H	Carlisle U	L0-1	0-1	14		11,147
23	27	CL	A	Sheffield W	W2-0	2-0	13	Sugrue, Currie	24,818
24	31	CL	A	Leeds U	L1-4	0-1	13	Currie (pen)	14,215
25	J 2	CL	H	Chelsea	W2-1	1-0	12	Hamilton, Currie	11,579
26	**7**	**FAC 3**	**H**	**Arsenal**	**W3-2**	**1-1**		**McDonald, Sugrue, Baxter**	**17,813**
27	14	CL	H	Portsmouth	D0-0	0-0	12		7,971
28	21	CL	H	Grimsby T	D0-0	0-0			7,342
29	**31**	**FAC 4**	**H**	**AFC Bournemouth**	**W2-0**	**1-0**		**Sugrue 2**	**21,175**
30	F 4	CL	H	Crystal Palace	L0-1	0-0			5,819
31	11	CL	H	Barnsley	W2-1	0-0	10	Currie 2 (1 pen)	7,480
32	**18**	**FAC 5**	**A**	**Notts Co**	**L0-1**	**0-1**			**17,487**
33	25	CL	H	Manchester C	D0-0	0-0	11		9,343
34	28	CL	A	Shrewsbury T	L0-1	0-0			3,043
35	M 3	CL	A	Cardiff C	L1-2	1-2	13	MacDonald	4,422
36	17	CL	A	Newcastle U	L1-3	1-1	18	Bell	30,386
37	20	CL	H	Derby Co	D0-0	0-0			5,735
38	24	CL	H	Fulham	L0-2	0-0	16		5,435
39	31	CL	H	Oldham Ath	W3-2	2-1	16	Bell, Sugrue, Otto	5,615
40	A 7	CL	A	Blackburn R	L0-1	0-1	17		4,910
41	14	CL	H	Cambridge C	D1-1	1-1	17	Otto	5,121
42	20	CL	A	Carlisle U	D1-1	0-1		Mowbray	5,674
43	25	CL	H	Sheffield W	W2-0	1-0		Hamilton, Currie	12,362
44	27	CL	A	Swansea C	L1-2	1-2		Wood	3,628
45	M 5	CL	H	Charlton Ath	W1-0	0-0	16	Otto	4,720
46	7	CL	A	Brighton & HA	L0-3	0-1	16		9,168
47	12	CL	H	Huddersfield T	D0-0	0-0	17		5,687

[5]Lost On Penalties

Av Home Att **8,464**

Goal Scorers

League (41): Currie 15 (3 pens), Otto 7, Hamilton 3, MacDonald 3, Sugrue 3, Baxter 2, Bell 2, Wood 2, Crawford 1, Mowbray 1, Roberts 1, Ward 1
FA Cup (5): Sugrue 3, Baxter 1, MacDonald 1
Milk Cup (1): Otto 1

1983-84

O'Hanlon	Wood	Ward	Otto	Baxter	Nattrass	Roberts	MacDonald	Currie	Sugrue	Bell	Mowbray	Kennedy	Hamilton	Crawford	Pears **(L)**	Gill	**REFEREE**	
1	2	3	4	5	6	7	8	9	10*	11	12						A Crickmore	1
1	**2**	**3**	**4**	**5**	**6**	**12**	**9**	**7**	**10**	**11***		**8**					**C Seel**	**2**
1	2	3	4	5	6	7	11	9	10			8					D Shaw	3
1	2	3	4*	5	6	7	11	9	10			8	12				K Hackett	4
1	2	3	9	5	6	7	11		10			8	4				H Holbrook	5
1	**2**	**3***	**4**	**5**	**6**	**7**	**11**	**9**	**10**		**12**	**8**					**N Ashley**	**6**
1	2	3	4	5	6	7*	11	9	10			8	12				D Scott	7
1	2	3	4	5	6		11	9	10	7		8*	12				D Brazier	8
1	2	8	4	5	6		11	9	10*	7	12		3				J Martin	9
1	2	3	4	5	6	7	11	9	10	8							P Tyldesley	10
1	2	8	4	5	6		11	9	10	7*	3		12				A Challinor	11
1	2	3	4	5	6		11	9	10	7	8						J Lovatt	12
1	2		4	5	6	7	11	9	10		3			8			F Roberts	13
1	2	7	4	5	6			9	10		3	8		11			D Allison	14
	2	7	4	5	6			9		10	3	8		11	1		JD Hough	15
	2	7	4	5	6			9†	12	11*	3†	8		10	1		C Downey	16
	2	7	4	5	6			9	10		3	8	12	11	1		AN Buksh	17
	2	4	9	5	6				10	7		8	3	11	1		A Robinson	18
	2		4	5	6			11	10	7	3	9	8		1		R Milford	19
	2		4	5	6		12	11	10*	7	3	9	8		1		J Key	20
1	2		9	5	6			11	10	7	3	8	4				G Napthine	21
1	2		9	5	6		12	11	10	7	3	8	4*				M Scott	22
1	2	7	4	5	6		9	11	10		3	8					K Barratt	23
1	2	8	9	5	6		7	11	10	12	3*		4				K Walmsley	24
1	2	8	9	5	6		7	11	10		3		8				T Jones	25
1	**2**		**4**	**5**	**6**		**9**	**11**	**10**		**3**	**8**	**7**				**M Heath**	**26**
1	2	12	4	5	6		9	11*	10		3	8	7				L Dilkes	27
	2	12	4	5	6		9		10	11	3	8	7*		1		A Banks	28
	2		**4**	**5**	**6**		**9**		**10**	**11**	**3**	**8**	**7**		**1**		**K Hackett**	**29**
	2		4	5	6		9	11	10		3	8	7		1		B Stevens	30
	2		4	5	6		9	11	10	12	3	8	7*		1		T Fitzharris	31
	2	**12**	**4**	**5**	**6**		**9**	**11**	**10***		**3**	**8**	**7**		**1**		**B Hill**	**32**
	2		4	5	6		9	11	10	12	3	8	7*		1		D Hutchinson	33
	2		4	5	6		9	11	10		3	8	7		1		L Robinson	34
	2		4	5	6		9	11	10	8	3		7*		1	12	L Burden	35
1	2		4	5	6		9	11	10	8	3		7*			12	J Worrall	36
1	2	11	4	5	6		9	12	10*	7	3	8					N Midgley	37
1	2		4	5	6		9	12	10	7*	3	8	11				D Richardson	38
1	2	4	9	5	6			12	10*	7	3	8	11				M Peck	39
1	2	4	9	5	6		12	11*		7	3	8	10				C Seel	40
1	2	4	9	5	6			12	10	7*	3	8	11				I Hendrick	41
1	2	4	9	5	6			11	10		3	8	7*	12			R Nixon	42
1	2	4	8	5	6		12	10	9		3		11*	7			D Allison	43
1	2	8	11	4	5			6	10	12	3			7*		9	D Letts	44
1	2		9	5	6			11	10		3	8	4			7	A Challinor	45
1	2		9	5	6			11	10		3	8†	4			7	D Axcell	46
1	2	11	9		6		12	5*	10		3	8	4			7	J Hough	47
30	**42**	26	**42**	41	**42**	7	24	35	39	21	33	30	26	8	12	4	League Appearances	
		+2S					+5S	+4S	+1S	+4S	+2S		+5S	+1S		+2S		
1	3	1S	3	3	3		3	2	3	1	3	3	3		2		FA Cup Appearances	
2	2	2	2	2	2	1+1S	2	2	2	1	1S	2					Milk Cup Appearances	

AYRESOME PARK

Official Address: Ayresome Park, Middlesbrough, Cleveland TS1 4PB. Telephone: 0642 819659/815996

Telegraphic: Football, Middlesbrough

Ground Capacity: 42,000

Record Attendance: 53,596 v. Newcastle U, Division 1, 27 Dec 1949

Record Receipts: £57,710 v. Barnsley, F.A. Cup Round 5, 14 Feb 1981

Size of Playing Area: 115yds × 75 yds

Season Tickets: Stands £76 (£56 Juniors/OAP), £66.00 (£49 Juniors/OAP), North Terrace: £66 (£43 Juniors/OAP), South Terrace £48 (£38 Juniors/OAP), Other gates £45 (£33 Juniors/OAP)

Executive Box Season Tickets: None

Cost of Stand Tickets: £4.20 £3.70 (£3.00 Juniors/OPA), Ground (South) £2.70 (£2.20 Juniors/OAP), Ground (West) £2.50 (£1.70 Juniors/OAP), £2.00 South Stand juniors.

Match and Ticket Information: Postal or personal applications two weeks prior to any match.

Car Parking: off-street near the ground; on-street around the ground.

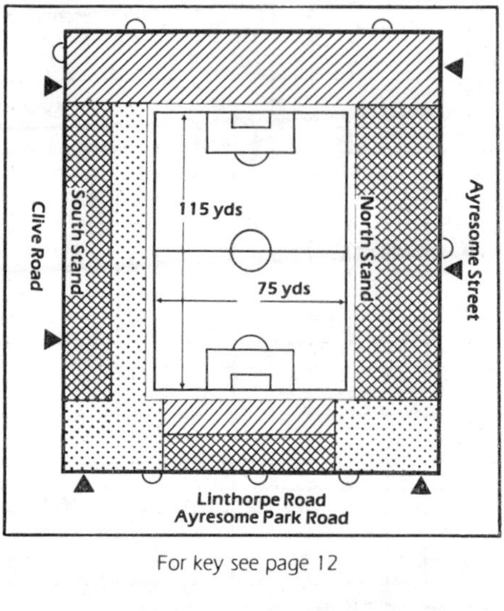

For key see page 12

How to get to the ground

From North: Use A19 (S.P. Middlesbrough) cross Tees Bridge and in 0.2m join A66, in 1.5m at roundabout take 3rd exit into Heywood Street, at end turn left into Ayresome Street for Middlesbrough F.C.

From South: Use A1, and A19 to junction with A1130. In 1m join A66, 1m farther at roundabout take 4th exit into Heywood Street, at end turn left into Ayresome Street to Middlesbrough F.C.

From West: Use A66 (S.P. Middlesbrough) 1.6m after Teeside Park Race Course at roundabout take 4th exit into Heywood Street, at end turn left into Ayresome Street for Middlesbrough F.C.

MILLWALL

Division 3

President
RJ Mellish

Chairman
Alan A Thorne

Directors
WJ Nelan
BA Thorne
BFL White FRJCS
JR Groser

Chief Executive
Tony Shaw

Secretary
Sylvia Shaw

Manager
George Graham

Coach
Theo Foley

Reserve & Youth Coach
Roger Cross

Chief Scout
Bob Pearson

Commercial Manager
Billy Neill (01-639 4590)

Physiotherapist
Brian Carnaby

Groundsman
Ernie Godden

The Lions roared on occasions during the 1983-84 season and a final Third Division position of ninth could have been worse. But since nothing great was achieved in any of the cup competitions to supplement this ordinary League fare it was not surprising that attendance records at the Den were not broken. In these recession days people will not rush to see the ordinary if they must pay a great deal for the pleasure and only something exceptional will lure them away from their television sets on cold winter afternoons. Millwall were never serious challengers for promotion and never looked likely relegation candidates so it was an undistinguished season, although there was promising 'team' building on and off the field which might mean a promotional challenge in 1985.

The cups in each case provided initial success. In the First Round of the Milk Cup Northampton were defeated in both legs for an aggregate in favour of Millwall of five goals to one. This brought West Bromwich to the Den for the first leg of the next round and goals from Neal (2) and Lowndes sent Albion back to the West Midlands with problems, which they did well to overcome in the return so that the London club did go out on aggregate (4-5). In the F.A. Cup Dartford put up stout resistence at the Den before bowing out (2-1) which meant a tie at home with Swindon, who played very well in an exciting match to oust the home team by the odd goal in five after matters had been level at half-time. The rest of the season involved a short acquaintance with the new Associate Members Cup and the need to complete the League programme.

The new season's hopes must rest on a similar staff to the one which finished in May 1984. Consistency can be expected from Lovell, Nutton and Kevin Bremner, but will the manager have anyone with flair? Supporters only wait and see.

WLM

Unfortunately, Millwall's kit sponsored by the LDDC did not arrive in time for a team photo to be taken at the beginning of the season. However, this action shot shows striker Dean Neal, watched by Kevin Bremner (left), shooting for goal against Charlton Athletic in a pre-season friendly.
Photo: Paul Dane

'THE LIONS'

Sponsored by
The London Docklands Development Corporation

Formed: 1885 **Turned Professional:** 1893 **Ltd Co:** 1894
Previous Names: 1885 Millwall Rovers 1889 Millwall Athletic
Previous Managers: H B Lipsham (signed as player c1909)-1921 1921-33 R Hunter 1933-6 W McCracken 1936-40 C Hewitt 1940-4 W Voisey 1944-8 J Cock 1948-56 C Hewitt 1957-58 R Gray 1958-9 J Seed 1959-61 J R Smith 1961-3 R Gray 1963-6 W Gray 1966-74 B Fenton 1974-7 G Jago 1978-80 G Petchey 1980 B Kitchener (Caretaker) 1980-2 P Anderson 1982 B Kitchener (Caretaker)
Honours: Division 3 (South) Champions 1927-8 Division 4 Champions 1961-2
League Career: Original members of Division 3 1920 Transferred to Division 3 (S) 1921 Promoted to Division Two 1927-8 Relegated to Division 3 (S) 1933-4 Promoted to Division 2 1937-8 Relegated to Division 3 (S) 1947-8 Relegated to Division 4 1957-8 Promoted to Division 3 1961-2 Relegated to Division 4 1963-4 Promoted to Division 3 1964-5 Promoted to Division 2 1965-6 Relegated to Division 3 1974-5 Promoted to Division 2 1975-6 Relegated to Division 3 1978-9
Colours: Royal blue shirts, white shorts, blue stockings
Change Colours: All red with white trim

CLUB RECORDS

Most Appearances for Club: Barry Kitchener: Football League 518 + 5s + F.A. Cup 29 + 2s + League Cup 42 **Total 589 + 7 subs**
Most Capped Player: Eamonn Dunphy, 22, Eire. **For England:** J R Smith and L Graham, 2
Record Goalscorer in a Match: Richard Parker, 5 v Norwich City (H) 6-1, Div 3 (S), 28.08.26
Record League Goalscorer in a season: Richard Parker, 37, Div 3 (S), 1926-7 **In all competitions:** Peter Burridge, 39, 1960-1 (League 36, F.A. Cup 2, League Cup 1)
Record League Goalscorer in a career: Derek Possee, 79, 1967-73 **In all competitions:** Derek Possee, 87 (League 79, F.A. Cup 4, League Cup 4)
Record Transfer Fee Received: £250,000 from Ipswich Town for Kevin O'Callaghan, Jan 1980
Record Transfer Fee Paid: £150,000 to Barnsley for Trevor Aylott, August 1982
Best Performances: League: 3rd Div 2 1971-2 **F.A. Cup:** Semi-Final (3) including 1937 when Millwall was the first Third Division Club to reach this stage **League/Milk Cup:** 5th Round, 1973-4, 1976-7
Most League Points: (3pts for win) 67, Div 3 1983-4 (2pts for win) 67, Div 3 1982-3 **Most League Goals:** 127, Div 3 (S) 1927-8
Record League Victory: 9-1 v Torquay United, Div 3 (S), 29 Aug 1927 9-1 v Coventry City, Div 3 (S), 19 Nov 1927
Record League Defeat: 1-8 v Plymouth Argyle

Club Statistician for the Directory: R Lindsay

Programme Editor

Price	**Number of Pages**
50p	20

Subscriptions
£16 per season

MILLWALL

PLAYERS NAME Ht Wt Birthdate	Honours	Birthplace Transfers	Clubs	APPEARANCES League	Milk Cup	F.A.C.	A.M.C.	GOALS League	Milk Cup	F.A.C.	A.M.C.
GOALKEEPERS											
Paul Sansome		New Addington	Crystal Palace (A)								
5-11 11.10 6.10.61		F	Millwall	63	3	1	5				
Peter Wells		Nottingham	Nottingham F. (A)	27		2					
6-1 13.4 13.8.56		£16,000	Southampton	141	3	12					
		F	Millwall	33	2	2					
DEFENDERS											
Nick Coleman		Crayford	Millwall (A)	1							
6.5.61											
David Cusack	Div. 4, 81	Rotherham	Sheffield Wed.	92+3	7	7		1			
6-1½ 13.12 6.6.56		£50,000	Southend U.	186	13	7		17		1	
		£30,000	Millwall	53	4	2		1			
Steve Lovell	W. (1)	Swansea	Crystal Palace (A)	68+6	10+	1+1		3	1		
5-9 11.13 16.7.60	FAYC. 77, 78		Stockport Co. (L)	12		1				1	
			Millwall	63	4	2	5	8		1	
Mickey Nutton		St John's Wood	Chelsea (A)	77+2	1	3					
5-11 10.12 3.10.59			Reading (L)	6							
		£65,000	Millwall	53	4	2	3	3			
Paul Robinson	E. Y. S.	Hampstead	Millwall (A)	56+3	4	6	3+2	2			
5-10 11.1 5.1.63	FAYC. 79										
Bill Roffey	Div. 2, 70	Stepney	Crystal Palace (A)	24							
5-11 12.13 6.2.50	Div. 2, 80	£5,000	Orient	224+4	16+1	18+1		8		1	
			Brentford (L)	13			1				
Lindsay Smith		Enfield	Colchester U. (A)	185+27	8+2	12+		16			
5-11 12.0 18.9.54			Charlton A. (L)	1							
			Millwall (L)	5							
			Cambridge U.	173+1	9	7+1		7			
			Lincoln C. (L)	5							
			Plymouth A.	76	4	14	3	5		1	1
Keith Stevens		Wimbledon	Millwall (A)	50+1	2	1	5				
5-11 11.1 21.6.64											
MIDFIELD											
Les Briley*		Lambeth	Chelsea (A)								
5-6 9.11 2.10.56		F	Hereford U.	60+1	3+1	2		2			
		£18,000	Wimbledon	59+2	4+1	8+1		2			
		£43,000	Aldershot	157	11	6	1	3			
		Player Exchange	Millwall				SL1				
Tony Kinsella	Ei. U.21 (2)	Orsett	Millwall (A)	55+6	2+1	4		1			
5-8 10.4 30.10.61	FAYC. 79		Tampa Bay Rowdies								
		£60,000	Ipswich T.	7+2	1	1					
		F	Millwall								
Alan McLeary	E. Y	London	Millwall (A)	25+8		2	5	1			
5-10 10.9 6.10.64											
David Martin	FAYC. 79	East Ham	Millwall (A)	129+9	8+2	7	4	6	3	1	
5-11 10.11 25.4.63											
Anton Otulakowski†	Div. 4, 81	Dewsbury	Ossett Trinity								
5-7 10.10 29.1.56			Barnsley	42		1		2			
		£60,000	West Ham U.	10+7							
		£50,000	Southend U.	161+2	12	9		8			
		£30,000	Millwall	47	3		3	9	1		
FORWARDS											
Kevin Bremner		Banff	Keith								
5-9½ 12.3 7.9.52		£40,000	Colchester U.	89+6	5+2	10		31	3	2	
			Birmingham C. (L)	3+1				1			
			Wrexham (L)	4				1			
			Plymouth A. (L)	5				1			
		£25,000	Millwall	58+1	4	2	4	21			
Nick Chatterton	Div. 2, 79	Norwood	Crystal Palace	142+9	15	15		31	3	2	
5-9 11.0 18.5.54		£100,000	Millwall	210+4	14	13	2	49	3	5	
Steve Lowndes	W. (2), U.21 (4)	Cwmbran	Newport Co.	200+8	10+	12		29	2		
5-7 10.7 17.6.60		£55,000	Millwall	20	4	1	3+1	3	1		
Dean Neal		Edmonton	Q.P.R. (A)	20+3	2			8	1		
5-10½ 12.0 5.1.61			Tulsa Roughnecks								
		£100,000	Millwall	84+12	4+2	4+1	4	35	4	1	
John Neal	E. S	London	Millwall (A)	3+3			2	1			
5-8½ 10.7 11.3.66											
Ed Sherringham	E. Y	London	Millwall (A)	4+3			1+2	1			
5-10½ 12.4 2.4.66											

APPRENTICES

Brian Horne, Paul Malcolm, Darren Morgan, Eamonn Ryan, Mike Marks, Steve Middleton, Martin Saltery, Neil Ruddock

MILLWALL

DIVISION THREE 9TH **FA CUP** 2ND ROUND **MILK CUP** 2ND ROUND

MATCH	DATE	COMPETITION	VENUE	OPPONENTS	RESULT	HALF TIME	L'GUE POS'N	GOALSCORERS	ATTENDANCE
1	A 28	CL	A	Brentford	D2-2	1-2		McNichol (og), Lowndes	6,224
2	29	MC 1	H	Northampton T	W3-0	1-0		Martin, Chatterton 2 (1 pen)	4,185
3	S 3	CL	H	Plymouth Ath	W1-0	0-0	9	Lovell	4,611
4	6	CL	H	Port Vale	W3-2	1-0		Chatterton 2 Bremner	4,918
5	10	CL	A	Hull C	L0-5	0-3	10		7,338
6	13	MC 1	A	Northampton T	W2-1	1-0		Otulokowski, Neal D	2,313
7	17	CL	H	AFC Bournemouth	W3-1	1-1	7	Otulokowski 2, Chatterton (pen)	4,272
8	19	CL	A	Southend U	L2-3	1-1	7	Otulokowski, Chatterton (pen)	4,272
9	24	CL	A	Oxford U	L2-4	1-2	9	Lowndes, Stride	5,543
10	O 1	CL	H	Sheffield U	L1-2	1-1	15	Otulokowski	5,601
11	4	MC 2	H	WBA	W3-0	2-0		Neal D 2, Lowndes	10,721
12	9	CL	H	Burnley	W2-0	1-0		Stride, Neal D	6,709
13	15	CL	A	Lincoln C	D2-2	2-1	11	Bremner, Neal D	3,190
14	18	CL	A	Rotherham U	L0-1	0-1			3,461
15	21	CL	H	Preston NE	W1-0	1-0		Neal D	5,243
16	25	MC 2	A	WBA	L1-5	0-1		Martin	13,311
17	29	CL	A	Gillingham	D3-3	1-2	15	Burke, Bruce (og), Chatterton	6,226
18	N 1	CL	H	Newport Co	D1-1	1-0		Bremner	4,352
19	5	CL	H	Wigan	W2-0	1-0	12	Nutton, Martin	3,850
20	12	CL	A	Bradford C	D3-3	0-1	12	Chatterton, Bremner 2	3,548
21	19	FAC 1	H	Dartford	W2-1	1-0		Massey, Cusack	4,931
22	26	CL	H	Scunthorpe U	W2-1	1-0	13	Bremner, Neal D	3,776
23	D 3	CL	A	Walsall	D1-1	1-0	12	Lovell	5,329
24	10	FAC 2	H	Swindon T	L2-3	1-1		Lovell (pen), Martin	4,597
25	17	CL	A	Exeter C	L2-3	0-2	13	Sparrow, Neal D	2,854
26	26	CL	H	Orient	W4-3	1-2	13	Sparrow, Bremner, Lovell (pen), Lowndes	5,161
27	27	CL	A	Wimbledon	L3-4	1-2	13	Otulokowski, Bremner, Downes (og)	5,667
28	30	CL	H	Bristol R	W1-0	0-0		Otulokowski	4,885
29	J 2	CL	A	Bolton W	L0-2	0-1	13		7,054
30	15	CL	H	Brentford	L1-2	0-1		Lovell (pen)	5,370
31	21	CL	H	AFC Bournemouth	D1-1	1-1	13	Sherringham	4,242
32	28	CL	H	Hull C	W1-0	1-0	10	Bremner	3,991
33	F 4	CL	A	Sheffield U	L0-2	0-1	13		9,916
34	11	CL	H	Oxford U	W2-1	1-1	11	Robinson, Massey	4,974
35	14	CL	A	Newport Co	D1-1	1-0		Martin	2,070
36	19	CL	H	Gillingham	D2-2	0-1		Neal D, Nutton	6,344
37	25	CL	A	Preston NE	D0-0	0-0	13		4,109
38	28	AMC 1	H	Gillingham	W4-3[1]	2-2		Neal, Martin, Sitton (og), Sherringham	2,364
39	M 3	CL	H	Rotherham U	W2-0	1-0	12	Neal J, Martin	2,985
40	6	CL	A	Wigan Ath	D0-0	0-0			3,212
41	10	CL	H	Bradford C	D0-0	0-0	13		3,269
42	13	AMC 2	H	AFC Bournemouth	D2-2§	0-0		White, Neal	2,099
43	17	CL	A	Burnley	L0-1	0-1	13		5,061
44	20	CL	A	Plymouth Arg	W1-0	0-0		Nutton	4,507
45	27	AMC SQF	H	Swindon T	W3-1	1-0		Emmanuel (og), Lovell (pen), Bremner	2,112
46	A 14	CL	H	Walsall	W2-0	0-0	11	Lovell (pen), Neal D	3,458
47	18	CL	H	Southend U	W4-0	1-0		Neal D 2, Bremner 2	3,345
48	21	CL	A	Orient	L3-5	2-2	12	Osgood (og), Lovell, Neal D	3,874
49	23	CL	H	Wimbledon	D1-1	0-1	12	Lovell	5,153
50	27	CL	A	Scunthorpe U	W1-0	0-0		Bremner	2,867
51	M 1	CL	H	Lincoln C	L0-2	0-0			2,825
52	5	CL	H	Bolton W	W3-0	2-0	9	Neal D 3	2,346
53	8	CL	A	Bristol R	L2-3	1-1		Robinson, Otulokowski	5,347
54	12	CL	H	Exeter C	W3-0	2-0	9	Bremner 3	2,898
55	14	CL	A	Port Vale	L0-1	0-1			2,299
56	17	AMC SSF	A	Plymouth Arg	W1-0	0-0		Lovell	4,531
57	21	AMC SF	A	AFC Bournemouth	L1-2	0-1		Cusack	4,058

[1]After Extra Time. §Lost 6-7 on Penalties, After Extra Time

Av Home Att 4,384

Goal Scorers

League (71): Bremner 15, Neal D 13, Lovell 7 (3 pens), Otulokowski 7, Chatterton 6 (2 pens), Lowndes 3, Martin 3, Nutton 3, Robinson 2, Sparrow 2, Stride 2, Burke 1, Massey 1, Neal J 1, Sherringham 1, opponents 4
FA Cup (4): Cusack 1, Lovell 1 (1 pen), Martin 1, Massey 1
Milk Cup (9): Neal D 3, Chatterton 2 (1 pen), Martin 2, Lowndes 1, Otulokowski 1
AMC (11): Lovell 2, Neal D 2, Bremner 1, Cusack 1, Sherringham 1, White 1, opponents 2

1983-84

Sansome	Lovell	Stride	Robinson	Nutton	Cusack	Bremner	Lowndes	Martin	Otulokowski	Chatterton	Massey	Neal D	Wells	White	McLeary	Burke (L)	Sparrow (L)	Cowley	Stevens	Sherringham	Neal J	Coleman	REFEREE	
1	2	3	4	5	6	7	8	9	10*	11	12												K Baker	1
1	**2**	**3***	**4**	**5**	**6**	**7**	**8**	**9**	**10**	**11**		**12**											**A Gunn**	**2**
1	2	3	4	5	6	7	8	9*	10	11		12											B Hill	3
1	2	3	4	5	6	7	8		10	11		9											I Borrett	4
	2	3	4*	5	6	7	8	12	10	11		9	1										L Dilkes	5
1	**2**	**3**		**5**	**6**	**7**	**8**		**10**	**11**		**9**		**4**									**M Heath**	**6**
1	2	3		5	6	7	8		10	11		9		4									DA Hedges	7
1	2	3		5	6	7	8*	12	10	11		9		4									D Letts	8
1	2	3		5	6	7	8		10	11		9		4									Alan Robinson	9
	2		3	5	6	12	7	9*	10	11		8	1	4									RG Milford	10
	2		**3**	**5**	**6**	**9**	**7**	**12**	**10**	**11**		**8**	**1**	**4**									**M James**	**11**
	2	3	10		6	9	7	5		11		8	1	4									K Barratt	12
	2	3	10*		6	9	7	5		11		8	1	4	12								NL Wilson	13
	2	3	10*		6	9	7	5		11		8	1	4	12								K Walmsley	14
	2	3		5	6	9	7	12		11		8*	1	4		10							H King	15
	2	**3**	**10***	**5**	**6**	**9**	**7**	**12**		**11**		**8**	**1**	**4**									**B Stevens**	**16**
	2		3	5	6	9	7	8		11			1	4		10							M Bodenham	17
	2		3	5	6	9	7†	8		11			1	4		10							H Taylor	18
	2	3		5	6	8	7	9		11			1	4		10							DJ Axcell	19
	2	3*		5	6	9	7	8		11	12		1	4		10							J Ashworth	20
	2		**3**	**5**	**6**	**8**		**9**		**11**	**7**	**10**	**1**		**4**								**B Scales**	**21**
	3		3	5	6	8		9		11	12	10*	1		4	7							EA Read	22
	2		3	5	6	8		9		11	10†		1		4	7							K Cooper	23
	2		**3**	**5**	**6**	**8**	**7**	**9**		**11**	**10**	**12**	**1**		**4***								**Alan Robinson**	**24**
	2		4*	5	6	8	7	12		11		9	1	10			3*						T Spencer	25
	2			4	5	8	7	4	10			9*	1	11	12		3						L Burden	26
	2			5	6	8		9*	10	7	12		1	11	4		3						J Martin	27
1	2			5	6	8	7	9	10*	12				11	4		3						J Hunting	28
1	2		3	5		8	7*	4	10	11	9				6			12					M Peck	29
1	2		4	5		8			10	11*	12				6		3		7	9			A Seville	30
1	2	3	11	5	6	8			10		7				4					9			T Bune	31
1	2	3	11	5	6	8		12	10		7				4					9*			M Taylor	32
1	2	3	11	5	6	8		9	10		7	12			4*								N Glover	33
1	2	3	11	5	6	8*		9	10		7	12			4								I Borrett	34
1	2	3	11	5	6	8		9	10		7*	12			4								R Bridges	35
1	2	3	11	5	6	8		9	10		7*	12			4								M Dimblebee	36
1	7	3	11	5	6			9	10			8			12				2	4*			P Holbrook	37
1	**4**	**3**	**11***	**5**	**6**			**9**				**8**		**12**	**10**				**2**	**13**	**7***		**D Axcell**	**38**
1	4	3	12	5	6			9	10			8			11				2		7*		L Shapter	39
1	4	3	11	5	6			9*	10			8			7				2		12		C Seal	40
1	4	3		5				9				8		10	7			6	2		11		G Napthine	41
1	**4**	**3**	**12**	**5**		**12**		**9***				**8**		**10**	**7***			**6**	**2**		**11**		**M James**	**42**
1	6	5		3		11		8*				10		7	9			4	2	12			J Key	43
1	4	3		5	6	11			10			10		9	7				2				J Bray	44
1	**4**		**12**	**5**	**6**	**8***			**10**			**9**		**11**	**7***				**2**	**12**		**3**	**K Barratt**	**45**
1	4	3		5	6*	8			10			9			7				2	12	11		D Letts	46
1	4	3	11	5	6	8			9			10			7*				2		12		E Read	47
1	4	3*	11	5	6	8			10			9		7					2		12		Alan Robinson	48
1	4		3*	5		8		6	10			9		11	7				2	12			C Thomas	49
1	4		3	5		8			10	2		9		11	7				6				J Worrall	50
1	4		3	5		8			10	2		9		11	7				6				A Gunn	51
1	4		3	5	6	8			10			9		11	7				2				D Hedges	52
1	4		3	5	6	8			10			9		11	7				2				A Crickmore	53
1	4		3	5	6	8			10	7*		9		11	12				2				T Spencer	54
1	4		3	5*	6	8			10	7		9		11	12				2				R Guy	55
1	**4**		**3**		**6**	**8**		**5**	**10**	**7**					**11**				**2**	**9**			**K Baker**	**56**
1	**4**		**3**		**6**	**8**		**5**	**10**	**7**		**9**			**11**				**2**				**J Martin**	**57**
31	**46**	28	32	43	39	41	20	26	33	26	8	29	15	27	24	7	5	2	17	4	3		League Appearances	
			+1S			+1S		+5S		+1S	+5S	+5S			+6S			+1S		+3S	+3S			
	2		2	2	2	2	1	2		2	2	1+1S	2		2								FA Cup Appearances	
2	4	3	3	4	4	4	4	1+2S	3	4		3+1S	2	3									Milk Cup Appearances	
5	5	2	3+2S	3	4	3+1S		4	3	2		4		2+1S	5			1	5	1+2S	2	1	AM Cup Appearances	

THE DEN

Official Address: The Den, Cold Blow Lane, London SE14 5RH. Telephone: 01-639 3143/4

Ground Capacity: 32,000

Record Attendance: 48,672 v. Derby County, F.A. Cup round 5, 20 Feb 1937

Record Receipts: £26,872 v. W.B.A., Milk Cup Round 2, 4 Oct 1983

Size of Playing Area: 112yds × 74 yds

Season Tickets: £103.50 to £126.50 (adults stand), £72.50 to £88.50 (OAP/juveniles stand); £69.00 (adult ground), £46.00 (juveniles/OAP ground); £260.00 (wing forecourt, 2 adults, 2 children); £175.00 (wing forecourt, 1 adult, 2 children)

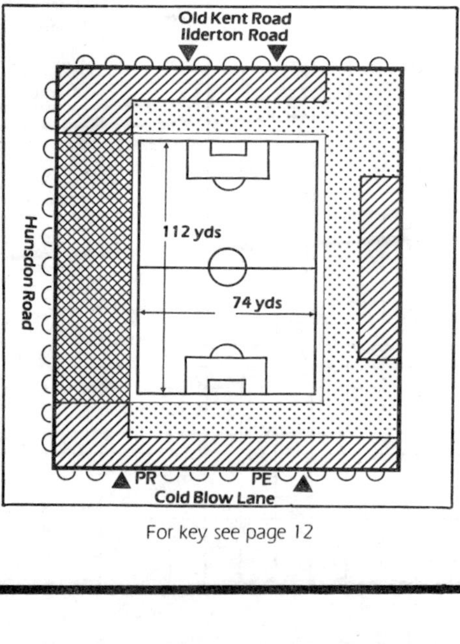

For key see page 12

Executive Box Season Tickets: V.P. Club £250.00 per annum (usual V.P. facilities and car park)

Cost of Stand Tickets: £4.50, £5.00, £5.50; **Terraces:** £3.00 (£2.00 juveniles/OAP)

Match and Ticket Information: Bookable 10-14 days in advance from club office

Car Parking: Good street parking. Also Car Park near the ground

How to get to the ground

From North: From Motorway M1 and A1 follow signs London A1 then City, then follow signs Shoreditch, Whitechapel. Then follow signs Ring Road, Dover to Cross Tower Bridge. In 1m at roundabout take 1st exit A2. In 1.8m turn left into Avonley Road then take 3rd turning right into Edric Road, at end turn right then turn left into Cold Blow Lane for Millwall F.C.

From East: Use A2 S.P. London. At New Cross follow signs City, Westminster, into Kender Street and at end keep forward into Avonley Road. Take 3rd turning right into Edric Road. At end turn right then turn left into Coldblow Lane for Millwall F.C.

From South: Use A20 and A21 S.P. London. At New Cross follow signs City, Westminster, into Kender Street, and end keep forward into Avonley Road then take 3rd turning right into Edric Road. At end turn right then turn left into Cold Blow Lane for Millwall F.C.

From West: From Motorway M4 and M3 take South Circular Road A205. Then follow signs Clapham, City A3 then signs Camberwell, New Cross and later Rochester A202 and in 0.8m turn left into Kender Street and at end forward into Avonley Road. Take 3rd turning right into Edric Road, at end turn right then turn left into Cold Blow Lane for Millwall F.C.

NEWCASTLE UNITED Division 1

President
F Braithwaite

Chairman
S Seymour

Directors
R Mackenzie (Vice Chairman)
J Rush AFC
W G McKeag
Sir George Bowman JP
E Dunn
G R Forbes

General Manager Secretary
R Cushing

Commercial Manager
G McDonnell (0632-322285)

Manager
J Charlton

Assistant Manager
J Harvey

Coach & Reserve Team Coach
W McFaul

Youth Team Coach
C Suggett

Physiotherapist, Chief Scout, Assistant Secretary and Groundsman:
To be appointed

The Magpies soared triumphantly back to the First Division, drawing huge crowds to St James' Park. Although promotion was not guaranteed until drawing at Huddersfield in their penultimate match, few doubted that Newcastle would return to the top.

Inspired by former England captain Kevin Keegan, who scored 28 League and Cup games in his final season as a player, Newcastle recovered from a shaky start, holding third place in the table for most of the second half of the season.

Manager Arthur Cox found another star in Peter Beardsley who captivated fans with skilful performances and 20 goals. Chris Waddle also played well, hitting 18 goals in a manner that promises well.

Beardsley was the third new face following left-back John Ryan (from Oldham) and forward David Mills (Sheffield Wednesday) who had previously played for the club on loan. Later Mr Cox signed centre-back Glenn Roeder from QPR.

Maximum points from five games in October firmly established the promotion challenge which was maintained throughout the season. The Magpies closed that month with a fabulous 5-0 win over close rivals, Manchester City, Beardsley scoring a spectacular hat-trick.

29,123 saw the opening home game of the season against Shrewsbury. Though Newcastle were surprisingly beaten, the locals remained loyal and on ten occasions there were crowds exceeding 30,000 at St James' Park. The best was 36,725 for a critical match with Sheffield Wednesday in April and the final average of 29,977 was the best in Division Two.

There was a scare at the end of April when Newcastle visited the bottom club Cambridge Utd who, the previous week, had established a new League record by playing 31 League matches without a win. Newcastle lost 0-1.

The Magpies recovered by thrashing Derby 4-0 before an ecstatic 35,850 home crowd a week later. Grimsby also won and, technically, could still catch Newcastle. Further shocks were in store in the penultimate match at Huddersfield. The Magpies conceded two goals mid-way through the first-half but then showed fine character in recovering through goals from Beardsley and Mills. That point assured promotion.

36,415 turned up for the final game against Brighton to salute the team's achievement and pay homage to Kevin Keegan who was playing his 500th, and final, game in League football. He responded by scoring a goal.

However, Newcastle were disappointing in the Cups being knocked out of the Milk Cup by Third Division Oxford United and taking an early FA Cup exit at Liverpool.

The season ended sadly when manager Arthur Cox, the architect of the success, fell into dispute with the board and left to take up a new appointment with Derby County. Jack Charlton, the former England defender and Middlesbrough and Sheffield Wednesday manager, succeeded him. TP

Back Row L to R: Chris Hedworth, Kevin Carr, Wesley Saunders, Martin Thomas, Malcolm Brown. **Middle Row:** Willie McFaul (Coach), Darren Melville, Ken Wharton, David McCreery, John Ryan, Neil McDonald, John Anderson, Ian Dawes, Jack Charlton (Manager). **Front Row:** John Carver, Paul Ferris, Peter Beardsley, Glenn Roeder, Steve Carney, Chris Waddle, Peter Haddock.

'THE MAGPIES'

Sponsored by **Scottish and Newcastle Breweries**

Formed: 1882 **Turned Professional:** 1889 **Ltd Co:** 1890
Previous Names: Until 1892 Newcastle East End
Previous Managers: Since 1946
George Martin Duggie Livingstone Charlie Mitten Norman Smith Joe Harvey Gordon Lee Richard Dinnis Bill McGarry Arthur Cox
Honours: Division 1: Champions 1904-5, 1906-7, 1908-9, 1926-7, Division 2: Champions 1964-5 F.A. Cup Winners: 1910, 1924, 1932, 1951, 1952, 1955 European Fairs Cup: Winners 1968-9 Anglo-Italian Cup: Winners 1973 Texaco Cup: Winners 1973-4, 1974-5.
League Career: Elected to Division 2 1893 Promoted to Division 1 1897-8 Relegated to Division 2 1933-4 Promoted to Division 1 1947-8 Relegated to Division 2 1960-1 Promoted to Division 1 1964-5 Relegated to Division 2 1977-8 Promoted to Division 1 1983-84
Colours: Black and white striped shirts, black shorts and black stockings with two white hoops on tops
Change Colours: All yellow

CLUB RECORDS

Most Appearances for Club: Jim Lawrence 432, 1904-22
Most Capped Player: Alf McMichael 40 N. Ireland **For England:** Malcolm Macdonald, 14
Record Goalscorer in a Match: Len Shackleton, 6 v Newport County, Div 2, 05.10.46 (his debut)
Record League Goalscorer in a season: Hughie Gallacher 36 Div 1, 1926-7
Record League Goalscorer in a career: Jackie Milburn 177 1946-57
Record Transfer Fee Received: £500,000 from Aston Villa for Peter Withe, May 1980
Record Transfer Fee Paid: £250,000 to West Bromwich Albion for John Trewick, Dec 1980
Best Performances: League: Champions (4) **F.A. Cup:** Winners(6) **League/Milk Cup:** Finalists 1975-6
Most League Points: (3 points for win) 80 Div 2, 1983-4 (2 points for win) 57 Div 2, 1964-5
Record League Victory: 13-0 v Newport County Div 2, 5 Oct 1946
Record League Defeat: 0-9 v Burton Wanderers Div 2, 15 Apr 1895
European Competitions Entered: European Fairs Cup: 1968-9, 1969-70, 1970-1 U.E.F.A. Cup:1977-78 Anglo-Italian Cup: Winners 1973

Club Statistician for the Directory: F. Evans

Programme Editor
Tony Hardisty

Price	Number of Pages
40p	24

Subscriptions
40p postage per home match

NEWCASTLE UNITED

PLAYERS NAME Ht Wt Birthdate	Honours	Birthplace Transfers	Clubs	APPEARANCES League	Milk Cup	F.A.C.	E. Cups	GOALS League	Milk Cup	F.A.C.	E. Cups
GOALKEEPERS											
Kevin Carr		Ashington	Burnley (A)								
6-2 13.6 6.11.58		F	Newcastle U.	149	5	9					
Martin Thomas	W. U.21(2)	Senghenydd	Bristol R. (A)	162 12	9						
6-1 13.0 28.11.59			Cardiff C. (L)	15	4						
			Southend U. (L)	6							
			Newcastle U.	26	2	1					
DEFENDERS											
John Anderson	Ei.(5), U.21(3),	Dublin	W.B.A. (A)								
5-11 11.6 7.11.59	Y	£40,000	P.N.E.	47+4	2	1					
		F	Newcastle U.	72+2	4	3		2			
Malcolm Brown	Div. 4, 80	Salford	Bury (A)	10+1							
6-2 13.0 13.12.56		F	Huddersfield T.	256	22	18		16	2	3	
			Newcastle U.								
Steve Carney		Wallsend	Blyth Spartans								
5-10 11.5 22.9.57		£3,000	Newcastle U.	119+9	4	9					
John Carver		Newcastle	Newcastle U. (A)								
5-8 10.8 16.1.65											
Jeff Clarke	Div. 2, 76	Pontefract	Manchester C.	13	2						
5-10½ 13.8 18.1.54		£100,000	Sunderland	178+3	14	15		6			
		F	Newcastle U.	53	2	2		1		1	
Peter Haddock		Newcastle	Newcastle U. (A)	46+4	1	6					
5-11 11.5 22.9.57											
Chris Hedworth		Wallsend	Newcastle U. (A)	3+1							
6-1 10.11 5.1.64											
Glen Roeder*	E. B(6)	Woodford	Orient (A)	107+8	8	13		4			
6-2½ 12.8 13.12.55		£250,000	Q.P.R.	157	13	11		17		1	
			Notts Co. (L)	4							
		£125,000	Newcastle U.	23							
John Ryan	E. U.21(1)	Oldham	Oldham A. (A)	77	6	2		8			
5-10 11.7 18.2.62			Newcastle U.	22	2	1		1			
Wes Saunders		Sunderland	Newcastle U.	58	4	3					
6-0 11.11 23.2.63											
MIDFIELD											
Paul Ferris	E. Y	Lisburn	Newcastle U. (A)	1+6		1					
5-8 10.8 10.7.65											
David McCreery†	N.I.(46), U.21(1),	Belfast	Manchester U. (A)	48+39	4	1		7	1		
5-6½ 10.7 16.9.57	Y, S	£200,000	Q.P.R.	56+1	8	1+1		4	1		
		£125,000	Tulsa Roughnecks								
		£80,000	Newcastle U.	63+3	4	1					
Terry McDermott	E.(25), U.23(1),	Kirkby	Bury (A)	83+7	5	5		8	1	2	
5-9 12.13 8.12.51	Div. 1, 77, 79, 80,	£25,000	Newcastle U.	55+1	4	10		6	2	2	
	82, ESC. 77,	£166,000	Liverpool	221+11	36	23		54	5	4	
	FC. 81, 82, Euro	£100,000	Newcastle U.	74	3	3		12	1	1	
	Cup 77, 78, 81										
Ken Wharton		Newcastle	Newcastle U.	140+14	6+1	10		14			
5-8 8.10 28.11.60											
FORWARDS											
Peter Beardsley		Newcastle	Carlisle U.	93+11	6+1	15		22		7	
5-8 11.4 18.1.61		£275,000	Vancouver W.								
			Manchester U. (L)								
			Vancouver W.								
		£150,000	Newcastle U.	34+1	2	1		20			
Neil McDonald	E. Y, S	Wallsend	Newcastle U. (A)	32+4		+1		4			
5-11 11.4 2.11.65											
Chris Waddle		Hepworth	Tow Law T.								
6-0 11.5 14.12.60		£10,000	Newcastle U.	134	5	10		33		3	

APPRENTICES

Ian Bogle, Paul Gascoigne, Steve Forster, Peter Harbach, Tony Haytor, Gary Kelly, Brian Kilford, Ian McKenzie, Tony Nesbit, Brian Tinnion, Stuart Dickinson, Paul Stephenson, Jeff Wrightson

NEWCASTLE UNITED

DIVISION TWO 3RD **FA CUP** 3RD ROUND **MILK CUP** 2ND ROUND

MATCH	DATE	COMPETITION	VENUE	OPPONENTS	RESULT	HALF TIME	L'GUE POS'N	GOALSCORERS	ATTENDANCE
1	A 27	CL	A	Leeds U	W 1-0	1-0		Dickinson (og)	30,806
2	29	CL	H	Shrewsbury T	L 0-1	0-1			29,123
3	S 3	CL	H	Oldham Ath	W 3-0	1-0	3	McDermott, Waddle, Mills	22,644
4	6	CL	A	Middlesbrough	L 2-3	0-1		Keegan, Mills	19,648
5	10	CL	A	Grimsby T	D 1-1	0-1	9	Keegan	9,000
6	17	CL	H	Crystal Palace	W 3-1	1-0	7	Ryan, Waddle, Keegan	22,774
7	24	CL	A	Barnsley	D 1-1	0-0	7	Waddle	14,085
8	O 1	CL	H	Portsmouth	W 4-2	3-0	4	Waddle 2, Keegan, Wharton	25,411
9	**5**	**MC 2**	**H**	**Oxford U**	**D 1-1**	**0-0**		**McDermott**	**21,161**
10	8	CL	H	Charlton Ath	W 2-1	0-1	4	Keegan 2	23,247
11	16	CL	A	Swansea C	W 2-1	1-0		Wharton, Mills	9,807
12	19	CL	A	Cardiff C	W 2-0	1-0		Keegan, Beardsley	9,926
13	**26**	**MC 2**	**A**	**Oxford U**	**L 1-2**	**0-2**		**Keegan**	**13,040**
14	29	CL	H	Manchester C	W 5-0	2-0	2	Beardsley 3, Keegan, Waddle	33,588
15	N 5	CL	H	Fulham	W 3-2	1-1	2	Keegan, Mills, Wharton	31,568
16	12	CL	A	Chelsea	L 0-4	0-2	3		30,628
17	19	CL	A	Sheffield W	L 2-4	1-1	4	McDermott, Keegan (pen)	41,134
18	26	CL	H	Cambridge U	W 2-1	1-0	3	Keegan, Beardsley	25,005
19	D 3	CL	A	Derby Co	L 2-3	2-0	4	Keegan, Waddle	18,691
20	10	CL	H	Huddersfield T	W 5-2	2-2	3	Keegan, Beardsley, Waddle 2, McDermott	25,652
21	17	CL	A	Brighton & HA	W 1-0	0-0	3	Waddle	13,896
22	26	CL	H	Blackburn R	D 1-1	0-1	3	Waddle	33,802
23	27	CL	A	Carlisle U	L 1-3	1-1	4	Waddle	14,756
24	31	CL	A	Oldham Ath	W 2-1	1-0	4	Keegan 2	8,518
25	J 2	CL	H	Barnsley	W 1-0	1-0	3	Waddle	29,833
26	**6**	**FAC 3**	**A**	**Liverpool**	**L 0-4**	**0-2**			**33,566**
27	21	CL	A	Crystal Palace	L 1-3	0-3	4	Beardsley	9,464
28	F 4	CL	A	Portsmouth	W 4-1	2-0		Keegan 2, Beardsley 2	18,686
29	11	CL	H	Grimsby T	L 0-1	0-1	5		28,526
30	18	CL	A	Manchester C	W 2-1	2-0	4	Beardsley, Keegan	41,767
31	25	CL	H	Cardiff C	W 3-1	2-0	4	Waddle, Keegan 2 (1 pen)	27,909
32	M 3	CL	A	Fulham	D 2-2	1-2	3	Beardsley, Keegan	12,290
33	10	CL	H	Chelsea	D 1-1	0-0	3	McDermott	36,504
34	17	CL	H	Middlesbrough	W 3-1	1-1	4	Beardsley, McDermott, Keegan	30,386
35	24	CL	A	Shrewsbury T	D 2-2	0-0	3	Johnson (og), Keegan	8,313
36	28	CL	H	Leeds U	W 1-0	1-0		Irwin (og)	30,877
37	31	CL	H	Swansea C	W 2-0	0-0	3	Wharton, Beardsley	27,306
38	A 7	CL	A	Charlton Ath	W 3-1	1-1	3	Waddle, McDermott, Beardsley	15,289
39	14	CL	H	Sheffield W	L 0-1	0-0	3		36,725
40	20	CL	A	Blackburn R	D 1-1	0-0		Trewick	19,196
41	23	CL	H	Carlisle U	W 5-1	2-0	3	Keegan 2, Waddle, Beardsley 2	33,386
42	28	CL	A	Cambridge U	L 0-1	0-1	3		7,720
43	M 5	CL	H	Derby Co	W 4-0	2-0	3	Keegan, Beardsley 2, Waddle	35,850
44	7	CL	A	Huddersfield T	D 2-2	2-2	3	Beardsley, Mills	25,101
45	12	CL	H	Brighton & HA	W 3-1	1-1	3	Keegan, Waddle, Beardsley	36,415

Av Home Att **29,977**

Goal Scorers

League (85): Keegan 27 (3 pens), Beardsley 20, Waddle 18, McDermott 6, Mills 5, Wharton 4, Ryan 1, Trewick 1, opponents 3
FA Cup (-): —
Milk Cup (2): Keegan 1, McDermott 1

1983-84

Carr	Anderson	Ryan	McCreery	Clarke	Carney	Keegan	McDonald	Mills	McDermott	Waddle	Wharton	Thomas	Trewick	Beardsley	Saunders	Haddock	Roeder	REFEREE	
1*	2	3	4	5	6	7	8	9	10	11	12							R Bridges	1
	2	3	4	5	6	7	8*	9	10	11	12	1						N Wilson	2
	2	3	4	5	6	7	8	9	10	11		1						A Challinor	3
	2	3	4	5	6	7	8*	9	10	11	12	1						K Hackett	4
	2	3	4	5	6	7		9	10	11	8	1						M Heath	5
	2	3	4	5	6	7		9	10	11	8*	1	12					N Midgley	6
	2	3	4	5*	6	7		9	10	11	8	1		12				K Walmsley	7
	2	3	4		6	7		12	10	11*	8	1		9	5			W Scott	8
	2	**3**	**4**		**6**	**7**		**12**	**10**	**9**	**11***	**1**		**8**	**5**			**N Glover**	**9**
	2	3	4		6	7		12	10	9	11*	1		8	5			P Tydesley	10
	2	3	4		6	7		12	10	11*	8	1		9	5			K Baker	11
	2	3	4		6	7			10	9	11	1		8	5			RG Milford	12
	2	**3**	**4**		**6**	**7**		**12**	**10**	**9**	**11***	**1**		**8**	**5**			**C Thomas**	**13**
	2	3	4		6	7			10	9	11	1		8	5			C Seel	14
	2	3	4		6	7		12	10	9	11	1		8	5*			D Richardson	15
	2	3	4*		6	7		12	10	9	11	1		8	5			H King	16
	2	3			6	7	4		10	9	11	1		8	5			JB Worrall	17
	2	3			6	7	4		10	9	11	1		8	5			T Mills	18
		3	4*		6	7	12		10	9	11	1		8	5	2		R Nixon	19
	2	3*	4		6	7		12	10	9	11	1		8	5			I Hendrick	20
	2		4		6	7		11	10	9	3	1		8	5			D Reeves	21
	2		4			7	12	11*	10	9	3	1		8	5		6	D Hutchinson	22
	2		4		11	7			10	9	3	1		8	5		6	T Fitzharris	23
	2	3	4			7	8		10	9*	11	1	12		5		6	D Shaw	24
	2	3	4			7			10	9	11	1		8	5		6	D Scott	25
	2	**3**	**4**			**7**	**12**		**10**	**9**	**11***	**1**		**8**	**5**		**6**	**K Hackett**	**26**
1	2	3	4	5		7			10	9	11			8			6	T Spencer	27
1	2	11*	4	5	12	7			10	9	3			8			6	D Axcell	28
1	2		4	5		7	11		10	9	3			8			6	D Allison	29
1	2		4	5		7			10	9	3		11	8			6	J Hunting	30
1	2		4	5		7			10	9	3		11	8			6	A Robinson	31
	2		4	5		7			10	9	3	1	11	8			6	E Read	32
1	2		4	5		7			10	9	3		11	8			6	J Hough	33
1	2		4		5	7			10	9	3		11	8			6	J Worrall	34
1	2		4		5	7			10	9	3		11	8			6	F Roberts	35
1	2		4		5	7			10	9	3		11	8			6	M Peck	36
1	2		4		5	7			10	9	3		11	8			6	R Dilkes	37
1	2		4		5	7			10	9	3		11	8			6	T Bune	38
1	2		4		5	7			10	9	3		11	8			6	C Seel	39
1	2		4		5	7			10	9	3		11*	8		12	6	J Key	40
1	2		4		5	7	11		10	9	3			8			6	N Midgley	41
1	2		4		5	7	11*		10	9	3			8		12	6	A Seville	42
1	2		4		5	7			10	9	3		11	8			6	D Richardson	43
1	2		4		5			8	10	9	3		11	7			6	J Lovatt	44
1	2		4		5	7			10	9	3		11	8			6	K Walmsley	45
19	41	22	40	14	32	41	10	10	**42**	**42**	38	23	14	34	16	1	23	League Appearances	
					+1S		+2S	+6S			+3S		+2S	+1S		+2S			
	1	1	1			1	1S		1	1	1	1		1	1		1	FA Cup Appearances	
	2	2	2		2	2		2S	2	2	2	2		2	2			Milk Cup Appearances	

ST. JAMES' PARK

Official Address: St. James' Park, Newcastle-upon-Tyne NE1 4ST. Telephone: (0632) 328361

Telegraphic: Football, Newcastle-upon-Tyne

Ground Capacity: 37,718

Record Attendance: 68,386 v. Chelsea, Division 1, 3 Sept 1980

Record Receipts: £83,000 v. Liverpool, (Kevin Keegan Farewell Match), 17 May 1984

Size of Playing Area: 115yds × 75 yds

Season Tickets: £80 (£60 juvenile), £105 (£70 juvenile), £110 (£70 juvenile), £125 (£75 juveniles) all seats; £50 (£25 juvenile) family enclosure; £63.50 (£40 juvenile) West Stand Centre Paddock

Executive Box Season Tickets: None available

Cost of Stand Tickets: £4.50, £5.50, £5.75, £6.50 (£3.50, £4.00, £4.00, £4.50 OAP/juveniles); **Terraces:** £2.80 (£1.50 OAP/juveniles); **Paddocks:** £3.00 (£1.50 OAP/juveniles) £3.50

Match and Ticket Information: Postal applications 14 days before each match, personal ten days before each

Car Parking: Parking on the north side of the ground. Also street parking is permitted.

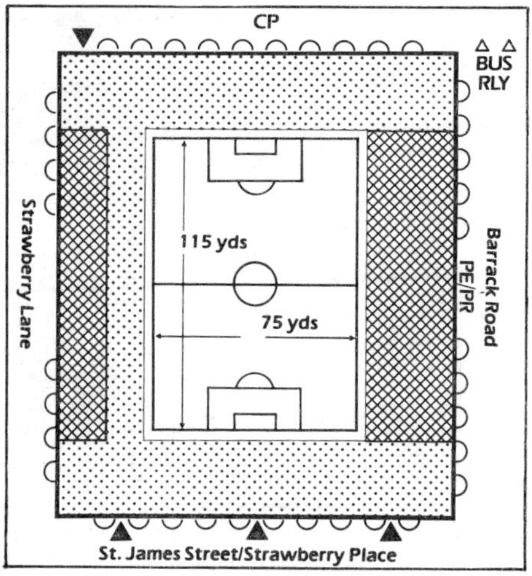

For key see page 12

How to get to the ground

From North: Use A1 into Newcastle then follow signs Hexham into Percy Street, then turn right into Leaze Park Road (or turn left then right into St. James' Street) for Newcastle United F.C.

From South: Use A1, A68 and then A6127, cross River Tyne and at roundabout take 1st exit into Mosley Street. (One-way keep to left hand lane into Neville Street. At end turn right into Clayton Street for Newgate Street. Then turn left into Leaze Park Road (one-way) turn left then right into St. James' Street for Newcastle United F.C.

From West: Use A69 (S.P. Newcastle) enter city centre then turn left into Clayton Street for Newgate Street. Then turn into Leaze Park Road (one-way) turn left then right into St. James' Street for Newcastle United F.C.

NEWPORT COUNTY Division 3

President
S Jenkins

Chairman
A O Menzies

Directors
J Ford
G P Prosser
J P Adams

Secretary
P Dauncey

Manager
Colin Addison

Assistant Manager
Bobby Smith

Physiotherapist
S Williams

Youth Development Officer/ Chief Scout
G E A Reynolds

Commercial Manager
P Jones (0633 277472)

After mounting a strong promotion challenge the previous season the 'Ironsides' were less successful this time round having sold their top scorer, Tynan to Plymouth and near the end of the season a further shock was announced to their fans when another prolific marksman, Aldridge, departed to Oxford. All clubs have cash-flow problems, but the supporters will only hope that Manager Colin Addison can find a suitable replacement so that another challenge can be made.

This was a season when a serious attempt at promotion was in fact spoiled by a mediocre start and an improvement in October and November was never enough to suggest a serious threat to the front-runners. The domestic cup competitions brought little excitement as compensation with an early departure from the Milk Cup at the hands of Torquay United, who won both legs, being a bad start. The F.A. Cup was better, although the two beaten teams in the first two rounds came from outside the League and the first opponents, Poole Town, forced a replay at Somerton Park after a goalless game in Dorset. Harrow Borough, subsequent Isthmian League Champions, were at home in the next round but gave the Gwent team few anxious moments. A visit to Plymouth in the Third Round produced an excellent draw with Aldridge scoring twice (as he had done at Harrow), but having done the hard work County failed at home and went out to the eventual semi-finalists by a single goal. With the Welsh Cup producing no fireworks and without success in the new Associate Members Cup it became a rather drab season, which the team had to complete with few exciting moments in the later stages.

There is plenty of talent at Somerton Park with Kendall in goal giving a sound lead and consistency coming from Oakes, Vaughan Jones, the veteran Relsih and Boyle in defence. The midfield has also been sound with Reid playing well, but there could be problems up front (as has been said already) if Neville Chamberlain and the others cannot find the net with regularity. The early matches will provide a guide to Manager Addison's and the team's chances.

WLM

Back Row L to R: Bobby Smith (Assistant Manager), Gary Emmanuel, Tony Pulis, John Lewis, Roy Carter, Mark Kendall, Trevor Matthewson, Mike Saxby, Neville Chamberlain, Phil Green, David Williams (Trainer-Coach). **Front Row:** Chris Lilygreen, Mike Pratt, John Relish, Terry Boyle, Colin Addison (Manager), Linden Jones, Kevin Kent, Ceri Williams, Tony Reid.

'THE IRONSIDES'

Formed: 1912 **Turned Professional:** 1912 **Ltd Co:** 1912
Previous Managers: Since 1946: Billy McCandless Tom Bromilow Fred Stansfield Bill Lucas Bobby Evans Bill Lucas Trevor Morris Les Graham Bob Ferguson Bill Lucas Brian Harris Dave Elliot Jimmy Scoular Colin Addison Len Ashurst
Honours: Champions Division 3(S) 1938-9
League Career: Original Members of Division 3 1920 Reverted to Division 3(S) 1921
Dropped out of the Football League 1931 Re-elected to Division 3(S) 1932
Promoted to Division 2 1938-9 Relegated to Division 3(S) 1946-7
Transferred to Division 3 1958 Relegated to Division 4 1961-2
Promoted to Division 3 1979-80
Colours: Amber shirts, black shorts, amber stockings
Change Colours: White shirts, black shorts, white stockings

CLUB RECORDS

Most Appearances for Club: Len Weare: Football League 526 + F.A. Cup 35 + League Cup 13 **Total 574**
Most Capped Player: Nigel Vaughan, 3, Wales **For England:** None
Record Goalscorer in a Match: Tudor Martin, 5 v Merthyr Tydfil (H, 10-0), Div 3(S), 10 Apr 1930
Record League Goalscorer in a season: Tudor Martin, 34, Div 3(S), 1929-30 **In All Competitions:** Tudor Martin 36 (45 League + 2 F.A. Cup), 1929-30
Record League Goalscorer in a career: Reg Parker, 99, 1948-54 **In All Competitions:** Reg Parker 109 (99 League + 10 F.A. Cup) 1948-54
Record Transfer Fee Received: £50,000 from Luton Town for Mark Aizlewood, Mar 1978
Record Transfer Fee Paid: £80,000 to Swansea City for Alan Waddle, Jan 1981
Best Performances: League: 4th Div 3 1982-3 **F.A. Cup:** 5th Round 1948-9 **League/Milk Cup:** Never past 3rd Round **Welsh Cup:** Winners 1979-80 **European Cup Winners Cup:** Quarter Final
Most League Points: 78 in Div 3, 1982-3 **Most League Goals:** 85, Div 4, 1964-5
Record League Victory: 10-0 v Merthyr Tydfil, Div 3 South, 10 Apr 1930
Record League Defeat: 0-13 v Newcastle United, Div 2, 5 Oct 1946
European Competitions Entered: European Cup Winners Cup 1980-1
Club Statistician for the Directory: Tony Ambrosen

Editorial
Richard Shepherd

Price	**Number of Pages**
40p	20

Subscriptions
Apply to club for rates

NEWPORT COUNTY

PLAYERS NAME Ht Wt Birthdate	Honours	Birthplace Transfers	Clubs	APPEARANCES League	Milk Cup	F.A.C.	A.M.C.	GOALS League	Milk Cup	F.A.C.	A.M.C.
GOALKEEPER											
Mark Kendall	W. U.21(1), S	Blackwood	Tottenham H. (A)	29	1	6					
6-0 12.4 20.9.58			Chesterfield (L)	9							
		£45,000	Newport Co.	161	10	12	1				
DEFENDERS											
Terry Boyle*†	W.(2), U.21(1),	Ammanford	Tottenham H. (A)								
5-10 12.4 29.10.58	Y, S	F	Crystal Palace	24+2		1		1		2	
			Wimbledon (L)	5							
		Player Exchange	Bristol C.	36+1	4	8			2		
		F	Newport Co.	73+1	2	6	1	1	1		
Linden Jones	W. U.21(3)	Tredegar	Cardiff C. (A)	143+2	10	4		2		1	
5-6 10.8 5.3.61		Player Exchange	Newport Co.	32			1				
Trevor Mattewson		Sheffield	Sheffield Wed. (A)	3		2					
6-1 12.5 12.2.65		F	Newport Co.	30+2		5	1				
John Relish		Liverpool	Chester (A)	10+1	3			1			
5-8 12.0 5.10.53			Newport Co.	286+16	18	12+	4E	7			
Mike Saxby	Div. 2, 82	Mansfield	Mansfield T. (A)	76+3	2	1+1		5			
6-2 13.0 12.8.57		£200,000	Luton T.	82	7	2		6	1		
			Grimsby T. (L)	10							
			Lincoln C. (L)	10				1			
			Newport Co.								
MIDFIELD											
Roy Carter	Div. 3, 76	Torpoint	Falmouth T.								
6-0½ 11.7 19.2.54			Hereford U.	64+7	9	4+1		9	3	1	
		£22,000	Swindon T.	193+7	22+	11		34	2	2	
			Torquay U. (L)	6				5			
			Bristol R. (L)	4				1			
		F	Torquay U.	21				3			
		F	Newport Co.	37+2		5	1	4			
Gary Emmanuel	W. U.23(1)	Swansea	Birmingham C. (A)	61+10	1	5		6			
5-9 11.3 1.2.54		£50,000	Bristol R.	59+6	4	3		2			
		Player Exchange	Swindon T.	109+2	6	12	2	8			
		F	Newport Co.								
Chris Lilygreen		Newport	Newport Co.	15+7			1	4			
5-9 9.8 9.6.65											
Tony Reid		Nottingham	Derby Co. (A)	27+3	2	1+1		1			
5-9 10.10 9.5.63			Scunthorpe U. (L)	6							
		F	Newport Co.	39+2	1	4	1	6			
John Lewis	W. U.21(1)	Tredegar	Pontllanfraith								
5-9 11.3 15.10.55		Player Exchange	Cardiff C.	135+5	10	10	1	9	1	1	
			Newport Co.	25				1			
Tony Pulls		Newport	Bristol R.	78+7	7+1	5		3		1	
5-10 11.8 16.1.58		F	Happy Valley (HK)								
		F	Bristol R.	44+1	3			2			
		F	Newport Co.								
FORWARDS											
Neville Chamberlain		Stoke	Port Vale (A)	133+8	7	10		33	3·	6	
5-7½ 11.5 22.1.60			Stoke C.	6							
			Newport Co. (L)	6				2			
			Plymouth A. (L)	7+4				3			
			Newport Co.								
Kevin Kent		Birmingham	W.B.A. (A)	1							
5-9 11.0 19.3.65		F	Newport Co.								
Mike Pratt		Newport	Newport Co.	3+3				2			
6-0 11.10 15.1.66											
Ceri Williams	W. Y	Tonyrefail	Newport Co.	16+7	1		1	2			
5-6 8.2 16.10.65											
NON-CONTRACT PLAYER 1984-85											
Phil Green				8+1				2			

Captains: Terry Boyle (team), John Relish (club)

NEWPORT COUNTY

DIVISION THREE 13TH **FA CUP** 3RD ROUND **MILK CUP** 1ST ROUND

MATCH	DATE	COMPE-TITION	VENUE	OPPONENTS	RESULT	HALF TIME	L'GUE POS'N	GOALSCORERS	ATTEN-DANCE
1	A 27	CL	H	Bristol R	W2-1	1-0		Vaughan, Aldridge	5,015
2	**30**	**MC 1**	**H**	**Torquay U**	**L2-3**	**1-1**		**Boyle, Aldridge**	**2,282**
3	S 3	CL	A	Wimbledon	L0-6	0-2			2,007
4	6	CL	A	Burnley	L0-2	0-0			6,719
5	10	CL	H	Bradford C	W4-3	2-1	12	Martinez, Aldridge, Vaughan 2 (1 pen)	2,462
6	**13**	**MC 1**	**A**	**Torquay U**	**L0-1**	**0-0**			**2,015**
7	17	CL	A	Walsall	L2-3	1-1	15	Vaughan (pen), Elsey	2,818
8	24	CL	H	Scunthorpe U	D1-1	0-0	15	Vaughan	2,679
9	27	CL	H	Preston NE	D1-1	1-0		Aldridge	2,542
10	O 1	CL	A	Rotherham U	W1-0	0-0	11	Aldridge	4,099
11	8	CL	H	Orient	D0-0	0-0	12		3,213
12	15	CL	A	Bolton W	W3-2	1-1	9	Farnworth (og), Reid, Carter	4,928
13	18	CL	H	Lincoln C	W1-0	1-0		Aldridge	3,450
14	22	CL	A	Exeter C	W2-1	0-1	6	Aldridge 2	3,970
15	29	CL	H	Port Vale	W2-1	1-0	5	Aldridge, Reid	3,829
16	N 1	CL	A	Millwall	D1-1	0-1		Aldridge	4,352
17	5	CL	H	Southend U	D1-1	1-0	6	Aldridge	3,769
18	12	CL	A	Hull C	D0-0	0-0	8		7,853
19	**20**	**FAC 1**	**A**	**Poole Town**	**D0-0**	**0-0**			**4,470**
20	**22**	**FAC 1R**	**H**	**Poole Town**	**W3-1**	**1-1**		**Oakes, Aldridge, Lewis**	**3,090**
21	26	CL	A	Oxford U	L0-2	0-2	10		6,330
22	D 3	CL	H	Wigan Ath	W5-3	1-1	9	Reid, Lewis, Aldridge 3	3,196
23	**10**	**FAC 2**	**A**	**Harrow Borough**	**W3-1**			**Aldridge 2, Chamberlain**	**2,500**
24	17	CL	H	Sheffield U	L0-2	0-0	11		4,295
25	26	CL	A	AFC Bournemouth	D1-1	0-1	12	Chamberlain	7,220
26	27	CL	H	Plymouth Arg	W2-0	1-0	9	Aldridge 2	5,154
27	31	CL	A	Brentford	L0-2	0-2	10		4,631
28	**J 7**	**FAC 3**	**A**	**Plymouth Arg**	**D2-2**	**1-0**		**Aldridge 2**	**6,789**
29	**10**	**FAC 3R**	**H**	**Plymouth Arg**	**L0-1**	**0-0**			**5,459**
30	14	CL	A	Bristol R	L0-4	0-2			6,041
31	22	CL	H	Walsall	W3-1	0-1		Chamberlain, Aldridge 2	4,375
32	F 4	CL	H	Rotherham U	L1-4	0-2		Aldridge (pen)	2,391
33	10	CL	A	Scunthorpe U	D3-3	3-2		Lilygreen, Jones V, Williams	2,879
34	14	CL	H	Millwall	D1-1	0-1		Aldridge	2,070
35	18	CL	A	Port Vale	L2-4	2-2	14	Jones V, Lilygreen	3,437
36	25	CL	H	Exeter C	W1-0	1-0	14	Aldridge	2,465
37	**28**	**AMC 1**	**H**	**Bristol R**	**L0-1**	**0-0**			**2,116**
38	M 3	CL	A	Lincoln C	W3-2	2-2	14	Reid 2, Oakes	1,780
39	6	CL	H	Wimbledon	D1-1	1-1		Pratt	2,538
40	10	CL	H	Hull C	D1-1	0-0	14	Jones V (pen)	2,813
41	17	CL	A	Orient	D2-2	1-1	14	Carter, Boyle	2,355
42	24	CL	H	Bolton W	L2-3	0-3	14	Micallef, Lilygreen	2,436
43	27	CL	H	Gillingham	W1-0	0-0		Carter	1,849
44	30	CL	A	Preston NE	L0-2	0-0			3,534
45	A 7	CL	H	Burnley	W1-0	0-0	12	Jones V	2,306
46	14	CL	A	Wigan Ath	L0-1	0-0	13		2,903
47	20	CL	A	Plymouth Arg	W1-0	0-0		Green	7,654
48	21	CL	H	AFC Bournemouth	W2-1	1-1	10	Reid (pen), Green	2,356
49	25	CL	A	Bradford C	L0-1	0-0			3,347
50	28	CL	H	Oxford U	D1-1	1-1	11	Carter	4,562
51	30	CL	A	Southend U	L1-3	0-2		Pratt	2,108
52	M 5	CL	A	Gillingham	L1-4	1-3	13	Micallef	3,073
53	7	CL	H	Brentford	D1-1	0-1	13	Lilygreen	2,154
54	12	CL	A	Sheffield U	L0-2	0-1	13		16,700

Av Home Att 3,158

Goal Scorers

League (58): Aldridge 20 (1 pen), Reid 6 (1 pen), Vaughan 5 (2 pens), Carter 4, Jones V 4 (1 pen), Lilygreen 4, Chamberlain 2, Green 2, Micallef 2, Pratt 2, Boyle 1, Elsey 1, Lewis 1, Martinez 1, Oakes 1, Williams 1, opponent 1
FA Cup (8): Aldridge 5, Chamberlain 1, Lewis 1, Oakes 1
Milk Cup (2): Aldridge 1, Boyle 1
AMC (-): —

1983-84

Kendall	Jones V	Relish	Bailey	Oakes	Boyle	Martinez	Aldridge	Woodruff	Vaughan	Elsey	Williams	Stroud	Reid	Jones G	Carter	Micallef	Lewis	Matthewson	Jones L	Lilygreen	Chamberlain (L)	Green	Pratt	Randell (L)	REFEREE	
1	2	3	4	5	6	7	8	9*	10	11	12														G Napthine	1
1	**2**	**3**	**4**	**5**	**6**	**7**	**8**	**9**	**10**	**11***	**12**														**D Brazier**	**2**
1	2	12	4		5		8	9*	3	7	11	6	10												J Bray	3
	2	3	7		6	9*	8		10	11	12	5	4	1											J Lovatt	4
	2	3	7*		5	9	8		10	11	12	6	4	1											J Martin	5
1	**2**	**3**	**7**	**5**	**6**	**9***	**8**		**10**	**11**		**12**	**4**												**T Bune**	**6**
1	2	3		5	6	7	8	9	10	11			4												L Dilkes	7
1	2	3		5	6	7	8	9	10	11*			4		12										A Seville	8
1	2	3		5	6	7	8		10	11		4			9										DA Hedges	9
1		3	4	5	6	7	8								10	9	11		2						DB Allison	10
1		3		5	6	7	8						4		10	9	11		2						T Spencer	11
1		3		5	6	7	8						4		10	9	11		2						J Key	12
1		3		5	6	7	8						4		10	9	11		2						V Callow	13
1		3		5	6	7	8						4		10	9	11		2						Alan Robinson	14
1		3		5	6	7	8						4		10	9*	11	12	2						A Crickmore	15
1		3		5	6		8	9					4		10		7	11	2						H Taylor	16
1		3		5	6		8	9					4*		10	7	11	12	2						R Nixon	17
1		3		5	6		8†						4		10	7	11	9	2						D Richardson	18
1		**10**		**5**	**6**	**12**	**8**						**4**		**9**	**7***	**11**	**3**	**2**						**E Read**	**19**
1				**5**	**6**	**7**	**8**						**4**		**10**	**9**	**11**	**3**	**2**						**E Read**	**20**
1		10		5	6	7*							4		9		11	3	2	12	8				AN Buksh	21
				5	6	7	8						4	1	10		11	3	2		9				C Downey	22
1	**2**			**5**	**6**	**7**	**8**						**4**		**10**		**11**	**3**			**9**				**T Bune**	**23**
1	2	12		5	6	7*	8						4		10		11	3			9				K Salmon	24
1	2			5	6		8						4		10	7	11	3			9				L Shapter	25
1		12		5	6		8						4		10	7	11	3	2		9*				M Robinson	26
1		10*		5	6		8	12					4		7	9	11	3	2						I Borrett	27
1	**2**	**3**			**5†**	**7**	**8**						**4**		**10**		**11**	**6**			**9**				**D Reeves**	**28**
1	**2**	**3**			**5**	**7**	**8**	**12**					**4**		**10**		**11**	**6***			**9**				**D Reeves**	**29**
1	2	3			5	7	8	9*					4		10		11			12					D Vickers	30
1		3*			5	2	8				11		4		6	10				7	9		12		M James	31
1	2	3			5	12	8				11		4*		10	9		6		7					D Letts	32
1	9				5		8				11		4		6	12	10	3	2	7*					P Willis	33
1	9	3*				12	8				11		4		5		10	6	2	7					R Bridges	34
1	9				6	7*					11		4		5	12	10	3	2	8					F Roberts	35
1	12			5	6		8*				11		4		9		10	3	2	7					A Ward	36
1	**9**			**5**	**6**						**11**		**4**		**8**		**10**	**3**	**2**	**7**					**A Seville**	**37**
1	8			5	6						12		4		9		11	3	2	7*				10	D Reeves	38
1	9			5	6			8*			7		4				11	3	2				12	10	K Baker	39
1	9			5	6						7*		4				11	3	2			8	12	10	E Scales	40
1	7			5	6		8*						4		9		11	3	2	12				10	D Hedges	41
1	4	12		5	6			8*							9	11		3	2	7				10	M Dimblebee	42
1	4	8		5	6										9	11		3	2	7				10	L Burden	43
1		8		5	6								4		9	11*		3	2	12		8		10	T Jones	44
1	8	11		5	6								4		12			3	2	7		9*		10	V Callow	45
1	2	7		3	4						11		6		9			5		12		8*		10	K Hackett	46
1	2	3		5	6						11		4		9			8		7*		12		10	T Holbrook	47
1	9*	3		4	5						12		6		11*			8	2			10		7	R Lewis	48
1		3		5	6						11*		4		9			8	2	12		7		10	I Hendrick	49
1		3		5	6						12		4		9	10		11	2	7*		8			E Read	50
1		3*		5	6						8				10	9		11	2	7			4		T Bune	51
1				5	6						11				4	8		3	2	7			9*	10	C Downey	52
1				5	6						12				4	8	11	3	2	7			9*	10	B Stevens	53
1				5	6	8					11				4	7*		3	2	12		9		10	T Fitzharris	54
43	24	30	5	37	45	18	28	9	7	7	15	4	37	3	37	22	25	30	32	15	6	8	3	15	League Appearances	
	+1S	+4S				+2S		+1S			+7S	+1S			+2S	+2S		+2S		+7S		+1S	+3S			
5	3	3		5	3	4+1S	5	1S					5	5	2	5	5		2		3				FA Cup Appearances	
2	2	2	2	2	2	2	2	1	2	2	1S	1S	1												Milk Cup Appearances	
1	1			1	1						1		1		1		1	1	1	1					AM Cup Appearances	

Also Played: Layton match 23, no.6. Mather match 44, no.12. Morse match 43, no.12.

SOMERTON PARK

Official Address: Somerton Park, Newport, Gwent. Telephone Newport (0633) 277543/277271/277472

Ground Capacity: 18,000 (1,200 seats)

Record Attendance: 24,268 v. Cardiff C, Division 3 (S), 16 Oct 1937

Record Receipts: £28,050 v. Carl Zeiss Jena, European Cup Winners Cup Quarter Final 2nd Leg, 18 Mar 1981

Size of Playing Area: 110yds × 75 yds

Season Tickets: Stand (Main Upper): £68.60; Lower: £43.20; Ground £36.00, (juveniles/OAPs £42.30, £32.40, £23.40 respectively)

Executive Box Season Tickets: Vice-Presidents Club £120 (£5 per match)

Cost of Stand Tickets: £3.20 (Main Upper); £2.40 (Main Lower), (OAP/juveniles £2.35 & £1.80 respectively); **Ground:** £2.00, (OAP/juveniles £1.30)

Match and Ticket Information: Seats can be purchased from Club Secretary.

Car Parking: Street parking under police control.

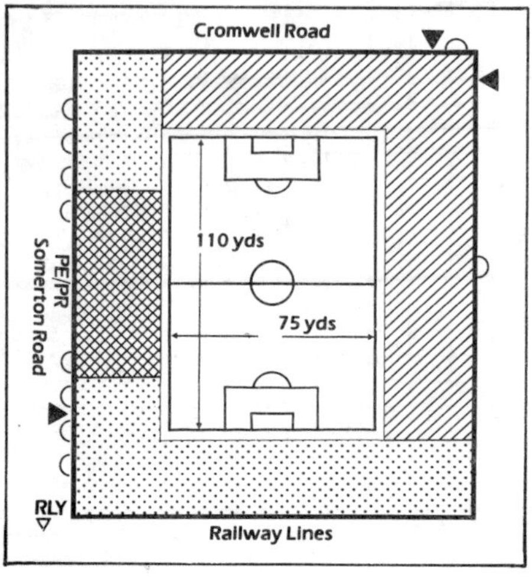

For key see page 12

How to get to the ground

From North and East: Use Motorway M4 until junction 24. Leave Motorway and follow signs Newport A48. In 1.8m turn left into Somerton Road B4237. In 0.4m turn right into Cromwell Road for Newport County F.C.
From West: Use Motorway M4 until junction 28. Leave Motorway and follow signs Newport A48. In 2.3m turn right A467. Cross Railway Bridge then turn right into A455 into Corporation Road. In 0.4m turn left into Cromwell Road for Newport County F.C.

NORTHAMPTON TOWN Division 4

Chairman
N J Ronson

Vice-Chairman
S Wilson

Directors
E P Northover
W M Griggs
D Bowen

Secretary/Director
Dave Bowen

Manager
Tony Barton

Physiotherapist/Assistant Manager
Richie Norman

Commercial Manager
G Moody (0604-712847)

Six new players were signed for the start of the season to replace those that were released at the end of 1983, and supporters hoped to see an improvement on last season's 15th position.

First came a defeat at Southern League Corby Town, in the Maunsell Cup, by 2 goals to 1. Next came an early exit from the Milk Cup by Millwall, and last season's skipper, Ian Phillips, in dispute over money, was transferred to Colchester. Meanwhile the League campaign had started, and the 'Cobblers' were creating something of a record; of their first 10 games 8 were drawn, including 6 on the trot. Defeat came in the twelfth game, at Crewe; in a close game, the Cobblers lost 2-3, and followed this by losing to the eventual champions, York City, at home 1-0.

In the FA Cup, it took 3 games to defeat non-league Waterlooville; after two 1-1 draws, the Southern League team were beaten 2-0. Then Northampton were drawn against another non league team, Alliance Premier side Telford, who drew at Northampton and then won the replay at Telford.

In an away match at Wrexham new striker Terry Austin netted his eighth goal for Northampton and his 100th competitive goal in football.

The team which had spent so much of the early part of the season on the 'fringe' of the promotion race suddenly tumbled down the league.

A 1-4 defeat at home to Aldershot was followed by a 3-5 defeat at Darlington, 1-5 at home to Blackpool and fans were so upset that the following game at home attracted only 1,109; the lowest home gate since joining the league in 1920.

If trouble on the field was not enough, trouble brewed off the field. A band of supporters expressed their feelings, so much so the directors put the club up for sale, threatening to close down if no buyers were imminent.

A crushing 0-6 defeat by neighbours Peterborough was the last straw for manager Clive Walker; he decided to forsake his '5-man back line' used all season and injected the team with youth; in the last three games three different players made their debuts, including Aidy Mann, who at 16 was the youngest player **ever** to appear for the Cobblers.

Re-election was avoided; the directors decided to keep the club going although they did state that if a buyer came along they would sell.

On the playing side, six players were given free transfers at the end of the season; five of these were seasoned campaigners, leaving the oldest player on the books 27 years old.

Manager Clive Walker resigned in May but took a position as coach to the youth team in an attempt to continue the flow of local talent that has passed through the club in recent years, like Phil Neal (Liverpool and England), John Gregory (QPR and England) and George Reilly (Watford).

The League Directory's Statistician for the Club

Back Row L to R: Paul Bancroft, Russell Lewis, Neil Brough, Wakeley Gage, Peter Gleasure, Michael Barnes, Ian Benjamin, Trevor Lee. **Front Row:** Ritchie Norman (Coach), Austin Hayes, Paul Shirtliff, Brian Mundee, Tony Barton (Manager), Ray Train (Captain), Philip Cavener, Frank Belfon, Clive Walker (Youth/Reserve Team Manager).

'THE COBBLERS'

Sponsored by **Manns Brewery**

Formed: 1897 **Turned Professional:** 1901 **Ltd Co:** 1901
Previous Managers: 1903-12 Herbert Chapman 1912-4 no manager 1920-5 Bob Hewison 1925-31 Jack Tresadern 1931-6 Jack English Snr 1936-7 Sid Puddefoot 1937-War Warney Cresswell War-1949 Tom Smith 1949-55 Bob Dennison 1955-9 Dave Smith 1959-63 Dave Bowen 1963 Jack Jennings (caretaker) 1963-7 Dave Bowen 1967-8 Tony Marchi 1968-9 Ron Flowers 1969-72 Dave Bowen 1972-3 Bill Baxter 1973-6 Bill Dodgin 1976-7 Pat Crerand 1977 Committee* 1977-8 John Petts 1978-9 Mike Keen 1979-80 Clive Walker 1980-1 Bill Dodgin 1981-4 Clive Walker
*Committee: 1 director, 1 coach, 2 senior players
Honours: Division Three Champions 1962-3
League Career: Original members of Division Three 1920 Transferred to Division 3(S) 1921
Relegated to Division 4 1957-8 Promoted to Division 3 1960-1
Promoted to Division 2 1962-3 Promoted to Division 1 1964-5
Relegated to Division 2 1965-6 Relegated to Division 3 1966-7
Relegated to Division 4 1967-8 Promoted to Division 3 1975-6
Relegated to Division 4 1976-7
Colours: White shirts with claret trim, claret shorts, white stockings
Change Colours: Yellow shirts with claret trim, yellow shorts and stockings

CLUB RECORDS

Most Appearances for Club: Tommy Fowler: Football League 521 + F.A. Cup 31 + League Cup 31 **Total 583**
Most Capped Player: E Lloyd, 12, Wales **For England:** None
Record Goalscorer in a Match: R. Hoten, 5 v Crystal Palace (h) 8-1, Div 3 South, 27.10.28
A. Dawes, 5 v Lloyds Bank (h) 8-1, F.A. Cup 1st Round, 26.11.32
Record League Goalscorer in a season: Cliff Holton, 36, Div 3, 1961-2 **In all competitions:** Cliff Holton, 39 (League 36, F.A. Cup 3), 1961-2
Record League Goalscorer in a career: Jack English, 135, 1948-60 **In all competitions:** Jack English, 143 (League 135, F.A. Cup 8)
Record Transfer Fee Received: £140,000 from Cambridge United for George Reilly, Nov 1979
Record Transfer Fee Paid: £40,000 to Brentford for Steve Phillips
Best Performances: League: 21st Div 1 1965-6 **F.A. Cup:** 5th Round 1933-4, 1949-50, 1969-70 **League/Milk Cup:** 5th Round 1964-5, 1966-7
Most League Points: 68 in Div 4, 1975-6
Record League Victory: 10-0 v Walsall, Div 4(S), 5 Nov 1927
Record League Defeat: 0-10 v Bournemouth, Div 3(S), 2 Sept 1939
Club Statistician for the Directory: Frank Grande

Programme Editor
John Morris

Price	**Number of Pages**
40p	20

Subscriptions
Please contact club

NORTHAMPTON TOWN

PLAYERS NAME Ht Wt Birthdate	Honours	Birthplace Transfers	Clubs	APPEARANCES League	Milk Cup	F.A.C.	A.M.C.	GOALS League	Milk Cup	F.A.C.	A.M.C.
GOALKEEPER											
Peter Gleasure	FAYC. 79	Luton	Millwall (A)	55	7	4					
5-11 12.13 8.10.60			Northampton T.	57	2	5	1				
DEFENDERS											
Michael Barnes		Reading	Reading (A)	29+5	2		1	2	1		
6-4 13.4 17.9.63											
Adrian Burrows		Sutton	Mansfield T.	77+1	6	1+2		6			
5-11 11.12 16.1.59		F	Northampton T.	88	6	5	1	4			
Wakeley Gage†		Northampton	Desborough T.								
6-4 13.7 5.5.58		£5,000	Northampton T.	173+2	10	14	1	13		2	
Russell Lewis		Neath	Everwarm								
5-10½ 13.3 15.9.56			Swindon T.	175+6	17	16		7	1	2	
		F	Northampton T.	45	2	5	1	4			
Brian Mundee		London	Hungerford T.								
5-10 10.12 12.1.66		F	Bournemouth	3+1	1	3					
		F	Northampton T.	33+3			1	1			
MIDFIELD											
Trevor Lee		London	Epsom & Ewell								
5-11 11.7 3.7.54			Millwall	99+9	10+	5		23	2	2	
		£15,000	Colchester U.	95+1	6	13		35	1	3	
		£90,000	Gillingham	43+4	3	2		14			
			Orient (L)	5							
		£5,000	Bournemouth	28+6	+1	+2		9		1	
			Cardiff C.	21				5			
		F	Northampton T.								
Paul Shirtliff		Barnsley	Sheffield Wed. (A)	7+2	1						
5-5 8.12 3.11.62			Northampton T.								
Ray Train*	Div. 2, 76	Nuneaton	Walsall (A)	67+6		5		11			
5-5 10.5 10.2.51	Div. 2, 78	£15,000	Carlisle U.	154+1	5	13		8		1	
		£80,000	Sunderland	31+1	4	1		1	2		
		£80,000	Bolton W.	49+2	3	3					
		£50,000	Watford	91+1	8+1	9		3			
		£10,000	Oxford U.	49+1	5+1	2+1	1		1		
			Bournemouth (L)	7		3					
		F	Northampton T.								
FORWARDS											
Paul Bancroft		Derby	Derby (A)								
5-10 12.0 10.9.64			Crewe A. (L)	21				3			
			Northampton T.								
Neil Brough		Byfield	Northampton T. (A)								
6-1 12.5 22.12.65											
Frank Belfon		Wellingborough	Northampton T.	38+10	2	4+1	1	10		2	
5-9 11.3 18.2.65											
Austin Hayes	Ei.(1), U.21(1)	London	Southampton (A)	22+9	2+1	4	+1E	5	1	1	
5-4½ 9.12 15.7.58		£25,000	Millwall	40+7	1	2		5			
			Northampton T.	40+3	2	5	1	8			

NON-CONTRACT PLAYERS 1984-85

John Arundel, Billy Douglas, Neil Freeman, Shane Geary, Garry Johnson, Steve Rutter, Adrian Sheerin, Steve Brown, Mark Bushell, Paul Jelley, Simon Morrice, Simon Richmond, Wayne Baptiste, Jim Hamill, David Johnson, Barry Leslie, Maurice Muir

APPRENTICE: Adrian Mann

NORTHAMPTON TOWN

DIVISION FOUR 18TH **FA CUP** 2ND ROUND **MILK CUP** 1ST ROUND

MATCH	DATE	COMPE-TITION	VENUE	OPPONENTS	RESULT	HALF TIME	L'GUE POS'N	GOALSCORERS	ATTEN-DANCE
1	A 27	CL	A	Chester C	D1-1	1-1		Belfon	1,680
2	**29**	**MC 1**	**A**	**Millwall**	**L0-3**	**0-1**			**4,185**
3	S 3	CL	H	Darlington	W2-0	1-0	6	O'Neill, Austin	2,009
4	6	CL	H	Tranmere R	D0-0	0-0			2,326
5	10	CL	A	Blackpool	W3-2	2-1	2	Gage, Belfon, Austin	3,216
6	**13**	**MC 1**	**H**	**Millwall**	**L1-2**	**0-1**		**Gage**	**2,312**
7	18	CL	H	Stockport Co	D0-0	0-0	6		3,189
8	24	CL	A	Rochdale	D1-1	1-0	8	O'Neill	1,402
9	27	CL	A	Halifax T	D2-2	1-0		Jeffrey, Syrett	1,519
10	O 1	CL	H	Chesterfield	D1-1	0-0	9	Belfon	2,733
11	9	CL	H	Reading	D2-2	2-1		Gage, Austin	3,835
12	15	CL	A	Colchester U	D2-2	1-1	12	Austin, O'Neill	1,964
13	18	CL	H	Torquay U	W2-1	1-1		Hayes, Tucker	2,573
14	22	CL	A	Crewe Alex	L2-3	0-2	11	Jeffrey, Gage	2,107
15	29	CL	H	York C	L1-2	1-1	14	Belfon	2,956
16	N 1	CL	A	Aldershot	L0-1	0-0			1,711
17	5	CL	H	Swindon T	W2-0	2-0	14	Austin 2	2,354
18	12	CL	A	Hereford U	D0-0	0-0	13		3,007
19	**19**	**FAC 1**	**H**	**Waterlooville**	**D1-1**	**0-1**		**Gage**	**2,627**
20	**23**	**FAC 1R**	**A**	**Waterlooville**	**D1-1[1]**	**0-0**		**Austin**	**3,500**
21	26	CL	A	Wrexham	W1-0	0-0	11	Austin	1,234
22	**28**	**FAC 1R2**	**H**	**Waterlooville**	**W2-0**	**1-0**		**O'Neill (pen), Mundee**	**3,534**
23	D 3	CL	H	Bristol C	W1-0	1-0	10	Belfon	2,823
24	**10**	**FAC 2**	**H**	**Telford U**	**D1-1**	**0-1**		**Austin**	**3,903**
25	**14**	**FAC 2R**	**A**	**Telford U**	**L2-3**	**0-1**		**Belfon, Jeffrey**	**3,320**
26	18	CL	H	Mansfield T	W2-1	0-1		Austin, Lewis	2,628
27	26	CL	A	Doncaster R	L0-1	0-0	10		3,127
28	27	CL	H	Peterborough U	W2-1	2-0	9	Jeffrey, Austin	6,464
29	31	CL	A	Hartlepool T	L0-2	0-1	10		1,706
30	J 2	CL	H	Bury	W1-0	1-0	8	O'Neill	2,525
31	14	CL	H	Chester C	W2-1	1-1	6	Lewis, Belfon	2,198
32	20	CL	A	Stockport Co	L0-1	0-0			1,846
33	F 4	CL	A	Chesterfield	L1-2	0-0	10	Hayes	3,280
34	11	CL	H	Rochdale	D1-1	0-0	11	Hayes	2,022
35	14	CL	H	Aldershot	L1-4	1-3		Belfon	1,573
36	18	CL	A	York C	L0-3	0-2	14		3,941
37	**21**	**AMC 1**	**A**	**Walsall**	**L1-3**	**1-0**		**Austin**	**3,190**
38	25	CL	H	Crewe Alex	W2-0	1-0	10	Gage, Hayes	1,696
39	28	CL	A	Darlington	L3-5	1-2		Martinez, Hayes 2	1,328
40	M 3	CL	A	Torquay U	L1-2	0-0	14	Martinez	1,926
41	6	CL	A	Swindon T	D0-0	0-0			2,608
42	10	CL	H	Hereford U	L0-3	0-0	15		1,592
43	17	CL	A	Reading	L0-3	0-2	15		3,475
44	20	CL	H	Blackpool	L1-5	0-3		O'Neill	1,318
45	24	CL	H	Colchester U	W3-1	1-1	15	Austin, Gage, Belfon	1,499
46	30	CL	A	Tranmere R	L0-1	0-0			1,839
47	A 7	CL	H	Halifax T	D1-1	0-0	16	Hayes	1,356
48	10	CL	A	Harltepool U	D1-1	0-1		Hayes	1,109
49	14	CL	A	Bristol C	L1-4	1-1	16	O'Neill (pen)	6,620
50	21	CL	H	Doncaster R	L1-4	1-3	17	Lewis	1,912
51	24	CL	A	Peterborough U	L0-6	0-3			3,481
52	28	CL	H	Wrexham	D3-3	3-1	18	Belfon, Gage, Austin	1,189
53	M 5	CL	A	Bury	W2-1	0-1	18	Mundee, Lewis	1,096
54	12	CL	A	Mansfield T	L1-3	1-0	18	Jeffrey	2,141

[1]After Extra Time

Av Home Att **2,393**

Goal Scorers

League (53): Austin 11, Belfon 9, Hayes 8, Gage 6, O'Neill 6 (1 pen), Jeffrey 4, Lewis 4, Martinez 2, Mundee 1, Syrett 1, Tucker 1
FA Cup (7): Austin 2, Belfon, 1, Gage 1, Jeffrey 1, Mundee 1, O'Neill 1 (1 pen)
Milk Cup (1): Gage 1
AMC (1): Austin 1

1983-84

Gleasure	Tucker	Forster	Gage	Lewis	Burrows	O'Neill	Jeffrey	Syrett	Belfon	Hayes	Austin	Mundee	Muir	Brough	Martinez (L)	Mann	Phillips	Brown	REFEREE	
1	2	3	4	5	6	7	8	9*	10	11	12								K Walmsley	1
1	2		4	5	6	8	7	9*	10	11	12						3		**A Gunn**	**2**
1	2	3	4	5	6	7	8		10	11	9								I Borrett	3
1	2	3	4	5	6	8	7*	12	10	11	9								D Reeves	4
1	2	3	4	5	6	8	7		10	11*	9	12							P Tyldesley	5
1	3	2	4	5*	6	8	7		10	11	9		12						**M Heath**	**6**
1	3	2	4	5	6	8	7	9	10	12			11*						Alan Robinson	7
1	3	2	4	5	6	8	7	9	10	11									GM Tyson	8
1	3	2		5	6	8	7	9	10		11	4							C Seel	9
1	3	2		5	6	8	7	4	10	11	9								TG Bune	10
1	8	2	4	5	6		7		10	11	9	3							LR Dilkes	11
1	3	2	4	5	6*	8	7		9	12	11	10							D Letts	12
1	6	2	4	3	5	8*	7		11	9	10	12							M Scott	13
1	3	2	4	5	6	8	7		9	10	11								A Robinson	14
1	3	2	4	5	6	8	7*		9	10	11	12							RS Lewis	15
1	11*	2	4	5	6	7	8		10	12	9	3†							D Hedges	16
1		2	4	5	6	8	7		10	11	9*	3		12					TA Jones	17
1		2	4	5	6	8	7		10	11	9	3							L Shapter	18
1	3	2	4	5	6	8	7*		10	11	9		12						**P Tyldesley**	**19**
1		2	4*	5	6	8	7		10	11	9	3	12						**A Buksh**	**20**
1		2	4	5	6	8	7		10*	11	9	3	12						R Banks	21
1		2	4	5	6	8	7			9	10	3	11						**A Buksh**	**22**
1		2	4	5	6	8	7		10*	11	9	3	12						A Ward	23
1		2	4*	5	6	8	7		10	11	9	3	12						**C Downey**	**24**
1		2	4	5	6*	8	7		10	11	9	3	12						**C Downey**	**25**
1		2	4	5	6	8	7		10	11	9	3							J Moules	26
1		2	4*	5	6	8	7		10	11	9	3	12						D Scott	27
1		2	4	5	6	8	7		10	11	9*	3	12						D Vickers	28
1	8	2	4	5	6		7		10	11	9*	3		12					N Wilson	29
1		2	4	5	6	8	7		10	11	9	3							E Read	30
1		2*	4	5	6	8	7		10	11	9	3	12						E Scales	31
1	2		4	5	6	8	7		10	11	9	3							A Saunders	32
1	10	2*	4	5	6	8	7			11	9	3	12						T Holbrook	33
1	2		4	5*	6	8	7		10	11	9	3	12						A Crickmore	34
1	2*	12	4		5	7	6		10	11	9	3	8						J Lovatt	35
1	9	2	4	5	6	8	7		10	11		3							N Midgley	36
1		2	4	5	6	8	7		10	11	9	3							**K Barratt**	**37**
1		2	4	5	6	8	7			10	9	3			11				A Buksh	38
1	4	2*		5	6	8	7		12	10	9	3			11				R Guy	39
1	4*	2		5	6	8	7			10	9	3	12		11				B Stevens	40
1		2	4	5	6	8	7			10	9	3			11				D Reeves	41
1		2	4	5	6	8	7			10	9*	3	12		11				L Burden	42
1		2	4	5		8	7		12	10	9	3	6*		11				M James	43
1		2	4	5	6	8	7		12	10	9*	3			11				D Axwell	44
1		2	4	3	5	8	7		10	6	9				11				N Ashley	45
1			4	5	6	8	7		2	10	9	3			11				D Scott	46
1	12	3	4*	2	5	8	7		10	6	9				11				L Shapter	47
1		3	4	2	5	8	7		10	6	9		12		11*				L Robinson	48
1		3	4	2	5*	8	7		12	6†	10	9	11						K Cooper	49
1	6		4	2	5	8	7		12	9	10	3	11*						C Downey	50
1	11	2	4	6	5	8				7	10	3			9				M Heath	51
1	11	3	4	2	5	8	12		10		9	6*		7					P Scott	52
1		3		2	5	8	4		10		9	6		7		11			T Mills	53
1		3		2	5		4		10	8	9	6		7		11*		12	R Banks	54
46	25	41	40	45	45	43	44	5	35	40	42	33	5	3	12	2		0	League Appearances	
	+1S	+1S					+1S	+1S	+5S	+3S	+1S	+3S	+10S	+2S				+1S		
5	1	5	5	5	5	5	5		4	5	5	4	1+4S						FA Cup Appearances	
2	2	1	2	2	2	2	2	1	2	2	1+1S		1S				1		Milk Cup Appearances	
1		1	1	1	1	1	1		1	1	1	1							AM Cup Appearances	

THE COUNTY GROUND

Official Address: County Ground, Abington Avenue, Northampton NN1 4PS. Telephone: Northampton (0604) 31553

Ground Capacity: 17,000 (1,400 seats)

Record Attendance: 24,523 v. Fulham, Division 1, 23 Apr 1966

Record Receipts: £25,000 v. Aston Villa, F.A. Cup Round 3

Size of Playing Area: 120yds × 75 yds

Season Tickets: A & D: £56.00, B C: £66 (OAP/under 14 £46, £56 respectively); Ground: £36, £31 (OAP/under 14); Family: £70 (1 adult, 1 child), £100 (2 adults, 1 child), £125 (2 adults, 2 children)

Executive Box Season Tickets: None on sale

Cost of Stand Tickets: £2.80, £3.20 (50p reductions OAP/under 14's); **Terraces:** £2.00 (30p reductions OAP/children)

Match and Ticket Information: No pre-match bookings

Car Parking: Ample street parking

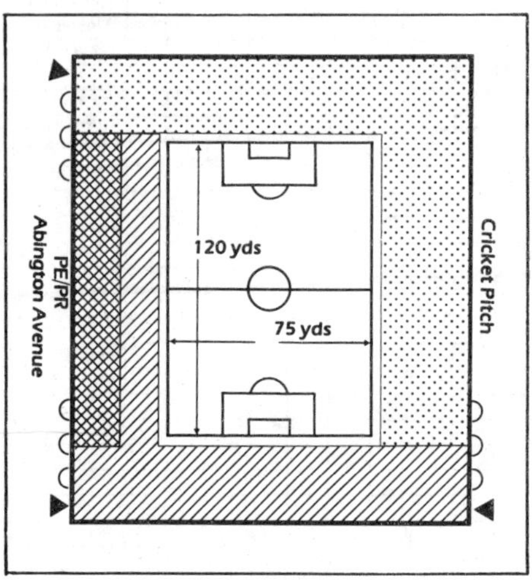

For key see page 12

How to get to the ground

From North and West: Use A45 into Northampton. Follow signs Kettering A43 into Kettering Road. In 0.9m turn right into Abington Avenue for Northampton Town F.C.
From East: Use A45 S.P. Northampton to Wilby. In 5.2m at roundabout forward. In 2.5m turn right then over crossroads into Abington Avenue for Northampton Town F.C.
From South: Use Motorway M1 until junction 15. Leave Motorway and follow signs Northampton A508. Follow signs Kettering A43 into Kettering Road. In 0.9m turn right into Abington Avenue for Northampton Town F.C.

NORWICH CITY Division 1

President
J L Hanly JP

Chairman
Sir Arthur Smith JP

Directors
G C Watling
D S McCall
E A Burrell
I D Coutts CBE
J A Jones
R T Chase

Secretary
Nigel Pleasants

Assistant Secretary
Jon Pollard

Commercial Manager
Nigel Mackay (0603-61511)

Manager
Ken Brown

Chief Coach
Mel Machin

Coach
Dave Stringer

Chief Scout
Ronnie Brooks JP

Physiotherapist
Tim Sheppard

Groundsman
Russell Allison

In a strange season Norwich City could feel that with some more luck trophies might have ended up on the Carrow Road sideboards instead of a final First Division position of 15th and elimination from both cup competitions at a time when the prospects of a Wembley trip seemed very good.

After a shaky start in the League the side settled into a middle of the table position which was only forsaken near the end of the campaign when there was nothing to arouse any ambitious thoughts, which might have been entertained if the cups had not produced so much promise followed by frustration. The Milk Cup typified this as first Cardiff City were comfortably beaten on aggregate. Sunderland came to Carrow Road in the Third Round and earned a replay at Roker Park, where goals from Bertschin gave City a good win. In the next round at Portman Road the veteran Mike Channon scored in the second half and a firm defence held out comfortably to deny Ipswich so that Aston Villa were to be faced at Carrow Road in the last eight. Villa had in fact lost an FA Cup Replay only a few days earlier at the same venue and had lost comfortably so the defeat on this occasion by two clear goals was a nasty shock. That Villa match had in fact started the FA Cup campaign and a Deehan goal at Villa Park (against his old club) earned a replay which was won at Carrow Road by three clear goals. White Hart Lane provided a tough challenge in Round Four but the match was goalless and City won the return at Carrow Road by the odd goal in three. This was the same score at Derby in the next round, but Derby scored that vital extra one to give Norwich a surprise knock-out blow. Sadly the League was now an anti-climax.

It is never easy to obtain good results at Norwich, but Ken Brown has the right players there and will not need too many new ones to mount a challenge in all competitions. Woods (in goal), Downs, Mendham, Deehan and Bertschin all shone at various times and also showed good consistency as did that marvellous veteran, Mike Channon, who gave an example to other players by giving of his best and showing that he also actually enjoyed doing it. WLM

Back Row L to R: Keith Bertschin, Dennis van Wyk, Jon Rigby, Chris Woods, Robert Rosario, Steve Bruce, John Devine. **Middle Row:** Mel Machin (Coach), Jeremy Goss, Mark Crowe, Paul Clayton, Dave Watson (Capt.), Ken Brown (Manager), Mick Channon, Peter Mendham, Greg Downs, Steve Goble, Tim Sheppard (Physio). **Front Row:** Tony Spearing, Paul Haylock, John Deehan, Mark Farrington, Louie Donowa, Gary Rowell, Mark Barham.

'THE CANARIES'

NORWICH CITY FC

Sponsored by **Poll and Withey Windows/ Hummel International**

Formed: 1905 **Turned Professional:** 1905 **Ltd Co:** 1905
Previous Managers: 1905-6 J W Bowman 1907-8 J McEwen 1908-10 A Turner 1910-5 J B Stansfield 1919-20 F C Buckley 1920-1 C O'Hagan 1921-6 A A Gosnell 1926-7 J B Stansfield 1927-8 C B Potter 1929-33 J Kerr 1933-7 T Parker 1937-8 R T Young 1938-9 R T Young & A J Jewell 1946-7 C H Spiers 1947-8 C H Spiers & D Lochhead 1948-50 D Lochhead 1950-5 N H Low 1955-7 T R Parker 1957-62 A Macauley 1962 B Reid 1962-3 G Swindin 1963-6 R Ashman 1966-9 L Morgan 1969-73 R Saunders 1973-80 J Bond
Honours: Division Two Champions 1971-2 Division Three (S) Champions 1933-4 Football League Cup Winners 1962
League Career: Original member of Division 3 1920 Transferred to Division 3(S) 1921 Promoted to Division 2 1933-4 Relegated to Division 3 1938-9 Promoted to Division 2 1959-60 Promoted to Division 1 1971-2 Relegated to Division 2 1973-4 Promoted to Division 1 1974-5 Relegated to Division 2 1980-1 Promoted to Division 1 1981-2
Colours: Yellow shirts with green pin stripe, green shorts with yellow trim, yellow stockings
Change Colours: White shirts with green pin stripe, white shorts, green stockings

CLUB RECORDS

Most Appearances for Club: Kevin Keelan, 1963-79: League 571 + Cup ties 110 **Total 681**
Most Capped Player: Martin O'Neill, 19, Northern Ireland **For England:** Dave Watson, 3
Record Goalscorer in a Match: Roy Hollis, 5 v Walsall (H) 8-0 Div 3(S), 29.12.51
Record League Goalscorer in a season: Ralph Hunt, 31, Div 3(S) 1955-6 **In All Competitions:** Terry Alcock, 37, 1962-3
Record League Goalscorer in a career: Johnny Gavin, 122 **In All Competitions:** Johnny Gavin 132 (League 122 + Cup 10) 1945-54, 1955-8
Record Transfer Fee Received: £1,000,000 from Manchester City for Kevin Reeves, Mar 1980 £1,000,000 from Nottingham Forest for Justin Fashanu, Aug 1981
Record Transfer Fee Paid: £300,000 to Hadjuk Split for Drazen Muzine, Sept 1980
Best Performances: League: 10th Div 1 1975-6 **F.A. Cup:** Semi-Final 1959 **League/Milk Cup:** Winners 1962
Most League Points: (3 pts for win) 71 in Div 2, 1981-2; (2 pts for win) 64 in Div 3(S), 1950-2 **Most League Goals:** 99, Div 3(S) 1952-3
Record League Victory: 10-2 v Coventry City, Div 3(S), 15 Mar 1930
Record League Defeat: 0-7 v Walsall (A), Div 3(S), 13 Sept 1930
Club Statistician for the Directory: Dave Pease

Programme Editor
Colin Benson

Price	**Number of Pages**
50p	28

Subscriptions
£18.00 from Programme Department N.C.F.C.

NORWICH CITY

PLAYERS NAME Ht Wt Birthdate	Honours	Birthplace Transfers	Clubs	APPEARANCES League	Milk Cup	F.A.C.	E. Cups	GOALS League	Milk Cup	F.A.C.	E. Cups
GOALKEEPER											
Chris Woods†	E. U.21(6). Y.	Boston	Nottingham F.		2						
6-2 12.8 14.11.59	Lg.C. 78	£250,000	Q.P.R.	63	8	1					
		£250,000	Norwich C.	136	14	13					
DEFENDERS											
Steve Bruce	E. Y	Corbridge	Gillingham	205 + 3	15	8		23	6	1	
6-0 11.2 31.12.60		£125,000	Norwich C.								
Mark Crowe	FAYC. 83	Southwold	Norwich C.	0 + 1							
5-10 10.10 21.1.65											
Greg Downs		Carlton	Norwich C. (A)	143 + 6	11	17		7			
5-9½ 10.7 13.12.58			Torquay U. (L)	1				1			
Dale Gordon		Gt. Yarmouth	Norwich C. (A)								
5-11 11.0 9.1.67											
Paul Haylock		Lowestoft	Norwich C. (A)	101 + 1	13	8 + 1		1			
5-8 11.0 24.3.63											
Tony Spearing	E. Y.	Romford	Norwich C.	4							
5-10 10.12 7.10.64	FAYC. 83										
Dave Watson*	E.(3). U.21(7)	Liverpool	Liverpool								
5-11½ 11.12 20.11.61		£100,000	Norwich C.	131	8	15		8	2	1	
MIDFIELD											
Mark Barham	E.(2). Y	Folkestone	Norwich C. (A)	109 + 6	14 +	8		11		1	
5-7 11.0 12.7.62											
John Devine	Ei.(11).	Dublin	Arsenal (A)	86 + 3	25	6					
5-10½ 12.0 11.11.58	U.21(2)		Norwich C.	31 + 1	4	5		3			
Jeremy Goss	FAYC. 83	Cyprus	Norwich C. (A)	+ 1							
5-9 10.9 11.5.65											
Peter Mendham		Kings Lynn	Norwich C. (A)	126 + 11	10 +	17		11		1	
5-10 11.6 9.4.60											
Dennis Van Wijk		Holland	Ajax								
5-10 11.2 16.2.62			Norwich C.	53 + 3	7	10		2		1	
FORWARDS											
Keith Bertschin	E. U.21(3). Y.	Enfield	Barnet								
6-1 11.8 25.8.56	FAYC. 75		Ipswich T.	19 + 13	1			8			
		£100,000	Birmingham C.	113 + 5	7 + 1	8 + 1		29	1	8	
		£200,000	Norwich C.	107 + 2	11	13		27	4	5	
Mick Channon	E.(46). U.23(9).	Orcheston	Southampton (A)	388 + 4	24	34 +		155	10	15	
6-0½ 12.11 28.11.48	FAC. 76. FL	£300,000	Manchester C.	71 + 1	10 +	3 + 1		24	4		
		£200,000	Southampton	119	4	6		27		1	
		F	Newcastle U.	4				1			
		F	Bristol R.	4 + 5	+ 1	1					
		F	Norwich C.	54 + 3	6	5		8	4	2	
Paul Clayton	FAYC. 83	Dunstable	Norwich C. (A)	3 + 4							
5-11 11.3 4.1.65											
John Deehan	E. U.21(7). Y.	Birmingham	Aston Villa (A)	107 + 3	13	7 + 1		42	2	3	
6-0 11.3 6.8.57	Lg.C. 77	£400,000	W.B.A.	44 + 3		2		5			
		£175,000	Norwich C.	96	9	13		45	1	2	
Lou Donowa	FAYC. 83	Ipswich	Norwich C. (A)	23 + 3	5 + 1	+ 1		4			
5-9 11.0 24.9.64											
Mark Farrington		Liverpool	Everton (A)								
6-0 11.8 15.6.65		F	Norwich C.	1 + 1							
Jon Rigby	FAYC. 83	Bury St. Edmunds	Norwich C. (A)	3 + 2							
6-2 11.2 31.1.65											
Robert Rosario		Hammersmith	Norwich C. (A)	6 + 2				2			
6-4 12.8 4.3.66											
Gary Rowell	E. U.21(1)	Seaham	Sunderland	229 + 25	19 +	15		88	7	4	
5-10 10.3 6.6.57			Norwich C.								

CONTRACT PLAYERS WITH NO FIRST TEAM APPEARANCES: Brendan McIntyre (MF), John Waddell (D)

NON-CONTRACT PLAYER 1984-85: Neil Ridley

APPRENTICE: Paul Kinnaird

NORWICH CITY

DIVISION ONE 14TH **FA CUP** 5TH ROUND **MILK CUP** 5TH ROUND

MATCH	DATE	COMPETITION	VENUE	OPPONENTS	RESULT	HALF TIME	L'GUE POS'N	GOALSCORERS	ATTENDANCE
1	A 27	CL	A	Sunderland	D1-1	0-0		Bertschin	17,057
2	31	CL	H	Liverpool	L0-1	0-1			23,859
3	S 3	CL	H	Wolverhampton W	W3-0	2-0	11	Bertschin, Deehan 2	13,713
4	6	CL	A	Luton T	D2-2	2-0		Channon, Mendham	11,095
5	10	CL	A	Aston Villa	L0-1	0-1	13		18,887
6	17	CL	H	Nottingham F	L2-3	2-2	17	Bertschin, Deehan (pen)	15,017
7	24	CL	A	Arsenal	L0-3	0-1	19		24,438
8	O 1	CL	H	Manchester U	D3-3	0-1	19	Bennett, Channon, Donowa	19,630
9	**4**	**MC 2**	**A**	**Cardiff C**	**D0-0**	**0-0**			**4,425**
10	15	CL	A	Watford	W3-1	0-1	17	Rostron (og), Devine, Donowa	12,745
11	19	CL	H	Leicester C	W3-1	1-1		Donowa, Bertschin, Channon (pen)	14,566
12	22	CL	A	West Ham U	D0-0	0-0	16		18,958
13	**26**	**MC 2**	**H**	**Cardiff C**	**W3-0**	**1-0**		**Channon 3**	**9,887**
14	29	CL	H	QPR	L0-3	0-2	16		16,532
15	N 5	CL	H	Southampton	W1-0	0-0	15	Bertschin	14,303
16	**9**	**MC 3**	**H**	**Sunderland**	**D0-0**	**0-0**			**12,400**
17	12	CL	A	Notts Co	D1-1	1-1	17	Barham	7,882
18	19	CL	H	WBA	W2-0	0-0	13	Downs, Barham	13,358
19	**22**	**MC 3R**	**A**	**Sunderland**	**W2-1**	**1-0**		**Bertschin 2**	**14,149**
20	26	CL	A	Everton	W2-0	0-0	11	Donowa, Bailey (og)	14,016
21	**30**	**MC 4**	**A**	**Ipswich T**	**W1-0**	**0-0**		**Channon**	**25,570**
22	D 3	CL	H	Tottenham H	W2-1	1-1	9	Bertschin, Channon	22,148
23	10	CL	A	Birmingham C	W1-0	1-0	7	Downs	9,971
24	17	CL	H	Coventry C	D0-0	0-0	9		16,646
25	26	CL	A	Stoke C	L0-2	0-1	10		12,049
26	27	CL	H	Ipswich T	D0-0	0-0	10		25,679
27	31	CL	A	Wolverhampton W	L0-2	0-0	10		10,725
28	J 2	CL	H	Arsenal	D1-1	0-0	10	Deehan	20,482
29	**7**	**FAC 3**	**A**	**Aston Villa**	**D1-1**	**1-1**		**Deehan**	**21,454**
30	**11**	**FAC 3R**	**H**	**Aston Villa**	**W3-0**	**1-0**		**Channon, Mendham, Bertschin**	**16,420**
31	14	CL	H	Sunderland	W3-0	3-0	10	Downs, Bertschin, Hareide	13,204
32	**17**	**MC 5**	**H**	**Aston Villa**	**L0-2**	**0-2**			**21,568**
33	21	CL	A	Notttingham F	L0-3	0-3	10		13,993
34	**28**	**FAC 4**	**A**	**Tottenham H**	**D0-0**	**0-0**			**37,792**
35	**F 1**	**FAC 4R**	**H**	**Tottenham H**	**W2-1**	**2-0**		**Van Wyk, Channon**	**26,811**
36	4	CL	A	Manchester U	D0-0	0-0	10		36,851
37	11	CL	H	Aston Villa	W3-1	0-0	9	Deehan 2, Channon	14,392
38	14	CL	A	QPR	L0-2	0-0			12,901
39	**18**	**FAC 5**	**A**	**Derby Co**	**L1-2**	**0-0**		**Deehan**	**25,793**
40	25	CL	H	West Ham U	W1-0	0-0	7	Deehan	16,294
41	M 3	CL	A	Southampton	L1-2	0-1	8	Deehan	17,456
42	14	CL	H	Notts Co	L0-1	0-0			13,230
43	17	CL	H	Luton T	D0-0	0-0	11		14,181
44	31	CL	A	Leicester C	L1-2	0-2	15	Deehan	11,278
45	A 7	CL	H	Watford	W6-1	3-1	13	Deehan 4 (2 pens), Downs, Devine	14,451
46	14	CL	A	WBA	D0-0	0-0	12		11,572
47	21	CL	H	Stoke C	D2-2	0-1	12	Rosario, Deehan	16,084
48	23	CL	A	Ipswich T	L0-2	0-1	13		23,135
49	28	CL	H	Everton	D1-1	0-1	13	Hareide	13,624
50	M 5	CL	A	Tottenham H	L0-2	0-1	14		18,874
51	7	CL	H	Birmingham C	D1-1	0-0	14	Watson	13,601
52	12	CL	A	Coventry C	L1-2	1-1	13	Deehan (pen)	14,007
53	15	CL	A	Liverpool	D1-1	1-1		Devine	38,837

Av Home Att **17,078**

Goal Scorers

League (48): Deehan 15 (4 pens), Bertschin 7, Channon 5 (1 pen), Donowa 4, Downs 4, Devine 3, Barham 2, Hareide 2, Bennett 1, Mendham 1, Rosario 1, Watson 1, opponents 2
FA Cup (7): Channon 2, Deehan 2, Bertschin 1, Mendham 1, Van Wyk 1
Milk Cup (6): Channon 4, Bertschin 2

1983-84

Woods	Devine	Downs	Mendham	Young	Watson	Barham	Van Wyk	Deehan	Bertschin	Bennett	Haylock	Channon	Donowa	Hareide	Pickering	Godbold	Clayton	Rigby	Rosario	Spearing	Farrington	Goss	REFEREE	
1	2	3	4	5	6	7	8	9	10	11													A Banks	1
1		3	4	5	6	7		9	10	11	2	8											D Axcell	2
1		3	4	5	6	7	11	9	10		2	8											D Vickers	3
1		3	4	5	6	7	11	9	10		2	8											A Gunn	4
1	12	3	4	5	6	7	11	9	10		2*	8											N Midgley	5
1	7	3	4		6		11	9	10		2*	8	12	5									EJ Scales	6
1	2	3	4	12	6		11*	10	9	7		8		5									H Taylor	7
1	7	3	4		6*				10	11	2	8	9	5	12								R Lewis	8
1	**7**	**3**	**4**	**6**					**10**	**11**	**2**	**8**	**9**	**5**									**K Baker**	**9**
1	10	3	4		6				9	11	2	8	7	5									M Bodenham	10
1	9	3	4		6				10	11	2	8	7	5									A Ward	11
1	9	3	4		6				10	11	2	8	7	5									D Brazier	12
1	**9**	**3**	**4**		**6**	**12**			**10**	**11***	**2**	**8**	**7**	**5**									**B King**	**13**
1	9	3	4		6	12			10	11*	2	8†	7	5									V Callow	14
1	9	3	4		6	11	12		10		2	8*	7	5									K Hackett	15
1	**9**	**3**	**4**			**11**		**6**	**10**		**2**	**8**	**7**	**5**									**D Reeves**	**16**
1	9	3	4		6	11		8	10		2		7	5									A Robinson	17
1	9	3	4		6	11	12	8	10		2		7	5*									C Downey	18
1		**3**	**4**		**6**	**11**	**10**	**5**	**9**		**2**	**8**	**7**										**N Wilson**	**19**
1		3	4		6	11	9	5	10		2	8	7										M Heath	20
1		**3**	**4**		**6**	**11**	**9**	**5**	**10**		**2**	**8**	**7**										**M Taylor**	**21**
1	2	3	4		6	11*	9	5	10			8	7			12							G Napthine	22
1		3	4		6		10	5	9		2	8	7	11									J Hough	23
1		3	4		6		11	5	10		2	8	7	9*			12						M James	24
1	9	3	4		6		11	5	10		2	8	7										F Roberts	25
1	9	3	4*		6		11	5	10		2	8	7	12									J Hunting	26
1	9	3	4		6		11	5	10		2	8*	7	12									K Cooper	27
1		3	4		6		11	9	10		2	8	7*	5			12						T Holbrook	28
1	**7**	**3**	**4**		**6**		**11**	**9**	**10**		**2**	**8**		**5**									**R Bridges**	**29**
1	**7**	**3**	**4**		**6**		**11**	**9**	**10**		**2**	**8***	**12**	**5**									**D Brazier**	**30**
1	7	3	4		6		11		10		2	8*	9	5			12						D Letts	31
1	**7**	**3**	**4**		**6**		**11**	**9**	**10**		**2**	**8**	**12**	**5**									**T Mills**	**32**
1	7	3	4				11*	9	10		2	8		5		12	6						R Guy	33
1	**7**	**3**	**4**		**6**		**11**	**9**	**10**		**2**	**8**		**5**									**J Worrall**	**34**
1	**7**	**3**	**4**		**6**		**11**	**9**	**10**		**2**	**8**		**5**									**J Worrall**	**35**
1	7	3	4		6		11	9	10		2	8		5									M Peck	36
1	5	3	4		6		11	9	10	12	2	8					7*						E Scales	37
1	5	3	4		6		11	9	10		2	8*					7	12					H King	38
1	**7**	**3***	**4**		**6**		**11**	**9**	**10**	**12**	**2**	**8**		**5**									**A Saunders**	**39**
1	7	3	4		6		11	9	10		2	8		5									J Ashworth	40
1		3	4		6		11	9		7	2	8		5				10					K Baker	41
1		3*	4		6		11	9		7	2	8	12	5				10					J Moules	42
1		3	4		6		11	9		7	2	8		5				10					M Scott	43
1	7	3	4		6			9		10*	2	8	11	5				12					P Tyldesley	44
1	7	3	4		6			9			2	8	11	5					10				J Bray	45
1	7	3	4		6		10				2	8	11	5					9				K Walmsley	46
1	2	3	4		6		10	9			12	8	11	5*					7				A Buksh	47
1	7	3			6		4*	9	8		2		11	5			12		10				A Challinor	48
1	7	3	4		6		11	9	10*		2	8		5					12				D Vickers	49
1	7	5	4		6		11*	9	10		2	8							12	3			Alan Robinson	50
1	7	5	4		6		11	9			2	8							10	3			A Gunn	51
1	7	5	4		6		11	9*			2								10	3	8	12	N Ashley	52
1	6	5	4				11	9	10		2	8	7							3*	12		V Callow	53
42	31	**42**	41	5	40	10	31	34	33	12	38	37	23	26	0	0	3	3	6	4	1	0	League Appearances	
	+1S			+1S		+1S	+2S			+1S	+1S		+2S	+2S	+1S	+2S	+4S	+2S	+2S		+1S	+1S		
5	5	5	5		5		5	5	5	1S	5	5	1S	5									FA Cup Appearances	
6	4	6	6	1	4	3+1S	3	4	6	2	6	6	5+1S	4									Milk Cup Appearances	

CARROW ROAD

Official Address: Carrow Road, Norwich NR1 1JE. Telephone: (0603) 612131. Information: (0603) 612591

Ground Capacity: 28,500

Record Attendance: 43,984 v. Leicester City, F.A. Cup Round 6, 30 Mar 1963

Record Receipts: £71,948 v. Tottenham Hotspur, F.A. Cup Round 4 Replay, 1 Feb 1984

Size of Playing Area: 114yds × 74 yds

Season Tickets: Stands: £50.00 to £80.00; Ground: £35.00

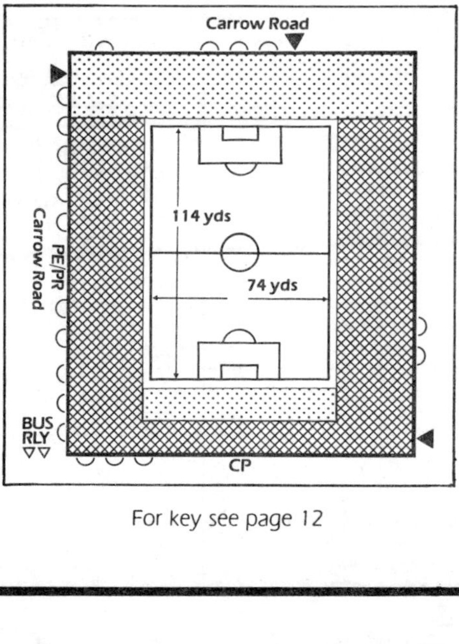

For key see page 12

Executive Box Season Tickets: Variable according to match

Cost of Stand Tickets: £3.50 to £5.00; **Terraces:** £2.50

Match and Ticket Information: Applications to Box Office 14 days before match with payment and SAE

Car Parking: Numerous private parks nearby. Multi-storey parks in Malt House Road and St. Andrews Street. Street parking nearby in Rover Road, Carrow Hill, Kerrison Road, Cousins Road and side streets off King Street. Coaches may park at Lower Clarence Road Car Park

How to get to the ground

From North: Use A140 to junction with Ring Road, then follow signs Yarmouth A47. In 3.5m at T road turn right. In 0.5m turn left into Carrow Road for Norwich City F.C.

From East: Use A47 S.P. Norwich on entering city, keep left into Ring Road for Carrow Road for Norwich City F.C.

From South and West: Use A11, A140 into Norwich and follow signs Yarmouth A47 into Ring Road, Carrow Road for Norwich City F.C.

NOTTINGHAM FOREST Division 1

President
H W Alcock FCA

Chairman
M Roworth

Directors
D C Pavis
G E McPherson JP
F Reacher
F T V Pell FCA, JP
J F Hickling
F A Allcock
I I Korn
W M Burrows

Secretary
Ken Smales

Assistant Secretary
Paul White

Commercial Manager
Dave Pullen (0602 820444)

Manager
Brian H Clough

Coach
Ron Fenton

Reserve Team Coach
Liam O'Kane

Chief Scout
Alan Hill

Physiotherapist
Tony Verity

Groundsman
Billy Gray

A nine match unbeaten run to end the 1982/83 season saw Nottingham Forest enter the 1983/84 campaign full of optimism. A first match home defeat by Southampton was immediately followed by an impressive 2-1 victory at Old Trafford ending Manchester United's sixteen month unbeaten home run.

An embarrassing 1st round Milk Cup defeat by 3rd Division Wimbledon was soon forgotten as Forest went to Holland and convincingly beat PSV Eindhoven in the UEFA Cup 2nd Round first leg thanks to a tense last minute penalty by Colin Walsh and a brilliant solo effort from Peter Davenport producing one of the finest goals ever scored in Forest's colours.

Mediocre league results put Forest in 11th place in mid-November with hopes of league honours rapidly disappearing. The UEFA Cup still provided hopes of winning a trophy even when the third round draw produced a difficult tie against Celtic. After being held to a 0-0 draw in Nottingham, few people rated the Reds' chances of making the quarter final. Forest can never be ruled out of any European tie and they gave their best performance of the season to defeat Celtic 2-1 in front of 65,000 fervent Scotsmen and 2,000 faithful Forest followers.

Another home defeat by Southampton eliminated Forest from the FA Cup in the 3rd Round for the third year running but, following this, their defences were rarely breached thanks to excellent performances by goalkeeper Hans van Breukelen and defenders Viv Anderson and future England prospect Chris Fairclough. Five consecutive away wins put Forest in 2nd place in the league in February but last minute goals by Arsenal and Wolves ended their championship dreams as they slipped to 4th, 10 points behind leaders Liverpool.

After defeating Sturm Graz in the UEFA Cup quarter final, two goals from Steve Hodge in the semi final sent Forest to Brussels with a 2-0 lead against holders Anderlecht. Confidence was shattered when a dubious penalty decision and a disallowed last minute goal went against Forest to give Anderlecht a 3-0 win and ruin captain Bowyer's dream of adding a UEFA Cup winners medal to his European Cup and European Cup Winners Cup medals.

League results were vital and away defeats at Coventry and Leicester were cancelled out by a fine 5-1 defeat of FA Cup finalists Watford and a 2-1 win at West Ham. The last match saw leading goal scorers Forest defeat championship contenders Manchester United to bring a final, creditable, 3rd place.

Back Row L to R: Gary Megson, Gary Mills, Mark Smalley, Chris Fairclough, Kenny Swain, Franz Carr, Steve Murray. **Middle Row:** Ronnie Fenton (Coach), Trevor Christie, Johnnie Metgod, Darren Heyes, Steve Sutton, Ronnie Sinclair, Paul Hart, Brian Clough (Manager). **Front Row:** Peter Davenport, Jim McInally, Steve Hodge, Ian Bowyer, Steve Wigley, Bryn Gunn, Colin Walsh.

'FOREST'

Sponsored by
Skol

Formed: 1865 **Turned Professional:** 1889 **Ltd Co:** 1982
Previous Managers: Until 1936, a secretary fulfilled the role of manager:
1889-97 Harry Radford 1897-1909 Harry Hallam 1909-12 F W Earp 1912-25 Bob Marsters
1925-9 Jack Baynes 1930-1 Stan Hardy 1931-6 Noel Watson 1936-9 Harold Wightman
1939-60 Billy Walker 1960-3 Andy Beattie 1963-8 Johnny Carey 1969-72 Matt Gillies
1972-3 Dave MacKay 1973-5 Allan Brown
Honours: Division 1 Champions 1977-8 Division 2 Champions 1906-7, 1921-2
Division 3 (S) Champions 1950-1 F.A. Cup Winners 1898, 1959
Football League Cup Winners 1977-8, 1978-9 Anglo Scottish Cup Winners 1976-7
European Cup Winners 1978-9, 1979-80 European Super Cup Winners 1979-80
League Career: Elected to Division 1 1892 Relegated to Division 2 1905-6
Promoted to Division 1 1906-7 Relegated to Division 2 1910-11 Promoted to Division 1 1921-2
Relegated to Division 2 1924-5 Relegated to Division 3 (S) 1948-9 Promoted to Division 2 1950-1
Promoted to Division 1 1956-7 Relegated to Division 2 1971-2 Promoted to Division 1 1976-7
Colours: Red shirts with white pin stripe, white shorts, red stockings
Change Colours: All yellow

CLUB RECORDS

Most Appearances for Club: Bobby McKinlay: Football League 614 + F.A. Cup 54 + League Cup 11 + Inter Cities Fairs Cup 6 **Total 685**
Most Capped Player: Martin O'Neill, 36, N Ireland. **For England:** Peter Shilton, 19
Record Goalscorer in a Match: A Higgins, 5 v Clapton (14-0) (A), F.A. Cup 1st Round, 1890
Record League Goalscorer in a season: Wally Ardron, 36 **All competitions:** Wally Ardron, 36 (all League), 1950-1
Record League Goalscorer in a career: Grenville Morris, 199 **All competitions:** Grenville Morris, 217 (League 199, F.A. Cup 18)
Record Transfer Fee Received: £1,250,000 from Manchester United for Gary Birtles, Oct 1980
Record Transfer Fee Paid: £1,250,000 to Coventry City for Ian Wallace, July 1980
Best Performances: League: As in Honours **Most League Points:** (3pts for win) 74, Div 1, 1983-4 (2pts for win) 70, Div 3 (S), 1950-1
Record League Victory: 12-0 v Leicester City, Div 1, 21 Apr 1909
Record League Defeat: 1-9 v Blackburn Rovers, Div 2, 10.4.37
European Competitions Entered: European Cup: 1978-9, 1979-80, 1980-1 **Fairs Cup:** 1961-2, 1967-8
UEFA Cup: 1983-4 **Super Cup:** 1979-80 **World Club Championship:** 1980-1
Club Statistician for the Directory: Andy Johnson

Programme Editor
John Lawson

Price	Number of Pages
40p	20

Subscriptions
Apply to club

NOTTINGHAM FOREST

PLAYERS NAME Ht Wt Birthdate	Honours	Birthplace Transfers	Clubs	APPEARANCES League	Milk Cup	F.A.C.	E. Cups	GOALS League	Milk Cup	F.A.C.	E. Cups
GOALKEEPERS											
Ron Sinclair		Stirling	Nottingham F. (A)								
5-9 11.12½ 19.11.64			Wrexham (L)	11			1 AMC				
Hans Segers		Holland	PSV Eindhoven								
5-11 11.0			Nottingham F.								
Steve Sutton		Derby	Nottingham F. (A)	25	2		2				
6-0 13.1½ 16.4.61			Mansfield T. (L)	8	1						
DEFENDERS											
Chris Fairclough†		Nottingham	Nottingham F. (A)	43+3	3	1	7+2				
5-11 11.12½ 12.4.64											
Bryn Gunn	E. Cup 80	Kettering	Nottingham F. (A)	112+2	11	7	1+2	1			
5-9 10.4 21.8.58											
Paul Hart		Manchester	Stockport Co.	88	7	5+1		5			
6-2 12.8 4.5.53		£30,000	Blackpool	143	7	6		17	1		
		£300,000	Leeds U.	191	17	11	4	16	1	1	2
		£50,000	Nottingham F.	36	2	1	9				
Johnny Metgod		Holland	Holland/Real Madrid								
6-4 13.0			Nottingham F.								
Mark Smalley	E. Y	Newark	Nottingham F. (A)	+2							
5-11 11.2½ 2.1.65											
Kenny Swain	E. Cup 82,	Birkenhead	Wycombe W.								
5-11 11.7 28.1.52	Div. 1, 81		Chelsea	114+5	6	7		26	1	2	
		£100,000	Aston Villa	148	12	10	8	2	1		
			Nottingham F.	73	6	2	10	2			
Des Walker		Hackney	Nottingham F. (A)	3+1							
5-11 11.3 26.11.65											
MIDFIELD											
Ian Bowyer*	Div. 1, 78,	Little Sutton	Manchester C. (A)	42+8	6+2	4	5+3	13	2		
5-11 11.2 6.6.51	FC. 70, 78, 79,	£25,000	Orient	75+3	5	5		18	2	2	
	E. Cup 79, 80	£40,000	Nottingham F.	222+17	31+	25	15	49	12	5	5
		£50,000	Sunderland	15	1			1			
		£50,000	Nottingham F.	104+2	6	2	10	11	1		1
Trevor Christie		Newcastle	Leicester C. (A)	28+3	1			8			
6-2 12.0 28.2.59		£60,000	Notts. Co.	158+29	19+	8+2		64	5	3	
			Nottingham F.								
Jim McInally		Glasgow	Celtic								
5-9 10.10			Nottingham F.								
Gary Megson		Manchester	Plymouth A. (A)	78	9	5		10			
5-10 11.6 2.5.59		£200,000	Everton	20+2		3		2		1	
		£30,000	Sheffield Wed.	123	13	12		13	1	5	
		£75,000	Nottingham F.								
Colin Walsh	S. U.21(5), S. Y	Hamilton	Nottingham F.	89+17	5+3	7	10	25		1	3
5-9 11.0 22.7.62											
FORWARDS											
Garry Birtles	E.(3), U.21(2)	Nottingham	Long Eaton U.								
5-11 11.8 27.7.56	B(1), Lg.C. 79,	£3,000	Nottingham F.	87	18	5	20	32	10	1	8
	E. Cup 79, 80,	£1,250,000	Manchester U.	57+1	2	4		11			
	ESC. 79	£275,000	Nottingham F.	58+1	5	2	5+2	22		4	
Peter Davenport		Birkenhead	Cammell Lairds								
5-10 11.1½ 24.3.61			Nottingham F.	52+4	3	1+1	8+1	25			2
Steven Hodge	E. U.21(6)	Nottingham	Nottingham F. (A)	78+1	5	1	10	18		1	4
5-8 10.8 25.10.62											
Gary Mills	E. U.21(2), Y. S.	Northampton	Nottingham F. (A)	50+8	7+3	3	4+2	8	2		
5-8 11.1 11.11.61	E. Cup 80	Seattle Sounders	Derby Co.	18	2	3		1			
		Seattle Sounders	Nottingham F.	5+2			2				
David Riley		Northampton	Keyworth U.								
5-9 10.10½ 8.12.60			Nottingham F.	0+1							
Steve Wigley		Ashton-u-Lyme	Curzon Ashton								
5-9 10.12 15.10.61			Nottingham F.	27+12	3	1	9	1			

CONTRACT PLAYERS WITH NO FIRST TEAM APPEARANCES: David Longhurst (MF), Franz Carr (F)

NON-CONTRACT PLAYERS 1984-85: Roy Campbell, Gareth Healey, Lloyd Bloomfield

APPRENTICES: Shaun Finney, Barry Fleming, James Fleming, Richard Gachagen, Patrick Kelly, Steven Murray, Russell Turley, Gary Andrews, Andy Bullingham, Brett Williams

NOTTINGHAM FOREST

DIVISION ONE 3RD **FA CUP** 3RD ROUND **MILK CUP** 2ND ROUND **UEFA CUP** SEMI-FINAL

MATCH	DATE	COMPETITION	VENUE	OPPONENTS	RESULT	HALF TIME	L'GUE POS'N	GOALSCORERS	ATTENDANCE
1	A 27	CL	H	Southampton	L0-1	0-0			14,626
2	29	CL	A	Manchester U	W2-1	0-1		Anderson, Davenport	43,005
3	S 3	CL	A	Liverpool	L0-1	0-0	15		31,376
4	7	CL	H	Aston Villa	D2-2	1-1		Davenport, Birtles	16,363
5	10	CL	H	QPR	W3-2	2-1	9	Hodge, Davenport, Hazel (og)	14,607
6	**14**	**UEFA 1**	**H**	**Vorwaerts**	**W2-0**	**1-0**		**Wallace, Hodge**	**14,994**
7	17	CL	A	Norwich C	W3-2	2-2	9	Walsh 3 (1 pen)	15,017
8	24	CL	H	Luton T	W1-0	0-0	7	Wallace	16,296
9	**28**	**UEFA 1**	**A**	**Vorwaerts**	**W1-0**	**0-0**		**Bowyer**	**18,000**
10	O 2	CL	A	Tottenham H	L1-2	1-0		Walsh	30,596
11	**4**	**MC 2**	**A**	**Wimbledon**	**L0-2**	**0-1**			**7,554**
12	16	CL	H	Notts Co	W3-1	3-1		Wallace, Bowyer, Davenport	26,658
13	**19**	**UEFA 2**	**A**	**PSV Eindhoven**	**W2-1**	**0-0**		**Davenport, Walsh (pen)**	**28,000**
14	22	CL	A	Arsenal	L1-4	0-2	11	Davenport (pen)	22,870
15	**26**	**MC 2**	**H**	**Wimbledon**	**D1-1**	**0-0**		**Wallace**	**13,718**
16	29	CL	H	Sunderland	D1-1	1-0	11	Thijssen	13,968
17	**N 2**	**UEFA 2**	**H**	**PSV Eindhoven**	**W1-0**	**0-0**		**Davenport**	**16,934**
18	5	CL	H	Wolverhampton W	W5-0	2-0	7	Birtles, Davenport (pen), Walsh, Hodge 2	13,855
19	12	CL	A	Everton	L0-1	0-1	11		17,546
20	D 19	CL	H	Ipswich T	W2-1	0-0	8	Birtles, Swain	14,979
21	**23**	**UEFA 3**	**H**	**Celtic**	**D0-0**	**0-0**			**32,017**
22	26	CL	A	Stoke C	D1-1	1-1	7	Walsh (pen)	11,655
23	D 4	CL	H	Leicester C	W3-2	2-0		Walsh, Bowyer, Thijssen	23,248
24	**7**	**UEFA 3**	**A**	**Celtic**	**W2-1**	**0-0**		**Hodge, Walsh**	**66,938**
25	10	CL	A	Watford	L2-3	1-3	11	Birtles 2	14,047
26	17	CL	H	West Ham U	W3-0	1-0	8	Hodge, Birtles, Walsh (pen)	14,544
27	26	CL	A	Birmingham C	W2-1	0-1	6	Birtles, Hodge	14,482
28	28	CL	H	Coventry C	W3-0	1-0		Davenport, Birtles 2	22,169
29	31	CL	H	Liverpool	L0-1	0-1	5		29,692
30	J 2	CL	A	Luton T	W3-2	3-1	4	Birtles, Hodge, Davenport	12,126
31	**7**	**FAC 3**	**H**	**Southampton**	**L1-2**	**0-0**		**Hart**	**19,721**
32	21	CL	H	Norwich C	W3-0	3-0	4	Thijssen, Hodge, Anderson	13,993
33	23	CL	A	Southampton	W1-0	1-0		Birtles	17,426
34	F 4	CL	H	Tottenham H	D2-2	1-1	4	Hodge, Walsh (pen)	21,428
35	8	CL	A	WBA	W5-0	1-0		Walsh (pen), McNaught (og), Bowyer, Birtles,	
								Anderson	11,020
36	11	CL	A	QPR	W1-0	1-0	2	Birtles	16,692
37	18	CL	A	Sunderland	D1-1	0-0	2	Anderson	15,958
38	25	CL	H	Arsenal	L0-1	0-0	3		20,045
39	M 3	CL	A	Wolverhampton W	L0-1	0-0	3		10,476
40	**7**	**UEFA QF1**	**H**	**Sturm Graz**	**W1-0**	**0-0**		**Hart**	**19,459**
41	14	CL	H	Everton	W1-0	0-0		Hodge	13,647
42	17	CL	A	Aston Villa	L0-1	0-0	3		16,270
43	**21**	**UEFA QF2**	**A**	**Sturm Graz**	**D1-1**[1]	**0-1**		**Walsh (pen)**	**25,000**
44	31	CL	A	Notts Co	D0-0	0-0	3		18,357
45	A 7	CL	H	WBA	W3-1	2-0	3	Walsh (pen), Anderson, Bowyer	15,245
46	**11**	**UEFA SF1**	**H**	**Anderlecht**	**W2-0**	**0-0**		**Hodge 2**	**22,681**
47	14	CL	A	Ipswich T	D2-2	1-0	3	Wigley, Davenport	15,429
48	17	CL	A	Coventry C	L1-2	0-1		Walsh	9,818
49	21	CL	H	Birmingham C	W5-1	2-0	3	Davenport 2, Walsh, Wallace, Bowyer	15,323
50	**25**	**UEFA SF2**	**A**	**Anderlecht**	**L0-3**	**0-1**			**36,000**
51	28	CL	H	Stoke C	D0-0	0-0	5		13,625
52	M 5	CL	A	Leicester C	L1-2	0-2	5	Davenport	16,600
53	7	CL	H	Watford	W5-1	3-0	5	Atkinson (og), Hodge, Davenport 2, Bowyer	13,732
54	12	CL	A	West Ham U	W2-1	1-1	4	Birtles, Davenport	18,468
55	16	CL	H	Manchester U	W2-0	1-0		Birtles, Anderson	23,651

[1] After Extra Time (Score After 90 mins 0-1)

Av Home Att 17,695

Goal Scorers

League (76): Birtles 15, Davenport 15 (2 pens), Walsh 13 (6 pens), Hodge 10, Anderson 6, Bowyer 6, Thijssen 3, Wallace 3, Swain 1, Wigley 1, opponents 3
FA Cup (1): Hart 1
Milk Cup (1): Wallace 1
UEFA Cup (12): Hodge 4, Walsh 3 (2 pens), Davenport 2, Bowyer 1, Hart 1, Wallace 1

1983-84

Van Breukelen	Anderson	Swain	Todd	Hart	Bowyer	Walsh	Wallace	Birtles	Hodge	Davenport	Wigley	Fairclough	Smalley	Thijssen	Sutton	Gunn	Walker	Mills	Riley	Wilson	REFEREE	
1	2	3	4	5	6	7*	8	9	10	11	12										G Courtney	1
1	2	3	4	5	6	7	8	9	10	11											R Bridges	2
1	2	3	4	5	6	7	8	9	10	11											J Lovatt	3
1	2	3	4	5	6	7	8	9	10	11											J Hough	4
1	2	3	4	5	6	7*	8	9	10	11	12										R Nixon	5
1	**2**	**3**	**4**		**6**	**7**	**8**		**10**	**9**	**11**	**5**								**12**		**6**
1	2	3	4		6	7*	8		10	9	11	5	12								E Scales	7
1	2	3	4	5	6	7	8	9	10		11										J Worrall	8
1	**2**	**3**	**4**	**5**	**6**	**11***	**8**	**9**	**10**		**7**					**12**						**9**
1	2	3	4	5	6	11	8	9	10		7										Alan Robinson	10
1	**2**	**3**	**4**	**5**	**6**	**11**		**9**	**10**	**8**	**7**										**M Bodenham**	**11**
1	2	3	4	5	6		8		11	9	7			10							N Midgley	12
1	**2**	**3**	**4**	**5**	**6**	**10**	**8**		**11**	**9**	**7**	**12**										**13**
1	2	3	4	5†	6		8		11	9	7			10							K Cooper	14
	2	**3**	**4**	**5**	**6**	**12**	**8**		**11**	**9**	**7**			**10***	**1**						**D Scott**	**15**
	2	3	4	5	6		8		11	9	7			10	1						N Ashley	16
	2	**3**	**4**	**5**	**6**	**11**	**8***	**12**	**10**	**9**	**7***	**12**			**1**						**Petrovic**	**17**
	2	3	4		6	12		9	11	8	7	5		10*	1						I Borrett	18
	2	3	4		6	12		9	11	8	7	5		10*	1						C Seel	19
	2	3		5	6	12		9	11	8	7	4		10*	1						A Saunders	20
	2	**3**		**5**	**6**	**11**	**12**	**9**	**10**	**8***	**7**	**4**			**1**							**21**
	2	3		5	6	11		9	7	10		4		8	1						DB Allison	22
	2	3		5	6	11		9		10	7	4		8	1						A Robinson	23
1	**2**	**3**		**5**	**6**	**11**		**9**	**8**	**10**	**7**	**4**									**Dalna**	**24**
1	2	3		5	6	11		9	8	10	7	4									J Deakin	25
1	2	3		5*	6	11	12	9	10	8	7	4									T Holbrook	26
1	2	3			6	11		9	8	10	7	5				4					D Richardson	27
1	2	3			6	11	12	9	8	10	7*	5				4					T Jones	28
1	2	3		5	6	11	12	9	8	10	7*	4									M Dimblebee	29
1	2	3		5	6	11	12	9	8	10*	7	4									D Axcell	30
1	**2**	**3**		**5**	**6**	**11**	**12**	**9**	**8**	**10**	**7***	**4**									**B Hill**	**31**
1	2	3		5	6	11	8	9*	10		12	4		7							R Guy	32
1	2	3		5	6	11	8	9*	10		12	4		7							K Salmon	33
1	2	3		5	6	11	8	9*	10	12		4		7							T Mills	34
1	2	3		5	6	11	8	9	10		12	4		7*							T Fitzharris	35
1	2	3		5	6	11	8	9	10			4		7							T Spencer	36
1	2	3		5	6	11	8	9	10		12	4		7*							I Hendrick	37
1	2	3		5	6	11	8	9	10		12	4		7*							D Owen	38
1	2	3		5	6	11	8*	9	10		12	4		7							D Scott	39
1	**2***	**3**		**5**	**6**	**11***	**8**	**9**	**10**	**12**	**7**	**4**				**13**					**Christov (CZ)**	**40**
1		3		5	6	11*	12	9	10	8	7	4					2				A Buksh	41
1		3		5	6	11		9	10	8	7	4					2				H King	42
1	**2**	**3**		**5**	**6**	**11**		**9**	**10**	**8**		**4**		**7**							**Yushka (SU)**	**43**
1	2	5		4	6	9	8	11*	7	10		3					12				K Warmsley	44
1	2	3		5	6	11			10	9	7	4						8*	12		G Tyson	45
1	**2**	**3**		**5**	**6**	**11**			**10**	**9**	**7**	**4**						**8**			**Brummeler (AUS)**	**46**
1	2	3		5	6	11			10	9	7						4	8			A Gunn	47
1	2	3		5	6	11			10	9	7	4						8			A Ward	48
1	2			5	6	11	8			9	7	4		10*		3		12			J Moules	49
1	**2**	**3**		**5**	**6**	**11**		**12**	**10***	**9**	**7**	**4**						**8**			**Guruceta (SP)**	**50**
1	2	3		5	6	11		12	8	9	7	4						10*			R Lewis	51
1	2	3		5	6			9	10	8	7	4						11			D Reeves	52
1	2	3		5	6	11		9*	8	10	7	4						12			P Willis	53
1	2	3		5	6	11		9	8	10	7	4									L Shapter	54
1	2	3			6	11	8	9		10	7	5				4					D Vickers	55
36	40	41	13	36	**42**	35	22	33	39	32	27	31	0	17	6	4	3	5	0		League Appearances	
						+3S	+5S	+1S		+1S	+8S		+1S				+1S	+2S	+1S			
1	1	1		1	1	1	1S	1	1	1	1	1									FA Cup Appearances	
1	2	2	2	2	2	1+1S	1	1	2	2	2			1	1						Milk Cup Appearances	
8	10	10	4	9	10	10	5+1S	5+2S	10	8+1S	9	7+2S		1	2	2S		2		1S	UEFA Cup Appearances	

CITY ROAD

Official Address: City Ground, Nottingham NG6 5FJ. Telephone: Nottingham (0602) 822202. Information Desk: (0602) 821122

Telegraphic: Forestball Nottingham

Ground Capacity: 35,000 (14,561 seats)

Record Attendance: 44,945 v. Manchester United, Division 1, 28 Oct 1967

Record Receipts: £132,000 v. Ajax, European Cup Semi-Final 1st Leg, 9 Apr 1980

Size of Playing Area: 115yds × 78 yds

Season Tickets: £56.00, £72.00, £82.00 (stands); £113.00 & £90.00 (Tandems of 1 adult and 1 juvenile); £42.00 (ground); £22.50 (juveniles/OAP)

Executive Box Season Tickets: Phone Commercial Office for details

Cost of Stand Tickets: £5.50, £5.00, £4.00 (Tandems £8.00 and £6.50); **Terraces:** £2.50 (adults), £1.30 (OAP/juveniles)

Match and Ticket Information: 14 days in advance (personal); 12 days (postal)

Car Parking: Space for 300 cars in East Stand car park plus street parking off Loughborough and Radcliffe Roads

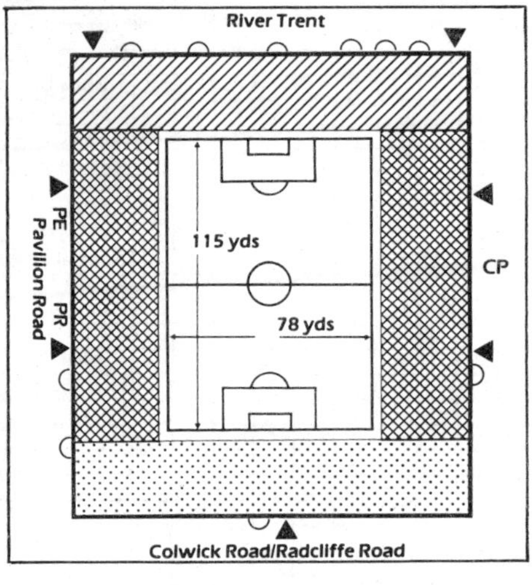

For key see page 12

How to get to the ground

From North: Use Motorway M1 until junction 26, leave Motorway and follow signs into Nottingham A610. Follow signs Melton Mowbray, Trent Bridge A606. Cross River and turn left into Radcliffe Road, then turn left into Colwick Road for Nottingham Forest F.C.
From East: Use A52 S.P. Nottingham into West Bridgeford, then turn right into Colwick Road for Nottingham Forest F.C.
From South: Use Motorway M1 until junction 24, leave motorway and follow signs Nottingham (South) to Trent Bridge, turn right into Radcliffe Road, then turn left into Colwick Road for Nottingham Forest F.C.
From West: Use A52 into Nottingham, then follow signs Melton Mowbray, Trent Bridge A606, cross river and turn left into Radcliffe Road, then turn left into Colwick Road for Nottingham Forest F.C.

NOTTS COUNTY Division 2

Chairman
J J Dunnett, MA, LLB(Cantab), MP

Directors
R Sweet
J Mounteney
J Sirrel

Company Secretary & Commercial Manager
Neal Hook, M Inst M (0602 861155)

Manager
Larry Lloyd

Reserve Team Coach
Michael Walker

Physiotherapist
John Short

At no time during the season did County seem likely to escape relegation from the First Division after a gallant spell of three seasons during which they were often out of their class. Cash resources have always been limited and Manager Jimmy Sirrel (now General Manager) has worked miracles whilst the tenuous hold on the top status has been maintained.

The recent League campaign never saw County out of the bottom three spots once the early flurries had ended — at least never for long. There were some gallant efforts such as a victory over Southampton at the Dell and a draw away to Manchester United, but consistency was missing and the final points tally was nine less than those gained by the last safe clubs Coventry and Stoke City, who had better goal differences. In the cups nothing startling was achieved. The Milk Cup Second Round was survived against Aldershot with comfortable wins in both legs and in the next round three draws against Birmingham City were followed by defeat in the third replay at Meadow Lane. The F.A. Cup did provide a good run with victories at Ashton Gate in a replay against Bristol City, another at Huddersfield in the Fourth Round, dismissal of Middlesbrough at home in the Fifth and finally defeat (again at Meadow Lane) in the last eight against Everton, the ultimate winners (1-2). A brave effort it was but not enough to bring consolation for other misfortunes.

So it will be back to the drawing board amidst hopes that the top status can be regained even though the resources to mount such a challenge and maintain it are very slender. With Christie away, this will not be easy and when the new season starts there will be some new faces to join the better known incumbents such as Richards and Goodwin. WLM

Back Row L to R: David Beaver, David Clarke, Tim Dalton, Seamus McDonagh, David Hunt, Pedro Richards. **Middle Row:** Michael Walker (Youth Team Coach), Mark Jones, Aki Lahtinen, Mick Leonard, Martin O'Neill, Rachid Harkouk, John Short (Physiotherapist). **Front Row:** Tristan Benjamin, Keith Downing, Justin Fashanu, Larry Lloyd (Manager), Simeon Hudson, Ian McParland, Mark Goodwin.

'THE MAGPIES'

Formed: 1862 (oldest League club) **Turned Professional:** 1885 **Ltd Co:** 1888
Previous Managers: Since 1946
Arthur Stollery Eric Houghton George Poyser Tommy Lawton Frank Hill Tim Coleman Eddie Lowe Jack Burkitt Andy Beattie Billy Gray Jimmy Sirrel Ronnie Fenton Jimmy Sirrel Howard Wilkinson Larry Lloyd
Honours: Division Two Champions 1896-7, 1913-4, 1922-3
Division Three (S) Champions 1930-1, 1949-50 Division Four Champions 1970-1
F.A. Cup Winners 1893-4
League Career: Founder member of Football League 1888 Relegated to Division 2 1892-3
Promoted to Division One 1896-7 Relegated to Division Two 1912-3
Promoted to Division One 1913-4 Relegated to Division Two 1919-20
Promoted to Division One 1922-3 Relegated to Division Two 1925-6
Relegated to Division Three (S) 1929-30Promoted to Division Two 1930-1
Relegated to Division Three (S) 1934-5 Promoted to Division Two 1949-50
Relegated to Division Three 1957-8 Relegated to Division Four 1958-9
Promoted to Division Three 1959-60 Relegated to Division Four 1963-4
Promoted to Division Three 1970-1 Promoted to Division Two 1972-3
Promoted to Division One 1980-1 Relegated to Division Two 1983-4
Colours: Black and white striped shirts, black shorts with white stripe, white stockings with black hoops on tops
Change Colours: All yellow with blue trim or all blue

CLUB RECORDS

Most Appearances for Club: Albert Irenmonger, 564, 1904-26
Most Capped Player: A Lahtinen, 10, Finland **For England:** None
Record Goalscorer in a Match:
Record League Goalscorer in a season: Tom Keetley 39, Div 3(S), 1930-1
Record League Goalscorer in a career: Les Bradd, 125, 1967-8
Record Transfer Fee Received: £150,000 from Wrexham for Mick Vinter, June 1979
Record Transfer Fee Paid: £600,000 to Orient for John Chiedozie, Aug 1981
Best Performances: League: 3rd Div 1 1890-1, 1900-1 **F.A. Cup:** Winners **League/Milk Cup:** 5th Round 1963-4, 1972-3, 1975-6
Most League Points: 69 in Div 4, 1970-1 **Most League Goals:** 107, Div 4, 1959-60
Record League Defeat: 1-9 v Blackburn Rovers, Div 1, 16 Nov 1889 1-9 v Aston Villa, Div 1, 27 Dec 1930
1-9 v Portsmouth, Div 2, 9 Apr 1927
Most Goals in a Match: Bob Jardine 5 v Burnley, Div 1, 27.10.1888
Dan Bruce 5 v Burslem Port Vale, Div 2, 26.02.1895
Paddy Mills 5 v Barnsley, Div 2, 19.11.27
Club Statistician for the Directory: H. Warsop

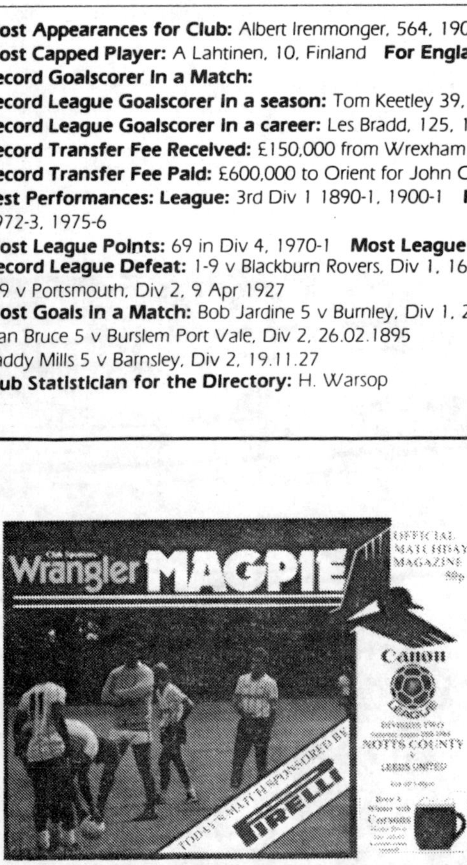

Programme Editor
Terry Bowles

Price	Number of Pages
50p	32

Subscriptions
£14 UK; £16 Europe; £20 elsewhere.

NOTTS. COUNTY

PLAYERS NAME Ht Wt Birthdate	Honours	Birthplace Transfers	Clubs	APPEARANCES League	Milk Cup	F.A.C.	E. Cups	GOALS League	Milk Cup	F.A.C.	E. Cups
GOALKEEPERS											
Richard Delton 5-10½ 11.10 14.10.65		London	Coventry C. (A)								
Mick Leonard 5-11 11.0 9.5.59		Carshalton	Epsom & Ewell								
			Halifax T.	69	6	1					
		£30,000	Notts. Co.	37	3	3					
Jim McDonagh 6-0 13.9 6.10.52	Ei.(16) Div. 2. 78	Rotherham	Rotherham U. (A)	121	5	9					
		£10,000	Bolton W.	161	13	10					
		£250,000	Everton	40	3	5					
		£90,000 + Player	Bolton W.	81	6	3		1			
			Notts. Co.	24	5	2					
DEFENDERS											
David Beaver 5-6½ 11.6 4.4.66		Kirkby-in-Ashfield	Notts. Co.								
Tristan Benjamin 6.0 11.1 1.4.57	E. Y	St. Kitts. W.I.	Notts. Co. (A)	208 + 15	20 +	8		4			
Simeon Hodson 5-10 11.2 5.2.66		Lincoln	Notts. Co. (A)	13							
Aki Lahtinen 5-11 11.3 4.4.66	Finland	Finland	Opsoulu								
		£61,000	Notts. Co.	23 + 8	2 + 1	1		2			
Pedro Richards* 5-8 10.8 1.11.56		Edmonton	Notts. Co. (A)	343 + 1	30 +	13		4			
Steve Sims 13.9 2.7.57	E. B(1). U.21(10). Y	Lincoln	Leicester C. (A)	78 + 1	5	3		3			
		£175,000	Watford	150 + 2	14	14	4 + 1	4	3		
		£50,000	Notts. Co.								
MIDFIELD											
Mark Goodwin 5-10 10.9 23.2.60	Div. 2. 80	Sheffield	Leicester C. (A)	69 + 22	3	4 + 1		8			
		£60,000	Notts. Co.	103 + 8	10	5 + 1		10			
Rachid Harkouk 6-0½ 12.5 19.5.56		Chelsea	Feltham								
			Crystal Palace	51 + 3	4 + 1	1 + 3		21	3		
		£100,000	Q.P.R.	15 + 5	3	1		3			
		£50,000	Notts. Co.	70 + 19	2	5 + 1		17			
David Hunt 5-11 11.0 17.4.59		Leicester	Derby Co. (A)	5							
		£30,000	Notts. Co.	230 + 5	19 +	13 +		15	3	1	
Mark Jones 5-11 12.2 21.12.65		Mansfield	Notts. Co. (A)	+ 2							
Martin O'Neill 5-10 11.3 1.3.52	N.I.(62) Div. 1. 78. Lg.C. 78. E. Cup 80. ESC. 79	Kilrea	Distillery								
		£15,000	Nottingham F.	264 + 21	34	28 +	15 +	48	8	3	1
		£250,000	Norwich C.	11				1			
		£275,000	Manchester C.	12 + 1	3						
		£150,000	Norwich C.	54 + 1	5	4		11	1		
			Notts. Co.	37 + 1	5	5		4			
FORWARDS											
David Clarke 5-10 11.0 3.12.64	E. Y	Nottingham	Notts. Co.	29 + 7	3 + 2	4			1		
Keith Downing 5-7½ 11.0 8.2.66		Oldbury	Notts. Co.								
Justin Fashanu 6-1 12.7 18.9.62	E. U.21(11). Y	Hackney	Norwich C. (A)	84 + 6	8	5		35	4	1	
		£1,000,000	Nottingham F.	31 + 1	4	1		3	1		
			Southampton (L)	9							
		£150,000	Notts. Co.	32	3	2		12		2	
John McCulloch 5-10 11.0 28.12.54	S. U.21(2)	Kilmarnock	Kilmarnock	108 + 8	18	8		14	3	1	
		£80,000	Notts. Co.	212 + 3	17	10 +		51	1	2	
Ian McParland 5-8 10.8 4.10.61		Edinburgh	Ormiston Primrose								
			Notts. Co.	26 + 20	1 + 2	1 + 1		3			
Alan Young 6-0 12.7 26.10.55	S. S Div. 2. 80	Kirkcaldy	Oldham A.	107 + 15	3	6		30	1	4	
		£250,000	Leicester C.	102 + 2	5	10		26	1	2	
		£160,000	Sheffield U.	23 + 3	4	2		7	3	3	
		£140,000	Brighton	25 + 1	2	1		12			
		£55,000	Notts. Co.								

APPRENTICES

Darren Davis (1 app), **Tony Dawes, Paul Smalley, Paul Barnes, Luke Betteridge, Wayne R. Fairclough, David J. Kevan, Tony Woods, Derek Yates**

Trevor Christie (now with Nottingham Forest) shared the Player of the Year award with John Chiedozie (now Tottenham H.)

NOTTS COUNTY

DIVISION ONE 21ST **FA CUP** 6TH ROUND **MILK CUP** 3RD ROUND

MATCH	DATE	COMPE-TITION	VENUE	OPPONENTS	RESULT	HALF TIME	L'GUE POS'N	GOALSCORERS	ATTEN-DANCE
1	A 27	CL	A	Leicester C	W4-0	2-0		O'Neill, Christie 3	14,838
2	30	CL	H	Birmingham C	W2-1	1-1		Harkouk 2	11,031
3	S 3	CL	H	Ipswich T	L0-2	0-0	6		9,023
4	6	CL	A	Coventry C	L1-2	1-0		Fashanu	10,912
5	10	CL	A	Watford	L1-3	1-2	11	Harkouk	12,763
6	17	CL	H	Arsenal	L0-4	0-2	16		10,217
7	24	CL	A	West Ham U	L0-3	0-1	18		20,613
8	O 1	CL	H	Everton	L0-1	0-1	20		7,949
9	**4**	**MC 2**	**A**	**Aldershot**	**W4-2**	**1-2**		**Kilcline, Christie 2, Fashanu**	**4,458**
10	16	CL	A	Nottingham F	L1-3	1-3		Christie (pen)	26,658
11	22	CL	H	Stoke C	D1-1	0-0	20	Kilcline	7,684
12	**25**	**MC 2**	**H**	**Aldershot**	**W4-1**	**2-0**		**Hunt 2, Christie 2**	**3,439**
13	29	CL	A	Tottenham H	L0-1	0-0	20		29,138
14	N 5	CL	A	WBA	L0-2	0-1	20		10,821
15	**8**	**MC 3**	**A**	**Birmingham C**	**D2-2**	**0-1**		**Harkouk, Chiedozie**	**10,484**
16	12	CL	H	Norwich C	D1-1	1-1	20	Fashanu	7,882
17	19	CL	A	Southampton	W2-0	1-0	19	Fashanu, Christie	15,009
18	**22**	**MC 3R**	**H**	**Birmingham C**	**D0-0[1]**	**0-0**			**8,268**
19	26	CL	H	Aston Villa	W5-2	2-0	18	Christie 2 (1 pen), Chiedozie 2, Harkouk (pen)	8,960
20	**29**	**MC 3R2**	**A**	**Birmingham C**	**D0-0[1]**	**0-0**			**9,678**
21	D 3	CL	A	QPR	L0-1	0-1	18		10,217
22	**5**	**MC 3R3**	**H**	**Birmingham C**	**L1-3**	**0-3**		**O'Neill**	**7,361**
23	10	CL	H	Sunderland	W6-1	3-1	18	Christie, Worthington, McParland, Chiedozie 2, Richards	7,123
24	17	CL	A	Liverpool	L0-5	0-3	18		22,436
25	26	CL	H	Luton T	L0-3	0-1	20		9,789
26	27	CL	A	Manchester U	D3-3	0-0	20	Christie (pen), Fashanu 2	41,544
27	31	CL	A	Ipswich T	L0-1	0-1	20		14,146
28	J 2	CL	H	West Ham U	D2-2	1-2	20	Christie, O'Neill	8,667
29	**8**	**FAC 3**	**H**	**Bristol C**	**D2-2**	**1-1**		**Christie 2 (1 pen)**	**11,042**
30	**10**	**FAC 3R**	**A**	**Bristol C**	**W2-0**	**0-0**		**Kilcline, McCulloch**	**16,107**
31	14	CL	H	Leicester C	L2-5	2-1	20	Chiedozie, Harkouk	10,607
32	21	CL	A	Arsenal	D1-1	0-1	20	Chiedozie	20,110
33	**F 1**	**FAC 4**	**A**	**Huddersfield T**	**W2-1**	**2-1**		**Kilcline, Harkouk**	**13,634**
34	4	CL	A	Everton	L1-4	1-3	20	McParland (pen)	13,016
35	11	CL	H	Watford	L3-5	2-3	21	Harkouk, Christie 2 (1 pen)	8,078
36	**18**	**FAC 5**	**H**	**Middlesbrough**	**W1-0**	**1-0**		**Chiedozie**	**17,487**
37	21	CL	H	Tottenham H	D0-0	0-0			7,943
38	25	CL	A	Stoke C	L0-1	0-1	21		11,725
39	M 3	CL	H	WBA	D1-1	0-0	21	Christie (pen)	7,373
40	**10**	**FAC 6**	**H**	**Everton**	**L1-2**	**1-1**		**Chiedozie**	**19,534**
41	14	CL	A	Norwich C	W1-0	0-0		O'Neill	13,230
42	17	CL	H	Coventry C	W2-1	0-0	21	O'Neill, Christie (pen)	6,564
43	24	CL	A	Birmingham C	D0-0	0-0	21		9,040
44	31	CL	H	Nottingham F	D0-0	0-0	21		18,357
45	A 7	CL	A	Wolverhampton W	W1-0	1-0	21	Hunt	7,481
46	14	CL	H	Manchester U	W1-0	0-0	21	Christie	13,911
47	21	CL	A	Luton T	L2-3	0-0	21	Christie, Chiedozie	8,181
48	28	CL	A	Aston Villa	L1-3	1-1	21	Chiedozie	13,059
49	M 1	CL	H	Wolverhampton W	W4-0	2-0		Chiedozie, Christie 2, Hunt	5,378
50	5	CL	H	QPR	L0-3	0-2	21		7,309
51	7	CL	A	Sunderland	D0-0	0-0	21		14,517
52	12	CL	H	Liverpool	D0-0	0-0	21		18,745
53	17	CL	H	Southampton	L1-3	1-1		Christie	6,035

[1]After Extra Time **Av Home Att 9,456**

Goal Scorers

League (50): Christie 19 (6 pens), Chiedozie 9, Harkouk 6 (1 pen), Fashanu 5, O'Neill 4, Hunt 2, McParland 2 (1 pen), Kilcline 1, Richards 1, Worthington 1
FA Cup (8): Chiedozie 2, Christie 2 (1 pen), Kilcline 2, Harkouk 1, McCulloch 1
Milk Cup (11): Christie 4, Hunt 2, Chiedozie 1, Fashanu 1, Harkouk 1, Kilcline 1, O'Neill 1

1983-84

McDonagh	Lahtinen	Worthington	Goodwin	Kilcline	Hunt	Chiedozie	Fashanu	Christie	Harkouk	O'Neill	McParland	McCulloch	Benjamin	Mair	Richards	Roeder **(L)**	Clarke	Leonard	Jones	Hodson	Armstrong **(L)**	Davis	**REFEREE**	
1	2	3	4	5	6	7*	8	9	10	11	12												R Milford	1
1	2	3	4*	5	6	7	8	9	10	11		12											TA Jones	2
1	2	3	4*	5	6	7	8	12	10	11		9											DB Allison	3
1	2	3	4	5	6	7	8		10	11		9											T Bune	4
1	2	3	4*	5	6	7	8	12	10	11		9											H King	5
1		3	4*	5	6	7	8	12	10	11		9	2										K Redfern	6
1		3		5	6	12		8*	10	4	7	9	2	11									M James	7
1		3	4	5	6	7		8	10	11		9*	2	12									TJ Holbrook	8
1		**3**	**4**	**5**	**6**	**7**	**9**	**8**	**10**	**11**			**2**										**E Read**	**9**
1		3	4	5*	6†	7	8†	9	10	11			2		12								N Midgley	10
1		3	4	5	6		8*	9	10	12			2	11	7								J Moulds	11
1		**3**	**4**	**5***	**6**	**8**		**9**		**10**	**12**		**2**	**11**	**7**								**D Shaw**	**12**
1		3	4	5	6	8		9		10	12		2*	11	7								JE Martin	13
1		6	8	3		10		11		7	12		2	9*	5	4							M Dimblebee	14
1		**3**	**2**	**5**		**8**		**9**	**4**	**10**	**11***				**7**	**6**	**12**						**R Bridges**	**15**
1		3	2		5	11	8	9	10	7					4	6							A Robinson	16
1		3	2		5	11	8	9	10	7					4	6							R Lewis	17
1		**3**	**2**		**5**	**11**	**8**	**9**	**10**	**7**					**4**	**6**							**J Worrall**	**18**
1		3	2		5	11	8	9	10	7					4	6							G Tyson	19
1		**3**	**2**		**5**	**11**	**8**	**9**	**10**	**7**					**4**	**6**							**B Stevens**	**20**
1		3	2		5	11	8	9	10	7			6		4								H Taylor	21
1		**3**	**2**		**5**	**11**	**8**	**9**	**10**	**7**	**12**		**6***		**4**								**P Willis**	**22**
1		3	2		5	11	8	9		7	10		6		4								R Tyldesley	23
1		3	2		5	11	8	9		7*	10	12	6		4								N Ashley	24
1		3	2	6	5	11	8	9	12	7		10*			4								T Mills	25
1		3	2	6	5	11	8	9	10*	7					4		12						D Owen	26
1		3	2	6	5	11	8*	9	10	7					4		12						C Downey	27
1		3	2*	6	5	11		9	10	7	12				4		8						G Courtney	28
1		**3**	**2**	**6**	**5**	**11**		**9**	**10***	**7**		**12**			**4**		**8**						**N Glover**	**29**
1		**3**	**2**	**6**	**5**	**11**		**9**	**10**	**7**		**8**			**4**								**N Glover**	**30**
1		3	2	6	5	11		9	10	7		8			4								D Hutchinson	31
		10*		6	5	11		9	12	7		8	2		4		3	1					A Crickmore	32
				6	**5**	**11**		**9**	**10**	**7***	**12**	**8**	**2**		**4**		**3**	**1**					**A Saunders**	**33**
			7	6	5	11			10		9*	8	2		4		3	1	12				F Roberts	34
1				6	5	11		9	10		7	8	2		4		3						D Richardson	35
				5	**6**	**11**		**9**	**10**	**7**		**8**	**2**		**4**		**3**	**1**					**B Hill**	**36**
			12	5	6	11		9	10*		7	8	2		4		3	1					R Nixon	37
			12	5	6	11		9	10		7*	8	2		4		3	1					K Barratt	38
	2			5	6	11		9	10*	7	12	8			4		3	1					R Banks	39
	2		**12**	**5**	**6**	**11**		**8**		**7**	**10***	**9**			**4**		**3**	**1**					**J Martin**	**40**
				5	6	11		9		7		8		10	4		3	1		2			J Moules	41
					6	11		9		7		8		10	4		3	1		2	5		K Redfern	42
			6			11		9		7		8		10	4		3	1		2	5		D Reeves	43
					6	11		10		7		9		8	4		5	1		2	3		K Walmsley	44
					6	11*		9		7	12	8		10	4		3	1		2	5		T Spencer	45
					6			9	12	7	11	8*		10	4		3	1		2	5		R Lewis	46
					6	11		8*	12	7	9			10	4		3	1		2	5		J Martin	47
					6	11			9	7	8			10	4		3	1		2	5		D Hedges	48
					6	11		9	12	7	8			10	4		3*	1		2	5		T Bune	49
					5	11		10	6	7	8			9	3			1		2	4		C Thomas	50
			6			11*		9	10	7	8			12	4			1		2	5	3	T Mills	51
			6		5	11		9	10	7	8				4		3	1		2			D Vickers	52
			6		5	11		9		7	8			10*	4		3	1	12	2			L Dilkes	53
24	6	24	27	24	39	39	17	36	27	37	15	20	15	15	33	4	18	18	0	13	10	1	League Appearances	
			+2S			+1S		+3S	+5S	+1S	+6S	+2S		+2S	+1S		+2S		+2S					
2	1	2	2+1S	5	5	5		5	4	5	1+1S	4+1S	2		5		4	3					FA Cup Appearances	
6		6	6	3	5	6	4	6	5	6	1+2S		3	1	5	3	1S						Milk Cup Appearances	

MEADOW LANE

Official Address: County Ground, Meadow Lane, Nottingham NG2 3HJ. Telephone: Nottingham (0602) 861155

Telegraphic: Notts County FC, Nottingham

Ground Capacity: 23,680

Record Attendance: 47,310 v. York City, F.A. Cup Round 6, 10 Mar 1955

Record Receipts: £63,505 v. Everton, F.A. Cup Round 6, 10 Mar 1984

Size of Playing Area: 117yds × 76 yds

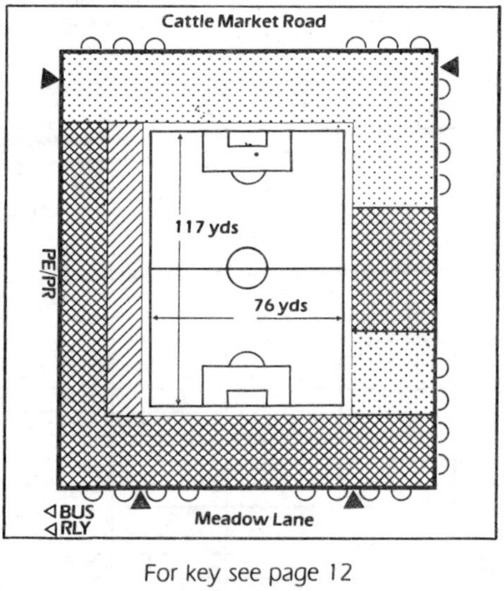

For key see page 12

Season Tickets: £90, £81, £75, £65, £50 (Stand), £35 Ground (£17.50 Juveniles/OAP).

Executive Box Season Tickets: Consult Commercial Manager

Cost of Stand Tickets: £4.50, £5.50, £2.50 (£1.50 Juveniles/OAP) (£1.00 Junior Magpies)

Match and Ticket Information: Applications by post (with remittance and SAE) or in person fourteen days before each match.

Car Parking: no street parking near ground but ample space in the City of Nottingham Corporation car park on the Cattle Market, Meadow Lane, 400 yards from the main entrances.

How to get to the ground

From North: Use Motorway M1 until junction 26, leave Motorway and follow signs into Nottingham A610. Follow signs Melton Mowbray, Trent Bridge A606. On nearside of River Trent turn left into Meadow Lane for Notts County F.C.
From East: Use A52 S.P. Nottingham to Trent Bridge, cross River and then turn right into Meadow Lane for Notts County F.C.
From South: Use Motorway M1 until junction 24, leave motorway and follow signs Nottingham (South) to Trent Bridge, cross River and then turn right into Meadow Lane for Notts County F.C.
From West: Use A52 into Nottingham, then follow signs Melton Mowbray, Trent Bridge A606, on nearside of River Trent turn left into Meadow Lane for Notts County F.C.

OLDHAM ATHLETIC Division 2

President
R Schofield

Chairman
I H Scott

Directors
D A Brierley (Vice Chairman)
R Adams
G T Butterworth
J Kershaw
D R Taylor
H Wilde

Secretary
T M Finn

Commercial Manager
A Hardy (061-652 0966)

Manager
Joe Royle

Coach
W Urmson

Chief Scout
C McDonald

Groundsman
H Wood

This was a bitterly disappointing season for the Latics and it wasn't until they defeated Grimsby in their penultimate match that they could be sure of maintaining Second Division status at Boundary Park.

They started well with a home win over Brighton but they managed to win only one of their next 13 League games and, by the middle of November, were third from bottom of the table.

Injuries to goalkeeper Andy Goram caused numerous problems for manager Joe Royle. He initially loaned Mark Grew from Leicester and later gave young Brian Parkin a run. With the situation growing tense towards the end of the season, the Oldham boss felt he needed the experience of Jeff Wealands, loaned from Manchester United.

More problems arose in attack. Roger Palmer was the only player able to get his name regularly on the scorers' list and in the end Mr Royle signed Mike Quinn from Stockport for £50,000.

Until the middle of February Oldham managed to keep a reasonable cushion of points between them and the real strugglers. Then a dismal run produced only one victory in 11 attempts and the warning bells began to clang loudly.

A 3-2 Boundary Park win over Portsmouth at the end of April was a real life saver because Derby also won and the Latics would otherwise have fallen into third-from-bottom place.

A useful three points from Burnley took away much of the pressure but there was still some concern when the Latics conceded an early goal at home to Grimsby in their penultimate game. Quinn equalised before the interval and, with just nine minutes to go, young Andrew Hodkinson scored his first League goal. And that meant Oldham had saved their Second Divison place.

There was not a lot to shout about in the Milk Cup, either. A 4-2 aggregate victory over Fourth Division Stockport County took them into a third round clash at Wimbledon. Though Oldham took an early lead, the Third Division side recovered well to win 3-1.

Their F.A. Cup hopes were killed at the first stage. Oldham had to travel to Shrewsbury Town where they were beaten by three clear goals.

Oldham's failure to produce the right sort of results soon hit gates. Towards the end of the season, attendances dropped to below the four thousand mark and it was only the 20,320 packed house, for the Easter derby with Manchester City, that enabled the club to return a final average League attendance figure of 6,213.

TP

Back Row L to R: Gary Hoolickin, Derrick Parker, Andy Goram, Brian Parkin, Alex Jones, Tony Henry. **Middle Row:** Ian Liversedge (Physiotherapist), John Bowden, Mike Quinn, Darron McDonough, Martin Buchan, Bob Colville, Willie Donachie, Billy Urmson (Asst Coach). **Front Row:** Nick Sinclair, Roger Palmer, Joe McBride, Joe Royle (Team Manager), Kenny Clements, Andy Hodkinson, Mark Ward. **Sitting:** Wayne Harrison, Andy Barlow, Andy Gorton, Steve Bullock, Jimmy Collins.

'THE LATICS'

Sponsored by **J.W. Lees & Co (Breweries) Ltd**

Formed: 1894 **Turned Professional:** 1899 **Ltd Co:** 1906
Previous Names: Pine Villa 1894-1899
Previous Managers: Since 1946
Bob Mellor Frank Womack Billy Wooton George Hardwick Ted Goodier Peter McKennan Norman Dodgin Jack Rowley Les McDowell Gordon Hurst Jimmy McIlroy Jack Rowley Jimmy Frizell
Honours: Division Three (N) Champions 1952-3 Division Three Champions 1973-4
League Career: Elected to Division Two 1907 Promoted to Division One 1909-10
Relegated to Division Two 1922-3 Relegated to Division 3(N) 1934-5
Promoted to Division Two 1952-3 Relegated to Division Three 1953-4
Relegated to Division Four 1957-8 Promoted to Division Three 1962-3
Relegated to Division Four 1968-9 Promoted to Division Three 1970-1
Promoted to Division Two 1973-4
Colours: Royal blue shirts with white trim on sleeves, white shorts with blue stripe, white stockings
Change Colours: Tangerine shirts, blue shorts, tangerine stockings

CLUB RECORDS

Most Appearances for Club: Ian Wood, 525, 1966-80
Most Capped Player: Albert Gray, 9, Wales
Record Goalscorer in a Match:
Record League Goalscorer in a season: Tom Davis, 33, Div 3(N), 1936-7
Record League Goalscorer in a career: Eric Gemmell, 110, 1947-54
Record Transfer Fee Received: £275,000 from Queens Park Rangers for Simon Stainrod, Nov 1980
Record Transfer Fee Paid: £200,000 to Manchester City for Kenny Clements, Sept 1979
Best Performances: League: 2nd Div 1 1914-5 **F.A. Cup:** Semi-Final 1913 **League/Milk Cup:** Never past 3rd Round
Most League Points: 62 in Div 3, 1973-4 **Most League Goals:** 95, Div 4, 1962-3
Record League Victory: 11-0 v Southport, Div 4, 26 Dec 1962
Record League Defeat: 4-13 v Tranmer Rovers, Div 3(N), 26 Dec 1935
Club Statistician for the Directory: D. Williams

Programme Editor
A. Hardy

Price	Number of Pages
40p	28

Subscriptions
No subscriptions

OLDHAM ATHLETIC

PLAYERS NAME Ht Wt Birthdate	Honours	Birthplace Transfers	Clubs	APPEARANCES League	Milk Cup	F.A.C.	E. Cups	GOALS League	Milk Cup	F.A.C.	E. Cups
GOALKEEPERS											
Andy Goram		Bury	W.B.A. (A)								
5-10 11.6 13.4.64			Oldham A.	63	3	2					
Andy Gorton											
6-0 12.0 23.9.66											
Brian Parkin		Birkenhead	Oldham A.	5							
6-1 12.0 12.10.65											
DEFENDERS											
Andrew Barlow											
5-8 9.10 24.11.65											
Martin Buchan	S.(34), U.23 (3),	Aberdeen	Aberdeen	129 + 2	6	15	11 + 1	10			1
5-10 12.2 6.3.49	Y, S.L.(1),	£125,000	Manchester U.	376	34	39		4			
	FAC. 77,		Oldham A.	24							
	Div. 2, 75										
Steven Bullock											
5-8 9.9 5.10.66											
Kenny Clements*		Manchester	Manchester C.	116 + 3	18	7					
6-1 12.6 9.4.55		£200,000	Oldham A.	181 + 1	9	7		2			
Willie Donnachie	S.(35), U.23(2),	Glasgow	Manchester C.	347 + 4	40	21		2			
5-9 11.5 5.10.51	FC. 76	£200,000	Portland Timbers								
		£200,000	Norwich C.	11	2						
		£200,000	Portland Timbers								
		F	Burnley	60	4	12	4 AMC	3			
Gary Hoolickin		Middleton	Oldham A.	128 + 2	16	4 + 1		2			
5-11 11.1 29.10.57											
John Hudson		Middleton	Manchester C								
5-5 9.2 25.11.64			Oldham A.	16 + 4		1					
Alex Jones		Blackburn	Oldham A. (A)	4							
6-0 11.6 27.11.64											
Nicky Sinclair		Manchester	Oldham A.	72 + 2	5			1			
5-11 11.7 3.1.60											
MIDFIELD											
John Bowden		Stockport	Oldham A.	60 + 7	5	2		5			
6-0 11.7 21.1.63											
Jimmy Collins				0 + 1							
5-8 9.7 27.12.66											
Tony Henry		Newcastle	Manchester C. (A)	68 + 11	7	3 + 1		6	6		
5-11 12.0 26.11.57		£125,000	Bolton W.	80	3	3		22	2		
		£21,000	Oldham A.	50 + 3	2	1		5			
Darren McDonough		Antwerp,	Oldham A.	122 + 5	10	3		14	1		
5-11 11.0 7.11.62		Belgium									
Mark Ward		Huyton	Everton (A)								
5-5 10.0 10.10.62			Northwich Victoria								
		£10,000	Oldham A.	42	3	1		6			
FORWARDS											
Bob Colville		Nuneaton	Oldham A.	4				1			
5-11 11.12 27.4.63											
Andy Hodkinson	E. S	Ashton-u-Lyne	Bolton W. (A)								
5-9 10.2 4.11.65		F	Oldham A.	3 + 1				1			
Joe McBride	S. U.21(1), S	Glasgow	Everton (A)	51 + 6	3	6		9	1	1	
5-8 10.8 17.8.60		£50,000	Rotherham U.	45	4	1		12			
		£45,000	Oldham A.	19 + 6				4			
Roger Palmer†		Manchester	Manchester C. (A)	22 + 9	3 + 3			9	1		
5-10 10.10 30.1.59		£70,000	Oldham A.	140 + 2	10	5		41			
Derrick Parker		Wallsend	Burnley (A)	5 + 1				2			
5-9½ 11.8 7.2.57		F	Southend U.	129	8	12		43	1	7	
		F	Barnsley	104 + 3	15	6		33	4	3	
		£40,000	Oldham A.	22 + 3	2	1		2			
Mike Quinn		Liverpool	Derby Co. (A)								
5-9½ 10.0 2.5.62		F	Wigan A.	56 + 13	5	3		19			
		F	Stockport Co.	62 + 1	5	2		39	2		
		£52,000	Oldham A.	14				5			

NON-CONTRACT PLAYERS 1984-85: Mark Kay, Darren Lyons, Godfrey Williams

APPRENTICE: Wayne Harrison

OLDHAM ATHLETIC

DIVISION TWO 19TH **FA CUP** 3RD ROUND **MILK CUP** 3RD ROUND

MATCH	DATE	COMPE-TITION	VENUE	OPPONENTS	RESULT	HALF TIME	L'GUE POS'N	GOALSCORERS	ATTEN-DANCE
1	A 27	CL	H	Brighton & HA	W1-0	0-0		Ward	5,750
2	S 3	CL	A	Newcastle U	L0-3	0-1	15		22,644
3	6	CL	A	Swansea C	D0-0	0-0			7,244
4	10	CL	H	Huddersfield T	L0-3	0-0	17		8,543
5	17	CL	A	Derby Co	D2-2	1-2	18	Palmer, McBride	12,521
6	24	CL	H	Sheffield W	L1-3	1-1	18	Heaton (pen)	9,269
7	27	CL	H	Charlton Ath	D0-0	0-0			3,679
8	O 1	CL	A	Cambridge U	L1-2	0-1	20	Turner (og)	2,696
9	**4**	**MC 2**	**A**	**Stockport Co**	**W2-0**	**2-0**		**McDonough, Parker**	**4,640**
10	8	CL	A	Shrewsbury T	L0-2	0-0	20		4,087
11	15	CL	H	Middlesbrough	W2-1	0-0	19	Ward, Hoolickin	5,000
12	22	CL	A	Blackburn R	L1-3	0-0	19	Palmer	5,863
13	**25**	**MC 2**	**H**	**Stockport Co**	**D2-2**	**0-2**		**McDonough, Palmer**	**3,540**
14	29	CL	H	Carlisle U	L2-3	1-1	19	Palmer 2	4,087
15	N 5	CL	H	Chelsea	D1-1	0-0	20	Palmer	5,807
16	**8**	**MC 3**	**A**	**Wimbledon**	**L1-3**	**1-1**		**Cross**	**4,624**
17	12	CL	A	Crystal Palace	L1-2	0-2	20	Cross	5,481
18	19	CL	H	Cardiff C	W2-1	1-0	20	Palmer, Parker	3,587
19	26	CL	A	Portsmouth	W4-3	4-0	18	Ward, Cross 2, Palmer	11,404
20	D 3	CL	H	Barnsley	W1-0	1-0	18	Heaton (pen)	5,475
21	13	CL	A	Grimsby T	L0-3	0-2			4,825
22	17	CL	H	Fulham	W3-0	1-0	16	Cross 2, Palmer	4,915
23	26	CL	A	Manchester C	L0-2	0-0	18		35,898
24	27	CL	H	Leeds U	W3-2	0-1	16	Bowden, McBride, Cross	8,393
25	31	CL	H	Newcastle U	L1-2	0-1	16	Henry	8,518
26	J 2	CL	A	Sheffield W	L0-3	0-0	16		18,690
27	**7**	**FAC 3**	**A**	**Shrewsbury T**	**L0-3**	**0-1**			**4,650**
28	14	CL	A	Brighton & HA	L0-4	0-1	16		10,203
29	21	CL	H	Derby Co	W3-0	2-0	15	Henry, Parker, Ward	4,564
30	F 4	CL	H	Cambridge U	D0-0	0-0	18		3,646
31	11	CL	A	Huddersfield T	W1-0	1-0	16	Quinn	8,162
32	18	CL	A	Carlisle U	L0-2	0-0	16		4,389
33	25	CL	H	Blackburn R	D0-0	0-0	17		6,855
34	M 3	CL	A	Chelsea	L0-3	0-1	18		12,736
35	10	CL	H	Crystal Palace	W3-2	2-1	16	Quinn, Ward, Palmer	4,138
36	17	CL	H	Swansea C	D3-3	2-2	16	Palmer, Henry, McBride	3,597
37	24	CL	A	Charlton Ath	L1-2	0-2	17	Ward	4,535
38	31	CL	A	Middlesbrough	L2-3	1-2	18	Quinn, Henry	5,615
39	A 7	CL	H	Shrewsbury T	L0-1	0-0	19		3,428
40	14	CL	A	Cardiff C	L0-2	0-1	19		4,657
41	20	CL	H	Manchester C	D2-2	1-1		Palmer, Quinn	20,320
42	24	CL	A	Leeds U	L0-2	0-0			9,576
43	28	CL	H	Portsmouth	W3-2	1-1	19	Colville, McBride, Palmer	3,558
44	M 5	CL	A	Barnsley	W1-0	1-0	19	Palmer	5,539
45	7	CL	H	Grimsby T	W2-1	1-1	18	Quinn, Hodkinson	4,156
46	12	CL	A	Fulham	L0-3	0-2	19		5,089

Av Home Att **6,213**

Goal Scorers

League (47): Palmer 13, Cross 6, Ward 6, Quinn 5, Henry 4, McBride 4, Heaton 2 (2 pens), Parker 2, Bowden 1, Colville 1, Hodkinson 1, Hoolicken 1, opponents 1

FA Cup (-): —

Milk Cup (5): McDonough 2, Cross 1, Palmer 1, Parker 1

1983-84

Goram	Hoolickin	Heaton	Bowden	Clements	Buchan	Ward	Henry	McDonough	Parker	Palmer	Humphries	Hudson	Sinclair	McBride	Cross	Grew **(L)**	Bromage **(L)**	Anderson	Quinn	Parkin	Wealands **(L)**	Jones	Hodkinson	Colville	**REFEREE**	
1	2	3	4	5	6	7	8	9	10*	11	12														R Nixon	1
1	2*	3	4	5	6	7	8	9	10	11	12														A Challinor	2
1	2*	3	4	5	6	7	8	9	12	11		10													B Stevens	3
1	6		4	5		7	8	9		10	12	3*	2	11											R Bridges	4
1		3	4	5	6	7	12	9	8*	10			2	11											K Hackett	5
1		3	4	5	6	7	8	9		10			2	11											G Courtney	6
1	3		4	5	6	7	12	9	8*	10			2	11											F Roberts	7
1	3		4	5	6	7	8	9		10			2	11											A Gunn	8
1	**3**		**4**	**5**	**6**	**7**		**9**	**8**	**10**	**11***	**12**	**2**												**M Robinson**	**9**
1	3*		4	5	6	7	2	9	8	10				11	12										B Hill	10
1	3		4	5	6	7	2	9		10				11	8										J Lovatt	11
1*	3		4	5	6	7	2	9	12	10				11	8										N Ashley	12
	3		**4**	**5**	**6**	**7**	**2**	**9**		**10**	**11**				**8**					**1**					**M Dimblebee**	**13**
	6		4	5		7	2	9	12	10				11*	8	1	3								M Heath	14
	3		4	5	2*	7	8	6	10	11					9	1		12							A Saunders	15
	3		**4***	**5**		**7**	**8**	**6**	**10**	**11**			**2**		**9**	**1**		**12**							**R Milford**	**16**
	4			5		7	8	6	10*	11	12		2		9	1	3								D Brazier	17
	4	3		5*		7	8	6	10	11			2	12	9	1									T Holbrook	18
	4	3		5		7	8	6	10	11			2		9	1									M James	19
1	4	3		5		7	8	6	10*	11			2	12	9										J Hough	20
1	4	3*	10	5		7	8	6		11			2	12	9										J Key	21
1	4		3	5		7	8	6		11	10		2		9										G Tyson	22
1	4		3	5		7	8	6		11	10		2*	12	9										K Walmsley	23
1	4	3*	2	5		7	8	6		11	10			12	9										C Seel	24
1	4		2	5		7	8	6		11	10*			3	9										D Shaw	25
1	4		2	5		7	8	6		11	10*			3	9			12							P Willis	26
1	**4**		**2**	**5**		**7**	**8**	**6**	**10**	**11***		**3**			**9**			**12**							**C Thomas**	**27**
1	4		2	5		7	8	6	10	11	12	3			9*										L Buksh	28
1	4		2	5		7	8	6	10	11		3			9										K Redfern	29
1	4		2	5		7	8	6	10*	11		3			12				9						K Hackett	30
1	2		4	5	3*	7	8	6	10	11		12							9						K Baker	31
	2		4	5		7	8	6	10	11		3							9	1					D Hutchinson	32
	2		4	5		7	8	6		11		3			10				9	1					A Seville	33
	2		4	5		7	8	6		11		3*		12	10				9	1					C Thomas	34
			4	5	2	7	8	6		10		3		11					9	1					M Scott	35
			4*	5	2	7	8	6		10		3		11	12				9	1					A Challinor	36
			4	5	6	7	8			10		3	2	11					9		1				J Ashwood	37
			4	5	3	7	8	6		10			2	11*	12				9		1				M Peck	38
			4*	5	3	7	12	6	8	10			2	11					9		1				A Saunders	39
				5	3	7	4		8*	10		11	2						9		1	6			C Downey	40
	6			5	3	7	4			10			2	11					9		1			8	T Mills	41
	6			5	3	7	4		9	10			2	11							1			8	J Bray	42
	6			5	3	7	4	2	9	10				11*							1		12	8	T Holbrook	43
	6			5	3	7	4	2	9	10									8		1		11		J Hunting	44
	2			5	3	7	4	6	9	10									8		1		11		N Ashley	45
	6				3	7	4	2	9	10											1	5	11	8*	L Burden	46
22	34	10	31	41	24	**42**	39	38	22	**42**	5	12	18	19	18	5	2	0	14	5	10	2	3	4	League Appearances	
							+3S		+3S		+5S	+1S		+6S	+4S			+2S					+1S			
1	1		1	1		1	1	1	1	1		1			1			1S							FA Cup Appearances	
1	3		3	3	2	3	2	3	2	3	2	1S	2		2	1		1S		1					Milk Cup Appearances	

Also Played: Bullock match 40, no.12. Collins match 46, no.12.

BOUNDARY PARK

Official Address: Boundary Park, Oldham, Greater Manchester. Telephone: 061-624 4972

Ground Capacity: 26,324

Record Attendance: 47,671 v. Sheffield Wednesday, F.A. Cup Round 4, 25 Jan 1930

Record Receipts: £44,998.30 v. Manchester City, Division 2, 20 April 1984

Size of Playing Area: 110yds × 74 yds

Season Tickets: £76.00 (stand), £47.50 (enclosure — adult; £28.50 juvenile/OAP), £43.50 (ground — adult, £28.50 juvenile/OAP)

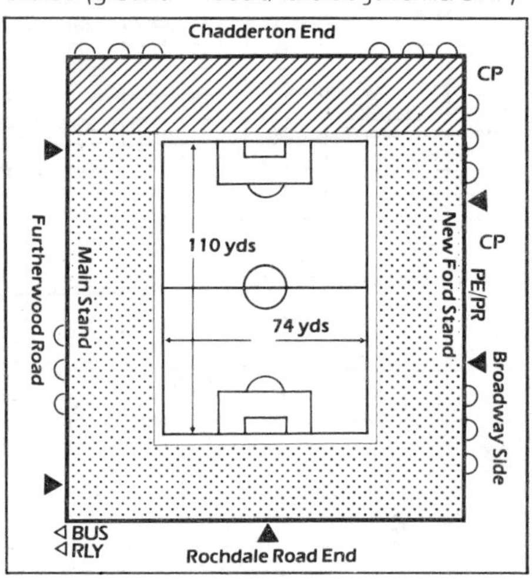

For key see page 12

Executive Box Season Tickets: V.P. Box £195.00, V.P. Stand £145.00

Cost of Stand Tickets: Centre £4.50, Wing £4.00, Juvenile/OAP £2.50; **Terraces:** Enclosures £2.50 (adult), £1.50 (juvenile/OAP), £2.30 (adult), £1.50 (child/OAP) Chadderton End

Match and Ticket Information: 12 days in advance postal or personal

Car Parking: Parking for 800 cars on site adjacent to ground

How to get to the ground

From North, East, South and West: Use Motorway M62 until junction 20, then A627 m to junction with A664. Leave Motorway and at roundabout take 2nd exit into Burnley Lane. In 0.3m turn left into Boundary Park Road for Oldham Athletic F.C.

ORIENT Division 3

Chairman
N Ovenden

Managing Director
B Winston

Directors
A Pincus
D L Weinrabe
A Harding
M Ovenden

Secretary
Miss Carol Stokes

Assistant Secretary
Mrs Sue Tilling

Manager
Frank Clark

Physiotherapist
Bill Songhurst

Commercial Manager
F Woolf (01-539 4483/4)

A position of eleventh in Division Three and instant removal from both major Cup competitions represents a very mediocre season for Orient and for Manager Frank Clark it is a case of hoping for better things in 1984-85. How many times can we hear that said? But again, we see a position of a friendly club with insufficient funds to buy players for a promotion challenge; bargain basement signings are the only chance.

In the League Orient started well enough and briefly held top place in mid-September but the state of affairs was flattering and inconsistency was the main characteristic of future matches. Few long runs without defeat were experienced and with this kind of form attendances were poor, which was not relieved by any kind of Cup run. Aldershot won the First Round tie of the Milk Cup on aggregate and at the same stage of the F.A. Cup Wimbledon visited Brisbane Road and survived by the odd goal in three in an exciting match. Home supporters would in the long run have preferred a dull match and victory. With the Associate Members Cup providing no fireworks the rest of the season was a struggle to keep interest alive.

With money scarce it can be assumed that faces will not change much at Brisbane Road and hopes for the coming season must rest on the premise that consistency shown by such people as Cornwell, Hales, Silkman and Godfrey will be repeated. The support locally is loyal and pleasant and they need Second Division football as their reward.

WLM

Back Row L to R: Bill Songhurst (Physiotherapist), Neil Banfield, Kevin Godfrey, Andy Sussex, Rhys Wilmot (on loan from Arsenal), Colin Foster, Pat Corbett, Mark McNeil, Pat Holland (Youth Coach), Jimmy Hallybone (Youth Coach). **Front Row:** Kevin Hales, Shaun Brooks, David Stride, John Cornwell, Frank Clark (Manager), Tommy Cunningham, Richard Cadette, Steve Castle, Barry Silkman.

'THE O'S'

Formed: 1881 **Turned Professional:** 1903 **Ltd Co:** 1906
Previous Names: 1881-86 Glyn Cricket and Football Club 1886-88 Eagle Football Club 1888-98 Orient Football Club 1898-1946 Clapton Orient 1946-67 Leyton Orient
Previous Managers: 1905-7 S Ormerod 1907-22 W Holmes 1923-8 P Proudfoot 1929-30 A Grimsdell 1930-1 P Proudfoot 1931-3 J Seed 1933-5 D Pratt 1935-9 P Proudfoot 1939-40 T Halsey 1940-5 W Wright 1945 W Hall 1945-6 W Wright 1946-8 C Hewitt 1948-9 N McBain 1949-56 A Stock 1956 L Gore (Caretaker) 1956-7 A Stock 1957-8 L Gore (Caretaker) 1958-9 A Stock 1961-3 J Carey 1963 L Gore (Caretaker) 1963-4 B Fenton 1964-5 L Gore (Caretaker) 1965 D Sexton 1965-6 L Gore (Caretaker) 1966-8 R Graham 1968-71 J Bloomfield 1971-26/8/77 G Petchey 12/8/77-27/8/77 J Bloomfield 23/9/81-12/10/81 P Went (20 days) 13/10/81-24/5/83 K Knighton
Honours: Division 3 Champions 1969-70
Division 3 (S) Champions 1955-56
League Career: Elected to Division 2 1905 Relegated to Division 3 (South) 1928-9 Promoted to Division 2 1955-6 Promoted to Division 1 1961-2 Relegated to Division 2 1962-3 Relegated to Division 3 1965-6 Promoted to Division 2 1969-70 Relegated to Division 3 1981-2
Colours: All red
Change Colours: All blue

CLUB RECORDS

Most Appearances for Club: Peter Allen: Football League 431 + F.A. Cup 25 + 24 League Cup **Total 480**
Most Capped Player: Tony Grealish, 8, Eire. **For England:** J Townrow, 2.
Record Goalscorer in a Match: Ron Heckman, 5 v Lovells Athletic (H) 7-1 1st Rnd F.A. Cup, 19.08.55
Record League Goalscorer in a season: Tom Johnston, 35, Div 2, 1957-8 **In all competitions:** Tom Johnston, 36, Football League 35 + 1 F.A. Cup **Total 36**
Record League Goalscorer in a career: Tom Johnston, 126 **In all competitions:** Tom Johnston, 128, Football League 126 + 2 F.A. Cup, 1956-8, 1959-61
Record Transfer Fee Received: £600,000 from Notts County for John Chiedozie, Aug 1981
Record Transfer Fee Paid: £150,000 to Tottenham Hotspur for Peter Taylor, Nov 1980
Best Performances: League: 22nd Div 1 1962-3 **F.A. Cup:** Semi-Final 1977-8 **League/Milk Cup:** 5th Round, 1963
Most League Points: 66 in Div 3, 1955-6 **Most League Goals:** 106, Div 3 (S) 1955-6
Record League Victory: 8-0 v Crystal Palace, Div 3, 12 Nov 1955
Record League Defeat: 1-7 v Torquay United (A), Div 3 (S), 16 April 1949, v Stoke City (A) Div 2, 7 Sept 1956

Club Statistician for The Directory: A Higgins

Programme Editor
Don Allen

Price	Number of Pages
50p	28

Subscriptions
Rates obtainable from shop manager

ORIENT

PLAYERS NAME Ht Wt Birthdate	Honours	Birthplace Transfers	Clubs	APPEARANCES League	Milk Cup	F.A.C.	A.M.C.	GOALS League	Milk Cup	F.A.C.	A.M.C.
GOALKEEPER											
**											
DEFENDERS											
Neil Banfield		London	Orient	6							
20.1.62											
Pat Corbett	E. Y	Hackney	Tottenham H. (A)	5				1			
6-0 11.0 12.2.63			Orient	43	2	1	1	1			
Tommy Cunningham*		London	Chelsea (A)								
6-0 11.3 7.12.55		F	Q.P.R.	27+3	1+1	3		2			
		£45,000	Wimbledon	99	11	6		12			
		£60,000	Orient	82	1	5		10	1		
Colin Foster		Chislehurst	Orient (A)	76+1	4	2		5	2		
6-4 13.10 16.7.64											
Kevin Hales		Dartford	Chelsea (A)	18+2		7		2			
5-7 10.4 13.1.61			Orient	43	2	1	1	2			
David Stride		Lymington	Chelsea (A)	35		2					
5-11 11.5 14.3.58		£90,000	Memphis								
		£25,000	Millwall	55		3	2				
			Orient								
MIDFIELD											
Shaun Brooks†	E. Y. S	London	Crystal Palace	47+7	6	4+2		4			
5-7 11.0 9.10.62			Orient	33+3		1	1	9			
Steve Castle		Ilford	Orient (A)								
17.5.66											
John Cornwell		Bethnal Green	Orient (A)	71+2	2	2		10	1		
13.10.64											
Barry Silkman	Div. 3. 76	London	Barnet								
5-8 10.13 29.6.52			Hereford U.	18+19	1	1		2			
		F	Crystal Palace	40+8	1	5		7			
		£53,000	Plymouth A.	14							
			Luton T. (L)	3							
		£60,000	Manchester C.	19	2			3			
		£50,000	Brentford	14	2			1			
		£5,000	Q.P.R.	22+1		2		2			
		£15,000	Orient	91+7	3	5	1	11			
FORWARDS											
Kevin Godfrey		Kennington	Orient (A)	144+15	6+1	15	1	31	1	2	
5-10 11.2 24.2.60											
Mark McNeil		Bethnal Green	Orient (A)	72+9	2	2+1	1	13			
5-10 10.5 3.12.62											
Andy Sussex		Islington	Orient (A)	56+5	+1	2	1	9			1

MONTHLY CONTRACT PLAYER 1984-85

Richard Cadette

NON-CONTRACT PLAYERS 1984-85

Terry Drew, Mike Barnes, Terry Drew, Mark Fackerell, Paul Rogan, Kevin Spires, Jimmy Tibbs

APPRENTICES

Lee Harvey (4 Subs Lg.), **Bob Quinell**

**Arsenal's young goalkeeper Rhys Wilmott has signed for Orient on loan for season 1984-85.

ORIENT

DIVISION THREE 11TH **FA CUP** 1ST ROUND **MILK CUP** 1ST ROUND

MATCH	DATE	COMPE-TITION	VENUE	OPPONENTS	RESULT	HALF TIME	L'GUE POS'N	GOALSCORERS	ATTEN-DANCE
1	A 27	CL	H	Bradford C	W2-0	2-0		Foster, Cunningham	2,675
2	**30**	**MC 1**	**A**	**Aldershot**	**L1-3**	**1-2**		**Houchen**	**1,978**
3	S 3	CL	A	Walsall	W1-0	0-0	5	Godfrey	3,003
4	7	CL	A	Lincoln C	L0-2	0-1			2,899
5	9	CL	H	Scunthorpe U	W1-0	1-0	2	Houchen	2,702
6	**13**	**MC 1**	**H**	**Aldershot**	**D3-3**	**1-2**		**Godfrey, Cornwell, Kitchen**	**2,236**
7	17	CL	A	Rotherham U	W1-0	0-0	1	Godfrey	5,518
8	23	CL	H	Bristol R	L0-1	0-1			4,206
9	O 1	CL	A	Wimbledon	D2-2	0-0	7	McNeil, Houchen	3,323
10	8	CL	A	Newport Co	D0-0	0-0	8		3,213
11	14	CL	H	Port Vale	W3-0	1-0		Hales, McNeil, Houchen (pen)	3,027
12	18	CL	H	Sheffield U	W2-0	1-0		Godfrey, Houchen	4,090
13	21	CL	A	Southend	L0-3	0-1			4,116
14	24	CL	H	Gillingham	D1-1	1-0		Silkman	4,013
15	29	CL	H	Exeter C	D2-2	1-1	7	Houchen (pen), Silkman	3,190
16	N 1	CL	A	Wigan Ath	W1-0	1-0		Cunningham	3,362
17	5	CL	A	Bolton W	L2-3	1-1	8	Godfrey, Houchen (pen)	5,859
18	12	CL	H	Brentford	W2-0	2-0	5	Godfrey, Brooks	3,650
19	**19**	**FAC 1**	**A**	**Wimbledon**	**L1-2**	**1-1**		**Smith (og)**	**4,330**
20	26	CL	A	Hull C	L1-2	0-0	7	Kitchen	6,857
21	D 3	CL	H	Preston NE	W2-1	0-1	6	Kitchen, McNeil	2,679
22	17	CL	H	Plymouth Arg	W3-2	1-2	6	McNeil, Cornwell 2	2,684
23	26	CL	A	Millwall	L3-4	2-1	5	Sussex, Kitchen, Godfrey	5,161
24	27	CL	H	AFC Bournemouth	W2-0	1-0	4	Cornwell, Sussex	4,077
25	31	CL	A	Oxford U	L2-5	1-4	7	Houchen (pen), Cornwell	11,126
26	J 2	CL	H	Burnley	L1-2	1-1	9	Houchen	4,470
27	7	CL	H	Walsall	L0-1	0-0	9		3,106
28	14	CL	A	Bradford C	L1-4	1-2	9	Cunningham	3,950
29	22	CL	H	Rotherham U	W2-1	2-0	7	Brooks, Houchen (pen)	2,204
30	27	CL	H	Wigan Ath	D0-0	0-0	7		2,123
31	F 4	CL	H	Wimbledon	L2-6	1-3	9	Kitchen, Corbett	3,377
32	11	CL	A	Bristol R	D0-0	0-0	10		4,741
33	18	CL	A	Exeter C	W4-3	1-1	10	Cunningham 3, Godfrey	2,347
34	**21**	**AMC 1**	**A**	**Brentford**	**L2-3**	**1-3**		**Kitchen 2**	**2,301**
35	26	CL	H	Southend U	W1-0	1-0		Brooks	3,001
36	M 3	CL	A	Sheffield U	L3-6	1-2	10	Silkman, Cornwell, Kitchen	10,021
37	6	CL	H	Bolton W	W2-1	0-0		Godfrey, Kitchen	2,449
38	10	CL	A	Brentford	D1-1	0-0	7	Kitchen	4,358
39	17	CL	H	Newport Co	D2-2	1-1	9	Godfrey, Silkman	2,355
40	31	CL	A	Gillingham	L1-3	0-1	10	Godfrey	3,090
41	A 7	CL	H	Lincoln C	D1-1	0-0	11	Brooks	2,174
42	9	CL	A	Port Vale	L0-2	0-2			3,169
43	14	CL	A	Preston NE	L1-3	0-0	12	Cornwell	3,144
44	21	CL	H	Millwall	W5-3	2-2	14	Cornwell, Kitchen 4	3,874
45	24	CL	A	AFC Bournemouth	L2-3	0-0		Kitchen (pen), Brooks	3,736
46	28	CL	H	Hull C	W3-1	1-1	13	Sussex 2, Brooks	3,020
47	M 1	CL	A	Scunthorpe U	L1-3	0-2		Brooks	2,284
48	5	CL	A	Burnley	W3-2	1-2	10	Sussex, Hales, Brooks (pen)	3,256
49	7	CL	H	Oxford U	L1-2	0-1	11	Brooks (pen)	5,655
50	12	CL	A	Plymouth Arg	L1-3	1-2	11	Sussex	7,664
								Av Home Att	**3,246**

Goal Scorers

League (71): Kitchen 12 (1 pen), Godfrey 10, Brooks 9 (2 pens), Houchen 9 (5 pens), Cornwell 7, Cunningham 6, Sussex 6, McNeil 4, Silkman 4, Hales 2, Corbett 1, Foster 1
FA Cup (1): Opponent 1
Milk Cup (4): Cornwell 1, Godfrey 1, Houchen 1, Kitchen 1
AMC (2): Kitchen 2

1983-84

Key	Cornwell	Corbett	Foster	Cunningham	Hales	Godfrey	Silkman	Houchen	Kitchen	McNeil	Roffey	Sussex	Brooks	Osgood	Harvey	Banfield	Wilkins **(L)**	Mancini	Shoemake	REFEREE	
1	2	3	4	5	6	7	8	9	10	11										L Shapter	1
1	**2**	**3**	**4**	**5**	**6**	**7**	**8**	**9**	**10***	**11**		**12**								**A Crickmore**	**2**
1	2	3	4	5	6	7	8	9		11	10									A Robinson	3
1	7	5	4		6*	10	8	9	12	11	2	3								T Jones	4
1	2	3	4	5	6	7	8	9		11	10									K Cooper	5
1	**2**	**3**	**4**	**5**	**6**	**7**	**8**	**9**	**12**	**11**	**10***									**K Baker**	**6**
1	2	3	4	5	6	7	8	9		11	10									I Hendrick	7
1	2	3	4*	5		7	8	9	10	11	6	12								TS Bune	8
1	2	3		5	4	7	8	9		11	6	10								C Thomas	9
1	2	3	8	5	6	7		9		11	10	4								T Spencer	10
1	2	3	8	5	6	7	4	9		11	10									ML James	11
1	2	3	8	5	6	7	4	9		11	10									MJ Taylor	12
1	2	3	8*	5	6	7	4	9		11	10		12							D Hedges	13
1	2	3		5	6*	7	4	9		11	10	8	12							B Hill	14
1	2	3		5	6	7	4	9		11	10*	8	12							A Seville	15
1	2	3	12	5	6	7*	4	9		11		8	10							J Hough	16
1	2	3		5	6	7	4	9		11†		8	10							D Owen	17
1	2*	3		5	6	7	4	9		11	12	8	10							M Bodenham	18
1	**2**	**3**		**5**	**6**	**7**	**4**	**9**	**10**		**11**		**8**							**D Reeves**	**19**
1	2	3		5	6	7	4	9	10		11		8							NL Wilson	20
1	2	3		5	6	7	4	9	12	11	10		8*							Alan Robinson	21
1	2	3			6	7		9	10	11	4	5	8							H Taylor	22
1	2	3			6	7		9	10	11	4	5	8							L Burden	23
1	2	3		5	6	7		9	10	11*	4	12	8							A Gunn	24
1	2	3		5	6	7		9		11	4	10	8							B Stevens	25
1	2	3		5	6	7	4	9	10		11		8							D Letts	26
1	2	3		5	6*	7	4	9	10		11	12	8							I Borrett	27
1	2	3		5	6	7	10	9		11	4		8							K Redfern	28
1	2	3		5	6		7	9	10	11	4		8							E Read	29
1	2	3		5	6	12	7	9*	10	11	4		8							J Martin	30
1	2	3		5	6	12	7	9	10	11	4		8*							J Hunting	31
1	2			5	6	9	7		10	11	4		8	3						J Bray	32
1	2			5	6	9	7		10*	11	4†	12	8	3						M Robinson	33
1		2			6	9	7	12	10	11*	4	5	8	3						M Bodenham	34
1	2				6	9	7	12	10	11*	4	5	8	3						H King	35
1	2	4			6	9	7		10	11*		5	8	3	12					J Lovatt	36
1	2	4			6	9	7	12	10	11*			8	3		5				D Brazier	37
1	2	4		5	6	9	7		10*	12	11		8	3						M Dimblebee	38
1	2	4		5	6	9	7		10			11	8	3						D Hedges	39
1	6	4		5		9	7		10			11	8	3		2				K Baker	40
1	6	4		5	2	9	7		10	12		11*	8				3			K Cooper	41
1	6	4		5	2	9	7		12			11	8*				3	10		K Barratt	42
1	6	4		5		9*	7		10			12	8			2	3	11		M Scott	43
1	6	4			2		7		10	11		9	8	5			3			Alan Robinson	44
	6	4			2		7		10	11		9	8	5			3		1	T Bune	45
	6*	4			2		7		10	11		9	8	5	12		3		1	V Callow	46
		4			2		7		10	11		9	8	5	12	6*	3		1	J Ashworth	47
1		4		3	6	11	8			9		10	7			2	5			R Nixon	48
1		4		5	2	6	7		10	11		9	8				3			L Shapter	49
		4		5	2	10	7*			11		9	8		12	6	3		1	A Seville	50
42	42	43	10	36	43	39	41	28	26	37	28	24	33	12	0	6	10	2	4	League Appearances	
			+1S			+2S		+2S	+3S	+2S	+1S	+5S	+3S		+4S						
1	1	1		1	1	1	1	1	1		1		1							FA Cup Appearances	
2	2	2	2	2	2	2	2	2	1+1S	2	1	1S								Milk Cup Appearances	
1		1			1	1	1	1S	1	1	1	1	1	1						AM Cup Appearances	

LEYTON STADIUM, BRISBANE ROAD

Official Address: Leyton Stadium, Brisbane Road, Leyton, London E10 5NE. Telephones: 01-539 2223/4

Telegraphic: The Orient Leyton E10

Ground Capacity: 26,500 (7,171 seats)

Record Attendance: 34,345 v. West Ham U, F.A. Cup Round 4, 25 Jan 1964

Record Receipts: £41,765.20 v. West Ham U, F.A. Cup Round 4, 26 Jan 1980

Size of Playing Area: 110yds × 75 yds

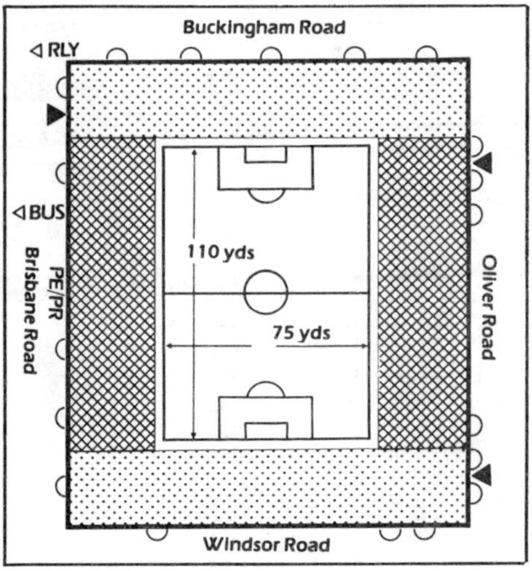

For key see page 12

Season Tickets: Stand (Main): £95, £75 (OAP/children) (Centre), £75 (£65 children/OAP) (Wing); Unreserved seats of Ground: £52 (£32 OAP, £25 children)

Executive Box Season Tickets: Double O' Directors Box, Seats £200

Cost of Stand Tickets: £5.50, £3.80; **Ground:** £2.60 (£1.60 OAP/Juveniles)

Match and Ticket Information: Bookable at least two weeks in advance.

Car Parking: Street parking around the ground. NCP five minutes from Brisbane Road (off Oliver Road).

How to get to the ground

From North and West: Use A406 North Circular Road (S.P. Chelmsford) to Edmonton, then in 2.6m at roundabout take 3rd exit A112 (S.P. Leyton). Pass Leyton Midland Road Station and in 0.5m turn right into Windsor Road, then turn left into Brisbane Road for Orient F.C.
From East: Use A12 (S.P. London then City) to Leytonstone and follow signs Hackney into Grove Road. At Leyton cross main road and forward into Ruckholt Road, then turn right then left into Leyton High Road and in 0.2m turn left into Buckingham Road then right into Brisbane Road for Orient F.C.
From South: Use A102M through Blackwall Tunnel and follow signs Newmarket A102 to join A11 to Stratford. Follow signs Stratford Station into Leyton Road A112, to Leyton Station then keep forward. In 0.4m keep left then turn right then left into Leyton High Road and proceed as from East.

OXFORD UNITED Division 2

President
The Duke of Marlborough

Chairman
I R Maxwell MC

Directors
W Black
G E Coppock
J Devaney
H Kimber
Miss G N Maxwell
I R C Maxwell
P D McGeough
P Reeves
W H Reeves
L Town

Secretary
Jim Hunt

Commercial Manager
F M Ward (0865-64615)

Manager
Jim Smith

Coach
Ray Graydon

Chief Scout
Maurice Evans

Physiotherapist
Ken Fish

Club Captain
Malcolm Shotten

Groundsman
L Bateman

One of Oxford's finest seasons on record included runs to the quarter-finals of the Milk Cup, the fifth round of the F.A. Cup and the Championship of the Third Division — only the second club to win that title for a second time.

Unbeaten in their opening nine League games, Oxford soared to the top of the table and were only occasionally dislodged throughout the season.

Their first major Cup victims were Second Division pacemakers Newcastle United. Even Kevin Keegan couldn't save the Geordies from a 1-2 defeat, and elimination from the Milk Cup, at The Manor.

Next came Leeds, fading giants 'tis true. After a 1-1 draw at Elland Road, Oxford coasted to an easy 4-1 win.

It seemed their chances of ousting Manchester United had gone after the sides had drawn 1-1 at The Manor. But Oxford held out for another draw at Old Trafford and then finally killed off the Reds in a third meeting at The Manor.

Oxford were leading Everton 1-0 in the quarter final with only nine minutes left then lapsed to give the Toffees an equaliser. That Cup run ended with a heavy defeat at Everton.

By then they were already through to the fourth round of the F.A. Cup, having disposed of Peterborough, Reading and Burnley. Fourth Division Blackpool were then beaten at The Manor but all the Cup excitement came to an end with a heavy defeat by Sheffield Wednesday in round five.

Manager Jim Smith faced problems when Andy Thomas broke a leg in January and he didn't find it easy to find a replacement. He eventually signed Peter Rhoades-Brown from Chelsea and, just to bolster his squad as the promotion battle warmed up, he secured the service's of that great former England defender Colin Todd, from Nottingham Forest.

Mr Smith also signed that prolific scorer John Aldridge from Newport for £70,000. Aldridge had scored 26 goals for Newport but an injury delayed his Oxford debut.

Oxford opened up such a large lead that promotion became a mere formality. It was hoped they might become the first club to break the 100 points barrier in League football but York City pipped them to that honour with Oxford quite content to end up with 95.

Remaining unbeaten in their final 13 games, Oxford repeated their 1968 Third Division Championship success, this time winning it with eight points to spare over Wimbledon.

Oxford were easily the best side in the Third Division, giving the indications that they will also be a power in Division Two in 1984/85.

Back Row L to R: John Aldridge, Neil Whatmore, Steve Hardwick, John Butcher, Gary Briggs, John Trewick, Bobby McDonald. **Middle Row:** Ken Fish (Trainer), Mick Vinter, David Langan, Peter Rhoades-Brown, Andy Thomas, David Fogg, Paul Hinshelwood, Steve Biggins, Trevor Hebberd, George Lawrence, Ray Graydon (Coach), Maurice Evans (Chief Scout). **Front Row:** Kevin Brock, Les Phillips, Malcolm Shotton, Jim Smith (Manager), Gary Barnett, Mark Jones, Sean Reck.

OXFORD UNITED F.C.

Sponsored by
BPCC

'THE U's'

Formed: 1896 **Turned Professional:** 1949 **Ltd Co:** 1949
Previous Names: Headington United (until 1960)
Previous Managers: Since 1962:
Arthur Turner Ron Saunders Gerry Summers Mike Brown Bill Asprey Ian Greaves
Honours: Division Three Champions 1967,8, 1983-4
League Career: Elected to Division Four 1962 Promoted to Division Three 1965
Promoted to Division Two 1968 Relegated to Division Three 1976 Promoted to Division Two 1984
Colours: Yellow shirts with blue trim, blue shorts, yellow stockings
Change Colours: All white

CLUB RECORDS

Most Appearances for Club: John Shuker, 480, 1962-77
Most Capped Player: Dave Roberts, 6(17), Wales **For England:** None
Record Goalscorer in a Match: No one more than four
Record League Goalscorer in a season: Colin Booth, 23, Div 4, 1964-5 **In all competitions:** Steve Biggins, 24 (League 19, F.A. Cup 2, Milk Cup 3)
Record League Goalscorer in a career: Graham Atkinson, 73, 1962-73 **In all competitions:** Peter Foley, 87, (League 70, F.A. Cup 9, League/Milk Cup 8) 1974-83
Record Transfer Fee Received: £100,000 from Watford for Les Taylor, Nov 1980
Record Transfer Fee Paid: £75,000 to Cardiff City for Andy McCulloch, July 1974
Best Performances: League: 8th Div 2 1972-3 **F.A. Cup:** 6th Round 1963-4 (best by Div 4 club) **League/Milk Cup:** 5th Round 1969-70, 1983-4
Most League Points: 95 in Div 3, 1983-4 **Most League Goals:** 91, Div 3, 1983-4
Record League Victory: 7-0 v Barrow, Div 4, 19 Dec 1964
Record League Defeat: 0-5 v Cardiff City, Div 2, 8 Feb 1969, v Cardiff City, Div 2, 12 Sept 1973

Club Statistician for the Directory: Mick Brown

Programme Editor
Mick Brown

Price	Number of Pages
50p	28

Subscriptions
£16.50 per season (U.K. postage paid); Overseas rates on request

OXFORD UNITED

PLAYERS NAME Ht Wt Birthdate	Honours	Birthplace Transfers	Clubs	APPEARANCES League	Milk Cup	F.A.C.	A.M.C.	GOALS League	Milk Cup	F.A.C.	A.M.C.
GOALKEEPER											
Steve Hardwick	E. Y. Div. 3. 84	Mansfield	Chesterfield	38	2	4					
5-11 13.0 6.9.56		£80,000	Newcastle U.	92	3	4					
		£20,000	Oxford U.	64	11	7					
DEFENDERS											
Gary Briggs	Div. 3. 84	Leeds	Middlesbrough (A)								
6-3 12.10 21.6.59		£12,500	Oxford U.	265+2	28	18	1	9			
David Fogg		Liverpool	Wrexham	159+2	4	13+					
5-10½ 11.8 28.5.51		F	Oxford U.	287+4	23+	16		16	2	2	
Paul Hinshelwood	Div. 2. 79.	Bristol	Crystal Palace	271+5	18	24		23	2	1	
6-0 12.6 14.5.56	Div. 3. 84.	F	Oxford U.	43	10	7	1		1		
	E. U.21(2).										
	FAYC. 72. Div. 3.										
	84. FC. 75										
David Langan	Ei.(15)	Dublin	Derby Co. (A)	143	6	6					
5-10 11.2 15.2.57		£350,000	Birmingham C.	92	6	4				1	
			Oxford U.								
Bobby McDonald	FAYC. 72.	Aberdeen	Aston Villa (A)	33+6	4	3		3			
5-10 12.1 13.4.55	Lg.C. 75.	£40,000	Coventry C.	161	11+	7		14		1	
	Div. 3. 84	£270,000	Manchester C.	96	5	10+		11	1	4	
			Oxford U.	39	10	7	1	4	3	4	
Malcolm Shotton*	Div. 3. 84	Newcastle	Leicester C. (A)								
6-3 13.12 16.2.57		F	Nuneaton B.								
		£15,000	Oxford U.	167	25	17	1	11	2	1	
MIDFIELD											
Steve Aries		Oxford	Oxford U.								
6.0 11.9 14.8.65											
Kevin Brock†	E. U.21(3). S	Middleton	Oxford U.	144+11	20+	12+		19	4	1	
5-9 10.12 9.9.62		Stoney									
Trevor Hebberd	Div. 3. 84	Winchester	Southampton (A)	69+28	9+1	4+3		7	3		
5-11½ 11.4 19.6.58			Bolton W. (L)	6							
			Leicester C. (L)	4							
		£80,000	Oxford U.	100	14	10	1	23		1	
Mark Jones		Berinsfield	Oxford U. (A)	87+18	9+2	5+1		7			
5-8 9.12 26.9.61											
Les Phillips		Lambeth	Birmingham C. (A)	36+6	7+1	1		3	1		
5-8 10.6 7.1.63		£5,000	Oxford U.	2+4							
Andy Thomas	Div. 3. 84	Oxford	Oxford U. (A)	76+19	13+	9		29	4	3	
6-0 10.10 16.12.62			Fulham (L)	3+1							
			Derby Co. (L)	0+1							
John Trewick	E. Y. S	Bedlington	W.B.A. (A)	84+12	10+	2		11			
5-10 10.13 3.6.57		£250,000	Newcastle U.	76+2	2	7		8			
			Oxford U.	3							
FORWARDS											
John Aldridge		Liverpool	South Liverpool								
5-11 10.4 18.9.58		£3,500	Newport Co.	159+11	11	12+		69	5	7	
		£78,000	Oxford U.	5+3				4			
Gary Barnett		Stratford	Coventry C. (A)								
5-5 9.4 11.3.63		F	Oxford U.	36+5	6+2	3	1	9			
			Wimbledon (L)	5				1			
Steve Biggins	Div. 3. 79. 84	Walsall	Hednesford T.								
6-0 11.12 20.6.54		£6,000	Shrewsbury T.	140+6	7	11		41	2	3	
		F	Oxford U.	43+9	11+	4+1	1	20	4	2	
Billy Hamilton	N.I.(35).	Belfast	Linfield								
6-1 12.0 9.5.57	U.23(1).	£25,000	Q.P.R.	9+3		1		2			
	Div. 3. 82	£38,000	Burnley	200	16	22	3	58	5	7	
		Player Exchange	Oxford U.								
George Lawrence	Div. 3. 84	London	Southampton (A)	7+3	2+1			1			
5-10 12.2 14.9.62		£45,000	Oxford U.	71	11	10		22	1	1	
Peter Rhoades-Brown	Div. 3. 84	Hampton	Chelsea (A)	86+10	4	7+2		4		1	
5-9 11.4 2.1.62			Oxford U.	19+1		2	1	4			

NON-CONTRACT PLAYERS 1984-85: Colin Fleet, Terry Muckelberg, Wayne Cooney, Stuart Fletcher, Jason Gay, Paul Griffiths, Duncan Mitchell, Gerry O'Loughlin, Paul Rayson

APPRENTICE: Sean Reck

OXFORD UNITED

DIVISION THREE 1ST **FA CUP** 5TH ROUND **MILK CUP** 5TH ROUND

MATCH	DATE	COMPE-TITION	VENUE	OPPONENTS	RESULT	HALF TIME	L'GUE POS'N	GOALSCORERS	ATTEN-DANCE
1	A 27	CL	H	Lincoln C	W3-0	1-0		Biggins, Whatmore, Lawrence	4,239
2	S 3	CL	A	Wigan Ath	W2-0	1-0	2	Briggs, Vinter	2,697
3	7	CL	A	Scunthorpe U	D0-0	0-0			3,516
4	10	CL	H	Burnley	D2-2	0-0	6	Thomas, Lawrence	5,637
5	17	CL	A	Gillingham	W3-2	3-1	3	Hebberd, Barnett, Biggins	3,370
6	24	CL	H	Millwall	W4-2	2-1	2	Lawrence 2, Barnett, Jones	5,543
7	28	CL	H	Walsall	W6-3	4-1		Lawrence 2, Thomas 2, Barnett 2	5,720
8	O 1	CL	A	Preston NE	W2-1	2-1	1	Thomas, Biggins	4,665
9	8	CL	H	Brentford	W2-1	0-0	1	Biggins 2	7,140
10	15	CL	A	Plymouth Arg	L1-2	1-0	1	Lawrence	2,990
11	19	CL	H	Bradford C	W2-0	1-0		Hebberd 2 (1 pen)	5,624
12	22	CL	A	AFC Bournemouth	L1-2	0-1	1	Barnett	4,758
13	29	CL	H	Hull C	D1-1	0-1	1	Lawrence	7,884
14	N 1	CL	A	Wimbledon	L1-3	0-2		Thomas	3,821
15	5	CL	H	Sheffield U	D2-2	1-1	3	Barnett, Biggins	7,514
16	12	CL	A	Port Vale	W3-1	1-0	2	Thomas, Hebberd 2 (1 pen)	3,927
17	26	CL	H	Newport Co	W2-0	2-0	1	Thomas, Vinter	6,330
18	D 2	CL	A	Southend U	W1-0	1-0		Biggins	2,559
19	17	CL	A	Rotherham U	W2-1	0-1	1	Whatmore 2	4,000
20	26	CL	H	Bristol R	W3-2	2-1	1	Vinter 2, Brock	12,748
21	27	CL	A	Bolton W	L0-1	0-0	1		11,059
22	31	CL	H	Orient	W5-2	4-1	1	Hebberd 2 (2 pens), Brock, Vinter 2	11,126
23	J 2	CL	A	Exeter C	L1-3	0-0	1	Barnett	4,557
24	14	CL	A	Lincoln C	D2-2	2-2	2	Hebberd, Vinter	3,345
25	F 4	CL	H	Preston NE	W2-0	0-0	3	Hebberd, Vinter	9,105
26	11	CL	A	Millwall	L1-2	1-1	4	Cusack (og)	4,974
27	15	CL	H	Wimbledon	W2-0	2-0	3	McDonald (pen), Morris (og)	7,640
28	25	CL	H	AFC Bournemouth	W3-2	1-1	3	Brock, Biggins, Rhoades-Brown	6,535
29	28	CL	A	Hull C	W1-0	1-0		Vinter	11,790
30	M 3	CL	A	Bradford C	D2-2	1-0	1	Rhoades-Brown, Biggins	7,322
31	6	CL	A	Sheffield U	W2-1	1-1		Biggins 2	17,914
32	10	CL	H	Port Vale	W2-0	2-0	1	Rhoades-Brown, McDonald (pen)	7,645
33	14	CL	H	Gillingham	L0-1	0-1			7,433
34	17	CL	A	Brentford	W2-1	0-1	1	Hebberd, Biggins	5,936
35	24	CL	H	Plymouth Arg	W5-0	2-0	1	Biggins 3, McDonald 2 (2 pens)	7,777
36	27	CL	A	Barnsley	D1-1	0-1		Jones	7,993
37	31	CL	H	Scunthorpe U	W1-0	1-0	1	Shotton	6,747
38	A 7	CL	A	Walsall	W1-0	0-0	1	Rhoades-Brown	10,163
39	14	CL	H	Southend U	W2-1	2-0	1	Biggins 2	7,538
40	20	CL	H	Bolton W	W5-0	4-0		Hebberd, Briggs, McElhinney (og), Biggins,	
								Aldridge	9,788
41	21	CL	A	Bristol R	D1-1	0-1	1	Aldridge	6,397
42	28	CL	A	Newport Co	D1-1	1-1	1	Aldridge	4,562
43	M 2	CL	H	Wigan Ath	D0-0	0-0			8,967
44	5	CL	H	Exeter C	D1-1	1-0	1	Briggs	8,056
45	7	CL	A	Orient	W2-1	1-0	1	Aldridge, Vinter	5,655
46	12	CL	H	Rotherham U	W3-2	1-1	1	Biggins, Lawrence, Vinter	9,852

A SPECIAL CUP TRIBUTE TO OXFORD UNITED ON PAGE 568

Av Home Att **7,682**

Goal Scorers

League (91): Biggins 19, Hebberd 11 (4 pens), Vinter 11, Lawrence 9, Barnett 7, Thomas 7, Aldridge 4, McDonald 4 (4 pens), Rhoades-Brown 4, Briggs 3, Brock 3, Whatmore 3, Jones 2, Shotton 1, oppenents 3

1983-84

Hardwick	Hinshelwood	Fogg	Thomas	Briggs	Shotton	Lawrence	Whatmore	Biggins	Hebberd	Brock	Vinter	Grant	McDonald	Barnett	Jones	Train	Trewick **(L)**	Rhoades-Brown	Todd	Phillips	Aldridge	Butcher	Gibson		**REFEREE**	
1	2	3	4	5	6	7	8	9	10	11															M Dimblebee	1
1	2		4	5*	6	7	8	9	10	11	12	3													MG Peck	2
1	2		4	5	6	7	8*	12	10	11	9	3													N Midgley	3
1	2		4	5	6	7		9	10	11	8		3												H Taylor	4
1	2		4	5	6	7		9	10	11			3	8*	12										R Lewis	5
1	2		4	5	6	7		9*	10	11			3	8	12										A Robinson	6
1	2		4	5	6	7		9	10	11			3*	8	12										A Crickmore	7
1	2		4	5	6	7		9	10	11			3	8											R Bridges	8
1	2		4	5	6	7		9	10	11			3	8											RG Milford	9
1	2		4	5	6	7		9	10	11			3	8											J Deakin	10
1	2		4	5	6	7		9	10	11			3	8											D Axcell	11
1	2*		4	5	6	7		9	10	11			3	8	12										K Salmon	12
1		2	4	5	6	7	9		10	11			3	8											L Shapter	13
1	2		4	5	6	7	9*		10	11			3	8	12										A Gunn	14
1	2		4		6		9	12	10	11*	8		3	7	5										JE Martin	15
1	2		4	5	6	7		8	10	11	9		3												J Key	16
1	2		4	5	6	7		8	10	11	9		3												A Buksh	17
1	2		4	5	6			8	10	11	9		3	7*	12										M James	18
1	2		4	5		7	12	8	10	11	9		3	6*											RA Banks	19
1	2		4	5	6	7		8	10	11	9		3												J Ashworth	20
1	2		4	5	6	7*	12	8	10	11	9		3												A Saunders	21
1	2		4	5	6	7	8		10	11	9	3													B Stevens	22
1	2		4*	5	6		8	12	10	11	9	3		7											R Milford	23
1	2			5	6	7		8	10	11	9		3			4									J Hough	24
1	2			5	6	7		12	8	10	9		3				4	11*							J Moules	25
1	2			5	6	7		12	8	10	9		3				4	11*							I Borrett	26
1	2			5	6	7		11	8	10	9*		3				4	12							A Seville	27
1	2			5	6	7	9*	8	10	4			3	12				11							G Napthine	28
1	2				6	7	8		10	4	9		3					11	5						D Scott	29
1	2			12	6	7	9	8	10	4			3					11*	5						M Heath	30
1	2			12	6	7		8	10	4	9		3					11*	5						D Owen	31
1	2			5		7		8	10	4			3	9				11	6						D Vickers	32
1	2*			5		7		8	10	4			3	9	12			11	6						M Robinson	33
1				5	2			8	10	4			3	9	7			11	6						J Martin	34
1	2				6			8	10	4*	9		3		7			11	5	12					A Ward	35
1	2				6			8	10	4	9		3		7			11*	5	12					A Challinor	36
1	2				6			8	10	4	9		3		7			11	5						K Cooper	37
1	2				6			8	10	4	9*		3		7			11	5		12				A Robinson	38
1	2				6			8	10	4	9		3		7			11	5						J Bray	39
1	2			5	6			8	10	4*			3		7			11		12	9				A Gunn	40
1	2				6			8	10	4	9*		3		7				5	11	12				L Burden	41
1	2			5	6			8	10	4			3		7			11			9				E Read	42
1	2			5	6	7		8*	10				3		4			11		12	9				M Taylor	43
1	2*	3		5	6	7		12	10	4				8	11						9				M Scott	44
1				5	6	2*		12	10	4	8				7			11		3	9				L Shapter	45
1	2			5	6	7		8	10	4	9		3					11*			12				D Axcell	46
46	43	3	23	36	43	34	11	35	**46**	45	25	4	39	18	13	1	3	19	12	2	5				League Appearances	
				+2S			+2S	+7S			+1S			+1S	+7S			+1S		+4S	+3S					

THE MANOR GROUND

Official Address: Manor Ground, Headington, Oxford. Telephone: (0865) 61503

Ground Capacity: 14,500

Record Attendance: 22,730 v. Preston North End, F.A. Cup Round 6, 29 Feb 1964

Record Receipts: £56,528 v. Manchester United, Milk Cup Round , 1984

Size of Playing Area: 112yds × 78 yds

Season Tickets: Stand: £89.00 adult, £53.50 juvenile/OAP; Ground £53.50 adult, £26.75 juvenile/OAP

Executive Box Season Tickets: Limited number of places. Details from club

Cost of Stand Tickets: £5.00 (adults), £3.00 (juvenile/OAP); **Terraces:** £3.00 (adults), £1.50 (juveniles/OAP)

Match and Ticket Information: Bookable 14 days in advance subject to availability

Car Parking: Street parking near ground

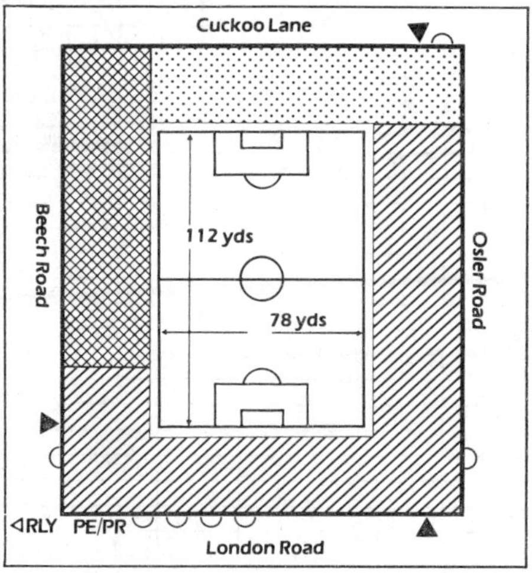

For key see page 12

How to get to the ground

From North: Follow signs Ring Road, London, A40, then at roundabout take 4th exit A420 S.P. Headington. In 0.8m turn right into Sandfield Road, then turn right into Beech Road to Oxford United F.C.
From East: Use Motorway M40 then A40 and at roundabout take 2nd exit A420 S.P. Headington. In 0.8m turn right into Sandfield Road, then turn right into Beech Road for Oxford United F.C.
From South: Use A34 then follow signs Bypass, London A4142, then at roundabout take 1st exit A420 S.P. Headington. In 0.8m turn right into Sandfield Road then turn right into Beech Road for Oxford United F.C.
From West: Use A420 into Oxford, then follow signs London along Headington Road. In 2m turn left into Sandfield Road then turn right into Beech Road for Oxford United F.C.

PETERBOROUGH UNITED Division 4

President
G H Woodcock

Chairman
W O'Neill Wilde

Vice-Chairman
J C Duddington

Directors
S E Nicholas
A H Hand
G H Woodcock
D E Ringham
S E Kendrick

General Manager/Secretary
A V Blades

Manager
John Wile

Club Coach/Physiotherapist
Bill Harvey

Commercial Manager
Ellis Stafford (0733 69760)

With John Wile, a well respected 'old boy', back at the club after a successful playing career at West Bromwich Albion, the season started with an air of optimism.

A well deserved draw at Stoke brought the First Division club to London Road but a good game was lost 1-2. However, the cup fighting spirit remained and only one more league game was lost before Christmas. The all conquering Oxford United knocked 'Posh' out of the FA Cup but when Colchester United were beaten on Boxing day the club moved into second place.

With fortunes swinging violently six games brought just three points, then an unbeaten run of another half dozen games lifted hopes again only to be dashed in a controversial defeat against Aldershot which frustrated Ray Hankin so much that he finished the evening dismissed for the fourth time in the season.

Promotion was now out of reach but a 6-0 victory over arch rivals and neighbours Northampton Town gave the season a happier end and, although supporters felt a little 'flat' as the season closed, it should be noted that 'Posh' finished in the 'magical' seventh position.

Only once in the last ten years has the club finishing seventh missed promotion the following year and not many people know that.

Mick Robinson, The League Directory's Statistician for the Club

Back Row L to R: Phillip Chard, Errington Kelly, Kenny Beech, Bryan Klug, Martin Pike, Trevor Quow. **Middle Row:** Jimmy Holmes (Assistant Manager), Alan Waddle, Neil Firm, David Seaman, Ray Hankin, Trevor Slack, Bill Harvey (Physio/Coach). **Front Row:** Gary Worrall, Patrick Rayment, John Wile (Manager), Francis Cassidy, David Johnson.

'THE POSH'

Formed: 1934 **Turned Professional:** 1934 **Ltd Co:** 1934
Previous Managers: 1934-6 Jock Porter 1936-7 Fred Taylor 1937-8 V Poulter 1938-48 Sam Maden 1948-50 Jack Blood 1950-2 Bob Gurney 1952-4 Jack Fairbrother 1954-8 George Swindon 1958-62 Jimmy Hagen 1962-4 Jack Fairbrother 1964-7 Gordon Clark 1967-9 Norman Rigby 1969-72 Jim Iley 1972-7 Noel Cantwell 1977-8 John Barnwell 1978-9 Billy Hails 1979-82 Peter Morris 1982-3 Martin Wilkinson
Honours: Champions, Div 4, 1960-1
League Career: Elected to Division 4 1960 Promoted to Division 3 1960-1 Demoted to Division 4 for financial irregularities 1968 Promoted to Division 3 1973-4 Relegated to Division 4 1978-9
Colours: Royal blue shirts, white shorts, blue stockings with white tops
Change Colours: All yellow with blue trim

CLUB RECORDS

Most Appearances for Club: Tommy Robson: Football League 440 + 42 sub + F.A. Cup 43 + 2 sub + 31 League Cup + 1 sub **Total 514 + 45 subs**
Most Capped Player: Tony Millington, 8, Wales **For England:** None
Record Goalscorer in a Match: Laxton, 6 v Rushden, F.A. Cup 3rd Qual. Round, 06.10.45
Record League Goalscorer in a season: Terry Bly, 52, Div 4, 1960-1 **In All Competitions:** Terry Bly, 54 (League 52, F.A. Cup 2) 1960-1
Record League Goalscorer in a career: Jim Hall, 122, 1967-75 **In All Competitions:** Jim Hall (League 122, F.A. Cup 11, League Cup 4)
Record Transfer Fee Received: £110,000 from Blackpool for Bobby Doyle, July 1979
Record Transfer Fee Paid: £60,000 to West Ham United for Bill Green, July 1978
Best Performances: League: 4th Div 3 1977-8 **F.A. Cup:** 6th Round, 1965 **League/Milk Cup:** Semi-Final 1966
Most League Points: 82 in Div 4, 1981-2 **Most Goals in Season:** 134, Div 4, 1960-1
Record League Victory: 8-1 v Oldham Athletic, Div 4, 26 Nov 1969; 7-0 v Barrow, Div 4, 9 Oct 1971
Record League Defeat: 0-6 v Notts County, Div 4, 30 Jan 1971
Club Statistician for the Directory: Mick Robinson

Programme Editor
Russell Plummer (Peterborough 68803)

Price	Number of Pages
40p	24

Subscriptions

PETERBOROUGH UNITED

PLAYERS NAME Ht Wt Birthdate	Honours	Birthplace Transfers	Clubs	APPEARANCES League	Milk Cup	F.A.C.	A.M.C.	GOALS League	Milk Cup	F.A.C.	A.M.C.
GOALKEEPER											
David Seaman†		Rotherham	Leeds U. (A)								
6-2 13.0 19.9.63		£4,000	Peterborough U.	83	8	5					
DEFENDERS											
Neil Firm*		Bradford	Leeds U. (A)	11+1							
6-3 13.7 23.1.58			Oldham A. (L)	9							
		£10,000	Peterborough U.	63+1	3+1	4	1	2			
Jimmy Holmes	Ei (30)	Dublin	Coventry C. (A)	122+6	9	11+		7			
5-9 11.7 11.11.53		£100,000	Tottenham H.	81	2	9		2			
			Vancouver WH								
		F	Leicester C.	2							
		F	Brentford	4							
		F	Torquay U.	25				3			
		F	Peterborough U.	20+1			1	2			
Pat Rayment		Peterborough	Peterborough U. (A)	24+5	1+2		+1	3			
5-11 12.3 11.4.65											
Trevor Slack	E. Y	Peterborough	Peterborough U. (A)	121	13	9	1	11			
6-2 12.2 26.9.61											
John Wile		Sherburn	Durham C.								
6-1½ 12.0 9.3.47			Sunderland								
			Peterborough U.	116+2	8	6		7			
		£30,000	W.B.A.	499+1	42	42		24	2	2	
		F	Peterborough U.	32	4	1		2			
MIDFIELD											
Ken Beech		Stoke	Port Vale (A)	169+6	9	11+		17	1	3	
5-7 10.2 28.5.63		£10,000	Walsall	78+1	4	6		5			
			Peterborough U.	38	2	1	1	3			
Francis Cassidy	FAYC 82	Watford	Watford (A)				+1				
5-9 10.12 20.8.64			Plymouth A. (L)	1							
Phil Chard		Corby	Nottingham F. (N-C)								
5-8 11.3 16.10.60			Peterborough U.	128+19	13+	7	1	17	1	1	
Bryan Klug	E. Y	Coventry	Ipswich (A)								
5-8 10.10 8.10.60			Wimbledon (L)	10+1							
		F	Chesterfield	27+7	3	1	1	2			
Martin Pike		South Shields	W.B.A. (A)								
5-9 10.11 21.10.64			Peterborough U	28+7	4	1		1	2		1
Trevor Quow*		Peterborough	Peterborough U. (A)	127+10	12+	8+1	1	13		2	1
5-6 10.4 28.9.60											
FORWARDS											
Ray Hankin	E. U.23(3), Y	Wallsend	Burnley (A)	110+2	12	5		37	4	1	
6-2 14.0 2.2.56		£180,000	Leeds U.	82+1	15	1		32	3		
		£300,000	Vancouver WH								
		£85,000	Middlesbrough	19+2	2	3		1	1		
		£10,000	Peterborough U.	25+2	2			7			
David Johnson	FAYC 82	Gloucester	Redhill								
5-8 10.10 26.12.62			Watford	4+3	1+1		1+1				
Errington Kelly		St Vincent	Ledbury T.								
5-8 11.7 8.4.58			Bristol R.	12+6				3			
			Lincoln C.	6+2							
			Bristol C.	4+1				1			
			Coventry C.								
			Peterborough U. (L)	11				7			
Alan Waddle		Wallsend	Halifax T.	33+6				4			
6-3 13.0 9.6.54			Liverpool	11+5	3	2	+1	1			
		£45,000	Leicester C.	11				1			
			Swansea C.	83+7	9	7		34	4	3	
			Newport Co.	27		+1	1	8			
			Hong Kong								
			Mansfield	14	1			4			
			Hartlepool U.	12				2			
			Peterborough U.	33		1		12			
Garry Worrall		Salford	Manchester U. (A)								
5-9 11.5 4.11.61			Peterborough U.	18+1			+1	2			

NON-CONTRACT PLAYERS 1984-85: Simon Haigh, Stuart Hicks, Patrick O'Keefe, Danny Reilly, Andy Kazimerow

*Neil Firm Club Captain, Trevor Quow Team Captain

PETERBOROUGH UNITED

DIVISION FOUR 7TH **FA CUP** 1ST ROUND **MILK CUP** 2ND ROUND

MATCH	DATE	COMPETITION	VENUE	OPPONENTS	RESULT	HALF TIME	L'GUE POS'N	GOALSCORERS	ATTENDANCE
1	A 27	CL	H	Hartlepool U	W3-1	2-0		Clarke, Buchanan, Benjamin	3,213
2	**30**	**MC 1**	**A**	**Crystal Palace**	**L0-3**	**0-1**			**3,975**
3	S 3	CL	A	Wrexham	D2-2	1-1	5	Clarke 2	1,680
4	6	CL	A	York C	L0-2	0-0			3,709
5	10	CL	H	Torquay U	W5-0	3-0	5	Turner (og), Hankin 2, Chard, Clarke	3,135
6	17	CL	A	Hereford U	L1-2	0-2	9	Slack	3,172
7	**14**	**MC 1**	**H**	**Crystal Palace**	**W3-0[4]**	**2-0**		**Hankin, Clarke, Quow**	**3,504**
8	24	CL	H	Mansfield T	W3-0	2-0	7	Buchanan 2, Chard (pen)	3,490
9	28	CL	H	Crewe Alex	W1-0	1-0		Benjamin	3,783
10	**O 5**	**MC 2**	**A**	**Stoke C**	**D0-0**	**0-0**			**11,085**
11	8	CL	H	Doncaster R	D1-1	0-1	6	Pike	4,400
12	15	CL	A	Halifax T	L1-2	0-1	9	Benjamin	1,079
13	18	CL	A	Rochdale	L1-2	0-1		Hankin	1,299
14	22	CL	H	Tranmere R	W2-0	0-0	10	Pike, Hankin	3,311
15	**26**	**MC 2**	**H**	**Stoke C**	**L1-2**	**0-1**		**Chard (pen)**	
16	29	CL	A	Bristol C	W1-0	0-0	6	Buchanan	7,380
17	N 2	CL	H	Reading	D3-3	2-2		Waddle, Chard (pen), Imlach	4,073
18	5	CL	A	Aldershot	L2-3	1-2	9	Quow, Clarke	1,856
19	12	CL	H	Chesterfield	W2-0	1-0	7	Quow, Waddle	3,807
20	**19**	**FAC 1**	**A**	**Oxford U**	**L0-2**	**0-1**			**6,343**
21	26	CL	H	Stockport Co	W2-0	1-0	6	Hankin 2	3,240
22	29	CL	A	Bury	D2-2	1-1		Chard (pen), Waddle	2,013
23	D 3	CL	A	Blackpool	W2-1	1-0	4	Quow, Benjamin	4,439
24	17	CL	A	Chester C	D1-1	0-1	5	Chard (pen)	1,191
25	26	CL	H	Colchester U	W2-0	0-0	2	Beech, Waddle	6,527
26	27	CL	A	Northampton T	L1-2	0-2	5	Waddle	6,464
27	31	CL	H	Swindon T	D1-1	1-0	7	Slack	4,140
28	J 2	CL	A	Darlington	L0-1	0-0	7		1,471
29	7	CL	H	Wrexham	L0-1	0-0	8		3,277
30	21	CL	H	Hereford U	D1-1	0-1	10	Bemjamin	2,559
31	28	CL	A	Torquay U	L0-1	0-0	10		1,461
32	F 4	CL	H	Bury	W2-1	1-0	8	Benjamin 2	2,507
33	11	CL	A	Mansfield T	D0-0	0-0	9		2,179
34	15	CL	A	Reading	D1-1	1-1		Waddle	2,986
35	18	CL	H	Bristol C	W4-1	1-1	8	Waddle 2, Hankin, Worrall	3,356
36	**21**	**AMC 1**	**A**	**Wrexham**	**L2-3[1]**	**1-0**		**Quow, Pike**	**1,018**
37	24	CL	A	Tranmere R	D0-0	0-0			1,763
38	M 3	CL	H	Rochdale	W2-0	0-0	8	Chapman (og), Wile	2,335
39	7	CL	H	Aldershot	L1-2	0-0		Wile	3,568
40	10	CL	A	Chesterfield	L0-1	0-1	8		2,853
41	17	CL	A	Doncaster R	D1-1	1-0	9	Chard (pen)	3,672
42	24	CL	H	Halifax T	W4-0	1-0	8	Benjamin, Worrall, Kelly, Chard	2,304
43	27	CL	A	Hartlepool U	D1-1	1-1		Kelly	1,689
44	A 1	CL	H	York C	L0-2	0-0			5,216
45	7	CL	A	Crewe Alex	W1-0	1-0	8	Beech	2,024
46	14	CL	H	Blackpool	W4-0	1-0	6	Kelly 2, Waddle, Beech	2,921
47	21	CL	A	Colchester U	D1-1	0-1	8	Holmes (pen)	1,746
48	24	CL	H	Northampton T	W6-0	3-0		Waddle 2, Holmes (pen), Kelly 2, Rayment	3,481
49	27	CL	A	Stockport Co	L1-4	0-3		Waddle	1,753
50	M 5	CL	H	Darlington	D2-2	0-1	7	Quow, Slack	1,925
51	7	CL	A	Swindon T	L0-2	0-0	7	Kelly	1,679
52	12	CL	H	Chester C	W1-0	0-0	10		1,461

[1]After Extra Time. [4]Won on Penalties

Av Home Att **3,402**

Goal Scorers

League (72): Waddle 12, Benjamin 8, Chard 7 (5 pens), Hankin 7, Kelly 7, Clarke 5, Buchanan 4, Quow 4, Beech 3, Slack 3, Pike 2, Holmes 2 (2 pens), Worrall 2, Wile 2, Imlach 1, Rayment 1, opponents 2

FA Cup (-): —

Milk Cup (4): Chard 1 (1 pen), Clarke 1, Hankin 1, Quow 1

AMC (2): Pike 1, Quow 1

1983-84

Seaman	Chard	Imlach	Benjamin	Wile	Slack	Beech	Pike	Clarke	Quow	Buchanan	Rayment	Hankin	Linton	Firm	Tydeman	Waddle	Holmes	Zenchuk	Worrall	Kelly (L)	Allen	Ippolito	REFEREE	
1	2	3	4	5	6	7	8	9*	10	11	12												A Buksh	1
1	2	3	4	5	6	7	8	9	10	11*	12												**E Reed**	2
1	2	3	4	5	6	7	8	9	10	11													R Dilkes	3
1	2*	3	4	5	6	7	8	9	10	11	12												DB Allison	4
1	2	3		5	6	4	8	11	10	7		9											J Moules	5
1	2	3	12	5	6	4*	8	11	10	7		9											MJ Heath	6
1	2	3	12	5	6	4	8	11	10	7*		9											**J Hough**	7
1	2	3	4	5	6		8	11	10	7		9†											KG Salmon	8
1	2	3	4	5	6		8	11	10*	7	12	9											R Lewis	9
1	2	3	4	5	6		8	11		7		9	10*	12									**R Banks**	10
1	2	3	4	5	6		8	11		7	9		10										D Hedges	11
1	2	3	4	5	6		8	11	10*	7			9	12									P Willis	12
1	2	3	4	5	6		7	11		8	12	9*	10										JM Key	13
1	2	3	4	5	6		8	11		7		9			10								C Downey	14
1	2	3	4	5	6		8	11		7*		9†	10									12	**A Ward**	15
1	2	3	4	5	6		7	11*		12		9			8	10							J Worrall	16
1	2	3	4	5	6		7	11		12		9			8	10*							G Napthine	17
1	2	3		5	6	4	7	11	10						8	9							M Bodenham	18
1	2	3	7	5	6	4	12	11*	10						8	9							D Letts	19
1	2	3	7	5	6	4	11*		10	12					8	9							**H King**	20
1	2		7	5	6	4			10			9			8	11	3						K Baker	21
1	2		7	5	6	4	12		10*			9			8	11	3						R Nixon	22
	2		7	5	6	4			10			9			8	11	3	1					G Tyson	23
1	2*		7	5	6	4	12		10			9			8	11	3						D Hutchinson	24
1	2		7*	5	6	4	12		10			9			8	11	3						H Taylor	25
1	2		7*	5	6	4	12		10			9†			8	11	3						D Vickers	26
1	2				6	4	7			10		9		5	8	11	3						E Scales	27
1	2	12			6	4	7			10		9		5	8*	11	3						K Hackett	28
1	2		12	5		4	7		10			9		6	8*	11	3						A Challinor	29
1	2	12	9	5		4	7*		10					6	8	11	3						T Mills	30
1	2	7	9	5	8	4	12		10*					6		11	3						T Holbrook	31
1	2	8	9	5	6	4			10					7		11	3						M Robinson	32
1	2	7		5	8	4			10*			9		6		11	3		12				J Lovatt	33
1	2	3	7	5		4*	12					9		6	8	10			11				D Reeves	34
1	2	3	7	5		4						9		6	8	10			11				A Gunn	35
	2	3			6	4	7*	9	10*	8	12			5			11		13		1		**D Richardson**	36
1	2	3	7	5		4						9		6	8	10			11				J Fitzharris	37
1		3	7	5		4	2				12	9		6	8	10*			11				M James	38
1	2	3	7	5		4		12				9†		6	8	10*			11				P Tyldesley	39
1	2	3	7		5	4		10	12			9		6	8*				11				I Hendrick	40
1	2	3	7		5	4		10				9			8		6		11				R Guy	41
1	2	3	7		5	4				12				6	8	10*			11	9			I Borrett	42
1	2	3*	7		5	4	8							6		9	12		11	10			K Walmsley	43
1	2		7	8	5	4						12		6		9*	3		11	10			J Moules	44
1					5	4	7				2†			6	8	9	3		11	10			N Midgley	45
1					6	4	7				2	12		5	8	9*	3		11	10			V Callow	46
1	2				5	4*	7		12					6	8	9	3		11	10			M Dimblebee	47
1					5	4	7		12		2			6	8	9*	3		11	10			M Heath	48
1					5	4	7		12		2			6	8	9	3*		11	10			D Allison	49
1		12			5	4	7		3		2			6	8*	9			11	10			R Lewis	50
1		3			5	4	7		8		2			6		9			11	10			A Seville	51
1		3	12		5	4	7		8		2			6		9*			11	10			A Buksh	52
45	38	29	31	32	39	38	28	17	24	13	8	25	3	24	29	33	20	1	18	11			League Appearances	
		+3S	+3S				+7S	+1S	+4S	+3S	+5S	+2S		+1S			+1S		+1S					
1	1	1	1	1	1	1	1		1	1S					1	1							FA Cup Appearances	
4	4	4	3+1S	4	4	2	4	4	2	4	1S	3	2	1S								1S	Milk Cup Appearances	
	1	1			1	1	1	1	1	1	1S			1			1		1S		1		AM Cup Appearances	

LONDON ROAD GROUND

Official Address: London Road Ground, Peterborough PE2 8AL. Telephone: Peterborough (0733) 63947

Ground Capacity: 28,000

Record Attendance: 30,096 v. Swansea Town, F.A. Cup Round 5, 20 Feb 1965

Record Receipts: £44,157.83 v. Manchester United,F.A. Cup Round 5, 20 Feb 1981

Size of Playing Area: 112yds × 76 yds

Season Tickets: Stands: £60 (centre), £55 (off centre), £45 (D), £20 (A. Wright Block for OAP), £40 (enclosure), £36 (Ground)

Executive Box Season Tickets: 4 boxes being built (already sold), £110 in the new executive suite for Vice Presidents (single)

Cost of Stand Tickets: D £2.70, £3.30 (off-centre—centre); **Terraces:** £2.00, Enclosure £2.20

Match and Ticket Information: tickets bookable fourteen days in advance.

Car Parking: ample parking available at ground.

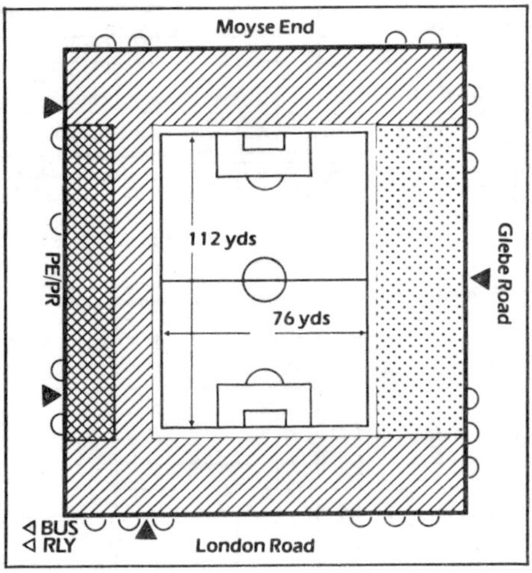

For key see page 12

How to get to the ground

From North and West: Use A1 then A47 S.P. Peterborough into town centre. Follow signs Whittlesey and cross river br into London Road for Peterborough United F.C.
From East: Use A47 into Peterborough town centre and follow signs Whittlesey and cross river br into London Road for Peterborough United F.C.
From South: Use A1 then A15 S.P. Peterborough into London Road for Peterborough United F.C.

PLYMOUTH ARGYLE Division 3

President
G H Gillan

Chairman
S W Dawe

Vice-Chairman
P D Bloom

Directors
R Burroughs, ARICS
G E Jasper
J E C Kent
B L Hooper

Secretary
Graham Little

Manager
John Hore

Club Coach
M Harvey

Commercial Manager
W E Pearce (0752 51041)

Amid scenes of great jubilation hundreds of Plymouth Argyle fans celebrated a joyous reprieve from relegation after the final fixture against Orient.

The season had proved to be a very eventful one; the first league victory was not achieved until late September, and after some very mixed results relegation was a distinct possibility after the Easter games, but with a final flourish ten out of a possible twelve points were gained from the remaining four matches.

The Milk Cup provided First Division opponents in Arsenal, after a previous victory against Swindon Town. The two games were keenly contested games with a 1-1 draw at Home Park, and a 0-1 defeat at Highbury. Against such illustrious opposition the team performed very well.

The 1983-84 season will always be remembered by the Argyle supporters for the club's F.A. Cup exploits.

The 1st Round was an away game against Southend United ending in a 0-0 draw; the home match was won by 'Argyle' by 2-0. Round 2 played at home to Barking proved to be a tough contest and victory by 2-1 was rather fortunate.

Round 3 proved to be very tight games against Newport County. The first match played at home was a closely fought contest with 'Argyle' equalising with a penalty in injury time, but winning the replay 1-0.

After defeating Darlington 2-1 in the following round West Bromwich Albion were to be the next opponents at The Hawthorns.

Excitement was now beginning to rise in the city, and thousands of supporters made the journey to the Midlands to see Tynan score the winning goal, which was a blow for Johnny Giles, newly appointed Albion manager.

History was made at this stage because the club had reached the 6th Round of the F.A. Competition for the very first time, and with the Quarter Final tie at home against Derby County hopes were high.

After an excellent game the teams finished with a blank score sheet; many supporters thought this was the end, but in the replay at the Baseball Ground Argyle emerged victors by 1-0 scored direct from a corner by Rogers.

A place in the semi-final had been won with opponents Watford to be played at Villa Park.

Well over twenty-five thousand supporters travelled from Plymouth and when the teams took the field it provided a very colourful sight with green and black scarfs and hats well in prominence, to be followed by showers of yellow and red confetti from the Watford supporters.

The match was closely fought with a 13th minute goal by Reilly settling it in Watford's favour.

The crowd of 45,000 conducted themselves in a very admirable way, a credit to both clubs with families enjoying a very entertaining afternoon.

So 1983-84 season comes to a close and the Plymouth Argyle supporters will be looking forward to a promotion challenge in 1984-85 season.

F.J. Lee, The League Directory's Statistician for the Club

Back Row: Martin Harvey (Team Coach), Adrian Burrows, John Uzzell, David Philp, Geoff Crudginton, Mike Ham, Gordon Nisbet, John Hore (Manager). **Front Row:** Mark Rowe, Andy Rogers, Kevin Hodges, Chris Harrison, Leigh Cooper (Capt.), Tommy Tynan, Russell Coughlin and Gordon Staniforth.

'ARGYLE' or 'THE PILGRIMS'

Formed: 1886 **Turned Professional:** 1903 **Ltd Co:** 1903
Previous Name: 1886-1903 Argyle Athletic Club
Previous Managers: 1903-5 Frank Brettell 1905-6 Bob Jack 1906-7 William Fullerton 1910-38 Bob Jack 1938-48 Jack Tresardern 1948-55 Jimmy Rae 1955-60 Jack Rowley 1960-1 George Taylor/Neil Dougall 1961-3 Ellis Studdard 1963 Vic Buckingham 1963-4 Andy Beattie 1964-5 Malcolm Allison 1965-8 Derek Ufton 1968-70 Billy Bingham 1970-2 Ellis Studdard 1972-7 Tony Waiters 1977-8 Mike Kelly 1978 Lenny Lawrence 1978-9 Malcolm Allison 1978-81 Bobby Saxton 1981-3 Bobby Moncur
Vic Buckingham was only with the club for six weeks during the summer of 1963 and never fielded an 'Argyle' team.
Lennie Lawrence was acting manager only for 5 games early in 1978. George Taylor and Neil Dougall worked together in 1960-1
Honours: Champions Division 3 (S) 1929-30, 1951-2 Champions Division 3 1958-9
League Career: Original Member of Division 3 1920 Reverted to Division 3 (S) 1921 Promoted to Division 2 1929-30 Relegated to Division 3 (S) 1949-50 Promoted to Division 2 1951-2 Relegated to Division 3 (S) 1955-6 Transferred to Division 3 1958 Promoted to Division 2 1958-9 Relegated to Division 3 1967-8 Promoted to Division 2 1974-5 Relegated to Division 3 1976-7
Colours: Green shirts with black trim, black shorts, green stocking with black and white tops
Change Colours: All Yellow

CLUB RECORDS

Most Appearances for Club: Sammy Black: Football League 470 + F.A. Cup 22 **Total 492**
Most Capped Player: Moses Russell, 20, Wales. **For England:** None
Record Goalscorer in a Match: Wilf Carter, 5 v Charlton Athletic, Div 2, 27.12.60
Record League Goalscorer in a season: Jack Cock, 32, 1926-7 **All competitions:** Wilf Carter (League 26, F.A. Cup 6), 1957-8, and Jack Cock (all League) 1926-7
Record League Goalscorer in a career: Sammy Black, 180 **All competitions:** Sammy Black, 184 (League 176, F.A. Cup 7) 1924-38
Record Transfer Fee Received: £250,000 from Everton for Gary Megson, Feb 1980
Record Transfer Fee Paid: £75,000 to Carlisle United for David Kemp, Sept 1979
Best Performances: League: 4th Div 2 1931-2, 1952-3 **F.A. Cup:** Semi-Final (as Third Div club)
League/Milk Cup: Semi-Final, 1965, 1974
Most League Points: 68 in Div 3 (S), 1929-30
Most League Goals: 107, Div 3 (S), 1925-6 107, Division 3 (S), 1951-2
Record League Victory: 8-1 v Millwall, Div 2, 16 Jan 1932
Record League Defeat: 0-9 v Stoke City, Div 2, 17 Dec 1980
Club Statistician for the Directory: F Lee

Programme Editor
Bill Pearce

Price	Number of Pages
50p	32

Subscriptions

PLYMOUTH ARGYLE

PLAYERS NAME Ht Wt Birthdate	Honours	Birthplace Transfers	Clubs	APPEARANCES League	Milk Cup	F.A.C.	A.M.C.	GOALS League	Milk Cup	F.A.C.	A.M.C.
GOALKEEPERS											
Geoff Crudgington	E. S	Wolverhampton	Wolverhampton W. (N-C)								
6-0 13.5 14.2.52			Aston Villa	4							
			Bradford C. (L)	1							
			Crewe A.	250	15	14					
		£20,000	Swansea C.	52	9	4					
		£40,000	Plymouth A.	219	12	21	3				
David Philp		Newquay	Plymouth A.				1				
5-11 11.8											
DEFENDERS											
Mike Ham		Plymouth	Plymouth A. (A)	10+1		1					
6-1 12.2 6.12.63											
Chris Harrison		Launceston	Plymouth A. (A)	287+4	19	23+1	4	6	1		
5-10 11.0 17.10.56											
Gordon Nisbet	E. U.23(1)	Wallsend	W.B.A.	136	8	13					
5-10 12.4 18.9.51		£30,000	Hull C.	190+3	11	10		1		1	
		£30,000	Plymouth A.	154	10	16	4	9	2		
John Uzzell		Plymouth	Plymouth A.	199+2	8	13	4	4		1	
5-10 11.13 31.3.59											
MIDFIELD											
Leigh Cooper		Reading	Plymouth A. (A)	172	8	20	4	14			
5-8 11.0 7.5.61											
Russell Coughlin		Swansea	Manchester C. (A)								
5-8 11.8 15.2.60		£40,000	Blackburn R.	22+2	1+1						
		£20,000	Carlisle U.	114+16	5	12		13	1		
		£20,000	Plymouth A.								
Clive Goodyear	Div 1, 82	Lincoln	Luton T.	85+5	5	4		4			
6-0 12.6 15.1.61			Plymouth A.								
Kevin Hodges		Bridport	Plymouth A. (A)	224+8	17+1	22	2+1	36		1	2
5-8 10.0 12.6.60											
Mark Rowe		Wadebridge	Plymouth A. (A)	32+8	3	4	2+1	1		1	
5-6 10.0 9.6.64											
FORWARDS											
Andy Rogers		Chatteris	Chatteris T.								
5-8 10.0 1.12.56			Peterborough U.	25+4	3			1			
		F	Hampton								
			Southampton	+5							
		£50,000	Plymouth A.	120+1	7	14	3+1	13		3	1
Gordon Staniforth	E. S	Hull	Hull C. (A)	7+5				2			
5-6 9.12 23.5.57		£10,000	York C.	128	7	6		33	2	4	
		£120,000	Carlisle U.	118+8	7	17		33	2	3	
			Plymouth A.	47+3	4	7+1	2	12	1	1	
Tommy Tynan		Liverpool	Liverpool (A)								
5-10 13.0 17.1.56			Swansea C. (L)	6				2			
		£10,000	Sheffield Wed.	89+2	12	4		31	5	1	
		£33,000	Lincoln C.	9							
		£25,000	Newcastle U.	168+15	11+	7+1		66	5	4	
		£55,000	Plymouth A.	35	4	10	2+1	12	1	3	4

NON-CONTRACT PLAYERS 1984-85: Mark Smith (3 Lg), **Nigel Menhenick, David Philp**

PLYMOUTH ARGYLE

DIVISION THREE 19TH **FA CUP** SEMI-FINAL **MILK CUP** 3RD ROUND

MATCH	DATE	COMPETITION	VENUE	OPPONENTS	RESULT	HALF TIME	L'GUE POS'N	GOALSCORERS	ATTENDANCE
1	A 27	CL	H	Wigan Ath	D0-0	0-0			3,730
2	S 3	CL	A	Millwall	L0-1	0-0	18		4,611
3	6	CL	A	Rotherham U	L0-2	0-1			4,488
4	10	CL	H	Gillingham	D1-1	0-0	20	Nisbet	3,192
5	17	CL	A	Lincoln C	L1-3	1-1	22	Tynan	3,003
6	24	CL	H	Preston NE	W1-0	0-0	20	Rogers	3,674
7	27	CL	H	Scunthorpe U	W4-0	2-0		Staniforth 2, Rowe, Rogers	3,821
8	O 1	CL	A	Burnley	L1-2	1-2	18	Flynn (og)	6,766
9	8	CL	A	AFC Bournemouth	L1-2	1-2	19	Pearson	3,759
10	15	CL	H	Oxford U	W2-1	0-1	16	Nisbet, Phillips	2,990
11	18	CL	H	Bristol R	D1-1	0-0		Phillips	4,896
12	22	CL	A	Hull C	W2-1	0-1	16	Smith L, Tynan	8,807
13	29	CL	H	Sheffield U	L0-1	0-0	16		5,458
14	31	CL	A	Port Vale	W1-0	1-0		Phillips	3,466
15	N 5	CL	A	Brentford	D2-2	1-1	15	Tynan, Hodges	4,183
16	12	CL	H	Bolton W	W2-0	1-0	14	Kellow, Phillips	4,624
17	D 3	CL	A	Bradford C	L0-2	0-0	14		2,955
18	17	CL	A	Orient	L2-3	2-1	14	Nisbet 2	2,684
19	26	CL	H	Exeter C	D2-2	1-0	14	Staniforth, Kellow	10,387
20	27	CL	A	Newport Co	L0-2	0-1	17		5,154
21	31	CL	H	Southend U	W4-0	1-0	14	Hodges, Clark (og), Tynan (pen), Rogers	2,978
22	J 2	CL	A	Walsall	L2-3	1-2	15	Smith L, Tynan	4,856
23	21	CL	H	Lincoln C	D2-2	1-0	15	Cooper 2	3,804
24	F 4	CL	H	Burnley	D1-1	0-0	15	Staniforth	5,104
25	11	CL	A	Preston NE	L1-2	0-2	17	Staniforth	4,370
26	14	CL	H	Port Vale	W3-0	0-0		Staniforth, Tynan 2	3,552
27	25	CL	H	Hull C	W2-0	1-0	15	Tynan (pen), Phillips	10,023
28	28	CL	A	Sheffield U	L0-2	0-1			9,541
29	M 3	CL	A	Bristol R	L0-2	0-1	17		5,619
30	6	CL	H	Brentford	D1-1	0-0		Phillips	4,332
31	17	CL	H	AFC Bournemouth	W1-0	1-0	17	Staniforth	7,325
32	20	CL	H	Millwall	L0-1	0-0			4,507
33	24	CL	A	Oxford U	L0-5	0-2	17		7,777
34	30	CL	H	Rotherham U	D1-1	0-0		Tynan	4,736
35	A 3	CL	A	Wigan Ath	D1-1	0-1		Tynan	2,757
36	7	CL	A	Scunthorpe U	L0-3	0-1	17		2,780
37	10	CL	H	Wimbledon	L1-2	1-0		Tynan	6,471
38	16	CL	A	Bolton W	L1-2	0-1		Tynan (pen)	3,266
39	20	CL	H	Newport Co	L0-1	0-0			7,654
40	21	CL	A	Exeter C	D1-1	0-1	19	Staniforth	6,870
41	28	CL	A	Wimbledon	L0-1	0-1	20		3,706
42	M 1	CL	A	Gillingham	L1-2	0-1		Chamberlain	3,103
43	5	CL	H	Walsall	W3-1	0-0	20	Rogers, Staniforth 2 (1 pen)	5,144
44	7	CL	A	Southend U	D1-1	1-0	20	Chamberlain	3,540
45	9	CL	H	Bradford C	W3-0	1-0		Smith L, Staniforth, Hodges	5,744
46	12	CL	H	Orient	W3-1	2-1	18	Chamberlain, Smith L, Hodges	7,664

A SPECIAL CUP TRIBUTE TO PLYMOUTH ARGYLE ON PAGE 568

Av Home Att **5,339**

Goal Scorers

League (56): Tynan 12 (3 pens), Staniforth 11 (1 pen), Phillips 6, Hodges 4, Nisbet 4, Rogers 4, Smith L 4, Chamberlain 3, Cooper 2, Kellow 2, Pearson 1, Rowe 1, opponents 2

1983-84

Crudgington	Nisbet	Uzzell	Harrison	Smith L	Forbes	Hodges	Phillips	Tynan	Staniforth	Rogers	Cooper	Rowe	Ham	Pearson	Kellow	Price (L)	Cassidy (L)	Smith M	Chamberlain (L)	Swiggs	Phild	REFEREE	
1	2	3	4	5	6	7	8	9	10	11												L Burden	1
1	2	3	4	5	6	7	8	9	10	11												B Hill	2
1	2	3	4†	5		7	8	9	10	11	6											J Bray	3
1	2	3	4	5		7	8*	9	10	11	6	12										E Read	4
1		3	4	5		7	2	9	10	11	6	8										J Lovatt	5
1	2	3		5		7		9	10	11	6*	8	4	12								R Milford	6
1	2	3	4	5		7		9	10	11	6	8										C Thomas	7
1	2	3*	4	5		7	12	9	10	11	6	8										JD Hough	8
1	2	3	4	5		7	11	9			6	8		10								R Lewis	9
1	2	3	4	5		7	11	9			6	8		10								J Deakin	10
1	2	3	4	5		7	11	9	12		6	8		10*								A Seville	11
1	2	3	4	5		7	11	9	10		6	8										P Tyldesley	12
1	2	3	4	5		7	11	9*	10		6	8		12								D Letts	13
1	2	3	4	5		7	11	9	10		6	8										D Owen	14
1	2	3	4	5		7	11	9	10*		6	8		12								M Taylor	15
1	2	3	4	5	6	7	11	9				8			10							B Stevens	16
1	2	3	4	5		7	11	9	12		6*	8			10							N Ashley	17
1	2	3	4	5		7	12		10	11	6	8*			9							M Taylor	18
1	2	3	4	5		7			10	11	6	8			9							T Bune	19
1	2	3	4	5		7	12		10	11	6	8			9*							M Robinson	20
1	2	3	4	5		7	8	9	12	11	6				10*							V Callow	21
1	2	3	4	5		7	8	9	10	11*	6				12							A Buksh	22
1		3	4	5		7	2	9†	10	11	6			8								J Martin	23
1	2	3	4	5		7	8		10	11	6			9*	12							C Downey	24
1	2	3	4	5		7	8		10	11	6	12			9*							A Challinor	25
1	2	3	4	5		7	8	9	10	11	6											L Burden	26
1	2	3	4	5		7	8	9	10	11	6											E Read	27
1	2	3	4			7*	8	9	10	11	6	12	5									R Bridges	28
1	2	3	4			7	8	9		11	6		5		10							H King	29
1	2	4				7	8	9		11	6		5			3	10					T Spencer	30
1	2	3	4	5		7	8	9	10	11	6											R Milford	31
1	2	3	4	5		7	8	9		11	6	10										J Bray	32
1	2		4	5*			8	9		11	6	7	12					3	10			A Ward	33
1	2		4	5		7	8	9	10	11	6							3				D Hedges	34
1	2		4	5*		7	8	9	10	11	6	12						3				J Lovatt	35
1	2	3	4	5		7	8	9	10*	11	6								12			L Dilkes	36
1	2		4	5		7	8	9	10*	11	6	3							12			K Cooper	37
1	2	3	4	5		7	8	9	10*	11	6								12			K Redfern	38
1	2	3	4	5		7	8	9	10	11	6											T Holbrook	39
1	2	3	4	5		7	8	9*	10	11	6								12			G Napthine	40
1	2	3	4	5		12	8		10	11*	6	7							9			A Gunn	41
1	2	3	4			7			10	11	6	5							9	8		K Salmon	42
1	2	3	4	5			8		10	12	6	7	11*						9			J Martin	43
1	2	3	4	5			8		10	11	6	7							9			C Downey	44
1	2	3	4	5		12	8		10	11	6	7*							9			R Lewis	45
1	2	3	4	5		7	8		10*	11	6								9	12		A Seville	46
46	44	42	44	42	3	41	39	35	36	36	43	24	5	5	8	1	1	3	7	1		League Appearances	
						+2S	+3S		+3S	+1S		+4S	+1S	+3S	+2S				+4S	+1S			

HOME PARK

Official Address: Home Park, Plymouth, Devon PL2 3DQ. Telephone: Plymouth (0752) 52561/2/3, 51041 (Lottery Shop)

Ground Capacity: 35,000

Record Attendance: 43,596 v. Aston Villa, Div 2, 10 Oct 1936

Record Receipts: £118,000 v. Derby Co., F.A. Cup Round 6, 3 Mar 1984

Size of Playing Area: 112yds × 75 yds

Season Tickets: Stand (Centre): £70, £50 (under 16/OAP), £55 (Wing), £40 (under 16/OAP); Ground: £30, £20 (under 16/OAP)

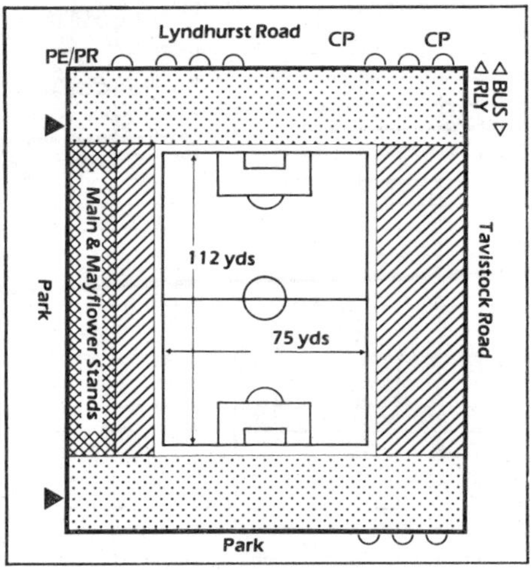

For key see page 12

Executive Box Season Tickets: None free

Cost of Stand Tickets: £4.50 (Centre), (£3.00 under 16/OAP), £3.50 (Wing), £2.50 (under 16/OAP); **Ground:** £2.00, £1.00 (under 16/OAP)

Match and Ticket Information: Grand Stand and Mayflower Stand tickets are available 2 to 3 weeks before each first-team game.

Car Parking : Car park (2,000 vehicles) adjoins ground.

How to get to the ground

From All Directions: Use A38 Plymouth bypass as far as the Tavistock Road A386, then branch left and follow signs Plymouth A386. In 0.7m turn right then left A3041 into Outland Road for Plymouth Argyle F.C.

PORTSMOUTH Division 2

Chairman
B J Deacon

Directors
J R Parkhouse
G G Gauntlett
D K Deacon
S W Sloan
Mrs J Deacon

Company Secretary
W B J Davis

Commercial Manager
L Allen (0705 731204)

Manager
Alan Ball

Chief Scout
D Healey

Having stormed into the Second Division with the support of fine Fratton Park attendances, the availability of money for players made 'Pompey' most people's favourites for a good season.

But on looking back, their first home match, against a very ordinary looking Middlesbrough, was lost in dismal fashion and sadly a trend was set for the Fratton Park regulars.

There was early season promise in the Milk Cup when a two goal lead was wasted against Aston Villa at home when late goals brought the visitors a 2-2 draw, and at Villa Park the First Division team only scraped through 3-2 after extra time.

'Pompey's' happiest moments were perhaps to be found against Grimsby Town whom they beat twice in the league and at home in the Third Round of the F.A. Cup. However, the dream draw of Southampton at home, although bringing a capacity crowd to Portsmouth, also brought the disappointment of a last minute defeat after good chances had been missed.

As it turned out, the investment in Tony Hateley certainly paid off for the club but at the time of his arrival it might have been more advantageous to have signed experienced quality defenders, as it was in this department that the club were forced to chop and change with disastrous results. The arrival of Baxter and the strong tackling Kennedy from Middlesbrough will certainly help and a solid and confident defence should give young Neil Webb a chance to show his obvious class and should also help Alan Knight return to top form in goal.

Portsmouth is a club well equipped to cope with life at the top. They have the support to keep solvent in the highest sphere, so it could be that Alan Ball is in the right place at the right time.

Back Row: N. Morgan, G. Stanley, R. Money, M. Baxter, M. Walsh, K. Dillon, M. Tait. **Standing:** K. Ball, S. McGarvey, B. Gilbert, A. Knight, A. Gosney, B. Doyle, M. Waldron, A. Biley. **Sitting:** C. Sullivan, P. Hardyman, P. Wood, A. Ball (Manager), D. Thomas (Youth Team Coach), G. Neave (Physiotherapist), N. Webb, M. Kennedy, P. Wimbleton.

'POMPEY'

Formed: 1898 **Turned Professional:** 1898 **Ltd Co:** 1898
Previous Managers: 1898-1901 Frank Brettell 1901-4 Robert Blyth 1904-8 Richard Bonney 1909-20 Robert Brown 1920-7 John McCartney 1927-47 John W Tinn 1947-52 J R (Bob) Jackson 1952-8 Eddie Lever 1958-61 Freddie Cox 1961 William Thompson 1961-70 George Smith 1970-3 Ron Tindall 1973-4 John Mortimore 1974 Ron Tindall 1974-7 Ian St John 1977-9 Jimmy Dickinson 1979-82 Frank Burrows 1982-4 Bobby Campbell
Honours: Division One Champions 1948-9, 1949-50 Division Three(S) Champions 1923-4 Division Three Champions 1961-2, 1982-3 F.A. Cup Winners 1939
League Career: Original members of Division 3 1920 Transferred to Division 3(S) 1921
Promoted to Division 2 1923-4 Promoted to Division 1 1926-7
Relegated to Division 2 1958-9 Relegated to Division 3 1960-1
Promoted to Division 2 1961-2 Relegated to Division 3 1975-6
Relegated to Division 4 1977-8 Promoted to Division 3 1979-80
Promoted to Division 2 1982-3
Colours: Royal blue shirts with white collars and cuffs, white shorts, red stockings
Change Colours: Red shirts with white collar and cuffs, red shorts and white stockings

CLUB RECORDS

Most Appearances for Club: Jimmy Dickinson (1946-65): Football League 764 + F.A. Cup 58 **Total 822**
Most Capped Player: Jimmy Dickinson, 48, England
Record Goalscorer in a Match: Alf Strange, 5 v Gillingham (h) 6-1 Div 3, 27.01.23
Peter Harris, 5 v Aston Villa (h) 5-2 Div 1, 03.09.58
Record League Goalscorer in a season: Billy Haines, 40, Div 2, 1926-7 **In All Competitions:** Billy Haines 43 (League 40, F.A. Cup 3) 1926-7
Record League Goalscorer in a career: Peter Harris, 194 **In All Competitions:** Peter Harris, 209 (League 194 + F.A. Cup 15) 1946-60
Record Transfer Fee Received: £1,000,000 from Inter Milan for Tony Hateley, June 1984
Record Transfer Fee Paid: £180,000 to Coventry City for Tony Hateley, June 1983
Best Performances: League: Champions (2) **F.A. Cup:** Winners **League/Milk Cup:** 5th Round 1967
Most League Points: 91 in Div 3, 1982-3 **Most League Goals:** 91, Div 4, 1979-80
Record League Victory: 9-1 v Notts County, Div 2, 9 Apr 1927
Record League Defeat: 0-10 v Leicester City, Div 1, 20 Oct 1928
Club Statistician for the Directory: Doug Robinson

Programme Editor
L. Allen

Price	Number of Pages
50p	24

Subscriptions
Available from club

PORTSMOUTH

PLAYERS NAME Ht Wt Birthdate	Honours	Birthplace Transfers	Clubs	APPEARANCES League	Milk Cup	F.A.C.	E. Cups	GOALS League	Milk Cup	F.A.C.	E. Cups
GOALKEEPERS											
Andy Gosney	E. Y	Southampton	Portsmouth (A)	1	1						
6-4 13.5 8.11.63											
Alan Knight	E. U.21(2), Y.	Balham	Portsmouth (A)	143	9	9					
6-1 13.1 3.7.61	Div. 3, 1983										
DEFENDERS											
Noel Blake		Jamaica	Aston Villa	4							
6-0 13.5 12.1.62			Shrewsbury T. (L)	6							
		£55,000	Birmingham C.	76	12	8		5			
		£150,000	Portsmouth								
Mike Baxter		Birmingham	P.N.E.	209+1	16	6		17	1		
6-1 12.0 30.12.56		£425,000	Middlesbrough	122	4	7		7		1	
			Portsmouth								
Billy Gilbert	E. U.21(11), Y, S,	Lewisham	Crystal Palace	235+2	19	15		3		1	
5-11 12.0 10.11.59	YC. 78, Div. 2, 78.		Portsmouth								
Richard Money	E. B(1).	Lowestoft	Lowestoft T.								
5-11½ 11.5 13.10.55	Div. 2, 82		Scunthorpe U.	165+8	10	6		4			
		£30,000	Fulham	106	4	6		3		1	
		£333,333	Liverpool	12+2	1	1					
			Derby Co. (L)	5							
		£100,000	Luton T.	44	4	1		1			
		£50,000	Portsmouth	16	4						
Colin Sullivan	E. U.23(2), Y.	Saltash	Plymouth A. (A)	225+5	14	12		7			
5-7 11.3 24.6.51	Div. 3, 83	£70,000	Norwich C.	154+3	16	9		3			
		£60,000	Cardiff C.	61+2	4	2		1			
			Hereford U. (L)	8							
		F	Portsmouth	94+1	3	4					
Mick Tait	Div. 2, 83	Wallsend	Oxford U. (A)	61+3	2+1	2		23	1		
5-11 12.5 30.9.56		£65,000	Carlisle U.	101+5	7	7		20		2	
		£150,000	Hull C.	29+4		1		3		1	
		£100,000	Portsmouth	150+3	13+	7		27		1	
Malcolm Waldron	E. B(1)	Emsworth	Southampton (A)	177+1	19	15	4	10			
6-0 12.4 6.9.56			Burnley	16							
		£60,000	Portsmouth	12							
MIDFIELD											
Kevin Dillon	E. U.21(1), Y.	Sunderland	Birmingham C. (A)	181+5	14	9		15	3		
6-0 11.0 18.12.59	Div. 3, 83	£200,000	Portsmouth	47	4	2		14	2		
Bobby Doyle	Div. 3, 83	Dumbarton	Dumbarton								
6-0 11.2 27.12.53		F	Barnsley	148+1	5	6		16			
		£20,000	Peterborough U.	130	18	8		10	2		
		£120,000	Blackpool	47+2	6	5		2			
		£90,000	Portsmouth	149	10	4		14	1		
Mike Kennedy*	Ei. U.21	Salford	Halifax T. (A)	74+2	2	6		4			
5-10 10.6 9.4.61		£50,000	Huddersfield T.	80+1	4+2	8		9			
		£100,000	Middlesbrough	68	4	7		5			
		£10,000	Portsmouth								
Gary Stanley		Burton	Chelsea (A)	105+4	5	4+1		15			
5-9 12.6 4.3.54		£300,000	Everton	52	7	2		1			
		£150,000	Swansea C.	60+12	4	1	2	3			
		F	Portsmouth	11+1							
Neil Webb	E. Y	Reading	Reading (A)	65+7	2	2		22			
6-1 11.12 30.7.63	Div. 3, 83	£87,500	Portsmouth	82	5	4		18	1		
Paul Wimbleton	E. S.	Havant	Portsmouth (A)	5+5							
5-8 10.6 13.11.64											
FORWARDS											
Alan Biley	Div. 3, 83	Leighton Buzzard	Luton T. (A)								
5-8½ 11.11 26.2.57	Div. 4, 74	F	Cambridge U.	160+5	12	5		75	4	3	
		£350,000	Derby Co.	47	2	2		19			
		£300,000	Everton	16+3				3			
			Stoke (L)	8				1			
		£100,000	Portsmouth	83	6	4		39	4	2	
Scott McGarvey	S. U.21(4)	Glasgow	Manchester U.	13+12				3			
6-0 11.5 22.4.63			Wolverhampton W. (L)	13				2			
		£85,000	Portsmouth								
Nicky Morgan		East Ham	West Ham U. (A)	14+7	1			2			
5-10½ 13.5 30.10.59		£50,000	Portsmouth	19+12	1+1	+1		10		1	

CONTRACT PLAYERS WITH LESS THAN TEN APPEARANCES: Kevin Ball (D) (1 Lg), **Paul Hardyman (D)** (2 + 1 Lg), **Paul Wood (F)** (7 + 1 Lg)

NON-CONTRACT PLAYERS 1984-85: Darren Angel, Brendan O'Connell, Gary Stroud. Mark Hateley was Player of the Year 1983-84

APPRENTICES: Tony Oliver, Martin Roderick, Lee Sandford, Bob Taylor

PORTSMOUTH

DIVISION TWO 16TH **FA CUP** 4TH ROUND **MILK CUP** 2ND ROUND

MATCH	DATE	COMPETITION	VENUE	OPPONENTS	RESULT	HALF TIME	L'GUE POS'N	GOALSCORERS	ATTENDANCE
1	A 27	CL	H	Middlesbrough	L0-1	0-1			17,547
2	**31**	**MC 1**	**A**	**Hereford U**	**L2-3**	**1-1**		**Hateley, Dillon (pen)**	**4,631**
3	S 3	CL	A	Fulham	W2-0	1-0	14	Hateley, Biley	10,672
4	6	CL	H	Barnsley	W2-1	1-0		Hateley, Webb	12,804
5	10	CL	H	Manchester C	L1-2	1-2	11	Morgan	18,852
6	**13**	**MC 1**	**H**	**Hereford U**	**W3-1**	**2-1**		**Biley, Webb, Dillon (pen)**	**8,363**
7	17	CL	A	Cardiff C	D0-0	0-0	10		9,033
8	24	CL	H	Shrewsbury T	W4-1	1-1	9	Hateley, Biley, Dillon (pen), Morgan	11,909
9	27	CL	A	Crystal Palace	L1-2	0-1		Biley	8,486
10	O 1	CL	A	Newcastle U	L2-4	0-3	12	Biley, Tait	25,411
11	**4**	**MC 2**	**H**	**Aston Villa**	**D2-2**	**1-0**		**Hateley, Gibson (og)**	**18,484**
12	8	CL	A	Brighton & HA	W1-0	1-0	8	Morgan	17,582
13	15	CL	H	Sheffield W	L0-1	0-0	10		16,335
14	**26**	**MC 2**	**A**	**Aston Villa**	**L2-3**[1]	**1-1**		**Biley, Dillon**	**20,898**
15	29	CL	A	Leeds U	L1-2	0-1	15	Morgan	16,254
16	N 1	CL	H	Cambridge U	W5-0	2-0		Hateley 3 (1 pen), Howe, Tait	10,852
17	5	CL	H	Grimsby T	W4-0	2-0	7	Hateley 3, Tait	12,906
18	12	CL	A	Carlisle U	D0-0	0-0	7		4,814
19	19	CL	A	Blackburn R	L1-2	1-0	10	Webb	5,551
20	26	CL	H	Oldham Ath	L3-4	0-4	14	Biley, Howe, Webb	11,404
21	D 3	CL	A	Huddersfield T	L1-2	0-1	15	Hateley	8,724
22	10	CL	H	Derby Co	W3-0	2-0	12	Biley, Dillon (pen), Morgan	11,834
23	17	CL	A	Swansea C	W2-1	0-1	10	Dillon, Biley	6,404
24	26	CL	H	Charlton Ath	W4-0	2-0	10	Hateley, Biley, Morgan, Webb	15,331
25	27	CL	A	Chelsea	D2-2	2-2	10	Hateley, Dillon	25,440
26	31	CL	H	Fulham	L1-4	1-2	10	Biley	15,649
27	J 2	CL	A	Shrewsbury T	L0-2	0-1	11		4,970
28	**7**	**FAC 3**	**H**	**Grimsby T**	**W2-1**	**0-0**		**Hateley, Morgan**	**12,707**
29	14	CL	A	Middlesbrough	D0-0	0-0	11		7,971
30	21	CL	H	Cardiff C	D1-1	0-1	11	Dillon (pen)	11,938
31	**28**	**FAC 4**	**H**	**Southampton**	**L0-1**	**0-0**			**36,000**
32	F 4	CL	H	Newcastle U	L1-4	0-2		Webb	18,686
33	11	CL	A	Manchester C	L1-2	1-0	14	Wood	23,138
34	18	CL	H	Leeds U	L2-3	2-1	14	Morgan, Hateley	13,911
35	25	CL	A	Cambridge U	W3-1	2-0	12	Biley, Hateley 2	4,359
36	M 3	CL	A	Grimsby T	W4-3	2-2	12	Hateley, Biley, Dillon 2	8,729
37	10	CL	H	Carlisle U	L0-1	0-0	13		10,748
38	17	CL	A	Barnsley	W3-0	1-0	11	Hateley, Biley, Webb	7,030
39	24	CL	H	Crystal Palace	L0-1	0-1	12		10,237
40	31	CL	H	Brighton & HA	W5-1	0-1	11	Webb, Doyle, Hateley, Biley, Dillon	12,724
41	A 7	CL	A	Sheffield W	L0-2	0-1	12		20,239
42	14	CL	H	Blackburn R	L2-4	2-0	15	Webb 2	8,915
43	21	CL	A	Charlton Ath	L1-2	1-0	15	Morgan	6,328
44	24	CL	H	Chelsea	D2-2	0-1		Biley, Dillon	19,267
45	28	CL	A	Oldham Ath	L2-3	1-1	15	Webb, Hateley (pen)	3,558
46	M 5	CL	H	Huddersfield T	D1-1	1-0	17	Hateley	7,738
47	9	CL	A	Derby Co	L0-2	0-0			10,181
48	12	CL	H	Swansea C	W5-0	2-0	16	Biley 3, Hateley, Morgan	7,359

[1]After Extra Time **Av Home Att 13,196**

Goal Scorers

League (73): Hateley 21 (2 pens), Biley 17, Webb 10, Dillon 9 (4 pens), Morgan 9, Tait 3, Howe 2, Doyle 1, Wood 1
FA Cup (2): Hateley 1, Morgan 1
Milk Cup (9): Dillon 3 (2 pens), Biley 2, Hateley 2, Webb 1, opponent 1

1983-84

Knight	Ellis	Sullivan	Doyle	Tait	Money	Webb	Dillon	Hateley	Biley	Rogers	Aizlewood	Morgan	Howe	McLaughlin	Thomas	Hindmarch (L)	Wimbleton	Ball K	Stanley	Wood	Waldron	Hardyman	Gosney	REFEREE	
1	2	3	4	5	6	7	8	9	10	11														A Crickmore	1
	2	3	4	5	6	7	8	9	10	11													1	**K Cooper**	**2**
1	2	12	4	5	3	7	8	9	10	11*	6													DH Brazier	3
1	2		4	5	3	7	8	9	10	11	6													KG Salmon	4
1	2		4	5	3	7	8		10	11	6	9												D Vickers	5
1	2		4	5	3	7	8	9	10	11	6													**M Bodenham**	**6**
1	2		4	5	3	7	8		10	11		9	6											VG Callow	7
1			4	5	3	7	8	9*	10	11	6	12		2										EJ Scales	8
1			4	5	3	7	8	9	10	11	6			2										IJ Borrett	9
1			4	5	3	7	8	9	10	11*	6	12		2										W Scott	10
1			4	5	3	7*	8	9	10	12	6	11		2										**J Moules**	**11**
1			4	5	3	7	8	9	10		6	11		2										C Downey	12
1			4	5	3	7	8	9	10		6	11		2										AW Ward	13
1			4	5	3	7	8	9	10	11	6*	12		2										**D Richardson**	**14**
1		3	4	5		7	8	9	10			11	6	2										GM Tyson	15
1		3	4	5		7	8	9	10	11			6	2										D Reeves	16
1		3	4	5		7	8	9	10	11		12	6	2*										R Lewis	17
1	12	3	4			7	8	9	10	11*	5†		6	2										G Courtney	18
1	12	3	4			7	8	9	10	11	5*		6	2										D Shaw	19
1	5	3				7	8	9	10	11		4	6	2										ML James	20
1		3	4	5		7	8	9	10				6	2	11									MG Peck	21
1		3	4	5		7	8	9	10*			12		2	11	6								A Buksh	22
1		3		5		7	8	9	10			12		2	11	6	4*							K Barratt	23
1	3			5		7	8	9	10		6	4		2	11									D Allison	24
1	3		4	5		7	8	9	10		6	12		2*	11									M Taylor	25
1	2*	3	4	5		7†	8	9	10		6	12			11									L Burden	26
1		3	4	5		7	8	9	10	12		6			11*			2						T Fitzharris	27
1	2	3	4	5		7	8	9*	10		6	12			11									**J Moules**	**28**
1	5	3	4				8				6	10		2	11*		12		7	9				L Dilkes	29
1		3	4	5			8	9	10		6	11		2					7*	12				A Gunn	30
1		3	4	5		7	8	9	10	11	6			2										**L Shapter**	**31**
1		3	4	5		7	8	9			6	10		2						11				D Axcell	32
1		3	4	5		7	8	9			6	10		2						11				K Hackett	33
1		3		5		7	8	9			6	10		2					4	11				T Bune	34
1		3		5		7	8	9	10		6	11		2					4					B Hill	35
1		3	4	5		7	8	9	10		6			2					11					J Worrall	36
1		3	4	5		7	8	9	10		6	12							11*		2			J Deakin	37
1		3	4	5		7	8	9	10					2					11		6			A Robinson	38
1		3	4	8		7		9	10		6*	11		2							5	12		K Baker	39
1		3	4		6	7	8	9	10						11				2		5			B Stevens	40
1		3	4		6	7		9	10					2	11				8		5			N Ashley	41
1		3	4	8	6	7		9	10*					2	11				12		5			A Ward	42
1			4	10	6	7	8*					9		2	12					11	5	3		K Cooper	43
1		3	4	11	6	7	8	9	10					2							5			M Bodenham	44
1		3	4	11	6	7		9	10					2	12				8*		5			T Holbrook	45
1		3	4	6		7	8	9	10					2						11	5			M Dimblebee	46
1		3	4	6		7		9	10					2						11	5	8		D Scott	47
1		3	4*	6		7		9	10			12		2	11				8		5			D Hedges	48
42	10	30	37	36	16	40	36	38	37	13	22	16	8	33	12	2	1	1	11	7	12	2		League Appearances	
	+2S	+1S								+1S		+9S			+2S		+1S		+1S	+1S		+1S			
2	1	2	2	2		2	2	2	2	1	2	1S		1	1									FA Cup Appearances	
3	2	1	4	4	4	4	4	4	4	3+1S	3	1+1S		2									1	Milk Cup Appearances	

FRATTON PARK

Official Address: Fratton Park, Portsmouth PO4 8RA. Telephone: Portsmouth (0705) 731204

Telegraphic: 'Pompey' Portsmouth

Ground Capacity: 36,000

Record Attendance: 51,385 v. Derby County,. F.A. Cup Round 6, 26 Feb 1949

Record Receipts: £122,000 v. Southampton, F.A. Cup Round 4, 28 Jan 1984

Size of Playing Area: 116yds × 73 yds

Season Tickets: Stand: £106.80; Ground £53.80

Executive Box Season Tickets: None

Cost of Stand Tickets: £5.60; **Terraces:** £2.80

Match and Ticket Information: South Stand (central section) bookable ten days in advance

Car Parking: Side-street parking only

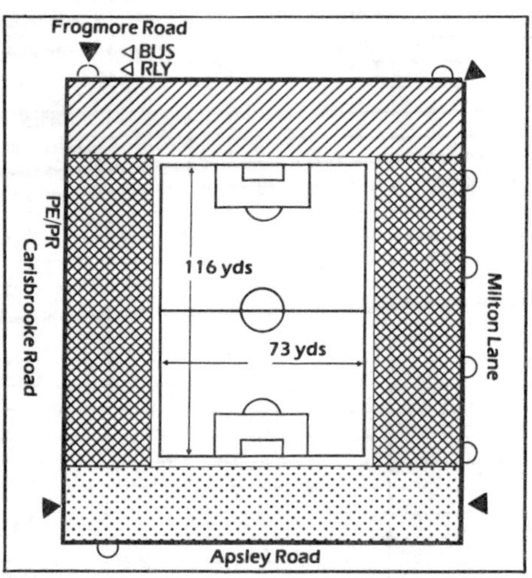

For key see page 12

How to get to the ground

From North and West: Use Motorway M27 and M275 and at end at roundabout take 2nd exit and in 0.2m at T road turn right A2047 into London Road. In 1.3m over railway bridge and turn left into Goldsmith Avenue. In 0.6m turn left into Frogmore Road for Portsmouth F.C.

From East: Use A27 then follow signs Southsea A2030. In 3m at roundabout turn left A288. Then turn right into Priory Crescent then take next turning right into Carisbrooke Road for Portsmouth F.C.

PORT VALE   Division 4

President
J Burgess

Chairman
J D Lloyd

Directors
D P McGrath
A McPherson
W T Bell

Secretary
P A Shaw

Assistant Secretary
Mrs A Cegielski

Commercial Manager
M Cullerton (0782-814134/5)

Manager
J Rudge

Youth Team Coach
G Barnett

Chief Scout
R Williams

Groundsman
R Fairbanks

When a club finishes in the penultimate position of their league it can fairly be said that they have experienced a poor season and this was the case with Port Vale, who return to the Fourth Division after only one season amongst better company. What a tragedy! As so often happens the Cup form provided little relief, but that is another story. The main result of the poor form was a change of management during the campaign with John McGrath being replaced as Manager by the Chief Coach, John Rudge. McGrath is astute enough to know that survival depends on a team's success.

At no time during the season did Port Vale seem likely to escape an early return to the lowest reaches of the League and some bad defeats were suffered as the team were really out of their class; no matches were won from 10th September 1983 until Boxing Day, when the promotion-chasing Sheffield United came to grief at Vale Park. During that bad run Burnley won by seven clear goals at Turf Moor and the stage was set for ultimate disaster, only Exeter City having a worse record in the Division. In the Cups Wrexham were well beaten in both legs of the Milk Cup First Round (aggregate 8-2 for Vale), but this brought Manchester United to Vale Park and at least a good gate was forthcoming, whilst the team played gallantly in both legs before losing (0-1 and 0-2). But in the F.A. Cup the First Round brought Lincoln City to Vale Park and they left with a win by the odd goal in three. There remained the fight to avoid the drop and it failed with the Associate Members Cup bringing no relief from the gloom.

Manager John Rudge has problems. That is an understatement! With only Hunter showing any consistency and the team being chopped and changed last season the supporters will hope that such a trend will not continue. They will also hope that the veteran Scot, Ally Brown, will do the same for Vale as he has done for W.B.A., Walsall and others. He has in his time lifted them and may do so again at Burslem.

WLM

Back Row L to R: Russel Bromage, Wayne Cegielski, Ally Brown, Phil Sproson, Barry Siddall, Chris Pearce, John Ridley, Derek Monaghan, Martyn Smith, Colin Tartt. **Front Row:** Terry Armstrong, Robbie Earle, Peter Griffiths, Geoff Hunter, Andrew Shankland, Alan Webb, Tommy Gore, Eamon O'Keefe.

PORT VALE F.C.

1876

'THE VALIANTS'

Formed: 1876 **Turned Professional:** 1885 **Ltd Co:** 1911
Previous Names: Burslem Port Vale (until 1913)
Previous Managers: Since 1946:
Billy Smith Gordon Hodgson Ivor Powell Freddie Steele Norman Low Freddie Steele Jackie Mudie Sir Stanley Matthews Gordon Lee Roy Sproson Colin Harper Bob Smith Dennis Butler Alan Bloor John McGrath
Honours: Division Three (North) Champions 1929-30, 1953-4 Division Four Champions 1958-9
League Career: Original member Division Two 1892 Not re-elected to Division Two 1896 Re-elected to Division Two 1898 Resigned from Division Two 1907 Returned to Division Two** 1919 Relegated to Division Three (North) 1929 Promoted to Division Two 1930 Relegated to Division Three (North) 1936 Transferred to Division Three (South) 1938 Transferred to Division Three (North) 1952 Promoted to Division Two 1954 Relegated to Division Three (South) 1957 Original members of Division Four 1958 Promoted to Division Three 1959 Relegated to Division Four 1965 Promoted to Division Three 1970 Relegated to Division four 1978 Promoted to Division Three 1983 Relegated to Division Four 1984
**Port Vale took over the fixtures of Leeds City — expelled from the League for irregularities — in October 1919.
Colours: White shirts with black trim, white shorts, black stockings
Change Colours: Yellow shirts, green shorts, yellow stockings

CLUB RECORDS

Most Appearances for Club: Roy Sproson, 1950-72 (League 761 + 5 subs + F.A. Cup 65 + League Cup 21) **Total** 831 + 5 subs
Most Capped Player: Sammy Morgan 7(18), Northern Ireland **For England:** None
Record Goalscorer in a Match: Stewart Littlewood, 6 v Chesterfield, Div 2, 24.09.32
Record League Goalscorer in a season: Wilf Kirkham, 38, Div 2, 1926-7 **In all competitions:** Wilf Kirkham, 41 (League 38, F.A. Cup 3)
Record League Goalscorer in a career: Wilf Kirkham, 154, 1923-9 & 1931-3 **In all competitions:** Wilf Kirkham, 165 (League 154, F.A. Cup 11)
Record Transfer Fee Received: £135,000 from Stoke City for Mark Chamberlain, 1982
Record Transfer Fee Paid: £40,000 to Bury for Peter Farrell, Nov 1978 £40,000 to Wolverhampton Wanderers for Ken Todd, Aug 1978 £40,000 to Crewe Alexandra for Paul Bowles, Sept 1979
Best Performances: League: 5th Div 2 1930-1 **F.A. Cup:** Semi-Finalists 1953-4 **League/Milk Cup:** Never past 2nd Round
Most League Points: 88 in Div 4, 1982-3 **Most League Goals:** 110, Div 4, 1958-9
Record League Victory: 9-1 v Chesterfield, Div 2, 24 Sept 1932
Record League Defeat: 0-10 v Sheffield United (H), Div 2, 10 Dec 1892 0-10 v Notts County, Div 2, 26 Feb 1895

Club Statistician for the Directory: Steve Askey

Programme Editor
Cowdall's Printing Co., 16 Flag Lane, Crewe.
(0270) 212389

Price	Number of Pages
50p	20

Subscriptions
No fixed rate

PORT VALE

PLAYERS NAME Ht Wt Birthdate	Honours	Birthplace Transfers	Clubs	APPEARANCES League	Milk Cup	F.A.C.	A.M.C.	GOALS League	Milk Cup	F.A.C.	A.M.C.
GOALKEEPERS											
Chris Pearce	W. Y. S	Newport	Wolverhampton W. (A)								
6-0 11.4 7.8.61		F	Blackburn R.								
		F	Rochdale	41	6	1					
		F	Port Vale	7	1						
Barry Siddall	E. Y	Ellesmere Port	Bolton W. (A)	137	10	11					
6-0½ 14.4 12.9.54			Sunderland	167	11	9					
			Darlington (L)	8							
			Port Vale	72	5	2	2				
			Blackpool (L)	7							
DEFENDERS											
Chris Banks		Stone	Port Vale								
5-8 10.8 12.11.65											
Wayne Cegielski*	W. U.21(2)	Bedwelty	Tottenham H. (A)								
6-0 12.0 11.1.56	FAYC. 74		Northampton T. (L)	11							
		F	Schalke Oy								
		F	Wrexham	150 + 12	7 + 1	10 +	2			1	
		F	Port Vale	82 + 1	5			4			
John Ridley		Consett	Port Vale	143 + 7	8	13		3		1	
6-1½ 12.6 27.4.52		£55,000	Leicester C.	17 + 7		2					
		£35,000	Chesterfield	121 + 3	9	6		8			
		F	Port Vale	62 + 9	4	2	1 + 1	6			
Phil Sproson		Trent Vale	Port Vale	226 + 4	13	11 +	2	18	2		
6-0 12.0 13.10.59											
Colin Tartt		Liverpool	Alsager T.								
5-11 17.7 23.11.50			Port Vale	171 + 4	5	8 + 2		7		2	
		£15,000	Chesterfield	185 + 1	15	12		7	2	1	
		£15,000	Port Vale	104 + 1	6	7	2	8			1
MIDFIELD											
Terry Armstrong		Barnsley	Huddersfield T. (A)	36 + 4							
5-10 12.2 10.7.58		F	Port Vale	91 + 2	6	6		12		1	
Russell Bromage		Stoke	Port Vale (A)	222 + 7	13	11	1	10	1		
5-11 11.5 9.11.59			Oldham A. (L)	2							
Tom Gore		Liverpool	Tranmere R. (N-C)								
5-7 11.8 26.11.53			Wigan A.	102	9	7		14	4	4	
		£20,000	Bury	118 + 1	4	9		15	1		
			Port Vale	33 + 3	4	1	2	2	1		
Peter Griffiths		Barnstaple	Bideford								
5-6 10.8 14.8.57		£15,000	Stoke C.	46 + 14	+ 3	1		5			
			Bradford C. (L)	2							
			Port Vale								
Geoff Hunter		Hull	Manchester U.								
5-9 10.5 27.10.59		F	Crewe A.	86 + 1	4	2		8	1		
		£10,500	Port Vale	127 + 2	9	7	2	8	1		
Eamon O'Keefe†	E.S-P(2), Ei.(1)	Manchester	Stalybridge Celt.								
5-7 11.5 13.10.53		£6,000	Plymouth A.								
		Hyde U.	Saudi Arabia/Mossley								
		£22,000	Everton	26 + 14	1	4		6	1	1	
		£65,000	Wigan A.	56 + 2	3			25	1		
			Port Vale	34 + 3	4	1	1	10	1		
FORWARDS											
Ally Brown	Div. 2, 71	Musselburgh	Leicester C.	93 + 8	11 +	7 + 1		32	1	2	
6-0 11.0 12.4.51		£60,000	W.B.A.	254 + 24	27	26 +		72	2	5	
		F	Crystal Palace	11							
		F	Walsall	37 + 1	7	1		13	2		
Robbie Earle		Stoke	Stoke C. (N-C)								
5-9 10.0 27.1.65		F	Port Vale	14 + 6	1 + 1		+ 1	1			
Martin Henderson	SPD.(1), SC.(1)	Kirkcaldy	Glasgow Rangers								
6-0 12.9 3.5.56	Div. 2, 80	£30,000	Leicester C.	72 + 12	3 + 1	5		12		4	
		£70,000	Chesterfield	87	4	3		23		1	
			Port Vale	27		1		7			
Andy Shankland		Stoke	Port Vale (A)	13 + 10	2			1			
5-8 9.0 8.4.64											
APPRENTICES: Les Evans, Eric Mountford, Adrian Reeves-Jones, Paul Sherwin											
Alan Webb		Wrockwardine	W.B.A. (A)	23 + 1			0 + 1				
5-9½ 12.0 1.1.63			Lincoln C. (L)	11							
Derek Monaghan	E. Y	Bromsgrove	W.B.A. (A)	14 + 5	2 + 1	1		2	1		
5-10 11.3 20.1.59											

PORT VALE

DIVISION THREE 23RD **FA CUP** 1ST ROUND **MILK CUP** 2ND ROUND

MATCH	DATE	COMPETITION	VENUE	OPPONENTS	RESULT	HALF TIME	L'GUE POS'N	GOALSCORERS	ATTENDANCE
1	A 27	CL	H	Scunthorpe U	D0-0	0-0			4,565
2	**31**	**MC 1**	**H**	**Wrexham**	**W3-1**	**1-1**		**Sproson 2, O'Keefe (pen)**	**3,916**
3	S 3	CL	A	Rotherham U	L1-2	1-1	17	O'Keefe	4,847
4	6	CL	A	Millwall	L2-3	0-1		Steel 2	4,918
5	10	CL	H	Bristol R	W2-0	1-0	16	Sproson, Steel	4,308
6	**13**	**MC 1**	**A**	**Wrexham**	**W5-1**	**4-1**		**Hunter, Gore, Newton 2, Steel**	**2,903**
7	17	CL	A	Wimbledon	L2-4	1-1	18	Newton 2	2,690
8	24	CL	H	Bradford C	L1-2	1-1	21	Fox	4,897
9	26	CL	H	Wigan Ath	D1-1	0-1		Bromage	4,655
10	O 1	CL	A	Walsall	L0-2	0-2	21		3,757
11	**3**	**MC 2**	**H**	**Manchester U**	**L0-1**	**0-1**			**19,855**
12	14	CL	A	Orient	L0-3	0-1			3,027
13	18	CL	A	Brentford	L1-3	0-1		Henderson	3,903
14	22	CL	H	Bolton W	L1-2	1-2	24	Tartt	4,269
15	**26**	**MC 2**	**A**	**Manchester U**	**L0-2**	**0-1**			**23,589**
16	29	CL	A	Newport Co	L1-2	0-1	24	Ridley	3,829
17	31	CL	H	Plymouth Arg	L0-1	0-1			3,466
18	N 5	CL	A	Exeter C	D1-1	1-1	24	Armstrong	3,301
19	12	CL	H	Oxford U	L1-3	0-1	24	O'Keefe	3,927
20	**19**	**FAC 1**	**H**	**Lincoln C**	**L1-2**	**0-2**		**Bright**	**3,647**
21	26	CL	A	Burnley	L0-7	0-6	24		6,353
22	D 3	CL	H	Gillingham	L0-1	0-1	24		3,086
23	17	CL	H	Lincoln C	L0-1	0-1	24		2,861
24	26	CL	A	Preston NE	L0-4	0-3	24		5,599
25	27	CL	H	Sheffield U	W2-0	1-0	24	O'Keefe, Young	7,034
26	31	CL	A	Hull C	L0-1	0-0	24		9,431
27	J 2	CL	H	AFC Bournemouth	W2-1	2-0	24	O'Keefe, Henderson	4,008
28	21	CL	H	Wimbledon	W2-0	1-0	24	O'Keefe, Bright	3,627
29	28	CL	A	Bristol R	D0-0	0-0	24		6,502
30	30	CL	H	Southend U	W2-1	1-0		Henderson, Ridley	3,636
31	F 4	CL	H	Walsall	L0-2	0-1	24		6,966
32	11	CL	A	Bradford C	D2-2	2-1	24	Henderson, Gore (pen)	5,340
33	14	CL	A	Plymouth Arg	L0-3	0-0			3,552
34	18	CL	H	Newport Co	W4-2	2-2	23	Henderson, Tartt, Young, Bright	3,437
35	**22**	**AMC 1**	**A**	**Hereford U**	**W1-0**	**1-0**		**Tartt**	**1,605**
36	25	CL	A	Bolton W	L0-2	0-1	23		5,818
37	M 3	CL	H	Brentford	W4-3	3-2	22	Gore (pen), Fox, O'Keefe 2	3,704
38	5	CL	H	Exeter C	D2-2	1-1		Henderson, Young	4,338
39	10	CL	A	Oxford U	L0-2	0-2	21		7,645
40	**13**	**AMC 2**	**A**	**Bristol R**	**L0-2**	**0-0**			**2,585**
41	19	CL	A	Southend U	W2-1	1-0		Bright, O'Keefe	2,080
42	31	CL	A	Wigan Ath	L0-3	0-3	21		3,163
43	A 2	CL	H	Rotherham U	L2-3	1-0		O'Keefe, Massey (pen)	3,705
44	9	CL	H	Orient	W2-0	2-0		Henderson, Hunter	3,169
45	14	CL	A	Gillingham	D1-1	0-0	22	Bright	3,323
46	17	CL	A	Scunthorpe U	D1-1	1-0		Sproson	2,952
47	21	CL	H	Preston NE	D1-1	0-0	23	O'Keefe (pen)	3,574
48	24	CL	A	Sheffield U	L1-3	0-2		Bright	14,385
49	28	CL	H	Burnley	L2-3	1-1	23	Bright, Young	3,061
50	M 5	CL	A	AFC Bournemouth	D1-1	1-1	23	Bright	3,305
51	7	CL	H	Hull C	W1-0	1-0	23	Bright	3,958
52	12	CL	A	Lincoln C	L2-3	1-1	23	Bright, Armstrong	1,372
53	14	CL	H	Milwall	W1-0	1-0		Fox	2,299
								Av Home Att	**4,023**

Goal Scorers

League (51): O'Keefe 10 (1 pen), Bright 9, Henderson 7, Young 4, Fox 3, Steel 3, Armstrong 2, Gore 2 (2 pens), Newton 2, Ridley 2, Sproson 2, Tarrt 2, Bromage 1, Hunter 1, Masse 1 (pen)
FA Cup (1): Bright 1
Milk Cup (7): Newton 2, Sproson 2, Gore 1, Hunter 1, O'Keefe 1 (1 pen), Steel 1
AMC (1): Tartt 1

1983-84

Siddall	Tartt	Bromage	Hunter	Sproson	Cegielski	Fox	Gore	Bright	O'Keefe	Armstrong	Steel	Pollard	Newton	White	Pearce	Shankland	Ridley	Henderson	Earle	Oakes	Thompson (L)	Young (L)	Massey (L)		REFEREE	
1	2	3	4	5	6	7	8	9*	10	11	12														N Glover	1
1	2	3	4	5	6	7	8	9*	10	11	12														**D Scott**	**2**
1	2	3	4	5			8		10	11	7	6	9												K Redford	3
1	2	3	4	5		12	8		10	11*	7	6	9												I Borrett	4
1	2	3	4	5		11	8		10		7	6	9												D Richardson	5
1	2	3	4	5		11	8		10		7	6	9												**J Deakin**	**6**
1	2	3	4	5		11	8		10		7	6	9												M Dimblebee	7
1	2	3	4	5	6	11	8		10	12	7*		9												R Guy	8
1		3	4	5	6	11	8	7	10			2	9												MP Scott	9
1	12	3	4	5	6	11		7	10	8		2*	9												JA Moules	10
1	2	3	4	5	6	11	8	12	10*				9				7								**V Callow**	**11**
		3	4	5	6	11	8	12	10*	7		2			1			9							ML James	12
	2	3	4	5	6		8		12	11*	7				1			9	10						E Read	13
	2		4	5	6	12	8		11		7				1	3*		9	10						J Ashworth	14
	2		4	5*	6	11	8		10		7				1	3	9		12						**G Tyson**	**15**
	2		4		6	11	8		10		7*			12	1	3	5		9						A Crickmore	16
	2		4		6	11	12	9	10						1	3	5		7*	8					D Owen	17
	2		4		6				10	9	7	5			1	3	8		11						C Thomas	18
	2		4		6	7			10	11	9	5			1	3	8								J Key	19
1	2*		4			11	3	12	10	9	7	5					6	8							**R Guy**	**20**
1		2	4		11		3*		10	9	7	5					6	8	12						EJ Parker	21
1		3	4	6	10					11	7	5					8	9			2				D Allison	22
1	2	3	4	5		7					10						8	9			6	11			L Dilkes	23
1	2†	3	4	5		11			12		7*	6					10	9				8			C Seel	24
1	2	3	4		6	11	7		10								5	9				8			R Banks	25
1	2	3	4		6	7	8	12	10								5	9*				11			A Saunders	26
1	2	3	4		6	11	7	12	10								5	9*				8			R Bridges	27
1		3	4	2	6	11	7	12	10								5	9				8*			R Nixon	28
1		3	4	2	6	11	7		10								5	9				8			R Lewis	29
1		3	4	2	6	11	7		10								5	9				8			I Hendrick	30
1		3	4	2	6	11	7	12	10*								5	9				8			N Wilson	31
1	2	3	4	6		11	7	10									5	9	12			8			K Walmsley	32
1			4	2	6	11	7	12	10							3	5	9*				8			L Burden	33
1	3		4	2	6	11	7	12	10								5	9*				8			F Roberts	34
1	2		4	5*	6	11	7	9	10			3					12					8			**A Crickmore**	**35**
1	2	3	4	5	6	11	7	9	10			12										8*			T Mills	36
1	2	3	4	5	6	11	7		10									9*	12			8			L Robinson	37
1		3	4	2	6	11	7		10								5	9*	12			8			M Peck	38
1		3	4	2	6	11	7	10	12								5	9*				8			D Vickers	39
1	2*	3	4*	10	6	11	7	9				12					5		13			8			**D Hedges**	**40**
1		3		2	6	11	7	9	10								5					8	4		C Downey	41
1		3		4	6	11		10				2				12	5	9	7*			8			A Challinor	42
1		3	4	2	6	11		12	10*								5	9				8	7		A Robinson	43
1		3	4	5	2	11	7		10								6	9					8		K Barratt	44
1		3	4	5	6		11	12	10			2						9*				8	7		I Borrett	45
1		3	4	5	6	10	7	9		11		2										8			M Dimblebee	46
1		3	4	5	6	12	7	9	10	11		2										8*			A Seville	47
1		3	4	5	2	11		9	10	7							6					8			K Redfern	48
1		3	4	5	2	11		9	10	7							6					8			B Stevens	49
1		3	4	5	2	11	12	9		7*							6	10				8			E Scales	50
1		3	4	5	2*	11	12	10		7							6	9				8			L Dilkes	51
1		3		5	12	11	4	9		7							6	10*	2			8			G Courtney	52
1				5	2	11	8	9		7		3					6		10			4			R Guy	53
39	21	38	42	38	38	37	33	17	34	18	14	17	7	0	7	6	30	27	8	1	2	28	4		League Appearances	
	+1S				+1S	+3S	+3S	+9S	+3S	+1S	+1S	+1S		+1S		+1S			+4S							
1	1		1			1	1	1S	1	1	1	1					1	1							FA Cup Appearances	
3	4	3	4	4	3	4	4	1+1S	4	1	2+1S	1	2		1	1	2		1S						Milk Cup Appearances	
2	2	1	2	2	2	2	2	2	1			1+1S					1+1S		1S			2			AM Cup Appearances	

VALE PARK

Official Address: Vale Park, Burslem, Stoke-on-Trent. Telephone: 0782 814134

Ground Capacity: 35,000

Record Attendance: 50,000 v. Aston Villa, F.A. Cup Round 5, 20 Feb 1960

Record Receipts: £45,873 v. Manchester United, Milk Cup Round 2, 3 Oct 1983

Size of Playing Area: 116yds × 76 yds

Season Tickets: Stand: £52, (£26 OAP/Agents/Juveniles); Ground: £31 (£15.50 OAP/Agents/Juveniles)

Executive Box Season Tickets: £125

Cost of Stand Tickets: £3 (£1.50 Juveniles/OAP); **Terraces:** £2 (£1 Juveniles/OAPs)

Match and Ticket Information: No advance bookings

Car Parking: Parking (ample) behind the Railway Stand on Hamil Road and on Lorne Street sides of ground.

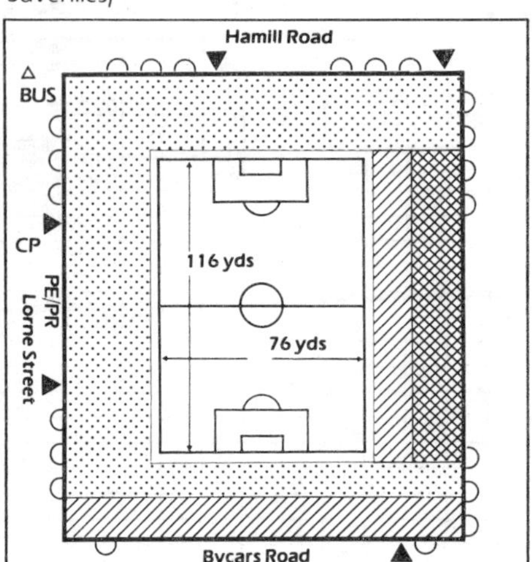

For key see page 12

How to get to the ground

From North: Use Motorway M6 until junction 16 then join A500 S.P. Stoke. In 5.9m branch left and at roundabout take 1st exit A50. In 0.4m turn right B5051 into Newcastle Street and at end over crossroads into Moorland Road. Shortly turn left into Hamil Road for Port Vale F.C.

From East: Use A50 or A52 into Stoke upon Trent then follow signs Burslem A50 into Waterloo Road. At Burslem crossroads turn right into Moorland Road. Shortly turn left into Hamil Road for Port Vale F.C.

From South and West: Use Motorway M6 until junction 15 then A5006 and A500. In 6.3m branch left and at roundabout take 3rd exit A50. In 0.4m turn right B5051 into Newcastle Street and at end over crossroads into Moorland Road. Shortly turn left into Hamil Road for Port Vale F.C.

PRESTON NORTH END Division 3

Chairman
Keith W Leeming

Directors
John T Garratt (Joint V President)
Malcolm J Woodhouse (Joint V President)
F Neil Bamber
Barney J Campbell
J N Duncan Catterall
Thomas WS Croft FCIOB
John Devol MBICSC
Jack Francis
Edward Griffiths BVsc, MRCVS
Michael J Riding AMIMI
J Ernest Wignall
John W Wilding
J Terence Worden

Company Secretary
Edward Griffiths BCsc, MRCVS

Club Secretary
Derek J Allan

Manager
Alan Kelly

Player/Coach
Tommy Booth

Commercial Manager
David Bradshaw
(0772-795919, 795465, 795156)

After the 'miracle' of escaping relegation to Division Four, at the end of the 1982-83, the club's dire financial state forced the club to release 18 of the first team squad in a desperate bid to cut costs and hope to re-sign them again on similar terms or reduced terms. Most of the team re-signed on new contracts, but several players signed for other clubs; Alex Bruce to Wigan Athletic, Don O'Riordan and Graham Bell to Carlisle United (Bell later joined Bolton Wanderers), Gordon Coleman to Bury, Gary Buckley to Chorley (later Bury), Simon Westwell to Chorley (after a trial at Blackpool) and Alan Gowling retired. No new players were signed until the start of the season, when ex-Everton David Jones signed (his brother Mark Jones also later signed), Geoff Twentyman was signed from non-league Chorley and Peter Houghton was signed from Wigan Athletic.

The season started well, the team being unbeaten in the first five games, but the club hit a bad patch in October and early November, when they lost a record eight league games in succession. A League Cup win over Tranmere Rovers was followed with two wins over Wolverhampton Wanderers in Round Two. A Third Round League Cup defeat at home to a strong Sheffield Wednesday was soon followed by defeat in the First Round of the F.A. Cup, 1-0 at Scunthorpe by a disputed penalty.

The club had slumped to 22nd in the table, but results picked up briefly. But the manager's (Gordon Lee's) fate was sealed after a 5-1 defeat in a friendly at Crewe on December 10th. After Gordon Lee was sacked, Alan Kelly was appointed caretaker manager, later made permanent. This proved very popular with both supporters and players. The team immediately went on the attack over Christmas, with a 4-0 home win over Port Vale and a 5-1 away win at Scunthorpe. The side now began to pick up points steadily to avoid relegation, but the club's financial problems reached a peak in February. Then a rescue deal was arranged with the local council, which cleared the club's debts. At this time admission prices rose by 30 per cent and various fund raising events have raised further money.

The lowest recorded league gate at home is now 3,146 at the game v. Orient on Saturday 14th April.

After several bad seasons the outlook is beginning to look more hopeful.

Lawrence Bland, The League Directory's Statistician for the Club

Back Row: Tommy Booth, David Jones, Andy McAteer, Glen Campbell, Peter Litchfield, Paul Wilkins, Paul Welsh, Jonathan Clark, Mike Farrelly. **Middle Row:** Dennis Loze (Physio), Richard Hunter, Darren Norris, Darren Whiteley, Geoff Twentyman, Mark Jones, Dale Rudge, Peter Horton, Andrew Murphy, Nigel Greenwood, Harold Sandells, Harry Hubbick (Kit Manager). **Front Row:** Damien Williams, Mark Walsh, Graham Houston, Chris Hunter, Alan Kelly (Manager), Duncan Crosbie, John Kelly, Willie Naughton, Paul Savage. **Squatting:** Tony Pemberton, Ian Stevens.

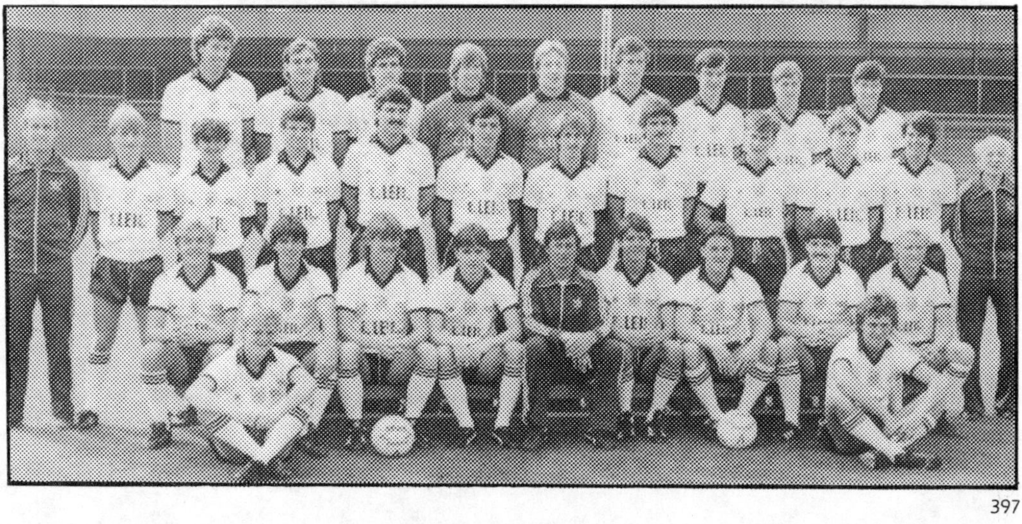

'THE LILLYWHITES' or 'NORTH END'

Sponsored by **Lombard Elizabethan Insurance**

Formed: 1881 **Turned Professional:** 1885 **Ltd Co:** 1893
Previous Managers: 1919 V Hayes 1924 T Lawrence 1925 F Richards 1927 A Gibson 1931 L Hyde 1936-7 T Muirhead 1943-53 W Scott 1953-4 Scot Symon 1954-6 F Hill 1956-61 C Britton 1961-8 J Milne 1968-70 R Seith 1970-3 A Ball Snr 1971 F Lord (caretaker) 1973-5 R Charlton 1975-7 H Catterick 1977-81 N Stiles 1981 T Docherty 1981-3 G Lee
Honours: Division One Champions *1888-89 (first winners), 1889-90
Division Two Champions 1903-4, 1912-13, 1950-51 Division Three Champions 1970-1
F.A. Cup Winners *1889, 1938
*League and F.A. Cup 'Double'
League Career: Original Member of Football League 1888 Relegated to Division 2 1900-1
Promoted to Division 1 1903-4 Relegated to Division 2 1911-2
Promoted to Division 1 1912-3 Relegated to Division 2 1913-4
Promoted to Division 1 1914-5 Relegated to Division 2 1924-5
Promoted to Division 1 1933-4 Relegated to Division 2 1948-9
Promoted to Division 1 1950-1 Relegated to Division 2 1960-1
Relegated to Division 3 1969-70 Promoted to Division 2 1970-1
Relegated to Division 3 1973-4 Promoted to Division 2 1977-8
Relegated to Division 3 1980-1
Colours: White shirts with navy blue trim, navy blue shorts, white stockings with navy blue rings
Change Colours: All yellow

CLUB RECORDS

Most Appearances for Club: Alan Kelly: Football League 447 + 65 Cup games **Total 512**
Most Capped Player: Tom Finney, 76, England
Record Goalscorer in a Match: Jimmy Ross, 8 v Hyde (h) 26-0 1st Round F.A. Cup, 15.10.1887
Record League Goalscorer in a season: Tom Harper, 37, Div 2, 1932-3 **In All Competitions:** Ted Harper 38 (League 37 + F.A. Cup 1), 1932-3
Record League Goalscorer in a career: Tom Finney, 187 **In All Competitions:** Tom Finney, 210 (League 187 + F.A. Cup 23 (1946-60)
Record Transfer Fee Received: £765,000 from Manchester City for Michael Robinson, June 1979
Record Transfer Fee Paid: £95,000 to Nottingham Forest for Steve Elliott, March 1979
Best Performances: League: Champions (2) **F.A. Cup:** Winners (2) **League/Milk Cup:** 4th Round 1963, 1966, 1972, 1981
Most League Points: 61 in Div 3, 1970-1, 1981-2 **Most League Goals:** 100, Div 2, 1927-28; 100, Div 1, 1957-8
Record League Victory: 10-0 v Stoke City, (H) Div 1, 14 Sept 1889
Record League Defeat: 0-7 v Blackpool (h), Div 1, 1 May 1948
Club Statistician for the Directory: L Bland

Programme Editor
Kath Bradshaw

Price	**Number of Pages**
40p	16

Subscriptions
40p per programme plus 20p for postage

PRESTON NORTH END

PLAYERS NAME Ht Wt Birthdate	Honours	Birthplace Transfers	Clubs	APPEARANCES League	Milk Cup	F.A.C.	A.M.C.	GOALS League	Milk Cup	F.A.C.	A.M.C.
GOALKEEPERS											
Glen Campbell		Leyland	P.N.E.	2							
5-11 11.10 26.2.65											
Peter Litchfield†		Manchester	Droylsden								
6-1 13.9 27.7.56		£3,000	P.N.E.	89	8	4					
DEFENDERS											
Tommy Booth*	E. U.23(4)	Manchester	Manchester C.	380+2	49+	27	25E	25	3	5	3E
6-2½ 13.5 9.11.49	ECWC. 70	£30,000	P.N.E.	73	1	1	1	2			
	Lg.C. 70, 76										
David Jones	E. U.21(1)	Liverpool	Everton (A)	79+7				1			
5-11 13.4 17.8.56			Coventry C.	8+3							
			Seiko Sports								
			P.N.E.	37			3	1			
Mark Jones		Liverpool	Runcorn								
5-11 12.0 16.9.60			P.N.E.	4							
Andy McAteer		Preston	P.N.E. (A)	158+2	12	6		5		1	
5-10 11.10 24.4.61											
Geoff Twentyman		Liverpool	Chorley								
6-1 12.10 10.3.59			P.N.E.	25+3			2+1	2			
Paul Welsh		Liverpool	Formby								
6-2 12.4 10.5.66			P.N.E.								
MIDFIELD											
Jon Clark	W. U.21(2),	Swansea	Manchester U. (A)	+1							
5-10 11.10 12.11.58	S	£50,000	Derby Co.	48+5	4	4		3			
		F	P.N.E.	52	5	1	1	5	1		
Mike Farrelly	E. Y. S	Manchester	P.N.E.	38+5	2+1		2	2			
5-11½ 11.11 1.1.62											
John Kelly	E. S	Bebbington	Cammell Lairds								
5-10 10.10 7.10.62			Tranmere R.	55+9	7	1		9	1		
			P.N.E.	85+8	7	3	2	20		1	
Dale Rudge		Wolverhampton	Wolverhampton W. (A)	23+4		1					
5-8 10.6 9.9.63			P.N.E.								
Mark Walsh	E. S U.18	Preston	P.N.E. (A)	56+6	5+1	2	2	2			
5-10 10.10 7.10.62											
FORWARDS											
Peter Houghton		Liverpool	South Liverpool								
5-11 12.7 30.11.54		£500	Wigan A.	169+16	18+	14		62	3	3	
			P.N.E.	30+2			2+1	10			
Graham Houston		Gibraltar	P.N.E.	64+33	5	5	1+2	6		1	
5-8 11.4 24.2.60											
Willie Naughton		Catrine	P.N.E. (A)	117+12	6	4	3	9	2		1
6-0 12.8 20.3.62											
Paul Wilkins		Hackney	Tottenham H. (A)								
6-2 12.0 20.3.64		F	Crystal Palace	9+4				3			
		F	P.N.E.								

NON-CONTRACT PLAYERS 1984-85

Stuart Cameron, Duncan Crosbie, David Despard, Gary Hyslop, Andy Lean, David Leaver, Steve Lillycrop, Andy Murphy, Giuseppe Paladino, Graham Rowlands, Ian Stevens

APPRENTICES

Nigel Greenwood, Darren Whiteley, Damien Williams

PRESTON NORTH END

DIVISION THREE 16TH **FA CUP** 1ST ROUND **MILK CUP** 3RD ROUND

MATCH	DATE	COMPE-TITION	VENUE	OPPONENTS	RESULT	HALF TIME	L'GUE POS'N	GOALSCORERS	ATTEN-DANCE
1	A 27	CL	A	AFC Bournemouth	W1-0	1-0		Houston	4,163
2	**30**	**MC 1**	**H**	**Tranmere R**	**W1-0**	**0-0**		**Kelly**	**3,231**
3	S 3	CL	H	Brentford	D3-3	1-2	7	Kelly 2, Sayer	3,799
4	6	CL	H	Southend U	W4-1	3-0		Sayer, Kelly, Elliott 2	3,967
5	10	CL	A	Sheffield U	D1-1	1-1	7	Sayer	12,441
6	**12**	**MC 1**	**A**	**Tranmere R**	**D0-0**	**0-0**			**2,986**
7	17	CL	H	Hull C	D0-0	0-0	9		6,661
8	24	CL	A	Plymouth Arg	L0-1	0-0	10		3,674
9	27	CL	A	Newport Co	D1-1	0-1		Elliott (pen)	2,542
10	O 1	CL	H	Oxford U	L1-2	1-2	13	Sayer	4,665
11	**4**	**MC 2**	**A**	**Wolverhampton W**	**W3-2**	**1-2**		**Hinnigan 2, Naughton**	**7,796**
12	8	CL	A	Gillingham	L0-2	0-1	14		3,725
13	15	CL	H	Wigan Ath	L2-3	0-1	18	Elliott (pen), Hinnigan	6,622
14	18	CL	H	Wimbledon	L2-3	2-2		Elliott 2	3,515
15	21	CL	A	Millwall	L0-1	0-1			5,243
16	**25**	**MC 2**	**H**	**Wolverhampton W**	**W1-0**	**0-0**		**Elliott**	**8,857**
17	29	CL	H	Lincoln C	L1-2	1-1	20	Clark	4,435
18	N 1	CL	A	Bristol R	L1-3	1-1		Farrelly	5,635
19	5	CL	A	Burnley	L1-2	0-2	22	Houghton	7,915
20	**8**	**MC 3**	**H**	**Sheffield W**	**L0-2**	**0-1**			**11,060**
21	12	CL	H	Rotherham U	W1-0	0-0	20	Hinnigan	3,915
22	**19**	**FAC 1**	**A**	**Scunthorpe U**	**L0-1**	**0-0**			**3,484**
23	26	CL	H	Exeter C	W2-1	1-1	18	Kelly 2	3,373
24	D 3	CL	A	Orient	L1-2	1-0	19	Jones D	2,689
25	17	CL	A	Bolton W	D2-2	1-2	21	Houghton, Farnworth (og)	6,275
26	26	CL	H	Port Vale	W4-0	3-0	18	Houghton 2, Elliott, Kelly	5,599
27	27	CL	A	Scunthorpe U	W5-1	1-0	15	Elliott 3, Houghton, Kelly	3,986
28	31	CL	H	Walsall	L0-1	0-0	18		6,226
29	J 2	CL	A	Bradford C	L2-3	1-1	18	Naughton, Kelly	6,405
30	14	CL	H	AFC Bournemouth	W2-0	0-0	15	Houghton, Clark	3,476
31	31	CL	H	Sheffield U	D2-2	0-1	16	Houghton, Farrelly	5,023
32	F 4	CL	A	Oxford U	L0-2	0-0	17		9,105
33	11	CL	H	Plymouth Arg	W2-1	2-0	16	Twentyman, Naughton	4,370
34	14	CL	H	Bristol R	W1-0	0-0	16	Clark	3,813
35	18	CL	A	Lincoln C	L1-2	1-1	16	Naughton	2,780
36	**22**	**AMC 1**	**A**	**Rochdale**	**W3-0**	**2-0**		**Elliott 3**	**1,300**
37	25	CL	H	Millwall	D0-0	0-0	16		4,109
38	M 3	CL	A	Wimbledon	D2-2	1-1	16	Booth, Hinnigan	2,524
39	6	CL	H	Burnley	W4-2	1-1		Elliott, Kelly, Hinnigan, Houghton	8,812
40	10	CL	A	Rotherham U	W1-0	1-0	15	Hinnigan	3,256
41	**13**	**AMC 2**	**A**	**Doncaster U**	**L1-2**	**0-1**		**Naughton**	**2,098**
42	17	CL	H	Gillingham	D2-2	0-2	15	Twentyman, Elliott	3,874
43	**20**	**AMC NQF**	**A**	**Hull C**	**L0-3**	**0-2**			**4,377**
44	24	CL	A	Wigan Ath	L0-1	0-1	16		4,470
45	30	CL	H	Newport Co	W2-0	0-0		Elliott, Kelly	3,534
46	A 3	CL	A	Brentford	L1-4	0-1		Houston	3,446
47	6	CL	A	Southend U	D1-1	0-0		Kelly	1,826
48	10	CL	A	Hull C	L0-3	0-1			8,134
49	14	CL	H	Orient	W3-1	0-0	16	Houghton, Kelly, Houston	3,144
50	21	CL	A	Port Vale	D1-1	0-0	16	Houghton	3,574
51	24	CL	H	Scunthorpe U	W1-0	0-0		Elliott	3,420
52	28	CL	A	Exeter C	L1-2	0-1	16	Elliott	2,005
53	M 5	CL	H	Bradford C	L1-2	1-1	16	Clark (pen)	3,242
54	7	CL	A	Walsall	L1-2	0-1	16	Kelly	3,273
55	12	CL	H	Bolton W	W2-1	1-1	16	Clark, Elliott	5,001
								Av Home Att	**4,547**

Goal Scorers

League (66): Elliott 16 (2 pens), Kelly 13 (1 pen), Houghton 10, Clark 5 (2 pens), Hinnigan 5, Sayer 4, Houston 3, Naughton 3, Farrelly 2, Twentyman 2, Booth 1, Jones D 1, opponent 1

FA Cup (-): —

Milk Cup (5): Hinnigan 2, Elliott 1, Kelly 1, Naughton 1

AMC (4): Elliott 3, Naughton 1

1983-84

Litchfield	Hinnigan	McAteer	Jones D	Booth	Lodge	Kelly	Sayer	Elliott	Naughton	Houston	Telfer	Bleasdale	Clark	Walsh	Farrelly	Twentyman	Houghton	Jones M	Murphy	Cameron	REFEREE	
1	2	3	4	5	6	7	8	9	10	11											H Bodenham	1
1	**2**	**3**	**4**	**5**	**6**	**7**	**8**	**9**	**10**	**11**											**G Courtney**	**2**
1	2	3*	4	5	6	7	8	9		11	12	10									T Mills	3
1	2	3	4	5	6	7	8	9		11*	12	10									A Saunders	4
1		3	4	5	6	7	8	9	12	11*		10	2								MP Scott	5
1		**3**	**4**	**5**	**6**	**7**	**8**	**9**		**11**		**10**	**2†**								**J Key**	**6**
1		3	4	5	6	7	8	9	12	11		10*	2								JD Hough	7
1	12	3	4*	5	6		8	9	10	11			2	7							RG Milford	8
1	3		4	5	6		8	9	10	11				7	2						DA Hedges	9
1	2	3	4	5*	6		8		10	11		12		7		9					R Bridges	10
1	**2**	**3**	**4**		**6**		**8**	**9**	**10**	**11**				**7**		**5**					**B Stevens**	**11**
1	2	3	4		6		8	9	10*	12			7			5	11				J Ashworth	12
1	2	3	4		6		8	9	10	12			7*			5	11				KA Redfern	13
1		3		5	6			9	12	7			10	8*	2	4	11				M Heath	14
1		3	4	5	6			9		7			10	8	2*	12	11				M Brown	15
1		**3**	**4**	**5**	**6**			**9**		**7**			**10**	**8**	**2**	**11**					**D Hutchinson**	**16**
1	3		4	5	6			9	12	7			10	8	2	11*					F Roberts	17
1	3		4	5	6			9	11	7			10*	8	2	12					VG Callow	18
1	3		4	5	6	7		9	8				10		2		11				P Willis	19
1	**2**	**3**	**4**	**5**	**6***	**7**	**12**	**9**	**8**				**10**			**11**					**J Jones**	**20**
1	2	3	4	5	6	7		9	8*				10			12	11				P Tyldesley	21
1	**2**	**3**	**4**	**5**	**6†**	**7**		**9**	**8**				**10**			**12**	**11***				**J Key**	**22**
1	2	3	4		6	7		9	8	12			10			5*	11				J Lovatt	23
1	2	3	4	5		7		9	8*	12			10	6			11				Alan Robinson	24
1	2	3	4	5		7		9	10	12				8	6*		11				K Hackett	25
1	2	3	4	5		7		9	10					8	6		11				C Seel	26
1	2	3*	4	5		7		9	10	12				8	6		11				G Napthine	27
1	3		4	5		7		9	10	12			2	8	6*		11				R Nixon	28
1	3		4	5		7		9	10				2	8	6		11				G Tyson	29
1	3		4	5*		7		9	10	12			2	8	6		11				N Ashley	30
1	3		4			7*		9	10	12			2	8	6	5	11				G Courtney	31
1	3		4			7		9	10	12			2	8*	6	5	11				J Moules	32
1	3	12	4			7		9	10				2	8	6	5	11*				A Challinor	33
1	3	12	4			7		9	10	11			2	8*	6	5					M Dimblebee	34
1	2	3	4		12			9	10	11			6	8	7*	5					K Baker	35
1	**2**	**3**	**4**					**9**	**10***	**12**		**7**	**6**	**8**	**11***	**5**	**13**				**R Bridges**	**36**
1	2	3		4				9	10	12			6	8*	7	5	11				P Holbrook	37
1	2	3		4*		8		9	10	12			6		7	5	11				T Bune	38
1	2	3	4			7		9	10	12			6		8	5	11*				A Saunders	39
1	2	3	4			7		9	10	12			6		8*	5	11				F Roberts	40
1	**2**	**3**	**4**			**7**	**12**	**9**	**10**	**8***				**6***		**5**	**11**		**13**		**M Heath**	**41**
1	2	3	4			7		9	10	12				6*	8	5	11				D Hutchinson	42
1	**2**	**3**	**4**	**5**		**7**	**6**	**9**	**10**	**12**					**8***	**13**	**11***				**K Redfern**	**43**
1	2	5	3	4		7		9	10	12				6	8		11*				J Hough	44
1	2	3	4	5		7	11	9	10	12				6*	8						T Jones	45
1	2	3	4			7	6*	9	10	11					8	5	12				L Shapter	46
1	2	3		5		7	6*	9	10	11				8		4	12				M Taylor	47
1	2	3	4		12	7		9	10	11				6*		5	8				G Napthine	48
1		3	4	5		7			10	12			6			9*	11	2	8		M Scott	49
1	2	3	4*	5†		7		9	12	11					6		10		8		A Seville	50
	3*			5		7		9	12	11			6		2	4	10		8	1	T Mills	51
1	3			5		7		9	12	11			6		2	4	10		8*		E Scales	52
1	4					7	8	9		11			6		2	5	10	3			L Robinson	53
1		3				7	8*	9	10	11			6		4	5		2	12		D Hedges	54
1		3		5				9	10	11			6		7	4	8	2			G Tyson	55
45	38	32	37	31	17	34	15	44	35	23	0	4	31	25	31	25	30	4	4	1	League Appearances	
	+1S	+2S			+2S				+7S	+18S	+2S	+1S				+3S	+2S		+1S			
1	1	1	1	1	1	1		1	1				1			1S	1				FA Cup Appearances	
5	3	5	5	4	5	3	3+1S	5	3		4		1	3	2	1	3				Milk Cup Appearances	
3	3	3	3	1		2	1+1S	3	3	1+2S		1	1	2	2	2+1S	2+1S		1S		AM Cup Appearances	

DEEPDALE

Official Address: Deepdale, Preston PR1 6RU. Telephone: 0772 795919; 0772 795465 & 795156 (Commercial Dept)

Ground Capacity: 25,000

Record Attendance: 42,684 v. Arsenal, Div 1, 23 Apr 1938

Record Receipts: £28,300 v. Blackburn Rovers, Div 2, 21 Apr 1981

Size of Playing Area: 112 × 78 yds

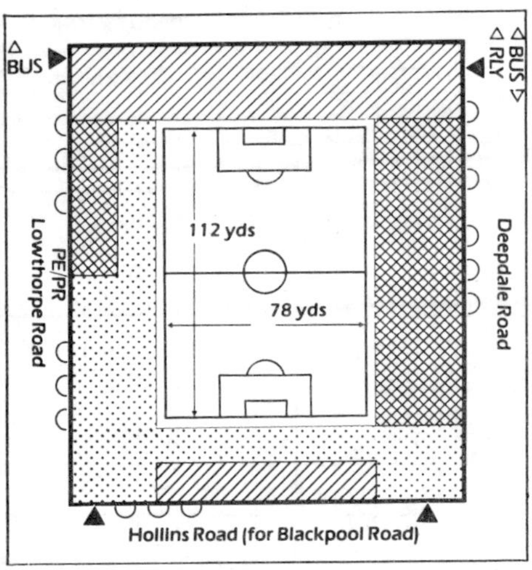

For key see page 12

Season Tickets: Pavilion: £60 (£44 Under 15/OAPs); West Stand: £54 (£27 Under 15/OAPs); Paddock £48 (£24 Under 15/OAPs); Ground £43 (£20 Under 15/OAPs)

Executive Box Season Tickets: None available

Cost of Stand Tickets: Pavilion: £3.50 (all); West Stand: £3.00 (£2.20 Under 15/OAPs); Paddock: £2.80 (£1.90 Under 15/OAPs); Ground: £2.50 (£1.50 Under 15/OAPs)

Match and Ticket Information: Postal applications with payment and SAE 14 days before match

Car Parking: Club park on Deepdale Road (West Stand) side of ground for 500 vehicles. Limited off-street parking

How to get to the ground

From North: Use Motorway M6 then M55 until junction 1, leave motorway and follow signs Preston A6. In 1.9m at crossroads turn left A5085 into Blackpool Road. In 0.8m turn right A6063 into Deepdale for Preston North End F.C.
From East and South: Use Motorway M6 until junction 31, leave motorway and follow signs Preston A59. In 1m at roundabout take 2nd exit into Blackpool Road. In 1.3m turn left A6063 into Deepdale for Preston North End F.C.
From West: Use Motorway M55 until junction 1, leave motorway and follow signs Preston A6. In 1.9m at crossroads turn left A5085 into Blackpool Road. In 0.8m turn right A6063 into Deepdale for Preston North End F.C.

QUEENS PARK RANGERS Division 1

President
Sir Stanley Rous CBE

Chairman
J A Gregory

Deputy-Chairman
A Williamson

Directors
C J Armstrong, FCA
B A V Henson, FCA
A Ingham
A Chandler
E W Saunders

Secretary
R J Phillips

Team Manager
Alan Mullery

Assistant Team Manager/Club Coach
Frank Sibley

Physiotherapist
D Butler

Commercial Director
A Ingham (01-740 7740 & 01-749 1890)

Rangers returned to the First Division in style and, though never really in contention for the Championship, kept close on the tails of the leaders and eventually finished high enough to qualify for the UEFA Cup.

Apart from the addition of Mike Fillery, a midfield player signed from Chelsea for £150,000, manager Terry Venables started the season with his Second Division championship side. But soon Terry Fenwick and Steve Wicks took over in the middle of the defence and the side began to play some very attractive football.

Though several opponents continued to criticise their Omniturf pitch, the more skilful sides looked quite at home on it. Liverpool, Luton and Nottingham Forest all won at Shepherd's Bush.

Mr Venables always maintained that playing on the plastic surface improved his players' skill — and they proved this, also, when playing away from home — but the club did take the point about the unnatural bounce of the ball and steps were taken at the end of the season to put this right.

Striker Simon Stainrod scored consistently throughout the season and, when he returned during the latter part, Clive Allen also hit peak form and earned himself a place in the England team.

Fenwick and Gregory also won England caps and Stainrod went on to the summer tour to South America, giving added credence to Mr Venables' claims about the skill in his side.

Rangers held a place among the top six clubs for the entire second half of the season and, close to the end, ran up six successive victories, a run that took them into third place and, briefly, gave them a technical chance of taking top place.

A couple of slips close to the end meant they had to satisfy themselves with fifth place but that was good enough to put them into the UEFA Cup.

In view of their success in the League, Rangers' Cup exploits were a disappointment. They did what was expected of them against Fourth Division Crewe Alexandra in the first-leg of their Milk Cup tie, cracking home eight goals at The Bush. But they then lost the return 0-3 and went out at Ipswich in the next round.

Their F.A. Cup hopes came to an end in the third round when they lost 1-2 away to Second Division Huddersfield Town.

Manager Venables left at the end of the season to take up the plum job in charge of Barcelona and Alan Mullery was chosen to succeed him. TP

Back Row L to R: Warren Neill, Gary Waddock, Mike Fillery, Alan McDonald, Wayne Fereday, Ian Stewart and Gary Micklewhite. **Middle Row:** David Butler (Physio), Jeremy Charles, Steve Wicks, Peter Hucker, Gary Chivers, Simon Stainrod, George Armstrong (Reserve Coach). **Front Row:** Alan Mullery (Manager), John Gregory, Clive Allen, Terry Fenwick (Captain), Ian Dawes, Frank Sibley (Assistant Manager).

'RANGERS' or 'R's'

Sponsored by **Guinness**

Formed: 1885 **Turned Professional:** 1898 **Ltd Co:** 1899
Previous Names: St Jude's 1885-7
Previous Managers: 1907-13 James Cowan 1913-20 James Howie 1920-5 E (Ned) Liddell 1925-31 R (Bob) Hewison 1931 John Bowman 1931-3 Archie Mitchell 1933-5 Michael T O'Brien 1935-9 William Birrell 1939-44 E (Ted) Vizard 1944-52 Dave Mangnall 1952-9 Jack Taylor 1959-68 Alec Stock 1968 Tommy Docherty 1969-71 Les Allen 1971-4 Gordon Jago 1974-7 Dave Sexton 1977-8 Frank Sibley 1978-9 Steve Burtenshaw 1979-80 Tommy Docherty 1980-4 Terry Venables
Honours: Champions Division 2 1982-3 Champions Division 3 (S) 1947-8 Champions Division 3 1966-7 Winners Football League Cup 1966-7
League Career: Original Members of Division 3 1920 Transferred to Division 3 (S) 1921 Promoted to Division 2 1947-8 Relegated to Division 3 (S) 1951-2 Transferred to Division 3 1958 Promoted to Division 2 1966-7 Promoted to Division 1 1967-8 Relegated to Division 2 1968-9 Promoted to Division 1 1972-3 Relegated to Division 2 1978-9 Promoted to Division 1 1982-3
Colours: Blue and white hooped shirts, white stockings with three blue hoops
Change Colours: Red shirts, black shorts, red stockings with four red bands on tops

CLUB RECORDS

Most Appearances for Club: Tony Ingham: Football League 514 + F.A. Cup 30 + League Cup 4 **Total 548** (1950-63)
Most Capped Player: Don Givens, 26, Eire. **For England:** Gerry Francis, 12
Record Goalscorer in a Match: Alan Wilks, 5 v Oxford United, 3rd Rnd League Cup, 10.10.67
Record League Goalscorer in a season: George Goddard, 37, Div 3 (S), 1924-30 **All competitions:** Rodney Marsh, 44 (League 30, F.A. Cup 3, League Cup 11), 1966-7
Record League Goalscorer in a career: George Goddard, 174 **All competitions:** George Goddard, 186 (League 174, F.A. Cup 12), 1926-34
Record Transfer Fee Received: £1,250,000 from Arsenal for Clive Allen, June 1980
Record Transfer Fee Paid: £400,000 to Leeds United for Tony Currie, Aug 1979
Best Performances: League: Runners Up 1975-6 **F.A. Cup:** Runners Up 1982 **League/Milk Cup:** Winners 1966-7 **UEFA Cup:** Quarter Finals
Most League Points: (2 pts for win) 67 in Div 3, 1966-7; (3 pts for win) 85, Div 2, 1982-3
Most League Goals: 111, Div 3, 1961-2
Record League Victory: 9-2 v Tranmere Rovers, Div 3, 3 Dec 1960
Record League Defeat: 1-8 v Mansfield Town, Div 3, 15 March 1965
1-8 v Manchester United, Div 1, 19 March 1969
European Competitions Entered: UEFA Cup 1976-7
Club Statistician for the Directory: Stewart Fell

Programme Editor
Ron Phillips

Price	Number of Pages
50p	24

Subscriptions
Full Season £20.00. Half-Season £11.00 (both U.K. postage paid). Full Season (European addresses) £25.00

QUEEN'S PARK RANGERS

PLAYERS NAME Ht Wt Birthdate	Honours	Birthplace Transfers	Clubs	APPEARANCES League	Milk Cup	F.A.C.	E. Cups	GOALS League	Milk Cup	F.A.C.	E. Cups
GOALKEEPERS											
Graham Benstead	E. Y	Woking	Q.P.R. (A)			1					
6-2 12.10 20.8.63											
Peter Hucker†	E. U.21(2)	London	Q.P.R. (A)	107	5	10					
6-4½ 13.0 28.10.59	Div. 2, 83										
DEFENDERS											
Gary Chivers		Stockwell	Chelsea (A)	128+5	8	7		4			
5-11 11.5 15.5.60			Swansea C.	10	1		2				
			Q.P.R.								
Ian Dawes	E. S	Croydon	Q.P.R. (A)	89	5	2		2			
5-8 10.12 22.2.63	Div. 2, 83										
Martin Duffield	E. Y	Park Royal	Q.P.R. (A)	0+1							
5-10 11.3 28.2.64			Bournemouth (L)	6	1			1			
Terry Fenwick*	E.(6), U.21(11),	Durham	Crystal Palace (A)	62+8	4+1	7					
5-10 10.11 17.11.59	Y, Div. 2, 79,	£100,000	Q.P.R.	135	9	12		20		2	
	Div. 2, 83,										
	FAYC. 77, 78										
Doug McClure	E. Y, S		Q.P.R. (A)								
5.9 11.4 6.9.64											
Alan McDonald	N.I. Y	Belfast	Q.P.R. (A)	5							
6-2½ 12.7 12.10.63			Charlton A. (L)	9	3						
Warren Neill	E. S,	Acton	Q.P.R. (A)	94+1	4+1	5+1		3			
5-10½ 12.5 21.11.62	Div. 2, 83										
Steve Wicks	E. U.21(1), Y,	Reading	Chelsea (A)	117+1	3	5		5		2	
6-2¾ 13.2 3.10.56	Div. 2, 83	£275,000	Derby Co.	24	1						
		£300,000	Q.P.R.	73	5+1	3					
		£250,000	Crystal Palace	14		5		1			
		£250,000	Q.P.R.	54		1		3			
MIDFIELD											
Mike Fillery	E. Y, S	Mitcham	Chelsea (A)	156+5	9	11		32	6	3	
5-10 11.2 17.9.60		£150,000	Q.P.R.	29+1	1+1	1		1			
John Gregory	E.(6), Div. 2, 83	Scunthorpe	Northampton T. (A)	187	8	7		8	1	1	
6-1 11.5 11.5.54		£40,000	Aston Villa	59+6	5	2	3+1	10	1		
		£250,000	Brighton	72	6	3		7			
		£300,000	Q.P.R.	113	8	8		31	3		
Gary Micklewight	Div. 2, 83	London	Manchester U. (A)								
5-8 9.10 21.3.61		F	Q.P.R.	84+7	8+1	5+1		10	3	1	
Mark O'Connor		Basildon	Q.P.R. (A)	2+1							
5-6 9.10 10.3.66			Exeter C. (L)	38				2			
Gary Waddock	Ei.(12), U.21(1),	Kingsbury	Q.P.R. (A)	141+12	11 +	13		7			
5-10 11.12 17.3.62	Div. 2, 83										
FORWARDS											
Gary Bannister	E. U.21(1)	Warrington	Coventry C. (A)	17+5	2	2		3			
5-8½ 11.3 22.7.60		£100,000	Sheffield W.	117+1	13	12		55	2	1	
			Q.P.R.								
Steve Burke	E. Y	Nottingham	Nottingham F. (A)								
5-10 10.8 29.9.60		£125,000	Q.P.R.	43+24	4+2	+3		5			
			Millwall (L)	7				1			
Jeremy Charles	W.(14), U.21(2)	Swansea	Swansea C. (A)	224+23	19	11	8	53	7	3	5
6-1¾ 13.8 26.9.59	WC.81, 83		Q.P.R.	10+2		1		5			
Wayne Fereday		Warley	Q.P.R. (A)	18+14	2	+2		6			
5-9½ 11.8 16.6.63											
Tony Sealy	Div. 2, 83	London	Southampton (A)	2+5	+1						
5-8½ 10.11 7.5.59		£50,000	Crystal Palace	16+8	+2	1		5			
			Port Vale (L)	17				6			
			Fulham (L)	5				1			
			Port Vale (L)	6				4			
		£75,000	Q.P.R.	57+6	3+1	1		18			
Simon Stainrod	E. Y,	Sheffield	Sheffield U.	59+8	1+1	1+1		14			
6-1½ 11.11 1.2.59	Div. 2, 83	£60,000	Oldham A.	69	3	1		21	1		
		£275,000	Q.P.R.	124+2	9	12		43	2	6	
Ian Stewart	N.I.(16), Y, S,	Belfast	Q.P.R.	47+7	3+3	2+1		2			
5-6½ 11.9 10.9.61	Div. 2, 83		Millwall (L)	10+1				3			

CONTRACTED PLAYERS WITH NO FIRST TEAM APPEARANCES: Martin Allen, Gary Cooper, David Kerslake, Alan Comfort

NON-CONTRACT PLAYERS 1984-85: Ken Lavender, Gavin Maguire, Gavin Peacock, Stuart Walton

APPRENTICES: Billy Beggs, Paul Davis, Steve Scott, Graham Westley, Gavin Maguire

QUEEN'S PARK RANGERS

DIVISION ONE 5TH **FA CUP** 3RD ROUND **MILK CUP** 3RD ROUND

MATCH	DATE	COMPETITION	VENUE	OPPONENTS	RESULT	HALF TIME	L'GUE POS'N	GOALSCORERS	ATTENDANCE
1	A 27	CL	A	Manchester U	L1-3	0-2		Allen	48,742
2	29	CL	A	Southampton	D0-0	0-0			19,522
3	S 3	CL	H	Aston Villa	W2-1	1-0	13	Stainrod, Withe (og)	16,922
4	6	CL	H	Watford	D1-1	1-1		Stainrod	17,111
5	10	CL	A	Nottingham F	L2-3	1-2	16	Dawes, Stainrod	14,607
6	17	CL	H	Sunderland	W3-0	1-0	13	Fenwick (pen), Stainrod, Allen	12,929
7	24	CL	A	Wolverhampton W	W4-0	3-0	9	Gregory, Allen 2, Stainrod	11,511
8	O 1	CL	H	Arsenal	W2-0	1-0	5	Gregory, Neill	26,293
9	**4**	**MC 2**	**H**	**Crewe Alex**	**W8-1**	**3-1**		**Stainrod 3, Waddock, Stewart, Allen, Micklewhite, McDonald**	**8,911**
10	15	CL	A	Ipswich T	W2-0	1-0	3	Stainrod, Gregory	17,959
11	22	CL	H	Liverpool	L0-1	0-0	6		27,140
12	**25**	**MC 2**	**A**	**Crewe Alex**	**L0-3**	**0-2**			**3,662**
13	29	CL	A	Norwich C	W3-0	2-0	3	Fenwick 2 (1 pen), Stainrod	16,532
14	N 5	CL	H	Luton T	L0-1	0-1	6		15,053
15	**9**	**MC 3**	**A**	**Ipswich T**	**L2-3**	**1-1**		**Stewart, Gregory**	**12,341**
16	12	CL	A	Coventry C	L0-1	0-1	9		11,755
17	19	CL	H	Birmingham C	W2-1	0-0	7	Stainrod, Fenwick	10,824
18	26	CL	A	Tottenham H	L2-3	1-1	10	Stainrod, Fenwick (pen)	38,789
19	D 3	CL	H	Notts Co	W1-0	1-0	8	Waddock	10,217
20	10	CL	A	WBA	W2-1	0-1	5	Fenwick, Stainrod	11,717
21	17	CL	H	Everton	W2-0	1-0	4	Charles 2	11,608
22	26	CL	A	Leicester C	L1-2	0-1	8	Fenwick (pen)	17,460
23	31	CL	A	Aston Villa	L1-2	0-0	9	Charles	19,978
24	J 2	CL	H	Wolverhampton W	W2-1	0-0	8	Wicks, Gregory	12,875
25	**7**	**FAC 3**	**A**	**Huddersfield T**	**L1-2**	**0-1**		**Gregory**	**7,984**
26	13	CL	H	Manchester U	D1-1	1-0		Fenwick	16,309
27	17	CL	H	Stoke C	W6-0	3-0		Stainrod, Gregory, Charles 2, Stewart, Fillery	9,320
28	F 4	CL	A	Arsenal	W2-0	0-0		Stewart, Fenwick	31,014
29	7	CL	H	West Ham U	D1-1	1-1		Stainrod	20,102
30	11	CL	H	Nottingham F	L0-1	0-1	5		16,692
31	14	CL	H	Norwich C	W2-0	0-0		Dawes, Waddock	12,901
32	25	CL	A	Liverpool	L0-2	0-1	6		32,206
33	M 3	CL	A	Luton T	D0-0	0-0	6		11,922
34	7	CL	A	Sunderland	L0-1	0-0			13,538
35	10	CL	H	Coventry C	W2-1	0-1	6	Stainrod, Allen	10,284
36	17	CL	A	Watford	L0-1	0-0	6		18,645
37	24	CL	H	Southampton	W4-0	2-0	6	Wicks, Micklewhite, Allen, Waddock	15,407
38	31	CL	A	West Ham U	D2-2	0-2	6	Allen 2	21,099
39	A 7	CL	H	Ipswich T	W1-0	0-0	4	Allen	12,251
40	14	CL	A	Birmingham C	W2-0	1-0	4	Gregory, Fenwick	10,255
41	21	CL	H	Leicester C	W2-0	1-0	4	Allen, Fereday	12,360
42	23	CL	A	Stoke C	W2-1	1-1	3	Allen, Fereday	13,935
43	28	CL	H	Tottenham H	W2-1	1-0	3	Fereday, Gregory	24,937
44	M 5	CL	A	Notts Co	W3-0	2-0	3	Allen 3	7,309
45	7	CL	H	WBA	D1-1	0-0	3	Fereday	14,418
46	12	CL	A	Everton	L1-3	0-1	3	Micklewhite	20,679
								Av Home Att	**15,818**

Goal Scorers

League (67): Allen 14, Stainrod 13, Fenwick 10 (4 pens), Gregory 7, Charles 5, Fereday 4, Waddock 3, Dawes 2, Micklewhite 2, Stewart 2, Wicks 2, Neill 1, Fillery 1, opponents 1
FA Cup (1): Gregory 1
Milk Cup (10): Stainrod 3, Stewart 2, Allen 1, Gregory 1, McDonald 1, Micklewhite 1, Waddock 1

1983-84

Hucker	Neill	Dawes	Waddock	Hazell	Roeder	Micklewhite	Flanagan	Allen	Stainrod	Gregory	Fillery	Fenwick	Stewart	Sealy	McDonald	Fereday	Wicks	Charles	Burke	REFEREE	
1	2	3	4	5	6	7	8*	9	10	11	12									J Bray	1
1	2	3	4	5		7	12	9	10	11	8*	6								B Hill	2
1	2	3	4	5		7		9	10	11*	8	6	12							D Hedges	3
1	2	3	4	5		7	12	9	10	11		6	8*							K Baker	4
1	2	3	4	5		7			10	11		6	8	9						R Nixon	5
1	2	3	4	5*		7		9	10	11		6	8	12						LM Robinson	6
1	2	3	4			7		9	10	11*		6	8	12	5					D Richardson	7
1	2	3	4			7		9	10	11		6	8		5					LC Shapter	8
1	**2**	**3**	**4**			**7**		**9**	**10**	**11**		**6**	**8**		**5**					**I Borrett**	**9**
1	2*	3	4			7		9	10	11		6	8		5	12				K Barratt	10
1		3	4			7		9	10	11		6	8		5	2				C Thomas	11
1		**3**	**4**			**7***		**9**	**10**		**11**	**6**	**8**	**12**	**5**	**2**				**K Hackett**	**12**
1	2	3	4			7		9	10	11†		6	8				5			L Burden	14
1	2	3	4			7		9	10	11		6	8				5			L Burden	14
1	**2**	**3**	**4**			**7**		**9***	**10**	**11**	**12**	**6**	**8**		**5**					**J Martin**	**15**
1	2	3	4*			7	12		10	11		6	8	9	5					R Guy	16
1	2	3	4			7			10		11	6	8	9			5			D Axcell	17
1	2	3	4			7	12		10*		11	6	8	9			5			N Ashley	18
1	2	3	4						10	11	7	6	8	9			5			MJ Taylor	19
1	2	3	4						10	11	7	6	9	8*			5	12		J Worrall	20
1	2	3	4						10	11	7	6	8				5	9		B Stevens	21
1	2	3	4						10	11	7	6	8				5	9		M Heath	22
1	2	3	4						10	11	7	6	8				5	9		A Banks	23
1	2	3	4*						10	11	7	6	8			12	5	9		M Bodenham	24
1	**2**	**3**	**4**						**10**	**11**	**7**	**6**	**8***			**12**	**5**	**9**		**K Barratt**	**25**
1	2	3	4						10	11	7	6	8				5	9		J Hunting	26
1	2	3	4			12			10	11	7	6	8				5	9*		A Robinson	27
1	2	3	4						10	11	7	6	8			12	5	9*		B Hill	28
1	2	3	4			12			9	11	7*	6	8			10	5			G Napthine	29
1	2	3	4						10	11	7	6	8			12	5	9*		T Spencer	30
1	3	2	6						11	9	7	5	8				4		10	H King	31
1	2	3	4						10	11	7*	6	8				5	9	12	D Shaw	32
1	2	3	4					12	10	11	7	6	8				5	9*		N Midgley	33
1	2	3	4			12		9	10	11†	7*	6	8				5			M Scott	34
1	2	3	4			7		9	10	11		6	8				5			A Gunn	35
1	2	3	4			7		9	10	11		6	8				5			K Hackett	36
1	2	3	4			7		9	10		8	6				11	5			T Bune	37
1	2	3	4			7		9	10		8	6				11*	5		12	M Dimblebee	38
1	2	3	10			11		7	8		6	5				9	4			J Deakin	39
1	2	3	4*			7		9	10	11	8	6				12	5			N Glover	40
1	2	3				7		9	10	11*	8	6				4	5		12	M Taylor	41
1	2	3				7		9	10	11	8	6				4	5			A Robinson	42
1	2	5				6		10	11	8	7*	4				9	3		12	J Martin	43
1	2	5				6		10	11	8	7	4				9	3			C Thomas	44
1	2	3				7		9	10	11	8	6				4	5			R Milford	45
1	2	3				7		9		11*	8	6	10			4	5	12		J Key	46
42	41	**42**	36	6	1	27	1	24	41	37	29	41	30	6	5	11	31	10	1	League Appearances	
						+3S	+4S	+1S			+1S		+1S	+2S		+6S		+2S	+4S		
1	1	1	1						1	1	1	1	1			1S	1	1		FA Cup Appearances	
3	2	3	3			3		3	3	2	1+1S	3	3	1S	3	1				Milk Cup Appearances	

LOFTUS ROAD

Official Address: Rangers Stadium, South Africa Road, London W12 7PA. Telephone: 01-743 0262/5

Telegraphic: Queu Pear

Ground Capacity: 27,500

Record Attendance: 35,353 v. Leeds U, Div 1, 27 Apr 1974

Record Receipts: £79,660 v. Tottenham H, FA Cup Round 3, 3 Jan 1981

Size of Playing Area: 112 × 72 yds

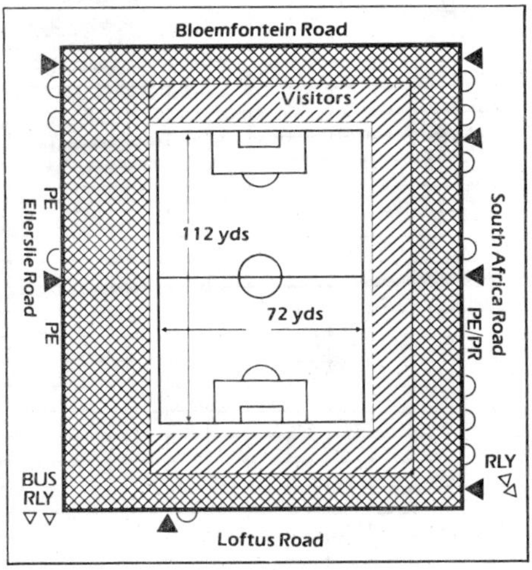

For key see page 12

Season Tickets: Stands: £84, £95, £105, £119, £143, £191; Terraces: £36

Executive Box Season Tickets: Negotiable with the office

Cost of Stand Tickets: £4.00, £5.00, £6.00, £8.00; Ground: £2.50, £3.00 (Visitors) (£1.50 Juveniles/OAPs)

Match and Ticket Information: Seats bookable one month in advance of each match

Car Parking: White City park, near ground, is recommended. Limited side-street parking available

How to get to the ground

From North: Use Motorway M1 and A406 North Circular Road as for Neasden. In 0.7m turn left then join A404 S.P. Harlesden then follow signs Hammersmith, pass White City Stadium and turn right into White City Road then turn left into South Africa Road for Queens Park Rangers F.C.
From East: Use A12, A406 then A503 then join Ring Road and follow signs Oxford to join A40 (M). In 2m branch left (S.P. The West) to join M41. At roundabout take 3rd exit A40 then join A4020 S.P. Acton. In 0.3m turn right into Loftus Road for Queens Park Rangers F.C.
From South: Use A206, A3 to cross Putney Bridge and follow signs to Hammersmith. Follow signs Oxford A219 to Shepherds Bush then join A4020 S.P. Acton. Then as East.
From West: Use Motorway M4 to Chiswick then A315 and A402 to Shepherds Bush, then join A4020 S.P. Acton. Then as East.

READING Division 3

Chairman
RG Smee

Directors
JH Brooks
J Campbell
MJ Lewis
R Tranter

Secretary
MJ Lewis

Manager
Ian Branfoot

Coach
Stewart Henderson

Youth Team Coach
Bobby Williams

Commercial Manager
Albert Moss (0734-57878)

Physiotherapist
Glen Hunter

Groundsman
Gordon Neate

Third place in the Fourth Division was a great boost for a club which a year ago was threatened with virtual extinction owing to the efforts of Mr Robert Maxwell to create a kind of hybrid club in their place to be located in Didcot. Instead the new board of the club led by ex-player Roger Smee resisted that utter nonsense and the real Reading always seemed likely to respond gratefully. The Third Division is really not good enough for a town the size of Reading, but at least promotion is a start in the right direction.

From the start of 1984 onwards promotion seemed almost certain and this was virtually clinched on 7th April when Bristol City were beaten at Elm Park (2-0) and the visiting supporters rioted in a probable attempt to cause the abandonment of the match. As their club also went up — and were likely to do so at the time — it is hard to see the logic in that behaviour. The Reading margin over local rivals Aldershot, who finished fifth, was seven points, so it can be seen that there were not too many anxieties before success was achieved. In the cups there was no success, the Milk Cup challenge being lost on away goals in a high scoring first round tie against Manchester United. Another United — from Oxford — beat the club at the Manor Ground in a Second Round F.A. Cup replay by three clear goals after Hereford had been beaten at Elm Park in the First Round by two clear goals.

Apart from the excellent achievement of promotion the season's highlight was the consistent goalscoring of Trevor Senior, a record-breaker in his own right, who could if he maintains his form bring the club further success. The consistency of Hicks, Sanchez and Richardson should be another bonus for the management.

W.L.M.

Back L to R: Glenn Hunter (Physio), Jerry Williams, Ken Price, Steve Wood, Trevor Senior, Martin Hicks (Skipper), Lawrie Sanchez, Dean Horrix, Colin Duncan, Stewart Henderson (Coach). **Front:** Stuart Beavon, Michael Gilks, Mark White, Gary Westwood, Ian Branfoot (Manager), Alan Judge, Derrick Christie, David Crown, Steve Richardson.

'THE ROYALS'

Sponsored by
Courage

Formed: 1871 **Turned Professional:** 1895 **Ltd Co:** 1895
Previous Managers: 1923-6 Arthur Chadwick 1926-31 Angus Wylie 1931-5 Joe Smith 1935-9 Billy Butler 1939 Johnny Cochrane 1939 Joe Edelston 1947-52 Ted Drake 1952-5 Jack Smith 1955-63 Harry Johnston 1963-9 Roy Bentley 1969-72 Jack Mansell 1972-7 Charlie Hurley 1977-84 Maurice Evans
Honours: Division 3(S) Champions 1925-6 Division 4 Champions 1978-9
League Career: Original Members Division 3 1920 Transferred to Division 3(S) 1921
Promoted to Division 2 1925-6 Relegated to Division 3(S) 1930-1
Transferred to Division 3 1958 Relegated to Division 4 1970-1
Promoted to Division 3 1975-6 Relegated to Division 4 1976-7
Promoted to Division 3 1978-9 Relegated to Division 4 1982-3
Promoted to Division 3 1983-4
Colours: White shirts with blue shoulders and yellow and blue trim, blue shorts and stockings
Change Colours: All yellow

CLUB RECORDS

Most Appearances for Club: Steve Death: Football League 471 + F.A. Cup 33 + League Cup 32 **Total 536**
Most Capped Player: Billy McConnell, 8, Northern Ireland **For England:** Herbert Smith 4
Record Goalscorer in a Match: Arthur Bacon, 6 v Stoke City (h) 7-3 Div 2, 03.04.31
Record League Goalscorer in a season: Ronnie Blackman, 39, Div 3(S) **In All Competitions:** Trevor Senior 41 (League 36, F.A. Cup 1, Milk Cup 4) 1983-4
Record League Goalscorer in a career: Ronnie Blackman, 158 **In All Competitions:** Ronnie Blackman 166 (League 158, F.A. Cup 8) 1946-54
Record Transfer Fee Received: £170,000 from Chelsea for Kerry Dixon, July 1983
Record Transfer Fee Paid: £50,000 to Charlton Athletic for Dave Shipperley, Sept 1979
Best Performances: League: 14th Div 2 1926-7 **F.A. Cup:** Semi-Final 1927 **League/Milk Cup:** 4th Round 1965, 1966, 1978
Most League Points: 82 in Div 4, 1983-4 **Most League Goals:** 112, Div 3(S), 1951-2
Record League Victory: 10-2 v Crystal Palace, Div 3(S), 4 Sept 1946
Record League Defeat: 1-8 v Burnley, Div 2, 13 Sept 1930
Club Statistician for the Directory: David Downs

Programme Editor
Colin Gunney

Price	**Number of Pages**
40p	28

Subscriptions
Please contact club

READING

PLAYERS NAME Ht Wt Birthdate	Honours	Birthplace Transfers	Clubs	Appearances League	Appearances Milk Cup	Appearances F.A.C.	Appearances A.M.C.	Goals League	Goals Milk Cup	Goals F.A.C.	Goals A.M.C.
GOALKEEPERS											
Alan Judge		Kingsbury	Luton T. (A)	11	1						
5-11 11.5 14.5.60		F	Reading	74	2	3	1				
Gary Westwood	E. Y	Barrow	Ipswich T. (A)								
6-0 13.0 3.4.63		F	Reading								
DEFENDERS											
Martin Hicks*	Div. 4, 79	Stratford-on-	Stratford T.								
6-3 13.6 27.2.57		Avon	Reading (N-C)								
		F	Charlton A.								
		£3,000	Reading	214+1	14	10		10			
Steve Richardson†		Slough	Southampton (A)								
5-5 10.3 11.2.62		F	Reading	73+1	3	3	1	1			
Mark White	Div. 4, 79	Sheffield	Sheffield U. (A)								
5-10 11.12 26.10.58		F	Reading	191+5	13+	9+1	1	3			
Jerry Williams		Didcot	Reading (A)	168+17	8	6	1	9	1		
5-11 11.10 24.3.60											
Steve Wood		Bracknell	Reading (A)	94+1	4	5		3			
6-1 12.7 2.2.63											
MIDFIELD											
Stewart Beavon		Wolverhampton	Tottenham H. (A)	3+1	+1						
5-6½ 10.6 30.11.58			Notts. Co. (L)	6							
			Reading	152+7	9+1	6	1	22	1		
Colin Duncan		Plymouth	Oxford U. (A)	188+1	14	6		6			
5-11 11.0 5.8.57		£60,000	Gillingham	83+2	6	6+1		5			
		F	Reading	33				2			
Ken Price		Dudley	Dudley T.								
5-10½ 11.3 26.2.54			Southend U.	1							
		F	Gillingham	247+8	15+	20+		79	7	4	
		£10,000	Reading	34+3		2		6		1	
Lawrie Sanchez	Div. 4, 79	Lambeth	Thatcham								
6-1 12.0 22.10.59		F	Reading	234+13	19+	14	1	26			
FORWARDS											
Derrick Christie		Bletchley	Northampton T. (A)	116+22	11+	4+2		18	2	1	
5-8 11.0 15.3.57		F	Cambridge U.	132+6	11+	3+1		19	2		
		F	Reading								
David Crown		Enfield	Walthamstow Av.								
5-10 11.4 16.2.58		£13,000	Brentford	44+2	4	3	1	8	1	1	
		Player Exchange	Portsmouth	25+3		2		2			
			Exeter C. (L)	6+1				3			
		F	Reading	45	2	3	1	7			
Mike Gilkes			Leicester C.								
5-7 10.10			Reading								
Dean Horrix		Taplow	Millwall (A)	65+7	5+1	3		19	3		
5-10 10.8		Player Exchange	Gillingham	7+7							
		£11,000	Reading	43	2	1	1	8		1	
Trevor Senior		Dorchester	Dorchester T.								
6-1½ 12.8 28.11.61		£20,000	Portsmouth	11	+2			2			
			Aldershot (L)	10				7			
		£30,000	Reading	45	2	2		36	4	1	

NON-CONTRACT PLAYERS 1984-85

Brian Benham, Frank Boahene, Colin Ferguson, Deane Foster, Simon Hargrave, Steve Head, Neville John, Mark Matthews (0+2), **Eddie O'Leary, Steve Smith, Mike Tune, Paul White**

READING

DIVISION FOUR 3RD **FA CUP** 2ND ROUND **MILK CUP** 1ST ROUND

MATCH	DATE	COMPE-TITION	VENUE	OPPONENTS	RESULT	HALF TIME	L'GUE POS'N	GOALSCORERS	ATTEN-DANCE
1	A 27	CL	A	Blackpool	L0-1	0-1			3,429
2	**30**	**MC 1**	**A**	**Colchester U**	**L2-3**	**1-2**		**Barnes, Senior**	**2,418**
3	S 3	CL	H	Stockport Co	W6-2	2-1	8	Sanchez, Tutty, Beavon, Senior 3	2,469
4	6	CL	H	Doncaster R	W3-2	2-2		Tutty, Senior, Horrix (pen)	3,688
5	10	CL	A	Rochdale	L1-4	1-1	11	Crown	1,199
6	**13**	**MC 1**	**A**	**Colchester U**	**W4-3**[3]	**1-2**		**Beavon, Senior 3**	**2,418**
7	17	CL	H	Chesterfield	D1-1	0-0	12	Senior	2,985
8	24	CL	A	Chester C	L1-2	1-1	16	Senior	1,367
9	27	CL	A	Bristol C	L1-3	1-0		Senior	6,322
10	O 1	CL	H	Darlington	W1-0	0-0	15	Barton (og)	2,422
11	9	CL	A	Northampton T	D2-2	1-2		Senior 2	3,835
12	14	CL	H	Crewe Alex	W5-0	3-0		Wood, Crown, Senior 2, Beavon	3,039
13	19	CL	H	Mansfield T	W4-0	3-0		Senior 3, Wood	3,551
14	22	CL	A	York C	D2-2	1-0	7	Crown, Beavon	4,315
15	29	CL	H	Swindon T	D2-2	0-2	10	Senior 2	5,918
16	N 2	CL	A	Peterborough U	D3-3	2-2		Horrix, Senior 2	4,073
17	5	CL	A	Colchester U	L0-3	0-2	12		2,433
18	12	CL	H	Wrexham	W4-1	0-1	10	Senior 2, Sanchez, Horrix	3,082
19	**19**	**FAC 1**	**H**	**Hereford U**	**W2-0**	**0-0**		**Senior, Horrix**	**4,453**
20	26	CL	A	Bury	W3-2	2-1	8	Sanchez, Horrix 2	2,220
21	D 2	CL	H	Halifax T	W1-0	0-0		Crown	3,930
22	**10**	**FAC 2**	**H**	**Oxford U**	**D1-1**	**0-0**		**Price**	**11,590**
23	**14**	**FAC 2R**	**A**	**Oxford U**	**L0-3**	**0-2**			**7,570**
24	17	CL	H	Hartlepool U	W5-1	3-1		Tutty, Price, Beavon, Wood, Lowe (og)	2,737
25	26	CL	A	Aldershot	D0-0	0-0	7		6,270
26	27	CL	H	Torquay U	D2-2	2-1	7	Senior, Horrix	4,910
27	30	CL	A	Tranmere R	W3-2	2-1		Beavon, Crown, Senior	2,716
28	J 2	CL	H	Hereford U	W3-1	1-0	4	Beavon, Crown, Senior	4,548
29	6	CL	A	Stockport Co	L0-3	0-0			1,751
30	14	CL	H	Blackpool	W2-0	0-0	3	Senior, Sanchez	4,923
31	21	CL	A	Chesterfield	L1-2	0-0		Senior	3,010
32	28	CL	H	Rochdale	D0-0	0-0			3,932
33	F 4	CL	A	Darlington	D1-1	1-1		Cartwright (og)	1,395
34	11	CL	H	Chester C	W1-0	0-0	4	Beavon	3,280
35	15	CL	H	Peterborough U	D1-1	1-1		Senior	2,986
36	18	CL	A	Swindon T	D1-1	1-0	4	Senior	4,659
37	**20**	**AMC 1**	**A**	**Southend U**	**L0-5**	**0-3**			**1,597**
38	25	CL	H	York C	W1-0	0-0	3	Sanchez	4,548
39	M 3	CL	A	Mansfield T	L0-2	0-0	4		1,950
40	7	CL	H	Colchester U	W1-0	0-0		Senior	3,360
41	10	CL	A	Wrexham	W3-0	1-0	3	Senior, Sanchez, Hicks	1,871
42	17	CL	H	Northampton T	W3-0	2-0	3	Senior 2, Horrix	3,475
43	23	CL	A	Crewe Alex	D1-1	1-1		Crown	2,435
44	A 7	CL	H	Bristol C	W2-0	2-0	3	Sanchez, Horrix	8,528
45	13	CL	A	Halifax T	W1-0	1-0		Sanchez	1,113
46	21	CL	H	Aldershot	W1-0	0-0	4	Senior	7,645
47	23	CL	A	Torquay U	D2-2	1-0	3	Senior, Duncan	2,525
48	28	CL	H	Bury	D1-1	1-1	4	Senior	4,307
49	M 1	CL	A	Doncaster R	W3-2	2-1		Senior, Price, Sanchez	4,972
50	5	CL	A	Hereford U	D1-1	0-0	4	Sanchez	3,611
51	7	CL	H	Tranmere R	W1-0	0-0	4	White	6,989
52	12	CL	A	Hartlepool U	D3-3	1-1	3	Senior 2, Duncan	1,214

[3]Lost on Away Goals

Av Home Att 4,532

Goal Scorers

League (84): Senior 36, Sanchez 10, Horrix 8 (1 pen), Beavon 7 (1 pen), Crown 7, Tutty 3, Wood 3, Duncan 2, Price 2, White 2, Hicks 1, opponents 3
FA Cup (3): Horrix 1, Price 1, Senior 1
Milk Cup (6): Senior 4, Barnes 1, Beavon 1
AMC (-): —

1983-84

Judge	Williams	Richardson	Beavon	Hicks	Barnes	Tutty	Horrix	Senior	Sanchez	Crown	White	Wood	Matthews	Price	Westwood (L)	Duncan	REFEREE	
1	2	3	4	5	6	7	8	9	10	11							D Owen	1
1	**2**	**3**	**4**	**5**	**6**	**7**	**8**	**9**	**10**	**11**							**M Scott**	**2**
1	2	3	4	5	6	7	8	9	10	11							KG Salmon	3
1	2	3	4	5	6	7	8	9	10	11							RG Milford	4
1	2	3	4	5	6*	7	8	9	10	11	12						A Saunders	5
1	**2**	**3**	**4**	**5**		**7***	**8**	**9**	**10**	**11**	**12**	**6**					**M Scott**	**6**
1	2	3	4	5			8	9	10	11	7	6					ML James	7
1	2	3*	4	5			8	9	10	11	7	6	12				JA Hendrick	8
1*	2		4	5			8	9	10	11	3	6	12	7			JC Deakin	9
	2		4	5			8	9	10	11	3	6			1	7	EA Read	10
	2		4*	5			8	9	10	11	3	6		12	1	7	LR Dilks	11
	2		4	5			8	9	10	11	3	6			1	7	JA Moules	12
	2		4	5			8	9	10	11	3	6			1	7	BT Stevens	13
	2		4	5			8	9	10	11	3	6			1	7	R Bridges	14
1	2		4	5			8	9	10	11	3	6				7	A Gunn	15
1	2*	12	4	5			8	9	10	11	3	6				7	G Napthine	16
1		2	4	5			8	9	10	11	3†	6				7	CJ Scales	17
1	12	2	4	5			8	9	10	11	3	6				7*	B Hill	18
1	**2**	**3**	**4**	**5**			**8**	**9**	**10**	**11**		**6**				**7**	**A Ward**	**19**
1	2	3	4	5			8	9*	10	11		6		12		7	D Shaw	20
1	2	3	4	5			8*	9	10	11		6		12		7	T Spencer	21
1	**2**	**3**	**4**	**5**				**9**	**10**	**11**		**6**		**8**		**7**	**J Moules**	**22**
1	**2***	**3**	**4**	**5**				**9**	**10**	**11**	**12**	**6**		**8**		**7**	**J Moules**	**23**
1		2	4	5		7			10	9	3	6		8		11	K Baker	24
1		2	4	5				9	10	11	3	6		8		7	C Downey	25
1	12	2		5		4	8	9	10	11*	3	6				7	I Borrett	26
1		2	4	5			8	9	10	11	3	6				7	P Tyldesley	27
1		2	4	5			8	9	10	11	3	6				7	Alan Robinson	28
1	12	2	4	5			8	9	10	11	3*	6				7	J Key	29
1	2	3	4	5			8	9	10	11		6				7	L Burden	30
1	3		4	5		2	8	9	10	11		6				7	N Midgley	31
1	2		4	5			8	9	10	11	3	6				7	K Cooper	32
1	2	10	4	5			8	9		11	3	6				7	R Banks	33
1	12	2	4	5			8	9	10	11	3	6*				7	L Shapter	34
1		2	4	5	6		8	9	10	11	3					7	D Reeves	35
1	2	3		5			8	9	10	11	6			4		7	M Heath	36
1	**2**	**3**	**4**		**5**	**7**	**8**		**10**	**11**	**6**			**9**			**E Scales**	**37**
1	2	3	12	5			8	9	10	11	6			4*		7	M Taylor	38
1	2	3	4	5			8	9	10	11	6					7	N Ashley	39
1	2	3		5			8	9	10	11	6			4		7	M Bodenham	40
1	2	3	12	5			8	9	10	11	7	6		4*			L Dilkes	41
1	2	3		5			8	9	10	11	7	6		4			M James	42
1	2	3		5			8	9	10	11	7	6		4			T Fitzharris	43
1	2	3		5			8	9	10	11	7	6		4			D Vickers	44
1	2	3		5			8	9	10	11	7	6		4			D Shaw	45
1	2	3	12	5			8	9	10	11	7*	6		4			M Robinson	46
1	2*	3	4	5	12			9	10		11	6		8		7	H King	47
1		2	4	5			8	9	10	11	3	6				7	M Dimblebee	48
1		2		5			8	9	10	11	3	6		4		7	M Scott	49
1	2			5			8	9	10	11	3	6		4		7	F Roberts	50
1	2		12	5			8	9	10	11*	3	6		4		7	J Moules	51
1	2			5			8	9	10	11	3	6		4		7	J Worrall	52
41	34	33	32	**46**	5	7	43	45	45	45	38	37	0	17	5	33	League Appearances	
	+4S	+1S	+4S		+1S						+1S		+2S	+3S				
3	3	3	3	3			1	3	3	3	1S	3		2		3	FA Cup Appearances	
2	2	2	2	2	1	2	2	2	2	2	1S	1					Milk Cup Appearances	
1	1	1	1		1	1	1		1	1	1			1			AM Cup Appearances	

ELM PARK

Official Address: Elm Park, Norfolk Road, Reading. Telephone: (0734) 507878/9-507880

Ground Capacity: 27,200

Record Attendance: 33,042 v. Brentford, F.A. Cup Round 5, 19 Feb 1978

Record Receipts: £25,972 v. Southampton, League Cup Round 4, 8 Nov 1978

Size of Playing Area: 112yds × 77 yds

Season Tickets: Stand A & E: £65.00, £45.00 (juveniles/OAP), B & D £67.00 & £47.00, 'C' £75.00 & £55.00. Ground: £45.00 (adults), £30 (juveniles/OAP)

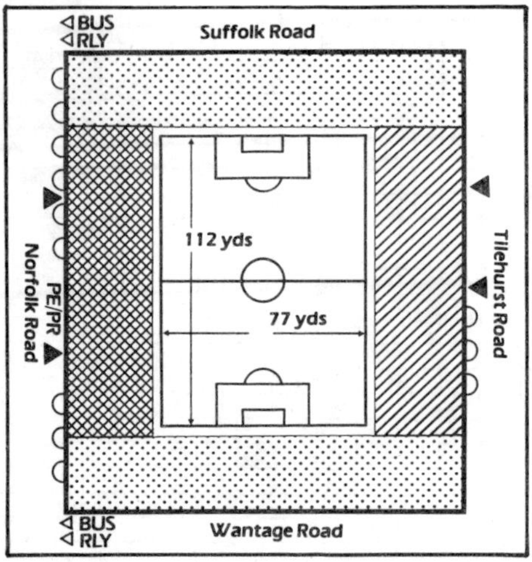

For key see page 12

Executive Box Season Tickets: £3,000 per season

Cost of Stand Tickets: A & E: £2.75, B & D £3.00, C £3.50; **Terraces:** £2.20

Match and Ticket Information: Stand tickets bookable 14 days in advance of match

Car Parking: Space for 300 cars in Norfolk Road and Tilehurst Road

How to get to the ground

From North: From Oxford use A423, A4074 and A4155 and cross railway bridge into Reading, then follow signs Newbury A4 into Castle Hill, then turn right into Tilehurst Road. In 0.7m turn right into Cranbury Road, then turn left then take 2nd left into Norfolk Road for Reading F.C.
From East: Use Motorway M4 until junction 10, leave Motorway and use A329 and A4 into Reading. Follow signs Newbury into Bath Road. Over railway bridge then take 3rd turning on right into Liebenrood Road. At tend turn left then right into Waverley Road, and turn right into Norfolk Road for Reading F.C.
From South: Use A33 into Reading then follow signs Newbury A4 into Bath Road. Over railway bridge then take 3rd turning on right into Liebenrood Road. At end turn left then right into Waverley Road and turn right into Norfolk Road for Reading F.C.
From West: Use Motorway M4 until junction 12, then leave Motorway and follow signs Reading A4. In 3.3m turn left into Liebenrood Road. At end turn left then right into Waverley Road and turn right into Norfolk Road for Reading F.C.

ROCHDALE — Division 4

President
FS Ratcliffe

Chairman
DF Kilpatrick

Directors
G Morris
CD Walkden
WAC Dromsfield

Secretary
WH Kenyon

Manager
Vic Halom

Reserve Team Manager
I Forsyth

Commercial Manager
G Bailey (0706-44648)

Groundsman
J Wilson

Rochdale were the Canon League's ninetieth placed club and once again needed a trip to the Annual General Meeting to plead for another chance. The plea was successful, so the club will be seen at Fourth Division grounds during the coming season making strenuous efforts to avoid such an ignominy again. Hope springs eternal, but the small band of faithful followers will be none too optimistic.

There is little that can be said about the campaign in favour of the team. It was a tough struggle for most of the season but the players did try hard to stem the tide flowing against them and at one stage it looked as if a position outside the bottom four would be achieved. In this final 'run-in' three clubs were in danger of finishing in one of those dreaded places apart from Chester and Hartlepool, who had been virtually doomed at an early stage. In the end it was Wrexham who finished twentieth beating Halifax on goal difference and Rochdale by two points. In the Cups there was also little joy at the outset when Stockport County won the Milk Cup First Round tie quite comfortably on aggregate. The F.A. Cup fortunes were better with good victories in the first two rounds over Crewe Alexandra (1-0 at home) and York City (2-0 at Bootham Crescent). After the latter excellent result hopes should have been high against Telford United, the F.A. Trophy holders, but the visitors played really well to win by four goals to one. Morale was not boosted by this and the rest of the season was tragedy.

Such form can lead to the inevitable scripted event happening and Jimmy Greenhoff's management career in the League ended — at least for the time being. His place was taken by Les Chapman, who will undoubtedly hope for better luck — and a few miracles. His playing staff was — and is — weak with only Conroy in goal having shown any consistency. Few will feel envious for his situation, but everyone will wish him luck — as they also did for Jimmy Greenhoff.

WLM

Back Row L to R: Dave Thompson, Steve Edwards, Ian McMahon, Les Lawrence, Steve Conroy, Keith Hanvey, Joe Cooke, Jim McCluskie. **Front Row:** Paul Heaton, Ged Keegan, Barry Diamond, Ian Griffiths, Les Chapman, Shaun Reid.
Photograph courtesy Rochdale Observer

'THE DALE'

Formed: 1907 **Turned Professional:** 1907 **Ltd Co:** 1910
Previous Managers: 1920-1 William Brodshaw 1921-2 No appointment made
1922-3 Thomas C Wilson 1923-30 Jack Peart 1930-30 Harry C Martin (caretaker)
1930-1 William Smith Cameron 1931-2 Vacant 1932-4 Herbert Hopkinson
1934-5 William H Smith 1935-7 Ernest Nixon (caretaker) 1937-8 Sam Jennings 1938-52 Ted Goodier
1952-2 Jack Warner 1953-8 Harry Catterick 1958-60 Jack Marshall
1960-7 Tony Collins 1967-8 Bob Stokoe 1968-70 Len Richley 1970-3 Dick Connor
1973-6 Walter Joyce 1976-7 Brian Green 1977-8 Mike Ferguson 1978-9 Peter Madden (caretaker)
1979-9 Doug Collins 1979-80 Bob Stokoe 1980-3 Peter Madden 1983-4 Jimmy Greenhoff
Honours: None
League Career: Elected to Division 3(N) 1921 Transferred to Division 3 1958
Relegated to Division 4 1958-9 Promoted to Division 3 1968-9
Relegated to Division 4 1973-4
Colours: White shirts, blue shorts, white stockings
Change Colours: White shirts with pencil green strip, blue shorts, white stockings

CLUB RECORDS

Most Appearances for Club: Graham Smith: Football League 316 + 1 sub + F.A. Cup 15 + League Cup 13 **Total 344 + 1 sub**
Most Capped Player: No Rochdale player has won an international cap
Record Goalscorer in a Match: Tommy Tippett, 6 v Hartlepool United (A, 8-2), Div 3(N), 21.04.30
Record League Goalscorer in a season: Albert Whitehurst, 44 **In All Competitions:** Albert Whitehurst (League 44, F.A. Cup 2) in 43 games, 1926-7
Record League Goalscorer in a career: Reg Jenkins, 119 **In All Competitions:** Reg Jenkins, 130 (League 119, F.A. Cup 5, League Cup 6) 1964-73
Record Transfer Fee Received: £40,000 + player from Norwich City for David Cross, Oct 1971
Record Transfer Fee Paid: £13,000 to Bury for Steve Johnson, July 1983
Best Performances: League: 9th Div 3 1969-70 **F.A. Cup:** 4th Round Replay 1970-1 **League/Milk Cup:** Runners-Up 1962 (4th Div Record)
Most League Points: 62 in Div 3(N), 1923-4 **Most League Goals:** 105, Div 3(N), 1926-7
Record League Victory: 8-1 v Chesterfield, Div 3(N), 18 Dec 1926
Record League Defeat: 1-9 v Tranmere Rovers, Div 3(N), 25 Dec 1931
Club Statistician for the Directory: S Birch

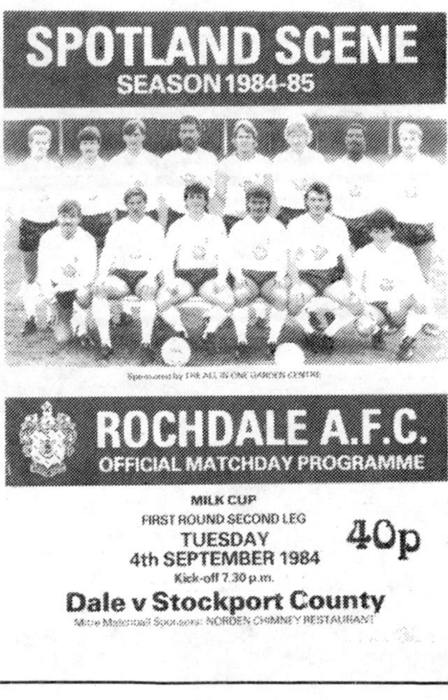

Programme Editor
Les Barlow

Price	Number of Pages
40p	20

Subscriptions
Please contact club

ROCHDALE

PLAYERS NAME Ht Wt Birthdate	Honours	Birthplace Transfers	Clubs	APPEARANCES League	APPEARANCES Milk Cup	APPEARANCES F.A.C.	APPEARANCES A.M.C.	GOALS League	GOALS Milk Cup	GOALS F.A.C.	GOALS A.M.C.
GOALKEEPERS											
Steve Conroy†	E. S	Chesterfield	Sheffield U. (A)	104	9	6					
6-0¾ 12.2 19.12.66		F	Rotherham U.	5							
		F	Rochdale	46							
Ian McMahon		Wells	Oldham A. (A)	2							
6-0 12.0 7.10.64			Rochdale	21							
DEFENDERS											
Les Chapman		Oldham	Oldham A.	75+1	5	1		9		1	
5-7 10.4 27.9.48		£20,000	Huddersfield T.	120+13	8	11		8		2	
		£10,000	Oldham A.	186+1	9	11		11		1	
		F	Stockport Co.	32	4	1		1			
		£10,000	Bradford C.	137+2	14+	6		3		1	
		F	Rochdale	44+1	2	3	1				
Steve Edwards		Birkenhead	Oldham A. (A)	77+3	5+1	2					
5-9 11.0 11.1.58		F	Crewe A.	57+1	4	1	3	1			
		F	Rochdale								
Keith Hanvey		Manchester	Manchester C.								
6-0 12.7 18.1.52		F	Swansea C.	11	2						
		F	Rochdale	121	6	13		10		1	
		£12,000	Grimsby T.	54		5		2			
		F	Huddersfield T.	205	16	14		14		1	
		F	Rochdale								
Bill Williams*		Littlesborough	Rochdale	65+5	4	3		2			
5-10 12.7 9.10.60											
MIDFIELD											
Peter Farrell		Liverpool	Bury	49+5	3+2	2		9			
5-7 10.7 10.1.57		£40,000	Port Vale	85+4	2	6		10			
		F	Rochdale	67+1	5	2	1	17		1	
Ian Griffiths		Birkenhead	Tranmere R.	110+6	9	9		5			
5-5 10.7 17.4.60			Rochdale	39+2	1+1	1	1	5	1		
Ged Keegan	E. U.21(1)	Manchester	Manchester C. (A)	32+5	4+1	0+1		2	1		
5-6 10.9 3.10.55		£25,000	Oldham A.	139+5	10	5		5			
		F	Mansfield T.	18		2		1			
		F	Rochdale	5							
Shaun Reid		Huyton	Rochdale	17							
5-8 11.8 13.10.65											
FORWARDS											
Barry Diamond			Barrow								
5-8 11.0			Rochdale								
Joe Cooke		Dominica W.I.	Bradford C. (A)	184+20	10+	15		62	5	4	
5-11 12.7 15.2.55		£40,000	Peterborough U.	18				5			
		£50,000	Oxford U.	71+1	5	2		13			
		£25,000	Exeter C.	17	3	1		3	2		
		£10,000	Bradford C.	61+1	6	4		6	2	4	
		F	Rochdale								
Paul Heaton		Hyde	Oldham A. (A)	124+12	9+2	4		28	2	1	
5-9 10.2 24.1.61			Rochdale	2+3							
Les Lawrence		Wolverhampton	Stourbridge								
6-3 11.0 18.5.57			Shrewsbury T.	10+4							
			Telford U.								
			Torquay U.	170+19	11+4	9+1		45	4	4	
			Weymouth								
			Port Vale	5+3	0+1						
		F	Aldershot	39	4	2	1	23	2		
		£15,000	Rochdale								
Jim McCluskie		Rossendale	Rochdale	4+1							
5-11 12.0 29.9.66											
David Thompson		Manchester		83+5	4+1	6+1	1	9			
5-9 11.6 27.5.62											

NON-CONTRACT PLAYERS 1984-85

Gary Broadbent, Eddie Burrows, Andy Dean, Mark Ennis (1 Lg), **Jim Blake** (2 Lg), **Ron Fairhurst, Simon Holden, Graham Hurst**

ROCHDALE

DIVISION FOUR 22ND **FA CUP** 3RD ROUND **MILK CUP** 1ST ROUND

MATCH	DATE	COMPETITION	VENUE	OPPONENTS	RESULT	HALF TIME	L'GUE POS'N	GOALSCORERS	ATTENDANCE
1	A 27	CL	H	Crewe Alex	W1-0	0-0		Farrell (pen)	1,673
2	**30**	**MC 1**	**H**	**Stockport Co**	**L0-3**	**0-2**			**1,839**
3	S 3	CL	A	York C	L0-2	0-0	14		2,772
4	6	CL	A	Wrexham	L1-5	0-2		Johnson	1,684
5	10	CL	H	Reading	W4-1	1-1	14	Farrell, Allatt 2, Johnson	1,199
6	**12**	**MC 1**	**A**	**Stockport Co**	**D2-2**	**1-0**		**Griffiths, Johnson**	**2,160**
7	17	CL	A	Colchester U	L0-4	0-2	17		1,955
8	24	CL	H	Northampton T	D1-1	0-1	18	Johnson	1,402
9	27	CL	H	Hartlepool U	W2-0	0-0		Farrell 2	1,381
10	O 1	CL	A	Swindon T	L1-2	0-1	17	Johnson	2,626
11	8	CL	A	Blackpool	W2-0	0-0	11	Farrell, Thompson S	3,126
12	15	CL	H	Chesterfield	L2-4	0-2	15	Allatt, Bellamy (og)	1,762
13	18	CL	H	Peterborough U	W2-1	1-0		Higgins, Doyle	1,299
14	22	CL	A	Darlington	L0-1	0-0	16		1,307
15	29	CL	H	Chester C	D1-1	0-0	15	Hamilton	1,481
16	N 1	CL	A	Mansfield T	L0-3	0-1			2,535
17	5	CL	H	Stockport Co	D2-2	1-1	19	Farrell (pen), Oates	1,682
18	12	CL	A	Tranmere R	D2-2	1-1	19	Farrell (pen), Johnson	2,455
19	**19**	**FAC 1**	**H**	**Crewe Alex**	**W1-0**	**1-0**		**Farrell**	**2,465**
20	26	CL	A	Aldershot	L1-2	0-0	21	Johnson	1,686
21	D 3	CL	H	Hereford U	D3-3	0-1	20	O'Connor, Higgins, Farrell	1,261
22	**13**	**FAC 2**	**A**	**York C**	**W2-0**	**1-0**		**Johnson 2**	**5,203**
23	17	CL	H	Bristol C	L0-1	0-0			1,496
24	26	CL	A	Bury	L1-3	1-1	20	Johnson	4,096
25	27	CL	H	Halifax T	D1-1	1-0	21	Higgins	1,896
26	31	CL	A	Torquay U	L2-4	1-1	22	Thompson S, Williams	1,887
27	J 2	CL	H	Doncaster R	D3-3	0-1	22	Thompson D, Thompson S 2	1,978
28	**7**	**FAC 3**	**H**	**Telford U**	**L1-4**	**1-1**		**Allatt**	**4,889**
29	14	CL	A	Crewe Alex	W1-0	1-0	21	Thomas	2,640
30	28	CL	A	Reading	D0-0	0-0	21		3,932
31	F 4	CL	H	Swindon T	D3-3	2-2		Griffiths, Thompson D, Allatt (pen)	1,297
32	11	CL	A	Northampton T	D1-1	0-0	20	Thompson S	2,022
33	14	CL	H	Mansfield T	D0-0	0-0			1,095
34	18	CL	A	Chester C	L0-1	0-0	21		1,423
35	**22**	**AMC 1**	**H**	**Preston NE**	**L0-3**	**0-2**			**1,300**
36	25	CL	H	Darlington	W2-0	0-0	19	Higgins, Allatt	1,048
37	M 3	CL	A	Peterborough U	L0-2	0-0	20		2,335
38	5	CL	A	Stockport Co	L1-2	1-0		McMahon	2,112
39	10	CL	H	Tranmere R	L2-3	0-2	21	Griffiths, Thompson D	1,263
40	13	CL	A	Bristol C	D1-1	1-0		O'Connor	6,996
41	17	CL	H	Blackpool	W1-0	0-0	20	Griffiths	3,115
42	24	CL	A	Chesterfield	L0-3	0-1	20		2,955
43	27	CL	H	York C	L0-2	0-0			1,756
44	31	CL	A	Hartlepool U	W2-1	1-0	19	Griffiths, O'Connor	1,245
45	A 7	CL	H	Wrexham	L1-2	1-2	20	Allatt	1,228
46	14	CL	A	Hereford U	L1-2	1-1	21	Allatt	2,686
47	17	CL	H	Colchester U	D0-0	0-0			1,020
48	21	CL	H	Bury	L0-2	0-0	20		2,027
49	23	CL	A	Halifax T	L0-5	0-2	21		1,422
50	28	CL	H	Aldershot	W3-1	2-1	20	Allatt, Griffiths, Thompson D	970
51	M 5	CL	A	Doncaster R	L0-3	0-2	21		3,396
52	7	CL	H	Torquay U	W1-0	0-0	20	Williams	1,042

Av Home Att 1,494

Goal Scorers

League (52): Allatt 8 (1 pen), Farrell 8 (3 pens), Johnson 7, Griffiths 5, Thompson S 5, Higgins 4, Thompson D 4, O'Connor 3, Williams 2, Doyle 1, Hamilton 1, McMahon 1, Oates 1, Thomas 1, opponent 1
FA Cup (4): Johnson 2, Allatt 1, Farrell 1
Milk Cup (2): Griffiths 1, Johnson 1
AMC (-): —

1983-84

Conroy	Oates	Chapman	Farrell	Higgins	Doyle	Thompson D	Hamilton	Johnson	Allatt	Greenhoff J	Williams	Griffiths	Thompson S	Thomas	Keenan	O'Connor	Greenhoff B	McMahon	Reid	Ennis	Blake	Heaton **(L)**	Humphreys **(L)**	McCluskie	REFEREE	
1	2	3	4	5	6	7	8	9	10	11															C Seel	1
1	**2**	**3**	**4**	**5**	**6**	**7**	**8**	**9**	**10**	**11***		**12**													**T Mills**	**2**
1	2	3	4	5		7	8	9	10	11	6														MP Scott	3
1	2	3	4	5†		7	8	9	10	11	6														L Robinson	4
1	2	3	4	5	6	7	8	9	10			11													A Saunders	5
1	**2**	**3**	**4**	**5**	**6**	**7**	**8**	**9**	**10**			**11**													**A Challinor**	**6**
1	2	3	4	5	6	7	8	9	10			11													C Downey	7
1	2	3	4		6	7	8†	9	10*		5	11	12												GM Tyson	8
1	2	5	6		4	11	7	9	10		3	8													TJ Holbrook	9
1	6	3	4	5			8	9	10		2	11	7												TW Ward	10
1	5	3	4	8	6	7		9*	11		2	10	12												G Courtney	11
1	5	3	4	12	6	7	8		9		2	11	10*												D Owen	12
1	5	3	4	9	6	7	8		10		2	11													JM Key	13
1	4	3		12	6	7	8	9	10		2	5		11*											M Peck	14
1	5	3	4	9	6	7	8		10*			11	12		2										KA Redfern	15
1	5	3	4	9	6	7*	8		10			11	12		2										D Hutchinson	16
1	5	3	4		6	7	8	9				11			2	10									R Bridges	17
1	5	3	4		6		8	9			7	11			2	10									K Barratt	18
1	**5**	**3**	**4**		**6**	**7**	**8**	**9**	**10**		**2**	**11**													**D Allison**	**19**
1	5	3	4		6	12	8	9	10		7	11			2*										M Dimblebee	20
1		3	4	5	6	7	8	9		11*	2					10	12								F Roberts	21
1		**3**	**4**	**7**	**6**		**8**	**9**	**10**		**5**		**11**				**2**								**M Robinson**	**22**
1		3	4	5	7	11	8	9	10*		5	12					2								R Nixon	23
1		6	8	4	5	7	9	11	10		3	12					2*								N Wilson	24
1	2	3		6		7	8	9*	10		5	11	12			4									M Heath	25
1	2	3	4*	6		7	8		10		5	11	9			12									D Reeves	26
1	2	3		5		7	8		9		6	11	4			10									A Saunders	27
1	**12**	**3**		**5**		**7**	**8**		**9**		**6***	**11**	**4**			**10**	**2**								**H Taylor**	**28**
1	6	3				7			4			11	9	8			2	5	10						H King	29
1	6	3				7		12	4			11	9	8			2*	5†	10						K Cooper	30
1	6	3				7		12	4			11	9	8				5	10	2*					G Tyson	31
1	6	3		5		7			4			11	9	10			2		8						A Crickmore	32
1	6	3*		5		7	12		4			11	9	8			2	10							C Seel	33
1	6	12		5		7	11		4*				9	8			2	3	10						J Ashworth	34
1	**6***	**3**	**10***		**4**	**7**	**8**		**9**			**11**		**12**		**13**	**2**	**5**							**R Bridges**	**35**
1	6	3	4	9		7	8		10			11					2	5							J Bray	36
1	6	3				7	8		10		2	11	9	4				5							M James	37
1		3	4			7	8		10		6	11		9				5			2				T Mills	38
1	6	3	4			7	8		10			11		9*		12		5			2				K Bakers	39
1	2	3				7	8		10		6	11				9		5	4						R Lewis	40
1	2	3	12			7*	8		10		6	11				9		5	4						G Napthine	41
1	6	3	7*				8					11	12			9		5	4			2	10		A Buksh	42
1	2	3				7*	8		10		6	11				9		5	4			12			N Ashley	43
1	2	3					8		10		6	11				9		5	4				7		J Key	44
1	2	5					7		11		4	8				10*		3	6			12	9		M Peck	45
1	2	3			5	7	8		10		6	11				9			4						D Hedges	46
1	2	3			6	7	8		10†			11	9					5	4						P Willis	47
1	2	3			6	9			10			11						5	4			8	7*	12	D Shaw	48
1	2	3			6		8		10			11	9					5	4*			12		7	R Nixon	49
1	2	3			6	7	8		10			11						5	4					9	F Roberts	50
1	2				6	7	8				4	11						5					10	9	A Seville	51
1	2	3			6	7					8	11*				12		5	4				10	9	G Courtney	52
46	42	44	24	20	24	39	38	17	40	4	27	39	13	10	5	12	8	21	17	1	2	2	6	4	League Appearances	
		+1S	+1S	+2S		+1S	+1S	+2S				+2S	+6S			+3S	+1S					+3S		+1S		
3	1+1S	3	2	2	2	2	3	2	3		3	2	2			1	2								FA Cup Appearances	
2	2	2	2	2	2	2	2	2	2	1		1+1S													Milk Cup Appearances	
1	1	1	1		1	1	1		1			1		1S		1S	1	1							AM Cup Appearances	

Also Played: Dean match 51, no.3.

SPOTLAND

Official Address: Spotland, Willbutts Lane, Rochdale OL11 5DR. Telephone: 0706 44648/9

Ground Capacity: 28,000

Record Attendance: 24,231 v. Notts County, F.A. Cup Round 2, 10 Dec 1949

Record Receipts: £8,834 v. Telford United, F.A. Cup Round 3, 7 Jan 1984

Size of Playing Area: 113yds × 75 yds

Season Tickets: Stand: £48.00; Ground: £35.00

Executive Box Season Tickets: £100.00 Stand Seat. Car Park, Bar, Refreshments

Match and Ticket Information: Seats bookable in advance.

Car Parking: At the Ground and in adjacent streets.

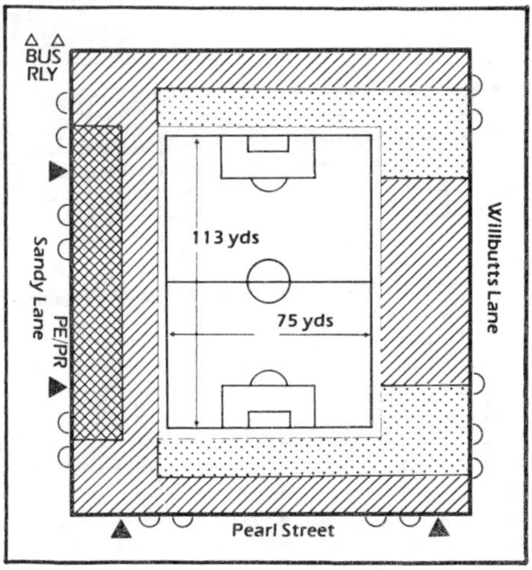

For key see page 12

How to get to the ground

From North: Use A680 S.P. Rochdale then turn right into Willbutts Lane for Rochdale F.C.
From East and West: Use Motorway M62 until junction 20 then follow signs Rochdale. In 1.5m at roundabout take 2nd exit into Roch Valley Way and in 1.5m turn right into Willbutts Lane for Rochdale F.C.

ROTHERHAM UNITED Division 3

Chairman
S Wood

Vice-Chairman
G Humphries

Directors
C R Wright
J Layden

Secretary
N Darnill

Player-Manager
George Kerr

Assistant Manager/Physiotherapist
A B Claxton

Chief Scout
A Turner

Commercial Manager
Commercial Department (0709 562434)

Demoted the previous season, it was natural that Rotherham United should hope for a quick return to the Second Division but after some moments of anxiety near the end the supporters were just glad that Third Division fare will still be seen next season at Millmoor; it could have been worse, although the team started well enough.

Eighteenth place is not something the supporters will find satisfying, but there could be remedies if silly home points are not thrown away next season and the team can also do better than the nineteen points collected from their travels. The defensive record (a loss of sixty four goals) could stand improvement and with Moore having departed early in the season there was an inevitable lack of goals, even though Kilmore as usual tried hard with some success. Manager George Kerr needs some bright new faces and a lot of luck.

Some success was enjoyed in the Cup campaigns and this particularly applied to the Milk Cup where with a start in the First Round victories were recorded over Hartlepool (1-0 on aggregate — too close), Luton Town (4-3 on aggregate with a 2-0 success away), Southampton (2-1 at Millmoor — excellent) and Wimbledon 1-0 at home — also good). This meant that a visit to Walsall stood between the Millers and the semi-final, but the West Midland club were playing very well at the time and won a very good match by four goals to two. The F.A. Cup also brought some early cheer with Hartlepool again (1-0 at the Victoria Ground in a replay) and Hull City being despatched — the latter by two goals to one at Millmoor. This meant that West Bromwich Albion were to be visitors in the Third Round and they managed a goalless draw at Millmoor before soundly thrashing the Millers in the replay at the Hawthorns (3-0). Survival was the objective for the rest of the season and this was achieved with eight points to spare over the twenty-first club.

George Kerr has some rebuilding to do with the Third Division Championship side of 1982 largely broken up. There are already several new faces and the experience of Stevenson in goal has been very useful. Others who helped the club to its occasional good moments were Kilmore (as mentioned already), Mitchell and Gooding. Cash is short but the determination exists for a real challenge for honours this coming season.

Standing Back Row L to R: Gerry Forrest, John Dungworth, Mike Trusson, Bobby Mimms, Nigel Johnson, Mike Pickering, Phil Crosby. **Standing Middle Row:** Barrie Claxton (Asst/Manager), Kevin Kilmore, Tony Simmons, Bobby Mitchell, Terry Donovan, Phil Walker, Andy O'Dell, Phil Henson (Youth Team Manager). **Seated Front Row:** Alan Birch, Mark Rhodes, Ian McInnes, George Kerr (Manager), Willie Raynes, John Durham, Mick Gooding.

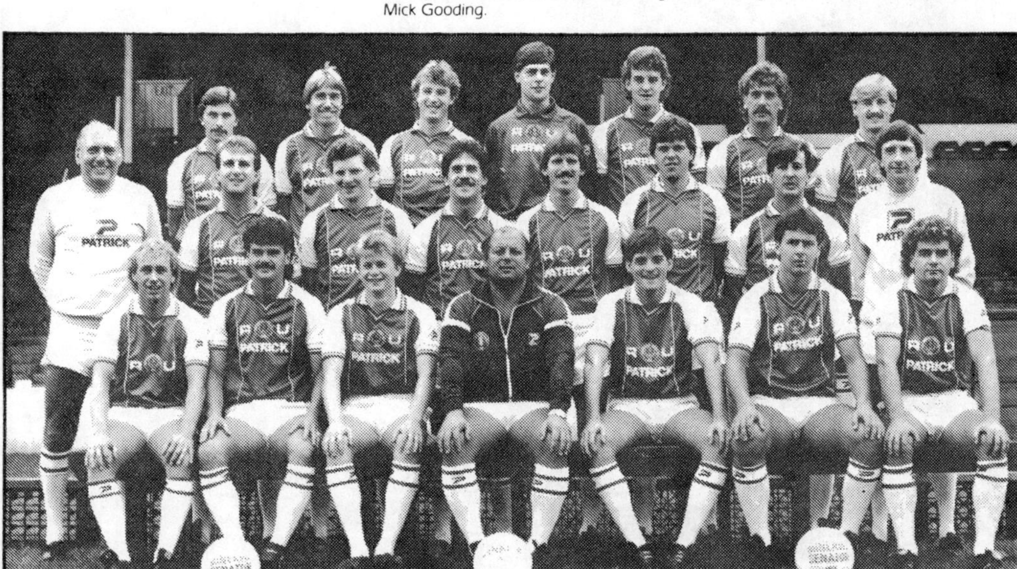

'THE MERRY MILLERS'

Formed: 1884 **Turned Professional:** 1905 **Ltd Co:** 1920
Previous Names: Thornhill United (1884), Rotherham County (1905) amalgamated in 1925 with Rotherham Town as Rotherham United
Previous Managers: Since 1946:
Reg Freeman Andy Smailes Tom Johnston Danny Williams Jack Mansell Tommy Docherty Jimmy McAnearney Jimmy McGuigan Ian Porterfield Emlyn Hughes
Honours: Division Three (N) Champions 1950-1 Division Three Champions 1980-1
League Career: Rotherham Town:Elected to Division 2 1893 Not re-elected to Division 2 1896
Rotherham County: Elected to Division 2 1919 Relegated to Division 3(N) 1923
Promoted to Division 2 1951 Relegated to Division 3 1968 Relegated to Division 4 1973
Promoted to Division 3 1975 Promoted to Division 2 1981 Relegated to Division 3 1983
Colours: Red shirts, white collar and sleeves, white shorts with red trim, red stockings
Change Colours: Yellow shirts with blue trim, blue shorts with yellow trim, yellow stockings

CLUB RECORDS

Most Appearances for Club: Danny Williams, 459, 1946-52
Most Capped Player: Harold Millership, 6, Wales **For England:** None
Record Goalscorer in a Match: No player has scored more than four goals
Record League Goalscorer in a season: Wally Ardon, 38, Div 3(N), 1946-7
Record League Goalscorer in a career: Gladstone Guest, 130, 1946-56
Record Transfer Fee Received: £100,000 from Sunderland for Dave Watson, Dec 1970
Record Transfer Fee Paid: £100,000 to Cardiff City for Ronnie Moore, Aug 1980
Best Performances: League: 3rd Div 2 1954-5 **F.A. Cup:** 5th Round 1952-3, 1967-8 **League/Milk Cup:** Finalists 1960-1
Most League Points: (2 pts for a win) 71, Div 3(N), 1950-1 **Most League Goals:** 114, Div 3(N), 1946-7
Record League Victory: 8-0 v Oldham Athletic, Div 3(N), 26 May 1947
Record League Defeat: 1-11 v Bradford City, Div 3(N), 25 Aug 1928**
**First match of the season. Rotherham United won their second match — at home!

Editorial
R. Finney

Price	**Number of Pages**
35p	16

Subscriptions
Apply to club

ROTHERHAM UNITED

PLAYERS NAME Ht Wt Birthdate	Honours	Birthplace Transfers	Clubs	APPEARANCES League	APPEARANCES Milk Cup	APPEARANCES F.A.C.	APPEARANCES A.M.C.	GOALS League	GOALS Milk Cup	GOALS F.A.C.	GOALS A.M.C.
GOALKEEPERS											
Bob Mimms		York	Halifax T. (A)								
6-6 12.4 12.10.63		£15,000	Rotherham U.	37	1	2					
Alan Stevenson	E. U.23(11),	Staveley	Chesterfield	104	4	8					
6-1 12.3 6.11.50	Div. 2, 73,	£50,000	Burnley	438	36	33					
	Div. 4, 70,	F	Rotherham U.	24	6	3	1				
	Div. 3, 82										
DEFENDERS											
Phil Crosby†	E. Y	Leeds	Grimsby T. (A)	34+5	3	1		1			
5-9 10.8 9.11.62			Rotherham U.	39	6	4	1				
Gerry Forrest	Div. 3, 81	Stockton	South Bank								
5-11 10.7 21.1.57			Rotherham U.	296	28	20	1	7			
Nigel Johnson		Rotherham	Rotherham U. (A)	54	7	4	1	1			
6-3 12.3 23.6.64											
Mike Pickering*		Huddersfield	Barnsley	100	6	3		1			
5-11 12.8 29.9.56			Southampton	44	3	4					
			Sheffield W.[1]	106+4	8+2	9		1			
			Rotherham U.	24							
MIDFIELD											
Alan Birch		West Bromwich	Walsall	158+13	9	9		23	1		
5-6 10.5 12.8.52		£25,000	Chesterfield	90	8	8		35	4	1	
		£200,000	Wolverhampton W.	13+2	2	1					
		£100,000	Barnsley	43+1	4	2		11	1		
			Chesterfield	30+2	4	3		5		2	
			Rotherham U.	14			1				1
Bobby Mitchell	Div. 3, 80	South Shields	Sunderland (A)	1+2							
5-10 11.0 4.1.55			Blackburn R.	17+12		2		6			
			Grimsby T.	142	16	8		6		1	
			Carlisle U.	2							
			Rotherham U.	46+7	7	5		2		1	
Andy O'Dell		Hull	Grimsby T. (A)	18+2	0+2	2					
5-8 10.8 2.1.63		F	Rotherham U.	15+2	5+1	3	0+1				
Mark Rhodes	Div. 3, 81	Sheffield	Rotherham U. (A)[2]	227+11	17+	16+		13	1		
5-9 10.11 26.8.57											
Mike Trusson	Div. 4, 82	Northolt	Plymouth A. (A)	65+8	12	1+1		15	4		
5-10 10.2 27.2.58			Sheffield U.	125+1	12	11		31			
			Rotherham U.	25			1	2			
FORWARDS											
Terry Donovan	Ei.(2), U.21(1)	Liverpool	Louth U.								
5-11 10.2 27.2.58			Grimsby T.	52+12	6	3		23	2	2	
		£75,000	Aston Villa	17		6		6	3		
			Oxford U. (L)	3							
		£25,000	Burnley	13+2		6					
			Rotherham U.	5+1							
John Dungworth		Rotherham	Huddersfield T. (A)[3]	18+5				1			
6-0 10.7 30.3.55		F	Oldham A.[4]	2+2							
			Aldershot	105	4	9		58			
		£100,000	Shrewsbury[5]	81+2	2	3		17			
		F	Mansfield T.	50+6	3+1	3		16			
		F	Rotherham U.	22			1	3			
Jon Durham		Rotherham	Rotherham U. (A)	3+3		2		1			
Mike Gooding		Newcastle	Bishop Auckland								
5-7½ 10.7 16.2.59			Rotherham U.	90+15	9	3		9	1		
			Chesterfield	12							
			Rotherham U.	24+2	6	5	1	7	2		
Kevin Kilmore	E. Y, Div. 3, 80	Scunthorpe	Scunthorpe U.	93+9	6+2	3		28	1		
5-9 11.10 11.11.59		£60,000	Grimsby T.	70+32	4	4+1		27			
		F	Rotherham U.	45	6	5	1	13	5	3	
Billy Raynes		Sheffield	Heanor T.								
5-8 10.4 30.10.64			Rotherham U.	11+3	5	3					
Tony Simmons	E. Y	Sheffield	Sheffield W. (A)	1+3							
5-10 11.3 9.2.65			Q.P.R.								
		F	Rotherham U.	18				8			
Phil Walker		Kirkby	Chesterfield	151+15	13	10		38	3	5	
6-0 12.1 27.1.57		Player Exchange	Rotherham U.	20+5	4+1	3		3	1		
			Cardiff C. (L)	2							

[1]**Mike Pickering played on loan with Norwich C.** (0+1) **Norwich C.** (4 Lg., 2 FAC), **Barnsley** (3)
[2]**Mark Rhodes played on loan with Darlington** (4) **Mansfield T.** (4)
[3]**John Dungworth played on loan with Barnsley** (2+1) [4]**Rochdale** (14, 3 g.) [5]**Hereford** (7, 3 g.)

NON-CONTRACT PLAYERS 1984-85: P. Henson (5 Lg., 1+2 FAC), **D. Battersby, P. Green, A. Morris, N. Pepper, K. Rimmington, M. Scott**

APPRENTICES: P. Emerson, J. Littlewood, P. McHale, J. Ramsford, M. Ash, C. Dule, K. Eley, M. Phillips, R. Warburton

ROTHERHAM UNITED

DIVISION THREE 18TH **FA CUP** 3RD ROUND **MILK CUP** 5TH ROUND

MATCH	DATE	COMPE-TITION	VENUE	OPPONENTS	RESULT	HALF TIME	L'GUE POS'N	GOALSCORERS	ATTEN-DANCE
1	A 27	CL	A	Southend U	D2-2	0-1		Moore, Kilmore	3,119
2	**30**	**MC 1**	**H**	**Hartlepool U**	**D0-0**	**0-0**			**4,384**
3	S 3	CL	H	Port Vale	W2-1	1-1	8	Moore, Kilmore	4,847
4	6	CL	H	Plymouth Arg	W2-0	1-0		Kilmore, McBride (pen)	4,488
5	10	CL	A	Exeter C	W1-0	1-0	3	Rhodes	3,193
6	**14**	**MC 1**	**A**	**Hartlepool U**	**W1-0**	**0-0**		**Gooding**	**2,321**
7	17	CL	H	Orient	L0-1	0-0	6		5,518
8	24	CL	A	Bolton W	L0-2	0-2	8		5,592
9	O 1	CL	H	Newport Co	L0-1	0-0	14		4,099
10	**4**	**MC 2**	**H**	**Luton T**	**L2-3**	**0-2**		**Gooding, Kilmore**	**4,035**
11	8	CL	H	Walsall	L0-1	0-0	15		3,540
12	15	CL	A	Scunthorpe U	W2-1	1-1	12	Gooding 2	3,139
13	18	CL	H	Millwall	W1-0	1-0		Stone	3,461
14	22	CL	A	Wimbledon	L1-3	0-1	14	Kilmore	2,579
15	**25**	**MC 2**	**A**	**Luton T**	**W2-0[1]**	**1-0**		**Walker, Kilmore**	**6,755**
16	29	CL	H	Bradford C	W1-0	0-0	12	Durham	4,506
17	N 1	CL	A	AFC Bournemouth	L2-4	1-2		Walker, Gooding	3,495
18	5	CL	H	Bristol R	D2-2	1-1	14	Gooding 2 (2 pens)	3,957
19	**8**	**MC 3**	**H**	**Southampton**	**W2-1**	**2-1**		**Rhodes, Mitchell**	**8,821**
20	12	CL	A	Preston NE	L0-1	0-0	16		3,916
21	**19**	**FAC 1**	**H**	**Hartlepool U**	**D0-0**	**0-0**			**3,325**
22	**23**	**FAC 1R**	**A**	**Hartlepool U**	**W1-0[1]**	**0-0**		**Kilmore**	**2,635**
23	26	CL	A	Gillingham	L2-4	0-2	16	Bruce (og), Raynes	4,052
24	**29**	**MC 4**	**H**	**Wimbledon**	**W1-0**	**1-0**		**Kilmore**	**6,946**
25	D 3	CL	H	Burnley	D1-1	1-1	15	Kilmore	5,544
26	**10**	**FAC 2**	**H**	**Hull C**	**W2-1**	**0-0**		**Kilmore 2**	**6,885**
27	17	CL	H	Oxford U	L1-2	1-0	16	Mitchell	4,000
28	26	CL	A	Sheffield U	L0-3	0-2	17		22,756
29	27	CL	H	Hull C	L0-1	0-1	18		6,298
30	31	CL	A	Wigan Ath	L1-2	1-1	20	Johnson	3,526
31	J 2	CL	H	Lincoln C	D1-1	0-0	20	Kilmore	4,595
32	**7**	**FAC 3**	**H**	**WBA**	**D0-0**	**0-0**			**8,142**
33	**11**	**FAC 3R**	**A**	**WBA**	**L0-3**	**0-0**			**12,107**
34	**18**	**MC 5**	**H**	**Walsall**	**L2-4**	**0-2**		**Kilmore 2**	**14,487**
35	22	CL	A	Orient	L1-2	0-2	20	Kilmore	2,204
36	F 4	CL	A	Newport C	W4-1	2-0	20	Kilmore, Gooding 2 (1 pen), Rhodes	2,391
37	11	CL	H	Bolton W	D1-1	1-1	18	Trusson	5,043
38	18	CL	A	Bradford C	L0-1	0-0	20		5,020
39	**21**	**AMC 1**	**H**	**Sheffield U**	**L0-1**	**0-1**			**3,396**
40	25	CL	H	Wimbledon	L1-2	0-1	20	Dungworth	3,141
41	M 3	CL	A	Millwall	L0-2	0-1	21		2,985
42	6	CL	A	Bristol R	L0-2	0-2			5,264
43	10	CL	H	Preston NE	L0-1	0-1	22		3,256
44	17	CL	A	Walsall	D2-2	1-0	22	Simmons, Dungworth	4,915
45	20	CL	A	Brentford	L1-2	0-1		Kilmore	3,391
46	30	CL	A	Plymouth Arg	D1-1	0-0		Simmons	4,736
47	A 2	CL	A	Port Vale	W3-2	0-1		Birch 3 (1 pen)	3,705
48	7	CL	H	Brentford	W4-0	2-0	20	Simmons, Trusson, Birch (pen), Mitchell	3,635
49	10	CL	H	Southend U	D0-0	0-0			3,722
50	14	CL	A	Burnley	D2-2	2-1	20	Kilmore, Birch (pen)	4,591
51	17	CL	H	AFC Bournemouth	W1-0	1-0		Simmons	3,937
52	21	CL	H	Sheffield U	L0-1	0-0	20		14,177
53	23	CL	A	Hull C	L0-5	0-3	22		9,799
54	28	CL	H	Gillingham	W3-0	2-0	19	Birch 2 (1 pen), Simmons	3,198
55	M 1	CL	H	Exeter C	W1-0	1-0		Birch	3,636
56	5	CL	A	Lincoln C	W1-0	0-0	18	Kilmore	2,140
57	7	CL	H	Wigan Ath	W4-1	2-0	18	Birch, Simmons 2, Dungworth	3,863
58	12	CL	A	Oxford U	L2-3	1-1	19	Kilmore 2	9,852
59	15	CL	H	Scunthorpe U	W3-0	2-0		Green (og), Birch, Simmons	4,298

[1]After Extra Time

Av Home Att **4,598**

Goal Scorers

League (57): Kilmore 13, Birch 10 (4 pens), Simmons 8, Gooding 7 (3 pens), Dungworth 3, Mitchell 2, Moore 2, Rhodes 2, Trusson 2, Durham 1, Johnson 1, McBride 1 (1 pen), Raynes 1, Stone 1, Walker 1, opponents 2

FA Cup (3): Kilmore 3

Milk Cup (10): Kilmore 5, Gooding 2, Mitchell 1, Rhodes 1, Walker 1

AMC (-): —

1983-84

Stevenson	Forrest	Crosby	O'Dell	Johnson	Trusson	Pickering	Kilmore	Moore	Mitchell	McBride	Rhodes	McEwan	Walker	Mimms	Gooding	Donovan	Seasman	Friar	Raynes	Stone	Durham	Dungworth	Simmons (L)	Birch	REFEREE	
1	2	3	4	5			8	9	10	11	12														C Downey	1
1	**2**	**3**	**4**	**5**			**8**	**9**	**10**	**11**	**12**														**R Guy**	**2**
1	2	3	4	5			8	9	10	11*	7	6													K Redfern	3
1	2	3	4*	5			8	9	10	11	7	6		12											J Bray	4
1	2	3	4	5			8*	9	10		7	6	12		11										B Stevens	5
1	**2**	**3**	**4***	**5**			**8**	**9**	**10**		**7**	**6**	**12**		**11**										**M Peck**	**6**
1	2	3	4	5			8		10		7*	6	12		11	9									IA Hendricks	7
1	2	3	4*	5			8		10		7	6			11	9	12								NJ Ashley	8
1	2	3	12	5			8*		10		4	6			7	9	11								DB Allison	9
1	**2**	**6**	**4**	**5**			**8**		**10**						**7**		**9**	**3**	**11**						**D Owen**	**10**
1	2	6	4	5			8		10*						7	12	9	3	11						D Scott	11
1	2			5			8		10			4			7	9	11	3		6					B Hill	12
1	2	3		5			8		10		12	4			7	9*	11			6					K Walmsley	13
1	2	3		5			8		10		11*	4	9		7					6	12				T Bune	14
1	**2**	**3**		**5**			**8**		**10**			**4**	**9**		**7**				**11**	**6**					**K Barratt**	**15**
1	2	3		5			8		10		12	4			7				11*	6	9				RF Nixon	16
1	2	3		5			8		10		12	4	9		7				11*	6					RG Milford	17
1	2	3	4	5			8*		10			6	9		7				11		12				N Smidgley	18
1	**2**	**6**	**7**	**5**					**10**		**4**		**9**		**8**			**3**	**11***						**G Tyson**	**19**
1	2	3	7	5					10		4		9		8				11*						P Tyldsley	20
1	**2**	**3**	**7**	**5**			**8***		**10**		**12**		**9**		**4**		**11**			**6**					**J Ashworth**	**21**
1	**2**	**3**	**7**	**5**			**8**		**10**				**9**		**4**		**11**			**6**					**N Glover**	**22**
1	6	3*	7	5			8		10		2		9		4		11†		12						D Reeves	23
1	**2**		**12**	**5**			**8**		**3**		**4**		**9**		**10**		**7***		**11**	**6**					**A Saunders**	**24**
1	2		7	5			8		3		4		9		10				11	6					T Jones	25
1	**2**		**7**				**8**		**3**		**4**		**9**		**10**				**11**	**6**					**R Nixon**	**26**
1	2		7				8		3		4		9		10				11*	6	12				R Banks	27
1	2*	5	7				8		3		4				10		9		12	6					J Worrall	28
	2	3	4	5			8		10						7		9			6					D Hutchinson	29
	2†	3		5			8		10				9		7				11	6					R Bridges	30
	2	6		5	4		8		10						7			3	11		9				D Shaw	31
	2	**6**		**5**	**4**		**8**		**10**						**7**			**3**	**11***		**9**				**J Hough**	**32**
	2	**6**		**5**	**4**		**8**		**10**						**7**			**3**	**11**		**9***				**J Hough**	**33**
		6	**2**	**5**			**8**		**10**		**4**		**9**		**7**			**3**	**11**						**G Napthine**	**34**
				5	4	6	8		3		10		12		7			2	11		9*				E Read	35
1	2			5	4	6	8		10		12	7	9		11			3							D Letts	36
1	2	3		5	4	6	8*		10		12	7			11							9			J Hunting	37
1	2	3		5	4	6	8		10		12	7*			11							9			C Seel	38
1	**2**	**3**	**12**	**5**	**4**	**6**	**8**								**10***				**11**			**9**			**L Dilkes**	**39**
1	2	3	12	5	4	6	8		10			7							11*			9			R Guy	40
1	2	3	11*	5	4	6	8		10			7							12			9			L Shapter	41
	2	3		5*	4	6	11		10		7			1								9	8		J Deakin	42
	2	3			5	6	11		10		4	12	8*	1								9	7		F Roberts	43
	2	3		5	4	6	11		10		7			1								9	8		K Salmon	44
	2	3		5	4	6	11		10		7			1								9	8		H King	45
	2	3		5	4	6	11		10					1								9	8	7	D Hedges	46
	2	3		5	4	6	11		10*		12			1								9	8	7	A Robinson	47
	2	3		5	4	6*	11		12		10			1								9	8	7	H Taylor	48
	2	3		5	4	6	11				10			1								9	8	7	T Fitzharris	49
	2	3		5	4	6	11		12		10			1								9*	8	7	J Lovatt	50
	2	3		5	4	6	11*		12		10			1								9	8	7	T Holbrook	51
	2	3		5	4	6	11		12		10			1								9*	8	7	N Midgley	52
	2	3		5	4	6	11		12		10*			1								9	8	7	R Banks	53
	2	3		5	4*	6	11		12		10			1								9	8	7	N Glover	54
	2	3		5	4	6	11				10			1								9	8	7	P Willis	55
	2	3		5	4	6	11*		12		10			1								9	8	7	J Ashworth	56
	2			5	4	6	11		3		10			1	12							9	8	7*	M Heath	57
	2			5	4	6	11		3		10			1	12							9*	8	7	D Axcell	58
	2	3		5	4*	6	11							1	10							9	8	7	E Scales	59
24	45	39	15	43	25	24	45	4	36	3	28	17	10	22	24	5	7	5	11	10	3	22	18	14	League Appearances	
			+2S						+7S		+8S	+1S	+5S		+2S	+1S	+1S		+3S		+3S					
3	5	4	3	4			5		5		1+1S		3		5		2	2	3	3	2				FA Cup Appearances	
6	6	6	5+1S	7			6	2	7	1	4+1S	2	4+1S		6		2	3	5	2					Milk Cup Appearances	
1	1	1	1S	1	1	1	1								1				1			1			AM Cup Appearances	

Also Played: Brown match 20, no.6. Green matches 1, 2, no.6. Henson matches 26, 27, no.5; 28, 29, no.11; 30, no.4. McFadzean matches 19, 20, no.12. McInnes matches 1, 2, no.7; 42, no.12. Rowe match 4, no.12.

MILLMOOR GROUND

Official Address: Millmoor Ground, Rotherham. Telephone: 0709 562434

Telegraphic: Holmes, Millmoor, Rotherham

Ground Capacity: 21,000

Record Attendance: 25,000 v. Sheffield U, Div 2, 13 Dec 1952

Record Receipts: £34,217 v. Sheffield W, Div 2, 4 May 1982

Size of Playing Area: 115 × 76 yds

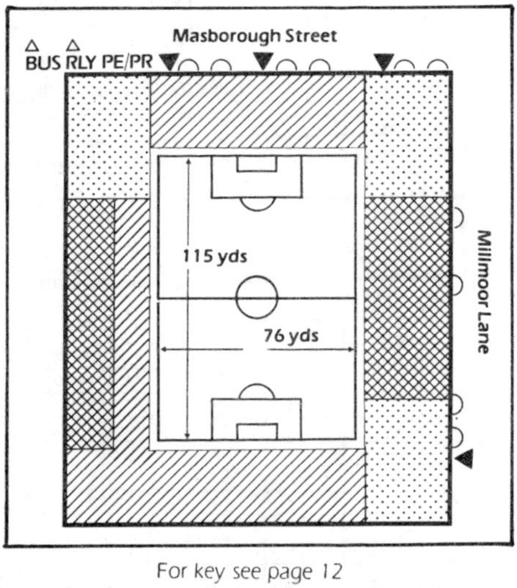

For key see page 12

Season Tickets: Main Stand: £70 (£46.50 Juveniles/OAPs); Millmoor Lane Stand: £50 (£36 Juveniles/OAPs); Enclosure: £44 (£28 Juveniles/OAPs); Ground: £38 (£28 Youths, £22 Juveniles/OAPs)

Cost of Stand Tickets: Main Stand: £4.00 (£2.50 Juveniles/OAPs); Millmoor Lane End Stand: £2.50 (£2.00 Juveniles/OAPs); Ground £2.00 (£1.50 Youths with identity cards, £1.20 Juveniles/OAPs); Enclosure £2.50 (£1.50 Juveniles/OAPs)

Match and Ticket Information: Seats can be reserved one month before match

Car Parking: There are parks within easy distance of the ground in Kimberworth Road and Main Street

How to get to the ground

From North: Use Motorway M1 until junction 34, leave Motorway and follow signs Rotherham A6109. Cross railway bridge and then turn right into Mill Moor Lane for Rotherham United F.C.
From East: Use A630 into Rotherham and then follow signs Sheffield into Masborough Street, then turn left into Mill Moor Lane for Rotherham United F.C.
From South and West: Use Motorway M1 until junction 24, leave Motorway and follow signs Rotherham A6178. At roundabout take 1st exit into Ring Road and at next roundabout take 1st exit into Masborough Street A6109. Take 1st turning left into Mill Moor Lane for Rotherham United F.C.

SCUNTHORPE UNITED Division 4

President
Sir Reginald Sheffield BT

Chairman
DJ Wraith

Directors
GJ Alston (Vice Chairman)
T Belton
P Cooper
G Pearson
AJ Clarke

Secretary
AD Rowing

Promotions Manager
S Roach (0724 848077)

Manager
F Barlow

Physiotherapist
P McLoughlin

Groundsman
R Barnes

To drop back into the Fourth Division only twelve months after gaining promotion may appear to the outsider as a lack of (a) foresight, (b) ambition or (c) quality players. The first two counts can be dispelled immediately and by the end of the season the third could also be discounted. The words 'by the end of the season' probably explain the reason for United's quick return.

Towards the end of the 1982/83 campaign manager Allan Clarke publicly stated that it would be a miracle if the 'Iron' were promoted considering the small squad at his disposal. Once the 'miracle' became reality he knew the injection of better class players was necessary if the 'Iron' were to prove a force in Division Three. Money was made available and two experienced players were acquired in John Green from Rotherham and Mike Brolly from Derby County. A third, Paul Longden, had arrived on a free transfer from Barnsley. All three were regulars during the Third Division campaign. Clarke knew more players were needed but refused to jeopardise the club's financial structure by paying 'inflated' prices.

The team made a good start, losing only once in the first six league matches before signs of the struggle ahead became apparent. A 0-4 defeat at Plymouth closely followed by a 1-6 home drubbing from Southend were to be the warning shots. A terrible league run followed with the previously safe defence now alarmingly leaking goals. The only bright spots were a tremendous 5-1 win over Wimbledon, a 2-0 defeat of Gillingham and victory in the early rounds of the FA Cup. The arrival of the new year coincided with an upsurge in the team's fortunes. Again it was the FA Cup which brought relief with three tremendous performances against Leeds (which twice broke the Old Show Ground gate receipts record) followed by an unlucky exit at West Bromwich. In the league, six consecutive draws showed United had improved the defence and victory over Bradford City – unbeaten in 17 games – set the revival into motion. Further 'new blood' had since arrived in the form of Mick Matthews, Alan Whitehead and Derek Bell and all three were part of the improved form. The club easily held its own to the season's end but unfortunately it was not quite enough to avoid relegation. There is little doubt the squad which ended the season would have comfortably held onto the club's newly won status if they had been together in August.

Special mention must be made of goalkeeper Joe Neenan who had a fabulous season and striker Steve Cammack who hit 25 goals for the second successive season. This was a fine achievement considering Cammack delayed an operation on a groin injury to help United's cause over the last four months.

The League Directory's Statistician for the Club

Back Row L to R: Phil McLoughlin (Physiotherapist), Chris Cowling, Alan Whitehead, Joe Neenan, John Green, Ian Webster, Neil Pointon, Eddie Edwards (Ex-Chief Scout). **Front Row:** Mike Brolly, Steve Cammack, Mick Matthews, Allan Clarke (Ex-Manager), Frank Barlow (Manager), Derek Bell, Mike Lester, Paul Longdon.

'THE IRON'

Sponsored by **Scunthorpe E.Z.**

Formed: 1904 **Turned Professional:** 1912 **Ltd Co:** 1912
Previous Managers: Since 1946: Leslie Jones Bill Corkhill Ron Suart Tony McShane Bill Lambton Frank Soo Dick Duckworth Freddie Goodwin Ron Ashman Ron Bradley Dickie Rooks Ron Ashman John Duncan
Honours: Division Three (North) Champions 1957-8
League Career: Elected to Division 3(N) 1950 Promoted to Division 2 1957-8 Relegated to Division 3 1963-4 Relegated to Division 4 1967-8 Promoted to Division 3 1971-2 Relegated to Division 4 1972-3 Promoted to Division 3 1982-3 Relegated to Division 4 1983-4
Colours: Sky blue shirts with claret 'V' and trim, sky blue shorts and stockings with claret trim
Change Colours: All yellow with green 'V' and trim

CLUB RECORDS

Most Appearances for Club: Jack Brownsword: Football League 600 + Cup 56 **Total 656**
Most Capped Player: No Scunthorpe player has won an international cap
Record Goalscorer in a Match: Barrie Thomas, 5 v Luton Town (h) 8-1, Div 3, 24.05.65
Record League Goalscorer in a season: Barrie Thomas, 31, Div 2, 1961-2 **In all competitions:** Barrie Thomas, 31 (all League)
Record League Goalscorer in a career: Barrie Thomas, 92 **In all competitions:** Barrie Thomas 95 (League 92, F.A. Cup 3) 1959-62, 1964-6
Record Transfer Fee Received: £60,000 from Grimsby Town for Kevin Kilmore, Sept 1979
Record Transfer Fee Paid: £25,000 to Notts County for Rick Green, August 1979
Best Performances: League: 4th Div 2 1961-2 **F.A. Cup:** 5th Round 1957-8, 1969-70 **League/Milk Cup:** Never beyond 3rd Round
Most League Points: 83 in Div 4, 1982-3 **Most League Goals:** 88, Div 3(N), 1957-8
Record League Victory: 8-1 v Luton Town, Div 3, 24 April 1965
Record League Defeat: 0-8 v Carlisle United, Div 3(N), 25 Dec 1952
Club Statistician for the Directory: M Girdham

Programme Editor
Martyn Girdham

Price	Number of Pages
40p	24

Subscriptions
Enquire from club shop

SCUNTHORPE UNITED

PLAYERS NAME Ht Wt Birthdate	Honours	Birthplace Transfers	Clubs	APPEARANCES League	Milk Cup	F.A.C.	A.M.C.	GOALS League	Milk Cup	F.A.C.	A.M.C.
GOALKEEPER											
Joe Neenan†		Manchester	York C. (A)	56	5	3					
6-3 11.13 17.3.59		Player Exchange	Scunthorpe U.	177	8	17	3				
DEFENDERS											
John Green		Rotherham	Rotherham U. (A)	247 + 1	21	17		8	2	2	
5-10 12.1 7.8.58			Scunthorpe U.	45		6	3	2			
Phil Longdon		Wakefield	Barnsley (A)	5							
5-7 10.3 28.9.62			Scunthorpe	43	2	5	3				
Neil Pointon		Church Warsop	Scunthorpe U. (A)	96	3	10	2	2			
5-10 12.10 28.11.64											
Alan Whitehead		Bury	Bury	98 + 1	6	10		13			
6-3 12.0 20.11.56		£75,000	Brentford	101 + 1	13	9		4			
		£35,000	Scunthorpe U.	15							
MIDFIELD											
Mike Brolly	S. S	Kilmarnock	Chelsea	7 + 1		1		1			
5-9 10.4 6.10.54		F	Bristol C.	27 + 3	2	1		2		1	
		£6,000	Grimsby T.	246 + 8	16	16		27	2	1	
		F	Derby Co.	41 + 1	5	3		4			
		F	Scunthorpe U.	40 + 1	2	6	3	5		1	1
Geoff Dey	E. Y	Chesterfield	Sheffield U. (A)								
5-8 11.0 11.1.64			Scunthorpe U.	12	2	5	1 + 1	1			
Mike Lester*		Manchester	Oldham A.	26 + 1	2			1			
5-9½ 11.8 1.5.56		£80,000	Manchester C.	2							
			Stockport Co. (L)	8 + 1	1			1			
		£10,000	Washington D.								
			Grimsby T.	45 + 3	3 + 1	0 + 1		10	2		
		£20,000	Barnsley	64	6	8		11		2	
			Exeter C.	18 + 1	4	1		6			
			Bradford C.	46 + 3	5	4		2		1	
		£7,000	Scunthorpe U.	44	2	5	2	6		1	
Mick Matthews		Hull	Wolverhampton W. (A)	72 + 4	4	2 + 1		7			
5-7½ 10.12 25.9.60		£5,000	Scunthorpe U.	25		1	3	1			
FORWARDS											
Derek Bell		Wyberton	Derby Co. (A)								
5-8 10.3 30.10.56			Halifax T.	104 + 8	4 + 3	4		21	2		
			Sheffield W. (L)	5				1			
			Barnsley	45 + 1	4	3		20	1	1	
			Lincoln C.	69 + 14	10 +	2 + 1		33	4		
			Chesterfield	15 + 2				3			
			Scunthorpe U.	19			3	5			3
Julian Broddie		Laughton	Sheffield U. (A)	1							
5-9 11.3 1.11.64			Scunthorpe U.	9 + 4	1	2		1			
Steve Cammack	E. Y	Sheffield	Sheffield U. (A)	21 + 15	1 + 1			5			
5-10 11.9 20.3.54			Chesterfield	95 + 18	7 + 1	4		21	3		
		£12,500	Scunthorpe U.	84	2	4		27		1	
		£29,000 + P/E	Lincoln C.	18	4 + 1	2 + 1		6		1	
		£3,000 + P/E	Scunthorpe U.	89 + 1	3	10	3	46		5	2
Chris Cowling		Scunthorpe	Scunthorpe U. (A)	94 + 13	5	10	2 + 1	17	1	3	
5-11½ 11.0 19.9.62											

NON-CONTRACT PLAYERS 1984-85

Steve Beaglehole, Ian Botham (7 + 2 Lg., 1 MC), **Linton Brown, David Hill** (1 + 1), **Paul Mable, Dean Meadows, Richard Parsmoor, Simon Shaw** (5), **Simon Steele** (5), **Sean Stobart, Ian Webster** (8 + 1 Lg., 5 FAC, 1 AMC)

SCUNTHORPE UNITED

DIVISION THREE 21ST **FA CUP** 4TH ROUND **MILK CUP** 1ST ROUND

MATCH	DATE	COMPETITION	VENUE	OPPONENTS	RESULT	HALF TIME	L'GUE POS'N	GOALSCORERS	ATTENDANCE
1	A 27	CL	A	Port Vale	D0-0	0-0			4,565
2	**30**	**MC 1**	**H**	**Doncaster R**	**D1-1**	**1-1**		**Cammack**	**4,295**
3	S 3	CL	H	Exeter C	W3-1	1-0	6	Lester, Cammack, Graham	2,768
4	6	CL	H	Oxford U	D0-0	0-0			3,516
5	9	CL	A	Orient	L0-1	0-1	12		2,702
6	**13**	**MC 1**	**A**	**Doncaster R**	**L0-3**	**0-2**			**4,377**
7	16	CL	H	Bolton W	W1-0	0-0	8	Cowling	4,406
8	24	CL	A	Newport Co	D1-1	0-0	11	Green	2,679
9	27	CL	A	Plymouth Arg	L0-4	0-2			3,821
10	30	CL	H	Southend U	L1-6	0-2		Holden (pen)	3,335
11	O 8	CL	A	Bradford C	D2-2	1-1	18	Leman, Lester	2,476
12	15	CL	H	Rotherham U	L1-2	1-1	19	Lester	3,139
13	18	CL	H	Wigan Ath	D0-0	0-0			2,345
14	22	CL	A	Bristol R	L1-4	1-1	19	Pointon	5,324
15	29	CL	H	Wimbledon	W5-1	2-1	17	Peters (og), Wilson 2 (1 pen), Cammack 2	2,347
16	N 1	CL	A	Sheffield U	L3-5	1-1		Dey, Broddle, Wilson	10,502
17	5	CL	H	Walsall	D0-0	0-0	18		2,932
18	12	CL	A	Lincoln C	L1-2	1-0	18	O'Berg	4,657
19	**19**	**FAC 1**	**H**	**Preston NE**	**W1-0**	**0-0**		**Cammack (pen)**	**3,484**
20	26	CL	A	Millwall	L1-2	0-1	19	Cammack	3,776
21	D 3	CL	H	AFC Bournemouth	L1-2	0-1	21	Cammack	2,344
22	**10**	**FAC 2**	**H**	**Bury**	**W2-0**	**2-0**		**Coleman (og), Cammack**	**3,246**
23	17	CL	H	Gillingham	W2-0	1-0	19	Cammack, Cowling	2,127
24	26	CL	A	Hull C	L0-1	0-1	22		18,461
25	27	CL	H	Preston NE	L1-5	0-1	22	Cammack	3,986
26	31	CL	A	Burnley	L0-5	0-3	23		7,632
27	J 2	CL	H	Brentford	D4-4	1-1	23	Graham, Cammack 2, Brolly	2,239
28	**7**	**FAC 3**	**A**	**Leeds U**	**D1-1**	**1-1**		**Cammack**	**17,130**
29	**10**	**FAC 3R**	**H**	**Leeds U**	**D1-1[1]**	**0-0**		**Dey**	**13,129**
30	**16**	**FAC 3R2**	**H**	**Leeds U**	**W4-2**	**2-1**		**Brolly, Cammack, Lester, Graham**	**13,312**
31	21	CL	A	Bolton W	D0-0	0-0	23		5,379
32	**F 1**	**FAC 4**	**A**	**WBA**	**L0-1**	**0-0**			**18,235**
33	3	CL	A	Southend U	D0-0	0-0			1,976
34	10	CL	H	Newport Co	D3-3	2-3		Brolly 2, Cammack	2,879
35	18	CL	A	Wimbledon	D1-1	0-0	22	Cammack (pen)	3,117
36	**21**	**AMC 1**	**H**	**Chesterfield**	**W2-1**	**1-1**		**Cammack, Brolly**	**2,507**
37	25	CL	H	Bristol R	D2-2	1-2	22	Cammack (pen), O'Berg	2,737
38	M 3	CL	A	Wigan Ath	L0-2	0-2	23		3,092
39	6	CL	A	Walsall	D1-1	1-0		Bell	4,735
40	10	CL	H	Lincoln C	D0-0	0-0	23		3,889
41	**13**	**AMC 2**	**H**	**Crewe Alex**	**D4-4[4]**	**1-0**		**Bell 3 (1 pen), Matthews**	**1,524**
42	17	CL	H	Bradford C	W2-1	1-0	20	Cammack, Matthews	3,274
43	**20**	**AMC NQF**	**H**	**Sheffield U**	**L2-3[1]**	**1-0**		**Matthews, Cammack**	**2,720**
44	27	CL	H	Sheffield U	D1-1	0-0		Bell	6,750
45	31	CL	A	Oxford U	L0-1	0-1	20		6,747
46	A 7	CL	H	Plymouth Arg	W3-0	1-0	21	Bell, Brolly, Cammack	2,780
47	11	CL	A	Exeter C	D1-1	1-0		Brolly	2,003
48	14	CL	A	AFC Bournemouth	D1-1	0-1	21	Cammack	3,501
49	17	CL	H	Port Vale	D1-1	0-1		Bell	2,952
50	21	CL	H	Hull C	W2-0	1-0	21	Bell (pen), Cammack	8,286
51	24	CL	A	Preston NE	L0-1	0-0			3,403
52	27	CL	H	Millwall	L0-1	0-0			3,403
53	M 1	CL	H	Orient	W3-1	2-0		Graham 2, Parkinson	2,284
54	5	CL	A	Brentford	L0-3	0-1	22		4,561
55	7	CL	H	Burnley	W4-0	2-0	21	Cammack 2 (1 pen), Cowling, Green	2,620
56	12	CL	A	Gillingham	D1-1	1-0	21	Cowling	3,513
57	15	CL	A	Rotherham U	L0-3	0-2			4,298

[1]After Extra Time. [4]Won 7-6 on Penalties, After Extra Time

Av Home Att **3,453**

Goal Scorers

League (54): Cammack 18 (3 pens), Bell 5 (1 pen), Brolly 5, Cowling 4, Graham 4, Lester 3, Wilson 3 (1 pen), Green 2, O'Berg 2, Broddle 1, Dey 1, Holden 1 (1 pen), Leman 1, Matthews 1, Parkinson 1, Pointon 1, opponent 1

FA Cup (9): Cammack 4 (1 pen), Brolly 1, Dey 1, Graham 1, Lester 1, opponents 1

Milk Cup (1): Cammack 1

AMC (8): Bell 3 (1 pen), Cammack 2, Matthews 2, Brolly 1

1983-84

Neenan	Longdon	Pointon	Brolly	Boxall	Hunter	Graham	Cammack	Cowling	Dey	Broddle	Webster	Green	Lester	Bell	Holden	O'Berg	Richardson	Matthews	Whitehead	Wilson **(L)**	Leman	Parkinson	Pratley **(L)**	Steele	REFEREE	
1	2	3*	4	5	6	7	8	9	10	11	12														N Glover	1
1	**2**	**3**	**4**	**5**	**6**	**7**	**8**	**9**	**11**				**10**												**A Saunders**	**2**
1	2	3	4		6	7	8	9	11			5	10												PA Tyldesley	3
1	2	3	4		6	7	8	9	11			5	10												N Midgley	4
1	2	3	4*		6	7	8	9	11	12		5	10												K Cooper	5
1	**2**	**3**	**4**		**6**	**7**	**8**	**9**	**11**	**5***			**10**		**12**										**V Callow**	**6**
1	2	3	4	7	6		8*	9	11			5	10		12										MP Scott	7
1	2	3	4	7	6			9	11*			5	10		8	12									A Seville	8
1	2	3	4	7*	6			9	11			5	10		8	12									C Thomas	9
1		3	4		6							5	10		8	7	2								RA Banks	10
1	2	3	7		6			9				5	10		8*	12				4	11				J Hough	11
1	2	3	7		6	12		9*				5	10			8				4	11				B Hill	12
1	2	3	7		6			9				5	10		8	11				4					JE Bray	13
1	2	3	7		6*			9		12		5	10		8	11				4†					L Burden	14
1	2	3	7				8	6		9		5	10			11				4					LR Dilkes	15
1	2	3					8	6	7	9		5	10			11				4					R Guy	16
1	2	3	7				8	6	4	9		5	10			11									K Walmsley	17
1	2	3	7				8	6	4	9		5	10			11									L Robinson	18
1	**2**	**3**	**7**				**8**	**6**	**4**	**9**		**5**	**10**			**11**									**J Key**	**19**
1	2	3	7			4	8			9	6	5	10			11									EA Read	20
1	2	3	7			4	8			9*	6	5	10			11			12						T Mills	21
1	**2**	**3**	**4**				**8**			**7**	**6**	**5**	**10**			**11**									**K Hackett**	**22**
1	2	3	4				8	7				5	10			11									M Heath	23
1	2	3	4				8	7				5	10			11		6							T Jones	24
1	2	3	12		4		8	7*				5	10			11		6							G Napthine	25
1	2	3	7		6	9	8					5	10			11		4							M Peck	26
1		3	7		6	9	8					5	10			11	2	4							D Owen	27
1		**3**	**7**			**9**	**8**		**4**		**6**	**5**	**10**			**11**	**2**								**J Worrall**	**28**
1	**2**	**3**	**7**			**9**	**8**		**4**		**6**	**5**	**10**			**11**									**J Worrall**	**29**
1	**2**	**3**	**7**			**9**	**8**		**4**		**6**	**5**	**10**			**11**									**G Tyson**	**30**
1	2	3	7			9	8					5	10			11		4	6						J Lovatt	31
1	**2**	**3**	**7**			**9**	**8**		**10**		**6**	**5**				**11**		**4**							**A Robinson**	**32**
1	2	3	7			9	8		10*	12	6	5		11				4							K Baker	33
1	2	3	7				8			11	6	5	10	9				4							P Willis	34
1	2	3	7				8		11		6	5	10	9				4							B Stevens	35
1	**2**	**3**	**7**				**8**		**11**		**6**	**5**	**10**	**9**				**4**							**K Redfern**	**36**
1	2	3	7				8				6	5	10	9		11		4							A Saunders	37
1	2	3	7			11	8					5	10	9				4					6		F Roberts	38
1	2	3	7			11	8					5	10	9				4					6		D Richardson	39
1	2	3	7			11	8					5	10	9				4					6		D Scott	40
1	**2**	**3**	**7**			**11**	**8**					**5**		**9**		**10***		**4**				**12**	**6**		**G Tyson**	**41**
1	2	3	7			11	8					5	10	9				4					6		N Wilson	42
1	**2**		**7**			**11**	**8**		**12**			**5**	**10**	**9***			**3**	**4**					**6**		**J Hunting**	**43**
1	2	3	7				8					5		9				4	10			11	6		H Taylor	44
1	2	3	7			12	8					5		9				4	10			11*	6		K Cooper	45
1	2	3	7			11	8					5		9				4	10				6		L Dilkes	46
1	2	3	7			11	8					5		9				4	10				6		R Lewis	47
1			7			11	8			3	2*	5	4	9					10			12	6		D Reeves	48
1	2	3	7			11	8					5	4	9					10				6		M Dimblebee	49
1	2	3	7			11	8					5		9				4	10			6			T Fitzharris	50
1	2	3	7			11	8					5		9				4	10			6			T Mills	51
1	2	3	7			11	8					5		9				4	10			6			J Worrall	52
	2	3				11	8					5		9		7		4	10			6		1	J Ashworth	53
	2	3				11	8	12				5		9*		7		4	10			6		1	I Borrett	54
	2	3				11	8	9				5				7		4	10			6		1	L Robinson	55
	2	3					8	9				5	10			7		4	10			6		1	Alan Robinson	56
	2	3	10*			6	8	9		12		5				7		4	11					1	E Scales	57
41	43	45	40	4	15	25	39	21	12	9	8	45	34	19	6	22	2	25	15	6	2	9	10	5	League Appearances	
			+1S			+2S		+1S		+4S	+1S				+1S	+3S						+1S				
6	5	6	6		1	4	6	1	5	2	5	5	5			6	1	1							FA Cup Appearances	
2	2	2	2	1	2	2	2	2	2	1			2		1S										Milk Cup Appearances	
3	3	2	3			2	3		1+1S		1	3	2	3		1	1	3				1S	2		AM Cup Appearances	

Also Played: Snow match 10, no.9. Hill match 10, no.11; 21, no.12. Botham matches 22, 23, 24, 25, no.9.

THE OLD SHOW GROUND

Official Address: Old Show Ground, Scunthorpe, South Humberside. Telephone: Scunthorpe 848077

Ground Capacity: 25,000

Record Attendance: 23,935 v. Portsmouth, F.A. Cup Round 4, 30 Feb 1954

Record Receipts: £28,612 v. Leeds United, F.A. Cup Round 3 Replay, Jan 1984

Size of Playing Area: 111yds × 73 yds

Season Tickets: Stand: £69.00 (£34.50 OAP/child); Ground: £50.60 (£25.30 OAP/child)

Executive Box Season Tickets: Adult £125, child £90 (Bar & Buffet – Buffet free)

Cost of Stand Tickets: £3.30 (£1.50 OAP/child); **Terraces:** £2.20 (£1.20 OAP/child)

Match and Ticket Information: No telephone bookings Ground. Can reserve until day of match unless otherwise notified in press (for seats by phoning office).

Car Parking: Club park adjacent to Ground for 40/50 vehicles. Ample street parking.

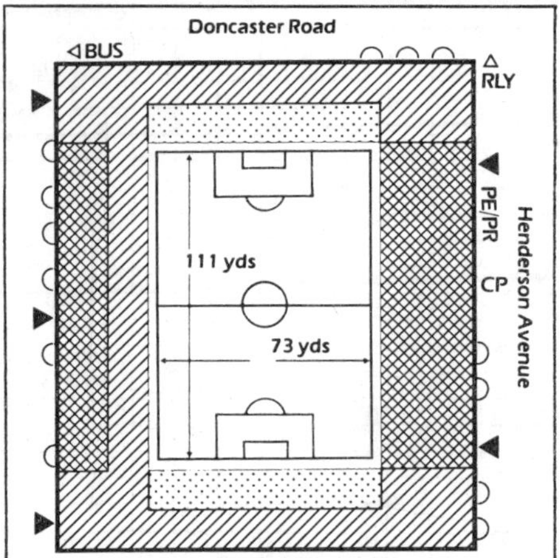

For key see page 12

How to get to the ground

From North and West: Use Motorway M180 to end of Motorway then join A161 and A18 S.P. Scunthorpe. At Motorway Terminal roundabout take 1st exit and at next take 2nd exit into Doncaster Road for Scunthorpe United F.C.

From East: Use A18 S.P. Scunthorpe into town centre and roundabout take 3rd exit into Ashby Road. In 0.8m at crossroads turn left into Doncaster Road for Scunthorpe United F.C.

From South: Use A1 then A1133 and A156 to Gainsborough then follow signs into Scunthorpe town centre on A159. At roundabout take 2nd exit into Ashby Road. In 0.8m at crossroads turn left into Doncaster Road for Scunthorpe United F.C.

SHEFFIELD UNITED Division 2

Chairman
R J Brealey

Directors
A H Laver
M Wragg
R Wragg M.Inst.B.M.
D Dooley (Associate)

Secretary
Jeff Smith

Manager
Ian Porterfield

Assistant Manager
John McSeveney

Club Coach
Jim McGuigan

Pools & Commercial Manager
T Burdass (0742 738995)

Third place in Third Division may not be the greatest achievement in the history of Sheffield United, but it does represent the end (or so supporters will hope) of one of the grimmest periods in the club's annals with a move upwards to the Second Division. By now most supporters' fingernails will have grown again after the harrowing wait all must have experienced that evening in May when Hull City went to Burnley needing to win by three clear goals to deny United their prize. Hull won by only two goals and up went the Blades.

With occasional slips the team did consistently mount a challenge with a talented squad which included in Edwards a dangerous man anywhere near goal. With McHale and Morris also determined the Blades were an attractive team to watch as their final tally of eighty six league goals will testify. A slightly uncertain defence (fifty-three goals conceded in the League) meant that there was that final traumatic match at Burnley to endure.

In the cups Bramall Lane did not have much to cheer with a narrow first round aggregate win against Bradford City (2-1) in the Milk Cup being followed by narrow defeat against Shrewsbury Town (3-4). The Third Round of the F.A. Cup was attained after a resounding First Round win at Wrexham (5-1), when Edwards scored four goals and a far narrower affair against Lincoln when the only goal of the whole tie was scored by Stancliffe in the second half of the replay at Bramall Lane. In the Third Round Birmingham returned to St. Andrews with a draw (two goals were shared) and won the replay by two clear goals leaving the Blades to concentrate on and win promotion.

So, are the great days returning to Bramall Lane? With some very useful players around Manager Ian Porterfield had a nicely balanced squad apart from some defensive lapses. Tomlinson is a most promising young goalkeeper and Edwards, McHale and Morris have already been mentioned favourably. Others to note are Arnott, Stancliffe and the veteran Joe Bolton. The future could be most interesting.

WLM

Atkin, Heffernan, Bolton, Waugh, Stancliffe, Tomlinson, West, Cockerill, Kenworthy. Middle Row: McSeveney (Coach), Arnott, Smith, Eckhardt, Peattie, Garner, Charles, McGuigan (Coach — not now with club). **Front Row:** Black, Cooper, McHale, Morris, Porterfield (Manager), Edwards, Brazil, Henderson, Philliskirk.

'THE BLADES'

Formed: 1899 **Turned Professional:** 1899 **Ltd Co:** 1899
Previous Managers: Since 1946
Ted Davison Reg Freeman Joe Mercer John Harris Arthur Rowley John Harris Ken Furphy Jimmy Sirrel Harry Haslam Martin Peters
Honours: Division One Champions 1897-8 Division Two Champions 1952-3 Division Four Champions 1981-2 F.A. Cup Winners 1898-9, 1901-2, 1914-5, 1924-5
League Career: Elected to Division Two 1892 Promoted to Division One 1893 Relegated to Division Two 1934 Promoted to Division One 1939 Relegated to Division Two 1949 Promoted to Division One 1953 Relegated to Division Two 1956 Promoted to Division One 1961 Relegated to Division Two 1968 Promoted to Division One 1971 Relegated to Division Two 1976 Relegated to Division Three 1979 Relegated to Division Four 1981 Promoted to Division Three 1982 Promoted to Division Two 1984
Colours: Red and white striped shirts, black shorts, red and white stockings
Change Colours: Yellow shirts and stockings with blue trim, white shorts

CLUB RECORDS

Most Appearances for Club: Joe Shaw, 629, 1948-66
Most Capped Player: Billy Gillespie, 25, Northern Ireland
Record Goalscorer in a Match: Harry Hammond 5 v Bootle, Div 2, 26.11.1892; Harry Johnson 5 v West Ham United, Div 1, 26.12.27
Record League Goalscorer in a season: Jimmy Dunne, 41, Div 1, 1930-1
Record League Goalscorer in a career: Harry Johnson, 205, 1919-20
Record Transfer Fee Received: £400,000 from Leeds United for Alex Sabella, May 1980
Record Transfer Fee Paid: £160,000 to River Plate for Alex Sabella, July 1982 £160,000 to Leicester City for Alan Young, Aug 1982
Best Performances: League: Champions (1) **F.A. Cup:** Winners (4) **League/Milk Cup:** 5th Round 1961-2, 1966-7, 1971-2
Most League Points: 96 in Div 4, 1981-2 **Most League Goals:** 102, Div 1, 1925-6
Record League Victory: 10-0 v Port Vale, Div 2, 10 Dec 1892 (away) 10-0 v Burnley, Div 1, 19 Jan 1929
Record League Defeat: 3-10 v Middlesbrough, Div 1, 18 Nov 1937
Club Statistician for the Directory: Andrew Trehearne

Programme Editor
Andy Daykin

Price	Number of Pages
50p	24

Subscriptions
£16.50 (post paid British Isles), £24.00 (postage overseas).

SHEFFIELD UNITED

PLAYERS NAME Ht Wt Birthdate	Honours	Birthplace Transfers	Clubs	APPEARANCES League	Milk Cup	F.A.C.	E. Cups	GOALS League	Milk Cup	F.A.C.	E. Cups
GOALKEEPERS											
Paul Tomlinson		Brierley Hill	Sheffield U.	30		5	3				
22.2.64											
Keith Waugh		Sunderland	Sunderland (A)								
6-1 12.0 27.10.56		F	Peterborough U.	195	22	10					
		£90,000	Sheffield U.	89	8	6	1				
DEFENDERS											
Bob Atkins		Leicester	Sheffield U.	21+3	2+1		2+1	3			
6-0½ 12.0 16.10.62											
Joe Bolton	Div. 2, 76	Birtley	Sunderland (A)	264+9	16	22		11			
5-11 12.2 2.2.55			Middlesbrough	59	2	3		1			
			Sheffield U.	45	2	5	3	1			
Paul Garner	E. Y, Div. 4, 82	Doncaster	Huddersfield T. (A)	96	8	2		2			
5-9 10.10 1.12.55		£60,000	Sheffield U.	248+3	8+1	14	3	7			2
Mike Henderson		Gosforth	Sunderland (A)	81+3	2	6		2			
5-10 11.6 31.3.56		£140,000	Watford	50+1	8+1	4					
			Cardiff C.	11							
			Sheffield U.	52+2	5	11	2				
Tony Kenworthy	E. Y, Div. 4, 82	Leeds	Sheffield U. (A)	250+4	15	15	1	34	1	1	
5-10 10.7 30.10.58											
Paul Smith		Rotherham	Sheffield U. (A)	9+1			1				
5-9 11.0 9.11.64											
Paul Stancliffe*	Div. 3, 81	Sheffield	Rotherham U. (A)	285	10	22		8		2	
6-0 11.10 5.5.58			Sheffield U.	43	4	5	2	1	2	1	
Gary West	E. Y	Scunthorpe	Sheffield U. (A)	50	1	6	2	1			
6-1 12.2 25.8.64											
MIDFIELD											
Kevin Arnott		Bensham	Sunderland (A)	132+1	7	6		16	1		
5-10 11.12 28.9.58			Blackburn R. (L)	17				2			
			Sheffield U.	53	7	5		7	1	1	
			Blackburn R. (L)	11+1				1			
			Rotherham U. (L)	9			2+1	2			
Gary Brazil		Tunbridge Wells	Crystal Palace (A)								
5-8½ 9.9 19.9.62		F	Sheffield U.	33+23	4+1	4+4		7		1	
Steve Charles	Div. 4, 82	Sheffield	Sheffield U.	110+11	11	9+1	3	9	1	1	1
5-9 10.7 10.5.60											
Glen Cockerill		Grimsby	Louth U.								
6-0 11.13 25.8.55			Lincoln C.	65+6	2	2		10			
		£111,000	Swindon T.	23+3	3			1			
		£140,000	Lincoln C.	114+1	16	6		25	1		
		£125,000	Sheffield U.	10				1			
Ray McHale		Sheffield	Chesterfield	123+1	10	8		27	2	1	
5-8 12.6 12.8.50		Player Exchange	Halifax T.	86	6	5		21			
			Swindon T.	171+2	22	21		33	4	6	
		£100,000	Brighton	9+2	2						
		£60,000	Barnsley	52+1	8	1		1			
		£20,000	Sheffield U.	54	7+1	7	3	1			
			Bury (L)	6							
FORWARDS											
Richard Cooper		London	Sheffield U. (A)	1+1							
5-10 10.8 7.5.65											
Keith Edwards†	Div. 4, 82	Stockton	Sheffield U.	64+6	2	3		29			
5-10 10.3 16.7.57		£60,000	Hull C.	130+2	9	10		57	1	5	
		£95,000	Sheffield U.	122+5	6+2	13	3	81	7	10	2
Colin Morris	Div. 4, 82	Blyth	Burnley (A)	9+1		0+1					
5-7 10.5 22.8.53			Southend	133	11	12		25	4	1	
		£111,111	Blackpool	87	6	7		26	3	3	
		£100,000	Sheffield U.	106	7+1	11	3	38	2	3	1
Tony Philliskirk		Sheffield	Sheffield U.	20+1	1	3	3	8			
6-1 11.2 10.2.65											

APPRENTICES: Paul Burgin, Richard Chapplow, Jimmy Flynn, Ken Geelan, Jimmy Pearson, Richard Shipston

SHEFFIELD UNITED

DIVISION THREE 3RD **FA CUP** 3RD ROUND **MILK CUP** 2ND ROUND

MATCH	DATE	COMPETITION	VENUE	OPPONENTS	RESULT	HALF TIME	L'GUE POS'N	GOALSCORERS	ATTENDANCE
1	A 27	CL	H	Gillingham	W4-0	1-0		Edwards 4	10,405
2	**30**	**MC 1**	**A**	**Bradford C**	**W1-0**	**0-0**		**Stancliffe**	**4,401**
3	S 3	CL	A	Lincoln C	W2-0	0-0	1	Trusson, Edwards	6,686
4	6	CL	A	Walsall	W2-1	1-1		Atkins, Morris	4,711
5	10	CL	H	Preston NE	D1-1	1-1	2	Edwards	12,441
6	**13**	**MC 1**	**H**	**Bradford C**	**D1-1**	**1-1**		**Edwards**	**8,658**
7	24	CL	H	Wigan Ath	D2-2	0-2	7	Edwards, Kenworthy	10,797
8	27	CL	H	Bradford C	W2-0	0-0		Trusson 2	10,040
9	O 1	CL	A	Millwall	W2-1	1-1	4	Edwards, Morris (pen)	5,601
10	**4**	**MC 2**	**A**	**Shrewsbury T**	**L1-2**	**1-0**		**Stancliffe**	**4,382**
11	8	CL	A	Hull C	L1-4	1-1	4	Morris (pen)	16,728
12	15	CL	H	AFC Bournemouth	W2-0	1-0	4	Heffernan, Morris (pen)	8,984
13	18	CL	A	Orient	L0-2	0-1			4,090
14	22	CL	H	Brentford	D0-0	0-0	5		9,848
15	**25**	**MC 2**	**H**	**Shrewsbury T**	**D2-2**	**1-0**		**Edwards, Arnott**	**9,399**
16	29	CL	A	Plymouth Arg	W1-0	0-0	4	Philliskirk	5,458
17	N 1	CL	H	Scunthorpe U	W5-3	1-1		Philliskirk 2, Brazil, Morris, Edwards	10,502
18	5	CL	A	Oxford U	D2-2	1-1	4	Edwards, Morris (pen)	7,514
19	8	CL	A	Burnley	L1-2	0-1		Morris	9,551
20	12	CL	H	Exeter C	D2-2	1-0	4	Philliskirk, Brazil	10,334
21	**19**	**FAC 1**	**A**	**Wrexham**	**W5-1**	**2-1**		**Edwards 4, Arnott**	**2,842**
22	26	CL	H	Southend U	W5-0	1-0	4	Philliskirk, Edwards 3, McHale	9,627
23	D 3	CL	A	Bristol R	D1-1	0-1	3	Morris (pen)	7,472
24	**10**	**FAC 2**	**A**	**Lincoln C**	**D0-0**	**0-0**			**7,554**
25	17	CL	A	Newport Co	W2-0	0-0	2	Edwards 2	4,295
26	**19**	**FAC 2R**	**H**	**Lincoln C**	**W1-0**	**0-0**		**Stancliffe**	**12,547**
27	26	CL	H	Rotherham U	W3-0	2-0	2	Philliskirk 2, Edwards	22,756
28	27	CL	A	Port Vale	L0-2	0-1	3		7,034
29	31	CL	H	Bolton W	W5-0	2-0	3	Morris 3 (1 pen), Bolton, Edwards	14,252
30	J 2	CL	A	Wimbledon	L1-3	0-0	3	Edwards	5,020
31	**7**	**FAC 3**	**H**	**Birmingham C**	**D1-1**	**0-1**		**Brazil**	**17,202**
32	**10**	**FAC 3R**	**A**	**Birmingham C**	**L0-2**	**0-0**			**10,888**
33	14	CL	A	Gillingham	L2-4	2-2	6	Sitton (og), Shaw (og)	5,408
34	21	CL	H	Burnley	D0-0	0-0	6		13,892
35	31	CL	A	Preston NE	D2-2	1-0	6	Edwards, Philliskirk	5,023
36	F 4	CL	H	Millwall	W2-0	1-0	5	Morris, Arnott	9,916
37	7	CL	H	Lincoln C	D0-0	0-0			9,765
38	11	CL	A	Wigan Ath	L0-3	0-2	5		5,079
39	**21**	**AMC 1**	**A**	**Rotherham U**	**W1-0**	**1-0**		**Morris**	**3,396**
40	25	CL	A	Brentford	W3-1	2-1	6	Morris (pen), Atkins, Edwards	5,100
41	28	CL	H	Plymouth Arg	W2-0	1-0		Charles, Morris	9,541
42	M 3	CL	H	Orient	W6-3	2-1	3	Edwards 3, Morris 2 (2 pens), Heffernan	10,021
43	6	CL	H	Oxford U	L1-2	1-1		Morris	17,914
44	10	CL	A	Exeter C	W2-1	0-0	4	Edwards, Morris	3,274
45	**13**	**AMC 2**	**H**	**Bradford C**	**W2-1**	**0-1**		**Charles, Garner**	**3,175**
46	17	CL	H	Hull C	D2-2	1-1	4	Arnott, Edwards	15,374
47	**20**	**AMC NQF**	**A**	**Scunthorpe U**	**W3-2[1]**	**0-1**		**Edwards 2, Garner**	**2,720**
48	24	CL	A	AFC Bournemouth	W1-0	1-0	3	Edwards	4,767
49	27	CL	A	Scunthorpe U	D1-1	0-0		Edwards (pen)	6,750
50	31	CL	H	Walsall	W2-0	1-0	2	Arnott, Edwards	13,227
51	A 7	CL	A	Bradford C	L1-2	1-0	2	Edwards	9,262
52	14	CL	H	Bristol R	W4-0	0-0	4	Stancliffe, Garner, Edwards 2	12,688
53	21	CL	A	Rotherham U	W1-0	0-0	3	Atkins	14,177
54	24	CL	H	Port Vale	W3-1	2-0		Cockerill, Morris (pen), Arnott	14,385
55	28	CL	A	Southend U	W1-0	0-0	3	Arnott	4,971
56	**M 2**	**AMC NSF**	**A**	**Hull C**	**L0-1**	**0-0**			**3,800**
57	5	CL	H	Wimbledon	L1-2	0-1	3	Morris	22,850
58	7	CL	A	Bolton W	L1-3	0-2	3	Edwards	9,036
59	12	CL	H	Newport Co	W2-0	1-0	3	Edwards, Arnott	16,700

[1]After Extra Time (Score after 90mins 2-2) — **Av Home Att 12,880**

Goal Scorers

League (86): Edwards 33 (2 pens), Morris 20 (9 pens), Philliskirk 8, Arnott 6, Atkins 3, Trusson 3, Brazil 2, Heffernan 2, Bolton 1, Charles 1, Cockerill 1, Garner 1, Kenworthy 1, McHale 1, Stancliffe 1, opponents 2
FA Cup (7): Edwards 4, Arnott 1, Brazil 1, Stancliffe 1
Milk Cup (5): Edwards 2, Stancliffe 2, Arnott 1
AMC (6): Edwards 2, Garner 2, Charles 1, Morris 1

1983-84

Waugh	Atkins	Garner	Arnott	Stancliffe	Henderson	Morris	Trusson	Edwards	McHale	Brazil	Heffernan	Bolton	Charles	Kenworthy	Philliskirk	Tomlinson	West	Ross	Smith	Cockerill	McGeeney	Walshaw	Eckhardt	REFEREE	
1	2	3	4	5	6	7	8	9	10	11														V Callow	1
1	**3**		**4**	**5**	**6**	**7**	**8**	**9**	**10**	**11**	**2**													**D Allison**	**2**
1	11		4	5	6	7	8	9	10		2	3												E Scales	3
1	11		4	5	6†	7	8	9	10		2	3												H King	4
1	11*		4	5	6	7	8	9	10	12	2	3												MP Scott	5
1	**12**		**4**	**5**	**6**	**7**	**8**	**9**	**10**	**11***	**2**	**3**												**A Seville**	**6**
1			4	5		7	8	9	10	12	2*	3	11	6										J Ashworth	7
1			4	5		7	8	9	10		2	3	11	6										D Richardson	8
1			4	5	6	7	8	9	10		2	3	11											RG Milford	9
1			**4**	**5**	**6**	**7**	**8**	**9**	**10**		**2**	**3**	**11**											**J Bray**	**10**
1			4	5	6	7	8	9	10		2	3	11											K Redfern	11
1			4	5	6	7	8	9	10		2	3	11											D Scott	12
1			4	5	6	7	8	9	10	12	2	3	11*											MJ Taylor	13
1			4	5		7	8	9	10		2	3		6	11									I Hendrick	14
1			**4**	**5**		**7**	**8***	**9**	**10**	**12**	**2**	**3**		**6**	**11**									**K Walmsley**	**15**
1			4	5		7		9	10	11	2	3		6	8									D Letts	16
1			4	5*	12	7		9	10	11	2	3		6	8									R Guy	17
1			4	5		7		9	10	11	2	3		6	8									JE Martin	18
1			4	5		7		9	10	11	2	3		6	8									RF Nixon	19
1			4	5		7		9	10	11	2	3		6	8									N Ashley	20
			8	**5**	**6**	**7**		**9**	**10**		**2**	**3**			**11**	**1**	**4**							**D Owen**	**21**
			8	5	6	7		9	10		2	3			11	1	4							PN Willis	22
			8	5	6	7		9	10	12	2	3			11*	1	4							J Moules	23
			8	**5**	**6**	**7**		**9**	**10**	**11**	**2**	**3**				**1**	**4**							**G Napthine**	**24**
			8	5	6	7		9	10		2	3			11	1	4							K Salmon	25
			8	**5**	**6**	**7**		**9**	**10**		**2**	**3**			**11**	**1**	**4**							**G Napthine**	**26**
			8	5	6	7		9	10		2	3			11	1	4							J Worrall	27
			8	5	6	7		9	10	12	2	3*			11	1	4							R Banks	28
			8	5	6	7		9	10	12	2	3			11*	1	4							M Robinson	29
			8	5	6	7		9	10		2	3			11	1	4							M James	30
			8	**5**	**6**	**7**		**9**	**10**	**12**	**2**	**3**			**11***	**1**	**4**							**C Downey**	**31**
			8	**5**	**6**	**7**		**9**	**10**	**11**	**2**	**3**				**1**	**4**							**C Downey**	**32**
		11	4		6	7		9	10		2	3			8	1	5							B Stevens	33
		11	4	5	2	7		9	10*	12		3			8	1	6							G Napthine	34
		11	4	5	2	7		9				3			8	1	6	10						G Courtney	35
		11	4	5*	2	7				12		3			8	1	6	10	9					N Glover	36
		11	4		5	7				12	2	3	6		8*	1		10	9					P Tyldesley	37
		11	4	5	6	7		9			2	3			8*	1		10	12					G Tyson	38
	8	**11**	**4**		**5**	**7**		**9**	**10**		**2**	**3**	**6**			**1**								**L Dilkes**	**39**
	8	11	4	5		7		9	10		2	3	6			1								L Burden	40
	8	11	4	5		7		9	10		2	3	6			1								R Bridges	41
	8	11	4	5		7		9	10	12	2	3	6*			1								J Lovatt	42
	8	11	4	5		7		9	10	12	2	3	6*			1								D Owen	43
	8	11	4	5		7		9	10		2	3				1	6							D King	44
		11	**12**	**5**		**7**		**9**	**10**		**2**	**3***	**4**		**8**	**1**	**6**							**A Saunders**	**45**
		11	4	5		7		9	10		2	3			8	1	6							M Heath	46
	12	**11**	**4**	**5***		**7**		**9**	**10**	**12**	**2**	**3**			**8***	**1**	**6**							**J Hunting**	**47**
	8	11	4	5				9	10	7	2	3				1	6							E Read	48
	12	11	4	5				9	10	7*	2	3				1	6			8				H Taylor	49
	7	11	4	5				9	10		2	3				1	6			8				J Hough	50
	7	11	4	5				9	10		2	3				1	6			8				A Banks	51
		11	4	5		7		9	10		2	3				1	6			8				K Baker	52
	12	11	4	5		7		9*	10		2	3				1	6			8				N Midgley	53
		11	4	5		7		9	10		2	3				1	6			8				K Redfern	54
		11	4	5		7		9	10		2	3				1	6			8				I Borrett	55
	8				**2**					**11**			**10**	**6**	**9**				**7**		**3**	**4**	**5**	**D Richardson**	**56**
	12	11	4	5*		7		9	10		2	3				1	6			8				G Courtney	57
	5	11*	4			7		9	10		2	3			12	1	6			8				F Roberts	58
		11	4	5		7		9	10		2	3				1	6			8				T Fitzharris	59
16	13	24	**46**	43	21	42	11	44	42	8	42	45	11	8	20	30	24	4	2	10				League Appearances	
	+3S				+1S					+11S					+1S				+1S						
			5	5	5	5		5	5	2+1S	5	5			3	5	5							FA Cup Appearances	
4	1+1S		4	4	3	4	4	4	4	2+1S	4	3	1	1	1									Milk Cup Appearances	
1	2+1S	3	2+1S	2	2	3		3	3	1–1S	3	3	3	1	3	3	2		1		1	1	1	AM Cup Appearances	

BRAMALL LANE

Official Address: Bramall Lane Ground, Sheffield S2 4SU. Telephone: Sheffield (0742) 738955/6/7

Telegraphic: United, Sheffield

Ground Capacity: 49,000 (15,300 seats)

Record Attendance: 68,287 v. Leeds U, FA Cup Round 5, 15 Feb 1936

Record Receipts: £65,092 v. Sheffield W, Div 3, 5 Apr 1980

Size of Playing Area: 117 × 75 yds

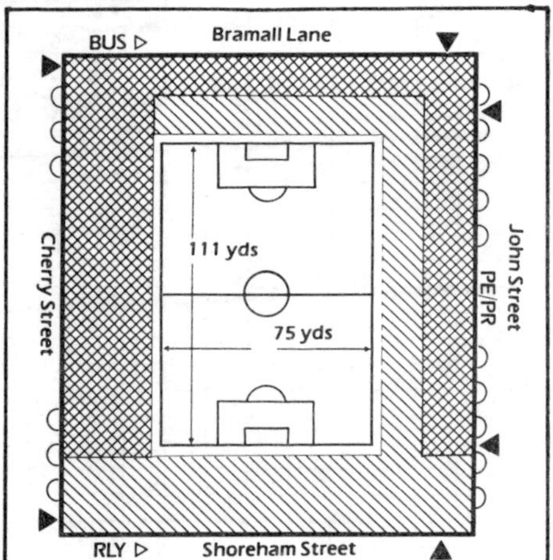

For key see page 12

Season Tickets: £105 (Main Bramall Lane and John Street) (£52.50 Juveniles/OAPs); £73.50 (rear of stands) (£42 Juveniles/OAPs); Terraces £63 (£36.75 Juveniles/OAPs); Ground: £52.50 (£31.50 Juveniles/OAPs)

Executive Box Season Tickets: None available. All sold

Cost of Stand Tickets: £5.00 (£2.50 Juveniles/OAPs), £6.00 Family Ticket (1 Adult, 1 Child); Ground: £2.50 (£1.50 OAPs, £1.00 Junior Blade); Terrace: £3.00 (£1.75 OAPs, £1.50 Junior Blade)

Match and Ticket Information: Tickets bookable fourteen days prior to each match

Car Parking: The ground is five minutes away from car parks in the City Centre. Side-street parking is ample

How to get to the ground

From North: Use Motorway M1 until junction 34. Leave Motorway and follow signs, Sheffield A6109. In 3.4m turn left and shortly at roundabout take 4th exit into Sheaf Street. Then at 2nd roundabout take 5th exit into St. Mary's Road (S.P. Bakewell). In 0.5m left into Bramall Lane for Sheffield United F.C.
From East and South: Use A57 from Motorway M1 (junction 31 or 33) then at roundabout take 3rd exit into Sheaf Street. Then at 2nd roundabout take 5th exit into St. Mary's Road and proceed as above.
From West: Use A57 (S.P. Sheffield) and at roundabout take 4th exit A6134 into Upper Hanover Street. Then at 2nd roundabout take 3rd exit into Bramall Lane.

SHEFFIELD WEDNESDAY Division 1

Chairman
H E McGee

Directors
M Sheppard JP, FCA (Vice-Chairman)
S L Speight
C Woodward
K T Addy
E Barron
G K Hulley

Secretary
R H Chester

Commercial Manager
D Woodhead (0742 337235)

Manager
Howard Wilkinson

Assistant Manager
Peter Eustace

Chief Scout
John Harris

Physiotherapist
Alan Smith

Groundsman
D Barber

Wednesday started the season with a new management team taking over from the departed Jack Charlton. Two ex Wednesday players were appointed, Howard Wilkinson as manager and Peter Eustace coach. After several near misses promotion was essential for the Owls.

Under Wilkinson's dedicated approach the Owls started off with a sound 1-0 victory at Swansea, a goal scored fittingly by Mike Lyons, ever an inspiring skipper. This opening victory started a club record opening season run of 15 league matches without defeat. During this fine opening spell they had a run of 8 consecutive wins in League and Milk Cup.

Their first defeat came at Crystal Palace in November after an undefeated run of 18 matches (League and Milk Cup) from the season's start.

The only time promotion hopes may have faltered slightly was at Christmas when two consecutive defeats, away at Grimsby, then at home to Middlesbrough, gave cause for a little apprehension. But these results were soon forgotten with a great display at in-form Carlisle, where only a freak last minute equaliser, due entirely to the gale blowing, denied them victory.

The highlights of the second half of the campaign were numerous. A 6-1 thrashing of Swansea, a brilliant win at Newcastle, outplaying and beating neighbours Barnsley for the third time in the season and also the Cups provided several highlights. Two good games against Liverpool in the Milk Cup quarter-finals, were followed by a good Cup run to the same stage, including a 3-0 victory at Oxford, where good opposition had previously done badly. Also the 'live' TV coverage of the Southampton 6th Round tie drew to Hillsborough the highest crowd for any of the 'ordinary' live games. Defeat by 5-1 in the replay was on balance of play a travesty of a result, but this seemed only to inspire Wednesday on to promotion.

The atmosphere during the home match v Crystal Palace was fabulous. Palace put up very physical resistance and the Owls struggled to make their superiority pay dividends. Then Cunningham was hauled down in the box and Mel Sterland gleefully sidefooted the penalty home. Hillsborough erupted. After 14 years the Owls were back in the 1st Division and it was fitting 'Zico' Sterland should get the clincher. Although every player did his bit during the season, 'Zico', a local lad, had a special rapport with the fans.

For a team dubbed as unadventurous and unexciting it might have been overlooked that the Owls actually won more league matches than any other in the 2nd Division and were never out of the top 2 all season. Indeed Chelsea only went top after playing the same number of games for the first time after the first match. Indeed the Owls lost the championship not on goal difference, but because Chelsea had scored more goals.

Mick Renshaw

Back Row L to R: Lawrie Madden, Gavin Oliver, Ian Hesford, Martin Hodge, Mark Smith, Mike Lyons. **Middle Row:** Peter Eustace (Assistant Manager), Gary Shelton, Peter Shirtliff, John Pearson, Lee Chapman, Imre Varadi, Nigel Worthington, Alan Smith (Physiotherapist). **Front Row:** Brian Marwood, Mel Sterland, Charlie Williamson, Howard Wilkinson (Manager), Pat Heard, Chris Morris, Andy Blair.

'THE OWLS'

Year Formed: 1867 **Turned Professional:** 1887 **Ltd Co:** 1899
Previous Managers: Since 1946: Eric Taylor (Secretary/Manager) Harry Catterick Vic Buckingham Alan Brown Jack Marshall Danny Williams Derek Dooley Steve Burtenshaw Len Ashurst Jack Charlton OBE
Honours: Champions Division 1 1902-3, 1903-4, 1928-9, 1929-30 Champions Division 2 1899-1900, 1925-6, 1951-2, 1955-6, 1958-9 F.A. Cup Winners 1896, 1907, 1935
League Career: Elected to Division 1 1892 Relegated to Division 2 1898-1899
Promoted to Division 1 1899-1900 Relegated to Division 2 1919-20 Promoted to Division 1 1925-6
Relegated to Division 2 1936-7 Promoted to Division 1 1949-50 Relegated to Division 2 1950-1
Promoted to Division 1 1951-2 Relegated to Division 2 1954-5 Promoted to Division 1 1955-6
Relegated to Division 2 1957-8 Promoted to Division 1 1958-9 Relegated to Division 2 1969-70
Relegated to Division 3 1974-5 Promoted to Division 2 1979-80 Promoted to Division 1 1983-4
Colours: Blue and white striped shirts, blue shorts, white stockings
Change Colours: Yellow shirts with blue trim, white shorts, yellow stockings with blue band

CLUB RECORDS

Most Appearances for Club: Andrew Wilson: Football League 502 + F.A. Cup 44 **Total 546**
Most Capped Player: Ron Springett, England, 33
Record Goalscorer in a Match: Douglas Hunt, 6 v Norwich City (7-0) (H), Div 2, 19.11.38
Record League Goalscorer in a season: Derek Dooley, 46 **All competitions:** Derek Dooley, 47 (League 46, F.A. Cup 1), 1951-2 (in 31 appearances)
Record League Goalscorer in a Career: Andrew Wilson, 200 **All competitions:** Andrew Wilson, 216 (League 200, F.A. Cup 16), 1900-20
Record Transfer Fee Received: £120,000 from Newcastle United for Tommy Craig, Jan 1975
Record Transfer Fee Paid: £200,000 to Budocnost for Ante Mirocevic, 1980
Best Performances: League: Champions (4) **F.A. Cup:** Winners (3) **League/Milk Cup:** 5th Round, 1982-3
European Fairs Cup: Quarter Final
Most League Points: (2pts for win) 62, Div 2, 1968-94 (3pts for win) 77, Div 2, 1983-4
Most League Goals: 106, Div 2, 1958-9
Record League Victory: 9-1 v Birmingham City, Div 1, 13 Dec 1930
Record League Defeat: 0-10 v Aston Villa, Div 1, 5 Oct 1912
European Competitions Entered: Fairs Cup 1961-62, 1963-64.

Club Statistician for the Directory: Mick Renshaw

Programme Editor
Roger Oldfield

Price	Number of Pages
50p	24

Subscriptions
£16.00 (League matches, 2nd class postage, U.K. included); £17.00 (League matches, surface mail to Europe); £20.00 (League matches, surface mail outside Europe); £32.00 (League matches, airmail outside Europe)

SHEFFIELD WEDNESDAY

PLAYERS NAME Ht Wt Birthdate	Honours	Birthplace Transfers	Clubs	APPEARANCES League	APPEARANCES Milk Cup	APPEARANCES F.A.C.	APPEARANCES E. Cups	GOALS League	GOALS Milk Cup	GOALS F.A.C.	GOALS E. Cups
GOALKEEPERS											
Ian Hesford	E. U.21(7)	Kenya	Blackpool (A)	202	14	13					
6-2 13.12 4.3.60		£40,000	Sheffield W.								
Martin Hodge		Southport	Plymouth A. (A)	43	1	1					
6-2 13.7 4.2.59			Everton[1]	25							
		£50,000	Sheffield W.	42	6	5					
David Redfern		Sheffield	Sheffield W.								
6-1 13.8 8.11.62											
DEFENDERS											
Ian Bailey		Middlesbrough	Middlesbrough (A)[2]	140+5	12	14+		11		1	
5-9 11.4 20.10.56		£80,000	Sheffield W.	35							
Mick Lyons*	E. U.23(5), B(1)	Liverpool	Everton (A)	364+26	37	34+		48	5	6	
6-1 13.2 8.12.51		£100,000	Sheffield W.	81	11	12		8		1	
Lawrie Madden		London	Arsenal (N-C)								
5-11 13.1 28.9.55			Mansfield (N-C)	9+1							
			Manchester Univ.								
			Charlton A.	109+4	4+2	8		7			
		£10,000	Millwall	44+3	2	1		1			
		F	Sheffield W.	38	6	5		1			
Gavin Oliver		Felling	Sheffield W.	5+5	0+2	1					
5-11 12.10 6.9.62			Tranmere R. (L)	17				1			
Peter Shirtliff		Chaplestown	Sheffield W. (A)	132	9+2	9		4			
6-2 12.10 6.4.61											
Mark Smith	E. U.21(5)	Sheffield	Sheffield W. (A)	216+1	23	25		14	1	2	
6-10½ 12.2 21.3.60											
Mel Sterland	E. U.21(7)	Sheffield	Sheffield W. (A)	123+4	12	14+1		11		1	
5-11 13.2 1.10.61											
Charles Williamson		Glasgow	Sheffield W.	61+1	1			1			
5-8 11.5 16.3.62			Lincoln C.	5			1AM				
Nigel Worthington	NI.(2), Y	Ballymena	Ballymena U.								
5-10 12.6 7.5.62			Notts. Co.	67	9	4		4			
			Sheffield W.	14				1			
MIDFIELD											
Andy Blair	S. U.21(5),	Bedworth	Coventry C. (A)	90+3	11	8		6	1	7	
5-9 10.9 18.12.59	ESC. 82	£300,000	Aston Villa	24+10	0+2	3					
			Wolverhampton W. (L)	10							
		£80,000	Sheffield W.								
Pat Heard	E. Y	Hull	Everton (A)	10+1							
5-10 11.0 17.3.60			Aston Villa	20+4	0+1			2			
			Sheffield W.	21+3	1	6		3			
Simon Mills	E. Y	Sheffield	Sheffield W.	1+2		1					
5-8 11.4 16.8.64											
Chris Morris	E. S	Dronfield	Sheffield W.	8+5	4	0+1		1	1		
5-8 11.6 24.12.63											
Gary Shelton†		Nottingham	Walsall (A)	12+12	0+1	2+2					
5-7 11.3 21.3.58		£80,000	Aston Villa	24	2+1			7			
			Notts. Co. (L)	8							
			Sheffield W.	87+2	8	12		10	2	2	
FORWARDS											
Lee Chapman	E. U.21(1)	Lincoln	Stoke C.	95+4	5	3		34	3		
6-1½ 13.0 5.12.59			Plymouth A. (L)	3+1							
			Arsenal	15+8	0+2			4		1	
			Sunderland	14+1		2		3			
			Sheffield W.								
Brian Marwood		Easington	Hull C. (A)	154+4	6+1	16	5	51			
5-7 9.13 5.2.60		£100,000	Sheffield W.								
David Mossman	E. S	Chesterfield	Sheffield W.								
5-11 12.2 27.7.64											
John Pearson	E. Y	Sheffield	Sheffield W. (A)	61+35	6+2	10+		22	1	1	
6-2 13.2 1.9.63											
Imre Varadi		Paddington	Letchworth G.C.								
5-8 11.1 8.7.59			Sheffield U.	6+4		2		4			
		£80,000	Everton	22+4		6		6			
		£100,000	Newcastle U.	81	4	5		39	1	2	
		£150,000	Sheffield W.	35+3	5	4		17			

NON-CONTRACT PLAYERS: Eddie Colton, Dylan Kerr

APPRENTICES: D. Bradshaw, M. Brookes, L. Coombes, D. Hazel, P. Showler, A. Smith, S. Chambers, T. Gregory, K. Pressman

[1]Martin Hodge played on loan for P.N.E. (28), Oldham (4), Gillingham (4). [2]Ian Bailey played on loan for Doncaster (9), Carlisle (7, 1g.), Bolton W. (5).

SHEFFIELD WEDNESDAY

DIVISION TWO 2ND **FA CUP** 6TH ROUND **MILK CUP** 5TH ROUND

MATCH	DATE	COMPETITION	VENUE	OPPONENTS	RESULT	HALF TIME	L'GUE POS'N	GOALSCORERS	ATTENDANCE
1	A 27	CL	A	Swansea C	W1-0	1-0		Lyons	10,900
2	29	CL	A	Derby Co	D1-1	0-1		Bannister	10,241
3	S 3	CL	H	Carlisle U	W2-0	1-0	1	O'Riordan (og), Bannister	14,544
4	6	CL	H	Cambridge U	W1-0	1-0		Varadi	14,947
5	10	CL	A	Charlton Ath	D1-1	1-1	1	Dowman (og)	6,904
6	17	CL	H	Chelsea	W2-1	0-1	1	Lyons, Megson	20,596
7	24	CL	A	Oldham Ath	W3-1	1-1	1	Varadi, Shelton, Sterland	
8	O 1	CL	H	Blackburn R	W4-2	1-1	1	Sterland, Bannister, Varadi, Lyons	16,849
9	**4**	**MC 2**	**H**	**Darlington**	**W3-0**	**3-0**		**Bannister, Morris, Madden**	**9,060**
10	8	CL	H	Leeds U	W3-1	1-0	1	Shelton, Pearson, Morris	26,814
11	15	CL	A	Portsmouth	W1-0	0-0	1	Megson	16,335
12	22	CL	A	Brighton & HA	W3-1	2-0	1	Shirtliff P, Madden, Bannister	14,827
13	**25**	**MC 2**	**A**	**Darlington**	**W4-2**	**0-1**		**Madden, Shelton, Bannister 2**	**3,615**
14	29	CL	H	Huddersfield T	D0-0	0-0	1		27,824
15	N 5	CL	H	Barnsley	W2-0	1-0	1	Smith, Sterland (pen)	27,491
16	**8**	**MC 3**	**A**	**Preston NE**	**W2-0**	**1-0**		**Varadi, Shelton**	**11,060**
17	11	CL	A	Fulham	D1-1	1-0		Cunningham	9,687
18	19	CL	H	Newcastle U	W4-2	1-1	1	Varadi 2, Cunningham, Bannister	41,134
19	26	CL	A	Crystal Palace	L0-1	0-0	1		11,263
20	**29**	**MC 4**	**A**	**Stoke C**	**W1-0**	**0-0**		**Bannister**	**18,653**
21	D 3	CL	H	Shrewsbury T	D1-1	1-0	1	Varadi	17,703
22	10	CL	A	Manchester C	W2-1	1-1	1	Varadi 2	41,862
23	17	CL	H	Cardiff C	W5-2	3-0	1	Varadi 2, Shelton, Bannister, Lyons	14,580
24	26	CL	A	Grimsby T	L0-1	0-0	1		16,197
25	27	CL	H	Middlesbrough	L0-2	0-2	1		24,818
26	31	CL	A	Carlisle U	D1-1	0-0	2	Megson	10,475
27	J 1	CL	H	Oldham Ath	W3-0	0-0	1	Varadi, Cunningham, Bannister	18,690
28	**7**	**FAC 3**	**H**	**Barnsley**	**W1-0**	**1-0**		**Pearson**	**29,638**
29	14	CL	H	Swansea C	W6-1	3-0	1	Lyons, Pearson, Toshack (og), Megson, Heard, Varadi	13,787
30	**17**	**MC 5**	**H**	**Liverpool**	**D2-2**	**1-1**		**Megson, Lawrenson (og)**	**49,357**
31	21	CL	A	Chelsea	L2-3	0-2	2	Smith, Bannister	35,147
32	**25**	**MC 5R**	**A**	**Liverpool**	**L0-3**	**0-1**			**40,485**
33	**30**	**FAC 4**	**H**	**Coventry C**	**W3-2**	**1-2**		**Shirtliff, Bannister, Sterland (pen)**	**26,154**
34	F 4	CL	A	Blackburn R	D0-0	0-0	2		16,158
35	11	CL	H	Charlton Ath	W4-1	1-0	2	Bannister, Shirtliff, Cunningham, Varadi	18,510
36	**18**	**FAC 5**	**A**	**Oxford U**	**W3-0**	**2-0**		**Varadi, Bannister 2**	**14,167**
37	25	CL	H	Brighton & HA	W2-1	1-0	1	Bannister, Varadi	21,614
38	M 3	CL	A	Barnsley	W1-0	1-0	2	Sterland (pen)	20,322
39	7	CL	H	Fulham	D1-1	0-0		Pearson	20,440
40	**11**	**FAC 6**	**H**	**Southampton**	**D0-0**	**0-0**			**43,030**
41	17	CL	A	Cambridge U	W2-1	1-0	2	Bannister, Varadi	5,562
42	**20**	**FAC 6R**	**A**	**Southampton**	**L1-5**	**1-2**		**Shirtliff**	**20,592**
43	31	CL	A	Leeds U	D1-1	0-0	2	Bannister	25,343
44	A 7	CL	H	Portsmouth	W2-0	1-0	2	Shelton, Sterland	20,239
45	10	CL	H	Derby Co	W3-1	1-0		Varadi 2, Sterland (pen)	21,792
46	14	CL	A	Newcastle U	W1-0	0-0	1	Shelton	36,725
47	21	CL	H	Grimsby T	W1-0	0-0	1	Sterland (pen)	25,828
48	25	CL	A	Middlesbrough	L0-2	0-1			12,362
49	28	CL	H	Crystal Palace	W1-0	0-0	1	Sterland (pen)	27,287
50	M 1	CL	A	Huddersfield T	W1-0	0-0		Lilis (og)	18,488
51	5	CL	A	Shrewsbury T	L1-2	0-0		Bannister	7,885
52	7	CL	H	Manchester C	D0-0	0-0			36,763
53	12	CL	A	Cardiff C	W2-0	0-0		Bannister, Cunningham	14,171
								Av Home Att	**24,238**

Goal Scorers

League (72): Varadi 17, Bannister 14, Sterland 8 (5 pens), Cunningham 5, Lyons 5, Shelton 5, Megson 4, Pearson 3, Shirtliff 2, Smith 2, Heard 1, Madden 1, Morris 1, opponents 4
FA Cup (8): Bannister 3, Shirtliff 2, Pearson 1, Sterland 1 (1 pen), Varadi 1
Milk Cup (12): Bannister 4, Madden 2, Shelton 2, Megson 1, Morris 1, Varadi 1, opponents 1

1983-84

Hodge	Sterland	Williamson	Shirtliff Peter	Lyons	Madden	Morris	Megson	Bannister	Pearson	Shelton	Varadi	Smith	Taylor	Oliver	Cunningham	Heard	Worthington	Mills	REFEREE	
1	2	3	4	5	6	7	8	9	10*	11	12								E Read	1
1	2	3	4	5	6	7*	8	9	10	11	12								D Reeves	2
1	2	3	4	5	6		7	8	10	11	9								H Taylor	3
1	2	3	4	5	6	12	8	9*	10	11	7								N Glover	4
1	2		4	5	6	12	7	8*	10	11	9	3							M Taylor	5
1	2	3		5	6		7	8	10	11	9	4							A Bridges	6
1	2	3		5	6	12	7	8*	10	11	9	4							G Courtney	7
1	2	3		5	6		7	8	10	11*	9	4	12						G Tyson	8
1	**2**	**3**		**5**	**6**	**9***	**7**	**8**	**10**	**11**		**4**	**12**						**G Napthine**	**9**
1	2	3		5	6	9	7	8	10	11		4							R Nixon	10
1	2		3	5	6	9	7	8	10*	11		4		12					AW Ward	11
1	2		3	5	6	9	7	8	10*	11		4	12						E Scales	12
1	**2**		**3**	**5**	**6**	**10**	**7**	**8**		**11**	**9***	**4**		**12**					**D Allison**	**13**
1	2		3	5	6	10	7	8		11	9	4							K Warmsley	14
1	2		3	5	6	10*	7	8		11	9	4	12						D Shaw	15
1	**2**		**3**	**5**	**6**	**10**	**7**	**8**		**11***	**9**	**4**	**12**						**J Jones**	**16**
1	2		3	5	6		7	8		11	9	4			10				A Gunn	17
1	2		3	5	6		7	8		11	9	4			10				JB Worrall	18
1	2*		3	5	6	12	7	8		11	9	4			10				B Hill	19
1	**2**		**3**	**5**	**6**	**10***	**7**	**8**	**12**		**9**	**4**				**11**			**K Baker**	**20**
1	2		3	5	6		7	8	10		9	4				11			D Richardson	21
1	2		3	5	6		7	8		11	9	4			10				A Saunders	22
1	2		3	5	6	12	7	8		11	9*	4			10				R Guy	23
1	2		3	5	6*		7	8		11	9	4			10	12			D Brazier	24
1	2		3	5	6	8	7			11	9	4*			10	12			K Barratt	25
1	2		3	5	6		7	8		11	9	4			10				N Midgley	26
1	2		3	5	6		7	8		11	9	4*			10	12			P Willis	27
1	**2**		**3**	**5**	**6**	**12**	**7**	**8**	**9***			**4**			**10**	**11**			**G Napthine**	**28**
1	2		3	5	6		7	8	9		12	4			10*	11			I Hendrick	29
1	**2**		**3**	**5**	**6**		**7**	**8**	**10**	**11**	**9**	**4**							**M Scott**	**30**
1	2		3	5	6		7	8	10	11	9*	4			12				B Stevens	31
1	**2**		**3**	**5**	**6**		**7**	**8**	**10**	**11**	**9**	**4**							**M Heath**	**32**
1	**2**		**3***	**5**	**6**		**7**	**8**	**10**	**11**	**9**	**4**			**12**				**D Hutchinson**	**33**
1	2			5	6		7	8	12	11	9	4		3	10*				R Nixon	34
1	2		3	5	6		7	8		11	9	4			10				A Robinson	35
1	**2**		**3**	**5**	**6**		**7**	**8**	**12**	**11**	**9**	**4**			**10***				**T Spencer**	**36**
1	2		3	5			7	8	12	11	9*	4			10		6		G Courtney	37
1	2		3	5			7*	8	9	11		4	12		10		6		M Peck	38
1	2		3	5			7*	8	12	11	9	4			10		6		L Robinson	39
1	**2**		**3**	**5**	**6**			**8**	**12**	**11**	**9***	**4**	**7**		**10**				**G Tyson**	**40**
1	2		3	5	4		7	8	12	11	9				10*		6		M Bodenham	41
1	**2**		**3**	**5**	**6**		**7**	**8**	**12**	**11**	**9**			**4**	**10***				**A Gunn**	**42**
1		2		5			7	8		11	9		3	4	10		6		D Richardson	43
1	2		3	5	4		7	8*	12	11	9				10		6		N Ashley	44
1	2		3	5	4		7		8	11	9				10		6		D Owen	45
1	2		3	5	6		7		8	11	9	4		12	10*				C Seel	46
1	2*		3	5	6		7		8	11	9			12	10		4		F Roberts	47
1	2		3	5	4		7		8	11	9				10		6		D Allison	48
1	2		3	5	4		7	12	8	11	9				10*		6		R Banks	49
1	2*		3	5	4		7	10	8	11	9				12		6		N Glover	50
1			3	5	4		7	8		11	9			2	10		6	12	V Callow	51
1		12	3	5	4		7	8		11*	9				10		6	2	T Holbrook	52
1	2		4	5	6		7	8	12	11	9*				10		3		R Milford	53
42	39	9	36	**42**	38	8	**42**	36	21	40	35	27	1	3	26	2	14	1	League Appearances	
		+1S				+5S		+1S	+6S		+3S		+4S	+3S	+2S	+3S		+1S		
5	5		5	5	5	1S	4	5	2+3S	4	4	4	1	1	4+1S	1			FA Cup Appearances	
6	6	1	5	6	6	4	6	6	3+1S	5	5	6	2S	1S		1			Milk Cup Appearances	

HILLSBOROUGH

Official Address: Hillsborough, Sheffield S6 1SW. Telephone: 0742 343123 (Club), 0742 343122 (Box Office)

Telegraphic: Wednesday, Sheffield 6

Ground Capacity: 50,174

Record Attendance: 72,841 v. Manchester City, F.A. Cup Round 5, 17 Feb 1934

Record Receipts: £192,162, Tottenham Hotspur v. Wolverhampton Wanderers, F.A. Cup Semi-Final, 11 Apr 1981

Size of Playing Area: 115yds × 75 yds

Season Tickets: N & S Stands (centre): £90.00 (adults), £55.00 (juveniles/OAP); N & S Stands (wings) £80.00 (adults), £40.00 (juveniles/OAP); Uncovered seating: £71.50 (adults), £38.00 (juveniles/OAP). New season ticket holders (uncovered excluded) pay £5 extra (adults), £2 extra (juveniles/OAP)

Cost of Stand Tickets: N & S (centre): £5.00 (adult), £3.50 (juvenile/OAP); N & S (wings) £4.50, £2.50; Uncovered £4.00, £2.50; **Terraces:** £2.50 (adult), £1.50 (juveniles/OAP)

Match and Ticket Information: South and North Stand. Applications not more than 3 weeks in advance subject to tickets being unsold. Payment and SAE must accompany application

Car Parking: Street parking is available plus park at training ground (Middlewood Road)

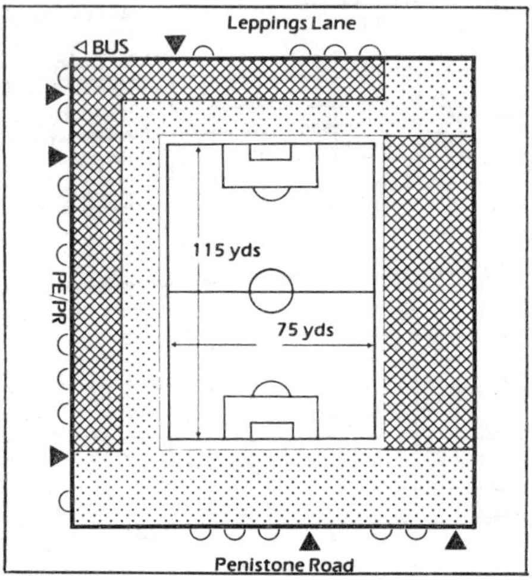

For key see page 12

How to get to the ground

From North: Use Motorway M1 until junction 34, leave Motorway and follow signs Sheffield A6109. In 1.5m at roundabout take 3rd exit A6102. In 3.2m turn left into Herries Road South for Sheffield Wednesday F.C.
From East and South: Use A57 from Motorway M1 (junction 31 or 33) then at roundabout junction with Ring Road take 3rd exit A610 into Princes of Wales Road. In 5.8m turn left into Herries Road South for Sheffield Wednesday F.C.
From West: Use A57 (S.P. Sheffield) then turn left A6101. In 3.8m at T road turn left A61 into Penistone Road for Sheffield Wednesday F.C.

SHREWSBURY TOWN Division 2

President
L Tudor-Owen

Chairman
H S Yates

Vice-Chairman
K R Woodhouse

Directors
L Tudor-Owen
A C Williams
F C G Fry
P W Newbrook

Secretary
M J Starkey

Player/Manager
Chic Bates

Pysiotherapist
Wayne Jones

Chief Scout
R Jukes

Commercial Manager
I Hookway (0743 56316)

Amongst the miracle clubs of Football can be counted Shrewsbury Town, who operate with a squad of some fifteen players throughout a season and earned an award in 1983 for reaching their highest ever League position — 9th. 'It cannot last' said the experts so 'Town' promptly responded by rising a further place up the League table to finish eighth in 1983-84 — their new record. If the winning of the Welsh Cup is added to that achievement it can be said that they had another really good season, so good in fact that one of the inspirations of their success — Manager Graham Turner — was lured to Villa Park in succession to Tony Barton during the close season.

Teams with small squads need a good start to any season so that morale can start and remain high and Shrewsbury did not actually lose for the first time in the League until their seventh match — away to Portsmouth (1-4). The club's character was then resoundingly demonstrated the very next time they played as Leeds United found to their cost when a single goal half-time lead for the visitors was transformed into a thrashing for them (5-1), Petts scoring a very clever hat-trick. For the rest of the programme there was never any lack of commitment and character as the team without making too serious a challenge for promotion did nevertheless usually give a very good account of itself.

In the cups — all three of them — results varied with a hard-won Second Round Milk Cup tie against Sheffield United (4-3 on aggregate) being followed by defeat at Walsall, which seemed less of a disgrace when the Saddlers' subsequent results were announced. The F.A. Cup had its good moments with Oldham Athletic (3-0) being dismissed at the Gay Meadow in Round Three followed by Ipswich Town the next time also at the Meadow (2-0). This meant a visit to Goodison Park in the Fifth Round and the eventual Cup Winners were too good and won by three clear goals. But at the end of the season there was no bare cupboard at the ground since the Welsh Cup returned to Shrewsbury for the first time since 1979 and for the fifth time in all after two tough legs against Wrexham (2-1 and 0-0); it is a shame that the best team in the competition could not play in Europe, but the rules ban Non-Welsh clubs.

That was a good season, but can the success be maintained? Can Chic Bates do as well as Graham Turner as Manager? These are imponderables, but the team of unknowns will lack nothing in determination. Ogrizovic will need to be replaced in goal, but for the record it is right to mention others in whom the supporters will place much faith — Williams, Cross, McLaren, Pearson, Griffin (the captain), McNally, Petts, Robinson, Stevens and Hackett. All are sound and committed and you can not ask for more.

WLM

Back Row: Derek Mann (Youth Coach & Physiotherapist), Steve Cross, Mark Bates, Paul Tester, Steve Perks, Andy Kerr, Ron Gren, Gary Stevens, Nigel Pearson, Colin Griffin, Chic Bates (Player Manager). **Front Row:** Paul Johnson, Colin Robinson, Wayne Williams, Gerry Nardiello, Ross Maclaren, Garry Hackett, Kevin Collins, Paul Petts, Bernard McNally.

'THE TOWN'

Sponsored by
Link 51

Formed: 1886 **Turned Professional:** 1905 **Ltd Co:** 1936
Previous Managers: Since 1950: Sammy Crooks Walter Rowley Harry Potts John Spuhler 1957-68 Arthur Rowley 1968-72 Harry Gregg 1972-4 Maurice Evans 1974-8 Alan Durban 1978 Richie Barker 1978-84 Graham Turner
Honours: Division Three Champions, Welsh Cup Winners (5)
League Career: Elected to Division 3(N) 1950 Reverted to Division 3(S) 1951 Joined Division 4 1958 Promoted to Division 3 1958-9 Relegated to Division 4 1973-4 Promoted to Division 3 1974-5 Promoted to Division 2 1978-9
Colours: Blue shirts with amber trim, amber shorts and stockings
Change Colours: All red or all white

CLUB RECORDS

Most Appearances for Club: Ken Mulhearn, 370 League + 22 F.A. Cup + 19 League Cup **Total 411**
Most Capped Player: Jimmy McLaughlin, 5 (Northern Ireland) **For England:** None
Record Goalscorer in a Match: Alf Wood, 5 v Blackburn Rovers (h) 7-1, Div 3, 07.10.71
Record League Goalscorer in a season: Arthur Rowley, 38, Div 3, 1958-9 **All Competitions:** Alf Wood: 40 (35 League + 2 F.A. Cup + 3 League Cup) (1971-2)
Record League Goalscorer in a career: Arthur Rowley, 152, 1958-65
Record Transfer Fee Received: £262,000 from Stoke City for Paul Maguire, Sept 1980
Record Transfer Fee Paid: £100,000 to Aldershot for John Dungworth, Nov 1979
Best Performances: League: 8th Div 2 1983-4 **F.A. Cup:** 6th Round 1978-9, 1981-2 **League/Milk Cup:** Semi-Final 1961 **Welsh Cup:** Winners 1891, 1938, 1977, 1979, 1984
Most League Points: 62 in Div 4, 1974-5 **Most League Goals:** 101, Div 4, 1958-9
Record League Victory: 7-0 v Swindon Town, Div 3(S), 6 May 1955
Record League Defeat: 1-8 v Norwich City, Div 3 South, 13 Sept 1952; v Coventry City, Div 3, 22 Oct 1963
Club Statistician for the Directory: Richard Stocken

Programme Editor
I. Hookway

Price	Number of Pages
40p	24

Subscriptions
Apply to club

SHREWSBURY TOWN

PLAYERS NAME Ht Wt Birthdate	Honours	Birthplace Transfers	Clubs	APPEARANCES League	Milk Cup	F.A.C.	E. Cups	GOALS League	Milk Cup	F.A.C.	E. Cups
GOALKEEPERS											
Ron Green		Birmingham	Alvechurch								
6-2 14.0 13.10.56		£2,000	Walsall	163	8	11	2				
			Shrewsbury T.								
Steve Perks		Shrewsbury	Shrewsbury T. (A)								
6-0 11.4 19.4.63											
DEFENDERS											
Mark Bates		Walsall	Walsall (A)	4		1					
5-10 10.6 25.4.65		F	Shrewsbury T.								
Kevin Collins		Birmingham	Shrewsbury T.	1							
5-9 11.0 21.7.64											
Colin Griffin	Div. 3, 79	Dudley	Derby Co. (A)								
6-0 11.7 8.1.56		£10,000	Shrewsbury T.	322+2	15	29		6			
Paul Johnson		Stoke	Stoke C. (A)	33+1							
5-9 11.3 25.5.59		£20,000	Shrewsbury T.	91+1	4	6+1		2			
Nigel Pearson		Nottingham	Heanor T.								
6-1 12.6 21.8.63		£5,000	Shrewsbury T.	65	5	3		1			
Wayne Williams		Telford	Shrewsbury T. (A)	82	5	3		4	1		
5-9 11.10 17.11.63											
MIDFIELD											
Chic Bates		West Bromwich	Stourbridge								
6-0 12.0 28.11.49		£5,000	Shrewsbury T.	160	9	14		45	2	5	
		£40,000	Swindon T.	50+13	5+1	4		15	1	2	
		£50,000	Bristol R.	26+3	5+1			4	2		
		£10,000	Shrewsbury T.	98+11	6	9		18	2	3	
Steve Cross	Div. 3, 79	Wolverhampton	Shrewsbury T. (A)	165+22	9	12		20	3	3	
5-11 10.4 22.12.59											
Ross McLaren*†		Edinburgh	Glasgow Rangers								
5-10 12.12 14.4.62		F	Shrewsbury T.	116+3	7	6		12	1	1	
Bernard McNally		Shrewsbury	Shrewsbury T. (A)	98+2	6	8		6			
5-7 9.11 17.2.63											
Paul Petts	E. Y	Hackney	Bristol R. (A)	12+1	+2						
5-9 10.11 27.9.61		£30,000	Shrewsbury T.	108+9	8	6		14			
FORWARDS											
Gary Hackett		Stourbridge	Bromsgrove R.								
5-7 10.8 11.10.62			Shrewsbury T.	29+2	3	3		3	1	1	
Gerardo Nardiello		Warley	Shrewsbury T. (A)	11+1				5			
5-11 11.0 5.5.66											
Colin Robinson		Birmingham	Mile Oak R.								
5-10 11.0 15.5.60			Shrewsbury T.	30+12	3	1+2		7		2	
Gary Stevens		Birmingham	Evesham U.								
6-2 12.0 30.8.54		£4,000	Cardiff C.	138+12	9	4+2		44	3		
		£20,000	Shrewsbury T.	67+6	4	3		6	1	1	
Paul Tester		Stroud	Cheltenham T.								
5-10 10.7 10.3.59			Shrewsbury T.	6+2							

NON-CONTRACT PLAYERS 1984-85

Salem Ahmed, Michael Brown, John Carmichael, Richard Green, Martin Hudson, Darren Hunting, Scott Maund, Neil Meredith, Jason Minton, Stephen Mullings, Ian Smith, Tony Spray

APPRENTICES

John Dale, David Goodall, Bob Goodwin, Tim Steele

SHREWSBURY TOWN

DIVISION TWO 8TH **FA CUP** 5TH ROUND **MILK CUP** 3RD ROUND

MATCH	DATE	COMPE-TITION	VENUE	OPPONENTS	RESULT	HALF TIME	L'GUE POS'N	GOALSCORERS	ATTEN-DANCE
1	A 27	CL	A	Grimsby T	D1-1	0-0		McNally	5,177
2	29	CL	A	Newcastle U	W1-0	1-0		Brown	29,123
3	S 3	CL	H	Crystal Palace	D1-1	0-0	6	MacLaren	3,849
4	6	CL	H	Cardiff C	W1-0	1-0		Bates	4,405
5	10	CL	A	Carlisle U	L0-1	0-0	9		3,164
6	17	CL	H	Barnsley	W3-2	2-1	5	McNally, Petts 2	3,867
7	24	CL	A	Portsmouth	L1-4	1-1	8	Cross	11,909
8	O 1	CL	H	Leeds U	W5-1	0-1	5	Robinson, Brown, Petts 3	6,289
9	**4**	**MC 2**	**H**	**Sheffield U**	**W2-1**	**0-1**		**Stevens, Brown**	**4,382**
10	8	CL	H	Oldham Ath	W2-0	0-0	5	Robinson, MacLaren	4,087
11	16	CL	A	Blackburn R	D1-1	0-1		MacLaren	5,777
12	22	CL	A	Fulham	D0-0	0-0	6		4,767
13	**25**	**MC 2**	**A**	**Sheffield U**	**D2-2**	**0-1**		**Hackett, Bates**	**9,399**
14	29	CL	A	Middlesbrough	L0-4	0-0	7		6,362
15	N 5	CL	H	Manchester C	L1-3	0-0	9	Cross	9,471
16	**8**	**MC 3**	**A**	**Walsall**	**L1-2**	**0-1**		**Williams**	**7,952**
17	12	CL	A	Huddersfield T	L0-1	0-1	11		8,798
18	19	CL	A	Brighton & HA	D2-2	0-1	12	MacLaren (pen), Petts	9,746
19	26	CL	H	Charlton Ath	D1-1	0-0	13	McNally	3,141
20	D 3	CL	A	Sheffield W	D1-1	0-1	12	Robinson	17,703
21	10	CL	H	Cambridge U	W1-0	0-0	10	Petts	2,457
22	17	CL	A	Derby Co	L0-1	0-0	11		11,265
23	26	CL	H	Chelsea	L2-4	1-0	13	Brown, MacLaren	7,582
24	27	CL	A	Swansea C	W2-0	0-0	11	Hackett, Stevens	7,706
25	31	CL	A	Crystal Palace	D1-1	0-1		Robinson	5,275
26	J 2	CL	H	Portsmouth	W2-0	1-0		Hackett, Brown	4,970
27	**7**	**FAC 3**	**H**	**Oldham Ath**	**W3-0**	**1-0**		**Stevens, MacLaren (pen), Robinson**	**4,650**
28	14	CL	H	Grimsby T	L1-2	1-1	10	Hackett	3,343
29	**28**	**FAC 4**	**H**	**Ipswich T**	**W2-0**	**0-0**		**Hackett, Robinson**	**11,110**
30	F 4	CL	A	Leeds U	L0-3	0-2	14		10,628
31	11	CL	H	Carlisle U	D0-0	0-0	13		3,439
32	**18**	**FAC 5**	**A**	**Everton**	**L0-3**	**0-1**			**27,106**
33	25	CL	A	Fulham	L0-3	0-0	16		5,149
34	28	CL	H	Middlesbrough	W1-0	0-0		Brown	3,043
35	M 3	CL	A	Manchester C	L0-1	0-0	14		20,144
36	10	CL	H	Huddersfield T	W1-0	0-0	12	Petts	3,627
37	13	CL	A	Barnsley	L0-3	0-1			5,576
38	17	CL	A	Cardiff C	L0-2	0-1	14		3,870
39	24	CL	H	Newcastle U	D2-2	0-0	15	Cross 2	8,313
40	30	CL	H	Blackburn R	W1-0	1-0		Cross	3,352
41	A 7	CL	A	Oldham Ath	W1-0	0-0	11	Bates	3,428
42	14	CL	H	Brighton & HA	W2-1	1-0	11	Nardiello 2	3,332
43	21	CL	A	Chelsea	L0-3	0-2	11		17,295
44	24	CL	H	Swansea C	W2-0	1-0		Cross 2	3,060
45	28	CL	A	Charlton Ath	W4-2	0-0	10	Cross 2, Nardiello, McNally	3,786
46	M 5	CL	H	Sheffield W	W2-1	0-0		MacLaren, Nardiello	7,885
47	7	CL	A	Cambridge U	L0-1	0-1			2,208
48	12	CL	H	Derby Co	W3-0	1-0		Nardiello, Bates (pen), MacLaren (pen)	5,562
								Av Home Att	**4,750**

Goal Scorers

League (49): Cross 9, Petts 8, MacLaren 7 (2 pens), Brown 5, Nardiello 5, McNally 4, Robinson 4, Bates 3 (1 pen), Hackett 3, Stevens 1
FA Cup (5): Robinson 2, Hackett 1, MacLaren 1 (1 pen), Stevens 1
Milk Cup (5): Bates 1, Brown 1, Hackett 1, Stevens 1, Williams 1

1983-84

Ogrizovic	Williams	Cross	MacLaren	Pearson	Griffin	McNally	Petts	Brown	Robinson	Hackett	Stevens	Bates	Johnson	Turner	Collins	Nardiello	Tester			REFEREE	
1	2	3	4	5	6	7	8	9	10	11*	12									A Saunders	1
1	2	3	4	6	7	5	8	9	10	11*	12									N Wilson	2
1	2	3	4	6	5	7	8*	9	10	11	12									TA Jones	3
1	2	3	4	6	5	7		9	10	11		8								A Banks	4
1	2	3	4	5	6	7		9*	10	11		8	12							K Redfern	5
1	2	3	4	5	6	7	8	9*	10	11	12									R Guy	6
1	2	3	4	5	6	7	8	9	10	11										EJ Scales	7
1	2	3	4	5	6	7	8	9	10	11										J Deakin	8
1	**2**	**3**	**4**		**6**	**7**	**8**	**9**	**10***	**11**	**5**						**12**			**J Bray**	**9**
1		2	4	5	6	7	8		10	11	9		3							B Hill	10
1		2	4	5			8	9	10	11	6	7	3							K Hackett	11
1	2	3	4	5		7	8	9	10	11*	6	12								B Stevens	12
1	**2**		**4**	**5**		**7**	**8**	**9**	**10**	**11***	**6**	**3**		**12**						**K Walmsley**	**13**
1	2	3	4	5		7	8	9	10	11	6									D Allison	14
1	2	3	4	5	6*	7	8	9	12	11	10									E Read	15
1	**2**	**3**	**4**	**5**		**7**		**9**	**10**	**11**	**6**	**8**								**N Midgley**	**16**
1	2	3	4	5		7*	8	9	10		6	11		12						J Worrall	17
1	2	3	4	5		7	8	9	10		6	11								J Moules	18
1	2	3	4	5		7	8	9	10*	12	6	11								R Dilkes	19
1	2	3	4	5		7	8	9	10	11	6									D Richardson	20
1	2	3	4	5		7	8	9	10	11	6									H King	21
1	2	3	4	5		7	8	9	10	11*	6	12								A Robinson	22
1	2	3	4	5*	6	7	8	10	12	11	9									I Hendrick	23
1	2	3	4		6	7	8	9		11	10			5						A Buksh	24
1	2	3	4		6	7*	8	10	12	11	9			5						J Ashworth	25
1	2		4	5	6	7*	8	10	12	11	9			3						T Fitzharris	26
1	**2**	**3**	**4**	**5**	**6**		**8**	**10***	**12**	**11**	**9**	**7**								**C Thomas**	**27**
1	2	3	4	5		7	8	10	6	11	9									R Nixon	28
1	**2**	**3**	**4**	**5**	**6**	**7**	**8**	**10***	**12**	**11**	**9**									**N Ashley**	**29**
1	2	3	4	5	6	7	8	10*	12	11	9									D Scott	30
1	2	3	4	5	6	7	8		10	11	9									R Bridges	31
1	**2**	**3**	**4**	**5**	**6**	**7**	**8**		**10***	**11**	**9**		**12**							**G Napthine**	**32**
1	2	10			6	7	8	9	12	11*	5		3	4						M James	33
1	2	10	4		6	7	8	9		11	5		3							L Robinson	34
1	2	10	4		6	7	8	9		11	5		3							A Challinor	35
1	2	10*	4		6	7	8	9	12	11	5		3							K Barratt	36
1	2	10	4		6	7	8	9		11	5		3							P Tyldesley	37
1	2	12	4	5	6	7	8*				9				3	10	11			A Crickmore	38
1	2	11	4		6	7					9	8	3	5		10				F Roberts	39
1	2	11	4		6	7					9	8	3	5		10*	12			C Thomas	40
1	2	11		5*	6	7					9	8	3	4		10	12			A Saunders	41
1	2	11	4		6	7					9	8	3	5		10				D Allison	42
1	2	11	4		6*	7			12		9	8	3	5		10				T Spencer	43
1	2	9	4			7	6				5	8	3			10	11			N Wilson	44
1	2	9	4			7	6				5		3	8		10	11			L Shapter	45
1	2	9	4			7*	6			12	5	8	3			10	11			V Callow	46
1	2	9	4			7	6		12	8	5*		3			10	11			D Brazier	47
1	2	9	4			7	6		12		5	8	3			10*	11			D Hutchinson	48
42	40	40	40	26	27	41	35	29	20	29	34	14	17	10	1	11	6			League Appearances	
		+1S							+10S	+2S	+4S	+2S	+1S	+1S			+2S				
3	3	3	3	3	3	2	3	2	1+2S	3	3	1	1S							FA Cup Appearances	
3	3	2	3	2	1	3	2	3	3	3	3	2					1S		1S	Milk Cup Appearances	

GAY MEADOW

Official Address: Gay Meadow, Shrewsbury. Telephone: (0743) 60111.

Ground Capacity: 16,800

Record Attendance: 18,917 v. Walsall, Div. 3, 26 Apr 1961

Record Receipts: £36,240 v. Ipswich Town, F.A. Cup Round 5, 13 Feb 1982

Size of Playing Area: 116yds × 76 yds

Season Tickets: Stand: £70.00 (£45 juveniles)

Executive Box Season Tickets: None

Cost of Stand Tickets: £4.00 (Centre), £3.50 (Station), £3.50 (Wakeman), £2,00 (pensioners & juniors); **Terraces:** £2.30 (£1.50 juveniles/OAPs) visitors £2.30 (All).

Car Parking: Park adjacent to ground and a free public car park five minutes away.

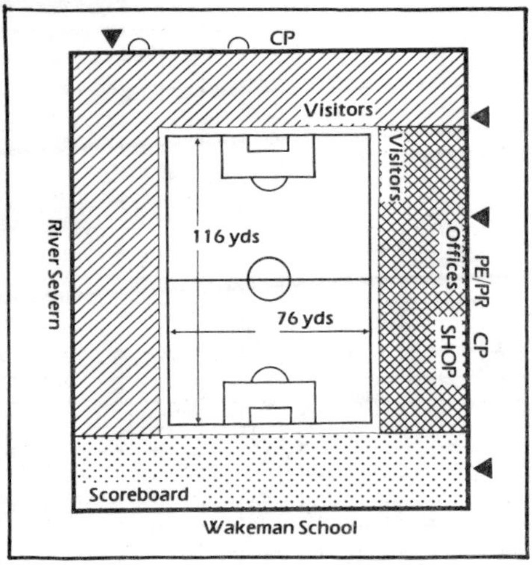

For key see page 12

How to get to the ground

From North: Use A49 or A53 and at roundabout take 2nd exit A5112 into Telford Way. In 0.8m at roundabout take 2nd exit. Then at T road turn right into Abbey Foregate A458 for Shrewsbury Town F.C.
From East: Use A5 then A458 into Shrewsbury and into Abbey Foregate for Shrewsbury Town F.C.
From South: Use A49 and follow signs Shrewsbury town centre then at end of Coleham Head turn right into Abbey Foregate for Shrewsbury Town F.C.
From West: Use A458 then A5 around Shrewsbury Ring Road, Roman Road, then turn left A49 into Hereford Road, and at end of Coleham Head turn right into Abbey Foregate for Shrewsbury Town F.C.

SOUTHAMPTON Division 1

Chairman
A A Woodford

Directors
F G L Askham FCA
E T Bates
B G W Bowyer TD, JP
J Corbett
Sir George Meyrick BMC

Secretary
Brian Truscott

Assistant Secretary
Barry Fox

Commercial Manager
Malcolm Price (0703 36617)

Manager
Lawrie McMenemy

Assistant Manager
John Mortimore

First Team Coach
Lew Chatterley

Reserve Team Coach
Frank Burrows

Physiotherapist
Bob Taylor

Southampton smashed all club records in runners-up position in the First Division behind Liverpool by just three points. They were also denied a place in the Wembley FA Cup Final by conceding a goal three minutes from the end of extra-time in the semi-final.

Lawrie McMenemy's careful team building over several years was this time concentrated on improving his defence. The team responded by not conceding a goal in their opening three matches.

New centre-back Ken Armstrong signed from Kilmarnock initially slotted in well with Mark Wright in the middle of defence. Another newcomer was former England centre-forward Frank Worthington from Sunderland.

The Saints started well, drawing at Liverpool and scoring an outstanding 3-0 home win over Manchester United early in the season.

Mr McMenemy is restricted by his very small first-team squad and injuries mean trouble. With such difficulties in November, he signed Birmingham's England under-21 international defender Mark Dennis and Wales international striker Alan Curtis, from Swansea.

Dennis settled in at left-back and the defence was restructured with Mick Mills on the right and Wright and Nick Holmes playing in the middle in front of sweeper Reuben Agboola. Curtis played only a few games before a back-to-form Steve Moran took over and Steve finished the season with a personal best tally of 25 League and Cup goals.

Four successive League victories in the new year – culminating in a spectacular televised 2-0 victory over Liverpool at The Dell – showed that the Saints would probably break their previous best placing of sixth in the First Division.

Heavy defeat at QPR brought reality but they finished with a magnificent unbeaten run of 10 League matches. The Saints won crushingly (8-2) against Coventry at The Dell and, in their next home game, crushed Spurs – with virtually a reserve team – by a five-goal margin.

A goalless draw at Birmingham put the Championship mathematically beyond reach but, by winning their final two games, Southampton overtook Manchester United and ended three points behind Liverpool.

Following the Milk Cup defeat by Third Division Rotherham United, Southampton started a fine run in the FA Cup although drawn away in all four rounds before the semi-final.

Having defeated Nottingham Forest in round three and neighbouring Portsmouth at the next stage, Southampton became Cup favourites following the shock exit of Manchester United and Liverpool.

A well-planned away win at Blackburn was followed by a 1-1 draw at Sheffield Wednesday, where the superb England goalkeeper Peter Shilton kept their interest alive. Southampton won the replay easily and held Everton to 0-0 in the Highbury semi-final until the 27th minute of extra-time when Adrian Heath scored Everton's winner.

TP

Back Row L to R: Eamonn Collins, Dennis Rofe, Mick Mills, Joe Jordan, Ivan Golac, Alan Curtis, Mark Dennis. **Middle Row:** Lew Chatterley (Trainer), Steve Moran, Peter Shilton, Mark Whitlock, Phil Kite, David Puckett, John Mortimore (Assistant Manager). **Front Row:** Danny Wallace, Mark Wright, Steve Williams, Lawrie McMenemy (Manager), Nick Holmes, Reuben Agboola, David Armstrong.

'THE SAINTS'

Sponsored by
Draper Tools

Formed: 1885 **Turned Professional:** 1894 **Ltd Co:** 1897
Previous Name: Southampton St. Mary's (until 1885)
Previous Managers: (Since 1946) Bill Dodgin (Sr) Sid Cann George Roughton Ted Bates
Honours: Division 3 (South): Champions 1921-22 Division 3: Champions 1959-60 F.A. Cup: Winners 1975-76
League Career: Original Members of Division 3 1920 Allocated to Division 3 (South) 1921 Promoted to Division 2 1922 Relegated to Division 3 (South) 1953 Original Members of New Division 3 1958 Promoted to Division 2 1960 Promoted to Division One 1966 Relegated to Division 2 1974 Promoted to Division 1 1978
Colours: Red and white striped shirts, black shorts, white stockings
Change Colours: Light and dark blue striped shirts, dark blue shorts, light blue stockings

CLUB RECORDS

Most Appearances for Club: Terry Paine 809 (League 713 + F.A. Cup 51, League Cup 37, E Fairs Cup 8) 1956-74
Most Capped Player: Mike Channon 45 (46) England **For England:** Mike Channon 45 (46)
Record Goalscorer in a Match: Derek Reeves 5 v. Newport County 1st Round Replay, Milk Cup (5-3), 1960
Record League Goalscorer in a season: Derek Reeves 39, Div 3 1959-60 in all competitions.
Record League Goalscorer in a career: Mike Channon 183 1966-77, 1979-82 **All Competitions:** Mike Channon 226 (League 183, F.A. Cup 17, League Cup 12, European Cup 4, UEFA 5, Texaco 5)
Record Transfer Fee Received: £300,000 from Manchester City for Mike Channon July 1977
Record Transfer Fee Paid: £600,000 to Middlesbrough for David Armstrong Aug 1981
Best Performances: League: 2nd Div 1 1983-4 **F.A. Cup:** Winners 1975-76 **League/Milk Cup:** Finalists 1978-79
Most League Points: (3 points for win) 77 Div 1 1983-84 (2 points for win) 61 Div 3 (S) 1921-22 & Div 3 1959-60
Record League Victory: 9-3 v Wolverhampton Wanderers Div 2, 8 Sept 1965 8-2 v Coventry City Div 1 28 Apr 1984
Record League Defeat: 0-8 v Tottenham Hotspur Div 2, 28 Mar 1936 0-8 v Everton Div 1 20 Nov 1971
European Competitions Entered: European Fairs Cup 1969-70 U.E.F.A. Cup 1971-72, 1981-82, 1982-83 European Cup-Winners Cup 1976-77

Club Statistician for the Directory: D. Buckle

Programme Editor
Malcolm Price

Price	Number of Pages
50p	32

Subscriptions
Apply to commercial department

SOUTHAMPTON

PLAYERS NAME Ht Wt Birthdate	Honours	Birthplace Transfers	Clubs	APPEARANCES League	Milk Cup	F.A.C.	E. Cups	GOALS League	Milk Cup	F.A.C.	E. Cups
GOALKEEPERS											
Phil Kite	E. Y	Bristol	Bristol R. (A)	96	12	8	2 AMC				
6-1½ 14.7 26.10.62											
Peter Shilton	E.(63), U.23(3), Div	Leicester	Leicester C. (A)	286	20	30		1			
6-0 14.0 18.9.49	2, 71, F.L. Div. 1,		Stoke C.	110	4	7					
	78, Lg.C. 79, EC.		Nottingham F.	202	26	18	24				
	79, 80, ESC. 79		Southampton	81	7	7	2				
Alistair Sperring	(Monthly)	Hayling Island	Southampton (A)		1						
6-2 13.3 26.10.63											
DEFENDERS											
Reuben Agboola		London	Southampton (A)	80+1	8	7	5				
5-10 11.2 30.5.62											
Steve Baker		Newcastle	Southampton (A)	21	1						
5-5 10.5 16.6.67			Burnley (L)	10			2AM				
Mark Dennis	E. U.21(3), Y	Streatham	Birmingham C. (A)	130	8	7	1	1			
5-9 10.8 2.5.61			Southampton	20		6					
Ivan Golac	Yug.	Yugoslavia	Southampton	143+1	13	12	3	4			
5-10 13.1 15.6.50			Bournemouth	9							
			Manchester C.	2							
			Southampton	11							
Mick Mills	E.(42), U.23(5), Y,	Godalming	Portsmouth (A)								
5-7½ 11.10 4.1.49	FAC. 78, F.L.,	F	Ipswich T.	588+3	43+	57		22	2	5	
	UEFA. 81	£50,000	Southampton	61	2	6		3			
Dennis Rofe	E. U.23(1)	Fulham	Orient (A)	170+1	7	11		6			
5-7 10.11 1.6.50		£112,000	Leicester C.	290	12	21		6			
		£80,000	Chelsea	58+1	2	1					
		F	Southampton	18+2	6		1	1			
Mark Whitlock		Portsmouth	Southampton (A)	24+1	1		1	1			
5-11½ 12.2 14.3.61			Grimsby T. (L)	7+1							
			Aldershot (L)	14							
Mark Wright	E.(1), U.21(4)	Dorchester,	Oxford U.	8+2							
6-3 12.1 1.8.63		Oxon	Southampton	71	7	7	2	3	1	1	1
MIDFIELD											
David Armstrong†	E.(3), U.23(2)	Durham	Middlesbrough (A)	357+2	27	29		59	6	8	
5-8 11.10 26.12.54	Div. 2, 74	£600,000	Southampton	124	9	8	5	38	3	2	1
Nick Holmes	FAC. 76	Southampton	Southampton (A)	375+6	26	37	10	53	5	2	
5-11 12.2 11.11.54											
Steve Williams*	E.(3), B.(4),	London	Southampton (A)	263+1	25+	27	10	17	3	3	3
5-11 10.11 12.7.58	U.21(14)										
FORWARDS											
Ian Baird		Southampton	Southampton (A)	15+2	1			3			
6-0 12.9 1.4.64			Cardiff C. (L)	12				6			
Alan Curtis	W.(30), U.23(1)	Rhondda	Swansea C.	244+4	12	14	5	72	6	7	
5-11 12.5 16.5.54	U.21(1)	£350,000	Leeds U.	28	2	1	4	5			
		£165,000	Swansea C.	82+8	5	3	2	21	1		
		£75,000	Southampton	8+1							
Ian Juryeff		Gosport	Southampton	0+2							
5-11 12.0 24.11.67			Mansfield T. (L)	12							
Steve Moran	E. U.21(2)	Croydon	Southampton	117+3	8+2	11	6	59	3	7	2
5-8 10.11 10.1.61											
David Puckett		Southampton	Southampton (A)	33+34	1+3		0+1	9	1		
5-7 10.5 29.10.60											
Danny Wallace	E. U.21(8), Y	London	Southampton (A)	78+7	8+1	7	0+3	23	1		
5-4½ 9.13 21.1.64											
Joe Jordan	S.(52), U.23(1)	Carluke	Morton	7+3				1			
6-0¾ 12.8 15.12.51	Div. 1, 74		Leeds U.	139+31	9+1	16+1	18+3		3	4	6
		Verona	Manchester U.	109	6	11+1	1		2	2	
		£150,000	Southampton								

CONTRACT PLAYERS WHO HAVE NO FIRST TEAM APPEARANCES

Duncan Burns, Barry Blanckley, Tim Dixon , David Baker, Kevan Brown, Stuart McManus, Eamonn Collins

APPRENTICES: Simon Bergara, Ian Straw, Dennis Wise, Mark Blake, Bob Carroll, Ian Hamilton, Paul Johnson, Craig Maskell, Phil Parkinson, Chris Wilder

SOUTHAMPTON

DIVISION ONE 2ND **FA CUP** SEMI-FINAL **MILK CUP** 3RD ROUND

MATCH	DATE	COMPE-TITION	VENUE	OPPONENTS	RESULT	HALF TIME	L'GUE POS'N	GOALSCORERS	ATTEN-DANCE
1	A 27	CL	A	Nottingham F	W1-0	0-0		Wallace	14,626
2	29	CL	H	QPR	D0-0	0-0			19,522
3	S 3	CL	H	Arsenal	W1-0	0-0	4	Baird	19,377
4	6	CL	A	Liverpool	D1-1	0-0		Mills	26,331
5	10	CL	A	Sunderland	W2-0	1-0	5	Moran 2	12,716
6	17	CL	H	Manchester U	W3-0	2-0	2	Williams 2, Armstrong D	20,674
7	24	CL	A	Aston Villa	L0-1	0-1	3		21,209
8	O 1	CL	H	Wolverhampton W	W1-0	0-0	2	Worthington	16,689
9	**4**	**MC 2**	**A**	**Carlisle U**	**L0-2**	**0-1**			**8,570**
10	22	CL	A	Luton T	L1-3	0-2	7	Armstrong D	12,389
11	**25**	**MC 2**	**H**	**Carlisle U**	**W3-0**	**1-0**		**Armstrong D, Foyle 2**	**12,438**
12	29	CL	H	Ipswich T	W3-2	1-2	5	Williams, Holmes, Moran	18,515
13	N 5	CL	A	Norwich C	L0-1	0-0	8		14,303
14	**8**	**MC 3**	**A**	**Rotherham U**	**L1-2**	**1-2**		**Armstrong D**	**8,821**
15	12	CL	H	WBA	W1-0	1-0	4	Moran (pen)	16,450
16	19	CL	H	Notts Co	L0-2	0-1	9		15,009
17	26	CL	A	Coventry C	D0-0	0-0	8		11,579
18	30	CL	A	Leicester C	L1-2	0-1		Worthington	14,181
19	D 3	CL	H	Stoke C	W3-1	2-1	6	Wallace, Armstrong D, Mills	15,301
20	10	CL	A	Tottenham H	D0-0	0-0	9		29,711
21	17	CL	H	Birmingham C	W2-1	1-1	6	Blake (og), Hagan (og)	16,288
22	26	CL	A	West Ham U	W1-0	0-0	4	Wallace	22,221
23	27	CL	H	Watford	W1-0	1-0	3	Armstrong D	20,659
24	31	CL	A	Arsenal	D2-2	0-1	4	Moran 2	27,596
25	J 2	CL	H	Aston Villa	D2-2	0-1	5	Moran, Armstrong D	18,963
26	**7**	**FAC 3**	**A**	**Nottingham F**	**W2-1**	**0-0**		**Moran 2**	**19,721**
27	21	CL	A	Manchester U	L2-3	2-2	6	Moran 2	40,371
28	23	CL	H	Nottingham F	L0-1	0-1			17,426
29	**28**	**FAC 4**	**A**	**Portsmouth**	**W1-0**	**0-0**		**Moran**	**36,000**
30	F 4	CL	A	Wolverhampton W	W1-0	0-0	6	Moran	9,943
31	11	CL	H	Sunderland	D1-1	1-0	6	Moran (pen)	16,968
32	**17**	**FAC 5**	**A**	**Blackburn R**	**W1-0**	**0-0**		**Armstrong D**	**15,357**
33	21	CL	A	Ipswich T	W3-0	3-0		Worthington, Moran, Armstrong D	14,934
34	25	CL	H	Luton T	W2-1	2-0	5	Wright, Armstrong D	17,947
35	M 3	CL	H	Norwich C	W2-1	1-0	5	Armstrong D, Puckett	17,456
36	**11**	**FAC 6**	**A**	**Sheffield W**	**D0-0**	**0-0**			**43,030**
37	16	CL	H	Liverpool	W2-0	1-0		Wallace 2	19,698
38	**20**	**FAC 6R**	**H**	**Sheffield W**	**W5-1**	**2-1**		**Williams, Oliver (og), Wright,**	
								Armstrong D, Moran	**20,592**
39	24	CL	A	QPR	L0-4	0-2	4		15,407
40	31	CL	A	Everton	L0-1	0-1	5		20,244
41	A 7	CL	H	Leicester C	D2-2	0-0	5	Wallace, Moran	17,445
42	**14**	**FAC SF**	**N**	**Everton**	**L0-1[1]**	**0-0**			**46,587**
43	17	CL	H	Everton	W3-1	0-0		Armstrong D 2, Moran	16,978
44	21	CL	H	West Ham U	W2-0	1-0	5	Holmes, Moran	20,846
45	24	CL	A	Watford	D1-1	0-1		Armstrong D	16,744
46	28	CL	H	Coventry C	W8-2	2-0	4	Armstrong D, Wallace 3, Moran 3,	
								Worthington	16,746
47	M 5	CL	A	Stoke C	D1-1	0-0	4	Holmes	12,131
48	7	CL	H	Tottenham H	W5-0	2-0	4	Pucket, Wallace 2, Armstrong D 2	21,141
49	12	CL	A	Birmingham C	D0-0	0-0	5		16,445
50	14	CL	A	WBA	W2-0	0-0		Puckett, Moran	10,365
51	17	CL	A	Notts Co	W3-1	1-1		Moran 2, Armstrong D	6,035

[1]After Extra Time

Av Home Att 17,434

Goal Scorers

League (66): Moran 21 (2 pens), Armstrong D 15, Wallace 11, Worthington 4, Holmes 3, Puckett 3, Williams 3, Mills 2, Baird 1, Wright 1, opponents 2
FA Cup (9): Moran 4, Armstrong D 2, Williams 1, Wright 1, opponents 1
Milk Cup (4): Armstrong D 2, Foyle 2

1983-84

Shilton	Agboola	Mills	Williams	Armstrong K	Wright	Holmes	Moran	Worthington	Armstrong D	Wallace	Baird	Baker	Foyle	Whitlock	Rofe	Juryeff	Dennis	Curtis	Puckett	Golac	Sperring	REFEREE	
1	2	3	4	5	6	7	8	9	10	11												G Courtney	1
1	2	3	4	5	6	7	8	9	10	11												B Hill	2
1	2	3	4	5	6	7		9	10	11	8											G Napthine	3
1	2	3		5	6	7		9*	10	11	8	4	12									T Holbrook	4
1	2	3	4	5	6	7	8	9	10	11												K Warmsley	5
1	2	3	4	5	6	7	8	9	10	11												L Shapter	6
1	2	3	4	5	6	7	8	9†	10	11												J Key	7
1	2	3	4	5	6	7	8	9	10	11												M James	8
1	**2**	**3**	**4**	**5**	**6**	**7**	**8**	**9**	**10**	**11**												**D Scott**	**9**
1	2		4	5	6	7	8		10	11	9	3										V Callow	10
1	**2**		**4**	**5**	**6**	**7**	**8**		**10**	**11**	**9***	**3**	**12**									**D Reeves**	**11**
1			4	5	6*	7	12	9	10	11		3	8	2								LM Robinson	12
1			4			6	8	9	10	11		3	7	5	2							K Hackett	13
	2				**6***	**7**	**8**	**9**	**10**	**11**		**3**	**12**	**5**	**4**						**1**	**G Tyson**	**14**
1	2		4	5		7	8	9	10	11		3		6								A Crickmore	15
1	2		4	5		7	8	9	10	11		3*	12	6								R Lewis	16
1			4*	5		7	8	9	10	11		3		6	2	12						D Owen	17
1			4	5		7	8	9	10	11		2		6		12	3*					R Nixon	18
1	6	2	4	5		7		9	10	11							3	8				E Scales	19
1	6	2	4	5		7		9	10	11							3	8				L Barratt	20
1	6	2	4	5		7		9*	10	11							3	8	12			D Vickers	21
1	5	2	6	4		7		9	10	11							3	8*	12			M Bodenham	22
1	6	2	4	5		7		9	10	11							3		8			E Read	23
1	6	2*	4		5	7	8	9	10	11							3		12			M Scott	24
1	6		4	5	2	7	8	9*	10	11							3		12			A Gunn	25
1	**6**	**2**	**4**		**5**	**7**	**8**	**9**	**10**	**11**							**3**					**B Hill**	**26**
1	4	2		5*	6	7	8	9	10	11							3		12			A Seville	27
1	4	2		5	6	7	8	9*	10	11							3		12			K Salmon	28
1	**6**	**2**	**4**		**5**	**7**	**8**	**9**	**10**	**11**							**3**					**L Shapter**	**29**
1	6	2	4		5	7	8	9	10	11							3					T Jones	30
1	6	2	4		5	7	8	9	10	11							3					A Buksh	31
1	**6**	**2**	**4**		**5**	**7**	**8**	**9**	**10**	**11**							**3**					**N Ashley**	**32**
1	5	2	4		6	7	8	9	10	11							3					D Axcell	33
1	5	2	4		6	7	8	9	10	11							3					K Cooper	34
1	6	2	4	5		7		9	10	11							3	8*	12			K Baker	35
1	**5**	**2**	**4**		**6**	**7**	**8**	**9**	**10**	**11**							**3**					**G Tyson**	**36**
1	5	2	4		6	7	8	9*	10	11							3		12			B Stevens	37
1	**5**	**2**	**4**		**6**	**7**	**8**	**9**	**10**	**11**							**3**					**A Gunn**	**38**
1	5	2			6*	7	8	9	10	11				12			3		4			T Bune	39
1		2*			6	7	8		10	11	9			5	12				4	3		K Redfern	40
1	5	2			6	7	8	9*	10	11							3		12	4		A Ward	41
1	**5**	**2**	**4**		**6**	**7**	**8**	**9**	**10**	**11**							**3**					**G Courtney**	**42**
1	6	2*			5	7	8	9	10	11							3	12		4		C Downby	43
1		2			6	7	8	9	10	11				5				4		3		C Thomas	44
1		2			6	7	8		10	11				5			3	9		4		H Taylor	45
1		2			6	7	8	9	10	11				5				4*	12	3		H King	46
1	3	2			6	7	8		10	11	9			5					12	4*		D Scott	47
1	4	2			6	7	8		10	11				5					9	3		G Napthine	48
1		2		5	6	7	8		10		11*		12	4					9	3		N Wilson	49
1	4	2		5		7	8		10	11				6					9	3		D Richardson	50
1	4	3		5		7	8		10	11				6					9	2		L Dilkes	51
42	33	34	27	26	29	**42**	33	34	**42**	41	6	8	2	15	2	0	20	8	7	11		League Appearances	
							+1S						+3S	+1S	+1S	+2S		+1S	+11S				
6	6	6	6		6	6	6	6	6	6							6					FA Cup Appearances	
2	3	1	2	2	3	3	3	2	3	3	1	2	2S	1	1						1	Milk Cup Appearances	

THE DELL

Official Address: The Dell, Milton Road, Southampton SO9 4XX. Telephone: 0703 39444/ 39633

Ground Capacity: 25,000

Record Attendance: 31,044 v. Manchester United, Division 1, 8 October 1969

Record Receipts: £71,202 v. Sheffield Wednesday, F.A. Cup Round 6 Replay, Mar 1984

Size of Playing Area: 110yds × 72 yds

Season Tickets: Stands: £116-£126; Ground: £53.00; Bench Seats: £78 & £85

Executive Box Season Tickets: None

Cost of Stand Tickets: Season ticket holders only; **Terraces:** £2.80 (adults), £1.50 (juveniles/ OAP)

Match and Ticket Information: No seats available. Room for 8,000 on terraces to be booked in advance

Car Parking: Street parking and nearby municipal parks

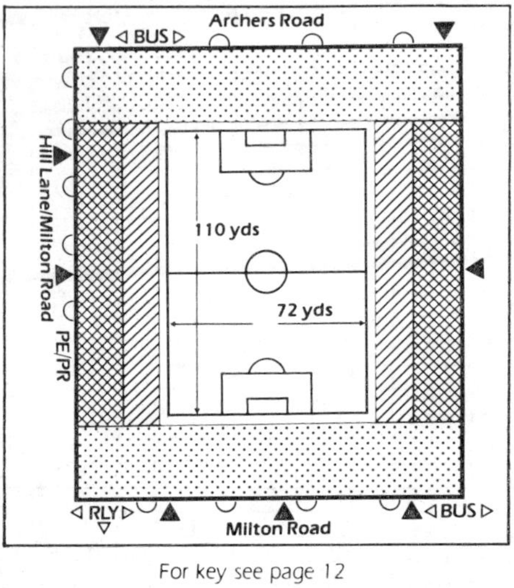

For key see page 12

How to get to the ground

From North: Use A33 S.P. Southampton into The Avenue then turn right into Northlands Road and at end turn right into Archers Road for Southampton F.C.

From East: Use Motorway M27 then A334 and follow signs Southampton A3024. Then follow signs The West into Commercial Road then turn right into Hill Lane and take 1st turning right into Milton Road for Southampton F.C.

From West: Use A35 then A3024 S.P. Southampton City Centre. Forward into Fourposts Hill then turn left into Hill Lane and take 1st turning right into Milton Road for Southampton F.C.

SOUTHEND UNITED Division 4

President
N J Woodcock

Chairman
A W A MacHutchon

Directors
N J Woodcock
F H Walton.
R F Moore
A H Gerschlik
V T Jobson

Secretary
K Holmes, F.A.A.I., F.Inst.C.M.

Manager
R F Moore

Club Coach
H Cripps

Physiotherapist
H Footman

Chief Scout
Bob Walls

Commercial Manager
S Jackson (0702 611350)

There were times during the recent season when it seemed that Third Division Football might remain at Roots Hall but a very bad slump after the New year saw the team sink gradually into the relegation zone where they remained finishing in twenty-second place with a points score of forty-four — five behind Brentford, who were the lowest survivors. This kind of form could lead to one inevitable result, which was that there was a different manager at the end of the season to the one who started it. Few will sympathise with a club which sacked one of their more successful managers, Dave Smith, in the close season and his successor must have known that anything other than complete success would lead to an early parting of the ways which was the fate of Peter Morris. In came Bobby Moore and his fate will be no better unless he can 'deliver'.

Morris had the impossible task of building a winning team with no cash resources at his disposal and morale was not helped by the team's immediate departure from both the major cup competitions. First, Wimbledon won a thrilling Milk Cup Round One tie on aggregate (6-5 after extra time), and in the F.A. Cup the future heroes Plymouth Argyle struggled to survive in a goalless match at Roots Hall before winning a First Round replay at Home Park by two clear goals. The Associate Members Cup did little to cheer the local support, so the fight for survival was all that was left to arouse interest and that was a failed effort.

Now Bobby Moore is in the 'hot seat' and for his next campaign he must hope that such men as Keeley (in goal), Stead, Collins, Fuccillo, Ferguson, Kellock and Whymark (the former Ipswich Town veteran) will be the right ones around whom a team can be built to bring a speedy return to the Third Division. It will be most interesting to see how they succeed. The Fourth Division is a bleak place and not one which attracts spectators to watch losing teams. WLM

Back Row L to R: Buster Footman (Physio), Jack Burkett (Youth Team Coach), Micky Stead, Greig Shepherd, Trevor Whymark, Micky Engwell, John Keeley, Brian Ferguson, Alan Rogers, Lil Fuccillo, Paul Clark, Bobby Moore (Manager), Harry Cripps (Coach). **Front Row:** Ron Pountney, John Gymer, Warren May, Glenn Pennyfather, Billy Kellock (Captain), Steve Philips, Adrian Owers, Steve Collins.

'THE SHRIMPERS'

Formed: 1906 **Turned Professional:** 1906 **Ltd Co:** 1919
Previous Managers: Since 1946:
Harry Warren Eddie Perry Frank Broome Ted Fenton Alvan Williams Ernie Shepherd
Geoff Hudson Arthur Rowley David Smith
Honours: Division Four Champions 1980-1
League Career: Original members of Division Three 1920 Allocated to Division Three (South) 1921
Original members of new Division Three 1958 Relegated to Division Four 1966
Promoted to Division Three 1972 Relegated to Division Four 1976 Promoted to Division Three 1978
Relegated to Division Four 1980 Promoted to Division Three 1981 Relegated to Division Four 1984
Colours: Blue shirts with white pinstripe on collar and cuffs, white shorts, blue stockings
Change Colours: Red shirts with white pinstripe, red shorts and stockings

CLUB RECORDS

Most Appearances for Club: Sandy Anderson, 451, 1950-63
Most Capped Player: George McKenzie, 9, Eire **For England:**
Record Goalscorer in a Match: Jimmy Shankley, 5 v Merthyr Town, Div 3(S), 01.03.30
Record League Goalscorer in a season: Jim Shankley, 31, Div 3(S), 1928-9; Sam McCrory, 31, Div 3(S), 1957-8
Record League Goalscorer in a career: Roy Hollis, 122, 1953-60
Record Transfer Fee Received: £120,000 from Crystal Palace for Peter Taylor, Oct 1973
Record Transfer Fee Paid: £111,111 to Blackpool for Derek Spence, Dec 1979
Best Performances: League: 3rd Div 3(S) 1930-1 **F.A. Cup:** Last sixteen 1920-1, 1925-6, 1951-2, 1975-6
League/Milk Cup: Never past 3rd Round
Most League Points: 69 in Div 3, 1981-2 **Most League Goals:** 92, Div 3(S), 1950-1
Record League Victory: 9-2 v Newport County, Div 3(S), 5 Sept 1936
Record League Defeat: 1-9 v Brighton, Div 3, 27 Nov 1965

Club Statistician for the Directory: P. Esdaile

Programme Editor
S. Jackson

Price	**Number of Pages**
40p	16

Subscriptions
£23.00/£24.00 per season

SOUTHEND UNITED

PLAYERS NAME Ht Wt Birthdate	Honours	Birthplace Transfers	Clubs	APPEARANCES League	Milk Cup	F.A.C.	A.M.C.	GOALS League	Milk Cup	F.A.C.	A.M.C.
GOALKEEPER											
John Keeley		Plaistow	Southend U. (A)	54	2	5	3				
5-0 12.3 27.7.61											
DEFENDERS											
Paul Clark	E. Y	Benfleet	Southend U. (A)	29+4	0+1	1		1			
5-10 12.5 14.9.58		£55,000	Brighton	69+10	8+1	4+1		9			
			Reading (L)	2							
		F	Southend U.	48+3	3	4+1		1			
Steve Collins		Stamford	Peterborough U. (A)	92+2	11	10		1			
5-8 11.4 21.3.62		£7,500	Southend U.	36			2				
Warren May		Rochford	Southend U.	27+9	1		1	3			
5-0½ 11.8 31.12.64											
Mike Stead†	Div. 4, 81	West Ham	Tottenham H. (A)	14+1							
5-8 11.7 28.2.57			Swansea C. (L)	5				1			
			Southend U.	242+1	15	15	3	5			
Chris Turner		St Neots	Peterborough U.	308+6	16+	33		37	3	3	
5-1 14.0 3.4.51		£100,000	Luton T.	30	4			5			
		£90,000	New England Teamen								
		F	Cambridge U.	15+4							
		F	Swindon T.	0+3							
		F	Cambridge U.	68+3	4	5		3			
		F	Southend U.	22			2	1			
MIDFIELD											
Jim Ferguson		Irvine	Mansfield T. (A)								
5-10 10.6 14.12.60			Newcastle U.	4+1				1			
			Hull C.	24+4							
			Goole T.								
			Southend U.	28+1				2			
Pasquale Fugillo	Div. 2, 82	Bedford	Luton T.	153+7				24			
5-11 11.4 2.5.56			Tulsa R.								
			Southend U.	19+4			1+1	2			
Billy Kellock*	S. S	Glasgow	Aston Villa (A)								
5-10 11.10 7.2.54		F	Cardiff C.	33+2		7		2			
		£5,000	Norwich C.	1+2							
		£30,000	Peterborough U.'	134	12	10		43	4	1	
		£30,000	Luton T.	2+5	1	0+1			2		
		£20,000	Wolverhampton W.	12				3			
		£20,000	Southend U.	40	1	1	3	6	1		3
Glen Pennyfather		Billericay	Southend U. (A)	96+5	3+1	6+3	2	9	1		1
5-8 10.4 11.2.63											
Ron Pountney	Div. 4, 81	Bilston	Walsall	1							
5-6 9.13 19.3.55			Port Vale								
			Bilston								
		£12,000	Southend U.	295+16	15+	22+	3	25	2	6	
FORWARDS											
Adrian Owers		Chelmsford	Southend U.	10+5							
5-8½ 9.11 26.2.65											
Steve Phillips		Edmonton	Birmingham C. (A)	15+5	2			1			
5-6 10.9 4.8.54			Torquay U. (L)	6							
			Northampton T.	50+1	3	1		8			
		£19,000	Brentford	156+1	5	4		65	1	3	
		£40,000	Northampton T.	75	7	4		29	3	2	
		£15,000	Southend U.	102	2+1	7	3	43	1	1	
Alan Rogers	Div. 3, 83	Plymouth	Plymouth A. (A)	107+10	13	7		5			
5-10 10.7 6.7.54		£15,000	Portsmouth	154+8	13+	9+2		15	2		
		£20,000	Southend U.	13							
Greig Shepherd		Edinburgh	Musselburgh								
6-1 12.0 29.9.60			Norwich C.	13+3	2			2			
			Southend U.	36+3	2	2	2	8	3		1
Trevor Whymark	E. (1), U.23 (7)	Burston	Diss T.								
6-0 11.0 4.5.50			Ipswich T.	249+11	20	21		74	9	2	
			Vancouver & S. Rotterdam								
			Derby Co. (L)	2							
		£80,000	Grimsby T.	83+10	5	5		16	1	1	
			Southend U.	19			2	3			2

NON-CONTRACT PLAYERS 1984-85: Andy Garwood, Jon O'Brien

APPRENTICES: Kirk Game, John Gymer (1+2 Lg., 1 g.), **Tony Rose, John Senden**

*Before joining Peterborough Billy Kellock played for Millwall (0 Apps), Chelmsford and Kettering

SOUTHEND UNITED

DIVISION THREE 22ND **FA CUP** 1ST ROUND **MILK CUP** 1ST ROUND

MATCH	DATE	COMPETITION	VENUE	OPPONENTS	RESULT	HALF TIME	L'GUE POS'N	GOALSCORERS	ATTENDANCE
1	A 27	CL	H	Rotherham U	D2-2	1-0		Phillips, Shepherd	3,114
2	**29**	**MC 1**	**H**	**Wimbledon**	**W1-0**	**0-0**		**Shepherd**	**2,572**
3	S 3	CL	A	Bristol R	L1-2	1-1	16	Ferguson	4,410
4	6	CL	A	Preston NE	L1-4	0-3		McDonough	3,967
5	10	CL	H	Wimbledon	D1-1	1-1	21	Shepherd	3,106
6	**13**	**MC 1**	**A**	**Wimbledon**	**L4-6[1]**	**1-2**		**Shepherd 2, Kellock, Phillips**	**1,967**
7	17	CL	A	Bradford C	D1-1	0-0	20	Phillips	2,574
8	19	CL	H	Millwall	W3-2	1-1	17	Kellock, McDonough, Phillips	4,272
9	24	CL	H	Walsall	D0-0	0-0	14		3,061
10	30	CL	A	Scunthorpe U	W6-1	2-0		Phillips 3, Pennyfather, Stead, Shepherd	3,335
11	O 15	CL	H	Exeter C	L0-3	0-1	17		2,342
12	18	CL	A	Burnley	L0-3	0-1			5,301
13	21	CL	H	Orient	W3-0	1-0		McDonough, Ferguson, Phillips	4,116
14	29	CL	A	Bolton W	L0-2	0-1	18		5,366
15	31	CL	H	Brentford	W6-0	2-0		Ferguson 2, Pennyfather 2, Phillips, Shepherd	2,902
16	N 5	CL	A	Newport Co	D1-1	0-1	17	Turner	3,769
17	11	CL	H	AFC Bournemouth	D0-0	0-0			3,277
18	**19**	**FAC 1**	**H**	**Plymouth Arg**	**D0-0**	**0-0**			**3,408**
19	**22**	**FAC 1R**	**A**	**Plymouth Arg**	**L0-2[1]**	**0-0**			**5,570**
20	26	CL	A	Sheffield U	L0-5	0-1	17		9,627
21	D 2	CL	H	Oxford U	L0-1	0-1			2,559
22	17	CL	H	Wigan Ath	W1-0	0-0	15	Shepherd	1,819
23	26	CL	A	Gillingham	L1-5	1-2	15	Phillips	5,511
24	27	CL	H	Lincoln C	W2-0	0-0	14	McDonough, Phillips	2,824
25	31	CL	A	Plymouth Arg	L0-4	0-1	16		2,978
26	J 2	CL	H	Hull C	D2-2	2-0	16	Fuccillo, Phillips	2,737
27	9	CL	H	Bristol R	L1-2	0-1		Kellock	2,564
28	28	CL	A	Wimbledon	L2-3	2-2	18	Pennyfather, Phillips	2,752
29	30	CL	A	Port Vale	L1-2	0-1		Phillips	3,636
30	F 3	CL	H	Scunthorpe U	D0-0	0-0			1,976
31	6	CL	H	Bolton W	L0-1	0-0			1,594
32	11	CL	A	Walsall	L0-4	0-1	20		8,156
33	14	CL	A	Brentford	D0-0	0-0			3,961
34	**20**	**AMC 1**	**H**	**Reading**	**W5-0**	**3-0**		**Pennyfather, Kellock 2 (1 pen), Turner, Whymark**	**1,597**
35	26	CL	A	Orient	L0-1	0-1			3,001
36	M 2	CL	H	Burnley	D2-2	1-1		Whymark, Phelan (og)	2,567
37	10	CL	A	AFC Bournemouth	L0-1	0-1	20		3,615
38	**13**	**AMC 2**	**A**	**Colchester U**	**W2-0**	**0-0**		**Whymark, Kellock**	**2,841**
39	19	CL	H	Port Vale	L1-2	0-1		Kellock	2,080
40	23	CL	A	Exeter C	D3-3	0-1		Ferguson, Phillips, Pountney	1,782
41	**A 3**	**AMC SQF**	**H**	**Bristol R**	**L1-2**	**1-1**		**Shepherd**	**1,480**
42	6	CL	H	Preston NE	D1-1	0-0		Kellock (pen)	1,826
43	10	CL	A	Rotherham U	D0-0	0-0			3,722
44	14	CL	A	Oxford U	L1-2	0-2	23	Shepherd	7,538
45	16	CL	H	Bradford C	W2-1	1-1		Whymark, Shepherd	2,033
46	18	CL	A	Millwall	L0-4	0-1			3,345
47	20	CL	H	Gillingham	W3-1	2-0		Fuccillo, Shepherd, Gymer	3,218
48	23	CL	A	Lincoln C	W2-1	1-1	20	Phillips, Kellock	1,834
49	28	CL	H	Sheffield U	L0-1	0-0	21		4,971
50	30	CL	H	Newport Co	W3-1	2-0		May, Whymark, Kellock	2,108
51	M 5	CL	A	Hull C	L1-2	1-2	21	Phillips	6,758
52	7	CL	H	Plymouth Arg	D1-1	0-1	22	May	3,540
53	12	CL	A	Wigan Ath	L0-1	0-1	22		3,335

[1] After Extra time **Av Home Att 2,822**

Goal Scorers

League (55): Phillips 16, Shepherd 8, Kellock 6 (1 pen), Ferguson 5, McDonough 4, Pennyfather 4, Whymark 3, Fuccillo 2, May 2, Gymer 1, Pountney 1, Stead 1, Turner 1, opponent 1

FA Cup (-): —

Milk Cup (5): Shepherd 3, Kellock 1, Phillips 1

AMC (8): Kellock 3 (1 pen), Whymark 2, Pennyfather 1, Shepherd 1, Turner 1

1983-84

Cawston	Stead	Collins	Ferguson	Yates	Clark	Pountney	Skivington	McDonough	Shepherd	Phillips	May	Pritchard **(L)**	Pennyfather	Cartwright **(L)**	Kellock	Peyton **(L)**	Turner	Moody	Keeley	Fuccillo	Whymark	Steggles **(L)**	Rogers	Wilkins **(L)**	REFEREE	
1	2	3	4	5	6	7	8	9	10	11															C Downey	1
1	**2**	**3**	**4**	**5**	**6***	**7**	**8**	**9**	**10**	**11**			**12**												**G Napthine**	**2**
1	2	3	4	5		7	8*	9	10		6		11												K Barratt	3
1	2	3	4	5		7		9	10		6		11	8											A Saunders	4
1	2	3		5	6	7		9	10	4				11	8										I Borrett	5
1		**3**			**5**	**7***		**9**	**10**	**12**	**6**		**4**	**11**	**8**										**Alan Robinson**	**6**
1	2	3	7	5	6			9	10	11			4		8										J Worrall	7
	2	3	4	5	6			9*	10	11†			7	12	8	1									D Letts	8
	2	3	7	5	6			9*	10	11			4	12	8	1									M Taylor	9
	2	3	7	5	6			9	10	11			4		8	1									R Banks	10
	2	3	7	5	6	11		9	10				4		8	1									J Martin	11
	2	3	7	5	6	11*	12	9	10				4		8	1									T Holbrook	12
	2	3	7					9	10	11			4		8	1	5	6							D Hedges	13
	2	3	7			12		9	10	11			4*		8	1	5	6							A Challinor	14
	2	3	7					9	10	11			4		8	1	5	6							J Bray	15
	2	3	7			8		9	10	11			4			1	5	6							R Nixon	16
	2		7	3		12		9	10	11			4		8*	1	5	6							D Reeves	17
	2	**3**	**7**			**12**		**9**	**10**	**11**			**4**		**8***		**5**	**6**	**1**						**M Bodenham**	**18**
	2	**3**	**7**		**12**	**8**		**9**	**10**	**11**			**4***				**5**	**6**	**1**						**M Bodenham**	**19**
	2	3	7				12	9	10	11			4*		8		5	6	1						PN Willis	20
	2	3	4			7		9*	10	11	12				8		5	6	1						M James	21
1	2	3	4			7		9	10	11					8		5	6							A Gunn	22
1	2	3	4			7		9	10*	11					8		5	6		12					A Ward	23
1	2	3	4			7		9		11	12				8		5*	6		10					M Bodenham	24
1	2	3	4		5	7		9	12	11					8			6		10*					V Callow	25
1	2	3	4		5	7		9		11					8			6		10					M Dimblebee	26
1	2	3	4*			7				11	12				8		5	6		10	9				D Letts	27
	2	3	9			7			8	11	12		4				5		1	10*	6				B Hill	28
	2*	3				7			9	11	12		4		8		5		1	10	6				I Hendrick	29
		3.	12			7			9	11	2		4		8*		5		1	10	6				K Baker	30
	2	3				7			9	11			4		8		5	6	1		10				K Salmon	31
	2	3	11			7			12	10			4*		8		5		1		9	6			D Owen	32
	2	3	4			7				11			10		8		5		1		9	6			C Thomas	33
	2	**3**	**10**			**7**				**11**			**4**		**8**		**5**		**1**		**9**	**6**			**E Scales**	**34**
	2	3	10			7				11	12		4		8		5		1		9	6*			H King	35
	2	3				7				11	12		4		8		5*	6	1	10	9				R Lewis	36
	2	3			6	7			12	11			4*		8		5		1	10	9				D Hedges	37
	2	**3**			**6**	**7**			**4**	**11**					**8**		**5**		**1**	**10**	**9**				**K Hackett**	**38**
	2	3			6	7			4*	11	12				8		5		1	10	9				C Downey	39
	2*		7		6	12			9	10			4		8		5	3	1				11		J Deakin	40
	2		**11**			**7**			**9**	**10**	**5**		**4**		**8**			**6***	**1**	**12**				**3**	**A Gunn**	**41**
	2				6*	7			9	10	5		4		8				1	12			11	3	M Taylor	42
	2					7			9	10	5	1	4		8			6		12			11*	3	T Fitzharris	43
	2				5	7			9	10			4		8			6*	1	12			11	3	J Bray	44
	2	3							9	4	5	1			8			6		10	7		11		A Buksh	45
	2	3							9	4	5	1			8			6		10	7		11		E Read	46
	2								9	4	5	1	3		8			6		10	7*		11		D Reeves	47
	2					12			9*	4	5	1	3		8			6		10			11		G Tyson	48
	2				7				9	4	5	1	3					6		10	8		11		I Borrett	49
	2				7				9	4	5	1	3		8					10	6		11		T Bune	50
	2				7				9*	4	5	1	3		8					10	6		11		D Allison	51
	2*	3			7				9	4	5	1			8					10	6		11		C Downey	52
		3	4*		7						5		2		8				1	10	6		11		P Willis	53
11	44	36	28	11	20	27	2	22	36	41	14	9	33	2	40	10	22	23	16	19	19	3	13	3	League Appearances	
			+1S			+4S	+2S		+3S		+8S			+2S						+4S						
	2	2	2		1S	1+1S		2	2	2			2		1		2	2	2						FA Cup Appearances	
2	1	2	1	1	2	2	1	2	2	1+1S	1		1+1S	1	1										Milk Cup Appearances	
	3	2	2		1	3			2	3	1		2		3		2	1	3	1+1S	2	1		1	AM Cup Appearances	

Also Played: Greaves match 3, no.12. Gymer match 47, 51, 52, no.12; 48, no.7; 53, no.9 Owers match 53, no.12. Angus match 6, no.2

ROOTS HALL

Official Address: Rock Hall Football Ground, Victoria Avenue, Southend-on-Sea. Telephone: Southend (0702) 340707

Ground Capacity: 32,000 (16,000 covered)

Record Attendance: 31,033 v. Liverpool, F.A. Cup Round 3, 10 Jan 1979

Record Receipts: £36,599 v. Liverpool, F.A. Cup Round 3, 10 Jan 1979

Size of Playing Area: 110 × 74 yds

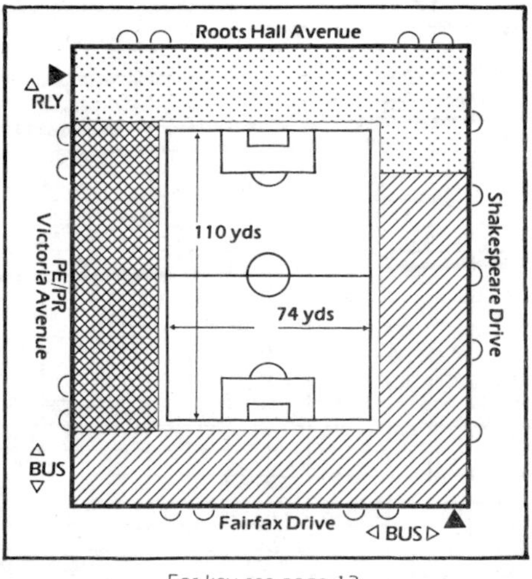

For key see page 12

Season Tickets: Stand (East) (Red/Yellow/Green): £80.00; (Blue): £65, (£45 OAP/juveniles); Paddock: £50, (£25 OAP/juveniles); North Bank & West Standing: £46, (£23 OAP/juveniles); South Bank Standing: £40, (£20 OAP/juveniles)

Executive Box Season Tickets: None available

Cost of Stand Tickets: £4.00; **Paddock:** £2.50, (£1.30 OAP/juveniles); Standing North Bank & West: £2.30, (£1.50 OAP/juveniles); South Bank Standing: £2.00, (£1.30 OAP/juveniles)

Match and Ticket Information: Seats can be bought fourteen days before match.

Car Parking: Two parks at the ground hold 700 vehicles (approximately). Ample street parking is available.

How to get to the ground

From North, East: Use A127 S.P. Southend, and then at roundabout take 3rd exit into Victoria Avenue for Southend United F.C.
From South: Use A13 S.P. Southend and then turn left into West Road and at end turn left into Victoria Avenue for Southend United F.C.

STOCKPORT COUNTY Division 4

President & Chairman
Alan Kirk

Directors
Dragan Lukic
Josh Lewis
Grahame White
Brian Taylor
Peter Snape MP

Chief Executive & Secretary
Terry McCreery, FAAI

Assistant Secretary & Commercial Manager
Peter Lamb (061 480 8888)

Office Secretary
Andrea Dawson

Meidcal Officers
Richard Hardman
Chris Martin

Manager
Eric Webster

Physiotherapist
Chris Wych, MCSP, SRP

Groundsman
Steve McArdle

No doubt about it, this was Stockport County's best season since 1972-73, although the cynics will say that their 12th place was hardly anything to get excited about.

The previous season had ended with a dark cloud hanging over the Edgeley Park boardroom, before Chairman/President Alan Kirk made sure that through the goodness of his own pocket and with a little help on the transfer market unpaid income tax bills were cleared and the club did not go under before it's Centenary Season.

Two new Directors joined the Board during the campaign, Brian Taylor (a successful Stockport solicitor) and Peter Snape MP, both of whom had been life-long supporters of the club.

On the playing front ever present 'keeper Mick Salmon was voted Player of the Year in his first season with the club. Top scorer . . . ? Well that honour fell to Mike Quinn for the second season in succession, although his £55,000 transfer to Oldham in mid-term looked to have left his 15 goal league tally a vulnerable target, but only centre-half Tommy Sword also managed to get into double figures.

Incredibly County failed to win any of their first six home games before a victory over Darlington in October turned the tide and yet from November to February County won seven consecutive league matches on their own ground to illustrate their topsy turvey form at home.

There were of course highlights in the season, including an incredible 3-0 win over promotion candidates Reading in January, as well as magnificent wins by the same scoreline at Rochdale in the Milk Cup and Crewe in Division Four.

Apart from a remarkable first-half performance at Oldham in the 2nd-round of the Milk Cup, County had little or no luck in the season's three major Cup competitions.

The FA Cup, never a happy hunting ground for the club in recent seasons, saw a disastrous 3-0 reverse at non-league Telford and after a spirited comeback at home to Crewe in the newly inaugurated Associate Members Cup County went out rather ignominiously 3-0 on penalties at Edgeley Park in a bizarre shoot-out.

Howard Jones
The League Directory's Statistician for the Club

Back Row L to R: Paul Hendrie, Dean Emerson, Andy Thorpe, Clive Evans, John Rutter. **Middle Row:** Steve Buxton, Steve Taylor, Steve Sherlock, Paul Bowles, Mick Salmon, Tommy Sword, Mike Power, Tony Coyle, Chris Wych (Physio). **Front Row:** John Kerr, Grahame White (Director), Eric Webster (Manager), Alan Kirk (Chairman/President), Brian Taylor (Director), Oshor Williams.

'COUNTY'

Formed: 1883 **Turned Professional:** 1891 **Ltd Co:** 1908
Previous Managers: 1900-11 Fred Stewart 1911-4 Harry P Lewis 1914-9 David Ashworth 1919-24 Albert Williams 1924-6 Fred Scotchbrook 1926-31 Lincoln Hyde 1931-2 No Manager 1932-3 Andrew Wilson 1933-4 No Manager 1934-6 Fred Westgarth 1936-8 Bob Kelly 1938-9 No Manager 1939-49 Bobbie Marshall 1949-52 Andy Beattie 1952-6 Dick Duckworth 1956-60 Willie Moir 1960-3 Reg Flewin 1963-5 Trevor Porteous 1965-6 Bert Trautmann 1966-6 Eddie Quigley 1966-9 Jimmy Meadows 1969-70 Walter Galbraith 1970-1 Matt Woods 1972-4 Brian Doyle 1974-5 Jimmy Meadows 1975-6 Roy Chapman 1976-7 Eddie Quigley 1977-8 Alan Thompson 1978-9 Mike Summerbee 1979-82 Jimmy McGuigan
Honours: Division 3(N) Champions, Division Four Champions
League Career: Elected to Division 2 1900 Failed Re-election 1904 Elected to Division 2 1905
Relegated to Division 3 (North) 1920-1 Promoted to Division 2 1921-2
Relegated to Division 3 (North) 1925-6 Promoted to Division 2 1936-7
Relegated to Division 3 (North) 1937-8 Transferred to Division 3 1958
Relegated to Division 4 1958-9 Promoted to Division 3 1966-7
Relegated to Division 4 1960-70
Colours: Royal blue and white striped shirts, blue shorts, blue stockings with three white bands at the top.
Change Colours: All green, with yellow stockings

CLUB RECORDS

Most Appearances for Club: Bob Murray, 1952-63: Football League 465 + F.A. Cup 27 + League Cup 3 **Total 495**
Most Capped Player: Harry Hardy (England) 1
Record Goalscorer in a Match: Joe Smith, 5 v Southport (h) 6-3, Div 3(N) 07.01.28
Joe Smith, 5 v Lincoln County (h) 7-3, Div 3(N) 15.09.28 Jack Connor, 5 v Workington (h) 6-0, Div 3(N) 08.11.52
Jack Connor, 5 v Carlisle United (h) 8-1, Div 3(N) 07.04.56
Record League Goalscorer in a season: Alf Lythgoe, 46 **All Competitions:** Alf Lythgoe, 46 League + 1 F.A. Cup = 47, 1933-4
Record League Goalscorer in a career: Jack Connor, 132 **All Competitions:** Jack Connor 132 League + 8 F.A. Cup = 140, 1951-6
Record Transfer Fee Received: £80,000 from Manchester City for Stuart Lee, Sept 1979
Record Transfer Fee Paid: £25,000 to Albion Rovers for Tony Coyle, Dec 1979
Best Performances: League: 17th Div 2 1905-6 **F.A. Cup:** 5th Round 1935, 1950 **League/Milk Cup:** 4th Round 1972-3
Most League Points: 64 in Div 4, 1966-7 **Most League Goals:** 115, Div 3(N), 1957-8
Record League Victory: 13-0 v Halifax Town, Div 3(N), 6 Jan 1934
Record League Defeat: 1-8 v Chesterfield, Div 2, 19 Apr 1902

Club Statistician for the Directory: Howard Jones

Programme Editor
Howard Jones

Price	Number of Pages
40p	12

Subscriptions
£19.00 per season (postage included), £24.00 (overseas — postage included)

STOCKPORT COUNTY

PLAYERS NAME Ht Wt Birthdate	Honours	Birthplace Transfers	Clubs	APPEARANCES League	Milk Cup	F.A.C.	A.M.C.	GOALS League	Milk Cup	F.A.C.	A.M.C.
GOALKEEPER											
Mike Salmon.		Leyland	Blackburn R.	1							
6-2 12.12 14.7.64			Chester (L)	16		2					
			Stockport Co.	46	4	1	1				
DEFENDERS											
Paul Bowles		Manchester	Crewe A. (A)	178	13	9		20	2	1	
6-1 12.11 31.5.57		£30,000	Port Vale	98	4	11		8			
		F	Stockport Co.	67	2						
John Rutter		Warrington	Wolverhampton W. (A)								
5-9 10.10 13.9.52		F	Bournemouth	2+2							
		£15,000	Exeter C.	31+1	2	2		1			
		F	Stockport Co.	346+3	25	15	1	10			
Steve Shercock		Birmingham	Manchester C. (A)								
5-9 11.8 10.5.59		F	Luton F.	2	1						
		F	Stockport Co.	182+5	13+	5		7			
Andy Thorpe		Stockport	Stockport Co.	251+2	16+	6	1	3			
5-11 12.0 15.9.60											
Tommy Sword*		Newcastle	Bishop Auckland								
6-2 14.0 12.11.57		£6,000	Stockport Co.	153+1	10	4		27			
MIDFIELD											
Dean Emerson		Salford	Stockport Co.	112	6	2	1	5	3		
5-8 10.8 27.12.62											
Clive Evans		Birkenhead	Tranmere R. (A)	175+3				27			
5-10 11.5 1.5.57		£25,000	Wigan A.	29+3				2			
		F	Crewe A.	26+2				7			
		F	Stockport Co.	31				7			
Paul Hendrie		Glasgow	Rob Roy								
5-6 10.3 27.3.55		F	Birmingham C.	19+4	3	3		1			
			Portland Timbers								
		F	Bristol R.	17+3		0+1		1			
		F	Halifax T.	187	8	11	1	12		1	
		F	Stockport Co.								
FORWARDS											
Steve Buxton		Birmingham	Wrexham	93+16	3+2	4	2	21			
5-5 9.8 13.3.60		F	Stockport Co.								
Tony Coyle		Glasgow	Albion R.	46				5			
5-10 11.12 17.1.60			Stockport Co.	153+3	3+1	2		18			
John Kerr		Birkenhead	Tranmere R. (A)	145+9	10	6+2		38	4	1	
5-11 12.5 23.11.59			Bristol C.	13+1	2	2		4			
		F	Stockport Co.	21			1	6			
Mike Power		Stockport	Stockport Co.	61+1	3+1	2		15			
6-0 12.0 3.10.61											
Steve Taylor	Div. 2, 78	Royton	Bolton W. (A)	34+6	7	1		16	4		
5-10 10.9 18.10.55	Div. 3, 82		Port Vale (L)	4				2			
		£40,000	Oldham A.	45+2		2		25			
		£50,000	Luton T.	15+5				1			
		£50,000	Mansfield T.	30+7	5	3		7	3		
		£35,000	Burnley	80+6	11+	12		37	1	5	
		F	Wigan A.	29+1	1	4	1	7		2	
		F	Stockport Co.								
Oshor Williams		Stockton	Middlesbrough (A)								
5-9½ 11.7 21.4.58			Manchester U.								
			Gateshead								
		£2,000	Southampton	4+2							
			Exeter C. (L)	2+1							
		£10,000	Stockport Co.	179+1	14	6		24	2	3	

NON-CONTRACT PLAYERS 1984-85

Neil McCreery, Mark Wroe, Paul Wroe

STOCKPORT COUNTY

DIVISION FOUR 12TH **FA CUP** 1ST ROUND **MILK CUP** 2ND ROUND

MATCH	DATE	COMPETITION	VENUE	OPPONENTS	RESULT	HALF TIME	L'GUE POS'N	GOALSCORERS	ATTENDANCE
1	A 27	CL	H	York C	L0-2	0-1			2,185
2	**30**	**MC 1**	**A**	**Rochdale**	**W3-0**	**2-0**		**Quinn 2 (1 pen), Sword**	**1,839**
3	S 3	CL	A	Reading	L2-6	1-2	24	Williams, Rutter	2,469
4	6	CL	A	Mansfield T	W2-1	0-1		Quinn, Sword	2,166
5	9	CL	H	Colchester U	D0-0	0-0	16		2,077
6	**12**	**MC 1**	**H**	**Rochdale**	**D2-2**	**0-1**		**Williams 2**	**2,160**
7	18	CL	A	Northampton T	D0-0	0-0	19		3,189
8	23	CL	H	Swindon T	L1-3	0-1		Williams	2,244
9	26	CL	H	Wrexham	D1-1	0-0		Williams	2,031
10	30	CL	A	Crewe Alex	W3-0	1-0		Quinn 3	2,955
11	**O 3**	**MC 2**	**H**	**Oldham Ath**	**L0-2**	**0-2**			**4,640**
12	8	CL	A	Chesterfield	L0-2	0-0	20		3,846
13	15	CL	H	Darlington	W2-0	0-0	17	Quinn, Williams	1,360
14	17	CL	H	Aldershot	D2-2	0-0		Williams, Emerson	1,935
15	22	CL	A	Chester C	W4-2	2-1	14	Quinn 2, Jones, Coyle	1,495
16	**25**	**MC 2**	**A**	**Oldham Ath**	**D2-2**	**2-0**		**Emerson 2**	**3,540**
17	29	CL	H	Blackpool	L1-2	1-1	16	Thorpe	2,602
18	N 1	CL	A	Bury	L1-2	0-1		Quinn	2,547
19	5	CL	A	Rochdale	D2-2	1-1	20	White, Quinn	1,682
20	11	CL	H	Halifax T	W4-0	1-0		Quinn 2, Sword 2	2,134
21	**19**	**FAC 1**	**A**	**Telford U**	**L0-3**	**0-1**			**2,470**
22	26	CL	A	Peterborough U	L0-2	0-1	17		3,240
23	D 2	CL	H	Torquay U	W2-1	2-0		Sword, Evans	1,874
24	10	CL	A	Aldershot	D1-1	1-0	13	Quinn	1,349
25	16	CL	H	Tranmere R	W2-1	2-0		Quinn, Williams	1,644
26	26	CL	A	Bristol C	L1-3	0-2	13	Sword	8,888
27	27	CL	H	Hereford U	W1-0	1-0	11	Evans	2,287
28	31	CL	A	Doncaster R	L1-2	0-1	12	Quinn	3,736
29	J 2	CL	H	Hartlepool U	W1-0	0-0	11	Jones	1,799
30	6	CL	H	Reading	W3-0	0-0		Kerr 2, Quinn (pen)	1,751
31	14	CL	A	York C	L1-3	1-1	10	Sword (pen)	3,750
32	20	CL	H	Northampton T	W1-0	0-0		Kerr	1,846
33	28	CL	A	Colchester U	D1-1	1-1	8	Sword	2,213
34	F 3	CL	H	Crewe Alex	L2-3	1-2		Coyle, Sword	2,775
35	11	CL	A	Swindon T	L1-2	0-0	12	Evans	3,032
36	13	CL	H	Bury	D1-1	1-1		Kerr	2,281
37	**22**	**AMC 1**	**H**	**Crewe Alex**	**D2-2[5]**	**0-0**		**Thorpe, Kerr**	**1,692**
38	24	CL	H	Chester C	W2-1	1-1		Evans 2	2,006
39	M 5	CL	H	Rochdale	W2-1	0-1		Kerr, Evans (pen)	2,112
40	9	CL	A	Halifax T	L0-2	0-2			1,261
41	16	CL	H	Chesterfield	W2-0	2-0		Sword (pen), Taylor	2,010
42	30	CL	A	Wrexham	W2-1	2-1		Taylor, Evans	1,252
43	A 6	CL	H	Mansfield T	L0-4	0-1			1,933
44	10	CL	A	Blackpool	D1-1	0-0		Taylor	3,971
45	14	CL	A	Torquay U	D1-1	1-1	12	Kerr	1,392
46	21	CL	H	Bristol C	D0-0	0-0	13		2,645
47	23	CL	A	Hereford U	L0-2	0-2	13		3,560
48	27	CL	H	Peterborough U	W4-1	3-0		Taylor 2, Coyle 2	1,753
49	M 2	CL	A	Darlington	L0-1	0-0			1,102
50	5	CL	A	Hartlepool U	W2-1	1-0	11	Taylor, Coyle	790
51	7	CL	H	Doncaster R	L0-2	0-1	11		2,993
52	12	CL	A	Tranmere R	L0-1	0-0	12		1,475

[5]Lost 0-3 on Penalties, After Extra Time

Av Home Att **2,094**

Goal Scorers

League (60): Quinn 15 (1 pen), Sword 9 (2 pens), Evans 7 (1 pen), Kerr 6, Taylor 6, Williams 6, Coyle 5, Jones 2, Emerson 1, Rutter 1, Thorpe 1, White 1

FA Cup (-): —

Milk Cup (7): Emerson 2, Quinn 2 (1 pen), Williams 2, Sword 1

AMC (2): Kerr 1, Thorpe 1

1983-84

Salmon	Rutter	Sherlock	Emerson	Sword	Evans	Thorpe	Jones	Quinn	Coyle	Ryan	Smith	Williams	Power	Bowles	White	Kerr	Leigh	Parker	Sutcliffe	Taylor	Ford	REFEREE	
1	2	3	4	5	6	7	8	9†	11				10									S Roberts	1
1	**2**	**11**	**4**		**10***	**3**	**6**	**9**		**7**		**8**	**12**								**5**	**T Mills**	**2**
1	3	11	4	5		2	6	9		7*	12	8	10									K Salmon	3
1	3	11	4	5		6	2	9			8	7	10									E Scales	4
1	3		4	5		6	2	9	11	12	8	7	10*									V Callow	5
1	**3**	**11**	**4**	**5***		**6**	**2**		**10**	**7**	**8**	**9**		**12**								**A Challinor**	**6**
1	2	3	4	5		6	8		11		7	9	10									A Robinson	7
1	2	3	4	5		6	10	9	11		8	7										N Wilson	8
1	3		4	5		2	10	9	11		8	7		6								K Walmsley	9
1	3		4	10		6	2	9	11		8	7		5								G Napthine	10
1	**3**		**4**	**10**		**6**	**2**	**9**	**11**		**8**	**7**		**5**								**M Robinson**	**11**
1	3		4	10		6	2	9	11		8	7		5								G Tyson	12
1	2	3	4	10		6	8	9	11			7		5								H Taylor	13
1	3	10	4	6		2		9	11		8	7		5								D Hutchinson	14
1	3		4	6		2	10	9	11		8	7		5								C Seel	15
1	**3**		**4**	**6**		**2**	**10**	**9**	**11**		**8**	**7**		**5**								**M Dimblebee**	**16**
1	3	12	4	6		2	10	9	11		8	7*		5								K Barratt	17
1	3	8	4	6		2	10	9	11		7			5								K Redfern	18
1	3	11	4	6		2	10	9	8					5	7							R Bridges	19
1	2	3		10		6	8	9	11		4			5	7							A Seville	20
1	**2**	**3**	**4**	**10**		**6**	**8**	**9**				**7**		**5**	**11**							**D Brazier**	**21**
1	3	12	4	6	8	2*	10	9				7		5	11							K Baker	22
1	2		4	6	8	3	10	9				7		5	11							G Courtney	23
1	2	3	4	10	11	6	8	9				7		5								J Ashworth	24
1	2	3	4	10	11	6	8	9				7		5								D Richardson	25
1	2	3	4	10	11	6	8	9				7		5								T Spencer	26
1	2	3	4	10	8	6		9	11			7		5								R Guy	27
1	2	3		4	8	6	10	9	11			7		5								D Allison	28
1	2	3	4	10	8	6	12	9	11			7		5*								J Bray	29
1	2	3	4	5	8	6		9	11			7				10						J Key	30
1	2	3	4	10	8	6	12		11*			7		5		9						G Napthine	31
1	3		4	10	8	6	2		11			7		5		9						A Saunders	32
1	3		4	10	8	6	2		11			7		5		9						D Reeves	33
1	3		4	10	8	6	2		11			7		5		9						D Owen	34
1	3		4	10	8	6	2		11*		7			5		9	12					M Bodenham	35
1	3		4	10	8	6	2				11	7		5		9						A Challinor	36
1	**3**		**4**		**8**	**6**	**2**		**11**		**7**			**5**		**9**	**12**	**10***				**F Roberts**	**37**
1	3		4	10*	8	6	2		11		7			5		9		12				K Walmsley	38
1	3		4		8	6	2		11		10	7		5		9						T Mills	39
1	3		4	10	8	6	2		11		7*			5		9			12			N Glover	40
1	3		4	6	8	2*	12		11		7			5		9				10		G Tyson	41
1	3		4	6	9	2	8		11		7			5						10		V Callow	42
1	3		4	5	8	2			11			7		6		9				10		M Robertson	43
1	3		4	6	8	2			11			7		5		9				10		M Peck	44
1	3		4	5	8	2			11			7		6		9				10		A Seville	45
1	3		4	5	8	2			11			7		6		9				10		D Scott	46
1	2	3	4	5	8				11			7		6		9				10		K Cooper	47
1		3	4	5	8	2			11			7		6		9				10		D Allison	48
1		3	4	5	8	6	2		11			7				9				10		N Wilson	49
1		3	4	5	8	2			11			7		6		9				10		C Seel	50
1		3	4	5	8	2			11			7		6		9†				10		K Baker	51
1		3	4	5	8	2	7		11*			12		6		9				10		D Richardson	52
46	41	24	44	45	31	45	32	24	38	1	19	36	5	38	4	21	0	0	0	12		League Appearances	
		+2S					+3S			+1S	+1S	+1S					+1S	+1S	+1S				
1	1	1	1	1		1	1	1				1		1	1							FA Cup Appearances	
4	4	2	4	3	1	4	4	3	3	2	3	4	1S	2+1S							1	Milk Cup Appearances	
1	1		1		1	1	1		1		1			1		1	1S	1				AM Cup Appearances	

EDGELEY PARK

Official Address: Edgeley Park, Hardcastle Road, Edgeley, Stockport, Cheshire SK3 9DD. Telephone: 061-480 8588

Ground Capacity: 16,500

Record Attendance: 27,833 v. Liverpool, F.A. Cup Round 5, 11 Feb 1950

Record Receipts: £19,382 v. Arsenal, League Cup Round 3, 22 Sept 1980

Size of Playing Area: 110yds × 75 yds

Season Tickets: Stand: £25 (OAP), £30 (Child), £37 (Ladies) £52 (Gentlemen).

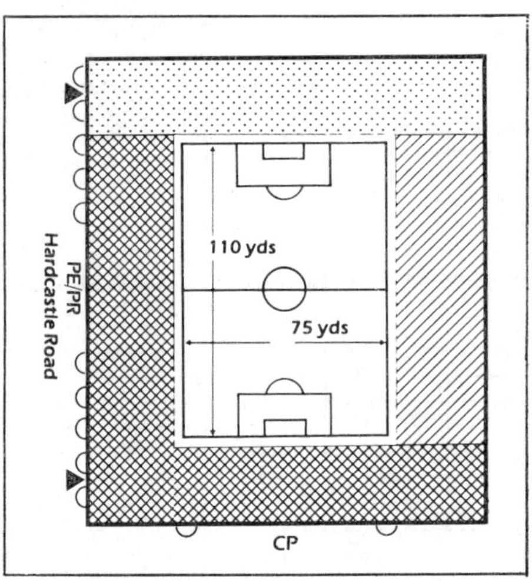

For key see page 12

Executive Box Season Tickets: 1. On application to the Assistant Secretary. 2. For match sponsorship — on application to Assistant Secretary.

Cost of Stand Tickets: Cheadle Stand £2.50 (Adults), £2.00 (OAP/Child); Main Stand £3.00 (All). **Terraces:** £2.00 (Adults), £1.50 (OAP/Child)

Match and Ticket Information: Seats can be reserved in the main stand by telephone or post (with remittance & SAE).

Car Parking: ample street parking around the ground.

How to get to the ground

From North, South and West: Use Motorway M63 until end then join A560 S.P. Stockport. In 0.4m turn right into Edgeley Road. In 1m turn right into Caroline Street for Stockport County F.C.
From East: Use A6 or A560 into Stockport town centre, then turn left into Greek Street. At roundabout take 2nd exit into Castle Street then turn left into Caroline Street for Stockport County F.C.

STOKE CITY — Division 1

Chairman
F Edwards

Directors
A W Clubb
G L Manning

Secretary
M J Potts

Manager
Bill Asprey

Club Coach
Tony Lacey

Commercial Manager
D H J Kernick (0782 45840)

The old cliché that this was a season of two halves seems most apt. Indeed it was not until the last match of the season that the club's fate was settled and First Division status retained.

The expectation of progress was very high as the 1983/84 campaign opened with supporters looking for the club to build on the advance of the previous season which saw them on the brink of European competition for a long time. It was also important that the modest success achieved had been by playing adventurous football led by Mark Chamberlain, Mickey Thomas and Sammy McIlroy.

New signings Paul Dyson, Robbie James, Robbie Savage and Dennis Tueart arrived at a cost of around £300,000 largely funded by the sale of Paul Bracewell to Sunderland. An unexpected change of style saw Manager Richie Barker embrace 'the percentage game' with its reliance on long balls out of defence. The surprising absence in the newcomers was a goalscorer as the ageing Tueart could not make any impact in Division One.

The new style did not appear to suit the playing resources of the team and whilst changes in patterns came regularly the team slumped towards Division Two when the directors terminated Barker in December with only the already doomed Wolverhampton Wanderers below them.

With Barker's assistant Bill Asprey given the manager's job to the end of the season there was no immediate transformation in fortunes but at least the club reverted to playing football. Mickey Thomas, a firm favourite with the fans, joined Chelsea in January but then came the masterstroke as Asprey tempted Alan Hudson back to the Potteries and Division One after years in the wilderness (NASL and Football Combination) – only on loan at first.

His first game against Arsenal on 28th January brought 3 points – only the second maximum return since October 1st – thus starting a breathtaking escape act and a run of 7 home wins. A fee of £22,500 brought him back fully and a 2-0 win over Liverpool in April gave the supporters the hope, credibility and belief for which they craved. Finishing the season with a 4-0 win over Wolves with Paul Maguire grabbing the lot was the cream on the cake. Other hopeful signs came when the club's youth team unluckily lost in the FA Youth Cup Final and Bill Asprey accepted a 2 year contract, fine reward for his efforts which had seen a gain of 33 points since Alan Hudson's return – one more than Liverpool in the same spell.

Wade Martin, The League Directory's Statistician for the Club

Back Row L to R: Phillip Heath, Brendan O'Callaghan, Paul Dyson, Peter Fox, Steve Bould, Robbie James, Carl Saunders. **Front Row:** Ian Painter, Chris Maskery, Mark Chamberlain, Bill Asprey (Manager), Sammy McIlroy (Captain), Alan Hudson, Steve Parkin.

Sponsored by
Ricoh

'THE POTTERS'

Formed: 1863 **Turned Professional:** 1885 **Ltd Co:** 1908
Previous Managers: 1875-82 Tom C Slaney 1882 Walter Cox 1882-90 Harry Lockett 1890-2 J Bradshaw 1892-5 A F Reeves 1985-7 J Rowley 1897-1908 A D Austerberry 1923 Jock Rutherford 1923-35 Tom Mather 1935-52 Bob McGrory 1952-60 Frank Taylor 1960-77 Tony Waddington 1977-8 George Eastham 1978 Alan A'court (Caretaker) 1978-81 Alan Durban 1981-3 Richie Barker
Honours: Division 2 Champions 1932-3, 1962-3 Division 3 (N) Champions 1926-7 Football League Cup Winners 1971-2
League Career: Founder Members of Football League 1888 Failed re-election 1890 Re-elected to Football League 1891 Relegated to Division 2 1906-7 Resigned from League 1908 Re-elected to Division 2 1919 Promoted to Division 1 1921-2 Relegated to Division 2 1922-3 Relegated to Division 3 (N) 1925-6 Promoted to Division 2 1926-7 Promoted to Division 1 1932-3 Relegated to Division 2 1952-3 Promoted to Division 1 1962-3 Relegated to Division 2 1976-7 Promoted to Division 1 1978-9
Colours: White shirts with thin red stripe and red sleeves, red shorts and stockings
Change Colours: White with thin blue stripe and blue sleeves, blue shorts and stockings.

CLUB RECORDS

Most Appearances for Club: Eric Skeels: Football League 495 + 11s + F.A. Cup 42 + 2s + League Cup 36 + 2s + UEFA Cup 1 + Texaco Cup 1 + 1s + Watney Cup 1 sub **Total 575 +17 subs**
Most Capped Player: Gordon Banks, 36, England
Record Goalscorer in a Match: Neville (Tim) Coleman, 7 v Lincoln C (8-0) (H), Div 2, 23.02.57 (Coleman played as an orthordox outside right in this match)
Record League Goalscorer in a season: Freddie Steele, 33 **All competitions:** Freddie Steele, 36 (League 33, F.A. Cup 3), 1936-7
Record League Goalscorer in a career: Freedie Steele, 142 **All competitions:** Freddie Steele, 161 (League 142, F.A. Cup 19)
Record Transfer Fee Received: £700,000 from Everton for Adrian Heath, Jan 1982
Record Transfer Fee Paid: £350,000 to Manchester United for Sammy McIlroy, Feb 1982
Best Performances: League: 4th Div 1 1935-6, 1946-7 **F.A. Cup:** Semi-Final 1899, 1971, 1972
League/Milk Cup: Winners 1971-2 **UEFA Cup:** First Round (2)
Most League Points: 63, Div 3 (N), 1926-7
Most League Goals: 92, Div 3 (N), 1926-7
Record League Victory: 10-3 v West Bromwich Albion, Div 1, 4 Feb 37
Record League Defeat: 0-10 v Preston North End, Div 1, 14 Sept 1889
European Competitions: UEFA Cup 1972-3, 1974-5

Club Statistician for the Directory: Wade Martin

Programme Editor & Publisher
Dudley Kernich

Price	Number of Pages
50p	20

Subscriptions
£27.50 for season's home matches in League plus one Milk Cup & one F.A. Cup (postage to U.K. and Scandinavia paid)

STOKE CITY

PLAYERS NAME Ht Wt Birthdate	Honours	Birthplace Transfers	Clubs	APPEARANCES League	Milk Cup	F.A.C.	E. Cups	GOALS League	Milk Cup	F.A.C.	E. Cups
GOALKEEPERS											
Mervyn Cawston	E. S. Div. 4. 81	Norwich	Norwich C. (A)	4							
6-2 13.4 4.2.57			Southend U. (L)	10							
			Newport Co. (L)	4							
			Gillingham	19	1	1					
		£8,500	Chicago Stings								
		£20,000	Southend U.	189	13	12					
		F	Stoke C.								
Peter Fox		Scunthorpe	Sheffield W. (A)	49		3					
5-10½ 12.4 5.7.57			Barnsley	1							
		£15,000	Stoke C.	181	11	8					
DEFENDERS											
George Berry	W.(5). FC. 80	W. Germany	Wolverhampton W. (A)	124	14	21		4		2	
6-0¾ 11.12 19.11.57		F	Stoke C.	35 + 4	2	2		5			
Steve Bould†		Stoke	Stoke C. (A)	50 + 4	4	1		2	1		
6-2½ 11.13 16.11.62			Torquay U. (L)	9		2					
Paul Dyson	E. U.21(4)	Birmingham	Coventry C. (A)	140	14	12		5			
6-2 13.7 27.12.59		£150,000	Stoke C.	38	5	1		2			
Chris Hemming		Newcastle-u-Lyme	Stoke C.								
5-9 11.3											
Neil Howells		Bishop Auckland	Stoke C. (A)								
5-11 12.4 8.1.66											
Brendan O'Callaghan	Ei.(7)	Bradford	Doncaster R.	184 + 3	15	10		65	10	2	
6-2½ 14.0 23.7.55		£40,000	Stoke C.	235 + 10	17	8		45	3		
Steve Parkin	E. Y. S	Mansfield	Stoke C. (A)	3							
5-6 10.7 7.11.65											
MIDFIELD											
Alan Hudson	E.(2). U.23(10).	London	Chelsea (A)	144 + 1				10			
5-10½ 11.6 21.6.51	ECWC.71		Stoke C.	105				9			
		£200,000	Arsenal	36							
		£120,000	Seattle Sounders								
			Chelsea								
		F	Stoke C.	16							
Robbie James	W.(27).	Swansea	Swansea C. (A)	386 + 8	21	19		99	6	5	
5-11 13.1 23.3.57	U.21(3)		Stoke C.	40	5	1		6	1		
Chris Maskery		Stoke	Stoke C. (A)	19 + 7	2 + 1	1 + 1					
5-7½ 10.8 25.9.64											
Sammy McIlroy*	NI.(75). U.23(1)	Belfast	Manchester U. (A)	320 + 22	25 +	35 +		57	6	6	
5-9½ 11.4 2.8.54	FAC.77. CS.78.			98 + 1	5	4		12			
	Div. 2. 75. S										
Neil Mountford		Stoke	Stoke C.								
5-8 10.10											
FORWARDS											
Mark Chamberlain	E.(7). U.21(4). S	Stoke	Port Vale (A)	90 + 6	4	10		17			
5-8½ 9.8 19.11.61		£35,000	Stoke C.	76 + 1	7	2		13			
Jon Chapman		Lincoln	Stoke C.								
6-2 12.0 26.10.65											
Phil Heath		Stoke	Stoke C. (A)	3 + 2				1			
5-9 11.5 24.11.64											
Ian Painter		Wombourne	Stoke C. (A)	52 + 4	1	3 + 1		12			
5-7 10.2 28.12.64											
Carl Saunders		Marston	Stoke C.	0 + 1							
5-8 10.12 26.11.64											

NON-CONTRACT PLAYER 1984-85

Tony Hughes

APPRENTICES

Carl Beeston, Darren Bishop, Aaron Callaghan, Ken O'Neill, Paul Reece, Stuart Roberts, Graham Shaw, David Sutton, Simon Ward, Terry Williams

STOKE CITY

DIVISION ONE 18TH **FA CUP** 3RD ROUND **MILK CUP** 4TH ROUND

MATCH	DATE	COMPETITION	VENUE	OPPONENTS	RESULT	HALF TIME	L'GUE POS'N	GOALSCORERS	ATTENDANCE
1	A 27	CL	A	Everton	L0-1	0-1			22,658
2	29	CL	H	WBA	W3-1	2-1		Painter 2, Maguire	16,156
3	S 3	CL	H	Manchester U	L0-1	0-0	14		23,704
4	6	CL	A	Birmingham C	L0-1	0-1			13,728
5	10	CL	A	Ipswich T	L0-5	0-3	20		16,315
6	17	CL	H	Watford	L0-4	0-1	20		12,691
7	24	CL	A	Leicester C	D2-2	2-2	20	Painter, Maguire	10,215
8	O 1	CL	H	West Ham U	W3-1	1-0	18	McAughtrie, Chamberlain M, Thomas	13,852
9	**5**	**MC 2**	**H**	**Peterborough U**	**D0-0**	**0-0**			**11,085**
10	15	CL	A	Sunderland	D2-2	1-1	19	James R 2	11,973
11	22	CL	A	Notts Co	D1-1	0-0	18	Bould	7,684
12	**26**	**MC 2**	**A**	**Peterborough U**	**W2-1**	**1-0**		**O'Callaghan, James**	**9,898**
13	29	CL	H	Coventry C	L1-3	1-2	19	Thomas	11,836
14	N 5	CL	H	Tottenham H	D1-1	1-1	19	Thomas	14,727
15	**8**	**MC 3**	**H**	**Huddersfield T**	**D0-0**	**0-0**			**14,175**
16	12	CL	A	Aston Villa	D1-1	0-1	18	Chamberlain M	19,272
17	19	CL	A	Liverpool	L0-1	0-0	18		26,529
18	**22**	**MC 3**	**A**	**Huddersfield T**	**W2-0**	**1-0**		**Bould, Maguire**	**14,191**
19	26	CL	H	Nottingham F	D1-1	1-1	19	Chamberlain M	11,655
20	**30**	**MC 4**	**H**	**Sheffield W**	**L0-1**	**0-0**			**18,653**
21	D 3	CL	A	Southampton	L1-3	1-2	21	James	15,301
22	10	CL	H	Luton T	L2-4	1-2	21	James 2 (1 pen)	10,329
23	17	CL	A	Wolverhampton W	D0-0	0-0	21		8,679
24	26	CL	H	Norwich C	W2-0	1-0	21	Maguire, James	12,049
25	31	CL	A	Manchester U	L0-1	0-0	21		40,164
26	J 2	CL	H	Leicester C	L0-1	0-1	21		13,728
27	**7**	**FAC 3**	**H**	**Everton**	**L0-2**	**0-0**			**16,462**
28	14	CL	H	Everton	D1-1	0-0	14	Heath P	7,935
29	17	CL	A	QPR	L0-6	0-3			9,320
30	21	CL	A	Watford	L0-2	0-0	21		14,076
31	28	CL	H	Arsenal	W1-0	0-0	21	Maguire (pen)	12,840
32	F 4	CL	A	West Ham U	L0-3	0-2	21		18,775
33	11	CL	H	Ipswich T	W1-0	0-0	20	Painter	10,315
34	18	CL	A	Coventry C	W3-2	1-1	20	Hampton, Chamberlain, O'Callaghan	9,752
35	25	CL	H	Notts Co	W1-0	1-0	20	Chamberlain	11,725
36	M 3	CL	A	Tottenham H	L0-1	0-1	20		18,271
37	10	CL	H	Aston Villa	W1-0	0-0	20	Painter	13,967
38	17	CL	H	Birmingham C	W2-1	1-0	19	Dyson, Bould	13,506
39	24	CL	A	WBA	L0-3	0-2	19		13,681
40	31	CL	H	Sunderland	W2-1	2-1	19	Painter, Dyson	11,047
41	A 7	CL	A	Arsenal	L1-3	0-0	19	Chamberlain	21,211
42	14	CL	H	Liverpool	W2-0	1-0	19	Painter, Russell	24,372
43	21	CL	A	Norwich C	D2-2	1-0	19	McIlroy, Chamberlain	16,084
44	23	CL	H	QPR	L1-2	1-1	20	Russell	13,735
45	28	CL	A	Nottingham F	D0-0	0-0	20		13,625
46	M 5	CL	H	Southampton	D1-1	0-0	20	Maguire	12,131
47	7	CL	A	Luton T	W1-0	1-0	20	Painter	9,807
48	12	CL	H	Wolverhampton W	W4-0	2-0	17	Maguire 4 (2 pens)	18,977

Av Home Att 13,870

Goal Scorers

League (44): Maguire 9 (3 pens), Painter 8, Chamberlain M 7, James 6 (1 pen), Thomas 3, Bould 2, Dyson 2, Russell 2, Hampton 1, Heath 1, McAughtrie 1, McIlroy 1, O'Callaghan 1

FA Cup (-): —

Milk Cup (4): Bould 1, James 1, Maguire 1, O'Callaghan 1

1983-84

Fox	Chamberlain N	Savage	James	Dyson	Bould	Griffiths	Painter	O'Callaghan	Thomas	Maguire	McIlroy	Berry	Chamberlain M	Hampton	Tueart	McAughtrie	Maskery	Heath	Parkin	Hudson	Hemmings	Russell **(L)**	REFEREE	
1	2	3	4	5	6	7*	8	9	10	11	12												G Tyson	1
1		3	4	5	2		7	9	10	11	8	6											M Peck	2
1		3	4	5	2		7	9	10	11	8	6	12										M Dimblebee	3
1	2	3	4	5	6		7	9	10*	12	8		11										C Downey	4
1	2		4	5			7	12	10	9	8*	6	11	3									K Salmon	5
1		3	4	5	2		7	9	10*	6	8		11		12								T Mills	6
1		12	4	5	2		7	9		10*	8		11	3		6							T Spencer	7
1			4	5			7	9	10		8	2	11	3		6							B Stevens	8
1			**4**	**5**			**7**	**9***	**10**	**12**	**8**	**2**	**11**	**3**		**6**							**R Banks**	**9**
1			4	5	2		7	9	10		8		11	3		6							D Richardson	10
1			4	5	2			9	10*		8		11	3	7	6	12						J Moules	11
1			**4**	**5**	**2**			**9**	**10†**		**8**		**11**	**3**	**7***	**6**	**12**						**A Ward**	**12**
1			4	5				9	10		8	2	11	3	7	6							D Scott	13
1			4	9	2			5	10	7	8		11	3		6							N Wilson	14
1			**4**	**9**	**2**			**5**	**10**	**7**	**8**		**11**	**3**		**6**							**D Hedges**	**15**
1			4*	9	2	10		5		7	8		11	3		6	12						M Scott	16
1		12	4*	9	2	10		5		7			11	3		6	8						A Challinor	17
1			**4**	**9**	**2**			**5**	**10**	**7**			**11**	**3**		**6**	**8**						**N Midgley**	**18**
1					2	12		5	10	7	4*	9	11	3		6	8						D Allison	19
1			**4**	**9**	**2**	**12**		**5**	**10**	**7**			**11***	**3**		**6**	**8**						**K Baker**	**20**
1			4	9	2			5	10				11	3		6	8	7					EJ Scales	21
1			4		2		9*		10	12	8	5	11	3		6	7						C Thomas	22
1			4		2		9	5	10		8		11	3		6	7						L Shapter	23
1			4	5	2		7	9		10	8		11	3		6							F Roberts	24
1			4	5	2		7	9		10	8		11	3†		6							J Key	25
1			4	5	2		7	9	10*	12	8		11	3		6							W Glover	26
1			**4**	**5**	**2**		**7**	**9**		**10**	**8***		**11**	**3**		**6**	**12**						**M Peck**	**27**
1			4	5	2		7			10	8		11			6	3	9					B Hill	28
1			4	5	2		7			10	8		11	12		6*	3	9					A Robinson	29
1			4	5	2		12	6*		9	8		11	3			10		7				D Axcell	30
1			4	5	2		7	6		9	8*		11				3	12		10			K Walmsley	31
1			4	5	2		7	6		9	8		11				3			10			R Milford	32
1			4	5	2		12	6		9	8		11*	3			7			10			J Worrall	33
1			4*	5	2		12	6		9	8		11	3			7			10			J Martin	34
1			4	5	2			6		9	8		11	3			7			10			K Barratt	35
1			4	5	2		12	6		9	8		11				7			10*	3		A Crickmore	36
1			4	5	2		10	6		12	8		11				7*				3	9	G Courtney	37
1			4	5	2		7	6			8		11	3						10		9	P Tyldesley	38
1				5			7	6		4	8		11	3			2			10		9	N Midgley	39
1			4	5	2		7	6		12	8		11	3						10		9*	R Guy	40
1			4	5	2		7*	6		12	8		11	3						10		9	I Borrett	41
1			4	5	2		7	6			8		11	3						10		9	E Read	42
1			4	5	2		7				8		11	3						10	6	9	A Buksh	43
1			4	5	2		7	6		12	8		11*	3						10		9	A Robinson	44
1			4	5	2		7	6		12	8		11*	3						10		9	R Lewis	45
1			4	5	2		7	6		12	8		11	3						10		9*	D Scott	46
1			4		2		7	6		10	8	5	11	3			12					9*	M James	47
1			4	5	2		7	6		9	8		11	3						10			C Thomas	48
42	3	5	40	38	38	3	30	37	16	24	39	8	39	31	2	17	16	3	1	16	3	11	League Appearances	
		+2S				+1S	+4S	+1S		+9S	+1S		+1S	+1S	+1S		+3S	+1S						
1			1	1	1		1	1		1	1		1	1		1	1S						FA Cup Appearances	
5			5	5	4	1S	1	5	5	3+1S	3	1	5	5	1	5	2+1S						Milk Cup Appearances	

VICTORIA GROUND

Official Address: Victoria Ground, Stoke-on-Trent. Telephone: Stoke-on-Trent (0782) 413511, (0782) 413961 (Ticket Office)

Telegraphic: Football, Stoke-on-Trent

Ground Capacity: 35,238

Record Attendance: 51,380 v. Arsenal, Div 1, 29 Mar 1937

Record Receipts: £43,000 v. Manchester C, Div 1, Sept 1981

Size of Playing Area: 116 × 75 yds

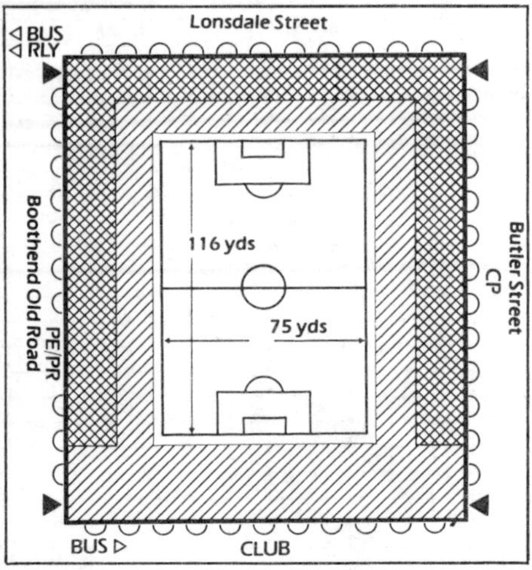

For key see page 12

Season Tickets: Main stands: £100 (£50 Juveniles/OAPs); Stoke-End: £80 (£40 Juveniles/OAPs); Ground: £50 (£26 Juveniles/OAPs)

Executive Box Season Tickets: Consult Secretary

Cost of Stand Tickets: £5.00 (£2.50 Juveniles/OAPs), £4.00 (advance price for Stoke-End stand); Ground: £2.50 (£1.30 Juveniles/OAPs)

Match and Ticket Information: Bookable two weeks before each match from ticket office

Car Parking: Surrounding streets

How to get to the ground

From North, West and South: Use Motorway M6 until junction 15, leave Motorway and follow signs Stoke A5006 then join A500. In 0.8m branch left and shortly at roundabout take 2nd exit into Campbell Road for Stoke City F.C.
From East: Use A50 into Stoke town centre and at crossroads turn left into Lonsdale Street for Campbell Road for Stoke City F.C.

SUNDERLAND — Division 1

Chairman
T Cowie, OBE

Vice-Chairman
J M Ditchburn

Directors
E M Evans
B Batey, FRICS
R S Murray, FCCA

General Manager/Secretary
G Davidson

Manager
Len Ashurst

Assistant Manager/Club Coach
Frank Burrows

Youth Development Officer
George Herd

Promotions Manager
C O'Donnell (0783 41280)

Physiotherapist
Stephen Mason, MCSP, SRP

What was in store for the supporters at the start of 1983/84 after Sunderland had won a trophy in the Isle of Man in a pre-season competition?

Had Alan Durban assembled a squad of players to bring the results needed for success at Roker Park after such a long wait in the League and Cup?

Alas, early results only told us that we were destined for a tough time; goals were scarce, without goals no points and that situation was not attracting the supporters. Yes, the early months of the season were anything but good.

The sun did begin to shine after we beat Liverpool at Anfield by a penalty goal and went eight games with only two defeats mostly by concentrating on defence. In fact we played at Southampton the ninety minutes with one forward and miraculously we won a point. Then things started to go against us after a shocking defeat in the FA Cup by Birmingham and many players could not lift themselves after that; they seemed to lose heart as did many supporters, so the attendances dropped to an average of 13,000.

But the shock was to come on March 2nd 1984 when Alan Durban was sacked; the reason given by the club Chairman 'Failing to get success'. Here they were sacking the manager when the team had only about twelve league games left and occupied a dangerous position in the bottom half of the table.

Three days after the sacking of Alan Durban came the news that former Sunderland player Len Ashurst would be the new manager, so all he could do was to wave a magic wand over the players on the books, as there was no money to buy others.

Anyway Len must have talked well to the players as he extracted something from them that Durban could not manage, but it was not until we won the last game of the season against Leicester that we could breathe again, remaining in Division 1.

Yet where do we find the answer to their dismal season? Blame the directors? Blame the Manager? The players? Are they too well paid, or are the supporters greedy for success? Perhaps we must go along with it all. Anyway maybe Len Ashurst can solve all in coming seasons.

So welcome in 1984/85 season.

Billy Simmons
The League Directory's Statistician for the Club

Back Row: Lemon, Walker, Berry, Duncan, Vennison, Proctor, O'Hagan. **Middle Row:** Hughes (Coach), Burgess, Herd (Coach), Pickering, Corner, Prudhoe, Turner, Chilton, West, Chisholm, Burrows (Asst Manager). **Front Row Sitting:** Gayle, Elliott, Atkins, Ashurst (Manager), Wylde, Bennett.

'THE ROKERITES'

Formed: 1879 **Turned Professional:** 1886 **Ltd Co:** 1906
Previous Names: Sunderland & District Teachers A.F.C.
Previous Managers: 1889-96 Tom Watson 1896-99 Robert Campbell 1905 28 Bob Kyle 1928-39 John Cochrane 1939-57 Billy Murray 1957-64 Alan Brown 1964-5 George Hardwick 1965-8 Ian McColl 1968-72 Alan Brown 1972-6 Bob Stokoe-Ian McFarlane (cartaker manager) 1976-78 Jim Adamson-D Merrington (caretaker manager) 1978-9 Billy Elliott 1979-81 Ken Knighton 1981 Mick Docherty 1981-4 Alan Durban
Honours: Division One Champions 1891-2, 1892-3, 1894-5, 1901-2, 1912-3, 1935-6 Division Two Champions 1975-6 F.A. Cup Winners 1937, 1973
League Career: Elected to Division 1 1890 Relegated to Division 2 1957-8 Promoted to Division 1 1963-4 Relegated to Division 2 1969-70 Promoted to Division 1 1975-6 Relegated to Division 2 1976-7 Promoted to Division 1 1979-80
Colours: Red and white striped shirts, black shorts, red stockings with white tops
Change Colours: Blue shirts with red trim, red shorts with white trim, blue stockings with red tops

CLUB RECORDS

Most Appearances for Club: Jim Montgomery: Football League 537 + F.A. Cup 39 **Total 576**
Most Capped Player: Billy Bingham, M Harvey (Northern Ireland), Charlie Hurley (Eire) 33 **For England:** Dave Watson 14
Record Goalscorer in a Match: C Buchan, N Sharkey 5
Record League Goalscorer in a season: Dave Halliday, 43 **In All Competitions:** Dave Halliday 43 (all League) 1928-9
Record League Goalscorer in a career: Charles Buchan, 209 **In All Competitions:** Charles Buchan 223 (League 209 + F.A. Cup 14) 1911-25
Record Transfer Fee Received: £275,000 from Manchester City for Dennis Tueart, Mar 1974
Record Transfer Fee Paid: £320,000 to San Lorenzo for Claudio Maranoni, Dec 1979
Best Performances: League: Champions (6) **F.A. Cup:** Winners (2) **League/Milk Cup:** Semi-Final 1963
Most League Points: 61 in Div 2, 1963-4 **Most League Goals:** 109, Div 1, 1935-6
Record League Victory: 9-1 v Newcastle U (A), Div 1, 5 Dec 1908 (half-time 1-1) — Newcastle went on to win the Championship
Record League Defeat: 0-8 v West Ham United, Div 1, 19 Oct 1968 v Watford, Div 1, 25 Sept 1982
European Competitions Entered: European Cup Winners Cup 1973-4

Club Statistician for the Directory: Billy Simmons

Programme Editor
Geoff Triggs

Price	**Number of Pages**
40p	24

Subscriptions
Contact commercial department

SUNDERLAND

PLAYERS NAME Ht Wt Birthdate	Honours	Birthplace Transfers	Clubs	APPEARANCES League	Milk Cup	F.A.C.	E. Cups	GOALS League	Milk Cup	F.A.C.	E. Cups
GOALKEEPERS											
Cameron Duncan		Shotts	Sunderland (N-C)								
6-0 11.8											
Mark Prudhoe		Durham	Sunderland (A)	7							
6-1 11.8			Hartlepool U. (L)	3							
Chris Turner	E. Y	Sheffield	Sheffield W. (A)	91	11	13					
5-10½ 11.11 15.9.58			Lincoln C. (L)	5		1					
		£80,000	Sunderland	153	11	6					
DEFENDERS											
Ian Atkins*	Div. 3, 79	Birmingham	Shrewsbury T. (A)	273+5	13	23		58	3	3	
5-10 11.0 16.1.57		Player Exchange	Sunderland	76+1	7	4		6			
Gary Bennett		Manchester	Manchester C.								
6-1 12.1 4.12.61		F	Cardiff C.	85+2	4	3		11			
Gordon Chisholm		Glasgow	Sunderland (A)	160+4	12+	8		9	2	2	
6-0¾ 12.0 8.4.60											
Shaun Elliott	E. B(3)	Hebden Bridge	Sunderland (A)	253+4	20	14		10			
6-0 11.6 26.1.58											
Nick Pickering	E.(1), U.21(8), Y	Newcastle	Sunderland (A)	118	10	6		11			
6-1 11.11 4.8.63											
Barry Venison	E. U.21(2), Y	Consett	Sunderland (A)	94+4	9	3+1		1			
5-10½ 11.12 16.8.64											
MIDFIELD											
Paul Atkinson	E. Y	Chester-Le-	Sunderland (A)	7+1				1			
5-9 10.10 19.1.66		Street									
Steve Berry		Gosport	Portsmouth (A)	26+2	2+1			2	1		
5-7 10.6 4.4.63			Sunderland								
David Corner		Sunderland	Sunderland (A)								
6-1¾ 12.13 15.5.66											
Paul O'Hagan	E. Y	Wallsend	Sunderland (A)								
6-0 11.10 25.9.65											
Mark Proctor	E. U.21(4), Y	Middlesbrough	Middlesbrough (A)	107+2	6	10		12	1	1	
5-10 11.9 30.1.61		£115,000	Nottingham F.	60+4	10	2		5	3	1	
		£115,000	Sunderland	45+1	4	2		2	1		
FORWARDS											
John Cooke	E. Y	Salford	Sunderland (A)	38+11	2	3+1		4	1		
5-8 11.0 25.4.62											
Howard Gayle	E. U.21( )	Liverpool	Liverpool	3+1							
5-10½ 10.9 18.5.58			Fulham (L)	14							
			Newcastle U. (L)	8							
		£50,000	Birmingham C.	45+1	5	2		9	2	2	
		£75,000	Sunderland								
David Hodgson	E. U.21(7)	Gateshead	Middlesbrough	116+9	6	9		16		4	
5-10 11.12 1.11.60	Div. 1, 83	£450,000	Liverpool	21+7	4+1	3	3+4	4	2	1	2
		£125,000	Sunderland								
Paul Lemon		Middlesbrough	Sunderland (A)								
5-10¾ 11.6½ 3.6.66											
Clive Walker	E. S	Oxford	Chelsea	168+30	9+1	14+		60	2	3	
5-8½ 11.4 26.5.57		£75,000	Sunderland								
Colin West		Wallsend	Sunderland (A)	68+11	8	2+1		10	2	2	
6-1½ 13.2 13.11.62											
Roger Wylde		Sheffield	Sheffield W. (A)	157+12	10	15		54	8	4	
6-1½ 12.0 6.3.54		£80,000	Oldham A.	109+4	8	4		51			

MONTHLY CONTRACT PLAYERS 1984-85: Stephen A. Berry, Robert Burgess, Tony Chilton

NON-CONTRACT PLAYERS 1984-85: Allan Hope, Bryan Robson (7 + 3 Lg. (3 g.), 0 + 1 (Milk Cup))

APPRENTICES

Gordon Armstrong, Paul Breen, John Cornforth, Tom Garside, Gerard Henry, Ian Howell, John Lewis, Mark Liddle, John McGonigal, John Moore, Mark Outterside, Dale White, David Woodcock

Player of the Year 1983-84: Paul Bracewell (now Everton)

SUNDERLAND

DIVISION ONE 13TH **FA CUP** 4TH ROUND **MILK CUP** 3RD ROUND

MATCH	DATE	COMPE-TITION	VENUE	OPPONENTS	RESULT	HALF TIME	L'GUE POS'N	GOALSCORERS	ATTEN-DANCE
1	A 27	CL	H	Norwich C	D1-1	0-0		West	17,057
2	29	CL	A	Aston Villa	L0-1	0-0			20,390
3	S 3	CL	A	Luton T	L1-4	0-0	19	West	10,846
4	7	CL	H	Wolverhampton W	W3-2	1-0		Rowell (pen), Daniel (og), Atkinson	12,961
5	10	CL	H	Southampton	L0-2	0-1	19		12,716
6	17	CL	A	QPR	L0-3	0-1	19		12,929
7	24	CL	H	Coventry C	W1-0	0-0	17	West	11,612
8	O 1	CL	A	Liverpool	W1-0	1-0	15	Rowell (pen)	29,534
9	**4**	**MC 2**	**A**	**Cambridge U**	**W3-2**	**1-0**		**Rowell 2, West**	**4,835**
10	15	CL	H	Stoke C	D2-2	1-1	16	Thomas (og), Rowell	11,973
11	22	CL	H	Manchester U	L0-1	0-1	17		26,826
12	**26**	**MC 2**	**H**	**Cambridge U**	**W4-3**	**3-2**		**Rowell 2 (1 pen), Proctor, Cooke**	**9,059**
13	29	CL	A	Nottingham F	D1-1	0-1	17	Rowell	13,968
14	N 5	CL	A	Arsenal	W2-1	1-0	17	West, Atkins	26,064
15	**9**	**MC 3**	**A**	**Norwich C**	**D0-0**	**0-0**			**12,400**
16	12	CL	H	Watford	W3-0	1-0	15	West, Proctor, Chisholm	15,407
17	19	CL	H	West Ham U	L0-1	0-0	16		19,921
18	**22**	**MC 3R**	**H**	**Norwich C**	**L1-2**	**0-1**		**West**	**14,149**
19	26	CL	A	Birmingham C	W1-0	0-0	16	Bracewell	11,948
20	D 3	CL	H	Ipswich T	D1-1	1-1	14	Rowell	15,555
21	10	CL	A	Notts Co	L1-6	1-3	15	Bracewell	7,123
22	18	CL	H	Leicester C	D1-1	0-0		Rowell	16,993
23	26	CL	A	Everton	D0-0	0-0	14		18,683
24	27	CL	H	WBA	W3-0	2-0	13	Robson, Bracewell 2	17,986
25	31	CL	H	Luton T	W2-0	0-0	12	Chisholm, Pickering	19,482
26	J 2	CL	A	Coventry C	L1-2	0-2	13	West	13,249
27	**7**	**FAC 3**	**A**	**Bolton W**	**W3-0**	**1-0**		**West, Chapman, Rowell**	**14,018**
28	14	CL	A	Norwich C	L0-3	0-3	14		13,204
29	**28**	**FAC 4**	**H**	**Birmingham C**	**L1-2**	**1-0**		**West**	**21,226**
30	F 4	CL	H	Liverpool	D0-0	0-0	16		25,646
31	8	CL	A	Tottenham H	L0-3	0-2			19,327
32	11	CL	A	Southampton	D1-1	0-1	16	Chapman	16,968
33	18	CL	H	Nottingham F	D1-1	0-0	15	Chisholm	15,958
34	25	CL	A	Manchester U	L1-2	1-1	16	Chapman	40,615
35	M 3	CL	H	Arsenal	D2-2	1-1	17	Proctor, Rowell (pen)	15,370
36	7	CL	H	QPR	W1-0	0-0		Fenwick (og)	13,538
37	17	CL	A	Wolverhampton W	D0-0	0-0	17		9,111
38	20	CL	A	Watford	L1-2	0-0		Rowell	16,231
39	24	CL	H	Aston Villa	L0-1	0-1	18		11,908
40	31	CL	A	Stoke C	L1-2	1-2	18	Atkins	11,047
41	A 7	CL	H	Tottenham H	D1-1	1-1	18	West	15,433
42	14	CL	A	West Ham U	W1-0	0-0	18	Chisholm	16,558
43	21	CL	H	Everton	W2-1	1-1	16	Robson, West	15,876
44	23	CL	A	WBA	L1-3	1-2	18	West	11,252
45	28	CL	H	Birmingham C	W2-1	1-0	15	James 2 (2 pens)	13,061
46	M 5	CL	A	Ipswich T	L0-1	0-1	15		17,657
47	7	CL	H	Notts Co	D0-0	0-0	16		14,517
48	12	CL	A	Leicester C	W2-0	2-0	13	Chapman, Robson	12,627

Av Home Att 16,608

Goal Scorers

League (42): West 9, Rowell 8 (3 pens), Bracewell 4, Chisholm 4, Chapman 3, Robson 3, Atkins 2, James 2 (2 pens), Proctor 2, Atkinson 1, Pickering 1, opponents 3

FA Cup (4): West 2, Chapman 1, Rowell 1

Milk Cup (8): Rowell 4 (1 pen), West 2, Cooke 1, Proctor 1

1983-84

Turner	Venison	Munro	Atkins	Chisholm	Proctor	Bracewell	Rowell	West	Pickering	Atkinson	Cooke	Elliott	James	Hindmarch	Walker	Robson	Chapman	Murray (L)	REFEREE	
	2	3	4	5	6	7	8	9	10	11									A Banks	1
	2	3	4	5	10	6*	8	9	7	11	12								J Deakin	2
	2	3	4	5	10		8	9	7	11		6							A Lewis	3
	2	3	4	5	10		8	9	6	11			7*	12					H Peck	4
	2	3	4	5	6	7	8	9	10	11*			12						K Walmsley	5
	2		4	5	6	7	8	9	10	11				3					LM Robinson	6
	2		4	5	6	7	8	9	10		12		11*	3					C Steel	7
	2		4	5	6	7	8	9	10			3	11						M Heath	8
	2		**4**	**5**	**6**	**7**	**8**	**9**	**10**			**3**	**11**						**C Downey**	**9**
	2		4	5	6	7	8	9	10			3	11						D Richardson	10
	2*		4	5	6	7	8	9	10		12	3	11						D Hutchinson	11
	2			**4**	**5**	**7**	**8**	**9**	**10**		**6**	**3**	**11**						**A Challinor**	**12**
	2			4	10	7	8	9	3		11	6		5					N Ashley	13
	2		4	5	10	7	8	9	3			6	11						D Hedges	14
	2		**4**	**5**	**10**	**7**	**8**	**9**	**3**			**6**	**11**						**D Reeves**	**15**
	2		4	5	10	7	8	9	3				11*	6	12				N Glover	16
	2		4	5	10	7	8	9	3				11	6					T Jones	17
	2		**4**	**5**	**10**	**7**	**8**	**9**	**3**				**11**	**6***		**12**			**N Wilson**	**18**
	2		4	5	8	7	10	11	3			6	9						LF Burden	19
	2		4	5	10	7	8	9	3			6	11						K Hackett	20
	2		4	5	10	7	8	9	3	12		6	11*						P Tyldesley	21
	2		4	5	10	7	8	9	3			6	11						T Fitzharris	22
	2		4	5†	10	7	8	9	3*	11		6	12						K Barratt	23
	2		4	5	10	7		9	3			6	11			8			J Key	24
	2		4	5	10	7		9	3			6	11*			12	8		A Robertson	25
		2	4	5	10*	7	11	9	3			6				12	8		E Scales	26
		2	**4**	**5**	**10**	**7**	**8**	**9**	**3**			**6**					**11**		**D Hutchinson**	**27**
	2		4		10	7	8	9	3			6		5			11		D Letts	28
	2		**4***	**5**	**10**	**7**	**8**	**12**	**3**			**6**	**11**				**9**		**D Richardson**	**29**
	2		4	5	10	7	8	9	3			6	11						J Hough	30
	2		4		10	7	8	9	3			6	11				5		J Bray	31
	2		4		10	7	8	9	3			6	11				5		A Buksh	32
	2		4	5	10	7	8		3			6	11				9		I Hendrick	33
	2		4	5	9	7	8	12	3			6	11*				10		H Taylor	34
	2	7	4	5	10		12	8*	3			6	11				9		R Dilkes	35
	2	7	4	5	10		8*	12	3			6	11				9		M Scott	36
	2		4	5	10	7	8		3			6	11				9		J Ashworth	37
	2	6*	4	5	10	7	8		3				11			12	9		K Cooper	38
	2		4	5	10	7	8*		3			6	11			12	9		K Walmsley	39
	2		4	5	10	7	12	8	3			6	11				9*		R Guy	40
	2			5	10	7	8	9	3			6	11			12		4*	G Worrall	41
	2		4	5		7		9	3			6	11	10		8			T Bune	42
	2		4		10	7		9	3			6	11	5		8			M Peck	43
	2		4	5*	8	7	12	9	3			6	11	10					T Jones	44
	2		4		10	7		9	3			6	11	5†		8			D Scott	45
	2		4	10*	12	7		9	3			6	11	5		8			A Ward	46
	2		4		10	7		9	3			6	11	5		8*	12		T Mills	47
	2		4	5	10	7		9	3			6				8	11		H King	48
42	41	9	40	36	40	38	31	36	**42**	7	1	33	32	12	0	7	14	1	League Appearances	
					+1S		+3S	+2S		+1S	+3S		+2S	+1S	+1S	+5S	+1S			
2	1	1	2	2	2	2	2	1+1S	2			2	1				2		FA Cup Appearances	
	4		3	4	4	4	4	4	4		1	3	4	1		1S			Milk Cup Appearances	

ROKER PARK

Official Address: Roker Park Ground, Sunderland. Telephone: Sunderland (0783) 40332

Ground Capacity: 37,683

Record Attendance: 75,118 v. Derby Co, FA Cup Round 6 replay, 8 Mar 1933 68,004 v. Newcastle U, Div 1, 4 Mar 1950.

Record Receipts: £63,211 v. Southampton, Div 1, 23 Aug 1980

Size of Playing Area: 113 × 74 yds

Season Tickets: Stand: £99 (centre), £86 (elsewhere); Ground: £45 (Adult), £37 (Juveniles/OAPs)

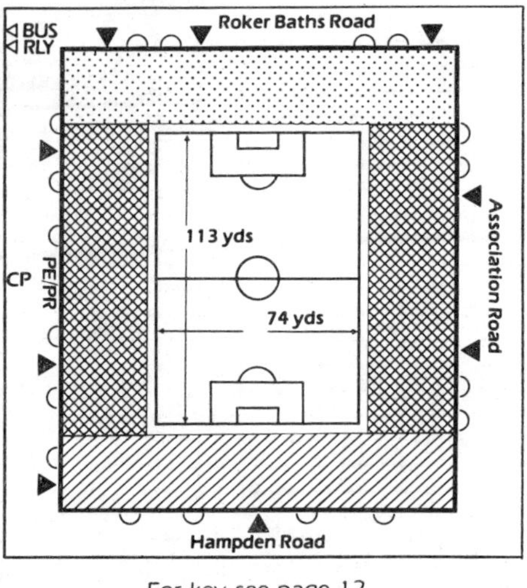

For key see page 12

Executive Box Season Tickets: None available (£3,700 for 8 seats when available including VAT)

Cost of Stand Tickets: £4.50 (increased prices occasionally charged for special games): Ground: £2.40 & £2.70 (Paddocks) (£1.50 Juveniles/OAPs)

Match and Ticket Information: Bookable ten days prior to a match

Car Parking: Parking for 1,500 cars 200 yards from ground

How to get to the ground

From North: Use A184 and A19 into Sunderland and at roundabout take 1st exit into Roker Avenue. In 0.2m turn left into Fulwell Road then turn right one-way and then left into Roker Baths Road for Sunderland F.C.
From South: Use A1 and A690 into Sunderland then follow signs Gateshead A1018 and cross Wearmouth Bridge. Then at roundabout take 4th exit into Roker Avenue. In 0.2m turn left into Fulwell Road then turn right one-way and then left into Roker Baths Road for Sunderland F.C.
From West: Use A1231 into Sunderland then at roundabout take 2nd exit shortly turn right into Sunderland Road for Southwick Road then at roundabout take 2nd exit into Roker Avenue. In 0.2 turn left into Fulwell Road then turn right one-way and then left into Roker Baths Road for Sunderland F.C.

SWANSEA CITY — Division 3

Joint Presidents
P E Holden
I C Pursey, MBE
E P Walters

Chairman
R G Jones

Vice-Chairman
T J Phillips, FCIOB

Directors
T J Phillips, FCIOB
P L W Owen, TD, QC, MA(Oxon)
D W A Rees, M Inst TT
P K Howard, MPS
H A Hyde, F Inst D
D V Savage
M T G Nurse
W C Floyd, JP
D J Sharpe

Chief Executive
M Struel

General Executive
David Morris

Manager
Colin Appleton

Club Coaches
Les Chappell
Colin Meldrum

Player Coach
Wyndham Evans

Commercial Manager
G Ford (0792 42182)

Even the most pessimistic home supporters, having watched the opening game of the season against Sheffield Wednesday, would have been hard-put to forecast the final positions of the two clubs. A hard fought game resulted in a win for Wednesday by the only goal of the match.

Nine months later, as Sheffield prepared for a term in Division One, the Vetch club licked its wounds and contemplated life in the Third. The irony of that situation was not lost on the club's supporters, for it was as recently as April 1979 that the Swans left that division en route for the First. En route, that is, for the fastest rise from the Fourth to the First in English League history. Now, for the second season in succession the club was to be relegated.

1983-84 was a season in which the club had three different managers and two chairmen. John Toshack, folk hero of the meteoric rise, and Malcolm Struel, his Chairman throughout that period, both resigned. Doug Livermore took over as manager for just five weeks, then Toshack came back for a further period, before new chairman, Doug Sharpe, wielded the axe. When 'Tosh' left for the second time, Les Chappell became caretaker manager. Despite his brave efforts, given his threadbare resources, he could not save the club from relegation.

The club's problems began long before Chappell became manager. Because of its precarious financial position Swansea City was forced to dispose of the core of its first team squad. Between July 1983 and March 1984 seven experienced internationals left the club. And, in addition to that, Colin Irwin, the club's record buy, and goalkeeper Jimmy Rimmer each played only a handful of games. Denuded of players like them, Alan Curtis, Leighton and Robbie James, Jeremy Charles and Bob Latchford, the club was forced to blood its youngsters; many too quickly. Then, whilst the side struggled and home crowds dwindled the financial position became exacerbated.

A few days after the end of the season Colin Appleton accepted the post of manager. But much needed to be done before the new term starts. To rekindle the flame of Vetch Field success would need to blend the youthful promise of the club's youngsters with mature experience. The job will not be a sinecure.

David Farmer, The League Directory's Statistician for the Club

Back Row L to R: Colin Meldrum (Coach), Chris Marustik, Wyndham Evans, Gary Richards, Roger Mullen, Mike Hughes, Jimmy Rimmer, Chris Sander, Pat McQuillan, Darren Gale, David Hough, Dudley Lewis, Les Chappell (Coach). **Front Row:** Anthony Cottey, Dean Saunders, Neil Robinson, Colin Pascoe, Mark Hughes, Colin Appleton (Manager), Nigel Stevenson, Jimmy Loveridge, Steve Mardenborough, Phil Williams.

'THE SWANS'

Formed: 1900 **Turned Professional:** 1912 **Ltd Co:** 1912
Previous Name: Swansea Town until Feb 1970
Previous Managers: 1912-4 Walter Whittaker 1914-5 William Bartlett 1919-26 Joe Bradshaw 1927-31 James Thompson 1934-9 Neil Harris 1939-47 Haydn Green 1947-55 Billy McCandless 1955-8 Ron Burgess 1958-65 Trevor Morris 1965-6 Glyn Davies 1967-9 Billy Lucas 1969-72 Roy Bentley 1972-5 Harry Gregg 1975-8 Harry Griffiths 1978-84 John Toshack
In addition B Watts-Jones, Joe Sykes, Walter Robins, Doug Livermore and Les Chappell all acted in a "caretaker" capacity for short periods
Honours: Champions Division 3(S) 1924-5, 1948-9 Welsh Cup Winners (8)
League Career: Original Members of Division 3 1920 Promotion to Division 2 1924-5
Relegated to Division 3(S) 1946-7 Promoted to Division 2 1948-9
Relegated to Division 3 1964-5 Relegated to Division 4 1966-7
Promoted to Division 3 1969-70 Relegated to Division 4 1972-3
Promoted to Division 3 1977-8 Promoted to Division 2 1978-9
Promoted to Division 1 1980-1 Relegated to Division 2 1982-3
Relegated to Division 3 1983-4
Colours: All white with black trim
Change Colours: Red shirts, black shorts and stockings

CLUB RECORDS

Most Appearances for Club: 'Wify' Milne: Football League 587 + F.A. Cup 44 + Welsh Cup 28 **Total 659**
Most Capped Player: Ivor Allchurch, 48, Wales **For England:** None
Record Goalscorer in a Match: Jack Fowler, 5 v Charlton Athletic, (6-1) Div 3, 27.09.24
Record League Goalscorer in a season: Cyril Pearce, 35, 1931-2 **In All Competitions:** Cyril Pearce 39 (League 35, Welsh Cup 4), 1931-2; Jack Fowler, 36 (League 28, F.A. Cup 8) 1924-5
Record League Goalscorer in a career: Ivor Allchurch, 166 **In All Competitions:** Ivor Allchurch, 189 (League 166, FA Cup 9, League Cup 4, Welsh Cup 10)
Record Transfer Fee Received: £370,000 from Leeds United for Alan Curtis, May 1979
Record Transfer Fee Paid: £340,000 to Liverpool for Colin Irwin, Aug 1981
Best Performances: League: 6th Div 1 1981-2 **F.A. Cup:** Semi-Finals 1926, 1964 **League/Milk Cup:** 4th Round 1964-5, 1976-7 **European Cup Winners Cup:** 2nd Round **Welsh Cup:** Winners (8)
Most League Points: 69 in Div 1, 1981-2 **Most League Goals:** 92, Div 4, 1976-7
Record League Victory: 8-0 v Hartlepool United, Div 4, 1 Apr 1978
Record League Defeat: 1-8 v Fulham, Div 2, 22 Jan 1938
European competitions entered: European Cup Winners Cup 1961-2, 1966-7, 1981-2, 1982-3
Club Statistician for the Directory: David Farmer

Programme Editor
Geoff Ford

Price

Number of Pages
24

Subscriptions
Please contact club

SWANSEA CITY

PLAYERS NAME Ht Wt Birthdate	Honours	Birthplace Transfers	Clubs	APPEARANCES League	Milk Cup	F.A.C.	A.M.C.	GOALS League	Milk Cup	F.A.C.	A.M.C.
GOALKEEPERS											
Jimmy Rimmer	E.(1), Div. 1, 81	Southport	Manchester U. (A)	34	3	6					
5-11 11.12 10.2.48	EC. 82		Swansea C. (L)	17							
		£40,000	Arsenal	124	10	12					
		£70,000	Aston Villa	229	23	12	13				
		£35,000	Swansea C.	14	2		2				
Mike Hughes†	W. Y	Swansea	Swansea C. (A)	21		2					
5-10½ 11.3 19.8.64											
Chris Sander	W. Y	Swansea	Swansea C. (A)	20							
5-11 11.4 11.11.62											
DEFENDERS											
Wyndham Evans (N-C)		Llanelli	Stoke C. (N-C)								
5-9½ 13.0 19.3.51			Swansea C.	366+5	18	11		19	1		
Dzemal Habziabdic	Yug.	Yugoslavia	Velez Mostar								
5-8¾ 10.11 25.7.53		£160,000	Swansea C.	87+2	4	1		2			
Mark Hughes	W. Y	Port Talbot	Bristol R.	64+1	9+1	3			3		
6-1 13.8 3.2.62			Torquay U. (L)	9		3		1	1		
Dudley Lewis	W. U.21(3)	Swansea	Swansea C. (A)	73	3	2	2	7			
5-10¾ 10.9 17.11.62											
Pat McQuillan		Belfast	Pembroke Boro								
5-11 11.0 27.6.61			Swansea C.	19		1					
Chris Marustik	W.(6), U.21(7)	Swansea	Swansea C. (A)	94+8	7	8	2	6			
5-8¾ 11.5 10.8.61	Y, S										
Roger Mullen	W. Y	Tonyrefail	Swansea C. (A)	+1							
5-10½ 11.12 29.3.66											
Gary Richards	W. Y	Swansea	Swansea C. (A)	48+2	2	2		1			
5-8½ 11.2 2.8.63											
Neil Robinson		Liverpool	Everton (A)	13+3	3	1		1			
5-8 10.6 20.4.57		£70,000	Swansea C.	109+9	5	2	2	7			
Nigel Stevenson*	W.(4), U.21(2)	Swansea	Swansea C. (A)	189+9	9	8	2	14			
6-2 12.0 2.11.58											
MIDFIELD											
Tony Cottey		Swansea	Swansea C. (A)	+1							
5-4 9.0 2.6.66											
David Hough	W. Y	Crewe		1+1							
5-10 11.2 20.2.66											
Ante Rajkovic	Yug.	Yugoslavia	Sarajevo								
5-11¾ 12.13 17.8.52		£100,000	Swansea C.	78	4	1		2			
FORWARDS											
Darren Gale	W. U.21(1)	Port Talbot	Swansea C. (A)	26+10	2	2	+2	6	1	1	
5-10½ 12.13 25.10.63											
John Loveridge	W. U.21(3), Y	Swansea	Swansea C. (A)	34+5	2+1	1		3	1		
5-8¾ 11.2 19.10.62											
Steve Mardenborough		Selly Oak	Coventry C.								
5-8 11.9 11.9.64			Wolverhampton W.	17		+1		2			
			Cambridge U. (L)								
			Swansea C.								
Colin Pascoe	W.(2), U.21(4)	Aberavon	Swansea C. (A)	33+6	2	1		3			
5-9½ 10.0 9.4.65	Y										
Dean Saunders		Swansea	Swansea C. (A)	14+5	+1			3			
5-8½ 10.0 21.6.64											

APPRENTICE

Phil Williams (1 app)

SWANSEA CITY

DIVISION TWO 21ST **FA CUP** 3RD ROUND **MILK CUP** 2ND ROUND

MATCH	DATE	COMPE-TITION	VENUE	OPPONENTS	RESULT	HALF TIME	L'GUE POS'N	GOALSCORERS	ATTEN-DANCE
1	**A24**	**ECWC1**	**H**	**Magdeburg**	**D1-1**	**0-0**		**Walsh**	**6,475**
2	27	CL	H	Sheffield W	L0-1	0-1			10,900
3	**31**	**ECWC1**	**A**	**Magdeburg**	**L0-1**	**0-1**			**25,000**
4	S 3	CL	A	Derby Co	L1-2	0-1	20	Latchford	9,711
5	6	CL	H	Oldham Ath	D0-0	0-0			7,244
6	10	CL	H	Brighton & HA	L1-3	0-2	21	Lake	7,643
7	17	CL	A	Huddersfield T	L0-1	0-1	22		10,116
8	24	CL	H	Cambridge U	W2-1	1-0	21	Curtis, Latchford	7,197
9	O 1	CL	A	Fulham	L0-5	0-1	22		7,253
10	**4**	**MC 2**	**H**	**Colchester U**	**D1-1**	**1-1**		**Gale**	**3,758**
11	8	CL	A	Manchester C	L1-2	1-1	22	Latchford	23,571
12	16	CL	H	Newcastle U	L1-2	0-1		Marustik	9,807
13	22	CL	A	Charlton Ath	D2-2	0-0	22	Stevenson, Loveridge	5,737
14	**25**	**MC 2**	**A**	**Colchester U**	**L0-1**	**0-1**			**5,204**
15	29	CL	H	Blackburn R	L0-1	0-0	22		10,588
16	N 5	CL	H	Carlisle U	D0-0	0-0	22		6,938
17	12	CL	A	Barnsley	L2-3	0-1	22	Lake, Gale	8,161
18	19	CL	H	Grimsby T	L0-1	0-1	22		6,178
19	22	CL	H	Chelsea	L1-3	1-3		Pascoe	7,848
20	26	CL	A	Middlesbrough	L0-1	0-1	22		6,804
21	D 3	CL	H	Crystal Palace	W1-0	1-0	22	Gale	6,304
22	6	CL	A	Chelsea	L1-6	0-3		Walsh	12,389
23	17	CL	H	Portsmouth	L1-2	1-0		Maddy	6,404
24	26	CL	A	Cardiff C	L2-3	1-2		Stanley (pen), Toshack	14,580
25	27	CL	H	Shrewsbury T	L0-2	0-0			7,706
26	31	CL	H	Derby Co	W2-0	0-0		Stevenson 2	6,578
27	J 2	CL	A	Cambridge U	D1-1	1-0		Richards	2,500
28	**7**	**FAC 3**	**A**	**Brighton & HA**	**L0-2**	**0-0**			**11,330**
29	14	CL	A	Sheffield W	L1-6	0-3		Marustik	13,787
30	18	CL	H	Huddersfield T	D2-2	1-1		Walsh 2	4,944
31	F 5	CL	H	Fulham	L0-3	0-0			7,350
32	11	CL	A	Brighton & HA	D1-1	0-0	21	Gale	11,979
33	15	CL	A	Leeds U	L0-1	0-0			10,031
34	25	CL	H	Charlton Ath	W1-0	1-0	21	Pascoe	5,222
35	M 3	CL	A	Carlisle U	L0-2	0-0	21		4,280
36	7	CL	A	Blackburn R	L1-4	1-2		Maddy	5,554
37	10	CL	H	Barnsley	W1-0	0-0	21	Marustik	4,864
38	17	CL	A	Oldham Ath	D3-3	2-2	21	McDonough (og), Saunders, Maddy	3,597
39	31	CL	A	Newcastle U	L0-2	0-0	21		27,306
40	A 7	CL	H	Manchester C	L0-2	0-2	21		6,261
41	14	CL	A	Grimsby T	L0-3	0-1	21		5,851
42	21	CL	H	Cardiff C	W3-2	1-2	21	Saunders 2, Walsh	10,275
43	24	CL	A	Shrewsbury T	L0-2	0-1			3,060
44	27	CL	H	Middlesbrough	W2-1	2-1		Walsh 2	3,628
45	M 5	CL	A	Crystal Palace	L0-2	0-2	21		5,318
46	7	CL	H	Leeds U	D2-2	0-1	21	Marustik (pen), Loveridge	5,498
47	12	CL	A	Portsmouth	L0-5	0-2	21		7,359
								Av Home Att	**7,113**

Goal Scorers

League (36): Walsh 6, Marustik 4 (1 pen), Gale 3, Latchford 3, Maddy 3, Saunders 3, Stevenson 3, Lake 2, Loveridge 2, Pascoe 2, Curtis 1, Richards 1, Stanley 1 (pen), Toshack 1, opponent 1

FA Cup (-): —

Milk Cup (1): Gale 1

ECW Cup (1): Walsh 1

1983-84

Rimmer	Robinson	Marustik	Charles	Stevenson	Lewis	Curtis	Stanley	Pascoe	Kennedy	Latchford	Richards G	Walsh	Maddy	Gale	Chivers	Lake	Hughes E	Loveridge	Saunders	McQuillan	Evans	Hughes M	Sander	Holtham	REFEREE	
1	**2**	**3**	**4**	**5**	**6**	**7***	**8**		**10**	**11***		**12**		**13**		**9**									**Fiedriksson (Swe)**	**1**
1	2*	3	4	5	6	7	8	9	10	11						12									E Read	2
1	**2**	**3**	**4**	**5**	**6**	**7**	**8**		**10**	**11***		**9**		**12**											**Konrath (F)**	**3**
1	2		4	5	6	7	8		10*	11	3	9	12												D Hutchinson	4
1	2		4	5	6	7	8		10	11	3	9*		12											B Stevens	5
1	4		5*		6	7	12			11	3		8	9	2	10									R Milford	6
1	2	3		5		7	9			11			8	12	4	10*	6								PN Willis	7
1		3		5		8	10	11		9	4			7	2		6								L Burden	8
1	7	3		5		8	2*	11		9	10			12	4		6								DA Hedges	9
1	**2**	**3**		**5**		**8**		**11**		**9**	**4**			**7**		**10**	**6**								**A Seville**	**10**
1		4		5	6					9	11	8	10		2	7	3								T Holbrook	11
1		3		5	4					9	11	8	10	12	2	7*	6								K Baker	12
1		8	4	5	6			11*			3		10	9			2	7	12						M James	13
1		**8**	**4**	**5**	**6***			**11**			**10**			**9**			**3**	**7**	**12**						**K Salmon**	**14**
1	12	8	4	5	6			11*		9	3						10	7							G Napthine	15
1	8	4	5		6			11		9	3		10*	7	2	12									LC Shapter	16
1		4	5		6			11		9	3		10	7	2	8									A Banks	17
1		8	4	5				11		9	3		10*	7	2	6									TG Bune	18
		8	4	5		7	6*	11		9	3			10	2	12							1		LM Robinson	19
		8		5	2	7	6	11*		9	3			10†				12					1		A Robinson	20
		3*		5	2		6	11		9		12	8	10		7							1		R Guy	21
		3		5	2		6	11		9		7	4*	10		8		12					1		JE Bray	22
		4		5	6		2					9	8			7		10*	12				1		K Barratt	23
		8		5	6		3	9			4	12	11*					7					1		E Read	24
		4		5	6		3				8	9		10*		11		7	12				1		A Buksh	25
		4		5	6			11			12			9		8*		7							A Crickmore	26
		4		5	6		10	11			8			9				7							D Vickers	27
		4		**5**	**6**		**2**	**11**			**8**			**9**				**7**							**L Burden**	**28**
		4		5	6			12		11			8	9				7							I Hendrick	29
		4		5	6			12			10	9	8					7*	11	3	2	1			R Bridges	30
		6			2			12			3	8	11	9		7*		10		3	2	1			V Callow	31
		2		5	6			11			8	10		9				7		3	2	1			M Dimblebee	32
		2		5	6			11			8	9*	12					10	7	3	2	1			D Owen	33
	7	2		5	6			11			8	10				12			9*	3	2	1			T Pascoe	34
	7	2		5	6			11			8	10				9*			12	3	2	1			N Glover	35
	2	7		5	6			11*				9	10						12	3	2	1			G Tyson	36
	8	2		5	6			11			8	9	10						7	3		1			C Downey	37
	8	2		5	6			11				9	10						7	3	4	1			A Challinor	38
	2			5	6			11			10					7			9		4	1		3	R Dilkes	39
	2	9		5	6			11			10								7		4	1		3	R Milford	40
	8	7		5	2			11			10								9	3	4	1			T Jones	41
	8	10		5	4			11			12	9							7	3	2*	1			B Stevens	42
	8	10		5	2			11			4	9							7	3		1			N Wilson	43
	4	8		5	6			11			2	9						10*	7	3		1			D Letts	44
		2		5	6						11	9						10	7	4		1		3	H Taylor	45
		2		5*	6						10	9						7	11	4		1		3	L Burden	46
		2			6			11			8	9						10*	7	5		1		3	D Hedges	47
14	17	38	10	37	37	9	14	29	3	18	32	22	18	16	10	14	7	16	14	19	17	21	7	6	League Appearances	
	+1S						+1S	+3S			+2S	+2S	+2S	+4S		+4S		+2S	+5S							
		1		1	1		1	1			1			1				1							FA Cup Appearances	
2	1	2	1	2	1	1		2		1	2			2		1	2	1	1S						Milk Cup Appearances	
2	2	2	2	2	2	2	2		2	2		1+1S		2S		1									ECWC Appearances	

Also Played: Guard matches 14, 15, no.2. Hughes R 15, 28, no.12. Morgan 18, 44, no.12; 23, no.11; 39, 40, 45, 46, no.8. Irwin 20, 21, 37, no.4. Toshack 24, 26, no.10; 28, 29, no.10*. Williams 47 no.12. Mullen 43, no.12. Hough 46, no.12; 47, no.4. Rajkovic 41, 42, no.6; 43, no.6*.

VETCH FIELD

Official Address: Vetch Field, Swansea. Telephone: Swansea (0792) 474114

Ground Capacity: 26,237

Record Attendance: 32,796 v. Arsenal, FA Cup Round 4, 17 Feb 1968

Record Receipts: £33,141 v. Manchester U, Div 1, 30 Jan 1982

Size of Playing Area: 110 × 70 yds

Season Tickets: Stands (centre): £85.50; (west): £76.00 (Family — 1 Adult, 1 Child — £103), OAP £45; Wing: £61 (£38 OAP): East: £85.50 (£103 Family, £45 OAP): New Stand (Quadrant): £69, £61; Terrace: £35.50 (£23 Juveniles/OAPs)

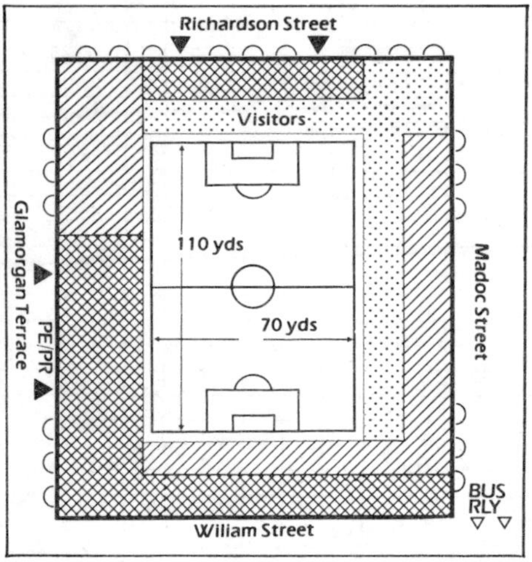

For key see page 12

Executive Box Season Tickets: None available

Cost of Stand Tickets: Centre: £4.50; East: £4.00 (£5.50 Family); West Stand: £4.00 (Adults), £5.50 (Family — 1 Adult, 1 Child); Wing Stand: £3.20 (£2.50 OAPs). **Terrace:** £2.00 (£1.50 Juveniles/OAPs), £3.00 (Family — 1 Adult, 1 Child); Enclosure: £4.00 (Family — 1 Adult, 2 Children)

Match and Ticket Information: Tickets are on sale at the ticket office in the ground, Vetch Field, two weeks before each match

Car Parking: Car Park 200 yards from ground in The Kingsway. There is also ample street parking

How to get to the ground

Five minutes walk from city bus station or take South Wales Transport Co Ltd from High Street General station to Lower Oxford Street. Car parking near ground at Quadrant.

SWINDON TOWN Division 4

President
W H Castle

Chairman
M E Earle

Vice-Chairman
B Hillier

Directors
T J R Kearsley
R Stephenson
W H Dore
L Smart
N Arkell
G Herbert
C Howard
D Alderton
C J Green

Admin Manager/Secretary
R J Jefferies

Commercial Manager
D Buswell (0793 22118)

Player/Manager
L Macari

Finance Manager
R A Morse

Assistant Manager/Club Coach
Harry Gregg

Youth Team Manager
John Trollope

Physiotherapist
Kevin Morris

The season was another disappointment to the dwindling band of regular supporters who have become accustomed in recent seasons to seeing their team promise promotion only to fall away from Christmas. There was some optimism at the start with the return of Alan Mayes and the signing of giant defender Nigel Gray and the experienced David Hockaday.

Sadly Mayes never really struck form whilst his old goalscoring partner Andy Rowland spent much of the season in defence replacing the injured Mike Graham. This gave Jimmy Quinn a chance to prove himself which he took in style with a burst of goalscoring which eventually brought him a call up into the Northern Ireland squad at the end of the season. Nigel Gray never really settled, although he did look as though he might find a place at left back before going on loan to Brentford. His centre half spot went to Simon Gibson, signed in October from Chelsea. Gibson impressed at the start but later in the season his form suffered and he unfortunately collected far too many disciplinary points which created problems at the centre of the defence, where Andy Rowland and Charlie Henry filled in. Rowland indeed seemed set on playing everywhere as he also stepped in, not for the first time, as goalkeeper when Jimmy Allan suffered a broken arm which has unfortunately ended his playing career.

The League programme began with a 4-0 win over Chester — one of three teams over which Town did the 'double'. Results against leading sides were reasonably good. York and Doncaster were both beaten at the County Ground, but it was against some of the bottom teams that Town struggled. Christmas brought the start of a run of eight games without a win and, as the team slipped down the table, attendances fell away alarmingly. Indeed, it was the F.A. Cup which brought some sparkle and cash. A remarkable 7-0 win at Kettering, a fine 3-2 victory at Millwall and a surprise 1-1 draw at Carlisle gave the County Ground two good gates as Carlisle were defeated 3-0 before Blackburn gained a fortunate 2-1 victory. A brief flurry in the Associate Members Cup, wins over Oxford and Walsall being tempered by the knowledge that those clubs had other priorities, was all that was left as the season dragged to a slow, uninspiring conclusion.

Tony Angell, The League Directory's Statistician for the Club

Back Row L to R: Charlie Henry, Simon Gibson, Alan Churchward, Nigel Gray, Scott Endersby, Andy Wollen, Mark Hughes. **Centre:** Harry Gregg (Assistant Manager), John Trollope (Youth Team Manager), Jamie Reynolds, Mark Gardiner, Martin Davison, Sean Prowse, Mike Graham, Dave Hockaday, Kevin Morris (Physiotherapist). **Front Row:** Paul Batty, Gary Nelson, Leigh Barnard, Lou Macari (Player Manager), Andy Rowland, Alan Mayed, Colin Bailie. **Seated:** Mark Payne, Sheldon Lee.

'THE ROBINS'

Formed: 1881 **Turned Professional:** 1894 **Ltd Co:** 1894
Previous Managers: The club did not actually have the post of manager before the 1933/4 season; the Secretary was in charge of team matters. This post was held for a great many years by Sam Allen who was appointed in 1902 and who still held the position on his death in 1946. In 1933 a team manager was appointed (Ted Vizard). He was replaced in 1939 by Neil Harris who continued until the wartime closure in 1940. The full list of modern day managers since Sam Allen's death is:
1945-53 Louis Page 1953-8 Maurice Lindley 1957-65 Bert Head 1965-9 Danny Williams
1969-71 Fred Ford 1971-2 Dave Mackay 1972-4 Les Allen 1974-8 Danny Williams
1978-80 Bob Smith 1980-83 John Trollope 1983-4 Ken Beamish
Honours: Football League Cup: Winners 1968-9 Anglo-Italian Trophy 1970
League Career: Elected to Division 3 1920 Transferred to Division 3 (S) 1921
Transferred to Division 3 1958 Promotion to Division 2 1962-3 Relegation to Division 3 1964-5
Promotion to Division 2 1968-9 Relegation to Division 3 1973-4 Relegation to Division 4 1981-2
Colours: Red shirts, white shorts, red stockings
Change Colours: Yellow shirts, blue shorts, yellow stockings

CLUB RECORDS

Most Appearances for Club: John Trollope: **Total 770**
Most Capped Player: Rod Thomas, 30, Wales. **For England:** Harold Fleming, 11
Record Goalscorer in a Match: Harry Morris, 5 v QPR (H) Div 3 (S) 6-2, 18 Dec 1927
Harry Morris, 5 v Norwich (A), Div 3 (S) 5-1 (A) 26 April 1930
Keith East, 5 v Mansfield (H) Div 3, 6-2, 20 Nov 1965
Record League Goalscorer in a season: Harry Morris, 47, Div 3 (S) **All competitions:** Harry Morris, 53 (League 47, F.A. Cup 6), 1926-7
Record League Goalscorer in a career: Harry Morris, 216 **All competitions:** Harry Morris, 230 (League 216, F.A. Cup 14), 1926-33
Record Transfer Fee Received: £175,000 from Chelsea for Alan Mayes, Dec 1980
Record Transfer Fee Paid: £150,000 to Southampton for David Peach, Mar 1980
Best Performances: League: 5th Div 2 1969-70 **F.A. Cup:** Semi-Finals 1910, 1912 **League/Milk Cup:** Winners (1) **Anglo-Italian Trophy:** Winners (1)
Most League Points: (3pts for win) 68, Div 4, 1982-3 (2pts for win) 64, Div 3, 1968-9
Most League Goals: 100, Div 3 (S), 1926-7
Record League Victory: 9-1 v Luton Town, Div 3 (S), 28 April 1921
Record League Defeat: 0-9 v Torquay United, Div 3 (S), 8 March 1952
European Competitions Entered: Anglo-Italian Trophy
Club Statistician for the Directory: Tony Angell

Programme Editor
R.J. Jefferies

Price	Number of Pages
45p	24

Subscriptions
£13.80 for season (postage included)

SWINDON TOWN

PLAYERS NAME Ht Wt Birthdate	Honours	Birthplace Transfers	Clubs	APPEARANCES League	Milk Cup	F.A.C.	A.M.C.	GOALS League	Milk Cup	F.A.C.	A.M.C.
GOALKEEPERS											
Jimmy Allan		Inverness	Swindon T. (A)	371	37	35					
6-0 12.0 10.11.53											
Scott Endersby +	E. Y	Lewisham	Ipswich T. (A)								
5-10 12.11 20.2.62		F	Tranmere R.	79	6	6					
			Swindon T.	37		5	3				
DEFENDERS											
Colin Baillie		Belfast	Swindon T. (A)	64 + 1	2	5	2	4			
5-11 10.11 31.3.64											
Simon Gibson	S. Y. S	Nottingham	Chelsea (A)								
6-2 13.2 10.12.64			Swindon T.	29		5	3	3			1
Nigel Gray		Fulham	Orient	233	8	20 +		3			
6-3 13.4 2.11.56			Charlton A. (L)	3							
		F	Swindon T.	15	1						
			Brentford (L)	16			1	1			
Charlie Henry		Acton	Swindon T. (A)	120 + 2	8	10	1	3		1	
5-11 12.8 13.2.62											
Andy Rowland*	E. Y	Derby	Derby Co. (N-C)								
5-10½ 12.1 8.9.54			Bury	169 + 5	19	10		58	8	4	
		£80,000	Swindon T.	222 + 1	19	19 +	3	75	5	8	
MIDFIELD											
Leigh Barnard		Worsley	Portsmouth (A)	71 + 8	4	6		8			
5-7½ 9.10 29.10.58			Peterborough U. (L)	1 + 3							
			Swindon T.	81 + 1	2 + 1	10	1	11		1	
Paul Batty		Edington	Swindon T. (A)	78 + 2	1	10	3	5		2	
5-7 10.11 9.1.64											
Lou Macari	S.(24), U.23(2),	Aberdeen	Celtic								
5-5½ 10.13 4.6.49	FAC. 77,	£200,000	Manchester U.	311 + 18	23 +	31 +	9E	78	2	8	
	Div. 2, 75,		Swindon T.								
	SD.1(4), SFAC.(2)										
Paul Richardson	E. Y,	Shirebrook	Nottingham F. (A)	198 + 23	9 + 1	16		18	2	1	
5-11 12.0 25.10.49	Div. 4, 82		Chester	28		5		2			
		£30,000	Stoke C.	124 + 3	10 +	3 + 1		10	1		
		£15,000	Sheffield U.	35 + 1	4	4		2	1		
			Blackpool (L)	4							
		F	Swindon T.	7	1						
FORWARDS											
Peter Coyne	E. S	Hartlepool	Manchester U. (A)	2				1			
5-9 10.7 13.11.58		F	Crewe A.	134	6 + 1	6		47	1	1	
		F	Hyde U.								
			Swindon T.								
David Hockaday		Billingham	Blackpool	131 + 16	18 +	10 +		23		2	
5-10 10.9 9.11.57			Swindon T.	32 + 4	2	5	3	3			
Alan Mayes	Div. 4, 78	London	Q.P.R. (A)								
5-7 10.10 11.12.53			Watford	110 + 23	11 +	5 + 3		31	4	1	
			Northampton T. (L)	10				4			
		£65,000	Swindon T.	89	15	8		38	9	4	
		£200,000	Chelsea	61 + 5	1	9		18		5	
		F	Swindon T.	34 + 5	1	1 + 1	3	17			3
Garry Nelson		Braintree	Southend U.	106 + 23	3 + 1	6 + 2		17	1		
5-10 11.10 16.1.61		£10,000	Swindon T.	35 + 1	2	3	3	4			1

APPRENTICES

Alan Churchward, Martin Davison, Mark Gardiner (1 Lg.), **Mark Hughes** (+1 Lg.), **Sheldon Lee, Mark Payne, James Reynolds, Richard Robinson, Andy Wollen**

SWINDON TOWN

DIVISION FOUR 16TH **FA CUP** 4TH ROUND **MILK CUP** 1ST ROUND

MATCH	DATE	COMPE-TITION	VENUE	OPPONENTS	RESULT	HALF TIME	L'GUE POS'N	GOALSCORERS	ATTEN-DANCE
1	A 27	CL	A	Chesterfield	L0-1	0-1			4,161
2	**30**	**MC 1**	**H**	**Plymouth Arg**	**W1-0**	**0-0**		**Hockaday**	**3,343**
3	S 3	CL	H	Chester C	W4-0	1-0	10	Nelson, Mayes 2 (1 pen), Rowland	2,891
4	6	CL	H	Halifax T	L2-3	0-2		Hockaday, Rowland	3,633
5	10	CL	A	Darlington	L0-1	0-0	20		1,091
6	**13**	**MC 1**	**A**	**Plymouth Arg**	**L1-4**	**0-1**		**Nelson**	**3,432**
7	17	CL	H	Blackpool	D0-0	0-0	19		2,867
8	23	CL	A	Stockport Co	W3-1	1-0		Mayes 2 (1 pen), Rowland	2,244
9	27	CL	A	Aldershot	L1-2	1-2		Mayes	2,644
10	O 1	CL	H	Rochdale	W2-1	1-0	14	Mayes, Quinn	2,626
11	8	CL	A	Crewe Alex	L0-2	0-1	16		2,111
12	15	CL	H	York C	W3-2	2-2	13	Emmanuel, Bailie, Barnard	2,517
13	17	CL	A	Tranmere R	L1-2	1-1		Mayes	2,543
14	22	CL	H	Colchester U	W2-1	0-1	13	Rowland, Hockaday	3,079
15	29	CL	A	Reading	D2-2	2-0	13	Mayes, Batty	5,918
16	N 1	CL	H	Hereford U	W3-0	3-0		Gibson, Mayes (pen), Barnard	3,645
17	5	CL	A	Northampton T	L0-2	0-2	13		2,354
18	12	CL	H	Hartlepool U	W3-2	1-1	11	Emmanuel, Rowland, Barnard	3,072
19	**19**	**FAC 1**	**A**	**Kettering T**	**W7-0**	**2-0**		**Gibson, Quinn 2, Rowland, Henry, Batty, Barnard**	**2,834**
20	26	CL	A	Mansfield T	D2-2	1-1	10	Quinn 2	3,327
21	D 3	CL	H	Doncaster R	W2-1	1-1	9	Quinn, Barnard	3,545
22	**10**	**FAC 2**	**A**	**Millwall**	**W3-2**	**1-1**		**Quinn 2, Batty**	**4,597**
23	17	CL	H	Bury	D0-0	0-0	9		3,551
24	26	CL	A	Torquay U	L0-1	0-0	11		2,837
25	27	CL	H	Wrexham	L0-1	0-1	13		4,298
26	31	CL	A	Peterborough U	D1-1	0-1	13	Quinn	4,140
27	**J 7**	**FAC 3**	**A**	**Carlisle U**	**D1-1**	**0-1**		**Rowland**	**5,778**
28	**10**	**FAC 3R**	**H**	**Carlisle U**	**W3-1**	**1-0**		**Quinn, Batty, Rowland**	**8,077**
29	14	CL	H	Chesterfield	L1-2	1-1	16	Batty	3,936
30	21	CL	A	Blackpool	D1-1	1-0	16	Emmanuel	3,474
31	24	CL	H	Bristol C	D1-1	0-0		Quinn	6,493
32	**28**	**FAC 4**	**H**	**Blackburn R**	**L1-2**	**1-0**		**Quinn**	**11,143**
33	F 4	CL	A	Rochdale	D3-3	2-2	16	Gibson, Mayes (2 pens)	1,297
34	8	CL	A	Chester C	W3-0	3-0		Nelson 2, Batty	880
35	11	CL	H	Stockport Co	W2-1	0-0	14	Mayes, Rowland	3,032
36	15	CL	A	Hereford U	L1-2	1-1		Barnard	2,002
37	18	CL	H	Reading	D1-1	0-1	15	Bailie	4,659
38	**22**	**AMC 1**	**A**	**Oxford U**	**W3-1**	**0-0**		**Quinn 2, Mayes**	**4,744**
39	25	CL	A	Colchester U	D0-0	0-0	15		2,448
40	M 3	CL	H	Tranmere R	D1-1	1-1	15	Nelson	2,595
41	6	CL	H	Northampton T	D0-0	0-0			2,608
42	10	CL	A	Hartlepool U	W1-0	1-0	13	Batty	1,274
43	**13**	**AMC 2**	**H**	**Walsall**	**W3-0**	**2-0**		**Gibson, Mayes 2 (1 pen)**	**2,705**
44	18	CL	H	Crewe Alex	W1-0	1-0		Hockaday	2,960
45	24	CL	A	York C	L0-2	0-1	13		3,341
46	**27**	**AMC SF**	**A**	**Millwall**	**L1-3**	**0-1**		**Nelson**	**2,112**
47	30	CL	A	Halifax T	L1-2	0-1		Quinn	1,008
48	A 7	CL	H	Aldershot	L0-2	0-0	15		2,834
49	14	CL	A	Doncaster R	L0-3	0-1	17		3,804
50	17	CL	H	Darlington	W1-0	1-0		Barnard	1,681
51	20	CL	A	Wrexham	W3-0	2-0		Gibson, Mayes (pen), Emmanuel	1,442
52	21	CL	H	Torquay U	L2-3	1-1	15	Mayes 2	2,197
53	29	CL	H	Mansfield T	D1-1	1-0		Bailie	1,941
54	M 5	CL	A	Bristol C	L0-1	0-0	16		12,786
55	7	CL	H	Peterborough U	W2-0	1-0	14	Barnard, Mayes	1,876
56	12	CL	A	Bury	L1-2	0-1	15	Mayes	1,214
								Av Home Att	**3,153**

Goal Scorers

League (58): Mayes 17 (6 pens), Barnard 7, Quinn 7, Rowland 6, Batty 4, Emmanuel 4, Nelson 4, Bailie 3, Gibson 3, Hockaday 3
FA Cup (15): Quinn 6, Batty 3, Rowland 3, Barnard 1, Gibson 1, Henry 1
Milk Cup (2): Hockaday 1, Nelson 1
AMC (7): Mayes 3 (1 pen), Quinn 2, Gibson 1, Nelson 1

1983-84

Allan	Henry	Baillie	Emmanuel	Gray	Graham	Hockaday	Richardson	Rowland	Mayes	Nelson	Quinn	Batty	Baddeley	Barnard	Endersby	Gibson	Andrews **(L)**	Hughes	Gardiner	Woodruff **(L)**	REFEREE	
1	2	3	4	5	6	7	8	9	10	11											I Hendrick	1
1	**2**	**3**	**4**	**5**	**6**	**7**	**8**	**9**	**10**	**11**											**D Vickers**	**2**
1	2	3	4	5	6	7	8	9	10	11											A Buksh	3
1	2*	3	4	5	6	7	8	9	10	11	12										J Moules	4
1		3	4	5	6	7	8	9	10	11		2									A Robinson	5
1	**5**	**2**	**4**		**6**	**7**		**9**		**11**	**10**	**8***	**3**	**12**							**T Holbrook**	**6**
1		2	4	5	6	7		9	12	11	10*		3	8							B Hill	7
1		2	4	5	6	7		9	10	11			3	8							N Wilson	8
1		2	4	5	6		7*	9	10	11		12	3	8							M Taylor	9
1*		2		5	6		7	9	10	11	12	4	3	8							TW Ward	10
		2	7	3	4		6	9	10	11		8	5		1						N Glover	11
	2	3	8		6			5	10	11	9	4		7	1						M Dimblebee	12
	2	3	8		6	12		5	10	11*	9	4		7	1						DB Allison	13
	2	3	8		6	7		9	10			4		11	1	5					A Crickmore	14
	2	3	8		6	7		9	10			4		11	1	5					A Gunn	15
	2	3	8		6	7		9	10			4		11	1	5					D Letts	16
	2*	3	8		6	7		9	10	11		4	12		1	5					TA Jones	17
	2*	3	8		6	7		9	10		12	4		11	1	5					K Salmon	18
	2	**3**	**8**		**6**	**7**		**9**			**10**	**4**		**11**	**1**	**5**					**B Stevens**	**19**
	2*	3	8		6	7		9	12		10	4		11	1	5					V Callow	20
	2	3	8		6	7			10		9	4		11	1	5					L Burden	21
	2	**3**	**8**		**6**	**7**			**10**		**9**	**4**		**11**	**1**	**5†**					**Alan Robinson**	**22**
	2	3	8		6	7*		12	10		9	4		11	1	5					K Cooper	23
	2	3	8		6	7		5	10		9	4		11	1						C Thomas	24
	2	3	8		6	7		5	10	12	9	4		11*	1						R Lewis	25
	2		8			7*		6	12	10	9	4	3	11	1	5					E Scales	26
	2		**8**			**7**		**6**		**10**	**9**	**4**	**3**	**11**	**1**	**5**					**T Mills**	**27**
	2		**8**			**7**		**6**		**10**	**9**	**4**	**3**	**11**	**1**	**5**					**T Mills**	**28**
	2		8			7		6	12	10	9	4	3	11*	1	5					J Deakin	29
	2		8			7		6		10	9	4	3	11	1	5					A Challinor	30
	2		8			7		6		10	9	4	3	11		5	1				C Downey	31
	2*		**8**			**7**		**6**	**12**	**10**	**9**	**4**	**3**	**11**	**1**	**5**					**K Baker**	**32**
			8	2				6	7	10	9	4	3	11	1	5					G Tyson	33
			8	2				6	7	10	9	4	3	11	1	5					A Robinson	34
			8	2		12		6	7	10	9	4	3	11*	1	5					M Bodenham	35
			8	2		12		6	7	10	9*	4	3	11	1	5					N Ashley	36
		8		2		7		6		10	9	4	3	11	1	5					M Heath	37
		2				**7**		**6**	**8**	**10**	**9**	**4**	**3**	**11**	**1**	**5**					**T Holbrook**	**38**
		2		5		7		6	8	10	9	4	3	11	1						I Borrett	39
		2	12		5	8		6	7*	10	9	4	3	11	1						A Buksh	40
		2	8		6	7		9		10		4*	3	11	1	5		12			D Reeves	41
	11	2	8		6	7		9		10		4	3		1	5					T Fitzharris	42
	2		**8**		**6**	**7**		**9**	**10**	**11**		**4**	**3**		**1**	**5**					**L Burden**	**43**
	2*	12	8		6	7		9	10	11		4	3		1	5					A Ward	44
		2	8		6	7		9	10	11		4*	3	12	1	5					R Banks	45
		2	**8**		**6**	**7**		**9**	**10**	**11**		**4**	**3**		**1**	**5**					**K Barratt**	**46**
		2	8		6	7		9	10*	11	12	4	3		1	5					A Saunders	47
		2	8		6	7		9	12	11*	10	4	3		1	5					H King	48
	3	2	8		6				10†	11	9	4		7	1	5					J Hough	49
	3	2	8		6				10	11	9	4		7	1	5					L Shapter	50
	3	2	8		6	12			10*	11	9	4		7	1	5					D Scott	51
	3	2	8		6				10	11	9	4		7	1	5					D Axell	52
	5	2	9		6					11	9	4	3	7	1				10		A Crickmore	53
	2	3	8		6	10				11	9	4	5	7	1						B Stevens	54
	2	3			6	7			10		9	4		11	1	5				8	A Seville	55
	2	3	8		6*	7			10		9	4		11	1	5†				12	J Lovatt	56
8	29	37	41	15	36	32	7	36	34	35	28	40	24	35	37	29	1	0	1	1	League Appearances	
		+1S	+1S			+4S		+1S	+5S	+1S	+4S	+1S	+1S	+1S				+1S		+1S		
	5	2	5		2	5		4	1+1S	3	5	5	3	5	5	5					FA Cup Appearances	
2	2	2	2	1	2	2	1	2	1	2	1	1	1	1S							Milk Cup Appearances	
	1	2	2		2	3		3	3	3	1	3	3	1	3	3					AM Cup Appearances	

THE COUNTY GROUND

Official Address: County Ground, Swindon, Wiltshire. Telephone: Swindon (0793) 22118/ 36170
Ground Capacity: 25,000 (6,500 seats)

Record Attendance: 32,000 v. Arsenal, F.A. Cup Round 3, 15 Jan 1972

Record Receipts: £56,024 v. Tottenham H, F.A. Cup Round 4, 26 Jan 1980

Size of Playing Area: 114 × 72 yds

Season Tickets: Stand (North): £58.50, (£37 OAP/juveniles); Stand (South): £55, (£37 OAP/juveniles); Ground (covered) £39, (£25 OAP/juveniles); Ground (uncovered) £37, (£21 OAP/juveniles)

Executive Box Season Tickets: Rendezvous Box: £68, (£40 OAP/juveniles); Vice President's Club: £172.50

Cost of Stand Tickets: (Main Stands) £3.00, (£1.70 OAP/juveniles); Ground (covered): £2.00, (£1.20 OAP/juveniles); Ground (uncovered): £1.80, (£1.20 OAP/juveniles); Rendezvous Box £3.50, (£2.20 OAP/juveniles)

Match and Ticket Information: Available three weeks in advance.

Car Parking: Corporation car park adjacent to the west end of ground off County Road.

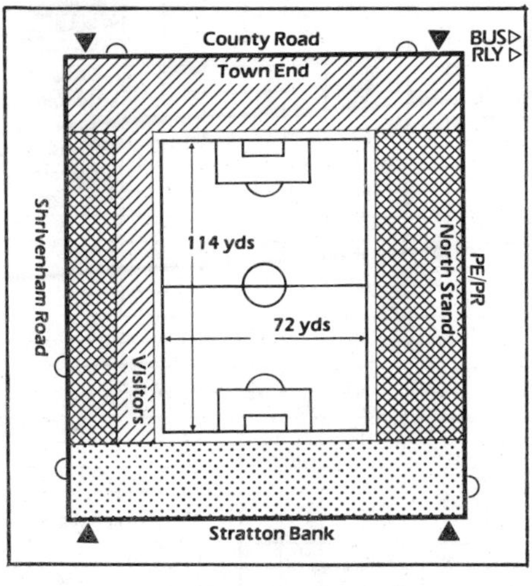

For key see page 12

TORQUAY UNITED Division 4

Chairman
L W Pope

Vice-Chairman
G J Harvey

Directors
D C Hair, M.R.C.V.S.
J H Perry
Lt-Col W J Elliott, M.B.E., F.C.I.S.
L W Leppington, E.R.D.
W W Rogers
J Farrell, O.B.E.
A J Boyce
S Latter
F M Mossley, T.D.
R Daniel
A Loze

Managing Director/Team Manager
D J Webb

Secretary
D J Easton

Club Coach
A Slough

Physiotherapist
W J Wright

Commercial Manager
M J Goulding (0803 39349)

For a team which had a very bad start to the season a final position of ninth — even in Division Four — with a final points total of sixty-seven was most creditable and if such an improvement can be maintained promotion can be a possibility at Plainmoor. Not only was the start bad but also Cup successes were few, so that the inevitable change of manager took place with Bruce Rioch making way for David Webb.

None of the first eight League matches was won and on the 24th September 1983 the club had the Herculean task of holding up the rest of the League. However, the First Round of the Milk Cup had seen 'The Gulls' win both legs against Newport County which brought a draw against Manchester City and some improvement in morale. Four League matches produced eleven points and a positional improvement, but that Manchester City tie saw a goalless draw at Plainmoor followed by a six-nil thrashing at Maine Road. but the team quickly shook off the effects of that disaster and took another eleven points from five matches. One victim in the League was Colchester United at Plainmoor, where a week earlier Colchester had in fact ended any F.A. Cup hopes with a First Round win (2-1). The form remained 'up and down' for a while but the players showed sufficient character to avoid allowing the season to 'fall flat' with the results already mentioned. If the defence had played better in away matches a real challenge might have been mounted, but at least there is something to encourage David Webb for the future.

In the new season David Webb will rely on the steady play of Impey, Barnes, Pugh and Anderson for his team building and this time he will hope that the team has a good start to the programme. He will need a great deal of luck and shrewdness to achieve promotion.

Back Row: Derek Fowler, Paul Thorpe, Jeremy Judd, Kenny Allen, Alan Gilson, Gary Perry, David Smith. **Middle Row:** David Webb (Manager), David Wakefield, Colin Barnes, Steve Pugh, Colin Anderson, Paul Compton, Dean Mooney, Gary Wright, Simon Malin, Brian Wilson (Assistant Manager/Coach). **Front Row:** Dean Whitehouse, Steve Carter, Derek Dawkins, John Impey (Capt.), Ben Laryea, Derek Hall.
Photo: Colin Bratcher

'THE GULLS'

Formed: 1898 **Turned Professional:** 1921 **Ltd Co:** 1921
Previous Names: Torquay Town (1910)
Previous Managers: Since 1946:
John Butler John McNeil Bob John Alex Massie Eric Webber Frank O'Farrell Allan Brown Jack Edwards Malcolm Musgrove Frank O'Farrell Mike Green Frank O'Farrell Bruce Rioch
Honours: None
League Career: Elected to Division Three (South) 1927 Original members of Division Four 1958 Promoted to Division Three 1960 Relegated to Division Four 1962 Promoted to Division Three 1966 Relegated to Division Four 1972
Colours: All blue, white stockings
Change Colours: All white

CLUB RECORDS

Most Appearances for Club: Dennis Lewis, 1947-59 (League 443 + F.A. Cup 30) **Total 473**
Most Capped Player: None
Record Goalscorer in a Match: Robin Stubbs, 5 v Newport County, Div 4, 19.10.63
Record League Goalscorer in a season: Sammy Collins, 40, Div 3(S), 1955-6 **In all competitions:** Sammy Collins, 42 (League 40, F.A. Cup 2)
Record League Goalscorer in a career: Sammy Collins, 204, 1948-58 **In all competitions:** Sammy Collins, 219 (League 204, F.A. Cup 15)
Record Transfer Fee Received: £80,000 from Tottenham Hotspur for Colin Lee, October 1977
Record Transfer Fee Paid: £25,000 to Exeter City for Vince O'Keefe, March 1980
Best Performances: League: 2nd Div 3(S) 1956-7 **F.A. Cup:** 4th Round 1948-9, 1954-5, 1970-1 **League/Milk Cup:** Never past 3rd Round
Most League Points: 67 in Div 4, 1983-4 **Most League Goals:** 89, Div 3(S), 1956-7
Record League Victory: 9-0 v Swindon Town, Div 3(S), 8 Mar 1952
Record League Defeat: 2-10 v Fulham, Div 3(S), 7 Sept 1931 2-10 v Luton Town, Div 3(S), 2 Sept 1933

Club Statistician for the Directory: John Lovis

Programme Editor

Price	**Number of Pages**
40p	16

Subscriptions

TORQUAY UNITED

PLAYERS NAME Ht Wt Birthdate	Honours	Birthplace Transfers	Clubs	APPEARANCES League	Milk Cup	F.A.C.	A.M.C.	GOALS League	Milk Cup	F.A.C.	A.M.C.
GOALKEEPER											
Kenny Allen		Thornaby	Hartlepool U. (N-C)	7							
6-4 13.8 12.1.57			Bath C.								
			Bournemouth	152	9	8					
		F	Torquay U.	11							
DEFENDERS											
Colin Anderson†		Newcastle	Burnley (A)	3+3							
5-8 10.0 26.4.62			Torquay U.	79+2	3	5	1	9		1	
Paul Compton		Stroud	Trowbridge T.								
6-1½ 13.1 6.6.63		£10,000	Bournemouth	64	5	2					
		F	Aldershot	13		2					
		F	Torquay U.	16			0+1				
Derek Dawkins		Luton	Leicester C. (A)	3							
5-9 10.0 28.5.57			Mansfield T.	73							
			Bournemouth	4							
			Torquay U.	14+2			1				
John Impey*		Exeter	Cardiff C. (A)	13+8		0+2				1	
6-0 11.12 11.8.54			Bournemouth	280+4	12	16+		7			
			Torquay U.	41	4	1	1				
Steve Pugh		Wolverhampton	Wolverhampton W. (A)								
5-9 10.7 1.2.65			Torquay U.	37+1	3	1	1	1			
MIDFIELD											
Derek Fowler			Torquay U.	7+1							
5-11 11.7 28.11.61											
Derek Hall			Coventry C. (A)								
5-9 10.7			Torquay U.	1							
Paul Thorpe			Torquay U.								
6-2 12.6											
David Wakefield		South Shields	Darlington (A)	7+15							
5-8 10.0 15.1.65			Torquay U.	10				1			
Dean Whitehouse		Mexborough	Barnsley (A)	1+1	0+1						
5-5 9.1 3.10.63			Torquay U.								
FORWARDS											
Colin Barnes		Luton	Barnet								
5-10 11.7 28.2.57			Torquay U.	35	2	1	1	8			
Steve Carter		Yarmouth	Manchester C. (A)	4+2							
5-8 10.10 23.4.53		F	Notts. Co.	172+16	10+3	10+2		21	3		
		Player Exchange	Derby Co.	32+1	1	1					
		F	Bournemouth	42+4	4	2	1+1	1			
Ben Laryea		Ghana	Maidenhead U.								
5-11 10.7 20.3.62			Torquay U.	1							

NON-CONTRACT PLAYERS 1984-85

John Berry (1 Lg.), **Tony Currie** (9 Lg.), **David Fifield, Graham Horn** (1 Lg.), **Mark Loram, Paul McCulloch, Martin Powell, Tony Stuart, David Webb, Gary Wright, Mark Young**

TORQUAY UNITED

DIVISION FOUR 9TH **FA CUP** 1ST ROUND **MILK CUP** 2ND ROUND

MATCH	DATE	COMPE-TITION	VENUE	OPPONENTS	RESULT	HALF TIME	L'GUE POS'N	GOALSCORERS	ATTEN-DANCE
1	A 27	CL	A	Halifax T	D2-2	1-1		Bishop, Hughes	1,448
2	**30**	**MC 1**	**A**	**Newport Co**	**W3-2**	**1-1**		**Little, Sims, Carter**	**2,282**
3	S 3	CL	H	Tranmere R	D1-1	0-0	17	Holmes (pen)	2,317
4	7	CL	H	Darlington	L0-1	0-1			2,038
5	10	CL	A	Peterborough U	L0-5	0-3	21		3,135
6	**14**	**MC 1**	**H**	**Newport Co**	**W1-0**	**0-0**		**Carter**	**2,015**
7	17	CL	H	Aldershot	L0-1	0-0	23		1,812
8	24	CL	A	Bristol C	L0-5	0-1	24		4,266
9	28	CL	A	Chester C	W2-1	1-0		Little, Barnes	1,356
10	O 1	CL	H	Doncaster R	W4-1	2-0	20	Sims 2, Holmes, Hughes	1,814
11	**5**	**MC 2**	**H**	**Manchester C**	**D0-0**	**0-0**			**6,439**
12	8	CL	H	Hartlepool U	D0-0	0-0			1,936
13	15	CL	A	Mansfield T	W3-1	2-0	18	Cooper, Sheridan 2	1,939
14	18	CL	A	Northampton T	L1-2	1-1		Sims	2,573
15	22	CL	H	Hereford U	D1-1	0-1	21	Holmes (pen)	1,951
16	**25**	**MC 2**	**A**	**Manchester C**	**L0-6**	**0-1**			**14,021**
17	29	CL	A	Wrexham	D2-2	0-2	21	Cooper, Barnes	1,505
18	N 2	CL	H	Chesterfield	D1-1	0-0		Cooper	1,542
19	5	CL	H	Bury	W2-0	2-0	18	Curle, Barnes	1,530
20	12	CL	A	York C	W3-2	2-1	15	Sims, Pugh, Young	4,609
21	**19**	**FAC 1**	**H**	**Colchester U**	**L1-2**	**0-1**		**Curle**	**2,126**
22	26	CL	H	Colchester U	W2-1	2-1	13	Curle 2 (2 pens)	1,364
23	D 2	CL	A	Stockport Co	L1-2	0-2		Cooper	1,874
24	17	CL	A	Blackpool	L0-1	0-0	14		3,955
25	26	CL	H	Swindon T	W1-0	0-0	14	Hughes	2,837
26	27	CL	A	Reading	D2-2	1-2	14	Hughes, Anderson	4,910
27	31	CL	H	Rochdale	W4-2	1-1	11	Anderson, Curle, Higgins (og), Sims	1,887
28	J 2	CL	A	Crewe Alex	L1-2	0-2	13	Cooper	2,489
29	7	CL	A	Tranmere R	L0-3	0-0	14		1,789
30	14	CL	H	Halifax T	D1-1	1-0	14	Curle	1,369
31	21	CL	A	Aldershot	L1-3	0-1	15	Bishop	1,543
32	28	CL	H	Peterborough U	W1-0	0-0	13	Sims	1,461
33	F 4	CL	A	Doncaster R	D1-1	1-1	15	Cooper	3,727
34	11	CL	H	Bristol C	W1-0	0-0	13	Sims	4,188
35	18	CL	H	Wrexham	W1-0	0-0	11	Sims	1,868
36	**21**	**AMC 1**	**A**	**Plymouth Arg**	**L1-5**	**0-2**		**Dawkins**	**3,962**
37	25	CL	A	Hereford U	D1-1	0-0	11	Anderson	1,978
38	M 3	CL	H	Northampton T	W2-1	0-0	10	Hughes, Squires	1,926
39	6	CL	A	Bury	D0-0	0-0			1,329
40	10	CL	H	York C	L1-3	0-0	12	Barnes	2,836
41	17	CL	A	Hartlepool U	L1-2	1-1	12	Compton	969
42	18	CL	A	Chesterfield	L2-3	2-0		Cooper, Squires	3,142
43	24	CL	H	Mansfield T	W1-0	0-0	14	Hall	1,447
44	A 7	CL	A	Darlington	W1-0	0-0	11	Cooper	1,322
45	14	CL	H	Stockport Co	D1-1	1-1	14	Compton	1,392
46	21	CL	A	Swindon T	W3-2	1-1	10	Hughes, Fowler, Barnes (pen)	2,197
47	23	CL	H	Reading	D2-2	0-1	11	Barnes 2 (1 pen)	2,525
48	28	CL	A	Colchester U	L0-3	0-2	13		1,226
49	M 2	CL	H	Chester C	W1-0	1-0		Wakefield	967
50	5	CL	H	Crewe Alex	W3-1	1-0	9	Hall, Barnes, Squires	1,167
51	7	CL	A	Rochdale	L0-1	0-0	9		1,042
52	12	CL	H	Blackpool	W1-0	1-0	9	Anderson	1,592

Av Home Att 1,900

Goal Scorers

League (59): Barnes 8 (2 pens), Cooper 8, Sims 8, Hughes 6, Curle 5 (2 pens), Anderson 4, Holmes 3 (2 pens), Squires 3, Bishop 2, Compton 2, Hall 2, Sheridan 2, Fowler 1, Little 1, Pugh 1, Wakefield 1, Young 1, opponent 1
FA Cup (1): Curle 1
Milk Cup (4): Carter 2, Little 1, Sims 1
AMC (1): Dawkins 1

1983-84

Turner	Collins	Holmes	Impey	Little	Carr	Hughes	Carter	Bishop	Sims	Anderson	Cooper	Pugh	Sheridan	Compton	Barnes	Squires	Currie	Curle **(L)**	Hall **(L)**	Wharton **(L)**	Lennox **(L)**	Allen	Wakefield	Dawkins	REFEREE	
1	2	3	4	5	6	7	8	9	10	11															J Ashworthy	1
1	**2**	**3**	**4**	**5**	**6**	**7**	**8**	**9**	**10**	**11**															**D Brazier**	**2**
1		3	4	5	6	7	8	11*	10	12	9														K Cooper	3
1		3	4	5*	6	7	8	12	10	11	9														D Letts	4
1	2	3	4†		6	7	8	9	10	11	12	5*													J Moules	5
1	**2**	**3**	**4**		**6**	**7**	**8**		**10**	**11**	**9**	**5**													**A Ward**	**6**
1	2	3	4		6	7*	8	9	10	11		5	12												B Stevens	7
1	2	3		5	6	7		9*	10	11		8	4												LM Robinson	8
1	2	3		5	6	7			10	11*		8	4		9										D Scott	9
1		3	4	5	6	7			10			2	8		9										J Martin	10
1		**3**	**4**	**5**	**6**	**7**			**10**		**11**	**2**	**8**		**9**										**D Hedges**	**11**
1		3	4	5	6	7			10		11	2	8		9										E Read	12
1		3	4†	5	6	12			10	7	11	2	8		9*										A Robinson	13
1		3	4	5	6	12			10	7	11	2	8*		9										M Scott	14
1	7	3	4	5*	6	12			10	11		2	8		9										T Spencer	15
1		**3**	**4**	**5**	**6**	**12**			**10**	**11**	**9**	**2**	**8**		**7***										**T Mills/S Caulkin**	**16**
1				5	6	4		12	10	11	9	2	8*		7										J Bray	17
1		3	4	5	6	7		8	10		9	2			11										L Burden	18
1		3	4	7	5	6			10		11	2			8			9							H King	19
1		3	4	5	6				10		9	2			11			8							LR Dilkes	20
1		**3**	**4**	**5**	**6**				**10**		**9**	**2**			**11**			**8**							**K Cooper**	**21**
1			4		6	5			10		9	2			11			8		3					J Deakin	22
1			4		6	5			10	12	9	2			11*			8		3					G Courtney	23
1			4		6	5			10	11		2			9			8		3	7				J Lovatt	24
1			4		6	5			10	11		2			9			8		3	7				C Thomas	25
1			4		6	5			10	11	12	2			9*			8		3	7				J Borrett	26
1			4		6	5			10	11	12	2			9*			8		3	7				D Reeves	27
1			4		6	5			10	11	12	2			9*			8		3	7				I Hendrick	28
1			4		6	5			10	11	9	2						8		3	7				R Banks	29
1			4		6	5			10		9	2			11			8		3	7				C Downey	30
1			4		6	5		12	10	11	9	2						8*			7				K Salmon	31
1			4		6	5		12	10	3	9	2			11*			8			7				T Holbrook	32
			4		6	12			10	3	9*	2			11			8		5	7	1			P Willis	33
1			4		6	5		9	10	3		2			11			8			7				V Callow	34
1			5		4	7		9	10	3		2			11			8						6	M Bodenham	35
1			**5**		**4**	**7**		**9***		**3**		**2**		**12**	**11**	**10**		**8**						**6**	**J Deakin**	**36**
1			5		4	7		11		3		8		6	10	9								2	N Midgley	37
1			5		4	7		11		3		2		6	10	9	8								B Stevens	38
1			5		4	7		11*		3		2		6	10	9	8							12	M Heath	39
1			5			7				3	9	4		6	10	11	8							2	R Milford	40
					6	7				3		2		5	10*	9						1	4	12	D Scott	41
1			5			12				3	9*	2		6		10	8						7	4	D Shaw	42
			5							3				6		9	10		11			1	7	2	J Martin	43
			5							3	9			6	10	8			11			1	7	2	T Fitzharris	44
			5							3	9			6	10	8	4		11			1	7	2	A Seville	45
			5			4				3	9			6	10	7			11			1		2	D Axcell	46
			5							3	9			6	10		4		11			1	7	2	H King	47
			5							3	9	10		6			4		11			1	7	2	J Hunting	48
			5							3	9	4		6	10	12			11			1	7	2	T Spencer	49
						5				3	9	2		6	10	8			11			1	7	4	K Cooper	50
			5			4				3	9	12		6	10	8*			11			1	7	2	G Courtney	51
			5							3	9*	7		6	10		4		11			1		2	J Bray	52
34	6 -	15	41	14	34	33	5	11	30	37	27	37	8	16	35	12	9	16	10	10	11	11	10	14	League Appearances	
						+5S		+4S		+2S	+4S	+1S	+1S			+1S								+2S		
1		1	1	1	1				1		1	1			1			1							FA Cup Appearances	
4	2	4	4	3	4	3+1S	2	1	4	3	3	3	2		2										Milk Cup Appearances	
1			1		1	1		1		1		1		1S	1	1		1						1	AM Cup Appearances	

Also Played: Fifield match 8, no.12. Rioch 9, no.12; 10, no.11. Smith 17, no.3. Berry 31, no.3. Horn 33, no.1. Bailey 41, no.8. Young **(L)** 20, 21, 22, 23, no.7. Arkwright **(L)** 43, 44, no.4. Fowler 52, no.12; 41, 42, no.11; 43, 46, 47, 48, no.8; 49, no.8*. Laryea 52, no.8. Rollings 3, 4, no.2.

PLAINMOOR

Official Address: Plainmoor Ground, Torquay, Devon TQ1 3PG. Telephone: Torquay (0803) 38666/7.

Ground Capacity: 22,000

Record Attendance: 21,908 v. Huddersfield, F.A. Cup Round 4, 29 Jan 1955

Record Receipts: £14,300 v. Sheffield Wednesday, F.A. Cup Round 4, 29 Jan 1983

Size of Playing Area: 112yds × 74 yds

Season Tickets: £55 (adult), £27.50 (juveniles/OAP)

Executive Box Season Tickets: £150 for one, £250 for two.

Cost of Stand Tickets: £3.00 (£1.50 juveniles/OAP), £2.00 (£1.00 juveniles/OAP)

Match and Ticket Information: Seat bookings accepted two weeks before each match. Postal applications must include remittance and sae.

Car Parking: some street parking. Coaches park at Lymington Road Coach Station.

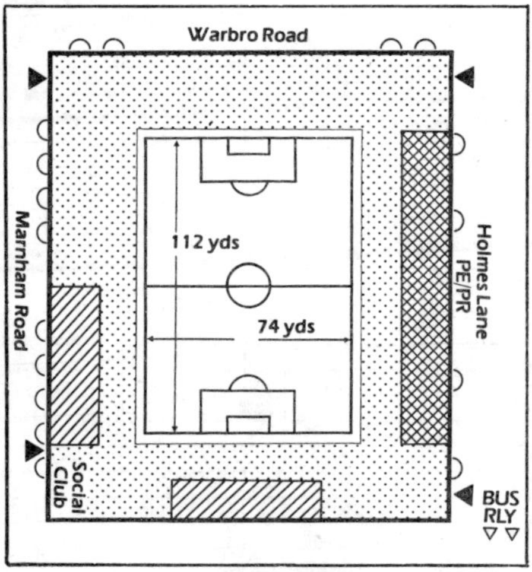

For key see page 12

How to get to the ground

From North: Use A38 then A380 to Kings Kerswell. In 1m at roundabout take 1st exit. In 1m turn left A3022 S.P. Babbacombe. In 0.8m turn left then right into Westhill Road and Warbro Road for Torquay United F.C.
From West: Use A380 into Torquay town centre then follow signs Teignmouth A379 into Lymington Road, then turn right into Upton Hill then keep forward into Bronshill Road. Take 2nd turning on left into Derwent Road and at end turn right then turn right again into Marnham Road for Torquay United F.C.

TOTTENHAM HOTSPUR Division 1

Chairman
I Scholar

Vice-Chairman
D A Alexiou

Directors
P Bobroff
F Sinclair

Financial Controller
D Peter

Secretary
P Day

Assistant Secretary
Peter Barnes

Manager
Peter Shreeves

Physiotherapist
Mike Varney

Chief Scout Consultant
W E Nicholson

Commercial Manager
M Rollo (01-808 0281)

Youth Team Coach
Keith Blunt

Spurs had just about the most extraordinary and contradictory season in their history which meant that they were never out of the news. They were in the news for several reasons and it might be best to summarise the most interesting of these:-

1. The club went 'public' in 1983. Apparently pressures on the Manager, Keith Burkinshaw, persuaded him to resign with effect from the end of the season, Peter Shreeves eventually being appointed as his successor.
2. Two Scottish players, Alan Brazil and Steve Archibald, were at loggerheads with the manager throughout the season and left the club in the summer.
3. The club won the UEFA Cup after a thrilling Final against Anderlecht of Belgium when a penalty 'shoot-out' decided the outcome, Tony Parks saving the final Anderlecht kick.
4. As a result of this successful campaign Spurs fans had spread devastation almost everywhere they went in Europe and helped to maintain the shocking reputation of English 'fans' for violent hooliganism.

All these matters made headlines and one wonders which ones the new directors liked least. In the League Spurs had a modest season by their own standards and finished in eighth place; they were thereabouts from the beginning of 1984 and found it difficult to do any better than that. In the domestic cups they struggled to beat Lincoln City in the Second Round of the Milk Cup (4-3 on aggregate) and then lost at White Hart Lane to Arsenal in the next round to two Charlie Nicholas goals. The F.A. Cup was little different with Fulham being beaten in the Third Round at White Hart Lane after a replay and another second match — this time at Norwich — accounting for the team in the next round. It needed that UEFA success to satisfy the shareholders — but what a success! It was applauded in most places because Burkinshaw is well-liked and it was a deserved reward for his many good years at White Hart Lane.

Peter Shreeves must now take over the reins and it is surprising that few uncommitted people would like to be in his position when his and the team's survival depends greatly on the reaction to results of a very aggressive board of young businessmen. The playing staff may see some changes with the two departures already mentioned and the fact that Crooks may not keep his place and Ardiles and Perryman cannot go on for ever. It can be hoped that the genius of Glenn Hoddle will be seen more often, whilst the consistency of Roberts and Hughton will again be badly needed; Parks in goal will be expected to challenge for an International place very soon.

The right ingredients for success exist but will they produce the right results?

Back Row L to R: G. O'Reilly, M. Falco, R. Clemence, G. Stevens, T. Parks, T. Galvin, P. Miller, J. Pratt (Reserve Team Manager). **Middle Row:** M. Varney (Physiotherapist), D. Thomas, C. Hughton, I. Crook, M. Bowen, O. Ardilles, A. Dick, G. Crooks, G. Roberts, J. Wallis (Trainer). **Front Row:** G. Mabbutt, M. Hazard, G. Hoddle, P. Shreeves (Manager), S. Perryman, G. Brooke, R. Cooke.

'THE SPURS'

Sponsored by
Holsten

Formed: 1882 **Turned Professional:** 1895 **Ltd Co:** 1898
Previous Name: Hotspur Football Club 1882-4
Previous Managers: 1895-8 Frank Brettell John Cameron Arthur Turner Fred Kirkham 1912-27 Peter McWillian 1927-30 Billy Minter 1930-5 Percy Smith 1935-8 Jack Tresadern 1938-45 Peter McWilliam 1945-9 Joe Hulme 1949-55 Arthur Rowe 1955-8 Jimmy Anderson 1958-74 Bill Nicholson 1974-6 Terry Neill 1976-84 Keith Burkinshaw
Honours: Division 1 Champions 1950-1, 1960-1 Division 2 Champions 1919-20, 1949-50 F.A. Cup Winners 1901 (only Non-League club to win), 1921, 1961, 1962, 1967, 1981, 1982 (no final has been lost) Football League Cup Winners 1970-1, 1972-3 European Cup Winners Cup Winners 1962-3 EUFA Cup Winners 1971-2
League Career: Elected to Division 2 1908 Promoted to Division 1 1908-9 Relegated to Division 2 1914-5 Promoted to Division 1 1919-20 Relegated to Division 2 1927-8 Promoted to Division 1 1932-3 Relegated to Division 2 1934-5 Promoted to Division 1 1949-50 Relegated to Division 2 1976-7 Promoted to Division 1 1977-8
Colours: White shirts, navy blue shorts, white stockings
Change Colours: All yellow

CLUB RECORDS

Most Appearances for Club: Steve Perryman: Football League 589 + 1 + F.A. Cup 61 + League Cup 57 + European Cups 55 + 1 + Anglo-Italian 2 + Charity Shield 1 + 1 **Total 768 + 3**
Most Capped Player: Pat Jennings, 68, N Ireland. **For England:** Jimmy Greaves, 42
Record Goalscorer in a Match: Jack Rowley, 7 v Luton T, Wartime South Regional Lg
In League or Cup: Ted Harper, 5 v Reading, (7-1) Div 2, 30.08.30
Alf Stokes, 5 v Birmingham City, (7-1) Div 1, 18.09.57
Les Allen, 5 v Crewe A, (5-1) 4th Round, F.A. Cup, 03.02.60
Record League Goalscorer in a season: Jimmy Greaves, 37, 1962-3 **All competitions:** Jimmy Greaves, 43 (League 37, European 6) 1962-3
Record League Goalscorer in a career: Jimmy Greaves, 220 **All competitions:** Jimmy Greaves, 267 (League 220, F.A. Cup 32, League Cup 5, European 10)
Record Transfer Fee Received: £850,000 for Steve Archibald, July 1984
Record Transfer Fee Paid: £800,000 to Aberdeen for Steve Archibald, May 1980
Best Performances: League: Winners (2) **F.A. Cup:** Winners (7) **League/Milk Cup:** Winners (2)
European Cup: Semi-Final **European Cup Winners Cup:** Winners **UEFA Cup:** Winners
Most League Points: (2pts for win) 70, Div 2, 1919-20 (3pts for win) 71, Div 1, 1981-2
Most League Goals: 115, Div 1, 1960-1
Record League Victory: 9-0 v Bristol Rovers, Div 2, 22.04.1977
Record League Defeat: 0-7 v Liverpool (A), Div 1, 2 Sept 1978
European Competitions Entered: European Cup 1961-2 European Cup Winners Cup 1962-3, 1963-4, 1967-8, 1981-2 UEFA Cup 1971-2, 1972-3, 1973-4, 1983-4

Club Statistician for the Directory: Andy Porter

Programme Editor
Leslie Yates

Price	Number of Pages
50p	28

Subscriptions
Subscription rate unavailable. Postal rate (in U.K.) 78p per programme
N.B. 'Spurs News' — a monthly publication — is available at £5.00 per annum (postage paid U.K.) or £7.00 per annum (surface postage paid). Apply to 'Spurs News', 748 High Road, Tottenham, London N17 0AP.

TOTTENHAM HOTSPUR

PLAYERS NAME Ht Wt Birthdate	Honours	Birthplace Transfers	Clubs	APPEARANCES League	Milk Cup	F.A.C.	E. Cups	GOALS League	Milk Cup	F.A.C.	E. Cups
GOALKEEPERS											
Ray Clemence	E.(61), U.23(4),	Skegness	Notts. Co. (N-C)								
5-11½ 12.9 5.8.48	Div. 1(5), FAC(2),		Scunthorpe U.	48		2					
	Lg.C., EC(3),		Liverpool	470	55	54					
	UEFAC.(2), ESC.		Tottenham H.	105	15	11	19				
Tony Parks	UEFAC. 84	Hackney	Tottenham H. (A)	19		3	5+1				
5-10½ 10.8 28.1.83											
DEFENDERS											
Mark Bowen	W. U.21(3),	Neath	Tottenham H. (A)	6+1		3					
5-8 11.2 7.12.63	Y, S										
Ian Culverhouse	E. Y	Bishops Stortford	Tottenham H. (A)	1+1							
5-9 11.1 22.9.64											
Chris Hughton	Ei.(10), U.21(1)	Forest Gate	Tottenham H.	182	23	23	23	10	1	1	3
5-7½ 11.5 11.12.58	FAC. 81, 82,										
	UEFAC. 84										
Paul Miller	FAC. 81, 82	Stepney	Tottenham H. (A)	136+2	13	24+	15	5		1	2
6-1 12.2 11.10.59	UEFAC. 84										
Graham Roberts	E.(5), UEFAC. 84	Southampton	Weymouth								
5-10 12.12 3.7.59	FAC. 81, 82	£30,000	Tottenham H.	111+9	10+	21	18+	14		2	3
Gary Stevens	E. U.21(1)	Hillingdon	Brighton (A)	120+13	9+1	15+		2		1	
5-11 11.10 30.3.62	UEFAC. 84	£350,000	Tottenham H.	37+3			9	4			
Danny Thomas	E.(2), U.21(5), S	Worksop	Coventry C. (A)	103+5	11+	8+1		5	1		
5-7 11.0 12.11.61	UEFAC. 84		Tottenham H.	26+1			7+1				
Simon Webster		Hinckley	Tottenham H. (A)	2+1							
6-0 11.0 20.1.64			Exeter C. (L)	26			3				
MIDFIELD											
Ossie Ardiles	Arg., W.C.78,	Argentina	Huracan								
5-6 9.10 3.8.52	FAC. 81,	£325,000	Tottenham H.	140	17	24	6	13	2	4	1
	UEFAC.84		Paris St. Germain	14				1			
			Tottenham H.	10+1	1	1	2+1				1
Gary Brooke	FAC. 81, 82	Bethnal Green	Tottenham H. (A)	48+21	4+1	4+8	6+1	14	1	1	1
5-6 10.5 24.11.60											
Alan Cockram		Kensington	Tottenham H.	2							
5-7 10.0 8.10.63											
Ian Crook		Romford	Tottenham H. (A)	7+1							
5-8 10.6 18.1.63											
Mike Hazard	FAC. 82	Sunderland	Tottenham H. (A)	55+9	8+2	7+3	15+	8	3	2	2
5-7 10.5 5.2.60	UEFAC. 84										
Carl Hoddle		Hayes	Tottenham H. (A)								
6-1 12.2											
Glen Hoddle	E.(19), B(2),	Hayes	Tottenham H. (A)	279+4	28	33+	13+	70	6	9	1
6-0 11.6 27.10.57	U.21(12), Y,										
	FAC. 81, 82										
Gary Mabbutt	E.(9), U.21(5), Y	Bristol	Bristol R. (A)	122+9	10	5+1		10	1	1	2
5-10 10.6 23.8.61	UEFAC. 84	£105,000	Tottenham H.	59	7	4+1	11+	12			1
Steve Perryman*	E.(1), U.23(17), Y,	Ealing	Tottenham H. (A)	589+1	57	61	55+	29	3	2	3
5-8 10.0 21.12.51	S, FAC. 81, 82,										
	Lg.C.(2), UEFA 72										
FORWARDS											
Clive Allen	E.(3), U.21(3), Y,	London	Q.P.R. (A)	43+6	5	1		32	2		
5-10 11.0 20.5.61	S, Div. 2, 83	£1,250,000	Arsenal								
		£1,250,000	Crystal Palace	25	4			9			
		£425,000 + P/E	Q.P.R.	83+4	7	8		40	1	7	
			Tottenham H.								
John Chiedozie	Nigeria	Owerri	Orient (A)	131+14	8	7		20	1	2	
5-7 11.0 18.4.60		£60,000	Notts. Co.	110+1	10	8		15	1	2	
			Tottenham H.								
Richard Cooke		Islington	Tottenham H. (A)	9	1	0+1	4+2	1			
5-7 9.7 4.9.65											
Garth Crooks	E. U.21(4),	Stoke	Stoke C. (A)	141+6	10+	3+2		48	4	1	
5-8 11.6 10.3.58	FAC. 81, 82	£600,000	Tottenham H.	99+4	17+	18	10+	38	5	8	6
			Manchester U. (L)	6+1				2			
Ally Dick	S. Y	Stirling	Tottenham H. (A)	13+1		2	3+1	2			
5-9 10.7 25.4.65	UEFAC. 84										
Mark Falco	E. Y	Hackney	Tottenham H. (A)	75+11	8+2	8	13+	27	1	2	9
6-0 12.0 22.10.60	UEFAC. 84										
Tony Galvin	Ei.(3), S, UEFAC.84	Huddersfield	Goole T.								
5-9 11.5 12.7.56	FAC. 81, 82	£30,000	Tottenham H.	113+3	12	19+	18	11	1	1	5

NON-CONTRACT PLAYERS 1984-85: S. Close, A. Edmonds, T. O'Shea, M. Poultney, T. Wilkinson, Danny Andrews, David Howells, Paul Moran, Gary Poole, Mark Poultney, Mark Stimson, Simon Toms

APPRENTICES: B. Conroy, P. Corder, S. Grenfell, D. Maddix, J. Moncur, J. Polston

TOTTENHAM HOTSPUR

DIVISION ONE 8TH **FA CUP** 4TH ROUND **MILK CUP** 3RD ROUND **UEFA CUP** WINNERS

MATCH	DATE	COMPETITION	VENUE	OPPONENTS	RESULT	HALF TIME	L'GUE POS'N	GOALSCORERS	ATTENDANCE
1	A 27	CL	A	Ipswich T	L1-3	0-1		Archibald	26,185
2	29	CL	H	Coventry C	D1-1	1-0		Hoddle (pen)	35,854
3	S 3	CL	H	West Ham U	L0-2	0-2	20		38,042
4	7	CL	A	WBA	D1-1	1-0		Roberts	14,989
5	10	CL	A	Leicester C	W3-0	2-0	15	Crooks, Mabbutt, Stevens	15,538
6	**14**	**UEFA 1**	**A**	**Drogheda**	**W6-0**	**3-0**		**Falco 2, Mabbutt 2, Crooks, Galvin**	**7,000**
7	17	CL	H	Everton	L1-2	0-2	18	Falco	29,125
8	24	CL	A	Watford	W3-2	0-1	16	Hoddle, Archibald, Hughton	21,056
9	**28**	**UEFA 1**	**H**	**Drogheda**	**W8-0**	**4-0**		**Falco 2, Roberts 2, Brazil 2, A'bald, H'ton**	**19,831**
10	O 2	CL	H	Nottingham F	W2-1	0-1		Stevens, Archibald	30,596
11	**5**	**MC 2**	**H**	**Lincoln C**	**W3-1**	**2-0**		**Archibald, Houghton (og), Galvin**	**20,241**
12	15	CL	A	Wolverhampton W	W3-2	2-1	9	Archibald 2, Falco	12,523
13	**19**	**UEFA 2**	**H**	**Feyenoord**	**W4-2**	**4-0**		**Archibald 2, Galvin 2**	**35,404**
14	22	CL	A	Birmingham C	W1-0	0-0	8	Archibald	19,016
15	**26**	**MC 2**	**A**	**Lincoln C**	**L1-2**	**0-1**		**Falco**	**12,088**
16	29	CL	H	Notts Co	W1-0	0-0	6	Archibald	29,138
17	**N 2**	**UEFA 2**	**A**	**Feyenoord**	**W2-0**	**1-0**		**Hughton, Galvin**	**54,600**
18	5	CL	A	Stoke C	D1-1	1-1	5	Falco	14,727
19	**8**	**MC 3**	**H**	**Arsenal**	**L1-2**	**0-1**		**Hoddle (pen)**	**48,200**
20	12	CL	H	Liverpool	D2-2	1-1	7	Archibald, Hoddle (pen)	45,032
21	19	CL	A	Luton T	W4-2	1-0	4	Cook, Archibald 2, Dick	17,275
22	**23**	**UEFA 3**	**A**	**Bayern Munich**	**L0-1**	**0-0**			**25,000**
23	26	CL	H	QPR	W3-2	1-1	4	Falco 2, Archibald	38,789
24	D 3	CL	A	Norwich C	L1-2	1-1	4	Dick	22,148
25	**7**	**UEFA 3**	**H**	**Bayern Munich**	**W2-0**	**0-0**		**Archibald, Falco**	**41,977**
26	10	CL	H	Southampton	D0-0	0-0	6		29,711
27	16	CL	H	Manchester U	L2-4	0-1	11	Brazil, Falco	33,616
28	26	CL	H	Arsenal	L2-4	1-1	11	Roberts, Archibald	38,756
29	27	CL	A	Aston Villa	D0-0	0-0	11		30,125
30	31	CL	A	West Ham U	L1-4	1-1	11	Stevens	30,939
31	J 2	CL	H	Watford	L2-3	0-2	12	Hughton, Hoddle (pen)	32,495
32	**7**	**FAC 3**	**A**	**Fulham**	**D0-0**	**0-0**			**23,398**
33	**11**	**FAC 3R**	**H**	**Fulham**	**W2-0**	**2-0**		**Roberts, Archibald**	**32,898**
34	14	CL	H	Ipswich T	W2-0	2-0	13	Roberts, Falco	25,832
35	21	CL	A	Everton	L1-2	0-1	12	Archibald	18,003
36	**28**	**FAC 4**	**H**	**Norwich C**	**D0-0**	**0-0**			**37,792**
37	**F 1**	**FAC 4R**	**A**	**Norwich C**	**L1-2**	**0-2**		**Falco**	**26,811**
38	4	CL	A	Nottingham F	D2-2	1-1	13	Falco, Hughton	21,428
39	8	CL	H	Sunderland	W3-0	2-0	9	Archibald 2, Perryman	19,327
40	11	CL	H	Leicester C	W3-2	1-0	7	Falco, Archibald, Galvin	24,810
41	21	CL	A	Notts Co	D0-0	0-0			7,943
42	25	CL	H	Birmingham C	L0-1	0-0	9		23,564
43	M 3	CL	H	Stoke C	W1-0	1-0	7	Falco (pen)	18,271
44	**7**	**UEFA QF1**	**H**	**Austria Vienna**	**W2-0**	**0-0**		**Archibald, Brazil**	**34,069**
45	10	CL	A	Liverpool	L1-3	1-2	7	Stevens	36,718
46	17	CL	H	WBA	L0-1	0-0	10		22,385
47	**21**	**UEFA QF2**	**A**	**Austria Vienna**	**D2-2**	**1-0**		**Brazil, Ardiles**	**21,000**
48	24	CL	A	Coventry C	W4-2	2-0	9	Brazil 2 (1 pen), Roberts, Hazard	12,803
49	31	CL	H	Wolverhampton W	W1-0	1-0	7	Hazard	19,296
50	A 7	CL	A	Sunderland	D1-1	1-1	8	Falco	15,433
51	**11**	**UEFA SF1**	**A**	**Hajduk Split**	**L1-2**	**1-0**		**Falco**	**35,000**
52	14	CL	H	Luton T	W2-1	1-0	7	Roberts, Falco	25,390
53	18	CL	H	Aston Villa	W2-1	2-1		Mabbutt, Roberts (pen)	18,668
54	21	CL	A	Arsenal	L2-3	0-1	7	Archibald 2	48,831
55	**25**	**UEFA SF2**	**H**	**Hajduk Split**	**W1-0**	**0-0**		**Hazard**	**43,969**
56	28	CL	A	QPR	L1-2	0-1	8	Archibald	24,937
57	M 5	CL	H	Norwich C	W2-0	1-0	7	Falco, Archibald	18,874
58	7	CL	A	Southampton	L0-5	0-2	8		21,141
59	**9**	**UEFA F1**	**A**	**Anderlecht**	**D1-1**	**0-0**		**Miller**	**40,000**
60	12	CL	H	Manchester U	D1-1	0-0	7	Archibald	39,790
61	**23**	**UEFA F2**	**H**	**Anderlecht**	**D1-1***	**0-0**		**Roberts**	**46,205**

*Won 4-3 on Penalties, After Extra Time

Av Home Att 28,754

Goal Scorers

League (64): Archibald 21, Falco 13 (1 pen), Roberts 6 (1 pen), Hoddle 4 (3 pens), Stevens 4, Brazil 3 (1 pen), Hughton 3, Dick 2, Hazard 2, Mabbutt 2, Cook 1, Crooks 1, Galvin 1, Perryman 1
FA Cup (3): Archibald 1, Falco 1, Roberts 1
Milk Cup (5): Archibald 1, Falco 1, Galvin 1, Hoddle 1 (1 pen), opponents 1
UEFA Cup (20): Falco 6, Archibald 5, Brazil 4, Galvin 4, Roberts 3, Hughton 2, Mabbutt 2, Ardiles 1, Crooks 1, Hazard 1, Miller 1

1983-84

Clemence	Thomas	Mabbutt	Roberts	Stevens	Perryman	Hazard	Archibald	Galvin	Hoddle	Brazil	Falco	Bowen	Hughton	Miller	Crooks	O'Reilly	Brooke	Price	Dick	Cook	Ardiles	Webster	Cockram	Parks	REFEREE	
1	2	3	4	5	6	7	8	9	10	11*	12														M Scott	1
1	3	7	4	5	6		8	9	10	11*	12	2													I Borrett	2
1	3	7	4	5	6			9	10*		8		2	12	11										J Hunting/D Nevin	3
1		7	4	5	6			9			8		3		11	2	10								D Hedges	4
1		7	4	5	6			9			8	12	2		11	3	10*								D Owen	5
1		**7**	**4**		**6**			**8**			**10**		**2**		**11**	**3**	**9**	**5**							**Amundson**	**6**
1		7	4		6			9		12	8		2		11*	3	10	5							EA Read	7
1		7	4	5	6		12	3	10	9	8		2				11*								A Challinor	8
1		**7**	**4**		**6**		**8**	**3**	**10**	**11**	**9**		**2***			**12**		**5**							**Briguglio**	**9**
1		7	4	5	6		8	3	10	11*	9		2				12								A Robinson	10
1		**7**	**4**	**5**	**6**	**12**	**8**	**3**	**10**		**9**		**2**				**11***								**A Gunn**	**11**
1		7	4*	5	6		8	3	10		9		2				11	12							RA Banks	12
1		**7**	**4**	**5**	**6**		**8**	**3**	**10**		**9**		**2**		**12**		**11***								**G Muro**	**13**
1		7	4	5	6		8	3	10		9		2			12									D Shaw	14
1		**7**	**4**	**5**	**6**		**8**	**3**	**10**		**9**		**2**		**12**						**11***				**N Midgley**	**15**
1		7	4	5	6		8	3	10		9		2		12		11*								J Martin	16
1	**3**	**7**	**4**	**5**	**6**		**8**	**11**	**10**	**12**	**9***		**2**												**Agnolin**	**17**
1	3	7*	4	5	6		8	11	10		9		2			12									N Wilson	18
1	**3**		**7**	**5**	**6**		**8**	**11**	**10**	**12**	**9**		**2**					**4***							**K Hackett**	**19**
1	3		4	5	6		8	11	10	12	9		2						7*						M Taylor	20
1	3		4	5	6		8		10		9		2						7	11					L Robinson	21
1	**3**		**4**	**5**	**6**	**7***	**8**		**10**	**13**	**9**		**2**				**12**		**11***						**Muro**	**22**
1	3		4	5	6		8		10		9		2						11	7					N Ashley	23
1	3		4	5	6		8		10		9		2			12			11	7*					G Napthine	24
1	**2**		**4**	**5**	**6**		**8**		**10**		**9**		**3***			**12**			**11**	**7**					**Delmer**	**25**
1	3		4	5	6		8*		10	11	9					2	12			7					K Barratt	26
1	3		4	5	6			7*	10	8	9					2			11		12				A Saunders	27
1			4	5	6		8		10	9	12		2*						11	3	7				R Lewis	28
1	3		4	5	6		8	7*	10	9	12		11			2									R Milford	29
1	10			5	6		8				9	3				2			11		7	4			T Spencer	30
1	2			4	6		8		10		9	2	3			5	12						11*		A Seville	31
1*			**4**	**2**	**6**	**11**			**10**	**8**	**9**	**3**				**5**	**7**			**12**					**T Bune**	**32**
			4	**2**	**6**		**8**	**11**	**10**		**9**	**3**		**5**						**7**				**1**	**T Bune**	**33**
			4	2	6		8	11	10*		9	3		5	12					7				1	G Thomas	34
		7	4	2	6		8	11	10		9	3		5										1	D Hutchinson	35
		7	**4**	**2**	**6**	**12**	**8**	**11**	**10**		**9***	**3**		**5**										**1**	**J Worral**	**36**
		7	**4**	**2**	**6**	**12**	**8**	**11**			**9***		**3**	**5**							**10**			**1**	**J Worral**	**37**
	12	7	4	2	6		8	11			9		3	5*							10			1	T Mills	38
			4	2	6		8	11	10		9		3	5							7			1	J Bray	39
			4	2	6		8	11	10		9		3	5					12		7*			1	K Childs	40
	2			5	6			11*	10	8	9		3	4							7			1	R Nixon	41
	2			4	6	12	8		10	9			3	5					11*	7				1	D Letts	42
			4	2	6	10				8	9		3	5			12		11*		7			1	A Crickmore	43
			4	**2**	**6**	**10***	**8**		**12**	**9**			**3**	**5**					**11**		**7**			**1**	**Sostaric (YUG)**	**44**
1	2		4	7	6	10	8			9			3	5	12				11*						T Jones	45
1	2	11	4	10	6	12	8			9			3	5*							7				D Axcell	46
1	**12**	**2**	**4**	**10**	**6**		**8**	**11**		**9***	**13**		**3**	**5**							**7***				**Prokop (EG)**	**47**
1	2		4	10	6	7	8	11		9			3	5											L Dilkes	48
	2		4	8	6	7		11		10	9		3	5										1	L Burden	49
	2		4	8*	6	7		11		10	9		3	5			12							1	G Worrall	50
	2	**10***	**4**		**6**	**7**	**8**	**11**			**9**		**3**	**5**	**12**									**1**	**Wurtz (F)**	**51**
	2	10	4	12	6	7	8	11*			9		3	5										1	M Bodenham	52
	2	10	4	12	6	7*	8	11			9		3	5										1	L Shapter	53
	2	7	4	12	6		8	9					3	5	11									1	J Hunting	54
	2	**12**	**4**	**10***	**6**	**7**	**8**	**11**			**9**		**3**	**5**										**1**	**Casarin (IT)**	**55**
	2	7		4	8	6	11	9			10		5	3										1	J Martin	56
	2	10		4	6		8	11			9*		3	5	12					7				1	Alan Robinson	57
1										10		3		5	11	4	8			7			9		G Napthine	58
	2	**12**	**3**	**8***	**6**	**7**	**11**	**9**			**10**		**5**	**4**										**1**		**59**
	2	7	4	10	6		8	11			9		3	5										1	M Taylor	60
	2	**6***	**4**	**10**		**7**	**8**	**11**			**9**		**3**	**5***					**12**		**13**			**1**		**61**
26	26	21	35	37	41	9	31	30	24	17	32	6	34	20	6	9	7	1	10	9	8	1	2	16	League Appearances	
	+1S			+3S		+2S	+1S			+2S	+4S	+1S		+1S	+4S	+3S	+5S	+1S	+1S		+1S					
1		2	4	4	4	1+2S	3	3	3	1	4	3	1	3		1	1			1+1S	1			3	FA Cup Appearances	
3	1	2	3	3	3	1S	3	3	3	1S	3		3		1S		1	1			1				Milk Cup Appearances	
7	7+1S	7+2S	12	9	11	6	11	9	5+1S	3+2S	10+1S		12	6	1+2S	1+2S	2+1S	2	3+1S	1	2+1S			5	UEFA Cup Appearances	

Also Played: Culverhouse match 41, no.12; 58, no.2. Crook match 14, no.11; 54, no.10; 58, no.6.

WHITE HART LANE

Official Address: 748 High Road, Tottenham, London N17. Telephone: 01-801 3411

Ground Capacity: 50,000

Record Attendance: 75,038 v. Sunderland, FA Cup Round 6, 5 Mar 1938

Record Receipts: Not divulged v. Anderlecht, UEFA Cup Final 2nd Leg, 23 May 1984

Size of Playing Area: 110 × 73 yds

Season Tickets: Stands: £125, £137.50, £150, £175, £200, £250; Ground: £60 (£30 Juvelines/OAPs)

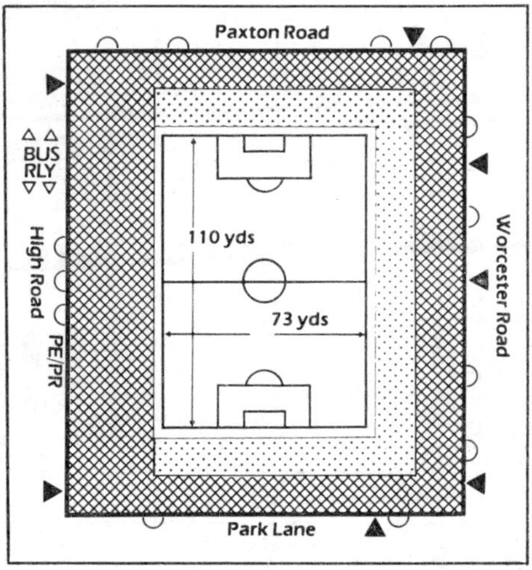

For key see page 12

Executive Box Season Tickets: Between £10,000 and £12,000 (all sold)

Cost of Stand Tickets: £5, £7, £8, £10; Family Section: £5 (£2); Ground: £3.00 (£1.50 Members of Junior Spurs Club)

Match and Ticket Information: Seats for League matches bookable three weeks in advance. Seats are available on match days at the Park Lane and Paxton Road ends

Car Parking: No street parking within a ¼ mile radius of the ground

How to get to the ground

From North, East, South and West: Use A406 North Circular Road to Edmonton then at traffic signals follow signs Tottenham A1010 into Fore Street for Tottenham Hotspur F.C.

TRANMERE ROVERS — Division 4

President
HB Thomas

Chairman
GA Gould

Directors
GL Baird
GJH Kemp
AJ Adams
GEH Jones
WR McAteer
FJ Williams
JJ Hulsgrove

General Manager Secretary
J Butterfield

Manager
Bryan Hamilton

Assistant Manager
Ray Mathias

Youth Team Coach
A Muir

Commercial Manager
W Rimmer (051 608 3677/4194)

Physiotherapist
Judith Foed

Groundsman
FR Davies

Tenth place in the League and sixty-six points was the final 'score' for Tranmere Rovers and for a struggling club that was not bad. In the major domestic cup competitions there was immediate elimination in both cases at the first time of asking, but The Rovers were the first finalists with Hull City in the Northern Section of the new Associate Members Cup, so again there were consolations. All this meant that it was a much better season for the club after the near-extinction and the poor final position of the previous year and Bryan Hamilton was one manager who was not shown the door by his employers.

In the League Rovers made a poorish start but an unbeaten spell of five matches in October steadied the team and from then onwards there was no need to fight against a need to apply for re-election. By this time too the Milk Cup challenge had come and gone (0-1 on aggregate against Preston North End), whilst the F.A. Cup campaign also ended early with a draw (1-1) at Prenton Park being followed at Bolton by a severe beating, the Trotters winning by four goals to one. The team could have been excused for allowing their form to slump but they showed the right attitude and won much respect for their fine form in the new Associate Members Cup. Ultimate defeat by Hull was no disgrace.

Bryan Hamilton must take a great deal of credit for the successes and must also hope that his popular team will do even better from now onwards. The retained list shows how satisfied the manager and board have been with the form and with this stability they will look for further good form from Burgess, Aspinall, Hilditch, Mungall and Palios — to mention just a few heroes. Uncommitted fans elsewhere will wish them all well.

WLM

Back Row: Ron Goodlass, Ray Woods, Nigel Adkins, Bob Wardle, Mark Ferguson, Mark Palios. **Middle Row:** John Aspinall, Colin Clarke, Mark Hilditch, Dave Philpotts, John Clayton, John Williams, Doug Anderson, Dave Higgins, Dave Burgess. **Front Row:** Andy Lee, Seamus Heath, Bryan Hamilton (Player Manager), Billy Rodaway (Captain), Ray Mathias (Player Coach), Steve Mungall, Neville Powell.

'THE ROVERS'

Sponsored by **Hugh Foulerton Cutlery Ltd**

Formed: 1883 **Turned Professional:** 1912 **Ltd Co:** 1920
Previous Names: None
Previous Managers: Since 1946:
Ernie Blackburn Noel Kelly Peter Farrell Walter Galbraith Dave Russell Jackie Wright Ron Yeats Peter King
Honours: Division Three (North) Champions 1937-8 Welsh Cup Winners 1934-5
League Career: Original members of Division Three (North) 1921 Promoted to Division Two 1938 Relegated to Division Three (North) 1939 Original members of Division Three 1958 Relegated to Division Four 1961 Promoted to Division Three 1967 Relegated to Division Four 1975 Promoted to Division Three 1976 Relegation to Division Four 1979
Colours: Blue shirts with red pinstripe, white shorts, white stockings with blue and red trim
Change Colours: All red

CLUB RECORDS

Most Appearances for Club: Harold Bell, 595*, 1946-64
Most Capped Player: Albert Gray, 3(22), Wales **For England:** None
Record Goalscorer in a Match: 'Bunny' Bell, 9 v Oldham Athletic, 26.12.35
Record League Goalscorer in a season: 'Bunny' Bell, 35, Div 3(N), 1933-4
Record League Goalscorer in a career: 'Bunny' Bell, 104, 1931-6
Record Transfer Fee Received: £120,000 from Cardiff City for Ronnie Moore, Feb 1979
Record Transfer Fee Paid: £20,000 to Charlton Athletic for Hugh McAuley, Aug 1978
Best Performances: League: 22nd Div 2 1938-9 **F.A. Cup:** 5th Round 1967-8 **League/Milk Cup:** 4th Round 1960-1, 1981-2
Most League Points: 66 in Div 4, 1983-4 **Most League Goals:** 111, Div 3(N), 1930-1
Record League Victory: 13-4 v Oldham Athletic, Div 3(N), 26 Dec 1935
Record League Defeat: 2-9 v. Q.P.R., Div 3, 3 Dec 1960
*Including League Record of 401 consecutive appearances.

Club Statistician for the Directory: Bernard Jones

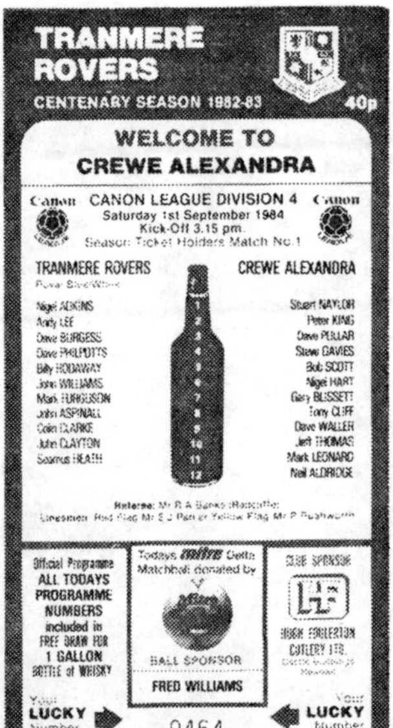

The programme is produced as one sheet folded three times and costs 40p

TRANMERE ROVERS

PLAYERS NAME Ht Wt Birthdate	Honours	Birthplace Transfers	Clubs	APPEARANCES League	Milk Cup	F.A.C.	A.M.C.	GOALS League	Milk Cup	F.A.C.	A.M.C.
GOALKEEPER											
Nigel Adkins		Birkenhead	Tranmere R. (A)	14							
-11 12.7 11.3.65											
DEFENDERS											
David Burgess†		Liverpool	Tranmere R.	136	12	8	5	1			
-10 11.2 20.1.60											
David Higgins		Liverpool	Tranmere R.	20			4				
-0 11.0 19.8.61											
Andy Lee	E. S	Liverpool	Liverpool (A)								
-7 10.8			Wrexham								
			Bangor C.								
			Stafford R.								
			Tranmere R.								
Steve Mungall		Bellshill	Motherwell	14+6							
-8 10.2 22.5.58		F	Tranmere R.	154+9	9+2	10+	3	5			
Billy Rodaway*	E. S	Liverpool	Burnley (A)	207+2	16	11					
-10 13.2 26.9.54		F	Peterborough	80+1	6	6					
			Blackpool	41	2	5					
John Williams		Liverpool	Tranmere R.	124+6	11	6		9			
-2 13.6 3.10.60											
Gary Williams		Nantwich	Tranmere R.	1							
-9½ 11.5 14.5.59		F	Djugarden								
		£40,000	Blackpool	30+1	4	2		2		1	
		£40,000	Swindon T.	37+1	2	2		3			
		F	Tranmere R.	50	2	1	5	3			
MIDFIELD											
John Aspinall		Birkenhead	Tranmere R.	73+4	5	6	3	19	1	2	
-10 11.1 15.3.59											
Ronnie Goodlass		Liverpool	Everton	31+4				2			
-7 11.9 6.9.53			Den Haag								
			Fulham	21+1				1			
			Scunthorpe U.	9							
			Hong Kong								
			Tranmere R.	18+2			4				
Seamus Heath			Wrexham	32	2	1	2+1	5			
-7 10.0											
Bobby Hutchinson		Glasgow	Montrose	41				8			
-9 11.4 19.6.53			Dundee U.	88				25			
			Hibernian	67				13			
			Wigan A.	35				3			
			Tranmere R.	35				6			
Mark Palios		Birkenhead	Tranmere R.	177+13	15	8		25			
-8 10.13 9.11.57		F	Crewe A.	114+4	1	4		23			
		F	Tranmere R.	32+3				4			
			Wigan A.	34+1				3			
			Tranmere R.	32+3				6			
			Mansfield T.	10				3			
			Tranmere R.								
FORWARDS											
Doug Anderson		Hong Kong	Port Glasgow								
-11½ 9.8 29.8.63			Oldham A.	4+5	0+1	0+1					
Colin Clarke		Newry	Ipswich T. (A)								
-11 12.10 30.10.62			Peterborough U.	76+6							
			Gillingham (L)	8							
			Tranmere R.								
John Clayton		Elgin	Derby Co. (A)	11				1			
-11 11.7 20.8.61			Hong Kong								
			Chesterfield	25+8	3+1	3		5			
Mark Ferguson		Liverpool	Tranmere R.	57+12	3	4	0+1	12			
-8 12.4 6.11.60											
Mark Hilditch		Royton	Rochdale	184+13	10	11	5	40	1	4	5
-11 11.8 20.8.60		F	Tranmere R.	39	2			8			
Neville Powell		Flint	Tranmere R. (A)	75+10	5	3+3	5	4			1
-8 10.1 2.9.63											
Ray Woods		Birkenhead	Tranmere R. (A)	3+4			1	2			
-9 10.4 7.6.65											

NON-CONTRACT PLAYERS 1984-85: Tony Clarke, Joe Craven, Tom Doherty, Paul Fitzpatrick, Bryan Hamilton, Mark Horgan, Steve Jones, Ron Kilshaw, Ian McMullen, Ray Mathias, Paul Proctor, Tony Sumner

TRANMERE ROVERS

DIVISION FOUR 10TH **FA CUP** 1ST ROUND **MILK CUP** 1ST ROUND

MATCH	DATE	COMPE-TITION	VENUE	OPPONENTS	RESULT	HALF TIME	L'GUE POS'N	GOALSCORERS	ATTEN-DANCE
1	A 27	CL	H	Bury	D1-1	0-0		Aspinall	2,133
2	**30**	**MC 1**	**A**	**Preston NE**	**L0-1**	**0-0**			**3,231**
3	S 3	CL	A	Torquay U	D1-1	0-0	18	Pallos	2,317
4	6	CL	A	Northampton T	D0-0	0-0			2,326
5	10	CL	H	Wrexham	W2-1	2-1	13	Aspinall, Hilditch	2,425
6	**12**	**MC 1**	**H**	**Preston NE**	**D0-0**	**0-0**			**2,986**
7	17	CL	A	Mansfield T	L0-1	0-0	15		2,002
8	23	CL	H	Hereford U	L0-1	0-0			1,984
9	26	CL	H	Colchester U	W2-1	1-0		Williams G, Ferguson	1,866
10	O 1	CL	A	Hartlepool U	W1-0	1-0	10	Aspinall	1,226
11	8	CL	A	Aldershot	D1-1	0-1	10	Brown	1,769
12	14	CL	H	Bristol C	W2-0	1-0		Williams G, Halliday (og)	2,518
13	17	CL	H	Swindon T	W2-1	1-1		Ferguson, Bailie (og)	2,543
14	22	CL	A	Peterborough U	L0-2	0-0	6		3,311
15	29	CL	H	Doncaster R	D1-1	1-0	7	Hilditch	2,789
16	N 1	CL	A	Darlington	L0-1	0-0			1,776
17	4	CL	A	Halifax T	W2-1	2-1		Philpotts, Williams G	1,735
18	12	CL	H	Rochdale	D2-2	2-2	9	Aspinall, Ferguson	2,455
19	**19**	**FAC 1**	**H**	**Bolton W**	**D2-2**	**1-1**		**Aspinall, Powell**	**5,497**
20	**22**	**FAC 1R**	**A**	**Bolton W**	**L1-4[1]**	**1-1**		**Allen**	**6,305**
21	26	CL	H	Crewe Alex	L2-3	1-3	12	Mathias, Aspinall	2,210
22	D 3	CL	A	Chesterfield	D3-3	2-1	12	Ferguson, Pallos, Williams J	2,796
23	15	CL	A	Stockport Co	L1-2	0-2	13	Hilditch	1,644
24	26	CL	H	Blackpool	W3-2	2-0	12	Hetzkie (og), Aspinall 2 (1 pen)	3,492
25	27	CL	A	York C	D1-1	0-1	12	Philpotts	6,357
26	30	CL	H	Reading	L2-3	1-2		Aspinall 2	2,716
27	J 2	CL	A	Chester C	D0-0	0-0	14		2,672
28	7	CL	H	Torquay U	W3-0	0-0	13	Hilditch 2, Aspinall	1,789
29	30	CL	H	Mansfield T	W1-0	0-0	13	Philpotts	1,482
30	F 3	CL	H	Hartlepool U	L0-1	0-1	13		1,774
31	7	CL	A	Bury	D0-0	0-0	12		1,502
32	11	CL	A	Hereford U	W1-0	0-0	10	Philpotts	2,188
33	13	CL	H	Darlington	L0-1	0-0			1,606
34	18	CL	A	Doncaster R	D1-1	0-0	12	Aspinall	3,781
35	**20**	**AMC 1**	**H**	**Halifax T**	**W2-0**	**0-0**		**Hutchinson, Hilditch**	**937**
36	24	CL	H	Peterborough U	D0-0	0-0			1,763
37	M 3	CL	A	Swindon T	D1-1	1-1	13	Bailie (og)	2,595
38	5	CL	H	Halifax T	W3-2	2-0		Hutchinson, Pallos, Aspinall	1,486
39	10	CL	A	Rochdale	W3-2	2-0	9	Powell, Hilditch, Aspinall	1,263
40	**12**	**AMC 2**	**H**	**Chester C**	**W4-1**	**1-0**		**Hilditch 3, Goodlass**	**2,116**
41	17	CL	H	Aldershot	W3-0	2-0	8	Hilditch, Hutchinson 2	1,761
42	**20**	**AMC NQF**	**H**	**Crew Alex**	**D0-0[4]**	**0-0**			**2,246**
43	24	CL	A	Bristol C	D1-1	0-0	9	Hutchinson	6,548
44	30	CL	H	Northampton T	W1-0	0-0		Aspinall	1,839
45	A 7	CL	A	Colchester U	W1-0	0-0	7	Pallos	1,679
46	14	CL	H	Chesterfield	L0-3	0-2	8		1,929
47	**17**	**AMC NSF**	**H**	**Burnley**	**W2-0[1]**	**0-0**		**Hilditch, Philpotts**	**3,968**
48	21	CL	A	Blackpool	W1-0	0-0	7	Hilditch	4,055
49	23	CL	H	York C	L0-1	0-1	7		3,527
50	28	CL	A	Crewe Alex	L0-3	0-1	8		2,066
51	M 5	CL	H	Chester C	D2-2	1-1	10	Philpotts (pen), Woods	1,592
52	7	CL	A	Reading	L0-1	0-0	10		6,989
53	12	CL	H	Stockport Co	W1-0	0-0	10	Woods	1,475
54	**18**	**AMC NF**	**A**	**Hull C**	**L1-4**	**0-1**		**Hutchinson**	**5,478**
55	21	CL	A	Wrexham	L1-5	0-2		Philpotts (pen)	1,858

[1]After Extra Time [4]Won 4-3 on Penalties, After Extra Time **Av Home Att** **2,137**

Goal Scorers

League (53): Aspinall, 14 (1 pen), Hilditch 8, Philpotts 6 (2 pens), Ferguson 4, Hutchinson 4, Pallos 4, Williams G 3, Woods 2, Brown 1, Mathias 1, Powell 1, Williams J 1, opponents 4

FA Cup (3): Allen 1, Aspinall 1, Powell 1

Milk Cup (-): —

AMC (9): Hilditch 5, Hutchinson 2, Goodlass 1, Philpotts 1

1983-84

Davies	McMahon	Burgess	Parry	Hamilton	Williams J	Powell	Aspinall	Hilditch	Allen	Williams G	Brown O	Pallos	Ferguson	Higgins	Mungall	Philpotts	Mathias	Greenwood (L)	Adkins	Goodlass	Woods	Wellings	Hutchinson		REFEREE	
1	2	3	4	5	6	7	8	9	10*	11	12														A Seville	1
1	**2**	**3**	**4***	**5**	**6**	**7**	**8**	**9**	**10**	**11**		**12**													**G Courtney**	**2**
1	2	3		5	6	7	8	9		11	10	4													K Cooper	3
1	2	3		5	6	7	8	9		11	10	4													D Reeves	4
1	2	3		5	6		8	9	12	11	10*	4	7												N Wilson	5
1	**2**	**3**		**5**	**6**		**8**	**9**		**11**	**10†**	**4**	**7**												**J Key**	**6**
1	2	3			6		8	9*	12	11	10	4	7	5											AN Buksh	7
1	2	3		5	6		8	9	12	11	10*	4	7												WH Glover	8
1	2	3	4	5*	6		8	9	10	11			7		12										MJ Heath	9
1	2	3	4		6		8	9	10	11			7		5										K Hackett	10
1	2	3	4*	12	6		8	9		11	10		7		5										E Scales	11
1	2	3	4	12	6*		8	9		11	10		7		5										MG Peck	12
1	2	3	4				8	9		11	10		7		5	6									DB Allison	13
1	2	3	4†	12			8*	9		11	10	5	7			6									C Downey	14
1	2	3	4				8	9		11	10	6	7			5									N Smidgley	15
1	2	3	4	12			8	9*		11	10	5	7			6									M Dimblebee	16
1	2	3					8		9	11	10	5	7	4*		6	12								H Taylor	17
1	2	3					8			11	10	4	7	5		6		9							K Barratt	18
1	**2**	**3**				**11**	**8**		**9**		**10**	**6**	**7**	**4**		**5**									**N Ashley**	**19**
1	**2**	**3**				**7**	**8**		**9**	**11**	**10**	**6***		**4**		**5**	**12**								**N Ashley**	**20**
1	2	3					8		12	11	10*		7	4		6	5	9							K Walmsley	21
	2	3			6	12	8	9				5*	7			4		10	1	11					M Robinson	22
1	2	3			6*	11	8	9	10			5	7			4					12				D Richardson	23
1	2	3				12	8	9	10				7*		6	4	5			11					J Hough	24
1	2	3				7	8	9					12		6	4	5			11		10*			G Tyson	25
1	2	3				7	8	9			12				6	4	5			11		10*			P Tyldesley	26
1	2	3				7	8	9			12				6	4	5			11		10			G Napthine	27
1	2	3				7	8	9							6	4	5			11		10			R Banks	28
1	2	3				7		9						5	6	4				11		10	8		T Jones	29
1	2	3			12	8		9						5	6	4				11		10*	7		A Challinor	30
1	2	3			6		7	9		11*				5		4				12		10	8		C Seel	31
1	2	3			6*		7	9		11				5		4				12		10	8		T Bune	32
1	2	3			6		7	9		11		12		5		4						10*	8		D Allison	33
1	2	3				7	8	9		6		6				4				11			10		L Dilkes	34
1	**2**	**3**				**7**	**8**	**9**		**5**		**6**				**4**				**11**			**10**		**M Heath**	**35**
1	2	3				7	8	9*		6	12	5		4						11			10		T Fitzharris	36
1	2*	3					8			5	10	6	7		9	4				11	12				A Buksh	37
1		3					8			5	12	6	7*	2	9	4				11			10		N Midgley	38
1		3				7	8	9*		5		6	12		2	4				11			10		K Baker	39
1	**2**	**3**				**7**	**8**	**9**		**5**				**6**		**4**				**11**			**10**		**I Hendrick**	**40**
1		3				7	8*	9		5			12	6	2	4				11			10		K Walmsley	41
1		**3**				**7**	**8**	**9**		**5**		**12**		**6***	**2**	**4**				**11**			**10**		**N Glover**	**42**
1		3					8	9		5		6	7	2		4				11			10		A Seville	43
1		3			12	7	8	9*		5		6			2	4				11			10		D Scott	44
1	12	3			9	7	8			5		6			2	4*				11			10		L Burden	45
1	9*	3				7	8			5		6	12		2	4				11			10		D Hutchinson	46
1	**11**	**3**				**7**		**9**		**5**		**6**		**8**	**2**	**4**							**10**		**D Hough**	**47**
1	11	3				7		9		5		6		8	2	4							10		A Saunders	48
1	11	3			4*	7		9		5		6	12	8	2								10		F Roberts	49
1		3				7	8	9		5		6	12	11*	2	4							10		J Key	50
	11	3				7	8	9		5*				6	2	4			1		12		10		M Peck	51
	3*			12		7	8	9		5				6	2	4			1		11		10		J Moules	52
1	11							9		5	12	6	8*	3	2	4					7		10		D Richardson	53
1	**8**	**3**				**7***		**9**		**5**			**12**	**6**	**2**	**4**				**11***	**13**		**10**		**P Willis**	**54**
	11	3			6	12		9		5				2	8	4			1		7*		10		A Robinson	55
42	39	44	9	6	18	22	40	39	6	37	15	25	21	20	25	34	6	3	4	18	3	9	21		League Appearances	
	+1S			+5S	+2S	+3S			+4S		+6S	+1S	+6S		+1S		+1S			+2S	+3S					
2	2	2				2	2		2	1	2	2	1	2		2	1S								FA Cup Appearances	
2	2	2	1	2	2	1	2	2	1	2	1	1+1S	1												Milk Cup Appearances	
5	4	5				5	3	5		5		2+1S	1S	4	3	5				4	1S			5	AM Cup Appearances	

PRENTON PARK

Official Address: Prenton Park, Prenton Road West, Birkenhead. Telephone: 051-608 3677/4194

Ground Capacity: 18,000

Record Attendance: 24,424 v. Stock City, F.A. Cup Round 4, 5 Feb 1922

Record Receipts: £16,392.90 v. Wolverhampton Wanderers, F.A. Cup Round 3, 8 Jan 1983

Size of Playing Area: 112yds × 74 yds

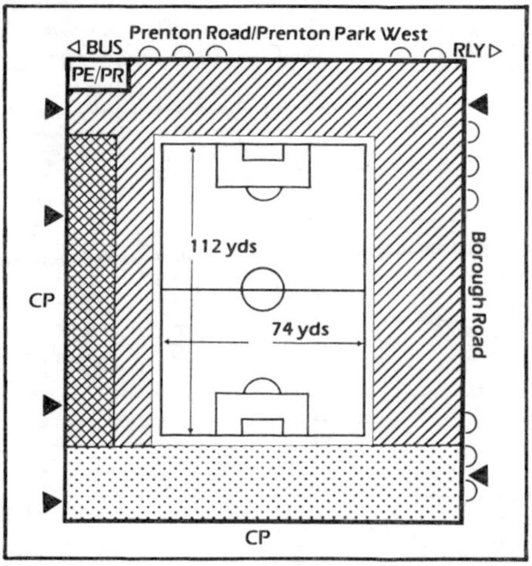

For key see page 12

Season Tickets: £40 (adults), £30 (juveniles/OAPs) for Ground; £52.50 (adults, £35 (juveniles/OAPs) Stands

Executive Box Season Tickets: £95.00

Cost of Stand Tickets: £3.00 (adults), £2.00 (juveniles/OAPs); **Terraces:** £2.00 (adults), £1,50 (juveniles/OAPs)

Match and Ticket Information: Not bookable in advance.

Car Parking: Large park at back of Stand. Also street parking.

How to get to the ground

From North: Use Mersey Tunnel and Motorway M53 until junction 3. Leave motorway and at roundabout take 1st exit A552. In 1.3m at crossroads turn right B5151 then turn left into Prenton Road for Tranmere Rovers F.C.
From South: Use Motorway M53 until junction 4, leave motorway and at roundabout take 4th exit B5151. In 2.5m turn right into Prenton Road for Tranmere Rovers F.C.

WALSALL Division 3

Chairman
K E Wheldon

Directors
J A Harris
R Homden
S E Boler

Secretary
John Westmancoat, FAAI

Commercial Department
(0922 22791)

Manager
Alan Buckley

Assistant Manager/Coach
Gary Pendrey

Physiotherapist
Fred Pedley

Chief Scout
Steve Joesbury

Groundsman
Roger Johnson

Commercial Manager
Refer to Secretary (0922 22791)

About the only thing which did not go right for Walsall in the past season was that their brilliant side was not rewarded with promotion to the Second Division, but the main consolation — a Semi-Final place in the Milk Cup — will have made sure that a mere sixth place in the Third Division eight points 'behind the pace' was no disaster.

For a long spell after the New Year Walsall actually led the division and it could be said that the Milk Cup run caused fixture congestion and a subsequent slump in League form, so it would be good to concentrate on the Milk Cup triumphs. These started with a two-legged tie against Blackpool, which was won narrowly on aggregate (4-3), the second leg at Walsall being decisive only two days after losing a league match at Bolton 1-8! In the second round Barnsley were the opposition and both legs were won; this led to a tie (once-off) against Shrewsbury at Fellows Park, which again provided a good win by the odd goal in three. A visit to Highbury to face Mighty Arsenal was the reward and most thought that the gate receipts would be a nice consolation for the journey, but the Saddlers felt no need to bow out just yet and after trailing unluckily at half-time they won with goals by Rees and Ally Brown. The last eight provided a tie at home to Rotherham United who went down by four goals to two and — incredibly — Walsall were a step away from Wembley. This step seemed to be quite realistic even against holders Liverpool after the first semi-final leg at Anfield where a brave two-all draw was earned, but Liverpool are not where they are for nothing and won at Walsall by two clear goals. In between these heroics by a strange coincidence Walsall went out of the F.A. Cup with a bad defeat (4-0) at Bournemouth, where more fun was to happen later!

Walsall have a good manager, Alan Buckley, and plenty of naturally talented players, Mower, Shakespeare (a good Midlands name), Hart, O'Kelly and Childs are a fine basis for a good side and there are others who will maintain the side's good skills in their play. Future prospects must be good.

Back Row L to R: P. Hart, R. O'Kelly, K. Mower, M. Kearns, S. Cherry, C. Brazier, D. Bamber, B. Caswell, G. Pendrey (Asst Manager). **Middle Row:** D. Preece, I. Handysides, C. Shakespeare, A. Buckley (Manager), G. Childs, P. Hawker, M. Rees. **Front Row:** P. Jones, B. Palgrave, M. Taylor, D. Kelly.

'THE SADDLERS'

Sponsored by **Highgate**

Formed: 1888 **Turned Professional:** 1888 **Ltd Co:** 1921
Previous Names: Walsall Swifts (1877) and Walsall Town (1879) amalgamated and played as Walsall Town Swifts until 1895
Previous Managers: 1921-6 J Burchell 1926-7 D Ashworth 1927-8 J Torrance 1928-9 J Kerr 1929-30 S Scholey 1930-2 P O'Rourke 1932-4 W G Slade 1934-7 Andy Wilson 1937-44 T Lowes 1944-51 Harry Hibbs 1951-2 G McPhee 1952-3 Brough Fletcher 1953-6 Frank Buckley 1956-7 John Love 1957-64 Bill Moore 1964 Alf Wood 1964-8 Ray Shaw 1968 Dick Graham 1968-9 Ron Lewin 1969-72 Bill Moore 1972-3 John Smith 1973 Jimmy McEwan (Caretaker) 1973 Ronnie Allen 1973-7 Doug Fraser 1977-8 Dave Mackay 1978 Alan Buckley (Caretaker) 1978 Alan Ashman 1978 Frank Sibley 1979-81 Alan Buckley 1981 Alan Buckley/Neil Martin (Joint Managers) 1981-2 Neil Martin
Honours: Division 4 Champions 1959-60
League Career: Elected to Division 2 1892 Failed to gain re-election 1895 Rejoined Division 2 1896 Failed re-election 1901 Elected as original member of Div 3 (N) 1921 Transferred to Division 3 (S) 1927 Transferred to Division 3 (N) 1931 Transferred to Division 3 (S) 1936 Joined Division 4 1958 Promoted to Division 3 1959-60 Promoted to Division 2 1960-1 Relegated to Division 3 1978-9 Relegated to Division 4 1978-9 Promoted to Division 3 1979-80
Colours: Red shirts, white shorts, red stockings
Change Colours: All blue

CLUB RECORDS

Most Appearances for Club: Colin Harrison: Football League 471 + Cup ties 55 **Total 526**
Most Capped Player: Mick Kearns, 15, Eire. **For England:** A Jones, 2
Record Goalscorer in a Match: Johnny Devlin, 5 v Torquay United (7-1) (H), Div 3 (S), 1.9.49
Record League Goalscorer in a season: Gilbert Alsop, 40, Div 3 (N) **All competitions:** Gilbert Alsop, 44 (League 40, F.A. Cup 4), 1934-5
Record League Goalscorer in a career: Tony Richards, 184, 1954-63 Colin Taylor, 184, 1958-63, 1964-8, 1969-73, 1973-8, 1979-84 **All competitions:** Alan Buckley, 204 (League 174, Cup 30)
Record Transfer Fee Received: £175,000 from Birmingham City for Alan Buckley, Oct 1978
Record Transfer Fee Paid: £175,000 to Birmingham City for Alan Buckley, June 1979
Best Performances: League: 6th Div 2 1898-9 **F.A. Cup:** 5th Round 1939, 1975, 1978, and last sixteen 1889 **League/Milk Cup:** Semi-Final 1983-4
Most League Points: (3pts for win) 75, 1983-4 (2pts for win) 65, 1959-60
Most League Goals: 102, Div 4, 1959-60
Record League Victory: 10-0 v Darwen, Div 2, 4.3.1899
Record League Defeat: 0-12 v Small Heath, Div 2, 17.12.1892 0-12 v Darwen, Div 2, 26.12.1896
Club Statistician for the Directory: M.A. Sergeant

Publisher & Advertising
Don Stanton with Permandos Advertising & Marketing, Shenstone, Lichfield, Staffs (0543 480940)

Price	**Number of Pages**
40p	16

Subscriptions
Apply club shop

WALSALL

PLAYERS NAME Ht Wt Birthdate	Honours	Birthplace Transfers	Clubs	APPEARANCES League	APPEARANCES Milk Cup	APPEARANCES F.A.C.	APPEARANCES A.M.C.	GOALS League	GOALS Milk Cup	GOALS F.A.C.	GOALS A.M.C.
GOALKEEPER											
Steve Cherry	E. Y	Nottingham	Derby Co. (A)	77	2	3					
5-11 11.0 5.8.60			Port Vale (L)	4	2						
DEFENDERS											
Colin Brazier	Lg.C. 80	Birmingham	Alvechurch								
6-1½ 10.13 6.6.57			Wolverhampton W.	69+9	1+3	1		2			
			Jacksonville M								
			Birmingham C.	10+1	4			1			
			Lincoln C.	9							
			Walsall	45	9	1	2	2			
Brian Caswell		Wednesbury	Walsall (A)	354+11	25	22	1	17		1	
5-10 10.7 14.2.56											
Peter Hart*	Div. 4, 80	Mexborough	Huddersfield T. (A)	208+2	14	5		7		1	
5-11 12.7 14.8.57			Walsall	180	15	7	2	9			
Phil Hawker	E. Y	Solihull	Birmingham C. (A)	34+1	2			1			
6-1 11.6 7.12.62		F	Walsall	16	2						
Kenny Mower†		Walsall	Walsall (A)	200+1	15	13	2	5			
6-0¾ 12.4 1.12.60											
Brian Palgrave			Walsall								
Gary Pendry	(N-C)	Birmingham	Birmingham C. (A)	287+17	21+	15+		4	1		
5-10 12.0 9.2.49		£30,000	W.B.A.	18							
		F	Torquay U.	12							
		F	Bristol R.	1							
		F	Walsall	8							
MIDFIELD											
Gary Childs	E. Y	Birmingham	W.B.A. (A)	2+1							
5-7 10.8 19.4.64			Walsall	27+3	5	1	2	2	1		1
Ian Handysides	E. Y	Jarrow	Birmingham C. (A)	44+18	6+1	2+2		2	5		
5-6 10.6 14.12.62			Walsall	17+1			2	4			
Paul Jones		Walsall	Walsall (A)	3+3	1		2				
5-9 10.4 6.9.65											
David Preece		Bridgend	Walsall (A)	95+4	11	5	1	5	4	1	
5-5 10.0 28.5.63											
Craig Shakespeare		Birmingham	Walsall (A)	70+7	10	2	2	10		1	
5-10 11.5 26.10.63											
Bob Taylor		Birmingham	Walsall								
5-5 10.3											
FORWARDS											
David Bamber		St Helens	Manchester Univ.								
6-3 13.10 1.2.59			Blackpool	81+5	6	7+1		29	5	2	
		£50,000	Coventry C.	18+1	2	0+1		3	1		
		£20,000	Walsall	9+1				3			
Alan Buckley	(N-C)	Mansfield	Nottingham F. (A)	16+2	0+1			1			
5-6 10.9 20.4.51		£20,000	Walsall	241	18	9		125	12	9	
		£175,000	Birmingham C.	24+4	1			8			
		£175,000	Walsall	160+16	10	10+	1+1	49	2	5	
David Kelly		Birmingham	Walsall	5+1			0+1	3			
5-11 11.1 25.11.65											
Richard O'Kelly		West Bromwich	Alvechurch								
5-10 11.8 8.8.57			Walsall	130+12	7+1	6+1	2	32	2		1
Mark Rees	E. S	Smethwick	Walsall (A)	117+26	10+	4+3		24	5		
5-0 11.10 13.10.61											

NON-CONTRACT PLAYERS 1984-85

Darren Callaghan, Sean Humphries, Mark Kavanagh, Nick Preece

APPRENTICES

Richard Beeton, Steve Clews, Carl Page, Leo Harrison, Mark Jones, Don Kelly

WALSALL

DIVISION THREE 6TH **FA CUP** 1ST ROUND **MILK CUP** SEMI-FINAL

MATCH	DATE	COMPETITION	VENUE	OPPONENTS	RESULT	HALF TIME	L'GUE POS'N	GOALSCORERS	ATTENDANCE
1	A 27	CL	A	Exeter C	W1-0	1-0		Hart	4,742
2	**30**	**MC 1**	**A**	**Blackpool**	**L1-2**	**0-1**		**Buckley**	**3,353**
3	S 3	CL	H	Orient	L0-1	0-0	13		3,003
4	6	CL	H	Sheffield U	L1-2	1-1		Summerfield	4,711
5	10	CL	A	Bolton W	L1-8	0-4	19	Brown	4,375
6	**13**	**MC 1**	**H**	**Blackpool**	**W3-1**	**1-1**		**Summerfield, Preece, O'Kelly**	**2,879**
7	17	CL	H	Newport Co	W3-2	1-1	16	Summerfield 2, O'Kelly	2,818
8	24	CL	A	Southend U	D0-0	0-0	16		3,061
9	28	CL	A	Oxford U	L3-6	1-4		Brown 2 (1 pen), Shakespeare	5,720
10	O 1	CL	H	Port Vale	W2-0	2-0	16	Summerfield, Shakespeare	3,757
11	**4**	**MC 2**	**H**	**Barnsley**	**W1-0**	**0-0**		**Rees**	**3,681**
12	8	CL	A	Rotherham U	W1-0	0-0	9	Brown (pen)	3,540
13	15	CL	H	Wimbledon	W4-0	1-0	7	O'Kelly, Rees 2, Brown	2,546
14	18	CL	H	AFC Bournemouth	W3-1	1-0		Brown (pen), O'Kelly 2	3,782
15	22	CL	A	Bradford C	D0-0	0-0	8		2,474
16	**25**	**MC 2**	**A**	**Barnsley**	**W2-0**	**1-0**		**Preece, Rees**	**7,844**
17	29	CL	H	Bristol R	W2-1	1-0	6	O'Kelly (pen), Rees	4,964
18	N 1	CL	A	Hull C	D2-2	0-2		O'Kelly, Brown	8,375
19	5	CL	A	Scunthorpe U	D0-0	0-0	9		2,932
20	**8**	**MC 3**	**H**	**Shrewsbury T**	**W2-1**	**1-0**		**Preece, Childs**	**7,952**
21	12	CL	H	Gillingham	W3-1	1-0	6	Brown 2, Preece	4,639
22	**19**	**FAC 1**	**A**	**AFC Bournemouth**	**L0-4**	**0-2**			**4,298**
23	26	CL	A	Wigan Ath	W1-0	0-0	5	Rees	3,485
24	**30**	**MC 4**	**A**	**Arsenal**	**W2-1**	**0-1**		**Rees, Brown**	**22,406**
25	D 3	CL	H	Millwall	D1-1	1-0	5	O'Kelly	5,329
26	17	CL	H	Brentford	W1-0	1-0	4	Brown (pen)	3,965
27	26	CL	A	Lincoln C	L1-2	1-0		O'Kelly	4,886
28	27	CL	H	Burnley	D1-1	0-0		Rees	8,131
29	31	CL	A	Preston NE	W1-0	0-0		Childs	6,226
30	J 2	CL	H	Plymouth Ath	W3-2	2-1		Hart, Summerfield, O'Kelly	4,856
31	7	CL	A	Orient	W1-0	0-0	3	Summerfield	3,106
32	14	CL	H	Exeter C	W4-1	1-1	1	Brown, Brazier, O'Kelly, Shakespeare	5,028
33	**18**	**MC 5**	**A**	**Rotherham U**	**W4-2**	**2-0**		**Rees 2, O'Kelly, Brown**	**14,487**
34	22	CL	A	Newport Co	L1-3	1-0	1	Rees	5,028
35	28	CL	H	Bolton W	W1-0	0-0	1	Shakespeare	7,812
36	F 4	CL	A	Port Vale	W2-0	1-0	1	Handysides, Preece	6,966
37	**7**	**MC SF**	**A**	**Liverpool**	**D2-2**	**1-1**		**Neal (og), Summerfield**	**31,073**
38	11	CL	H	Southend U	W4-0	1-0	1	Hart, Handysides, Preece, Brown (pen)	8,156
39	**14**	**MC SF**	**A**	**Liverpool**	**L0-2**	**0-1**			**19,591**
40	18	CL	A	Bristol R	L2-4	1-3	1	Childs, Buckley	5,643
41	**21**	**AMC 1**	**H**	**Northampton T**	**W3-1**	**0-1**		**Childs, Handysides, O'Kelly**	**3,190**
42	25	CL	H	Bradford C	L1-2	1-0	2	Handysides	6,013
43	M 3	CL	A	AFC Bournemouth	L0-3	0-1	4		3,913
44	6	CL	H	Scunthorpe U	D1-1	0-1		Handysides	4,735
45	10	CL	A	Gillingham	W3-1	1-0	3	Summerfield 2, Shakespreare	4,544
46	**13**	**AMC 2**	**A**	**Swindon T**	**L0-3**	**0-2**			**2,705**
47	17	CL	H	Rotherham U	D2-2	0-1	3	Shakespeare, Buckley	4,915
48	24	CL	A	Wimbledon	L0-2	0-1	4		4,057
49	27	CL	H	Hull C	W2-1	1-0		Bamber 2	6,851
50	31	CL	A	Sheffield U	L0-2	0-1	4		13,227
51	A 7	CL	H	Oxford U	L0-1	0-0	5		10,163
52	14	CL	A	Milwall	L0-2	0-0	5		3,458
53	21	CL	H	Lincoln C	L0-1	0-0	6		3,660
54	23	CL	A	Burnley	W2-0	1-0	6	Brown, Kelly	3,953
55	28	CL	H	Wigan Ath	W3-0	0-0	6	Mower, Kelly, O'Kelly	3,286
56	M 5	CL	A	Plymouth Arg	L1-3	0-0		Kelly	5,144
57	7	CL	H	Preston NE	W2-1	2-0		Brazier, O'Kelly	3,273
58	12	CL	A	Brentford	D1-1	1-1		Bamber	5,281

Av Home Att **4,814**

Goal Scorers

League (68): Brown 13 (5 pens), O'Kelly, 12 (1 pen), Summerfield 8, Rees 6, Shakespeare 6, Handysides 4, Bamber 3, Hart 3, Kelly 3, Preece 3, Brazier 2, Buckley 2, Childs 2, Mower 1
FA Cup (-): —
Milk Cup (17): Rees 5, Preece 3, Brown 2, O'Kelly 2, Summerfield 2, Buckley 1, Childs 1, opponent 1
AMC (3): Childs 1, Handysides 1, O'Kelly 1

1983-84

Kearns	Hawker	Mower	Shakespeare	Sinnott	Hart	Rees	Brown	Summerfield	Preece	Brazier	Buckley	Green	Bates	Jones	O'Kelly	Caswell	Godden **(L)**	Childs	Bamber	Handysides	Kelly	REFEREE	
1	2	3	4	5	6	7	8	9	10*	11	12											D Letts	1
1	**2**	**3**	**4***	**5**	**6**	**7**	**8**	**9**	**10**	**11**	**12**											**J Worrell**	**2**
	2	3	4	5	6	7		9	8	11	10	1										A Robinson	3
	6	3	4*	5	2	7	8	9	10	11	12	1										H King	4
		3	4	5	6		8	9	10	11	7*	1	2	12								G Tyson	5
	5	**3**	**4**		**2**	**12**	**8**	**9**	**7**	**6**	**10**	**1**			**11***							**T Jones**	**6**
	5	3	4		2	12	8	9	7	6	10*	1			11							L Dilkes	7
		3	4		6	7	8*	9	10	5	12	1			11	2						MJ Taylor	8
		3	4		6	7	8	9	10	5	12	1			11*	2						A Crickmore	9
		3	4		6	7	8	9	11	5	10	1				2						JA Moules	10
1		**3**	**4**		**6**	**7**	**8**	**9**		**5**	**11**				**10**	**2**						**F Roberts**	**11**
		3	4		6	7	8		10	5					9	2	1	11				D Scott	12
		3	4		6	7	8		10	5					9	2	1	11				PA Tydesley	13
		3	4		6	7	8		10	5					9	2	1	11				A Banks	14
		3	4		6	7	8*	12	10	5					9	2	1	11				N Glover	15
1		**3**	**4**		**6**	**7**		**9**	**10**	**5**				**8**		**2**		**11**				**G Courtney**	**16**
		3	4		6	7		9	10	5					8	2	1	11				R Guy	17
		3	4		6*	7	8	12	10	5					9	2	1	11				A Challinor	18
		3	4		6		8	9	10	5					7	2	1	11				K Walmsley	19
1		**3**	**4***		**6**	**7**	**8**	**12**	**10**	**5**					**9**	**2**		**11**				**N Midgley**	**20**
1		3	4		6	7	8	12	10	5					9	2*		11				I Hendrick	21
1		**3**	**4***		**6**	**7**	**8**	**9**	**10**	**5**					**12**	**2**		**11**				**D Hedges**	**22**
1		3	4		6	7	8	12	10*	5					9	2		11				JM Key	23
1		**3**	**4**		**6**	**7**	**8**		**10**	**5**					**9**	**2**		**11**				**L Burden**	**24**
1	5	3	4		6	7	8	12	10						9	2		11*				K Cooper	25
1		3	4		6	7*	8	11	10	5			2	12	9							J Hunting	26
1		3	4		6	7	8	12	10	5					9	2		11*				K Hackett	27
	2	3	4		6	7	8*	12	10	5		1			9			11				R Bridges	28
	3*		4		6	7	8	10		5	12	1			9	2		11				R Nixon	29
		3	4		6	7*	8	10		5	12	1			9	2		11				A Buksh	30
		3	4		6	12	8	10		5		1			9*	2		11		7		I Borrett	31
		3	4		6	12	8	10	11	5		1			9*	2				7		D Reeves	32
		3	**4**		**6**	**7**	**8**		**11**	**5**		**1**			**9**	**2**		**10**				**G Napthine**	**33**
		3	4		6	7	8		10*	5		1			9	2		11		12		M James	34
1		3	4		6	7	8	11	10*	5						2		12		9		T Ward	35
		3	4		6		8	12	10	5		1			9	2		11*		7		N Wilson	36
		3	**4**		**6**	**7**	**8**	**12**	**10**	**5**		**1**			**9**	**2**		**11***				**N Ashley**	**37**
		3	4		6	7*	8	11	10	5		1			9			12		2		D Owen	38
		3	**4**		**6**	**7**	**8**	**11**	**10**	**5**		**1**			**9**	**2**						**J Hunting**	**39**
		3	4		6	7*	8			5	12	1			9	2		11		10		Alan Robinson	40
		3	**4**		**6**					**5**	**10***	**1**		**8**	**9**	**2**		**11**		**7**	**12**	**K Barratt**	**41**
		3	4		6	12	8		10	5		1			9	2*		11		7		R Milford	42
1		3	4		6	7	8	12	10	5					9*			11		2		M Dimblebee	43
1		3	4*		6		8	9	10	5					12	2		11		7		D Richardson	44
1		3	4		6			9	10	5					8	2		11		7		R Lewis	45
		3	**4***		**6**				**10**	**5**	**12**	**1**	**2**	**9**	**8**			**11**		**7**		**L Burden**	**46**
		3	4		6	7		8		5	12				9	2*	1	11		10		K Salmon	47
		3	4		6			8	10	5	12				2		1	11*	9	7		M Bodenham	48
		3	4		6		8		10	5					2		1	11	9	7		B Hill	49
		3	4		6		8*	12	10	5					11	2	1		9	7		J Hough	50
		3	4		6		8	12	10	5					11	2*	1		9	7		A Robinson	51
			4		6		8		10	5					11	2	1	3	9*	7	12	D Letts	52
		3	4		6*		12		10	5					8	2	1	11	9	7		J Worrall	53
	6	3	4				8		10	5				7	11	2	1				9	P Willis	54
	6	3	4		2		8		10	5				7*	11		1		12		9	J Ashworth	55
	6	3	4		2	7†		12	10	5					11		1		8*		9	J Martin	56
	6	3	4		2	7			10	5					11		1		8		9	D Hedges	57
		3	4*		6	7			10	5					11	2	1	12	8		9	A Gunn	58
10	11	44	46	4	45	29	37	21	41	45	4	17	2	2	39	32	19	27	9	17	5	League Appearances	
						+4S	+1S	+12S			+9S			+2S	+1S			+3S	+1S	+1S	+1S		
1		1	1		1	1	1	1	1	1					1S	1		1				FA Cup Appearances	
5	2	8	8	1	8	7+1S	7	5+2S	7	8	2+1S	3		1	6	6		4				Milk Cup Appearances	
		2	2		2				1	2	1+1S	2	1	2	2	1		2		2	1S	AM Cup Appearances	

FELLOWS PARK

Official Address: Fellows Park, Walsall, West Mildands. Telephone: 0922 22791

Telegraphic: Walsall F.C., Walsall

Ground Capacity: 24,100

Record Attendance: 25,433 v. Newcastle United, Div 2, 29 Aug 1961

Record Receipts: £40,714 v. Liverpool, Milk Cup Semi-Final, 2nd leg, 14 Feb 1984

Size of Playing Area: 113yds × 73 yds

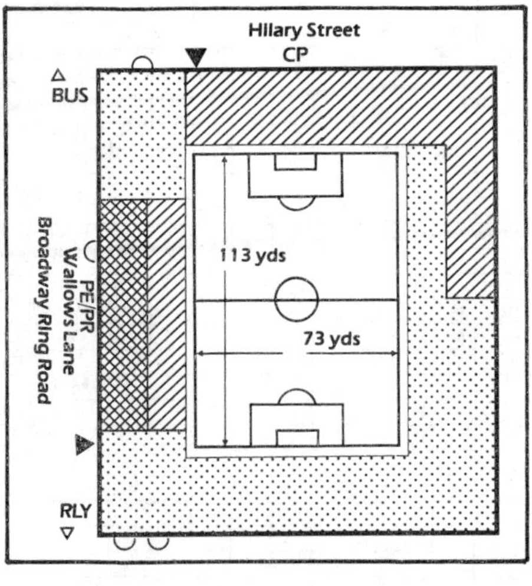

For key see page 12

Season Tickets: Stand: £60.00, Ground: £28.00

Executive Box Season Tickets: £145

Cost of Stand Tickets: £3.50; **Terraces:** £2.00

Match and Ticket Information: Seats bookable at any time by postal, telephone or personal application.

Car Parking: car park for 100 vehicles in Hillary Street, side-street parking available.

How to get to the ground

From North: Use A461 S.P. Walsall then join A4148 Broadway North around Ring Road into Broadway West for Walsall F.C.
From East, South, West: Use Motorway M6 until junction 9, leave motorway and follow signs Walsall A461, then turn right A4148 into Broadway West for Walsall F.C.

WATFORD Division 1

Chairman
E John

Vice-Chairman
G A Smith

Directors
E Harrowell
Bertie Mee
J Reid
H M Stratford, J.P.

Chief Executive & Company Secretary
Eddie Plumley, F.A.A.I.

General Manager
Graham Taylor

Marketing Manager
Caroline Gillies, M.Inst. M, M.I.P.R.

Public Relations Officer
Ed Coan

Club Coaches
John Ward
Tom Walley
Steve Harrison

Physiotherapist
Billy Hails

Club Captain
Wilf Rostron

Commercial Manager
M Sullivan (0923 25761)

A first Wembley appearance was one more landmark to confound the now dwindling band of detractors still blinkered or bigoted enough to deride a breezy attacking approach which continues to combine forthright entertainment with unprecedented success.

Luther Blissett's departure and a cascade of injuries prefaced a poor start to the League programme, punctuated by an outrageously impudent UEFA Cup run, Kaiserslautern and especially Levski Spartak, in Sofia, being beaten against all the odds. Such were the fitness problems that four captains were appointed by late September and twenty-nine players used in four months. With so many unfit or ineligible four young reserves actually played in European matches without previous first team experience.

With two League matches won out of fifteen, comprehensive defeat in Prague coincided with a diminishing casualty list and some shrewd raids on the transfer market, including the signing of a young Scot seen as future scoring potential. Maurice Johnston himself had more immediate ambitions, completing an eight-minute hat-trick at Wolverhampton on his third appearance. By the end of February his tally was seventeen in twenty matches, the team – now a settled one – had surged up the table with a free-scoring sequence of ten wins in thirteen League games and Wembley looked a distinct possibility.

The FA Cup run started against Luton with an exhilarating replayed local derby of eleven goals, during which both sides lost a two-goal lead. Such was the momentum by now that Charlton (away), Brighton (at home) and Birmingham (away) were all seen off at the first attempt with two goals to spare, and in an unusually open and entertaining semi-final Plymouth's unexpectedly worthy resistance was overcome.

The season's latter stages brought more injuries and an uncharacteristic dearth of goals – Johnston's exceptional contribution apart – and Wilf Rostron's controversial suspension meant that Les Taylor led a remarkably young Cup Final side as its fifth captain of the season. An occasion notable for integrity and fair play (essential ingredients of the Watford scheme of things) left Everton with the prize, but Graham Taylor has the satisfaction of a unique achievement in taking a club from 4th Division to 1st and establishing it there. By brilliantly astute management he has assembled much promising talent, with John Barnes the jewel in the crown, and as a perfect reflection of the manager's own personality the team is youthful, jaunty and utterly positive.

TG Jones
The League Directory's Statistician for the Club

Back Row L to R: Alan Paris, Lee Sinnott, Steve Sims, George Reilly, Steve Sherwood, Richard Jobson, Paul Franklin, Jimmy Giligan, Steve Terry. **2nd Row:** Billy Hails (Physiotherapist), Tom Walley (coach), Luther Blissett, Kenny Jackett, John Barnes, Sean Griffith, Dereck Williams, David Bardsley, Jan Lofiman, Paul Atkinson, John Ward (coach), Steve Harrison (coach). **3rd Row:** Worrell Sterling, Ian Richardson, Maurice Johnston, Nigel Callaghan, Graham Taylor (Manager), Wilf Rostron, Neil Price, Gary Parker, Les Taylor. **Front Row:** Cliff Powell, Bruce Andrews, Nigel Gibbs, Richard Sendall, Malcolm Allan.

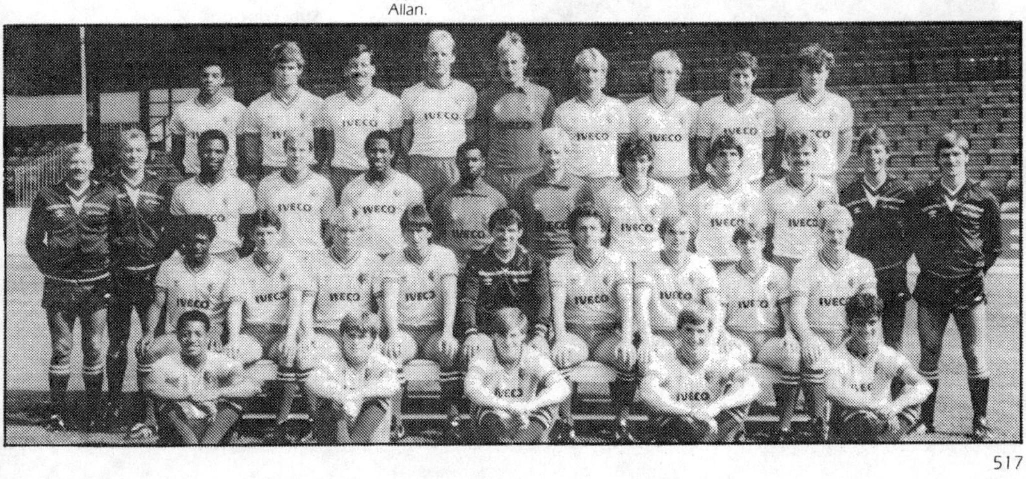

'THE HORNETS'

Sponsored by
Iveco

Formed: 1891 **Turned Professional:** 1897 **Ltd Co:** 1909
Previous Names: West Herts until merger with Watford St. Mary's in 1898
Previous Managers: 1903 Johnny Goodall 1910 Harry Kent 1926 Fred Pagnam 1929 Neil McBain 1938 Billy Findlay 1947 Jack Bray 1948 Eddie Hapgood 1950 Ron Gray 1951 Haydn Green 1952 Len Goulden 1955 Johnny Paton 1956 Len Goulden 1956 Neil McBain 1959 Ron Burgess 1963 Bill McGarry 1964 Ken Furphy 1971 George Kirby 1973-7 Mike Keen
Honours: Champions Division 3 1968-9 Champions Division 4 1977-8
League Career: Original Members of Division 3 1920 Transferred to Division 3 (S) 1921 Relegated to Division 4 1958 Promoted to Division 3 1959-60 Promoted to Division 2 1968-9 Relegated to Division 3 1971-2 Relegated to Division 4 1974-5 Promoted to Division 3 1977-8 Promoted to Division 2 1978-9 Promoted to Division 1 1981-2
Colours: Yellow shirts with black and red trim, red shorts, red stockings with black and yellow tops
Change Colours: White shirts, black shorts, black stockings with red and yellow tops

CLUB RECORDS

Most Appearances for Club: Duncan Welbourne: Football League 404 + 7 + F.A. Cup 28 + League Cup 17 + 1 **Total 449 + 8 subs**
Most Capped Player: Gerry Armstrong, 21, Northern Ireland. **For England:** Luther Blisset, 5 + 4 subs
Record Goalscorer in a Match: Eddie Mummery, 5 v Newport County (8-2) (H), Div 3 (S), 05.01.24
Dennis Westcott, 5 v Q.P.R. (5-1) (A), London League, 01.11.41 (as guest player)
Record League Goalscorer in a season: Cliff Holton, 42 **All competitions:** Cliff Holton, 48 (League 42, F.A. Cup 6)
Record League Goalscorer in a career: Tommy Barnett, 148 **All competitions:** Tommy Barnett, 161 (League 145, F.A. Cup 16, Div 3 (S) Cup 3)
Record Transfer Fee Received: £1,000,000 from A.C. Milan for Luther Blissett, June 1983
Record Transfer Fee Paid: £550,000 to A.C. Milan for Luther Blissett, July 1984
Best Performances: League: Runners-Up 1982-3 **F.A. Cup:** Runners-Up 1983-4 **League/Milk Cup:** Semi-Final 1978-9 **UEFA Cup:** 3rd Round 1983-4
Most League Points: (2pts for win) 71, Div 4, 1959-60 (3pts for win) 80, Div 2, 1981-2
Most League Goals: 92, Div 4, 1959-60
European Competitions Entered: UEFA Cup 1983-4

Club Statistician for the Directory: Trefor Jones

Programme Editor & PRO
Ed Coan

Price	Number of Pages
50p	20

Subscriptions
£15.00 (home programmes), £30.00 (home and away)

WATFORD

PLAYERS NAME Ht Wt Birthdate	Honours	Birthplace Transfers	Clubs	APPEARANCES League	Milk Cup	F.A.C.	E. Cups	GOALS League	Milk Cup	F.A.C.	E. Cups
GOALKEEPERS											
Steve Sherwood	Div. 4. 78	Selby	Chelsea (A)	16	1						
6-4 14.7 10.12.53			Millwall (L)	1							
			Brentford (L)	62	2	2					
		£4,000	Watford	189	21	21	6	1			
Derick Williams	E. Y	Sunderland	Watford (A)								
5-11 11.10 5.10.65											
DEFENDERS											
David Bardsley	E. Y	Manchester	Blackpool (A)	45	4	2		1	1		
5-10 10.0 11.9.64		£150,000	Watford	25		7					
Paul Franklin	FAYC. 82	Ilford	Watford (A)	25	1	5	4				
6-0 11.8 5.10.63											
Nigel Gibbs	FAYC. 82	St. Albans	Watford (A)	2+1			4				
5-7 10.2 20.11.65											
Neil Price	FAYC. 82	Hemel	Watford (A)	7+1		2	2				
5-9 10.10 15.2.64		Hempstead	Plymouth A. (L)	1							
Wilf Rostron*†	E. S	Sunderland	Arsenal (A)	12+5	1	1		2			
5-7 11.1 29.9.56		£40,000	Sunderland	75+1	4	4		17			
		£150,000	Watford	160+6	13+	16+	6	13	1	2	3
Lee Sinnott	E. Y	Pelsall	Walsall (A)	40	3	4		2			
6-1 11.9 12.7.65		£100,000	Watford	19+1		2					
Steve Terry		Clapton	Watford (A)	57	8	7	2+1	4	1		
6-1½ 13.3 14.6.62											
MIDFIELD											
Paul Atkinson	E. Y	Pudsey	Oldham A. (A)	139+4	9+1	5		11			
5-10 11.5 14.8.61		£175,000	Watford	8+3		0+2					
Kenny Jackett	W.(12).	Watford	Watford (A)	133+1	17+	13	5	10	1		
5-10½ 11.3 5.1.62	U.21(2). Y										
Richard Jobson		Hull	Burton A.								
6-1 12.2 9.5.63		£15,000	Watford	24+2	2			3			
Alan Paris		Slough	Slough T.								
6-0 11.6 16.8.64			Watford								
Gary Porter	E. Y	Sunderland	Watford (A)	2							
5-5 9.10 6.3.66	FAYC. 82										
Les Taylor		North Shields	Oxford U. (A)	219	16	3		15	1		
5-8 11.7 4.12.56		£105,000	Watford	128+4	9	16	1	10	3		
FORWARDS											
John Barnes	E.(12). U.21(3)	Jamaica	Sudbury Court								
5-11 11.10 7.9.63	FAYC. 82		Watford	116+1	10	14	6	34	2	1	
Luther Blissett	E.( ). U.21	Jamaica	Watford	222+24	26+	17		95	13	3	
5-10½ 11.13 1.2.58		£1,000,000	A.C. Milan								
		£550,000	Watford								
Nigel Callaghan	E. U.21(9)	Singapore	Watford (A)	135+6	12+	15+	6	26	1	1	1
5-9 10.9 12.9.62											
Jimmy Gilligan	E. Y	Hammersmith	Watford (A)	13+4	1+1	2	3+1	6	1		2
6-2 11.7 24.1.64	FAYC. 82		Lincoln C. (L)	0+3							
Maurice Johnston	S.(3). U.21	Glasgow	Partick Thistle	85	10+1	9		40	5	8	
5-9 10.6 30.4.63		£200,000	Watford	28+1		7		20		3	
Jan Lohman	Hol. U.21	Dussen, Hol.	Lokeren								
5-10 11.2 18.2.56		£25,000	Watford	46+6	1	5+1	1	5		3	
George Reilly		Bellshill	Corby T.								
6-3 13.5 14.9.57			Northampton T.	124+3	13	4		46	9		
		£140,000	Cambridge U.	136+2	7	8		36	1	2	
		£100,000	Watford	27	1	7		8			
Ian Richardson	FAYC. 82	Ely	Watford (A)	4+3	1+1			2			
5-8½ 10.6 5.5.64											
Worrell Sterling	FAYC. 82	Bethnal Green	Watford (A)	9+4			0+1	1			
5-8 10.8 8.6.65											

NON-CONTRACT PLAYER 1984-85: Sean Griffiths

APPRENTICES: Malcolm Allen, Jason Polak, Richard Sendall

WATFORD

DIVISION ONE 11TH **FA CUP** FINALISTS **MILK CUP** 2ND ROUND **UEFA CUP** 3RD ROUND

MATCH	DATE	COMPETITION	VENUE	OPPONENTS	RESULT	HALF TIME	L'GUE POS'N	GOALSCORERS	ATTENDANCE
1	A 27	CL	H	Coventry C	L2-3	0-1		Barnes, Jobson	15,333
2	30	CL	H	Ipswich T	D2-2	2-2		Lohman, Callaghan	15,388
3	S 3	CL	A	Birmingham C	L0-2	0-1	18		11,931
4	6	CL	A	QPR	D1-1	1-1		Barnes	17,111
5	10	CL	H	Notts Co	W3-1	2-1	14	Reilly, Palmer, Barnes	12,763
6	**14**	**UEFA 1**	**A**	**Kaiserslautern**	**L1-3**	**1-1**		**Gilligan**	**19,906**
7	17	CL	A	Stoke C	W4-0	1-0	12	Lohman, Barnes 2, Jobson	12,691
8	24	CL	H	Tottenham H	L2-3	1-0	15	Rostron, Callaghan (pen)	21,056
9	**28**	**UEFA 1**	**H**	**Kaiserslautern**	**W3-0**	**2-0**		**Richardson 2, Melzer (og)**	**21,457**
10	O 1	CL	A	WBA	L0-2	0-2	16		14,456
11	**4**	**MC 2**	**A**	**Huddersfield T**	**L1-2**	**0-0**		**Barnes**	**10,631**
12	15	CL	H	Norwich C	L1-3	0-1	18	Terry	12,745
13	**19**	**UEFA 2**	**H**	**Levsky Spartak**	**D1-1**	**0-1**		**Rostron**	**16,139**
14	22	CL	H	Everton	L0-1	0-1	19		13,571
15	**25**	**MC 2**	**H**	**Huddersfield T**	**D2-2**	**2-1**		**Gilligan, Sims**	**13,006**
16	28	CL	H	West Ham U	D0-0	0-0			14,559
17	**N 2**	**UEFA 2**	**A**	**Levsky Spartak**	**W3-1[1]**	**1-1**		**Callaghan, Rostron, Richardson**	**60,000**
18	5	CL	H	Leicester C	D3-3	2-1	18	Callaghan, Richardson 2	15,807
19	12	CL	A	Sunderland	L0-3	0-1	19		15,407
20	19	CL	A	Manchester U	L1-4	0-2	20	Callaghan	43,111
21	**23**	**UEFA 3**	**H**	**Sparta Prague**	**L2-3**	**0-2**		**Rostron, Gilligan**	**15,590**
22	26	CL	H	Luton T	L1-2	1-1	20	Callaghan	17,791
23	D 3	CL	A	Wolverhampton W	W5-0	3-0	19	Johnston 3, Reilly 2	11,906
24	**7**	**UEFA 3**	**A**	**Sparta Prague**	**L0-4**	**0-4**			**38,000**
25	10	CL	H	Nottingham F	W3-2	3-1	19	Johnston, Reilly, Callaghan	14,047
26	17	CL	A	Arsenal	L1-3	0-1	19	Johnston	25,104
27	26	CL	H	Aston Villa	W3-2	2-0		Gilligan 2, Barnes	18,226
28	27	CL	A	Southampton	L0-1	0-1			20,659
29	31	CL	H	Birmingham C	W1-0	0-0		Johnston	14,359
30	J 2	CL	A	Tottenham H	W3-2	2-0	17	Johnston 2, Barnes	32,495
31	**7**	**FAC 3**	**A**	**Luton T**	**D2-2**	**2-2**		**Barnes, Johnston (pen)**	**15,007**
32	**10**	**FAC 3R**	**H**	**Luton T**	**W4-3[1]**	**2-1**		**Callaghan, Reilly, Barnes, Johnston**	**20,586**
33	14	CL	A	Coventry C	W2-1	1-1	16	Sherwood, Reilly	13,307
34	21	CL	H	Stoke C	W2-0	0-0	13	Reilly, Johnston	14,076
35	**28**	**FAC 4**	**A**	**Charlton Ath**	**W2-0**	**1-0**		**Johnston, Reilly**	**22,392**
36	F 1	CL	A	Liverpool	L0-3	0-3	13		20,746
37	4	CL	H	WBA	W3-1	0-0	12	Johnston, Gilligan 2	14,240
38	11	CL	A	Notts Co	W5-3	3-2	11	Jackett, Callaghan 2, Reilly, Johnston	8,078
39	**18**	**FAC 5**	**H**	**Brighton & HA**	**W3-1**	**2-0**		**Reilly, Johnston, Jackett**	**28,000**
40	21	CL	A	West Ham U	W4-2	1-1		Johnston, Barnes 2, Callaghan	19,241
41	25	CL	H	Everton	D4-4	1-0	8	Barnes 2, Johnston, Rostron	16,982
42	M 3	CL	A	Leicester C	L1-4	1-1	9	Rostron	13,295
43	**10**	**FAC 6**	**A**	**Birmingham C**	**W3-1**	**1-0**		**Barnes 2, Taylor**	
44	17	CL	H	QPR	W1-0	0-0	9	Rostron	18,645
45	20	CL	H	Sunderland	W2-1	0-0		Johnston 2	16,231
46	24	CL	A	Ipswich T	D0-0	0-0	7		14,956
47	31	CL	H	Liverpool	L0-2	0-0	9		21,293
48	A 7	CL	A	Norwich C	L1-6	1-3	10	Johnston	14,451
49	**14**	**FAC SF**	**N**	**Plymouth Arg**	**W1-0**	**1-0**		**Reilly**	**43,858**
50	17	CL	H	Manchester U	D0-0	0-0			20,764
51	21	CL	A	Aston Villa	L1-2	1-1	11	Sterling	16,110
52	24	CL	H	Southampton	D1-1	1-0		Johnston	16,744
53	28	CL	A	Luton T	W2-1	2-0	10	Callaghan, Johnston	12,594
54	M 5	CL	H	Wolverhampton W	D0-0	0-0	10		13,534
55	7	CL	A	Nottingham F	L1-5	0-3	11	Johnston	13,732
56	12	CL	H	Arsenal	W2-1	1-1	11	Johnston, Reilly	22,007
57	**19**	**FAC F**	**N**	**Everton**	**L0-2**	**0-1**			**100,000**

[1] After Extra Time

Av Home Att **16,515**

Goal Scorers

League (68): Johnston 20, Barnes 11 (1 pen), Callaghan 10 (1 pen), Reilly 8, Gilligan 4, Rostron 4, Jobson 2, Lohman 2, Richardson 2, Jackett 1, Palmer 1, Sherwood 1, Sterling 1, Terry 1
FA Cup (15): Barnes 4, Johnston 4, Reilly 4, Callaghan 1, Jackett 1, Taylor 1
Milk Cup (3): Barnes 1, Gilligan 1, Sims 1
UEFA Cup (10): Richardson 3, Rostron 3, Gilligan 2, Callaghan 1, opponent 1

1983-84

Sherwood	Rice	Rostron	Taylor	Sims	Bolton	Callaghan	Gilligan	Terry	Lohman	Barnes	Jobson	Franklin	Reilly	Sterling	Patching	Jackett	Palmer	Sinnott	Richardson	Atkinson	Johnson	Bardsley	Price	Johnston	REFEREE	
1	2	3	4	5*	6	7	8	9	10	11	12														H Taylor	1
1	2	3	4		5	7			10	8		6	9	11											B Stevens	2
1	2	3				7		5*	11	8	12	6	9		4	10									R Guy	3
1		11		5		7			10	8	4	6	9			3	2								K Baker	4
1		11		5		7	12		10*	8	4	6	9			3	2								H King	5
1	**12**	**11**		**5***		**7**	**9**	**12**	**10**	**8**	**4**	**6**				**3**	**2***								**Fredriksson**	**6**
1		11				7		5	10	8	4	6	9			3	2								T Mills	7
1		11				7	12	5	10	8	4		9*			6	2	3							A Challinor	8
1		**3**			**6**	**7**	**9**	**5**		**11**	**4**					**10**	**2**		**8**						**V Butenko**	**9**
1		11			4	8	10*	3		9	6					7	2	5	12						T Jones	10
		3			**6**	**7**		**5**		**11**	**4**		**9**			**10**	**2**		**8**						**R Nixon**	**11**
	2	10			12	7		5		8	4		9			6		3			11*				M Bodenham	12
1		**3**			**6**	**7**	**9**	**5**		**8***	**4**					**10**	**2**		**11**		**12**				**Konrath**	**13**
1		11			6	7	9	5†			4					10	2	3			8				K Redfern	14
1		**3**		**5**		**7**	**9**			**8**	**4**	**6**				**10***	**2**		**12**		**11**				**T Bune**	**15**
1		11		5	10	7				9	4	6					2	3	8						B Hill	16
1		**6**		**3**	**7**	**9**				**11**	**8**	**4**					**2**		**10**				**5**		**Fredriksson**	**17**
1		10		5	4	7				11		6	9				2	3	8						A Gunn	18
1	2	3	4	5	10	7				11		6	9						8						N Glover	19
1		10	4	5		7				9	11	6					2	3						8	G Napthine	20
1		**3**	**4**	**5**		**7**	**12**			**9**	**13**	**6**				**10***			**8**		**11***				**Schmiohubner**	**21**
1		10		5		7				11	4	6	9									2	3	8	D Hedges	22
1		10		5		7				11		6	9*			4						2	3	8	R Bridges	23
1		**10**		**3**		**9**				**11**	**6***	**4**		**13**		**5**			**4**				**5***		**Tokat**	**24**
1		10		5		7				11		6	9†			4						2	3	8	JC Deakin	25
1		10		5		7				11		6	9*			4		12				2	3†	8	C Thomas	26
1		3	4	5		7	9			11		6				10						2		8	J Martin	27
1		3	4	5		7				11		6	9*			10				12		2		8	E Read	28
1		3	4	5		7				11		6	9			10						2		8	D Brazier	29
1		3	4	5		7				11		6	9			10						2		8	A Seville	30
1		**3**	**4**	**5**		**7**				**11**		**6**	**9**			**10**						**2**		**8**	**A Gunn**	**31**
1		**3**	**4**	**5**		**7**				**11**		**6**	**9**			**10**						**2**		**8**	**A Gunn**	**32**
1		3	4	5		7				11		6	9			10						2		8	L Shapter	33
1		3	4	5		7				11		6	9			10						2		8	D Axcell	34
1		**3**	**4**	**5**		**7**				**11**		**6**	**9**			**10**						**2**		**8**	**M Bodenham**	**35**
1		3	4	5		7				11		6	9*			10				12		2		8	L Robinson	36
1		3		5		7	9			11	4*	6				10				12		2		8	D Vickers	37
1		3	4			7		5		11*		6	9	12		10						2		8	R Richardson	38
1		**3**	**4**			**7**		**5**		**11**		**6**	**9***			**10**				**12**		**2**		**8**	**R Lewis**	**39**
1		3	6	4		8				10		5				7				11		2		9	A Richardson	40
1		3	4	5		7				9		6				10				11		2		8	V Callow	41
1		3	4	5		7*				9				12		10	6					2		8	D Allison	42
1		**3**	**4**			**7**		**5**		**11**		**6**	**9**			**10**						**2**		**8**	**T Bune**	**43**
1		3	4			7		5		11			9			10		6	8*			2		12	K Hackett	44
1		3	12			7		5		11			9	4*		10		6				2		8	K Cooper	45
1		3	4			7	9	5		11						10		6				2		8	M James	46
		3	4			7				10			9			5		6	12	11*		2		8	T Holbrook	47
1			4			7		5		10			9			3		6	12	11*		2		8	J Bray	48
1		**10**	**4**			**7**		**5***		**11**	**12**		**9**					**6**				**2**	**3**	**8**	**J Worrall**	**49**
1		6	4			7	9			10				11				5				2	3	8	K Barratt	50
1		3	4				9*			10			5	7				6		11		2	12	8	I Hendrick	51
1		3	4			7		5		10			9	11				6				2		8	H Taylor	52
1		10†	4			7		5		9*				12				6		11		2	3	8	R Milford	53
1		11	4			7	12	5						9*		3		6		10				8	A Gunn	54
1			4			7	9	5						11		3		6		10				8	P Willis	55
1	2*		4			7		5		11			9			10		6					3	8	E Read	56
1			**6**			**8**		**4**		**11**			**9**			**7**		**3**		**12**		**2**	**5***	**10**	**J Hunting**	**57**
40	6	39	26	22	7	41	9	17	7	39	11	24	27	7	1	31	10	19	4	8	2	25	7	28	League Appearances	
			+1S		+1S		+3S				+2S			+3S				+1S	+3S	+3S			+1S	+1S		
7		6	7	3		7		4		7	1S	5	7			6		2		2S		7	2	7	FA Cup Appearances	
1		2		1	1	2		1		2	2	1	1			2	2		1+1S		1S				Milk Cup Appearances	
6	1S	6	1	4	3	6	3+1S	2+1S	1	6	5+1S	4		1S		5	4		5		2		1		UEFA Cup Appearances	

Also Played: Steele matches 11, 12, 47, no.1. Porter match 23, no.12; 42, no.11. Gibbs matches 54, 55, no.2; 56, no.12.

VICARAGE ROAD

Official Address: Vicarage Road Stadium, Watford WD1 8ER. Telephone: Watford (0923) 30933 (office), 44930 (information)

Ground Capacity: 28,500

Record Attendance: 34,099 v. Manchester U, FA Cup Round 4, 3 Feb 1969

Record Receipts: £74,505 v. Brighton & Hove A, FA Cup Round 5, 18 Feb 1984

Size of Playing Area: 113 × 73 yds

Season Tickets: Stands: £157, £145, £133, £121, £113, £97.50; Ground: £68.50 (South), £57.00 (Rest), £42.00 (Under 16)

Executive Box Season Tickets: 1981 Club: £400 (includes special club room and seat)

Cost of Stand Tickets: £6.50, £6.00, £5.50, £4.00; **Terraces:** £3.00, £2.50; **Family Terrace:** £2.50 (Adults), £1.50 (Children)

Match and Ticket Information: Stand tickets bookable ten days before each match. Visiting terrace supporters are guided by police to special visitors' enclosure

Car Parking: Parking at ground for season ticket holders only. There are several multi-storey parks nearby

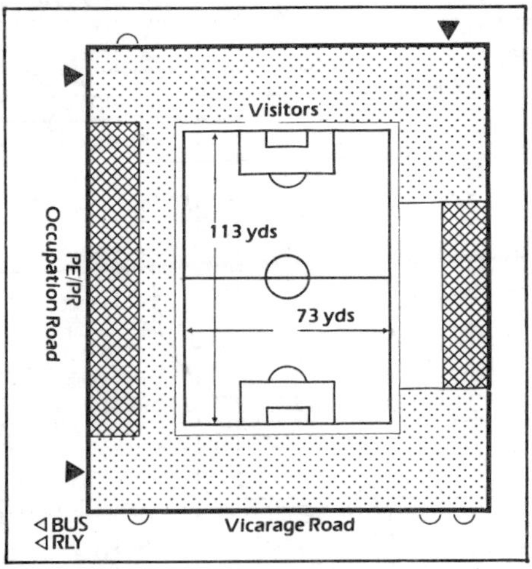

For key see page 12

How to get to the ground

From North: Use Motorway M1 until junction 6. Leave motorway and follow signs Watford A405/A41 and A411. Follow signs Slough A412 and in 0.7m turn left into Harwoods Road. At end at T road turn left into Vicarage Road for Watford F.C.

From East and South: Use Motorway M1 until junction 5. Leave Motorway and follow signs Watford A41 and A412. Then follow signs Slough A412 and in 0.7m turn left into Harwoods Road. At end at T road turn left into Vicarage Road for Watford F.C.

From West: Use A412 S.P. Watford and pass Croxley Green Station then in 0.9m turn right into Harwoods Road. At end at T road turn left into Vicarage Road for Watford F.C.

WEST BROMWICH ALBION Division 1

President
J W Gaunt

Vice-President
F T D Hall

Chairman
J S Lucas

Directors
C Edwards
A Everiss JP
D B Boundy (Vice Chairman)

Secretary/Commercial Manager
G Dimbleby (021-553 5472)

Assistant Secretary
R Fairfax

Accountant
M Rollason

Statistician
T Matthews

Manager
J Giles

Coaches
N Hunter
N Stiles

Physiotherapist
George Wright

Sales Executive
E Adkins

Commercial Assistant
J Stokes

Reserve and Youth Coach
N Stiles

Chief Scout
B Harris

Lottery Manager
T Cardall

Youth Development
R Horobin

Junior Thostles Club
M Sippitts

Groundsman
J Wheeler

For the second time in three seasons Albion found themselves battling to stay in the First Division having looked all set for a good cup run with the possibility of a Wembley appearance.

Honestly speaking Albion were not really relegation material: they started off their League programme with two defeats, picked up a little immediately after that and when ten games had been completed they were lying a comfortable 10th in the table, five points behind the leaders Manchester United and 15 points ahead of bottom club Leicester City.

Suddenly the form-rate dropped; there were signs of inconsistency creeping in and at the turn of the year, after a sad Milk Cup k.o. by neighbours Aston Villa, Albion had nose-dived down the table and were only five points above the relegation zone, yet at the same time they were just 11 behind the top dogs Liverpool. Tony Morley arrived from Villa Park and he settled in quickly, scoring on his debut, but now there was a sense of uneasiness drifting through the ranks.

Albion struggled to beat two Third Division sides, Rotherham and Scunthorpe, in the FA Cup, and Manager Ron Wylie was now unpopular with the supporters.

Nottingham Forest at The Hawthorns in mid-February slammed Albion 5-0. The warning lights were blazing and a week later Wylie was out and back to The Hawthorns after a break of seven years came Johnny Giles, who recruited to the coaching staff former England internationals Norman Hunter and Nobby Stiles.

Their arrival could not prevent Albion crashing out of the FA Cup to underdogs Plymouth Argyle and even at this stage in the season relegation looked a strong possibility, although the manager and his players never really thought about the dreaded drop.

In March, on the transfer deadline, Giles signed two talented midfielders, Steve Hunt (from Coventry) and Paddy Grealish, a Republic of Ireland international, from Brighton – and straight away Albion began to pull round, winning three games in a row at Tottenham, and at home to Stoke and championship contenders Manchester United.

However, only one win came in the next six matches and it was a last-ditch effort (against Luton Town at home) which finally kept Albion in Division One.

On reflection Johnny Giles returned to The Hawthorns just a month too late. He had only a couple of days with the players prior to that 5th round FA Cup-tie with Plymouth and had he been there perhaps even a week then I believe Albion would have progressed further in the competition. Still, we can't relive the past. And now with the squad of players available West Bromwich Albion could be a good force in 1984/85.

Tony Matthews
The League Directory's Statistician for the Club

Back Row L to R: Michael Parry, Garry Thompson, Martyn Bennett, Paul Barron, Tony Godden, Ken McNaught, Barry Cowdrill, Michael Forsyth, Gary Robinson. **Centre Row:** Gary Leonard, Joe Tortolano, Clive Whitehead, Cyrille Regis, Steve Mackenzie, Nicky Cross, Wayne Ebanks, Michael Lewis. **Front Row:** Nobby Stiles (Coach), Alistair Robertson, Derek Statham, Gary Owen, John Giles (Manager), Steve Hunt, Tony Grealish, Tony Morley, George Wright (Physio).

'THROSTLES' 'BAGGIES' or 'ALBION'

Sponsored by **West Midland Health Authority**

Formed: 1879 **Turned Professional:** 1885 **Ltd Co:** 1892
Previous Managers: From the time that the club turned professional, no manager was appointed until 1948. Secretary/Managers before that time were: 1885-7 Thomas Foster 1887-90 Louis Ford 1890-2 Louis Ford/W Pierre Dix 1892-4 Henry 'Swin' Jackson 1894-5 E Stephenson 1892-95 Clement Keys 1896-1902 W Frank Heaven 1902-48 Fred Everiss 1948-52 Jack Smith 1952 Jesse Carver, Manager/Coach 1953-9 Vic Buckingham 1959-61 Gordon Clark 1961-3 Archie Macauly 1963-7 Jimmy Hagen 1967-71 Alan Ashman 1971-5 Don Howe 1975-7 Jonny Giles 1977 Ronnie Allen 1978-1981 Ron Atkinson 1981-2 Ronnie Allen 1982-4 Ron Wylie
Honours: Champions Division 1 1919-20 Champions Division 2 1901-2, 1910-1 F.A. Cup Winners 1888, 1892, 1931, 1954, 1968 Football League Cup Winners 1966
League Career: Founder Members of Football League 1888 Relegated to Division 2 1900-1 Promoted to Division 1 1901-2 Relegated to Division 2 1903-4 Promoted to Division 1 1910-1 Relegated to Division 2 1926-7 Promoted to Division 1 1930-1 Relegated to Division 2 1937-8 Promoted to Division 1 1948-9 Relegated to Division 2 1972-3 Promoted to Division 1 1975-6
Colours: Navy blue and white stripes, white shorts and stockings
Change Colours: Yellow shirts with navy blue pin striped hoops and trim, navy blue shorts, yellow stockings

CLUB RECORDS

Most Appearances for Club: Tony Brown: Football League 561 + 13 + F.A. Cup 53 + 1 + League Cup 46 + 1 + European competitions 16 + 1 + Charity Shield 1 Other Senior competitions 27 **Total 704 + 16 subs**
Most Capped Player: Stuart Williams, 33, Wales **For England:** Jesse Pennington, 25
Record Goalscorer in a Match: Jimmy Cookson, 6 v Blackpool (6-3), Div 2, 17.09.27
Record League Goalscorer in a season: W G Richardson, 39 **All competitions:** W G Richardson, 40 (39 League, F.A. Cup 1), 1935-6
Record League Goalscorer in a career: Tony Brown, 218 **All competitions:** Tony Brown 278 (League 218, F.A. Cup 27, League Cup 16, European competitions 8, Other Senior competitions 9), 1963-79
Record Transfer Fee Received: £1,500,000 from Man Utd for Bryan Robson, Oct 1981
Record Transfer Fee Paid: £748,000 to Man City for Peter Barnes, July 1979
Best Performances: League: Champions 1919-20 **F.A. Cup:** Winners (5) **League/Milk Cup:** Winners (1) **EUWC:** Quarter Final **UEFA Cup:** Quarter Final **Charity Shield:** Runners-Up
Most League Points: (2pts for win) 60, Div 1, 1929-30
Most Goals in Season: 105, Div 2, 1929-30
Record League Victory: 12-0 v Darwen, Div 1, 4 Apr 1892
Record League Defeat: 3-10 v Stoke City, Div 1, 4 Feb 1937
European Competitions Entered: European Cup Winners Cup 1968-9 UEFA 1978-9, 1979-80, 1981-2

Club Statistician for the Directory: Tony Matthews

Programme Editors
Gordon Dimbleby & Tony Matthews

Price	Number of Pages
50p	24

Subscriptions
Subscriptions on request to club shop

WEST BROMWICH ALBION

PLAYERS NAME Ht Wt Birthdate	Honours	Birthplace Transfers	Clubs	APPEARANCES League	Milk Cup			GOALS League	Milk Cup		
GOALKEEPERS											
Paul Barron†		London	Slough T.								
6-2 13.5 16.9.53			Plymouth A.	44	4	4					
		£60,000	Arsenal	8							
		£140,000	Crystal Palace	90	13	5					
		£60,000	W.B.A.	62	4	6					
Tony Godden		Gillingham	Ashford T.								
6-0½ 13.0 2.8.55			W.B.A.	205	21	18	12				
			Luton T. (L)	12							
			Walsall (L)	19							
DEFENDERS											
Martyn Bennett	E. S	Birmingham	W.B.A. (A)	95+1	7	10		4			
6-0 12.12 4.8.61											
Barry Cowdrill		Birmingham	Sutton Coldfield								
5-11 11.4 3.1.57		£5,000	W.B.A.	49+2	6+1	5				1	
Wayne Ebanks		Birmingham	W.B.A.	6+1							
5-10 11.5 2.10.64											
Mike Forsyth	E. Y	Liverpool	W.B.A. (A)	8		1				1	
5-11 11.2 20.3.66											
Gary Leonard		Newcastle	W.B.A. (A)								
5-10 12.0 28.11.65											
Ken McNaught*	EC. 82, ESC.82,	Kirkcaldy	Everton (A)	64+2	10	10		3			
5-11 11.1 11.1.55	Div. 1, 81		Aston Villa	207	17	13	14	8			2
		£125,000	W.B.A.	42	4	4		1			
Alistair Robertson	S. Y, S	Phillipstown	W.B.A. (A)	447+2	43	32+	12	8	1		1
5-11 12.2 9.9.52											
Derek Statham	E.(3), B(2), FAYC.	Wolverhampton	W.B.A. (A)	224+1	24	22	12	4	1	1	
5-5½ 11.1 24.3.59	76, U.21(6), Y										
Joe Tortolano		Wolverhampton	W.B.A.								
5-5½ 11.5											
Clive Whitehead	E. Y	Birmingham	Bristol C.	209+20	17+	10		10	2	2	
5-10½ 11.4 24.11.55		£100,000	W.B.A.	77+1	6	8		3	1	2	
MIDFIELD											
Tony Grealish	E.(37), Y	Paddington	Orient (A)	169+2	6+1	17		10			
5-7 11.7 21.9.56			Luton T.	78	5	3		2			
			Brighton	95+5	7	13		6		2	
			W.B.A.	11							
Steve Hunt	E.(2)	Birmingham	Aston Villa (A)	4+3				1			
5-7 10.10 8.7.56			New York C.								
			Coventry C.	178+7	17	14		26	3	4	
			W.B.A.	12				2			
Mickey Lewis	E. Y	Birmingham	W.B.A.	21+2	3+1	4					
5-6 10.6 15.2.65											
Steve Mackenzie	E. B(1), U.21(3),	Romford	Crystal Palace (A)								
5-10 11.3 23.11.61	Y, FAYC. 78	£250,000	Manchester C.	56+2	11	8		8		2	
		£650,000	W.B.A.	56+1	9+2	6	2	9	1	1	
Gary Owen	E. B(9), U.21(22)•,	St. Helens	Manchester C. (A)	101+2	8	7	5	19	2	2	
5-9 11.3 7.7.58	Y, FLg.XI	£465,000	W.B.A.	168	24	11+	4	19	2	3	
Gary Robson		Durham	W.B.A. (A)	5+4	1						
5-5 10.11 6.7.65											
FORWARDS											
Nicky Cross		Birmingham	W.B.A. (A)	53+28	4+2	4	0+1	10	2		
5-9 11.2 7.2.61											
Tony Morley	E.(6), B(2),	Ormskirk	P.N.E. (A)	78+6	8	6+1		15	3	2	
5-8½ 11.8 26.8.54	U.23(1), Y, EC.82,	£100,000	Burnley	78+13	3+1	3+2		5	1	1	
	Div. 1, 81	£200,000	Aston Villa	128+9	14	8	20+	25	3	1	5
	ESC. 82	£80,000	W.B.A.	26		4		4		2	
Mike Perry		Wimbledon	W.B.A. (A)	14+6	2	1		5			
5-10 11.4 4.4.64											
Cyrille Regis	E.(4), B(3),	French Guyana	Hayes								
6-0 13.4 9.2.58	U.21(6)	£5,000	W.B.A.	226+4	27+	25	10	81	16	10	3
Gary Thompson	E. U.21(6)	Birmingham	Coventry C. (A)	127+7	12+	11		38	7	4	
6-0 12.9 7.10.59		£225,000	W.B.A.	49	4	4		20	3	1	

APPRENTICES

Karl Addis, Steve Bell, Darren Carmell, Hector Wynter, Lionel Dobbins, Ian Hathaway, Mark Housego, Andy Thompson

•Record number of U.21 caps

WEST BROMWICH ALBION

DIVISION ONE 17TH **FA CUP** 5TH ROUND **MILK CUP** 4TH ROUND

MATCH	DATE	COMPETITION	VENUE	OPPONENTS	RESULT	HALF TIME	L'GUE POS'N	GOALSCORERS	ATTENDANCE
1	A 27	CL	A	Aston Villa	L3-4	3-3		Zondervan, Thompson, Regis	29,522
2	29	CL	A	Stoke C	L1-3	1-2		Cross	16,156
3	S 3	CL	H	Leicester C	W1-0	1-0	16	Whitehead	12,016
4	7	CL	H	Tottenham H	D1-1	0-1		Regis	14,989
5	10	CL	A	Everton	D0-0	0-0	17		15,548
6	17	CL	H	West Ham U	W1-0	0-0	14	Thompson	15,161
7	24	CL	A	Ipswich T	W4-3	2-2	10	Zondervan, Regis, Perry, Thompson (pen)	16,611
8	O 1	CL	H	Watford	W2-0	2-0	7	Regis, Thompson	13,585
9	**4**	**MC 2**	**A**	**Millwall**	**L0-3**	**0-2**			**10,721**
10	15	CL	A	Manchester U	L0-3	0-2	11		42,221
11	22	CL	A	Coventry C	W2-1	1-0	9	Regis, Perry	13,441
12	**25**	**MC 2**	**H**	**Millwall**	**W5-1**	**1-0**		**Thompson 2, Regis 2, Owen (pen)**	**13,311**
13	29	CL	H	Birmingham C	L1-2	0-1	12	Perry	20,224
14	N 5	CL	H	Notts Co	W2-0	1-0	10	McNaught, Luke	10,821
15	**8**	**MC 3**	**A**	**Chelsea**	**W1-0**	**0-0**		**Thompson**	**22,932**
16	12	CL	A	Southampton	L0-1	0-1	12		16,450
17	19	CL	A	Norwich C	L0-2	0-0	14		13,358
18	26	CL	H	Wolverhampton W	L1-3	0-0	15	Thompson	17,947
19	**30**	**MC 4**	**H**	**Aston Villa**	**L1-2**	**1-1**		**Regis**	**31,114**
20	D 3	CL	A	Arsenal	W1-0	0-0	12	Monaghan	22,271
21	10	CL	H	QPR	L1-2	0-1	12	Morley	11,717
22	18	CL	A	Luton T	L0-2	0-1			11,566
23	26	CL	H	Liverpool	L1-2	0-1	15	Morley	25,139
24	27	CL	A	Sunderland	L0-3	0-2	15		17,986
25	31	CL	A	Leicester C	D1-1	0-0	15	Thompson	15,146
26	J 2	CL	H	Ipswich T	W2-1	1-1	15	Owen, Thompson	11,199
27	**7**	**FAC 3**	**A**	**Rotherham U**	**D0-0**	**0-0**			**8,142**
28	**11**	**FAC 3R**	**H**	**Rotherham U**	**W3-0**	**0-0**		**Thompson, Morley 2**	**12,107**
29	14	CL	H	Aston Villa	W3-1	0-0	12	Thompson 2, Regis	20,399
30	21	CL	A	West Ham U	L0-1	0-0	16		17,213
31	**F 1**	**FAC 4**	**H**	**Scunthorpe U**	**W1-0**	**0-0**		**Luke**	**18,235**
32	4	CL	A	Watford	L1-3	0-0	17	Zondervan	14,240
33	8	CL	H	Nottingham F	L0-5	0-1	17		11,020
34	11	CL	H	Everton	D1-1	0-0	17	Perry	10,313
35	**18**	**FAC 5**	**H**	**Plymouth Arg**	**L0-1**	**0-0**			**23,795**
36	25	CL	H	Coventry C	D1-1	0-0	19	Cross	10,900
37	28	CL	A	Birmingham C	L1-2	0-2		Mackenzie	16,780
38	M 3	CL	A	Notts Co	D1-1	0-0	18	Cross	7,373
39	17	CL	A	Tottenham H	W1-0	0-0	18	Regis	22,385
40	24	CL	H	Stoke C	W3-0	2-0	17	Mackenzie, Hunt, Morley	13,681
41	31	CL	H	Manchester U	W2-0	1-0	16	Mackenzie, Regis	27,954
42	A 7	CL	A	Nottingham F	L1-3	0-2	16	Thompson	15,245
43	14	CL	H	Norwich C	D0-0	0-0	17		11,572
44	21	CL	A	Liverpool	L0-3	0-3	18		35,320
45	23	CL	H	Sunderland	W3-1	2-1	16	Regis, Hunt, Thompson	11,252
46	28	CL	A	Wolverhampton W	D0-0	0-0	16		13,208
47	M 5	CL	H	Arsenal	L1-3	1-2	17	Thompson	13,566
48	7	CL	A	QPR	D1-1	0-0	17	Thompson	14,418
49	12	CL	H	Luton T	W3-0	0-0	15	Morley, Regis, Mackenzie	12,400
50	14	CL	H	Southampton	L0-2	0-0			10,365
								Av Home Att	**14,781**

Goal Scorers

League (48): Thompson 13 (1 pen), Regis 10, Mackenzie 4, Morley 4, Perry 4, Cross 3, Zondervan 3, Hunt 2, Luke 1, McNaught 1, Monaghan 1, Owen 1, Whitehead 1
FA Cup (4): Morley 2, Luke 1, Thompson 1
Milk Cup (7): Regis 3, Thompson 3, Owen 1 (1 pen)

1983-84

Barron	Webb	Whitehead	Zondervan	McNaught	Bennett	Joi	Thompson	Regis	Owen	Cross	Robson	Robertson	Cowdrill	Perry	Lewis	Luke	Monaghan	Forsyth	Mackenzie	Morley	Ebanks	Statham	Grealish	Hunt	REFEREE	
	2	3	4*	5	6	7	8	9	10	11	12														N Ashley	1
		3		5	6	7	8	9	10	11	4	2													M Peck	2
		3	2	5	6	7	8	9	10	11	4														D Scott	3
		2	4	5	6	7*	8	9	10	11			3	12											D Hedges	4
		2	4	5	6		8	9	10	12	7*		3	11											P Willis	5
		2	4	5	6		8	9	10	11*			3	12	7										N Wilson	6
		2	4	5	6		8	9		11	10*		3	12	7										J Moules	7
	2	10	4	5	6		8	9		11*			3		7										T Jones	8
		2	**4**	**5***			**8**	**9**		**11**	**10**		**3**		**7**				**12**						**M James**	**9**
		2	4	5	6		8	9	10	11			3		7										A Challinor	10
		2	7	5	6		8	9*	10		12		3	11	4										E Read	11
		2	**4**	**5**	**6**		**8**	**9**	**10***	**12**			**3**	**11**	**7**										**B Stevens**	**12**
		2	7	5	6*		8	9	10	12			3	11	4										D Hutchinson	13
		2	7	5			8		10			6	3	11	4	9									M Dimblebee	14
		2	**4**	**5**			**8**		**10**			**6**	**3**	**9**	**7**	**11**									**Alan Robinson**	**15**
		2	4*	5			8		10	12	7	6	3	9		11									E Crickmore	16
		2	4	5		7	8		10	12		6	3	9*		11									C Downey	17
		2	9	3		7	10		8			4	5	11*		6	12								K Hackett	18
		2	**4**	**5**		**7**	**8**	**9***	**10†**	**11**		**6**	**3**						**12**						**C Thomas**	**19**
	2		4	5			8		11				3			7	9	6	10						T Bune	20
	2		4	5	6		8		10				3	12			9		11*	7					J Worrall	21
			2	5		7†		9		10			3		8	4		6		11					M Taylor	22
	2		4	5		7		9		10*			3	12	8			6		11					H King	23
			4	5			8	9	10	12			3		7			6		11	2*				J Key	24
		2	4	5	6	7	8	9	10				3							11					T Mills	25
		2	4*	5	6		8	9	10	12			3		7					11					J Lovatt	26
		2		**5**	**6**		**8**	**9**	**10***	**4**			**3**		**7**	**12**				**11**					**J Hough**	**27**
		2		**5**	**6**		**8**	**9**	**10**				**3**		**7**	**4**				**11**					**J Hough**	**28**
		2	7	5	6		8	9	10				3			4				11					A Ward	29
		2	7	5		12	9	10	8*			6	3			4				11					I Borrett	30
		2	**7**	**5**			**8**	**9**					**3**		**10**	**4**		**6**		**11**					**Alan Robinson**	**31**
		2	4	5		7	8	9					3		10			6		11					D Vickers	32
		2	4	5		7	8	9*							10			6	12	11		3			T Fitzharris	33
		2	4	5		7				12				9				6*	10	11		3			D Reeves	34
		2	**4**	**5**	**6**	**7**	**8**							**9***		**12**			**10**	**11**		**3**			**P Willis**	**35**
			4	5	6	7	8			9									10	11	2	3			P Tyldesley	36
			4	5	6	7	8			9									10	11	2	3			L Shapter	37
		2	4	5	6	7	8			9									10	11		3			R Banks	38
		2		5	6		8	9											10	11		3	7	4	D Axcell	39
		2		5	6*		8	9											10	11	12	3	7	4	N Midgley	40
		2		5	6		8	9											10	11		3	7	4	D Letts	41
		2		5	6		8	9											10	11		3	7	4	G Tyson	42
				5	6		8			9									10	11	2	3	7	4	K Walmsley	43
		2		5	6		8	9											10	11		3	7	4	K Redfern	44
		2		5	6		8	9		12									10	11		3*	7	4	T Jones	45
		2		5	6		8†	9											10	11		3	7	4	J Hough	46
		2		5	6		8	9		12									10	11		3	7*	4	J Worrall	47
		2		5			8	9										6	10	11	7	3		4	R Milford	48
		2		5	6			9		8									10	11		3	7	4	K Hackett	49
		2		5	6					8					9				10	11	3*		7	4	D Richardson	50
2	5	34	29	**42**	29	15	37	30	20	16	5	6	22	8	14	8	2	8	18	26	6	16	11	12	League Appearances	
						+1S				+9S	+2S			+5S			+1S		+1S		+1S					
		4	2	4	3	1	4	3	2	1			3	1	3	2+2S		1	1	4		1			FA Cup Appearances	
		4	4	4	1	1	4	3	3	2+1S	1	2	4	2	3	1			2S						Milk Cup Appearances	

lso Played: Kent match 34, no.8; 50, no.12. Smith match 9, no.6. Child match 8, no.12.

THE HAWTHORNS

Official Address: The Hawthorns, West Bromwich B71 4LF. Telephone: 021 525 8888 (6 lines) (Club); 021 553 5472 (Ticket Office)

Ground Capacity: 39,159 (12,500 seats)

Record Attendance: 64,815 v. Arsenal, F.A. Cup Round 6, 6 Mar 1937

Record Receipts: £79,494.76 v. Tottenham Hotspur, League Cup Semi-Final, 3 Feb 1982

Size of Playing Area: 115yds × 75 yds

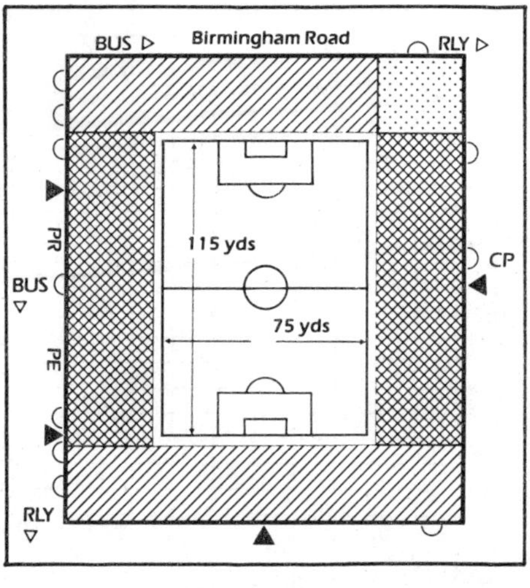

For key see page 12

Season Tickets: Stands: £65.00 to £96.00; Ground: £40.00 to £44.00 (Reductions for juveniles/OAP)

Cost of Stand Tickets: £3.70, £4.00, £4.30, £4.50, £5.00, £5.50, £6.00; **Terraces:** £2.50 & £2.70 (juveniles/OAP £1.50 & £1.60)

Match and Ticket Information: Six weeks in advance for Centre & Wing stands by post with remittance & SAE. Telephone only two days before for tickets to be collected not less than 30 minutes before kick-off. Limited availability of unreserved seats (Door E1) on day of match

Car Parking: Street parking in some areas within 10 minutes walk of ground

How to get to the ground

From all directions: Use Motorway M5 until junction 1. Leave motorway and follow signs Birmingham A41 into Loop Road for West Bromwich Albion F.C.

WEST HAM UNITED Division 1

Chairman
L C Cearns

Directors
W F Cearns
B R Cearns, FCIS
J Petchey
M W Cearns

Chief Executive & Secretary
Eddie Chapman, FAAI

PRO
Jack Helliar

Manager
John Lyall

Chief Scout
E Bailey

Commercial Manager
B C Blower (01-472 7352)

Although the pre-season results were disappointing, the aim at Upton Park was to finish in the top six and qualify for a place in Europe. The optimism was well founded as the opening day brought a 4-0 win over Birmingham with new signings Steve Walford and Steve Whitton settling in well.

The Hammers won their first five games including a thrilling London derby at Tottenham and a remarkable game with Coventry; after missing a penalty and going 2-0 behind, an incredible burst of scoring saw Hammers score three goals in three minutes to demoralise their visitors. The clash with Liverpool in October was long awaited but after a terrific display from the Merseysiders it was apparent that West Ham would not be challenging them for the title. The Milk Cup scoring record was broken as the luckless Bury were the victims of a 10-0 rout, Tony Cottee scoring four. Tougher opposition was to follow, however, as Everton knocked Hammers out at Goodison after extra time in a replay.

December brought home wins over London rivals Arsenal and Spurs, and West Ham now second in the league went into 1984 in high spirits. The joy of a 1-0 FA Cup win over Wigan was shortlived as an injury to Alan Devonshire forced him to miss the rest of the season, a blow which proved costly. Further injuries were soon to decimate the side as Bonds, Brooking, Martin, Pike and Whitton missed most games throughout January and February. The youngsters who deputised, however, did a good job as Crystal Palace were knocked out of the Cup and Coventry, Stoke and West Bromwich were beaten in the league. In a black day for West Ham on 18th February a weakened side were well beaten in the FA Cup by Birmingham and a pitch invasion brought shame to the club. Despite brilliant displays by Trevor Brooking in his farewell season the team began to struggle; successive away games at Leicester and Liverpool saw the defence concede ten goals. The home faithful became frustrated as former favourites Pop Robson and Mervyn Day became surprise winners at Upton Park with Sunderland and Aston Villa respectively. Creditable draws at Old Trafford and Highbury were gained but the season ended on a sad note with a home defeat by cup finalists Everton. Trevor Brooking in his last game for the club deserved better.

Back Row L to R: Paul Hilton, Billy Bonds, Tony Gale, Tom McAlister, John Vaughan, Phil Parkes, Alvin Martin (capt.), Steve Walford, Dave Swindlehurst. **Middle Row:** Paul Brush, Keith McPherson, Greg Campbell, Ray Stewart (vice-capt.), Steve Whitton, Alan Devonshire, George Parris, Alan Dickens, Neil Orr. **Front Row:** Warren Donald, Frank Lampard, Paul Allen, Tony Cottee, Bobby Barnes, Geoff Pike, Paul Goddard.

'THE HAMMERS'

Sponsored by
AVCO

Formed: 1900 **Turned Professional:** 1900 **Ltd Co:** 1900
Previous Managers: 1900-31 Syd King 1931-50 Charlie Paynter 1950-61 Ted Fenton 1961-74 Ron Greenwood
Honours: Champions Division 2 1957-8, 1980-1 F.A. Cup Winners 1964, 1975, 1980
League Career: Elected to Division 2 1919 Promoted to Division 1 1922-3 Relegated to Division 2 1931-2 Promoted to Division 1 1957-8 Relegated to Division 2 1977-8 Promoted to Division 1 1980-1
Colours: Claret shirts with sky blue sleeves and trim, white shorts and stockings
Change Colours: White shirts with three claret stripes down sleeves, blue shorts with three claret stripes, blue stockings

CLUB RECORDS

Most Appearances for Club: Billy Bonds: Football League 601 + 1 + F.A. Cup 41 + 1 + League/Milk Cup 60 + European Cup Winners Cup 15 **Total 717 + 2 subs**
Most Capped Player: Bobby Moore, 108, for England
Record Goalscorer in a Match: Geoff Hurst, 6 v Sunderland (8-0), Div 1, 19.10.68
Record League Goalscorer in a season: Vic Watson, 42 **All competitions:** Vic Watson, 50 (League 42, F.A. Cup 8), 1929-30
Record League Goalscorer in a career: Vic Watson, 298 **All competitions:** Vic Watson, 326 (League 298, F.A. Cup 28)
Record Transfer Fee Received: £225,000 from Birmingham City for Alan Curbishley, June 1979
Record Transfer Fee Paid: £800,000 to Q.P.R. for Paul Goddard, August 1979
Best Performances: League: 6th Div 1 1926-7 **F.A. Cup:** Winners (3) **League/Milk Cup:** Runners Up 1966, 1981 **European Cup Winners Cup:** Winners 1965
Most League Points: (2pts for win) 66, Div 2, 1980-1
Most Goals in a Season: 101, Div 2, 1931-2
Record League Victory: 8-0 v Rotherham United, Div 2, 8 March 1958
8-0 v Sunderland, Div 1, 19 Oct 1968
Record League Defeat: 2-8 v Blackburn Rovers (H), Div 1, 26 Dec 1963
European Competitions Entered: European Cup Winners Cup (4) 1964-5, 1965-6, 1975-6, 1980-1
Club Statistician for the Directory: John Northcutt (Secretary of West Ham Statisticians Group, 7 Bells Chase, Great Baddow, Chelmsford, Essex)

Programme Editor
Colin Benson

Price	Number of Pages
50p	28

Subscriptions
£26.00 for season (postage paid U.K.), £32.00 for season (postage paid Europe)

WEST HAM UNITED

PLAYERS NAME Ht Wt Birthdate	Honours	Birthplace Transfers	Clubs	APPEARANCES League	Milk Cup	F.A.C.	E. Cups	GOALS League	Milk Cup	F.A.C.	E. Cups
GOALKEEPERS											
Tony McAllister		Clydebank	Sheffield U. (A)	63	6	2					
6-0 12.13 10.12.52		£15,000	Rotherham U.	159	12	14					
		£50,000	Blackpool	16	4						
		F	Swindon T.	1							
			Bristol R. (L)	13							
		F	West Ham U.	3	1						
Phil Parkes	E.(1). B(1).	Sedgeley	Walsall	52	1	7					
6-3 14.9 8.8.50	U.23(6).	£15,000	Q.P.R.	344	27	27	8				
	Div. 2. 73.	£500,000	West Ham U.	223	33	18	6				
	FAC. 80.										
	Div. 2. 81										
DEFENDERS											
Billy Bonds	E. U.23(2).	Woolwich	Charlton Ath. (A)	95	3	2		1			
6-0½ 13.2 17.9.46	FAC. 75. 80.		West Ham U.	601 + 1	60	41 +	15	45	6	2	3
	Div. 2. 81										
Paul Brush	FAC. 80	London	West Ham U. (A)	126 + 7	12 +	12	1 + 3				
5-11 11.12 22.2.58	Div. 2. 81										
Tony Gale	E. U.21(1)	London	Fulham (A)	277	22	16		19	2		
6-1½ 12.4 19.11.59											
Frank Lampard	E.(2). U.23(4). Y.	West Ham	West Ham U. (A)	545 + 5	54	43	15	18	1	2	1
5-11 12.9 20.9.48	FAC. 75. 80.										
	Div. 2. 81										
Mick McGiven		Newcastle	Sunderland	107 + 6	3	2		9		1	
6-0 11.3 7.2.51		£25,000	West Ham U.	46 + 2	2	3					
Alvin Martin	E.(12). Y.	Bootle	West Ham U. (A)	203 + 2	34	14	6	15	3		
6-1 13.0 29.7.58	FAC. 80.										
	Div. 2. 81										
Neil Orr	S. U.21(7).	Greenock	Morton	180 + 6	10	14		1			
5-10 12.2 13.5.59	SD. 1(1)	£400,000	West Ham U.	61 + 6	8	2 + 2		1	1		
Ray Stewart	S.(7). U.21(12).	Perth	Dundee U.	44	8	1	1	4			
5-11 12.0 7.9.59	FAC. 80.	£430,000	West Ham U.	202	33	18	6	40	10	5	1
	Div. 2. 81										
Steve Walford	E. Y. FAC. 79	Highgate	Tottenham H. (A)	1 + 1							
6-1 11.7 5.1.58		£25,000	Arsenal	64 + 13	5	5		3	1		
		£175,000	Norwich C.	93	8	7		2			
		£165,000	West Ham U.	41	5	4		2			
MIDFIELD											
Paul Allen	E. Y.(23—Record).	Aveley	West Ham U.	111 + 3	16 +	10 +	1 + 1	3	2	1	
5-7 9.12 28.8.62	FAC. 80.										
	Div. 2. 81										
Alan Devonshire	E.(9). B(1).	London	Southall								
5-10½ 11.0 13.4.56	FAC. 80.	£5,000	West Ham U.	269 + 3	34	18	4	24	2	1	
	Div. 2. 81										
Alan Dickens	E. Y.	Plaistow	West Ham U. (A)	19 + 6	0 + 1	1		6			
5-11 12.0 3.9.64											
Warren Donald		Uxbridge	West Ham U. (A)	1 + 1							
5-7 10.1 7.10.64											
Paul Hilton	E. S.	Oldham	Bury	136 + 12	2 + 3	16					
6-1 11.6 8.10.59		£75,000	West Ham U.	7 + 1							
Geoff Pike	FAC. 80.	Clapton	West Ham U.	225 + 15	33 +	16 +	6	30	2	2	1
5-6 11.3 28.9.56	Div. 2. 81										
FORWARDS											
Bobby Barnes	E. Y.	Kingston	West Ham U. (A)	13 + 9	1 + 1	3 + 1	0 + 1	3		1	
5-7 11.0 17.12.62											
Tony Cottee	E. Y.	West Ham	West Ham U. (A)	40 + 7	4	4		20	4		
5-8 11.5 11.7.65											
Paul Goddard	E.(1). U.21(8).	Harington	Q.P.R. (A)	63 + 7	4 + 1						
5-8 11.8 12.10.59	Div. 2. 81	£800,000	West Ham U.	117 + 3	21	6	6	43	8		2
Dave Swindlehurst	E. U.21(1). Y.	Edgware	Crystal Palace	221 + 16	17	22		73	3	4	
6-2 13.3 6.1.56	Div. 2. 79	£41,000	Derby Co.	110	8	7		29	3		
		£200,000	West Ham U.	44 + 1	5	4		16	1	1	
Steve Whitton		London	Coventry C. (A)	64 + 10	2 + 2	3		21			
6-0 12.7 4.12.60		£175,000	West Ham U.	22	3	1		5			

CONTRACT PLAYERS WHO HAVE NO FIRST TEAM APPEARANCES

John Vaughan (G), **Keith McPherson** (D), **Kevin Keen** (MF), **Gerhard Ampofo** (D), **David Matthews** (MF), **George Parris** (MF), **Andy Skinner** (MF), **Greg Campbell** (F), **Steve Potts** (F)

APPRENTICES

Paul McMenemy, Andy Parr, Alan Spiers, Dean Crumpton, Eamonn Dolan, Trevor Lake

Player of the Year 1983-84 Trevor Brooking (retired)

WEST HAM UNITED

DIVISION ONE 9TH **FA CUP** 5TH ROUND **MILK CUP** 4TH ROUND

MATCH	DATE	COMPE-TITION	VENUE	OPPONENTS	RESULT	HALF TIME	L'GUE POS'N	GOALSCORERS	ATTEN-DANCE
1	A 27	CL	H	Birmingham C	W4-0	3-0		Cottee 2, Martin, Swindlehurst	19,792
2	29	CL	A	Everton	W1-0	0-0		Walford	20,375
3	S 3	CL	A	Tottenham H	W2-0	2-0	1	Whilton, Swindlehurst	38,042
4	6	CL	H	Leicester C	W3-1	1-1		Walford, Swindlehurst, Cottee	22,131
5	10	CL	H	Coventry C	W5-2	3-2	1	Swindlehurst 3, Whitton 2	22,195
6	17	CL	A	WBA	L0-1	0-0	1		15,161
7	24	CL	H	Notts Co	W3-0	1-0	1	Brooking, Goddard, Stewart (pen)	20,613
8	O 1	CL	A	Stoke C	L1-3	0-1	1	Stewart (pen)	13,852
9	**5**	**MC 2**	**A**	**Bury**	**W2-1**	**1-0**		**Goddard, Orr**	**8,050**
10	15	CL	H	Liverpool	L1-3	0-2	2	Devonshire	32,555
11	22	CL	H	Norwich C	D0-0	0-0	3		18,958
12	**25**	**MC 2**	**H**	**Bury**	**W10-0**	**5-0**		**Cottee 4, Brooking 2, Devonshire 2, Martin, Stewart (pen)**	**10,896**
13	28	CL	A	Watford	D0-0	0-0			14,559
14	N 5	CL	H	Ipswich T	W2-1	2-1	3	Swindlehurst 2	20,682
15	**8**	**MC 3**	**H**	**Brighton**	**W1-0**	**0-0**		**Swindlehurst**	**17,082**
16	12	CL	A	Wolverhampton W	W3-0	0-0	2	Brooking, Swindlehurst, Cottee	12,062
17	19	CL	A	Sunderland	W1-0	0-0	2	Swindlehurst	19,921
18	27	CL	H	Manchester U	D1-1	0-0		Swindlehurst	23,355
19	**30**	**MC 4**	**H**	**Everton**	**D2-2**	**1-1**		**Mountfield (og), Pike**	**19,702**
20	D 3	CL	A	Aston Villa	L0-1	0-0	2		21,297
21	**6**	**MC 4R**	**A**	**Everton**	**L0-2**	**0-0**			**21,609**
22	10	CL	H	Arsenal	W3-1	1-0	2	Brooking, Whyte (og), Pike	25,118
23	17	CL	A	Nottingham F	L0-3	0-1	3		14,544
24	26	CL	H	Southampton	L0-1	0-0	5		22,221
25	27	CL	A	Luton T	W1-0	0-0	4	Cottee	16,343
26	31	CL	H	Tottenham H	W4-1	1-1	3	Cottee, Martin, Stewart, Brooking	30,939
27	J 2	CL	A	Notts Co	D2-2	2-1	3	Stewart (pen), Swindlehurst	8,667
28	**7**	**FAC 3**	**H**	**Wigan Ath**	**W1-0**	**1-0**		**Stewart (pen)**	**16,000**
29	14	CL	A	Birmingham C	L0-3	0-1	3		10,334
30	21	CL	H	WBA	W1-0	0-0	3	Cottee	17,213
31	**28**	**FAC 4**	**A**	**Crystal Palace**	**D1-1**	**0-1**		**Swindlehurst**	**27,590**
32	**31**	**FAC 4R**	**H**	**Crystal Palace**	**W2-0**	**1-0**		**Gilbert (og), Barnes**	**27,127**
33	F 4	CL	H	Stoke C	W3-0	2-0	4	Barnes, Cottee, Stewart (pen)	18,775
34	7	CL	A	QPR	D1-1	1-1	3	Cottee	20,102
35	11	CL	A	Coventry C	W2-1	1-0	3	Bamber (og), Cottee	13,271
36	**18**	**FAC 5**	**A**	**Birmingham C**	**L0-3**	**0-2**			**29,570**
37	21	CL	H	Watford	L2-4	1-1		Swindlehurst, Barnes	19,241
38	25	CL	A	Norwich C	L0-1	0-0	4		16,294
39	M 3	CL	A	Ipswich T	W3-0	1-0	4	Hilton, Butcher (og), Cottee	17,297
40	10	CL	H	Wolverhampton W	D1-1	1-1	3	Cottee	18,111
41	17	CL	A	Leicester C	L1-4	0-1	5	Stewart (pen)	13,533
42	31	CL	H	QPR	D2-2	2-0	4	Pike, Cottee	21,099
43	A 7	CL	A	Liverpool	L0-6	0-4	6		38,359
44	14	CL	H	Sunderland	L0-1	0-0	6		16,558
45	17	CL	H	Luton T	W3-1	2-0		Cottee 2, Martin	15,430
46	21	CL	A	Southampton	L0-2	0-1	6		20,846
47	28	CL	A	Manchester U	D0-0	0-0	7		44,124
48	M 5	CL	H	Aston Villa	L0-1	0-1	9		17,390
49	7	CL	A	Arsenal	D3-3	3-2	7	Whitton 2, Hilton	33,347
50	12	CL	H	Nottingham F	L1-2	1-1	8	Stewart (pen)	18,463
51	14	CL	H	Everton	L0-1	0-1			25,452
								Av Home Att	**21,247**

Goal Scorers

League (60): Cottee 15, Swindlehurst 13, Stewart 7 (6 pens), Whitton 5, Brooking 4, Martin 3, Barnes 2, Hilton 2, Pike 2, Walford 2, Devonshire 1, Goddard 1, opponents 3

FA Cup (4): Barnes 1, Stewart 1 (1 pen), Swindlehurst 1, opponent 1

Milk Cup (15): Cottee 4, Brooking 2, Devonshire 2, Goddard 1, Martin 1, Orr 1, Pike 1, Stewart 1 (1 pen), Swindlehurst 1, opponent 1

1983-84

Parkes	Stewart	Walford	Bonds	Martin	Devonshire	Whitton	Cottee	Swindlehurst	Brooking	Pike	Orr	Goddard	Dickens	Allen	Lampard	Donald	Brush	Barnes	Hilton	REFEREE	
1	2	3	4	5	6	7	8	9	10*	11	12									Alan Robinson	1
1	2	3	4	5	6	7	8	9		11	10									P Tyldesley	2
1	2	3	4	5	6	7	8	9	10	11										J Hunting/D Nevin	3
1	2	3	4	5	6	7	8	9	10	11										L Burden	4
1	2	3	4	5	6	7	8	9	10	11										A Crickmore	5
1	2	5	3	4	6		9	10	7	11	8*	12								N Wilson	6
1	2	3	4	5	6		8	9	10	11		7								M James	7
1	2	3	4	5	6	7		9	10	11		8								B Stevens	8
1	**2**	**3***	**4**	**5**	**6**	**7**		**9**	**10**	**11**	**12**	**8**								**M Heath**	**9**
1	2	3	4	5	6	7	12	9	10	11		8*								LC Shapter	10
1	2	3	4	5	6	7*	8	9	10	11			12							D Brazier	11
1	**2**	**3**	**4***	**5**	**6**		**8**	**9**	**10**	**11**	**12**			**7**						**D Letts**	**12**
1	2	3	4	5	6		8	9	10		11			7						B Hill	13
1	2	3	4*	5	6		8	9		11	7		10		12					T Bune	14
1	**2**	**4**		**5**	**6**		**8**	**9**	**10**	**11**	**7**				**3**					**M Scott**	**15**
1	2	4		5	6		8	9	10	11	7				3					J Deakin	16
1	2	4		5	6	7	8	9	10	11					3					T Jones	17
1	2	4		5	6	7	8	9	10	11					3					C Thomas	18
1	**2**	**4**		**5**	**6**	**7**	**8**	**9**	**10**	**11**					**3**					**A Gunn**	**19**
1	2	4		5	6	7	12	9	10	11	8*				3					N Glover	20
1	**2**	**4**		**5**		**7**	**8***	**9**	**10**	**11**	**6**		**12**		**3**					**T Mills**	**21**
1	2	4		5	6	7		9†	10	11	8				3					E Read	22
1	2	4		5	6	7		9	10		8		12		3					T Holbrook	23
1	2	4		5	6	9	8		10		7		11		3*	12				M Bodenham	24
1	2	4		5	6	7	9		10		8						3	11		K Baker	25
1	2	4		5	6	7	8	9	10		11						3			T Spencer	26
1	2	4		5	6	7	8	9	10		11						3			G Courtney	27
1	**2**	**4**		**5**	**6***	**7**	**8**	**9**	**10**		**11**						**3**	**12**		**A Seville**	**28**
1	2	4		5		9	11	10	6		7						3	8		D Hedges	29
1	2	4					8	9	10	11	5				3		6	7		I Borrett	30
1	**2**	**4**					**8**	**9**	**10**	**11**	**5**			**12**	**3**		**6***	**7**		**J Hunting**	**31**
1	**2**	**4**					**8**	**9**	**10**	**11***	**5**			**12**	**3**		**6**	**7**		**J Hunting**	**32**
1	2	4					8	9			5		11	10	3		6	7		R Milford	33
1	2	4					8	9			5		11	10	3		6	7		G Napthine	34
1	2	4					8	9			5		11	10	3		6	7		L Burden	35
1	**2**	**4**	**12**				**8**	**9**			**5**		**11**	**10**	**3**		**6***	**7**		**G Courtney**	**36**
1	2	5	4				10	11					8	7	3			9	6	Alan Robinson	37
1	2	5	4				8	9					11	10	3			7	6	J Ashworth	38
1	2	5	4				8	9	10		7			11	3				6	J Bray	39
1	2	5	4				8	9	10		6		12	11	3			7*		E Read	40
1	2	5	4				8	9	10	11	6*			7	3			12		D Richardson	41
1	2	3	4	5			8	9	10	11	6			7						M Dimblebee	42
1	2	3	4	5		9	8		10	11	6			7						D Hutchinson	43
1	2		4	5			8	9	10	11	6*			7	3			12		T Bune	44
1	2	3	4	5			8	9	10	11				7				6		D Reeves	45
1	2	3	4	5			8	9	10	11				7				6*	12	C Thomas	46
1	2	3	4	5			8		10	11	9			7					6	K Hackett	47
1	2*	3	4				9	10	8	11	6	12		7					5	B Hill	48
1	2	5	4			11	8		10		9			7			3		6	R Lewis	49
1	2	5	4			11	8		10	12	9			7			3*		6	L Shapter	50
1	2	5	4			9	8	12	10	11*	3			7		6				M Taylor	51
42	**42**	41	27	29	22	22	37	35	35	27	28	3	7	19	17	1	10	11	7	League Appearances	
							+2S	+1S		+1S	+1S	+2S	+3S		+1S	+1S		+2S	+1S		
4	4	4	1S	1	1	1	4	4	3	2	4		1	1+2S	3		4	3+1S		FA Cup Appearances	
5	5	5	2	5	4	3	4	5	5	5	2+2S	1	1S	1	3					Milk Cup Appearances	

BOLEYN GROUND, UPTON PARK

Official Address: Boleyn Ground, Green Street, Upton Park, London E13. Telephone: 01-472 2740

Ground Capacity: 35,500

Record Attendance: 42,322 v. Tottenham H, Div 1, 17 Oct 1970

Record Receipts: £98,663 v. Crystal Palace, FA Cup Round 4 replay, 31 Jan 1984

Size of Playing Area: 110 × 72 yds

Season Tickets: Stands: £90, £100. Ground: £66

Executive Box Season Tickets: £315 per person

Cost of Stand Tickets: £6.50, £6.00, £5.50 (Upper Tier); £6.50, £6.00, £4.50 (Lower Tier); **Ground:** East Terrace: £3.50 (Adults and Children), North & South Banks: £2.50 (Adults), £1.50 (Children)

Match and Ticket Information: Advance bookings personally or by post are accepted three weeks before each League match. Stand ticket prices are increased by £1 for every match involving Liverpool or Manchester United

Car Parking: Ample side-street parking available

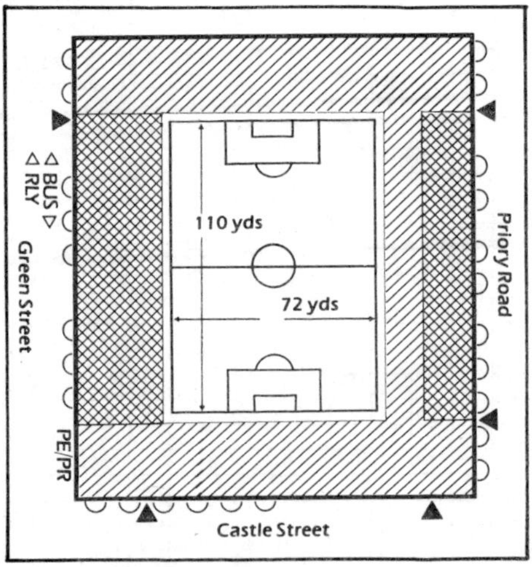

For key see page 12

How to get to the ground

From North and West: Use A406 North Circular Road, then A104 to Leytonstone, then follow A114 to Forest Gate Station and shortly at T road turn left then shortly turn right B167 into Green Street for West Ham United F.C. **From East:** Use A13 (S.P. London) then at crossroads turn right A117. In 0.9m at crossroads turn left A124. In 0.6m turn right into Green Street for West Ham United F.C. **From South:** Use Blackwall Tunnel and A13 to Canning Town, then follow signs East Ham A124. In 1.7m turn left into Green Street for West Ham United F.C.

WIGAN ATHLETIC Division 3

President
AD Horrocks

Chairman
B Heathcote

Directors
A Barrington
JA Bennett
T Hitchen

Secretary
JA Bennett

Deputy Secretary
Lynda Fillingham

Manager
Harry McNally

Coach
Kenny Banks

Reserve Team Manager
Mick Clarke

Youth Team Coach
Dave Crompton

Chief Scout
Mick Worswick

Commercial Manager
Christine Matthews (0492 44433)

Physiotherapist
Duncan Colquoun

Groundsman
Billy Mitchell

In a season of no great distinction the Latics were still a tough side to beat and could take some satisfaction from the fact that they finished in fifteenth position in the Third Division with sixty-one points. Relegation was only a brief threat in December 1983, but the team showed plenty of guts and soon rose to a position of safety and miantained it. For this the manager was given a vote of confidence by his board and the directors may be congratulated for keeping calm even when events were not running in their favour.

Seven matches without defeat in the League from 17th September 1983 virtually removed any need for anxiety and the players were then able to coast through the rest of the season with some good results coming their way. Amongst the teams to lose at Springfield Park were the promoted clubs Wimbledon and Sheffield United, but the cup form was mixed with an early exit from the Milk Cup giving the team a sad start; Bury won both legs of the First Round tie. The F.A. Cup was a different matter and the team played well to remove Bradford City after a replay (4-2) at Springfield Park. In the Second Round Whitby Town of the Northern League were tough opponents but a second-half goal saw the home team through for a match at Upton Park in the Third Round. Wigan played most gallantly to lose by a single goal. The new Associate Members cup did not bring success.

In this undistinguished season the manager had good support from the veteran Tunks in goal, Butler, Walsh, Methven, Cribley and Langley and will hope for something similar in the new season so that — if anything — a better position can be won. The facilities at Wigan are good and a successful team would be an added bonus.

WLM

Back Row L to R: Mick Clarke (Reserve Team Coach), Kevin Langley, Graham Barrow, Steven Walsh, Colin Methven, Roy Tunks, Billy Stewart, Stephen Johnson, Paul Comstive, Mike Newell, Alex Cribley. **Front Row:** David Crompton (Reserve Team Coach), Ray Redshaw, Alex Bruce, Paul Cook, Tony Kelly, Harry McNally (Manager), John Butler, David Lowe, Wayne Aspinall, Neil Bailey, Kenny Banks (Trainer).

'THE LATICS'

Formed: 1932 **Turned Professional:** 1932 **Ltd Co:** 1932
Previous Names: None
Previous Managers: Ted Goodier Allan Brown Gordon Milne Ian McNeill Larry Lloyd Bobby Charlton (acting) Harry McNally
Honours: None
League Career: Elected to Division Four 1978 Promoted to Division Three 1982
Colours: Royal blue shirts and shorts, white stockings
Change Colours: Yellow shirts and stockings, green shorts

CLUB RECORDS

Most Appearances for Club: Peter Houghton: Football League 164 + 15S + F.A. Cup 14 + Leauge/Milk Cup 16 + 1S **Total 194 + 16 Subs**
Most Capped Player: None **For England:** None
Record Goalscorer in a Match: No one more than three goals
Record League Goalscorer in a season: Les Bradd, 19, Div 4, 1981-2. In all competitions: Les Bradd, 20 (League 19, League Cup 1)
Record League Goalscorer in a career: Peter Houghton, 62, 1978-83. In all competitions: Peter Houghton, 68 (League 62, F.A. Cup 3, League Cup 3)
Record Transfer Fee Received: £135,000 from Sunderland for Joe Hinnigan, Feb 1980
Record Transfer Fee Paid: £65,000 to Everton for Eamonn O'Keefe, Jan 1982
Best Performances: League: 15th Div 3 1983-4 **F.A. Cup:** 4th Round 1979-80 **League/Milk Cup:** 4th Round 1981-2
Most League Points: 91 in Div 4, 1981-2 **Most League Goals:** 80, Div 4, 1981-2
Record League Victory: 7-2 v Scunthorpe United; Div 4 (A), 12 Mar 1982
Record League Defeat: 2-6 v Bradford City, Div 3, 27 Dec 1983 0-5 v Bristol Rovers, Div 3, 26 Feb 1983

Club Statistician for the Directory: G. Lea

Programme Editor
Mrs Linda Fillingham

Price	Number of Pages
50p	24

Subscriptions
Apply to club

WIGAN ATHLETIC

PLAYERS NAME Ht Wt Birthdate	Honours	Birthplace Transfers	Clubs	APPEARANCES League	Milk Cup	F.A.C.	A.M.C.	GOALS League	Milk Cup	F.A.C.	A.M.C.
GOALKEEPERS											
Roy Tunks		W. Germany	Rotherham U. (A)	138	9	8					
6-1 13.11 21.1.51			York C. (L)	4							
		£7,000	P.N.E.	277	20	16					
		F	Wigan A.	119	7	7	1				
Billy Stewart			Liverpool (A)								
5-11 11.7 1.1.65		F	Wigan A.								
DEFENDERS											
Wayne Aspinall		Wigan	Wigan A. (A)	7							
5-10 10.7 10.12.64											
John Butler†		Liverpool	Prescot Cables								
5-11 11.7 7.2.62		£100	Wigan A.	79+3	2+1	6	1	7			
Paul Comstive		Southport	Blackburn R.	3+3							
6-1 12.7 25.11.61			Rochdale (L)	9	1		1	2			
			Wigan A.	29	1	4	1	2			
Alex Cribley		Liverpool	Liverpool								
5-11½ 12.9 1.4.57		F	Wigan A.	144+2	9+1	10	1	2			
Tony Kelly		Prescot	Liverpool (A)								
5-10 11.9 1.10.64			Wigan A.	27+2		1	1	2			
Colin Methven*		India	East Fife	144	16	8		14			
6-2 12.7 10.12.55		£30,000	Wigan A.	209+1	15	15	1	14	3		1
Steve Walsh		Preston	Wigan A.	73	2	3	1	1			
6-2 11.10 7.10.62											
MIDFIELD											
Neil Bailey		Billinge	Burnley (A)								
5-9 11.0 26.9.58		F	Newport Co.	129+5	8	9		7			
		F	Wigan A.	16+7		2+1	0+1	1			
Graham Barrow		Chorley	Altrincham								
6-2 13.7 13.6.54		£10,000	Wigan A.	110+1	7	6	1	18	3		
Kevin Langley		St Helens	Wigan A. (A)	71+3	4	6	1	3			
6-1 9.0 24.5.64											
FORWARDS											
Alex Bruce	S. U.23(1)	Dundee	P.N.E. (A)	55+7	1	3		22			
5-8 11.0 23.12.52		£150,000	Newcastle U.	16+4				3			
		Player Exchange	P.N.E.	288+13	23+	16		135	7	6	
		F	Wigan A.	32+4		4		7		2	
Steve Johnson		Liverpool	Altrincham								
6-0 12.9 22.6.57			Bury	139+15	8+1	14+		52	5	4	
		£13,000	Rochdale	17+2	2	2		7	1	2	
			Wigan A.	21				7			
David Lowe	E. Y	Liverpool	Wigan A. (A)	62+6	1	3+1		14			
5-11 11.0 30.8.65											
Mike Newell		Liverpool	Crewe A.	3							
6-0 11.0 27.1.65		F	Wigan A.	5+4							
Ray Redshaw		Manchester	Horwich R.								
5-4 10.0											

WIGAN ATHLETIC

DIVISION THREE 15TH **FA CUP** 3RD ROUND **MILK CUP** 1ST ROUND

MATCH	DATE	COMPE-TITION	VENUE	OPPONENTS	RESULT	HALF TIME	L'GUE POS'N	GOALSCORERS	ATTEN-DANCE
1	A 27	CL	A	Plymouth Arg	D0-0	0-0			3,730
2	**30**	**MC 1**	**H**	**Bury**	**L1-2**	**1-1**		**Methven**	**3,071**
3	S 3	CL	H	Oxford U	L0-2	0-1	19		2,697
4	6	CL	H	Exeter C	D1-1	1-0		Taylor	2,669
5	10	CL	A	AFC Bournemouth	W1-0	1-0	15	Houghton	3,161
6	**13**	**MC 1**	**A**	**Bury**	**L0-2**	**0-1**			**2,558**
7	17	CL	H	Brentford	W2-1	0-1	12	Taylor, Bruce	3,034
8	24	CL	A	Sheffield U	D2-2	2-0	12	Lowe, Cribley	10,797
9	26	CL	A	Port Vale	D1-1	1-0		Bruce	4,655
10	O 1	CL	H	Hull C	D1-1	0-1	10	Taylor (pen)	4,858
11	8	CL	H	Lincoln C	W2-0	0-0	7	Taylor (pen), Comstive	3,864
12	15	CL	A	Preston NE	W3-2	1-0	6	Taylor, Bruce, Bailey	6,622
13	18	CL	A	Scunthorpe U	D0-0	0-0			2,345
14	22	CL	H	Gillingham	L1-2	0-2	11	Bruce	4,189
15	29	CL	A	Burnley	L0-3	0-2	14		7,410
16	N 1	CL	H	Orient	L0-1	0-1			3,362
17	5	CL	A	Millwall	L0-2	0-1	16		3,850
18	12	CL	H	Wimbledon	W3-2	0-0	15	Bruce, Barrow, Langley	3,470
19	**19**	**FAC 1**	**A**	**Bradford C**	**D0-0**	**0-0**			**4,559**
20	26	CL	H	Walsall	L0-1	0-0	15		3,485
21	**28**	**FAC 1R**	**H**	**Bradford C**	**W4-2**	**0-1**		**Taylor 2, Bruce 2**	**4,741**
22	D 3	CL	A	Newport Co	L3-5	1-1	16	Taylor (pen), Walsh, Lowe	3,196
23	**10**	**FAC 2**	**H**	**Whitby T**	**W1-0**	**0-0**		**Taylor (pen)**	**4,820**
24	17	CL	A	Southend U	L0-1	0-0	17		1,819
25	26	CL	H	Bolton W	L0-1	0-0	16		10,045
26	27	CL	A	Bradford C	L2-6	0-3	19	Butler, Lowe	5,176
27	31	CL	H	Rotherham U	W2-1	1-1	17	Bruce, Taylor	3,526
28	**J 7**	**FAC 3**	**A**	**West Ham U**	**L0-1**	**0-1**			**16,000**
29	21	CL	A	Brentford	W1-0	0-0	16	Comstive	3,972
30	27	CL	A	Orient	D0-0	0-0	15		2,123
31	F 4	CL	A	Hull C	L0-1	0-1	16		6,841
32	11	CL	H	Sheffield U	W3-0	2-0	15	Johnson 2, Barrow	5,079
33	18	CL	H	Burnley	W1-0	1-0	15	Barrow	7,509
34	**21**	**AMC 1**	**A**	**Bury**	**L0-1**	**0-1**			**1,613**
35	25	CL	A	Gillingham	L0-3	0-1	17		4,013
36	M 3	CL	H	Scunthorpe U	W2-0	2-0	15	Johnson 2	3,092
37	6	CL	H	Millwall	D0-0	0-0			3,212
38	10	CL	A	Wimbledon	D2-2	1-0	16	Johnson, Lowe	2,565
39	17	CL	A	Lincoln C	W1-0	1-0	16	Barrow	2,030
40	20	CL	H	AFC Bournemouth	L1-3	1-0		Kelly	2,910
41	24	CL	H	Preston NE	W1-0	1-0	15	Kelly	4,470
42	27	CL	A	Bristol R	L1-2	1-1		Lowe	7,072
43	31	CL	H	Port Vale	W3-0	3-0	15	Lowe, Butler 2	3,163
44	A 3	CL	H	Plymouth Arg	D1-1	1-0		Johnson	2,757
45	7	CL	A	Exeter C	D1-1	1-0	15	Barrow	2,412
46	14	CL	H	Newport Co	W1-0	0-0	14	Lowe	2,903
47	17	CL	H	Bristol R	D0-0	0-0			2,665
48	21	CL	A	Bolton W	W1-0	1-0	13	Johnson	6,142
49	23	CL	H	Bradford C	L0-1	0-1	13		3,470
50	28	CL	A	Walsall	L0-3	0-0	14		3,286
51	M 2	CL	A	Oxford U	D0-0	0-0			8,967
52	7	CL	A	Rotherham U	L1-4	0-2	15	Bruce	3,863
53	12	CL	H	Southend U	W1-0	1-0	15	Lowe	3,335
								Av Home Att	**3,898**

Goal Scorers

League (46): Lowe 8, Bruce 7, Johnson 7, Taylor 7 (3 pens), Barrow 5, Butler 3, Comstive 2, Kelly 2, Bailey 1, Cribley 1, Langley 1, Houghton 1, Walsh 1
FA Cup (5): Taylor 3 (1 pen), Bruce 2
Milk Cup (1): Methven 1
AMC (-): —

1983-84

Tunks	Cribley	Comstive	Butler	Walsh	Methven	Bruce	Barrow	Lowe	Taylor	Houghton	Langley	Williams	Bailey	Kelly	Kilner	Newell	Johnson	Aspinall	Schofield	REFEREE	
	2	3	4	5	6	7	8	9	10	11										L Burden	1
	2	**3**	**4**	**5**	**6**	**7**		**9**	**10**	**11**	**8**									**J Lovatt**	**2**
	2	3	4	5	6	7		9	10	11	8*	12								M Peck	3
	2	3	4	5	6	7	8	9	10		11									G Tyson	4
	2	3	4	5	6		8	9	10	11	7									A Buksh	5
	2	**3**	**4**	**5***	**6**		**8**	**9**	**10**	**11**	**7**							**12**		**M Dimblebee**	**6**
	2	5	6	3	4	12	8	9	10	11*	7									F Roberts	7
	2	3	4	5	6	11	8	9	10		7									J Ashworth	8
	2	3	4	5	10	11	7*	8	9	12	6									MP Scott	9
	2	3	4	5	6	8		9	10	11	7									KP Barratt	10
	2	5*	6	3	4	11	8	10	9		7		12							M Heath	11
	2	3	4	5	6	11	8	9*	10		7		12							KA Redfern	12
	2	3	4	5	6*	11	8	9	10		7		12							JE Bray	13
	2	5	6	3	4*	11	8	9	10		7		12							G Napthine	14
	2	3	4	5	6	11	8	9	10*		7		12							A Saunders	15
	6	3	4	5		11	8	9	10		7		2							JD Hough	16
	6	3	4	5†		11	8	9	10		7		2							JD Axcell	17
	2	3	9	5	6	11	8		10		7		4							V Callow	18
	5	**3**	**2**		**6**	**11**	**8**	**9**	**10**		**7**		**4**							**J Lovatt**	**19**
	5	3	4			11	8	9	10		7		6	2						JM Key	20
	4	**3***	**9**	**5**		**11**	**8**	**12**	**10**		**7**		**6**	**2**	**1**					**J Lovatt**	**21**
	4	3*	9	5		11	8	12	10		7		6	2						C Downey	22
	2	**3**	**4**	**5**	**6**	**11**	**8**	**9***	**10**		**7**		**12**							**T Jones**	**23**
	4	3	9	5		11	8		10		7		6	2						A Gunn	24
	2	3	9	5	6	11	8	12	10		7		4*							R Nixon	25
	2	3*	4	5	6	11	8	9	10		7			12	1					P Willis	26
	2		4	5	6	11	8	9	12		7			3	1	10*				R Bridges	27
	2	**3**	**4**	**5**	**6**	**11**	**8**	**9**	**10**		**7**									**A Seville**	**28**
	5	3†	4*		6	11	8	9	10		7		12	2						A Robinson	29
	2	3			6	11	8	9*	10		7		4	5		12				J Martin	30
		3	4	5	6	11*	8	9	10		7		12	2						H Taylor	31
		3	4	5	6	11	8		10		7			2			9			G Tyson	32
	5		6	3	4	11	8		9		7			2			10			K Redfern	33
	4	**3**	**9**	**5**	**6**	**11**	**8**		**10**		**7**		**12**	**2***						**K Walmsley**	**34**
	2	3	4	5	6*	11			10		7		8	12			9			J Moules	35
	2	3		5	6	11*		12	10		7		8	4			9			F Roberts	36
	2			5	6	12	8	11	10*		7		3	4			9			C Seal	37
	2	3		5	6	11*	8	10			7			4		12	9			L Shapter	38
		3	2	5	6		8	10			7			4		11	9			J Bray	39
		3	2	5	6		8	10			7			4		11	9			G Courtney	40
	2			3	4	11*	8	10			7			6		12	9	5		J Hough	41
	2		11	5	6		8	10			7			4	1		9	3		C Thomas	42
	2		11	4	5		8	10			7			6			9	3		A Challinor	43
	2		11	5	6		8	10			7			4			9	3		J Lovatt	44
	2		11	5	6		8	10					7	4			9	3		M James	45
	2		11*	3	4	12	8	10			7		5	6	1		9			K Hackett	46
	2		11	5	6		8	10			7		3	4			9			J Key	47
	2		11	5	6		8	10			7			4			9	3		N Ashley	48
	2		11	5		12	8	10			7			4		6	9	3*		M Peck	49
	6		2	5			8	10			7		3	4		11*	9		12	J Ashworth	50
	2		3	5	6	11	8	10			7			4			9			M Taylor	51
	2		11	5	6	10	8*				7		3	4		12	9			M Heath	52
	5	3	2		6	11	8	10			7			4			9			P Willis	53
2	44	29	41	42	39	32	42	37	29	5	44	0	16	27	4	5	21	7	0	League Appearances	
						+4S		+3S	+1S	+1S		+1S	+7S	+2S		+4S			+1S		
	4	4	4	3	3	4	4	3+1S	4		4		2+1S	1	1					FA Cup Appearances	
	2	2	2	2	2	1	1	2	2	2	2							1S		Milk Cup Appearances	
	1	1	1	1	1	1	1		1		1		1S	1						AM Cup Appearances	

SPRINGFIELD PARK

Official Address: Springfield Park, Wigan. Telephone: 0942 44433

Telegraphic: Springfield Wigan

Ground Capacity: 30,000

Record Attendance: 27,500 v. Hereford United, 2 Dec 1953

Record Receipts: £29,169 v. Aston Villa, League Cup Round 4, 1 Dec 1981

Size of Playing Area: 117yds × 73 yds

Season Tickets: Stand: £63.00, Ground: £36.00

Executive Box Season Tickets: £230 for seat in glass-enclosed area with buffet facilities at Half-Time and Full-Time with Licensed Bar

Cost of Stand Tickets: £3.00; **Terraces:** £2.00

Match and Ticket Information: Stand tickets bookable 14 days in advance

Car Parking: On ground and nearby

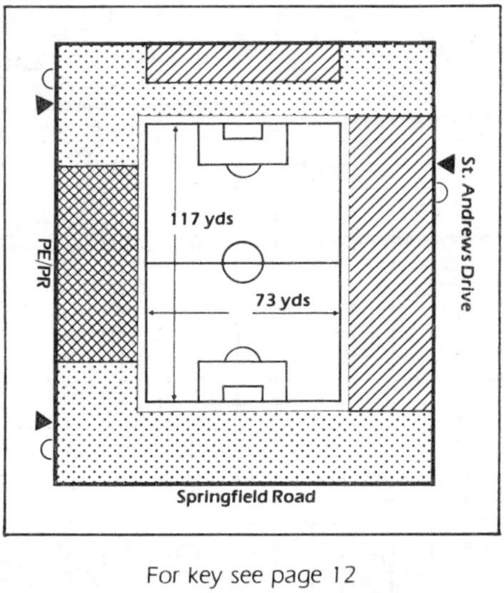

For key see page 12

How to get to the ground

From North: Use Motorway M6 until junction 27. Leave motorway and follow signs Wigan A5209. In 0.3m turn right B5206. In 1.1m turn left B5375. In 4.6m turn left into Springfield Road for Wigan Athletic F.C.

From East: Use A557 S.P. Wigan into town centre then turn left into Market Street and at end turn left into Parsons Walk B5375. In 0.7m turn right into Springfield Road for Wigan Athletic F.C.

From South: Use Motorway M6 until junction 25. Leave motorway and follow signs into Wigan A49. Turn left into Market Street and at end turn left into Parsons Walk B5375. In 0.7m turn right into Springfield Road for Wigan Athletic F.C.

WIMBLEDON Division 2

President
Rt Hon Sir Michael Havers, QC, MP

Chairman
B Reynolds

Vice-Chairman
G M Dell

Directors
P Cork
G M Dell
E C Gush
Q Spicer (Company Secretary)
S Hammam (Managing Director)

Chief Executive
Alan Batsford

Secretary
Adrian Cook

Manager/Club Coach
Dave Bassett

Physiotherapist
Derek French

Commercial Manager
Eric Willcocks (01-946 6311)

These amazing Dons changed divisions for the sixth year in succession! After winning the Fourth Division Championship in 1983, Wimbledon took runners-up spot in Division Three to get up into the Second Division for the first time.

Playing simple, but effective, football Dave Bassett's team scored 114 goals in 55 League and Cup games, Alan Cork leading the way with 32. Glyn Hodges weighed in with 19 with Stewart Evans adding 14.

Though the Dons scored a lot of goals, they also conceded quite a few. They went down 0-4 at Walsall and 1-5 at Scunthorpe in October when they were no more than on the fringe of the promotion race.

At one point their erratic form seemed to rule out serious promotion hopes. They remained unbeaten in their first 13 home League and Cup games but then crashed 1-4 to Burnley at Plough Lane.

It wasn't until the end of January that the Dons began to shape up as real promotion material. A run of three wins, including a 6-2 success at Orient, saw them tuck themselves in behind then leaders Walsall. But Hull, Oxford, Sheffield United and Bristol Rovers were all playing well and were closely on their heels.

Their hopes took a dive when they went down 1-4 at home to Hull City, one of their closest rivals, in April. But the Dons showed their character by winning their next three games.

Wimbledon's critical test came at the beginning of May when they had to travel to Sheffield United. The Dons were in second place with Sheffield lying immediately behind them and the Blades had been beaten only once at home in the League.

A huge crowd of 22,850 turned up for an enthralling game. The Dons looked in an unassailable position when goals from Evans and Cork put them 2-0 in front with less than ten minutes to play. Two minutes later United scored and with the huge crowd roaring them on, laid seige to Wimbledon's defence.

But the most criticised department of their team held tight and the prospects of Second Division football then looked very bright indeed.

The Dons then complicated the issue by losing at home to Gillingham two days later and it wasn't until they had won their final match at Burnley that they could be sure they would be going up.

Wimbledon's finest individual performance of the season, though, came in the second round of the Milk Cup when they outplayed Nottingham Forest to win 2-0 in the first leg at Plough Lane and then completed the job by drawing at the City Ground.

Another club record was achieved when Glyn Hodges, after several under-21 appearances, played in Wales' last two games of the season. He became the first Wimbledon player ever to appear in a full international match. TP

Back Row L to R: Mick Smith, Phil Driver, Stewart Evans, Dave Beasant, Colin Caulfield, Steve Hatter, Alan Cork, Glyn Hodges. **Middle Row:** John Kay, Steve Ketteridge, Mark Morris, Wally Downes, Kevin Gage, David Wintersgill. **Front Row:** Andrew Sayer, Steve Galliers, Phil Handford, Nigel Winterburn, Paul O'Berg.

'THE DONS'

Formed: 1889 **Turned Professional:** 1964 **Ltd Co:** 1964
Previous Name: Wimbledon Old Centrals 1899-1905
Previous Managers: 1977-8 Allen Batsford 1978-81 Dario Gradi
Honours: Champions, Division 4, 1982-3
League Career: Elected to Division 4 1977-8 Promoted to Division 3 1978-9 Relegated to Division 4 1979-80 Promoted to Division 3 1980-1 Relegated to Division 4 1981-2 Promoted to Division 3 1982-3 Promoted to Division 2 1983-4
Colours: Royal blue shirts with yellow trim, blue shorts with yellow trim, blue stockings
Change Colours: Yellow shirts and shorts with blue trim, yellow stockings

CLUB RECORDS

Most Appearances for Club: John Leslie: Football League 242 + 11 + F.A. Cup 14 + 2 + League Cup 20 + 1 **Total 276 + 14**
Most Capped Player: Glyn Hodges, 2, Wales **For England:** None
Record Goalscorer in a Match:
Record League Goalscorer in a season: Alan Cork, 32, Div 3, 1983-4 **In All Competitions:** Alan Cork, 32 (League 28 + F.A. Cup 2 + Milk Cup 2), 1983-4
Record League Goalscorer in a career: Alan Cork, 94, 1977-84 **In All Competitions:** Alan Cork, 106 (League 94 + F.A. Cup 6 + Milk Cup 6), 1977-84
Record Transfer Fee Received: £70,000 from Crystal Palace for Steve Galliers, Oct 1981
Record Transfer Fee Paid: £45,000 to Queen's Park Rangers for Tommy Cunningham, Mar 1979
Best Performances: League: 1st Div 3 1983-4 **F.A. Cup:** 4th Round 1974-5 **League/Milk Cup:** 4th Round 1979-80, 1983-4
Most League Points: 98 in Div 4, 1982-3 **Most League Goals:** 96, Div 4, 1982-3
Record League Victory: 6-0 v Newport County, Div 3, 3 Sept 1983
Record League Defeat: 0-8 v Everton, League Cup 2nd Round, 29 Aug 1978
Club Statistician for the Directory: S King

Programme Editor
Eric Willcocks

Price	Number of Pages
50p	24

Subscriptions
Home matches weekly per season £20.00 (postage included). Home and away matches weekly per season £31.00 (postage included).

⁄VIMBLEDON

⁄AYERS NAME t Wt Birthdate	Honours	Birthplace Transfers	Clubs	APPEARANCES League	Milk Cup	F.A.C.	A.M.C.	GOALS League	Milk Cup	F.A.C.	A.M.C.
OALKEEPER											
ave Beasant			Edgware T.								
3 13.0 20.3.59			Wimbledon	174	10	6	1				
EFENDERS											
eve Hatter	Div. 4, 83	London	Fulham (A)	25+1	+1	4		1			
2 13.0 21.10.58			Exeter C. (L)	11				1			
			Wimbledon	67+1	6	2	1	3			
hn Kay		Sunderland	Arsenal (A)	13+1							
10 11.6 29.1.64			Wimbledon								
ark Morris*	Div. 4, 83	Morden	Wimbledon	98	10	6	1	7			
) 11.10 26.9.62											
ick Smith	Div. 4, 83	Sunderland	Lincoln C.	20+5	2						
0½ 11.9 28.10.58		£12,500	Wimbledon	150+2	7	8		11		2	
igel Winterburn†		Nuneaton	Birmingham C. (A)								
10 10.7 11.12.63		F	Oxford U.								
		F	Wimbledon	43	6	2	1	1			
avid Wintersbick		York	Wolverhampton W. (A)	3+1							
10 11.2 19.9.65											
IDFIELD											
ally Downes	Div. 4, 83	London	Wimbledon (A)	171+4	15+	7+1	1	15		1	
10 10.11 9.6.61											
evin Gage	E. Y.	London	Wimbledon (A)	48+24	1+1	2+2		9			
9 11.2 21.4.64	Div. 4, 83										
eve Galliers	Div. 4, 83	Fulwood	Chorley								
5 9.7 21.8.57		£1,500	Wimbledon	148+7	17+	13+		10	2		
		£70,000	Crystal Palace	8+5							
		£15,000	Wimbledon	69+1	8	4		3	2		
il Handford		Chatham	Gillingham (A)	29+3	2	1	+1	1		1	
7 10.4 18.7.64		£5,000	Wimbledon								
eve Ketteridge	Div. 4, 83	Stevenage	Derby Co. (A)								
3½ 10.7 7.11.59		£3,000	Wimbledon	201+7	17	10	1	28	2	1	
ul O'Berg		Hull	Bridlington Trinity								
5 9.4 8.5.58			Scunthorpe U.	117+13	3+3	16	1	25		2	
RWARDS											
an Cork		Derby	Derby Co.								
) 12.0 8.10.59			Lincoln C. (L)	5							
			Wimbledon	198+2	20	16		95	6	6	
il Driver		Huddersfield	Luton T.								
0 10.12 10.8.59			Wimbledon	7+9				3			
		£20,000	Chelsea	25+19	+1	+1		4			
		F	Wimbledon	+2							
ewart Evans	Div. 4, 83	Maltby	Rotherham U. (A)								
3 11.5 15.11.60		F	Gainsborough T.								
		£7,000	Sheffield U.								
		F	Wimbledon	102+3	8	3	1	30	2		
ul Fishenden		Hillingdon	Wimbledon	21+16	1+1	2+1	1	13			
) 10.12 2.8.63											
yn Hodges	W.(2), U.21(1), Y	Streatham	Wimbledon (A)	129+14	8+1	5+2	+1	31	3		
) 12.3 30.4.63											
ndy Sayer		Brent	Wimbledon								
) 10.12 6.6.66											

ON-CONTRACT PLAYER 1984-85

lin Caulfield

PRENTICES

ndrew Clement, Gary Flore, John Gannon, Ian Hazel, Paul Jones, Andy Sayer (1Lg., 1AMC), **Kevin Wedderburn**

WIMBLEDON

DIVISION THREE 2ND **FA CUP** 2ND ROUND **MILK CUP** 4TH ROUND

MATCH	DATE	COMPE-TITION	VENUE	OPPONENTS	RESULT	HALF TIME	L'GUE POS'N	GOALSCORERS	ATTEN-DANCE
1	A 27	CL	A	Bolton W	L0-2	0-0			3,992
2	**29**	**MC 1**	**A**	**Southend U**	**L0-1**	**0-0**			**2,572**
3	S 3	CL	H	Newport Co	W6-0	2-0	10	Cork 3 (1 pen), Evans 2, Ketteridge	2,007
4	6	CL	H	AFC Bournemouth	W3-2	2-0		Cork, Hodges, Downes	2,345
5	10	CL	A	Southend U	D1-1	1-1	8	Cork	3,106
6	**12**	**MC 1**	**H**	**Southend U**	**W6-4**[1]	**2-1**		**Cork, Ketteridge 2, Galliers, Evans, Hodges**	**1,967**
7	17	CL	H	Port Vale	W4-2	1-1	4	Evans, Ketteridge, Morris, Hodges	2,690
8	24	CL	A	Exeter C	W3-0	1-0	3	Fishenden 2, Gage	3,046
9	27	CL	A	Hull C	L0-1	0-0			9,633
10	O 1	CL	H	Orient	D2-2	0-0	5	Corbett (og), Peters	3,323
11	**4**	**MC 2**	**H**	**Nottingham F**	**W2-0**	**1-0**		**Galliers, Hodges**	**7,554**
12	8	CL	H	Bristol R	D1-1	0-0	5	Hatter	3,462
13	15	CL	A	Walsall	L0-4	0-1	8		2,546
14	18	CL	A	Preston NE	W3-2	2-2		Smith, Hodges, Ketteridge	3,515
15	22	CL	H	Rotherham U	W3-1	1-0	4	Morris, Fishenden, Cork	2,579
16	**25**	**MC 2**	**A**	**Nottingham F**	**D1-1**	**0-0**		**Evans**	**13,718**
17	29	CL	A	Scunthorpe U	L1-5	1-2	9	Cork	2,347
18	N 1	CL	H	Oxford U	W3-1	2-0		Hodges, Cork 2	3,821
19	5	CL	H	Bradford C	W4-1	1-0	5	Cork 2, Evans, Hodges	2,408
20	**8**	**MC 3**	**H**	**Oldham Ath**	**W3-1**	**1-1**		**Hodges, Cork, Fishenden**	**4,624**
21	12	CL	A	Wigan Ath	L2-3	0-0	7	Fishenden, Cork	3,470
22	**19**	**FAC 1**	**H**	**Orient**	**W2-1**	**1-1**		**Cork 2**	**4,330**
23	**29**	**MC 4**	**A**	**Rotherham U**	**L0-1**	**0-1**			**6,946**
24	D 3	CL	H	Lincoln C	W3-1	1-0	7	Hodges 2 (1 pen), Ketteridge	2,434
25	**10**	**FAC 2**	**A**	**Brentford**	**L2-3**	**1-1**		**Peters, Downes**	**5,666**
26	17	CL	H	Burnley	L1-4	1-2	9	Cork	2,883
27	24	CL	A	Brentford	W4-3	1-2		Evans 2, Morris, Cork	6,689
28	27	CL	H	Millwall	W4-3	2-1	7	Smith, Cork 2, Evans	5,667
29	31	CL	A	Gillingham	W1-0	1-0	4	Cork	5,024
30	J 2	CL	H	Sheffield U	W3-1	0-0	4	Smith, Cork 2	5,020
31	7	CL	A	Bradford C	L2-5	2-3	5	Cork, Downes	4,563
32	14	CL	H	Bolton W	W4-0	1-0	4	Cork, Downes, Hodges, Evans	2,955
33	21	CL	A	Port Vale	L0-2	0-1	5		3,627
34	28	CL	H	Southend U	W3-2	2-2	2	Evans, Peters, Hodges	2,752
35	F 4	CL	A	Orient	W6-2	3-1	2	Thomas 2, Gage, Cork 2, Hodges	3,377
36	11	CL	H	Exeter C	W2-1	0-1	2	Gage, Hodges	3,013
37	15	CL	A	Oxford U	L0-2	0-2			7,640
38	18	CL	H	Scunthorpe U	D1-1	0-0	2	Ketteridge	3,117
39	**21**	**AMC 1**	**A**	**Colchester U**	**L1-2**	**1-2**		**Fishenden**	**1,888**
40	25	CL	A	Rotherham U	W2-1	1-0	1	Fishenden, Cork	3,141
41	M 3	CL	H	Preston NE	D2-2	1-1	2	Cork, Fishenden	2,524
42	6	CL	A	Newport Co	D1-1	1-1		Cork	2,538
43	10	CL	H	Wigan Ath	D2-2	0-1	2	Fishenden, Evans	2,565
44	17	CL	A	Bristol R	D1-1	0-0	2	Thomas	5,383
45	24	CL	H	Walsall	W2-0	1-0	2	Cork, Downes	4,057
46	31	CL	A	AFC Bournemouth	W3-2	2-2	3	Hodges, Galliers, Ketteridge	3,538
47	A 7	CL	H	Hull C	L1-4	0-2	3	Hodges	4,495
48	10	CL	A	Plymouth Arg	W2-1	0-1		Hatter (pen), Nisbett (og)	6,471
49	14	CL	A	Lincoln C	W2-1	0-1	2	Evans, Hodges	1,986
50	21	CL	H	Brentford	W2-1	1-0	2	Ketteridge, Hodges	5,487
51	23	CL	A	Millwall	D1-1	1-0	2	Peters	5,153
52	28	CL	H	Plymouth Arg	W1-0	0-0	2	Winterburn	3,706
53	M 5	CL	A	Sheffield U	W2-1	1-0	2	Evans, Cork	22,850
54	7	CL	H	Gillingham	L1-3	1-0	2	Gage	6,009
55	12	CL	A	Burnley	W2-0	2-0	2	Fishenden, Hodges	3,340

[1] After Extra Time

Av Home Att 3,443

Goal Scorers

League (97): Cork 28 (1 pen), Hodges 16 (1 pen), Evans 12, Fishenden 8, Ketteridge 7, Downes 4, Gage 4, Morris 3, Peters 3, Smith 3, Thomas 3, Hatter 2 (1 pen), Galliers 1, Winterburn 1, opponents 2
FA Cup (4): Cork 2, Downes 1, Peters 1
Milk Cup (12): Hodges 3, Cork 2, Evans 2, Galliers 2, Ketteridge 2, Fishenden 1
AMC (1): Fishenden 1

1983-84

Beasant	Peters	Winterburn	Galliers	Morris	Hatter	Evans	Ketteridge	Sayer	Hodges	Fishenden	Gage	Cork	Downes	Driver	Smith	Thomas	Thompson **(L)**	Shanks	Dibble	REFEREE	
1	2	3	4	5	6	7	8	9*	10	11	12									T Mills	1
1	**2**	**3**	**4**	**5**	**6**	**7**	**8**		**10**	**11**	**9**									**G Napthine**	**2**
1	2	3	4	5	6	7	8		11			9	10							J Bray	3
1	2	3	4	5	6	7*	8		11			9	10	12						D Axcell	4
1	2	3	4	5	6	7	8		11*			9	10	12						I Borrett	5
1	**2**	**3**	**4**	**5**	**6**	**7**	**8**		**12**			**9**	**10**	**11***						**Alan Robinson**	**6**
1	2	3	4	5	6	7*	8		11		12	9	10							M Dimblebee	7
1	2	3	4	5	6	7	8		11*	9	12		10							J Deakin	8
1	2	3	4	5	6	7	8		11*		12	9	10							N Midgley	9
1	2	3*	4	5	6	7	8		11		12	9	10							C Thomas	10
1	**2**	**3**	**4**	**5**	**6**	**7**	**8**		**11**			**9**	**10**							**M Bodenham**	**11**
1	2	3	4	5	6	7	8		11		12	9	10*							M Taylor	12
1	2*	3	4	5	6	7	8		11		12	9	10							PA Tyldesley	13
1	2	3		4	6	7	8		11	9	12		10		5*					M Heath	14
1	2	3		5	6	7	8		11	9	4*	12	10							T Bune	15
1	**2**	**3**	**4**	**5**	**6**	**7**	**8**		**11**			**9**	**10**							**D Scott**	**16**
1	2*	3		5	6	7	8		11	12		9	10			4				LR Bilkes	17
1	2	3	4	5	6	7*	8		11			9	10				12			A Gunn	18
1	2	3	4	5	6	7	8		11			9	10*				12			T Spencer	19
1	**2**	**3**	**4**	**5**	**6**	**7**	**8***		**11**	**12**		**9**	**10**							**R Milford**	**20**
1	2		4	5		7			11*	8		9	10		6	3	12			V Callow	21
1	**2**	**3**	**4**	**8**	**6**	**7**			**11**			**9**	**10**		**5**					**D Reeves**	**22**
1	**2**	**11**	**4**	**3**	**6**	**7**	**8**		**10**			**9**	**12**		**5***					**A Saunders**	**23**
1	2	3	4	5	6	7	8		11	12		9	10*							E Crickmore	24
1	**2**	**3**	**4**	**5**	**6**	**7***	**8**		**11**	**12**		**9**	**10**							**R Bridges**	**25**
1		3	4	2	6	7	8		11	10		9			5					J Ashworth	26
1		3		2	6	7	8		11			9	10		5	4				J Moules	27
1		3		2	6	7	8		11			9	10		5	4				J Martin	28
1		3	4	2	6	7*	8			12		9	10		5	11				D Hedges	29
1		3	4	2	6	7	8					9	10		5	11				M James	30
1		3	4*	2†	6	7	8		12			9	10		5	11				T Fitzharris	31
1	2	3	4	6		7	8		11			9	10		5					K Barratt	32
1	2	3	4			7	8		11		12	9	10		5			6*		R Nixon	33
1	2	3	4		6	7	8		11			9	10		5					B Hill	34
1	2	3			6	7	8		11		10	9			5	4				J Hunting	35
1	2	3			6	7	8		11		10	9			5	4				D Brazier	36
1	2	3		5	6	7	8		11*	12		9	10†			4				A Seville	37
1	2	3	4		6	7	8		11*	12		9	10		5					B Stevens	38
1	**2†**	**3**		**5**	**6**	**7**	**8**	**12**	**13**	**11**		**9***	**10***			**4**				**M Taylor**	**39**
1	2	3	4		6	7*	8		12	11		9	10		5					R Guy	40
1	2	3	4		6	12	8		11	7	10*	9			5					T Bune	41
1		3	4	2	6	7	8		12	11*	10	9			5					K Baker	42
1		3	4	2	6	7	8		11	12		9	10		5*					L Shapter	43
1	2	3*		8	6	7			11		12	9	10		5	4				M Robinson	44
1	2	3		6		7			11	12	8	9*	10		5	4				M Bodenham	45
1	2		4	6		7	8		11	12		9*	10		5	3				A Robinson	46
1	2	3	4	6		7	8		11	12		9	10*		5					D Axcell	47
1	2	3	4	5	6	7	8		11	12	10*	9								K Cooper	48
1	2	3	4	5	6	7	8		11		10	9								D Richardson	49
1	2	3	4	5	6		8		11*	7	10	9							12	R Milford	50
1	2	3	4	5	6	7	8		11		10	9								C Thomas	51
1	2	3	4	5	6	7	8				10	9				11				A Gunn	52
1	2	3	4	5	6	7	8			11*	10	9			12					G Courtney	53
1	2	3*	4	5	6	7	8		11	12	10	9								E Read	54
1			4	6	12	7	8	9*	11	10	2				5	3				T Mills	55
46	37	43	36	39	39	44	43	2	39	12	14	41	32	0	23	15	0	1	0	League Appearances	
					+1S	+1S			+3S	+11S	+10S	+1S		+2S	+1S		+3S		+1S		
2	2	2	2	2	2	2	1		2	1S		2	2		1					FA Cup Appearances	
6	6	6	6	6	6	6	6		5+1S	1+1S	1	5	4+1S	1	1					Milk Cup Appearances	
1	1	1		1	1	1	1	1S	1S	1		1	1			1				AM Cup Appearances	

PLOUGH LANE

Official Address: Plough Lane Ground, Dunsford Road, Wimbledon, London SW19. Telephone: 01-946 6311

Telegraphic:

Ground Capacity: 15,000

Record Attendance: 18,000 v. H.M.S. Victory, F.A. Amateur Cup Round 3, 1934-35

Record Receipts: £30,609 v. Leeds United, F.A. Cup Round 4 replay at Selhurst Park, 1974-5

Size of Playing Area: 110yds × 73 yds

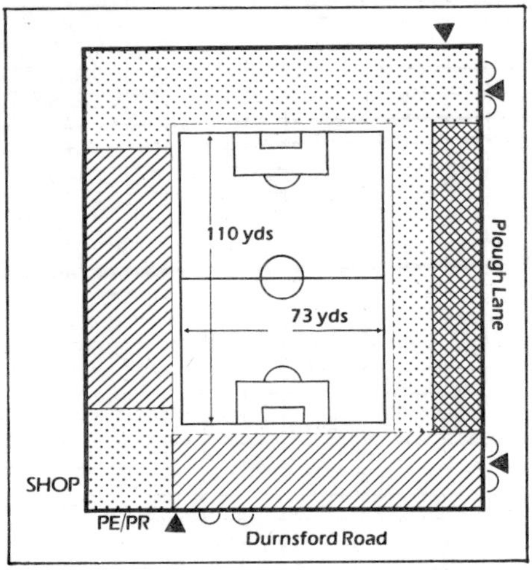

For key see page 12

Season Tickets: £85, £102, £153 (OAP half price) (£51 for OAP/Juveniles in least expensive seats)

Executive Box Season Tickets: No

Cost of Stand Tickets: £5.00, £6.00, £9.00 (half price OAP/Juveniles); Ground: £3.00 (£1.50 OAP/Juveniles)

Match and Ticket Information: available 14 days prior to important matches.

Car Parking: on ground and in streets quarter-mile from ground.

How to get to the ground

From North and West: Use A205 South Circular Road to Wandsworth, forward around one way system then follow signs Earlsfield A217 into Garratt Lane. In 1.6m turn right into Summerstown leading into Plough Lane for Wimbledon F.C.

From South: Use A24 to South Wimbledon Station then in 0.2m turn left into Haydons Road A218. In 0.8m turn right into Plough Lane for Wimbledon F.C.

From East: Use South Circular Road A205 then A24 S.P. Wimbledon to Clapham South Station then turn right B237 into Nightingale Lane. In 2m at T road turn left A217 then shortly turn right into Summerstown leading into Plough Lane for Wimbledon F.C.

WOLVERHAMPTON WDRS Division 2

President
J R Ireland

Chairman
A D Dougan

Directors
D Hope
R J Hipkiss
(Joint Vice Chairmen)
J Starkey
W J Smith jnr

Chief Executive
E Woodward

Secretary
Peter Redfern

Commercial Manager
J A Witherington (0902 23166)

Manager
Tommy Docherty

Coach
Jim Barron

Reserve & Youth Team Manager
Frank Upton

Chief Scout
Sammy Chapman

Physiotherapist
D Conyerd

Groundsman
Bill Pilbeam

Following an opening 1-1 draw with Liverpool, Wolves had to wait until late November to record their first league victory. The Wanderers were then comfortably bottom of the Division and had set a club 'record' of 19 matches without a win (including three from the end of the previous season).

Only five further wins followed in the entire season but strangely these included Liverpool (away), Nottingham Forest and Everton. Following Christmas, hopes were raised as victories against Everton (3-0), Norwich (2-0) and Liverpool (1-0) were interspersed by two drawn F.A. Cup games against Coventry and an unlucky defeat at Q.P.R. Unfortunately, things were soon back to normal and at the end of the season further club 'worsts' were fewest wins, points and goals in a season of 42 League matches.

To make matters worse Peter Daniel was sacked in April for refusing to play out of position and a number of players accused the club of failing to pay promotion bonuses for the previous season. Mel Eves and Wayne Clarke played through the season on weekly contracts after failing to agree terms.

Although a number of youngsters joined the club, the only major signings were Tony Towner from Rotherham United and Danny Crainie from Celtic. Andy Gray was the most expensive of the players to leave but despite the use of Andy Blair and Scott McGarvey on loan, the playing staff was just not strong enough.

Manager Graham Hawkins had little chance of success with the squad at his disposal and little money to spend so his sacking, when relegation was mathematically certain, was inevitable. His successor, Tommy Docherty, is a man with many ups and downs in his career. However, his best achievements have been with young players, which is where the Wolves future lies.

Everyone with the club's interests at heart must hope that those successes can be reproduced at Molineux.

Les Smith, The League Directory's Statistican for the Club.

Back Row L to R: Tommy Langley, John Humphrey, Alan Dodd, John Pender, Tim Flowers, Geoff Palmer, Mark Buckland, Joe Jackson, Stuart Watkiss. **Middle Row:** Sammy Chapman (Chief Scout), Ian Cartwright, Martin Bayly, Danny Crainie, Sammy Troughton, Tony Evans, Paul Butler, Dennis Conyerd (Physiotherapist). **Front Row:** Paul Dougherty, Frank Upton (Youth Team Coach), Neville Hamilton, Tommy Docherty (Manager), Tony Towner, Jim Barron (Assistant Manager), Alan Ainscough.

'THE WOLVES'

Formed: 1877 **Turned Professional:** 1888 **Ltd Co:** 1892
Previous Names: In 1880, St Luke's, Blakenall combined with The Wanderers to become Wolverhampton Wanderers (1923) Ltd until 1982 when a new company was formed
Previous Managers: 1927-44 Major Frank Buckley 1944-8 Ted Vizard 1948-64 Stan Cullis 1964-5 Andy Beattie 1965-8 Ronnie Allen 1968-76 Bill McGarry 1976-8 Sammy Chung 1978-82 John Barnwell 1982 Ian Greaves 1982-4 Graham Hawkins
Honours: Champions Division 1 1953-5, 1957-8, 1958-9 Champions Division 2 1931-2, 1976-7 Champions Division 3(N) 1923-4 F.A. Cup Winners 1893, 1908, 1949, 1960 Football League Cup Winners 1973-4, 1979-80 Texaco Cup Winners 1970-1
League Career: Founder Members of Football League 1888 Relegated to Division 2 1905-6
Relegated to Division 3(N) 1922-3 Promoted to Division 2 1923-4
Promoted to Division 1 1931-2 Relegated to Division 2 1964-5
Promoted to Division 1 1966-7 Relegated to Division 2 1975-6
Promoted to Division 1 1976-7 Relegated to Division 2 1981-2
Promoted to Division 1 1982-3 Relegated to Division 2 1983-4
Colours: Old gold shirts with black trim, black shorts, old gold stockings with black hoops
Change Colours: All white

CLUB RECORDS

Most Appearances for Club: Derek Parkin: Football League 500 + 1 + F.A. Cup 45 + 1 + League Cup 35 + European Cup 15 **Total 595 + 2 subs**
Most Capped Player: Billy Wright, 105, England
Record Goalscorer in a Match: Jack Brodie, 5 v Stoke City, 22.02.1890 Tom Phillipson, 5 v Bradford City, (H, 7-2), Div 2, 25.12.26
Billy Harthill, 5 v Notts County, (H, 5-1), Div 2, 12.10.29 and v Aston Villa, (H, 5-2), Div 1, 03.09.34
Record League Goalscorer in a season: Dennis Westcott, 37, Div 1, 1946-7 **In All Competitions:** Dennis Westcott, 43 (League 32, F.A. Cup 11), 1938-9
Record League Goalscorer in a career: Bill Harthill, 164, 1928-35 **In All Competitions:** John Richards, 190 (League 144, F.A. Cup 24, League Cup 18, European competitions 4), 1969-83
Record Transfer Fee Received: £1,000,000 from Manchester City for Steve Daley, Sept 1979
Record Transfer Fee Paid: £1,175,000 to Aston Villa for Andy Gray, Sept 1980
Best Performances: League: Champions Div 1 (3) **F.A. Cup:** Winners (4) **League/Milk Cup:** Winners (2) **European Cup:** Quarter Final **European Cup Winners Cup:** Semi-Final **U.E.F.A. Cup:** Runners Up
Most League Points: 75 in Div 2, 1982-3 **Most League Goals:** 115, Div 2, 1931-2
Record League Victory: 10-1 v Leicester City, Div 1, 15 April 1938
Record League Defeat: 1-10 v Newton Heath, Div 1, 15 Oct 1892
European Competitions Entered: European Cup 1958-9, 1959-60 European Cup Winners Cup 1960-1 U.E.F.A. Cup 1971-2, 1973-4, 1974-5, 1980-1
Club Statistician for the Directory: Les Smith

Programme Editor
Eric Woodward

Price	**Number of Pages**
50p	24

Subscriptions
Please consult club

WOLVERHAMPTON W.

PLAYERS NAME Ht Wt Birthdate	Honours	Birthplace Transfers	Clubs	APPEARANCES League	Milk Cup	F.A.C.	E. Cups	GOALS League	Milk Cup	F.A.C.	E. Cups
GOALKEEPER											
John Burridge†	Div. 2, 79	Workington	Workington (A)	27	1	4					
5-10½ 12.3 3.12.51	FC. 77	£10,000	Blackpool	134	10	4					
		£100,000	Aston Villa	65	9	6					
			Southend U.	6							
		£50,000	Crystal Palace	88	7	7					
		£200,000	Q.P.R.	39	4	2					
		£80,000	Wolverhampton W.	74	3	5					
DEFENDERS											
Mark Buckland		Cheltenham	AP Leamington								
5-10 12.0			Wolverhampton W.	13+2							
Alan Dodd		Stoke	Stoke C. (A)	349+7	25	18		3			
5-10¾ 12.3 20.9.53		£40,000	Wolverhampton W.	68	2	5		3			
John Humphrey		Paddington	Wolverhampton W.	107	4	2		3			
5-9½ 10.13 31.1.61											
Geoff Palmer*	E. U.23(2),	Cannock	Wolverhampton W. (A)	381+5	31	38+	6E	13	2		
5-10 10.5 11.7.54	Div. 2, 77,										
	FC. 74, 80										
John Pender	Ei. Y	Luton	Wolverhampton W. (A)	81	5	2		2			
6-0½ 12.3 19.11.53											
Stuart Watkiss		Wolverhampton	Wolverhampton W.	2							
6-2 13.2 8.5.66											
MIDFIELD											
Martin Bayly		Dublin	Wolverhampton W. (A)	7							
5-8 10.7 14.9.66											
Ian Cartwright		Birmingham	Wolverhampton W. (A)	23+2				1			
5-8½ 10.12 13.11.64											
Paul Dougherty		Leamington	Wolverhampton W. (A)	5							
5-2 10.0 12.5.66											
Neville Hamilton		Leicester	Leicester C. (A)	4							
5-8 10.0 19.4.60		£25,000	Mansfield T.	84+5	5+1	5		4	1		
		F	Rochdale	34+1	5+2	3+1	1AM	4			
Joe Jackson		Wolverhampton	Wolverhampton W. (A)	1							
5-0 11.9 22.4.66											
FORWARDS											
Paul Butler		Stockton	Wolverhampton W. (A)	1+10	+2						
5-7 10.4 9.6.64			Hereford U. (L)	16			1AM	2			
Danny Crainie	SPD. 82	Glasgow	Celtic	18+6	+3	+1		7	1		
5-8 10.5	S. U.21(1)	£20,000	Wolverhampton W.	27+1		3		3			
Tony Evans		Liverpool	Formby								
5-8 11.6			Blackpool	4+2							
		F	Cardiff C.	120+4	6+1	8	6E	47	6	4	1E
		£120,000	Birmingham C.	62+4	5	1+1		28	3	1	
		F	Crystal Palace	19+2	1	+1		7			
			Wolverhampton W.								
Tommy Langley	E. U.21(1), B.(3),	Lambeth	Chelsea (A)	129+13	4	6		40	1	2	
5-11 10.7 8.2.58	Y, S		Q.P.R.	24+1	3			8	1		
			Crystal Palace	54+5	5+1	5+1		9	1	1	
			AEK Athens								
			Coventry C. (L)	2							
Sammy Troughton		Lisburn, NI	Glentoran								
5-10 11.3 27.3.64			Wolverhampton W.	17		3		2			

NON-CONTRACT PLAYERS 1984-85

Stephen Blackwell, Cavan Chapman, Norman Dougherty, John Graham, John Hathaway, David Heywood, Roger Preece, Richard Smith, Darren Wright

APPRENTICES

Tim Flowers, Graham Rodger (1 Lg.), **Derek Ryan**

WOLVERHAMPTON WANDERERS

DIVISION ONE 22ND **FA CUP** 3RD ROUND **MILK CUP** 2ND ROUND

MATCH	DATE	COMPETITION	VENUE	OPPONENTS	RESULT	HALF TIME	L'GUE POS'N	GOALSCORERS	ATTENDANCE
1	A 27	CL	H	Liverpool	D1-1	1-0		Palmer (pen)	26,249
2	29	CL	H	Arsenal	L1-2	1-1		Clarke	18,571
3	S 3	CL	A	Norwich C	L0-3	0-2	21		13,713
4	7	CL	A	Sunderland	L2-3	0-1		Towner, Eves	12,961
5	10	CL	H	Birmingham C	D1-1	1-1	21	Eves	15,933
6	17	CL	A	Luton T	L0-4	0-1	21		10,975
7	24	CL	H	QPR	L0-4	0-3	21		11,511
8	O 1	CL	A	Southampton	L0-1	0-0	21		16,589
9	**4**	**MC 2**	**H**	**Preston NE**	**L2-3**	**2-1**		**Clarke 2**	**7,790**
10	15	CL	H	Tottenham H	L2-3	1-2	21	Gray 2	12,523
11	23	CL	H	Aston Villa	D1-1	0-1		Clarke	13,202
12	**25**	**MC 2**	**A**	**Preston NE**	**L0-1**	**0-0**			**8,857**
13	29	CL	A	Manchester U	L0-3	0-3	22		41,880
14	N 5	CL	A	Nottingham F	L0-5	0-2	22		13,855
15	12	CL	H	West Ham U	L0-3	0-0	22		12,062
16	19	CL	H	Coventry C	D0-0	0-0	22		11,419
17	26	CL	A	WBA	W3-1	0-0	22	Crainie 2, Clarke	17,947
18	D 3	CL	H	Watford	L0-5	0-3	22		11,905
19	10	CL	A	Leicester C	L1-5	1-4	22	Clarke	10,969
20	17	CL	H	Stoke C	D0-0	0-0	22		8,679
21	26	CL	A	Ipswich T	L1-3	0-1	22	Clarke (pen)	14,477
22	27	CL	H	Everton	W3-0	1-0	22	Eves, Crainie, Clarke	12,761
23	31	CL	H	Norwich C	W2-0	0-0	22	Troughton, Towner	10,725
24	J 2	CL	A	QPR	L1-2	0-0	22	Dawes (og)	12,875
25	**7**	**FAC 3**	**A**	**Coventry C**	**D1-1**	**1-1**		**Clarke**	**15,817**
26	**10**	**FAC 3R**	**H**	**Coventry C**	**D1-1**	**0-0**		**Eves**	**19,204**
27	14	CL	A	Liverpool	W1-0	1-0	22	Mardenborough	23,335
28	**16**	**FAC 3R2**	**A**	**Coventry C**	**L0-2**	**0-2**			**18,003**
29	21	CL	H	Luton T	L1-2	1-1	22	Pender	11,594
30	F 4	CL	H	Southampton	L0-1	0-0	22		9,943
31	11	CL	A	Birmingham C	D0-0	0-0	22		14,319
32	18	CL	H	Manchester U	D1-1	1-0	22	Traighton	20,676
33	25	CL	A	Aston Villa	L0-4	0-1	22		18,257
34	M 3	CL	H	Nottingham F	W1-0	0-0	22	Hart (og)	10,476
35	10	CL	A	West Ham U	D1-1	1-1	21	McGarvey	18,111
36	17	CL	H	Sunderland	D0-0	0-0	22		9,111
37	24	CL	A	Arsenal	L1-4	0-2	22	McGarvey	18,612
38	31	CL	A	Tottenham H	L0-1	0-1	22		19,296
39	A 7	CL	H	Notts Co	L0-1	0-1	22		7,481
40	14	CL	A	Coventry C	L1-2	1-1	22	Livingstone	8,246
41	21	CL	H	Ipswich T	L0-3	0-2	22		6,611
42	23	CL	A	Everton	L0-2	0-1	22		17,185
43	28	CL	H	WBA	D0-0	0-0	22		13,208
44	M 1	CL	A	Notts Co	L0-4	0-2			5,378
45	5	CL	A	Watford	D0-0	0-0	22		13,534
46	7	CL	H	Leicester C	W1-0	1-0	22	Smith	7,405
47	12	CL	A	Stoke C	L0-4	0-2	22		18,977
								Av Home Att	**12,004**

Goal Scorers

League (27): Clarke 6 (1 pen), Crainie 3, Eves 3, Gray 2, McGarvey 2, Towner 2, Troughton 2, Livingstone 1, Mardenborough 1, Palmer 1 (1 pen), Pender 1, Smith 1, opponents 2
FA Cup (2): Clarke 1, Eves 1
Milk Cup (2): Clarke 2

1983-84

Burridge	Humphrey	Palmer	Smith	Pender	Dodd	Daniel	Rudge	Eves	Gray	McGarvey (L)	Towner	Clarke	Livingstone	Cartwright	Buckland	Hibbitt	Bradshaw	Bennett	Coy	Blair (L)	Mardenborough	Crainie	Troughton	Bayly	REFEREE	
1	2	3	4	5	6	7	8	9	10		12														A Ward	1
1	2	3	4	5	6	7		9	10*		12	8													A Challinor	2
1	2	3	4	5	6	8		9			7	12	10												D Vickers	3
1	2	3		5	6	8	11	10			7	12	9*	4											M Peck	4
1	2	3		5	6	8*	4	9	10		11		12	7											C Thomas	5
1	2	3*		5	6		4	9	10		11		8	7		12									D Letts	6
1	2	3	4	5	6				10		12	8	9*	7											D Richardson	7
	2				6	4			10		12	8		9		7	1	3	5						M James	8
	2				**6**	**4**		**10***			**11**	**8**				**7**	**1**	**3**	**5**		**12**				**B Stevens**	**9**
	2	10			6	4*	12		9		11	8				7	1	3	5						R Banks	10
	2	10	4		6		11		9			8				7	1	3	5						J Worrall	11
	2	**10**	**4**		**6**		**11***		**9**			**8**				**7**	**1**	**3**	**5**						**D Hutchinson**	**12**
	2	10*	4		6		11					8				7	1	3	5	9					G Courtney	13
	2				6		12		9			8				7	1	3*	5	4	10	11			I Borrett	14
	2			5	6		12					8		9		7	1	3*		4	10	11			J Deakin	15
	2			5	6		3					8		9		7	1			4	10	11			RF Nixon	16
	2	12		3	4		5					11		8		6	1			7	10*	9			K Hackett	17
	2			5	6		3					8		9		7	1			4*	10	11			R Bridges	18
	2*			5	6		3					8		9		7	1			4	10	11			N Midgley	19
1		3		5	6	2		12				8		9*		7				4	10	11			L Shapter	20
1		3		5	6	2		10			12	8		9						4		11	7*		D Reeves	21
1	2	3		5	6			10			7	8								4		11	9		N Ashley	22
1	2	3		5*	6			10			7	8		4								11	9		K Cooper	23
1	4	3			6	2		10			7	8		5								11	9*		M Bodenham	24
1	**2**	**3**		**5**	**6**	**4**		**10**			**7**	**8**										**11**	**9**		**J Martin**	**25**
1	**2**	**3**		**5**	**6**	**4**		**10**			**7**	**8**										**11**	**9**		**J Martin**	**26**
1	2	3		5	6	4					7	8									10	11	9		A Saunders	27
1	**2**	**3**		**5**	**6**	**4**		**10**			**7**	**8***									**12**	**11**	**9**		**D Shaw**	**28**
1	2	3		5	6	4		10			7	8										11	9		H King	29
1	2	3		5	6	4					7*	8				12					10	11	9		T Jones	30
1		12		5	6	4					7	8			2	3						11	9		G Napthine	31
1		12		5	6	4		10			7	8			2*	3						11	9		D Brazier	32
1		3		5	6	4		10			7	8			2							11	9		N Wilson	33
1		3		5	6		4			10	7	8			2							11	9		D Scott	34
1		3		5	6		4			10	7	8			2							11	9		E Read	35
1		3		5		4				10	7	8			2							11	9		J Ashworth	36
1		3			6	4				10	7	8			2	12						11	9*		D Axcell	37
1		3		5	6	4				10	7	8*			2	12						11	9		L Burden	38
1		3		5	6					10	7		12	4	2*	8						11	9		T Spencer	39
1		3		5	6		10				12	8*	9	4	2	7						11			M Dimblebee	40
1		3*			6		12			10	8		9		2	7						11		4	R Guy	41
1	3			5	6					10	11		9		2	7							8	4	C Seel	42
1	2		3	5	6					9	7		10			8								4	J Hough	43
1	2		3	5	6					9	7		10*		12									4	T Bune	44
1	2		3	5	6			10*		9	7					8						12		4	A Gunn	45
1			8	5	6		3			9			10		2							7		4	D Shaw	46
1	2		8	5	6		3			9			10*		12							7		4	C Thomas	47
32	28	27	11	34	41	19	15	14	9	13	25	29	11	16	13	19	10	6	5	10	9	27	17	7	League Appearances	
		+3S					+4S	+1S			+6S	+2S	+2S		+2S	+4S						+1S				
3	3	3		3	3	3		3			3	3									1S	3	3		FA Cup Appearances	
	2	1	1		2	1	1	1	1		1	2				2	2	2	2		1S				Milk Cup Appearances	

Also Played: Kellock matches 1, 3, no.11*; 2, no.11. Matthews matches 7, 8, no.11; 9, no.9; 11, no.12. Wintersgill match 16, no.12; 26, no.10. Butler matches 12, 17, 21, 22, no.12. Jackson match 44, no.8. Rodger match 41, no.5. Watkiss match 36, no.6; 37, no.5. Dougherty matches 43, 44, 45, 46, 47, no.11.

MOLINEUX

Official Address: Molineux Grounds, Wolverhampton WV1 4QR. Telephone: 0902 711457/ 711432 (Ticket Office), 0902 712181 (Admin Office)

Telegraphic: Wanderers Wolverhampton

Ground Capacity: 38,000

Record Attendance: 61,315 v. Liverpool, F.A. Cup Round 5, 11 Feb 1939

Record Receipts: £80,839 v. Swindon Town, League Cup Semi-Final, 12 Feb 1980

Size of Playing Area: 115yds × 72 yds

Season Tickets: Stand: £90.00, £75.00 (adults), £35.00 (juveniles/OAPs in New Stand); Ground: £35.00 (adults), £17.50 (juveniles/OAPs)

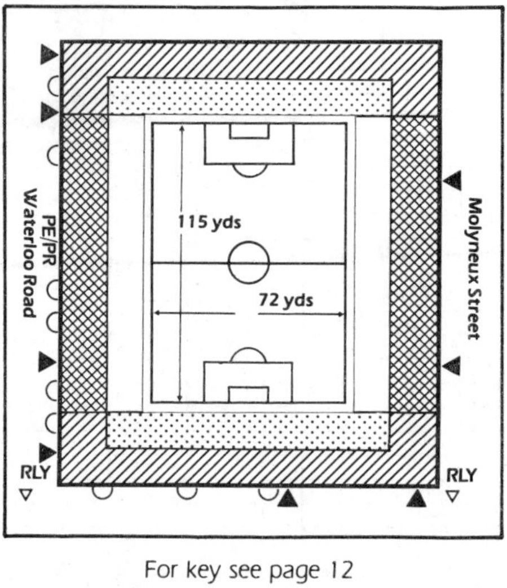

For key see page 12

Executive Box Season Tickets: £5,000 per annum

Cost of Stand Tickets: £4.00; **Terraces:** £2.00 (juveniles/OAPs half-price)

Match and Ticket Information: Seats available by post with payment & SAE one month before each match.

Car Parking: available around "The West Park", in side streets and at the Molineux Hotel.

How to get to the ground

From North: Use Motorway M6 until junction 12, leave Motorway and follow signs Wolverhampton A5 then A449 and at roundabout take 2nd exit into Waterloo Road then turn left into Molineux Street for Wolverhampton Wanderers F.C.

From East: Use Motorway M6 until junction 10, leave Motorway and follow signs Wolverhampton A454. Then at crossroads turn right into Stratford Street. In 0.2m turn left into Ring Road. Then at next crossroads turn right into Waterloo Road and shortly turn right into Molineux Street for Wolverhampton Wanderers F.C.

From South: Use Motorway M5 until junction 2, leave motorway and follow signs Wolverhampton A4123 turn right then shortly turn left into Ring Road. In 1m turn left into Waterloo Road and shortly turn right into Molineux Street for Wolverhampton Wanderers F.C.

From West: Use A454 S.P. Wolverhampton and at roundabout turn left into Ring Road, then turn left into Waterloo Road and shortly turn right into Molineux Street for Wolverhampton F.C.

WREXHAM

Division 4

President
F Wellum

Chairman
W Pryce Griffiths

Vice-Chairman
G Mytton

Directors
C Griffiths
F J Tomlinson
F Wellum
N Dickens
G Dickens
J Scott

Secretary
S Gandy

Assistant Secretary
Miss M Pike

Manager
Bobby Roberts

Physiotherapist
George Showell

Commercial Manager
S R Slater (0978 352536)

After all the traumatic experiences at the racecourse in the last few seasons to escape re-election to the fourth division at the last gasp and finish fifth from the bottom was perhaps a triumph in itself.

Bobby Roberts the manager was himself in a precarious position until the last few weeks of the seaon. But after a vote of confidence given to him by the board of directors the team seemed to gather confidence and obtained eight points out of a possible twelve to steer clear of the dreaded bottom four. In their final two home league games they scored a total of nine goals after losing six home league games in succession.

The team as a whole showed a complete lack of confidence in 83/84, especially at home, and the attendances plummeted to an all time low, with just over 1,000 for the Colchester game. With such a small staff Roberts could not put enough pressure on his team as the reserve strength was inadequate.

Since Bobby Roberts took over in June 1982 drastic financial cuts have been made. With no cash available for new players to boost the playing staff he has had to work on a shoestring with free transfer and loan players. However, in 83/84 the directors did manage to come up with £10,000 for Jim Steel who had impressed the club when on loan from Oldham the previous season. Injuries also did not help, but when at full strength the team did show promise, albeit in spasms. Jack Keay and Steve Wright as central defenders, young Shaun Cunnington at full back, Simon Hunt in midfield, and Andy Edwards all showed good form. The hard working Jim Steel and impressive goalscorer David Gregory give hope for the future. If one or two experienced players can be found to strengthen the squad, there **may** be signs of a recovery.

Wrexham FC are fortunate in having such an enthusiastic supporters club with their members perhaps showing an example to the rest of the club.

Perhaps we can look forward hopefully to the future and better times may be on the way. It is very sad to compare 1977/78 (when the Third Division championship was won, and the club seemed to be on its way to great days.) and the situation now. Bobby Roberts has said that teams used to fear coming to the Racecourse. Let's hope those days return soon.

Such is the irony of soccer that when struggling to survive in the Fourth Division, Wrexham should have become the first club to quality for Europe in 1984/85. They reached the final of the Welsh Cup and with fellow finalists Shrewsbury being an English club, Wrexham automatically qualified for the European Cup Winners Cup. Unfortunately they lost 2-1 on aggregate.

Gareth M Davies
The League Directory's Statistician of the Club

Back Row L to R: S. Cunnington, J. Keay, S. Wright, S. Parker, J. Steel, M. Williams, K. Rogers. **Front Row:** T. Evans, A. Edwards, J. Muldoon, J. King, N. Salathiel, B. Horne, D. Gregory.

'THE ROBINS'

Formed: 1873 **Turned Professional:** 1912 **Ltd Co:** 1912
Previous Managers: 1921-9 Charles Hewitt 1929-31 Jack Baynes 1932-6 Captain Logan 1936-8 Ernest Blackburn 1938-40 Tommy Morgan 1940-9 Tom W Williams 1949-50 Leslie J McDowall 1951-4 Peter Jackson 1954-7 Clifford Lloyd 1957-9 John Love 1960-1 Billy Morris 1961-5 Ken Barnes 1965-5 Billy Morris 1966-7 Jack Rowley 1967 Cliff Lloyd 1967-8 Alvan Williams 1968-77 John Neal 1977-81 Arfon Griffiths 1981-2 Mel Sutton 1982- Bobby Roberts
Honours: Division Three Champions, Welsh Cup Winners (21)
League Career: Original members of Division 3 (N) 1921 Transferred to Division 3 1958
Relegated to Division 4 1959-60 Promoted to Division 3 1961-2
Relegated to Division 4 1963-4 Promoted to Division 3 1969-70
Promoted to Division 2 1977-8 Relegated to Division 3 1981-2
Relegated to Division 4 1982-3
Colours: Red shirts with white trim, navy blue shorts, white stockings
Change Colours: Sky blue shirts, white shorts, sky blue stockings

CLUB RECORDS

Most Appearances for Club: Arfon Griffiths, **586 + 6 subs** (not including Cup Ties)
Most Capped Player: Joey Jones (Wales) 29 **For England:** None
Record Goalscorer in a Match: 7 v Tranmere Rovers (H), 9-0, Football League North, 25.09.43
Record League Goalscorer in a season: Tommy Bamford, 44, Div 3(N), 1934-5
Record League Goalscorer in a career: Tommy Bamford, 175, 1929-35
Record Transfer Fee Received: £300,000 from Manchester United for Mickey Thomas, Nov 1978; £300,000 from Manchester City for Bobby Shinton, July 1979
Record Transfer Fee Paid: £210,000 to Liverpool for Joey Jones, Oct 1978
Best Performances: League: 15th Div 2 1978-9 **F.A. Cup:** 6th Round 1973-4, 1977-8 **League/Milk Cup:** 5th Round 1961, 1978 **Welsh Cup:** Winners (21), Runners Up (19) This is a record number of victories and appearances in the Final
European Cup Winners Cup: Quarter Final 1975-6
Most League Points: 61 in Div 4, 1969-70, 1977-8 **Most League Goals:** 106, Div 3(N) 1932-3
Record League Victory: 10-1 v Hartlepool, Div 4, 3 March 1962
Record League Defeat: 0-9 v Brentford, Div 3, 15 Oct 1963
European Competitions Entered: European Cup Winners Cup: 1972-3, 1975-6, 1978-9, 1979-80

Club Statistician for the Directory: Gareth Davies

Programme Editors
David Roberts, Phil Jones & Geraint Perry (Supporters' Association) with Malcolm K. Davies (Adlink Advertising, Hawarden)

Price	Number of Pages
40p	20

Subscriptions
Apply to club for details

WREXHAM

LAYERS NAME t Wt Birthdate	Honours	Birthplace Transfers	Clubs	Appearances League	Appearances Milk Cup	Appearances F.A.C.	Appearances A.M.C.	Goals League	Goals Milk Cup	Goals F.A.C.	Goals A.M.C.
OALKEEPER											
tuart Parker		Nantwich	Wrexham	10	1	1					
·1 12.9 17.9.65											
EFENDERS											
haun Cunnington		Bourne	Wrexham	43+3	1	1	3				
·9 11.0 4.1.66											
ackie Keay*	Div. 3, 79.	Glasgow	Celtic								
0 12.6 14.6.60	WC. 79	F	Shrewsbury T.	152+3	7	15		20		2	
		£18,000	Wrexham	75	3	2	1	5		1	
ake King	Div. 3, 79.	Glasgow	Shrewsbury T.	304+2	14	26		20		1	
·10 11.0 29.1.55	WC. 79	F	Wrexham	77+1	2	3	3	5	1		
evin Rogers	W. Y. S	Mertlye	Aston Villa (A)								
·9 11.3 23.9.63		F	Birmingham C.	8+1							
		F	Wrexham								
avid Salathiel	W. S	Wrexham	4								
			Crewe A.	64+1	4	3					
			Wrexham								
eil Salathiel	W. Y. S	Wrexham	Wrexham	4			2				
7 10.0 19.11.62			Crewe A.	64+1	4	3					
			Wrexham	29							
teve Wright			Colchester U.	112+5	8	13+		2			
0 11.0 16.8.59			Lapf Jard								
			Wrexham	37	1	1					
IIDFIELD											
avid Gregory†		Peterborough	Chatteris T.								
9 11.6 6.10.51			Peterborough U.	125+17	10+	13+		32	2	6	
		£55,000	Stoke C.	22+1	1	1		3		1	
			Blackburn R. (L)	5	1			3	1		
		£30,000	Bury	50+2	2	4		13	1	6	
		£30,000	Portsmouth	64+10	7	4		18	2	1	
		F	Wrexham	83+2	4	3	3	23		1	1
arry Horne		St. Asaph	Liverpool Univ.								
10 12.3 18.5.63			Rhyl								
			Wrexham								
mon Hunt		Chester	Wrexham	102+6	5+2	4	3	18	2	1	
6 10.1 17.11.62											
m Muldoon		Clatterbridge	Wrexham	48+9	2	3	1+1	7		1	
7½ 11.0 21.11.64											
like Williams	W. Y	Mancot	Chester C. (A)	38+3				3			
10 11.0 6.2.65		F	Wrexham								
ORWARDS											
ndy Edwards		Wrexham	Wrexham	27+16	2	1	2+1	7			
8 11.6 28.3.65											
m Steel		Dumfries	Oldham A. (A)	101+7	8+1	6		24	1		
3 11.6 4.12.59			Wigan A. (L)	2				2			
			Wrexham (L)	9				6			
		£5,000	Port Vale	27+1	1+1	+1		6	1		
			Wrexham	21		3					

ONTRACTED PLAYERS 1984-85

evin Rogers, Michael Williams

ON-CONTRACT PLAYERS 1984-85

areth Barnes, Kevin Jones, Paul Nicoll, Gary Pugh, David Rielly, Steve Scott, David Williams

WREXHAM

DIVISION FOUR 20TH **FA CUP** 1ST ROUND **MILK CUP** 1ST ROUND

MATCH	DATE	COMPE-TITION	VENUE	OPPONENTS	RESULT	HALF TIME	L'GUE POS'N	GOALSCORERS	ATTEN-DANCE
1	A 27	CL	A	Doncaster R	L0-3	0-1			2,035
2	**31**	**MC 1**	**A**	**Port Vale**	**L1-3**	**1-1**		**Evans**	**3,916**
3	S 3	CL	H	Peterborough U	D2-2	1-1	19	Coleman, Hunt	1,680
4	6	CL	H	Rochdale	W5-1	2-0		Arkwright 2, Hunt, Gregory, Edwards	1,684
5	10	CL	A	Tranmere R	L1-2	1-2	16	Keay	2,425
6	**13**	**MC 1**	**H**	**Port Vale**	**L1-5**	**1-4**		**King**	**2,903**
7	16	CL	H	Bristol C	W3-1	1-0	8	Edwards, Gregory, Hunt	1,731
8	24	CL	A	Aldershot	D1-1	1-1	12	Gregory	2,007
9	26	CL	A	Stockport Co	D1-1	0-0		Heath	2,031
10	O 1	CL	H	Halifax T	W1-0	0-0	8	Hunt	5,472
11	8	CL	H	Hereford U	D0-0	0-0	9		3,190
12	15	CL	A	Hartlepool U	D1-1	1-0	11	Arkwright	982
13	18	CL	H	Blackpool	L0-1	0-1			2,005
14	22	CL	A	Bury	L0-2	0-1	19		2,320
15	29	CL	H	Torquay U	D2-2	2-0	19	Jones, King	1,505
16	N 1	CL	A	York C	L2-3	2-2		Edwards, Hunt	5,641
17	5	CL	H	Mansfield T	L2-3	0-2	22	Hunt, King	1,633
18	12	CL	A	Reading	L1-4	1-0	22	Keay	3,082
19	**19**	**FAC 1**	**H**	**Sheffield U**	**L1-5**	**1-2**		**Coleman**	**2,842**
20	26	CL	H	Northampton T	L0-1	0-0	22		1,234
21	D 17	CL	A	Chesterfield	D1-1	1-0	22	Coleman	2,616
22	26	CL	H	Chester C	W2-0	1-0	22	Arkwright, King	5,756
23	27	CL	A	Swindon T	W1-0	1-0	20	Edwards	4,298
24	31	CL	H	Darlington	D1-1	1-1	20	Gregory	2,200
25	J 2	CL	A	Colchester U	D1-1	0-1	19	Muldoon	3,182
26	7	CL	A	Peterborough U	W1-0	0-0	17	Gregory	3,277
27	14	CL	H	Doncaster R	L1-2	1-1	18	Gregory (pen)	2,266
28	21	CL	A	Bristol C	L1-2	0-1	18	Gregory	6,441
29	F 4	CL	A	Halifax T	D1-1	1-0	18	Gregory	1,184
30	11	CL	H	Aldershot	D1-1	1-1	18	King	1,898
31	18	CL	A	Torquay U	L0-1	0-0	20		1,868
32	**21**	**AMC 1**	**H**	**Peterborough U**	**W3-2**[1]	**0-1**		**Steel, Arkwright, Gregory**	**1,018**
33	25	CL	H	Bury	W3-0	1-0	18	Muldoon 2, Buxton	1,874
34	28	CL	H	York C	D0-0	0-0			1,199
35	M 3	CL	A	Blackpool	L0-4	0-2	18		3,798
36	6	CL	A	Mansfield T	W4-3	1-1		Buxton 2, Gregory 2	1,986
37	10	CL	H	Reading	L0-3	0-1	19		1,871
38	**14**	**AMC 2**	**H**	**Exeter C**	**W2-0**	**1-0**		**Edwards, Baker**	**834**
39	17	CL	A	Hereford U	L0-3	0-1	19		2,570
40	24	CL	H	Hartlepool U	L1-4	1-2	19	Gregory	1,181
41	30	CL	H	Stockport Co	L1-2	1-2		Gregory (pen)	1,252
42	**A 3**	**AMC SOF**	**A**	**AFA Bournemouth**	**L0-2**	**0-1**			**1,909**
43	7	CL	A	Rochdale	W2-1	2-1	19	Hunt, Gregory	1,228
44	14	CL	H	Crewe Alex	L0-1	0-0	20		2,102
45	20	CL	H	Swindon T	L0-3	0-2			1,442
46	21	CL	A	Chester C	L0-1	0-0	21		3,486
47	28	CL	A	Northampton T	D3-3	1-3	22	Keay, Muldoon, Gregory (pen)	1,189
48	M 5	CL	H	Colchester U	L0-2	0-0	22		1,016
49	8	CL	A	Darlington	D2-2	1-0		Todd (og), Hunt	1,123
50	12	CL	H	Chesterfield	W4-2	1-0	22	Bellamy (og), Gregory, Edwards 2	1,039
51	15	CL	A	Crewe Alex	D1-1	1-0		Gregory	1,811
52	21	CL	H	Tranmere R	W5-1	2-0		Gregory 3 (1 pen), Hunt, Edwards	1,858

[1]After Extra Time

Av Home Att **2,078**

Goal Scorers

League (59): Gregory 19 (4 pens), Hunt 9, Edwards 7, Arkwright 4, King 4, Muldoon 4, Buxton 3, Keay 3, Coleman 2, Heath 1, Jones 1, opponents 2
FA Cup (1): Coleman 1
Milk Cup (2): Evans 1, King 1
AMC (5): Arkwright 1, Baker 1, Edwards 1, Gregory 1, Steel 1

1983-84

Parker	Hunt	Evans	King	Keay	Cunnington	Arkwright	Gregory	Edwards	Buxton	Heath	Muldoon	Wardle **(L)**	Coleman **(L)**	Baker	Wright	Jones	Salathiel	Sturridge **(L)**	Millington	Steel	Sinclair	Bater	**REFEREE**	
1	2	3	4	5	6	7	8	9	10*	11	12												D Richardson	1
1	**2**	**11**	**4**	**5**	**6**	**7**	**10**	**9**		**3**	**8**												**D Scott**	**2**
	4	12	2	6	3	7	10	9*		11	8	1	5										R Dilkes	3
	4		2	6	3	7	10	12		11	8*	1	5	9									L Robinson	4
	6		2	3	4	7	11	12		5	10	1	9	8*									N Wilson	5
	4		**2**	**6**		**7**	**10**	**9**		**11**	**8**	**1**	**5**									**3**	**J Deakin**	**6**
	4	8	2	6.	3		10	9		11		1	5		7								DV Allison	7
	4		2	6	3	8	10	9*		11	12	1	5		7								D Vickers	8
	4		2	6	3	8	10	9		11		1	5		7								K Walmsley	9
	4		2	6	3	8	10	12	9*	11		1	5		7								TW King	10
	4		2	6		8	10	9		11	3	1	5		7								IA Hendrick	11
	4		2	6		8	10	9		11		1	5		7	3							T Mills	12
	4		2	6		8	10	9		11		1	5		7	3							H Taylor	13
	7		2	8			11	10	6*	9	12	1	3		4	5							A Saunders	14
	4	9	2	6	8			12			10	1	5	11	7	3*							J Bray	15
	4	11	2	6	3		12	9			8	1	5	10*	7								PN Willis	16
1	4	11	2	6	3	12		9			7		5	10*	8								N Glover	17
1	4		2	6	3	10	8	9		11	12		5*		7								B Hill	18
1	**4**		**2**		**3**	**8**	**10**	**9**		**11†**	**6**		**5**		**7**								**D Owen**	**19**
1	4	6*	2		3		10	9		11	8		5	12	7								RA Banks	20
1	4		2	6	3	8	10				12		5*		7		11	9					E Scales	21
1	4		2	6	3	8	10			5					7		11	9					T Holbrook	22
1	4		2	6	3		10	9		8	5				7		11*	12					R Lewis	23
	4		2	6	3	8	10			5					7		11	9	1				J Hough	24
	7		2	3	4	8	9			5	10				6		11		1				J Hedges	25
	4		2	6	3	8	10			5	9				7		11		1				A Challinor	26
	4		2	6	3	8	10			5					7		11		1	9			K Cooper	27
	4		2	6	3	8	10			5					7		11		1	9			J Moules	28
	4		2	5	3	7	8			11					6		9		1	10			J Worrall	29
	4*		2		3	7	8		12	11	5				6		9		1	10			R Guy	30
	4		2		3	7	8		6	11	5						9		1	10			M Bodenham	31
1	**4**		**2**		**3**	**7**	**8**	**12**	**6***	**11**	**13**			**5***			**9**			**10**			**D Richardson**	**32**
	4		2		3	7	8		12	11*	5				6		9		1	10			J Key	33
1	12		2	4	3	7	8		11		5*				6		9			10			K Barratt	34
1		4*	2	5	3	7	8	12	11						6		9			10			K Hackett	35
			2	4	3	7	8		11	5					6		9		1	10			J Ashworth	36
	12		2	5	3	7	8		11*	4					6		9		1	10			L Dilkes	37
	4	**7***	**2**		**3**	**12**	**8**	**5**		**12**				**11***	**6**		**9**		**1**	**10**			**R Banks**	**38**
	4		2	5	3*		8	7	11		12				6		9		1	10			D Brazier	39
	5	12	2		3		8	7	11					4	6*		9		1	10			T Jones	40
	4		2		3		8	7	11	5	6						9			10	1		V Callow	41
	4		**2**	**5**	**3**		**8**	**6***	**11**	**12**	**7**						**9**			**10**	**1**		**C Downey**	**42**
	4		2		3		8		11		6			7	5		9			10	1		M Peck	43
	4		2		3		8	12	11	5	6			7			9			10*	1		C Thomas	44
	4		2	7	3		8		11	5	6				10		9				1		D Scott	45
	4		2	5	3		8		11		6				7		9			10	1		N Glover	46
	4		2	5	3	6*	8	7		11	12						9			10	1		P Scott	47
	4		2	5	3	7*	8	12		11	6						9			10	1		T Fitzharris	48
	4			5	3		8	11	10		7				6		2			9	1		C Seel	49
	4	12		5	3		8	10	11		7				6		2			9*	1		D Allison	50
	4		9	5	3		8	10	11		7				6		2				1		D Hutchinson.	51
	4		2	5	3		8	10			7				6		11			9	1		A Robinson	52
9	42	7	44	38	42	28	43	22	18	32	25	13	17	8	37	4	29	3	13	21	11		League Appearances	
	+2S	+3S				+1S	+1S	+7S	+2S		+7S			+1S				+1S						
1	1		1		1	1	1	1		1	1		1		1								FA Cup Appearances	
1	2	1	2	2	1	2	2	2		2	2	1	1									1	Milk Cup Appearances	
1	3	1	3	1	3	1+1S	3	2+1S	2	1+2S	1+1S			2	1		3		1	3	1		AM Cup Appearances	

THE RACECOURSE GROUND

Official Address: Racecourse Ground, Mold Road, Wrexham. Telephone: Wrexham (0978) 262129

Telegraphic: Football Wrexham

Ground Capacity: 30,000

Record Attendance: 34,445 v. Manchester United, F.A. Cup Round 4, 26 Jan 1957

Record Receipts: £25,107 v. Anderlecht, European Cup-Winners Cup Quarter-Final, 17 Mar 1976

Size of Playing Area: 117yds × 75 yds

Season Tickets: (juveniles/OAP in brackets) Border and Yale Stand: £62.70 (£38), Mold Rd £52.25, (£38.00), Plas Coch Stand £52.25, (£38.00), Ground: £41.80 (£29) (Bench); £31.35 (£19.00)

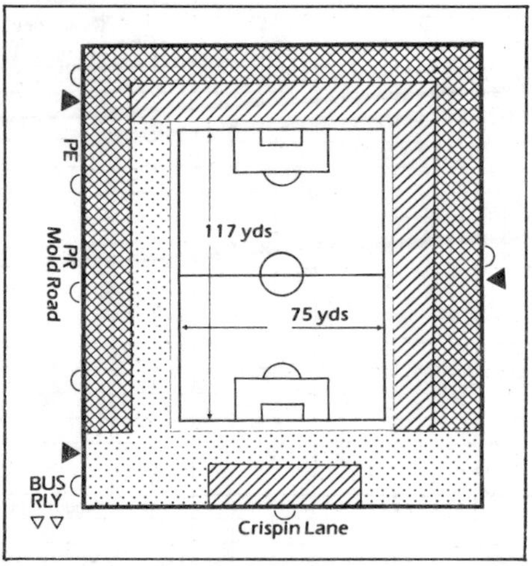

For key see page 12

Executive Box Season Tickets: None

Cost of Stand Tickets: £3.30, £3.00, £2.80, £2.20, £1.70; **Terraces:** £1.80 (£1.00 juveniles/OAP)

Match and Ticket Information: Stand seats bookable in advance.

Car Parking: Berse Field main car park plus parking ground at St. Marks, Bodlyfryd Square, Eagles Meadows, Old Guild Hall, Hill Street, Holt Street and Town Hall (Hill Street).

How to get to the ground

From North and West: Use A483 and Wrexham bypass until junction with A541 then branch left and at roundabout follow signs Wrexham into Mold Road for Wrexham F.C.
From East and South: Follow signs into Wrexham on A534 or A525 then follow signs A541 into Mold Road for Wrexham F.C.

YORK CITY

Division 3

President
F H Magson

Chairman
M D B Sinclair

Directors
D M Craig,
JP, BSC, FICE, FI Mun E, FCI, ARB, M Cons E
B A Houghton
R B Strachan, MA, LLB, FCIS
C Webb
E B Swallow

Club Secretary
Tom Hughes

Medical Officer
Dr A I MacLeod

Player Manager
Denis Smith

Club Coach
Viv Busby

Physiotherapist
John Simpson

Sales Executive
J Miller (0904 24447)

Whilst all other teams were huffing and puffing York City occupied themselves almost exclusively with one objective — the top position in the Fourth Division. That they were successful can be judged from a few relevant statistics:—

1. They were the first League team ever to score more than one hundred points — 101 to be exact. Even by the old scoring method they would have reached seventy points.
2. The attack scored ninety-six goals.
3. The defence conceded thirty-nine goals — less than one per match.
4. From 29th October 1983 they were never off the top spot in the table.

In short, their fans were given a lesson in efficiency and the hopes for the future in the higher division must be good. Cup runs did not hamper their progress as the Milk Cup challenge ended with a narrow First Round aggregate defeat against Grimsby Town (2-3). The F.A. Cup ended in the Second Round with a surprise home defeat by Rochdale. This followed a First Round against Macclesfield which went to a replay at Bootham Crescent (won 2-0) after a goalless draw.

What happens next? The team under the management of Denis Smith is well-based with sound goalkeeping from Roger Jones well backed up by Senior, Hay, Sbragia and MacPhail in defence. The midfield is well led by Ford and Crosby and the strike force of Walwyn and Byrne looks very powerful. They should make a few defences worry in the Third Division.

W.L.M.

Back Row L to R: Viv Busby (Coach), Nick Murphy, Ricky Sbragia, Alan Hay, Keith Houchen, Mike Astbury, Roger Jones, John MacPhail, Keith Walwyn, Chris Evans, Derek Hood, Gerry Delahunt (Physio). **Middle Row:** Sean Haslegrave, Malcolm Crosby, Steve Senior, John Byrne, Denis Smith (Manager), Hugh Atkinson, Gary Nicholson, Gary Ford, Alan Pearce, Brian Chippendale. **Front Row:** Richard Gill, Glen Liddle, Stuart McKenzie, Neil Smallwood, Michael King, Martin Butler, Steve Rodgers.

'THE MINSTERMEN'

Formed: 1922 **Turned Professional:** 1922 **Ltd Co:** 1922
Previous Managers: 1929-36 John Collier 1936-50 Tom Mitchell 1950-2 Dick Duckworth 1952-3 Charlie Spencer 1953-4 Jim McCormick 1956-60 Sam Bartram 1960-7 Tom Lockie 1967-8 Joe Shaw 1968-75 Tom Johnston 1975-7 Wilf McGuinness 1977-80 Charlie Wright 1980-1 Barry Lyons
Honours: Champions Division Four 1983-4
League Career: Elected to Division 3(N) 1929 Transferred to Division 4 1958 Promoted to Division 3 1958-9 Relegated to Division 4 1959-60 Promoted to Division 3 1964-5 Relegated to Division 4 1965-6 Promoted to Division 3 1970-1 Promoted to Division 2 1973-4 Relegated to Division 3 1975-6 Relegated to Division 4 1976-7 Promoted to Division 3 1983-4
Colours: Red shirts with white trim, white shorts with red stripe, red stockings
Change Colours: White shirts with red trim, black shorts, black stockings with red and white tops

CLUB RECORDS

Most Appearances for Club: Barry Jackson: Football League 481 + F.A. Cup 35 + League Cup 22 **Total 538**
Most Capped Player: Peter Scott, 7, Northern Ireland **For England:** None
Record Goalscorer in a Match: Alf Patrick, 5 v Rotherham United (6-1) Div 3, 20.11.48
Record League Goalscorer in a season: Bill Fenton, 31, Div 3(N), 1951-2 & Arthur Bottom, 1955-6, Div 3(N)
Record League Goalscorer in a career: Norman Wilkinson, 125, 1954-66
Record Transfer Fee Received: £120,000 from Carlisle United for Gordon Staniforth, Oct 1979
Record Transfer Fee Paid: £18,000 to Bournemouth for Micky Cave, Aug 1974
Best Performances: League: 15th Div 2 1974-5 **F.A. Cup:** Semi-Final Replay 1954-5 (as a Third Division club)
League/Milk Cup: 5th Round 1961-2
Most League Points: 101 in Div 4, 1983-4 **Most League Goals:** 96, Div 4, 1983-4
Record League Victory: 9-1 v Southport, Div 3(N), 2 Feb 1957
Record League Defeat: 0-12 v Chester, Div 3(N), 1 Feb 1936
Club Statistician for the Directory: David Batters

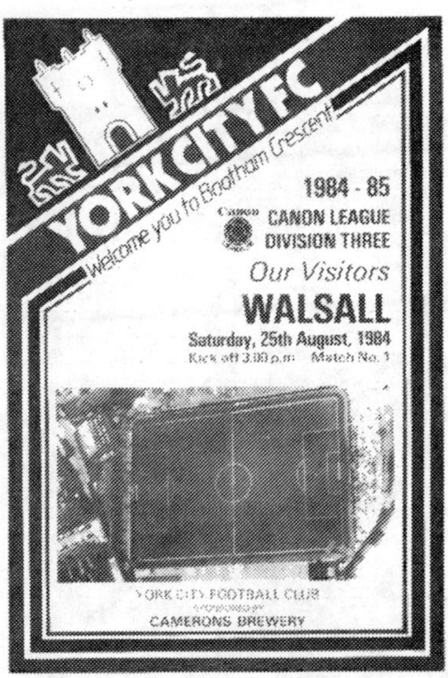

Programme Editor
Tom Hughes

Price	**Number of Pages**
40p	20

Subscriptions
£22.50 (home & away)

YORK CITY

				APPEARANCES				GOALS			
PLAYERS NAME **Ht Wt Birthdate**	**Honours**	**Birthplace Transfers**	**Clubs**	**League**	**Milk Cup**		**A.M.C.**	**League**	**Milk Cup**	**F.A.C.**	**A.M.C.**
GOALKEEPERS											
Mike Astbury		Leeds	York C. (A)	25	1	1					
5-11 13.0 22.1.64											
Roger Jones*	E. U.23(1).	Upton	Portsmouth (A)								
5-11 13.0 8.11.46	Div. 3, 75	F	Bournemouth	160	8	8					
	Div. 4, 84	£30,000	Blackburn R.	242	15	15					
		£50,000	Newcastle U.	5							
		F	Stoke C.	101	8	3					
		£20,000	Derby Co.	59	3	3					
			Birmingham C. (L)	4							
		F	York C.	83	3	6	1				
DEFENDERS											
Chris Evans	Div. 4, 84	Rhondda	Arsenal (A)								
5-10 11.2 13.10.62		F	Stoke C.								
		F	York C.	62 + 3	2	4 + 1	1				
Alan Hay	Div. 4, 84	Dunfermline	Bolton W. (N-C)								
5-11¾ 12.0 28.11.58			Bristol C.	72 + 2	4 + 2	4		1			
			York C.	84	4	7		2			
John McPhail†	Div. 4, 82,	Dundee	Dundee	64 + 4	11	5					
6-0½ 12.3 7.12.55	Div. 4, 84	£30,000	Sheffield U.	135	9	8		7		1	
		F	York C.	57 + 1	2	3	1	12			
Ricky Sbragia	Div. 4, 84	Lennoxtown	Birmingham C. (A)	14 + 1				1			
6-0 11.0 26.5.56		£15,000	Walsall	77	2	5		4			
		£35,000	Blackpool	24 + 2	1			1			
		F	York C.	91	4	7		5			
Steve Senior	Div. 4, 84	Sheffield	York C. (A)	60 + 9	2	6	1	3			
5-8½ 11.4 15.5.63											
MIDFIELD											
Hugh Atkinson	Ei. U.21	Dublin	Wolverhampton W. (A)	38 + 8	1	4		3			
6-0 11.9 8.11.60			York C.								
Brian Chippendale		Bradford	Bradford C. (A)								
5-10 10.11 29.10.64			York C.	+ 4		1	+ 1				
Malcolm Crosby	Div. 4, 84	South Shields	Aldershot (A)	272 + 22	11	18 +		23	2	2	
5-9 11.3 4.7.54		Player Exchange	York C.	88 + 4	2	10	1	4			
Gary Ford	Div. 4, 84	York	York C. (A)	230 + 7	12	20	1	40	2	4	
5-8 11.10 8.2.61											
Sean Haselgrave	Div. 4, 84	Stoke	Stoke C.	106 + 7	9 + 2	7 + 1		5	1	1	
5-8 10.7 7.6.51		£35,000	Nottingham F.	5 + 2				1			
		£20,000	P.N.E.	111 + 2	4	5		2			
		F	Crewe A.	78 + 4	4	3		1		1	
		F	York C.	24 + 2	1 + 1		+ 1				
Derek Hood	Div. 4, 84	Washington	W.B.A. (A)								
5-11 12.8 17.12.58	FAYC. 76	F	Hull C.	20 + 4	3	4					
			York C.	183 + 1	6	12		20			
Gary Nicholson		Newcastle	Newcastle U. (A)	7 + 5	3						
5-7½ 9.11 4.11.60		£10,000	Mansfield T.	74 + 3	5	3 + 1	1				
			York C.								
FORWARDS											
John Byrne	Div. 4, 84	Manchester	York C. (A)	157 + 8	6 + 2	10 +	1	53	2	3	
6-0 12.4 1.2.61											
Keith Houchen		Middlesbrough	Chesterfield (N-C)								
6-2 11.4 25.7.60			Hartlepool U.	160 + 10	8	4 + 1		65	1		
		£25,000	Orient	74 + 2	3	3		20	2		
		£15,000	York C.	1 + 6			+ 1	1			
Alan Pearce		Middlesbrough	York C.	17 + 1				5			
5-8 11.6 25.10.65											
Keith Walwyn	Div. 4, 84	Jamaica, W.I.	Winterton R.								
6-1 13.2 17.2.56			Chesterfield	3	+ 1	1 + 1	+ 1	2			
		£4,000	York C.	130	6	8	1	69	1	4	

NON-CONTRACT PLAYERS 1984-85

Viv Busby, Martin Butler, Nicholas Murphy, Neil Smallwood

YORK CITY

DIVISION FOUR 1ST **FA CUP** 2ND ROUND **MILK CUP** 1ST ROUND

MATCH	DATE	COMPE-TITION	VENUE	OPPONENTS	RESULT	HALF TIME	L'GUE POS'N	GOALSCORERS	ATTEN DANC
1	A 27	CL	A	Stockport Co	W2-0	1-0		McPhail, Byrne	2,185
2	**30**	**MC 1**	**H**	**Grimsby T**	**W2-1**	**1-0**		**Ford, Pollard**	**3,505**
3	S 3	CL	H	Rochdale	W2-0	0-0	2	Ford, Walwyn	2,772
4	6	CL	H	Peterborough U	W2-0	0-0		Pollard, Byrne	3,709
5	10	CL	A	Chesterfield	L1-2	0-1	1	Walwyn	4,041
6	**13**	**MC 1**	**A**	**Grimsby T**	**L0-2[1]**	**0-0**			**3,529**
7	17	CL	H	Chester C	W4-1	3-1	1	Byrne 3, McPhail	3,037
8	24	CL	A	Darlington	D0-0	0-0	1		2,181
9	27	CL	A	Doncaster R	D2-2	1-0		Byrne, Walwyn	4,996
10	O 1	CL	H	Blackpool	W4-0	1-0	1	Walwyn 2, Byrne 2	4,058
11	7	CL	H	Colchester U	W3-0	1-0		McPhail, Pollard (pen), Walwyn	6,207
12	15	CL	A	Swindon T	L2-3	2-2	1	Walwyn 2	2,517
13	18	CL	A	Bristol C	L0-1	0-1			10,837
14	22	CL	H	Reading	D2-2	0-1	2	Pollard, Sbragia	4,315
15	29	CL	A	Northampton T	W2-1	1-1	1	Walwyn 2	2,959
16	N 1	CL	H	Wrexham	W3-2	2-2		Sbragia, Pollard 2 (1 pen)	5,641
17	5	CL	A	Crewe Alex	W3-0	0-0	1	Byrne, Walwyn 2	2,785
18	12	CL	H	Torquay U	L2-3	1-2	1	Hood, Ford	4,609
19	**19**	**FAC 1**	**A**	**Macclesfield**	**D0-0**	**0-0**			**3,407**
20	**22**	**FAC 1R**	**H**	**Macclesfield**	**W2-0**	**1-0**		**Sbragia, Byrne**	**4,963**
21	26	CL	A	Hartlepool U	W3-2	1-2	1	Byrne 2, Sbragia	2,012
22	D 3	CL	H	Aldershot	W2-0	1-0	1	Byrne, Pearce	3,951
23	**13**	**FAC 2**	**H**	**Rochdale**	**L0-2**	**0-1**			**5,203**
24	17	CL	H	Hereford U	W4-0	2-0	1	Pearce, Byrne, Ford 2	2,722
25	26	CL	A	Halifax T	W2-1	1-1	1	Walwyn 2	2,457
26	27	CL	H	Tranmere R	D1-1	1-0	1	Senior	6,357
27	31	CL	A	Bury	W3-1	3-0	1	Walwyn, Byrne 2	3,864
28	J 2	CL	H	Mansfield T	W2-1	1-1	1	Ford, Hay	5,682
29	14	CL	H	Stockport Co	W3-1	1-1	1	Hood (pen), McPhail, Walwyn	3,750
30	21	CL	H	Chesterfield	W1-0	1-0	1	Byrne	4,782
31	F 5	CL	A	Blackpool	L0-3	0-2	1		6,010
32	11	CL	H	Darlington	W2-0	1-0	1	McPhail, Ford	4,773
33	18	CL	H	Northampton T	W3-0	2-0	1	Walwyn, Pollard (pen), Byrne	3,941
34	**21**	**AMC 1**	**H**	**Hull C**	**L1-2**	**1-0**		**Senior**	**5,674**
35	25	CL	A	Reading	L0-1	0-0	1		4,548
36	28	CL	A	Wrexham	D0-0	0-0			1,199
37	M 3	CL	H	Bristol C	D1-1	0-0	1	Phillipson-Masters (og)	5,096
38	6	CL	H	Crewe Alex	W5-2	1-1		Shragia, Pearce, Walwyn 2, Byrne	4,106
39	10	CL	A	Torquay U	W3-1	0-0	1	Ford, Walwyn, Byrne	2,836
40	17	CL	A	Colchester U	W3-1	2-0	1	McPhail, Walwyn, Pearce	3,032
41	24	CL	H	Swindon T	W2-0	1-0	1	Walwyn, Ford	3,341
42	27	CL	A	Rochdale	W2-0	0-0		Byrne 2	1,756
43	A 1	CL	A	Peterborough U	W2-0	0-0		McPhail, Byrne	5,216
44	8	CL	H	Doncaster R	D1-1	1-1		Ford	11,297
45	14	CL	A	Aldershot	W4-1	1-0	1	McPhail, Houchen, Byrne, Pearce	5,071
46	18	CL	A	Chester C	D1-1	1-1		Hood	1,750
47	20	CL	H	Halifax T	W4-1	3-0		Byrne 3, Walwyn	7,123
48	23	CL	A	Tranmere R	W1-0	1-0	1	Ford	3,527
49	28	CL	H	Hartlepool U	W2-0	0-0	1	Walwyn 2	6,063
50	M 5	CL	A	Mansfield T	W1-0	0-0	1	McPhail	3,355
51	7	CL	H	Bury	W3-0	2-0	1	Byrne, Hood, Ford	8,023
52	12	CL	A	Hereford U	L1-2	0-2	1	McPhail	4,333

[1]After Extra Time **Av Home Att** **4,984**

Goal Scorers

League (96): Byrne 27, Walwyn 25, Ford 11, McPhail 10, Pollard 6 (3 pens), Pearce 5, Hood 4 (1 pen), Sbragia 4, Hay 1, Houchen 1, Senior 1, opponents 1
FA Cup (2): Byrne 1, Sbragia 1
Milk Cup (2): Ford 1, Pollard 1
AMC (1): Senior 1

1983-84

Jones	Senior	Hay	Sbragia	McPhail	Hood	Ford	Crosby	Walwyn	Byrne	Pollard	Haselgrave	Astbury	Evans	Busby	Pearce	Chippendale	Houchen	REFEREE	
1	2	3	4	5	6	7	8	9	10	11								S Roberts	1
1	**2**	**3**	**4**	**5**	**6***	**7**	**8**	**9**	**10**	**11**	**12**							**D Richardson**	**2**
1	2	3	4	5		7	8	9	10	11	6							M Scott	3
1	2	3	4	5		7	8	9	10	11	6							D Allison	4
	2	3	4	5		7	8	9	10	11	6	1						J Ashworth	5
	2	**3**	**4**	**5**		**7**	**8**	**9**	**10***	**11**	**6**	**1**	**12**					**P Tyldesley**	**6**
	2	3	4	5		7	8	9	10	11	6	1						MG Peck	7
1†	2	3	4	5		7*	8	9	10	11	6		12					TA Jones	8
1	2	3	4	5		7	8	9	10	11	6							JD Hough	9
1	2	3	4	5		7	8	9	10	11	6							A Saunders	10
1	2	3	4	5		7	8	9	10	11	6							R Guy	11
	2	3	4	5		7	8	9	10	11	6	1						M Dimblebee	12
	6	3†	4	5		7	8	9*	10	11		1	2	12				K Cooper	13
1	6	3	4	5	12	7	8	9	10	11			2*					R Bridges	14
1	2*	3	4	5	6	7	8	9	10	11			12					RS Lewis	15
1	3		4	5	6	7	8	9*	10	11			2	12				PN Willis	16
1	2		4	5	6	7	8*	9	10	11			3	12				T Holbrook	17
1	8	3	4	5	6	7		9	10	11			2					LR Dilkes	18
1	**2**	**3**	**4**	**5**	**6**	**7**	**8**		**10**	**11**				**9**				**A Seville/Holland**	**19**
1	**2**	**3**	**4**	**5**	**6**	**7**	**8**		**10**	**11***			**12**	**9**				**D Richardson**	**20**
1	9	3	4	5	6	7	8		10				2		11*	12		C Seel	21
1	2	3	4	5		7	8	9	10		6*		12		11			D Scott	22
1	**2**	**3**	**4**	**5**	**6**	**7**	**8**	**9**	**10**	**11**								**M Robinson**	**23**
1	2	3	4	5	6	7	8	9	10						11			G Courtney	24
1	2	3	4	5	6	7*	8	9	10	11						12		A Challinor	25
1	6	3	4	5		7	8	9	10				2		11			G Tyson	26
1	2	3	4	5	6*	7	8	9	10	11						12		K Baker	27
1	2	3	4	5	6	7	8	9	10	11*					12			K Redfern	28
1	2	3	4	5	6	7	8	9	10						11			G Napthine	29
1	2	3	4	5	6	7*	8	9	10	11	12							D Richardson	30
1	2	3	4	5	6	7	8	9	10	11								T Tyldesley	31
1	2	3	4	5	6	7	8	9	10	11		1						L Robinson	32
1	3		4	5	6	7	8	9	10	11			2					N Midgley	33
1	**3**		**4**	**5**	**6**	**7**	**8***	**9**	**10**	**11***	**12**		**2**		**13**			**T Mills**	**34**
1	3		4	5	6	7	8	9	10	11*	12		2					M Taylor	35
1	2	3	4	5	6	7	8	9	10						11			K Barratt	36
1	2	3	4	5	6	7	8	9	10						11			I Hendrick	37
1	2	3	4	5	6	7		9	10		8				11			D Allison	38
1	2	3	4	5	6	7		9	10		8				11			R Milford	39
1	2	3	4	5	6	7		9	10		8				11			T Spencer	40
1	2	3	4	5	6	7		9	10		8				11			R Banks	41
1	2	3	4	5	6	7		9	10	12	8				11*			N Ashley	42
1	2	3	4	5	6	7		9	10	11	8							J Moules	43
1	2	3	4	5	6	7		9	10		8				11			K Walmsley	44
1	2*	3	4	5	6	7		9	10		8				11		12	D Axcell	45
1		3	4	5	6	7		9	10		8		2		11			N Wilson	46
1		3	4	5	6	7		9	10	11	8*		2				12	M Scott	47
1		3	4	5	6	7		9	10	11	8*		2				12	F Roberts	48
1		3	4	5	6	7		9	10	11*	8		2				12	L Dilkes	49
1		3	4	5	6	7	8	9*	10	11			2				12	N Glover	50
1		3		5	4	7		9	10		8		2		11	12	6*	J Hunting	51
1		3	4	5	6	7		9	10*		8		2		11		12	B Hill	52
1	39	42	45	**46**	33	**46**	31	45	**46**	29	24	5	16	0	17	0	1	League Appearances	
					+1S					+1S	+2S		+3S	+3S	+1S	+4S	+6S		
3	3	3	3	3	3	3	3	1	3	3			1S	2				FA Cup Appearances	
	2	2	2	1	2	2	2	2	2	2	1+1S	1	1S					Milk Cup Appearances	
	1		1	1	1	1	1	1	1	1	1S		1		1S			AM Cup Appearances	

BOOTHAM CRESCENT

Official Address: Bootham Crescent, York. Telephone: York (0904) 24447/32190

Telegraphic: City Football York

Ground Capacity: 13,500

Record Attendance: 28,123 v. Huddersfield Town, F.A. Cup Round 6, 5 Mar 1938

Record Receipts: £17,300 v. Hull City, Div 4, 19 Apr 1983

Size of Playing Area: 115yds × 75 yds

Season Tickets: Stand, Main: £80.00; Popular: £60 (40 junior/OAP)

Executive Box Season Tickets: None

Cost of Stand Tickets, Terraces: £2.00 (£1.00 juniors/OAP)

Match and Ticket Information: On sale fourteen days before each match.

Car Parking: ample parking in side streets.

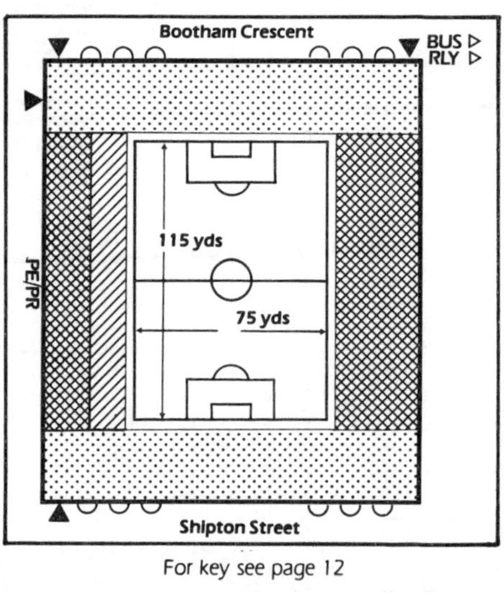

For key see page 12

How to get to the ground

From North: Use A1 then A59 S.P. York. Cross railway bridge and in 1.9m turn left into Water End. At end turn right A19 (S.P. City Centre). In 0.4m turn left into Bootham Crescent for York City F.C.
From East: Use A1079 into York City Centre and follow signs Thirsk A19 into Bootham. Cross railway bridge and then take 2nd turning on right into Bootham Crescent for York City F.C.
From South: Use A64 S.P. York into city centre and follow signs Thirsk A19 into Bootham. Cross railway bridge and then take 2nd turning on right into Bootham Crescent for York City F.C.
From West: Use B1224 S.P. York into city centre and follow signs Thirsk A19 into Bootham. Cross railway bridge and then take 2nd turning on right into Bootham Crescent for York City F.C.

LIVERPOOL HONOURS

Player	European	Domestic	Representative
Bruce Grobbelaar	European Cup 84	Div 1-82, 83, 84. Milk Cup 82, 83, 84	
Gary Gillespie			Scotland U-21 (8)
Alan Hanson (Scottish honour with Partick Thistle)	European Cup 78, 81, 84	Div 1-79, 80, 82, 83, 84. League Cup 81 Milk Cup 83, 84. Scottish Div 1 (1)	Scotland (21) Scotland U-23 (3)
Alan Kennedy	European Cup 81,84	Div 1-79, 80 82, 83, 84 League Cup 81 Milk Cup 82, 83, 84	England (2), England U-23 (6), England 'B' (7)
Mark Lawrenson	European Cup 84	Div 1-82, 83, 84. Milk Cup 82, 83, 84	Eire (25)
Phil Neal	European Cup 77, 78, 81, 84. European Super Cup 77	Div 1-76, 77, 79, 80, 82, 83, 84. League Cup 81. Milk Cup 82, 83, 84	England (50), England 'B' (1), Football League (1)
Phil Thompson	European Cup 78, 81. UEFA Cup 76. European Super Cup 77	Div 1-73, 76, 77, 79, 80, 82, 83, League Cup 81 Milk Cup 82. FA Cup 74	England (42), England U-23 (2)
Craig Johnston	European Cup 84	Div 1-82, 83, 84. Milk Cup 83, 84	England U-21 (2)
Sammy Lee	European Cup 81, 84	Div 1-82, 83, 84. League Cup 81. Milk Cup 82, 83, 84	England (14), England U-21 (6), England Youth
Steve Nicol	European Cup 84	Div 1-84	Scotland U-21 (14)
Ronnie Whelan	European Cup 84	Div 1-82, 83, 84. Milk Cup 82, 83, 84	Eire (7), Eire U-21 (1)
John Wark (with Ipswich Town)	UEFA Cup 81	FA Cup 78, FA Youth Cup 75	Scotland (28), Scotland U-21 (9)
Kenny Dalglish (Scottish honours with Celtic)	European Cup 78, 81, 84. European Super Cup 77	Div 1-79, 80, 82, 83, 84. League Cup 81 Milk Cup 82, 83, 84. Scottish Premier (1), Scottish Div 1 (5), Scottish Cup (4), Scottish League Cup (1)	Scotland (93), Scotland U-23 (4), Scotland Youth (8)
Ian Rush	European Cup 84	Div 1-82, 83, 84. League Cup 81. Milk Cup 82, 83, 84	Wales (20), Wales U-21 (2), Wales Schools
Mike Robinson	European Cup 84	Div 1-84. Milk Cup 84	Eire (16)
Paul Walsh (with Luton Town)			England (5) England U-21 (7), England Youth

LIVERPOOL'S CUP SEASON

P 24 W 16 D 7 L 1 F 45 A 13 HOME P 10 W 7 D 3 L 0 F 24 A

Cup Goalscorers (45)

Milk Cup (25):	Rush 8 (1 pen), Souness 5 (1 pen), Robinson 3, Whelan 3, Dalglish 2, Nicol 2, Hodgson, Neal (pen) 1
FA Cup (4):	Rush 2, Robinson, Johnston
European Cup (16):	Rush 5, Dalglish 3, Robinson 2, Whelan 2, Johnston, Lee, Neal, 1 og
Cup 'Ever Presents':	Bruce Grobbelaar, Alan Kennedy, Alan Hansen, Sammy Lee (24)
Top Cup Goalscorer:	Ian Rush 15

DATE	COMPETITION	VENUE	OPPONENTS	RESULT	HALF TIME	GOALSCORERS	ATTEN DANC
S 14	EC 1:1	A	Odense	W1-0	1-0	Dalglish	28,00
28	EC 1:2	H	Odense	W5-0	3-0	Robinson 2, Dalglish 2, Clausen (og)	14,98
O 5	MC 2:1	A	Brentford	W4-1	1-1	Rush 2, Robinson, Souness	17,85
19	EC 2:1	H	Athletico Bilbao	D0-0	0-0		33,06
25	MC 2:2	H	Brentford	W4-0	1-0	Souness (pen), Dalglish, Hodgson, Robinson	9,09
N 2	EC 2:2	A	Athletico Bilbao	W1-0	0-0	Rush	50,00
9	MC 3	A	Fulham	D1-1	0-0	Rush	20,14
22	MC 3:R	H	Fulham	D1-1†	0-0	Dalglish	15,78
29	MC 3:2R	A	Fulham	W1-0†	0-0	Souness	20,90
D 20	MC 4	A	Birmingham C	D1-1	1-0	Souness	17,40
22	MC 4:R	H	Birmingham C	W3-0	1-0	Nicol, Rush 2 (1 pen)	11,63
J 6	FAC 3	H	Newcastle U	W4-0	2-0	Robinson, Rush 2, Johnston	33,56
17	MC 5	A	Sheffield W	D2-2	1-1	Nicol, Neal (pen)	49,35
25	MC 5:R	H	Sheffield W	W3-0	1-0	Rush 2, Robinson	40,48
29	FAC 4	A	Brighton	L0-2	0-0		19,05
F 7	MC SF:1	H	Walsall	D2-2	1-1	Whelan 2	31,07
14	MC SF:2	A	Walsall	W2-0	1-0	Rush, Whelan	19,59
M 7	EC QF:1	H	Benfica	W1-0	0-0	Rush	39,09
21	EC QF:2	A	Benfica	W4-1	2-0	Whelan 2, Johnston, Rush	80,00
25	MC Final	N	Everton	D0-0†	0-0		100,00
28	MC Final:R	N	Everton	W1-0	1-0	Souness	52,08
A 11	EC SF:1	H	Dinamo Bucharest	W1-0	1-0	Lee	36,94
25	EC SF:2	A	Dinamo Bucharest	W2-1	1-1	Rush 2	60,00
30	EC Final	A	AS Roma	W*1-1†	1-1	Neal	69,69

Average Home Attendance: 26,572 Best Home Attendance: 40,485 Average Away Attendance: 34,756 Best Away Attendance: 80,00

Note: The European Cup Final was counted as an away game as it was played on Liverpool's opponents home ground and the result a full time being 1-1, is recorded as a draw although Liverpool won 4-2 on penalties (scored by Neal, Souness, Rush and Kennedy)

EVERTON'S CUP SEASON

P 19 W 11 D 6 L 2 F 29 A 10 HOME P 7 W 5 D 2 L 0 F 15 A

Cup Goalscorers (29)

Milk Cup (16):	Heath 4, Sharp 3, Sheedy 3, Richardson 2, Irvine, King, Reid, Steven
FA Cup (13):	Gray 3, Sheedy 3, Heath 2, Irvine, Reid, Richardson, Sharp, opponent 1
Cup 'Ever Presents':	Neville Southall, Kevin Ratcliffe (19)
Top Cup Goalscorers:	Adrian Heath, Kevin Sheedy (6)

DATE	COMPETITION	VENUE	OPPONENTS	RESULT	HALF TIME	GOALSCORERS	ATTEN DANC
O 5	MC 2:1	A	Chesterfield	W1-0	1-0	Sharp	10,71
26	MC 2:2	H	Chesterfield	D2-2	1-0	Heath, Steven	8,06
N 9	MC 3	H	Coventry C	W2-1	0-0	Heath, Sharp	9,08
30	MC 4	A	West Ham U	D2-2	1-1	Reid, Sheedy	19,70
D 6	MC 4:R	H	West Ham U	W2-0	0-0	King, Sheedy	21,68
J 7	FAC 3	A	Stoke C	W2-0	0-0	Gray, Irvine	16,46
18	MC 5	A	Oxford U	D1-1	0-0	Heath	14,33
24	MC 5:R	H	Oxford U	W4-1	2-0	Richardson, Sheedy, Heath, Sharp	31,01
28	FAC 4	H	Gillingham	D0-0	0-0		22,38
31	FAC 4:R	A	Gillingham	D0-0†	0-0		15,33
F 6	FAC 4:2R	A	Gillingham	W3-0	3-0	Sheedy 2, Heath	15,94
15	MC SF1	H	Aston Villa	W2-0	1-0	Sheedy, Richardson	40,00
18	FAC 5	H	Shrewsbury T	W3-0	1-0	Irvine, Reid, Griffin (og)	27,10
22	MC SF2	A	Aston Villa	L0-1	0-0		42,42
M 10	FAC 6	A	Notts C	W2-1	1-1	Richardson, Gray	19,53
25	MC Final	N	Liverpool	D0-0†	0-0		100,00
28	MC Final:R	N	Liverpool	L0-1	0-1		52,08
A 14	FAC SF	N	Southampton	W1-0†	0-0	Heath	46,58
M 19	FAC Final	N	Watford	W2-0	1-0	Sharp, Gray	100,00

Average Home Attendance: 22,751 Best Home Attendance: 40,006 Average Away Attendance: 19,306 Best Away Attendance: 42,42

Note: *Original referee injured during the game

1983-84

AWAY P 11 W 7 D 3 L 1 F 19 A 9 NEUTRAL P 3 W 1 D 2 L 0

Grobbelaar	Neal	Kennedy	Lawrenson	Hansen	Dalglish	Lee	Rush	Robinson	Souness	Johnston	Nicol	Hodgson	Whelan	Gillespie	REFEREES
1	2	3	4	6	7	8	9	10	11	5					Gudmundsson
1		3	4	6	7	8	9	10	11	5	2				Bastian
1		3	4	6	7	8	9	10	11	5	2				J Martin
1	2	3	4	6	7	8	9	10	11	5					Bergamon
1	2	3	4	6	7	8		10	11	5		9			P Tydesley
1	2	3	4	6	7	8	9	10*	11		5	12			Prokop
1	2	3	4	6	7	8	9	10	11		5				K Baker
1	2	3	4	6	7	8	9	10*	11	12	5				F Roberts
1	2	3	4	6		8	9	10	11	7	5*		12		G Napthine
1	2	3	4	6	7	8	9		11	10	5				B Hill
1	2	3	4	6	7*	8	9		11	10	5	12			K Hackett
1	2	3	4	6		8	9	7	11	10	5				K Hackett
1	2	3	4	6		8	9	7	11	10	5				M Scott
1	2	3	4	6		8	9	7	11	10	5				M Heath
1	2	3	4	6		8	9	7	11*	10	5		12		B Stevens
1	2	3		6		8	9	7*		10	5	12	11	4	N Ashley
1	2	3	4	6		8	9		11	10		7	5		J Hunting
1	2	3	4	6	12	8	9	7*	11	10			5		Fahnler
1	2	3	4	6	7	8	9		11	10			5		Roth
1	2	3	4	6	7	8	9	12	11	10*			5		Alan Robinson
1	2	3	4	6	7	8	9		11	10			5		Alan Robinson
1	2	3	4	6	7	8	9		11	10			5		Daina
1	2	3	4	6	7*	8	9	12	11	10*	12		5		Pauly
1	2	3	4	5	7*	8	9	12	11	10	12		5		Friedrickson
13	12	13	12	13	8	13	12	8+1	12	11+1	9	2+2	4+1	1	Milk Cup
2	2	2	2	2		2	2	2	2	2	2		+1		FA Cup
9	8	9	9	9	9	9	9	5+2	9	8	1+2	+1	5		European Cup

1983-84

AWAY P 8 W 4 D 3 L 1 F 11 A 5 NEUTRAL P 4 W 2 D 1 L 1 F 3 A 1 1,800 MINUTES OF CUP FOOTBALL

Southall	Harper	Bailey	Ratcliffe	Higgins	Reid	Steven	Heath	Sharp	Richardson	Sheedy	King	Irvine	Stevens	Mountfield	Gray	Johnson	Curran	REFEREES
1	2	3	4	5	6	7	8	9	10	11								H Taylor
1	2	3	4	5		10	8	9	6	11		7						M Peck/E Hart*
1	2	3	4	5	12	6*	8	9		11	10	7						A Challinor
1			3	5	6		8	9		11	10	7	2	4				T Mills
1			3	5	6		8	9		11	10	7	2	4				A Gunn
1		3	4		6		8	9		11		7	2	5	10			M Peck
1	3		4		6		8	9		11		7	2	5		10*		J Hunting
1	3		4		6		8	9	10	11		7	2	5				P Willis
1	3		4		6		8	9		11		7	2	5	10			E Courtney
1		3	4		6		8	9*	10	11		7	2	5	12			I Barrett
1		3	4		6		8		10	11		7	2	5	9			R Lewis
1		3	4		6		8	9	10	11		7	2	5				A Saunders
1		3	4		6		8*			11	10	7	2	5	9			G Napthine
1		3	4		6		8	9		11	10	7	2	5				K Hackett
1		3	4		6			9	8	11		7	2	5	10			J Martin
1		3	4		6		8	9	10	11*		7	2	5				Alan Robinson
1		3	4		6		8	9	10		12	7*	2	5				Alan Robinson
1		3	4		6	10*	8	12	11				2	5	9		7	G Courtney
1		3	4		7	6	8	10	11				2	5	9			J Hunting
11	5	7	11	5	9+1	3	11	11	6	11	4+1	10	8	8	0			Milk Cup
8	1	7	8		8	2	7	5+1	5	6	1	6	8	8	7+1	1		FA Cup

OXFORD UNITED'S RECORD BREAKING CUP SEASON

P 19 W 8 D 8 L 3 F 27 A 22 HOME P 12 W 7 D 3 L 2 F 21 A 14

Cup Goalscorers (27)
Milk Cup (16): Biggins 3, Brock 3, Lawrence 2, McDonald 2, Thomas 2, Vinter 2, Hinshelwood 1, Whatmore 1
FA Cup (10): McDonald 4 (2 pens), Biggins 2, Brock 1, Lawrence 1, Vinter 1, Scott (Burnley) og
Associates Cup (1): Baillie (Swindon Town) og
Cup 'Ever Present': Malcolm Shotton (19)
Top Cup Goalscorer: Bobby McDonald 6 (2 pens)

Note: Apart from the cup ties which they lost against Everton and Sheffield Wednesday, only Manchester United scored First Half goals against Oxford United.

DATE	COMPETITION	VENUE	OPPONENTS	RESULT	HALF TIME	GOALSCORERS	ATTENDANCE
A 31	MC 1:1	H	Bristol C	D1-1	0-0	Brock	3,924
S 12	MC 1:2	A	Bristol C	W1-0	1-0	Thomas	5,163
O 5	MC 2:1	A	Newcastle U	D1-1	1-0	Biggins	21,167
26	MC 2:2	H	Newcastle U	W2-1	2-0	Whatmore, Thomas	13,040
N 9	MC 3	A	Leeds U	D1-1	1-0	Vinter	13,349
19	FAC 1	H	Peterborough U	W2-0	1-0	Biggins, McDonald	6,343
23	MC 3:R	H	Leeds U	W4-1	3-0	Brock, Biggins, Vinter, Lawrence	13,389
29	MC 4	H	Manchester U	D1-1	1-1	McDonald	13,711
D 7	MC 4:R	A	Manchester U	D1-1[1]	0-0	Brock	27,459
10	FAC 2	A	Reading	D1-1	0-0	Biggins	11,590
14	FAC 2:R	H	Reading	W3-0	2-0	Brock, Vinter, McDonald	7,570
19	MC 4:R2	H	Manchester U	W2-1[1]	1-1	Lawrence, Biggins	13,912
J 7	FAC 3	A	Burnley	D0-0	0-0		11,672
11	FAC 3:R	H	Burnley	W2-1	1-0	Lawrence, Scott (og)	10,497
18	MC 5	H	Everton	D1-1	0-0	McDonald	14,333
24	MC 5:R	A	Everton	L1-4	0-2	Hinshelwood	31,011
28	FAC 4	H	Blackpool	W2-1	1-0	McDonald (2 pens)	10,759
F 18	FAC 5	H	Sheffield W	L0-3	0-2		14,167
22	AMC 1	H	Swindon T	L1-3	0-0	Baillie (og)	4,744

Average Home Attendance: 10,532 Best Home Attendance: 14,333 Average Away Attendance: 17,344 Best Away Attendance: 31,011

[1]After Extra Time

PLYMOUTH ARGYLE'S CUP SEASON

P 18 W 10 D 4 L 4 F 25 A 12 HOME P 11 W 7 D 3 L 1 F 22 A 9

Cup Goalscorers (25)
Milk Cup (5): Nisbet 2, Smith, Staniforth, Tynan
FA Cup (11): Tynan 3 (1 pen), Rogers 2, Hodges, Rowe, Smith, Uzzell, Staniforth, opponent
Associates Cup (9): Tynan 4, Hodges 2, Phillips, Rogers, Smith
Cup 'Ever Presents': John Uzzell
Top Cup Goalscorer: Tommy Tynan 8

DATE	COMPETITION	VENUE	OPPONENTS	RESULT	HALF TIME	GOALSCORERS	ATTENDANCE
A 30	MC 1:1	A	Swindon T	L0-1	0-0		3,343
S 13	MC 1:2	H	Swindon T	W4-1	1-1	Smith, Staniforth, Tynan, Nisbet	3,432
O 4	MC 2:1	H	Arsenal	D1-1	1-0	Nisbet	20,983
25	MC 2:2	A	Arsenal	L0-1	0-1		22,640
N 19	FAC 1	A	Southend U	D0-0	0-0		3,408
22	FAC 1	H	Southend U	W2-0	0-0	Stead (og), Tynan	5,570
D 10	FAC 2	H	Barking	W2-1	1-1	Rowe, Smith	4,754
J 7	FAC 3	H	Newport Co	D2-2	0-1	Hodges, Tynan (pen)	6,789
10	FAC 3:R1	A	Newport Co	W1-0	0-0	Rogers	5,549
28	FAC 4	H	Darlington	W2-1	1-1	Uzzell, Staniforth	8,918
F 18	FAC 5	A	W.B.A.	W1-0	0-0	Tynan	23,795
21	MC 1	H	Torquay U	W5-1	2-0	Tynan 2, Hodges 2, Rogers	3,962
M 1	FAC 6	H	Derby Co	D0-0	0-0		34,365
14	FAC 6:R	A	Derby Co	W1-0	1-0	Rogers	26,906
26	AMC 2	H	Brentford	W2-0	0-0	Tynan 2	2,308
A 14	FAC SF	N	Watford	L0-1	0-1		43,858
24	AMC SQF	H	Exeter C	W2-1	1-0	Smith, Phillips	3,715
M 17	AMC SSF	H	Millwall	L0-1	0-0		4,531

Average Home Attendance: 8,929 Best Home Attendance: 34,365 Average Away Attendance: 13,922 Best Away Attendance: 26,906

1983-84

AWAY P 7 W 1 D 5 L 1 F 6 A 8 1,770 MINUTES OF CUP FOOTBALL

Hardwick	Hinshelwood	Grant	Thomas	Briggs	Shotton	Lawrence	Whatmore	Biggins	Hebberd	Brock	Vinter	McDonald	Barnett	Fogg	Jones	Train	Trewick	Rhoades-Brown	Butcher	REFEREES
1	2	3	4*	5	6	7	8	9	10	11	12									E Scales
1	2		4	5	6	7		9	10	11	8*	3	12							L Burden
1	2		4	5	6	7		9	10	11		3	8							N Glover
1			4	5	6	7	9*		10	11		3	8	2	12					C Thomas
1	2		4		6	7*		9	10	11	8	3	12		5					D Richardson
1	2		4	5	6	7		8	10	11	9	3								H King
1	2		4	5	6	7		8	10	11	9	3								M Bodenham
1	2		4	5	6	7		8*	10	11	9	3			12					C Downes
1	2		4	5	6	7		8	10	11	9	3								K Redfern
1	2		4	5	6	7		8	10	11	9	3								J Moules
1	2		4	5	6*	7	12		10	11	9	3	8							J Moules
1	2		4	5	6	7	8*	12	10	11	9	3								T Spencer
1	2			5	6	7	8*	12	10	11	9	3	4							P Willis
1	2			5	6	7		8	10	11	9	3	4							J Deakin
1	2			5	6	7	12	8	10*	11	9	3				4				J Hunting
1	2			5	6	7		8		11	9	3	10*			12	4			P Willis
1	2			5	6	7	8			10	9	3					4	11		J Bray
1	2			5	6	7	12	8	10	4	9	3						11*		T Spencer
	2			5	6		8	9	10			3	7			4		11	1	T Holbrook
11	10	1	9	10	11	11	3+1	9+1	10	11	8+1	10	3+2	1	1+2	1+1	1			Milk Cup
7	7		3	7	7	7	2+2	4+1	6	7	7	7	3				1	2		FA Cup
	1			1	1		1	1	1			1	1			1		1	1	AM Cup

1983-84

AWAY P 6 W 3 D 1 L 2 F 3 A 2 NEUTRAL P 1 W 0 D 0 L 1 F 0 A 1

Crudgington	Nisbett	Uzzell	Harrison	Smith	Swiggs	Forbes	Smith, M	Hodges	Phillips	Tynan	Staniforth	Rogers	Cooper	Rowe	Ham (L)	Chamberlain, N	Pearson	Kellow	REFEREES
1	2	3	4	5		6		7	8	9	10	11							D Vickers
1	2	3	4	5				7		9	10	11	6	8					T Holbrook
1	2	3	4	5				7	12	9	10	11*	6	8					T Spencer
1	2	3	4	5				7	11	9	10		6	8			12		Alan Robinson
1	2	3	4	5				7	11	9			6	8				10	M Bodenham
1	2	3	4	5				7	11	9			6	8				10	M Bodenham
1	2	3		5				7	6	9*	12	11		8	4			10	T Spencer
1	2	3	4	5				7	8	9	10	11	6						D Reeves
1		3	4	5		8*		7	2	9	10	11	6				12		D Reeves
1	2	3	4	5				7	8	9	10	11	6						R Millford
1	2	3	4	5				7	8	9	10	11	6						P Willis
1	2	3	4	5*				7	8	9	10	11	6						J Deakin
1	2	3	4	5				7	8	9	10	11	6						B Stevens
1	2	3	4	5				7	8	9	10	11	6						B Stevens
1	2	3*	4		13		12		8	9		11	6	7*	5	10			J Hunting
1	2	3	4	5				7	8	9	10	11	6						J Worrall
	2	3*	4	5	9			12	8			13	6	11	7	10*			D Letts
1	2	3	4	5				7*	8	12	10	11	6*	13		9			K Baker
4	4	4	4	4				4	2+1	4	4	3	3	3			+1		Milk Cup
10	9	10	9	10		1		10	10	10	7+1	8	9	3	1		+1	3	FA Cup
3	4	4	4	3	1+1		+1	2+1	4	2+1	2	3+1	4	2+1	2	3			AM Cup

No1 v Exeter City, David Philp

DATE: SATURDAY NOV. 26th 1983 MATCH: LEAGUE DIV I

	IPSWICH TOWN		LIVERPOOL
MISTAKE AT FOREST 1.	LAST WEEK PAUL COOPER EVER-PRESENT THIS SEASON AND 30 NEXT MONTH - LEFT FOOTED YOUNG FOR A GOALKEEPER	1.	BRUCE GROBBELAAR PLAYING HIS 79th CONSECUTIVE LEAGUE MATCH - HAS NOT MISSED ONE SINCE DEBUT IN AUG 1981.
2.	GEORGE BURLEY STILL ONLY 27 BUT IT WILL BE TEN YEARS NEXT MONTH SINCE HE MADE HIS DEBUT. STILL TIME FOR SCOTLAND?	OWN GOAL HERE 2 YEARS AGO 2.	PHIL NEAL WINNER OF 50 ENGLAND CAPS WHICH MAY BE HIS FINAL TOTAL - COULD GO ON TO WINNING SIDE - UP AGAINST GALLY?
3.	STEVE McCALL EVER PRESENT AT LEFT BACK BECAUSE GERNON IS STILL RECOVERING (STITCHES OUT) LEFT FOOTED NO GOALS THIS SEASON	3.	ALAN KENNEDY EVER PRESENT THIS SEASON WHEN HE HAS BEEN CLOSE TO A FULL CAP. SCORER OF VITAL GOALS. BUT NONE THIS SEASON
- 4	TREVOR PUTNEY PUTNEY HAS HAD A THIGH STRAIN BUT SHOOK IT OFF. MORE TREATMENT THIS MORNING	4	MARK LAWRENSON SCORER OF TWO GOALS FOR REPUBLIC LAST WEEK BUT NONE FOR LIVERPOOL THIS SEASON LAST ONE EXACTLY A YEAR AGO.
5.	KEVIN STEGGLES KEEPS HIS PLACE EVEN THOUGH OSMAN IS FREE FROM SUSPENSION - "TWO STEADY DISPLAYS" SAYS FERGIE	5.	STEVE NICOL SIZE 12 BOOTS BIGGEST IN DIV ONE! 21 YEAR OLD SCOT WHO HAS PLAYED LAST 7 GAMES ON LEFT SIDE OF MIDFIELD
6	TERRY BUTCHER SCORED IN HIS LAST TWO MATCHES - WITH ENGLAND IN LUXEMBOURG AND FOR IPSWICH AT FOREST - CAPTAIN?	X 6	ALAN HANSEN HAS NOT SCORED A LEAGUE GOAL FOR MORE THAN THREE YEARS (v NORWICH AUG 1980) PLAYS OUT FROM BACK
7.	JOHN WARK JOINT TOP SCORER WITH 10. HAS 93 IN THE LEAGUE FOR IPSWICH IN 278 GAMES. BUT WANTS TO GET AWAY	259th LG 7.	GALLACHER/BAKER KENNY DALGLISH SCORED AGAINST FULHAM ON TUESDAY BUT ALSO GAVE AWAY EQUALISER. NOW LOOKS FOR 100th LGE GOAL. 3 PRD FINNEY
* 8.	MARK BRENNAN 18 YEAR OLD ENGLAND YOUTH INT PLAYING ONLY HIS THIRD LEAGUE GAME TODAY ANOTHER IPSWICH YOUTH PRODUCT	8.	SAMMY LEE EVER PRESENT THIS SEASON BUT HIS ONLY SENIOR GOAL WAS FOR ENGLAND. SKIMMED HERE ON WINNER LAST SEASON.
BOCKET X 9.	PAUL MARINER STILL OFFICIALLY ON TRANSFER LIST - HAS HAD HIS ADMIRERS AT LIVERPOOL OVER THE YEARS. 10 GOALS THIS SEASON	9.	IAN RUSH 16 GOALS FOR LIVERPOOL THIS SEASON PUTS HIM ON COURSE FOR 30 AGAIN (3rd YEAR). 10 GOALS IN THE LAST 7 GAMES
10	ERIC GATES CAME OFF TRANSFER LIST EARLIER THIS YEAR - WILL WARK AND MARINER FOLLOW SUIT?	10	RONNIE WHELAN [crossed out] APR 23rd LAST LGE APP PELVIC OP
11.	KEVIN O'CALLAGHAN EVER PRESENT THIS SEASON AFTER BEING AN ALMOST PERMANENT SUB BEFORE HAS SHOWN BENEFIT MADE WINNER v LIVERPOOL HERE LAST SEASON AS SUB	11.	GRAEME SOUNESS COULD BE QUITE A CONTEST IN CENTRE OF MID BETWEEN HIM AND WARK. (SCOTS INT)
12	MICH D'AVRAY WINNER LAST SEASON HERE	12	David HODGSON
	ROBIN TURNER		
	BOBBY FERGUSON 'RIGHT BALL IN' BEAT THOMSON AIR		JOE FAGAN
	CHARLIE WOODS		RONNIE MORAN
	TOMMY EGGLESTON		ROY EVANS

REFEREE: MARTIN BODENHAM (BRIGHTON)

LINESMEN: PLAYED GOOD ADVANTAGE AT OXFORD v LEEDS

GOALS: IF IPSWICH SCORE :- OF THE 13 GOALS LIVERPOOL HAVE CONCEDED THIS SEASON, 5 HAVE BEEN PENS AND 5 BY MID OR DEF AND ONLY 3 BY STRIKERS STAPLETON, ARCHIBALD, G. ROBERTS.

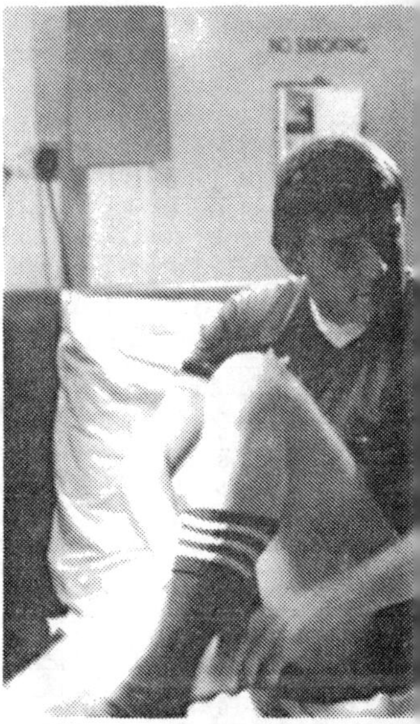

Before John Motson takes up his position to commentate on BBC's 'Match of the Day' programmes he always completes a very thorough 'Match Board' so he is fully prepared for the game ahead.

Both sides of John's board for the Ipswich Town v Liverpool Canon League game can be seen here and it is easy to understand how important statistics and records are for his preparation.

So for those readers who enjoy playing around with figures and indeed searching out pre-match relevant points of interest as John does (Steve Nicol wears size 12 boots, the biggest in the First Division!) we are inviting you to submit your own 'Match Boards' for any match that is scheduled to be televised this season.

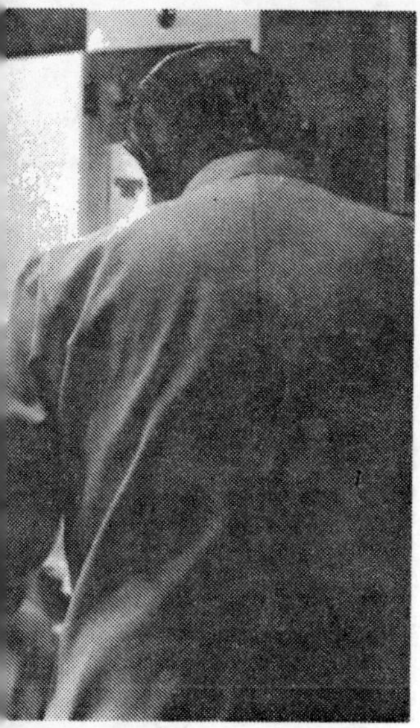

John Motson has been 'in love' with the game since he was a lad and even now, despite a very busy schedule, he regularly plays for the commentators' eleven on Sundays. Here you can see his worried look as he waits for the go-ahead for the big game after a strenuous 'medical'!

LIVERPOOL HAVE LOST ON FIVE OF THEIR LAST NINE VISITS TO PORTMAN ROAD IN THE LEAGUE

THIS INCLUDES THE LAST TWO SEASONS WHEN IPSWICH HAVE WON 2-0. 1-0. (3 IN A ROW?)

HOWEVER LIVERPOOL HAVE WON HERE IN MILK CUP IN LAST TWO SEASONS, 2-0. 2-1.

LIVERPOOL WENT TOP TWO WEEKS AGO AND ARE 6-4 ON TO WIN THEIR 15th CHAMPIONSHIP

IPSWICH ARE 12th IN THE TABLE HAVING LOST 6 OF THEIR LAST 9 LEAGUE MATCHES

BOTH CLUBS IN MILK CUP NEXT WEEK - LIVERPOOL AT FULHAM (TUES). IPSWICH HOME TO NORWICH (WED)

SINCE THE CHARITY SHIELD, LIVERPOOL HAVE LOST ONLY 2 OUT OF 22 MATCHES (MANOTT SUSPENDED).

THEY HAVE KEPT CLEAN SHEETS IN 12 OF THOSE GAMES AND ARE UNBEATEN IN LAST 12 (W8 D4)

THE CROWD FOR THIS MATCH LAST SEASON WAS 24.342 (AVERAGE THIS SEASON 18.500 HERE)

IF LIVERPOOL WIN TODAY THEY GO FOUR POINTS CLEAR AT THE TOP - ALBEIT FOR ONLY 24 HOURS

IPSWICH SCORERS: WARK 10. MARINER 10. GATES 6. O'CALLAGHAN 2.

BURLEY 1. OSMAN 1. BUTCHER 1. TURNER 1.

LIVERPOOL SCORERS: RUSH 16 (+2 FOR WALES). ROBINSON 9. DALGLISH 8. SOUNESS 3.

NICOL 2. HODGSON 1. JOHNSTON 1

The senders of the best three, in John Motson's opinion, will be sent next year's League Club Directory free of charge.

Entries should be sent to: The Editorial Office, The League Club Directory, 4 Rosen Court, Turners Drive, Thatcham, Newbury, Berkshire RG13 4DF.

ASSOCIATE MEMBERS' CUP 1983-4

The Associate Members' Cup was introduced during the latter weeks of the 1983/84 season for Third and Fourth Division clubs. The tournament was organised on a regional basis with the winners' of the Northern and Southern finals meeting to decide the ultimate winners of the trophy.

There were no replays. Where scores were level after extra-time, ties were decided on penalties.

The first round was played on a straight knockout basis but there was an early incentive to play attacking football. *The two losing clubs in the second round of both regional competitions, who had scored the highest number of goals in the first two rounds, also earned a place in the quarter-finals.

Northern Section Results

First round

Bradford City	3	Hartlepool	2
Burnley	2	Bolton	1
Bury	1	Wigan	0
Chester	2	Blackpool	1
Lincoln	0	Doncaster	2
Mansfield	1	Darlington	3
Rochdale	0	Preston	3
Rotherham	0	Sheffield United	1
Scunthorpe	2	Chesterfield	1
Stockport	2	Crewe	2

(Crewe won 3-0 on penalties)

Tranmere	2	Halifax	0
York	1	Hull	2

Second round

Burnley	2	Darlington	1
Doncaster	2	Preston	1
Hull	1	Bury	0
Scunthorpe	4	Crewe	4

(Crewe won 7-6 on penalties)

Sheffield United	2	Bradford City	1
Tranmere	4	Chester	1

Quarter-finals

Doncaster	1	Burnley	3
Hull	3	Preston*	0
Scunthorpe*	2	Sheffield United	3
Tranmere	0	Crewe	0

(Tranmere won 4-3 on penalties)

Semi-finals

Hull	1	Sheffield United	0
Tranmere	2	Burnley	0

Final

Hull	4	Tranmere	1

National Final

Hull	1	Bournemouth	2

Southern Section Results

First round

Bournemouth	4	Aldershot	0
Brentford	3	Orient	2
Colchester	2	Wimbledon	1
Exeter	3	Bristol City	0
Hereford	0	Port Vale	1
Millwall	4	Gillingham	3
Newport	0	Bristol Rovers	1
Plymouth	5	Torquay	1
Oxford	1	Swindon	3
Southend	5	Reading	0
Walsall	3	Northampton	1
Wrexham	3	Peterborough	2

Second round

Bristol Rovers	2	Port Vale	0
Colchester	0	Southend	2
Millwall	2	Bournemouth	2

(Bournemouth won 7-6 on penalties)

Plymouth	2	Brentford	0
Swindon	3	Walsall	0
Wrexham	2	Exeter	0

Quarter-finals

Bournemouth	2	Wrexham	
Millwall*	3	Swindon	
Plymouth	2	Exeter*	1
Southend	1	Bristol Rovers	2

Semi-finals

Bournemouth	1	Bristol Rovers	0
Plymouth	0	Millwall	1

Final

Bournemouth	2	Millwall	1

THE CENTRAL LEAGUE 1983-4

For reserve teams of Midland and Northern League Clubs

Division One	P	W	D	L	Goals For	Goals Agt	Pts
Liverpool	30	18	7	5	57	33	61
Manchester United	30	17	6	7	64	34	57
Aston Villa	30	16	6	8	50	29	54
Nottingham Forest	30	14	10	6	60	38	52
Everton	30	16	3	11	53	35	51
West Bromwich Albion	30	14	7	9	46	35	49
Newcastle United	30	14	7	9	44	37	49
Derby County	30	11	7	12	45	42	40
Stoke City	30	11	6	13	52	59	39
Sheffield Wednesday	30	11	5	14	52	61	38
Blackburn Rovers	30	10	6	14	38	46	36
Sheffield United	30	10	6	14	38	59	36
Sunderland	30	9	3	18	36	54	30
Leeds United	30	7	7	16	37	51	28
Bolton Wanderers	30	8	3	19	35	68	27
Burnley	30	5	9	16	19	45	24

Division Two	P	W	D	L	Goals For	Goals Agt	Pts
Bradford City	30	18	5	7	64	38	59
Huddersfield Town	30	17	2	11	58	49	53
Coventry City	30	15	6	9	54	30	51
Manchester City	30	15	5	10	60	36	50
Notts County	30	15	4	11	61	40	49
Barnsley	30	13	10	7	52	41	49
Oldham Athletic	30	13	6	11	46	44	45
Port Vale	30	12	6	12	37	46	42
Wolverhampton Wanderers	30	11	8	11	36	38	41
Chesterfield	30	10	9	11	40	42	39
Blackpool	30	12	3	15	51	70	39
Grimsby Town	30	10	8	12	53	46	38
Middlesbrough	30	9	9	12	44	63	36
Rotherham United	30	10	1	19	39	62	31
Preston North End	30	8	6	16	38	71	30
Wigan Athletic	30	6	4	20	40	57	22

THE FOOTBALL COMBINATION 1983-4

For reserve teams of League Clubs in the South

	P	W	D	L	Goals For	Goals Agt	Pts
Arsenal	42	29	8	5	96	30	66
Watford	42	28	6	8	94	50	62
Chelsea	42	25	5	12	84	38	55
Queens Park Rangers	42	23	9	10	80	37	55
West Ham United	42	21	11	10	105	50	53
Southampton	42	20	12	10	75	51	52
Tottenham Hotspur	42	21	8	13	110	64	50
Norwich City	42	20	10	12	78	45	50
Luton Town	42	19	11	12	78	54	49
Ipswich Town	42	20	8	14	67	53	48
Leicester City	42	18	9	15	96	63	45
Brighton & Hove Albion	42	19	7	16	74	65	45
Fulham	42	17	6	19	71	73	40
Millwall	42	17	6	19	60	77	40
Birmingham City	42	16	5	21	75	83	37
Swansea City	42	15	5	22	70	95	35
Charlton Athletic	42	11	11	20	46	88	33
Oxford United	42	11	10	21	56	87	32
Bristol Rovers	42	9	6	27	60	112	24
Crystal Palace	42	5	12	25	32	101	22
Swindon Town	42	6	8	28	42	111	20
Reading	42	3	5	34	31	153	11

FIAT PERFORMANCE OF THE WEEK AWARDS, 1983-84

DATE	PERFORMANCE	COMPETITION
27.08.83	Watford 2 **Coventry City 3**	Division 1
03.09.83	**Wimbledon 6** Newport County 0	Division 3
10.09.83	**Bolton Wanderers 8** Walsall 1	Division 3
17.09.83	Stoke City 0 **Watford 4**	Division 1
24.09.83	Wolves 0 **Q.P.R. 4**	Division 1
01.10.83	Liverpool 0 **Sunderland 1**	Division 1
05.10.83	Leeds United 0 **Chester City 1**	Milk Cup
15.10.83	West Ham United 1 **Liverpool 3**	Division 1
22.10.83	Hull City 1 **Plymouth Argyle 2**	Division 3
29.10.83	Aston Villa 2 **Arsenal 6**	Division 1
02.11.83	Levski Spartak 1 **Watford 3**	U.E.F.A. Cup
12.11.83	York City 2 **Torquay United 3**	Division 4
19.11.83	Southampton 0 **Notts County 2**	Division 1
26.11.83	W.B.A. 1 **Wolves 3**	Division 1
29.11.83	Arsenal 1 **Walsall 2**	Milk Cup
10.12.83	**Coventry City 4** Liverpool 0	Division 1
17.12.83	Chelsea 2 **Grimsby Town 3**	Division 2
31.12.83	Portsmouth 1 **Fulham 4**	Division 2
07.01.84	**Bournemouth 2** Manchester United 0	F.A. Cup
14.01.84	Liverpool 0 **Wolves 1**	Division 1
21.01.84	Ipswich Town 1 **Birmingham City 2**	Division 1
28.01.84	**Shrewsbury Town 2** Ipswich Town 0	F.A. Cu
03.02.84	Exeter City 0 **Bradford City 2**	Division
07.02.84	Liverpool 2 **Walsall 2**	Milk Cu
18.02.84	W.B.A. 0 **Plymouth Argyle 1**	F.A. Cu
25.02.84	Nottingham Forest 0 **Arsenal 1**	Division
02.03.84	Grimsby Town 3 **Portsmouth 4**	Division
10.03.84	Birmingham City 1 **Watford 3**	F.A. Cu
14.03.84	Derby County 0 **Plymouth Argyle 1**	F.A. Cu
21.03.84	**Manchester United 3** Barcelona 0	E.C.W.C
31.03.84	Manchester City 0 **Charlton Athletic 1**	Division
07.04.84	Wimbledon 1 **Hull City 4**	Division
14.04.84	**Stoke City 2** Liverpool 0	Division
21.04.84	Blackpool 0 **Tranmere Rovers 1**	Division
28.04.84	**Cambridge United 1** Newcastle United 0	Division
05.05.84	Sheffield United 1 **Wimbledon 2**	Division
09.05.84	Anderlecht 1 **Tottenham Hotspur 1**	U.E.F.A. Cu

FIAT/FLESA CLUB OF THE YEAR AWARDS — 198

First: Watford Second: Liverpool Third: Shrewsbury Town Fourth: Hull City

PLAYER'S AWARDS 1983-84

Football Writers Footballer of the Year: Ian Rush.

PFA Player of the Year: Ian Rush (Liverpool).

PFA Young Player of the Year: Paul Walsh (Luton Town).

PFA Merit Award: Bill Nicholson.

The following four teams were selected by the Professional Footballers' Association to represent the divisions of the Football League.

Division One: Peter Shilton (Southampton), Mike Duxbury (Manchester United), Mark Lawrenson (Liverpool), Alan Hansen (Liverpool), Kenny Sansom (Arsenal), Bryan Robson (Manchester United), Graeme Souness (Liverpool), Glenn Hoddle (Tottenham Hotspur), Ian Rush (Liverpool), Kenny Dalglish (Liverpool), Frank Stapleton (Manchester United).

Division Two: Alex Williams (Manchester City), Mel Sterland (Sheffield Wednesday), Mike McCarthy (Manchester City), Mick Lyons (Sheffield Wednesday), Joey Jones (Chelsea), Gary Megson (Sheffield Wednesday), Jimmy Case (Brighton & Hove Albion), Tony Grealish (Brighton & Hove Albion), Kerry Dixon (Chelsea), Kevin Keegan (Newcastle United), Mark Hateley (Portsmouth).

Division Three: David Felgate (Lincoln City), Gordon Nisbet (Plymouth Argyle), Steve Bruce (Gillingham), Malcolm Shotton (Oxford United), Bobby McDonald (Oxford United), Trevor Hebberd (Oxford United), Kevin Brock (Oxford United), Brian Flynn (Burnley), Keith Edwards (Sheffield United), Billy Hamilton (Burnley), Colin Morris (Sheffield United).

Division Four: Roger Jones (York City), Chris Price (Hereford United), Colin Greenall (Blackpool), John MacPhail (York City), Steve Richardson (Reading), Ian Snodin (Doncaster Rovers), Jimmy Harvey (Hereford United), Trevor Quow (Peterborough United), Trevor Senior (Reading), John Byrne (York City), Keith Walwyn (York City).

BELL'S SCOTCH WHISKY FOOTBALL MANAGERS AWARDS — SEASON 1983/84

BELL'S MANAGER OF THE YEAR: Joe Fagan (Liverpool)
SPECIAL AWARDS: Howard Kendall (Everton); **Alex Ferguson** (Aberdeen)

DIVISIONAL MANAGERS OF THE SEASON

The Football League named as Divisional Managers of the Season: **John Neal** of Chelsea in Division Two; **Jim Smith** of Oxford United in Division Three; and **Denis Smith** of York City in Division Four.

SEPTEMBER Manager of the Month

JOHN LYALL		West Ham United
Divisional Awards		
Div 2	Howard Wilkinson	Sheffield Wed.
Div 3	Jim Smith	Oxford United
Div 4	Jim Iley	Bury

OCTOBER Manager of the Month

RON ATKINSON		Manchester United
Div 2	John Neal	Chelsea
Div 3	Alan Buckley	Walsall
Div 4	Cyril Lea	Colchester United

NOVEMBER Manager of the Month

KEN BROWN		Norwich City
Div 2	Howard Wilkinson	Sheffield Wed.
Div 3	Alan Buckley	Walsall
Div 4	Denis Smith	York

DECEMBER Manager of the Month

JIM SMITH		Oxford United
Div 1	Lawrie McMenemy	Southampton
Div 2	Bob Stokoe	Carlisle
Div 4	Terry Cooper	Bristol City

JANUARY Manager of the Month

GRAHAM TAYLOR		Watford
Div 2	Chris Cattlin	Brighton
Div 3	Alan Buckley	Walsall
Div 4	Billy Bremner	Doncaster Rovers

FEBRUARY Manager of the Month

HOWARD KENDALL		Everton
Div 2	David Booth	Grimsby Town
Div 3	John Hore	Plymouth Argyle
Div 4	Len Walker	Aldershot

MARCH Manager of the Month

JOE FAGAN		Liverpool
Div 2	Arthur Cox	Newcastle
Div 3	Ian Porterfield	Sheffield United
Div 4	John Newman	Hereford United

APRIL Manager of the Month

TERRY VENABLES		Queen's Park Rangers
Div 2	John Neal	Chelsea
Div 3	Dave Bassett	Wimbledon
Div 4	Denis Smith	York City

CANON LEAGUE FIXTURES 1984-5

DIVISION ONE

	ARSENAL	ASTON VILLA	CHELSEA	COVENTRY	EVERTON	IPSWICH	LEICESTER	LIVERPOOL	LUTON	MAN UTD	NEWCASTLE	NORWICH	NOTT'M FOR	Q.P.R.	SHEFF WED	SOUTHAMPTON	STOKE	SUNDERLAND	TOTTENHAM	WATFORD	WEST BROM	WEST HAM
ARSENAL		10.11	25.08	02.02	06.10	12.01	16.03	08.09	01.12	23.02	04.09	06.04	13.04	17.11	27.04	06.05	22.09	20.10	01.01	22.12	15.12	02.03
ASTON VILLA	16.02		08.09	25.08	16.03	02.02	02.03	15.12	06.05	06.10	22.12	20.10	05.09	27.04	06.04	17.11	13.04	01.12	22.09	12.01	01.01	03.11
CHELSEA	19.01	09.02		03.11	**31.08**	27.10	29.09	01.12	13.04	29.12	16.02	23.03	01.01	06.04	06.05	09.03	15.12	27.08	27.04	13.10	17.11	15.09
COVENTRY	29.09	19.01	23.02		09.02	10.11	01.09	06.05	06.04	15.09	13.10	28.08	17.11	09.03	27.10	15.12	01.01	13.04	01.12	23.03	27.04	29.12
EVERTON	23.03	13.10	22.12	08.09		04.09	03.11	09.03	01.01	27.10	12.01	27.04	15.12	06.05	01.12	22.09	17.11	06.04	25.08	02.02	13.04	16.02
IPSWICH	15.09	29.09	02.03	16.02	29.12		09.02	27.04	28.08	01.09	23.03	01.01	06.04	13.10	13.04	01.12	06.05	15.12	17.11	03.11	20.10	19.01
LEICESTER	13.10	27.10	02.02	23.12	23.02	08.09		06.04	15.12	10.11	25.08	17.11	27.04	01.12	09.03	01.01	12.01	06.05	13.04	05.09	22.09	23.03
LIVERPOOL	09.02	11.05	04.05	04.12	20.10	24.11	26.12		29.12	**31.03**	20.04	19.01	02.03	01.09	29.09	10.11	23.02	15.09	16.03	08.04	06.10	27.08
LUTON	04.05	08.12	22.09	26.12	09.04	30.03	11.05	04.09		20.04	03.11	16.02	12.01	23.03	13.10	08.09	25.08	02.03	02.02	20.10	18.12	24.11
MAN UTD	**02.11**	23.03	05.09	12.01	02.03	22.12	16.02	22.09	17.11		08.09	01.12	06.05	15.12	01.01	13.04	06.04	27.04	20.10	25.08	02.02	13.10
NEWCASTLE	29.12	01.09	10.11	16.03	15.09	06.10	19.01	**18.11**	23.02	09.02		15.12	20.10	13.04	27.08	27.04	01.12	01.01	06.05	02.03	06.04	29.09
NORWICH	26.12	09.03	06.10	30.03	24.11	08.04	20.04	25.08	10.11	04.05	11.05		02.02	27.10	23.02	12.01	08.09	16.03	22.12	22.09	05.09	08.12
NOTT'M FOR	29.08	29.12	10.04	20.04	11.05	26.12	25.11	**28.10**	16.09	08.12	09.03	29.09		09.02	19.01	23.02	06.10	01.09	10.11	04.05	16.03	30.03
Q.P.R.	20.04	24.11	26.12	20.10	08.12	16.03	04.05	22.12	06.10	11.05	22.09	02.03	08.09		10.11	02.02	04.09	23.02	12.01	30.03	25.08	08.04
SHEFF WED	**25.11**	26.12	08.12	02.03	04.05	22.09	20.10	02.02	16.03	09.04	30.03	03.11	25.08	16.02		04.09	22.12	06.10	08.09	20.04	12.01	11.05
SOUTHAMPTON	08.12	20.04	20.10	11.05	30.03	04.05	09.04	16.02	09.02	28.08	24.11	15.09	03.11	29.09	29.12		16.03	19.01	06.10	26.12	02.03	01.09
STOKE	30.03	27.08	11.05	08.04	20.04	08.12	15.09	03.11	19.01	26.12	04.05	09.02	23.03	29.12	01.09	13.10		29.09	02.03	24.11	16.02	20.10
SUNDERLAND	09.03	04.05	30.03	22.09	26.12	11.05	08.12	12.01	27.10	24.11	08.04	13.10	23.12	03.11	23.03	25.08	02.02		04.09	16.02	08.09	20.04
TOTTENHAM	08.04	30.03	24.11	04.05	19.01	20.04	27.08	**12.10**	29.09	09.03	08.12	01.09	16.02	15.09	09.02	23.03	27.10	29.12		11.05	03.11	26.12
WATFORD	01.09	15.09	16.03	06.10	29.09	23.02	29.12	01.01	09.03	19.01	27.10	13.04	01.12	28.08	17.11	06.04	27.04	10.11	15.12		07.05	09.02
WEST BROM	11.05	08.04	20.04	24.11	27.08	09.03	30.03	23.03	01.09	29.09	26.12	29.12	13.10	19.01	15.09	27.10	10.11	09.02	23.02	08.12		04.05
WEST HAM	27.10	23.02	12.01	04.09	10.11	25.08	06.10	13.04	27.04	**15.03**	02.02	06.05	22.09	01.01	15.12	22.12	09.03	17.11	06.04	08.09	01.12	

Dates in **bold** indicate matches to be televised live

DIVISION TWO

	BARNSLEY	BIRMINGHAM	BLACKBURN	BRIGHTON	CARDIFF	CARLISLE	CHARLTON	CRYSTAL PAL	FULHAM	GRIMSBY	HUDDERSFIELD	LEEDS	MAN CITY	MIDDLESBRO	NOTTS CO	OLDHAM	OXFORD	PORTSMOUTH	SHEFFIELD UTD	SHREWSBURY	WIMBLEDON	WOLVES
BARNSLEY		27.04	01.01	09.03	15.09	27.08	27.10	23.03	01.12	19.01	13.04	13.10	06.04	16.02	29.12	01.09	15.12	09.02	03.11	17.11	06.05	29.09
BIRMINGHAM	24.11		13.10	23.03	04.05	15.09	20.04	09.02	29.12	26.12	29.09	11.05	16.02	08.12	09.03	19.01	27.10	18.09	08.04	03.11	01.09	30.03
BLACKBURN	08.04	16.03		10.11	18.09	01.09	24.11	19.01	09.02	15.09	29.12	26.12	02.03	20.04	30.03	20.10	23.02	04.05	08.12	06.10	29.09	11.05
BRIGHTON	20.10	06.10	16.02		09.02	19.01	08.04	15.09	29.09	08.12	01.09	20.04	03.11	24.11	28.08	29.03	16.03	26.12	11.05	02.03	29.12	04.05
CARDIFF	12.01	01.12	13.04	08.09		17.11	25.08	06.05	09.03	27.10	27.04	12.09	22.09	02.02	17.03	10.11	06.04	06.10	22.12	01.01	15.12	23.02
CARLISLE	30.03	12.01	23.12	25.08	20.04		03.05	13.10	03.11	09.03	27.10	16.02	08.09	26.12	24.11	11.05	02.02	08.12	22.09	04.09	23.03	08.04
CHARLTON	02.03	17.11	27.04	01.01	19.01	30.11		06.04	13.10	29.12	28.08	03.11	15.12	22.03	01.09	15.09	07.05	29.09	16.02	20.10	13.04	09.02
CRYSTAL PAL	07.10	08.09	25.08	12.01	09.12	17.03	26.12		27.10	11.05	10.11	22.09	02.02	04.05	08.04	25.11	26.01	20.04	30.03	06.11	24.02	09.03
FULHAM	04.05	04.09	08.09	02.02	20.10	23.02	16.03	02.03		20.04	06.10	30.03	22.12	22.09	11.05	08.12	12.01	08.04	26.12	25.08	10.11	24.11
GRIMSBY	25.08	05.04	12.01	07.05	02.03	20.10	04.09	15.12	17.11		01.01	08.09	13.04	21.12	23.02	06.10	22.09	16.03	02.02	01.12	27.04	10.11
HUDDERSFIELD	22.09	02.02	04.09	22.12	24.11	02.03	30.03	16.02	23.03	09.04		20.10	12.01	03.11	20.04	26.12	25.08	11.05	04.05	08.09	13.10	08.12
LEEDS	16.03	15.12	06.04	17.11	29.12	10.11	23.02	13.04	27.08	09.02	09.03		01.01	27.10	19.01	29.09	27.04	15.09	06.10	06.05	01.12	01.09
MAN CITY	26.12	10.11	27.10	23.02	30.03	09.02	11.05	29.09	01.09	27.08	15.09	08.04		09.03	08.12	04.05	06.10	24.11	20.04	16.03	19.01	29.12
MIDDLESBRO	10.11	06.05	17.11	27.04	29.09	06.04	06.10	01.12	13.04	01.09	23.02	02.03	20.10		09.02	29.12	01.01	19.01	16.03	15.12	18.09	15.09
NOTTS CO	04.09	20.10	22.09	14.04	14.10	27.04	22.12	01.01	16.12	03.11	17.11	25.08	06.05	08.09		02.03	01.12	16.02	12.01	02.02	06.04	23.03
OLDHAM	21.12	25.08	09.03	22.09	15.02	15.12	12.01	27.04	06.05	23.03	06.04	02.02	01.12	02.10	27.10		17.11	03.11	08.09	13.04	01.01	13.10
OXFORD	11.05	02.03	03.11	13.10	26.12	29.09	08.12	29.12	15.09	30.03	19.01	24.11	23.03	08.04	04.05	20.04		01.09	20.10	16.02	09.02	19.09
PORTSMOUTH	08.09	13.04	01.12	06.04	23.03	06.05	02.02	17.11	01.01	13.10	15.12	12.01	27.04	25.08	10.11	23.02	22.12		02.10	22.09	09.03	27.10
SHEFFIELD UTD	23.02	01.01	06.05	15.12	01.09	13.04	10.11	18.09	06.04	29.09	01.12	23.03	17.11	13.10	15.09	09.02	09.03	29.12		27.04	27.10	19.01
SHREWSBURY	20.04	23.02	23.03	27.10	09.04	29.12	09.03	01.09	19.01	04.05	09.02	08.12	13.10	11.05	29.09	18.09	10.11	30.03	24.11		15.09	26.12
WIMBLEDON	08.12	22.12	02.02	02.10	11.05	06.10	22.09	04.11	16.02	24.11	16.03	04.05	25.08	30.03	26.12	08.04	08.09	20.10	02.03	12.01		20.04
WOLVES	02.02	22.09	15.12	01.12	03.11	01.01	08.09	20.10	27.04	16.02	06.05	22.12	04.09	12.01	06.10	16.03	13.04	02.03	25.08	06.04	17.11	

DIVISION THREE

	BOURNEMOUTH	BOLTON	BRADFORD CITY	BRENTFORD	BRISTOL CITY	BRISTOL ROV	BURNLEY	CAMBRIDGE	DERBY	DONCASTER	GILLINGHAM	HULL	LINCOLN	MILLWALL	NEWPORT	ORIENT	PLYMOUTH	PRESTON	READING	ROTHERHAM	SWANSEA	WALSALL	WIGAN	YORK
BOURNEMOUTH		16 03	26 04	24 11	15 12	02 02	06 10	06 04	25 08	22 09	01 01	12 01	09 03	06 05	16 02	21 12	26 01	27 10	23 02	08 09	02 10	13 04	06 11	23 10
BOLTON	13 10		06 05	27 04	05 03	25 08	02 03	22 12	12 01	02 02	24 11	08 09	03 11	15 12	13 04	01 01	22 09	20 10	23 03	26 01	16 02	02 10	06 04	06 11
BRADFORD CITY	01 12	29 12		23 03	20 10	13 02	20 04	25 08	10 11	26 12	02 03	03 10	11 05	03 11	22 09	02 02	30 03	06 03	04 05	08 04	26 01	08 09	12 01	13 10
BRENTFORD	20 04	01 12	06 10		23 02	26 12	05 03	02 02	30.03	02 10	20 10	11 05	10 11	16 03	26 01	25 08	08 04	04 05	29 12	12 02	22 09	12 01	08 09	27 10
BRISTOL CITY	04 05	23 10	09 03	03 11		10 11	29 12	26 01	12 02	30 03	13 10	08 04	01 12	02 03	12 01	22 09	26 12	20 04	11 05	02 10	08 09	02 02	25 08	23 03
BRISTOL ROV	29 09	05 01	18 09	06 04	13 04		19 01	01 01	06 10	20 10	07 05	27 10	09 02	24 11	15 12	27 04	23 02	01 09	15 09	16 03	22 12	06 11	05 03	16 02
BURNLEY	23 03	27 10	24 11	23 10	06 05	?? ??		13 04	26 01	12 01	06 11	22 09	13 10	27 04	02 10	16 02	25 08	23 02	09 03	02 02	15 12	22 12	01 01	06 04
CAMBRIDGE	26 12	11 05	05 01	29 09	15 09	08 04	10 11		01 12	05 03	19 01	30 03	12 02	01 09	23 02	16 03	04 05	18 09	20 04	29 12	27 10	06 10	19 10	09 02
DERBY	05 01	01 09	13 04	07 11	19 09	23 03	15 09	27 04		03 11	06 04	20 10	29 09	16 02	22 12	15 12	13 10	19 01	09 02	02 03	06 05	06 03	24 11	01 01
DONCASTER	09 02	29 09	06 04	16 02	06 11	08 03	01 09	23 10	22 02		22 12	16 03	14 09	18 09	27 04	06 05	26 10	05 01	19 01	07 10	24 11	01 01	14 12	14 04
GILLINGHAM	09 04	20 04	27 10	09 03	16 03	29 12	29 03	08 09	26 12	11 05		12 02	04 05	06 10	25 08	12 01	02 10	01 12	23 10	10 11	02 02	22 09	26 01	23 02
HULL	01 09	19 01	16 02	22 12	01 01	02 03	09 02	06 11	09 03	13 10	18 09		05 01	06 04	24 11	13 04	23 03	15 09	29 09	03 11	23 10	15 12	27 04	06 05
LINCOLN	20 10	23 02	22 12	13 04	27 04	22 09	16 03	03 10	02 02	25 01	15 12	25 08		06 03	07 11	06 04	08 09	06 10	27 10	12 01	01 01	06 05	16 02	24 11
MILLWALL	29 12	04 05	23 02	13 10	27 10	20 04	30 11	12 01	02 10	12 02	23 03	12 03	23 10		02 02	09 09	11 05	10 11	09 04	29 03	25 08	26 01	22 09	09 03
NEWPORT	18 09	10 11	09 02	15 09	01 09	04 05	12 02	03 11	11 05	01 12	05 01	20 04	30 03	29 09		20 10	29 12	08 04	26 12	05 03	13 10	02 03	23 03	20 01
ORIENT	11 05	09 04	29 09	05 01	09 02	30 11	18 09	13 10	04 05	29 12	01 09	10 11	26 12	19 01	09 03		23 10	12 02	30 03	20 04	23 03	03 11	02 03	15 09
PLYMOUTH	15 09	09 02	06 11	01 01	05 04	03 11	05 01	15 12	16 03	02 03	16 02	06 10	19 01	21 12	06 05	05 03		29 9	01 09	20 10	27 04	24 11	13 04	18 09
PRESTON	02 03	09 03	23 10	15 12	24 11	12 01	03 11	16 02	08 09	25 08	27 04	26 01	23 03	13 04	01 01	02 10	02 02		13 10	22 09	06 11	06 04	06 05	21 12
READING	03 11	06 10	15 12	06 05	22 12	26 01	20 10	24 11	22 09	08 09	06 03	02 02	02 03	01 01	06 04	07 11	12 01	16 03		25 08	13 04	16 02	03 10	27 04
ROTHERHAM	19 01	15 09	01 01	18 09	16 02	13 10	29 09	06 05	27 10	23 03	13 04	23 02	01 09	06 11	23 10	24 11	09 03	09 02	05 01		06 04	27 04	22 12	15 12
SWANSEA	12 02	18 09	15 09	09 02	18 01	11 05	04 05	25 02	29 12	20 04	29 09	05 03	09 04	05 01	17 03	06 10	01 12	30 03	10 11	26 12		20 10	03 11	01 09
WALSALL	10 11	12 02	19 01	01 09	29 09	30 03	11 05	23 03	23 10	08 04	09 02	04 05	29 12	15 09	27 10	23 02	20 04	26 12	18 09	01 12	09 03		13 10	05 01
WIGAN	30 03	26 12	01 09	19 01	05 01	23 10	09 04	09 03	20 04	04 05	15 09	01 12	18 09	09 02	06 10	27 10	10 11	29 12	12 02	11 05	23 02	16 03		29 09
YORK	05 03	29 03	17 03	02 03	06 10	02 10	26 12	22 09	08 04	11 11	03 11	29 12	20 04	20 10	08 09	26 01	12 02	11 05	01 12	04 05	12 01	25 08	02 02	

DIVISION FOUR

	ALDERSHOT	BLACKPOOL	BURY	CHESTER	CHESTERFIELD	COLCHESTER	CREWE	DARLINGTON	EXETER	HALIFAX	HARTLEPOOL	HEREFORD	MANSFIELD	NORTHAMPTON	PETERBOROUGH	PORT VALE	ROCHDALE	SCUNTHORPE	SOUTHEND	STOCKPORT	SWINDON	TORQUAY	TRANMERE	WREXHAM
ALDERSHOT		23 03	13 10	01 09	05 01	09 02	26 12	29 09	15 09	19 01	01 12	11 05	23 10	09 03	18 09	10 11	12 02	23 02	27 10	30 03	20 04	09 04	04 05	29 12
BLACKPOOL	06 10		20 10	29 09	09 02	19 01	09 04	15 09	01 09	05 01	29 12	20 04	01 12	27 10	30 03	18 09	26 12	16 03	23 02	10 11	12 02	04 05	05 03	11 05
BURY	16 03	09 03		19 01	29 09	15 09	10 11	05 01	09 02	01 09	08 04	23 10	20 04	23 02	11 05	26 12	29 03	27 10	06 10	12 02	18 09	01 12	29 12	04 05
CHESTER	12 01	02 02	08 09		27 10	20 10	06 03	23 02	16 03	06 10	11 05	13 02	30 03	22 09	05 04	20 04	01 12	25 08	26 01	04 05	29 12	10 11	03 10	26 12
CHESTERFIELD	25 08	22 09	02 02	02 03		03 11	04 05	06 10	20 10	16 03	12 02	02 10	26 12	12 01	29 12	05 03	11 05	26 01	08 09	01 12	09 04	20 04	10 11	30 03
COLCHESTER	22 09	08 09	26 01	08 03	22 02		10 05	15 03	06 10	26 10	09 11	26 12	12 02	01 02	01 12	28 12	19 04	11 01	25 08	23 10	03 05	02 10	29 03	08 04
CREWE	06 04	01 01	13 04	23 10	05 12	21 12		06 05	27 04	23 11	01 02	08 09	26 01	06 11	23 02	22 03	27 10	16 02	02 10	09 03	13 10	25 08	12 01	22 09
DARLINGTON	02 02	27 01	25 08	03 11	23 03	13 10	29 12		02 03	09 03	02 10	29 03	09 04	08 09	20 04	04 05	23 10	22 09	21 01	11 05	02 12	12 02	26 12	10 11
EXETER	26 01	12 01	22 09	13 10	09 03	23 03	01 12	27 10		23 02	30 03	29 12	03 10	25 08	15 12	08 04	10 11	08 09	01 02	20 04	24 10	26 12	11 05	13 02
HALIFAX	08 09	25 08	12 01	23 03	13 10	25 02	19 04	19 10	03 11		26 12	03 05	10 11	25 01	05 03	30 11	08 04	01 02	21 09	29 12	10 05	30 03	12 02	02 10
HARTLEPOOL	27 04	06 05	02 01	22 12	19 09	13 04	29 09	16 02	07 11	06 04		13 10	27 10	15 12	09 02	19 01	15 09	24 11	24 10	05 01	01 09	09 03	23 03	23 02
HEREFORD	23 12	24 11	06 03	19 09	16 02	06 04	19 01	07 11	06 05	15 12	16 03		06 10	27 04	01 09	29 09	05 01	13 04	01 01	15 09	09 02	23 02	20 10	27 10
MANSFIELD	06 03	27 04	24 11	07 11	06 04	19 09	15 09	01 01	16 02	13 04	02 03	23 03		22 12	19 01	05 01	01 09	15 12	06 05	09 02	29 09	13 10	03 11	20 10
NORTHAMPTON	20 10	02 03	03 11	09 02	01 09	29 09	30 03	19 01	05 01	15 09	16 04	01 12	30 04		26 12	12 02	18 09	06 10	17 03	09 04	10 11	29 12	21 04	05 03
PETERBOROUGH	16 02	07 11	19 12	01 01	06 05	27 04	03 11	24 11	04 05	24 10	22 09	12 01	08 09	02 04		02 03	09 03	03 10	13 04	13 10	23 03	02 02	25 08	26 01
PORT VALE	13 04	15 02	06 04	23 11	22 10	06 05	06 10	15 12	01 01	27 04	08 09	02 02	25 08	01 10	27 10		16 03	22 12	05 11	23 02	09 03	26 01	22 09	12 01
ROCHDALE	02 10	06 04	06 11	27 04	21 12	24 11	02 03	05 03	13 04	01 01	26 01	25 08	12 01	16 02	20 10	13 10		06 05	15 12	23 03	03 11	22 09	02 02	08 09
SCUNTHORPE	03 11	13 10	02 03	04 01	15 09	31 08	18 09	08 02	19 01	09 11	04 05	22 03	12 02	10 05	29 12		08 03	26 12	29 03	23 10	09 04	30 11		
SOUTHEND	02 03	03 11	23 03	14 09	18 01	04 01	11 02	01 09	28 09	08 02	04 03	08 04	29 12	13 10	10 11	29 03	03 05	19 10		17 09	26 12	11 05	01 12	19 04
STOCKPORT	05 11	12 04	01 10	14 12	27 04	04 03	19 10	21 12	24 11	06 05	25 08	25 01	22 09	01 01	16 03	03 11	05 10	06 04	15 02		25 02	12 01	07 09	01 02
SWINDON	24 11	02 10	16 02	06 05	01 01	15 12	16 03	28 04	05 03	22 12	12 01	22 09	02 02	13 04	07 10	20 10	23 02	06 11	06 04	27 10		08 09	26 01	25 08
TORQUAY	01 01	15 12	27 04	13 04	24 11	16 02	05 01	18 09	06 04	06 11	20 10	03 11	16 03	06 05	29 09	15 09	09 02	05 03	22 12	.01 09	19 01		02 03	06 10
TRANMERE	15 12	23 10	06 05	16 02	13 04	06 11	01 09	06 04	21 12	17 09	06 10	08 03	22 02	23 11	05 01	09 02	29 09	01 01	26 04	19 01	14 09	27 10		16 03
WREXHAM	06 05	22 12	15 12	06 04	06 11	01 01	09 02	13 04	18 09	16 02	03 11	02 03	09 03	23 10	15 09	01 09	19 01	27 04	24 11	29 09	05 01	23 03	13 10	